C0:CF01809

TURFGRASS

AGRONOMY

A Series of Monographs

The American Society of Agronomy and Academic Press published the first six books in this series. The General Editor of Monographs 1 to 6 was A. G. Norman. They are available through Academic Press, Inc., 111 Fifth Avenue, New York, NY 10003.

1. C. EDMUND MARSHALL: The Colloid Chemical of the Silicate Minerals. 1949
2. BYRON T. SHAW, *Editor*: Soil Physical Conditions and Plant Growth. 1952
3. K. D. JACOB, *Editor*: Fertilizer Technology and Resources in the United States. 1953
4. W. H. PIERRE and A. G. NORMAN, *Editors*: Soil and Fertilizer Phosphate in Crop Nutrtion. 1953
5. GEORGE F. SPRAGUE, *Editor*: Corn and Corn Improvement. 1955
6. J. LEVITT: The Hardiness of Plants. 1956

The Monographs published since 1957 are available from the American Society of Agronomy, 677 S. Segoe Road, Madison, WI 53711.

7. JAMES N. LUTHIN, *Editor*: Drainage of Agricultural Lands. 1957
8. FRANKLIN A. COFFMAN, *Editor*: Oats and Oat Improvement. 1961
9. A. KLUTE, *Editor*: Methods of Soil Analysis. 1986
   Part 1—Physical and Mineralogical Methods. Second Edition.
   A. L. PAGE, R. H. MILLER, and D. R. KEENEY, *Editor*: Methods of Soil Analysis. 1982
   Part 2—Chemical and Microbiological Properties. Second Edition.
10. W. V. BARTHOLOMEW and F. E. CLARK, *Editors*: Soil Nitrogen. 1965
    (Out of print; replaced by no. 22)
11. R. M. HAGAN, H. R. HAISE, and T. W. EDMINSTER, *Editors*: Irrigation of Agricultural Lands. 1967
12. FRED ADAMS, *Editor*: Soil Acidity and Liming. Second Edition. 1984
13. E. G. HEYNE, *Editor*: Wheat and Wheat Improvement. Second Edition. 1987
14. A. A. HANSON and F. V. JUSKA, *Editors*: Turfgrass Science. 1969
15. CLARENCE H. HANSON, *Editor*: Alfalfa Science and Technology. 1972
16. J. R. WILCOX, *Editor*: Soybeans: Improvement, Production, and Uses. Second Edition. 1987
17. JAN VAN SCHILFGAARDE, *Editor*: Drainage for Agriculture. 1974
18. G. F. SPRAGUE and J. W. DUDLEY, *Editors*: Corn and Corn Improvement, Third Edition. 1988
19. JACK F. CARTER, *Editor*: Sunflower Science and Technology. 1978
20. ROBERT C. BUCKNER and L. P. BUSH, *Editors*: Tall Fescue. 1979
21. M. T. BEATTY, G. W. PETERSEN, and L. D. SWINDALE, *Editors*: Planning the Uses and Management of Land. 1979
22. F. J. STEVENSON, *Editor*: Nitrogen in Agricultural Soils. 1982
23. H. E. DREGNE and W. O. WILLIS, *Editors*: Dryland Agriculture. 1983
24. R. J. KOHEL and C. F. LEWIS, *Editors*: Cotton. 1984
25. N. L. TAYLOR, *Editor*: Clover Science and Technology. 1985
26. D. C. RASMUSSON, *Editor*: Barley. 1985
27. M. A. TABATABAI, *Editor*: Sulfur in Agriculture. 1986
28. R. A. OLSON and K. J. FREY, *Editors*: Nutritional Quality of Cereal Grains: Genetic and Agronomic Improvement. 1987
29. A. A. HANSON, D. K. BARNES, and R. R. HILL, JR., *Editors*: Alfalfa and Alfalfa Improvement. 1988
30. B. A. STEWART and D. R. NIELSEN, *Editors*: Irrigation of Agricultural Crops. 1990
31. JOHN HANKS and J. T. RITCHIE, *Editors*: Modeling Plant and Soil Systems, 1991
32. D. V. WADDINGTON, R. N. CARROW, and R. C. SHEARMAN, *Editors*: Turfgrass, 1992

TURFGRASS

**D. V. Waddington, R. N. Carrow, and
R. C. Shearman, co-editors**

Managing Editor: S. H. Mickelson

Editor-in-Chief ASA Publications: G. A. Peterson

Editor-in-Chief CSSA Publications: P. S. Baenziger

Editor-in-Chief SSSA Publications: R. J. Luxmoore

Number 32 in the series
AGRONOMY

American Society of Agronomy, Inc.
Crop Science Society of America, Inc.
Soil Science Society of America, Inc.
Publishers
Madison, Wisconsin USA
1992

Copyright © 1992 by the American Society of Agronomy, Inc.
Crop Science Society of America, Inc.
Soil Science Society of America, Inc.

ALL RIGHTS RESERVED UNDER THE U.S. COPYRIGHT ACT
OF 1976 (P. L. 94-553)

Any and all uses beyond the limitations of the "fair use" provision
of the law require written permission from the publishers and/or
author(s); not applicable to contributions prepared by officers or employees of the U.S. Government as part of their official duties.

American Society of Agronomy, Inc.
Crop Science Society of America, Inc.
Soil Science Society of America, Inc.
677 South Segoe Road, Madison, WI 53711 USA

Library of Congress Cataloging-in-Publication Data

Turfgrass / D.V. Waddington, R.N. Carrow, and R.C. Shearman, co-
editors.
     p.   cm. — (Agronomy : no. 32)
   Includes bibliographical references and index.
   ISBN 0-89118-108-3
   1. Turfgrasses. 2. Turf management. I. Waddington, D.V.
(Donald V.) II. Carrow, Robert N. III. Shearman, Robert C.
IV. Series.
SB433.T82 1992
635.9'642—dc20
                              91-46525
                                 CIP

Printed in the United States of America

CONTENTS

SECTION II. TURFGRASS PHYSIOLOGY

4 **Ecological Aspects of Turf Communities**   129

T. L. WATSCHKE AND R. E. SCHMIDT

5 **Energy Relations and Carbohydrate Partitioning in Turfgrasses**   175

RICHARD J. HULL

6 **Salinity and Turfgrass Culture**   207

M. ALI HARIVANDI, JACK D. BUTLER, AND LIN WU

7 **Physiological Effects of Temperature Stress**   231

J. M. DiPAOLA AND J. B. BEARD

SECTION IV. MANAGEMENT

13 Energy Conservation and Efficient Turfgrass Maintenance   473

PHILIP BUSEY AND JOHN H. PARKER

14 Integrated Pest Management   501

ARTHUR H. BRUNEAU, JOHN E. WATKINS, AND RICK L. BRANDENBURG

15 Turfgrass Management Operations   535

S. T. COCKERHAM AND J. A. VAN DAM

16 Plant Growth Regulators and Turfgrass Management   557

T. L. WATSCHKE, M. G. PRINSTER, AND J. M. BREUNINGER

SECTION V. RESEARCH METHODS

FOREWORD

The American Society of Agronomy serves agronomy and agronomists over a broad range of specialties, and with a variety of media. Agronomy has been defined as the theory and practice of field crop production and soil management. It is applied not only to plant and soil interactions for food and fiber production, but also to other operations involving plant growth and soil management. Turfgrass management and science, the subject of this volume, is an example of agronomy in action off the farm. *Turfgrass* is a successor to a successful earlier monograph, *Turfgrass Science*. It joins the ranks of outreach publications of the American Society of Agronomy. It will be a technical reference for years to come, and will serve the full gamut of research, teaching, and technical personnel who work with turf.

Donald N. Duvick, *president,* ASA
Gary H. Heichel, *president*, CSSA
William W. McFee, *president*, SSSA

PREFACE

Since the early 1950s, a tremendous expansion has occurred in the turfgrass industry. Dramatic increases in areas planted to turfgrasses and in personnel required to establish and maintain these areas have occurred. The demand for educational programs in turfgrass management increased, and turfgrass programs were initiated or expanded at many universities and colleges. Agronomy Monograph 14, *Turfgrass Science*, published in 1969, provided students, teachers, researchers, grounds managers, golf course superintendents, and others with a much needed up-to-date source of information dealing with historical, technical, and applied aspects of turfgrass science and management. The monograph became a widely accepted textbook and reference book. More copies of monograph 14 (more than 16 200 copies in 21 years) have been sold than any other monograph in the series published by ASA. This monograph, *Turfgrass*, updates some topics from monograph 14 and presents detailed discussions on additional topics. As such, it complements information contained in the earlier monograph and various turfgrass textbooks and reference books.

The monograph was completed after many years of planning, writing, reviewing, rewriting, editing, and procrastinating. In the fall of 1980, Victor B. Youngner accepted the appointment as editor for a new turfgrass monograph. Much of the first year was spent in obtaining opinions and suggestions from the membership of CSSA Division C-5 (Turfgrass Science) for the development of the monograph. Based on many responses from the members, it was concluded that the monograph should be an entirely new book emphasizing basic science rather than the "how-to-do-it" approach. It was visualized that the monograph would serve as a technical reference for turfgrass researchers, teachers, extension workers, advanced students, and trained professionals, and that it would not duplicate any of the excellent texts that had become available since the publication of the earlier monograph. Chapter topics were developed and senior authors were obtained by fall of 1982. Following the sudden depth of V. B. Youngner in April 1984, Victor A. Gibeault assumed editorial leadership in June 1984. Dr. Gibeault relinquished these duties in November 1986. In December 1986, ASA President Robert G. Gast appointed Donald V. Waddington as editor and Robert N. Carrow and Robert C. Shearman as associate editors. At this time the emphasis of the monograph was reassessed, and after several changes, a concentrated effort was made to bring the monograph to completion.

The monograph is divided into five sections: I. The Turfgrass Industry section includes chapters covering historical aspects of research and education, the current status of the industry, and artificial turf; II. Turfgrass Physiology includes chapters on ecological aspects, energy relations and carbohydrate partitioning, and stresses due to salinity, temperature, shade, and traffic; III. Soils and Water covers soils and amendments, nutrition, fertilization, water requirements, and irrigation; IV. Management section includes chapters on energy conservation and efficient maintenance, integrated pest management, turfgrass management operations, and plant growth regulators; and V. Research Methods addresses research techniques related to field and controlled-environment research, diseases, insects, weeds, and breeding. Authors of previously submitted chapters had the opportunity to update their manuscripts and new and delinquent authors submitted their chapters. Finally, the time and efforts of many people over this 12-yr period have resulted in the publishing of this monograph.

We appreciate the contributions of those who helped bring the monograph to completion: those who assisted in planning, previous editors Vic Youngner and Vic Gibeault, reviewers of manuscripts, managing editor Sherri Mickelson and others of the ASA Headquarters Staff, and especially the authors.

Donald V. Waddington, *co-editor*
Department of Agronomy
The Pennsylvania State University
University Park, Pennsylvania

Robert N. Carrow, *co-editor*
Agronomy Department
University of Georgia, Georgia Stn.
Griffin, Georgia

Robert C. Shearman, *co-editor*
Department of Agronomy
University of Nebraska
Lincoln, Nebraska

CONTRIBUTORS

James B. Beard	Professor, Turfgrass Stress Physiology, Department of Soil and Crop Sciences, Texas A&M University, College Station, TX 77843
Rick L. Brandenburg	Associate Professor and Extension Entomologist, Department of Entomology, North Carolina State University, Raleigh, NC 27695-7613
J. M. Breuninger	Technical Service and Development Representative, DowElanco, 3841 North Freeway Boulevard, Sacramento, CA 95834-1929
Arthur H. Bruneau	Associate Professor and Extension Specialist (Turf), Department of Crop Science, North Carolina State University, Raleigh, NC 27695-7620
Glenn W. Burton	Research Geneticist, USDA-ARS, Coastal Plain Experiment Station, P.O. Box 748, Tifton, GA 31793-0748
Philip Busey	Associate Professor of Environmental Horticulture, University of Florida, Fort Lauderdale Research and Education Center, 3205 College Avenue, Fort Lauderdale, FL 33314
Jack D. Butler	Professor of Horticulture-Emeritus, Department of Horticulture, Colorado State University, Fort Collins, CO 80523
Robert N. Carrow	Professor of Agronomy, Agronomy Department, University of Georgia, Georgia Station, Griffin, GA 30223-1797
S. T. Cockerham	Superintendent of Agricultural Operations, University of California, Riverside, 1060 Pennsylvania Avenue, Riverside, CA 92507
J. M. DiPaola	Associate Professor of Crop Science, North Carolina State University, Raleigh, NC 27695-7620
A. E. Dudeck	Professor of Turfgrass Science, Department of Environmental Horticulture, University of Florida, Gainesville, FL 32611-0512
Fred V. Grau	(Deceased) P.O. Box AA, College Park, MD 20740
M. Ali Harivandi	Turfgrass, Soils and Water Specialist, University of California Cooperative Extension, 224 West Winton Avenue, Room 174, Hayward, CA 94544
Wayne W. Huffine	(Deceased) Turfgrass Consultant, 1502 North Washington, Stillwater, OK 74075
Richard J. Hull	Professor of Plant Physiology, Plant Sciences Department, 145 Greenhouse, University of Rhode Island, Kingston, RI 02881
Norman W. Hummel, Jr.	Associate Professor of Turfgrass Science, Department of Floriculture and Ornamental Horticulture, Cornell University, Ithaca, NY 14853
B. J. Johnson	Professor of Agronomy, Agronomy Department, University of Georgia, Georgia Station, Griffin, GA 30223-1797
Howard E. Kaerwer	Turfgrass Consultant, HEK Consulting, 12800 Gerard Drive, Eden Prairie, MN 55346
W. R. Kneebone	Professor Emeritus, Department of Plant Sciences, University of Arizona, 2491 North Camino de Oeste, Tucson, AZ 85745-9630
D. M. Kopec	Associate Extension Specialist—Turf, Plant Science Department, University of Arizona, Tucson, AZ 85721
C. F. Mancino	Assistant Professor, Department of Plant Sciences, University of Arizona, Tucson, AZ 85721
David P. Martin	Director of Research, ChemLawn Services Corporation, 8275 North High Street, Columbus, OH 43235

Chauncey A. Morehouse	Professor Emeritus of Physical Education, Pennsylvania State University, 621 Old Farm Lane, State College, PA 16803
T. R. Murphy	Associate Professor of Agronomy, Extension Agronomy Department, University of Georgia Cooperative Extension Service, Georgia Station, Griffin, GA 30223-1797
Jack J. Murray	Turfgrass Consultant, 9602 Hammock Drive, Bradenton, FL 34202
John H. Parker	Professor of Chemistry and Environmental Science, Chemistry Department, Florida International University, Miami, FL 33199
C. H. Peacock	Associate Professor of Crop Science, Turf, Department of Crop Science, North Carolina State University, Raleigh, NC 27695-7620
A. Martin Petrovic	Associate Professor of Turfgrass Science, Department of Floriculture and Ornamental Horticulture, Cornell University, Ithaca, NY 14853
M. G. Prinster	Associate Research Scientist, ChemLawn Services Corporation, 2985 Sweetwater Church Road, Douglasville, GA 30134
Roger H. Ratcliffe	Research Entomologist, USDA-ARS, Germplasm Quality and Enhancement Laboratory, BARC-East, Beltsville, MD 20705. Currently Research Entomologist, USDA-ARS, Insect and Weed Control Research Unit, Department of Entomology, Purdue University, West Lafayette, IN 47907
Eliot C. Roberts	Director, The Lawn Institute, P.O. Box 108, Pleasant Hill, TN 38578
Carl D. Sawyer	Research Associate, Department of Plant Sciences, University of Rhode Island, Kingston, RI 02881
R. E. Schmidt	Professor of Turfgrass Science, CSES Department, Virginia Polytechnic Institute and State University, Blacksburg, VA 24061-0404
G. L. Schumann	Assistant Professor of Plant Pathology, Department of Plant Pathology, University of Massachusetts, Amherst, MA 01003
R. C. Shearman	Head and Professor, Department of Agronomy, University of Nebraska, Lincoln, NE 68583-0915
C. Richard Skogley	Professor Emeritus—Agronomy, Plant Sciences Department, University of Rhode Island, Kingston, RI 02881
Thomas R. Turner	Associate Professor of Agronomy, Department of Agronomy, University of Maryland, College Park, MD 20742
J. A. Van Dam	Turfgrass Advisor Emeritus, Cooperative Extension, University of California, 3627 Palm Crest Drive, Highland, CA 92346
Donald V. Waddington	Professor of Soil Science, Department of Agronomy, The Pennsylvania State University, University Park, PA 16802
John E. Watkins	Professor and Extension Plant Pathologist, Department of Plant Pathology, University of Nebraska-Lincoln, Lincoln, NE 68583-0722
T. L. Watschke	Professor of Turfgrass Science, 116 Agricultural Sciences and Industry Building, The Pennsylvania State University, University Park, PA 16802
James R. Watson	Vice President, Agronomist, The Toro Company, 8111 Lyndale Avenue South, Minneapolis, MN 55420
H. T. Wilkinson	Professor of Plant Pathology and Agronomy, University of Illinois, Urbana, IL 61801
Lin Wu	Professor of Environmental Horticulture, Department of Environmental Horticulture, University of California, Davis, CA 95616

Conversion Factors for SI and non-SI Units

Conversion Factors for SI and non-SI Units

To convert Column 1 into Column 2, multiply by	Column 1 SI Unit	Column 2 non-SI Unit	To convert Column 2 into Column 1, multiply by
Length			
0.621	kilometer, km (10^3 m)	mile, mi	1.609
1.094	meter, m	yard, yd	0.914
3.28	meter, m	foot, ft	0.304
1.0	micrometer, μm (10^{-6} m)	micron, μ	1.0
3.94×10^{-2}	millimeter, mm (10^{-3} m)	inch, in	25.4
10	nanometer, nm (10^{-9} m)	Angstrom, Å	0.1
Area			
2.47	hectare, ha	acre	0.405
247	square kilometer, km^2 (10^3 m)^2	acre	4.05×10^{-3}
0.386	square kilometer, km^2 (10^3 m)^2	square mile, mi^2	2.590
2.47×10^{-4}	square meter, m^2	acre	4.05×10^3
10.76	square meter, m^2	square foot, ft^2	9.29×10^{-2}
1.55×10^{-3}	square millimeter, mm^2 (10^{-3} m)^2	square inch, in^2	645
Volume			
9.73×10^{-3}	cubic meter, m^3	acre-inch	102.8
35.3	cubic meter, m^3	cubic foot, ft^3	2.83×10^{-2}
6.10×10^4	cubic meter, m^3	cubic inch, in^3	1.64×10^{-5}
2.84×10^{-2}	liter, L (10^{-3} m^3)	bushel, bu	35.24
1.057	liter, L (10^{-3} m^3)	quart (liquid), qt	0.946
3.53×10^{-2}	liter, L (10^{-3} m^3)	cubic foot, ft^3	28.3
0.265	liter, L (10^{-3} m^3)	gallon	3.78
33.78	liter, L (10^{-3} m^3)	ounce (fluid), oz	2.96×10^{-2}
2.11	liter, L (10^{-3} m^3)	pint (fluid), pt	0.473

To convert Column 1 into Column 2, multiply by	Column 1 SI Unit	Column 2 non-SI Unit	To convert Column 2 into Column 1, multiply by
Mass			
2.20×10^{-3}	gram, g (10^{-3} kg)	pound, lb	454
3.52×10^{-2}	gram, g (10^{-3} kg)	ounce (avdp), oz	28.4
2.205	kilogram, kg	pound, lb	0.454
0.01	kilogram, kg	quintal (metric), q	100
1.10×10^{-3}	kilogram, kg	ton (2000 lb), ton	907
1.102	megagram, Mg (tonne)	ton (U.S.), ton	0.907
1.102	tonne, t	ton (U.S.), ton	0.907
Yield and Rate			
0.893	kilogram per hectare, kg ha^{-1}	pound per acre, lb acre^{-1}	1.12
7.77×10^{-2}	kilogram per cubic meter, kg m^{-3}	pound per bushel, bu^{-1}	12.87
1.49×10^{-2}	kilogram per hectare, kg ha^{-1}	bushel per acre, 60 lb	67.19
1.59×10^{-2}	kilogram per hectare, kg ha^{-1}	bushel per acre, 56 lb	62.71
1.86×10^{-2}	kilogram per hectare, kg ha^{-1}	bushel per acre, 48 lb	53.75
0.107	liter per hectare, L ha^{-1}	gallon per acre	9.35
893	tonnes per hectare, t ha^{-1}	pound per acre, lb acre^{-1}	1.12×10^{-3}
893	megagram per hectare, Mg ha^{-1}	pound per acre, lb acre^{-1}	1.12×10^{-3}
0.446	megagram per hectare, Mg ha^{-1}	ton (2000 lb) per acre, ton acre^{-1}	2.24
2.24	meter per second, m s^{-1}	mile per hour	0.447
Specific Surface			
10	square meter per kilogram, m^2 kg^{-1}	square centimeter per gram, cm^2 g^{-1}	0.1
1000	square meter per kilogram, m^2 kg^{-1}	square millimeter per gram, mm^2 g^{-1}	0.001
Pressure			
9.90	megapascal, MPa (10^6 Pa)	atmosphere	0.101
10	megapascal, MPa (10^6 Pa)	bar	0.1
1.00	megagram per cubic meter, Mg m^{-3}	gram per cubic centimeter, g cm^{-3}	1.00
2.09×10^{-2}	pascal, Pa	pound per square foot, lb ft^{-2}	47.9
1.45×10^{-4}	pascal, Pa	pound per square inch, lb in^{-2}	6.90×10^3

(continued on next page)

Conversion Factors for SI and non-SI Units

To convert Column 1 into Column 2, multiply by	Column 1 SI Unit	Column 2 non-SI Unit	To convert Column 2 into Column 1, multiply by
Temperature			
$1.00\ (K - 273)$	Kelvin, K	Celsius, °C	$1.00\ (°C + 273)$
$(9/5\ °C) + 32$	Celsius, °C	Fahrenheit, °F	$5/9\ (°F - 32)$
Energy, Work, Quantity of Heat			
9.52×10^{-4}	joule, J	British thermal unit, Btu	1.05×10^{3}
0.239	joule, J	calorie, cal	4.19
10^{7}	joule, J	erg	10^{-7}
0.735	joule, J	foot-pound	1.36
2.387×10^{-5}	joule per square meter, $J\ m^{-2}$	calorie per square centimeter (langley)	4.19×10^{4}
10^{5}	newton, N	dyne	10^{-5}
1.43×10^{-3}	watt per square meter, $W\ m^{-2}$	calorie per square centimeter minute (irradiance), $cal\ cm^{-2}\ min^{-1}$	698
Transpiration and Photosynthesis			
3.60×10^{-2}	milligram per square meter second, $mg\ m^{-2}\ s^{-1}$	gram per square decimeter hour, $g\ dm^{-2}\ h^{-1}$	27.8
5.56×10^{-3}	milligram (H_2O) per square meter second, $mg\ m^{-2}\ s^{-1}$	micromole (H_2O) per square centimeter second, $\mu mol\ cm^{-2}\ s^{-1}$	180
10^{-4}	milligram per square meter second, $mg\ m^{-2}\ s^{-1}$	milligram per square centimeter second, $mg\ cm^{-2}\ s^{-1}$	10^{4}
35.97	milligram per square meter second, $mg\ m^{-2}\ s^{-1}$	milligram per square decimeter hour, $mg\ dm^{-2}\ h^{-1}$	2.78×10^{-2}
Plane Angle			
57.3	radian, rad	degrees (angle), °	1.75×10^{-2}

Electrical Conductivity, Electricity, and Magnetism

To convert Column 2 into Column 1, multiply by	Column 1 SI Unit	Column 2 non-SI Unit	To convert Column 1 into Column 2, multiply by
10	siemen per meter, $S\ m^{-1}$	millimho per centimeter, $mmho\ cm^{-1}$	0.1
10^4	tesla, T	gauss, G	10^{-4}

Water Measurement

To convert Column 2 into Column 1, multiply by	Column 1 SI Unit	Column 2 non-SI Unit	To convert Column 1 into Column 2, multiply by
9.73×10^{-3}	cubic meter, m^3	acre-inches, acre-in	102.8
9.81×10^{-3}	cubic meter per hour, $m^3\ h^{-1}$	cubic feet per second, $ft^3\ s^{-1}$	101.9
4.40	cubic meter per hour, $m^3\ h^{-1}$	U.S. gallons per minute, $gal\ min^{-1}$	0.227
8.11	hectare-meters, ha-m	acre-feet, acre-ft	0.123
97.28	hectare-meters, ha-m	acre-inches, acre-in	1.03×10^{-2}
8.1×10^{-2}	hectare-centimeters, ha-cm	acre-feet, acre-ft	12.33

Concentrations

To convert Column 2 into Column 1, multiply by	Column 1 SI Unit	Column 2 non-SI Unit	To convert Column 1 into Column 2, multiply by
1	centimole per kilogram, $cmol\ kg^{-1}$ (ion exchange capacity)	milliequivalents per 100 grams, $meq\ 100\ g^{-1}$	1
0.1	gram per kilogram, $g\ kg^{-1}$	percent, %	10
1	milligram per kilogram, $mg\ kg^{-1}$	parts per million, ppm	1

Radioactivity

To convert Column 2 into Column 1, multiply by	Column 1 SI Unit	Column 2 non-SI Unit	To convert Column 1 into Column 2, multiply by
2.7×10^{-11}	becquerel, Bq	curie, Ci	3.7×10^{10}
2.7×10^{-2}	becquerel per kilogram, $Bq\ kg^{-1}$	picocurie per gram, $pCi\ g^{-1}$	37
100	gray, Gy (absorbed dose)	rad, rd	0.01
100	sievert, Sv (equivalent dose)	rem (roentgen equivalent man)	0.01

Plant Nutrient Conversion

To convert Column 2 into Column 1, multiply by	Column 1 Elemental	Column 2 Oxide	To convert Column 1 into Column 2, multiply by
2.29	P	P_2O_5	0.437
1.20	K	K_2O	0.830
1.39	Ca	CaO	0.715
1.66	Mg	MgO	0.602

1   Turfgrass Science—Historical Overview

ELIOT C. ROBERTS

The Lawn Institute
Pleasant Hill, Tennessee

WAYNE W. HUFFINE

1502 North Washington
Stillwater, Oklahoma

FRED V. GRAU

P.O. Box AA
College Park, Maryland

JACK J. MURRAY

9602 Hammock Drive
Bradenton, Florida

Nature! . . . . She is the universal artist, creating the greatest contrasts from the simplest material, while achieving, without seeming to strive for it, an ultimate perfection. . . . . Each of her works has its own peculiar quality; everyone of her manifold appearances symbolizes a single concept and yet somehow blending they achieve unity. One must obey nature's laws even while he denies them; he is forced to produce with her aid even when he imagines that he is able to work against her.

"Nature"—A Poetic Fragment
Johann Wolfgang von Goethe
[Stites, 1940)

Turfgrasses, an integral part of landscape ecological systems worldwide, are one of nature's many assets. They, along with other landscape plants, provide humankind with living form to enhance our environment and improve on nature's natural features. They are both a thing of service and beauty.

The concept of turf as we know it today probably had its origin when man started to domesticate animals. They were herded or tethered to prevent escape and their grazed grounds might well have been the first play and sports turf. The natural landscape of the savannah in Africa, with scattered trees throughout extensive grassy plains, could have influenced our early ancestors in such ways that even today we feel most comfortable in an environment emulating the savannah, according to Falk (1977). This drive to maintain

Copyright © 1992 ASA-CSSA-SSSA, 677 S. Segoe Rd., Madison, WI 53711, USA. *Turfgrass—*
Agronomy Monograph no. 32.

lawns is evident through suburbia and rural towns alike and is noted even in the inner city.

The classic "Dance of the Nymphs," painted by Jean Baptiste Corot in 1951, was romantically inspired by mythology and seemingly performed on an "island" of turf. The mythical field of Mars, "Campus Martius," as described by Zimmerman (1964) where Roman youths performed exercises, rode horses, and drove chariots, perhaps evolved into our present stadia with manicured turf. These and other agronomic accomplishments were attributed to Ceres, the Goddess of Agriculture.

Turf in the modern concept may be natural, live grass or artificial. Natural grasses probably evolved in geological time during the Cretaceous and early Tertiary period, some 70 million yr ago, according to Harlan (1956), but the fragments of these fossils are scant. One rich fossil deposit of grassland flora, dating from the lower Miocene and later, is known from the Great Plains. Artificial turf was an outgrowth of the development of plastics in the 1950s and has found a place on sports fields where use intensity or growing conditions do not favor natural grass.

I. EARLY REFERENCES TO GRASS AND GARDENS

Numerous references to grass are to be found in the Bible. Genesis 1:11–12 reveals the benevolent nature of creation: "And God said: let the earth bring forth grass. . . . And the earth brought forth grass. . . ." In the fifth book of Moses (Deuteronomy 8:7) is the promise, "And I will send grass in thy fields for thy cattle, that thou mayest eat and be full." Solomon proclaims (Proverbs 19:12), "The King's wrath is as the roaring of a lion; but his favor is as dew upon the grass." Man's brief span is seen by the Psalmist (Psalm 10:3–15) as the ephemeral life of the flower: "As for man, his days are as grass: as a flower of the field, so he flourisheth. For the wind passeth over it and it is gone: and the place thereof shall know it no more." Similar expressions were made by Isaiah (Isaiah 40:6–8) and Peter (1 Peter 1:24), both devout naturalists.

While the Scriptures frequently refer to plants and their production, there are only a few references by name or location to gardens, as pointed out by MacKay (1950). Six gardens are listed in the Old Testament and two in the New Testament. These were somewhat like our present subtropical botanical gardens. They were predominantly gardens of trees that also provided a source of water. The earliest gardens, according to Rohde (1927) were divided into four parts by four rivers coming from a common source. As depicted in the Hindu Vedas, the accounts of Emperor Babar are pictured in the design of the famous garden carpets of Persia. The garden design in these carpets shows rectangular beds of flowers and grass, cypress and fruit trees, with a rectangular pool in the center from which flowed four streams. Gardens of Biblical times, with the exception of the Garden of Eden and Ezekiel's paradise, were associated with wealth and stories of them are steeped in mysticism and splendor. The association of lawns and gardens with better life styles holds today. Only now the cost is well within the means of most people.

II. EARLY USE OF TURF IN ASIA

Malone (1934) reports that vast pleasure gardens and magnificent palaces have been the most expensive luxuries of China's emperors. Emperor Wu Ti (157–87 B.C.) of the Han Dynasty had 30 000 slaves to care for his extensive grounds and buildings. The rarest trees and plants were assembled from throughout his entire empire that extended from Korea to Central Asia.

The simplest rectangular Eastern garden design is vividly shown in the Persian garden carpets that date back to the days of the ancient Kingdom of Assyria. Rohde (1927) describes one of the most famous of all garden carpets as made for Chosroes of Persia about 531–579 A.D. This garden represented the plan of a royal pleasure garden.

Firdawsi, the great Iranian poet, who wrote his "Shah nama" or "History of Kings" about the year 1000 A.D. described the beauties of nature as he wrote of an area along the Caspian Sea:

Mazanderan is the bower of spring
Tulips and hyacinths abound
On every lawn; and all around
Blooms like a garden in its prime
Fostered by that delicious clime.
(Wilber, 1962)

The Taj Mahal and garden, as Goethe (1955) relates, symbolize the romance that exists among garden lovers everywhere. The Agra garden, designed by some unknown landscape-artist dominated the thoughts of Shah Jahan, the Grand Mogul and his love for his wife Mumtza-i-Mahal.

Sports frequently occupied the day for Akbar, 1556–1605 A.D., the Great Emperor of Hindustan, according to Malleson (1891). Sometimes he would devote the early morning hours to field sports and late evenings to the game of chaugau or polo.

III. TURFGRASS CULTURE IN EUROPE

Rohde (1927) reveals that the rectangular garden plots portrayed in Persian garden carpets were common for centuries in the gardens of western Europe. The greatest influence came with the Crusades, when every class of society in Europe was brought into contact with the East.

A part of the classical gardens of Europe was probably devoted to lawns, although the first references to that effect only became available during medieval times. To this fact, Dawson (1949) pays a fitting tribute in his statement, "All lawn lovers should be grateful to Miss Eleanour Sinclair Rohde, who has searched the literature and brought together the early references on lawns in a fascinating article," in *Nineteenth Century and After*, 1928 CIV, 200.

Lawns seem to be sort of a living fossil according to some writers. In early times when wild beasts roamed the forests and both were close to the dwellings, the householder grazed his animals close to the house. This grazing system was an act of survival for both the man and his animals. The closely cropped grass became a symbol which exists today as a basis for landscaping around homes, businesses, in parks, and other places of beauty. It also served as a playground for young and old.

Bowls, a sport that has come to us from the crown heads of Europe, is played on turfgrass. Monro (1953) found that the association of bowls and war dates back hundreds of years. The game was so popular with the military personnel of England and France in the 1300s that it had to be forbidden, as it interfered with their practice of archery. Bowling on the green was the sport in which Sir Francis Drake was engaged when, in 1588, he was advised of the approach of the Spanish Armada. The original bowling green was the forerunner of our modern golf green.

Golf is played today on the highest quality turf possible. The game originated in the low countries (Holland's Kolf), and spread to England, Scotland, and the USA. It originated long before mowers existed to keep the grass clipped short. Mowing was done by sheep which, through a combination of close cropping and "treading" created favorable conditions for the game. As the game became more popular, there were times when putting on greens was delayed while the impediments were being brushed away.

Cricket, a British game, has persisted for centuries and has been carried to nearly every country, colony, or protectorate occupied by the British ruling class. The demands for perfection in the "pitch," the principal playing surface, place great stress on the grasses. The surface must be firm to the point of hardness and mowed as closely as mowers will cut. Just as cricket has been taken to the far corners of the earth, the British established fine lawns and exquisite botanical gardens wherever they went.

IV. LAWNS AND SPORTS TURF IN THE USA

The term *turfgrass* has been popularized in the USA only within the past 50 yr. For some time it carried an unfavorable connotation, especially when associated with horse racing and gambling at the track. Until the mid-1940s, the word portrayed an image of "golf turf," the playground of the idle rich.

The village green of ancient times has become the square or the park in many of our older towns. In early days, the green was grazed by sheep and goats, and the well-knit turf was pleasing to mothers who brought their little ones out for a stroll and some sunshine. With houses surrounding the village green, the turfed area was a natural meeting place for gossip and news, as well as for romance.

Turfgrass has been a part of the romantic West, too. As early as 1200 A.D., the inhabitants of the Midwest, the prehistoric Plains Indians, used sod strips to cover a framework of poles and brush matting to make comfortable dwellings. The sod was probably stripped from the buffalo-gramagrass prairies. Methods used to cut and lift the sod are unknown.

The sod house was typical of the early settlements in the West. About 1886, the sod house shown in Fig. 1-1 was built in Custer County, Nebraska.

Fig. 1-1. J. Cramer Sod House Home. Lillian Custer County, Nebraska. Nebraska State Historical Society.

Many homesteaded in dwellings such as this. The walls were blocks of sod with joints overlapped. The roof was "shingled" with strips of sod, probably buffalograss. These "soddies" were cool in summer and warm in winter, but unfortunately, during heavy rains, the sod became saturated and continued to drip inside for several days after the rain had stopped.

The Plains Indians engaged in several sports, all of which were played on grass sod. One that has been modified to meet modern civilized concepts is lacrosse, a popular game in Canada and at many American universities. The Indians played it on the grassed plains, both on foot and horseback. The game would often cover many miles during the course of a day. Much of the excitement of early day sports has been captured in the painting of Indians Playing Ball by the American artist and traveler George Catlin in 1932 (Fig. 1-2).

The first airport built in the USA was located in College Park, MD. It has had turf runways since its beginning. Turfgrasses were the only covering for airport runways until aircraft became too large and heavy. Then it became necessary to install concrete to support the heavy loads and provide

Fig. 1-2. Indians playing ball by George Catlin.

a better-wearing surface. Rural areas still use turfed runways for small aircraft and gliders.

With few exceptions, burial grounds have been covered with turf. The
Memorial Gardens of today remind us of an extensive turfed park beauti-
fully landscaped. Markers are flush with the ground or countersunk to facilitate the operation of maintenance equipment.

V. TURFGRASS RESEARCH

The first turf research, as revealed by Olcott (1890), appears to have
been conducted in the Olcott Turf Gardens in Connecticut in 1885 and tests
were continued until the death of J.B. Olcott in 1910. The next organized
turf research efforts were started in 1890 at the Rhode Island Agricultural
Experiment Station and by Beal at Michigan State University.

Initially, most of the research that could be related to turf was a by-
product of pasture and forage investigations. Many scientists at state colleges and universities and with the USDA (Table 1-1) have contributed to

Table 1-1. Turfgrass teaching, research, and extension throughout the USA.

KEY:
  State, *Location*
    EI—Early and previous investigators   EL—Extension leaders
    CLR—Current leaders—Research   TC—Turf conferences initiated
    AP—Academic program   RI—Research initiated

Alabama, *Auburn Univ.*
    EI—D. Sturkie; CLR—R. Dickens, T. Cope, P. Cobb; AP—B.S. program, Agrono-
    my, and graduate study; EL—C. Ward; TC—1960; RI—1927
Alaska, *Univ. of Alaska*
    EI—H. Hodgson, A. Kallio, A. Wilton, R. Taylor; CLR—W. Mitchell, R. Taylor, L.
    Klebesadel; AP—None; EL—F. Wooding, J. McKendrick, W. Mitchell, R. Taylor, L.
    Klebesadel; TC—None; RI—1950
Arizona, *Univ. of Arizona*
    EI—S. Fazio, J. Folkner, A. Baltensperger, W. Kneebone, I. Pepper; CLR—C. Mancino,
    D. Kopec; AP—B.S. program, Agronomy, and graduate study; EL—D. Kopec;
    TC—1953; RI—1949
Arkansas, *Univ. of Arkansas*
    EI—A. Davis, C. Murdock; CLR—J. King; AP—B.S. program, Agronomy, and gradu-
    ate study; EL—J. King; TC—1971; RI—1959
California, *Univ. of California, Davis*
    EI—L. Currier, R. Hagan, J. Madison, W. Davis; CLR—L. Wu; AP—B.S. program,
    ornamental horticulture, and graduate study; EL—None; TC—1951; RI—1951
  Univ. of California, Riverside
    EI—V. Stoutemeyer, P. Miller, R. Endo, V. Youngner; CLR—V. Gibeault; AP—B.S.
    program, Plant Sciences, and graduate study; EL—V. Gibeault; TC—1949; RI—1948
Colorado, *Colorado State Univ.*
    EI—G. Beach, J. Fults, J. Butler; CLR—A. Koski; AP—B.S. program, Horticulture,
    and graduate study; EL—A. Koski; TC—1954; RI—Early 1940s
Connecticut, *Univ. of Connecticut*
    EI—J. Olcott; CLR—W. Dest; AP—B.S. program, Plant Science, and graduate study;
    EL—W. Dest; TC—None; RI—1885

(continued on next page)

Table 1-1. Continued.

Delaware, *Univ. of Delaware*
  EI—W. Mitchell, C. Phillips; CLR—None; AP—B.S. program, Plant Science; EL—
  S. Barton; TC—1968; RI—1965
Florida, *Univ. of Florida*
  EI—R. Bair, G. Nutter, E. Burt, G. Horn, C. Peacock; CLR—A. Dudeck, P. Busey,
  J. Cisar, G. Snyder, T. Freeman; AP—B.S. program, Ornamental Horticulture, and
  graduate study; EL—B. McCarty; TC—1953; RI—1945
  Lake City Community College
  EI—G. Nutter, J. Cheesman; CLR—J. Piersol; AP—Two-yr program, B.S. program;
  TC—None; RI—None
Georgia, *Univ. of Georgia*
  EI—G. Burton, R. Burns; CLR—R. Carrow, K. Karnok, B. Johnson, L. Burpee; AP—
  B.S. program, Agronomy, and graduate study; EL—G. Landry, T. Murphy; TC—1946
  at Tifton, 1970 at Athens; RI—1946 at Tifton, Mid-1960s at Athens
Hawaii, *Univ. of Hawaii*
  EI—R. Voss, D. Watson, W. McCall; CLR—C. Murdoch; AP—B.S. program, Hor-
  ticulture, and graduate study; EL—C. Murdoch; TC—1965; RI—1963
Idaho, *Univ. of Idaho*
  EI—R. Ensign; CLR—None; AP—B.S. program, Plant Science; EL—None; TC—NTC
  Regional; RI—1970
Illinois, *Univ. of Illinois*
  EI—A. Lang, J. Pieper, F. Weinard, J. Butler, A. Turgeon; CLR—D. Wehner, T. Fer-
  manian; AP—B.S. program, Horticulture, and graduate study; EL—T. Fermanian,
  M. Shurtleff, H. Wilkinson; TC—1960; RI—1934
  Southern Illinois Univ.
  EI—H. Portz; CLR—K. Diesburg; AP—B.S. program, Agronomy, and graduate study;
  EL—None; TC—None; RI—Unknown
Indiana, *Purdue Univ.*
  EI—M. Clevitt, G. Hoffer, G. Mott, W. Daniel, R. Freeborg; CLR—C. Throssell; AP—
  B.S. program, Agronomy, and graduate study; EL—J. Lefton; TC—1937; RI—1942
Iowa, *Iowa State Univ.*
  EI—V. Stoutemeyer, H. Lantz, E. Roberts, E. Cott, N. Hummel, W. Knoop; CLR—
  N. Christians, C. Hodges, M. Agnew; AP—B.S. program, Horticulture, and gradu-
  ate study; EL—M. Agnew; TC—1932; RI—1931
Kansas, *Kansas State Univ.*
  EI—J. Zahnley, L. Quinlan, R. Keen, R. Carrow; CLR—J. Nus; AP—B.S. program,
  Horticulture, and graduate study; EL—L. Leuthold; TC—1950; RI—Late 1920s
Kentucky, *Univ. of Kentucky*
  EI—E. Fergus, J. Spencer; CLR—R. Buckner, A. Powell; AP—B.S. program, Agrono-
  my, and graduate study; EL—A. Powell; TC—1972; RI—1948
Louisiana, *Louisiana State Univ.*
  EI—T. Pope, T. Koske, E. Barrios; CLR—J. Frye; AP—B.S. program, Horticulture;
  EL—None; TC—1963; RI—1960
Maine, *Univ. of Maine*
  EI—R. Struchtemeyer, V. Holyoke; CLR—None; AP—B.S. program, Plant and Soil
  Environmental Sciences; EL—V. Holyoke; TC—1962; RI—1958
Maryland, *Univ. of Maryland*
  EI—R. Thomas, E. Cory, E. Deal, J. Hall, A. Powell, M. Welterlan; CLR—P. Der-
  noeden, T. Turner, M. Carroll; AP—Two-yr program, B.S. program, Agronomy, and
  graduate study; EL—T. Turner; TC—1928; RI—1931
Massachusetts, *Univ. of Massachusetts*
  EI—L. Dickinson, J. Cornish, E. Roberts, J. Troll, R. Carrow, D. Waddington, K.
  Hurto, W. Torello; CLR—R. Cooper, G. Schuman; AP—Winter school, 2-yr program,
  B.S. program, Agronomy, and graduate study; EL—R. Cooper; TC—1931; RI—1927

(continued on next page)

Table 1-1. Continued.

Michigan, *Michigan State Univ.*
EI—R. Cook, J. Tyson, M. McCool, J. Beard, K. Payne, J. Kaufmann; CLR—P. Rieke,
D. Branham, J. Vargas, J. Rogers; AP—Two-yr program, B.S. program, Agronomy,
and graduate study; EL—P. Rieke; TC—1930; RI—1929

Minnesota, *Univ. of Minnesota*
EI—H. Hayes, H. Schultz, G. Blake, D. Taylor; CLR—D. White, P. Larsen; AP—
B.S. program, Horticulture, and graduate study; EL—D. White; TC—1964; RI—1936

Mississippi, *Mississippi State Univ.*
EI—L. Wise, D. Johnson, C. Ward; CLR—J. Krans, G. Coats, D. Basingame, M. Goat-
ley; AP—B.S. program, Agronomy, and graduate study; EL—J. Perry, D. Nagel;
TC—1960; RI—1956

Missouri, *Univ. of Missouri*
EI—J. Whitten, E. Brown, D. Hemphill, R. Taven; GLR—J. Dunn, D. Minner, D.
Sleper; AP—B.S. program, Horticulture, and graduate study; EL—D. Minner;
TC—1960; RI—1910

Montana, *Montana State Univ.*
EI—G. Evans; CLR—G. Evans; AP—B.S. program, Plant and Soil Science; EL—O.
McCarver; TC—None; RI—During the 1920s

Nebraska, *Univ. of Nebraska*
EI—F. Keim, F. Grau, A. Dudeck, R. Shearman; CLR—T. Riordan, E. Kinbacher;
AP—B.S. program, Horticulture, and graduate study; EL—Open; TC—1962; RI—1927

Nevada, *Univ. of Nevada*
EI—R. Ruf, R. Post; CLR—D. Bowman; AP—None; EL—D. Bowman; TC—None;
RI—1965

New Hampshire, *Univ. of New Hampshire*
EI—L. Higgins, W. Knoop, C. Warren; CLR—J. Roberts; AP—B.S. program, Plant
Biology; EL—J. Roberts; TC—1965; RI—1961

New Mexico, *New Mexico State Univ.*
EI—C. Watson; CLR—A. Baltensperger, C. Glover; AP—B.S. program, Agronomy
and Horticulture; EL—C. Glover; TC—1955; RI—1954

New Jersey, *Rutgers Univ.*
EI—H. Sprague, E. Evaul, G. Musgrave, R. Engel, R. White; CLR—C. Funk, R. Duell,
H. Indyk; AP—B.S. program, Agronomy, and graduate study; EL—H. Indyk;
TC—1929; RI—1924

New York, *Cornell Univ.*
EI—J. Cornman, R. Smiley, H. Tashiro, J. Kaufmann; CLR—A. Petrovic, N. Hummel; AP—B.S. program, Ornamental Horticulture, and graduate study; EL—N. Hummel; TC—1947; RI—1947

North Carolina, *North Carolina State Univ.*
EI—J. Harris, W. Gilbert, G. Blake; CLR—J. DiPaola, A. Bruneau, L. Lucas, C. Pea-
cock; AP—B.S. program, Agronomy, and graduate study; EL—A. Bruneau; TC—1963;
RI—1961

North Dakota, *North Dakota State Univ.*
EI—J. Carter, K. Larson, I. Dietrich; CLR—None; AP—B.S. program, Horticulture
and Forestry; EL—None; TC—1985; RI—1962, project closed

Ohio, *Ohio State Univ.*
EI—F. Welton, G. McClure, R. Davis, R. Miller, D. Martin, J. Wilkinson; CLR—J.
Street, K. Danneburger, H. Niemczyk; AP—B.S. Program, Agronomy, and gradu-
ate study; EL—J. Street; TC—1938; RI—Early 1920s

Oklahoma, *Oklahoma State Univ.*
EI—W. Elder, R. Chessmore, W. Huffine, D. Brede, R. Green; CLR—J. Barber; AP—
B.S. program, Horticulture, and graduate study; EL—M. Kenna; TC—1946; RI—1948

(continued on next page)

Table 1-1. Continued.

Oregon, *Oregon State Univ.*
EI—H. Schoth, R. Cowan, N. Goetze; CLR—T. Cook; AP—B.S. program, Horticulture; EL—T. Cook; TC—1948; RI—1930

Pennsylvania, *Pennsylvania State Univ.*
EI—H. Musser, F. Grau, A. Cooper, A. Perkins, J. Harper; CLR—J. Duich, T. Watschke, D. Waddington, P. Sanders, P. Heller, P. Landschoot; AP—Winter school, B.S. program, Agronomy, and graduate study; EL—P. Landschoot; TC—1929; RI—1929

Rhode Island, *Univ. of Rhode Island*
EI—L. Kinney, H. Wheeler, J. DeFrance, F. Howard, R. Wakefield, J. Jagschitz, T. Kerr, C. Skogley; CLR—D. Duff, R. Hull, N. Jackson, M. Sullivan; AP—B.S. program, Agronomy, and graduate study; EL—B. Ruemmele; TC—None; RI—1890

South Carolina, *Clemson Univ.*
EI—P. Alexander, F. Ledeboer; CLR—R. Mazur, L. Miller; AP—B.S. program, Horticulture, and graduate study; EL—L. Miller; TC—1963; RI—1959

South Dakota, *South Dakota State Univ.*
EI—W. Macksam; CLR—None; AP—B.S. program, Horticulture and Forestry; EL—None; TC—1985; RI—1955, project closed

Tennessee, *Univ. of Tennessee*
EI—J. Underwood; CLR—L. Callahan, T. Samples; AP—B.S. program, Ornamental Horticulture, and graduate study; EL—T. Samples; TC—1947; RI—1938

Texas, *Texas A&M Univ.*
EI—G. Warner, R. Potts, A. Crain, J. Watson, E. Holt, G. McBee; CLR—J. Beard, W. Menn, M. Engelke, G. Horst, R. Duble, W. Knoop; AP—B.S. program, Agronomy, and graduate study; EL—R. Duble, W. Knoop; TC—1946; RI—1940

Utah, *Utah State Univ.*
EI—H. Peterson, K. Allred; CLR—W. Campbell; AP—B.S. program, Plant Science; EL—P. Rasmussen; TC—1964; RI—1958

Vermont, *Univ. of Vermont*
EI—G. Wood, W. Way; CLR—None; AP—B.S. program, Plant and Soil Science; EL—N. Pellett; TC—1965; RI—1959, project closed

Virginia, *Virginia Polytechnic Inst. and State Univ.*
EI—L. Carrier, A. Smith, R. Blaser, L. Taylor; CLR—R. Schmidt, J. Hall, D. Chalmers, H. Couch; AP—B.S. program, Agronomy, and graduate study; EL—J. Hall, D. Chalmers; TC—1957; RI—1910-1915

Washington, *Washington State Univ.*
EI—A. Law, R. Goss; CLR—W. Johnson, S. Brauen, G. Stahnke; AP—B.S. program, Agronomy, and graduate study; EL—G. Stahnke; TC—1948; RI—1942

West Virginia, *West Virginia Univ.*
EI—M. Hoover; CLR—None; AP—B.S. program, Plant and Soil Science; EL—None; TC—1967; RI—1930, project closed

Wisconsin, *Univ. of Wisconsin*
EI—F. Burcalow, E. Nielsen, D. Smith, J. Sund, R. Love, R. Newman; CLR—W. Kussow; AP—B.S. program, Soil Science; EL—D. Rohweder; TC—1959; RI—1920

Wyoming, *Univ. of Wyoming*
EI—L. Ayres; CLR—None; AP—None; EL—None; TC—None; RI—Since 1962, project closed

USDA Cooperating with USGA, *Arlington, VA*
EI—J. Monteith; CLR—None; AP—None; EL—None; TC—None; RI—1920, project closed

USDA-BARC, *Beltsville, MD*
EI—J. Monteith, F. Juska, A. Hanson, J. Murray, N. O'Neill; CLR—None; AP—None; EL—None; TC—None; RI—1941, project closed 1989

this continuing effort. These pioneer workers were concerned with the evaluation of products and practices, with teaching and extension, and with securing operating funds. These early turfgrass scientists learned much from visiting and inspecting sports fields, golf courses, and landscape plantings where problems existed. Meeting and working with greenkeepers (now golf course superintendents) aided the learning process. Opportunities to exchange ideas at turf conferences and seminars stimulated interest in this new area of research specialization. These excursions into the field helped develop a strong tie between research and extension. Although this tie is the recognized strength of federal and state funded agricultural programs, turf specialists often ignored official regulations and protocol to learn and be of service.

When serious problems were encountered in the early 1900s with the establishment and maintenance of turf on golf courses, primarily in the Northeast, two USDA scientists, C.V. Piper and R.A. Oakley, were called upon for assistance. As a result, several experiments were initiated on golf courses and in 1916 the USDA established the Arlington, VA, Turf Gardens where the Pentagon now stands. In 1920, the U.S. Golf Association (USGA) established its Green Section and joined with the USDA in an advisory and research role. These cooperative turf studies were directed primarily toward meeting the requirements of golf.

The first listing of turf in the Agricultural Appropriations Act of the Federal Government appeared for the year of 1901–

> . . . . and the Agricultural Experiment Stations are hereby authorized and directed to cooperate with the Secretary of Agriculture in establishing and maintaining experimental grass stations, for determining . . . . the best native and foreign species for reclaiming overstocked ranges and pastures, for renovating worn-out lands, for binding drifting sands and washed lands, and *for turfing lawns* and *pleasure grounds* . . . . seventeen thousand dollars: Provided.

In addition, the Appropriations Act for 1901 specified that $6000 of the amount appropriated be used to purchase and collect seed, roots, and specimens for distribution to experiment stations.

To assure further the distribution of these funds, the Act also provided that not more than $6000 of the amount appropriated be expended for salaries in Washington, D.C. Although federal allocations of funds for research including turf were made, it was not until the end of World War II that most agricultural experiment stations initiated turf research programs.

Today, the USDA-ARS, and almost every state agricultural experiment station is involved to some extent in turfgrass research (Table 1–1).

In September 1976, a survey was sent to turfgrass representatives in each of the 50 states to determine research activity (Beard, 1979). The distribution of professional man-year equivalents in research by region of the USA and cool- vs. warm-season turfgrass during 1974 to 1976 were determined (Table 1–2). Northeastern and southeastern regions were conducting a greater level of research than would be expected based on population (Table 1–3). Eleven states indicated no professional man-year equivalents devoted to turfgrass research. A summary of research activities divided into seven major problem-subject areas (Table 1–4) reveals that 35% of turfgrass research was

Table 1-2. Distribution of professional man-year equivalents (MYE) in research by region and by cool- vs. warm-season turfgrasses during 1974 to 1976 (Beard, 1979).

	Professional MYE in research			Percentage of U.S. population in each region
	Season		Regional total	
Region	Cool	Warm		
Northeastern	22.0 (32.0)†	2.9 (4.3)	24.9 (36.3)	28.9%
Southeastern	5.3 (7.6)	13.3 (19.4)	18.6 (27.0)	24.6%
North Central	15.4 (22.4)	1.5 (2.2)	16.9 (24.6)	28.9%
Western	7.2 (10.5)	1.1 (1.6)	8.3 (12.1)	17.7%
Total	49.9 (72.5)	18.8 (27.5)	68.7‡	

† Numbers in parentheses represent percentages.
‡ United States total MYE.

involved with pest problems. Cultivar improvement ranked second with 17% and soils ranked third with 14%.

A more recent evaluation of turfgrass research effort by area of concern has been made by Wehner and Murray (1987) (Table 1-5). The number of people working in turfgrass science varies from less than one full-time position in some of the western states to more than five positions in Virginia, Florida, and Texas.

The world's first turf research station was established in England on the St. Ives estate at Bingley, Yorkshire, in 1929. Under the able direction of R.B. Dawson, this station has achieved a world-wide reputation for its turf research. In New Zealand, turf investigations were started in 1932. Also about that time work began in New South Wales, Australia. In 1935, turf research was underway in Queensland; in 1936 in Victoria; and in 1948 in western Australia. In South Africa, turf research was pioneered by C.M. Murray of Capetown. By 1906, Dr. Murray had established grass greens at the Royal Cape Golf Course. As early as 1891 or 1892, a few grass greens had been put down in Durban. The first South African Golf Championship was played on grass greens in 1909 in the Transvaal. The Univ. of Witwatersrand, Frankenwald Turf Research Station in Johannesburg and the Roodeplaat Experiment Station at Pretoria are actively engaged in turf research.

VI. TURFGRASS EXTENSION EDUCATION

Cooperative Extension Service activities have been important to poultry, dairy, beef, sheep, field and forage crops, vegetable, and fruit production since before 1934. The need for educational assistance at turfgrass installations was recognized prior to the 1940s, particularly by those who managed golf courses, "greenkeepers" at that time.

A group of greenkeepers from the Philadelphia, PA area prevailed upon officials at Pennsylvania State College to hire a full-time extension agronomist to assist in solving turf-related problems. In 1935, Dr. Fred V. Grau became the first full-time extension turfgrass specialist in the country. Also, at that

Table 1-3. Professional man-year equivalents devoted to turfgrass research during 1974 to 1976 (Beard, 1979).

| State† | Man-year equivalents | | | Percentage of U.S. population (ranking) |
| | Season | | | |
	Cool	Warm	Total	
Virginia	5.2	1.6	6.8	2.3% (13)
Rhode Island	4.0		4.0	0.4% (39)
USDA	2.2	1.8	3.9	--
Florida	0.2	3.7	3.9	3.8% (8)
Texas	1.1	2.7	3.8	5.7% (3)
California	2.8	0.7	3.5	9.9% (1)
Pennsylvania	3.3		3.3	5.6% (4)
Georgia	0.7	1.9	2.6	2.3% (14)
Ohio	2.3		2.3	5.1% (6)
Washington	2.2		2.2	1.6% (22)
New Jersey	2.2		2.2	3.5% (9)
Michigan	2.1		2.1	4.3% (7)
Massachusetts	2.0		2.0	2.8% (10)
Nebraska	1.6	0.4	2.0	0.7% (35)
Minnesota	1.7		1.7	1.9% (19)
Mississippi	0.2	1.4	1.6	1.1% (29)
Illinois	1.4	0.1	1.5	5.3% (5)
Missouri	0.8	0.7	1.5	2.3% (15)
South Carolina	0.8	0.7	1.5	1.3% (26)
Indiana	1.4		1.4	2.5% (12)
Iowa	1.4		1.4	1.4% (25)
Kansas	0.8	0.4	1.2	1.1% (30)
Arizona	0.8	0.4	1.2	1.0% (32)
Kentucky	1.1		1.1	1.6% (23)
Arkansas	0.8	0.2	1.0	
New York	1.0		1.0	
North Carolina	0.5	0.5	1.0	
Vermont	0.8		0.8	
Alabama	0.3	0.5	0.8	
Tennessee	0.4	0.4	0.8	
Idaho	0.8		0.8	
Oklahoma	0.2	0.5	0.7	
Maryland	0.4	0.2	0.7	
Wisconsin	0.7		0.7	
New Hampshire	0.6		0.6	
Colorado	0.4		0.4	
Montana	0.2		0.2	
Connecticut	0.2		0.2	
Delaware	0.2		0.2	
South Dakota	0.1		0.1	

† States without professional turfgrass researchers: Alaska, Hawaii, Louisiana, Maine, New Mexico, North Dakota, Oregon, Utah, West Virginia, and Wyoming.

time in Pennsylvania there were three county agricultural extension agents involved in turf work. The plans of work developed by these men proved to be of great value and set the stage for increased activity across the country following World War II.

Table 1-4. Distribution of professional man-year equivalents of turfgrass research within seven major areas during 1974 to 1976 (Beard, 1979).

| Research area | Professional man-year equivalents | | | |
| | Season | | | |
	Cool	Warm	Total	Percentage
Pests	17.3	6.9	24.2	35.2
Cultivar improvement	8.7	3.1	11.7	17.1
Soils	8.1	1.9	10.0	14.6
Establishment	5.7	2.4	8.1	11.8
Physiology and ecology	5.5	2.4	7.9	11.4
Culture practices	4.4	1.8	5.8	8.4
Research techniques	0.8	0.2	1.0	1.5

In 1935, soil testing was in its infancy and although methods were crude, they were effective when interpreted by trained personnel. Testing turfgrass root zone soils for acidity and available nutrients became an important diagnostic aid for sports turf problems.

Identification of grasses and weeds ranked high on the agenda for the early extension turf specialists. The educational value to turf managers was immense. At that time, research data was lacking in many subject areas and chemical pesticides, fertilizers and sophisticated construction, maintenance, grooming and renovation equipment had not been developed. At times there was more commiserating than factual guidance.

One of the greatest benefits that evolved from these pioneering efforts was the development of harmonious collaboration between research and extension specialists. Problems encountered in the field were reviewed with experiment station staff and research efforts adjusted to meet new needs. Winter turf conferences and summer field days were initiated jointly by extension and research specialists with enthusiastic response by the turf manager.

Cooperative extension programs in turfgrass today have become standard in most states. With many improved and elite turfgrasses, specialized equipment, and an array of proven chemicals for many purposes, the extension specialist's responsibilities are greatly different now than in the past.

VII. ACADEMIC COURSES AND SHORT COURSES

In 1927, the University of Massachusetts, under the direction of Professor Lawrence S. Dickinson, initiated an educational program to advance the profession of greenkeeping (Roberts, 1956). The early success of this effort was, in large measure, due to Dickinson's understanding of the basic needs of grounds superintendents.

Courses of study at Massachusetts were designed for 8- to 10-wk, 2-, and 4-yr curricula. The shorter the time devoted to class-room instruction, the greater the importance of field experience in the selection of students for the curriculum. The job done in the classroom emphasized the natural factors of plant and soil science that influence maintenance practices and

Table 1–5. Turfgrass research effort by area of concern (Wehner & Murray, 1987).

| Location | Scientist man-years | | Percentage of effort | | | | | | | | | |
	Program†	Research	Turf-grass breeding	Cultivar evaluation	Soil fertility and chemistry	Soil physics and modification	Soil and water pollution	Turf-grass physiology	General mgt. studies	Weed research	Disease research	Insect research
Alabama	2.20	0.90	15	10	0	0	0	20	10	40	3	2
Arizona	0.80	0.65	20	20	25	0	15	5	10	0	0	5
Arkansas	2.50	1.90	0	25	10	0	0	0	25	35	5	0
California												
Davis	1.80	0.75	0	0	10	50	10	10	10	10	0	0
Riverside	2.80	1.90	20	25	0	0	5	10	20	10	5	5
Colorado	1.50	0.30	0	10	25	0	5	0	60	0	0	0
Connecticut	2.00	0.50	0	0	0	0	0	0	100	0	0	0
Delaware	1.80	1.10	0	10	10	20	30	0	10	10	10	0
Florida												
Ft. Lauderdale	4.30	3.40	20	9	4	0	13	0	15	15	10	15
Gainesville	3.20	1.80	6	5	40	0	5	0	5	5	18	14
Georgia												
Athens	2.40	0.30	0	0	0	0	0	0	100	0	0	0
Experiment	1.95	1.75	0	5	0	5	0	25	25	40	0	0
Idaho	0.50	0.22	0	0	20	0	0	0	40	0	25	15
Illinois												
Urbana	2.30	1.00	0	5	20	10	5	20	20	10	5	5
Carbondale	0.70	0.30	0	20	20	10	0	20	20	3	3	3
Indiana	2.20	0.85	5	15	10	20	0	5	10	15	15	5
Iowa	2.75	1.30	0	10	0	0	0	0	15	0	75	0
Kansas	1.00	0.50	0	15	25	30	0	5	10	0	15	0
Kentucky	1.30	0.60	10	25	5	0	0	0	20	20	10	10
Louisiana	2.00	1.80	0	5	35	35	0	25	0	0	0	0
Maine	0.30	0.00	--‡	--	--	--	--	--	--	--	--	--
Maryland												
USDA	1.90	1.90	30	20	15	0	0	5	20	2	5	2
College Park	4.25	1.25	0	20	20	0	0	15	15	5	10	15

State	Total†											
Massachusetts	2.30	0.80	0	20	10	0	0	5	35	20	10	0
Michigan	3.75	1.90	10	15	15	5	0	10	20	5	20	0
Minnesota	2.70	1.70	--‡	--‡	--‡	--‡	--‡	--‡	--‡	--‡	--‡	--‡
Mississippi	2.44	1.84	0	6	0	0	0	6	12	31	10	34
Missouri	0.97	0.39	25	25	0	0	0	25	25	0	0	0
Montana	0.30	0.15	0	5	0	5	0	0	90	0	0	0
Nebraska	3.20	2.10	25	10	10	5	0	25	10	10	5	0
Nevada	0.45	0.05	--‡	--‡	--‡	--‡	--‡	--‡	--‡	--‡	--‡	--‡
New Hampshire	1.00	0.60	--‡	--‡	--‡	--‡	--‡	--‡	--‡	--‡	--‡	--‡
New Jersey	3.50	2.20	15	20	10	0	0	10	20	10	5	10
New Mexico	0.90	0.50	30	20	30	0	0	0	10	10	0	0
New York	4.10	2.10	0	10	10	5	5	0	0	10	30	30
North Carolina	4.40	2.20	0	7	0	0	0	30	30	7	22	4
North Dakota	0.30	0.00	--‡	--‡	--‡	--‡	--‡	--‡	--‡	--‡	--‡	--‡
Ohio	3.40	1.30	0	10	10	0	0	50	20	10	0	0
Wooster	1.00	1.00	0	5	0	0	0	0	0	0	0	95
Oklahoma	1.00	0.45	0	5	15	5	0	0	25	40	10	0
Oregon	0.75	0.05	--‡	--‡	--‡	--‡	--‡	--‡	--‡	--‡	--‡	--‡
Pennsylvania	4.90	2.16	15	12	15	10	0	10	9	13	13	2
Rhode Island	4.20	2.35	2	5	8	0	0	10	50	20	5	0
South Carolina	2.00	1.06	10	10	30	20	0	0	20	10	0	0
South Dakota	0.35	0.20	0	50	0	0	0	0	50	10	0	0
Tennessee	1.25	0.85	0	5	0	20	0	20	10	35	5	5
Texas	8.25	5.22	20	5	4	4	0	20	12	10	15	10
Vermont	0.55	0.25	0	50	0	0	0	50	0	0	0	0
Virginia	5.75	3.05	10	15	10	10	0	20	10	15	10	0
Washington	3.30	2.40	0	10	35	10	0	5	8	10	20	2
Wisconsin	1.30	0.80	0	20	10	10	0	0	20	25	15	5

† Total of scientist man-years in turfgrass research, teaching and extension.
‡ Indicate data not reported.

that truly determined how successful various operations would be. Such schools were the place to prepare people interested in fine turf for the education that comes day by day on the golf course or in grounds maintenance.

In those early courses, Professor Dickinson also lectured on good business practices. Individuals with a good understanding of how grass grows, and how to grow it, will have increased confidence and a greater feeling for the importance of their work. Such people are better able to consider other related aspects of their positions, such as good business practices, record keeping, and maintaining a sound professional outlook.

The Stockbridge 2-yr turf major at Massachusetts required a 6-mo on-the-job training period. A satisfactory grade for this activity was necessary for graduation. The objective was to gain experience that would relate to classroom instruction in aboriculture, agricultural engineering, turfgrass science, soil science, entomology, pathology, ornamental horticulture, and business management.

Dickinson leaned away from an active career in turf research and placed emphasis on instruction (Roberts, 1957). He said, "There is and always has been a great need for men who know how to evaluate research information so that it can be put to its best use. Since there is great variation from one location to another, it's not an easy matter to predict how grasses will respond to the specific treatments researchers recommend. The kind of information which will, in the long run, be of most value is that which leads to a better fundamental understanding of the functions of the plant itself. The personal factor, the superintendent for example, is not scientifically controlled. We try to fill the gap between the researcher and the superintendent." Dickinson's philosophy has been perpetuated by faculty Geoffrey Cornish and Eliot Roberts, who were his close associates, and later by Joseph Troll.

About the time that turfgrass instruction was initiated at Massachusetts, Rutgers University, Penn State University, and Michigan State University started programs in this area. In the late 1920s and early 1930s, faculty at these four universities were leaders in turfgrass education and they developed the model other programs successfully followed.

From the late 1930s to the mid-1950s, seven universities recognized the need for courses and specialization in turfgrass science: Ohio State, Kansas State, and Purdue in the Midwest; Washington State and Oregon State in the Northwest; Maryland in the Northeast; and Florida in the Southeast. In the late 1950s and 1960s, more educational opportunities in turf management opened in the east at Cornell University, Clemson University, Virginia Tech, and Lake City Community College in Florida. In the Midwest, Iowa State and Oklahoma State Universities and the Universities of Missouri and Wisconsin made advances in the area of turfgrass teaching. Also, Cal-Poly in Pomona, CA in the Farwest and Mississippi State University in the southern region joined the ranks of leading institutions of turfgrass instruction.

Most Land Grant Universities offer a course or two in turfgrass science and have a faculty advisor for students interested in careers in grounds management. Many offer well-balanced curricula at short course, or 2-yr levels as well as at the 4-yr level. Programs for graduate study in turfgrass science are available at most of these universities. Community colleges in many regions feature programs in ornamental horticulture that provide 2-yr associate degrees in turfgrass science.

VIII. CROP SCIENCE SOCIETY OF AMERICA DIVISION C-5

Interest in turfgrass research and maintenance problems increased in the late 1930s. Dr. Fred V. Grau reported that a concern of agronomists for turfgrass was evident even at the Fourth International Grasslands Tour in Europe in 1937. By the mid-1940s, research was underway at some 20 agricultural experiment stations.

In a letter dated 1 Aug. 1945, to G.G. Pohlman, Secretary-Treasurer of the American Society of Agronomy (ASA), Grau said, "I have hopes that some day there may be a turf section at Society meetings." By December 1945, a petition had been filed with I.J. Johnson, Secretary Special Project Committee for ASA, for consideration by ASA of a plan to establish "an annual Turf Conference as a part of the ASA meeting and a symposium on turf research as a part of the Crop Section program." This petition was supported by 19 letters from turfgrass scientists throughout the country. As a consequence of these requests, ASA established a permanent Turfgrass Committee that functioned actively from 1946 to 1955. Thirty men (Table 1-6) served on this committee. Objectives were to: report progress made in the science of turfgrass culture, serve as a clearinghouse for research information, develop research priorities, and monitor the increasing growth and importance of the turfgrass commodity in the United States.

During this period, F.V. Grau was chairperson. The accomplishments of this group served as strong justification for the development of comprehensive turfgrass research across the country. In addition, a turfgrass research

Table 1-6. Members of the American Society of Agronomy Turfgrass Committee from 1946 to 1955.

Member	Period served	Member	Period served
F.V. Grau†	1946–1955	W.V. Kell	1948–1950
H.B. Musser	1946–1955	C.R. Runyan	1948–1950
M.E. Farnham	1946–1951	W.H. Daniel	1952–1955
H.R. Albrecht	1946	R.M. Hagan	1952–1955
O.J. Noer	1947–1955	J.A. DeFrance	1953–1955
A.E. Rabbitt	1947–1953	R.E. Engel	1953–1955
R.H. Morrish	1947–1952	M.H. Ferguson	1953–1955
H.A.Schoth	1947–1952	G.C. Nutter	1953–1955
H.B. Sprague	1947–1952	H.H. Rampton	1953–1955
E.B. Cale	1947–1950	J.R. Watson	1953–1955
G.H. Jones	1947–1950	B.P. Robinson	1953–1954
G.O. Mott	1947–1950	J.C. Harper	1953 and 1955
C.K. Hallowell	1948–1955	J.H. Boyce	1953
G.W. Burton	1948–1952	V.T. Stoutemyer	1954–1955
K.L. Anderson	1948–1951; 1955	A.G. Law	1955

† Chair, 1946 to 1955.

Table 1-7. Chair of the American Society of Agronomy Turfgrass Research Groups in the crops section from 1946 to 1963.

Section or division	Chair	Year
Section V	F.V. Grau	1946
	H.R. Albrecht	1947
	H.B. Sprague	1948
	H.B. Musser	1949
	G.O. Mott	1950
	R.E. Engel	1951
Division XI	R.R. Davis	1952
	M.H. Ferguson	1953
	W.H. Daniel	1954
	J.R. Watson	1955
	C.G. Wilson	1956
	G.C. Nutter	1957
	W.W. Huffine	1958
	H.B. Musser	1959
	R.E. Engle	1960
	V.B. Youngner	1961
	R.R. Davis	1962
	F.V. Juska	1963
Division C-5		
Turf section—Applied Agronomy	F.V. Grau	1947
	F.V. Grau	1948
	F.V. Grau	1949
	G.W. Burton	1950
	C.K. Hallowell	1951

section (V) was set up to feature research reports. An active program was supported from 1946 to 1951, when a reorganization changed the name to Division XI. This division functioned from 1952 to 1963 when another reorganization changed the name to Division C-5, in the Crop Science Society of America (CSSA).

Also, in the mid-1940s, ASA set up a practical turf session in the Applied Division. Appropriate reports were presented at this session from 1947 to 1951 when a reorganization placed emphasis on Land Use and Management (Division XIV). This division is designated now as A-2 in ASA. Current turfgrass research reports are presented at sessions of Division C-5 (CSSA), Division A-2 (ASA), and several other divisions of CSSA, ASA, and SSSA.

The 1946 action by ASA established a direct link between the leading agronomic science organization in the USA and the various groups concerned with applied turf management. These included associations of turf managers as well as groups representing business and commerce. Furthermore, scientists from public and private sectors were encouraged to meet for the purpose of integrating research activities and harmonizing the future development of a comprehensive national turf program. Leaders in the turf field have been able to maintain direct contact with one another through membership in ASA and CSSA. Chairpersons of the turfgrass science research groups are listed in Table 1-7 and division chairpersons, ASA Fellows, and numbers of papers presented each year are presented in Table 1-8.

Table 1-8. American Society of Agronomy (ASA) and Crop Science Society of America (CSSA) turfgrass section or division chair, ASA Representatives, ASA and CSSA Fellows, and number of papers presented annually.

Year	No. of papers presented	Chair	ASA representative	Div. members elected as fellows
1941	--	--	--	H.B. Sprague, ASA
1946	6	F.V. Grau	--	
1947	16	H.R. Albrecht	--	
1948	17	H.B. Sprague	--	
1949	12	H.B. Musser	--	G.W. Burton, ASA
1950	10	G.O. Mott	--	
1951	7	R.E. Engel	--	H.R. Albrecht, ASA
1952	7	R.R. Davis	--	
1953	6	M.H. Ferguson	--	R. Blaser, ASA
1954	6	W.H. Daniel	--	
1955	15	J.R. Watson	--	G.O. Mott, ASA
1956	16	C.G. Wilson	--	
1957	16	G.C. Nutter	--	
1958	16	W.W. Huffine	--	D.G. Sturkie, ASA
1959	22	H.B. Musser	--	
1960	17	R.E. Engel	--	
1961	11	V.B. Youngner	E.C. Roberts	
1962	22	R.R. Davis	E.C. Roberts	
1963	14	F.V. Juska	E.C. Roberts	W.H. Daniel, ASA A.A. Hanson, ASA
1964	36	N.R. Goetze	W.H. Daniel	
1965	24	E.C. Roberts	W.H. Daniel	
1966	25	J.B. Beard	W.H. Daniel	E. Holt, ASA F.V. Juska, ASA
1967	32	C.Y. Ward	R.R. Davis	R.R. Davis, ASA K. Payne, ASA
1968	34	J.A. Simmons	R.R. Davis	V.B. Youngner, ASA
1969	25	R.E. Schmidt	R.R. Davis	R.E. Engle, ASA F.V. Grau, ASA W.W. Huffine, ASA C.Y. Ward, ASA
1970	25	W.B. Gilbert	J.B. Beard	
1971	33	G.C. Horn	J.B. Beard	J.B. Beard, ASA E.C. Roberts, ASA
1972	29	R.W. Miller	J.B. Beard	
1973	33	P.E. Rieke	W.W. Huffine	
1974	41	L.M. Callahan	W.W. Huffine	
1975	38	J.F. Shoulders	W.W. Huffine	
1976	40	A.E. Dudeck	K. Payne	
1977	31	J.H. Dunn	K. Payne	J.F. Shoulders, ASA
1978	32	W.R. Kneebone	K. Payne	
1979	45	A.J. Powell	P.E. Rieke	J.R. Watson, ASA L. Wise, ASA
1980	41	D.B. White	P.E. Rieke	A. Baltensperger, ASA
1981	40	A.J. Turgeon	P.E. Rieke	
1982	44	R.W. Duell	J.H. Dunn	
1983	56	R.C. Shearman	J.H. Dunn	
1984	59	D.P. Martin	J.H. Dunn	C.R. Funk, ASA

(continued on next page)

Table 1-8. Continued.

Year	No. of papers presented	Chair	ASA representative	Div. members elected as fellows
1985	72	R.N. Carrow	A.E. Dudeck	†
1986	65	D.V. Waddington	A.E. Dudeck	D.V. Waddington, ASA
				P.E. Rieke, CSSA
				R.E. Schmidt, CSSA
1987	69	B.J. Johnson	A.E. Dudeck	
1988	81	T. Riordan	R.C. Shearman	A.J. Turgeon, ASA
				R.C. Shearman, CSSA
				B.J. Johnson, CSSA
1989	107	N.E. Christians	R.C. Shearman	R.C. Shearman, ASA
				B.J. Johnson, ASA
				A.L. Turgeon, CSSA
1990		T.L. Watschke	R.C. Shearman	

† In 1985, all living previously elected ASA Fellows listed above were elected Fellows of the Crop Society of America.
Other ASA and CSSA Honors and Awards to C-5 Members:
  Agronomic Service Award: 1973, W.H. Daniel; 1977, J.R. Watson.
  ASA President: 1914, C.V. Piper; 1962, G.W. Burton; 1970, R.E. Blaser; 1990, A.A. Baltensperger.
  CSSA President: 1973, R.R. Davis; 1986, J.B. Beard
  Fred V. Grau Turfgrass Science Award: 1987, J.R. Watson; 1988, J.B. Beard; 1989, J.J. Murray.

IX. INTERNATIONAL TURFGRASS SOCIETY

The basis for establishing an International Turfgrass Research Conference was developed in the fall of 1966 when Bjarne Langvad of Sweden visited J.B. Beard in East Lansing, MI. Such a conference was needed to facilitate the international exchange of information on turfgrass science. Researchers and educators were to participate. The objective was to have a meeting with a least 20 turf specialists attending. The first International Conference was held in 1969 in Harrogate, England. There were 83 registered attendees, representing 13 countries and 99 papers. As a result of the success of this conference, The International Turfgrass Society was established. Its objective was to foster the advancement of all aspects of turfgrass science.

The second international conference was held in 1973 at Virginia Polytechnic Institute and State University in the USA. There were 247 registrants, representing 15 countries and 80 papers. The third conference was held in 1977 in Munich, Germany with 229 registrants from 17 countries, and 95 papers. The fourth conference was held at the Ontario Agricultural College, University of Guelph in Ontario, Canada. There were 239 registrants from 21 countries and 81 papers. The fifth conference was held in 1985 in Avignon, France. There were 94 papers. The sixth conference was held in 1989 in Tokyo, Japan with 829 registrants from 17 countries, and 99 papers. Members of the International Turfgrass Society Executive Committee and Editors of Research Conference Proceedings are presented in Table 1-9.

Table 1-9. Executive committee members and conference proceedings editors serving the International Turfgrass Society.

Executive committee	First conference (1969)	Second conference (1973)
President	J.B. Beard, USA	R.R. Davis, USA
Vice president	B. Langvad, Sweden	B. Langvad, Sweden
Secretary	J.R. Escritt, England	J.R. Escritt, England
Past president	--	J.B. Beard, USA
Directors	--	W.H. Daniel, USA
		C.M. Switzer, Canada
		J.P. van der Horst, Germany
Treasurer	J.R. Watson, USA	R.E. Schmidt, USA
Historian	--	--
Editor conference proceedings	J.R. Escritt, England	E.C. Roberts, USA

	Third conference (1977)	Fourth conference (1981)
President	P. Boeker, Germany	C.M. Switzer, Canada
Vice president	J.P. van der Horst, Netherlands	H. Vos, Netherlands
Secretary	F.B. Ledeboer, USA	F.B. Ledeboer, USA
Past president	R.R. Davis, USA	P. Boeker, Germany
Directors	R.E. Engle, USA	W.A. Adams, United Kingdom
	K. Ehara, Japan	K. Ehara, Japan
	A.C. Ferguson, Canada	W.W. Huffine, USA
	R.L. Morris, United Kingdom	P. Mansat, France
	W. Skirde, Germany	D.K. Taylor, Canada
Treasurer	R.E. Schmidt, USA	R.E. Schmidt, USA
Historian	J.B. Beard, USA	J.B. Beard, USA
Editor conference proceedings	J.B. Beard, USA	R.W. Sheard, Canada

	Fifth conference (1985)	Sixth conference (1989)
President	P. Mansat, France	Y. Maki, Japan
Vice president	H. Vos, Netherlands	W.A. Adams, United Kingdom
Secretary	J.F. Shoulders, USA	J.F. Shoulders, USA
Past president	C.M. Switzer, Canada	P. Mansat, France
Directors	W.A. Adams, United Kingdom	J.R. Watson, USA
	Y. Maki, Japan	F. Lemaire, France
	T.R. Siviour, Australia	A. van Wijk, Netherlands
	R.W. Sheard, Canada	P. McMaugh, Australia
	J.L. Watson, USA	
Treasurer	R.E. Schmidt, USA	R.E. Schmidt, USA
Historian	J.B. Beard, USA	J.B. Beard, USA
Editor conference proceedings	F. Lemaire, France	H. Takatoh, Japan

	Seventh conference (1993)	
President	J.R. Watson, USA	
Vice president	W.A. Adams, United Kingdom	
Secretary	J. Hall, USA	
Past president	Y. Maki, Japan	
Directors	F. Lemaire, France	
	A. van Wijk, Netherlands	
	P. McMaugh, Australia	
	W. Meyer, USA	
	H. Yanagi, Japan	
Treasurer	R.E. Schmidt, USA	
Historian	J.B. Beard, USA	
Editor conference proceedings	--	

X. TURFGRASS ASSOCIATIONS, FOUNDATIONS, INSTITUTES, AND COUNCILS

Of major importance to the advancement of the turfgrass industry during the past 60 yr has been the development of linkages between academic programs and research and the business leaders and turf managers who have provided the products and demonstrated the practices that have resulted in high-quality sports and landscape turf. Many turfgrass associations, foundations, institutes, and councils have contributed to this process. Four of these serve to illustrate accomplishments in this area.

A. O. J. Noer Turfgrass Research Foundation

In recognition of a long and distinguished career as agronomist for the Milwaukee Sewerage Commission, O.J. Noer was honored by the creation of a turfgrass research foundation bearing his name. Funds contributed by Milorganite distributers across the country have been used to sponsor research on turf problems of concern to golf course superintendents and turf managers across the USA.

B. Musser International Turfgrass Foundation

Upon Professor H.B. Musser's death, a memorial to this Pennsylvania State University turfgrass pioneer, educator, and scientist was established. The foundation bearing his name was dedicated to advance turfgrass science through graduate education. Funding from a variety of sources has been used to help sponsor turfgrass research at land grant universities throughout the country.

C. Better Lawn and Turf Institute

The Better Lawn and Turf Institute was formed in 1955 by a group of turfgrass seedsmen as a nonprofit business league. Objectives were to evaluate research data worldwide and formulate recommendations for improved cultural practices on lawns and sports turf. Release of lawn-related information to other communicators (garden writers, editors, radio and television graden shows, county agents, and other horticultural consultants) helps provide a resource of technically accurate copy for public education. Robert Schery, founder of the Institute, directed this information service for more than 30 yr.

D. United States Golf Association Green Section

The USGA in 1945 obtained the services of its first Green Section Agronomist and Director. At that time, the USDA at Beltsville, MD, had a collaborative agreement with the USGA. F.V. Grau, having completed 10 yr as extension turfgrass specialist at Pennsylvania State University, provided the necessary leadership to develop both research and education programs. The USGA has distinguished itself in service and education to member golf clubs by staffing highly qualified turf agronomists who interpret research findings for the production of high-quality golf course turfs.

In addition, turfgrass associations and councils at state and regional levels have in recent years provided leadership in obtaining funding for turf research of local importance. The sponsorship of turf conferences and trade shows, in which various products are exhibited, has become a major means for generating needed revenue for this purpose. Close liaison with the land grant university system has been important for the success of these organizations. They also function as a means for recognizing turf managers and research scientists and educators. Some funds are put to good use in the development of professionalism within the sponsoring organization, including the granting of scholarships to worthy students.

Trade shows provide a favorable setting for business transactions, and for turf managers to view latest developments in the industry by bringing together the attendees and distributors of products and services. Also, many turf field days feature trade shows as a means of bringing turfgrass science and practice closer together. As early as 1936, the University of Massahcusetts staged exhibits of turf maintenance equipment in its field house. Now the Golf Course Superintendents Association of America and other national superintendents and managers associations use the best convention and show facilities available for their annual meetings. Each year more than 50 major state turf conferences and trade shows are held in the USA and Canada. Usually, only Alaska, Arkansas, Delaware, Montana, Nevada, North Dakota, Rhode Island, Utah, Vermont, and West Virginia have not listed state events. In addition, more than 12 regional and national organizations schedule turfgrass conferences and shows, usually at different locations each year.

The following state, regional, and national conferences and shows are listed regularly in the trade journals:

1. State Conferences and Trade Shows

Alabama Turfgrass Association Turf Conference
Arizona Turf and Landscape Conference and Trade Exhibit
California Professional Turf and Landscape Exposition
  • Southern Turfgrass Council Annual Turf and Landscape Institute
  • Turfgrass/Landscape Equipment and Materials Educational Exposition
Colorado—Rocky Mountain Turfgrass Conference
Connecticut—Professional Turf and Landscape Conference
Florida Turf-Grass Association Annual Conference and Show
Georgia Annual Turfgrass Conference
  • Southeastern Turfgrass Annual Conference
Hawaii Turfgrass Conference
Indiana—Midwest Turf Conference
Iowa Turfgrass Conference
Kansas—Central Plains Turfgrass Foundation Conference

Kentucky Turfgrass Conference
Louisiana Turfgrass Association Annual Conference and Short Course
Maine Winter Turf Conference
Maryland Turfgrass Council Annual Meeting
Massachusetts Turfgrass Conference and Industrial Show
Michigan Turfgrass Conference
Minnesota—Horticultural Industries Conference and Turfgrass Short Course
Mississippi Turfgrass Association Annual Convention
  • Turfgrass Association Short Course
Missouri Lawn and Turf Conference
Nebraska Turfgrass Conference and Trade Show
New Brunswick (Canada) Turf Seminar
New Hampshire Turfgrass Conference
New Jersey Turfgrass Expo
New Mexico—Southwest Turfgrass Conference
New York Professional Turf and Landscape Conference
  • Professional Turf and Plant Conference
  • State Turfgrass Association Conference and Trade Show
North Carolina Annual Turfgrass Conference
Ohio Turfgrass Foundation Annual Meeting
Oklahoma Turf Conference
Ontario (Canada) Annual Landscape Congress
Pennsylvania—Capital Area Turf School
  • Turf and Grounds Maintenance School
  • Eastern Pennsylvania Turf Conference and Trade Show
  • Western Pennsylvania Turf Conference and Trade Show
  • Penn State Golf Turf Conference
South Carolina—Clemson Annual Turfgrass Conference
South Dakota Turfgrass Conference
Tennessee Turfgrass Conference
Texas Turfgrass Conference
Virginia Turfgrass Conference and Trade Show
Wisconsin—Golf Turf Symposium
  • Green Industry Conference
  • Turfgrass Association Annual Meeting
  • University of Wisconsin Turfgrass Conference
Wyoming Turf Conference

2. Regional, National, and International Conferences and Trade Shows

Agri-Turf Irrigation Exposition and Conference
American Society of Golf Course Architects Annual Meeting
American Sod Producers Association Midwinter Conference
  • Summer Conference
Associated Landscape Contractors of America Annual Meeting and Trade
    Exhibit
Canadian Turfgrass Conference and Show

Golf Course Association Annual Conference
Golf Course Builders of America
Golf Course Superintendents Association of America International Turfgrass
    Conference and Show
National Institute on Park and Grounds Management
National Institute on Park and Grounds Management Athletic Turf Manage-
    ment Seminar
North Central Regional Turfgrass Conference and Show
Northwest Turfgrass Conference
Professional Grounds Management Society Annual Conference and Trade
    Show
Professional Lawn Care Association of America Annual Conference and
    Show
Sports Turf Managers Association Conference
Southern Turfgrass Conference

XI. TURFGRASS SCIENCE TEXTS

One of the measures of technical validity within any field of endeavor is the quality of the books published on the subject. Texts concerned with turfgrass science, grounds management and related topics are listed in Table 1-10. Starting in 1931 with Professor Dickinson's book entitled *The Lawn*, considerable progress has been made. Following *Dawson's Practical Lawncraft* in 1939, the first turf science text published in the USA was *Turf Management* by Professor Musser of Penn State University. This release in 1950 coincided with a new emphasis on turfgrass science that followed World War II.

As research findings were published in scientific journals, increasing need was realized for texts that further amplified this new information. Practical interpretations were developed that have helped in the utilization of a wealth of research results. These texts have been of great value in helping to make Turfgrass Management courses popular with students across the USA and Canada.

The *Turfgrass Science* Monograph (1969) has been the most popular of the monograph publications of ASA. By September 1988, 15 953 copies had been sold.

XII. SUMMARY

The history of turfgrass science provides worthwhile insight concerning the discovery of a new technology and the extension of this information in practical turf management. In many ways, it illustrates the philosophy of research and extension programming to meet needs of humankind on a national level. From this start, even international programs have developed and become strengthened.

Table 1–10. Turfgrass science texts.

Dickinson, L.S. 1931. The lawn. Orange Judd Publ. Co., New York.

Dawson, R.B. 1939. Dawson's practical lawncraft. Crosby Lockwood Staples and Son, London (Revisions: 1945, 1947, 1949, 1954, 1959, 1968, 1977 [revision by R. Hawthorn].)

Musser, H.B. 1950. Turf management. McGraw-Hill Book Co., New York. (Second edition, 1962.)

Conover, H.S. 1953. Grounds maintenance handbook. Tennessee Valley Authority. (Second edition: 1958 by F.W. Dodge Corp., New York.)

Schery, R.W. 1961. The lawn book. Macmillan Publ. Co., New York. (Revised in 1973 as A perfect lawn—The easy way.)

Wise, L.N. 1961. The lawn book. Bowen Press, Decatur, GA.

Greenfield, I. 1962. Turf culture. Leonard Hill, London.

Couch, H.B. 1962. Diseases of turfgrasses. Reinhold Publ. Corp., New York.

Hanson, A.A., and F.V. Juska (ed.). 1969. Turfgrass science. Agron. Monogr. 14, ASA, Madison, WI.

Vengris, J. 1969. Lawns: Basic factors, construction and maintenance of fine turf areas. Thomson Publ., Fresno, CA (Third edition, 1982. J. Vengris and W. Torello.)

Sprague, H.B. 1970. Turf management handbook. The Interstate Printers and Publ., Danville, IL. (Second edition, 1976.)

Madison, J.H. 1971. Practical turfgrass management. Van Nostrand Reinhold Co., New York.

Madison, J.H. 1971. Principles of turfgrass culture. Van Nostrand Reinhold Co., New York.

Beard, J.B. 1973. Turfgrass science and culture. Prentice-Hall, Englewood Cliffs, NJ.

Couch, H.B. 1973. Diseases of turfgrasses. Robert E. Kreiger Publ. Co., Huntingdon, NY.

Schery, R.W. 1976. Lawn keeping. Prentice-Hall, Englewood Cliffs, NJ.

Sanders, P.O. 1977. Microscopic identification of common turfgrass pathogens, A turf managers guide. Pennsylvania Turf Counc., Bellefonte, PA.

Beard, J.B., J.M. DiPaola, D. Johns, Jr., and K.J. Karnok. 1979. Introduction to turfgrass science and culture: Laboratory exercises. Burgess Publ. Co., Minneapolis.

Daniel, W.H., and R.P. Freeborg. 1979. Turf managers' handbook. Harvest Publ. Co., Cleveland, OH. (Second edition, 1987.)

Turgeon, A.J. 1980. Turfgrass management. Reston Publ. Co., Reston, VA. (Revised, 1985.)

Niemczyk, H.D. 1981. Destructive turf insects. HDN Publ., Wooster, OH.

Vargas, J.M., Jr. 1981. Management of turfgrass diseases. Burgess Publ. Co., Minneapolis.

Beard, J.B. 1982. Turfgrass management for golf courses. Burgess Publ. Co., Minneapolis.

Shetler, D.J., P.R. Heller, and P.D. Irish. 1983. Turfgrass insect and mite manual. Pennsylvania Turfgrass Counc., Bellefonte, PA. (Revised, 1988.)

Smiley, R.W. (ed.). 1983. Compendium of turfgrass diseases. Am. Phytopathol. Soc., St. Paul.

Emmons, R.D. 1984. Turfgrass science and management. Delmar Publ., Albany, NY.

Shurtleff, M.C., T.W. Fermanian, and R. Randell. 1987. Controlling turfgrass pests. Prentice-Hall, Englewood Cliffs, NJ.

Tashiro, H. 1987. Turfgrass insects of the United States and Canada. Cornell Univ. Press, Ithaca, NY.

Welterlen, M.S. 1987. Laboratory manual for turfgrass management. Prentice-Hall, Englewood Cliffs, NJ.

Decker, H.F., and J.M. Decker. 1988. Lawn care—A handbook for professionals. Prentice Hall, Englewood Cliffs, NJ.

Continuing records of advances in turfgrass science are being kept by CSSA Division C-5 and by the International Turfgrass Society. The Lawn Institute maintains files on lawns and sports turf history and provides insights from time to time. The January 1990 issue of *Harvests* quarterly newsletter was released as a special report on the history of lawns. The value of understanding where we've been and how we reached our current status is well recognized in charting future progress.

REFERENCES

Beard, J.B. 1979. Turfgrass research—Present and future. p. 11–16. *In* Post 1976 Turfgrass Industry challenges in research, teaching and continuing education. Bicentennial Symp. C-5 Div. CSSA and A-2 Div. ASA, Houston, TX. November 1976. Turfgrass Div. (C-5), CSSA, Madison, WI.

Dawson, R.B. 1949. Practical lawn craft. Crosby Lockwood and Son, London.

Falk, J.H. 1977. The Frenetic life forms that flourish in suburban lawns. Smithsonian (April) 8:90–96.

Goethe, C.M. 1955. Garden philosopher. The Keystone Press, Sacramento, CA.

Harlan, J.R. 1956. Theory and dynamics of grassland agriculture. D. Van Nostrand Co., Princeton, NJ.

MacKay, A.I. 1950. Farming and gardening in the bible. Rodale Press, Emmaus, PA.

Malleson, G.B. 1891. Rulers of India. Akbar Oxford at the Clarendon Press.

Malone, C.B. 1934. History of the Peking summer palaces under the Ch'ing Dynasty. Illinois Studies Social Sci. Vol. XIX nos. 1–2. Univ. of Illinois, Champaign.

Monro, J.P. 1953. Bowls encycloapeadia. Wilke and Co. Ltd., Melbourne, Australia.

Olcott, J.B. 1890. Annual report. Connecticut Agric. Exp. Stn.

Roberts, E.C. 1956. Course in turf management marks 30th year. The Golf Course Reporter. (September–October) 24(7):20, 21, 24, 25, and 27.

Roberts, E.C. 1957. Dickinson taught superintendents how to use tools of research. Golfdom (February) 1957:30–31, 70.

Rohde, E.S. 1927. Garden-craft in the bible. Herbert Jenkins, London.

Stites, R.S. 1940. The arts and man. McGraw-Hill Book Co., New York.

Wehner, D., and J. Murray. 1987. Turfgrass research in the United States. ASPA Turf Newsl. (November–December) 1987:6–8.

Wilber, D.H. 1962. Persian gardens and garden pavilions. Charles E. Tuttle Co., Tokyo, Japan.

Zimmerman, J.E. 1964. Dictionary of classical mythology. Harper and Row Publ., New York.

2

The Turfgrass Industry

JAMES R. WATSON

The Toro Company
Minneapolis, Minnesota

HOWARD E. KAERWER

12800 Gerard Drive
Eden Prairie, Minnesota

DAVID P. MARTIN

ChemLawn Services Corporation
Columbus, Ohio

Turfgrass is used in many different ways and under many different conditions. As a result, the multi-billion dollar industry is many-faceted, and encompasses diverse facilities and services. Personnel range from production workers to specialized individuals with skills in many academic disciplines. They are employed at all levels and in all aspects of the industry.

Nutter (1965) suggested that by definition, the *turfgrass industry* encompasses the production and maintenance of specialized grasses and other ground covers required in the development and management of facilities for utility, beautification, and recreation. He further suggested that the industry involves turfgrass science and technology, business management, manpower development, and the manufacturing and marketing of turfgrass products and services.

Turfgrass plays a major role in our daily life and in our pursuit of happiness. Turfgrass, from a beautification standpoint, provides a canvas for landscaped areas contributing to aesthetic appeal and adding to economic value. Recreational facilities include an array of sports fields, golf courses, parks, and lawns. They provide the environment for athletic endeavors, exercise and physical conditioning, therapeutic diversion, and healthful outlets for a growing population. Turfgrass, grown primarily for utility turf, provides functional value including dust control, erosion control, and glare reduction, and, thus can serve as a safety factor on air fields and highway rights-of-way (DiPaola et al., 1986). Facilities such as golf courses, parks, playgrounds, and sports fields serve all three functions—beautification, recreation, and utility—and most provide at least two of the major functions. Collectively, turfgrass facility development, maintenance, and utilization represent a major

Copyright © 1992 ASA-CSSA-SSSA, 677 S. Segoe Rd., Madison, WI 53711, USA. *Turfgrass—* Agronomy Monograph no. 32.

factor in our way of life and contribute substantially to the economic and aesthetic values of personal property and to our communities.

The underlying theme for the turfgrass industry emphasizes "facilities for people" rather than the earlier agronomic concept that envisioned turf production as the major objective. Use and appearance are prime considerations for turfgrass. To best serve a particular function, the turf should be, first, suitable for the use for which it is intended; and secondly, aesthetically appealing. Emphasis on use and appearance concepts relates production and maintenance of turfgrasses to their roles in the economy. This approach might be called the *facility concept* (Nutter & Watson, 1969).

This facility concept not only applies to the people who use the turfgrass facility but also to those who are indirectly exposed to it. For example, professional and amateur sports functions may draw thousands of spectators to a site and millions more people observe these events and facilities through the medium of television. Golf courses, parks, and similar land areas provide visual pleasure (aesthetic appeal) to passers-by as well as to those using the facility.

There also is increasing emphasis on the conditioning and grooming of turfgrass for competitive reasons, commercial appeal, and public relations. Resorts, commercial buildings, and office and apartment complexes use well-groomed turfgrass and attractively landscaped grounds as sales tools. Golf courses compete for player appeal on the basis of the turf condition and grooming. The well-groomed residential lawn is an ever-increasing mark of status.

Thus, the turfgrass industry is seen as an indispensable service industry revolving around specialized grasses and ground covers for the health, welfare, and general betterment of an ever-growing population. To some, however, turfgrass remains an industry based on luxury and affluence. Turfed areas that reduce toxic residuals, moderate temperature extremes, control erosion, and provide safe playing conditions, physical conditioning, recreational diversion from mental stress, and the healthy use of leisure time are not luxuries. They are essential to our lifestyle. These are the precepts upon which the turfgrass industry builds and services its facilities (Nutter & Watson, 1969).

I. EVOLUTION AND DEVELOPMENT

A particular industry may be defined as the accumulative effect of systematic and distinct endeavor in a recognized craft or art, especially one that employs several people, requires capital, and engages in profit-making enterprises. Turfgrass maintenance and utilization in its entirety, or as any of its several segments, including manufacturers of supplies, materials, and equipment, may be described as an industry.

The turfgrass industry is a close-knit group of academic, commercial, professional, managerial, and administrative segments. Most segments are highly specialized and articulate their needs to each other for support and development of new and innovative products, programs, and procedures. Turfgrass managers continually seek answers to the pressures arising from the expanding and intensive use of turfgrass facilities dedicated to a growing and more demanding populace. Both academic and commercial organizations have responded to these needs and have provided the technical and personnel support required to produce high-quality, use-directed turfgrass with substantial economic value.

A. Historical

The origin of the turfgrass industry closely parallels the history of turf usage, particularly golf. While the time or date for the care and management of turfgrass facilities or the manufacture of any specific turfgrass product cannot be fixed with any degree of accuracy, it could be argued that the seeds of a fledgling turfgrass equipment manufacturing industry began to grow when Edwin Budding of Stroud, Gloucestershire, England invented and patented the first reel-type lawn mower in 1830 (Beard, 1973, 1982). Some people may believe that this segment really had its beginnings when Ransomes began production of Budding's mower in 1832. Others may claim that the golf industry was launched in 1618 when the first feather ball was invented; or in 1848 when the gutta percha ball was developed; or in 1898 when the modern golf ball was patented by Coburn Haskell (Ward-Thomas et al., 1976). Excellent chronological reviews of the history and development of golf as a game, golf architects and their courses, evolution of the golf ball and golf clubs, turf research locations and workers, evolution and current role of the controlling associations, and early equipment use and practices have been presented by Beard (1982, p. 1-26), Cornish and Whitten (1981), Huffine and Grau (1969), Nutter and Watson (1969), and Ward-Thomas et al. (1976). In general, the turfgrass industry evolved slowly and has grown steadily with only temporary interruptions (Beard, 1982; Watson, 1984). The industry, as we know it today, began its expansion in the early 1950s.

Historically, golf course development and maintenance has set the pace for the growth of the turfgrass industry. Technical advances and industrial development within the turfgrass industry are due, in large part, to the manufacture, distribution, and servicing of products associated with the maintenance of golf courses. Turfgrass science, as an academic discipline, evolved by borrowing from other longer established, basic sciences. Likewise, the first equipment and products used in turf maintenance were borrowed from the farm; or, as in the case of the reel mower, adapted from the carpet industry. After hand scythes and cradles were abandoned to horse-drawn machines, the sickle bar mower was brought from the hay field to mow large turf areas, parks, and golf courses. The first grasses planted on turf facilities were those common to local pastures. There were no specialty fertilizers, only barnyard manures, natural compost, guano, fish and bone products, and certain early chemical fertilizers such as ammonium salts and nitrate of soda (a natural product from Chile). The only weed control in those early days was hand weeding, and irrigation was nonexistent. These early practices seem a long way removed from the specialized turfgrass cultivars, complex chemicals, specialized hydraulically operated mowing equipment, and sophisticated, computer-controlled automatic irrigation systems used in turfgrass management today.

Although golf courses have led the development of the turfgrass industry, maintenance of residential and commercial lawns has had the most accelerated growth of any segment of the industry in recent years. Other segments, in particular sports fields, also have continued to expand in number, job opportunities, size of budgets, and the technical and professional qualifications of their managers.

The future progress, especially in the reduction of maintenance costs, probably will come from new equipment currently under development, from new grasses, and from new pesticides and improved fertilizers. The impetus for change, however, will come from expectations and standards of maintenance expected and demanded by the public (users and spectators) as interpreted through the turf facility manager. The socio-economic values of turfgrass for a more organized and knowledgeable society have influenced and will continue to influence the direction of the turfgrass industry. Further, better understanding of the positive environmental values of turfgrass plus societal concerns about nonreplaceable resources, parental concern about safety, and requirements for sports activities will influence the industry.

B. Institutional Role in Education and Research

The need for specialized training and for research activities directed toward solving the increasing number of unique problems associated with turfgrass and its use became apparent as the growth of turfgrass facilities accelerated. Academic training in basic biology, botany, chemistry, genetics, and plant physiology as well as in the applied sciences of horticulture, agronomy, entomology, plant pathology, plant breeding, and others provided background for the initial educational thrust. Research information borrowed from closely related disciplines and interpreted for turfgrass helped to solve the less complex problems. research was and is spurred by the end user as well as the facility manager. Initially, golf course superintendents and commercial organizations recognized the need for academic support of their endeavors. This recognition focused attention on specific turfgrass problems affecting the industry. This effort evolved prior to specific college curricula directed toward turfgrass education and research. The need for more accurate information and academic programs to provide the research and teaching necessary to support industry requirements developed rapidly during the late 1940s and early 1950s. Currently, they are the key binding agent to efficient advancement of turfgrass utilization. The turfgrass industry continues to support academic programs for its own good and the welfare of the public, which benefits from these activities.

1. Research.

Selection of superior grasses for a particular turfgrass application was launched soon after the turn of the century. Early selections were made by choosing individual plants that displayed desirable characteristics. Some of the early plots were those established in 1860 at Michigan State University (Beard, 1982) and at the Rhose Island experimental station in 1890 by J. B. Alcott. The first federally (USA) appropriated funds to support turfgrass research were granted in 1901. Internationally, C. M. Murray, of Capetown, South Africa, established test plots in 1906. The first turfgrass research station was established in 1929 at the St. Ives Estate, Bingley, Yorkshire under the direction of R. B. Dawson. John Escritt succeeded Dawson as director and in the late 1970s, upon Escritt's retirement, Peter Hayes became director. Test plots were established in 1932 and 1935, in New Zealand and Australia, respectively (Beard, 1982; Watson, 1984).

Joseph Valentine, superintendent of Merion Cricket Club in Philadelphia, Marshall Farnham, superintendent of Philadelphia Country Club, and others prevailed upon Ralph D. Hetzel, president of The Pennsylvania State College to provide funds for support of turfgrass research in 1928. Professor H. B. Musser, a legume breeder, was directed to initiate the turfgrass research activity (J.M. Duich, 1987, personal communication). He was succeeded by J. M. Duich in 1959. Penn State continues to have one of the larger research facilities devoted to turfgrass research. Other early programs were located at the University of Massachusetts, Michigan State University, Purdue University, University of Florida, Texas A&M University, Rutgers, and at the University of California, Los Angeles.

Glen Burton, a forage and legume breeder in the south, recognized the need for improved bermudagrasses for turfgrass purposes. He began to breed and select superior fine-leafed bermudagrasses for turf in the late 1940s and early 1950s. He effected crosses between *Cynodon transvaalensis* Burtt-Davy and *C. dactylon* (L.) Pers. The first of these hybrids was released as 'Tiflawn' (No. 57) and 'Tiffine' (No. 127) in the early 1950s. These were followed by 'Tifgreen' (No. 328), 'Tifway' (No. 419), and 'Tifdwarf'. The latter cultivar was a natural cross selected from a green on the Florence, South Carolina Country Club and brought to Tifton by J. B. Moncrief, a U. S. Golf Association (USGA) Green Section agronomist assigned to the Southeast.

By the mid- to late 1960s, most of the states were conducting some type of turfgrass research. Although public support of turf research is declining today, major efforts by the private sector continue to provide funding. A number of companies and foundations support turfgrass research projects. And, in 1982 the USGA launched a 10-yr program to support turfgrass research at land grand universities. This program is specifically directed toward reduction in water use and maintenance costs. The program is guided by William Bengeyfield who chairs a research committee composed of Paul Rieke, Victor Gibeault, James Watson, Charles Smith, Howard Kaerwer, Tom Burton, and Jerry Faubel. Marvin Ferguson and James Moncrief also served on the committee prior to their deaths. James Prusa, former director of education for the Golf Course Superintendents Association of America (GCSAA) served until 1987.

2. Education

The first vocational course directed toward specialized training in turfgrass management was the Stockbridge Winter School, founded in 1927 at the University of Massachusetts under the direction of L. S. Dickinson. The Winter course is a concentrated 56 d vocational-type course. Its success, then and now, is evidenced by the large percentage of its graduates who became leaders, especially in golf course management. Consistent academic leadership has been a major factor contributing to the success of this course and the 2-yr program established later at the University of Massachusetts. E. C. Roberts succeeded Dickinson; he, in turn was followed by J. Troll who retired in 1986 and was succeeded by R. J. Cooper.

In 1957, 2-yr technical turfgrass courses were established at Penn State under the direction of H. B. Musser and J. Duich; at Michigan State under J. King, J. B. Beard, and K. T. Payne in 1967; and, at Lake City, FL under G. Nutter and J. Chessman. By the 1960s, numerous vocational and technical institutes were being established across the USA to fill a gap for advanced technical training at a level between high school and college curriculums. These schools, along with the 4-yr and graduate colleges and universities have supplied the qualified, well-trained manpower required for the explosive growth of turf facilities following World War II and they continue to do so today.

By the late 1940s, early 1950s, 4-yr and graduate curricula directed toward academically trained scholars in turfgrass science were being offered by a number of land grant universities including Penn State, Cornell, Michigan State, Purdue, Texas A&M, Rutgers, and the University of Rhode Island.

The impetus for graduate programs during this early period came primarily from the USGA Green Section. This organization, under the direction of F. V. Grau, provided 3-yr fellowships for a number of current leaders in the turfgrass field. Among them were W. Daniel, J. Duich, J. Harper, G. Nutter, R. Schmidt, and J. Watson. Today, a number of universities offer 4-yr and graduate courses specifically designed to train turfgrass scientists.

C. Commercial Role in Education and Research

The commercial segments of the turfgrass industry have often cooperated with university personnel to establish, maintain, and improve teaching and research efforts at universities and vocational-technical institutes across the country. In addition, their research efforts and advice have aided in focusing educational and technical efforts toward the needs of the industry. Through their business and technical associations, as well as individual effort, members of this segment of the industry provide a collective front for lobbying and supporting the needs of the academic institutions. Funding and, perhaps more importantly, the incentives to encourage researchers and scholars to explore the basic and applied sciences such as genetics, turfgrass breeding, physiology, pathology, entomology, chemistry, engineering, and business management have been provided by commercial organizations. Grants from associations, corporations, golf and sports clubs, and from individuals have raised substantial financial support for university research and teaching programs. They also have provided resources for scholarships, work-study programs, and part-time employment. Students not only receive financial support but also have an opportunity to explore the practical and applied aspects of the turfgrass industry.

Industry efforts directed toward keeping public and government bodies informed of the practical and aesthetic value of turfgrass to society and the environment provide recognition for the contributions of turfgrass to our lifestyle and the economic value of our communities. The industry as well as individuals have benefited through the efforts of the academic institutions. Many students from turfgrass programs at universities and vocational-technical institutions have entered the industry and are active in all segments and levels.

The commercial segment of the turfgrass industry has had a major impact on the continuing education of individuals associated with allied and related segments of the industry. This segment has affected nonprofessionals who are primarily interested in the quality of their lawns and aesthetic improvement of their environment. This is accomplished through industry or commercial seminars, sales meetings, conferences, product shows, and sales and service calls. Manufacturers, processors, and suppliers have used sales brochures, advertisements in turfgrass oriented magazines, public service articles, and advertisements as effective communication tools in publications read by the general public. Equally as important, professional employees working in turfgrass-related industries constitute a substantial educational and extension force that works with all segments of the turfgrass industry. All together the management, sales, marketing, distribution, manufacturing, and production as well as the research and technical service personnel of the supporting commercial organizations constitute a substantial segment of the turfgrass educational and research industry.

All turfgrass businesses are supported either directly or indirectly by internal research. Through the efforts of corporate research, most new innovative and improved products are developed. This group provides experts to solve customer problems, evaluate turf needs, and provide training for sales staffs to make them more effective in servicing their customer's needs.

To supply products to the turfgrass industry, commercial organizations spend millions of research dollars annually. research efforts are directed primarily toward improved grasses, new products, or product improvement. The research and development department of a major supplier may be structured to conduct basic and applied research (chemical industry) or applied product evaluation (chemical, fertilizer, and turfgrass varieties). Research on new materials, for example, plastics, is conducted by the chemical company supplying the basic product, as is metalurgical research conducted by the supplier or manufacturer who provides new castings, steel, or rubber. Research efforts of equipment companies are directed toward new product development that incorporates innovative design concepts, new materials, new manufacturing or molding concepts, and more efficient performance.

The size and extent of research facilities as well as the number of personnel engaged in various types of research is a function of the type of product, the structure of the organization, and its method of marketing the product. Research staffs per company, may vary from one or two to several hundred. Some organizations that supply products to the industry choose to operate without research personnel. These organizations must depend upon either university research or the research efforts of their basic suppliers.

D. Continuing Education

Data flow from university and commercial research centers provides the basis for current academic information for teaching purposes and an extensive continuing educational effort. Local, state, regional, national, and international turf conferences are held on a periodic basis. These conferences, shows, and special seminars, provide the opportunity for continual updating of all turfgrass industry personnel and serve to keep the industry abreast of current technologies and new products.

The certification program of the GCSAA is an outgrowth of recognition by the members of this organization of the need for, and the role of, continuing education in their profession. Originally conceived by S. Metsker of Colorado as a means of certifying professional status, the program has evolved to a level requiring academic training for base level entry and continuing education credits obtained by participation in accredited seminars and qualified turfgrass conference programs. The program assures a continuing supply of college-trained superintendents who keep abreast of technological advances in all aspects of their field.

Through the combined education and research efforts of the universities, associations, and commercial organizations, the turfgrass industry is supplied with the most in-depth, up-to-date information of any agricultural commodity group.

II. INDUSTRY ORGANIZATION

The turfgrass industry is composed of many functional segments and personnel representing various levels of skill, experience, educational background, and training. Turfgrass production and maintenance, facility management, product manufacture, distribution procurement, and utilization along with facility design and construction are all interrelated segments of this broad industry. To categorize or group the various components into an overall industry composition is an arbitrary effort. One plausible approach is that suggested originally by Nutter and Watson (1969) wherein they propose a composition based on function and manpower.

A. Function

Functionally, the turfgrass industry is composed of four rather distinct segments or branches. These are: (i) the *facilities* branch that deals with the management and maintenance of turfgrass sites; (ii) the *manufacturing* branch, which provides the products used in the care and maintenance of turfgrass; including the equipment (mowers, cultivators, aerators, irrigation system components, sweepers, seeders, spreaders, and sprayers); the fertilizers and soil conditioners, the plant materials; and the chemicals for disease, insect, and weed control; (iii) the *service* segment that designs and constructs; distributes, sells, and applies products and services; and in short, implements the development and utilization of both products and facilities; and (iv) the educational or *institutional* branch that includes schools, colleges, the extension service (federal, state, and county), and research experiment stations (federal, state, and private) (Nutter & Watson, 1969).

A detailed composition by branches is given in Table 2-1, but is not intended to be all inclusive or restrictive.

This expanded view represents an overall concept of the turfgrass industry. Because of the specialized nature of the more highly organized segments such as golf, lawn care, seed trade, and sports turf, among others, it seems appropriate to consider all the many segments or facets as one—*the turfgrass industry.*

B. Personnel

Nutter and Watson (1969) presented an in-depth review of factors that led to the development of specialized condensed college curricula, rather than apprenticeship, of the men and women associated with the turfgrass industry.

The most valuable resource in any industry is its personnel. Likewise, the progress and status of an industry may be evaluated by the stage of development of its manpower profile. The personnel profile outlines the vertical classification of personnel within the industry.

The personnel required to staff and service the turfgrass industry is diverse in its training, education, and experience. Opportunities abound for advancement within and between all segments of the industry. One may choose a finite field of endeavor (e.g., golf course superintendent), in which case advancement opportunity but not responsibility or salary, is lateral rather than vertical.

The personnel resources of the turfgrass industry may be categorized into seven occupations or levels of personnel utilizations. They are professional, managerial, supervisory, technician or specialist, production, sales and marketing personnel, and trainee. Table 2-2 illustrates the personnel profile as described. The examples given are not intended to be all-inclusive or restrictive (Nutter & Watson, 1969).

Demand for ever-higher turfgrass grooming standards, advancing technology, increased research knowledge, information dissemination, and labor costs are factors forcing the turfgrass industry toward more and more effective and efficient utilization of its manpower.

Table 2-1. Functional composition of the turfgrass industry. (Adapted from Nutter and Watson, 1969.)

Branch 1 — Turfgrass Facilities

Airports
Athletic fields
Bowling and croquet greens
Campuses (college and university)
Cemeteries, memorial gardens, and synagogues
Churches
Courthouses and governmental buildings
Exposition and fairgrounds
Garden apartments and condominiums
Golf courses and driving ranges
Grass tennis courts
Highway rights-of-way, interchanges, and medians
Hospitals
Hotels and motels
Housing projects and subdivisions
Industrial parks
Lawns (residential and commercial)
Military bases
Mobile home villages
Parks and playgrounds
Race tracks
Resorts
Retirement villages
Schools
Sports fields
Zoos and botanical gardens

Branch 2 — Manufacturing

Equipment (mowers, trimmers, cultivars-aerators, spikers and slicers, sprayers sprinklers, and spreaders)
Fertilizers
Irrigation system components
Plant growth regulators
Pesticides (herbicides, fungicides, and insecticides)
Seed, sod, stolons, sprigs and other landscape-related plant material (trees, flowers, and shrubs)
Special products (soil components, amendments)
Supplies (hoes, rakes, tools, miscellaneous)

Branch 3 — Servicing

Architects and designers
Consultants (business and technical)
Contract services (lawn and landscape maintenance companies, lawn care companies)
Distributors and retailers (all products)
Information service organizations (USGA Green Section, National Golf Foundation, Freshwater Society and others)
Publications
Research organizations
Salesmen
Service laboratories (soil testing, chemical, water, and similar)
Trade and professional organizations

Branch 4 — Institutions

Colleges, universities
Extension service (county, state, and federal)
Vocational-technical schools
U.S. Department of Agriculture

Table 2-2. Turfgrass industry personnel profile. (After Nutter and Watson, 1969.)

1. Managerial
   a. Superintendents
      Cemetery
      College and university grounds
      Golf course
      Government grounds
      Park and Recreation areas
      School maintenance
   b. Managers
      Air field
      Athletic stadium
      Lawn service
      Lawn and a garden supply
      Golf course
      Irrigation service and supply
      Pest control service
      Seed production
      Sports turf field
      Sod production manager
   c. Other turf facility supervisors, specialists, and managers
2. Production personnel (the work force)
   a. Semi-skilled maintenance workers
   b. Skilled equipment operators
   c. Specialized operations worker
   d. General (utility) worker
   e. Reserve labor
3. Professional
   a. Practicing turf agronomists, horticulturists, and other scientifically
      trained personnel
   b. Professional turf consultant — private, industry, or university
   c. Turfgrass business and administrative personnel
   d. Turfgrass education personnel — college teacher, extension service
      specialists, industry product or development specialists
   e. Turfgrass equipment designers and engineers
   f. Turfgrass facility architects (golf course and landscape)
   g. Turfgrass irrigation design engineers
   h. Turfgrass research personnel and scientists
   i. Turfgrass trade and professional organizations personnel
4. Sales and marketing (may be selected from any of the above classifications)
   a. Market specialists (those who analyze, survey, and project)
   b. Manufacturers' representative
   c. Product demonstrator and exhibit specialist
   d. Salesmen for turfgrass materials, supplies, and equipment
5. Supervisory
   a. Assistant golf course superintendent (may be managerial in larger
      operations)
   b. Assistant grounds maintenance superintendent
   c. Foremen
      Turf maintenance
      Landscape maintenance
      Landscape planting
      Pest control services
   g. Other supervisory personnel
6. Technician or specialist
   a. Technicians
      Turf irrigation

(continued on next page)

Table 2-2. Continued.

Sod harvesting
Turf planting
Turf laboratory
Turf research
Fertilizer
b. Specialists
Turf chemical (pest control)
Turf sprayer operator
Other related technical personnel
Equipment mechanics
7. Trainee and apprentice
a. Equipment operators
b. Semi-skilled maintenance workers
c. Specialized operations worker
d. General (utility) worker
e. Reserve labor

III. INDUSTRY COMPONENTS AND INTERACTIONS

Growth and development of the various components of the U.S. turfgrass industry has closely paralleled the growth and development of the golf industry. Golfer demand for superior playing conditions has necessitated improved operational efficiencies, minimized labor costs and expanded performance, and higher quality turfgrass. This demand was the impetus for key developments in grasses, chemicals, materials, and golf maintenance equipment and practices.

Advancements thus generated are quickly adapted for use on general turfgrass sites and, with modification, on home lawns.

Suppliers and equipment manufacturers have responded to the needs of the golf course superintendent to permit continued upgrading and improvement of his maintenance practices so that personnel, including labor costs, have remained 60 to 70% of the maintenance budget (Prusa & Beditz, 1985). An 18-hole golf course today employs an average of 8 to 10 maintenance personnel during the peak season and 3 to 5 during the remainder of the year. Not too many years ago, 25 to 30 or more employees were needed to maintain 18 holes.

The development of 2,4-D [(2,4-dichlorophenoxy) acetic acid] and related compounds in the early 1940s provided the industry with specific and highly effective postemergence control of broadleaf weeds. The subsequent development of preemergence compounds for control of weedy grasses provided the means to maintain dense, weed-free turf with minimal labor; in contrast to earlier tedious and labor-intensive hand weeding.

Likewise, the development of specific fungicides and insecticides when used properly made possible the maintenance of virtually disease-free turf and reduced insects as a factor in turfgrass growth and human annoyance. In both cases, turf quality was enhanced and playing time on improved surfaces extended.

Similarly, development of synthetic, slow-release fertilizers that performed like natural organics permitted the extension of the interval between feedings and contributed to a further reduction in the labor component of turfgrass cultural practices.

Development of vigorous, disease resistant and stress-tolerant turfgrasses also helped to reduce maintenance costs. The improved turfgrasses available today survive adversity and stress much better than earlier types; and, thereby, produce better playing surfaces. They have created an ever-increasing demand for more services, more innovative products, and better playing conditions.

Costs for maintenance today would be prohibitively expensive without continuing development of greater capacity equipment, more efficient fertilizers and pesticides, and superior turfgrasses. Although budgets for some 18-hole courses range from as low as $50 000 to as high as $400 000 or more annually, new courses are being added each year and the number of golfers continues to increase, ensuring continued growth. The research programs of today bode well for future reductions in maintenance costs, which in turn will help to maintain a balance between operational costs and abilities to support play.

There are no accurate figures available to describe the extent and value of the entire turfgrass industry. In fact, there is a lack of uniform agreement as to the constituents or segments that should be included. Specific dollar values for the land, buildings, and for all other assets of the various facilities likewise are difficult to assess and will not be attempted. Perhaps they are meaningless anyway, since the values change from year to year depending on the accounting procedures, tax rates (if any), age of the facility, its classification, the rate of inflation, and other financial factors.

It is meaningful, however, to present sources of information describing significant segments of the industry; and, where available, statistics describing known production and sale of products, number of facilities, and other pertinent information.

Statistical data describing the *basic* industries that manufacture, produce, and process products for the turfgrass industry are generally available. Categories that will be reviewed include equipment, chemicals, fertilizers, seed, and sod.

Supporting organizations that design, construct, and establish turfgrass facilities, along with those who advise and consult, play a major role in the industry. Their contributions to the aesthetic value, maintenance, and the use of current products is substantial. Most organizations have relatively small corporate staffs and are privately owned; therefore, little financial or performance data are available. Some estimate of business volume could be extrapolated from an analysis of the utilization component such as golf course activity. Included in this grouping are landscape and golf course architects, construction and irrigation contractors, hydroseeders, consultants, and specialty engineers such as irrigation designers.

The organizations that market, sell, and distribute the basic products also represent a significant component of the turfgrass industry. Again, information on their activity, numbers, and financial status is limited and can be obtgained only through extrapolation.

Industry segments that use and service turfgrass facilities provide limited data that may be useful in developing a financial profile for their activity. Included in this group are the golf, lawn care, and sports turf components.

Again, as with the composition of the industry, an arbitrary selection and grouping of components will serve to illustrate the nature and extent of the industry and the many interactions between components, functions, and services that exist.

Table 2–3 depicts industry interactive relationships. The complexity and the crossover relationships within the industry are illustrated. Also illustrated is the difficulty associated with efforts to focus on any particular segment of the industry independent of the others. This intermingling of functions, products, suppliers, and usage is an advantage for those associated with the industry but a definite disadvantage from the standpoint of creating emphasis and political influence. Too often the various segments talk only to their primary interest group and to others within the industry, not to the general public or the political entities who would be helpful in obtaining full recognition and understanding of the importance of this industry.

A. Equipment

Equipment for maintenance of turfgrass areas is usually classified as either *commercial* or *consumer*. Commercial equipment has greater capacity and durability, and consequently is more expensive. It is the equipment used to maintain large turfgrass facilities like golf courses, parks, cemeteries, and school grounds. Consumer equipment is designed primarily for maintenance of residential lawns. Use of consumer equipment for maintenance of large areas becomes expensive as it is not designed nor constructed to run for 8 h every day.

Statistics are virtually unavailable for most segments of the turfgrass equipment industry. Most manufacturing companies of specialized maintenance equipment are closely held, privately owned, or owned by conglomerates that are not required to divulge sales and earnings for these divisions. However, the Toro Company, a publically held company, registered sales of $406.7 million in 1985. This represented a 20.8% increase over the previous year and a 20.2% increase from fiscal 1983. A product-line breakdown of sales and percentage increases is given for the years 1983 to 1986 (Anonymous, 1985a) (Table 2–4).

1. Commercial

If one assumes that the Toro Company sales volume accounts for 5 to 10% of the commercial mowing equipment sales, then the size of the *commercial segment* of the turfgrass mowing equipment industry would approach $1 to 2 billion. Similarly, if Toro irrigation sales represent 10 to 30% of the industry, this segment would approach $278 to 830 million.

Table 2–3. Interactive industry relationships.

Utilization

1. Sports facilities	5. Golf courses	8. Roadways
2. Cemeteries	6. Governmental facilities	9. Schools and universities
3. Commercial and industrial turf	7. Parks and playgrounds	10. Home lawns
4. Condominiums and apartment turfs		

Manpower

Design, construction, and related industries	Services and service industry	Institutional activities	Manufacturing and production industry	Distribution
Architects	Lawn care	Research	Chemical	Wholesale
Golf	Grounds management	Extension	Equipment and machine	Retail
Landscape	Contract	Teaching	Fertilizer	
General	Custodial		Seed	
Contractors	Private		Sod	
Construction	Consultants			
Golf builders	Independent			
Maintenance	Commercial			
Speciality	University			
Irrigation	Irrigation			
Drainage	Associations			
Engineers				
Civil				
Drainage				
Irrigation				
Nurseries				
Plant material				
Design				
Construction				
Maintenance				

Table 2-4. The Toro Company sales, 1985

Sales by product line	Years ended:				
	31 July 1985	27 July 1984	29 July 1983	Percent change, 1985–1984	Percent change, 1984 1983
	—— dollars in millions ——			—— % ——	
Consumer lawn equipment	$128.5	118.4	115.8	8.5	2.2
Snow removal equipment	43.3	37.3	25.1	16.1	48.6
Professional turf equipment	84.8	68.4	60.6	24.0	12.9
Turf irrigation equipment	80.2	56.1	39.5	43.0	42.0
Total	$336.8	$280.2	$241.0	20.2	16.3

2 Consumer

Reliable estimates of sales for the lawn and garden equipment segment are published every year by the Outdoor Power Equipment Institute (OPEI). The OPEI is the national trade association representing manufacturers of such consumer power equipment as walk-behind and riding lawn mowers, garden tractors, tillers, snow throwers, shredders, grinders, and their major components. Annual finished goods retail sales are more than $3 billion.

This trade organization obtains data from its member companies. Although not all manufacturers are institute members, the data are considered valid and provide an acceptable estimate for this segment of the equipment industry. Table 2-5 from Nutter and Watson (1969) shows OPEI member shipments of power mowers, tillers, snow throwers, and riding garden tractors for the years 1946 through 1967. Similar information for the years 1970 through 1985 is shown in Table 2-6 (Anonymous, 1986a).

The data in Tables 2-5 and 2-6 indicate a mature, through consistent market for these products. total OPEI member sales for 1985 were approximately $2.25 billion. Thus, turfgrass maintenance equipment sales in 1985 could be estimated at an approximate range of $3.5 to 4.0 billion. If sales of sprayers, spreaders, and other specialized equipment were added, it seems likely that the turfgrass equipment business in 1985 could have approached $5 billion.

B. Seed

The turfgrass seed business is a vital and necessary part of the turfgrass industry. Although somewhat fragmented, it is nevertheless, an orderly business. The seed industry is composed of those persons and businesses that develop, produce, process, package, market, and distribute seed. Companies that specialize in the handling of seed are the conduits between the producer and consumer. Individual companies may conduct all or most of the functions while other copmanies may limit their activities.

Seed production fluctuates from year to year. Factors affecting annual production include anticipation of consumer demand, carry-over inventories,

Table 2-5. Annual shipments by U.S. manufacturers of four power equipment items for the period 1946 through 1967 as compiled by the Outdoor Power Equipment Institute. (Courtesy: The Toro Co., Minneapolis.) (Adapted from Nutter and Watson, 1969.)

	Units shipped			
Year	Power lawn mowers	Motor tillers	Rotary snow throwers	Riding garden tractors
1946	139 018	N/A†		
1947	362 000	31 051		
1948	397 000	15 176		
1949	529 000	11 006		
1950	1 080 000	17 211		
1951	1 241 000	26 098		
1952	1 155 000	41 498		
1953	1 275 000	67 922		
1954	1 802 000	75 082		
1955	2 750 000	N/A		
1956	3 200 000	N/A		
1957	3 266 000	129 0796	12 000	
1958	3 841 000	173 348	18 000	12 643
1959	4 200 000	251 778	20 000	27 047
1960	3 800 000	315 406	40 000	43 486
1961	3 500 000	277 048	75 000	67 124
1962	4 000 000	317 264	175 000	90 000
1963	3 900 000	306 090	200 000	100 000
1964	4 100 000	291 945	160 000	125 000
1965	4 500 000	340 000	165 000	175 000
1966	4 900 000	325 000	185 000	250 000
1967	4 900 000	350 000	185 000	275 000

† N/A = Information is not available.

cost considerations, and weather inconsistencies during the production year and the preceding year. Introductions of new or improved cultivars substantially affect production of a particular cultivar. Replacement of former cultivars is a continuing, on-going practice that ensures quality seed and improved, high-quality turfgrasses.

Cowan (1969) has reported on the production, processing, and shipment of seed and cultivar maintenance.

Seed production of cool-season grasses is centered in Oregon and Washington because of favorable climate. Oregon alone grows about 300 000 acres of grass seed within the Willamette Valley plus a substantial acreage east of the Cascades. Seed species produced in the Pacific Northwest includes Kentucky bluegrass (*Poa pratensis* L.), rough bluegrass (*Poa travialis* L.), perennial (*Lolium perenne* L.) and annual ryegrass (*L. multiflorum* Lam.), creeping (*Agrostis palustris* Huds.) and Colonial bentgrass (*A. tenuis* Sibth.), fine-leafed fescues {red (*Festuca rubra* L.), chewings (*F. rubra* var. *commutata* Gaud.), hard [*F. ovina* var. *duriuscula* (L.) Koch] and sheep (*F. ovina* L.)}, and tall fescue (*F. arundinacea* Schreb). Cool-season grass seed is also grown in northern Idaho, northern Minnesota, and the Peace River Valley region of Canada. Bermudagrass seed (common) is grown in the Imperial Valley of California and in southwestern Arizona. Centipedegrass [*Eremochloa ophiuroides* (Monro) Hackel] seed is grown almost exclusively

Table 2-6. OPEI Annual shipments by U.S. manufacturers of selected equipment. 1970 through 1985. Compiled by the Outdoor Power Equipment Institute. (Courtesy: The Toro Company.)

Model		Walk-behind power mowers	Lawn tractors/riding mowers	Riding garden tractors	Rotary tillers	Snow throwers
1970	Unit shipments‡	4 900 000	674 500	275 500	400 000	245 000
	F.O.B. value§#	N/A¶	N/A	N/A	N/A	N/A
1971	Unit shipments	4 800 000	630 000	245 500	400 000	265 000
	F.O.B. value	N/A	N/A	N/A	N/A	N/A
1972	Unit shipments	5 200 000	680 000	250 000	450 000	315 000
	F.O.B. value	N/A	N/A	N/A	N/A	N/A
1973	Unit shipments	6 400 000	920 000	305 000	575 000	300 000
	F.O.B. value	N/A	N/A	N/A	N/A	N/A
1974	Unit shipments	6 000 000	1 020 000	325 000	845 000	227 253
	F.O.B. value	$404.8	$332	$270	$111	$32.3
1975	Unit shipments	4 700 000	640 000	230 000	1 200 000	156 800
	F.O.B. value	$396.7	$253.4	$250	$205.2	$34.8
1976	Unit shipments	4 900 000	690 000	210 000	780 000	165 434
	F.O.B. value	$451.5	$300.5	$246	$135.8	$36.8

		Front engine	Rear engine			
1977	Unit shipments	5 000 000	403 800	266 200	215 000	633 000	267 950
	F.O.B. value	$469.5	$202.1	$111.4	$261	$109.7	$60
1978	Unit shipments	5 400 000	477 100	272 900	219 000	571 000	416 000
	F.O.B. value	$547.6	$256.4	$126.6	$282.2	$116.2	$94.3
1979	Unit shipments	5 900 000	515 000	343 000	254 000	571 300	1 118 000
	F.O.B. value	$656.0	$331	$182	$365	$125	$250
1980	Unit shipments	5 700 000	494 000	314 000	220 000	667 000	1 577 000
	F.O.B. value	$701	$345	$185	$351	$159	$397
1981	Unit shipments	4 600 000	370 000	250 000	151 000	501 000	344 700
	F.O.B. value	$606	$291	$162	$266	$138	$98
1982	Unit shipments	4 600 000	393 000	261 000	146 000	497 000	95 000
	F.O.B. value	$674	$359	$190	$280	$143	$27
1983	Unit shipments	4 400 000	415 000	276 000	129 000	408 000	264 000
	F.O.B. value	$695	$395	$205	$275	$132	$91
1984	Unit shipments	4 950 000	502 000	354 000	152 000	399 000	348 000
	F.O.B. value	$742	$482	$278	$311	$197	$122
1985	Unit shipments	5 193 000	458 000	355 000	147 000	362 000	421 000
	F.O.B. value	$792	$535	$287	$303	$181	$144

† The model year is 1 September through 31 August for all products listed except snow throwers. The snow thrower model year begins March and ends February.
‡ The U.S. estimate does not make an adjustment for units exported.
§ Dollar amounts indicate F.O.B. factory shipment value.
¶ N/A = Information is not available.
# Amounts in millions of dollars.

in southern Georgia and bahiagrass (*Paspalum notatum* Fluegge) seed is imported with limited production in Florida. Limited production of buffalograss [*Buchloë* dactyloides (Nutt.) Engelm.] seed is available from growers located from Nebrasks to Oklahoma. Minor quantities of cool-season grass seed are imported from Europe as are seed of other turfgrasses from around the world. Zoysiagrass (*Zoysia* spp.) seed is produced in Korea and the People's Republic of China

1. Production and Processing

Farmer-growers who specialize in turfgrass seed production have the responsibility to plant, maintain, and harvest seed crops. They are responsible for maintaining fields free of other crops, off-type plants, and especially weeds and pests. Depending on the contractual arrangement, either the grower-producer or the owner of the cultivar will hold title to the seed through the conditioning process.

The burning of crop residue following harvest has been a common practice in all seed production areas. Burning controls insects and diseases and stimulates plants to produce seed by thinning the stands. Objections to this economically desirable procedure raised by environmentalists have been overcome through research and controlled burning procedures.

Conditioning of seed consists of cleaning the seed to remove chaff, other inert material, weed and other crop seed, and undeveloped, immature and dead or nonviable seed. The equipment used for this process is primarily based on sizing, gravity flow, mechanical agitation, and air movement. It is highly effective and efficient.

Conditioning is performed in facilities licensed by the state in which the seed is grown. These facilities may be the property of the grower, a privately held seed-cleaning company, or a seed company that will ultimately own and market the seed.

2. Storage

Seed must be stored to meet market demands throughout any given year since only one crop of seed is produced annually. Storing seed inventories helps to guide production levels and provide reasonably uniform availability but may be costly for the owner. The distributor or wholesaler may store seed at the farm, or at a central warehouse. Storage facilities must be cool and preferably designed for good air movement. When beneficial endophytic fungi are present within grass seed, cold storage is required to maintain viability of the fungus for more than 1 yr.

Storage conditions can affect seed germination. For this reason, federal seed control regulations requires that seed be tested for germination every 9 mo and that test results be present on each seed label or container. State regulations also must be met if they vary from the federal standard.

3. Classes of Seed

State certified and licensed seed analysts conduct germination and purity tests after seed has been conditioned. Seed-testing laboratories may be publicly or privately owned. Seed qualified to enter commercial channels must meet federal and state standards; and, in the case of privately owned cultivars, the standards and specifications established by the owner.

Title to seed may be transferred to the individual or organization that will package, distribute, and market the seed only after all tests have been conducted and the standards established for the particular lot.

Seed normally enters commercial channels as a single cultivar, as a blend of two or more cultivars of a particular species, or sometimes as a mixture of two or more species. Seed standards may be warranted by the seller, by the individual, or by the organization taking title from the grower-producer.

Proprietary cultivars are named, improved, and genetically true-to-type. Proprietary cultivars are usually owned by or licensed to a seed company or group of companies who determine annual market needs and then, either grow or contract for production with a grower or growers. In either case, the owner determines quality standards, establishes quantities to be produced and agrees, in the case of a contract grower, to a predetermined price. Usually the agreements with a grower specify that all production will be sold to the contracting organization. An example of a proprietary cultivar is Baron Kentucky Bluegrass, developed by Barenbrug Holland B.V. It is licensed to Loft Seed Company for production and marketing in the USA. Kenblue Kentucky bluegrass is a nonproprietary cultivar released by the Kentucky Agriculture Experiment Station and available to any organization wishing to produce and market it.

Proprietary cultivars may be legally protected from unauthorized reproduction through the Plant Variety Protection Act which was authorized by the U.S. Congress in 1970. Plant Variety Protection (PVP) may be obtained for unique, genetically reproducable true-to-type (proprietary) cultivars. One may apply for PVP in two ways: (i) as a class of certified seed, in which case the cultivar can be sold *only* if it is certified; and (ii) receive PVP without certification. In this latter case, the owner may elect to sell the cultivar as certified or not certified, thus providing flexibility in marketing and protection for the owner against adversity that might preclude certification. The Plant Variety Protection Office is a division of the USDA, Agricultural Service located at Beltsville, MD. Vegetatively propagated cultivars can be protected by the U.S. Patent Office.

Contracting firms maintain and supply the basic seed stock of proprietary cultivars to the farmer-grower. They also employ field representatives to supervise the planting, verify isolation requirements, and inspect the fields for disease, insects, weeds, other crops, and off-type plants. In addition, the field representative advises growers on specialized cultural practices such as irrigation, pesticide application, and harvest.

Grass seed of undesignated or unimproved lineage is called *common*. It is often grown as a speculative crop by the farmer-producer. Seed stock may come from his own supply or someone elses production, or from a state crop improvement association. When a proprietary or nonproprietary improved cultivar is in surplus supply, the excess may be sold without identification as common seed if permission is received from the owner of the cultivar. Common seed must still meet certain standards of germination and purity even though genetic purity is not guaranteed.

Common seed is sold by the grower into normal trade channels at a negotiated price. The buyer will assume all responsibility for further sales and marketing activity beyond the normal grower functions.

Certified seed is grown in fields inspected by a state-certifying agency for genetic purity, and also must meet standards established for germination and freedom from weeds and other crop seeds. To be entered into the certification schemes, the seed stock used to produce certified seed must also be monitored and meet specifications adapted for each species. Through interagency agreement, seed certified by any one state agency is generally accepted throughout the USA. However, individual state agencies have the option to modify the standards acceptable for seeds entering a particular state. A few agencies such as Virginia, Maryland, and Pennsylvania have, in recent years, exercised their option.

Premium seed is an unofficial classification. even though every effort may be made to produce seed of a cultivar to meet high pre-established standards, not all seed will be of the same quality due to environmental, soil, and management vagaries. Premium seed that may be given a specific brand name or title represents seed lots selected because they meet an exceptionally high standard of quality. Usually they are grown at a premium price, have been given extra processing, and have been identified through tests to represent exceptional quality. These lots are often more expensive to purchase and usually are in short supply.

Sod quality seed may be certified or noncertified seed. However, it must meet higher standards of quality than the average certified seed lot. Up to 10 times greater quantities of seed than normal are examined by seed analysts for purity and germination. Substantially greater limitations are placed on the presence of hard-to-control grass and broad-leafed species considered to be weeds in turf. Germination standards also may be increased.

Special labels are used on seed sold as "branded" products to fill specific needs such as athletic field mixes, playground mixes, shady lawn mixes, or other applications. These formulas usually will contain grasses known to provide superior performance under the conditions for which they have been selected. Blended and promoted by the producer or marketer, these products usually represent the top of their product line and include the best combinations of species and cultivars currently available for specific or designated use. Some branded and promoted products have poor turf performance when they contain inferior, nonadapted, poor-quality seed.

4. Improvement

The seed industry constantly strives to improve the quality and performance of turfgrasses. Plant breeders employed by domestic and foreign seed companies, by the USDA and by state experiment stations conduct on-going programs that lead to a continuing flow of improved cultivars. Primary effort is directed toward development of improved proprietary varieties. Registration for PVP may or may not be sought. Proprietary cultivars are marketed more intensively and their production is more tightly controlled, therefore, they usually command a premium price.

Nonproprietary turfgrasses, which often are older cultivars released by experiment stations or common, unimproved, unnamed grasses, constitute more than 50% of total Kentucky bluegrass production (D. Jacklin, 1986, personal communication).

5. Distribution

Seed flows through trade channels in many ways. Proprietary controlled cultivars are marketed by their owner or his licensee. Nonproprietary seed may be sold directly to a distributor, to an end user, or to a broker, who in turn may sell to a distributing organization or to a seed company. Most seed follows this latter path. The seed company assumes the financial risks incurred from the time they purchase and take title of the seed from the grower, through the storage period, packaging, and marketing.

Seed may be sold in bulk, in bags, or in small boxes or plastic bags. Seed destined for the professional trade usually moves through a distributor, while seed packaged for general or nonprofessional trade follows a two-step process from the distributor to a retail dealer to the end user.

Seed sold to homeowners is usually packaged in attractively labeled boxes, while seed distributed to the professional trade will move in 50-lb bags in units of several bags per order.

6. Value

Available seed supply vs. demand has a direct influence on pricing. This is especially true for the nonproprietary cultivars and common types. Seed prices of proprietary cultivars do not fluctuate as much since production costs are under contract control.

The 1985 seed production (Table 2–7) provides insight into the volume of seed used each year even though it represents only one season. Shortages occurred in Kentucky bluegrass and creeping bentgrass seed supplies in 1985. Further, there was an over-supply of fine fescue and turf-type perennial ryegrass seed. These two phenomena distorted the market according to personal communications from R. Newman (1986), W. Rose (1986), and N. Rothwell (1986).

C. Sod

Sod is one of the two turfgrass commodities or products that are produced rather than manufactured; the other is seed.

The cultivated sod industry evolved in response to the need for rapid turfgrass cover and establishment, first in sports fields, and later to meet

Table 2-7. Turfgrass seed production in 1985.

	Production	Estimated Proprietary
	t	%
Kentucky bluegrass	25 000	65
Perennial ryegrass	27 000	67
Annual ryegrass	57 000	
Fine fescue		
U.S. production	10 500	5
Canadian production imported to the USA	N/A	N/A
Tall fescue (used for turf)		
Missouri and other eastern states	32 500	0
Oregon and other western states	11 500	80
Creeping bentgrass	2 300	90
Colonial bentgrass	1 500	--
Bermudagrass	6 600	--

† Total crop of 38 500 t, of which 85% went for turf-related use.

the need created by the explosive growth of single and multiple family dwellings. The first sod was cut from pastures. As an increasing demand for higher quality turf on lawns and playing fields developed and as improved vegetative cultivars became available, producers, marketers, landscape contractors, and direct customers turned to cultivated sod or "sprigs" produced by dividing sod into pieces of turf containing stolons, crowns, and rhizomes. Once launched, the cultivated sod industry grew rapidly with some 900 growers producing sod on 24 000 ha by the late 1960s. Farms averaged 73 ha with the wholesale value of sod in production at that time estimated at $100 million (Nutter & Watson, 1969).

Initially, the cultivated sod industry developed in the region of adaptation of cool-season turfgrasses. Kentucky bluegrass is currently the most widely grown cool-season grass for sod purposes. Major centers of production are located in Rhode Island, Maryland, New York, New Jersey, Ohio, Michigan, California, Illinois, Wisconsin, Minnesota, Missouri, and Colorado. The cool-season turfgrass sod industry remains concentrated in these general regions (D. H. Fender, 1986, personal communication).

There are some 1430 growers producing sod on approximately 50 000 ha according to a 1982 USDA census (D. H. Fender, 1986, personal communication) (Table 2-8). Value of the industry (exclusive of land, buildings, and other fixed assets) is estimated at $210 million.

Cultivated sod is produced on both organic and mineral soils. Normally, the same fields are used continuously with a crop being harvested every 1 to 2 yr, then reseeded and brought back into production. With nylon sod

Table 2-8. Comparison of producers and areas of cultivated sod marketed in USA in 1969 and 1982 (Courtesy: D.A. Fender, Rolling Meadow, IL.)

	1969	1982
Total no. of cultivated sod producers	900	1 430
Total area marketed annually, ha	2 400	50 000

netting in California, a crop is produced in 6 to 9 mo. Care is taken to maintain the production fields as free of weeds and other contaminants as is possible through both chemical and mechanical means.

Cultivated sod is produced from seed or sprigs to produce solid covers of grass turf. High-quality seed or sprigs are demanded by the producers and the latest cultivars are usually planted. Most sod production using cool-season grasses is seed established. Kentucky bluegrass is the dominant species used. Specialty sod may also contain improved turf-type perennial ryegrass (*Lolium perenne* L.), tall fescue (*Festuca arundinacea* Schreb.), fine fescue (*Festuca rubra* L. and *F. rubra* var. *commutata* Gaud.), and rough bluegrass (*Poa trivialis* L.). Nearly all cool-season grass sod is lifted and installed intact. Creeping bentgrass sod, which is produced in a limited volume, may be installed either as intact sod or divided into sprigs. Many golf courses grow their own bentgrass sod using soil mixtures similar to that used on areas where the sod will be placed.

Warm-season grass sod production is concentrated in Florida, Georgia, Texas, and California. The industry in Florida began with the production and sale of common St. Augustinegrass [*Stenotaphrum secundatum* (Walter) Kuntze]. The industry turned to the improved cultivars as they became available and their advantages were recognized.

Most warm-season grass sod production uses the improved cultivars of hybrid bermudagrass. Because they are sterile, sprigs are used for increase of these grasses. Centipedegrass [*Eremochloa ophiuroides* (Munro) Hackel], *Paspalum vaginatum*, and zoysiagrass (*Zoysia* spp.) sod is also produced. Centipedegrass seed is used to grow sod, however, *P. vaginatum* and most zoysiagrass sod is increased from sprigs. Buffalograss sod production is still in its infancy and originates from seed.

Hybrid bermudagrass (*Cynodon* spp.) cultivars were marketed initially as sprigs and stolons. Today, almost as much sod as sprigs of the improved, fine-leafed hybrid bermudagrasses is marketed according to pioneer producer, R. Jensen (1986, personal communication). Jensen also reported there is a continuing trend toward increased use of sod.

Although centipedegrass seed is normally the principal means for establishing lawns to this grass, Jensen indicated a definite trend toward centipedegrass sod production. He was aware of the sale of some 112 ha in the spring and early summer of 1986 in south Georgia alone.

Small acreages of bahiagrass sod are produced in Florida and *Paspalum vaginatum* sod and sprigs are produced in California. Zoysiagrass sod is primarily grown within the central states transition belt.

Sod production is a cyclical business and lags housing starts by a 6- to 8-mo period. It is sold direct to landscape contractors and through garden stores, nurseries and similar consumer outlets. Some nurseries grow 0.5 to 2.5 ha of sod for direct sale. These areas are not normally used in industry statistics.

The growth and development of this industry is another example of industry interaction. Initially, sod was harvested by hand using specially adapted hand tools. Cutting of 200 m^2 per day was considered to be "a good day's work'' until use of a tractor-mounted blade doubled the amount that could be harvested daily. Production once again doubled and tripled with introduction of a motorized Ryan sod cutter. Currently, under favorable conditions, integrally powered units with conveyors are able to harvest as much as 17 000 m^2 of sod daily (R. Jensen, 1986, personal communication). The development and manufacture of equipment in response to a need for more rapid harvesting techniques spurred sod production of ever increasing volumes.

Table 2-9 includes the estimated sale of sod on a state by state basis (Gibeault & Cookerham, 1985). Roberts (1986) estimated the sod segment of the turfgrass industry at $70 million.

D. Chemical

The chemical industry is another significant component of the turfgrass industry. Their products include fungicides, insecticides, herbicides, and nematicides, in addition to growth regulators, surfactants, amendments, and paints used to line and mark sports fields.

A common tie within the industry is the ability to manufacture and formulate useful turf-oriented products from raw chemical stocks. Multi-national organizations that generate millions of dollars in sales and smaller companies that generate only a few thousand dollars are involved in the research, manufacturing, formulating, packaging, labeling, and marketing of these products. Turfgrass chemical suppliers may manufacture the basic ingredients to formulate their branded compound or they may sell the active ingredient to another firm to be formulated or repackaged under their own or another label.

Chemicals labeled for use on turfgrass increasingly are the low sales volume agricultural trade with or without significant formulation changes. This is a result of the high research and registration costs involved in developing and introducing new chemical products. In some instances, a new turf care or pest control product may be introduced prior to its agricultural counterpart because livestock feeding studies and residual tolerance research have not been completed or required.

1. Regulation

The chemical industry is under strict regulatory control. In addition to determining product efficacy, the developer of a new chemical pesticide also must evaluate the product for safety to people as well as animals and plants. These procedures take years of research and a huge outlay of funds. Estimates range from 7 to 10 yr and $25 to 40 million. As the time and the money required for registration of chemical pesticides increases, it seems likely that an increasing percentage of new products ultimately cleared for turfgrass use may have to come from products originally developed for the higher volume general agricultural market.

Table 2-9. Annual turfgrass maintenance costs for eight turfgrass categories in 50 states in 1982. Includes sales of sod by state (After Gibeault and Cockerham, 1985.)

State	Home lawns	Golf courses	Parks	Schools	Lawns	Cemeteries	Highways	Airports	State total	Sod sales
AL	197.6	15.6	1.3	6.7	34.3	5.5	10.8	6.4	278.2	4.0
AK	15.1	0.5	0.9	0.5	2.5	0.4	0.8	0.5	21.2	0.0
AZ	350.6	21.6	22.4	11.7	60.1	9.7	18.9	11.2	506.2	2.4
AR	169.2	11.9	10.9	5.7	29.3	4.7	9.2	5.5	246.4	3.1
CA	648.9	124.2	47.7	24.9	128.0	20.6	40.1	23.9	1 058.3	30.4
CO	477.0	9.9	30.0	15.7	80.3	12.9	25.2	15.0	666.0	28.9
CT	467.5	39.4	30.5	15.9	81.8	13.2	25.6	15.2	689.1	4.4
DE	40.0	5.6	2.7	1.4	7.4	1.2	2.3	1.4	62.0	0.4
Wash. DC	40.0	1.7	2.5	1.3	6.7	1.1	2.1	1.2	56.6	0.0
FL	732.2	75.1	49.4	25.8	132.5	21.3	41.6	24.7	1 093.6	50.0
GA	331.7	45.2	22.9	12.0	61.4	9.9	19.2	11.4	513.7	8.7
HI	200.7	16.5	13.0	6.8	34.9	5.6	10.9	6.5	294.9	0.0
IA	467.5	37.7	30.4	15.9	62.0	13.0	20.7	15.2	662.4	3.3
ID	15.1	4.3	1.2	0.6	3.3	0.5	1.0	0.6	26.6	1.8
IL	600.1	99.5	42.7	22.3	114.5	18.4	35.9	21.3	954.7	15.9
IN	552.8	37.4	35.5	18.6	64.6	15.3	28.3	16.2	768.7	6.2
KA	458.1	29.2	29.4	15.3	78.7	12.7	24.7	14.7	662.8	4.4
KY	297.6	24.5	19.3	10.1	51.8	8.3	16.3	9.7	437.6	1.9
LA	303.2	11.5	18.9	9.9	50.7	8.2	15.9	9.5	427.8	2.6
MA	486.5	36.9	31.4	16.4	84.2	13.6	26.4	15.7	711.1	0.4
MD	514.9	18.3	32.2	16.8	86.3	13.9	27.1	16.1	725.6	12.8
ME	20.1	14.9	2.1	1.1	5.6	0.9	1.8	1.0	47.5	0.0
MI	675.9	60.8	44.6	23.3	119.7	19.3	37.5	22.3	1 003.4	17.9
MN	505.4	35.3	32.9	17.2	88.3	14.2	27.7	16.5	737.5	16.8
MO	325.0	29.4	21.3	11.2	57.3	9.2	18.0	10.7	482.1	8.3
MS	269.2	11.2	16.9	8.8	45.4	7.3	14.2	8.5	381.5	5.1
MT	15.1	4.1	1.2	0.6	3.6	0.5	1.0	0.6	26.2	0.8
NC	337.3	39.2	22.6	11.8	60.6	9.8	19.0	11.3	511.6	0.9

(continued on next page)

Table 2-9. Continued.

State	Home lawns	Golf courses	General						State total	Sod sales
			Parks	Schools	Lawns	Cemeteries	Highways	Airports		
ND	19.5	14.9	2.1	1.1	5.5	0.9	1.7	1.0	46.7	0.0
NE	166.6	22.6	10.4	5.5	28.0	4.5	8.8	5.2	251.6	4.3
NH	101.5	10.5	6.7	3.5	18.0	2.9	5.6	3.4	152.1	0.0
NJ	514.9	50.7	34.2	17.9	91.9	14.8	28.8	17.1	770.3	17.3
NM	107.0	6.8	6.9	3.6	18.5	3.0	5.8	3.4	155.0	1.9
NV	60.0	7.6	4.0	2.1	10.9	1.7	3.4	2.0	91.7	0.0
NY	732.7	130.4	52.0	27.2	139.5	22.5	43.7	26.0	1 174.0	13.2
OH	590.6	63.8	39.5	20.7	106.0	17.1	33.2	19.8	890.7	9.5
OK	357.0	13.1	22.3	11.6	59.8	9.6	18.7	11.1	503.2	3.1
OR	467.5	10.6	28.9	15.1	77.4	12.5	24.3	14.4	650.7	4.8
PA	675.9	66.8	44.6	22.3	119.7	19.3	37.5	22.3	1 009.4	5.4
RI	200.7	7.4	12.6	6.6	33.9	5.5	10.6	6.3	283.6	9.0
SC	280.5	21.7	18.1	9.5	48.6	7.8	15.2	9.1	410.5	0.3
SD	19.5	15.1	2.1	1.1	5.6	0.9	1.8	1.0	47.1	0.7
TN	314.6	24.6	20.3	10.6	54.6	8.8	17.1	10.2	460.8	1.1
TX	647.5	40.6	41.8	21.8	112.0	18.0	35.1	20.9	937.7	31.0
UT	41.7	4.6	2.9	1.5	7.7	1.2	2.4	1.4	63.4	3.0
VA	552.8	26.9	34.8	18.2	93.4	15.0	29.3	17.4	787.8	4.5
VT	19.5	7.8	1.6	0.9	4.4	0.7	1.4	0.8	37.1	0.0
WA	514.9	15.1	32.0	16.7	85.8	13.8	26.9	16.0	721.2	6.1
WI	533.8	39.5	34.9	18.2	93.5	15.1	29.3	17.4	781.7	12.1
WV	163.5	15.8	10.8	5.6	28.8	9.0	9.0	5.4	247.9	0.1
WY	15.1	3.2	1.1	0.6	2.9	0.5	0.9	0.6	24.9	1.0
	$16 602.6	$1 481.5	$1 081.4	$571.2	$2 881.7	$476.3	$912.7	$545.0	$24 552.4	$359.6
Employed directly	54 200	38 700	42 200	28 000	113 000	23 300	44 700	26 700	371 000	9 400
Total Employed	380 400									

Table 2-10. Pesticides sold to the turfgrass industry in 1984.

Type of chemical	dollars (thousands)
Herbicides—postemergence	716 000
Herbicides—preemergence	404 000
Fungicides	57 700
Insecticides	29 300
Wetting agents	7 640
Growth regulators	5 370
Total	$1 220 010

Environmental concerns must always be fully considered. Products must meet the exact standards established by the federal Environmental Protection Agency (EPA). They also must clear through various state agencies before they are ready for manufacture and introduction to the market. Once on the market, a chemical product is subject to review and reapproval as new evidence becomes available on its efficacy and safety. Alarmists and environmental extremists who attack the use of chemicals invest little or nothing in documented research; yet, their unwarranted actions jeopardize future development and use of essential and highly beneficial chemicals.

2. Labeling

The label *must* contain detailed instructions on the use of the product, specific identification of the pests controlled, the grasses upon which the product can be used, as well as detailed safety instructions and warnings concerning the degree of danger and how to treat misuse or abusive use of the product. A label must be developed for each product to meet government regulatory requirements. A consumer is legally required to follow these regulations and instructions when using the product.

3. Value

In 1984, sales of $3 to 4 billion were estimated (Table 2–10).

While the estimate of more than $3 billion is impressive, there are other classes of chemical products used on turfgrass that are not included in the six categories in Table 2–10 and for which sales estimates are not available.

Much can be done to control pests through management and grass breeding. Safe chemical pesticides do allow for prevention or curative control of diseases, insects, weeds, and other pests that are known to cause economic and aesthetic damage to turfed areas.

E. Fertilizer

The fertilizer segment of the turfgrass industry is a speciality business that serves the professional and nonprofessional markets. The industry has undergone many technical and economic changes during the past 40 yr. It evolved out of the agricultural fertilizer industry as the need for specially compounded materials was recognized. Soil tests and research on nutrient response indicated the need to provide high N, low P, and high K analysis in complete fertilizers. This special nutrient requirement and the desirability of slowly available N sources provided the initial impetus for the separation of speciality turfgrass fertilizers from those compounded for agriculture.

Comprehending the need for slowly available N sources to supplement the natural organic materials (processed sewage sludge, vegetable meals, and bonemeal) provided the stimulus and investment required to launch this segment of the fertilizer industry. The DuPont Company (Wilmington, DE) led the way with their ureaformaldehyde product in the late 1940s. Subsequently others, notably Hercules (New York City) and Borden (Carson, CA), followed suit with similar products; then, came isobutylidene diurea (IBDU) from Japan to be followed later by the S-coated ureas (SCU) developed by the National Fertilizer Development Center, Tennessee Valley Authority (TVA). These N sources provided the means for producing slowly available blends and complete fertilizers compounded specifically for turfgrass.

Increased knowledge of nutrient utilization by turfgrasses, and the nutritional and physiological role that particular elements play in plant metabolic activities, the development of higher N content of synthetic N sources, and the development of triple superphosphate, diammonium phosphate (DAP), and monoammonium phosphate (MAP) allowed for higher analysis fertilizer. However, throughout the 1950s and early 1960s, organic and organic-based turfgrass fertilizers were compounded with descending ratios—high N, low K; and some complete fertilizers followed suit; e.g., 6-3-0, 8-6-2, 10-6-4. In the mid-1960s, as a result of continued research on nutrient response and refinement of soil tests, fertilizer grades were changed to place more emphasis on N and K and less on P, and fertilizers with 4-1-2 and 4-1-3 ratios became available. Notable in more recent years (1970-1980s) has been the emphasis placed on the role of K for improved quality and stress tolerance.

Another innovation of the turfgrass industry was specialty products containing both fertilizer and pesticides. Herbicides and insecticides are commonly used in these products, and the most widely used of this group is a combination of fertilizer and preemergence herbicides, especially for crabgrass (*Digitaria* spp.) and annual bluegrass (*Poa annua* L.) control.

The ability of the fertilizer industry to respond to the nutritional needs of the turfgrass and incorporate technological advancements into their products is an example of a response that has created industry growth.

Fertilization is the process of supplementing basic nutrients present in the soil. The capability to blend or mix products to provide balance as well as the correct amount needed to ensure healthy growth is a trademark of this industry. Emphasis on particle size, spreadability, and N release characteristics, and the role of K have been important developments in the turfgrass industry.

The fertilizer industry consists of organizations that range in size from the large vertically integrated corporations, which sell worldwide, to the small facilities that mechanically blend separate ingredients and service only a local market.

Branded lawn fertilizers were once sold primarily to homeowners and to select professional customers like the golf courses and others that demanded high-quality turf. As the need for quality turf increased, demand for specific turfgrass formulas, to meet the increasing quest for improved quality, came from the entire turfgrass industry. The more recent explosive expansion of the lawn care and the lawn maintenance industries, where the application of fertilizer is an intrinsic part of the sales programs, has provided a further boost to the fertilizer industry.

Fertilizer moves through several channels to the end user. The retail customer normally purchases through garden stores, nurseries, hardware and general merchandise stores, as well as through discount centers and, on occasion, from farm supply outlets.

The professional customer may purchase fertilizer from national manufacturing companies or from their distributors, from a regional or local fertilizer manufacturer or blender, or from outlets that serve the nonprofessional. Many of the outlets that serve the professional customers, also provide soil testing services.

The volume of total fertilizer used by the various segments of the turf industry is hard to estimate because of the diversity of companies servicing these markets and the overlap with farm fertilizers used on turfgrass. During 1981, the Kline Report estimated turf fertilizers used during that year at $99 200 000 (Kline and Co., 1986a).

Based on 1982 fertilizer use, Harvey J. Stangel & Associates estimated production of 1 464 000 000 t of nonfarm fertilizer products, not including manures or activated sludge (H. J. Stangel, 1986, personal communication). Of this quantity, 53.7% was sold at retail for lawns, 16.1% was used by lawn services, 14.3% by golf courses, 14.3% for gardens, nursery, and greenhouse use and 1.6% for miscellaneous uses.

Undoubtedly, the percentage applied by the lawn service industry has increased substantially since 1982.

IV. AFFILIATED FUNCTIONS AND SERVICES

There are several functional and service organizations affiliated with the turfgrass industry. They individually and collectively are a major contributing factor to the industry, especially those segments concerned with the design, construction, and development of facilities and those associated with product distribution. Eight significant components are reviewed in this section.

A. Architects

Golf course and landscape architects play a significant role in the turfgrass industry. The architect designs and specifies construction procedures and materials including plants to be used on specific sites. Once the specifications have been developed, the architects, in conjunction with their client or his representative, coordinates the negotiations and letting of bids to contractors or subcontractors. Major jobs often will be let to a general constractor who may then sublet various parts of the job to specialty contractors, for example, irrigation system installers. Another major optional role for the architect is that of monitoring contractor performance against specifications for materials and construction procedures. Monitoring also may be performed by the client, the owner's representative, or the general contractor who may represent the client or the general contractor in accordance with prior contractual arrangements.

There are no estimates as to the number of landscape architects of firms associated with the turfgrass industry. Few specialize solely in turfgrass design and installation. Rather, turfgrass is usually treated as a part of the overall landscape.

Golf course architects, on the other hand, deal directly with turfgrass as the major component of their endeavors. These highly specialized architects are concerned with three major components: (i) strategy of play; (ii) artistic design and layout, and (iii) agronomic aspects associated with turfgrass culture.

The American Golf Course Architects Society lists 87 members for 1986. There are probably an additional 50 golf course architects and individuals who design or remodel golf courses.

Golf architects generally operate as sole proprietors. Early in their careers, they often are associated with an established architectural firm. Some are loosely affiliated with other architects, contractors, land planners and, in some limited cases, real estate developers. Golf course architects are paid on a negotiated fixed fee or percentage basis. Although far more common outside the USA and Canada, a few golf architects may be associated with a specific "home" course and are responsible for keeping the course strategically sound from a playing standpoint, and current from an agronomic standpoint. Occasionally, clubs may employ golf architects to develop long-range plans for orderly course and grounds improvement and updating.

The volume of business generated by landscape and golf course architects can be only roughly estimated. If approximately 300 new golf courses are constructed annually, and if architectural fees average $100 000 per course, then the annual fees generated would approach $30 million. Add fees generated for feasibility studies, remodeling, consulting, and other specialized programs and the figure could well approach $40 to 50 million annually. Landscape architect fees for all turf-related jobs could generate at least this amount or more. The value of this overall segment is estimated to approach $100 million.

B. Associations

Associations are often an overlooked component of the turfgrass industry. They are made up of organizations and individuals affiliated

Table 2-11. National associations affiliated with the turfgrass industry.

American Cemetery Association
American Institute of Maintenance
American Land Development Association
American Landscape Contractors of America
American Seed Trade Association
American Society of Golf Course Architects
American Society of Irrigation Consultants
American Society of Landscape Architects
American Sod Producers Association
Club Managers Association of America
The Fertilizer Institute
Golf Course Builders of America
Golf Course Superintendents Association of America
The International Turfgrass Society
The Irrigation Association
The Lawn Institute
Musser International Turfgrass Foundation
National Agricultural Chemicals Association
National Association of Industrial and Office Parks
National Association of Public Golf Courses
National Catholic Cemetery Conference
National Golf Foundation
National Institute on Parks and Grounds Management
National Landscape Association
National Parks and Conservation Association
National Recreation and Parks Association
National Sports Turf Council
National Water Supply Improvement Association
O. J. Noer Research Foundation
Outdoor Power Equipment Institute
Professional Grounds Management Society
The Professional Lawn Care Association of America
Potash and Phosphate Institute
Society of Commercial Seed Technologists
Sports Turf Managers Association
Sprinkler Irrigation Association
U.S. Golf Association
U.S. Golf Association, Green Section

through a common interest in product, mission, or service. They provide beneficial information to professionals and nonprofessionals involved in the use and management of turfgrass and bring together groups of individuals who benefit from the mutual exchange of ideas. In addition to the national associations (Table 2-11) there are many state, regional, and local associations that devote their energies to the advancement of specific areas of the turfgrass industry.

Officers, directors, and employees of these organizations range from strictly volunteer workers to highly paid executive directors. Association membership, numbers of employees, responsibility, and objectives vary substantially between organizations. Collectively, they represent a significant component of the industry. While no dollar value has been determined, some associations handle millions of dollars annually from their designated or related activities.

Associations generate funds from membership dues, donations, golf tournaments, shows, educational conferences, and the expanding sale of merchandise. Funds are used to support organization activities, sponsor research and scholarship, and defray operating expenses.

C. Turfgrass Publications

While many publications carry occasional articles relating to turf management and use, only a few devote a major portion of their content to the turfgrass industry. These publications serve as the vehicle for informing the industry through articles, editorials, and advertising. They are extremely influential in interpreting the industries' orientation, economic trends, and in presenting new concepts and scientific advances to industry personnel. Table 2-12 lists turfgrass industry publications.

D. Consultants

Independent, commercial, and university turfgrass consultants advise and counsel architects, contractors, developers, manufacturers, publishers, property owners, suppliers, and professional turf managers. They provide information on product development and performance, site planning, development and construction, and turfgrass facilities management and maintenance. They serve as specialty reviewers, editors, and writers for trade journals and other publications. Consultants may be employed on a regular basis or for specific projects. In the southern USA, often they are engaged on a regular basis to advise on the control and prevention of pests such as nematodes, insects, and weeds.

Consultants are a valuable industry resource. They are specialists and knowledgeable in specific areas of turfgrass science. No estimates of the dollar value generated from their services and activities is available.

Table 2-12. Turfgrass-related publications.

Agronomy Journal	American Society of Agronomy 667 S. Segoe Road Madison, WI 53711
American Cemetery	Kates-Boylston Publ., Inc. 1501 Broadway New York, NY 10036
American Lawn Applicator or ALA	Gie, Inc. 4012 Bridge Avenue Cleveland, OH 44113
American School & University	North American Publishing Co. 401 N. Broad St. Philadelphia, PA 19108

(continued on next page)

Table 2-12. Continued.

The Catholic Cemetery	National Catholic Cemetery Conference 701 N. River Road Des Plaines, IL 60016
Crop Science	Crop Science Society of America, Inc. 677 S. Segoe Rd. Madison, WI 53711
Greenmaster	Canadian Golf Course Superintendents Assoc. 698 Wiston Rd., Suite 32 Toronto, ON, Canada M6N 3R3
Green Section Record	United States Golf Assoc. Golf House Far Hills, NJ 07931
Grounds Maintenance	Intertec Publications P.O. Box 12901 Overland Park, KS 66212
Harvests	The Lawn Institute P.O. Box 108 Pleasant Hill, TN 38578
Irrigation Age	Webb Publications 1999 Shepard Road St. Paul, MN 55116
Landscape & Irrigation	Gold Trade Publications P.O. Box 156 Encino, CA 91426
Landscape Management (formerly *Weeds, Trees, & Turf*)	Edgell Communications, Inc. Publications 7500 Old Oak Blvd. Cleveland, OH 44130
Lawn Care Industry	Edgell Communications, Inc. Publications 120 West Second St. Duluth, MN 55802
Landscape Trades	Horticultural Publ. Div. Landscape Ontario Horticultural Trades Assoc. 1293 Matheson Blvd. Mississauga, ON, Canada L4W 1R1
Soil Science Society of America Journal	Soil Science Society of America 677 S. Segoe Rd. Madison, WI 53711
Southern Golf	Brantwood Publications Northwood Plaza Station Clearwater, FL 33519
Sports Turf	Gold Trade Publications P.O. Box 156 Encino, CA 91426
Sports Turf Research Institute Journal	Sports Turf Research Inst. Bingley, St. Ives West Yorkshire, UK
Sports Turf Review	New Zealand Turf Culture Inst. 25 Trent Ave. Palmerston North, NZ

E. Contractors and Builders

Construction and establishment of new turfgrass areas requires skilled personnel and often specialized equipment. Soil mixes for golf greens and sports fields must provide rapid drainage and a firm, yet resilient surface to ensure player safety, especially on sports turf. The engineering of grades, drainage, determination of soil mix, and establishment specifications are the responsibility of the landscape or golf course architect. The contractor is responsible for implementing the specifications.

In some cases on commercial or industrial projects, the owner or manager of the property may contract directly with the construction firm. In other cases, small jobs may be undertaken by a lawn maintenance firm, a landscape nursery, or by crews of the general contractor. In most instances, responsibilities of the construction contractor also will include the seeding and establishment of the grass along with the first month or so of maintenance.

Contractors also will reroute play areas, update landscape, rebuild greens, and incorporate other design changes on golf courses when specified by the golf course architect; or they may perform these activities under supervision of the golf course superintendent or golf professional. Renovation and improvement of turf areas, especially sports fields and golf courses, where drainage is the major problem, often is handled by contracting firms that specialize in drainage improvement without complete rebuilding of the turf.

F. Garden Nursery Trade Involvement with Turf

Garden centers and nurseries may engage in design and construction activities in addition to their normal retail sales of trees, shrubs, flowering plants, and grass seed. They are primarily equipped to handle individual landscapes and small to moderate sized commercial jobs. They do not compete directly with those firms that specialize in the construction of larger complexes.

G. Distribution

Turfgrass products are moved through various channels and in various ways from the manufacturer or product source to the customer or end user. The most important channel for products is through a local or regional sales oriented organization referred to as a distributor. The distributor may stock, warehouse, finance, provide credit service, market, and sell products. They are able to provide efficient and timely delivery of products because they, or their authorized sale and service dealers, are located in close proximity to the turfgrass facility. They are able to purchase in large volumes and secure transportation economies, maintain technically competent sales and service organizations, and serve as liaison between the manufacturer or supplier and the end user.

Distributors of turfgrass products may be "full" line (handle machinery, fertilizer, seed, chemicals, and other more specialized products) or may elect to concentrate on only one or two product lines. Some may supply products to specialized segments (e.g., golf courses or sports turf) while others supply a broad spectrum of customers. Distributors may serve a small sector (metropolitan area) or a large geographic region. Distributorships may be publicly owned stock companies, or as in most cases, closed stock or privately owned corporations.

Turfgrass distributors are the primary conduit for the sale of products, supplies, and materials. They distribute to the end user and provide sales, marketing, and technical information originating from manufacturers and suppliers. The manufacturer supplies the distributor with product and marketing information, technical support, product warranty, and service support; and, in the case of machinery, with backup and slow-moving parts. Additionally, the manufacturer may provide product information and training for the distributor's sales and service personnel. In some cases, they sponsor technical service meetings for the distributor's customers. As a result, distributors and their sales and service personnel are an excellent customer source of information for problem solving, product utilization, and development of new products. They likewise serve as a source of information for the manufacturer on the need for new products and specialty items.

Machinery, chemical, fertilizer, and seed distributors have unique sales, marketing, storage, and financing requirements. One organization may elect to handle all of these lines or only one or two. In either case, they must provide for the specialized handling and sales of each product line.

1. Machinery

Distributors of machinery, including mowers, cultivators, irrigation equipment, and the many specialized units used on turfgrass facilities, have the greatest financial investment in inventory. Additionally, they must provide easy and timely parts availability and service capability. They should be located in close proximity to their customer or have access to a dealer who will service outlying areas.

Machinery distributors often handle two types of equipment, each of which is sold to different types of customers or end users. *Commercial* equipment is sold directly to the end user by a specialized sales force capable of demonstrating the equipment on the customer's facility. These salesmen are required to know equipment capabilities, limitations, and service requirements. This is called one-step distribution. *Consumer* or homeowner-type equipment is sold by a distributor (wholesaler) to a retail *dealer*, who in turn sells to the end user. This is called two-step distribution. The sales force handling these lines is more sales and marketing oriented than product oriented, although general product knowledge is an essential requirement. Dealers are located in strategic shopping areas throughout metro areas and in each community throughout major trading areas. Proximity to the customer is a major key to success.

Whether distribution is separate or combined into a single house; service, technical backup, inventory of whole goods, parts, and adequate finance programs, including customer credit, are essential to successful machinery distribution.

2. Chemicals

Because of the breadth of the kinds of chemicals available, distribution channels are broad and varied. A manufacturer and sometimes the formulator and packager may market the product directly to the professional consumer, but in most cases, they will distribute through an intermediary who services the professional customer. Products packaged and labeled for nonprofessional (homeowner) use are usually packaged in smaller containers and sold through retail outlets. The retail outlet may buy directly from the manufacturer, formulator, or from a distributor. Chemicals generally have a high unit cost and require special handling and storage conditions away from other products. Chemical distributors must provide these and also have adequate financial resources and well-trained sales staffs. Some distributors may concentrate on a limited class or number of chemicals and become local specialists in handling these products. In some instances, they may provide for custom application of these and other chemicals. Other firms handle a broad line of chemicals, other products, and simple package goods for a broad range of customers.

Chemicals are a highly competitive item, requiring innovative marketing and personalized sales techniques. Nevertheless, some chemical manufacturers continue to sell direct, by phone or catalogue.

3. Fertilizer

Distribution of fertilizer products packaged for retail sales are handled by the specialized fertilizer distributor or by the large turf supply houses.

The advent and subsequent broad distribution of bulk fertilizer mixing plants provided a means of serving general agricultural needs in an efficient and economic manner. Ease of blending to meet formula requirements, short trucking distances, the ability to use the facilities when agricultural demand is low and low production costs have been reasons for bulk blended fertilizers entering the turfgrass market.

The mixing plant may formulate to the customer's specifications, truck the fertilizer directly to the site, and spread it onto the turfgrass. This is a specialized form of distribution unique to the fertilizer industry.

While the above distribution pattern is true for much of the turfgrass fertilizer sold today, there continues to be a substantial market for special analysis materials for use on golf courses and other turf facilities, which require above-average turf quality. In most instances, chemically combined formulas are manufacturered in centrally located, high volume facilities by corporations able to make the sizable investment that is required. These firms will usually sell through a distributor who assumes the credit risk and who delivers products locally from his own warehouse or distribution point.

Liquid fertilizers are often used by lawn care companies and as the nutrient source for fertigation. Concentrated solutions or soluble dry products may be mixed with water to meet formula requirements, or they may be sold directly for customer dilution. In either case, the liquid material is pumped into tank trucks or mixed in the tank, transported to the site and sprayed directly onto the turf. In the case of fertigation, dry materials or previously mixed liquid fertilizer is supplied to the customer's tanks for dispersion in the irrigation system. Because of the ease of application when using proper equipment, many of the landscape and lawn care companies use liquid formulas in their operation.

4. Seed

Seed is primarily purchased and used by turf managers during favorable planting seasons, usually the spring and fall. Thus, seed sales are highly seasonable with storage and timely delivery being key marketing considerations.

Seed volume needed for new construction sites may run from one thousand to several thousand kilograms. These large one customer sales often are handled by a seed company on a direct sale basis. Sales to individual facility managers for repair and reconstruction purposes usually amount to only 100 to 300 kg. These accounts are serviced by a distributor organization that also handles other products and maintains regular customer contact. This system allows for more calls offering seed to customers at reduced sales expense.

Seed companies provide sales, marketing, and technical training for distributor personnel. They, in turn, pass this information on to their customers. In a few instances, the seed company may sell directly to turf facility managers through their own sales organization. In these instances, they usually carry fertilizer and chemical lines to share the sales cost load.

5. Value

No information is available on the extent or size of distribution segment of the turfgrass industry. There are at least 150 major distributors who handle nationally known major product lines and at least an equal number who may be classed as specialty or local distributors. Distributor sales volume may range from several thousands to several millions of dollars annually. Assuming $30 million annual sales for the major distributors and $2 million for the smaller businesses, then sales approach $4.5 billion, for the major and $300 million for the smaller organizations or an estimated volume level approaching $5 billion. These sales more likely exceed $6 billion.

H. Nurseries

Nurseries, garden centers, and other service outlets engaged in the retail sale of plant materials and gardening products will usually handle turf equipment, chemicals, fertilizer, and seed. These products are designed and packaged for use by homeowners, or maintenance operators of small turf facilities. Package size (and equipment size) as well as instructions for use and safety precautions will be adapted for handling by lay operators caring for smaller turfgrass areas. In most instances, the retail operator will purchase for resale from an authorized distributor or wholesaler thereby implementing the two-step system of distribution. These firms handle most of the turfgrass products purchased by the retail trade along with hardware and discount outlets.

There are no estimates of the value of the service contribution or products sold by this significant segment of the industry. They further indicate the complexity of the turfgrass industry, for although they contribute only indirectly to the industry, they nevertheless are a significant interactive component whose role cannot be ignored.

V. USE OF TURFGRASS FACILITIES

Usage of turfgrass facilities is the common thread that brings all the components of the industry together. This commonality of interest spans all segments and reaches into those areas not specifically reviewed in this chapter. In addition to the many facilities that use turfgrass (Table 2-1), there are groups that foster continuing development of youth programs to ensure future players and participants. Among these are the many baseball leagues, and the community organized soccer, football, rugby, tennis, and related programs. The National Golf Foundation (NGF) has sponsored college level teaching programs for many years for those interested in golf.

Usage also provides the initiative for continuing expansion of green spaces within communities. The combination of all green spaces ensures that cities and towns have adequate places for recreational activity and enjoyment of leisure time. Green spaces also are valuable adjuncts to cities and towns for other reasons. For example, they provide oxygen, become sinks for CO_2, help to purify runoff and groundwater, cleanse the atmosphere of many pollutants and metabolize pollutants and particulate matter dispersed upon grass.

The total acreage of green spaces within a community or a metropolitan area is variable and depends upon several factors. These factors include budgets, availability of space, local laws governing set-aside portions of housing and commercial land developments, and flood plains subject to infrequent flooding. Parks, playgrounds, school grounds, sports fields, and home lawns make up a substantial portion of a community's green spaces. Golf courses, boulevards, highway interchanges and roadsides, airports, commercial and industrial lawns, memorial cemeteries, and lawns around condominiums and apartment complexes likewise are an integral part of the green space.

Maintenance standards and costs are extremely variable from city to city and may range from only mowing to complete application of all cultural practices. Most of the controlling organizations for these facilities operate independently of each other and often are supported entirely by patrons. Parks, school grounds, highways, and similar tax-supported facilities are exceptions, although some of these facilities may benefit from individual financial contributions, volunteer labor, and donated supplies and materials. Those facilities that are well maintained and properly groomed are used to a greater extent than poorly maintained sites. Total expenditures for management and maintenance as well as the numbers of individuals that use the various types of turfgrass facilities are unavailable.

Three areas, namely golf courses, lawn care, and sports turf have been selected as examples to illustrate the many facets of turfgrass facility utilization.

A. The Golf Industry

Golf has played a key role in developing the turfgrass industry. It has been the most organized segment internationally, nationally, statewide, and locally. It also attracted manufacturers, suppliers, and distributors of turf-related products to the business opportunities offered; and thus, became the nucleus or core—the trend setters for the industry. Through the USGA, its affiliated clubs and allied associations, GCSAA, NGF, The Professional Golfers Association (PGA), American Society of Golf Course Architects, and others, the golf industry has provided the largest amount of private sector financial support for turfgrass research of any segment of the industry.

1. Organizations and Historical Growth

The renowned Royal and Ancient Golf Club of St. Andrews, Scotland, originated in 1754 and has been in continuous operation ever since (Farley, 1931; Nutter & Watson, 1969; Cornish & Whitten, 1981; Ward-Thomas et al., 1976). Various golf-related organizations have evolved to support, articulate on-going needs, and govern the game. For instance, the USGA was organized in 1894, the PGA in 1916, the Green Section of the USGA in 1920, and the GCSAA in 1926. The American Society of Golf Course Architects was founded in 1946. The turfgrass section of the American Society of Agronomy (ASA) was formed in 1947 primarily to support turfgrass management for golf courses. In 1955, this ASA division evolved into the C-5, Turfgrass Division of the Crop Science Society of America (CSSA) and began to broaden its perspectives to include all types of turfgrass facilities. The International Turfgrass Society, organized by J. B. Beard, J. R. Escritt, B. Langvad, and J. R. Watson in 1969 was not specifically directed to golf but was supportive. The American Sod Producers Association (ASPA) was organized in 1967 and the Golf Builders of America in 1971. Both were involved in golf turfgrass, although the former to a limited extent.

These organizations provided the leadership and have been responsible, to a large extent, for developing the golf industry as it exists today through their effort on the play of the game, turfgrass research, and the development and application of cultural practices.

The first *official* American golf club was organized in 1888 as St. Andrews in Yonkers, NY over a century after the St. Andrews, Scotland, golf club was organized. It should be noted, however, that a golf club was founded in Charleston, SC in 1786 and that the first North American clubs were Canadian; the Royal Montreal formed in 1873 and the Royal Quebec founded in 1874 (Cornish & Whitten, 1981; Ward-Thomas et al., 1976). Gibson (1958) related that 40 additional golf courses were built in the USA by 1895 for a total of 80 (Nutter & Watson, 1969).

The number of U.S. golf courses grew rapidly in the early 20th century. By 1920, there were 477 member clubs in the USGA. Growth of golf in America was explosive during the next decade and by 1931 there were some 5700 golf courses in the USA. The depression of the 1930s closed many courses, but growth was again rapid following World War II. There were more than 10 000 courses and 11 million golfers by 1970. By 1984, there were more than 13 000 golf courses in North America and some 17.5 million golfers (Heuber, 1984; Nutter & Watson, 1969).

2. Worldwide

Golf courses are a major amenity for housing developments and resorts. They are an essential entity for developing tourist trade, especially in countries that depend upon tourism as a major source of income. Estimates of the number of courses in the major golfing countries are shown in Table 2-13. The list is incomplete and numbers are based on best available information. New courses are added worldwide at an average rate of 150 to 200 each year. This is down from the 400 to 450 annually in the 1960s and early 1970s prior to the energy crisis in 1973 to 1974. Nevertheless, it is enough to classify the golf segment of the industry domestically and internationally as one of growth.

3. Facilities

The growth in golf facilities has been consistently upward since 1946. Hueber (1984) reported a total of 12 278 golf facilities and 13 181 golf courses in the USA. Some facilities have more than one golf course which accounts for the discrepancy in numbers.

The number of facilities in the USA for selected years from 1932 (the earliest year for which statistics are available) through 1984 as compiled by the NGF are listed in Table 2-14. Included in the numbers are regulation, executive, and par-3 facilities.

Eckhoff (1986) reported in March 1986 that growth in facilities completed, new course construction, and remodeling of existing courses continued upward during 1985. Further, he indicated that there was every reason to believe that the trend would continue through 1986 and beyond.

Table 2-13. Number of golf courses worldwide.†

Africa		Pacific and Far East	
Ivory Coast	3	Australia	1600
Israel	1	China	6
Morocco	7	Fiji	6
Saudi Arabia	3	Guam	1
South Africa	280	Hong Kong	7
Tunisia	5	India	130
Zambia	1	Indonesia	30
Zimbabwe	14	Japan	1600
Caribbean		Malaysia	40
Grand Cayman	1	New Caledonia	2
Jamaica	21	New Zealand	360
Puerto Rico	11	Philippines Is.	25
Trinidad	3	Singapore	15
Virgin Is.	4	South Korea	43
West Indies	24	Taiwan	40
Central America		Tahiti	3
Costa Rica	3	Thailand	3
Guatemala	2	Scandanavia	
Honduras	2	Denmark	51
Nicaragua	1	Finland	15
Panama	3	Iceland	25
Europe		Sweden	180
Austria	21	South America	
Belgium	18	Argentina	55
Czechoslovakia	7	Bolovia	2
France	150	Brazil	35
Greece	5	Chile	7
Hungary	1	Colombia	35
Italy	66	Ecuador	3
Netherlands	45	Paraguay	2
Portugal	20	Peru	7
Spain	100	Venezuela	21
Switzerland	29	United Kingdom	
W. Germany	225	England	1600
Yugoslavia	7	Ireland	260
North America		No. Ireland	80
Canada	1500	Scotland	460
Mexico	126	Wales	100
USA	13181		

† 1986 estimates based on data from National Golf Foundation; Toro International; Ron Fream, golf architect; The World Atlas of Golf (Ward-Thomas).

4. The Golfer

To provide support for the more than 13 000 existing courses in the USA and to sustain the anticipated annual growth in numbers of courses, there must be a corresponding increase in the number of golfers. For in the final analysis, it is the golfer who provides the financial resources needed for perpetual support of this continuously expanding segment of the turfgrass industry.

According to Hueber (1984) there was an estimated 1.25% increase in the number of golfers and a 2.5% increase in the number of rounds played in 1984. This translates to more than 18 million golfers playing more than 445 million rounds of golf in 1984. Hueber further projected that the number

Table 2-14. Growth in golf facilities in the USA—1931 through 1984. The National Golf Foundation (Heuber, 1984; Nutter & Watson, 1969).

Year	Facility total	Private	Daily fee	Municipal	Year	Facility total	Private	Daily fee	Municipal
1931†	5 691	4 448	700	532	1963	7 477	3 615	2 868	994
1934	5 727	4 155	1 006	566	1964	7 893	3 764	3 114	1 105
1937	5 196	3 489	1 070	637	1965	8 323	3 887	3 368	1 068
1939	5 303	3 405	1 119	699	1966	8 672	4 016	3 483	1 173
1941	5 209	3 188	1 210	711	1967	9 336	4 166	3 960	1 210
1946	4 817	3 018	1 076	723	1968	9 615	4 269	4 110	1 236
1947	4 870	3 073	1 061	736	1969	9 926	4 459	4 192	1 275
1948	4 901	3 090	1 076	735	1970	10 188	4 619	4 248	1 321
1949	4 926	3 068	1 108	750	1971	10 494	4 720	4 404	1 370
1950	4 931	3 049	1 141	741	1972	10 665	4 787	4 484	1 394
1951	4 970	2 996	1 214	760	1973	10 896	4 720	4 710	1 466
1952	5 026	3 029	1 246	75$	1974	11 134	4 7$5	4 878	1 541
1953	5 056	2 970	1 321	765	1975	11 370	4 770	5 014	1 586
1954	5 076	2 878	1 392	806	1976	11 562	4 791	5 121	1 650
1955	5 218	2 807	1 534	877	1977	11 745	4 847	5 203	1 695
1956	5 358	2 801	1 692	865	1978	11 885	4 872	5 271	1 742
1957	5 553	2 887	1 832	834	1979	11 966	4 848	5 340	1 778
1958	5 745	2 986	1 904	855	1980	12 005	4 839	5 372	1 794
1959	5 991	3 097	2 023	871	1981	12 035	4 789	5 428	1 818
1960	6 385	3 236	2 254	895	1982	12 140	4 798	5 494	1 848
1961	6 623	3 348	2 363	912	1983	12 197	4 809	5 528	1 860
1962	7 070	3 503	2 636	931	1984	12 278	4 831	5 566	1 881

† 1931 is the earliest year for which golf facility statistics are available. Includes regulation, executive, and par-3 facilities.

of golfers will grow to an estimated 21.2 million by the year 2000, thus assuring continued basic financial resources for the anticipated growth of the golf industry.

A summary profile of the 1985 American golfer (Beditz, 1985) indicated that four times as many males played golf as did females. Among golfers, the majority were between the ages of 20 and 49 yr. The greatest percentage of U.S. golfers resided in the North Central region; and, the lowest number in the Southern region. From a socioeconomic standpoint, the greatest number of golfers were college educated, profesisonally employed, and came from households with yearly incomes over $40 000.

For purposes of analysis, golfers were classified into four groups based on the number of times they played during the past 12 mo (Table 2-15).

Table 2-15. Golfer classification based on number of rounds played annually. (Anonymous, 1985d).

Golfer type	No. of times played	Percentage of all golfers	Golfers, millions
Infrequent	1–2	21	4.3
Occasional	3–7	28	5.5
Average	8–24	27	5.5
Avid	>25	24	4.9

5. The Course

A survey of 2 309 golf courses in late 1984 by the GCSAA and the NGF provides statistical data on the acreage and cost of maintaining America's golf courses. Projecting the financial data obtained from the sample, Beditz et al. estimated that $1.7 billion is spent each year for golf course maintenance, and that the nation's courses had a maintenance equipment inventory valued at more than $1.8 billion (Prusa & Beditz, 1985).

The survey showed that golf course maintenance costs vary significantly both between and within facility types and regions. For example, 50% of all private 18-hole regulation length courses spend at least $207 006 per year while 25% spent at least $291 573 per year to maintain their courses. The upper 25% of courses in the West, South Central, Mountain, and Pacific regions spend approximately $400 000 per year. Beditz et al. (Prusa & Beditz, 1985) summarized the variation in costs by stating "there is no single standard for golf course maintenance costs." They recognized that factors such as facility type, size, region, quality of maintenance, and the number of rounds played must be considered when comparing a specific facility's costs with the figures developed in this survey.

According to this survey, the average hole on a regulation 18-hole course contains tees of 200 m^2 (2156 ft^2), fairways of 1.1 ha (2.8 acres), and greens of 518 m^2 (5579 ft^2). The average 18-hole course consists of 60 ha (133 acres) and the average 9-hole course contains 28 ha (62 acres). (These are median values that indicate that 50% of the samples are above and 50% below the stated figures.)

Key financial information indicated by the 1985 survey shows the following:

Operating Costs
- Annual maintenance costs at private 18-hole regulation courses exceed those at municipal and daily fee courses by 14.6 and 71.6%, respectively.
- Operating costs at private and municipal 9-hole regulation courses were greater than public fee by almost 30%.
- Operating costs at executive and par-3 courses were more than four times greater for 18-hole than 9-hole courses.

Capital Expenditures
- Both 9 and 18-hole municipal courses budget more for capital project expenditures than private or daily fee courses.
- Private 18-hole courses spend 4.7% more than municipal and 60.4% more than daily fee courses for maintenance equipment.

Inventory Values
- Private 18-hole courses have invested 13.7% more than municipal and 48.6% more than daily fee courses in equipment inventory.
- The West led all other regions in inventory values for each type of 18-hole regulation facility.

- Inventories of equipment and supplies at 9-hole daily fee facilities were greater than either private (2%) or municipal (11.5%) facilities.
- For executive and par-3 courses, inventory values for 18-hole courses were three times higher than those of 9-hole courses.

6. Management Organization

Management structure of a golf course is a function of the class of course, for example, a private, municipal, public fee, or a combination of any of these.

Public fee courses are often owned and managed by an individual or a group of individuals. These courses may or may not have a board of directors. When a board does exist, it is often a fixed nonrotating group whose major interest is to establish policies that guide and direct the managerial functions toward club profit. The superintendent normally reports to the owner or designated chief executive officer.

Municipal courses are operated most often by the park department of the municipality. They may be treated as a separate department or their operation may be an integral part of the municipal park and recreation department.

Private golf clubs, historically have been run by an elected board of directors. Each member of the board has assumed responsibilty for a major function, for example, the green chairman, house chairman, or golf chairman. The operational head for each major function under this arrangement is the golf course superintendent, the club manager, and the golf professional.

In an effort to improve operational efficiencies, several private clubs have, in recent years, employed a general manager or chief executive officer who has overall responsibility for the operation of the club. In this structure, the three functional department heads report to the general manager. Some general managers also may serve as a department head, for example, as the golf course superintendent or the club manager.

Management Companies. An even more recent development in club management has been the assumption of operating responsibilities by a club management organization. These organizations may build the golf course, purchase it, or, simply manage a part or all of the facility under a contractual arrangement. Some of these organizations like the pioneer, Club Corporation of America, operate internationally. They own or manage city clubs as well as golf clubs. Other organizations like American Golf tend to specialize in the management of daily fee golf courses. Still others, like developers Kindred and Company, Houston, TX, and PGA Tour Investment Corp., Jacksonville, FL, take equity positions in the club and manage it for themselves and the other owners. The major thrust of these groups is management efficiency and operational profit for their organizations and the club.

7. Asset Value

The grounds, buildings, equipment, furniture, and other assets of the nation's golf courses are valued in the billions of dollars. These values are not included in the total estimate of the industry value. Their greatest value, however, lies in their contribution to the nation's green spaces and as healthy and aesthetically appealing places for wholesome play and relaxation.

B. Lawn Care Industry

The rapid development of the industrialized world in the last century has produced a dramatic shift from an agrarian society to an industrial, urbanized population. That development, concomitant with dramatic population growth, has resulted in the existence of more than 85 million households in the USA primarily in an urban setting. Concurrent with this degree of growth has been a dramatic increase in income, leisure time, and recreational pursuits. These factors made it possible for most households to expand use of turfgrasses and ornamental plants and to pay for service companies to provide professional care for their grounds and plant material.

The residential marketplace may be divided arbitrarily into several categories and services for lawn care practices. They are as follows: those who (i) mow only, (ii) perform all their own lawn maintenance functions (the true do-it-yourself [DIY] segment), (iii) employ private gardeners, (iv) perform mowing maintenance, (v) perform landscape maintenance, and (vi) professional lawn care companies.

The mowing and landscape maintenance companies may apply fertilizers and pesticides to turfgrasses on properties they service, or may subcontract this work to other firms in the business. The professional lawn care industry may be narrowly defined as a service business that provides fertilization and pest control for a large segment of residential and commercial customers at a price many homeowners and proprietors can afford.

1. History

Historically, most residential lawns were mowed and maintained by the occupant, except for a small segment of upper income households that may have employed individual gardeners for their ornamental landscape plants and turfgrass maintenance. Increasing attention to lawn maintenance by DIY homeowners resulted in several companies supplying a large array of excellent products for this market. Companies such as O.M. Scott and Sons, Chevron Chemical Company (Ortho brand), and others sold excellent DIY products and the green industry in American suburbia was underway. Through the 1950s and 1960s, additional companies specializing in landscape and mowing maintenance became increasingly popular as the public demanded and was willing to pay for additional services.

The growth of an urban population, the increasing interest of home-owners in professional and leisure activities, the availability of discretionary funds, the recognition of aesthetic and economic value of landscapes, and the desire for a dark green, high-quality lawn gave rise to the professional lawn care service industry in the late 1960s. Dramatic growth in the volume of business and number of companies offering their service occurred during the decade of the 1970s and continued into the 1980s.

The professional lawn care industry most likely had its first developments in landscape maintenance companies and in small part-time or full-time businesses that applied fertilizers and pesticides to the lawns of a group of customers in their local area. Companies such as Lawn Doctor, Lawn-A-Mat, and Lawn King started in the Newark, NJ area in the late 1960s. Lawn Doctor is a franchise operation that evolved out of a hardware store owned by Anthony Giordano in 1967. Paul and Richard Duke, who operated Duke's Nursery in western Ohio, started fertilizing lawns and providing pest control in the late 1960s. In 1969, they formed ChemLawn Corporation. This organization has grown over the years to become the leader of the industry and, by far, the largest lawn care company. ChemLawn reported lawn care revenues in excess of $292 million in 1986 (Anonymous, 1986c).

2. Programs

Lawn care companies offer programs with three to six applications annually, depending on the complexity and geographic location. Most companies apply a combination of N, P, and K fertilizer in each application. Micronutrients may be applied on a periodic basis depending on turfgrass species, seasonal conditions, and geographic location.

Pest control is a key and integral part of lawn care success. A weed-free lawn is most important to customers and failure to eliminate weeds is a primary cause of customer complaints. Insects are the second most prevalent pest problem in residential turfs. The professional applicator must be able to control both surface and soil insects to be successful. Diseases are major problems in some locations but not all. Diseases may be addressed on a special treatment basis rather than a typical program application. Most successful companies will have separate programs for different conditions (e.g., sun vs. shade), different turfgrasses (e.g., warm vs. cool season) and customers (e.g., old vs. new).

A generalized program for Kentucky bluegrass in the humid, cool-season North is presented in Table 2-16 and a program for bermudagrass in the Southern USA is found in Table 2-17.

Most firms operating a professional lawn care service also provide additional customer service calls and product applications to their lawns. Supplemental services include aeration, dethatching, liming, mulching, pruning, vegetation control, and renovation, which are offered on an additional fee basis.

The Professional Lawn Care Association of America (PLCAA) (Anonymous, 1985c) conducted an operating performance survey in 1984. There were 55 firms reporting key performance measures, including a category on chemical supply purchase data. The largest chemical expenditure averaged over all firms was for fertilizers, followed by preemergent herbicides, insecticides,

Table 2-16. Generalized commercial lawn care program for established Kentucky bluegrass in the humid, cool-season north.

Category	Treatment dates			
	1 Mar. – 15 May	15 May – 15 July	15 July – 15 Sept.	15 Sept. – 15 Nov.
	kg ha^{-1}			
N	36.6–48.8	36.6–6.0	24.4–48.8	61.0–85.4
P	4.9–12.2	4.9–14.6	3.9–5.9	7.3–14.6
K	9.8–24.4	9.8–29.3	5.9–12.2	12.2–39.0
Broadleaf herbicide[†]	X			X
Preemergent herbicide[†]	X			
Insectcide, surface insects[†]		X		
Insecticide, soil insects[†]			X	
Miscellaneous products and services	X	X	X	X

[†] Pesticides are applied only when pest pressures dictate. Fungicides for disease control are less frequently applied on a programmed basis.

and postemergent herbicides (Table 2-18). Data were projected by 1985 and 1986 from the State of the Industry Survey by *Lawn Care Industry* magazine (Table 2-18). This data includes chemical lawn care and landscape maintenance information (Anonymous, 1985b, 1986d).

3. Value and Volume

There are approximately 49.8 million owner-occupied, single-family detached households (SFDH) in the USA. Approximately 35.5 million of these SFDH are prime target customers for the lawn care industry. Prime target customers for the professional lawn care industry may be defined as single family residences with family income of more than $20 000. A comparison of single family households that do no lawn care, the DIY group,

Table 2-17. Generalized commercial lawn care program for established bermudagrass in the southern USA.

Category	Treatment dates				
	15 Feb. – 1 Apr.	1 Apr. – 7 June	7 June – 7 Aug.	7 Aug. – 1 Oct.	1 Oct. – 10 Nov.
	kg ha^{-1}				
N	61.0–85.4	61.0–85.4	48.8–73.2	48.8–73.2	36.6–48.8
P	19.5–29.3	9.8–14.6	4.9–9.8	14.6–24.4	12.2–14.6
K	39.0–61.0	29.3–43.9	24.4–36.6	29.3–48.8	24.4–32.2
Fe		X			
Insecticide[†]			X		
Herbicide preemergent[†]	X	X			
Herbicide grasses[†]		X	X		
Herbicide, broadleaf[†]	X	X			X
Miscellaneous products and services	X	X	X	X	X

[†] Pesticides are applied only when pest pressures dictate. Fungicides for disease control are less frequently applied on a programmed basis.

Table 2-18. Chemical supply purchase estimates for the professional lawn care and landscape maintenance industries for 1984 and 1985 from two surveys.

Product category	Total purchases			Projected expenditures
	1984†	1985‡	1983§	1983§
		%		
Granular fertilizer	33.0	33.3	32.0	$113
Preemergence herbicides	18.9	15.7	19.2	67.9
Liquid fertilizer	14.9	15.5	14.6	51.7
Insecticides	14.5	10.6	11.5	40.5
Postemergence herbicides	9.7	8.2	8.1	28.5
Grass seed	2.3	9.0	8.7	30.8
Fungicides	2.2	4.0	2.7	9.7
Soil amendments	1.0	3.4	2.8	9.9
Plant growth regulators	--	0.3	0.4	1.3
Other	3.4	--	--	--

† Anonymous, 1985e. For chemical lawn care only.
‡ Anonymous, 1985b. Includes professional lawn care and landscape maintenance.
§ Anonymous, 1986d. Includes professional lawn care and landscape maintenance.

and those that hire a professional company (Fig. 2-1) clearly illustrates a nonmature industry with substantial opportunity for growth.

The professional lawn care industry has grown dramatically since the late 1960s. Reliable estimates of total revenue by professional lawn care companies are difficult to obtain and vary considerably. One survey listed the chemical lawn care industry revenue at $932 million for 1985 (Anonymous, 1986d); another survey using a broader definition places the industry closer to $2.0 billion (Kline, 1986a); and still others indicate an industry smaller than $900 million. It also was reported that 1985 revenues for the landscape maintenance industry totaled $1.3 billion (Anonymous, 1986d).

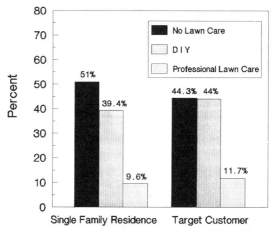

Fig. 2-1. Estimated percentage of single family residences and target customers that do no chemical lawn care, do-it-yourself (DIY), or hire a professional company. (Courtesy: The ChemLawn Corp., Columbus, OH.)

Table 2-19. Estimated do-it-yourself lawn care sales by product category for 1984 in manufacturers and consumer dollars (Anonymous, 1985b).

Lawn product category	Manufacturers, $	Consumer, $
Fertilizers	$385 000 000	$480 000 000
Herbicides	80 000 000	165 000 000
Insecticides	20 000 000	42 000 000
Fungicides	800 000	1 500 000
Total	$485 800 000	$688 500 000

4. Number of Companies

There were approximately 950 lawn care companies holding membership in PLCAA in 1989. A Kline Report estimated total active lawn care companies at 5500 (Kline, 1986b). The industry giant is ChemLawn Corporation, headquartered in Columbus, OH, with 1.6 million residential customers and 1986 revenue of $292.4 million (Anonymous, 1986c). These numbers included only the 180 or more company-owned branches. With franchise sales included, the revenue and customer numbers would be considerably larger. Total company customers and revenues for 1986 for all service lines (again not including franchises) were $1.9 million and $353.6 million, respectively (Anonymous, 1986c).

Tru-Green Corporation (purchased by Waste Management, Inc. in 1988) in Alpharetta, GA is the second largest lawn care company with 1985 revenues of approximately $38 million (Anonymous, 1986e) and estimated 1988 revenues of $200 million due to numerous acquisitions. Lawn Doctor of Matawan, NJ is probably the largest franchise lawn care company with 275 franchises and revenues for 1986 estimated at $33 million (Weidner, 1986). Forty-three professional lawn care companies in the USA had gross receipts of more than $1 million in 1984 (Anonymous, 1985b), while the number of $1-million copmanies grew to 57 in 1985 (Anonymous, 1986e).

Another important lawn care group is the large number of household occupants who do their own fertilization and pest control. Many products are available through retail outlets. Accurate revenue figures for this segment are also difficult to obtain. One report placed the DIY lawn care sales for 1984 at $485.8 million in manufacturers' dollars and $688.5 million in consumer dollars (Sullivan & Tarantola, 1985). These figures are probably low compared to actual sales. The DIY lawn care segment remains a large and important component of lawn care and the turfgrass industry (Table 2-19).

Many professional lawn care firms have diversified. They offer tree and shrub care, aeration, mowing maintenance, and other services. The professional lawn care, DIY, mowing maintenance, and other companies, both large and small, are important to the service oriented U.S. economy and help substantially to keep America green.

C. Sports Turfgrass

Sports fields may be defined as those areas prepared and maintained for games and other recreational activities. Most are planted to grass while a limited number of major league and university fields designated for baseball, football, and sometimes soccer and rugby use synthetic surfaces.

In comparison to golf, sports turf is a much larger, loosely affiliated and basically unorganized (except for the Sports Turf Managers Association) segment of the turfgrass industry. Sports turf has been described by Dr. F.V. Grau, President of the Musser International Turfgrass Foundation, as an emerging giant. To realize its full potential, the sports turf industry needs to establish standards for playing surfaces (natural grass and artificial surfaces). Further, there is a need to develop and insist that architects provide sound specifications for design and construction of sports fields. Too many fields are not properly drained and have seedbeds that are too shallow (< 40 cm) to effect proper water movement. Too many contractors and architects further complicate and disrupt water movement into (infiltration), through (percolation), and out of (drainage) the seedbed by planting sod grown in a different soil texture than that of the seedbed. Finally, there is a need to develop clear and responsible lines of communication between all parties involved in the administration, construction, and maintenance of sports fields.

Among the games and sports activities generally included in sports turf are: baseball, bocce ball, cricket, croquet, field hockey, football, golf, lacrosse, lawn bowling, polo, rugby, soccer, and softball.

Participants, spectators, and television audiences are included in the overall numbers associated with sports fields. It is indeed, a large segment of the turfgrass industry and a major contributing factor to our way of life.

1. History and Evolution

Outdoor games and sports events have been played and observed almost as long as people have lived in communities. On the North American continent, the Indians initially played on open areas near their villages and later developed playing fields and stadiums designated specifically for sports. Many local sports events in the USA were and are played on pastures, village greens, and on dual purpose parks and playgrounds. These areas received little or no maintenance other than an occasional mowing. University and professional sports organizations began to improve the construction, management and turf maintenance at their facilities in the late 1950s and early 1960s. Currently, there are thousands of playing fields, sports facilities, and dual purpose park areas available. Maintenance and quality of playing surfaces vary from poor to excellent.

Intensive use of playing fields increased the need for researchers to improve the playing quality of turfgrass facilities, especially for the growing number of organized sports. The modestly maintained playing field, constructed of native soil and planted to common, unimproved grasses, was incapable of supporting the traffic to which it was being subjected.

2. Research

Research was initiated in Europe and in the USA during the late 1950s and early 1960s to solve problems associated with production of quality and safe playing fields. Research launched and sponsored by sports organizations and institutions in Europe was directed toward development of methods for construction and maintenance of superior and safe playing surfaces as well as selection and breeding of more traffic-tolerant grasses. Efforts in the USA were directed initially toward improving putting green soils and superior grasses for golf turf.

Sports turf research programs and recommendations based on European studies have been published in Proceedings of the International Turfgrass Research Conference. Among those specifically relating to sports turf are: Escritt (1970) and Langvad and Weibull (1970) in the first proceedings; Daniel et al. (1974), Fisher and Ede (1974), Petersen (1974), and Skirde (1974) in the second proceedings; Blake (1980), Boekel (1980), Franken (1980) and van Wijk and Beuving (1980) in the third proceedings; Adams (1981) in the fourth proceedings, and Canaway (1985) in the fifth proceedings. Much of the more recent research has been published in the *Journal of the Sports Turf Research Institute:* for example, Bell et al. (1985); Baker et al. (1988a, b).

Basic information on methods and materials for golf green construction in North America was developed by Ferguson et al. (1960). Expansion of this work and research on sand particle sizes by S. W. Bingaman, H. Kohnke, W. H. Daniel, R. P. Freeborg, and M. J. Robey at Purdue University led to pioneer studies of techniques and procedures for improving sports turf. Daniel and Robey used their research to develop specifications for Prescription Athletic Turf (PAT) playing fields (Daniel et al., 1974). The PAT system along with the European "cell" system and other modified root-zone systems represent current state-of-the-art for development and maintenance of sports turf.

Construction of soil matrix for intensively used playing fields involves the use of high percentages (75–80%) of medium sand (0.25 – 0.50 mm). Architects and site construction contractors familiar with the technique of building these fields often base the cost of construction on intensity of use and available funds.

Information describing proper construction and maintenance of athletic facilities has been available since the late 1960s but has generally not reached those responsible for care and management of sports fields. This situation is gradually changing. Knowledgeable private consultants and state extension personnel are available to work with interested school and park boards, athletic directors, coaches, concerned parents, and facility managers. Design, construction, reconstruction, remodeling, and proper maintenance of sports turf are among the areas supported by consultants. Architects, construction contractors, and specialists in amending soils, improving and installing drainage and irrigation systems and establishing or renovating fields to improved traffic-tolerant grasses are available to assist in improving sports fields.

A key factor in emerging interest in sports turf at the para-professional levels is the recognition that athletic field maintenance requires personnel skilled in grounds management and that the job can no longer be handled on a part-time basis by a member of the custodial staff. The increased recognition of the healthful benefits of active recreation and physical fitness has substantially increased the awareness of the general public and professional recreation directors to the need for adequate and safe playing fields. Professional sports managers and color telecasting of major sporting events likewise has had a major impact on the public perception of "what's good and what's bad" about playing fields. While the public may use only the color (green) as the major criteria for quality; this awareness, nevertheless, has stimulated interest in providing quality turfgrass for all levels of sporting events.

3. Associations

Public awareness and the desire for improving turf facilities on the part of individuals and sports organizations has provided the impetus for expanding the Sports Turf Managers Association. A publication named *Sports Turf*, launched in 1985, is devoted to advocating proper utilization and management of athletic facilities.

The Sports Turf Managers Association was organized in 1981 by: Harry Gill, Milwaukee, WI; George Toma, Kansas City, KS; Dick Ericksen, Minneapolis; Bill Daniel, Purdue, IN, and others. The major objective of this group was to support communication between professional turf managers and provide information for interested non-professionals that would lead to improved playing fields. This association was incorporated in 1985 and employed Kent Kurtz as executive director. It is anticipated that membership will approach 500 plus by the end of 1986 (R. Ericksen, 1986, personal communication; K. Kurtz, 1986, personal communication).

The National Sports Turf Council was organized in 1986 by F. Grau, J. Murray, D. Waddington, T. Turner, B. Shank, E. Roberts, and others. This group, whose efforts are directed toward dissemination of reliable information for developing safe sports turf, elected F. V. Grau as chair. This organization initially operated as a tax exempt entity under the umbrella of the Musser International Turfgrass Foundation.

Sports turfgrass seemingly parallels golf turfgrass in many respects, although it is currently served by far fewer organizations and associations than is golf. Decades ago, golf turfgrass managers were secretive about their activities and the techniques used to produce good turfgrass. The same was true of sports field managers until the late 1970s and early 1980s. This reluctance to share ideas for the betterment of sports turf is gradually being overcome. Sports organizations and publications are expanding their efforts to develop better communications and establish forums for exchange of information.

4. Synthetic Turf

In the early 1960s, the Houston Astrodome was constructed. It was the first closed dome stadium built to permit play under all weather conditions. It was evident that the fully air-conditioned structure would need events beyond football and baseball to generate the funds to defray costs of construction and maintenance. The playing field was originally planted to Tifgreen bermudagrass. The turf grew satisfactorily and supported play until the dome was painted, ostensibly to protect players eyes against the sun. This painting caused a substantial light reduction, causing the turfgrass leaves to elongate and become soft. The weak turfgrass resulting could not support play.

A synthetic turf named *Astroturf* was introduced into the Astrodome as the new playing surface. This material permitted expansion of revenue-producing events without causing serious damage to the playing surface. Cost of maintenance of the synthetic surface, although originally touted as minimal, has since proven to be as great or greater than that for natural grass surfaces. Cleaning, repair of burn spots from cigarettes and tears, and looseness are the major maintenance cost factors. The surface must be replaced on a 5 to 7 yr basis. It lacks the resilience of natural turf and produces more wear and tear on the athletes, causing concerns about career longevity by athletes, agents, and team managers (G. Toma, 1986, personal communication).

Seventeen national football league teams currently play home games on synthetic surfaces while 11 have natural turf. Six National League baseball teams have natural grass and six play in stadiums with synthetic covers. In the American League, 10 baseball teams play on natural grass and four on synthetic surfaces (G. Toma, 1986, personal communication; S. Wightman, 1986, personal communication). Toma believes there will be a trend back to natural turfgrass to alleviate player concerns over shortened years of play.

Synthetic covers allow multiple use of stadiums to support events unrelated to those normally perceived as sports. Events such as rock concerts generate funds for the stadium owners and help to justify financing of much needed civic arenas.

Nevertheless, there is a marked need for research that may lead to the development of an environment suitable for the growth of turfgrass within closed, and partially domed stadiums.

5. Sports Facilities

It is impossible to identify the number of sports fields that exist in North America or to accurately estimate the funds expended for their upkeep. S. Wightman (1986, personnal communication) estimated that the city of Denver, CO, with a population of approximately 600 000, had 250 recreation fields, including practice fields at each of its 10 high schools, and a consolidated stadium for inter-school games. One may assume similar estimated for cities of comparable size.

K. Kurtz (1986, personal communication) and B. Shank (1986, personal communication) estimate there are between 15 000 and 20 000 school districts and an equal number of park systems in the USA. There are some 1200 4-yr colleges in the USA and 70 in Canada with intramural facilities and varsity practice and playing fields. There are also more than 660 community colleges and an unknown number of junior colleges that compete in sports activities.

A conservative estimate of the area involved in school districts is approximately 160 000 to 200 000 ha. Add colleges, universities, junior colleges, and private sports facilities and a minimal figure of 450 000 ha is reasonable (B.L. Shank, 1986, personal communication).

6. Participants

The number of participants in various organized sports events serves as another indication of the size of the sports turf segment of the turfgrass industry. Statistics indicate more than 2.2 million youngsters are involved in Little League baseball and more than 1 million in other baseball and softball leagues. More than 22 million adults play softball in at least 173 000 amateur softball leagues. Several million youngsters play organized soccer (the fastest growing sport) in the USA (K. Kurtz, 1986, personal communication). Millions more use these facilities for non-organized recreational sports activities.

Kurtz (1986, personal communication) estimates the number of high school and college football players in excess of 1.5 million. In addition, there are approximately 0.75 million soccer players; and 35 000 participants using more than 80 full-size croquet courts in the USA.

7. Economic Value

It is apparent there is a dearth of information dealing with the economic value of sports turf and there is every indication that it will take time before reliable data can be gathered. It is encouraging to note the increasing activity directed toward accumulating statistical data by the affiliated and supportive associations, publications, organizations, and individuals.

Obviously sports turf is a multimillion dollar segment of the industry even though statistical data and an overall controlling agency is lacking. Spectator fees, television revenues, equipment, fertilizer and chemical sales, soil amendments, irrigation system components and contractor installation fees, special drainage installation fees, and the development and sale of improved wear-resistant grasses contribute to the economic value of sports turf.

Undoubtedly, the recreational and aesthetic value of sports turf facilities in the USA exceed their actual material value.

VI. TURFGRASS SURVEYS

Turfgrass associations, trade organizations, corporations, marketing consulting firms, agricultural extension services, and trade publications provide turfgrass survey data from time to time. Unfortunately, there has been no attempt to standardize nor develop a nationwide survey encompassing the entire turfgrass industry. No attempt will be made to combine nor interpret the various surveys. Rather it is suggested that interested individuals contact the appropriate organizations to obtain the latest information available from them.

Several turfgrass associations have provided estimates covering what is believed to be reasonable approximations of the dollars spent to maintain turfgrass acreages within their states (Table 2-9).

While there is no consistency in the way these figures were developed, the totals are impressive and provide some idea of the importance of the turfgrass industry to the economy of the respective states. As an example, turfgrass ranks as the third largest crop in Virginia (R.E. Schmidt, 1983, personal communication), and only beef cattle (*Bos taurus*) and cotton (*Gossypium hirsutum* L.) exceed the gross value of turfgrass in Texas (R.L. Duble, 1983, personal communication). Data from the Rhode Island Department of Economic Development for 1980 indicates turf maintenance expenditures of $48.3 million, the value of fish landings at $46.1 million, and for crops and livestock sold, at $32.4 million (C.R. Skogley, 1983, personal communication). The 1982 replacement cost for the South Carolina turfgrass acreage would have amounted to $1.5 billion (A.R. Mazur, 1983, personal communication). Newman (1983, personal communication) estimated 1983 replacement cost for Wisconsin at $200 million. The North Carolina Turfgrass Survey of 1986 reported that the state had 846 000 ha of maintained turf and that the total maintenance expense for this turf was $733.8 million (J.M. DiPaola, 1988, personal communication).

Roberts (1986) has compiled selected data and commentary from nine trade journals and from state and national turfgrass surveys conducted since 1980. Information is included on the turfgrass industry, sod industry, golf turf, grounds management, DIY lawn care, the lawn care industry, and industry surveys.

Gibeault and Cockerham (1985) have prepared a summary which suggests that 340 000 people make their living within the turfgrass industry and that the expenditure for maintenance in 1982 amounted to $24.5 billion. A breakdown of this figure is presented in Table 2-9. Further details on the analysis of the industry by state can be obtained by contacting the turf specialist or the Extension Service of the appropriate state experiment station. Gibeault and Cockerham (1985) hypothesized the value of turfgrass within a typical city of 170 000 by stating, "$12 million on turf alone significantly affects the economy of the city. Multiplier effects, obviously, extend that many fold. Turf is important to this city—aesthetically, economically, and socially."

VII. SUMMARY

The turfgrass industry is a broad interrelated specialized group of individuals and organizations who share a common interest in the production, maintenance, and utilization of the nation's green spaces. Nevertheless, it is difficult to obtain reliable and accurate information on the various segments. This reflects, in part, the complexity of the interactive relationships and, in part, the immaturity and privacy of the industry.

Turfgrass surveys contribute to the knowledge and understanding of the size and types of turfgrass within a state. Surveys could provide a basis for development of national data; however, the lack of standardization renders them of value only to the specific entity surveyed. Thus, they do not contribute to a reliable estimate of the total value of the industry.

If one accepts the estimates for the various segments of the industry, as developed in this chapter, it would appear that an overall value of some $25 billion is a reasonable estimate for this industry. To be more accurate, values, perhaps, should be stated as a range, for example, $20 to $30 billion.

Regardless of the dollar values assigned or estimated, the true value of the turfgrass industry cannot be measured in monetary terms. Too often these values are relatively meaningless and unrelated. The true value of the industry lies in the contribution that all types of green spaces make to our way of life. In this respect, they are a national treasure that must be protected and expanded.

ACKNOWLEDGMENT

Many individuals contributed to the preparation of this material. The authors wish to thank the following for their assistance with the compilation of this chapter.

James B. Beard, Texas A&M University, College Station
R. L. Duble, Texas A&M University, College Station

Evolution and Development:
Dick Ericksen, grounds superintendent, HHH Metrodome, Minneapolis, MN
Kent Kurtz, executive director, Sports Turf Managers Assoc., Ontario, CA
Bruce Shank, editor, Sports Turf, Goldtrade Publications, Encino, CA
George Toma, H.S. Truman Sports Complex, Kansas City, MO
Chip Toma, head groundkeeper, Kansas City Chiefs, Kansas City, MO
Steve Wightman, field manager, Mile High Stadium, Denver, CO

Sod Industry:
Douglas H. Fender, American Sod Producers Association, Rolling Meadows, IL
J. S. Fickle, Mallinckrodt, Inc., St. Louis, MO
Ray Jensen, Tifton Turf, Tifton, GA

Seed Industry:
Doyle Jacklin, Jacklin Seed Co., Post Falls, ID
Bill Rose, Turf-Seed, Inc., Hubbard, OR
Norman Rothwell, Rothwell Seeds, Ltd., Lindsey, ON, Canada
Harry Stalford, International Seed Co., Halsey, OR

R. Newman, Univ. of Wisconsin, Madison, WI
Bill Meyer, Turf-Seed, Inc., Hubbard, OR
H. Schutte, Midcontinent Seed Co., Marshall, MO
P. Hodges, H & H Seed Co., Yuma, AZ

Lawn Care Industry:
C. R. Skogley, Univ. of Rhode Island, Kingston, RI
T. Skogley, Vander Have Oregon, Inc., Albany, OR

Fertilizer Industry:
H. J. Stangel, Highland Park, NJ

Turfgrass Surveys:
A. R. Mazur, Clemson Univ., Clemson, SC
Dick Schmidt, Virginia Polytechnic Univ., Blacksburg, VA
J. M. DiPaola, North Carolina State Univ., Raleigh, NC.

REFERENCES

Adams, W. 1981. Soils and plant nutrition for sportsturf. Perspectives and prospects. p. 167–179. *In* R.W. Sheard (ed.) Proc. 4th Int. Turfgrass Res. Conf., Guelph, ON, Canada. 19–23 July. Int. Turfgrass Soc., and Ontario Agric. Coll., Univ. of Guelph, ON, Canada.

Anonymous. 1985a. Annual report of the Toro Company. Kendrick B. Melrose, President. The Toro Co., Minneapolis, MN.

Anonymous. 1985b. Chemical applicators help industry hit new heights. p. 20–21. Lawn Care Ind. 9(5):20–21.

Anonymous. 1985c. 1985 Operating performance ratios for the professional lawn care association. Professional Lawn Care Assoc. of Am., Marietta, GA.

Anonymous. 1985d. Seven companies join million-dollar makers. Lawn Care Ind. 9(5):14–15.

Anonymous. 1986a. Annual report on outdoor power equipment production. Outdoor Power Equipment Inst., Washington, DC.

Anonymous. 1986b. Annual report. Oregon Fine Fescue Commission, Salem, OR.

Anonymous. 1986c. A matter of leadership. ChemLawn Corp. Ann. Rep. 1986. ChemLawn Corp., Columbus, OH.

Anonymous. 1986d. State of the industry. Lawn Care Ind. 10(6):1–4.

Anonymous. 1986e. Million dollar list grows to 57! Lawn Care Ind. 10(8):12–16.

Baker, S.W., A.R. Cole, and S.L. Thornton. 1988a. The effect of reinforcement materials on the performance of turf grown on soil and sand rootzones under simulated football-type wear. J. Sports Turf Res. Inst. 64:107–119.

Baker, S.W., A.R. Cole, and S.L. Thornton. 1988b. Performance standards and the interpretation of playing quality for soccer in relation to rootzone composition. J. Sports Turf Res. Inst. 64:120–132.

Beard, J.B. 1973. Turfgrass science and culture. Prentice-Hall, Englewood Cliffs, NJ.

Beard, J.B. 1982. Turfgrass management for golf courses. The United States Golf Assoc. Burgess Publ. Co., Minneapolis.

Beditz, J. 1985. Golf participation in the United States. Natl. Golf Foundation and Market Facts, North Palm Beach, FL and Chicago, IL, respectively.

Bell, M.J., S.W. Baker, and P.M. Canaway. 1985. Playing quality of sports surfaces: A review. J. Sports Turf Res. Inst. 61:26–45.

Blake, G. 1980. Proposed standards and specifications for quality of sand for sand-soil-peat mixes. p. 195–203. *In* J.B. Beard (ed.) Proc. 3rd Int. Res. Turfgrass Conf., Munich, Germany. 11–13 July 1977. Int. Turfgrass Soc., ASA, CSSA, and SSSA, Madison, WI.

Boekel, P. 1980. Some physical aspects of sports turfs. p. 437–441. *In* J.B. Beard (ed.) Proc. 3rd Int. Res. Turfgrass Conf., Munich, Germany. 11–13 July 1977. Int. Turfgrass Soc., ASA, CSSA, and SSSA, Madison, WI.

Canaway, P.M. 1985. Playing quality construction and nutrition of sports turf. p. 45–56. *In* F. Lemaire (ed.) Proc. 5th Int. Turfgrass Conf., Avignon, France. 1–5 July. Inst. Nat. de la Recherche Agron., Paris.

Cornish, G.S., and R.E. Whitten. 1981. The golf course. The Ruttledge Press, New York.

Cowan, J.R. 1969. Seed. p. 425–441. *In* A.A. Hanson and F.V. Juska (ed.) Turfgrass science. Agron. Monogr. 14. ASA, Madison, WI.

Daniel, W.H., R.P. Freeborg, and M.J. Robey. 1974. Prescription athletic turf system. p. 277–280. *In* E.C. Roberts (ed.) Proc. 2nd Int. Turfgrass Res. Conf., Blacksburg, VA. 19–21 June 1973. ASA and CSSA, Madison, WI.

DiPaolo, J., J.B. Beard, and J.R. Watson. 1986. Turf and its contributions to the quality of life. p. 00. *In* Proc. Massachusetts Turfgrass Conf., Univ. of Massachusetts, Amherst.

Eckhoff, H.C. 1986. And the boom goes on. Florida Golf Week, 20 March.

Escritt, J.R. 1970. Sports ground construction. p. 554–558. *In* J.R. Escritt (ed.) Proc. 1st Int. Turfgrass Res. Conf., Harrogate, England. 15–18 July 1969. Sports Turf Res. Inst., Bingley, England.

Farley, G.A. 1931. Golf course common sense. Farley Libraries, Cleveland Heights, OH.

Ferguson, M.H., L. Howard, and M.E. Bloodworth. 1960. Laboratory methods for evaluation of putting green soil mixtures. USGA J. Turf Manage. 13(5):30–32.

Fisher, G.C., and A.N. Ede. 1974. Vertical band soil additive methods for established turf. p. 281–286. *In* E.C. Roberts (ed.) Proc. 2nd Int. Turfgrass Res. Conf., Blacksburg, VA. 19–21 June 1973. ASA and CSSA, Madison, WI.

Franken, H. 1980. Soil conditioning by synthetic media. p. 443–449. *In* J.B. Beard (ed.) Proc. 3rd Int. Turfgrass Conf., Munich, Germany. 11–13 July 1977. Int. Turfgrass Res. Soc., and ASA, CSSA, and SSSA, Madison, WI.

Gibeault, V.A., and S.T. Cockerham. 1985. Turfgrass water conservation. Publ. 21405. Univ. of California, Riverside.

Gibson, N.H. 1958. The encyclopedia of golf. A.S. Barnes and Co., New York.

Hueber, D.B. (ed.) 1984. Statistical profile of golf in the United States. Nat. Golf Foundation, North Palm Beach, FL.

Huffine, W.W., and F.V. Grau. 1969. p. 1–9. *In* A.A. Hanson and F.V. Juska (ed.) Turfgrass science. Agron. Monogr. 14. ASA, Madison, WI.

Kline, C.H., and Co., 1986a. Report. C.H. Kline and Co., Fairfield, NJ.

Kline, C.H., and Co. 1986b. Strategic opportunities in chemical service businesses. Lawn Care Ind. 10(8):5–15.

Langvad, B., and W. Weibull. 1970. Soil heating under sports turf in Sweden. p. 252–257. *In* J.R. Escritt (ed.) Proc. 1st Int. Turfgrass Res. Conf., Harrogate, England. 15–18 July 1969. Sports Turf Res. Inst., Bingley, England.

Nutter, G.C. 1965. Turfgrass is a 4 billion dollar industry. Turf-Grass Times 1(1):1.

Nutter, G.C., and J.R. Watson. 1969. The turfgrass industry. p. 9–24. *In* A.A. Hanson and F.V. Juska (ed.) Agron. Monogr. 14. ASA, Madison, WI.

Petersen, M. 1974. Construction of sports grounds based on physical soil characteristics. p. 270–276. *In* E.C. Roberts (ed.) Proc. 2nd Int. Turfgrass Res. Conf., Blacksburg, VA. 19–21 June 1973. ASA and CSSA, Madison, WI.

Prusa, J., and J. Beditz (ed.) 1985. Golf course maintenance report. Natl. Golf Foundation and Golf Course Superintendents Assoc. of Am., North Palm Beach, FL and Lawrence, KS, respectively.

Roberts, E.C. 1986. Lawn and sports turf industry—characteristics and statistics. Harvest 32:4.

Skirde, W. 1974. Soil modification for athletic fields. p. 261–269. *In* E.C. Roberts (ed.) Proc. 2nd Int. Turfgrass Res. Conf., Blacksburg, VA. 19–21 June 1973. ASA and CSSA, Madison, WI.

Sullivan, L.J., and J.V. Tarantola. 1985. Consumer markets for pesticides and fertilizers 1984. C.H. Kline and Co., Fairfield, NJ.

van Wijk, A., and J. Beuving. 1980. Playing conditions of grass sports fields: A soil technical approach. p. 451–459. *In* J.B. Beard (ed.) Proc. 3rd Int. Res. Turfgrass Conf., Munich, Germany. 11–13 July 1977. Int. Turfgrass Soc., and ASA, CSSA, and SSSA, Madison, WI.

Ward-Thomas, P., H.W. Wind, C. Price, and P. Thomson. 1976. The world atlas of golf. Mitchell Beazley Ltd., London.

Watson, J.R. 1984. The turfgrass industry—past, present and future. Proc. Golf Course 84. Cambridge, England.

Weidner, T. 1986. Newark market report. Am. Lawn Applicator 7(6):42, 46, 60.

3 Artificial Turf

CHAUNCEY A. MOREHOUSE

621 Old Farm Lane
State College, Pennsylvania

Artificial turf was not the result of efforts to achieve a uniform playing surface for competitive sports but was originally developed as a playground surface for city children. During the 1950s, the Ford Foundation attempted to find ways to improve the physical fitness of young people. In comparing all aspects of the physical examination records of young men inducted into the armed forces from all parts of the USA, it was determined that the young persons from small towns and rural areas were more fit than those from the cities. The researchers deduced that these differences in fitness were the result of the available playground areas and the ways in which the young people played as children.

Youngsters from the country and small towns had ample grassy areas to run and play on without fear of falling and seriously injuring themselves. On the other hand, the city children had only limited areas on which to play and these were covered with asphalt or concrete surfaces which were hard and abrasive so falls often resulted in painful injuries. Consequently, it was concluded that the city children played with greater caution and their levels of fitness were lower.

In the early 1960s, the Ford Foundation's Education Facilities Laboratory was working with Chemstrand, a subsidiary of Monsanto Corporation, on the use of synthetic fibers for carpeting in school buildings. Being aware of the fitness studies of the Foundation, Dr. Harold Gores, President of the Educational Facilities Laboratory, requested Chemstrand to develop a suitable playing surface system for city children which would withstand heavy play, be easy to maintain, and would retain its playing characteristics year round for a number of years. In 1964, under the Ford Foundation's sponsorship, a synthetic grass surface called Chemgrass was installed in the fieldhouse of Moses Brown School in Providence, RI.

In 1965, the Houston Astrodome, touted as the eighth wonder of the world, was completed. This indoor sports facility was to have natural turf as a playing surface but it was soon discovered that baseball outfielders were unable to track fly balls because of the glare from the sunlight through the transparent panels in the roof of the dome. To solve this problem the panels were painted to eliminate the glare, but as a consequence the grass would not grow properly under the low artificial light and heavy usage.

Copyright © 1992 ASA-CSSA-SSSA, 677 S. Segoe Rd., Madison, WI 53711, USA. *Turfgrass—* Agronomy Monograph no. 32.

Astrodome operator, Judge Roy Hofheinz, approached Monsanto and asked if its Chemgrass could be used as a synthetic surface for the dome. By April 1966 Monsanto had manufactured and installed AstroTurf on the baseball infield and in midsummer the outfield of the dome was covered with synthetic turf. Early that fall the artificial turf field for tackle football was completed. The addition of more than 4.9 km (3 mi) of zippers made it possible to remove the turf and its underpad, which was installed directly over the earth floor. Removing the turf and underpad allowed rodeos, circuses, midget automobile races, and cattle shows on the floor of the dome.

I. TURF SYSTEMS

A. Three Original Turfs

The first outdoor AstroTurf[1] fields were installed in Memorial Stadium in Seattle, WA and at Indiana State University in Terre Haute, IN in 1967. In 1968, the 3M Company of St. Paul, MN introduced Tartan Turf as a complement to Tartan track surfaces which were initially installed in 1961. Soon after that the American Built-Rite Company of Boston began installing Poly-Turf.

The substructures of permanent or heavy duty athletic fields consist of stable compacted earth over which a layer of crushed stone is placed and covered by a layer of asphalt graded to provide good drainage. The asphalt was sealed to prevent water infiltration and any subsequent frost upheaval. The shock-absorbing underpad system of AstroTurf is glued to the asphalt. This underpad is a closed-cell, synthetic elastomeric foam made by incorporating a chemical blowing agent into the foam latex or plastisol. The blades of synthetic grass are made of 500 denier nylon 6-6 ribbon knitted into a high-strength polyester backing. The fabric panels of turf, 3.6 to 4.5 m (12–15 ft) wide, are bonded together by glueing onto a reinforcing tape, sewing, or some other technique. A schematic diagram of a typical installation for a heavy duty athletic field is shown in Fig. 3–1.

The underpad of the Tartan Turf consisted of a polyurethane foam base, 16-mm (5/8-in.) thick, laid over a special urethane-formulated adhesive that provided a bond to the asphalt subbase. Another coat of urethane adhesive was then spread over the foam base and the 13 mm (0.5 in.) carpet-like nylon surface was then laid down. The Tartan Turf had round, crimped, threadlike nylon six pile fiber in contrast to the more flat grass-like blades used in AstroTurf and many of the other synthetic surfaces.

In contrast, Poly-Turf's construction was a three component system. The base layer was a shock-absorbing underpad of closed-cell foam material similar to that used with AstroTurf. The middle layer designed to spread forces of impact over a greater area consisted of solid virgin vinyl. The top layer was comprised of blades of polypropylene fibers that were longer than

---

[1] AstroTurf Industries, formerly a subsidiary of Monsanto Company, was recently purchased by Balsam Company AG of Steinhagen, Germany.

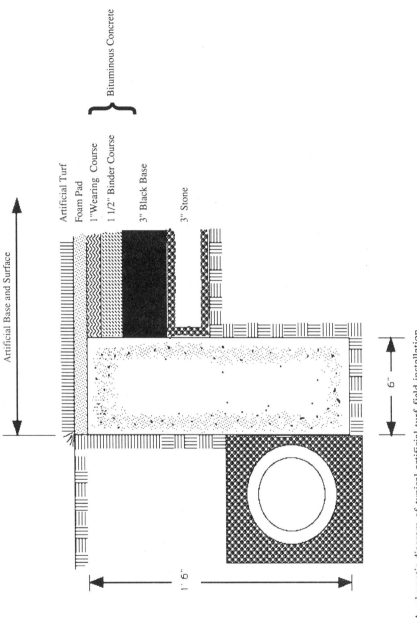

Fig. 3-1. A schematic diagram of typical artificial turf field installation.

either the AstroTurf or Tartan fibers. In the USA, Tartan Turf and Poly-Turf were manufactured within a few years after the original installation of AstroTurf in Houston, however, by 1976 both 3M and American Built-Rite had discontinued marketing synthetic turf fields. There are few fields, if any, where these two turf systems are still in use.

B. Other Turf Systems

Although the three types of turf previously described first appeared in the USA, European companies were also developing synthetic fields, which used somewhat different types of installations. The bonded turf-pad system was commony used, which was laid on top of permeable asphalt without glueing. The special porous backing material allows the water to percolate through the turf and drain away laterally through the aggregate subbase. The Poligrass Division of J.F. Adolff in Germany has used this type of installation combined with a special geotextile pad quite successfully for several years in outdoor installations for soccer and field hockey. This special geotextile pad keeps dust and small particles of soil from working their way up through the turf to the surface. The current permeable installations of Poligrass are fixed at the sides to curbing using metal concrete nails. They also may include a golf-green type sprinkling system installed at the sides to wet down the surface, which is frequently done for field hockey competition, and a side drainage system that readily handles run-off of excessive water on the surface.

Sand-filled turf systems were invented by an American, Frederick T. Haas, Jr., in 1976. The concept was first applied and developed in England but since 1983 sand-filled fields have been installed in the USA. In general, this system consists of some type of a shock-absorbing underpad that is loose-laid on an asphalt subbase, the carpet surface is laid over this underpad. The major difference in the surface is that the synthetic blades of grass are longer than nonsand-filled systems and the spaces between the blades are filled with a silica sand to within 6 mm (0.25 in.) of the top of the fibers, thus keeping the synthetic fiber blades of grass upright. Omniturf, one of the more widely known sand-filled surfaces, uses 25 mm (1.0 in.) long 10 000 denier polypropylene fibers tufted into a polypropylene backing. Because of the weight of the sand, it is not necessary to bond the fabric to the underpad in these sand-filled installations.

Several other companies entered the synthetic turf market during the 1970s and 1980s. A list of these companies with a general description of the turf manufactured appears in Table 3–1.

II. TURF CHARACTERISTICS

A. Knitted vs. Tufted Turfs

In general, most grasslike surfaces are either knitted or tufted, although a few are woven. These are procedures that are routinely used in the carpet

Table 3–1. Manufacturers and trade names for artificial surfaces.†

Product	Manufacturer	Description
All-Pro Turf	All-Pro Turf	3.6-m width tufted fabric polypropylene face yarn and synthetic backing yarns
AstroTurf Stadium Surface	AstroTurf Industries, Inc. (A wholly owned subsidiary of Monsanto until sold in 1988 to Balsam Sportstatenbau of Germany)	4.5-m width fabric employing 55.5 tex (500 den) nylon-6,6 pile ribbon and high-strength polyester backing yarns
Clubturf	Clubturf, UK	Woven polypropylene turf
Gras	Fieldcrest/Karastan	Woven fabric with textured nylon-6 face ribbon, synthetic yarns in backing
Grass Sport 500	Chevron	Polypropylene turf-polyurethane pad system for sport use
Instant Turf	Instant Turf Industries, Inc.	Polyolefin synthetic turf products for consumer and recreational use
Lancer	Lancer Enterprises, Inc.	Light-duty recreational surfaces using polypropylene or polyester face yarns, for consumer and marine applications
Omniturf	Sportec International, Inc.	Sand-filled surface using 1-in. long 10 000 denier polypropylene fibers tufted into a woven polypropylene backing coated with polyurethane
Playfield	Playfield Industries, Inc.	Tufted product using Chevron Polyloom II polypropylene yarn
Poligras	J.F. Adolff AG, Germany	Knitted polypropylene pile fabric supplied with a bonded underpad
Poly-Turf	Sports Surfaces International Ltd., UK	Nylon-6 tufted fabric installed with nitrile rubber-poly (vinyl chloride) pad
Superturf	Cam-Turf, Inc.	Tufted product using polypropylene yarn and a synthetic backing
Marubeni-Toray GS-2	Mitsubishi Trading Co., Japan	Tufted nylon-6 fabric using woven polyester backing

† This table was adapted and modified from Hamner and Orofino (1982).

industry, and therefore, artificial turf companies that have been more successful and have the greatest tenure in artificial turf are those that have been closely aligned with the carpet manufacturing industry. The prime examples are AstroTurf Industries, a subsidiary of Monsanto whose Chemstrand (now Textiles) Division has been making carpet fibers for many years, and Poligras, a Division of J.F. Adolff, a company in Germany that has been involved in the textile business since 1932.

In the tufted surface, the fibers are inserted into the backing by a series of needles each of which forms a loop or tuft as the fiber penetrates the backing. The looped tufts formed as a result of this process are then cut to provide the individual blades of the grass-like surface.

In contrast to the tufting process, the knitting process is somewhat more complex. The fibers in this technique are fed through the knitting needles of a knitting machine and each individual fiber is knotted into the backing fabric. This provides a surface of high strength and firmer binding of the fibers to the backing. Because the knitting process is more complex, the knitted artificial turfs are more expensive than the tufted artificial turf and in general are more durable.

B. Backing and Durability

Both knitted and tufted surfaces use a backing that is a fiber-forming polymer of considerable strength usually a polyester or a polypropylene. Although not visible in the finished product, the backing material is an essential component of the surface since it is responsible for holding the fibers together. This backing provides mechanical strength and dimensional stability of the surface and prolongs the life of the surface. A typical artificial surface should have a service life of at least 5 yr. Many installations have been used for 8 to 10 yr or longer without requiring replacement.

C. Underpadding

The underpad material is primarily designed for shock absorption. In the case of athletic fields used for tackle football, this padding is usually a closed-cell foam. These types of material, usually polyvinylchloride or polyethylenes, provide good energy absorption and the cost is reasonable. However, this underpad must be resistant to water absorption otherwise the foam padding would deteriorate in a couple of years, particularly in climates with freezing temperatures. The underpad must not only absorb shock but also must possess proper rebound characteristics for the ball and should not be so soft that players' leg muscles fatigue quickly when running on the surface. For the athletic fields in which shock-absorbency was a prime consideration, the early surfaces were usually nonpermeable, and therefore, runoff drainage for outdoor surfaces was provided for by the field camber or slope.

In sports such as baseball, soccer, and field hockey, the attenuation of shock is not so important. In fields designed specifically for these sports, a light underpad, which is permanently bonded to the carpet is often used. Many of the outdoor fields now being installed for these three field sports are permeable surfaces that allow the water to drain through the artificial turf system into a special drainage system installed under the surface. Sometimes these permeable fields may also include a supplementary drainage system at the edges to accommodate excessive water.

Permeable systems may include a closed-cell foam underpad with small holes punched through it after manufacture thus allowing the water to flow vertically downward through the system. In other instances, a geotextile fabric laid down under the turf allows water to easily drain through it in a vertical direction. This fabric also prevents dust and particles from working their way upward to the surface of the turf. A provision is then made for the water that has drained vertically through the surface to be drained away horizontally.

The Poligras Division of Adolff Company of Germany has recently been successful in laying their surface with a geotextile fabric underpad directly over a gravel substructure. This gravel substructure, however, must be carefully levelled and prepared or the carpet surface will be uneven, a condition that could hinder play especially in a sport such as field hockey where a smooth surface is essential.

D. Substructure

In general, the substructure under the shock-absorbing padding material consists of a fine finished layer of asphalt that provides a smooth and consistent base for the surface. Concrete could be used but this is unusual because the concrete is cost prohibitive. In climates where the artificial surface will be subject to freezing and thawing a coarse layer of asphalt, 102 to 152 mm (4-6 in.) thick, is put down before the final layer of finish asphalt. This coarse layer will prevent the surface from heaving and the asphalt from cracking under adverse weather conditions. A bottom base of crushed stone may also be recommended when the earth is not thoroughly compacted and solid.

III. MAINTENANCE

Although artificial turf fields generally require much less maintenance than natural grass fields, it is a fallacy to expect that no maintenance is necessary. AstroTurf Industries have outlined three simple rules for their surfaces: (i) keep it clean; (ii) do not abuse it with vehicular traffic, heavy static loads, fireworks or open flames; and (iii) make all repairs promptly (AstroTurf Industries, no date). These guidelines are appropriate for all other artificial surfaces as well. Certainly every company should provide consultive services, if repairs are needed or when complicated situations arise with which one does not know how to deal.

A. Routine Cleaning

To maintain a clean artificial turf field, it is important to remove all litter left behind by users and spectators. Accesses to the field should be designed so that a minimum of mud and soil particles are brought onto the field. Loose soil should be picked up as soon as possible before it begins to accumulate and work its way down between the fibers of the surface.

Although electrically powered vacuum sweepers may be used to remove dust and light trash from the surface of a field, to maintain the field in optimum condition it should be washed periodically with a generous amount of clean water. A fire hose using maximum pressure and full flow will flush away loose dust and blast away dirt particles embedded in the carpet. For hosing down a nonpermeable field, AstroTurf Industries (no date) recommends starting at the crown and directing the flow of water toward the sides of the field while working first down one side and then up the other side of the field. Treated water is recommended for this washing because untreated and polluted water often contains many dissolved minerals. After evaporation, such water will leave a noticeable film on the surface of the synthetic fibers that will detract from the appearance of the field.

Vacuum-type cleaning machines may also be employed to remove loose trash, small scraps of paper, dirt, dust, and other debris from a synthetic surface. A combination vacuum-brush type of machine is highly recommended for cleaning these surfaces. The sweeper should have synthetic fiber bristles at least 50.0 to 65.0 mm long (2–2.5 in.) with a maximum bristle diameter of 0.75 mm (0.030 in.). There should be no metal fibers in the brush to prevent damage to the turf. These fibers may also fall out and remain in the turf possibly injuring the players. The brush of the sweeper should not be set so low that it digs into the pile fiber or its backing. The best results will be obtained if the brush is set so it just touches the top of the surface. The brush will then agitate the fibers to loosen and dislodge dirt so that it is readily picked up by the suction of the machine.

Loose debris and surface dust should be removed as often as necessary depending on the amount of use. Generally a thorough wet cleaning once or twice a year is sufficient. Excessive brushing with heavy duty equipment may damage the synthetic surface and the underpadding.

B. Soiled Turf

Low-sudsing household detergents with plenty of hot water will remove most of the soils that occur on artificial turf. Whenever a detergent is used, whether it be with a carpet scrubber in the case of a heavily soiled surface or a sponge mop for a lightly soiled turf, the surface should be thoroughly rinsed with generous amounts of clean water after scrubbing or mopping.

More stubborn stains such as those from motor oil and grease, asphalt, chewing gum, lipstick, shoe polish, suntan oil, can usually be removed with dry cleaning fluid (perchlorethylene). All types of stains should be removed as soon as possible because fresh spills are always much easier to clean up than ones that have dried or hardened. In general, most cleaners that are suitable for cleaning household or commercial carpets may be used on artificial turf. The more reputable companies will offer advice and assistance in cleaning in cases of difficult circumstances.

C. Field Markings

If desired, permanent in-laid markings may be placed on the field when it is installed. This is probably not the best procedure unless a field is to be used for only one sport. Since most synthetic fields are multipurpose, the maintenance personnel will probably be responsible for marking the field at various times.

Very temporary markings may be achieved by applying the same white chalk dust (e.g., No. 32 Field White, Charles A. Wagner Co., Philadelphia, PA) as used on natural grass fields. A wet application may be used by making a slurry as a result of mixing the dust with water. The main problem with chalk dust markings is that they tend to be picked up on the shoes of players and tracked to other unmarked portions of the field. They also are easily washed away or spread by water. In fact, they may be completely obliterated by a hard rainstorm. The only advantage of dry markings on fields is that they are inexpensive.

More permanent markings are put down with paints. A top-quality water-based acrylic latex exterior paint such as Sherwin Williams A-100 SuperWhite Paint will provide satisfactory results. These markings will remain visible under relatively hard use for a reasonable length of time (at least one season if particularly heavy use areas are periodically touched up). AstroTurf Industries also recommends William Zinsser BIN (Bullseye) White Paint that is an alcohol-based lacquer and readily available in most paint stores for touch-up painting, especially if the surface is damp.

These semipermanent paints are quite readily removed by brushing the striped area with a solution of mild detergent followed by a thorough flushing with a high pressure water hose. Excess water may be picked up by a commercial water vacuum pick-up machine.

In applying markings, three precautions should be noted. First, *do not apply paints to a surface when it is wet.* The paint will spread and the markings will not be at all well defined. Second, *do not apply paint too heavily.* Light applications will be quite visible and remain that way for a sufficient length of time. Excessive layers of paint become caked and crusty making the surface more abrasive. The excess paint also gets down among the fibers, making it much more difficult to remove. Finally, *be sure to give the paint time to dry thoroughly before using the field.* Wet paint will easily be tracked over all parts of the field, however, after it is thoroughly dried the markings will be quite permanent.

In addition, to both temporary and semipermanent paints for field markings, standard and special paints are available. It is suggested that the manufacturer of the synthetic turf be contacted for specific suggestions of the type of paint to be used if permanent markings are desired.

D. Minor Repairs

Artificial turf fields should be inspected on a regular basis just like natural grass fields. Minor damage may become a major problem if not repaired soon after it is discovered. Regluing or resewing of seams that have become loose may be easily accomplished by a user's maintenance staff if simple directions provided by the turf manufacturer are followed. Even small tears in the surface of 152 mm (6 in.) or less may be readily repaired by competent maintenance workers. On the other hand, manufacturers should be contacted for major repairs, since these will probably require replacement of entire sections of turf.

To be certain to identify areas where minor repairs are needed, a routine inspection of the entire field is recommended at least once or twice a year. All seams should be carefully inspected and loose areas noted and repaired. All panels of fabric should be scrutinized carefully for any rips or tears and the condition of the underpadding and surface assessed. In situations where a field receives heavy use or is five or more years old, more frequent inspections than twice a year are warranted.

E. Protection Against Damage from Static Loading

Synthetic surfaces are not designed to accommodate long-term static loads. Such loads usually exist when playing fields are used for commencement exercises, assemblies, convocations, rock concerts, and even circuses.

Long-term static loads should not exceed 1.2 to 1.4 kPa (250–300 lb ft^{-2}) to ensure that the turf is not damaged as a result of special events. Sheets of plywood, 19-mm (¾-in.) thick with linear dimensions (1.22 × 2.44 m (4 × 8 ft) are recommended for use as load spreaders. However, the loads should not be placed too near the edges of these plywood sheets and a polyethylene sheet with a thickness of at least 0.15 mm (6 mils) should be laid over the turf beneath the load spreaders to avoid staining and soiling of the surface. If chairs are to be placed directly on the surface, be certain that all of the legs have plastic or rubber tips that will not damage the turf. Heavy wheeled equipment should not be allowed on the turf and any open flames should be prohibited. Although most synthetic surfaces are difficult to ignite and do not burn rapidly, open flames can easily cause major damage to the surface. For this reason, smoking by spectators or participants should not be allowed when they are on the surface of a synthetic field.

F. Watering Synthetic Fields

Wetting of fields may be done for several reasons. In hot weather, the temperature of a synthetic surface becomes quite high. This has been noted in several studies that will be cited in a subsequent section of this chapter. Evaporation of 1.2 L m^{-2} (slightly more than 1 qt yd^{-2}) per hour will be sufficient to cool the surface down to a level near that of natural grass (AstroTurf Industries, no date, p. 24). Wetting the field in this manner will also reduce the abrasiveness and decrease the probability of more serious injuries.

In the case of international competition in field hockey, it is required that the surface be wetted for official competition to provide a more effective playing surface. The dampened surface reduces the ball bounce enhancing skillful play. A hose with a flow meter or a watering truck should be used unless the field is equipped with a special sprinkling system. About 8000 to 10 000 L (approximately 2000–2500 gallons) of water spread evenly over a field hockey playing surface, 105 × 64 m (345 × 210 ft) will be sufficient for efficient play.

If the field is to be watered, be certain that the water is distributed evenly over the entire area being used. The amounts of water recommended will be sufficient to dampen but not enough to soak the surface or leave puddles of water standing on it. When the recommended quantity of water is applied, the field will remain damp for at least one-half of the game, even under favorable evaporative conditions (i.e., elevated air temperature and brisk air movement).

IV. ENVIRONMENTAL CONDITIONS AND ARTIFICIAL TURF

One of the potential problems with artificial turf is related to heat, particularly in warm climates during late summer, when tackle football practice normally begins. Often times football players, particularly young high school boys, do not become heat acclimatized prior to the beginning of practice and synthetic surfaces tend to re-radiate heat to a much greater extent than natural grass surfaces.

Buskirk et al. (1971) conducted a study in which air temperatures, surface temperatures, and net radiation over natural and synthetic grass surfaces were compared. Thermocouples were positioned in and above both types of surface at various heights. These fields were in the same locale so both sets of thermocouples were subjected to similar environmental microclimates (see Fig. 3-2). Air temperatures recorded above the synthetic surface averaged 3.5 to 4.5 °C (6–8 °F) higher than those measured over the natural grass

Fig. 3-2. Thermocouple trees with black globe placed on artificial turf. Instrument in center is pyroheliometer. (From Buskirk et al., 1971.)

surfaces over a 2-wk period of observations. However, the surface temperatures of the artificial turf were as much as 19.5 to 27.8 °C (35–50 °C) higher than the surface temperatures on the natural grass surface, particularly on the bright sunny days. At midday on some days during this investigation, the temperature of the artificial playing field reached 60 °C (140 °F). During early morning hours of a clear day, the turf temperature was below that of the natural grass, however, the synthetic turf temperature increased rapidly after sunrise. It should be noted that this study was conducted on an open field with air movement. The differences in air and surface temperatures over the two types of turf would probably have been much larger, if the investigation had been conducted in an enclosed stadium. The net radiations as detected by a pyroheliometer were quite similar over the two surfaces during the observation period. These results were confirmed by Koon et al. (1971) in a similar type study conducted at about the same time as the study by Buskirk et al. (1971). In addition, Koon et al. (1971) reported that a properly wetted synthetic field exhibited surface temperatures quite similar to those of nearby natural grass. Likewise, Kandelin et al. (1976) reported a maximum surface temperature of a synthetic field of 59 °C (138.2 °F) with a corresponding air temperature of 33.1 °C (91.5 °F).

To study the elevated surface temperature more thoroughly, Buskirk et al. (1971) had two individuals walk around on the artificial surface wearing cleated shoes with inner soles fitted with thermocouples. The foot-insole interface temperatures as recorded by the thermocouples were lower than those recorded by the thermocouples at the cleat-surface interface. This situation creates a heat transfer from the surface through the inner soles to the sole of the foot where the heat must be dissipated by the blood flow. This relative heat gain contributes to greater physiological heat stress that may ultimately result in serious heat problems such as heat stroke, which could lead to death if proper precautions are not taken. However, Ramsey (1982) concluded that in terms of psychometric components that relate to potential heat strain, the microclimates above natural and synthetic turf surfaces are similar. In this study, air velocity, wet and drybulb, and globe temperature (WGTB) was calculated to assess the heat stress. The differences in the measurement locations and the measured variables may have led to these contradictory conclusions. One of the precautions that can be taken when the air temperature is high is wet down the artificial turf periodically during games and practice sessions as mentioned in a previous section of this chapter.

V. TESTS OF PHYSICAL PROPERTIES

The introduction of artificial turf created several controversies with regard to inherent dangers to players in various sports and the impact of this new type of surface on the performances of these sports. Many of these questions have yet to be answered satisfactorily even though several tests have been developed to assess the physical properties of synthetic turfs. Some investigations were also designed to compare the characteristics of artificial and natural grass surfaces.

A. Shock Attenuation

From the standpoint of player safety, the capability of a playing surface to absorb shock is of prime importance. This is particularly true in the case of tackle football because of the higher incidence of more serious injuries. In cases of other field sports, such as soccer, field hockey, and baseball, shock attenuation receives a lower priority.

Typically, shock absorption of athletic fields has been measured by dropping missiles of various masses in free-fall onto the surface being evaluated and measuring the deceleration or stopping force and time during the impact. Because $F = ma$, for a given missile mass (m) the deceleration (a) is proportional to the stopping force (F). The kinetic energy involved in the impact is expressed by the formula, $T = 1/2\, mv^2$, where T equals the kinetic energy, m is the mass of the impacting object and v is the velocity of the missile at the moment of impact. The impact energy of the falling missile is expressed by the relationship, Impact Energy $= wv^2/2g$, with w equal to the weight of the missile and g equal to the acceleration due to gravity. The velocity, v, of the falling object is a function of the height, h, from which it is dropped. In physics this relationship is expressed by the formula, $V^2 = 2gh$, where g is the acceleration due to gravity. Most often, deceleration or negative acceleration of the falling mass is measured by a piezoelectric accelerometer, a crystal device that is sensitive to changes in velocity and generates an electrical charge or voltage output as a result of these changes. During an impact, the resulting electrical signal is recorded as an acceleration-time curve by using an oscilloscope or personal computer. Figure 3–3 shows a typical curve recorded from such an impact. Instantaneous accelerations

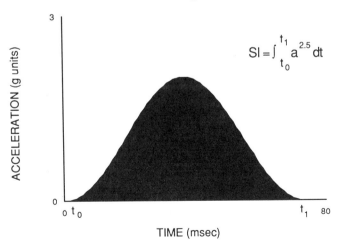

Fig. 3–3. Simulated acceleration-time history of an impact.

in *g*-units are on the vertical axis and time in milliseconds is on the horizontal axis. The apex of the acceleration-time curve that is approximately the point of the maximum acceleration experienced by the falling missile is usually referred to as the G_{max}. High accelerations may be endured for only short periods while lower accelerations may be tolerated by the human body for extended periods. This relationship of tolerance to G_{max} values in relation to time for impacts to the human head is depicted in the Wayne State Tolerance Curve for Cerebral Concussions (Gurdjian et al., 1966), which is shown in Fig. 3-4. The area to the right and above this curve indicates the combination of G_{max} and time duration of an impact that is likely to produce a head injury in an average adult. The area to the left and below the line represents a relatively safe condition as far as trauma to the human head is concerned.

Gadd (1966) experimented with an impulse-integration procedure that resulted in an exponential weighting taking into account the fact that lower acceleration-time pulses have only a small contribution to make to an injury but that higher levels of acceleration make a much greater contribution to the potential for injury. Gadd (1966) fitted this integration function to the Wayne State Tolerance Curve for head impacts and arrived at an exponential weighting of 2.5. The result, known as the Gadd Severity Index (Fig. 3-3), made it possible to compare irregular curves and curves of different

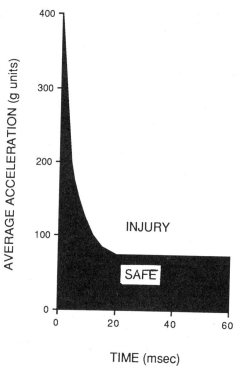

Fig. 3-4. Wayne State Tolerance Curve for Threshold of Cerebral Concussion. The average acceleration indicated on the ordinate is the mean of several G_{max} values.

shapes in terms of the injury-producing potentials of impacts to the head. The Gadd Severity Index (SI) is calculated in the following manner:

$$SI = \int_{t_0}^{t_1} a^{2.5} \, dt.$$

Where t_0 and t_1 are the onset and end of the acceleration, respectively, and a equals the instantaneous acceleration at any time during impact. Gadd (1966) originally established a criterion of 1000 as the SI at which an impact to an unprotected head of an adult would have a 50% chance of causing a cerebral concussion. Later Gadd (1971) set a higher value of 1500 for an impact to the head protected by a helmet.

The F-8 Committee on Sports Equipment and Facilities of the American Society of Testing and Materials (ASTM) has developed a standard impact absorption test method for evaluating artificial turf designated as F-355-86 (1986). In this standard, three procedures are specified. Procedure A uses a cylindrical metal missile with a flat, circular impacting surface of 129 cm^2 (20 in.^{2}) and a mass of 9.072 kg (20 lb). Procedure B employs a metal hemispherical shaped missile with a radius of 82.6 mm (3.25 in.) and a mass of 6.804 kg (15 lb). For Procedure C, the impacting missile is an ANSI Z90 metal headform (Type C) of 5.0 kg mass (11.0 lb) with a specified geometry and an impact velocity appropriate for the end use of the surface being tested. A photograph of the F-355 apparatus is shown in Fig. 3–5. Any one of these missiles is dropped in free-fall onto the test specimen and the

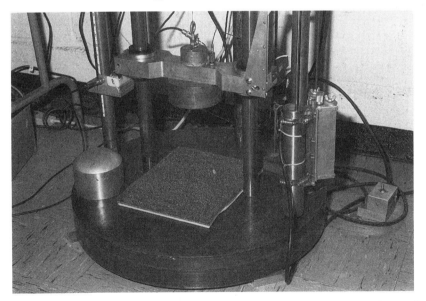

Fig. 3–5. ASTM F-355 apparatus. A sample of artificial turf is in place ready to be impacted. The missile for Procedure A is attached to the missile carriage. The Procedure B missile is shown on the left.

acceleration-time history, impact and rebound velocities, and the displacement-time history are recorded with appropriate instrumentation. In the laboratory, the test specimen is placed on a massive rigid anvil; however, a portable apparatus with the same missile specifications may be used in a field impact test on an installed surface. This standard is only a method of test, and at the present time, no minimum values for G_{max} or SI are given in the standard. This type of apparatus has been used to compare the shock-attenuation characteristics of different artificial surfaces and contrast the shock absorption of artificial surfaces with natural grass surfaces in several unpublished studies.

Bowers and Martin (1974) used a 7.25 kg (16 lb) indoor shot put on which a linear accelerometer was mounted to measure the shock-attenuation characteristics of athletic fields. This shot was suspended 32.75 cm (12.5 in.) above the surface being impacted and released in free-fall. The testing was done on four surfaces: (i) a dry natural grass surface that was covered with Kentucky bluegrass (*Poa pratensis* L.) cut to a height of approximately 3.8 cm (1.5 in.), (ii) a new AstroTurf surface glued to a 5-yr-old underpad, (iii) an old AstroTurf surface (1969 vintage) that had been used for 5 yr with its 5-yr-old underpad, and (iv) an asphalt surface on a walkway. The researchers reported G_{max} values of 150, 122, 286, and 5500 g for the impacts to the sod, new AstroTurf, old AstroTurf, and asphalt, respectively. Reported stopping times (times to G_{max}) were 14.5, 11.4, 7.6, and 6.1 s, respectively. Use and exposure to variable weather conditions were the factors responsible for deterioration of the AstroTurf over the 5-yr period. Bowers and Martin (1974) concluded that the new AstroTurf surface of that time approximated, but did not equal, a grass field in impact absorption characteristics and that there was a significant decrease in the shock-attenuation characteristics of the field over a 5-yr period.

Tests of shock attenuation of artificial surfaces have been conducted in Europe, in particular Germany and the Netherlands for nearly 20 yr. The Federal Institute for Sport Science (Bundesinstitut für Sportwissenschaft) initiated this research through funds awarded to the Otto Graf Building Research Institute in Stuttgart. This research led to the development of a special apparatus called the Stuttgart Artificial Athlete (Kunstlichen Sportler Stuttgart) designed primarily for functional testing of sport floors in gymnasiums and artificial track surfaces. This apparatus, now being used for testing artificial fields, uses a 50 kg (110 lb) weight dropped from a height of 3 cm (1.2 in.) onto a soft spring (50 Da N cm^{-1}). The force vs. time history of this impact is recorded and also the deformation at distances up to 20 cm in two directions at right angles to each other depending on the type of surface. The details of this test apparatus and procedures are contained in the German Standards Institute (Deutsches Institut für Normung) Standard, DIN 18035 Part 6 (1975).

A modification of the Stuttgart Artificial Athlete is the Berlin Artificial Athlete (Kunstlichen Sportler Berlin). This apparatus employs a 20 kg (45 lb) weight dropped from a height of 5.5 cm (2.2 in.) onto a spring with a specified stiffness (20 kN cm^{-1}). The force exerted by the foot of the device is measured and compared to the maximum force (650 Da N) which results from impacting a rigid surface. Results are expressed in terms of percentage of force absorption. Some typical values of force reductions are: concrete, 0%; tumbling mat, 90%; and wooden gymnasium floors, 50 to 70%. The International Hockey Federation (FIH) is using a Berlin Artificial Athlete as a test of impact response for artificial turf and requires a 40 to 65% force reduction on a wet surface (FIH, 1987). This standard impact attenuation is required for field hockey pitches that are certified by the FIH for international competition.

The Netherlands Sports Federation (NSF) employs an apparatus similar to the Berlin Artificial Athlete but uses a different type of spring. It has been claimed by some individuals that there is no correlation between the results obtained using the Berlin Athlete Tester and NSF Sports Flooring Tester; however, no published information is available on such a comparison. This seems to be a question that needs to be researched since the two apparatus are so similar.

The philosophy underlying the ASTM F-355-86 Standard and the three tests for shock attenuation developed in Europe are quite different. In the USA, the principal sport being played on most artificial turf fields is American tackle football. Because of the number of times players fall or are thrown to the playing field quite forcefully, the incidence of injury is high in modern football. Therefore, preventing injuries is a prime consideration not only in the design of artificial turf systems but also in the evaluation of their effectiveness. As a consequence, the values for G_{max} or SI in laboratory and field tests are extremely important. In other words, the protective function of the field on which American tackle football is to be played must be satisfied. The same protective function should be given major consideration when evaluating a multipurpose playground or playfield that is to be used exclusively by children.

On the other hand, in Europe the most popular field sports are soccer (European football) and field hockey. Neither of these sports involves an overwhelming number of violent impacts with the field surface from falls. Consequently, the player performance requirements or sports function of the artificial fields are usually considered to be of primary importance. Therefore, impact response tests have been designed to evaluate these characteristics of the artificial turf.

Running and jumping on various artificial and natural athletic field surfaces may have significant effects on the various joints; ankle, knee, hip, spine, and on the musculature of the lower extremity and trunk. Such effects have yet to be evaluated. Research is needed to ascertain how and to what degree athletes of various skill levels are able to use the body to attenuate the shock of normal impacts of the feet on athletic surfaces during competition. To obtain such data would require highly sophisticated instrumentation in tightly controlled environments. Such investigations have yet to be undertaken undoubtedly because of the enormity of the problems involved.

B. Shoe-Turf Interface

The interface between various types of sport shoes and artificial turf has been the subject of several studies. The knee and ankle injuries that have reached near epidemic proportions, particularly in tackle football, have been the underlying incentive for undertaking many of these investigations. The basic mechanism that results in many of these lower extremity joint injuries, according to most medical experts, is that the foot becomes fixed as a result of excessive traction and the shoe becomes "locked" into the turf when changing directions. The momentum of the body then places considerable stress on the ligaments of the joints, which frequently leads to severe sprains or even ruptured ligaments. Of course, it should be noted that not all injuries to knee and ankle joints can be blamed on the athletic surface. Often these injuries occur as a result of contact with other competitors during play. In these circumstances, the injuries may be more severe because of the increased impact energy resulting from the greater running velocity of players on high-quality turf fields. In some instances, the lower extremity becomes wedged between another player and the turf making it impossible to withdraw the foot and leg. In such cases, the knee or ankle would be injured regardless of the type of turf.

During the first few years following the introduction of artificial turf, it was not uncommon for visiting football teams to be provided with special shoes for play because the traditional seven-cleated football shoes used on natural grass were inappropriate. On natural grass, these longer cleats are able to penetrate the grass and soil providing maximum friction or traction, however, these cleats are not able to penetrate the tough polypropylene or polyester backing of the artificial turf. The situation, which may be visualized as a player standing on seven short stilts, does not provide adequate traction.

Much of the data in the earliest investigations involved gathering subjective opinions from players after they performed various types of exercises in different models of shoes. W.E. Brennan (unpublished interim report, Chemstrand Company, 1966) employed this methodology and from these subjective evaluations concluded that multi-cleated, rubber or molded-soled shoes with cleats 12.7 mm (0.5 in.) or less in length were best for playing field sports on artificial turf.

In 1969, Vinicki and Rogers (unpublished data, but cited in Morehouse & Morrison, 1975) developed a drag test that consisted of a weighted shoe (81.2 kg or 180 lb) being dragged across a surface at a rate of 25.4 cm min^{-1} (10 in. min^{-1}) by a cable connected to an Instron load cell. The apparatus used by Vinicki and Rogers (1969, unpublished data) is shown in Fig. 3–6. Different shoes and turfs could be easily fitted onto the simulated foot and sample platform, respectively. This early study of the "grip potential" of different types of shoes on various surfaces led to two conclusions. First, traction of a shoe depended on the composition and configuration of its sole, and second, the grip of a shoe on a particular surface when it was dry did

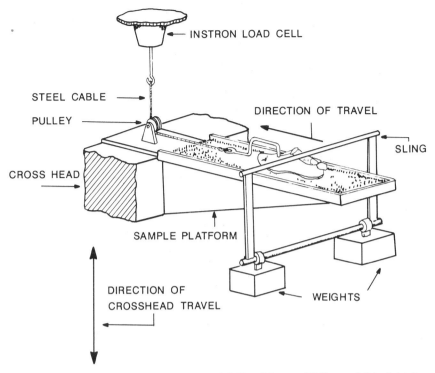

Fig. 3-6. Drag test apparatus developed by Vinicki and Rogers (1969, unpublished data).

not reflect the performance of the same shoe on the same turf under wet conditions.

Niebel et al. (unpublished research report of the Penn State Sports Research Institute, 1973) built a simulated leg apparatus to investigate the relationship of shoe design to playing surface. This apparatus allowed for loading of a pendulum that was swung to impact a weighted leg with simulated hinged ankle joint and ball and socket hip joint. A shoe was fitted on a cast aluminum foot and was forced across the playing surface when struck by the pendulum. The maximum force transmitted from the shoe to the surface was monitored by a three-dimensional strain gauge dynamometer and recorded on a strip chart recorder. Utilizing this apparatus, which is shown in Fig. 3-7, Niebel et al. (1973) arrived at conclusions similar to the earlier studies. The shoe-turf interface is a very complex phenomenon depending not only on the composition and configuration of the sole of the shoe, the type of surface and whether that surface is dry or wet but also on the weight placed upon the sample shoe. Data in a report by B.W. Niebel et al. (1973, unpublished data) revealed that one turf offered greater resistance under dry conditions while another surface provided better traction when wet using the same shoe. It was also discovered that the cleated shoes tended to offer less resistance force than the noncleated shoes on all synthetic turf surfaces tested (only three surfaces were available at that particular time).

Fig. 3-7. Apparatus for assessing shoe-turf interface under dynamic conditions (Niebel et al., 1973, unpublished data).

Morehouse et al. (unpublished research report, Penn State Sports Research Institute, 1974) conducted a field study comparing football player performances consisting of running specific football practice drills while alternately wearing cleated and noncleated shoes on artificial and natural grass playing surfaces. No differences due to shoe type were found between the mean times of players in an agility run, 9.15 m (10-yd) sprint and 36.6 m (40-yd) sprint while wearing cleated and noncleated shoes on an artificial grass surface. These timed performances were better, however, when players wore cleated in contrast to noncleated shoes on the natural turf. Since similar mean running times were achieved when wearing cleated and noncleated shoes on artificial turf, noncleated shoes were recommended for use on artificial turf. As previously mentioned (p. 106), cleats may become "locked" in the turf creating greater torsional forces that place more stress on the ligaments of the joints of the lower extremities. This recommendation was the same as that arrived at earlier by W.E. Brennan (unpublished data, 1966). A similar recomendation for soccer play on artificial turf resulted from an investigation conducted in Gothenberg, Sweden. The conclusions from this study were, that players should not use cleated shoes for play on artificial turf, and that when playing on natural grass, shoes with 6 to 10 cleats were preferred (Statens Naturvadsverket, 1977).

Krahenbuhl (1974) conducted a study quite similar to the investigation by Morehouse et al. (unpublished data, 1974), which has already been described. In this investigation, university students ran an obstacle course on artificial turf and natural grass wearing three different types of shoes. The artificial turf was a different brand from that used in Morehouse's study and by the Swedish researchers. However, Krahenbuhl (1974) reported results that were similar to the other studies. Subjects were able to move more quickly on the artificial turf as compared to the grass surface regardless of the type of shoes worn, and the fastest movement times were obtained when the subjects wore either tennis shoes or soccer style footwear.

The traditions associated with field sports, particularly tackle football and soccer, are quite strong. Even at present, 10 to 15 yr after the cited research, noncleated shoes for participation in field sports played on an artificial surface are not fully accepted by coaches and athletic administrators, despite the fact that at least four independent investigations have arrived at the same conclusion.

The torque generated at the shoe-turf interface appears to be a more important factor than linear traction in terms of risk of injury because most lower extremity joint injuries involve a rotational torque. Bonstingl et al. (1975) investigated the torque generated on the simulated leg (tibia) using a modification of the apparatus of Niebel et al. (unpublished report, 1973). The weighted pendulum struck an arm that pivoted the weighted shoe on a sample surface. The maximum torque was measured by recording the output from a system of strain gauges attached to the metal leg. The amount of torque developed with cleated shoes on synthetic grass was highly correlated with the "effective cleat surface area." The "effective cleat surface area" was defined as the total cleat area in actual contact with the sample of artificial surface. The relationship between torque developed at the shoe-turf interface and the effective cleat surface area is shown in Fig. 3-8 (Bonstingl et al., 1975).

More recently, additional investigations of the torque generated between the shoes and synthetic surfaces have been conducted but these studies were designed to determine the most effective shoes to use on artificial turf as opposed to evaluating the turf (Culpepper & Nieman, 1983; Andreasson et al., 1986). These studies also involved weighting the shoes but with much less weight, 44.5 to 400.3 N (10–90 lb) by Culpepper and Nieman (1983) and 241 N (54.2 lb) by Andreasson et al. (1986) as compared to 667.2 to 1067.5 N (150–240 lb) by Bonstingl et al. (1975).

In summary, there is no best shoe for all performers on all surfaces under all conditions. Although some valuable information has been gathered as a result of several investigations, the shoe-turf interface is complex. Among the factors involved are the type of surface and whether it is wet or dry, the composition and configuration of the outsole of the shoe, the type of stance (toe or full foot) which also determines the "effective cleat surface area," and the weight of the player. All of these variables contribute to the torque and traction forces and ultimately may affect player performances.

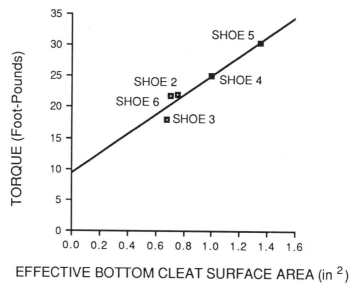

Fig. 3–8. Relationship of torque to effective cleat surface area in the toe stance position. (From Bonstingl et al., 1975.)

C. Resiliency and Ball Rebound

The resiliency of a surface has a noticeable effect on player performances in field sports. Not only does it have an effect on player movements but it also affects the muscular fatigue experienced by the athlete and the ball response during play. Resilience may be defined as the ability of a material to recover its size and shape after deformation. In a sport such as tackle football, shock attenuation is an important characteristic of any playing field whether artificial or natural grass. However, in general, as shock attenuation increases, penetration or deformation also increases. If penetration of the players' feet into the surface becomes too great, the players' movements are slower much as they would be if they were running in soft sand. These soft surfaces also lead to fatigue of the muscles of the lower extremity, and ultimately affect foot and ankle stability. Under these conditions, the athlete is at greater risk of sustaining an injury during participation. In essence, when developing an ideal playing surface of natural or synthetic materials, one is confronted with a compromise between safety and function.

In the ASTM F355-86 standard (1986) a simple method for determining resiliency of the playing surface is proposed. Since the coefficient of restitution may be simply defined as the ratio of the rebound velocity to the impact velocity, using the F355 drop apparatus, it is relatively easy to measure the velocity of the falling missile just prior to impact and immediately after impact during its rebound. This can be accomplished by the use of photoelectric cells, light-emitting diodes or a laser beam; perhaps the three most common methods for obtaining these velocities. Since the metal missile used in the F-355 apparatus is quite inelastic, the resulting coefficient of restitution obtained from the rebound and impact velocities is quite characteristic of the surface impacted. It should be noted, however, that the drop height of the missile will have a pronounced influence on the coefficients of restitution of artificial surfaces since the turf is a heterogeneous system consisting of fibers, backing, and underpadding. Therefore, coefficients of restitution determined as the ratio of impact to rebound velocities vary with the amount of impact energy. This method, however, does provide a rather simple and inexpensive procedure for estimating the coefficient of restitution of an artificial surface.

The functional test corresponding to the coefficient of restitution, used primarily in European countries including England, is the ball rebound or *rebound resilience test*. Rebound resilience, as defined in Part 2 of the British Sports Council Specification for Artificial Surfaces (1984), is a measure of the height or bounce of a ball (soccer) after impact with the surface. More specifically, it is the ratio of the rebound height to the drop height (Bell et al., 1985). The apparatus used for the Sports Council's test includes three 1-m long (39.37 in.) tubes that fit together and are mounted on a tripod base. The ball release mechanism that fits on top of the uppermost tube permits the ball to be released without an impulse or spin. The release mechanism includes a series of hinges and levers and is activated by pulling a string. The release height is exactly 3 m (118.01 in.) and a scale on the side of the upright is marked off in 3 cm (7.6 in.) intervals or 1% of the drop height so that the rebound height of the ball can be measured as a percentage of the original drop height. This measurement probably should be determined by using some objective device such as portable video equipment, but a British report (Winterbottom, 1985) states that trained operators usually can achieve a precision of mean values within 1%.

The type of ball used and the pressure to which it is inflated influence considerably the ball rebound measurements. A study by Holmes and Bell (1985) using 17 different types of soccer balls inflated at pressures between 59.0 and 108.5 kPa (9–16 lb in.$^{-2}$) revealed a difference in rebound ranging from 54.4 to 68.8% at an inflation pressure of 108.5 kPa and 49.4 to 63.8% at 59 kPa. Winterbottom (1985) reported that a study using only four different types of soccer balls reported a difference in rebound ranging from 14 to 18.9%. Concrete, natural grass, open pile artificial turf and sand-filled artificial turf surfaces were included in this investigation. All of the balls were inflated to a pressure of 69 kPa (10 lb in.$^{-2}$). The mean percentage of ball rebound from these four types of surfaces are shown in Table 3-2.

Note that the ball rebounds from the sand-filled and the open pile surfaces were 8 and 15% greater, respectively, than from the grass surfaces. These data were obtained from only one surface of each type, therefore, the variabilities created by the different types of ball were reasonably small (coefficients of variation ranging from 2.50–3.87%). The variabilities of ball rebound would have been much greater, if data had been gathered from different soccer pitches with both natural and artificial turfs. This same group (Winterbottom, 1985) conducted similar ball rebound tests on nine natural and 27 artificial turf fields in England. Tests were conducted at the

Table 3-2. Mean ball rebound of four types of soccer balls from four different surfaces.†

Type of surface	Ball rebound, %
Concrete	57.5 (3.87)‡
Artificial turf (Prepared substructure—open pile)	45.8 (2.50)
Artificial turf (Prepared substructure—sand-filled)	43.0 (2.94)
Grass	39.8 (2.99)

† Values derived from data in Winterbottom (1985).
‡ Standard deviations in parentheses.

goalmouth, in the center circle, and in the wing areas of the fields. On only one of the nine grass fields was the range of the ball rebound below 30%. For artificial turf, the variation among similar areas on the same turf was much smaller; the maximum range being 4%. Although the grass surfaces are much less consistent in ball bounce, in general, soccer players prefer to play on natural turf, presumably because the lower ball rebound makes it somewhat easier to control the ball. The artificial turf alters the skill techniques of the game to some degree due to the higher ball rebound. It should be noted that the soccer ball rebounds reported on a wet artificial turf ranged from 8 to 45% less than the rebounds conducted on the same fields when they were dry. For artificial surfaces, the wear and accompanying flattening of the pile fibers, compaction of the sand in sand-filled surfaces and hardening or compaction of the shock pad are at least some of the factors that would tend to increase ball rebound with time and use.

Lush (1985) conducted ball rebound and impact tests on the pitches of the Melbourne Cricket Ground in Australia. The ball rebound tests involved dropping new, old (used for 85-overs), and very old (used for considerably more than 85-overs) cricket balls from a height of 4.6 m (15.1 ft) and recording the rebound height in millimeters. The Clegg impact soil tester (Clegg, 1978) was employed in the impact tests. The hammer used had a mass of 0.5 kg (1.1 lb) with a flat impacting surface area of 20 cm^2 (3.1 in.^{2}) and was dropped in free-fall from a height of 0.3 m (11.8 in.). The mean peak accelerations at the wicket benches were 84 G ($S_{\overline{X}} = \pm 6$ G) before preparation of the first pitch of the season. These mean peak acceleration values increased to 376 G ($S_{\overline{X}} = \pm 14$ G) and to 605 G ($S_{\overline{X}} = \pm 26$ G) by the day before competitive play began. Lush reported a correlation of 0.725 and 0.825 between the mean impact values and the rebound of new and very old balls, respectively. Lush (1985) concluded that impact tests like the Clegg Tester could be used to assess natural sports turfs, but appropriate hammer weights for different sport activities would need to be determined by comparing impact values with some performance variables.

The FIH has adopted a test of ball rebound for field hockey similar to that used by the British Football Association for soccer (International Hockey Federation, 1987). In this test, a field hockey ball rather than a soccer ball is dropped vertically from a height of 1.5 m (59.0 in.) onto the artificial surface. To satisfy the FIH standard the ball must rebound at least 120 mm (4.7 in.) and not more than 300 mm (11.8 in.). These rebound heights correspond to a percentage of rebound of 8 to 20%. Currently, FIH states that the only ball that may be used for this test is the Kookaburra Dimple ball manufactured by A.G. Thompson of Australia. All measurements for this test are made from the surface to the underside of the ball and the surface must be wetted according to FIH specifications (3 L of water m^{-2} or 0.3 quarts of water ft^{-2}).

The field hockey competition is always played on wet turf to reduce the bounce of the ball; therefore, both laboratory and field tests are carried out using wet turfs. Contrary to the soccer players, field hockey players prefer artificial turf over natural grass because the synthetic surfaces are much more even and consistent than natural grass surfaces. Therefore, field hockey skills using the small ball are much easier to execute on the artificial turf as contrasted with natural grass.

D. Ball Roll

In addition to ball rebound, a ball roll test has also been used as a functional test for soccer and field hockey. The ball roll test measures the resistance offered by the turf to a rolling ball. For soccer, a ball inflated to 69 kPa (10 lb in.$^{-2}$) is rolled from a vertical height of 1 m (39.37 in.) down a ramp inclined at 45 degrees to the surface. The ramp consists of a channel with side rails 110 mm (4.33 in.) apart mounted on a sturdy frame. The ball contacts only the top edges of the side rails so as to cause as little friction as possible.

Initially, the distance that the ball rolled was measured in this test. For natural grass fields, this distance ranged from 5 to 12 m (16.5–39.6 ft) on nine soccer fields tested by the British Sports Council (Winterbottom, 1985). When the corresponding tests were conducted on artificial surfaces, the rolling distance ranged from 11 to 27 m (36.3–89.1 ft) when dry and 10 to 30 m (33.0–99.0 ft) when wet. Because of the rolling distances involved, the test has been modified and instead of measuring the distance traveled by the ball after it leaves the ramp, the deceleration of the ball is measured by using three photoelectric cells positioned at 1 m (39.37 in.) intervals. The first photoelectric cell is placed precisely 1 m (39.37 in.) from the bottom of the ramp. Using the recorded times from the three photoelectric cells, it is possible to calculate the ball deceleration using the following formulas:

$$V_1 = [S/(t_2 - t_1)] \ (\text{m s}^{-1}) \quad \text{and} \quad V_2 = [S/(t_3 - t_2)] \ (\text{m s}^{-1})$$

where

V_1 and V_2 = average velocities between photoelectric cells 1 and 2 and 2 and 3, respectively.

t_1, t_2, and t_3 = the recorded times at which the first, second, and third light beams are broken, respectively.

S = distance between each of the photoelectric cells (1 m or 39.37 in.).

With the average velocities, V_1 and V_2, the deceleration of the ball can be determined from the following:

$$a = [(V_2^2 - V_1^2)/2S] \ (m \ s^{-2}).$$

The calculated ball deceleration is assumed to be relatively constant and theoretically inversely proportional to the rolling distance. A deceleration of 1.0 m s^{-2} (3.3 ft s^{-2}) is equivalent to a distance of 6 m (19.8 ft) and a deceleration of 0.5 m s^{-2} (1.65 ft s^{-2}) is approximated by a rolling distance of 12 m (30.6 ft). The major problem with this test is that the results are influenced by several factors, the primary ones being the field camber and slope, direction of the pile fibers, and the wind direction. To provide more reliable results, the British Sports Council (1984) requires that five deceleration measurements be taken both with and against the direction of the pile fibers in three different locations on the field. The means of each set of five measurements (a total of six means) are calculated and these mean deceleration values must be between 1.50 and 0.45 m s^{-2} (5.0 and 1.5 ft s^{-2}) for national competition in soccer. For regional play the acceptable range is 20 to 0.35 m s^{-2} (6.6 to 1.116 ft s^{-2}). All field test measurements must take into account the slope of the field and the wind direction.

The ball roll test specified by FIH for field hockey allows for alternate tests. The standard inclined plane described in Part 2 of the British Sports Council Standards for Artificial Turf (1984) may be used, in which case, the ball shall not roll <5 m (16.5 ft) or more than 15 m (49.5 ft). These minimum and maximum distances correspond to ball deceleration values of approximately 1.25 m s^{-2} (4.13 ft s^{-2}) and 0.40 m s^{-2} (1.32 ft s^{-2}). The British Sports Council Standard specifies only that the ball used in this test shall be an outdoor hockey ball.

The alternative test permitted by FIH is one specified by the Netherlands Sports Federation (NSF-F8). In this test a standard blow is administered to a ball by means of a pendulum device. Following this blow, the ball shall not travel <30 m (99 ft) nor more than 40 m (132 ft).

To satisfy the FIH requirements for surface uniformity, the ball in either of these tests may not deviate more than three degrees on either side of the center line of the apparatus during its roll. In all a total of nine tests are conducted on a wet surface. Three of these measurements are performed in the same direction as the pile fibers, three directly against the grain of the turf and three at right angles to the first two sets of tests (International Hockey Federation, 1987).

Several tests described in this section have been developed as laboratory tests of materials and are not particularly suitable as field tests. Perhaps this is because the purposes of most research investigations have been to compare the characteristics of artificial turf with natural grass and to attempt to determine the differences among artificial turfs. This direction of research has continued in spite of the fact that artificial turfs are actually systems consisting of three essential elements; substructure, shock pad, and carpet. The substructure as an essential element of a complete system has an important influence on the performance characteristics of the turf system. Therefore, from a practical standpoint field tests are essential to provide a realistic evaluation of turf systems that will change with age, usage, and environmental conditions.

Tests should also be developed for specific sports because the requirements of different sports vary. Tackle football needs a surface with different characteristics than one designed for soccer. A laboratory or field test designed to evaluate running tracks may not be completely appropriate for the evaluation of artificial turf fields designed for field hockey. What is needed is a thorough analysis of the most important requirements of various sports. Based on the results of these analyses, specific tests should then be developed to evaluate the turfs' essential characteristics.

Finally, efforts should be made to correlate the results of different tests already available. These tests have been developed by different laboratories in three or four countries. As the number of international competitions increase, it would be quite advantageous to have facilities with artificial turf that satisfy certain minimum international standards.

VI. TURF-RELATED INJURIES

One of the on-going controversies associated with artificial turf fields since they were first installed is the effect of these surfaces on the incidence of injuries, particularly knee and ankle injuries in football. Although coaches, administrators, players, and researchers were concerned about injuries long before the introduction of synthetic turfs, they seemed to be prone to regard injuries as inevitable. These early studies of injuries were done mainly in the USA and dealt with injuries in tackle football. However, similar investigations have been conducted in England and Europe on soccer injuries. Most of these earlier studies were surveys concerned with frequency and type of injuries and the body parts that were injured most often. Only a few of these early studies dealt with ways in which rules and playing techniques might be modified in an attempt to reduce the incidence of injuries.

After the introduction of artificial turf, many studies were concerned with rates and seriousness of injuries but only limited efforts were made to establish either the direct or indirect causes of the injuries. In these investigations, the emphasis was placed on comparisons between the incidence and severity of injuries on artificial and natural turfs. It is difficult to interpret many of these studies because what was classified as an injury varied from player to player and study to study. Also, few researchers attempted to analyze injuries using sound epidemiological procedures. Samples were not random but were restricted in terms of geographical region and skill levels of participants. Rates of exposure were not calculated and few attempts were made to ascertain the possible causes of the injuries. For purposes of analysis it is necessary to define injuries, classify them according to severity, and at least estimate the exposure rates so that a denominator is available for the estimation of incidence.

In 1975, the National Athletic Injury/Illness Reporting System (NAIRS), a computerized data reporting system designed specifically for sports injuries, provided definitions of injury severity that have been used subsequently by many investigators (Alles et al., 1980). A reportable injury was defined as any injury that caused cessation of an athlete's customary participation for at least 1 d following the injury. Brain concussions serious enough to require observation before return to play and any dental injuries were also recorded as reportable injuries. A minor injury was a reportable injury with which the athlete was able to return to normal participation within 1 wk from the day of initial occurrence. A significant injury was one where the time loss from either practice or games exceeded 7 d. Significant injuries were classified further into three categories. Those injuries that kept the athlete from regular participation for a period of from 8 to 21 d were defined as moderate and the term major was assigned to injuries that prevented a return to normal participation within 21 d. Finally, a classification of severe was the classification given to permanently disabling injuries of societal importance such as quadriplegia, amputation, and death. NAIRS was also designed so that injuries were reported as they occurred on a weekly basis together with exposure data and most probable causes.

In addition to the factors of sampling, severity, exposure rates, and probable causes, in interpreting injury data for sports one should recognize that the occurrence of injuries is often cyclic in nature. Data from a single season may not present a true picture of the situation because such a limited period of data collection often leads to erroneous conclusions. Such conclusions may be either overestimations or underestimations of the true situation. All of these aspects should be considered when interpreting the results of published studies of athletic injuries.

A. Football Injuries

One of the first comparisons of injuries sustained on artificial and natural grass fields was released by a manufacturer soon after artificial turf was first used by colleges. This report claimed that there was a reduction in knee and ankle injuries when playing on artificial turf (Monsanto Company, unpublished report, 1968). A thorough analysis of this report reveals how it was possible to conclude that artificial turf was associated with fewer football injuries. In 1967, survey questionnaires were sent to 542 National Collegiate Athletic Association (NCAA) member institutions; 185 completed questionnaires were returned. The number of knee and ankle injuries, the severity of these injuries, and the number of games played during the season were provided. From these responses, a standardized injury rate (average number of injuries per game) was calculated and compared to the injury rate of those schools that played football on artificial turf. The standardized rate for NCAA schools competing on grass fields was 0.362 knee and ankle injuries per game compared to 0.058 injuries per game for schools playing on artificial turf. From these results, it was concluded that for each knee and ankle injury on synthetic turf there were approximately six injuries of a similar nature sustained on natural grass. Of the 69 games played on artificial turf, only 11 games involved college teams. Of the remaining games, 52 involved high school teams and six were games between professional teams. Injury rates for different football populations cannot be compared. In fact, it has been noted that within the college population, ankle and knee injuries vary with geographical region (Monsanto Company, unpublished report, 1968). It is interesting to note that those schools returning the questionnaire reported in response to a direct question that more than 50% of the knee and ankle injuries were definitely or possibly turf related.

In a study involving only 26 high school teams, Bramwell et al. (1972) reported that the injury rate for games played on synthetic surfaces was significantly higher than the rate for games played on natural grass. The injury rates were calculated based on 228 football games, of which 80 games were played on fields with artificial turf and the remaining 148 games were played on natural grass. Of the 80 games played on artificial turf, 41 were on dry fields and 39 on wet fields. Of the games played on natural grass, 88 were on dry fields and 60 on wet fields. These investigators reported injury rates of 0.52 and 0.76 injuries per game on natural and synthetic surfaces, respectively. Rates were also reported for both wet and dry fields on both types of surfaces. For natural grass, the rates were 0.53 and 0.50 injuries per game on dry and wet fields, respectively. In the case of artificial turf, the number of injuries per game on the dry and wet surfaces were 0.93 and 0.61, respectively. It is assumed that the lower incidence of injuries on the wet fields was due to the lower coefficient of friction between the shoes and the turf due to the water. However, if the wet surface is frozen, it might result in a higher incidence of injuries because of shock absorbency of the surface.

The numbers of severe injuries sustained on the two types of surfaces were also reported for this investigation (Bramwell et al., 1972). Severe injuries were defined as "those resulting from the inability to participate in two or more subsequent games" (Bramwell et al., 1972, p. 167). A total of 31% of the injuries sustained on artificial turf and 34% of the injuries on natural grass were classified as severe. Of the 19 severe injuries on artificial turf, 17 or 89% occurred when the surfaces were dry but only 59%, 14 of 26 injuries, sustained on natural grass occurred on dry fields. Although these results may be questioned since they were based on only one season of data and involved a limited number of schools in one very restricted geographical area, they do seem to indicate that the wetting of artificial surfaces may perhaps help to reduce more serious injuries.

Kretzler (1971) also reported fewer knee injuries on artificial turf (0.181 injuries per game) when it was wet as compared to a dry surface (0.375 injuries per game). Kretzler further reported that over a period of 4 yr, 1968 to 1971 inclusive, the rates of knee and ankle injuries on artificial turf were 0.312 and 0.170, respectively and the corresponding rates on natural grass fields for similar types of injury were 0.298 and 0.149 injuries per game, respectively. These results indicate the existence of small differences in rates of occurrence of knee and ankle injuries due to difference in type of field surface. Kretzler (1971) concluded that there was little or no difference be-

Table 3-3. Comparative rates of injury by gradient categories for professional football teams on natural grass and artificial turf.†

Gradient classification	Type of surface	
	Natural grass	Artificial turf
1. Major and minor injuries	2.00	2.70
2. Reinjury	0.59	0.49
3. Two or more missed games	0.76	0.78
4. Hospitalization	0.38	0.36
5. Surgery	0.33	0.26

† Data taken from J. Grippo (1973, unpublished data).

tween the incidence of injury in football on artificial turf and natural grass when the same population playing on the same field was studied.

A 3-yr study of injuries sustained by all 26 teams of the National Football League (NFL) was conducted by Stanford Research Institute (J. Grippo, unpublished data, 1973). To analyze the effects of turf on the injury rates in professional football, the investigators differentiated injuries in terms of gradients rather than by frequency alone. Gradient 1 included the incidence of both major and minor injuries, Gradient 2 the incidence of reinjury, Gradient 3 injuries causing two or more missed games, Gradient 4 injuries requiring hospitalization, and Gradient 5 injuries requiring surgery. The analysis of the data for Gradient 1, both major and minor injuries, indicated that the number of injuries per game was 2.0 on natural turf and 2.7 on synthetic turf. This difference was statistically significant ($P < 0.001$) indicating a lower injury rate on natural grass. For the other four gradients, however, there was no statistically significant difference between the injuries per game on natural grass and artificial turf. The actual rates per game as included in this report are shown in Table 3-3. The percentages of playing time on natural and artificial turfs were 56.3 and 43.7%, respectively.

Bortolin (1970) conducted a very limited study, in which only seven high schools participated, involving a comparison of injuries occurring on natural and artificial surfaces. A total of only 63 games were included in the analysis, 30 of which were played on artificial turf and the remaining 33 on natural grass. Of the total number of injuries reported, 60.6% occurred on artificial turf and 39.4% on natural turf. In this study, a serious injury was defined as one which required surgery, hospitalization, or full restriction of participation for five or more days following the occurrence of the injury. Based on this definition of serious, Bortolin (1970) reported that 5.8% of the injuries sustained on the artificial turf were classified as serious while 23.1% of the total number of injuries which occurred on the natural grass were serious. Based on these data, he concluded ". . .that the number of serious football injuries can be appreciably reduced by participating on artificial turf in preference to natural turf." (Bortolin, 1970, p. 62–63). One should keep in mind that this was a limited study and that no effort was made to determine how many of the serious injuries that occurred on either the synthetic or the natural surfaces were turf related. Also, Bortolin (1970) failed to describe the quality or condition of any of the fields in this study.

Although Bortolin's conclusions regarding serious injuries are contrary to the results of other studies involving comparisons of injuries on artificial and natural grass fields, he did report that abrasions accounted for a greater portion of the artificial turf injuries (Bortolin, 1970). The greater number of these injuries occurred at the elbow. Larson and Osternig (1974) stated a similar concern over the lesser number of cases of prepatellar and olecranon bursitis reported by Pacific-8 Conference teams that had home fields of natural grass as compared to teams that had artificial surfaces in their home stadiums. In both of these articles, the authors stressed the need to protect both the elbows and the knees using special protective pads to help dissipate the energy of impact and reduce the effects of greater surface friction of the artificial turf. It may be noticed when observing games on artificial turf that many players currently are using extra protective pads not only on the knees and elbows but also on the hands. More recent studies of the effectiveness of these supplementary pads have not been found in the published literature.

Alles et al. (1979) reported on 3 yr of NAIRS injury data for college football that pertained to the controversy concerning differences in injury rates on artificial and natural grass surfaces. These authors reasoned that injuries may be caused by surface hardness resulting in head concussions, surface friction differences are revealed by abrasions and differences in the shoe-turf interface may be associated with knee and ankle sprains. Therefore, these three different types of injuries were analyzed in an effort to compare the effects of the characteristics of the two types of surfaces.

Alles et al. (1979) reported that neither surface hardness nor surface friction of artificial fields created an added risk of injury among college football players. It should be noted that the authors analyzed significant injuries only (1 wk or more of missed practice time) and that it is unlikely that an abrasion would be classified as significant unless it became infected. The shoe-turf interface, on the other hand did appear to contribute to a greater injury rate per 1000 athlete exposures. According to Alles et al. (1979), a team might expect one additional knee sprain and one more significant ankle sprain on the average if all games and practices were held on an artificial turf field instead of on a natural grass field. This conclusion was derived from a combination of a chi-square test and a test of a critical interval that suggests that a more controlled study of this problem may be warranted.

Powell (1987) compared the injury rates of all NFL teams over 6 yr (1980–1985) on artificial and natural grass surfaces involving 11 400 player-seasons. He reported higher injury rates per team-game on synthetic surfaces, ranging from 1.94 to 2.36 on three different types of surfaces, as compared to grass fields (1.78 injuries per team-game). These data included 1520 team-games on natural grass fields and 1776 team-games on artificial turf surfaces. Based on the data from this study, Powell (1987) concluded that if an NFL team was to play its entire 20-game season (including preseason games) on artificial turf it could expect to incur one or two additional significant or major knee or ankle injuries and from one to four more reportable injuries than if it played all its games on a grass surface. The definitions of reportable, significant and major injuries were those used by NAIRS that have been described previously.

B. Soccer Injuries

There have been at least three rather extensive investigations carried out in England and Europe comparing injuries in soccer played on artificial and grass surfaces. One of these studies conducted in England (Winterbottom, 1985) involved 1125 soccer games on natural grass and 889 games on artificial turf. A study 2 yr later included 49 games played on natural grass and 153 games on a synthetic surface. In both of these studies, injury rates were reported as the number of player exposures per reportable injury where a reportable injury was defined as one that kept a player from participation for 4 d or longer.

The injury rates reported in the initial study conducted during the 1978 season were 1:80 on the natural grass and 1:90 on artificial turf. In games played during the 1980 season, the injury rates reported were 1:49 and 1:56 for games played on natural grass and artificial turf, respectively.

In 1983, the Federation of Ball Games in Berlin in Germany conducted a study comparing the injuries sustained on natural grass fields, synthetic turf pitches and hard porous surfaces (e.g., red shale fields) (W. Lavin, unpublished data, 1984). A total of 784 injuries were reported by the soccer teams that played in all districts of the city of Berlin. To make valid comparisons of incidence of injury on the three different types of fields because of the varying number of fields of each type, coefficients of injury were calculated based on 1000 h of field use per year. These injury coefficients were 2582 for natural grass, 1863 for hard porous surfaces, and 400 for synthetic turf. In this study, the higher numerical value of the coefficient indicated a relatively higher injury rate.

The available literature in which injuries sustained on natural grass and artificial turf are compared indicate that if both major and minor are included, the incidence of injury is somewhat higher on the synthetic surfaces than on natural grass. However, there is considerable evidence in the studies described to indicate that a much greater number of abrasions and burns occur when playing football on artificial surfaces as compared to natural grass. The nylon and polypropylene fibers and the exposed loose sand in sand-filled surfaces cause more burns and abrasions because they are naturally more abrasive. On sliding contact these more abrasive materials create higher skin temperatures due to friction that cause burns and abrasions. A considerable number of these abrasions occur at the knees and elbow joints and most can be prevented by the use of supplementary protective padding. When abrasions are sustained, they must receive careful attention by medical support personnel so they do not become infected. When infected the abrasion, usually classified as minor, may become a major injury.

C. Summary of Results of Injury Studies

The majority of the investigations have reported only small differences in the injury rates between artificial and natural turf fields when only the more serious injuries were considered. In football, the rates of injury reported have been slightly greater on the artificial surfaces while soccer has been associated with lower incidences of injury. The wetting of artificial surfaces appears to help reduce the number of injuries that are sustained, because of the lower coefficient of friction between shoes and the turf. Likewise, the use of noncleated shoes on the synthetic surfaces may aid in reducing injuries, however, except for the Berlin soccer study (Lavin, 1984) the objective data to support this supposition are limited.

One final point should be made regarding the interpretation of injury rates associated with artificial turf and natural grass surfaces, which was also mentioned by Kretzler (1971) and Merritt and Thomson (1978). One should recognize that there is much greater variation among different types of natural grass fields than between grass and artificial surfaces. On the one hand, a grass field may be quite lush and green with a smooth, dense, well-maintained turf growing on moist soil and used only a few times during a season. On the other hand, a natural grass field may be rough, stony, severely compacted, sun-baked, or primarily soil, perhaps even frozen solid in the northern climates during the latter part of the fall season. Unfortunately, most of the published comparative injury data have involved fields that were at least moderately well maintained, received only limited use, and had adequate grass cover. In future studies involving comparisons of natural grass and artificial surfaces, researchers should describe in some detail the nature of the grass fields and the types and characteristics of the soils underneath. If great variation exists in the quality of these fields, attempts should be made to classify them as poor, adequate, or excellent playing surfaces.

VII. USAGE

One aspect of artificial turf fields that should be taken into account when comparisons are made with natural turf fields is the increased use that can be made of a facility. An artificial playing surface may be used by more types of events for more hours each day and several more weeks each year than natural grass fields particularly in northern climates. However, the assumption must be that this increased utilization is appropriate and does not abuse the surface.

Leach (1979) compared the use of an artificial surface in Atwood Stadium in Flint, MI to the use of the same facility with a natural grass surface. In the 1967 to 1968 school year prior to the installation of the artificial surface, the field was used for only 19 football games. The remainder of the time the field was not used for any activity. In the 9 yr following the installation of artificial turf during the summer of 1968, an average of 332 events per year were held on the field. In addition to the football games, the field was used for soccer, rugby, softball, concerts, band practices, and band competitions. The estimated cost per participant hour for the facility with the synthetic turf was reduced by 75 to 80% over the cost per participant hour when the field of natural turf was used solely for football. These figures included mainly maintenance costs, inasmuch as Leach (1979) reported that most of the installation costs were recovered over a 9-yr period by renting the facility and charging admission to various events. Leach further stated that his data indicated "that one synthetic field could handle the same amount of activity as 17 grass fields." This statement, however, considered only usage and did not seem to take into account the problems of scheduling.

In 1977, the Swedes (Statens Naturvardsverket, 1977) reported that 2 yr after artificial turf was installed in Valhalla Stadium in Gothenberg the field was still in good condition after having received 5761 h of use with an average utilization time of 7.9 h per day. This one soccer field was able to be used 12.5 times longer than when the same field had a natural grass surface (average 0.6 h per day).

The British Sports Council (1975) monitored the use of synthetic field installations in environments of high demand in England. They reported that up to 35 soccer games per week could be played on fields with artificial turf when floodlighting was available. In contrast, the Council stated the normal rule was that no more than three football matches involving adults should be played per week on a typical grass field. Based on these data, the British Sports Council (1975, p. 21) estimated that one artificial turf field was equivalent in total use to approximately 11 grass fields.

Artificial fields in the St. Louis Soccer Park have been used for more than 1200 games per year in contrast to the fields with natural turf in the same park where considerably fewer games can be played. In fact, to maintain a top-quality natural turf only 50 soccer games per year are normally played on the main field (Anonymous, 1987).

These documented reports provide quite convincing evidence that artificial playing fields can be used much more extensively than fields with natural turf. However, it must be recognized that use is only one factor that must be considered when deciding on the most appropriate type of surface for an athletic field.

VIII. FACTORS TO CONSIDER IN THE CHOICE OF A PLAYING SURFACE

The decision to install an artificial or a natural surface on a playing field is usually quite difficult for most institutions or communities. Too frequently the final decision is based primarily on hearsay, limited experience, and the biased opinion of some outspoken individual in the decision-making group. The ultimate decision should not be made until a thorough analysis of several factors and their interactions has been carried out for a given situation.

One of the primary factors to be considered is the amount or cost of available land. If suitable land area is lacking and an extensive and varied

Table 3-4. Comparison of factors influencing choice of natural or artificial turf.

Factor	Type of surface	
	Natural grass	Artificial turf
Initial construction costs	Lower initial cost	Higher cost of installation
Replacement	Less cost	Higher cost
Maintenance costs	Higher cost of adequate maintenance	Lower maintenance costs
Field life	Indefinitely given proper maintenance. May require resodding	Limited to 10 to 15 yr of heavy usage
Repairs	Relatively continuous depending on weather conditions	Sporadic repairs depending on use
Usage	Limited number of games	Number of games limited only by schedule
Weather conditions	Limited use under adverse weather conditions	May be used under all but most adverse weather conditions
Consistency	Playing surface may be quite variable	Very consistent playing surface
Versatility	Limited activities (e.g., football, soccer, and other field sports)	Multipurpose use (e.g., band practice, concerts). Can be used in covered stadiums
Playability	Preferred by soccer and football players when field conditions and weather are good	Preferred by field hockey because of consistency
Injuries	Fewer minor injuries. Incidence of serious injury controversial	Greater incidence of burns and abrasions. Incidence of serious injury controversial

program of sports and other ancillary programs must use the facility, then maximum use must be anticipated. If this situation exists, perhaps an artificial surface will better satisfy the needs than a natural grass field.

On the other hand, if sufficient land is readily available at a reasonable cost, several natural grass fields may be more feasible than a single artificial turf facility. Economic factors also must be considered in the initial stages. Will it be better to make a larger initial investment at the time of installation and save in later years with reduced annual maintenance costs? Will it be easier to support a higher annual budget that includes more extensive maintenance than to raise a sizeable amount of money for installation of a field? Must a loan or a bond issue be floated, and if so, will the high cost of interest be a problem? Cost estimates presented by Indyk (1987) indicated that construction costs of a synthetic turf field would be about four times the costs for a properly constructed natural turf field.

A number of other factors should be considered as the analysis continues such as: (i) the number and types of events that will be scheduled in the facility, (ii) local climate, (iii) flexibility of the schedule, (iv) the availability of maintenance personnel, and (v) availability of other facilities. Table 3-4 includes not only these factors but some additional aspects that will have a direct effect on the participants.

It is unlikely that one could anticipate all of the factors that it might be necessary to consider in a situation, however, the final decision must be made carefully following a thorough and objective analysis of all the pertinent factors. In one community or educational institution an artificial playing surface may be more appropriate while in another situation a natural grass field may be a better decision. There is a legitimate place for both natural and synthetic surfaces in sports competition.

IX. SUMMARY

Although sports competition at professional, college, and high school levels have been played in several field sports for nearly 20 yr on synthetic surfaces, a great deal of controversy still exists concerning the use of artificial turf. Many players personally dislike playing on the synthetic surfaces because it is too hard, others seem to prefer this type of surface because they can run faster. Certainly as players have become bigger and stronger and are able to run faster, the greater energy involved in collisions between players creates a situation for more frequent and perhaps more severe injuries. These circumstances warrant additional research comparing the injury rates on the two types of surfaces. However, these studies must include prospective injury data that are carefully defined as to severity and probable cause. In addition, data collection must continue for several consecutive years involving several teams at the same skill level playing in different geographical regions under various environmental conditions. Further, the characteristics of the fields on which the competition is conducted must be described in detail, identifying such factors as age, condition, and substructure in the case of artificial surfaces and maintenance, ground cover and soil characteristics for natural grass fields. Such comprehensive and complex investigations would require appreciable financial support over the course of the study to alleviate the controversy of artificial vs. natural turf.

The International Fédération Internationale de Football (Soccer) Association (FIFA) discourages international competition on artificial grass pitches because its characteristics require a noticeable modification in the techniques of playing skills by players. The FIH, on the other hand, requires that international competition be played on artificial fields that have been wetted because its uniformity offers a much better surface on which to execute field hockey skills. Different games have different requirements, and it is suggested that greater efforts be made by manufacturers to attempt to modify the synthetic surfaces so that the requirements of each game are more adequately satisfied. Also purchasers of artificial surfaces must realize that multi-purpose installations will not adequately meet the needs of highly skilled players in several sports.

To achieve greater uniformity among surfaces and ensure adequate durability, testing programs and scientific standards should be developed. Although several tests currently exist, most of these have been developed by different research laboratories in various countries. There is a need to conduct scientifically designed round-robin tests on an international basis among qualified test laboratories to standardize and publicize valid and reliable tests for both laboratory and field situations.

Certainly artificial turf can provide several advantages over many natural grass fields. Among these are: (i) its consistent flatness or planarity with no holes, humps, ruts, depressions, (ii) the relatively consistent traction on all parts of the playing surface under all but the more adverse weather conditions, (iii) the uniform resilience over the entire playing field, and (iv) the increased durability making increased utilization possible under many weather conditions and in areas where field space is at a premium. In addition, the maintenance costs may be lower for synthetic fields than natural grass because no fertilizer, seed, sod, watering, and mowing are required. These artificial surfaces do require periodic cleaning that can be done quite quickly. However, if stains from shoe polish, tobacco juice, blood, gum, and other items are prevalent, the time required for cleaning will be increased to a considerable extent.

Certainly one of the major deterrents to the installation of artificial fields, particularly by small colleges and public schools is the initial cost of purchase and installation. One may expect synthetic fields to provide satisfactory service for a minimum of 5 yr and perhaps up to 10 yr but the initial cost of installation for most fields will exceed $500 000. The cost will probably be greater in colder climates where a more expensive substructure is required. This represents a substantial investment for a community for a facility that will be used by only a limited portion of the population. The interest costs on any loans and the higher cost of replacement of an artificial turf field in contrast to natural turf are also disadvantages.

Finally, most participants in field sports, except perhaps field hockey, would probably prefer to compete on a natural grass field if it is soft, has an abundance of grass with few weeds, no holes and ruts, and is well maintained. However, such fields are only available in areas where there is an abundance of space, well-trained maintenance personnel, and an enlightened athletic administration. Since these ideal situations are quite limited, there will probably always be a place for artificial turf in athletics. The controversy that currently exists over its use will continue unless adequate financial support is made available to qualified objective and disinterested researchers for well-controlled studies. There is no simplistic solution to this complex problem.

REFERENCES

Alles, W.F., J.W. Powell, W. Buckley, and E.E. Hunt, Jr. 1979. The National Athletic Injury/Illness Reporting System 3-year findings of high school and college football injuries. J. Orth. Sports Phys. Ther. 1(2):103–108.

Alles, W.F., J.W. Powell, W.E. Buckley, and E.E. Hunt, Jr. 1980. Three year summary of NAIRS football data. Athletic Training 15(2):98–100.

American Society of Testing and Materials. 1986. Standard test method for shock-absorbing properties of playing surface systems and materials. ANSI/ASTM F355-86. ASTM, Philadelphia.

Andreasson, G., U. Lindenberger, P. Renstrom, and L. Peterson. 1986. Torque developed at simulated sliding between sport shoes and an artificial turf. Am. J. Sports Med. 14(3):225–230.

Anonymous. 1987. St. Louis Park carries torch for U.S. soccer. Sportsturf 3(3):14–19.

AstroTurf Industries, Inc. 1981. Technical topics; key ideas, concepts and facts on the history and use of synthetic playing surfaces. AstroTurf Industries, Dalton, GA.

AstroTurf Industries, Inc. No date. Owner's manual: The care and maintenance of AstroTurf surfaces. AstroTurf Industries, Dalton, GA.

Bell, M.J., S.W. Baker, and P.M. Conaway. 1985. Playing quality of sports surfaces: A review. J. Sports Turf Res. Inst. 61:26–45.

Bonstingl, R.W., C.A. Morehouse, and B.W. Niebel. 1975. Torques developed by different types of shoes on various playing surfaces. Med. Sci. Sports 7:127–131.

Bortolin, J.J. 1970. A comparison of high school football game injuries occurring on artificial and natural turf. M.S. thesis. Univ. of Oregon, Eugene.

Bowers, K.D., Jr., and R.B. Martin. 1974. Impact absorption, new and old AstroTurf at West Virginia University. Med. Sci. Sports 6(3):217–221.

Bramwell, S.T., R.K. Requa, and J.G. Garrick. 1972. High school football injuries: A pilot comparison of playing surfaces. Med. Sci. Sports 4:166–169.

British Sports Council. 1984. Specification for artificial sports surfaces, Part 2. The British Sports Counc., London.

Buskirk, E.R.,E.R. McLaughlin, and J.L. Loomis. 1971. Microclimate over artificial turf. J. Health, Phys. Ed., Rec. 42(9):29–30.

Clegg, B. 1978. An impact soil tester for low cost roads. p. 58–85. *In* Proc. 2nd Conf. of the Road Engineers of Asia and Australia.

Culpepper, M.I., and K.M.W. Nieman. 1983. An investigation of the shoe-turf interface using different types of shoes on Poly-Turf and Astro-Turf: Torque and release coefficients. Ala. J. Med. Sci. 20(4):387–390.

Deutsches Institut für Normung. 1975. Teil 6 Sportplatze; Kunstoff-Flachen (Part 6 Sporting grounds; artificial surfaces). DIN 18035. 1975. Deutsches Inst. für Normung, Cologne, Germany.

Gadd, C.W. 1966. Use of a weighted impulse criterion for estimating injury hazard. p. 164–174. *In* Proc. 10th Stapp Car Crash Conf., SAE, New York.

Gadd, C.W. 1971. Tolerable severity index in whole-head non-mechanical impact. p. 809–816. *In* Proc. 15th Stapp Car Crash Conf. SAE, New York.

Gurdjian, E.S., V.L. Roberts, and L.M. Thomas. 1966. Tolerance curves of acceleration and intracranial pressures and protective index in experimental head injury. J. Trauma 6(5):600–604.

Hamner, W.F., and T.A. Orofino. 1982. Recreational surfaces. p. 922–936. *In* Kirk-Othmer (ed.) Encyclopedia of Chem. Tech., Vol. 19, 3rd ed. John Wiley and Sons, New York.

Holmes, G., and M.J. Bell. 1985. The effect of football type and inflation pressure on rebound resilience. J. Sports Turf Res. Inst. 61:132–135.

International Hockey Federation. 1987. International Hockey Federation handbook of requirements for synthetic hockey pitch surfaces. Fed. Int. de Hockey, Brussels, Belgium.

Indyk, H.W. 1987. The real economics of athletic field construction. Sports Turf Mgr. 3(3):1–2.

Kandelin, W.W., G.S. Krahenbuhl, G.S. Schact, and C.A. Schact. 1976. Athletic field microclimates and heat stress. J. Safety Res. 8:106–111.

Koon, J.L., E.W. Rochester, and M.K. Howard. 1971. Environmental studies with artificial turf and grass surfaces. *In* Am. Soc. Agric. Eng., Pullman, WA. 27–31 June.

Krahenbuhl, G.S. 1974. Speed of movement with varying footwear conditions on synthetic turf and natural grass. The Res. Quart. 45(1):28–33.

Kretzler, H.H. 1971. Artificial turf and football injuries. *In* Natl. Conf. Medical Aspects of Sports. Am. Med. Assoc., New Orleans, LA. Annual Safety Education Review. AAHPER Press, Washington, DC.

Larson, R.L., and L.R. Osternig. 1974. Traumatic bursitis and artificial turf. J. Sports Med. 2(4):183–188.

Leach, R. 1979. Synthetic turf multiplies stadium use. Am. School Univ. 52(3):28–29.

Lush, W.M. 1985. Objective assessment of turf cricket pitches using an impact hammer. J. Sports Turf Res. Inst. 61:71–79.

Merritt, S.C., and J.M. Thomson. 1978. The effect of artificial turf on injury rate in football—A review. Can. J. Appl. Sports Sci. 3:79–84.

Morehouse, C.A., and W.E. Morrison. 1975. The artificial turf story: A research review. Penn State HPER Ser. No. 9. College of Health, Physical Education and Recreation, Penn State Univ., University Park, PA.

Powell, J.W. 1987. Incidence of injury associated with playing surfaces in the National Football League 1980–1985. Athletic Training 22(3):202–206, Fall.

Ramsey, J.D. 1982. Environmental heat from synthetic and natural turf. Res. Quart. Exercise Sport 53(1):82–85.

Statens Naturvardsverket. 1977. Fotballsplan med knonstgras-Valhalla idrotsplats i Göteborg. SNV PM846.17120 Statens naturvardsverk Fack. 171 20 Solna, Sweden 08/98 1800. (In Swedish, summary in English.)

Winterbottom, W. Sir (ed.). 1985. Artificial grass surfaces for association football: Report and recommendations. The British Sports Counc., London.

UNPUBLISHED REFERENCES

Brennan, W.E. 1966. AstroTurf shoe and cleat study. Interim Rep. 816404-533-055 IC-D3247. Chemstrand Div. of Monsanto Co., St. Louis.

Grippo, J. 1973. National Football League injury study, 1969–1972. Unpublished report of Stanford Res. Inst. submitted to the Office of the Commissioner, Natl. Football League. SRI Rep. MSD-1961.

Lavin, W. 1984. Case study Berlin: Injury comparison on various sports surfaces. An unpublished report available from J.F. Adolff A.G., Sporte Poligras, Postfach 1109, D-7150 Backnang, Germany.

Monsanto Company. 1968. Survey of football knee and ankle injuries, 1967. Unpublished report of the Monsanto Co., St. Louis.

Morehouse, C.A., R.C. Nelson, W. Morrison, R. Shapiro, and J. Palmgren. 1974. Performances of football players wearing cleated and non-cleated shoes on artificial and natural grass playing surfaces. Unpublished research report of the Penn State Sports Res. Inst. submitted to Uniroyal Consumer Products, Div. of Uniroyal Inc., Naugatuck, CT.

Niebel, B.W., C.A. Morehouse, R.W. Bonstingl, and D.A. Zwigart. 1973. The influence of outsole design, outsole compound, and playing surface material on foot traction. Unpublished research report of the Penn State Sports Res. Inst. submitted to Uniroyal Consumer Products, Div. of Uniroyal Inc., Naugatuck, CT.

4 Ecological Aspects of Turf Communities

T. L. WATSCHKE

Penn State University
University Park, Pennsylvania

R. E. SCHMIDT

VPI & SU
Blacksburg, Virginia

The interactions between turfgrasses, their management, and the environment are complex and dynamic, and any ecological discussion concerning turfgrass communities is strongly influenced by these interactions. Environments are dictated largely by climate, edaphic, and geographic factors. However, unlike naturally occurring climax vegetation, turfgrasses persist only in settings managed by humans. Human endeavor is an intrinsic part of the turfgrass ecological system. Without the activities of people, turf communities would disappear because those cultural conditions that favor the competitive nature of turfgrasses over other plant species would not exist.

In early times, turfgrass communities evolved when people cleared forests and regrowth was prevented by domestic animal grazing. Modern turfgrass communities reflect intensive human management practices that control the natural tendency of grasses.

This chapter presents a discussion of the ecological aspects of management on environment and the subsequent development of turfgrass communities.

I. ECOLOGICAL ASPECTS OF ESTABLISHING TURFGRASSES

A. Environmental Conditions

The principle environmental factors that influence the establishment of turf species are temperature, moisture, light, wind, edaphology, and geography. Edaphic and geographic factors are the most stable. The other factors are constantly changing. Climatic and environmental conditions are usually predictable for different seasons and locations. Therefore, general recommendations for optimum turfgrass establishment times for different turfgrass species in the various climatic regions have been developed. Cultural practices such as seedbed preparation method, mulching practices, seed-

Copyright © 1992 ASA-CSSA-SSSA, 677 S. Segoe Rd., Madison, WI 53711, USA. *Turfgrass—*
Agronomy Monograph no. 32.

ing rates, and supplemental irrigation can facilitate turfgrass establishment, even in ecological settings that are less than ideally suited for turfgrasses.

B. Types of Turfgrass Communities Desired

At the outset, it is important that adapted turfgrass species be selected because established turf is intended to be more or less permanent. In choosing turfgrass species, consideration must be given to the species' tolerance of climate, environmental stresses, potential uses, and anticipated cultural levels.

Based on climatic adaptation, turfgrass species have been placed into four categories; grasses adapted for the cool humid region, warm humid region, cool arid region, and warm arid region (Ward, 1969). Although these categories are broad and regional boundaries are not absolute, species cultured outside their region of adaptation usually require special management attention. The major turfgrasses adapted to the cool humid regions, and irrigated areas of the cool arid region are species of *Agrostis, Poa, Festuca*, and *Lolium*. In the warm humid and irrigated areas of the warm arid regions, the major adapted turfgrasses are species of *Cynodon, Zoysia, Stenotaphrum, Eremochloa, Paspalum, Festuca*, and *Agropyron*; in the non-irrigated warm arid regions, species of *Buchloë* and *Bouteloua* are adapted.

Within a climatic region, species should be selected that are tolerant to the varying environmental stresses. For example, terraces and slopes facing south are warmer and drier than those facing north. Species with heat and drought tolerance should be selected for south-facing slopes (McKee et al., 1965; Ward, 1969). In north China, more than 130 species of Gramineae and Leguinosae from North America and the Mediterranean have been introduced and evaluated for acclimatization (Hu et al., 1989). They found *Buchloë* spp. to be the most adapted to the cold and aridity. In the cool humid regions, *Festuca* spp. tolerate well-drained, shaded areas better than *Kentucky* bluegrass (*Poa pratensis* L.) or perennial ryegrass (*Lolium perenne* L.), which are more suited to full sun settings (Juska et al., 1965; Blaser et al., 1961, p. 5–19). *Poa trivialis* is a shade-tolerant grass adapted to wet soils.

It has been shown that tolerances to environmental stresses also vary between cultivars of the same species. Kentucky bluegrasses that have been selected from warm rather than cool regions were generally more tolerant of high temperatures because of lower NO_3-N absorption and higher carbohydrate levels (Watschke et al., 1970).

Turfgrasses are established for many purposes including aesthetics, soil stabilization, and recreation. The anticipated intensity of cultural practices and the use that the turf will receive are factors that should be considered in species selection. Grasses selected for golf putting greens must tolerate frequent close mowing. Excellent wear tolerance and recuperative potential are important for turfgrasses used on sports fields. Grasses selected for highway slopes should persist under harsh xeric conditions with little maintenance yet produce extensive root systems.

Turfgrasses are, in essence, communities of plants that may be a monostand, which consists of a single cultivar, or a polystand, which is composed of two or more cultivars of the same species (blends) or of different species (mixtures) (Beard, 1973). Although polystand communities may not provide the uniform turf textural quality and growth responses of monostands, they do offer advantages. Properly formulated polystand communities provide a wider range of environmental stress and pest tolerance than monostand communities. Deterioration of turf stands are less likely to occur from disease and insect infestation in polystands (Beard, 1973; Madison, 1971).

Funk and Dickson (1981) indicated that performance of turfgrass polystands is determined by their relative cultivar composition, which may shift with time. Grasses best adapted to their subjected environment eventually dominate the polystand community. These authors reported that the cv. Brunswick and Touchdown comprised 68% and 23% of the plant population 7 yr after being established in a blend of 38 Kentucky bluegrasses in New Jersey.

In highway slope stablization, it is necessary to alter species components to obtain rapid vegetative cover at various seasons to minimize erosion (Blaser, 1963; Blaser & Woodruff, 1968; Duell & Schmidt, 1974; Schmidt & Blaser, 1969a; Woodruff et al., 1972). The differential seedling vigor associated with seasonal environmental changes must be considered in designing these mixtures (Wright et al., 1978a). Parks and Henderlong (1967) showed considerable differences existed in the germination and seedling growth rate of 10 common turfgrasses. Species ratios and seeding rates should be adjusted to provide proper plant succession, allowing a shift from faster establishing temporary species to slower establishing perennial species.

Botanical composition of polystands of perennial species is also influenced by the environment at planting time. Hall (1980) found August through September and March through April seeding dates of tall fescue (*Festuca arundinacea* Schreb.)-Kentucky bluegrass mixtures enhanced the tall fescue component when compared to October and November seeding dates.

C. Propagation Sources

Propagation of turfgrass can be accomplished with seed or vegetative plant parts. Seed is the most convenient propagating material in that it is easily stored and transported. Vegetative planting materials, such as stolons, sprigs, plugs, and sod, must be used for propagating those grasses that do not produce viable seed or that cannot be reproduced genotypically from seed. Sod from grasses normally established from seed may also be used to obtain turf and stabilize soil quickly.

The environment to which propagation material is exposed prior to establishment has an influence on its viability. Seed is a living organism and continues to respire using its stored organic food. Seed viability is affected principally by temperature and moisture conditions during storage. Cool temperatures and low humidity conserve stored organic food enabling seed to remain viable for longer periods.

Vegetative propagules are more perishable than seeds. Propagules must be handled with more care from harvest time to planting. If these harvested plant parts are packed together, they may overheat and reduce storage life or ability to propagate (Darrah & Powell, 1977; King, 1970; King & Beard, 1972). Temperature may be the most critical factor in storage of vegetative material in that it not only increases respiration rate but also enhances microbial activity (Bailey, 1940).

Several factors have been associated with sod heating: soil temperature at harvest, amount of leaf area present, N nutritional level, and soil moisture content (Beard, 1969, 1973). Darrah and Powell (1977) concluded that the detrimental effects of temperature on stored sod can be reduced by harvesting in early morning, removing excess clippings, and lowering N fertility.

D. Soil Preparation

In preparation for planting turfgrasses, it is imperative that adequate surface and subsurface drainage are provided to ensure optimum edaphic conditions for establishment, and to allow for future maintenance of the site. Inadequate drainage may result in poor soil gaseous exchange, which can cause poor turf establishment. Adequate surface grading and installation of internal drainage may be required to compensate for extreme cases of slow saturated soil moisture flow (Marsh, 1969). The unsaturated soil moisture and nutrient holding capacity of most topsoil enhances the environment for turfgrass establishment (Wright et al., 1978a). If the available topsoil is not of proper physical characteristics for turfgrass production, or when heavy traffic is anticipated (such as occurs on sports fields or golf greens), it is usually necessary to modify the soil to meet the anticipated use requirements. In general, fine-textured soils that are subjected to compaction should be modified with sand and organic matter to create an environment conducive for turf production (Radko, 1974; Schmidt, 1980; Swartz & Kardos, 1963; Waddington et al., 1974).

For rapid establishment of turfgrasses, proper soil pH and an adequate supply of soil nutrients are essential. Many researchers have concluded that P application is especially important for rapid seedling development in new turfgrass stands (McVey, 1968; Blaser et al., 1975; Turner & Waddington, 1983). Juska et al. (1965) reported that P fertilization was necessary on acid soil when seeding nonacid tolerant grasses such as 'Merion' Kentucky bluegrass, but was not as beneficial for acid-tolerant species, such as creeping red fescue (*Festuca rubra* L.). Vegetative establishment of zoysiagrass (*Zoysia japonica* Steud.) (Juska & Murray, 1974) and St. Augustinegrass [*Stenotaphrum secundatum* (Walter) Kuntze] (Wood & Duble, 1976) have also been enhanced with P fertilization.

To create a good nutrient environment for turfgrass species and to encourage deep rooting, it has been recommended that lime and P be incorporated into the top 10 to 15 cm of soil (Musser & Perkins, 1969a; Beard, 1973;

Turgeon, 1980). However, King and Skogley (1969) reported better establishment for a Kentucky bluegrass-creeping red fescue mixture with surface applied P rather than that incorporated into the upper 10 cm of soil. It has also been documented that N fertility improves turfgrass establishment (King & Skogley, 1969).

When steep slopes, such as highway corridor cuts and fills, are to be established with turf species, the grading and construction procedures can alter the microenvironment (Goss et al., 1970; Green et al., 1973; Wischmeier, 1973; Wright et al., 1975). A rough, loose, and undulated soil surface will permit precipitation to infiltrate rapidly, thus conserving soil moisture and reducing water runoff and erosion (Wright et al., 1978a). The roughness of the surface permits sloughing of loose soil that covers seeds and creates a more favorable moisture situation, which stimulates germination, seedling growth, and rate of vegetative cover (Perry et al., 1975). Stairstep grading of steep slopes further encourages precipitation infiltration and impedes surface water movement to minimize erosion and sedimentation. This grading technique helps create a favorable environment for establishing vegetation on harsh xeric conditions (Blaser & Perry, 1975; Green et al., 1974; Perry et al., 1975; Wright et al., 1975).

E. Soil Contact with Seeds or Vegetative Propagules

Covering seeds with soil moderates the temperature surrounding them, enhances moisture conditions for germination, and decreases injury due to drying (Musser & Perkins, 1969b). Ensuring good seed-soil contact through light rolling after seeding ensures more successful establishment by shortening germination time, which may allow seedling turf to be more competitive with germinating weed species. If seeds are planted too deeply, the developing seedling may exhaust carbohydrates within the seed endosperm and die before leaves emerge and manufacture photosynthate (Forbes & Ferguson, 1948; Madison, 1966; Murphy & Arny, 1939; Plummer, 1943). Also, seeds that require light for germination such as Kentucky bluegrass (Anderson, 1947; Hendricks et al., 1968; Nelson, 1927) and zoysiagrass (Portz et al., 1981; Yeam et al., 1981) should not be planted too deeply. Small seeded species should not be planted deeper than 6 to 12 mm, while species with large seeds may be covered to approximately 20 mm (Madison, 1966).

The process by which seed is applied by a stream of pressurized water is referred to as hydroseeding (Hottenstein, 1969). This technique does not provide intimate seed/soil contact, and depends upon applying a suitable mulch (e.g., wood cellulose fiber) to create a favorable environment for seed germination. Hydroseeding is most successful in regions or seasons where rainfall is uniformly distributed over the establishment period.

It is also imperative that vegetative propagules have good soil contact to ensure rapid rooting during establishment. When sprigs are planted in rows, they should be lightly topdressed with soil, leaving about 50% of the leaf tissue above the soil surface (Beard, 1973). Sprig-soil contact may be accomplished by topdressing or pressing the sprigs into the soil with a steel mat or a straight disk-like roller. Stolons have been established successfully when applied simultaneously with suitable mulching material by means of a hydroplanter equipped with a gear-type pump (Schmidt, 1967).

F. Mulching Materials

One of the most effective cultural practices used to enhance turfgrass establishment is mulching. Mulches reduce surface soil compaction resulting from the impact of raindrops or irrigation (Adams, 1966; Ellison, 1944), reduce runoff, and increase infiltration rate (Alderfer & Merkle, 1943; Duley, 1939; Duley & Kelley, 1939; Mannering & Meyer, 1963). Mulches conserve soil moisture by moderating soil temperatures and reducing evaporation (Harris & Yao, 1923; McGinnies, 1960). Barkley et al. (1965) reported that straw mulch applied at 2800 kg ha^{-1} lowered temperatures by 7 °C and preserved an average of 35% more moisture in the upper inch of soil than when no mulch was used.

In regions of limited rainfall where supplemental irrigation is not available, cereal grains are often planted the season prior to establishing the desirable grasses. After the cereal grain is harvested in the fall, a 15 to 20 cm stubble is left to enhance moisture retention during the winter, and desirable permanent grasses are seeded into this stubble the following spring (Musser & Perkins, 1969b).

Most mulching materials are applied to the soil surface and may be broadly classified as: (i) textured, (ii) chemical, and (iii) covers (mesh, blankets, and tarps). The best mulches for turf establishment are textured materials such as straw, hay, pine needles, wood cellulose fiber, recycled paper, and shredded woodbark. These materials moderate temperatures, most conserve moisture, and some stabilize soil. Wright et al. (1975) recommended that straw tacked with wood cellulose fiber or finely ground paper applied with a hydromulcher provided an excellent mulch that was resistant to wind movement on highway right-of-way slopes.

The chemical mulches such as polyvinyl, polyvinyl acetate, pectin, and elastomeric polymer emulsions have been used in specialized situations (Hottenstein, 1969). Barkley et al. (1965) reported that a dark colored emulsion mulch used in mid-summer conserved moisture, but caused soil temperatures to rise unfavorably and reduced seedling stands when compared to a nonmulch treatment. Perry et al. (1975) and Wright et al. (1975) reported that chemical binders and soil stabilizers did not control erosion, moderate temperatures, or conserve soil moisture as well as straw or wood cellulose fiber mulches.

Some woven net materials, such as jute nets, are suitable for aiding in the establishment of vegetation in ditches used as waterways (Wright et al., 1978b). Although most net mulches control some erosion, they only slightly enhance the microenvironment for successful turfgrass establishment (Beard, 1966a; Dudeck et al., 1966; Gilbert & Deal, 1964; Swanson et al., 1966). Wright et al. (1978b) reported that on steep slopes where nets fail to make good contact with the soil, water may flow under the net resulting in erosion and establishment failure.

Clear polyethylene covers with small holes on 10-cm centers to permit infiltration of water have been used to enhance microenvironments for seedling establishment of fine turf areas under suboptimal temperatures. These covers limit evaporation and permit solar radiation to warm the soil (Beard, 1973). Because of heat buildup, plastic covers should not be used when temperatures are optimum or higher (Schmidt, 1961). Covers have been used to improve winter survival and hasten spring green-up on putting greens (Cooper, 1982; Roberts, 1986).

G. Irrigation

Once newly sown seeds have imbibed water they are prone to injury from moisture stress. Imbibition of water by seeds generally decreases as soil moisture tensions increase (Phillips, 1968) causing germination of most plant species to decrease (Ayers, 1952; Evans & Strickler, 1961; Hughes et al., 1966; Hunter & Erickson, 1952; McGinnies, 1960). Species vary in their rate of germination and seedling development under moisture stress (Wright, 1978a). Strains of grasses with superior establishing characteristics germinate faster and produce larger seedlings when subjected to low soil moisture tension (Kneebone, 1957; Wright et al., 1978a).

Wright (1978a) reported that the germination of perennial ryegrass and Abruzzi rye (*Secale cereale* L.) seeds were less influenced by high soil moisture tension than annual ryegrass (*Lolium multiflorum* Lam.), tall fescue, or Kentucky bluegrass. These authors indicated that these competitive differences could be reduced when establishment was in soil containing adequate moisture, and if aggressive species were seeded at a lower rate.

Many of the turfgrasses that must be propagated vegetatively are susceptible to desiccation during establishment. Woodle (1954) reported that planting bermudagrass (*Cynodon* spp.) propagules in late winter or early spring when the grass is dormant was generally most successful. Late spring or early summer establishments may be successful if moisture is adequate and sprigs are properly handled. Chamblee and Gooden (1981) concluded that dormant bermudagrass sprigs tolerated desiccation better than nondormant sprigs.

Depending on weather conditions, supplemental irrigation will generally enhance turfgrass seedling development, even when mulched adequately (Barkley et al., 1965). Irrigating dormant bermudagrass has been beneficial in establishment in the spring (Hughes et al., 1962). Newly seeded or vegetatively propagated turf may benefit from a light irrigation several times a day to maintain adequate moisture near the soil surface until the grass is well rooted into the soil (Marsh, 1969).

H. Pest Control

Often areas scheduled for turfgrass establishment contain pests that potentially compete with the desirable turfgrass species. Pests such as weed seeds, undesirable vegetation, soil-borne disease organisms, insects, and nematodes may need to be eliminated or controlled prior to the establishment of turfgrasses. Fumigants such as methyl bromide or chloropicrin have been used to control troublesome organisms.

Weeds are generally the pest that gives the most competition to turf seedlings. Undesirable plant seeds and vegetative propagules remaining in the soil prior to planting may become the dominant species. Competition from weeds in the turf establishment area may be lessened by frequent tillage to destroy the weeds or by using chemicals prior to planting. In addition to fumigants, nonselective herbicides and selective preemergence herbicides may be used to control infestation. Glyphosate [N-(phosphonomethyl) glycine] is the principal nonselective systemic herbicide that is used to control actively growing perennial grasses (Baird et al., 1973; Burt, 1980; Jagschitz, 1978; Klingman & Murray, 1978). Its main advantages are that the chemical is capable of translocating to control below ground propagules, and it has essentially no soil residual. Successful establishment can occur as soon as foliage turns brown, usually within 7 to 10 d.

Selective preemergence herbicides have been used to reduce competition of certain undesirable plants arising from weed seed infested soil. Siduron [1-(2-methylcyclohexyl)-3-phenylurea] applications have successfully controlled smooth crabgrass [*Digitaria ischaemum* (Schreb.) Muhl.] and other annual grasses during establishment of perennial cool-season turfgrasses without phytotoxicity to nontargeted species (Jagschitz & Skogley, 1966; Kerr, 1969; Lewis & Gilbert, 1966).

Several preemergence herbicides have been used to control weedy grasses in newly sprigged warm-season turfgrasses. Portz et al. (1981) reported preemergence applications of siduron reduced weed competition without phytotoxic effects to zoysiagrass established from seed. These authors also found that simazine [2-chloro-4,5-bis(ethylamino)-s-triazine] and siduron alone or in combination could selectively reduce weed infestation when establishing zoysiagrass vegetatively. Simazine and atrazine [2-chloro-4-(ethylamino)-6-(isopropylamino)-s-triazine] applications following sprigging of centipedegrass [*Eremochloa ophiuroides* (Munro) Hackel] and St. Augustinegrass satisfactorily controlled grassy weeds and increased percent of ground cover (Johnson, 1973a, 1974). Sequential treatment of DCPA (dimethyl tetrachloroterephthalate) followed with monosodium methanearsonate (MSMA) + 2,4-D (2,4-dichlorophenoxy) acetic acid gave good weed control and enhanced 'Tifway' bermudagrass establishment (Johnson, 1973b).

Seeding and sprigging rates of the desirable turfgrass species influence the competition of weeds in newly established turf areas. Brede and Duich (1981) reported less annual bluegrass (*Poa annua* L.) encroachment when several Kentucky bluegrasses were separately sown at 388 or 1033 rather than at 64 or 194 pure live seeds dm^{-2}. Johnson (1973b) reported the invasion of grassy weeds decreased with the higher sprigging rate for bermudagrass.

I. Establishment During Renovation

Deterioration of turfgrass communities sometimes occurs because species are unadapted to the prevailing environmental conditions. If the environment cannot be favorably modified to improve turf quality by adjusting cultural practices, then renovation is necessary.

Soil related factors that frequently lead to the need for complete turf renovation are compaction, poor drainage, or contamination from various toxic chemicals. Regrading, installation of drainage systems, intensive tillage, or modification of soil texture may be necessary. Use of activated charcoal may be used to nullify the harmful effects of some chemical contamination such as herbicides (Jagschitz, 1968, 1974, 1977; Johnson, 1976b).

If soil related problems are not the cause of the turfgrass deterioration, complete establishment procedures may not be essential. Turf that has been extensively damaged by wear, disease, or insects or that has been invaded by nonselectively controlled weeds can be renovated by eliminating the existing vegetation with a nonselective herbicide such as glyphosate (Jagschitz, 1978) and re-establishing without tilling the soil.

Hall et al. (1981) reported that in a no-till creeping bentgrass (*Agrostis stolonifera* L.) putting green renovation study, glyphosate applied up to 6 d after overseeding controlled the undesirable turf without injury to several newly sown cool-season grasses. Glyphosate has also been used successfully to convert bermudagrass turf to both cool season (Johnson, 1976a) and vegetatively propagated warm-season turfgrasses (Johnson, 1976c).

Once the undesirable vegetation has been destroyed, the newly planted seed or vegetation propagules must have good soil contact for successful establishment. This may be accomplished by removing the excess thatch and debris and seeding with a disk seeder. Turf established from sprigs or sod will require light cultivation of the soil before planting to ensure a good establishment environment.

Siduron has been used to selectively control bermudagrass (Lewis & Gilbert, 1966) and in converting bermudagrass to bentgrass turf (Siviour & Schultz, 1981). This technique involves overseeding bentgrass in the fall into the bermudagrass turf and applying several applications of siduron in the spring as the bermudagrass breaks winter dormancy. However, Siviour and Schultz (1981) found that bermudagrass cultivars differ in their susceptibility to siduron.

Trees and shrubs often affect turfgrass adaptation by influencing light quality and intensity, soil moisture, and air movement patterns. Pruning or removing trees and shrubs in addition to reestablishing adapted turf species are frequently necessary to correct the problem.

II. ECOLOGICAL ASPECTS OF SEEDLING TURF STANDS

A. Inherent Seedling Competition

As early as 1898, Beal (1898) showed that the commercial lawn seed mixtures of the time (containing temporary and permanent species) produced inferior turf compared to establishing with plantings of separate species. Turfgrass plants within a community affect and are affected by surrounding plants within the community (Beard, 1973). Each plant has a minimum survival requirement for light, water, gases, and nutrients. The supply of these growth factors can be direct as far as moisture and nutrients are concerned, but the others can only be indirectly influenced by cultural practices (Turgeon, 1980). The intensity of cultural operations can influence the efficiency with which turfgrass communities use resources. A critical level of supply of any particular resource must be available, under uniform conditions, to achieve a desired turfgrass response. Within a concentration range above this level, which Turgeon (1980) referred to as an adequate range, additional supplies of a resource may cause little further response. Concentrations of a particular resource outside of the adequate range can either limit or cause some other factor to become limiting. It has been generally recognized that plants that dominate a seedbed will also remain dominant in the mature stand (Milthorpe, 1961). For more than 50 yr, ryegrasses, because of rapid germination and vigorous seedling growth, have been recognized as being able to dominate in the seedbed (Chippendale, 1932). Davies and Thomas (1928) demonstrated annual ryegrass seedling vigor. Lapp (1943) showed that, when heavily seeded, temporary grasses suppressed permanent species and allowed weed invasion as the turf cover thinned. Erdmann and Harrison (1947) found that both annual ryegrass and redtop (*Agrostis alba* L.) inhibited the establishment of Kentucky bluegrass and chewings fescue (*Festuca rubra* var. commutata Gaud.). They concluded, that when a quick cover was not essential, desired species should be seeded alone. Rhodes (1968b) found that annual ryegrass dominated tall fescue when used as a companion crop. Engel and Trout (1980) reported that perennial ryegrasses were slightly less competitive than annual ryegrass, while redtop was a very weak competitor. High seeding rates were found to be futile for the purpose of better establishment. Madison (1966) reported that high seeding rates resulted in dense initial stands that declined in density as the stand matured.

Once established, ryegrasses tiller rapidly (Blaser et al., 1956a, b), a trait of species that successfully compete during establishment (Rhodes, 1969). Kentucky bluegrasses are slow to germinate and have relatively low seedling vigor. Seedling comparisons of ryegrass to Kentucky bluegrass have shown that ryegrass produced more than 30 times more dry mass approximately 7 wk after planting (Blaser et al., 1956a). Seedling growth rate is quite variable among cool season turfgrasses. Although ryegrasses have a high seedling relative growth rate, annual bluegrass has been shown to have the highest relative seedling growth rate when compared to 132 other species (Grime & Hunt, 1975).

Seedling mortality plays an important role in seedbed competition and is a major influence on mature stand composition. Brede (1982) defined field survival as the ratio of seedlings to seeds planted. He found that over several planting dates during a season that annual bluegrass, Kentucky bluegrass, and perennial ryegrass had 72, 46, and 76% field survival, respectively. From this research, it appears that seed size is not highly associated with field survival. Field survival varied least with weather, while leaf mass per shoot varied the most. Seedling growth of perennial ryegrass was more closely associated with weather than was growth of the other two species.

Brede (1982) also determined that there was no advantage to preimbibing the seed of Kentucky bluegrass for seedling survival or development. In addition, he conducted experiments to determine the degree to which annual bluegrass, perennial ryegrass, and Kentucky bluegrass would compete interspecifically. Results obtained showed that annual bluegrass and perennial ryegrass had reduced growth when the seeding rate was doubled while Kentucky bluegrass demonstrated no self-limiting effects over the course of the 6-wk experiment. When various mixtures were seeded, Kentucky bluegrass reduced perennial ryegrass, but not to the extent that perennial ryegrass was self-limiting. Perennial ryegrass reduced annual bluegrass growth compared to annual bluegrass alone (seeded at a noncompetitive rate). The field survival of Kentucky bluegrass was reduced when perennial ryegrass or annual bluegrass seedlings were present.

In studies by Erdmann and Harrison (1947), perennial ryegrass was shown to be inhibitory to Kentucky bluegrass seedling and mature growth. Grasses contain coumarin, which can act as a germination inhibitor and is also partly responsible for the pleasant odor of freshly cut grass (Hart & Schuetz, 1972). Grasses vary in their sensitivity to coumarin. A 100 mg L^{-1} treatment of coumarin was required to decrease germination of annual bluegrass and perennial ryegrass, while 0.1 mg L^{-1} decreased Kentucky bluegrass germination (Brede, 1982). However, the low concentration caused reductions in shoot and root growth of all three species.

In a study to determine whether allelopathic effects have been responsible for reduced field survival of Kentucky bluegrass, Brede (1982) reported that the germination of Kentucky bluegrass was lower in the presence of annual bluegrass seedlings. Extracts from mature annual bluegrass had no effect. Root and shoot growth of all three species were affected by nearby seedlings of the others, with Kentucky bluegrass having the greatest sensitivity. In other mixture studies with Kentucky bluegrass and perennial ryegrass, the generalization that species dominating in the seedbed will dominate the mature stand did not apply. Touchdown Kentucky bluegrass, although weak in the seedbed, later dominated mixed stands. Allelopathic effects have also been shown in warm season grasses (Rasmussen & Rice, 1971). In their work, secondary metabolites in excretions of *Sporobulus pyramidatus* were inhibitory to bermudagrass and buffalograss [*Buchloë dactyloides* (Nutt.) Engelm.].

Not all allelopathic effects have a negative impact on the receptor. Of the 84 measurements made by Brede (1982) to determine the presence of allelopathy, about one-half showed significant effects on one or more of the species. He determined that about one half of those showed significant effects that were beneficial to the receptor. Regardless of whether the effects are construed to be beneficial or detrimental, most are very subtle. Muller (1969) found that, even though allelopathic effects may be subtle, their cumulative presence over the long term may be quite significant in the ecology of mixtures.

All turfgrass communities are dynamic, and at best, can be referred to as semi-stable in their composition. Beard (1973) stated that "The composition of a turfgrass community is generally in a constant state of change but the rate of change varies greatly depending on the age of the community as well as the environmental and cultural conditions to which it is exposed." The introduction of management can have a significant affect in adjusting or maintaining the desired composition of a turfgrass community even though the stability of the composition can, from time to time, be affected by uncontrollable environmental factors.

B. Establishment Date

Cool season grasses are best established in late summer or early spring to take advantage of favorable growth response-environment interactions. Late summer seedings are usually preferred over early spring because competition from summer annual weeds is reduced. In addition to summer annual competition, poor establishment may occur in late spring because air and soil temperatures increase and soil moisture levels commonly decrease. As a result, developing seedlings require more irrigation and certain pathogens (*Pythium* and *Rhizoctonia*), which are more pervasive at this time of year, may require fungicide applications. Mid to late fall seedings can be risky, especially for slow germinating species such as Kentucky bluegrass. In a tall fescue-Kentucky bluegrass establishment study, Hall (1980) reported plots seeded after September in Maryland had a decline in sod strength and root development when measured the following spring. Grass plants that are not well rooted before soils freeze are frequently more prone to damage from frost heaving and desiccation. Grasses sown after soil temperatures become low enough to inhibit germination (dormant seeding) may successfully establish the following spring if winter temperatures do not fluctuate high enough to cause germination. Morrish and Harrison (1948) showed that dormant seeding was successful where soil drainage was poor and competition from summer annual weeds was a problem.

Establishment of warm season grasses is best accomplished in late spring or early summer, which is the time period to obtain the most favorable match of inherent growth response with environment (Madison, 1971). Later establishment dates generally do not provide sufficient time for adequate establishment before temperatures drop to critical levels (except in the most southern regions of the USA) (Musser & Perkins, 1969b).

Blaser et al. (1956a, b) also found that seeding date can markedly affect the establishment rate of different species. Establishment rates varied primarily as a response to temperature and its effect on germination time and initial seedling growth rate. Creeping red fescue, with a higher optimum temperature for germination and seedling development, would be expected to have a competitive advantage over Kentucky bluegrass if a mixture of the two were seeded in late spring or early fall. Brede (1982) found perennial ryegrass seedlings to be most vigorous when planting was done during May through July. He also found that higher temperatures and lower precipitation were associated with an increase in the leaf/root and crown mass ratio.

C. Soil Reaction and Fertility

Turfgrass responses to soil pH and nutrient status have been studied from the botanical composition aspect and also in relation to growth and persistence of individual turfgrass species. Hartwell and Damon (1917) and later Garner and Damon (1929) demonstrated that bentgrass established better and competed favorably with Kentucky bluegrass when soil conditions were more acidic. Musser (1948) concluded that low acidity and high levels of available P greatly enhanced the establishment of Kentucky bluegrass. In a pH competition study using Kentucky bluegrass, fine fescue, and bentgrass seedlings, Roberts (1959) found that bentgrass encroached into Kentucky bluegrass turf on unlimed plots, Kentucky bluegrass encroached into the others when the soil was limed to a pH of 6.5, and fescue was not aggressive regardless of pH. He concluded that the originally seeded species will maintain dominance if the pH is suitable for that species.

Nutrient deficiencies can hinder seedling growth of any species, but most establishment methods eliminate the possibility of such problems. Even though pH and nutrients are most often in the recommended range for establishment, seedlings vary in their nutrient-absorbing capability (Beeson et al., 1947). Low N levels in the seedbed have been shown to increase the ultimate amount of creeping red fescue in a Kentucky bluegrass-creeping red fescue mixture (Roberts & Markland, 1967).

D. Mowing

Mowing management in the seedbed can greatly influence seedling development and influence the competitive abilities of species in turfgrass mixtures. Generally, mowing height should be adjusted as to not remove more than one-third of the existing leaf-blade (Frazier, 1960). In seedling stands, this often means that the first mowing occurs when plants are in the two to four leaf stage depending on species. Severe defoliation of seedling turf discourages seedling development and usually thins the stand, which results in weed invasion. The morphology and seedling growth rate of different species can result in significant mowing-species interactions in young turfgrass stands.

Brede and Duich (1984) found that the final composition of Kentucky bluegrass-perennial ryegrass mixtures could be altered by mowing management in the seedling stage. By using close mowing after both species had emerged, bluegrass was favored. Initial height of cut depended upon seedbed soil conditions (e.g., eveness and wetness). A 2-wk time interval between seeding and mowing coincided with an estimated 50% ground cover when 50 to 75% of the seed mixture was Kentucky bluegrass. A 50:50 stand of Kentucky bluegrass to perennial ryegrass was obtained from a 50:50 pure line seed ratio when this early mowing management was used. However, without early mowing, a 95:5 seed ratio of Kentucky bluegrass to perennial ryegrass was required to achieve a 50:50 seedling stand ratio. In subsequent research, Brede and Brede (1988) found significant early mowing effects on seedling stands of tall fescue and annual ryegrass. They concluded that their clipping treatments accounted for one-fourth to one-half the variability in seedling growth rate of annual ryegrass and tall fescue. Waiting 6 wk after seeding before clipping favored annual ryegrass, but a single, close clipping (<7 mm) within 3 d of annual ryegrass emergence favored the tall fescue. Similar results have been reported by Brede (1987) for other species. Clearly, mowing management can significantly influence the inherent seedling growth rate-environment interaction and more research is needed.

III. ECOLOGICAL ASPECTS OF MATURE TURF STANDS

Grime (1980) in a chapter on an ecological approach to management of amenity grassland concluded that information concerning the distribution, life-histories, phenology, reproductive biology, and physiology of herbaceous plants could be used to classify species, cultivars, and populations with respect to their ecological strategies. Recognition of such strategies provides insight into the processes controlling the population dynamics of vegetation and could provide management guidelines. The ecology of mature turfgrass communities is strongly influenced by management. So much so, that turfgrass stands are adapted to environmental conditions through the cultural manipulation of species competition.

A. Competition of Species

A turfgrass community has been defined as "an aggregation of individual turfgrass plants that have mutual relationships with the environment as well as among the individual plants" (Beard, 1973). Most often the turfgrass community is composed of a polystand of species that are competing for light, water, nutrients, carbon dioxide, oxygen, and space. Seasonal growth patterns, growth habit and rate, and stress tolerance influence the competitive ability of each species. Soil physical properties (porosity, texture, and moisture-holding capacity, etc.) and chemical properties (pH, nutrient status, and ion exchange capacities) also affect plant competition. Above all, management factors (fertilization, irrigation, mowing, and pest control) have a profound influence on the competitive abilities of the individual components of a turfgrass community. When the turfgrass stand is composed of the same cultivar (monostand), competition is particularly keen as the requirements for growth and growth habit are the same. Donald (1963) concluded that mixtures should have a potentially higher quality than would a monoculture of any component of the mixture.

As in the seedbed, plant competition also alters the composition of mature stands of turfgrass. Ultimately, the interaction of the factors mentioned previously causes the evolution of a turfgrass community in which the shoots per unit area remains somewhat stable in number due to an equilibrium between newly emerging shoots and older dying tillers. The time frame from planting to plant community stability is variable (Garner & Damon, 1929, p. 1–22; Van Dersal, 1936).

B. Seasonal Growth Pattern

Seasonal growth patterns differ with different turfgrass species. Ryegrasses and fine leaf fescues tend to have more rapid growth in the cool, moist, spring and fall (Schmidt & Blaser, 1967b) while Kentucky bluegrass, tall fescue, and the bentgrasses have more uniform growth rates throughout the season. Consequently, ranking for growth rate of grasses is meaningless without considering the time of the year, climate, and management factors. Differences in growth rate have also been associated with photoperiod (Eggens, 1979). At 10 h of daylength, Kentucky bluegrass and annual bluegrass did not differ in tillering rate. However, at 15 h of daylight, annual bluegrass tillered faster. Brede (1982) found a four times faster annual bluegrass shoot production compared to Kentucky bluegrass when daylight was increased. Plants are able to compete by adapting to existing conditions (Daubenmire, 1968).

C. Growth Habits

Growth habit (clump-type, creeping, or spreading) profoundly influences competitive ability. Clump or bunch-type species, when seeded sparsely are not as competitive as when more heavily seeded. Lateral growth occurs by initiation and development of basal tillers. Therefore, rate of tillering determines lateral competitive ability. Relative growth rate has also been used to assess competitive ability in relation to tillering rate (Grime & Hunt, 1975). The competitive ability of ryegrasses based upon tillering rate has been discussed by Rhodes (1969). He showed that rapid lateral tiller production was a distinct competitive advantage. Brede (1982) examined relative tillering rate and found it to be closely related to relative growth rate. He found an exponential growth response for 6 wk after transplanting of single shoots of Kentucky bluegrass, perennial ryegrass, and annual bluegrass. Leopold and Kriedeman (1975) state that exponential growth proceeds only if intraspecific interaction is very small. Brede (1982) also found that seasonal responses occurred (perennial ryegrass tillered more than annual bluegrass in early summer, but the reverse was true in early fall). In general, perennial ryegrass produced tillers faster than Kentucky bluegrass. Annual bluegrass and its tillering rate declined rapidly. Therefore, growth potential for a given plant is important in the initial colonization of a sward, but as the density increases, growth habit, adaptation to stress, disease resistance, and other factors become dominant in determining the ultimate semi-stable composition of the stand. In studies conducted by Dickson and Funk (1979), 'Jamestown' chewings fescue dominated a mixture with 'Fylking' Kentucky bluegrass until summer drought weakened it, at which point the Fylking began to dominate.

Creeping species (stoloniferous) have the advantage of spreading by aboveground vegetative propagules. New plants arising from stolon buds can rapidly establish into areas of poor density (Davis, 1958; Juska & Hanson, 1959; Musser, 1948). Spreading species (rhizomatous) can compete through the emergence of rhizome tillers into voids in the stand. Some species spread by both stolons and rhizomes, which increases their competitive ability. Usually, stoloniferous species outcompete rhizomatous species (e.g., creeping bentgrass encroachment into Kentucky bluegrass). Basal tillering, bunch-type species are generally more competitive if they also perpetuate themselves with seed (e.g., annual bluegrass). The prolific seed producing capability of annual bluegrass often allows it to compete successfully with creeping bentgrass, a stoloniferous species.

The aboveground and belowground competitive effects of perennial ryegrass and Kentucky bluegrass were studied in field research studies conducted by Brede (1982). He partitioned (by using plexiglas cells) roots and tops in various combinations and found that interaction aboveground affected growth belowground and vice versa. Kentucky bluegrass was more competitive when the interaction was confined aboveground. Perennial ryegrass had increased competitive ability when the interaction was confined to below the ground. The belowground competitive ability of ryegrasses has been shown to be related to superior water and nutrient uptake by the ryegrass root system (King, 1971; Milthorpe, 1961); and traditionally, species with relatively high tillering rates tend to dominate a stand. However, Brede (1982) found that, although Touchdown Kentucky bluegrass ranked lowest in relative tillering rate in his partitioning studies, it ultimately became the dominant species. He concluded that consistent growth (less seasonal fluctuation) and a sustained interaction with the other species allowed the Touchdown to dominate.

D. Tolerance of Natural Stresses

The composition of any turfgrass community is dramatically influenced by environmental conditions. Extremes in the environment can cause rapid changes in population dynamics. Typically, temperature extremes cause the most dramatic and sudden changes in population. The geographic distribution of cool and warm season grasses is primarily the result of temperature adaptation. Most semi-tropical species do not become established in northern latitudes due to direct low temperature kill during winter (Chalmers & Schmidt, 1979). Temperature species do not persist, or at least do not compete favorably, in southern latitudes, in part due to poor initiation of bud development (Youngner, 1961), and also because of metabolic factors (low CO_2 fixation and increased respiration rates).

Temperate species vary markedly in their tolerance to environmental conditions. Beard (1966b) found a significant variability in species tolerance to cold. Superior cold tolerance was found for rough bluegrass and creeping bentgrass and poor tolerance was found for 'Astoria' colonial bentgrass (*Agrostis tenuis* Sibth.) and 'Pennlawn' creeping red fescue. Creeping bentgrass had better survival than Astoria colonial bentgrass when exposed to ice covers (Beard, 1965b). In other research on ice damage (Beard, 1964), it was shown that creeping bentgrass was more tolerant than either Kentucky bluegrass or annual bluegrass. For Kentucky bluegrass, the presence of slush, followed by compaction and freezing, caused more damage than when a snow layer existed between the plants and an ice sheet (Beard, 1965a).

Tolerance of high temperature primarily depends upon the ability of a particular plant to cool itself. Reradiation, convention, and transpiration are the principal means by which plants dissipate energy. Reradiation is primarily operational when incident radiation is nonexistent (at night) or when convectional cooling is low and transpiration is restricted. Convectional cooling of turfgrass canopies can be free or forced (due to wind). The amount of cooling is related to the size, shape, and orientation of the canopy and to the flow rate of air (Gates, 1965). Leaf thickness is inversely proportional to heating and cooling (Ansari & Loomis, 1959); therefore, fine textured turfgrasses could be expected to have lower energy conversion efficiency than more coarsely textured species (Beard, 1973). Transpirational cooling is facilitated by low humidity, wind, and adequate soil moisture (Ansari & Loomis, 1959).

All turfgrasses have different optimum ranges for shoot growth, tillering, leaf number, leaf width, leaf length, leaf area, new leaf appearance, and root growth (Beard, 1973). Temperature optima for any of these growth responses are not necessarily related to optimum turfgrass quality. In general, optimum temperatures for root and rhizome growth are lower than for shoot growth. Diurnal fluctuations in temperatures in the microclimate of any turfgrass sward result in transitory periods when optimum conditions may exist for a particular component of the stand for a short period that would favor its competitiveness, but any advantage may be negated over the next increment of time as the conditions change and optimum conditions exist for another component of the stand. Temperature plays an important and dynamic role in the interaction of plants in any sward, but the morphological and physiological responses of any given plant are very complex and also influenced by factors other than temperature. An excellent review of turfgrass responses to temperature has been prepared by Beard (1973).

Adaptation to soil moisture conditions can allow particular species to dominate a stand. Bentgrasses, rough bluegrass, and annual bluegrass are more tolerant of poor drainage than Kentucky bluegrass, ryegrasses, and fine fescues (Davis & Martin, 1949; Dahl, 1934; Radko, 1956; Rhoades, 1964, 1967). With the exception of annual bluegrass, cool season grasses tolerate drought conditions through dormancy and then recovery when soil moisture becomes available. Annual bluegrass has no such dormancy mechanism, therefore, once permanently wilted, it dies. Tall and hard fescue (*Festuca longifolia* Thuill.) are the most tolerant cool season species of dry conditions.

In a study to determine submersion tolerance by several cool season grasses, Beard and Martin (1970) found that creeping bentgrass was superior while Merion Kentucky bluegrass and annual bluegrass were intermediate. Pennlawn red fescue was quite intolerant. They recommended that tolerant species should be used in areas where flooding was likely. Submersion tolerance was related to water temperature, in that, as temperature increased, submersion tolerance decreased. Buffalograss and bermudagrass have also shown excellent submersion tolerance (Parker & Whitfield, 1941; Porterfield, 1945). Submerged grasses have also been shown to be more tolerant when the water is moving compared to stagnant (Davis & Martin, 1949).

Light often becomes a selective environmental parameter. Turfgrasses vary in their response to light quality, duration, and intensity. The complete elimination of light due to materials left on turf may alter turf composition. Rhizomatous species could recover after removal of the light excluding material while bunch-type turfs would not recover (Beard, 1973). More often than not, total light exclusion can be alleviated rather easily, but shade of varying degrees often favors the competitiveness of one species over another.

It has been estimated that approximately one-fourth of all turf is grown in association with some shading from some source (Beard, 1973). The effects of shading on plant growth are not limited to those associated with decreased light intensity. Beard (1973) listed the following shade environmental conditions: (i) altered light quality, (ii) moderation of the extremes in diurnal and seasonal temperatures, (iii) restricted wind movement, (iv) increased relative humidity, (v) increased CO_2, and (vi) tree root competition for water and nutrients.

Trees vary in their shading capability. Canopy size at maturity, crown densities, and spacing all interact to influence the amount of shade. Tree canopies that allow sun flects generally allow better growth of turfgrasses beneath them than canopies that do not permit sun flecks (Evans, 1956). Alteration of light quality in the shade is primarily a function of whether the light reaching the turf is characterized as being transmitted or reflected. Transmitted or reflected light is reduced in the amount of photosynthetically active wavelengths it contains (Schull, 1929; Beard, 1965c). Most of the light under very dense deciduous canopies has been transmitted and is of poor quality for photosynthesis (Vezina & Boulter, 1966). Therefore, relatively thick stands of maple (*Acer* spp.) or oak (*Quercus* spp.) cause extremely difficult growing conditions for most turf species.

Adaptation to shade has not been extensively studied. In most shade research, altered morphology is frequently found (Blackman & Black, 1959; Juska, 1963; Juska et al., 1969). Total growth from shoots and roots has been shown to decrease in severe shade, but bentgrasses vary in their tolerance (Reid, 1933). In a study with 11 bentgrasses, Juska (1963) reported varietal differences in shade tolerance, but concluded that the varieties that had the best quality in sunlight also had the best quality in shade. Varietal differences in shade tolerance also occur in Kentucky bluegrass. Vargas and Beard

(1981) found that 'Nugget' was more tolerant than 'Kenblue.' Mitchell (1954), working with ryegrasses, concluded that roots were more severely affected by shade than tops. In a subsequent study, shading was also shown to decrease tillering in ryegrasses (Mitchell & Coles, 1955). Whitcomb (1972) has studied grass and tree root interactions and concluded that tree roots reduce growth and vigor of most grasses even when water and nutrients are maintained at optimum levels. He indicated that allelopathy may be involved. Beard (1965c) found that mixtures of species under shade provided a higher quality turf than most species established alone. He also concluded that disease activity, not light, moisture, or nutrient deficiencies was more important in influencing grass adaptation to shade. Rhizome and stolon tillers of turf grown in shade have been shown to grow more upright (Laughman, 1941; McBee & Holt, 1966). As a result of morphological anatomical and physiological changes, shaded turfgrasses may have reduced heat, drought, cold, and wear tolerance compared to unshaded turf. Beard (1973) has published a table showing the relative shade tolerance of cool- and warm-season grasses with red fescue ranking excellent and Kentucky bluegrass poor for the cool season species and St. Augustine ranking excellent and bermudagrass poor for the warm season species.

E. Turfgrass Influence on Microclimate

The microclimate surrounding turfgrass plants is more dynamic than the macroclimate above the sod, and is more extreme during the warm than cold seasons (Sprague et al., 1955). Welterlen and Watschke (1981) developed several techniques for monitoring the microclimate of turf swards. The most expedient and reliable method of temperature determination was to use thermocouples inserted into grass crowns. They found that sod acted as a heat source during periods of high reradiation and as a cold source when radiation was low. Plants had a direct influence on their surrounding environment. Plant communities moderate temperature extremes above and below the soil surface when compared to bare soil. Within a plant canopy, temperatures usually are lower and relative humidity higher in the canopy than at its surface (Denmead, 1972).

Short- and long-wave radiation from the sun may be reflected, reradiated, or absorbed by the plant community. Radiation absorption of a turf canopy is dictated by leaf area, leaf angle, leaf orientation, and leaf color. Grasses of light color or shiny leaf surfaces have a higher degree of reflecting capability (albedo) than dull or darker colored grasses. Vertical oriented leaves absorb less heat than those oriented horizontally (Idso et al., 1966; Denmead, 1972).

Short wave radiation, the main component absorbed, normally decreases with depth in the canopy. Sensible and latent heat decrease with increased canopy depth. The degree to which temperature is lower is influenced by incident radiation, leaf density, and canopy height. At midday, incident radiation is greatest. At this time, canopy temperatures may increase with canopy depth, especially when foliage is dense enough to sharply decrease radiation infiltration (Denmead, 1972).

It has been well documented that soil temperature extremes are greater at low heights of cut than at high (Beard, 1973). McKee et al. (1965) related deterioration of grass communities due to high soil surface temperatures, when the vegetation cover was < 30 to 40% of the soil surface. Since thermal properties of a soil are related to soil moisture conductivity, a dry soil surface will exhibit higher maximums and lower minimum temperatures than a wet one (Denmead, 1972). Grasses that have a high water use rate are more likely to reduce the soil conductivity and be subjected to more extreme temperature variance than those with low water use rates.

Convection and transpiration results in leaf cooling. Convection induces temperature gradients in the aboveground foliage that results in leaf energy loss. Energy loss by convection is related to the leaf's size and boundary layer thickness. Small leaves cool more readily than larger ones (Idso et al., 1966; Raschke, 1960). Transpiration cools foliage by latent heat transfer due to the water's ability to change from liquid to the gaseous state (Wiegand & Namken, 1966). The importance of transpiration in cooling foliage appears to vary with climate and geography (Clum, 1926). Transpiration is more important in hot-dry climates while convection is more important in cool humid regions for foliage heat exchange.

In Colorado, moisture stress increased summer midday canopy temperatures about 1.7 °C for each 10% reduction in evapotranspiration (Feldhake et al., 1984). In Georgia, leaf temperatures were highly correlated with transpiration under most conditions (Pallas & Harris, 1964). Baker (1929) and Watson (1934) indicated that evaporation, not transpiration, was the major factor lowering leaf temperature, since large leaf temperature changes occur in seconds. Raschke (1960) inferred that as plant resistances to transpiration proceeded less transpirational and more convectional heat exchange occurred.

Modifying the microenvironment to prolong the growing season or protect plants from adverse weather has been successful in turfgrass culture. Soil warming with electric heating cables, heated air ducts, or running hot water through pipes has protected turf against frost and freezing (Baltensperger, 1961, 1962; Beard, 1973; Daniel, 1970; Fisher, 1974; Janson, 1970; Langvad, 1970; Madison, 1971). However, operational expenses of these fuel energy-dependent practices are often economically unfeasible. Other less costly cultural methods have been more popular.

Applications of soil topdressing to turf areas in late autumn have aided in preventing winter desiccation (Beard, 1973). Snow fences, brush, or straw mulches create a thermal barrier by increasing snow coverage on turf areas, thus reducing injury from cold and desiccation (Beard, 1973; Madison, 1971). Dark colored materials such as soot and organic fertilizer are effective in absorbing solar radiation and melting the accumulated snow the following spring (Madison, 1971).

Moderation of winter temperatures and conservation of soil moisture of turf areas has been obtained with covers made from various materials (Ledeboer & Skogley, 1967; Watson, 1966, 1968; Watson & Wicklund, 1962;

Watson et al., 1960). Synthetic fiber cloth, plastic shade screens, and wood fiber covers provide protection from desiccation and cold temperatures.

Although clear polyethylene covers do not have good insulation properties, they are capable of creating a "greenhouse" effect by reducing the convection loss of radiant energy input. Because the clear plastic permits more radiation to reach the soil surface than more opaque covers, the clear covers are more effective in enhancing rapid early spring greenup as well as providing protection against frost. Covers have good insulation characteristics conserve soil heat in autumn, but inhibit the soil from warming in the spring. Use of clear polyethylene covers in Virginia has extended bermudagrass growth up to 60 d in autumn and enhanced post dormancy growth 30 d earlier in the spring.

Removal of the covers, especially those of clear plastic, is imperative when ambient temperatures become high and cause excessive heat to build up in the turf canopy (Madison, 1971). A fungicide should be applied prior to installing any of the protective mulches to prevent injury from pathogens that may be increased in the microenvironment created by these covers (Beard, 1973).

F. Allelopathy

Ahlgren and Aamodt (1939) concluded that root competitive effects may be occurring between species as the result of exudates. Allelopathic responses have been documented in warm season grasses and strong evidence has recently been shown in cool season species (Brede, 1982). Allelopathic compounds can exist in any plant part, but tend to be in highest concentration in leaves and seeds (Rice, 1974). Decaying plant debris is the principle means of release of such compounds although they can be leached or secreted from roots. Rice (1974) has classified inhibitor compounds and listed mechanisms of action on adjacent plants. Rovira (1969) has identified some of the factors that influence the quantity of inhibitors produced. Identification and extraction of a potentially allelopathic compound from a given plant does not mean it is excreted in the field or, even if it is, that there is any ecological significance (Putman & Duke, 1978). In a field study with annual bluegrass, perennial ryegrass, and Kentucky bluegrass, Brede (1982) concluded that allelopathy, which was both beneficial and detrimental, was an important contributing factor in the interaction of these three species. The allelopathic effects began at germination and continued throughout the development of the mature stand.

G. Cultural Influence

1. Mowing

Mowing is the cultural practice that influences most other management practices. It provides the desired uniformity and appearance of the turfgrass sward. Responses vary across species when a portion of the turfgrass plant is removed during mowing. Turgeon (1980) stated that "from a purely botanical standpoint, mowing is detrimental to turfgrasses. It causes a temporary cessation of root growth, reduced carbohydrate production and storage, creates ports of entry for disease-causing organisms, temporarily increases water loss from cut leaf ends, and reduces water absorption by the roots."

Beard (1973) stated that after mowing any species, a dense canopy should remain to intercept most of the sunlight. This is good ecological sense from the standpoint of maintaining turfgrasses in a uniform growth mode that should preclude invasion by undesirable species. As stated in the seedling ecology portion of this chapter, in general, only one-third of the existing leaf blade should be removed (Frazier, 1960). Plants with a procumbent growth habit and numerous small leaves are more competitive under close mowing than upright, large leaved plants.

Morphology is important to determine optimum cutting height. Both stem and leaf characteristics influence mowing height tolerance (Beard, 1973; Bredakis, 1959). Stoloniferous low growing species such as creeping bentgrass and bermudagrass can tolerate closer mowing than bunch-type erect growing species such as tall fescue and annual ryegrass (Davis, 1958; Laird, 1930; Funk & Engel, 1963). In Davis, CA, Madison (1962b) found that bermudagrass, mowed at 1.25 cm, invaded dense clumps of tall fescue more slowly than when mowed at 4.40 cm. Poor invasion at closer mowing was attributed to stolon removal.

Generally, increased cutting height increases vigor (Schmidt et al., 1967). Cutting lower than a given species can tolerate may cause the turf to become weak and less vigorous (Beach, 1963). Mowing too closely (scalping) can cause stand thinning that may change the composition of the sward. Annual bluegrass invasion into Kentucky bluegrass has been shown to be enhanced by close mowing (Davis, 1958; Funk et al., 1966, p. 7–21). Youngner (1959) found that annual bluegrass increased in bermudagrass when the sward was mowed at 1.25 cm compared to 1.91 cm. A study by Bogart and Beard (1973) revealed that the optimum cutting height for annual bluegrass was 2.54 cm when grown in a monostand and shoot density was used as the measure of potential competitiveness.

Mowing above the optimum height for maximum competitiveness can also be detrimental. A condition known as *puffiness* can occur with strongly stoloniferous species like creeping bentgrass (Engel, 1966). Puffiness may result in scalping and contribute to problems associated with excessive thatch accumulation.

Turf usage can also influence mowing height (Radko, 1968) and the competitive abilities of individual species are often compromised. Cutting height can influence the bounce and distance that a ball rolls in sports such as golf, bowling, and tennis (Langvad, 1968; Throssell, 1981). Schmidt and Blaser (1969a) state that when morphology and use are considered together, two concepts are important in determining the least detrimental clipping practices: "(1) closeness of clipping or leaf area left after mowing, and (2) height of canopy before it is mowed."

Ideally, turfgrasses should be allowed to rest between mowings. Madison (1962b) found that when bentgrass was given 2 or 3 d to recuperate between mowings, vigor was increased. Regrowth vigor is related to the photosynthetic potential of the clipped plants and their ability to use stored carbohydrate.

Mowing frequency can also influence plant competition, but usually not as significantly as cutting height. Maintenance height and use dictate frequency. In general, frequency increases as height decreases (Beard, 1973). Studies by Madison (1960, 1962a) have shown that as bentgrass mowing height is lowered from 13 to 6 mm, mowing frequency must be significantly increased to maintain recuperative potential and vigor. Mowing frequency is affected by the type of grass, moisture, fertility, height, temperature, and light. Plant responses to increased frequency are varied, but in most cases a more prostrate growth habit develops (Leukel et al., 1934) and shoot density increases (Juska, 1961b). These two responses occur if the frequency is not excessive. If the frequency becomes excessive, leaf area balance is destroyed resulting in decreased shoot growth, root growth, chlorophyll content, and recuperative potential (Beard, 1973). Therefore, proper mowing frequency can significantly improve competitiveness of desirable species while improper frequency can reduce competitiveness considerably.

Vertical mowing is another maintenance practice that can affect growth and vigor of turfgrasses. Although vertical mowing and grooving are frequently used for thatch removal, turfgrass species exhibit differential responses to the resulting vegetation thinning. Increases in shoot density have been observed on Kentucky bluegrass (Schery, 1966). Shallow vertical mowing of golf course putting greens during peak annual bluegrass seedhead production periods has been used to decrease the amount of newly produced seed that shatters onto the surface of the green. Shallow vertical mowing has also been used on putting greens as a means of stimulating bud break on creeping bentgrass stolons as a means of promoting a more leafy surface.

2. Soil Cultivation

Soil compaction indirectly affects the growth of turfgrasses and, as a result, can significantly alter plant competition. The reduced pore space resulting from compaction has a profound influence on oxygen diffusion and physically restricts rooting. Waddington and Baker (1965) found that all species tested produced fewer root laterals under conditions of poor aeration but roots were thicker. However, creeping bentgrass and goosegrass [*Eleusine indica* (L.) Gaertn.] maintained good root growth at all oxygen diffusion rates tested while Kentucky bluegrass root penetration decreased under conditions of low oxygen diffusion. Carrow (1980) has shown a 43% reduction in Kentucky bluegrass shoots in August when compaction was heavy due to repetitive mowing patterns. In a survey of New Zealand race course turf, Field and Murphy (1989) found that perennial ryegrass (preferred species) was most competitive under conditions of low compaction, lower height of cut, and high fertilizer K. Conversely, rough bluegrass (less desired species) was favored by high relative compaction, closer C/N ratio, and lower pH.

Soil compaction and the resulting decrease in pore space can be overcome by core cultivation (aeration). Aeration improves the movement of air and water into compacted soils and has been found to improve rooting (Engel, 1951) and increase shoot density (Madison & Hagan, 1962). Consequently, the competitiveness of species that ordinarily grow poorly under conditions of low O_2 diffusion can be improved by periodic aeration.

Often times, topdressing with soil is performed along with mechanical aeration practices. Topdressing provides a source of microbial activity at the upper surface of thatch, which aids in thatch control and the release of organic N for plant utilization, and topdressing also provides a medium for the rooting of new plants that have initiated from stolon buds. The overall vigor and competitiveness of the stand are improved, which decreases the possibility of encroachment by weeds into the voids created by the mechanical disturbance to the site.

3. Fertilization and pH Control

Pellett and Roberts (1963) indicated that turfgrass nutritional status is particularly important during periods of environmental stress. High N fertility levels have been associated with cool-season turfgrass resistance to high temperature (Carroll, 1943; Juska & Hanson, 1967; Lucanus et al., 1960; Pellett & Roberts, 1963; Watschke & Waddington, 1975).

Large amounts of N available to temperate turfgrasses under conditions that support rapid utilization of nonstructural carbohydrates (Green & Beard, 1969) may subsequently inhibit root development (Oswalt et al., 1959; Snyder & Schmidt, 1974; Troughton, 1957). Increased top growth may enhance transpiration (Oswalt et al., 1959) to levels higher than the associated impaired root system can provide moisture, thus causing severe drought symptoms (Funk et al., 1966, 1957, p. 71-76).

Others (Dunn, 1981; Hanson & Juska, 1961; Ledeboer & Skogley, 1963; Powell et al., 1967a; Powell et al., 1967b; Schmidt & Breuninger, 1981; Snyder & Schmidt, 1974) have shown increased carbohydrate content, increased root development, or improved turf quality when cool-season grasses were fertilized heavily with N in the fall. Snyder and Schmidt (1974) reported that foliar applications of Fe enhanced root development and lessened the effects of desiccation associated with high N fertilization.

Liberal fertilization may be detrimental to turfgrasses grown under low light intensity. Reduction of nonstructural carbohydrates and growth, especially roots, have been reported for both bermudagrass and bentgrass grown under reduced light when fertilized heavily with N (Burton & Devane, 1952; Schmidt & Blaser, 1967, 1969b).

Potassium fertility has been correlated with cool-season turfgrass resistance to high temperatures (Pellett & Roberts, 1963). Davidson (1969), with perennial ryegrass, and Schmidt and Breuninger (1981), with Kentucky bluegrass, found that K fertility enhanced recovery from drought irrespective of N and P fertility status. However, recovery was inhibited with heavy N fertilization when soil P content was low.

Fertilization has also been shown to influence environmental stress on warm-season turfgrasses. Bermudagrass recovery from winter injury has been enhanced with N fertilization when adequate K was concurrently applied (Gilbert & Davis, 1967, 1971; Juska & Murray, 1974).

Since grasses vary in their response to nutrition, fertility can influence the botanical composition of a polystand. Skogley and Ledeboer (1968) indicated that Kentucky bluegrasses respond more to N fertility than creeping red fescue. The population of Kentucky bluegrass generally increases in mixtures with red fescue, redtop (Juska et al., 1956), or tall fescue (Juska et al., 1955, 1956, 1969a; Schmidt et al., 1967) under high N fertility. Schmidt and Taylor (1981) reported that high N fertility increases the portion of Kentucky bluegrass in mixtures with perennial ryegrass. Adams et al. (1974) indicated that although both Kentucky bluegrass and perennial ryegrass tillering was enhanced with increased N fertility, Kentucky bluegrass had a higher N requirement for a given rate of top growth.

In a turfgrass polystand grown in Great Britain, annual bluegrass increased with increased increments of N while colonial bentgrass decreased and perennial ryegrass stayed constant (Adams, 1980). Dest and Allison (1981) reported that frequent but small increments of N maintained the highest level of leaf tissue P. Phosphorus fertility has been shown to be associated with improving annual bluegrass density and survival during summer stress (Dest & Allison, 1981; Juska & Hanson, 1969; Sprague & Burton, 1937).

Crabgrass infestations were reported to lower summer turf quality of Kentucky bluegrass grown under low fertility (Dunn et al., 1981; Schmidt et al., 1967). However, Burns (1981) found crabgrass infestation was most serious in tall fescue that was fertilized during the summer.

Applications of N during late fall and winter to mixed warm-cool season turfgrass polystands have permitted the cool-season species to dominate in the spring and the warm-season species in the summer (Hawes, 1980). Kneebone and Pepper (1981) reported that P deficiency increased with N fertilizer on annual ryegrass and several perennial ryegrasses overseeded in the fall on bermudagrass.

The influence of fertility on disease susceptibility of turfgrass varies with the specific pathogen. Rust (*Puccinia* spp.), dollarspot (*Sclerotinia homoeocarpa*) (Britton, 1969), red thread (*Laetisaria fuciformis*) (Couch, 1962), and pythium (*Pythium aphanidermatum*) (Freeman, 1974) are less serious with adequate fertility. Major diseases that are more serious with liberal fertility are fusarium blight (*Fusarium roseum* and *F. nivale*), gray snow mold (*Typhula incarnata*), brownpath (*Rhizoctonia solani*), take-all patch (*Gaeumannomyces graminis*), powdery mildew (*Erysiphe graminis*), and diseases caused by *Helminthosporium* spp. (Britton, 1969). Beard et al. (1973) reported that heavy applications of soluble N stimulated the development of fairy rings (*Marasmius oreades*). Juska and Murray (1974) found that damage caused by a *Helminthosporium* spp. and *Sclerotinia homoeocarpa* was less severe on bermudagrass fertilized with K.

Differences in turfgrass adaptation to acidic soil conditions may also influence the dominance of species in a turfgrass polystand. Beard (1973) has listed the optimum soil pH ranges for the commonly used turfgrass species. Murray and Foy (1980) indicated that cultivars of certain species also vary widely in tolerance to acid soil. They reported that Kentucky bluegrass cv. Majestic, Victa, Pennstar, Touchdown, and Fylking were more tolerant of acidity than Kenblue, Windsor, and South Dakota Common. Although tall fescue was more tolerant than Kentucky bluegrass, cultivars of both species differed significantly in tolerance to acid soil.

4. Irrigation

Water moisture exchange between the plant and atmosphere is related to a reciprocal exchange of energy transfers. The microenvironment influences the water exchange rate; at the same time the water exchange affects the microenvironment.

In general, energy exchanges correlate with the diurnal cycle of net radiation. Leaves are warmer during the day and cooler at night (Ansari & Loomis, 1959). The rate of energy exchange is a response of leaf structure and placement on the plant as well as the energy gradient between the plant and microenvironment. Leaves within a canopy are shielded by fluctuations of wind and light intensity (Ansari & Loomis, 1959).

When soil surfaces are wet, energy is used in the evaporation of water from the soil and transpiration from the foliage; thus the water vapor in the plant canopy increases (Denmead, 1972). If a negative water gradient exists between the canopy and atmosphere, the water will exchange to the atmosphere. The latent heat energy required to exchange this water into the atmosphere cools the leaf surface. Lack of soil water reduces transpiration and causes an increase of leaf temperature (Ansari & Loomis, 1959), but reduces the water gradient between the leaves and microenvironment.

At night when ambient temperature is reduced and humidity level is near saturation, the water gradient is reduced and condensation forms on the leaf surface. Not only does this affect the period of leaf wetness, but also reduces the rate of heat transfer.

Water use of a turf increases as atmospheric evaporational demand increases. Generally, evapotranspiration demands increase with solar radiation and are highest in early to mid summer and lowest during the winter (Ansari & Loomis, 1959; Ekern, 1966; Feldhake et al., 1983; Harrold & Driebelis, 1955; Richards & Weeks, 1963). Kneebone and Pepper (1982) reported that in Tucson, AZ, during April, May, and June as air temperatures increased and humidity declined, turf water consumption increased. However, during July and August, air temperatures were moderated by frequent rain showers and water consumption decreased. Evapotranspiration rates may also be significantly reduced in areas with frequent morning and evening fog (Youngner et al., 1981).

Irrigation can be used to moderate turf canopy temperatures and influence dominance of species. During hot weather when turf begins to wilt, a light syringing will reduce leaf temperatures and restore turgidity (Van Den Brink & Carolus, 1965). Turfgrass temperature has been shown to be 1 to 6 °C lower than air in studies conducted by Duff and Beard (1966) when syringing and air movement were controlled over bentgrass. More recently, DiPaola (1984) found that, in the absence of wilt, bentgrass canopy temperatures were not significantly altered 1 h after syringing regardless of water volume or timing. After 2 yr, supplemental irrigation on a mixed Kentucky bluegrass, creeping red fescue, and bentgrass turf caused bentgrass to dominate, while on comparable nonirrigated plots, the Kentucky bluegrass and creeping red fescue dominated (Watson, 1950). Youngner et al. (1981) reported that turf irrigated most frequently had the highest infestation of undesirable grasses such as annual and rough bluegrass.

Water also influences species dominance because water requirements of turfgrasses vary. Grasses with deep root systems can be sustained for longer periods of drought than grasses with shallow root systems. Warm-season grasses generally produce deeper root systems than cool-season grasses. Tall fescues produce an intermediate root system and can tolerate drought better than most of the commonly used cool-season grasses. Bermudagrass, zoysiagrass, tall fescue, and fine fescues are considered to have a high tolerance to drought. Kentucky bluegrass, perennial ryegrass, and St. Augustine have intermediate tolerances to drought. The bentgrasses are classified as low drought tolerant grasses.

Species and cultivars differ in water consumption rate (Welton & Wilson, 1931; Burton et al., 1957; Brian et al., 1981; Kneebone & Pepper, 1982). Cool-season grasses consume more water than warm-season grasses (Kneebone & Pepper, 1982; Feldhake et al., 1983; Brian et al., 1981; Marsh et al., 1980, p. 20–21, 32–33). Brian et al. (1981) reported that warm-season grasses with a vertical growth habit had a higher growth and water consumption rate than those with a decumbent growth habit. Grasses that grow most rapidly usually have the highest water consumption when water is available. Although tall fescue is drought tolerant, it has a high capacity to consume water. Youngner et al. (1981) showed that although Kentucky bluegrass was influenced by drought more severely than tall fescue. Tall fescue consumed more water than bluegrass. From experiments conducted in Tucson, AZ, Kneebone and Pepper (1982) concluded that when bermudagrass was overseeded with annual ryegrass the turf provided year-round green color with less water consumption than tall fescue. Brian et al. (1981) proposed that if water consumption be the criterion, the cool-season grasses should not be selected for warm semiarid areas.

Certain cultural practices influence the rate of water consumption. Turfgrass water consumption generally increases with soil water availability (Brian et al., 1981; Ekern, 1966; Mantell, 1966; Marsh et al., 1980, p. 20–21, 32–33); Tovey et al., 1969). Irrigation regimes that permit turfgrasses to temporarily wilt caused a significant decrease in growth and water use (Doss et al., 1964; Feldhake, 1979; Mantell, 1966). Increasing cutting height increases turf water consumption (Feldhake et al., 1983; Madison & Hagan, 1962). Brian et al. (1981) showed that a higher cutting height of cool-season grasses permanently increased water consumption, whereas, the raising of the cutting height of warm-season grasses only temporarily affected water use.

Stimulation of grass foliar growth with N fertilization increases water use rate (Feldhake et al., 1983; Krogman, 1967; Mantell, 1966; Watschke & Waddington, 1975). Dull mower, intense traffic, and certain diseases, such as rust, that damage the leaf epidermis may also increase water consumption of turf (Beard, 1973).

Free water or high relative humidities are required for activity of certain fungal pathogens on turfgrass leaves (Cochrane, 1958). In humid areas, foliar diseases are more prevalent than in semi-arid regions because extended wet periods caused by frequent dew formations and rains (Menzies, 1967). Endo (1972) indicated that prolonged periods of foliage wetness increased turf diseases spread by spores (gray leaf spot, copper spot, rust, and the leaf spot stage of various *Helminthosporium*-incited diseases). On the other hand, diseases caused by *Sclerotinia homoecarpa* (Couch & Bloom, 1960) *Pythium ultimum* (Moore & Couch, 1963) and *Fusarium roseum* pp. (Endo & Colbaugh, 1974) are favored by drought stress.

Nonpotable reclaimed water, or salt waters are often the sources available for turf irrigation. Water containing more than 650 mg kg^{-1} soluble salts may be potentially hazardous to turf growth. This hazard may be offset by maintaining high soil water, leaching with large amounts of irrigation water, and ensuring good soil drainage. Where salt accumulation cannot be avoided, only salt-tolerant grasses should be used. Weeping alkaligrass [*Puccinellia distans* (L.) Parl.] has been shown to be a highly salt tolerant cool season grass that may be used for athletic and residential turf. Of the other cool season turfgrasses, creeping bentgrass is considered to have good salt tolerance while tall fescue and perennial ryegrasses have medium salt tolerance (Beard, 1973).

Cultivars of red fescue and perennial ryegrass have been shown to respond differently to salt spray (Humphreys, 1981). Tolerance of red fescues to salts was independent of growth rate or response to drought. Both drought and salt-tolerant perennial turfgrasses had slow relative growth rates. The warm-season turfgrasses that exhibit good salt tolerance are bermudagrass, zoysiagrass, and St. Augustinegrass (Beard, 1973).

5. Pest Control

One definition of turfgrass management is, the creation of environmental conditions that favor the competitive nature of desired species over all others. Through this favored competition, pests of all types have a reduced ability to influence the composition and quality of a turfgrass sward. Inevitably, pests become part of the managed ecosystem. Controlling competition from them becomes a combination of cultural and pesticidal programs.

The need to control weeds may often arise because of stand losses resulting from other pests (diseases, insects, and nematodes). Weeds have long been recognized as indicators of unfavorable environmental conditions. For example, compaction, poor drainage, unfavorable soil pH, poor soil structure, and shade allow weeds to encroach. From a cultural standpoint, improper mowing height, irrigation mismanagement, inappropriate fertilizer rates and timings, poor disease and insect control, poorly timed cultivation, and misapplication of pesticides, fertilizers, and lime can all lead to weed encroachment.

Since growth rate has shown the strongest relationship to competitive ability over the years, the importance of N fertilization in the control of weeds has long been recognized. Levy and Madden (1931) noted the importance of fertility, soil moisture, pH, compaction, and aeration on the efficacy of early chemical weed control applications. Early research with preemergence herbicides showed that turf composition, density, quality, and mowing practices determined herbicide effectiveness (Roberts et al., 1966). They found that where preemergence herbicides were not used, favorable conditions for bluegrass growth allowed natural composition to account for about 70% control. Murray et al. (1983) found a positive correlation for increased control of dandelion (*Taraxacum officinale* Weber) and crabgrass (*Digitaria ischaemum* Schreb. Muhl.) with increased N levels. Increasing P fertility has been shown to decrease crabgrass and dandelion encroachment into Kentucky bluegrass, while limed turf tended to favor dandelion encroachment (Turner et al., 1979). Johnson and Bower (1982) found that it was possible to substitute a certain quantity of fertilizer for herbicides to maintain a good quality turf.

Although the positive effects of herbicides on turf weed competition are well documented, some evidence has been found that herbicide use can cause potentially detrimental side effects. Gaskin (1964) and Callahan (1972) have shown injury to desired species from preemergence applications. Injury to fine fescue from DCPA applications has been widely reported by many researchers for several years. Injury as a result of preemergence herbicide use has not, however, been reported to result in increased weed encroachment.

Recently, the concept of breeding for herbicide resistance has received some research attention. Lee and Wright (1981) reported progress in developing selections of chewings fescue and creeping bentgrass that have negligible seedling mortality when treated with aminotriazole (3-amino-1,2,4-triazole).

Reducing disease and insect pests to maintain turfgrass competitiveness is most effectively accomplished by combining cultural and chemical programs. Plant breeders have also been successful in developing improved resistance to many diseases, particularly the leaf spot organisms. Insect resistance, however, has not met with as much success, but progress has been made. Kindler and Kinbacher (1975) showed differential cultivar resistance of Kentucky bluegrass to bluegrass billbug (*Sphenophorus patvulus* Gyllenhal). Similar results have been found by Funk and Ahmad (1983) and Lindgren et al. (1981). Perennial ryegrass cultivars exhibit substantial variability in response to sod webworm (*Parapediasia* spp.) larvae feeding (Mazur et al., 1981).

The degree to which various grass species are susceptible to pests may be negated by altering the composition of the sward therefore making the availability of a particular host more diffuse. Research in California (Gibeault et al., 1980) has shown that mixes of Kentucky bluegrass and perennial ryegrass significantly reduced Fusarium blight activity. Plots of bluegrass monocultures were more seriously blighted.

Endophytic fungi associated with certain perennial ryegrasses, tall fescues, hard fescues, and chewing's fescue recently have been attributed to resistance of certain insects and improved turf vigor (Funk et al., 1983). It is anticipated that as techniques are developed to introduce endophytic fungi into turfgrasses that pesticide requirements will be reduced.

At present, a host of chemicals (i.e., pesticides and growth regulators) exist that are effective in controlling pests and manipulating plant growth. The use of growth regulators is covered with Chapter 16 of this monograph.

H. Overseeding of Warm-Season Grasses

Grime (1980) stated that an ecological approach to management involved the integration of information concerning species distribution, life history, and phenology. No management strategy exemplifies this statement more than the practice of overseeding warm-season species with cool-season species to provide year-round growth and aesthetic quality in a turfgrass stand.

Bermudagrass, a warm-season species, is an important turfgrass in the southern USA. However, this species becomes dormant when temperatures drop to 12 to 15 °C. In the northern limits for warm-season species, bermudagrass may remain dormant up to 7 mo from autumn to spring. In the lower southern USA, the warm-season species are usually dormant for about 3 mo during the winter. Therefore, cool-season turfgrasses are overseeded in the autumn to provide active turf during the winter to obtain pleasing color and to maintain good playing surfaces by preventing wearing of the dormant grass (Schmidt, 1970; Ward et al., 1974).

In the lower South, other wearm-season grasses such as St. Augustinegrass, bahiagrass, centipedegrass, and zoysiagrass have been successfully overseeded with cool-season turfgrasses (Meyers & Horn, 1970).

Overseeding with cool-season species too early in the fall often results in failure because of the warm-season grass competition and high incidence of disease (Ward et al., 1974; Meyers & Horn, 1970). The best date for overseeding varies with geographical location. Ward et al. (1974) reported that the optimum time for overseeding bermudagrass was 15 to 20 d prior to the first killing frost date. Later, overseedings were slow to become established and more easily damaged by freezing. Overseeding in early October was shown to be superior to mid-September overseeding in Virginia (Schmidt, 1970). In Florida, late November overseeding provided satisfactory winter turf (Meyers & Horn, 1968).

Seedbed preparation prior to overseeding temperate grasses into a warm-season turf influences the uniformity and stand of the winter turf (Ward et al., 1974). The germination and initial development of the seeds were enhanced when competition of the warm-season species was reduced and when the seeds had good contact with the soil (Schmidt, 1970).

In Florida, seedbed preparation of coarse textured warm-season turf-grasses such as St. Augustinegrass, centipedegrass, and bahiagrass usually consist of scalping and removal of clippings (Meyers & Horn, 1970).

Late aeration prior to overseeding has been found to permit seeds to accumulate in the holes created by the tines and poor germination patterns resulted (Meyers & Horn, 1970; Schmidt & Blaser, 1962). Best results have been found when bermudagrass has been vertically mowed in two or three directions just prior to overseeding and the site has been topdressed after seeding with 1 or 2 mm of soil similar in texture to the growing media (Meyers & Horn, 1970; Schmidt, 1970; Schmidt & Blaser, 1962; Ward et al., 1974).

The best overseeded species have been found to provide good density and color during the cold winter months, tolerate heavy traffic, and provide a gradual transition to bermudagrass in the spring (Meyer & Horn, 1970; Schmidt & Blaser, 1962; Schmidt, 1970; Ward et al., 1974). Selection of over-seeded grass species has been found to be strongly influenced by ultimate use (wear tolerance and ball roll performance on golf putting surfaces) (Batten et al., 1981; Dudeck & Peacock, 1981).

Although annual ryegrass is the species most rapid to establish in the fall of the year, its use for winter turf has been limited because of intolerance to low-temperature tolerance, coarseness of texture, susceptibility to disease, and lack of persistence during the transition to bermugrass in the spring (Meyers & Horn, 1970; Schmidt & Blaser, 1962; Ward et al., 1974). Perennial ryegrasses have been established about as fast as annual ryegrass, withstand wear, tolerate close mowing, have a medium to fine texture, and a gradual spring transition. In monostands as well as polystands, perennial ryegrasses have consistently provided desirable winter turf on putting greens (Batten et al., 1981; Ward et al., 1974) and other turf areas (Schmidt & Shoulders, 1980) throughout southeastern USA. The fine-textured, lower growing turf-type cultivars that also possess relatively good heat tolerance have been found to provide the best winter turf quality (Schmidt & Shoulders, 1980). Some varieties, such as Manhattan, have been found to shred when mowed in late spring (Ward et al., 1974). This undesirable characteristic is more noticeable with heavy seeding rates but has been offset with adequate N fertilization (Schmidt & Shoulders, 1980).

Fine fescues have been found to establish slower in the autumn than ryegrasses, but maintain a high level of turf quality in winter and persist until early summer (Schmidt & Shoulders, 1980). Bentgrasses are slow to establish and have not provided acceptable turf until the following spring when they become more vigorous (Ward et al., 1974).

Kentucky bluegrasses are slow to germinate and have not been found to establish an acceptable monostand of winter turf (Ward et al., 1974), nor do they enhance the performance of polystands (Schmidt & Shoulders, 1980). Rough bluegrass is comparable to red fescue in speed of establishment and has provided acceptable turf during the winter (Ward et al., 1974; Batten et al., 1981). However, it has been found to be inferior when the transition is rapid in the spring due to high temperature (McBee, 1970; Schmidt & Blaser, 1961; Schmidt & Shoulders, 1980). In Mississippi (Ward et al., 1974) and

Texas (Batten et al., 1981) rough bluegrass has been found to be a desirable component in polystands.

Ward et al. (1974) concluded that mixtures containing several species should be used for overseeding. In Texas, polystands consistently provided better overseeded turf than monostands under adverse environments (Batten et al., 1981). Mixtures containing 80% perennial ryegrass and 20% rough bluegrass had the highest winter putting green quality in two out of three years in these studies. In Virginia, it was found that a mixture of 65% perennial ryegrass, 30% fine fescue, and 5% bentgrass composed of cultivars that do well in monostands was considered superior for winter golf green turf (Schmidt & Shoulders, 1980).

Semitropical grasses used for turf other than golf greens are frequently coarse textured and mowed high. For these turf areas, coarser-textured temperate grasses have been found to be more compatible as winter turf than finer-textured grasses (Meyers & Horn, 1970). Perennial ryegrasses have provided satisfactory winter turf on dormant bermudagrass tees, fairways, and lawns.

Because of the high incidence of seedling mortality in overseeding situations, it has been found that high seeding rates are required. This is especially true when a dense turf is desired under close frequent mowings. Low seeding rates have resulted in thin, stemmy, coarse stands while excessive seeding rates have produced dense overcrowded turf that may result in disease infestation (Ward et al., 1974). Seeding rates that have provided satisfactory monostands of winter golf putting turf are 15 to 25 kg of *Lolium* spp. ha^{-1}; 8 to 15 kg of *Festuca* spp. ha^{-1}; 0.6 to 2.1 kg of *Agrostis* spp. ha^{-1}; 4 to 7 kg of *Poa* spp. ha^{-1} (Batten et al., 1981; Dudeck & Peacock, 1981; Schmidt & Shoulders, 1980; Ward et al., 1974). Ward et al. (1974) estimated that 10 to 15 million seeds ha^{-1} for monostands of *Lolium* cultivars and 20 to 25 million seed ha^{-1} of small-seeded species such as rough bluegrass should be used. For overseeding turf areas other than putting greens, satisfactory results were obtained with 4.9 to 7.35 kg of perennial ryegrass ha^{-1} (Schmidt & Shoulders, 1980).

Thatch buildup by vigorous bermudagrass impedes the development of temperate grasses that are overseeded for winter turf (Ward et al., 1974). Results of studies conducted by Schmidt and Shoulders (1972) show that the removal of thatch by frequent summer cultivation subsequently improved the overseeded winter turf quality.

Annual bluegrass and certain diseases can reduce turf quality on overseeded warm-season turf species. Although most overseeded species compete with annual bluegrass, those species with quick establishment ability such as perennial ryegrass and rough bluegrass, have had less annual bluegrass encroachment (Batten et al., 1981; Bingham et al., 1969; Menn & McBee, 1971; Schmidt & Shoulders, 1980). Annual bluegrass infestation may be further controlled with low rates of preemergence herbicides in conjunction with the competition of the overseeded winter turf (Bingham et al., 1969).

Damping-off caused by *Rhizoctoria, Fusarium,* and *Pythium* spp. often reduces turf density of grasses overseeded for winter turf (Meyers & Horn,

1970). Freeman (1970, 1974) found that the severity of *Pythium* infection could be reduced by a high rate of N. Use of fungicide treated seed and applications of appropriate fungicides immediately after overseeding has been found to enhance seedling emergence.

Adequate nutrition is needed to obtain best winter turf quality. Nitrogen has been found to have the most influence on winter turf quality. Soluble N rates of 50 kg of N ha^{-1} each month have been found to provide excellent winter golf putting turf in Florida and Mississippi (Meyers & Horn, 1970; Ward et al., 1974). Application of 50 kg of N ha^{-1} every 2 mo from October to May resulted in acceptable winter golf tee turf quality, while application of this rate of N applied only in October and December produced poor turf quality (Schmidt & Shoulders, 1980). Schmidt and Shoulders (1972) reported that excessive winter N fertilization caused a reduction of overseeded cool-season grasses in the spring, but stimulated early bermudagrass post-dormancy development. Therefore, fertilization did not significantly affect total coverage in late spring.

IV. RESEARCH NEEDS

It appears quite clear that turfgrass breeding programs will continue to develop new germplasm (for all species) at a rapid, if not accelerated, rate for the foreseeable future. By the Year 2000, a significant percentage of maintained turf will be comprised of plant material that was not commercially available prior to 1980. This new germplasm may be more disease tolerant, insect resistant, drought tolerant, thrive when fertility is low, produce less thatch, have deeper roots, tolerate more shade, tolerate more traffic, tolerate closer mowings, be compatible in mixtures or blends, compete with weeds, persist in compacted soils, or have other desirable attributes.

The challenge for research is obvious. A great need exists for continued emphasis on applied management studies to better understand the growth responses of these new plant introductions. It is very likely that much of the research previously conducted on subjects across the management spectrum will need to be repeated using the new cultivars. Ecological studies designed to determine the basis for competitive differences between species or cultivars require time and resources, but is necessary before reliable recommendations for establishment and maintenance can be formulated.

In addition to the challenge of understanding new germplasm, our ability to impose significant management influence on the natural ecology of a turfgrass ecosystem will continue to increase. Development of low dose, highly efficacious fertilizer sources, and new equipment innovations will provide managers with the ability to significantly alter what might typically be considered as the "natural course of events" in traditional plant ecology. Turfgrass research has made substantial contributions over the past several decades, but the future needs are far greater than what has been accomplished to date.

V. SUMMARY

The management practices available to the turfgrass manager and the ability to substantially control the turfgrass environment create an ecological situation unique in nature. Much of the ecological research conducted in turfgrass science occurred prior to 1970. This earlier work provided a better understanding of how management practices such as fertilization, mowing, irrigation, and pest control impacted the population dynamics of turfgrass communities. Since that time, most of the research has been focused on a better understanding of the plant physical characteristics that influence plant competition. Research on germination time, seedling growth and development, tillering rate, and the effect of plant growth regulators on morphology has received emphasis. As new germplasm continues to be developed and released and chemical and mechanical tools are innovated or improved, the need for increased research in turfgrass ecology is more essential than ever before.

REFERENCES

Adams, J.E. 1966. Influence of mulches on runoff, erosion, and soil moisture depletion. Soil Sci. Soc. Am. Proc. 30:110-114.

Adams, W.A., P.J. Bryan, and G.E. Walker. 1974. Effects of cutting height and nitrogen nutrition on growth pattern of turfgrasses. p. 131-144. In E.C. Roberts (ed.) Proc. 2nd Int. Turfgrass Res. Conf., Blacksburg, VA. 19-21 June 1973. ASA and CSSA, Madison, WI.

Adams, W.A. 1980. Effects of nitrogen fertilization and cutting height on the shoot growth, nutrient removal and turfgrass composition of an initially perennial ryegrass dominant sports turf. p. 343-350. In J.B. Beard (ed.) Proc. 3rd Int. Turfgrass Res. Conf., Munich, Germany. 11-13 July 1977. Int. Turfgrass Soc., and ASA, CSSA, and SSSA, Madison, WI.

Ahlgren, H.L., and O.S. Aamodt. 1939. Harmful root interactions as a possible explanation for effects noted between various species of grasses and legumes. J. Am. Soc. Agron. 31:982-985.

Alderfer, and R.B., and F.G. Merkle. 1943. The comparative effects of surface application vs. incorporation of various mulching material on structure, permeability, runoff and other soil properties. Soil Sci. Soc. Am. Proc. 8:79-86.

Anderson, A.M. 1947. Some factors influencing the germination of seed of Poa compressa L. Proc. Assoc. Off. Seed Anal. 37:134-143.

Anderson, L.G., and W.R. Kneebone. 1969. Differential responses of Cynodon dactylon (L.) Pers. selection to three herbicides. Crop Sci. 9:599-601.

Ansari, A.Q., and W.E. Loomis. 1959. Leaf temperatures. Am. J. Bot. 46:713-717.

Ayers, A.D. 1952. Seed germination as affected by soil moisture and salinity. Agron. J. 45:82-84.

Bailey, C.H. 1940. Respiration of cereal grains and flaxseed. Plant Physiol. 15:257-274.

Baird, D.D., S.C. Phatak, R.P. Upchurch, and G.F. Begeman. 1973. Glyphosate activity on quackgrass as influenced by mowing and rhizome density. Proc. NEWSS 27:13-20.

Baker, F.S. 1929. Effect of excessively high temperatures on coniferous reproduction. J. For. 27:949-975.

Baltensperger, A.A. 1961. Prolonged wintergreeness of bermudagrass by use of plastic covers and electrical soil heating. p. 40-44. In Arizona Agric. Exp. Stn. Rep. 203.

Baltensperger, A.A. 1962. Reduced dormancy of bermudagrass by soil heating. 1962 report of turfgrass research. p. 18-22. In Arizona Agric. Exp. Stn. Rep. 212.

Barkley, D.G., R.E. Blaser, and R.E. Schmidt. 1965. Effect of mulches on microclimate and turf establishment. Agron. J. 57:189-192.

Batten, S.M., J.B. Beard, D. Johns, A. Almodares, and J. Eckhardt. 1981. p. 83-94. In R.W. Sheard (ed.) Proc. 4th Int. Turfgrass Res. Conf., Guelph, ON, Canada. 19-23 July. Int. Turfgrass Soc., Ontario Agric. Coll., Univ. of Guelph, Guelph, ON.

Beach, G.A. 1963. Management practices in the care of lawns. p. 42–45. *In* Proc. 10th Rocky Mtn. Reg. Turf. Conf.

Beal, W.J. 1898. Lawn-grass mixtures as purchased in the market, compared with a few of the best. Proc. Soc. Prom. Agric. Sci. 1898:59–63.

Beard, J.B. 1964. Effects of ice, snow, and water covers on Kentucky bluegrass, annual bluegrass, and creeping bentgrass. Crop Sci. 4:638–640.

Beard, J.B. 1965a. Effects of ice covers in the field on two perennial grasses. Crop Sci. 5:139–140.

Beard, J.B. 1965b. Bentgrass (*Agrostis* spp.) varietal tolerance to ice cover injury. Agron. J. 57:313.

Beard, J.B. 1965c. Factors in the adaptation of turfgrass to shade. Agron. J. 57:457–459.

Beard, J.B. 1966a. A comparison of mulches for erosion control and grass establishment on light soil. Mich. Agric. Exp. Stn. Q. Bull. 48(3):369–376.

Beard, J.B. 1966b. Direct low temperature injury of nineteen turfgrasses. Mich. Agric. Exp. Stn. Q. Bull. 48(3):377–383.

Beard, J.B. 1973. Turfgrass: Science and culture. Prentice-Hall, Englewood Cliffs, NJ.

Beard, J.B., and D.P. Martin. 1970. Influence of water temperature on submersion tolerance of four grasses. Agron. J. 62:257–259.

Beard, J.B., and P.E. Rieke. 1969. Producing quality sod. p. 442–461. *In* A.A. Hanson and F. Juska (ed.) Turfgrass science. Agron. Monogr. 14. ASA, Madison, WI.

Beard, J.B., J.M. Vargas, Jr., and P.E. Rieke. 1973. Influence of nitrogen fertility on *Tricholoma* fairy ring development in Merion Kentucky bluegrass (*Poa pratensis* L.). Agron. J. 65:994–995.

Beeson, K.C., L. Gray, and M.B. Adams. 1947. The adsorption of mineral elements by forage plants: 1. The phosphorus, cobalt, manganese, and copper content of some grasses. Agron. J. 39:356–362.

Bingham, S.W., R.E. Schmidt, and C.K. Curry. 1969. Annual bluegrass in overseeded bermudagrass putting green turf. Agron. J. 61:908–911.

Blackman, G.E., and J.N. Black. 1959. Physiological and ecological studies in the analysis of plant environment. XI. A further assessment of the influence of shading on the growth of different species in the vegetative phase. Ann. Bot. N.S. 23(89):51–63.

Blaser, R.E. 1963. Principles for making up seed mixtures for roadside seeding. Natl. Acad. Sci. Highway Res. Bull. 1120:79–84.

Blaser, R.E., J.T. Green, Jr., and D.L. Wright. 1975. Establishing vegetation for erosion control in the Piedmont region. Chapter 7. *In* Special national EPA handbook on erosion control. USEPA, Washington, DC.

Blaser, R.E., W.I. Griffith, and T.H. Taylor. 1956a. Seedling competition in compounding forage seed mixtures. Agron. J. 48:118–123.

Blaser, R.E., and H.D. Perry. 1975. Establishing vegetation for erosion control along highways in the Appalachian region. Chapter 8. EPA-440/9-75-006. USEPA, Washington, DC.

Blaser, R.E., T. Taylor, W. Griffith, and W. Skirdle. 1956b. Seedling competition in establishing forage plants. Agron. J. 48:1–6.

Blaser, R.E., G.W. Thomas, C.R. Brooks, G.J. Shoop, and J. Martin, Jr. 1961. Turf establishment and maintenance along highway cuts. Roadside Development Highway Res. Board, Washington, DC.

Blaser, R.E., and J.M. Woodruff. 1968. The need for specifying two or three step seeding and fertilization practices for establishing sod on highways. Natl. Acad. Sci., Highway Res. Board, Washington, DC. 246:44–49.

Bogart, J.E., and J.B. Beard. 1973. Cutting height effects on the competitive ability of annual bluegrass (*Poa annua* L.). Agron. J. 65:513–514.

Bredakis, E.J. 1959. Interaction between height of cut and various nutrient levels on the development of turfgrass roots and tops. M.S. thesis, Univ. of Massachusetts, Amherst.

Brede, A.D. 1982. Interaction of three turfgrass species. Ph.D. diss. The Pennsylvania State University, University Park (Diss. Abst. 82-28866).

Brede, A.D. 1987. Isolated plot techniques for studying seedling growth of turfgrasses. Agron. J. 79:5–8.

Brede, A.D., and J.L. Brede. 1988. Establishment clipping of tall fescue and companion annual ryegrass. Agron. J. 80:27–30.

Brede, A.D., and J.M. Duich. 1981. Annual bluegrass encroachment affected by Kentucky bluegrass seeding rate. Proc. NEWSS 35:307–311.

Brede, A.D., and J.M. Duich. 1984. Initial mowing of Kentucky bluegrass-perennial ryegrass seedling turf mixtures. Agron. J. 76:711–714.

Brian, L.B., B. Bravdo, I. Bushkin-Harav, and E. Rawitz. 1981. Water consumption and growth rate of eleven turfgrasses as affected by mowing height, irrigation frequency, and soil moisture. Agron. J. 73:85–90.

Britton, M.P. 1969. Turfgrass disease. p. 288–335. *In* A.A. Hanson and F.V. Juska (ed.) Turfgrass science. Agron. Monogr. 14. ASA, Madison, WI.

Burns, R.E. 1981. Time of fertilizer application as it affects quality of tall fescue turf. p. 285–291. *In* R.W. Sheard (ed.) Proc. 4th Int. Turfgrass Res. Conf., Guelph, ON, Canada. 19–23 July. Int. Turfgrass Soc., and Ontario Agric. Coll., Univ. of Guelph, Guelph, ON.

Burt, E.O. 1980. Glyphosates for torpedograss and bermudagrass control. p. 257–262. *In* J.B. Beard (ed.) Proc. 3rd Int. Turfgrass Res. Conf., Munich, Germany. 11–13 July 1977. Int. Turfgrass Soc., and ASA, CSSA, and SSSA, Madison, WI.

Burton, G.W., and E.H. DeVane. 1952. Effect of rate and method of applying different sources of nitrogen upon the yield and chemical composition of bermudagrass. Agron. J. 44:128–132.

Burton, G.W., G.M. Prine, and J.E. Jackson. 1957. Studies of drought tolerance and water use of several southern grasses. Agron. J. 49:498–503.

Callahan, L.M. 1972. Phytotoxicity of herbicides to a Penncross bentgrass green. Weed Sci. 20:387–391.

Carroll, J.C. 1943. Effects of drought, temperature, and nitrogen on turf grasses. Plant Physiol. 18:19–36.

Carrow, R.N. 1980. Influence of compaction on three turfgrass species. Agron. J. 72:1038–1042.

Chalmers, D.R., and R.E. Schmidt. 1979. Bermudagrass survival as influenced by deacclimation, low temperatures, and dormancy. Agron. J. 71:947–949.

Chamblee, D.S., and D.T. Gooden, III. 1981. Desiccation, temperature, and degree of dormancy of sprigs influence on establishment of coastal bermudagrass. Agron. J. 73:872–876.

Chippendale, H.G. 1932. The operation of interspecific competition in causing delayed growth of grasses. Ann. Appl. Biol. 19:221–242.

Clum, H.H. 1926. The effect of transpiration and environmental factors on leaf temperatures. I. Transpiration. Am. J. Bot. 13:194–216.

Cochrane, V.E. 1958. Physiology of fungi. John Wiley and Sons, New York.

Cooper, R.J. 1982. Protecting turf from winter injury. Golf Course Mangae. 1982 (December):30–32.

Couch, H.B., and J.R. Bloom. 1960. Influence of environment on disease of turfgrasses. II. Effect of nutrition, pH, and soil moisture on *Sclerotinia* dollarspot. Phytopathology 50:761–763.

Couch, H.B. 1962. Diseases of turfgrasses. Reinhold Publ. Corp., New York.

Dahl, A.S. 1934. The relation between rainfall and injuries to turf season 1933. Greenskeepers Rep. 2(2):1–4.

Daniel, W.H. 1970. Soil warming in North America. p. 235–237. *In* J.R. Escritt (ed.) Proc. 1st Int. Turfgrass Res. Conf., Harrogate, England. 15–18 July 1969. Sports Turf Res. Inst., Bingley, England.

Darrah, C.H., and A.J. Powell, Jr. 1977. Post harvest heating and survival of sod as influenced by pre-harvest and harvest management. Agron. J. 69:283–287.

Daubenmire, R. 1968. Plant communities. A textbook of plant synecology. Harper and Row, New York.

Davidson, R.L. 1969. Effects of soil nutrients and moisture on root/shoot ratios in *Lolium perenne* L. and *Trifolium repens* L. Ann. Bot. 33:571–577.

Davies, W., and M.T. Thomas. 1928. The behavior of grasses in the seed year, when sown in pure plots: establishment, rate of growth, and palatability. Welsh J. Agric. 4:206–221.

Davis, A.G., and B.F. Martin. 1949. Observations on the effect of artificial flooding on certain herbage plants. J. Br. Grassl. Soc. 4:63–64.

Davis, R.R. 1958. The effect of other species and mowing height on persistence of lawn grasses. Agron. J. 50:671–673.

Denmead, O.T. 1972. The microclimate of grass communities. *In* V.B. Youngner and C.M. McKell (ed.) The biology and utilization of grasses. Academic Press, New York.

Dest, W.M., and D.W. Allison. 1981. Influence of nitrogen and phosphorus fertilization on the growth and development of *Poa annua* L. (annual bluegrass). p. 325–332. *In* R.W. Sheard (ed.) Proc. 4th Int. Turfgrass Res. Conf., Guelph, ON, Canada. 19–23 July. Int. Turfgrass Soc., Ontario Agric. Coll., Univ. of Guelph, Guelph, ON.

Dickson, W.K., and C.R. Funk. 1979. Performance of Kentucky bluegrass cultivars, selections, blends, and mixtures in a regional test at New Brunswick, NJ. Rutgers Turfgrass Proc. 10:110–118.

DiPaola, J.M. 1984. Syringing affects on the canopy temperature of bentgrass greens. Agron. J. 76:951–953.

Donald, C.M. 1963. Competition among crop and pasture plants. Adv. Agron. 15:1–118.

Doss, B.D., O.L. Bennett, and D.A. Ashley. 1964. Moisture use by forage species as related to pan evaporation and net radication. Soil Sci. 98:322–327.

Dudeck, A.E., and C.H. Peacock. 1981. Effects of several overseeded ryegrasses on turf quality, traffic tolerance and ball roll. p. 75–82. *In* R.W. Sheard (ed.) Proc. 4th Int. Turfgrass Res. Conf., Guelph, ON, Canada. 19–23 July. Int. Turfgrass Soc., Ontario Agric. Coll., Univ. of Guelph, Guelph, ON.

Dudeck, A.E., N.P. Swanson, and A.R. Dedrick. 1966. Protecting steep construction slopes against water erosion. II. Effect of selected mulches on seedling stand, soil temperature, and moisture relations. p. 38. *In* Agronomy abstracts. ASA, Madison, WI.

Duell, R.W., and R.M. Schmidt. 1974. Grass varieties for roadsides. p. 541–550. *In* E.C. Roberts (ed.) Proc. 2nd Int. Turfgrass Res. Conf., Blacksburg, VA. 19–21 June 1973. ASA and CSSA, Madison, WI.

Duff, D.T., and J.B. Beard. 1966. Effects of air movement and syringing on the microclimate of bentgrass turf. Agron. J. 58:495–497.

Duley, F.L. 1939. Surface factors affecting the rate of intake of water by soil. Soil Sci. Soc. Am. Proc. 4:60–64.

Duley, F.L., and L.L. Kelley. 1939. Effect of soil types, slope and surface condition on intake of water. Nebraska Agric. Exp. Stn. Res. Bull. 112.

Dunn, J.H., C.J. Nelson, and R.D. Winfrey. 1981. Effects of mowing and fertilization on quality of ten Kentucky bluegrass cultivars. p. 293–301. *In* R.W. Sheard (ed.) Proc. 4th Int. Turfgrass Res. Conf., Guelph, ON, Canada. 19–23 July. Int. Turfgrass Soc., Ontario Agric. Coll., Univ. of Guelph, Guelph, ON.

Eggens, J.L. 1979. The response of some Kentucky bluegrass cultivars to competitive stresses from annual bluegrass. Can. J. Plant Sci. 59:1123–1128.

Ekern, P.C. 1966. Evapotranspiration by bermudagrass sod, *Cynodon dactylon* L. Pers. in Hawaii. Agron. J. 58:387–390.

Ellison, W.D. 1944. Studies of raindrop erosion. Agric. Eng. 25:131–136, 181–182.

Endo, R.M. 1972. The turfgrass community as an environment for the development of facultative fungai parasites. p. 172–202. *In* V.B. Younger and C.M. McKell (ed.) Physiological ecology—The biology and utilization of grasses. Academic Press, New York.

Endo, R.M., and P.F. Colbaugh. 1974. Fusarium blight of Kentucky bluegrass in California. p. 325–327. *In* E.C. Roberts (ed.) Proc. 2nd Int. Turfgrass Res. Conf., Blacksburg, VA. 19–21 June 1973. ASA and CSSA, Madison, WI.

Engel, R.E. 1951. Studies of turf cultivation and related subjects. Ph.D. diss. Rutgers Univ., New Brunswick, N.J.

Engel, R.E. 1966. A comparison of Colonial and creeping bentgrass for 1/2 and 3/4 inch turf. p. 45–58. *In* 1966 Report on Turfgrass Res. at Rutgers University. New Jersey Agric. Exp. Stn. Bull. 816.

Engel, R.E., and R.J. Aldrich. 1955. Control of annual bluegrass (*Poa annua*) in fairway-type turf. Proc. NEWCC 9:353–355.

Engel, R.E., and J.R. Trout. 1980. Seedling competition of Kentucky bluegrass, red fescue, colonial bentgrass, and temporary grasses. p. 379–389. *In* J.B. Beard (ed.) Proc. 3rd Int. Turfgrass Res. Conf., Munich, Germany. 11–13 July 1977. Int. Turfgrass Soc., and ASA, CSSA, and SSSA, Madison, WI.

Erdmann, M.H., and C.M. Harrison. 1947. The influence of domestic ryegrass and redtop upon the growth of Kentucky bluegrass and chewings fescue in lawn turf mixtures. Agron. J. 39:682–689.

Evans, G.C. 1956. An area survey method of investigating the distribution of light intensity in woodlands, with particular reference to sunflecks. J. Ecol. 44:391–427.

Evans, W.F., and F.C. Stickler. 1961. Grain sorghum seed germination under moisture and temperature stresses. Agron. J. 53:369–372.

Feldhake, C.M. 1979. Measuring evapotranspiration of turfgrass. M.S. thesis. Colorado State Univ., Fort Collins.

Feldhake, C.M., R.E. Danielson, and J.D. Butler. 1983. Turfgrass evapotranspiration. 1. Factor influencing rate in urban environments. Agron. J. 75:824–830.

Feldhake, C.M., R.E. Danielson, and J.D. Butler. 1984. Turfgrass evapotranspiration. II. Responses to deficit irrigation. Agron. J. 76:85–89.

Field, T.R.O., and J.W. Murphy. 1989. Ecological analysis of racetrack turf species. p. 147–149. *In* H. Takatoh (ed.) Proc. 6th Int. Turfgrass Res. Conf., Tokyo. 31 July–5 Aug. Jpn. Soc. Turfgrass Sci., Tokyo.

Fisher, G.G. 1974. Heating turf by underground warm air. p. 215–220. *In* E.C. Roberts (ed.) Proc. of the 2nd Int. Turfgrass Res. Conf., Blacksburg, VA. 19–21 June 1973. ASA and CSSA, Madison, WI.

Forbes, I., and M.H. Ferguson. 1948. Effects of strain difference, seed treatment, and planting depth on seed germination of *Zoysia* spp. J. Am. Soc. of Agron. 40:725–732.

Frazier, S.L. 1960. Turfgrass seedling development under measured environment and management conditions. M.S. thesis. Purdue Univ., W. Lafayette, IN.

Freeman, T.R. 1970. Diseases of turfgrasses in warm-humid regions. p. 340–345. *In* Proc. 1st Int. Turfgrass Res. Conf., Harrogate, England. 15–18 July 1969. Sports Turf Res. Inst., Bingley, England.

Freeman, T.R. 1974. Influences of nitrogen fertilization on severity of *Pythium* blight of ryegrass. p. 335–338. *In* E.C. Roberts (ed.) Proc. 2nd Int. Turfgrass Res. Conf., Blacksburg, VA. 19–21 June 1973. ASA and CSSA, Madison, WI.

Funk, C.R., and S. Ahmad. 1983. The bluegrass billbug: Susceptibility of bluegrasses to damage. NY State Turf. Assoc. Bull. 117:842–843.

Funk, C.R., and W.K. Dickson. 1981. Composition and performance of a Kentucky bluegrass blend and turf maintenance. Rutgers Turf Proc. 12:74–77.

Funk, C.R., and R.E. Engel. 1963. Effect of cutting height and fertilizer on species composition and turf quality ratings of various turfgrass mixtures. p. 47–56. *In* Rutgers Turf Short Course in Turf. Manage.

Funk, C.R., R.E. Engel, and P.M. Halesky. 1966. Performance of Kentucky bluegrass varieties as influenced by fertility level and cutting height. New Jersey Agric. Exp. Stn. Bull. 816.

Funk, C.R., R.E. Engel, and P.M. Halesky. 1967. Summer survival of turfgrass species as influenced by variety, fertility, and disease incidence. New Jersey Agric. Exp. Stn. Bull. 818.

Funk, C.R., P.M. Halisky, M.C. Johnson, M.R. Siegel, A.V. Stewart, S. Ahmad, R.H. Hurley, and I.E. Harvey. 1983. An endophytic fungus and resistance to sod webworm: Association in *Lolium perenne* L. Bio/Technology (April) 1983:189–191.

Garner, E.S., and S.C. Damon. 1929. The persistence of certain lawn grasses as affected by fertilization and competition. Rhode Island Agric. Exp. Stn. Bull. 217.

Gaskin, T.A. 1964. Effect of preemergence crabgrass herbicides on rhizome development in Kentucky bluegrass. Agron. J. 56:340–342.

Gates, D.M. 1965. Heat transfer in plants. Sci. Am. 213:76–84.

Gibeault, V.A., R. Autio, S. Spaulding, and V.B. Youngner. 1980. Mixing turfgrass controls Fusarium blight. Calif. Turf. Culture 30:9–11.

Gilbert, W.B., and D.L. Davis. 1967. Relationships of potassium nutrition and temperature stresses on turfgrass. p. 52. *In* Agronomy abstracts. ASA, Madison, WI.

Gilbert, W.B., and D.L. Davis. 1971. Influence of fertility ratios on winter hardiness of bermudagrass. Agron. J. 63:591–593.

Gilbert, W.B., and E.E. Deal. 1964. Temporary ditch liners for erosion control and sod establishment. p. 101. *In* Agronomy abstracts. ASA, Madison, WI.

Goss, R.L., R.M. Blanchard, and W.R. Melton. 1970. The establishment of vegetation on non-topsoiled slopes in Washington. Final Rep. Y-1009. Prepared jointly by Washington State Highway Commission and Washington State University Agric. Res. Center in cooperation with Fed. Highway Administration. Dep. of Agron. and Soils, Washington State Univ., Pullman.

Green, D.G., and J.B. Beard. 1969. Seasonal relationship between nitrogen nutrition and soluble carbohydrates in leaves of *Agrostis palustris*. Agron. J. 61:107–111.

Green, J.T., Jr., R.E. Blaser, and H.D. Perry. 1973a. Establishing persistent vegetation on cuts and fills along West Virginia highways. Final Rep. West Virginia Dep. of Highways and U.S. Dep. of Transportation, Fed. Highway Admin., Bureau of Public Roads. Project 26, Phase II. Agron. Dep. Virginia Polytech. Inst. and State Univ., Blacksburg.

Green, J.T., Jr., H.D. Perry, J.M. Woodruff, and R.E. Blaser. 1974. Suitability of cool and warm season species for dormant winter seedings. p. 551–568. *In* E.C. Roberts (ed.) Proc. 2nd Int. Turfgrass Res. Conf., Blacksburg, VA. 19–21 June 1973. ASA and CSSA, Madison, WI.

Grime, J.P. 1980. An ecological approach to management. p. 13–35. *In* I.H. Rorison, and R. Hunt (ed.) Amenity grassland: An ecological perspective. John Wiley and Sons, New York.

Grime, J.P., and R. Hunt. 1975. Relative growth rate: Its range and adaptive significance in a local flora. J. Ecol. 63:393–422.

Hall, J.R., III. 1980. Effect of cultural factors on tall fescue-Kentucky bluegrass sod quality and botanical composition. p. 367–378. *In* J.B. Beard (ed.) Proc. 3rd Int. Turfgrass Res. Conf., Munich, Germany. 11–13 July 1981. Int. Turfgrass Soc., and ASA, CSSA, and SSSA, Madison, WI.

Hall, J.R., III, J.S. Coartney, and R.E. Schmidt. 1981. Effect of companion grass and other factors upon the speed and quality of putting green renovation. p. 543. *In* R.W. Sheard (ed.) Proc. 4th Int. Turfgrass Res. Conf., Guelph, ON. 19–23 July. Int. Turfgrass Soc., Ontario Agric. Coll., Univ. of Guelph, Guelph, ON.

Hanson, A.A., and F.V. Juska. 1961. Winter root activity in Kentucky bluegrass (*Poa pratensis* L.). Agron. J. 53:372–374.

Harris, F.S., and H.H. Yao. 1923. Effectiveness of mulches in preserving soil moisture. J. Agric. Res. 23:727–742.

Harrold, L.L., and F.R. Driebelis. 1955. Evaluation of agricultural hydrology by monolith lysimeters. USDA Tech. Bull. 1179. U.S. Gov. Print. Office, Washington, DC.

Hart, H., and R.D. Schuetz. 1972. Organic chemistry: A short course. Houghton Mifflin Co., Boston.

Hartwell, B.L., and S.C. Damon. 1917. The persistence of lawn and other grasses as influenced especially by the effect of manures on the degree of soil acidity. Rhode Island Agric. Exp. Stn. Bull. 170.

Hawes, D.T. 1980. Response of warm and cool season turfgrass polystands to nitrogen and topdressing. p. 65–74. *In* J.B. Beard (ed.) Proc. 3rd Int. Turfgrass Res. Conf., Munich, Germany. 11–13 July 1977. Int. Turfgrass Soc., and ASA, CSSA, and SSSA, Madison, WI.

Hendricks, S.B., V.B. Toole, and H.A. Borthwick. 1968. Opposing actions of light in seed germination of *Poa pratensis* and *Amaranthus arenicola*. Plant Physiol. 43:2033–2028.

Hottenstein, W.L. 1969. Highway roadsides. p. 603–637. *In* A.A. Hanson and F.V. Juska (ed.) Turfgrass science. Agron. Monogr. 14. ASA, Madison, WI.

Hu, Shu-liang, P. Dong, and L. Dong. 1989. Studies on the introduction and acclimatization of Graminae and Leguminosae. p. 151–152. *In* H. Takatoh (ed.) Proc. 6th Int. Turfgrass Res. Conf., Tokyo, Japan. 31 July–5 Aug. Jpn. Soc. Turfgrass Sci., Tokyo.

Hughes, H.D., M.E. Heath, and D.S. Metcalfe. 1962. Forages. The Iowa State Univ. Press, Ames.

Hughes, T.D., J.F. Stone, W.W. Huffine, and J.R. Gingrich. 1966. Effect of soil bulk density and water pressure on emergence of grass seedlings. Agron. J. 58:549–553.

Humphreys, M.O. 1981. Response to salt spray in red fescue and perennial ryegrass. p. 47–54. *In* R.E. Sheard (ed.) Proc. 4th Int. Turfgrass Res. Conf., Guelph, ON. 19–23 July. Int. Turfgrass Soc., and Ontario Agric. Coll., Univ. of Guelph, Guelph, ON.

Hunter, J.R., and A.E. Erickson. 1952. Relation of seed germination to soil moisture tension. Agron. J. 44:107–109.

Idso, S.B., D.G. Baker, and D.M. Gates. 1966. The energy environment of plants. Adv. Agron. 18:171–218.

Jagschitz, J.A. 1968. Use of charcoal to deactivate herbicide residue in turfgrass seedbeds. Proc. NEWSS 22:401–408.

Jagschitz, J.A. 1974. Use of activated charcoal to nullify the harmful effects of chemicals in turfgrass. p. 319–409. *In* E.C. Roberts (ed.) Proc. 2nd Int. Turf. Res. Conf., Blacksburg, VA. 19–21 June. ASA and CSSA, Madison, WI.

Jagschitz, J.A. 1977. Protecting turfgrass seedling from chemical residues with activated charcoal. Proc. NEWSS 31:371–376.

Jagschitz, J.A. 1978. Turfgrass renovation with cocodylic acid, glyphosate and paraquat. Proc. NEWSS 32:317 (Abstract).

Jagschitz, J.A. 1979. Mowing turfgrass with chemicals. URI Turf Res. Rev. (Spring).

Jagschitz, J.A., and C.R. Skogley. 1966. Turfgrass response to seedbed and seedling applications of preemergence and broadleaf herbicides. Proc. NEWSS 20:551–560.

Janson, L.E. 1970. Theoretical investigation of artificial heating of the topsoil. p. 243–251. *In* Proc. 1st Int. Turfgrass Res. Conf., Harrogate, England. 15–18 July 1969. Sports Turf Res. Inst., Bingley, England.

Johnson, B.J. 1973a. Establishment of centipedegrass and St. Augustinegrass with aid of chemicals. Agron. J. 65:959–962.

Johnson, B.J. 1973b. Herbicides, sprigging rates and nitrogen treatments for establishment of Tifway bermudagrass. Agron. J. 65:969–972.

Johnson, B.J. 1974. Herbicide influence on rate of establishment of warm-season turfgrasses. p. 365–371. *In* E.C. Roberts (ed.) Proc. 2nd Int. Turfgrass Res. Conf., Blacksburg, VA. 19–21 June 1973. ASA and CSSA, Madison, WI.

Johnson, B.J. 1976a. Timing of glyphosate for conversion of bermudagrass turf to tall fescue. Crop Sci. 16:597–598.

Johnson, B.J. 1976b. Effect of activated charcoal on herbicide injury during establishment of centipedegrass. Agron. J. 68:802–805.

Johnson, B.J. 1976c. Renovation on turfgrasses with herbicides. Weed Sci. 24:467–472.

Johnson, B.J., and H.G. Bower. 1982. Management of herbicide on rhizome development in Kentucky bluegrass turf. Agron. J. 74:845–850.

Juska, F.V. 1961a. Pre-emergence herbicides for crabgrass control and their effects on germination of turfgrass species. Weeds 9:137–144.

Juska, F.V. 1961b. Frequency and height of cutting bluegrass. p. 1–2. *In* Proc. 2nd Missouri Lawn and Turf Conf.

Juska, F.V. 1963. Shade tolerance of bentgrasses. Golf Course Rep. 31(2):28–34.

Juska, F.V., J.F. Corman, and A.W. Hovin. 1969a. Turfgrasses under cool humid conditions. p. 491–512. *In* A.A. Hanson and F.V. Juska (ed.) Turfgrass science. Agron. Monogr. 14. ASA, Madison, WI.

Juska, F.V., and A.A. Hanson. 1959. Evaluation of cool-season turfgrasses alone and in mixtures. Agron. J. 51:597–600.

Juska, F.V., and A.A. Hanson. 1967. Effect of nitrogen sources, rates, and time of application on the performance of Kentucky bluegrass turf. Am. Soc. Hortic. Sci. 90:413–419.

Juska, F.V., and A.A. Hanson. 1969. Nutritional requirements of *Poa annua* L. Agron. J. 61:466–468.

Juska, F.V., A.A. Hanson, and E.J. Erickson. 1965. Effects of phosphorus and other treatments on the development of red fescue, Merion, and common Kentucky bluegrass. Agron. J. 57:75–78.

Juska, F.V., A.A. Hanson, and A.W. Hovin. 1969b. Kentucky 31 tall fescue—a shade tolerant turfgrass. Weeds, Trees, Turf. 8(1):34–35.

Juska, F.V., A.A. Hanson, and A.W. Hovin. 1969c. Evaluation of tall fescue *Festuca arundinacea* Schreb., for turf in the transition zone of the United States. Agron. J. 61:625–628.

Juska, F.V., and J.J. Murray. 1974. Performance of bermudagrass in the transition zone as affected by potassium and nitrogen. p. 149–154. *In* E.C. Roberts (ed.) Proc. 2nd Int. Turfgrass Res. Conf., Blacksburg, VA. 19–21 June 1973. ASA and CSSA, Madison, WI.

Juska, F.V., J. Tyson, and C.M. Harrison. 1955. The competitive relationship of Merion bluegrass as influenced by various mixtures, cutting heights, and levels of nitrogen. Agron. J. 47:513–518.

Juska, F.V., J. Tyson, and C.M. Harrison. 1956. Field studies on the establishment of Merion bluegrass in various seed mixtures. Mich. Q. Bull. 38:678–690.

Kerr, H.D. 1969. Selective grass control with siduron. Weed Sci. 17(2):181–186.

Kindler, S.D., and E.J. Kinbacher. 1975. Differential reaction of Kentucky bluegrass cultivars to the bluegrass billbug, *Sphenophorus parvulus* Gyllenhal. Crop Sci. 15:873–874.

King, J.W. 1970. Factors affecting the heating and damage of Merion Kentucky bluegrass (*Poa pratensis* L.) sod under simulated shipping conditions. Ph.D. Diss. Michigan State Univ., East Lansing.

King, J. 1971. Competition between established and newly sown grass species. J. Br. Grassl. Soc. 26:221–229.

King, J.W., and J.B. Beard. 1972. Postharvest cultural practices affecting the rooting of Kentucky bluegrass sods grown on organic and mineral soils. Agron. J. 64:259–261.

King, J.W., and C.R. Skogley. 1969. Effect of nitrogen and phosphorus placements and rates on turfgrass establishment. Agron. J. 61:4–6.

Klingman, D.L., and J.J. Murray. 1978. Use of herbicides for renovation of turf. Proc. NEWSS 32:316 (Abstract).

Kneebone, W.R. 1957. Selection for seedling vigor in native grasses under artificial moisture stress. p. 55. *In* Agronomy abstracts. ASA, Madison, WI.

Kneebone, W.R., and I.L. Pepper. 1981. Differential uptake of phosphorus by cultivars of *Lolium perenne* L. p. 553–554. *In* R.W. Sheard (ed.) Proc. 4th Int. Turfgrass Res. Conf., Guelph, ON, Canada. 19–23 July. Int. Turfgrass Soc., Ontario Agric. Coll., Univ. of Guelph, Guelph, ON.

Kneebone, W.R., and I.L. Pepper. 1982. Consumptive water use by subirrigated turfgrasses under desert conditions. Agron. J. 74:419–423.

Krogman, K.K. 1967. Evapotranspiration by irrigated grass as related to fertilizer. Can. J. Plant Sci. 47:281–287.

Laird, A.S. 1930. A study of the root systems of some important sod-forming grasses. Univ. of Florida Agric. Exp. Stn. Bull. 211. p. 1–27.

Langvad, B. 1970. Soil heating under sports turf in Sweden. p. 252–257. In J.R. Escritt (ed.) Proc. 1st Int. Turfgrass Res. Conf., Harrogate, England. 15–18 July 1969. Sports Turf Res. Inst., Bingley, England.

Langvald, B. 1968. Ball-bouncing and ball-rolling as a function of mowing height and kind of soil have been studied at Weibullsholm. Weibulls Grastips. 10:355–357.

Lapp, W.S. 1943. A study of factors affecting the growth of lawn grasses. Proc. Penn. Acad. Sci. 17:117–148.

Laugham, D.G. 1941. The effect of light on growth habit of plants. Am. J. Bot. 28:951–956.

Ledeboer, F.B., and C.R. Skogley. 1963. Effects of various nitrogen sources timing, and rates on quality and growth rate of cool-season turfgrasses. Agron. J. 55:243–246.

Ledeboer, F.B., and C.R. Skogley. 1967. Plastic screens for winter protection. Golf Superintendent 35:22–23.

Lee, H., and C.E. Wright. 1981. Effective selection for animotriazole tolerance in Festuca and Agrostis turfgrasses. p. 41–46. In R.W. Sheard (ed.) Proc. 4th Int. Turfgrass Res. Conf., Guelph, ON, Canada. 19–23July. Int. Turfgrass Soc., and Ontario Agric. Coll., Univ. of Guelph, Guelph, ON.

Leopold, A.C., and P.E. Kriedeman. 1975. Plant growth and development. McGraw-Hill, New York.

Leukel, W.A., J.P. Camp, and J.M. Coleman. 1934. Effect of frequent cutting and nitrate fertilization on the growth behavior and relative composition of pasture grasses. Florida Agric. Exp. Stn. Bull. 269. p. 1–48.

Levy, E.B., and E.A. Madden. 1931. Weeds in lawns and greens—competition effects and control by treatment with chemical sprays. N.Z. J. Agric. 42:5(10):16–17.

Lewis, W.M., and W.B. Gilbert. 1966. The effect of siduron on crabgrass and goosegrass control and the establishment of five warm season and three cool season turfgrasses. Proc. South. Weed Conf. 19:150–154.

Lindgren, D.T., R.C. Shearman, A.H. Bruneau, and D.M. Schaaf. 1981. Kentucky bluegrass cultivar response to bluegrass billbug, Sphenophorus parvulus Gyllenhal. HortScience 16(3):339.

Lucanus, R., K.J. Mitchell, G.G. Pritchard, and D.M. Calder. 1960. Factors influencing survival of strains of ryegrass during the summer. N.Z. J. Agric. Res. 3:185–193.

Madison, J.H. 1960. The mowing of turfgrass. I. The effect of season, interval, and height of mowing on the growth of Seaside bentgrass turf. Agron. J. 52:449–452.

Madison, J.H. 1962a. Turfgrass ecology. Effects of mowing, irrigation and nitrogen treatments of Agrostis palustris Huds., 'Seaside' and Agrostis tenuis Sibth., 'Highland' on population, yield, rooting, and cover. Agron. J. 54:407–412.

Madison, J.H. 1962b. The effect of management practices on the invasion of lawn turf by bermudagrass (Cynodon dactylon L.). Proc. Am. Soc. Hortic. Sci. 80:559–564.

Madison, J.H. 1966. Optimum rates of seeding turfgrasses. Agron. J. 58:441–443.

Madison, J.H. 1971. Principles of turfgrass culture. Van Nostrand Reinhold Co., New York.

Madison, J.H., Jr., and R.H. Hagan. 1962. Extraction of soil moisture by Merion bluegrass (Poa pratensis L. 'Merion') turf as affected by irrigation frequency, mowing height, and other cultural operations. Agron. J. 54:157–160.

Mannering, J.V., and L.D. Meyer. 1963. The effect of various rates of surface mulch on infiltration and erosion. Soil Sci. Soc. Am. Proc. 27:84–86.

Mantell, A. 1966. Effect of irrigation frequency and nitrogen fertilization on growth and water use of kikuyagrass lawn (Pennisetum clandestinum Hockst.). Agron. J. 58:559–561.

Marsh, A.W. 1969. Soil water-irrigation and drainage. p. 151–186. In A.A. Hanson and F.V. Juska (ed.) Turfgrass science. Agron. Monogr. 14. ASA, Madison, WI.

Marsh, A.W., R.A. Strokman, S. Spaulding, V. Youngner, and V.G. Gibeault. 1980. Turfgrass irrigation research at the University of California. July/August 1980.

Mazur, G.C., R. Funk, W.K. Dickson, R.F. Bara, and J.M. Johnson-Cicalese. 1981. Reaction of perennial ryegrass varieties to sod webworm larvae. Rutgers Turfgrass Proc. 12:85–91.

McBee, G.C. 1970. Performance of certain cool season grasses in overseeding studies on a Tifgreen bermudagrass golf green. Texas A&M Univ., Texas Agric. Exp. Stn. Prog. Rep. 2457.

McBee, G.G., and E.C. Holt. 1966. Shade tolerance studies on bermudagrass and other turf-grasses. Agron. J. 58:523–525.

McKee, W.H., A.J. Powell, R.B. Cooper, and R.E. Blaser. 1965. Microclimate conditions found on highway slope facings as related to adaptation of species. Natl. Acad. Sci. Highway Res. Bull., Highway Res. Rec. 93:38–43.

McGinnes, W.J. 1960. Effects of moisture stress and temperature on germination of six range grasses. Agron. J. 52:159–162.

McMaugh, P.A. 1971. Control encroachment of *Agrostis* spp. sward by warm season turfgrasses. J. Sports Turf Res. Inst. 47:33–40.

McVey, G.R. 1968. How seedlings respond to phosphorus. Weeds, Trees, Turf 7(6):18–19.

Menn, W.G., and G.C. McBee. 1971. An evaluation of various cool-season grasses and grass mixtures in overseeding a Tifgreen bermudagrass golf green. Texas A&M Univ., Texas Agric. Exp. Stn. Prog. Rep. 2878.

Menzies, J.D. 1967. Plant diseases related to irrigation. p. 1058–1064. *In* R.M. Hagan et al. (ed.) Irrigation of agricultural lands. Agron. Monogr. 11. ASA, Madison, WI.

Meyers, H.G., and G.C. Horn. 1968. Selection of grasses for overseeding. p. 15–47. *In* Proc. Univ. Florida Turfgrass Management Conf.

Meyers, H.G., and G.C. Horn. 1970. The two-grass system in Florida. p. 110–117. *In* J.R. Escritt (ed.) Proc. 1st Int. Turfgrass Res. Conf., Harrogate, England. 15–18 July 1969. Sports Turf Res. Inst., Bingley, England.

Milthorpe, F.L. 1961. The nature and analysis of competition between plants of different species. *In* Mechanisms in biological competition. Symp. of the Soc. for Exp. Biol., No. XV. Academic Press, New York.

Mitchell, K.J. 1954. Influence of light and temperature on growth of ryegrass (*Lolium* spp.). III. Pattern and rate of tissue formation. Physiol. Planta 7:51–65.

Mitchell, K.J., and S.T.J. Coles. 1955. Effects of defoliation and shading on short-rotation ryegrass. N.Z. J. of Sci. Tech. Sec. A 36(6):586–604.

Moore, L.D., and H.B. Couch. 1963. Influence of environment on diseases of turfgrasses. III. Effect of nutrition, pH, soil temperature, air temperature, and soil moisture on *Pythium* blight of highland bentgrass. Phytopathology 53:53–57.

Morrish, R.H., and C.M. Harrison. 1948. The establishment and comparative wear resistance of various grasses and grass-legume mixtures to vehicular traffic. Agron. J. 40:168–179.

Muller, C.H. 1959. Allelopathy as a factor in ecological process. Vegetation 18:348–357.

Murphy, R.P., and A.C. Arny. 1939. The emergence of grass and legume seedlings planted at different depths in five soil types. J. Am. Soc. of Agron. 31:17–28.

Murray, J.J., and C.D. Foy. 1980. Lime responses of Kentucky bluegrass and tall fescue cultivars on an acid aluminum-toxic soil. p. 175–183. *In* J.B. Beard (ed.) Proc. 3rd Int. Turfgrass Res. Conf., Munich, Germany. 11–13 June 1977. Int. Turfgrass Soc., and ASA, CSSA, and SSSA, Madison, WI.

Murray, J.J., D.L. Klinman, R.G. Nash, and E.A. Woolson. 1983. Eight years of herbicide and nitrogen fertilizer treatments on Kentucky bluegrass (*Poa pratensis*) turf. Weed Sci. 31:825–831.

Musser, H.B. 1948. Effects of soil acidity and available phosphorus on population changes in mixed Kentucky bluegrass-bentgrass turf. Agron. J. 40:614–620.

Musser, H.B. 1962. Turf management. McGraw-Hill Book Co., New York.

Musser, H.B., and A.T. Perkins. 1969a. Guide to seedbed preparation. p. 462–489. *In* A.A. Hanson and F.V. Juska (ed.) Turfgrass science. Agron. Monogr. 14. Am. Soc. Agron., Madison, WI.

Musser, H.B., and A.T. Perkins. 1969b. Guide to planting. p. 447–490. *In* A.A. Hanson and F.V. Juska (ed.) Turfgrass science. Agron. Monogr. 14. ASA, Madison, WI.

Nelson, A. 1927. The germination of *Poa* spp. Ann. Appl. Biol. 14(2):157–174.

Oswalt, D.T., A.R. Bertrand, and M.R. Teel. 1959. Influence of nitrogen fertilization and clipping on grass roots. Soil Sci. Soc. Am. Proc. 23:288–290.

Pallas, J.E., Jr., and D.G. Harris. 1964. Transpiration, stomatal activity, and leaf temperature of cotton plants as influenced by radiant energy, relative humidity, and soil moisture tension. Plant Physiol. 39:1. iii(Abstract).

Parker, J.M., and C.J. Whitfield. 1941. Ecological relationships in playa lakes in the southern great plains. Agron. J. 33:125–129.

Parks, O.C., and P.R. Henderlong. 1967. Germination and seedling growth rates of ten common turfgrasses. Proc. W. Va. Acad. Sci. 39:132–140.

Pellett, H.M., and E.C. Roberts. 1963. Effects of mineral nutrition on high temperature induced growth retardation of Kentucky bluegrass. Agron. J. 55:473–476.

Perry, H.D. 1978. Culture of crownvetch (*Coronilla varia* L.) for slope stabilization. Ph.D. diss., Virginia Polytechnic Inst. and State Univ., Blacksburg.

Perry, H.D., D.L. Wright, and R.E. Blaser. 1975. Project 40: Producing vegetation on highway slopes concurrently with and subsequent to highway construction. Final Rep. Agron. Dep. Virginia Polytech. Inst. and State Univ., Blacksburg.

Phillips, R.E. 1968. Water diffusivity of germinating soybeans, corn, and cottonseed. Agron. J. 60:568–591.

Plummer, A.P. 1943. The germination and early seedling development of twelve range grasses. J. Am. Soc. of Agron. 35:19–34.

Porterfield, H.G. 1945. Survival of buffalograss following submersion in playas. Ecology 26:98–100.

Portz, H.L., J.J. Murray, and D.Y. Yeam. 1981. Zoysiagrass (*Zoysia yaponica* Steud.) establishment by seed. p. 113–122. *In* R.W. Sheard (ed.) Proc. 4th Int. Turfgrass Res. Conf., Guelph, ON, Canada. 19–23 July. Int. Turfgrass Soc., and Ontario Agric. Coll., Univ. of Guelph, Guelph, ON.

Powell, A.J., R.E. Blaser, and R.E. Schmidt. 1967a. Physiological and color aspects of turfgrasses with fall and winter nitrogen. Agron. J. 59:303–307.

Powell, A.J., R.E. Blaser, and R.E. Schmidt. 1967b. Effect of nitrogen on winter root growth of bentgrass. Agron. J. 59:529–530.

Putman, A.R., and W.B. Duke. 1978. Allelopathy in agroecosystems. Ann. Rev. Phytopathol. 16:431–451.

Radko, A.M. 1956. Hurricane damage in the northeast. USGA J. Turf Manage. 9(3):13–16.

Radko, A.M. 1968. Grooming your golf course is important. USGA Green Sect. Rec. 6(2):1–4.

Radko, A.M. 1974. Refining green section specifications for putting green construction. p. 287–297. *In* E.C. Roberts (ed.) Proc. 2nd Int. Turfgrass Res. Conf., Blacksburg, VA. 19–21 June 1973. ASA and CSSA, Madison, WI.

Raschke, K. 1960. Heat transfer between the plant and the environment. Ann. Rev. Plant Physiol. 11:111–126.

Rasmussen, J.A., and E.L. Rice. 1971. Allelopathic effects of *Sporobolus pyramidatus* on vegetation patterning. Am. Midl. Nat. 86:309–326.

Reid, M.E. 1933. Effects of shade on the growth of velvet bent and metropolitan creeping bent. Bull. USGA Green Sect. 13:131–135.

Rhoades, E.D. 1964. Inundation tolerance of grasses in flooded areas. Trans. ASAE 7(2):164–169.

Rhoades, E.D. 1967. Grass survival in flooded pool areas. J. Soil Water Conserv. 22:19–21.

Rhodes, I. 1968b. The growth and development of some grass species under competitive stress. 3. The nature of competitive stress and characters associated with competitive ability during seedling growth. J. Br. Grassl. Soc. 23:330–335.

Rhodes, I. 1969. The yield, canopy structure, and light interception of two ryegrass varieties in mixed culture and monoculture. J. Br. Grassl. Soc. 24:123–127.

Rice, E.L. 1974. Allelopathy. Academic Press, New York.

Richards, S.J., and L.V. Weeks. 1963. Evapotranspiration for turf measured with automatic irrigation equipment. Calif. Agric. 17(7):12–13.

Roberts, E.C. 1959. Changes in turfgrass cover, density, and frequency can be controlled. Golf Course Rep. 27(6).

Roberts, E.C., and F.E. Markland. 1967. Fertilizing helps turf crowd out weeds. Weed, Trees, Turf

Roberts, E.C., and F.E. Markland, and H.M. Pellet. 1966. Effects of bluegrass stand and watering regime on control of crabgrass with preemergence herbicides. Weeds 14:157–161.

Roberts, J.M. 1986. Influence of protective covers on reducing winter desiccation of turf. Agron. J. 78:145–147.

Rovira, A.D. 1969. Plant root exudates. Bot. Rev. 25:35–37.

Schery, R.W. 1966. Remarkable Kentucky bluegrass. Weeds, Trees, Turf 5(10):16–17.

Schmidt, B.L. 1961. Methods of controlling erosion on newly seeded highway backslopes in Iowa. Iowa Highway Res. Board Bull. 24.

Schmidt, R.E. 1967. Hydraulic vegetative planting of turfgrasses. Golf Superintendent 35( ):10–69.

Schmidt, R.E. 1970. Overseeding cool season turfgrasses on dormant bermudagrass for winter. p. 124–129. *In* J.R. Escritt (ed.) Proc. 1st Int. Turfgrass Res. Conf., Harrogate, England. 15–18 July 1969. Sports Turf Res. Inst., Bingley, England.

Schmidt, R.E. 1980. Bentgrass growth in relation to soil properties of typic hapludalfs soil variously modified for a golf green. p. 205–214. *In* J.B. Beard (ed.) Proc. 3rd Int. Turfgrass Res. Conf., Munich, Germany, 11–13 June 1977. Int. Turfgrass Soc., and ASA, CSSA, and SSSA, Madison, WI.

Schmidt, R.E., and R.E. Blaser. 1961. Cool season grasses for winter turf on bermuda putting greens. USGA J. Turf Manage. 14(5):25–29.

Schmidt, R.E., and R.E. Blaser. 1962. Establishing winter Bermuda putting turf. USGA J. Turf Manage. 15(5):30–32.

Schmidt, R.E., and R.E. Blaser. 1967a. Effect of temperature, light, and nitrogen on growth and metabolism of 'Cohansey' bentgrass (*Agrostis palustris* Huds.). Crop Sci. 7:447–451.

Schmidt, R.E., and R.E. Blaser. 1967b. Evaluation of turfgrasses for Virginia. Res. Div. V.P.I. Bull. 12.

Schmidt, R.E., and R.E. Blaser. 1969a. Ecology and turf management. p. 217–239. *In* A.A. Hanson and F.V. Juska (ed.) Turfgrass science. Agron. Monogr. 14. ASA, Madison, WI.

Schmidt, R.E., and R.E. Blaser. 1969b. Effect of temperature, light, and nitrogen on growth and metabolism of 'Tifgreen' bermudagrass (*Cynodon* spp.). Crop Sci. 9:5–9.

Schmidt, R.E., R.E. Blaser, and M.T. Carter. 1967. Evaluation of turfgrass for Virginia. Virginia Polytech. Inst. and State Univ. Res. Bull. 12.

Schmidt, R.E., and J.M. Breuninger. 1981. The effect of fertilization on recovery of Kentucky bluegrass turf from summer drought. p. 333–340. *In* R.W. Sheard (ed.) Proc. 4th Int. Turfgrass Res. Conf., Guelph, ON, Canada. 19–23 July. Int. Turfgrass Soc., and Ontario Agric. Coll., Univ. of Guelph, Guelph, ON.

Schmidt, R.E., and J.F. Shoulders. 1972. Winter turf development on dormant bermudagrass as influenced by summer cultivation and winter N fertilization. Agron. J. 64:435–437.

Schmidt, R.E., and J.F. Shoulders. 1980. Seasonal performance of selected temperate turfgrasses overseeded on bermudagrass turf for winter sports. p. 75–86. *In* J.B. Beard (ed.) Proc. 3rd Int. Turf. Res. Conf., Munich, Germany. 11–13 July 1977. Int. Turfgrass Soc., and ASA, CSSA, and SSSA, Madison, WI.

Schmidt, R.E., and L.H. Taylor. 1981. Botanical composition and turf quality of perennial ryegrass (*Lolium perenne* L.) Kentucky bluegrass (*Poa pratensis* L.) mixtures. p. 551–552. *In* R.W. Sheard (ed.) Proc. 4th Int. Turfgrass Res. Conf., Guelph, ON, Canada. 19–23 July. Int. Turfgrass Soc., and Ontario Agric. Coll., Univ. of Guelph, Guelph, ON.

Schull, C.A. 1929. A spectrophotometric study of reflection of light from leaf surfaces. Bot. Gaz. 87(5):583–607.

Siviour, T.R., and G.F. Schultz. 1981. Investigations into varied responses of couch (*Cynodon dactylon*) to field applications of Siduron. p. 546. *In* R.W. Sheard (ed.) Proc. 4th Int. Turfgrass Res. Conf., Guelph, ON, Canada. 19–23 July. Int. Turfgrass Soc., and Ontario Agric. Coll., Univ. of Guelph, Guelph, ON.

Skogley, C.R., and F.B. Ledeboer. 1968. Evaluation of several Kentucky bluegrasses and red fescue strains maintained as lawn turf under three levels of fertility. Agron. J. 60:47–49.

Snyder, V., and R.E. Schmidt. 1974. Nitrogen and iron fertilization of bentgrass. p. 176–185. *In* E.C. Roberts (ed.) Proc. 2nd Int. Turfgrass Res. Conf., Blacksburg, VA. 19–21 June 1973. ASA and CSSA, Madison, WI.

Sprague, H.B., and G.W. Burton. 1937. Annual bluegrass (*Poa annua* L.) and its requirements for growth. New Jersey Agric. Exp. Bull. 630.

Sprague, V.G., A.V. Havens, A.M. Decker, and K.E. Varney. 1955. Air temperatures in the microclimate at four latitudes in the northeastern U.S. Agron. J. 47:42–44.

Swanson, N.P., A.R. Dedrick, and A.E. Dudeck. 1966. Protecting steep construction slopes against erosion. I. Effects of selected mulches on seed, fertilizer, and soil loss. p. 40. *In* Agronomy abstracts. ASA, Madison, WI.

Swartz, W.E., and L.T. Kardos. 1963. Effects of compaction on physical properties of sand-soil-peat mixtures at various moisture contents. Agron. J. 55:7–10.

Tovey, R., J.S. Spencer, and D.C. Muckel. 1969. Turfgrass evapotranspiration. Agron. J. 61:863–867.

Throssell, C.S. 1981. Management factors affecting putting green speed. M.S. thesis. The Pennsylvania State Univ., University Park.

Troughton, A. 1957. The underground organs of herbage grasses. Bull. 44. Commonwealth Bureau Pasture Field Crops, Hurley, Berkshire, England.

Turgeon, A.J. 1980. Turfgrass management. Prentice-Hall Co., Reston, VA.

Turner, T.R., and D.V. Waddington. 1983. Soil test calibration for establishment of turfgrass monostands. Soil Sci. Soc. Am. J. 47:1161–1166.

Turner, T.R., D.V. Waddington, and T.L. Watschke. 1979. The effect of soil fertility levels on dandelion and crabgrass encroachment of Merion Kentucky bluegrass. Proc. NEWSS 33:280–286.

Van den Brink, C., and R.L. Carolus. 1965. Removal of atmospheric stresses from plants by overhead sprinkler irrigation. Michigan Agric. Exp. Stn. Bull. 47. p. 358–363.

Van Dersal, W.R. 1936. The ecology of a lawn. Ecology 17:515–527.

Vargas, J.M., Jr., and J.B. Beard. 1981. Shade environment—Disease relationships of Kentucky bluegrass cultivars. p. 391–395. In R.W. Sheard (ed.) Proc. 4th Int. Turfgrass Res. Conf., Guelph, ON, Canada. 19–23 July. Int. Turfgrass Soc., and Ontario Agric. Coll., Univ. of Guelph, Guelph, ON.

Vezina, P.E., and D.W.K. Boulter. 1966. The spectral composition of near ultra violet and visible radiation beneath forest canopies. Can. J. Bot. 44:1267–1284.

Waddinton, D.V., and J.H. Baker. 1965. Influence of soil aeration on the growth and chemical composition of three grass species. Agron. J. 57:253–258.

Waddington, D.V., T.L. Zimmerman, G.J. Shoop, L.T. Kardos, and J.M. Duich. 1974. Soil modification for turfgrass areas. I. Physical properties of physically amended soils. Pennsylvania State Univ., Coll. of Agric. Agric. Exp. Stn., University Park. Prog. Rep. 337.

Ward, C.Y. 1969. Climate and adaptation. p. 27–79. In A.A. Hanson and F.V. Juska (ed.) Turfgrass science. Agron. Monogr. 14. ASA, Madison, WI.

Ward, C.Y., E.L. McWhirter, and W.R. Thompson, Jr. 1974. Evaluation of cool-season turf species and planting techniques for overseeding bermudagrass golf greens. p. 480–495. In E.C. Roberts (ed.) Proc. 2nd Int. Turfgrass Res. Conf., Blacksburg, VA. 19–21 June 1973. ASA and CSSA, Madison, WI.

Watschke, T.L. 1974. Growth regulation of Kentucky bluegrass with commercial and experimental growth regulators. p. 474–479. In E.C. Roberts (ed.) Proc. 2nd Int. Turfgrass Res. Conf., Blacksburg, VA. 19–21 June 1973. ASA and CSSA, Madison, WI.

Watshcke, T.L., F.W. Long, and J.M. Duich. 1979. Control of Poa annua by suppression of seedheads with growth regulators. Weed Sci. 27:224–231.

Watshcke, T.L., R.E. Schmidt, and R.E. Blaser. 1970. Responses of some Kentucky bluegrasses to high temperature and nitrogen fertility. Crop Sci. 10:372–376.

Watschke, T.L., and D.V. Waddington. 1975. Effect of nitrogen fertilization on the recovery of 'Merion' Kentucky bluegrass from scalping and wilting. Agron. J. 67:559–562.

Watson, A.N. 1934. Further studies on the relation between thermal emissivity and plant temperatures. Am. J. Bot. 21:605–609.

Watson, J.R. 1950. Irrigation compaction on established fairway turf. Ph.D. thesis. Pennsylvania State Univ., University Park.

Watson, J.R., Jr. 1966. Frost protection. p. 68–74. In Proc. 20th Annu. Northwest Turfgrass Conf.

Watson, J.R., Jr. 1968. Blankets to protect golf greens against winter injury. p. 61. In Agronomy abstracts. ASA, Madison, WI.

Watson, J.R., Jr., H. Kroll, and L. Wicklund. 1960. Protecting golf greens against winterkill. Golf Course Rep. 28(7):10–16.

Watson, J.R., Jr., and L.W. Wicklund. 1962. Plastic covers protect greens from winter damage. Golf Course Rep. 30(9):30–38.

Welterlen, M.S., and T.L. Watschke. 1981. Techniques for thermocouple placement and the automation of temperature measurements in the microenvironment of Kentucky bluegrass. Agron. J. 73:808–812.

Welton, F.A., and J.D. Wilson. 1931. Water-supplying power of the soil under different species of grass and with different rates of water application. Plant Physiol. 6:485–493.

Whitcomb, E.C. 1972. Influence of tree root competition on growth response of cool-season turfgrasses. Agron. J. 64:355–359.

Wiegand, C.L., and L.N. Namken. 1966. Influence of plant moisture stress, solar radiation, and air temperature on cotton leaf temperature. Agron. J. 58:582–586.

Wischmeier, W.H. 1973. Conservation tillage to control water erosion. p. 133–141. In Conservation tillage Natl. Conf. Soil Conserv. Soc. of Am., March. Anheny, IA.

Wood, J.R., and R.L. Duble. 1976. Effects of nitrogen and phosphorus on establishment and maintenance of St. Augustinegrass. Texas Agric. Exp. Stn. RR-3368C.

Woodle, H.A. 1954. Coastal bermudagrass. Clemson Agric. Coll. Bull. 374.

Woodruff, J.M., J.T. Green, Jr., and R.E. Blaser. 1972. Weeping lovegrass for highway slopes in the Virginias. Natl. Acad. Sci. Highway Res. Bd. Highway Res. Rec., Washington, DC. 411:7-14.

Wright, D.L., R.E. Blaser, and J.M. Woodruff. 1978a. Seedling emergence as related to temperature and moisture tension. Agron. J. 70:709-712.

Wright, D.L., H.D. Perry, and R.E. Blaser. 1978b. Persistent low maintenance vegetation for erosion control and aesthetics in highway corridors. p. 553-583. *In* Reclamation of drastically disturbed lands. ASA, Madison, WI.

Wright, D.L., H.D. Perry, J.T. Green, Jr., and R.E. Blaser. 1975. Manual for establishing a vegetative cover in highway corridors of Virginia. Virginia Polytech. Inst. and State Univ., Blacksburg.

Yeam, D.Y., J.J. Murray, and H.L. Portz. 1981. Physiology of seed germination in zoysiagrass (*Zoysia japonica* Steud.). p. 467-476. *In* R.W. Sheard (ed.) Proc. 4th Int. Turfgrass Res. Conf., Guelph, ON, Canada. 19-23 July. Int. Turfgrass Soc., and Ontario Agric. Coll., Univ. of Guelph, Guelph, ON.

Youngner, V.B. 1959. Ecological studies on *Poa annua* in turfgrasses. J. Br. Grassl. Soc. 14:233-237.

Youngner, V.B. 1961. Population-density studies on cool-season turfgrasses grown in a subtropical climate. J. Br. Grassl. Soc. 16:222-225.

Youngner, V.B., A.W. Marsh, R.A. Strohman, V.A. Gibeault, and S. Spaulding. 1981. Water use and turf quality of warm-season and cool-season turfgrasses. p. 251-258. *In* R.W. Sheard (ed.) Proc. 4th Int. Turfgrass Res. Conf., Guelph, ON, Canada. 19-23 July. Int. Turfgrass Soc., and Ontario Agric. Coll., Univ. of Guelph, Guelph, ON.

5

Energy Relations and Carbohydrate Partitioning in Turfgrasses[1]

RICHARD J. HULL

University of Rhode Island
Kingston, Rhode Island

Since Dr. Youngner (1969) reviewed the subject of growth and development in the original monograph on turfgrass science, several reviews have appeared (Beard, 1973; Madison, 1971; Turgeon, 1985). While another analysis could be prepared based upon the advances that have occurred since the last review, it may be better to concentrate on energy relations and carbohydrate partitioning rather than turfgrass growth and development in general. These aspects of turfgrass biology have never been reviewed even though they have become a major focus of much contemporary research in crop physiology.

In some respects, closely mowed turf is a simple biological system. Apart from the period of establishment, which is a short time in the life of a turf, turfgrasses do little more than capture energy and use it to maintain and replace tillers and roots. Unlike most plant populations, which undergo profound ontogenetic changes during their seasonal growth cycle, properly managed turfgrasses mostly process energy for leaf production and maintenance. In an established turf, there is little seed germination, almost no flower induction, anthesis, fertilization, or seed production, and limited seasonal dormancy. The more complex aspects of turfgrass biology involve responses to environmental and biological stresses, interactions between plants and microorganisms comprising the turf community, and acquisition and cycling of water and nutrients for maintenance of the turf ecosystem. These subjects have been assigned to other chapters in this monograph.

For these reasons, this chapter emphasizes the energy relations that support the growth and development of a turfgrass stand. Even though energy flow is a primary activity in turfgrass growth and development, reports that address this subject area in turfgrasses are limited. Beard (1985) highlighted this fact in his review of turfgrass physiological research reported between 1981 and 1985, in which only 6 out of 61 papers were viewed as addressing turfgrass energy dynamics. Consequently, it will be necessary to draw from the broader physiological literature to develop the subject. Hopefully, this exercise will identify gaps and serve to stimulate research aimed at improving our understanding of this important subject.

---

[1] Contribution no. 2480 of the Rhode Island Agric. Exp. Stn., Kingston, RI 02881.

Copyright © 1992 ASA-CSSA-SSSA, 677 S. Segoe Rd., Madison, WI 53711, USA. *Turfgrass—Agronomy Monograph no. 32.*

I. PHOTOSYNTHESIS

A discussion of turfgrass energy relations might logically begin with photosynthesis, the ultimate energy capture and assimilation process. Currently, two basic pathways for photosynthetic CO_2 fixation have been identified. The first, originally described in algae and later in higher plants by Melvin Calvin and his associates (Bassham & Calvin, 1957), is commonly referred to as the reductive pentose phosphate cycle or C-3 pathway. C-3 refers to the number of carbon atoms present in the first stable metabolite resulting from CO_2 assimilation: 3-phosphoglyceric acid (PGA). The general reaction can be summarized as:

$$RuBP + CO_2 \rightarrow 2\ PGA.$$

RuBP is ribulose 1,5-bisphosphate, a five-carbon sugar that functions as the acceptor molecule and initial reductant for CO_2 (Bassham & Buchanan, 1982).

Later two research groups, one in Hawaii (Kortschak et al., 1965) and the other in Australia (Hatch & Slack, 1966), identified an alternate CO_2-assimilation pathway in sugarcane (*Saccharum officinarum* L.). The first stable metabolite in this pathway was a dicarboxylic anion containing four carbon atoms: oxaloacetate (OAA). The fixation reaction involves the carboxylation of phosphoenol-pyruvate (PEP) by a bicarbonate anion:

$$PEP + HCO_3^- \rightarrow OAA + H_2PO_4^-.$$

This pathway is called the *photosynthetic dicarboxylic acid cycle* or the C-4 pathway. Here HCO_3^- rather than CO_2 is the immediate substrate for the carboxylating enzyme: PEP carboxylase. In the cytoplasm of photosynthetic cells, CO_2 is in equilibrium with HCO_3^-. Under physiological conditions, this equilibrium favors a HCO_3^- concentration many times greater than that of CO_2. A C-4 route of CO_2 assimilation ultimately releases its fixed CO_2 within bundle sheath cells that surround the vascular bundles of leaves. There the CO_2 is reassimilated via the C-3 pathway (Ray & Black, 1979).

The benefit of the C-4 pathway lies in the high efficiency by which PEP carboxylase assimilates HCO_3^- and the capacity of the pathway for concentrating CO_2 within the chloroplasts of bundle sheath cells. There the less-efficient CO_2 assimilating enzyme of the C-3 pathway (RuBP carboxylase) will function more efficiently in the presence of elevated CO_2. Thus, the C-4 pathway serves as a preliminary CO_2 trap and transport system. Plants having the C-4 pathway ultimately depend on the C-3 cycle for CO_2 assimilation and reduction.

In C-4 plants, all leaf cells containing green chloroplasts are arranged radially around the vascular bundles. Frequently, there are several tiers of mesophyll cells, the most centripetal of which abut the single circle of bundle sheath cells surrounding each vascular bundle. This organization of photosynthetic cells is referred to as Kranz leaf anatomy in contrast to the less-ordered, more random distribution of mesophyll cells around the mostly chloroplast-deficient bundle sheath cells of C-3 plants. In C-4 photosynthesis, the outer mesophyll cells serve as antennae to capture and metabolize CO_2 from the CO_2-depleted atmosphere within grass leaves (e.g., $< 200 \ \mu L/L$). The resulting four-carbon anions malate or aspartate, which are synthesized directly from OAA, are transported to the bundle sheath cells adjacent to the conducting cells of the vascular bundles. There the four-carbon anions are decarboxylated, releasing CO_2 that accumulates to higher concentrations (0.8–1.9 mM) and is reassimilated and reduced in the C-3 pathway (Ray & Black, 1979).

The major reason RuBP carboxylase is a less-efficient CO_2 assimilating enzyme is that oxygen competes with CO_2 for the binding site of the enzyme. The O_2 is reduced and combines with RuBP to form one molecule of PGA and one molecule of phosphoglycolate (P-glycolate):

$$RuBP + O_2 \rightarrow PGA + \text{P-glycolate}.$$

This oxygenase activity of the enzyme reduces the CO_2-fixing efficiency by 50% or more (Lorimer, 1981). The P-glycolate in turn is metabolized via the glycolate oxidation cycle according to the net reaction:

$$2 \ \text{P-glycolate} + O_2 \rightarrow PGA + CO_2 + H_2PO_4^-.$$

The utilization of O_2 and liberation of CO_2 has led to the glycolate oxidation cycle being viewed as a respiratory pathway. Because P-glycolate is a photosynthetic product and made only in the light, the O_2 uptake and CO_2 release associated with P-glycolate metabolism is called *Photorespiration* (Ogren & Chollet, 1982).

Photorespiration releases CO_2 at the same time photosynthesis is fixing it. The net result of these two concurrent processes is a reduction in CO_2 exchange rate (CER). Photorespiration also causes an increase in the CO_2 compensation concentration (Γ) or the CO_2 concentration at which photosynthetic fixation and respiratory release are exactly equal and the plant causes no change in the atmospheric CO_2 concentration in which it is growing. C-4 plants exhibit little if any photorespiration. Because C-4 plants fix CO_2 via the PEP carboxylase enzyme, which does not exhibit competition between CO_2 and O_2, no P-glycolate is made that can be metabolized via photorespiration. In C-4 plants, the RuBP carboxylase is confined to the bundle sheath cells where elevated CO_2 concentrations favor the fixation of CO_2 rather than O_2. Any glycolate that may be produced through RuBP oxygenase activity in bundle sheath cells will be metabolized to CO_2 and PGA. The CO_2 is refixed via PEP carboxylase in the mesophyll cells before it can be lost to the atmosphere. If low levels of photorespiration occur in C-4 plants, they are never detected as a CO_2 release in the light.

This description of photosynthetic metabolism was presented to establish a basic understanding of the differences between C-3 and C-4 plants. To

Table 5-1. The CO_2 compensation concentration (Γ) of selected turfgrass and weed species and the photosynthesis type correlated with those values.

Plant species	Γ	Photosynthesis Type	Reference
	μL/L		
Cool-season turfgrasses			
Agrostis palustris Huds. (creeping bentgrass)	47	C-3	Krans et al., 1979
Agrostis tenuis Sibth. (colonial bentgrass)	65	C-3	Krans et al., 1979
Festuca arundinacea Schreb. (tall fescue)	45-69	C-3	Chen et al., 1970; Morgan & Brown, 1979
Festuca rubra L. (red fescue)	70	C-3	Krans et al., 1979
Lolium perenne L. (perennial ryegrass)	60	C-3	Krans et al., 1979
Poa annua L. (annual bluegrass)	46	C-3	Krans et al., 1979
Poa pratensis L. (Kentucky bluegrass)	55	C-3	Krans et al., 1979
Poa trivalis L. (rough bluegrass)	67	C-3	Krans et al., 1979
Warm-season turfgrasses			
Buchloë dactyloides (Nutt.) Engelm. (buffalograss)	<10	C-4	Krenzer et al., 1975
Cynodon dactylon (L.) Pers. (bermudagrass)	4-8	C-4	Chen et al., 1970; Krans et al., 1979
Eremochloa ophiuroides (Munro) Hackel (centipedegrass)	7	C-4	Krans et al., 1979
Paspalum notatum Fluegge (bahiagrass)	5-8	C-4	Chen et al., 1970; Krans et al., 1979
Stenotaphrum secundatum (Walter) Kuntze (St. Augustinegrass)	7	C-4	Krans et al., 1979
Zoysia japonica Steud. (zoysiagrass)	8	C-4	Krans et al., 1979
Turf weeds			
Cyperus esculentus L. (yellow netsedge)	15	C-4	Chen et al., 1970
Digitaria sanguinalis (L.) Scop. (large crabgrass)	1	C-4	Chen et al., 1970
Eleusine indica (L.) Gaertn. (goosegrass)	5	C-4	Chen et al., 1970
Mollugo verticillata L. (carpetweed)	24-40	Int.†	Sayre et al., 1979
Panicum dichotomiflorum Michx. (fall panicum)	<10	C-4	Krenzer et al., 1975
Paspalum dilatatum Poir. (dallisgrass)	2	C-4	Chen et al., 1970
Plantago lanceolata L. (buckhorn plantain)	43	C-3	Chen et al., 1970
Portulaca oleracea L. (common purslane)	2	C-4	Sayre et al., 1979

† Intermediate between C-3 and C-4.

appreciate why turfgrasses respond as they do to environmental variables such as temperature, light intensity, and CO_2 or O_2 concentrations, these photosynthetic distinctions must be understood.

Most turfgrasses (Krans et al., 1979) and some common turf weeds (Chen et al., 1970; Krenzer et al., 1975) have been identified as either C-3 or C-4 plants (Table 5-1). The C-3 and C-4 classification was based on leaf anatomy and CO_2 compensation concentration. Grasses exhibiting Kranz leaf anatomy and a CO_2 compensation concentration of 10 μL/L or less are regarded as C-4 plants. Plants not possessing Kranz anatomy and having a CO_2 compensation concentration >40 μL/L are classified as C-3 plants.

These data do not constitute proof of the CO_2 assimilation pathway. Only short-term $^{14}CO_2$-labeling experiments can do that, but the association between Kranz anatomy and a low CO_2 compensation concentration with C-4 photosynthesis is good.

Identifying plants having C-4 photosynthesis based on leaf anatomy is easy. It requires only the light microscopic observation of free-hand leaf sections. Carbon dioxide compensation concentration is no more difficult to measure, but it does require an infrared CO_2 analyzer. Care must be taken to make measurements on grasses growing under favorable conditions (Krans et al., 1979).

The path of CO_2 assimilation and the distribution of C-3 and C-4 enzymes between mesophyll and bundle sheath cells have been described for bermudagrass [*Cynodon dactylon* (L.) Pers.] and purple nutsedge (*Cyperus rotundus* L.) (Black et al., 1973). These limited observations support conclusions drawn from an analysis of leaf anatomy and CO_2-compensation concentration, namely that warm-season turfgrasses and summer weeds are all C-4 plants while cool-season grasses and spring or fall weeds exhibit C-3 photosynthesis (Table 5–1).

II. PHOTOSYNTHETIC EFFICIENCY

The physiological significance of a plant's photosynthetic CO_2 reduction pathway becomes apparent when its response to midsummer conditions is considered. The CER of several turfgrasses under high light and warm temperatures are summarized in Table 5–2. While the exact conditions under which these measurements were made varied, and in some cases the values reported are the average of several cultivars or experimental treatments, it is clear that CER of C-4 grasses is higher than that of C-3 grasses. This is true for grasses grown under controlled environments or in the field, and whether CER is expressed on a unit leaf area or standard land area basis.

The capacity of C-4 grasses to maintain a high CER during periods of elevated temperature when C-3 grasses suffer a decline gives the warm-season grasses a decided advantage. During mid-summer, when efficiency of energy capture for growth and maintenance of C-3 grasses becomes limiting, C-4 grasses are able to capture solar energy at their optimum efficiency (Ehleringer & Bjorkman, 1977). This difference in energy status between C-3 and C-4 grasses explains the aggressive growth of crabgrass in a heat stressed cool-season turfgrass sod. Warm-season turfgrasses grown in the South are most vigorous and exhibit their highest turf quality during the summer months while cool-season grasses, even when grown in the North, produce the best turf during spring and autumn (Beard, 1973).

High photorespiratory rates contribute most to the decline in CO_2 assimilation by cool-season grasses when grown under high temperatures. If the CER is measured at 2% O_2 instead of the atmospheric concentration of 21% O_2, the CER of C-3 grasses increases by an average of 45% while

Table 5-2. Carbon exchange rates (CER) of selected C-3 and C-4 grasses.

Grass	CER	Reference
	mg CO_2/(dm^2 h)	
Expressed on a leaf surface basis		
Cynodon dactylon (L.) Pers. (bermudagrass C-4)	82	Chen et al., 1970
Eleusine indica (L.) Gaertn. (goosegrass C-4)	77	Chen et al., 1970
Poa pratensis L. (Kentucky bluegrass C-3)	15–18	Krans & Beard, 1980; Wilkinson et al., 1975
Festuca rubra L. (red fescue C-3)	13–23	Krans & Beard, 1980; Wilkinson et al., 1975
Festuca arundinacea Schreb. (tall fescue C-3)	28–31	Chen et al., 1970; Morgan & Brown, 1979
Expressed on a turf area basis		
Cynodon dactylon (L.) Pers. (bermudagrass C-4)	36	Karnok & Beard, 1983
Eremochloa ophiuroides (Munro)Hackel (centipedegrass C-4)	35	Walker & Ward, 1974
Poa pratensis L. (Kentucky bluegrass C-3)	14–26	Karnok & Augustin, 1981; Mehall et al., 1974
Stenotaphrum secundatum (Walter) Kuntze (St. Augustinegrass C-4)	41–62	Karnok & Beard, 1983; Peacock & Dudeck, 1984

the O_2 concentration has no effect on the CER of C-4 grasses (Morgan & Brown, 1979). This differential O_2 sensitivity between C-3 and C-4 grasses is linked to the tendency of RuBP carboxylase to assimilate O_2 when CO_2 is in short supply. Because C-3 plants depend upon RuBP carboxylase as their primary CO_2 trapping enzyme, they are more susceptible to O_2 inhibition than are C-4 plants that use the O_2 insensitive enzyme PEP carboxylase as their CO_2 trap.

Supraoptimal temperatures favor the binding of O_2 to the reaction sites of the enzyme more than it does CO_2 mostly because of the declining concentration of dissolved CO_2 in solution as the temperature increases. Hall and Keys (1983) determined that elevated temperatures did not alter the oxygenase to carboxylase ratio if the O_2 and CO_2 concentrations were held constant (0.34 mM and 14 μM, respectively). When the O_2 and CO_2 concentrations were allowed to decrease as temperature increased, the oxygenase to carboxylase activity ratio increased 2.2 fold (i.e., 0.25 at 10 °C to 0.56 at 35 °C). While both CO_2 and O_2 become less soluble in water as the temperature increases, the CO_2 concentration is most critical because it is generally equal to or less than the Km-CO_2 for the carboxylase enzyme. The Km of an enzyme for a specific substrate is the concentration of that substrate which will support one-half the maximum reaction rate of the enzyme. This means that even a small reduction in CO_2 concentration will markedly decrease RuBP carboxylase activity. Oxygenase activity is also reduced but not by as much. Also, the exact concentrations of these gases in the stroma of illuminated chloroplasts, where CO_2 is being consumed and O_2 is released, are difficult to measure.

C-4 plants avoid these problems of gas solubility by trapping CO_2 in the HCO_3^- form via PEP carboxylase and increasing the CO_2 concentration in bundle sheath cells where RuBP carboxylase can operate under near-optimum conditions. This increased photosynthetic efficiency under conditions of high light and elevated temperature also makes C-4 plants more efficient in their use of water (Black et al., 1969). Because more CO_2 passes through open stomata per unit time into C-4 leaves, less water is lost for each gram of CO_2 assimilated. Thus, C-3 grasses transpire about 650 g water for each gram of dry matter produced and C-4 grasses use only 300 g per gram of dry matter (Shantz & Piemeisel, 1927). While turf managers are not interested in dry matter production per se, this difference in water use efficiency is reflected in a lower evapotranspiration rate for warm-season turfgrasses when compared to that of cool-season grasses (Biran et al., 1981; Kneebone & Pepper, 1982; Youngner et al., 1981). The CO_2 gradient between substomatal intercellular space and the ambient atmosphere is greater for illuminated leaves of C-4 grasses than it is for C-3 leaves (El-Sharkawy & Hesketh, 1965). Consequently, equivalent CO_2 flux rates can be sustained when the stomatal resistance of the C-4 grass is greater than that of the C-3. This will result in less water loss and a greater water use efficiency.

An additional distinction between C-4 photosynthesis over the C-3 pathway is the efficiency by which plants use N (Brown, 1978). Nitrogen use efficiency is expressed as the quantity of dry matter produced per unit of N present in the tissue (Gerloff, 1976). A nutrient efficiency value can be derived from the N content of leaf tissue by the equation:

N use efficiency (mg dry matter/mg N) = 1000/mg N/g dry matter.   [1]

Photosynthetic N use efficiency is defined as the CO_2 fixed per unit of N in a unit leaf area or leaf mass. Both expressions of nutrient use efficiency normally show C-4 grasses to be more efficient in their use of leaf N than C-3 grasses (Hallock et al., 1965; Wilson & Haydock, 1971). Nitrogen content of leaf tissues for several C-3 and C-4 grasses is summarized in Table 5–3.

The basis for greater N efficiency in C-4 grasses has been linked to a smaller allocation of leaf N to the CO_2 carboxylating enzyme, RuBP carboxylase (Brown, 1978). In most C-3 plants, RuBP carboxylase is the most abundant protein comprising more than 50% of total leaf N. By comparison, the leaves of C-4 plants allocate only 10 to 15% of their protein to RuBP carboxylase in bundle sheath cells. The primary CO_2 trapping enzyme, PEP carboxylase, in mesophyll cells is almost as large as RuBP carboxylase but it constitutes only about 10% of leaf protein. Thus, the N investment in CO_2 assimilating enzymes in C-4 plants is about one-half of what it is in C-3 plants. This relationship constitutes a major economy in the quantity of N required to do the work of photosynthesis in C-4 plants.

An alternative or companion theory explaining the greater N use efficiency in C-4 plants was proposed by Moore and Black (1979). Based

Table 5-3. Leaf N content of selected turfgrasses.

Turfgrass	Leaf N	Reference
	mg/g dry wt.†	
	C-3 Grasses	
Festuca rubra. var. *commutata* Gaud. (chewings fescue)	48.4	Turner & Waddington, 1983
Agrostis palustris Huds. (creeping bentgrass)	49.2	Waddington et al., 1978
Festuca rubra L. (creeping red fescue)	39.4	Waddington et al., 1975
Poa pratensis L. (Kentucky bluegrass)	37.6	Goss & Law, 1967
	35.5	Hall & Miller, 1974
	42.0	Hull & Smith, 1974
	55.9	Turner & Waddington, 1983
	42.9	Waddington et al., 1975
Lolium perenne L. (perennial ryegrass)	39.8	Sills & Carrow, 1983
	53.6	Turner & Waddington, 1983
Festuca arundinacea Schreb. (tall fescue)	30.1	Hallock et al., 1965
	C-4 Grasses	
Paspalum notatum Fluegge (bahiagrass)	13.6	Impithuksa et al., 1984
Cynodon dactylon (L.) Pers. (bermudagrass)	25.4	Hallock et al., 1965
Digitaria macroglossa Henr. and *Paspalum dilatatum* Poir. dallisgrass)	13.1	Colman & Lazenby, 1970

† Most values presented are averages of several experimental treatments or cultivars.

on analyses of isolated mesophyll cells and bundle sheath strands from large crabgrass [*Digitaria sanguinalis* (L.) Scop.] leaves, they determined that the enzymes required for nitrate (NO_3) reduction and assimilation were segregated between the two cell types. Both nitrate and nitrite (NO_2) reductases were concentrated exclusively in the mesophyll cells while the ammonium (NH_4)-assimilating enzymes, glutamine synthetase and glutamate synthase, were present in both cell types. The NO_3-reducing enzymes being confined to mesophyll cells permits these cells to function as NO_3 traps just as they do to trap CO_2. The heavy demand for reducing equivalents required to reduce NO_3 can most easily be met by mesophyll cells that are more readily illuminated and more highly endowed with the electron transport components needed for the synthesis of adequate NADPH (Mayne, 1971). The O_2 released during the photosynthetic generation of reducing potential will be less inhibitory to CO_2 fixation in mesophyll cells than it would be in bundle sheath cells where RuBP carboxylase is situated. The amino acids resulting from NO_3 metabolism in mesophyll cells also serve as transport vehicles for CO_2 and N to bundle sheath cells. This division of labor for NO_3 reduction and assimilation between cell types of C-4 leaves may contribute to the greater N use efficiency in warm-season grasses.

A comparative study between *Panicum* spp. that include C-3, C-4, and plants with characteristics of both C-3 and C-4 photosynthesis (intermediate plants) did not show a strong correlation between C-4 photosynthesis and increased N use efficiency (Wilson & Brown, 1983; Brown & Wilson, 1983). Nitrogen use efficiency of grasses generally increased slightly as temperature increased. The relative availability of N exerted a more complex effect on the efficiency of N use. Low N reduced the relative growth rate, CER, and leaf expansion rate of C-4 grasses less than it did that of C-3 or intermediate species. However, other growth factors such as specific leaf weight, leaf area expansion rate, and the partitioning of dry matter to stem or other organs that contain less N can negate the positive influence of C-4 photosynthesis on N use efficiency.

A recent study compared the N use efficiency of two morphologically and ecologically similar annual weeds, redroot pigweed (*Amaranthus retroflexus* L.) and common lambsquarters (*Chenopodium album* L.) that are C-4 and C-3 dicotyledons, respectively (Sage & Pearcy, 1987a, b). Lambsquarters contained 50% more N per unit leaf area than pigweed. At high N, N use efficiency, expressed either as net assimilation rate per unit N or relative growth rate per unit N, was greater for the C-4 pigweed than the C-3 lambsquarters. At low applied N, lambsquarters had a higher N use efficiency than pigweed. Leaf partitioning coefficients were similar for both plants grown at high N levels but, when cultured at low N, the pigweed partitioned more photosynthetic product to leaf area than did lambsquarters. The leaves of low N pigweed contained less N per unit area, often exhibited deficiency symptoms, and became necrotic. This resulted in low CERs and a decreased N use efficiency. Similar observations were made by Wilson and Brown (1983) on N-deprived *Panicum maximum*, the most typical C-4 grass they studied.

These findings led to the general conclusion that leaf expansion rate is less tightly linked to leaf N content in C-4 plants. C-3 plants require greater amounts of carboxylating enzyme per unit of functional leaf surface. If the N necessary to synthesize that enzyme is lacking, less leaf surface is produced. Thus C-3 plants normally will contain more N on a leaf area basis than will C-4 plants, especially when available N is limiting. This means that C-4 plants will exhibit greater N use efficiency when N is abundant and reduced N efficiency when the N supply is inadequate.

These conclusions were generally confirmed by Sinclair and Horie (1989) in their review of plant dry matter accumulation during vegetative growth of soybean [*Glycine max* (L.) Merr.], rice (*Oryza sativa* L.), and maize (*Zea mays* L.) as a function of leaf N content, CO_2 assimilation rate, and crop radiation use efficiency. They concluded that maize (C-4) allocated more carbon to leaf area production at all N levels than did soybean or rice (C-3) and this resulted in greater radiation use efficiency by the C-4 plant. For any rate of N supply, an optimum leaf N content exists that supports maximum growth and that optimum N level is lower for C-4 plants.

The implications of such findings for turfgrass nutrition have never been studied but it appears that N should be managed differently for C-3 and C-4 grasses. Stimulating leaf growth in C-3 turfgrasses will result in greater N loss from the plants when that growth is removed during mowing. Warm-season grasses probably can tolerate lower N rates to support equivalent growth, but care must be taken to avoid a N-deficient condition that would reduce the efficiency of N use. This may be especially true during mid-summer heat when the demands for photosynthate will be maximum. Reduced photosynthetic efficiency caused by insufficient N likely will result in greater vulnerability to pathogen attack and thinning of the stand. By comparison, cool-season grasses might suffer less from low N during mid-summer because leaf growth will be depressed by supraoptimal temperatures and N-deprived C-4 weeds should be less competitive. This may be a fertile area for future research in turfgrass management.

The obvious advantages of C-4 photosynthesis for greater heat tolerance, reduced water use, and increased N use efficiency of turfgrasses has thus far prompted little research directed to breeding cool-season grasses that possess C-4 characteristics. The potential for such genetic manipulation is limited because most turfgrass genera are either C-3 or C-4 with no intermediate species having been identified. A very different situation exists in the genus *Panicum* (Morgan & Brown, 1979) where both C-3 and C-4 species are present and at least three intermediate species have been identified. These intermediate species have more variable ploidy levels ($2n-6n$) than do the C-3 species that are all tetraploid or the C-4 species that are diploid or tetraploid (Bouton et al., 1981). These findings suggest that ploidy level may be involved in photosynthetic efficiency possibly due to past interspecific hybridization.

Garret (1978) discovered that a doubling of ploidy in various perennial ryegrass cultivars lowered the Km-CO_2 of purified RuBP carboxylase by about one-half (51 and 22 μM CO_2 for the diploid and tetraploid, respectively) without affecting the inhibitory binding affinity of O_2. This finding was confirmed by Rathnam and Chollet (1980) who compared leaf mesophyll protoplasts isolated from isogenic diploid and tetraploid cultivars of perennial ryegrass. Atmospheric O_2 levels inhibited photosynthetic CO_2 fixation of the diploid cells by 36% and that of tetraploid cells by 27%. Both cell cultures exhibited equal capacity for metabolizing added glycolate and glycine to liberate CO_2, thereby demonstrating unimpaired photorespiratory metabolism. However, the tetraploid cells when exposed to 10.5 μM CO_2 and 21% O_2 incorporated 18.4% of fixed carbon into glycolate, while the diploid cells shunted 37% of their photosynthetically fixed carbon to glycolate. Later studies by McNeil et al. (1981) demonstrated that the kinetic properties of carefully isolated and activated RuBP carboxylase from the two genotypes were in fact identical: Km-CO_2 = 9.8 and 9.1 μM CO_2 for the diploid and tetraploid, respectively. Thus, it appears that differences in the capacity to assimilate CO_2 between these perennial ryegrasses is due to some mechanism other than the Km-CO_2 of the carboxylase enzyme. Genetic potential for increased photosynthetic efficiency exists but it will more likely be linked to CO_2 transport and mechanisms for its concentration at the carboxylating sites.

A further indication of the potential for increased photosynthetic efficiency in a turfgrass species was offered by a series of investigations at the University of Missouri initiated with a report by Randall et al. (1977).

They observed a 69% increase in CER of a decaploid tall fescue genotype over that of 10 hexaploid types. This greater photosynthetic rate of the decaploid plants was associated with a greater specific activity of RuBP carboxylase and a somewhat lower activity of photorespiratory enzymes. In a later comparison of tall fescue ploidy levels ranging from $4n$ to $10n$, Byrne et al. (1981) noted a decrease in diffusive resistance to CO_2 flux and an increase in CER with increasing ploidy level. Vein size of leaves tended to decrease (i.e., larger percentage of minor veins) and mesophyll cell volume increased as ploidy level and CER increased. Joseph and Randall (1981) studying a similar range of tall fescue genotypes found the concentration of RuBP carboxylase and its percentage of total leaf protein increased with ploidy level and CER. Specific activity of the carboxylase did not increase significantly with ploidy. They concluded that polyploidization increased selectively the allocation of total leaf protein for the synthesis of RuBP carboxylase and this was best correlated with increased CER.

When Krueger and Mikles (1981) compared the Photosystem I electron transport activities of the decaploid tall fescue with a hexaploid (Kentucky-31), they found the electron transport activity to be consistently higher in the decaploid. They suggested that the increased ATP production associated with greater photosynthetic electron transport might contribute to the greater CER of the decaploid plants. However, when they compared 24 genotypes ranging from $2n$ to $10n$, no correlation between polyploidy and photosynthetic activity was found. They concluded that simple increases in gene mass did not explain increased photosynthetic activity in tall fescue. Rather, specific genes that may be expressed more at one ploidy level than another could account for greater electron transport and phosphorylation rates and these genes should be transferable to and expressed by other ploidy levels thereby increasing their photosynthetic efficiency.

These studies show at least one important consideration in the search for improved turfgrasses, namely that physiological efficiency is under genetic control and the potential exists for cultivar improvement at the physiological level. For such improvement to occur, much greater research emphasis must be given to the physiology and biochemistry underlying turfgrass performance than has already occurred.

III. ENERGY PARTITIONING

Research into the mechanisms and regulation of photosynthate partitioning in plants has enjoyed renewed activity since 1980 and has been the subject of several reviews (Geiger & Giaquinta, 1982; Thorne, 1985; Ho, 1988; Lucas & Madore, 1988). By comparison, the distribution of energy within grasses maintained as a closely mowed turf has received little attention. What follows is a fragmentary picture pieced together from those few studies that bear directly or indirectly on the subject of energy partitioning in turf.

Early seedling growth and development are critical during turf establishment. Most turfgrass species have small seeds so the energy supply available for seedling establishment is limited. Pregermination for 48 h on blotters soaked with water or a solution of gibberellic acid (GA$_3$) markedly increased the germination rate and total germination percentage of Italian ryegrass (*Lolium multiflorum* Lam.) and Kentucky 31 tall fescue (Dudeck & Peacock, 1986). Such pregermination treatments mobilize sugars from endosperm starch and initiate embryo growth so the seed is capable of more rapid radicle extension and quicker establishment than normal seeding procedures. By accelerating the seedling establishment process, pregermination should reduce vulnerability to desiccation and other adverse conditions.

Krans and Beard (1980) monitored changes in energy distribution for seedling development of 'Pennlawn' red fescue and 'Merion' Kentucky bluegrass. This study is unique to the turf literature in that mass distributions, CER, dark respiration, and photosynthate partitioning were all measured for 70 d following seedling emergence. Photosynthetic rates of both red fescue and Kentucky bluegrass were high during the first 7 d of growth, averaging 95 and 118% greater than the CER recorded for the remaining 63 d. During the initial week, dark respiration was twice its later rate reflecting a time of rapid growth. The high CERs coinciding with elevated respiration rates were surprising and were not explained by the authors. Aoyagi and Bassham (1986) have observed low levels of some enzymes for C-4 photosynthesis in seedling leaves of C-3 wheat (*Triticum aestivum* L.). They suggested that a modified C-4 pathway could serve to concentrate CO$_2$ in the chloroplasts of mesophyll cells and contribute to enhanced photosynthetic efficiency. While their case for a significant C-4 pathway in wheat was not supported by the data, it does open the possibility for such a mechanism to be operative in seedlings of other C-3 grasses. The data of Krans and Beard (1980) may indicate such a transient C-4 phase in small-seeded cool-season turfgrasses that could provide an initial increase in available energy during seedling establishment. This additional energy would result from depressed photorespiration; a phenomenon that easily could be tested experimentally.

The seedling grass was clipped weekly at a 7.5-cm height following the fourth week of growth (Krans & Beard, 1980). Under those conditions, roots constituted about one-third of plant dry weight, a condition that was constant after 21 d of growth. Photosynthate partitioning to roots of red fescue, measured as percent distribution of carbon-14 (^{14}C) 24 h following exposure to ^{14}CO$_2$, declined over a 56-d period from 27 to 10% of assimilated carbon. The allocation of current photosynthate to roots declined more rapidly in Kentucky bluegrass (within 42 d) to <10% of assimilated carbon. Similar values for carbon partitioning to roots in mature Kentucky bluegrass turf during summer conditions have been reported (Hull & Smith, 1974; Hull, 1976). Apparently, the source to sink relationship between roots and shoots of closely mowed grasses is determined early during the establishment of cool-season turf.

The stem fraction, which consisted of leaf sheath and crown tissues, constituted about 25% of the plant dry weight throughout the 70 d observed (Krans & Beard, 1980). The percentage of current photosynthate allocated to the stem tissues increased from 20 to 26% during the first week after emergence to more than 50% by week 3 in Kentucky bluegrass and week 5 in red fescue. Established Kentucky bluegrass turf grown under field conditions also allocated 50% of current photosynthate to the stem fraction during the spring but lesser amounts at other times of the year (Hull & Smith, 1974).

Leaf blades comprised almost 60% of the seedling dry weight, but this declined to about 40% by Week 5 and remained constant thereafter (Krans & Beard, 1980). Photosynthate retention in leaf blades 24 h after exposure to $^{14}CO_2$ exhibited a pattern similar to that for dry weight distribution. This condition was similar to the percentage of current photosynthate recovered in leaves of mature Kentucky bluegrass turf during late May (Hull & Smith, 1974).

These studies indicated that seedling stands of cool-season turfgrasses mowed at 7.5 cm achieved a pattern of current photosynthate distribution within 42 to 49 d that is similar to that observed in vigorously growing mature turf. Cool-season turfgrasses maintained under growth chamber conditions ($23°C/14$ h d $\times$ $16°C/10$ h night, $600\mu M$ m^{-2} s^{-1} PPFD) exhibited a photosynthate partitioning pattern similar to that observed in the field during late May in the Northeast (Krans & Beard, 1980).

Tiller initiation was observed at the three-leaf stage in red fescue and at the five-leaf stage in Kentucky bluegrass or 21 to 28 d after seedling emergence (Krans & Beard, 1980). Tillers emerged only from buds in leaf axils of fully expanded leaves. Rhizome initiation followed tiller emergence in red fescue but both lateral shoots appeared concurrently in Kentucky bluegrass. Rhizomes became a stronger sink for current photosynthate in Kentucky bluegrass than they did in red fescue but they never received more than 5% of assimilated ^{14}C. Although Krans and Beard (1980) suggested that rhizomes constitute a strong sink for photosynthate and have priority over roots in the partitioning of photoassimilated carbon, it is questionable if that is so in a turf except during establishment. Twenty-four hours after exposure to $^{14}CO_2$, rhizomes in mature Kentucky bluegrass stands never contained more than 0.5% of the ^{14}C recovered in the turfgrass plants (Hull, 1987). Krans and Beard (1985) observed values >5% but they were studying individual plants growing in sand-filled pots. Photosynthate allocation to subterranean stems is probably greatly restricted when their growth is physically confined by conditions in a dense sod. Valid samples of living rhizomes rarely were collected from mature stands of Merion Kentucky bluegrass (Hull & Smith, 1974; Hull, 1981) although rhizomes generally were present in Baron Kentucky bluegrass sod. Intraspecific differences in rhizome production within established turfs are suggested and may partially explain differences in rates of injury recovery and wear tolerance.

The amount of energy allocated to lateral shoot growth is influenced by turf management practices. Low cutting height and frequent mowing, which reduce the photosynthetic product available to the plant, result in a suppression of rhizome growth by Kentucky bluegrass (Eggens, 1981; Juska & Hanson, 1961). Low cutting heights frequently produce a turf containing greater numbers of small plants (Ledeboer, 1974; Madison & Hagan, 1962). Mowing tall fescue at a 2.5 cm height produced a sod of plants with fewer tillers than were present on uncut plants (Laude & Fox, 1982). In the same study, Russian wild rye (*Elymus junceus* Fisch.) produced more tillers per plant when mowed at a 0.5 to 5.0 cm height than did uncut plants. The number of tiller buds in the axils of leaf sheaths was three times greater in Russian wildrye than in tall fescue and this probably accounted for the difference in tillering response to mowing. Higher cut promoted increased tillering in tall fescue and leaf blade width was negatively correlated ($r = -0.67$) with tillering rate (Asay et al., 1977). Maximum tillering of six genotypes occurred at a 22/12 °C day/night temperature and declined sharply when temperature was increased. These results are encouraging for the development of superior turf-type tall fescues but indicate that high temperature suppression of tillering may be a problem when tall fescue is grown in the transition zone.

The pattern of energy transfer to lateral shoots of turfgrass plants has received little study. Photosynthate will translocate from parent culms to stolons of bermudagrass at any time that growth is occurring (Forde, 1966a). The sink strength for photosynthate is directly related to stolon size. Culms that have emerged from stolons will also transport photosynthate to the parent stem. Photoassimilate movement from one stolon to another occurs rarely in intact plants growing in full light. However, darkening or partial defoliation of a stolon can induce photoassimilate movement from an adjacent intact and illuminated stolon. In a companion study, Forde (1966b) traced photosynthate between tillers of perennial ryegrass plants. He noted substantial intertiller transport even when no tillers were defoliated. Similar results were reported by Clifford et al. (1973) in Italian ryegrass and St.-Pierre and Wright (1972) in timothy (*Phleum pratense* L.). Grasses used in these studies were not managed as closely mowed turf, but they indicate substantial potential for lateral transfer of energy between all components (tillers, rhizomes, stolons, and roots) which constitute turfgrass plants. This may impart considerable plasticity to turf stands by permitting energy exchange between plant organs in response to mowing, mechanical injury, or disease. It also may explain why sod-forming turfgrasses (those producing rhizomes or stolons) often maintain greater turf density and tend to recover more quickly from injury than do turfs composed of bunch-type grasses (Turgeon, 1985). The significance of photosynthate exchange between culms of a closely mowed turf is a subject for further research. Since the potential for such energy exchange clearly exists, breeding for this capacity in turfgrasses may markedly enhance their performance in the turf environments.

Root growth in turfgrasses has received somewhat more attention than has lateral shoot production. Early in seedling development, roots of Kentucky bluegrass and red fescue constitute a significant sink for current photosynthate (Krans & Beard, 1980). Once an established Kentucky bluegrass turf is present, approximately 5 to 10% of current photosynthate is allocated to roots of vigorously growing grass (Hull, 1976; Hull & Smith, 1974). This varies substantially with the season, being less during midsummer and early autumn (Hull, 1981; Mehall et al., 1984) when a 0.5 to 3% allocation to roots is typical. During the winter, before the ground freezes, Kentucky bluegrass roots can acquire more than 15% of current photosynthate (Hull, 1976; Hull & Smith, 1974). Winter root growth of cool-season grasses has been reported from several places (Hanson & Juska, 1961; Powell et al., 1967; Stuckey, 1941) and in a rhizotron study, Koski et al. (1988) observed that between January and June, accumulated degree-days accounted for 95% of the variation in root growth of 'Baron' Kentucky bluegrass. Nevertheless, the regulation of photosynthate partitioning to roots of turfgrass plants has received little attention. Hanson and Branham (1987) noted that four plant growth regulators that inhibited shoot growth elicited varied responses in the translocation of ^{14}C-photosynthate to roots of 'Majestic' Kentucky bluegrass. Given the importance of this phenomenon to the success of a turfgrass stand, it is likely that energy partitioning to roots will become an important area of future turfgrass research.

An interesting interaction between root growth and N fertility has been identified. During the growing season, elevated N levels have a negative impact on root growth of cool-season grasses (Adams et al., 1974; Goss & Law, 1967; Madison, 1962). This is reflected in decreased partitioning of photosynthate to the roots of heavily fertilized turf (Hull, 1976, 1981, 1987; Hull & Smith, 1974). The energy demand imposed by NO_3 reduction and the assimilation of NH_4 (Miflin, 1980) uses carbohydrates in the roots and stimulates vegetative shoot growth. This shunting of energy to the shoots detracts from energy available for root growth. This effect seems to be negated during the winter when low air temperatures depress shoot growth but photosynthesis continues, sometimes at CERs equal to those observed in mid-summer (R.J. Hull, 1974, unpublished data). Under these conditions, carbohydrates are produced in the leaves and are translocated to roots 2 to 10 times more rapidly than during the growing season (Hull & Smith, 1974). During this time, no effect of N nutrition on photosynthate transport to roots is observed (Powell et al., 1967; Hull & Smith, 1974). If high rates of N are applied during the winter months (1.0 kg 100 m^{-2} month^{-1}), root growth is inhibited (Powell et al., 1967). Apparently the energy demand required to metabolilze N absorbed by roots in the winter does not subside enough to maintain root growth.

Root growth of warm-season grasses is less inhibited by midsummer conditions (DiPaola et al., 1982) than is that of cool-season grasses. The average daily root extension rate of St. Augustinegrass [*Stenotaphrum secundatum* (Walter) Kuntze] and bermudagrass observed in rhizotron studies at Texas A&M University was five times greater than that reported for creeping bentgrass (Beard & Daniel, 1965). Rooting depth of both species exceeded 70 cm but over three-quarters of the root mass was confined to the upper 20 cm of soil. Fall root growth declined rapidly as the soil cooled but continued for about 30 d after shoot growth ceased. During the winter, no root growth was observed although roots appeared healthy and capable of functioning.

In March, when new leaf growth was first observed, roots of both species rapidly turned brown (Di Paola et al., 1982). New root initiation occurred from both nodes of stems and crowns 1 d and 14 d after the rapid root decline of bermudagrass and St. Augustinegrass, respectively. For both species, the reestablishment of an effective root system was delayed about 21 d. Later investigations extended this observation of a spring root decline to seven warm-season turfgrass species (Sifers et al., 1985). However, continued observations demonstrated that spring root decline did not occur every year, only during 4 of 8 yr studied. Root death was noted only during those years when soil warming was rapid and shoot greening occurred early or followed a cold winter. When shoot growth was delayed by cold spring conditions and greening was slow, no root decline was observed. This interaction of root death and temperature induced shoot growth was confirmed under controlled conditions (Sifers et al., 1985).

Sifers et al. (1985) explained this sudden root death phenomenon as a diversion of stem carbohydrates from roots to emerging shoots during rapid green-up resulting in an energy deficit in the roots such that death occurred. This could explain the situation; however, it is difficult to visualize a carbohydrate deficiency occurring in rhizomes and stolons that contain 15 to 25% nonstructural carbohydrates (Smith, 1968). Most C-4 grasses accumulate starch in their lateral stems and crown tissues (Bender & Smith, 1973) but starch must be mobilized before it can serve as an energy source for growth. This mobilization involves the induction of hydrolytic enzymes, a process which itself is under hormonal control. When conditions favorable for shoot growth occur rapidly, it is likely that energy demand may exceed the capacity of starch-storing tissues to deliver because of a lag in the mobilization process. When warming conditions occur slowly and growth demands for reserve energy are modest, the mobilization of starch has time to proceed and is able to meet the needs of both shoot growth and root maintenance. Thus, the induction of hydrolytic activity in storage organs more than the actual supply of carbohydrates available for growth may explain spring root decline in warm-season grasses.

Leaf and shoot growth are the processes of most direct interest to the turf manager. The maintenance of a uniform stand of grass that has the properties appropriate for recreational activities while it is aesthetically pleasing is the goal of turfgrass culture. Oddly the rate at which grass leaves grow is poorly correlated with turf quality (Mehall et al., 1984). This is only superficially surprising because leaf growth, when sufficient to replace senescent leaves and those damaged by insects, disease, or wear, will not improve turf quality further by occurring at a greater rate. Nevertheless, a healthy turf of good quality is normally composed of grass plants that maintain a constant rate of leaf growth.

The pattern of seasonal leaf growth for cool-season turfgrasses as measured by rate of clipping production is illustrated in Fig. 5-1 and 5-2 (E.S. Hesketh and R.J. Hull, 1986, unpublished data). A bimodal curve is frequently observed with maximum leaf growth occurring in the spring

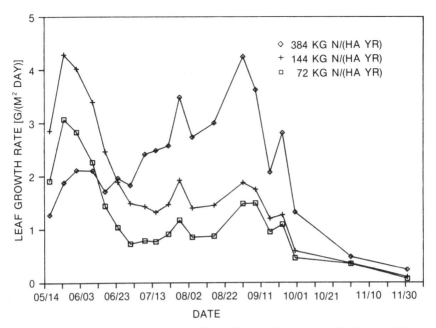

Fig. 5-1. Seasonal clipping growth rates of Baron Kentucky bluegrass fertilized at three N rates.

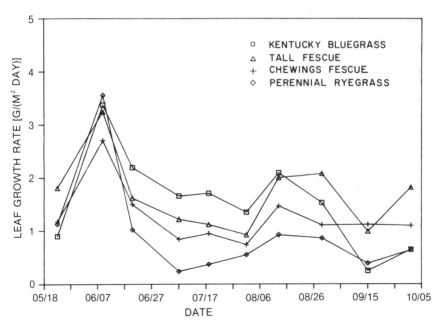

Fig. 5-2. Seasonal clipping growth rates of four cool-season turfgrasses after receiving a single N application on 14 May.

followed by a depressed growth rate in mid-summer and resumption of rapid growth in late summer and early autumn. Similar results have been reported by Landschoot and Waddington (1987) and Woolhouse (1981). Elevated N fertility increases leaf growth but does not eliminate the bimodal seasonal pattern (Fig. 5-1). Because heavily fertilized turf is often more susceptible to disease, the increased leaf growth expected from high fertilizer rates is sometimes not realized. This was the case for Baron Kentucky bluegrass that received 384 kg of N/ha but exhibited severe stripe smut injury in the spring (Fig. 5-1). The bimodal pattern of leaf growth is not a function of making fertilizer applications in the spring and fall although certainly the judicious use of N can reduce the mid-summer decline. When the entire seasonal allotment of fertilizer was applied at one time on 14 May, an initial burst of leaf growth occurred but this was followed by the expected bimodal pattern even though no fertilizer was applied in the fall (Fig. 5-2). A similar pattern was observed for the four cool-season turfgrasses studied.

This pattern of leaf growth can be explained on the basis of plant energy status. C-3 grasses sustain high rates of photorespiration during the intense light and elevated temperatures of mid-summer (Watschke et al., 1972). This diversion of photosynthetic energy into the nonproductive glycolate oxidation pathway can reduce CER by 35 to 50% or more (Morgan & Brown, 1979). A greatly reduced photosynthetic efficiency coupled with increased maintenance respiration caused by high temperatures forces cool-season grasses to compromise growth rates of leaves and roots during the mid-summer season. Additional stresses imposed at this time (e.g., drought possibly aggravated by photoinhibition) (Kyle et al., 1984) will often result in the death of leaf tissue and cause the grass to enter an inactive state. This condition is sometimes referred to as summer dormancy. This is a misnomer in that the grass is under no internal inhibition and will resume growth whenever favorable conditions return. Possibly those conditions that depress leaf growth during mid-summer also promote a growth inhibiting hormonal change, but there is no direct evidence for this. Preventing drought stress and maintaining adequate N fertility will reduce the summer decline in leaf growth by maintaining a positive photosynthesis/respiration ratio. The plant may achieve this in part by shunting additional N to the synthesis of more RuBP carboxylase but this remains to be shown.

Warm-season grasses experience no mid-summer leaf growth decline if drought and nutrient stresses are avoided (Morgan & Brown, 1983b). The lack of photorespiration in C-4 grasses removes a major physiological constraint to maintaining a favorable energy balance during summer conditions. Consequently, CERs on a turf area basis are directly related to photosynthetic photon flux density and leaf area index (Morgan & Brown, 1983a). These observations reemphasize the significance of incorporating traits for increased photosynthetic efficiency and the maintenance of a positive energy balance into the breeding programs of cool-season turfgrasses.

IV. CARBOHYDRATE DYNAMICS

Nonstructural carbohydrates constitute the energy currency within turfgrass plants. Growth, differentiation, and maintenance are purchased with carbohydrates obtained from current photosynthate or that banked in storage organs. The recognition of this central role played by carbohydrates in the energy economy of plants has resulted in their determination in numerous studies of turfgrass management and physiology (Beard, 1973). The total nonstructural carbohydrate (TNC) content of tissues is often used as an indicator of the physiological status of turfgrasses (Sheffer et al., 1979). The impact of N fertility (Green & Beard, 1969; Duff, 1974; Walker & Ward, 1974; Westhafer et al., 1982; Zanoni et al, 1969), supraoptimal temperatures (Duff & Beard, 1974; Watschke et al., 1972; Youngner & Nudge, 1976) and partial defoliation (Sheffer et al., 1979; Youngner & Nudge, 1976) on the soluble carbohydrate content of turfgrasses has been reported. Conditions that favor rapid growth and metabolic activity result in a lower TNC level than conditions that tend to depress growth while permitting near-maximum photosynthetic rates. The latter condition causes an accumulation of carbohydrates normally in the form of glucose or fructose polymers.

Smith (1968, 1972) classified grasses native and introduced to North America on the basis of the nonstructural polysaccharides that accumulate in their stem bases. Grasses of a tropical or subtropical origin (C-4, warm-season grasses) accumulate glucose polymers (starch) or sucrose. Temperate zone grasses (C-3, cool-season grasses) accumulate mostly fructose polymers (fructans) along with small amounts of starch and sucrose. Some C-3 grasses do accumulate starch (Bender & Smith, 1973) or sucrose (Borland & Farrar, 1985) in their stem bases but most cool-season turfgrasses concentrate fructans in their vegetative tissues. The degree of fructan polymerization varies between cool-season grass genera. Smith extracted tissues with an ethanol concentration series ranging from 0 to 95% and found that all fructans were removed from perennial ryegrass and tall fescue tissues in 65% ethanol (Smith & Grotelueschen, 1966; Smith, 1972). By comparison, Kentucky bluegrass and redtop (*Agrostis alba* L.) contained more highly polymerized fructans that could be extracted only with dilute ethanol solutions or pure water. These fractions contained long-chain fructan molecules consisting of about 260 fructose units while the fructans in ryegrass and tall fescue were short-chains consisting of 26 fructose molecules or less. The degree of fructan polymerization is not a reliable criterion for classifying grasses because elevated temperatures tend to inhibit fructan biosynthesis and reduce the size of fructan molecules (Smith, 1968). In addition, the degree of polymerization depends on the plant tissue analyzed; stem bases contain larger molecules than leaf blades or upper internodes (Smith, 1967, 1972). The degree of fructan polymerization is often different in the region of leaf cell division and elongation from that in fully expanded tissue (Spollen & Nelson, 1988). Nevertheless, it is often useful to regard warm-season grasses as starch accumulators and cool-season grasses as fructan accumulators.

Diurnal TNC variation in Kentucky bluegrass leaves exhibited a mid-day peak followed by a decline (Sheffer et al., 1979). Upper leaf blades were sampled every 2 h between 0400 and 2000 h on 18 Sept. 1974. During that day, solar irradiance declined sharply at 1200 h and recovered somewhat at 1600 h. The TNC content of leaves paralleled these changes in light energy but exhibited a 2-h lag. Other studies, in which grass leaves were analyzed during a constant light period, demonstrated an almost linear increase in TNC for up to 16 h (Sicher et al., 1984; Wagner et al., 1986). A steady accumulation of TNC during periods of light is the norm and this build up of photosynthetic products in leaves has been proposed as an explanation for the frequently observed decline in photosynthesis occurring during mid-day (Neales & Incoll, 1968; Nafziger & Koller, 1976). A gradual diurnal decline in CO_2 assimilation has been observed in Kentucky bluegrass turf at several times during the growing season (Hull, 1981). While other explanations for diurnal changes in CER have been proposed, the high concentration of various carbohydrates in photosynthetically active leaves is likely to be a contributing factor. During periods of darkness, the TNC is mobilized and translocated from the leaf blades to sheath, crown, and rhizome tissues (Hull, 1981, 1987). By the end of the dark period, leaf carbohydrate levels normally have returned to their concentration of the previous morning (Sicher et al., 1984). Consequently, grass leaves do not serve as permanent or long-term storage sites for TNC and any polymeric carbohydrates found in leaf tissues are the result of temporary accumulation occurring when photosynthesis exceeds export.

The major TNC found in turfgrass shoots consists of the monsaccharides glucose and fructose, the disaccharide sucrose, various oligosaccharides of the β-(2-6)-linked polyfructosylsucrose type (i.e., short-chain fructans), starch, and long-chain fructans (Smith, 1972; Westhafer et al., 1982) (Table 5-4).

Table 5-4. Nonstructural carbohydrate content of selected turfgrasses.

Turfgrass	Plant part	Reducing sugars	Nonreducing sugars	Fructans	Starch
			mg/g dry wt.		
Kentucky bluegrass	Leaf	40.1	35.3	98.0	--†
	Stem	29.1	19.4	141.1	--
	Root	25.6	7.1	42.3	--
Annual bluegrass	Leaf	40.6	60.6	61.0	--†
	Stem	24.6	36.1	69.2	--
	Root	6.9	28.5	18.3	--
Creeping bentgrass	Leaf	48.9	22.4	110.3	--†
	Stem	49.8	11.9	100.8	--
	Root	30.0	15.2	12.6	--
Perennial ryegrass	Leaf	51.0	50.0	47.0	--‡
	Stem	54.0	14.0	65.0	--
	Root	12.0	70.0	75.0	--
Centipedegrass	Stolon	6.8	51.5	--	152.2§

† Westhafer et al. (1982).
‡ Adams et al. (1974).
§ Walker and Ward (1974).

In most grasses, early photosynthetic product is partitioned between sucrose and starch during periods of light. The regulatory compound fructose 2,6-bisphosphate controls the flow of photosynthetically derived triose phosphates to sucrose by inhibiting the enzyme fructose 1,6-bisphosphatase that catalyzes the first irreversible reaction leading to sucrose (Stitt, 1987). When sucrose accumulates in the cytosol of leaf mesophyll cells because synthesis exceeds transport from the cells, fructose 2,6-bisphosphate is synthesized from fructose-6-phosphate. This blocks further sucrose synthesis, causing triose phosphates to accumulate in the chloroplasts and become channelled toward the synthesis of starch (Preiss, 1982).

In warm-season turfgrasses, this dichotomy in carbon partitioning between starch and sucrose appears to be fairly simple with starch accumulating when metabolic sinks become weakened due to inhibited growth (Walker & Ward, 1974) or when photosynthate production exceeds demand (Winstead & Ward, 1974). However, because C-4 grasses are highly efficient in exporting photosynthate from leaves (Hofstra & Nelson, 1969), starch rarely accumulates in leaves but concentrates mostly in storage organs.

Cool-season grasses exhibit a more complex pattern of photosynthate partitioning between TNC fractions. The initial dichotomy in carbon flow between sucrose and starch occurs but because C-3 grasses are less efficient than C-4 grasses in transporting photosynthate from mesophyll cells to sieve tube elements, they have a greater tendency to accumulate sucrose within the cytosol of their mesophyll cells. The fructose 2,6-bisphosphate control site would inhibit further sucrose synthesis, shunting triose phosphates to starch within the chloroplasts. The resulting accumulation of large starch grains within the chloroplasts causes internal shading or membrane distortion that will reduce the CER and lower the efficiency of photosynthetic energy conversion.

To accommodate this condition, most cool-season grasses have developed a mechanism for TNC storage within leaf cells. Sucrose is transported from the cytosol to the vacuoles of mesophyll cells where concurrently the enzyme sucrose-sucrose-fructosyltransferase (SST) is induced. SST catalyzes the transfer of a fructose moiety from one sucrose molecule to another producing a trisaccharide having one glucose and two fructose units (Housley & Pollock, 1985; Pollock, 1984; Wagner et al., 1983). An additional enzyme fructan-fructan-fructosyltransferase (FFT) catalyzes the transfer of a fructose from a trisaccharide or sucrose to another trisaccharide to produce a longer chain-length fructan (Housley & Daughtry, 1987; Pontis & del Campillo, 1985). Fructans are synthesized within vacuoles thereby removing sucrose from the cytosol and reducing its concentration to levels that will not cause the inhibition of further sucrose synthesis (Housley & Pollock, 1985; Pollock & Chatterton, 1988).

With the onset of darkness, the SST levels decline and fructan hydrolase activity increases. This promotes the hydrolysis of fructans to monosaccharides (Wagner et al., 1986) that exit the vacuoles and become substrates for sucrose synthesis. The sucrose in turn is transported to sieve tube elements where it is translocated from the leaves to sites of growth or storage. Within the leaf bases, translocated sucrose provides fructose units for the synthesis of fructans that are stored until remobilized to support additional growth (Hogan & Hendrix, 1986). Thus, the synthesis of temporary fructan pools within leaf blades provides a buffer against potentially inhibitory concentrations of sucrose and starch and are readily mobilized for transport when photosynthesis ceases.

This sequence of carbon flux through various carbohydrate fractions has yet to be demonstrated in turfgrasses but evidence for a similar pathway was reported by Hull and Smith (1974). Following the distribution of ^{14}C incorporated photosynthetically into Kentucky bluegrass turf, they observed a pattern of photosynthate flow from ethanol extractable mono- and disaccharides to water-soluble polymeric fructans and insoluble residues. This labeling sequence was noted in both leaf blades and leaf sheath/crown tissues.

Research into the reasons for the higher CERs of the decaploid tall fescue compared to those of the hexaploid types prompted a comprehensive analysis of photosynthate flow through carbohydrate fractions in the leaves of these grasses (Randall et al., 1985). Sucrose was the principal CO_2 assimilation product and its rate of synthesis was 7.76 and 4.94 mmol/g fresh wt. per h in the leaves of decaploid and hexaploid plants, respectively. The total sucrose pool, however, was 23% larger and free fructose was three times greater in the hexaploid leaves (Wong et al., 1983). Fructans are synthesized in tall fescue leaves and comprise 1 to 2% of leaf dry weight. The hexaploid plants accumulated more fructans than the decaploids. Pulse-chase experiments involving $^{14}CO_2$ labeling showed the decaploid to translocate about 79% of its fixed ^{14}C from the exposed leaf tissue within 24 h while the hexaploid exported 49% (Wong & Randall, 1985). Of the total ^{14}C recovered from the entire plant, the decaploid retained 40% in the labeled leaf with 10, 33, and 29% recovered in other leaves, stem bases, and roots, respectively. The hexaploid retained 91% of fixed ^{14}C in the labeled leaf with 4, 3, and 2% recovered in other leaves, stem bases, and roots, respectively. The more efficient removal of photosynthetic product from leaf cells through rapid translocation likely contributes to the greater photosynthetic activity of the decaploid tall fescue. These experiments do not permit a resolution of the cause-and-effect question. Does reduced feedback inhibition due to efficient translocation explain the greater CERs of the decaploid plants or does a higher CER result in greater sucrose synthesis that stimulates increased translocation (Randall et al., 1985)? Most available evidence favors the former explanation.

Fructan biosynthesis is favored by conditions that inhibit growth but permit photosynthesis to continue. Reducing the temperature of *Lolium temulentum* L. from 20 to 5 °C at the beginning of the light period resulted in sucrose and fructan accumulation in leaf blades and sheaths (Pollock, 1984). SST activity was stimulated by the onset of low temperatures. Smith (1968) noted that cool temperatures sharply increased the fructan content of timothy leaves, stems, and roots while having little effect on the levels of simple sugars and starch. Pontis and del Campillo (1985) suggest that the water soluble character of fructans and their apparent capacity to be transformed readily from long- to short-chain polymers may impart frost hardiness to plants that accumulate them. The ability to alter the cytoplasmic solute potential and thereby achieve osmotic adjustments could contribute significantly to stress tolerance.

Turfgrasses have been shown to increase their TNC content when subjected to certain stresses. Youngner and Nudge (1976) observed an increase in nonstructural carbohydrates in stem and leaf bases of Kentucky bluegrass when air or soil temperatures were reduced to 10 °C. It probably is safe to assume that fructans contributed to the TNC increase. Duff and Beard (1974) noted an increase in the water-soluble carbohydrate (fructan) fraction in creeping bentgrass leaf tissue from plants grown at supraoptimal temperatures (30–40 °C). Again growth was probably inhibited more than CO_2 fixation and fructans accumulated. Respiration rates increased with temperature but photosynthesis, measured as O_2 evolution, increased more. Consequently, the carbon needed for a TNC increase was available and fructan accumulation may have provided some protection against high-temperature injury.

C. J. Nelson and his students, in a series of detailed experiments conducted at the University of Missouri, studied the carbohydrate fluxes supporting leaf growth in tall fescue. As in all grasses, leaf blade growth results from a meristematic zone located at the base of the blade near the ligule (Schnyder & Nelson, 1978). As these cells elongate and differentiate, they are displaced from the zone of cell division and blade growth occurs (Schnyder et al., 1987). Under continuous light, leaf blades elongated at a near steady rate for several days. During diurnal cycles, leaf elongation rates were lower in the dark periods (Wilhelm & Nelson, 1978) but when plants were grown at high irradiance and the temperature of the tiller bases was held constant, leaf growth was 60% greater in darkness (Volenex & Nelson, 1984). An analysis of the various components of leaf blade extension resulted in a model that explained patterns of leaf growth (Schnyder et al., 1988). Photosynthate translocates to the region of cell division and elongation as sucrose where it is unloaded from sieve tubes and synthesized into low molecular weight fructans within the vacuoles of elongating cells. These fructans, along with sucrose and monosaccharides, contribute to a decreased osmotic potential that causes water influx, increased turgor, and cell enlargement. As cells grow, the solute concentration is diluted by water deposition (Schnyder & Nelson, 1988) and the synthesis of insoluble polymeric materials results in a gradual loss of turgor. This loss occurs especially during darkness when the influx of new substrate is reduced. Newly elongated cells undergo a diurnal fluctuation in dry matter content, which builds during the light and declines in darkness when these cells contribute energy to the adjacent meristematic and elongating cells.

These studies were not conducted on tall fescue managed as a closely mowed turf but the basic energy relations described between the various leaf tissues probably is the same. How leaf growth is influenced by the length of the fully expanded blade is not clear, but since the energy supply for the meristematic and elongating tissues depends in part upon photosynthate produced in the blade, a positive relationship between cutting height and leaf growth rate would be expected.

Mobilization of fructans in stem bases can be induced by defoliation. Yamamoto and Mino (1982) observed a sharp decrease in the fructan (phlein) concentration in stem bases of orchardgrass (*Dactylis glomerata* L.) within one day after mowing which removed most leaf tissue. The fructan hydrolase (phleinase) and invertase activities increased rapidly as did the concentration of fructose. Fifteen days after defoliation, the hydrolytic enzyme activities declined and the fructan concentration increased. A 57 000 molecular weight protein was extracted from orchardgrass stems and it was found to attack not only the β-2,6 linkages but also the β-2,1 linkages at branch points (Yamamoto & Mino, 1985). The enzyme exhibited no capacity to hydrolyze sucrose. Although the time between mowings and the extent of defoliation are different for turfgrass and forage crop management, it is interesting to speculate that mowing may induce a fructan hydrolase in the crowns of turfgrasses making fructans available to support regrowth. Because the impact of a routine mowing on the photosynthate partitioning within turfgrass plants appears to be minimal and of short duration (Hull, 1987), recovery from mowing probably makes little or no demands on the reserve fructans in leaf bases and stems. Observations of short-term fluctuations in fructan levels following mowing should answer this question.

The application of N fertilizers to turf has long been known to lower the TNC concentration of leaf and crown tissues. Green and Beard (1969) observed a decline in polymeric carbohydrates in the leaf blades of Merion Kentucky bluegrass and Toronto creeping bentgrass following the application of N fertilizers at several rates. Monosaccharides failed to exhibit a consistent response to N additions. Zanoni et al. (1969) noted a season-long depression in the TNC concentrations of intact shoots from Merion Kentucky bluegrass and three bentgrass species when normal N rates were compared to turf receiving no N. Several authors found that elevated N fertility depressed fructan levels in stem and leaf bases more than any other carbohydrate fraction (Adams et al., 1974; Duff, 1974; Hull & Smith, 1974; Westhafer et al., 1982).

This consistent response to N fertility likely results from the increased shoot growth stimulated by N and the additional demand on photosynthetic energy required to reduce and assimilate N. Thus, those carbohydrate fractions that represent photosynthate in excess of need will be most affected by N additions. Monosaccharides, which constitute a biochemical currency in energy demanding reactions, may actually increase when metabolic rates are stimulated (Green & Beard, 1969; Hull & Smith, 1974). Sucrose, the primary transport vehicle for carbon and energy within turfgrass plants, will also be influenced little by most rate changes in growth or metabolism except during periods of declining activity when sucrose may accumulate in vacuoles prior to the induction of fructan biosynthesis. Careful analysis of the TNC profile may provide insight into the metabolic status of turfgrasses and the extent to which growth may be limited by energy supply.

V. CONCLUSION

This chapter has presented an overview of the energy dynamics within turfgrass plants covering both diurnal and seasonal cycles. The picture that emerges is not as simple as might originally have been supposed. The capture, transformation, transport, and eventual use or storage of energy in the form of organic molecules is influenced by the genetic potential of the plant and its capacity to respond to environmental signals. Many details of this sequence are poorly understood for plants generally, let alone for turfgrasses. However, in order for turfgrass science to capitalize on the advances being made in basic plant physiology, biochemistry, and genetics, it is important that their relevancy to turfgrass culture and improvement be studied.

In assembling the materials for this chapter, I had to research grasses other than turfgrasses and plants maintained other than as a turf. Many questionable extrapolations may have resulted, but wherever possible studies were selected involving turfgrasses or at least grasses closely related to those used for turf. Much of the work cited was conducted by persons whose choice of a turfgrass species was prompted by physiological or morphological considerations rather than any potential impact the research might have on turfgrass culture. In short, there is a great need for more basic research on turfgrasses maintained in a turf environment. This need can be met only by enlisting the talents of cell biologists, biochemists, and physiologists to study turfgrasses. Significant advances in such areas as increased efficiency in the use of environmental inputs from light to micronutrients, greater tolerance of physical or environmental stresses ranging from supraoptimal temperatures to wear, and improved resistance to the assault of pests whether from insects, pathogens, or weeds can be made only through the systematic applications of all the science available. This chapter is intended to highlight the many deficiencies in our understanding of the energetics underlying turfgrass growth and development. I hope it will stimulate students to take up the challenge to satisfy them. Certainly, progress has been made. Most of the research presented in this chapter could not have been included in the 1969 turfgrass monograph. It is sobering to realize how little of this information is the product of turfgrass research programs.

REFERENCES

Adams, W.A., P.J. Bryan, and G.E. Walker. 1974. Effects of cutting height and nitrogen nutrition on growth pattern of turfgrasses. p. 131–144. *In* E.C. Roberts (ed.) Proc. 2nd Int. Turfgrass Res. Conf., Blacksburg, VA. 19–21 June 1973. Int. Turfgrass Soc., ASA and CSSA, Madison, WI.

Aoyagi, K., and J.A. Bassham. 1986. Appearance and accumulation of C_4 carbon pathway enzymes in developing wheat leaves. Plant Physiol. 80:334–340.

Asay, K.H., A.G. Matches, and C.J. Nelson. 1977. Effect of leaf width on responses of tall fescue genotypes to defoliation treatment and temperature regimes. Crop Sci. 17:816–818.

Bassham, J.A., and M. Calvin. 1957. The path of carbon in photosynthesis. Prentice-Hall, Englewood Cliffs, NJ.

Bassham, J.A., and B.B. Buchanan. 1982. Carbon dioxide fixation pathways in plants and bacteria. p. 141-189. *In* Govindjee (ed.) Photosynthesis, Vol. II. Development, carbon metabolism, and plant productivity. Academic Press, New York.

Beard, J.B. 1973. Turfgrass: Science and culture. Prentice-Hall, Englewood Cliffs, NJ.

Beard, J.B. 1985. Turfgrass physiology research: 1981-85. p. 81-104. *In* F. Lemaire (ed.) Proc. 5th Int. Turfgrass Res. Conf., Avignon, France. 1-5 July. Int. Natl. de la Recherche Agron., Paris.

Beard, J.B., and W.H. Daniel. 1965. Effect of temperature and cutting on the growth of creeping bentgrass (*Agrostis palustris* Huds.) roots. Agron. J. 57:249-250.

Bender, M.M., and D. Smith. 1973. Classification of starch- and fructosan-accumulating grasses as C-3 or C-4 species by carbon isotope analysis. J. Br. Grassl. Soc. 28:97-100.

Biran, I., B. Bravdo, I. Bushkin-Harav, and E. Rowitz. 1981. Water consumption and growth rate of 11 turfgrasses as affected by mowing height, irrigation frequency, and soil moisture. Agron. J. 73:85-90.

Black, C.C., W.H. Campbell, T.M. Chen, and P. Dittrich. 1973. The monocotyledons: Their evolution and comparative biology. III. Pathways of carbon metabolism related to net carbon dioxide assimilation by monocotyledons. Q. Rev. Biol. 48:299-313.

Black, C.C., T.M. Chen, and R.H. Brown. 1969. Biochemical basis for plant competition. Weed Sci. 17:338-344.

Borland, A.M., and J.F. Farmer. 1985. Diel patterns of carbohydrate metabolism in leaf blades and leaf sheaths of *Poa annua* L. and *Poa jemtlandica* (Almq.) Richt. New Phytol. 100:519-531.

Bouton, J.H., R.H. Brown, J.K. Bolton, and R.P. Campagnoli. 1981. Photosynthesis of grass species differing in carbon dioxide fixation pathways. VII. Chromosome numbers, metaphse I chromosome behavior, and mode of reproduction of photosynthetically distinct *Panicum* species. Plant Physiol. 67:433-437.

Brown, R.H. 1978. A difference in N use efficiency in C_3 and C_4 plants and its implications in adaptation and evolution. Crop Sci. 18:93-98.

Brown, R.H., and J.R. Wilson. 1983. Nitrogen response of *Panicum* species differing in CO_2 fixation pathways. II. CO_2 exchange characteristics. Crop Sci. 23:1154-1159.

Byrne, M.C., C.J. Nelson, and D.D. Randall. 1981. Ploidy effects on anatomy and gas exchange of tall fescue leaves. Plant Physiol. 68:891-893.

Chen, T.M., R.H. Brown, and C.C. Black. 1970. CO_2 compensation concentration, rate of photosynthesis, and carbonic anhydrase activity of plants. Weed Sci. 18:399-403.

Clifford, P.E., C. Marshall, and G.R. Sagar. 1973. The reciprocal transfer of radiocarbon between a developing tiller and its parent shoot in vegetative plants of *Lolium multiflorum* Lam Ann. Bot. 37:777-785.

Colman, R.L., and A. Lazanby. 1970. Factors affecting the response of tropical and temperate grasses to fertilizer nitrogen. p. 393-397. *In* M.J.T. Norman (ed.) Proc. XI Int. Grassl. Congr., Surfers Paradise, Queensland, Australia. 13-23 Apr. Univ. Queensland Press, St. Lucia, Queensland.

DiPaola, J.M., J.B. Beard, and H. Brawand. 1982. Key events in the seasonal root growth of Bermudagrass and St. Augustinegrass. HortScience 17:829-831.

Dudeck, A.E., and C.H. Peacock. 1986. Pregermination of Italian ryegrass and tall fescue seed. Crop Sci. 26:177-179.

Duff, D.T. 1974. Influence of fall nitrogenous fertilization on the carbohydrates of Kentucky bluegrass. p. 112-119. *In* E.C. Roberts (ed.) Proc. 2nd Int. Turfgrass Res. Conf., Blacksburg, VA. 19-21 June 1973. ASA and CSSA, Madison, WI.

Duff, D.T., and J.B. Beard. 1974. Supraoptimal temperature effects upon *Agrostis palustris*. Part II. Influence on carbohydrate levels, photosynthetic rate, and respiration rate. Physiol. Plant 32:18-22.

Eggens, J.L. 1981. Response of *Poa pratensis* L. (Kentucky bluegrass) and *Poa annua* L. (Annual bluegrass) to mowing and plant competition. p. 123-128. *In* R.W. Sheard (ed.) Proc. 4th Int. Turfgrass Res. Conf., Guelph, ON, Canada. 19-23 July. Int. Turfgrass Soc., and Ontario Agric. Coll., Univ. fo Guelph, Guelph, ON.

Ehleringer, J., and O. Bjorkman. 1977. Quantum yields for CO_2 uptake in C_3 and C_4 plants: Dependence on temperature, CO_2, and O_2 concentration. Plant Physiol. 59:86-90.

El-Sharkawy, M.A., and J.D. Hesketh. 1965. Photosynthesis among species in relation to characteristics of leaf anatomy and CO_2 diffusion resistances. Crop Sci. 5:517-521.

Forde, B.J. 1966a. Translocation in grasses. 1. Bermudagrass. N. Z. J. Bot. 4:479-495.

Forde, B.J. 1966b. Translocation in grasses. 2. Perennial ryegrass and couch grass. N. Z. J. Bot. 4:496–514.

Garrett, M.K. 1978. Control of photorespiration at RuBP carboxylase/oxygenase level in ryegrass cultivars. Nature (London) 274:913–915.

Geiger, D.R., and R.T. Giaquinta. 1982. Translocation of photosynthate. p. 345–386. In Govindjee (ed.) Photosynthesis. Vol. II. Development, carbon metabolism, and plant productivity. Academic Press, New York.

Gerloff, G.C. 1976. Plant efficiencies in the use of nitrogen, phosphorus and potassium. p. 161–173. In M.J. Wright (ed.) Plant adaptation to mineral stress in problem soils. Spec. Publ., Cornell Univ. and New York Agric. Exp. Stn., Ithaca.

Goss, R.L., and A.G. Law. 1967. Performance of bluegrass varieties at two cutting heights and two nitrogen levels. Agron. J. 59:516–518.

Green, D.G., and J.B. Beard. 1969. Seasonal relationships between nitrogen nutrition and soluble carbohydrates in the leaves of Agrostis palustris Huds., and Poa pratensis L. Agron. J. 61:107–111.

Hall, J.R., and R.W. Miller. 1974. Effect of phosphorus, season, and method of sampling on foliar analysis of Kentucky bluegrass. p. 155–171. In E.C. Roberts (ed.) Proc. 2nd Int. Turfgrass Res. Conf., Blacksburg, VA. 19–21 June 1973. ASA and CSSA, Madison, WI.

Hall, N.P., and A.J. Keys. 1983. Temperature dependence of the enzymic carboxylation and oxygenation of ribulose 1,5-bisphosphate in relation to effects of temperature on photosynthesis. Plant Physiol. 72:945–948.

Hallock, D.L., R.H. Brown, and R.E. Blaser. 1965. Rleative yield and composition of Ky. 31 fescue and coastal bermudagrass at four nitrogen levels. Agron. J. 57:539–542.

Hanson, A.A., and F.V. Juska. 1961. Winter root activity in Kentucky bluegrass (Poa pratensis L.). Agron. J. 53:372–374.

Hanson, K.V., and B.E. Branham. 1987. Effects of four growth regulators on photosynthate partitioning in 'Majestic' Kentucky bluegrass. Crop Sci. 27:1257–1260.

Hatch, M.D., and C.R. Slack. 1966. Photosynthesis by sugarcane leaves. A new carboxylation reaction and pathway of sugar formation. Biochem. J. 101:103–111.

Ho, L.C. 1988. Metabolism and compartmentation of imported sugars in sink organs in relation to sink strength. Ann. Rev. Plant Physiol. Plant Mol. Biol. 39:355–378.

Hofstra, G., and C.D. Nelson. 1969. A comparative study of translocation of assimilated ^{14}C from leaves of different species. Planta 88:103–112.

Hogan, M.E., and J.E. Hendrix. 1986. Labeling of fructans in winter wheat stems. Plant Physiol. 80:1048–1050.

Housley, T.L., and C.S.T. Daughtry. 1987. Fructan content and fructosyl-transferase activity during wheat seed growth. Plant Physiol. 83:4–7.

Housley, T.L., and C.J. Pollock. 1985. Photosynthesis and carbohydrate metabolism in detached leaves of Lolium temulentum L. New Phytol. 99:499–507.

Hull, R.J. 1976. A carbon-14 technique for measuring photosynthate distribution in field grown turf. Agron. J. 68:99–102.

Hull, R.J. 1981. Diurnal variation in photosynthate partitioning in Kentucky bluegrass turf. p. 509–516. In R.W. Sheard (ed.) Proc. 4th Int. Turfgrass Res. Conf., Guelph, ON, Canada. 19–23 July. Int. Turfgrass Soc., and Ontario Agric. Coll., Univ. of Guelph, Guelph, ON.

Hull, R.J. 1987. Kentucky bluegrass photosynthate partitioning following scheduled mowing. J. Am. Soc. Hortic. Sci. 112:829–834.

Hull, R.J., and L.M. Smith. 1974. Photosynthate translocation and metabolism in Kentucky bluegrass turf as a function of fertility. p. 186–195. In E.C. Roberts (ed.) Proc. 2nd Int. Turfgrass Res. Conf., Blacksburg, VA. 19–21 June 1973. ASA and CSSA, Madison, WI.

Impithuksa, V., W.G. Blue, and D.A. Graetz. 1984. Distribution of applied nitrogen in soil-pensacola bahiagrass components as indicated by nitrogen-15. Soil Sci. Soc. Am. J. 48:1280–1285.

Joseph, M.C., and D.D. Randall. 1981. Photosynthesis in polyploid tall fescue. II. Photosynthesis and ribulose-1,5-bisphosphate carboxylase of polyploid tall fescue. Plant Physiol. 68:894–898.

Juska, F.V., and A.A. Hanson. 1961. Effects of interval and height of mowing on growth of Merion and common Kentucky bluegrass (Poa pratensis L.). Agron. J. 53:385–388.

Karnok, K.J., and B.J. Augustin. 1981. Growth and carbon dioxide flux of Kentucky bluegrass (Poa pratensis L.) during sod establishment under low light. p. 517–526. In R.W. Sheard (ed.) Proc. 4th Int. Turfgrass Res. Conf., Guelph, ON, Canada. 19–23 July. Int. Turfgrass Soc., and Ontario Agric. Coll., Univ. of Guelph, Guelph, ON.

Karnok, K.J., and J.B. Beard. 1983. Effects of gibberellic acid on the CO_2 exchange rates of bermudagrass and St. Augustinegrass when exposed to chilling temperatures. Crop Sci. 23:514-517.

Kneebone, W.R., and I.L. Pepper. 1982. Consumptive water use by sub-irrigated turfgrasses under desert conditions. Agron. J. 74:419-423.

Kortschak, H.P., C.E. Hartt, and G.O. Burr. 1965. Carbon dioxide fixation in sugarcane leaves. Plant Physiol. 40:209-213.

Koski, A.J., J.R. Street, and T.K. Danneberger. 1988. Prediction of Kentucky bluegrass root growth using degree-day accumulation. Crop Sci. 28:848-850.

Krans, J.V., and J.B. Beard. 1980. The effects of stage of seedling development on selected physiological and morphology parameters in Kentucky bluegrass and red fescue. p. 89-95. In J.B. Beard (ed.) Proc. 3rd Int. Turfgrass Res. Conf., Munich, Germany. 11-13 July 1977. Int. Turfgrass Soc., and ASA, CSSA, and SSSA, Madison, WI.

Krans, J.V., and J.B. Beard. 1985. Effects of clipping on growth and physiology of 'Merion' Kentucky bluegrass. Crop Sci. 25:17-20.

Krans, J.V., J.B. Beard, and J.F. Wilkinson. 1979. Classification of C_3 and C_4 turfgrass species based on CO_2 compensation concentration and leaf anatomy. HortScience 14:183-185.

Krenzer Jr., E.G., D.N. Moss, and R.K. Crookston. 1975. Carbon dioxide compensation points of floweriung plants. Plant Physiol. 56:194-206.

Krueger, R.W., and D. Miles. 1981. Photosynthesis in fescue. III. Rate of electron transport in a polyploid series of tall fescue plants. Plant Physiol. 69:1110-1114.

Kyle, D.J., I. Ohad, and C.J. Arntzen. 1984. Membrane protein damage and repair: Selective loss of quinone-protein function in chloroplast membranes. Proc. Natl. Acad. Sci. USA 81:4040-4074.

Lancschoot, P.J., and D.V. Waddington. 1987. Response of turfgrass to various nitrogen sources. Soil Sci. Soc. Am. J. 51:225-230.

Laude, H.M., and R.E. Fox. 1982. Tillering differences after close clipping in Russian wildrye and tall fescue. Crop Sci. 22:978-980.

Ledeboer, F.B. 1974. Responses of several densely seeded turfgrasses to variable close cutting in the greenhouse. p. 452-457. In E.C. Roberts (ed.) Proc. 2nd Int. Turfgrass Res. Conf., Blacksburg, VA. 19-21 June 1973. ASA and CSSA, Madison, WI.

Lorimer, G.H. 1981. The carboxylation and oxygenation of ribulose 1,5-bisphosphate. Ann. Rev. Plant Physiol. 32:349-383.

Lucus, W.J., and M.A. Madore. 1988. Recent advances in sugar transport. p. 35-84. In J. Preiss (ed.) The biochemistry of plants. Vol. 14. Carbohydrates. Academic Press, San Diego.

Madison, J.H. 1962. Turfgrass ecology. Effects of mowing, irrigation, and nitrogen treatments of Agrostis palustris Sibth., 'Highland' on population, yield, rooting, and cover. Agron. J. 54:407-412.

Madison, J.H. 1971. Principles of turfgrass culture. van Nostrand Reinhold Co., New York.

Madison, J.H., and R.M. Hagan. 1962. Extraction of soil moisture by Merion bluegrass (Poa pratensis L. 'Merion') turf, as affected by irrigation frequency, mowing height, and other cultural operations. Agron. J. 54:157-160.

Mayne, B.C. 1971. Spectral, physical, and electron transport activities in the photosynthetic apparatus of mesophyll cells and bundle sheath cells of Digitaria sanguinalis (L.) Scop. Plant Physiol. 47:600-605.

McNeil, P.H., C.H. Foyer, D.A. Walker, I.F. Bird, M.J. Cornelius, and A.J. Keys. 1981. Similarity of ribulose-1,5-bisphosphate carboxylates of isogenic diploid and tetraplois ryegrasses (Lolium perenne L.) cultivars. Plant Physiol. 67:530-534.

Mehall, B.J., R.H. Hull, and C.R. Skogley. 1984. Turf quality of Kentucky bluegrass cultivars and energy relations. Agron. J. 76:47-50.

Miflin, B.J. 1980. Nitrogen metabolism and amino acid biosynthesis in crop plants. p. 255--296. In P.S. Carlson (ed.) The biology of crop productivity. Academic Press, New York.

Moore, R., and C.C. Black, Jr. 1979. Nitrogen assimilation pathways in leaf mesophyll and bundle sheath cells of C_4 photosynthesis plants formulated from comparative studies with Digitaria sanguinalis (L.) Scop. Plant Physiol. 64:309-313.

Morgan, J.A., and R.H. Brown. 1979. Photosynthesis in grass species differing in carbon dioxide fixation pathways. II. A search for species with intermediate gas exchange and anatomical characteristics. Plant Physiol. 64:257-262.

Morgan, J.A., and R.H. Brown. 1983a. Photosynthesis and growth of Bermudagrass swards. I. Carbon dioxide exchange characteristics of swards mowed at weekly and monthly intervals. Crop Sci. 23:347-352.

Morgan, J.A., and R.H. Brown. 1983b. Photosynthesis and growth of Bermudagrass swards. II. Growth patterns as estimated by harvest and gas exchange techniques. Crop Sci. 23:352-357.

Nafziger, E.D., and H.R. Koller. 1976. Influence of leaf starch concentration on CO_2 assimilation in soybean. Plant Physiol. 57:560-563.

Neales, T.F., and L.D. Incoll. 1968. The control of leaf photosynthesis rate by the level of assimilate concentration in the leaf: A review of the hypothesis. Bot. Rev. 34:107-125.

Ogren, W.L., and R. Chollet. 1982. Photorespiration. p. 191-230. In Govindjee (ed.) Photosynthesis. Vol. II. Development, carbon metabolism, and plant productivity. Academic Press, New York.

Peacock, C.H., and A.E. Dudeck. 1984. Physiological response of St. Augustinegrass to irrigation scheduling. Agron. J. 76:275-279.

Pollock, C.J. 1984. Sucrose accumulation and the initiation of fructan biosynthesis in Lolium temulentum L. New Phytol. 96:527-534.

Pollock, C.J., and N.J. Chatterton. 1988. Fructans. p. 109-140. In J. Preiss (ed.) The biochemistry of plants. Vol. 14. Carbohydrates. Academic Press, San Diego.

Pontis, H.G., and E. del Campillo. 1985. Fructans. p. 205-227. In P.M. Dey and R.A. Dixon (ed.) Biochemistry of storage carbohydrates in green plants. Academic Press, London.

Powell, A.J., R.E. Blaser, and R.E. Schmidt. 1967. Effect of nitrogen on winter root growth of bentgrass. Agron. J. 59:529-530.

Preiss, J. 1982. Regulation of the biosynthesis and degradation of starch. Ann. Rev. Plant Physiol. 33:431-454.

Randall, D.D., C.J. Nelson, and K.H. Asay. 1977. Ribulose bisphosphate carboxylase: Altered genetic expression in tall fescue. Plant Physiol. 59:38-41.

Randall, D.D., C.J. Nelson, D.A. Sleper, C.D. Miles, C.F. Crane, R.W. Krueger, J.H.H. Wong, and J.W. Poskuta. 1985. Photosynthesis in allopolyploid Festuca. p. 409-418. In P.W. Ludden and J.E. Burris (ed.) Nitrogen fixation and CO_2 metabolism. Elsevier Sci. Publ. Co., Amsterdam.

Rathnam, C.K.M., and R. Chollet. 1980. Photosynthetic and photorespiratory carbon metabolism in mesophyll protoplasts and chloroplasts isolated from isogenic diploid and tetraploid cultivars of ryegrass (Lolium perenne L.). Plant Physiol. 65:489-494.

Ray, T.B., and C.C. Black. 1979. The C_4 pathway and its regulation. p. 77-101. In M. Gibbs and E. Latzko (ed.) Encyclopedia of plant physiology. Vol. 6. Photosynthesis II, Photosynthetic carbon metabolism and related processes. Springer-Verlag, Berlin.

Sage, R.F., and R.W. Pearcy. 1987a. The nitrogen use efficiency of C_3 and C_4 plants. I. Leaf nitrogen, growth, and biomass partitioning in Chenopodium album (L.) and Amaranthus retroflexus (L.). Plant Physiol. 84:954-958.

Sage, R.F., and R.W. Pearcy. 1987b. The nitrogen use efficiency of C_3 and C_4 plants. II. Leaf nitrogen effects on the gas exchange characteristics of Chenopodium album (L.) and Amaranthus retroflexus (L.). Plant Physiol. 84:959-963.

Sayre, R.T., R.A. Kennedy, and D.J. Pringnitz. 1979. Photosynthetic enzyme activities and localization in Mollugo verticillata populations differing in the levels of C_3 and C_4 cycle operation. Plant Physiol. 64:293-299.

Schnyder, H., and C.J. Nelson. 1987. Growth rates and carbohydrate fluxes within the elongation zone of tall fescue blades. Plant Physiol. 85:548-553.

Schnyder, H., and C.J. Nelson. 1988. Diurnal growth of tall fescue leaf blades. I. Spatial distribution of growth, deposition of water, and assimilate import in the elongation zone. Plant Physiol. 86:1070-1076.

Schnyder, H., C.J. Nelson, and J.H. Coutts. 1987. Assessment of spatial distribution of growth in the elongation zone of grass leaf blades. Plant Physiol. 85:290-293.

Schnyder, H., C.J. Nelson, and W.G. Spollen. 1988. Diurnal growth of tall fescue leaf blades. II. dry matter partitioning and carbohydrate metabolism in the elongation zone and adjacent expanded tissue. Plant Physiol. 86:1077-1083.

Schantz, H.L., and L.N. Piemeisel. 1927. The water requirement of plants at Akron, Colorado. J. Agric. Res. 34:1093-1189.

Sheffer, K.M., T.L. Watschke, and J.M. Duich. 1979. Carbohydrate sampling in Kentucky bluegrass turf. Agron. J. 71:301-304.

Sicher, R.C., D.F. Kremer, and W.G. Harris. 1984. Diurnal carbohydrate metabolism of barley primary leaves. Plant Physiol. 76:165-169.

Sifers, S.I., J.B. Beard, and J.M. DiPaola. 1985. Spring root decline (SRD): Discovery, description and causes. p. 777-778. *In* F. Lemaire (ed.) Proc. 5th Int. Turfgrass Ref. Conf., Avignon, France. 1-5 July. Int. Turfgrass Soc. Inst. Natl. de la Recherche Agron., Paris.

Sills, M.J., and R.N. Carrow. 1983. Turfgrass growth, N. use, and water use under soil compaction and N fertilization. Agron. J. 75:488-492.

Sinclair, T.R., and T. Horie. 1989. Leaf nitrogen, photosynthesis, and crop radiation use efficiency: A review. Crop Sci. 29:90-98.

Smith, D. 1967. Carbohydrates in grasses. II. Sugar and fructosan composition of the stem bases of bromegrass and timothy at several growth stages and in different plant parts at anthesis. Crop Sci. 7:62-67.

Smith, D. 1968. Classification of several native North American grasses as starch or fructosan accumulators in relation to taxonomy. J. Br. Grassl. Soc. 23:306-309.

Smith, D. 1972. Carbohydrate reserves of grasses. p. 318-333. *In* V.B. Youngner and C.M. McKell (ed.) The biology and utilization of grasses. Academic Press, New York.

Smith, D., and R.D. Grotelueschen. 1966. Carbohydrates in grasses. I. Sugar and fructosan composition of the stem bases of several northern-adapted grasses at seed maturity. Crop Sci. 6:263-266.

Spollen, W.G., and C.J. Nelson. 1988. Characterization of fructan from mature leaf blades and elongation zones of developing leaf blades of wheat, tall fescue, and timothy. Plant Physiol. 88:1349-1353.

St.-Pierre, J.C., and M.J. Wright. 1972. Distribution of ^{14}C photosynthates in timothy (*Phleum pratense* L.) during the vegetative stage of growth. Crop Sci. 12:191-194.

Stitt, M. 1987. Fructose 2,6-bisphosphate and plant carbohydrate metabolism. Plant Physiol. 84:201-204.

Stuckey. I. 1941. Seasonal growth of grass roots. Am. J. Bot. 28:486-491.

Thorne, J.H. 1985. Phloem unloading of C and N assimilates in developing seeds. Ann. Rev. Plant Physiol. 36:317-343.

Turgeon, A.J. 1985. Turfgrass management. Reston Publ. Co., Reston, VA.

Turner, T.R., and D.V. Waddington. 1983. Soil test calibration for establishment of turfgrass monostands. Soil Sci. Soc. Am. J. 47:1161-1166.

Volenec, J.J., and C.J. Nelson. 1984. Carbohydrate metabolism in the leaf meristems of tall fescue. I. Relationship to genetically altered leaf elongation rates. Plant Physiol. 74:590-594.

Waddington, D.V., T.R. Turner, and J.M. Duich. 1975. Response of cool-season turfgrasses to liquid applications of fertilizer. Pennsylvania Agric. Exp. Stn., University Park. Progress Rep. 350.

Waddington, D.V., T.R. Turner, J.M. Duich, and E.L. Moberg. 1978. Effect of fertilization on Penncross creeping bentgrass. Agron. J. 70:713-718.

Wagner, W., F. Keller, and A. Wiemken. 1983. Fructan metabolism in cereals: Induction in leaves and compartmentation in protoplasts and vacuoles. Z. Planzenphysiol. 112:359-372.

Wagner, W., A. Wiemken, and P. Matile. 1986. Regulation of fructan metabolism in leaves of barley (*Hordeum vulgare* L. cv. Gerbel). Plant Physiol. 81:444-447.

Walker, R.H., and C.Y. Ward. 1974. Influence of N and K nutrition on net photosynthesis, dark respiration, and carbohydrates in centipedegrass. p. 196-208. *In* E.C. Roberts (ed.) Proc. 2nd Int. Turfgrass Res. Conf., Blacksburg, VA. 19-21 June 1973. ASA and CSSA, Madison, WI.

Watschke, T.L., R.E. Schmidt, E.W. Carson, and R.E. Blaser. 1972. Some metabolic phenomena of Kentucky bluegrass under high temperature. Crop Sci. 12:87-90.

Westhafer, M.A., J.T. Law, Jr., and D.T. Duff. 1982. Carbohydrate quantification and relationships with N nutrition in cool-season turfgrasses. Agron. J. 74:270-274.

Wilhelm, W.W., and C.J. Nelson. 1978. Leaf growth, leaf aging and photosynthetic rate of tall fescue genotypes. Crop Sci. 18:769-772.

Wilkinson, J.F., J.B. Beard, and J.V. Krans. 1975. Photosynthetic-respiratory responses of 'Merion' Kentucky bluegrass and 'Penlawn' red fescue at reduced light intensities. Crop Sci. 15:165-168.

Wilson, J.R., and R.H. Brown. 1983. Nitrogen response of *Panicum* species differing in CO_2 fixation pathways. I. Growth analysis and carbohydrate accumulation. Crop Sci. 23:1148-1153.

Wilson, J.R., and K.P. Haydock. 1971. The comparative response of tropical and temperate grasses to varying levels of nitrogen and phosphorus nutrition. Aust. J. Agric. Res. 22:573-587.

Winstead, C.W., and C.Y. Ward. 1974. Persistence of southern turfgrasses in a shade environment. p. 221–230. *In* E.C. Roberts (ed.) Proc. 2nd Int. Turfgrass Res. Conf., Blacksburg, VA. 19–21 June 1973. ASA and CSSA, Madison, WI.

Wong, J.H.H., and D.D. Randall. 1985. Translocation of photoassimilate from leaves of two polyploid genotypes of tall fescue differing in photosynthetic rates. Physiol. Plant. 63:445–450.

Wong, J.H.H., D.D. Randall, and C.J. Nelson. 1983. Photosynthesis in tall fescue: IV. Carbon assimilation pattern in two genotypes of tall fescue differing in net photosynthesis rates. Plant Physiol. 72:16–21.

Woolhouse, A.R. 1981. Nitrogenous fertilizers for sports turf. p. 303–312. *In* R.W. Sheard (ed.) Proc. 4th Int. Turfgrass Res. Conf., Guelph, ON, Canada. 19–23 July. Int. Turfgrass Soc., and Ontario Agric. Coll., Univ. of Guelph, Guelph, ON.

Yamamoto, S., and Y. Mino. 1982. Carbohydrate metabolism in the stem base of orchardgrass (*Dactylis glomerata* L.) after cutting. J. Jpn. Soc. Grassl. Sci. 28:8–13.

Yamamoto, S., and Y. Mino. 1985. Partial purification and properties of phleinase induced in stem base of orchardgrass after defoliation. Plant Physiol. 78:591–595.

Youngner, V.B. 1969. Physiology of growth and development. 187–216. *In* A.A. Hanson and F.V. Juska (ed.) Turfgrass science. Agron. Monogr. 14. ASA, Madison, WI.

Youngner, V.B., and F.J. Nudge. 1976. Soil temperature, air temperature, and defoliation effects on growth and nonstructural carbohydrates of Kentucky bluegrass. Agron. J. 68:257–260.

Youngner, V.B., A.W. Marsh, R.A. Strohman, V.A. Gibeault, and S. Spaulding. 1981. Water use and turf quality of warm-season and cool-season turfgrasses. p. 251–257. *In* R.W. Sheard (ed.) Proc. 4th Int. Turfgrass Res. Conf., Guelph, ON, Canada. 19–23 July. Int. Turfgrass Soc., and Ontario Agric. Coll., Univ. of Guelph, Guelph, ON.

Zanoni, L.J., L.F. Michelson, W.G. Colby, and M. Drake. 1969. Factors affecting carbohydrate reserves of cool-season turfgrasses. Agron. J. 61:195–198.

6 Salinity and Turfgrass Culture

M. ALI HARIVANDI

Univ. of California Coop. Extension
Hayward, California

JACK D. BUTLER

Colorado State University
Ft. Collins, Colorado

LIN WU

University of California
Davis, California

Salinity causes problems in turfgrass culture that are difficult and expensive to correct. Turfgrass growth and management problems associated either directly or indirectly with salinity continue to increase. This increase is due to several factors: (i) rapid population growth (and thus increase of turfgrass acreage) in arid and semiarid regions where soil and water salinity problems and strong water resource competition are common; (ii) development of turfgrass facilities near bodies of salt water; (iii) use of various salts for deicing highways, sidewalks, and airport runways.

Saline soils usually contain a mixture of salts. Sodium, Ca, Mg, and K are the most common cations found in high concentrations in saline soils. In such soils the dominant anions are generally chlorides, sulfates, carbonates, and bicarbonates. In studies of salt effects on plant growth, it is important to realize that under field conditions, a complex mixture of ions may exist. Although laboratory investigation of the effects of individual ions and specific cation-anion combinations is essential, field studies are required for accurately determining plant responses.

Turfgrass salinity damage may be directly attributed to soluble salts in the soil, but it is often related to a combination of soil physical and chemical factors such as osmotic stress, wet soil conditions and dispersed soil particles. Soils contaminated by Na salts often drain poorly, and are prone to compaction.

Various approaches may be successful in correcting the adverse turfgrass-growing conditions associated with salinity. In most cases, salts continue to concentrate over time and thus long-term solutions to salt problems must be sought.

Copyright © 1992 ASA-CSSA-SSSA, 677 S. Segoe Rd., Madison, WI 53711, USA. *Turfgrass—Agronomy Monograph no. 32.*

I. SOURCES OF SALINITY

The primary source of soluble salts is soil parent material, from which salts are released through weathering (Bresler et al., 1982; Richards, 1954). In humid areas, salts are continually leached from the root zone and so are less likely to be a problem than in arid regions. Salt-affected soils occur naturally in arid and semiarid regions where precipitation is insufficient to leach salts downward through the soil profile. Salt-contaminated soils also occur near sea coasts as a result of tidal action and airborne salt disposition, or where water tables are shallow and highly saline. Where salinization occurs, it is often an ongoing process resulting from combinations of insufficient precipitation, inadequate irrigation, poor drainage, irrigation with poor-quality water, or the upward movement of salts caused by high water tables. If the amount of water from irrigation plus natural precipitation exceeds evapotranspiration, salt movement is generally downward. If evapotranspiration exceeds irrigation and precipitation inputs, salt movement is generally upward. In the latter case, salts drawn to the soil surface may accumulate to injurious levels.

Salt-affected soils may contain Na ion or soluble salts. The U.S. Salinity Laboratory (Rhoades & Bernstein, 1971; Richards, 1954) has divided salt-contaminated soils into three groups:

1. Saline Soils—The saturated extract of these soils has an electrical conductivity (EC_e) >4 dS m^{-1}, and an exchangeable sodium percentage (ESP) below 15. The pH of these soils is ordinarily below 8.5. Saline soils are often referred to as "white alkali," and are recognized by the white salt crust that forms at their surface as the soil dries. With adequate water and drainage, these soils can be desalinized by leaching.

2. Saline-Sodic Soils—The saturation extract of these soils has an EC_e >4 dS m^{-1}, and an ESP >15. Soil pH is seldom above 8.5. If existing soluble salts are leached downward while the exchangeable Na in the soil profile remains constant, soil properties are likely to closely resemble those of the next group, the sodic soils. As long as soluble salts are present, however, these soils are more similar to saline than sodic soils in both appearance and physical properties.

3. Sodic Soils—This category applies to soils in which the EC_e is <4 dS m^{-1} and the ESP exceeds 15. Soil pH is generally above 8.5. These soils are often referred to as "black alkali" and do not exhibit a white surface crust when dry. High levels of Na combined with low levels of Ca and Mg cause dispersion of clay particles in these soils. This situation results in structureless soils with low water and air permeability.

Water is often the carrier of salts, since those released from rocks or soil by natural weathering move with its flow. The salt volume and composition of surface water, including water in rivers, streams, lakes and reservoirs, varies from place to place, season to season, and year to year. Groundwaters do not vary as markedly with time as surface waters, unless "disturbed" by man (Bresler et al., 1982; Richards, 1954).

In coastal areas, where pumping can deplete aquifers faster than they are naturally replenished, seawater may intrude into fresh water aquifers, increasing their soluble salt content. In Florida, for example, salt water intrusion into wells used for irrigating turfgrasses is a significant problem. This phenomenon, first reported during the 1920s, has increased in seriousness since 1960 due to population flux and increased demands for fresh water (Parker, 1975). Total soluble salts as high as 14 000 mg kg^{-1} are reported from wells in some areas due to salt intrusion (Peacock & Dudeck, 1985b).

Sewage effluent use has recently added a new dimension to turfgrass irrigation. Turfgrass irrigation with reclaimed water is attractive due to fresh water shortages and rising costs, increased availability of quality reclaimed water, and the need to properly handle effluent water. However, sewage effluent water must be evaluated for its potential contribution to salinity and heavy metals buildup in soil. Some effluent waters are so saline that use of them would prohibit turfgrass growth. In addition to salinity buildup, soil permeability can be reduced by the high Na content of some effluent waters.

The principal measurements used by the U.S. Salinity Laboratory (Richards, 1954) to determine water quality vis a vis salinity or sodicity are:

1. Salinity Hazard—The four categories of hazard are based on total salt concentration. Category 1, or *low* salinity hazards, applies to water with an EC_w of 0.25 dS m^{-1} or less. Category 2, *medium* salinity hazard, denotes waters with an EC_w of 0.25 to 0.75 dS m^{-1}. Waters assigned to Category 3, *high* salinity hazard, have an EC_w of 0.75 to 2.25 dS m^{-1}, while Category 4, *very high* salinity hazard, is reserved for waters with EC_w's above 2.25 dS m^{-1}.

2. Sodium Hazard—The amount of exchangeable Na in a soil affects its physical properties. When Na concentration is high relative to that of the combined Ca and Mg, soil tilth and water permeability decrease markedly. The sodium adsorption ratio (SAR) reflects the relative concentrations of Na to Ca plus Mg $\{SAR = Na^+/[(Ca^{2+} + Mg^{2+})/2]^{1/2}\}$. Thus, SAR provides an acceptable measure of irrigation water quality with regard to Na. Category 1, or *low* Na waters, have an SAR below 10. Category 2, *medium* Na waters, have SARs between 10 and 18. Category 3, *high* Na waters are those with SARs between 18 and 26, while waters with SARs >26 are classified as *very high* Na waters, or Category 4.

The above classification of water quality has been for average use conditions in general. Rhoades (1972) pointed out that the conventional approaches of water quality assessment were inadequate: "The suitability of an irrigation water needs to be evaluated on the basis of the specific conditions under which it will be used including crops being grown, soil properties, irrigation management, cultural practices, and climatic conditions." He later developed a method for assessing the suitability of water for irrigation (Rhoades, 1975, 1982), and suggested that since the effects of exchangeable Na on swelling and dispersion are counteracted by high electrolyte concentration, the soil sodicity (permeability) hazard cannot be assessed independently of electrolyte concentration (salinity). Soils vary in their permeability

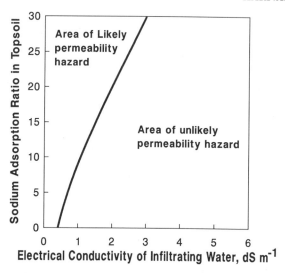

Fig. 6-1. Threshold values of sodium adsorption ratio of topsoil and electrical conductivity of infiltrating water for maintenance of soil permeability (Rhoades, 1983).

response to exchangeable Na and electrolyte concentration, making it difficult to specify universally applicable critical levels of SAR and EC_w. Values given (Fig. 6-1) are estimates for arid-land soils (Rhoades, 1983). Permeability hazard is assessed by ascertaining whether the SAR-EC_w combination falls to the left (problem likely) or right (no problem likely) of the threshold line. Even at low soil SAR permeability problems may occur, where rainfall leaches the surface soil nearly free of salts or very pure waters are used for irrigation (Fig. 6-1).

Quality of irrigation water is only one factor affecting soil salinity, sodicity, or both. Successful long-term use of saline irrigation water also depends on soil characteristics, water management, and turfgrass species.

An additional source of salinity problems in turfgrass culture is the large quantity of salt, primarily NaCl, applied to highways and other paved surfaces for snow and ice removal. Hutchinson (1970) reported that average annual application rates of 8000 to 14 000 kg km^{-1} of salt are common on roadways in several states. Hanes et al. (1970) determined that several states applied more than 18 000 kg km^{-1} of deicing salt (NaCl) per season per lane on some highways. The brine flowing from such treated surfaces can increase salt concentrations in adjacent soils, making them unsuitable for growth of turfgrasses and other vegetative covers essential for erosion control (Brod & Preusse, 1980; Butler et al., 1974; Cordukes, 1970; Greub et al., 1985; Hughes et al., 1975; Hutchinson, 1970; Nowicki et al., 1985; Roberts & Zykura, 1967). Salt concentrations of 20 000 mg kg^{-1} are typical in sparsely vegetated areas. Soluble salt concentrations were noted up to 50 000 mg kg^{-1} in soil from medians of some roads (Hutchinson, 1970).

Fertilizer may also be a source for salinity buildup in turfgrass culture (Beard, 1973; Madison, 1971), particularly with higher application rates of soluble sources. Animal manure, often used as an organic additive to soil, is another potential source of salinity (Oster et al., 1984). Applying sewage sludge to modify fine-textured soils can also create salt problems. Although sludge application may improve turfgrass establishment by improving a soil's physical properties and providing nutrients, sludge may also increase soil salinity and chloride content (Epstein et al., 1976). More data are needed on the effects of sludge related to salinity buildup in different soils.

II. THE NATURE OF SALINITY EFFECTS AND TURFGRASS TOLERANCE MECHANISMS

Excess soluble salts in the turfgrass root zone may affect growth by osmotic inhibition of water absorption (physiological drought), by specific effects of the constituent ions in the saline media (which may involve direct toxicity or a variety of nutritional effects), or by a combination of the two.

Plants experience restricted water uptake in saline solutions due to increased osmotic pressure. Sensitivity varies widely with plant species and mechanisms of salinity response. Experiments to determine response of bermudagrass (*Cynodon* spp.) to increasing salinity suggest that salinity tolerance in this species may involve several processes. Tolerance may be facilitated by the shunting of photosynthate from top to root growth and carbohydrate storage, by osmotic adjustment through ionic substitution and redistribution, or by increased concentration of organic acids in the cell sap (Ackerson & Youngner, 1975). Results from a study (Peacock & Dudeck, 1985a) that exposed the highly salt-tolerant bermudagrass and seashore paspalum (*Paspalum vaginatum* Swartz.) to increasing salinity, suggested that salt-tolerant grasses maintain as small a differential between leaf and solution osmotic potential as possible to conserve energy while protecting against salt stress. A salt exclusion tolerance mechanism was suggested when salt-tolerant creeping bentgrass (*Agrostis palustris* Huds.) took up less salt than nontolerant genotypes (Wu, 1981). Another series of studies (Torello, 1985) showed salt-tolerant species and cultivars greatly reduced salt (NaCl) uptake, and retained higher K, Mg, and Ca levels than salt-sensitive ones. Salt-tolerant types accumulated from 8 to 15 times more proline than did salt-sensitive cultivars. Proline is an amino acid often found to accumulate in salt, as well as drought-resistant plants. Proline accumulations apparently stabilize internal osmotic imbalances and protect enzyme systems and organelle functions normally disrupted in salt-sensitive plants (Levitt, 1972).

Turfgrasses absorb constituent ions of a saline solution to varying degrees, making both toxic ion accumulations, inadequate absorption of some essential nutrients, or both, possible. Such toxic or nutritional effects cannot be predicted from analysis of the saline solution. Although changes in the solution may cause responses usually associated with toxicity, such effects may arise partly from the accompanying change in solution osmotic potential. Partitioning of effects into osmotic and specific ion components is difficult. In general, increasing soil salinity increases osmotic stress within the plant, leading eventually to physiological drought (Levitt, 1972). In creeping bentgrass, however, no relationship between osmotic resistance, drought survival, and salinity has been found (Wu & Huff, 1983).

Accumulation of one or more salts in a turfgrass plant can limit the normal uptake of one or several essential nutrients causing mineral deficiencies. Increased concentrations of Na and Ca in tops and roots of 'Santa Ana' bermudagrass corresponded with decreased concentrations of K and Mg when NaCl and $CaCl_2$ were used in the culture solution (Ackerson & Youngner, 1975). When K_2SO_4 was applied, K concentrations increased in tops and roots while Ca and Mg decreased. This was not unexpected since uptake and translocation of other cations are commonly suppressed by large K supplies (Cain, 1955; Emmert, 1961; Shear et al., 1953). Since total inorganic concentrations did not change greatly with increasing amounts of NaCl and $CaCl_2$ in the culture media, it was suggested that a substitution mechanism may be preventing toxic buildup of mineral elements to facilitate osmotic adjustment in bermudagrass (Ackerson & Youngner, 1975). Although K decreased while Na increased with increased NaCl in a more recent study, the total concentration of K plus Na was again unaffected (Dudeck et al., 1983). Additionally, it was suggested that Na may actually substitute for K in bermudagrass nutrition.

In seashore paspalum, another warm-season grass, tissue Cl and Na contents increased with increasing salinity, while tissue content of Ca, Mg, and K decreased (Dudeck & Peacock, 1985a). Potassium content was most sharply decreased in concentration.

Treatment with NaCl resulted in greater Na concentration for various organs of creeping bentgrass (Chetelat & Wu, 1986). Organ tissue partitioning of Na was suggested as a source of salinity tolerance in creeping bentgrass. The highest Na concentration was in the roots, the lowest in young leaves and leaf blades. Chloride concentrations were similarly distributed throughout the plant, but were lower in concentration than Na. Tissue K and Ca decreased and Na to K ratio increased in the presence of increased NaCl.

In contrast to creeping bentgrass, weeping [*Puccinellia distans* (L.) Parl.] and Lemmon [*P. lemmoni* (Vasey) Scribn.] alkaligrasses irrigated with varying concentrations of synthetic sea water (Table 6–1) accumulated more Cl than Na in their leaf tissues (Harivandi et al., 1982a). As sea-water concentration increased, leaf Na and Cl concentrations both increased, but the rate of increase was higher for Cl. Increased Na accumulation also occurred in several cool-season grasses, including the alkaligrasses, grown in media with relatively high NaCl content (Hughes et al., 1975). Addition of NaCl to the soil led to decreased leaf Ca and Mg, but did not affect K (Table 6–2).

Harivandi et al. (1983) reported varying concentrations of common soluble salts (Cl and SO_4 salts of Na, K, Ca, and Mg) on salt accumulation patterns within weeping and Lemmon alkaligrass indicated that as concentration of salt solution increased, tissue ion accumulation increased. Cations applied as Cl salts accumulated to higher levels than those applied as SO_4 salts. When NaCl was applied, less Na accumulated than Cl, while more Na than

Table 6-1. Ionic composition of the instant ocean synthetic sea salt solution at 15 °C.†

Ion	Concentration	Ion	Concentration
	mg kg^{-1}		mg kg^{-1}
Cl	18 400	MoO$_4$	0.7
Na‡	10 200	S$_2$O$_3$	0.4
SO$_4$	2 500	Li	0.2
Mg	1 200	Rh	0.1
K	370	I	0.07
Ca	370	EDTA§	0.05
HCO$_3$	140	Al	0.04
H$_3$BO$_3$	25	Zn	0.02
Br	20	V	0.02
Sr	8	Co	0.01
PO$_4$	1	Fe	0.01
Mn	1	Cu	0.003

† Analysis by Aquarium Systems Inc., Eastlake, OH.
‡ SAR = 57.6 (Calculated from the analysis given by Aquarium Systems) (Harivandi et al., 1982a).
§ Ethylenediaminetetraacetic acid.

SO$_4$ accumulated with application of Na$_2$SO$_4$. Cation and anion generally accumulated to the same level with KCl applications, but more K accumulated than SO$_4$ with K$_2$SO$_4$ treatments. There was no clear ion accumulation pattern after CaCl$_2$ application. Calcium accumulated to higher levels than SO$_4$ with CaSO$_4$ treatments. More Mg accumulated than either Cl or SO$_4$ after MgCl$_2$ and MgSO$_4$ were applied. Chloride accumulation was greatest in combination with Na, when considered solely from the standpoint of accompanying cation. Chloride accumulation when combined with K, Ca, and Mg decreased in that order. Two months' exposure to 0.168 mol L^{-1} or more of SO$_4$ salts, or 0.112 mol L^{-1} or more of Cl salts, resulted in death of established Lemmon and weeping alkaligrass stands.

Other data suggested that several cool-season grasses experience Cl stress when Cl in blade tissue is approximately 15 000 mg kg^{-1} of dry matter (Cordukes, 1970). Chloride levels above 30 000 mg kg^{-1} of dry matter in these turfgrasses required immediate elimination of Cl uptake to prevent loss of the turf.

Five turfgrass species, common bermudagrass [*Cynodon dactylon* L. (Pers.)], Kentucky bluegrass (*Poa pratensis* L.), 'Alta' tall fescue (*Festuca arundinacea* Schreb.), 'Seaside' creeping bentgrass, and weeping alkaligrass, were studied for their tolerance to Na (Lunt et al., 1964). None of these grasses was found to be particularly sensitive, and the researchers suggest that all could be grown in soils with an ESP of 15 or less. Weeping alkaligrass and Seaside creeping bentgrass, the most tolerant in this study, would probably grow at soil ESP levels up to 30. The possibility of Ca deficiency was not discussed in this report. It has been suggested that increasing SAR at low salinity levels may reduce Ca concentration to nutritionally inadequate levels, or achieve high values of SAR while keeping Ca nutritionally adequate without also increasing salinity to high levels (Rhoades, 1983). Further in-

Table 6-2. Mineral composition of forage for five grass species as affected by NaCl addition (Hughes et al., 1975).

Species	NaCl added to soil	P	K	Ca	Mg	Si	Fe	Mn	Zn	Cu	B	Na	Al
						mg kg^{-1}							
Agropyron cristatum (L.) Gaertn.	0	2 700	20 200	6 800	2 300	16 000	141	338	77	15	148	501	105
	20 000	2 900	25 400	4 600	1 700	11 400	170	350	70	17	147	4 745	94
Agropyron smithii Rydb.	0	2 700	22 900	4 600	1 800	14 000	79	215	47	15	75	298	45
	20 000	3 000	26 400	3 500	1 400	6 700	78	137	48	17	54	2 640	39
Lolium perenne L.	0	3 400	25 200	7 000	3 100	19 200	156	440	66	19	165	1 692	131
	20 000	2 900	19 200	5 200	1 600	18 000	317	334	48	12	104	10 395	302
Poa pratensis L.	0	3 400	23 300	5 300	2 800	16 700	251	245	63	19	137	435	207
	20 000	2 900	21 200	3 900	2 300	12 500	372	150	48	15	106	5 073	233
Puccinellia distans (L.) Parl.	0	2 600	22 000	4 000	2 300	18 100	362	270	37	17	99	490	278
	20 000	2 800	23 300	3 400	1 800	11 000	152	336	37	14	83	5 615	112
LSD 0.05		500	5 600	800	500	3 100	179	84	11	5	28	2 878	149

vestigation is needed to establish critical Na levels for normal turfgrass growth, apart from possible Ca-deficiency effects.

As stated above, changes in solution composition may cause either toxic/nutritional problems or osmotic stress. Hayward and Wadleigh (1949) suggested that both components play a role in plant response to salinity. They stated that a species' salt tolerance depends on at least three attributes: (i) the plant's capacity to increase the osmotic potential of its tissue fluid to compensate for increases in substrate osmotic potential; (ii) the plant's capacity to regulate ion intake to increase its own osmotic potential while still avoiding accumulation of ions to a toxic level; and (iii) the inherent ability of the plant's protoplasm to resist deleterious effects of accumulated ions. Although the question of nutrient imbalances resulting from salinity stress is not directly addressed by these attributes, the second attribute may be regarded as an indirect means of regulating nutrient imbalances in a saline substrate.

A. Boron Toxicity

Although B is an essential turfgrass nutrient, excessive levels may be present in the root zone (Deal & Engel, 1965; Oertli et al., 1961). Soils with high native concentration of B occur primarily in arid and semiarid regions (Peryea & Bingham, 1984). Turf soils exposed to B in groundwater and treated sewage effluent water may develop elevated levels of this element (Butler et al., 1985; Donaldson et al., 1979). Boron toxicity in turfgrasses has not been intensively studied. The limited data available suggest that B does not create an insurmountable problem for turf since it accumulates in leaf tips that are routinely removed by mowing. (Boron damage is a major concern for other landscape plants grown with turf.) When five turfgrass species were grown in media with varying concentrations of B, little decline in turfgrass growth was observed even at high B concentrations. Differences in tip necrosis were negligible when the grass was clipped frequently (Oertli et al., 1961). Since B accumulated in leaf tips, where concentrations were approximately 10 times those in other parts of the leaf, clipping allowed tolerance of B levels that would normally cause plant damage. Before clipping, tip burn, the classic B-induced injury, was readily observed and correlated with high B analyses. Plants that were rapid B accumulators were first to show injury. The rate of B accumulation was: common bermudagrass < Japanese lawngrass (*Zoysia japonica* Steud.) < Kentucky bluegrass < Alta tall fescue < perennial ryegrass (*Lolium perenne L.*) < creeping bentgrass (Oertli et al., 1961).

Bernstein (1967, p. 51–65) indicated that marginal levels of B in irrigation water may not be immediately toxic, but continued use of such water can lead to intolerable soil B buildup. Boron is difficult to leach, requiring roughly twice as much water to leach as soluble salts (Oster et al., 1984). In work with high-B sewage effluent on golf greens, B concentrations were as high as 7.8 mg kg^{-1} in both water and soil (Donaldson et al., 1979). The high B level in soil was associated with high B content of effluent irrigation water. In this work of rather short duration (20 mo), the high B water caused no apparent injury to Seaside creeping bentgrass grown on loam soil. Overall visual appearance and playability of the greens remained excellent. Grass clippings did not indicate B concentrations high enough to cause leaf burn or necrotic tissue. In this study, researchers attributed the low B concentrations in clippings to rapid plant growth and frequent removal of clippings.

Available data indicate that most turfgrasses will grow normally at soil B levels as high as 10 mg kg^{-1} (Oertli et al., 1961). Although some injury, in the form of leaf tip burn, may occur, this tissue can be removed with regular mowing. Further field tests are needed to evaluate the maximum levels of tolerance to B for high cut turfgrass, and especially where clippings are not removed from the sward.

III. SALINITY EFFECTS ON TURFGRASS GROWTH

The degree of salt tolerance of a turfgrass can be estimated from plant growth responses to increasing salinity. Salinity conditions cause a wide variety of turfgrass growth and adaptations. Salinity effects on pattern and degree of shoot and root growth have been extensively studied (Chetelat & Wu, 1986; Dudeck et al., 1983; Horst & Beadle, 1984; Horst & Taylor, 1983; Rozema & Visser, 1981; Torello & Symington, 1984; Youngner & Lunt, 1967).

Water uptake in saline conditions is reduced by osmotic stress, and the uptake of some essential elements, such as K, may be depressed by competitive absorption of other elements, such as Na. As a compensatory adaptive mechanism to osmotic water and nutrient stress under saline conditions, a turfgrass may enlarge its water- and ion-absorbing root surface, thus increasing its root biomass (Dudeck et al., 1983; Parker, 1975; Torello & Symington, 1984; Youngner & Lunt, 1967). Sodium and Cl may reduce plant growth by their influence on photosynthesis (Rozema & Visser, 1981). Top growth of bermudagrass grown in solutions containing 0, 0.08, 0.16, 0.24, and 0.32 mol L^{-1} NaCl and 0, 0.16, 0.32, 0.48, and 0.64 mol L^{-1} CaCl$_2$ decreased significantly with each increment of salt in the solution (Youngner & Lunt, 1967). Root weight to top weight ratios increased with increased salinity, with the highest root weights obtained at intermediate to high salt levels. The authors offered the following explanations for their results: (i) maintenance of a high photosynthetic rate despite retardation of top growth; (ii) reduced percentage defoliation resulting from top growth retardation; or (iii) a differential response of tops and roots to growth hormones. In a later study, Dudeck et al. (1983) observed differential growth of tops and roots of bermudagrass and reported that top growth decreased by 22%, while root growth increased by 270% at the high salt (NaCl) level of 9.9 dS m^{-1}. Top growth decreased linearly in all cases. Root growth increased to a maximum point and then declined (Fig. 6–2). The concurrent increased root growth and decreased top growth may allow bermudagrass to survive osmotic and nutritional stresses caused by salinity. It was also reported (Dudeck & Peacock, 1985a) that seashore paspalum cultivars and experimental varieties differed in growth response to varying concentrations of synthetic sea water. FSP-1

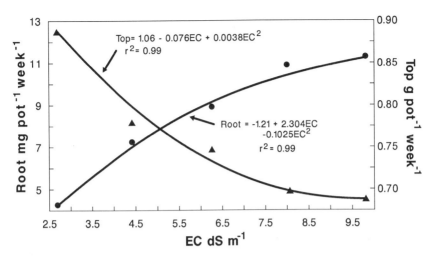

Fig. 6-2. Composite of growth responses of tops and roots of eight bermudagrass cultivars as influenced by NaCl (Dudeck et al., 1983).

was superior to other cultivars and experimental lines tested. Its crown growth was unaffected, top growth decreased gradually to a 50% yield reduction at 28.6 dS m^{-1}, root growth increased with increased salinity to a maximum at 15.7 dS m^{-1}. Both top and root growth decreased sharply in cv. Adalayd, Futurf, and FSP-2. In a subsequent study, Peacock and Dudeck (1985b) reported top growth of Adalayd and FSP-1 decreased when exposed to salinity. Root growth of Adalayd decreased, but rooting in FSP-1 increased to a maximum of 15.7 dS m^{-1} before decreasing.

Creeping bentgrass growth can be affected by increased salt stress (Tiku & Snaydon, 1971; Wainwright, 1981). Working with two creeping bentgrass clones with different salinity tolerances, Chetelat and Wu (1986) concluded that elongation of the plant's longest root is less inhibited by NaCl than growth of the entire root system, and that root elongation provides a better comparison of salinity tolerance than growth of the entire root system. In fact, root elongation was shown to be less strongly influenced by overall photosynthetic production of the shoots than was total root dry weight. The preferential elongation of roots might enable bentgrass to use potentially less saline water from greater soil depths.

Variation was minimal among cultivars of three cool-season turfgrasses for both leaf initiation and leaf length in response to increasing NaCl (Torello & Symington, 1984). Increasing NaCl levels reduced the extent of leaf production for all cultivars. The percentage reduction in leaf initiation and leaf length compared to control treatments was greater for Kentucky bluegrass than for the salt-tolerant red fescues (*Festuca rubra* L.) and alkaligrasses, with differences arising at the 0.043 mol L^{-1} NaCl concentration. All cultivars but one showed a reduction in root numbers as salinity increased, with little variation between alkaligrass and Kentucky bluegrass cultivars. Root initiation, however, increased for 'Dawson' red fescue between 0.017 and 0.085 mol L^{-1} NaCl concentrations.

Horst and Taylor (1983) observed a salt level × cultivar interaction for Kentucky bluegrass cultivar seedlings grown in saline solutions. Several cultivars had higher blade fresh weights at 7500 mg kg^{-1} salt (NaCl and $CaCl_2$) than at two higher salt levels. Seedling leaf blade fresh weight and seedling leaf blade length had negative responses to increased salt concentration, averaging a loss of approximately 0.023 g in blade weight and 0.0037 m in blade length for each 1000 mg kg^{-1} increase in salt concentration. Growth of Kentucky bluegrass cultivars was reduced by 50% at concentrations of 7500 mg kg^{-1}, by 75% at 12 500 mg kg^{-1} and stopped at approximately 15 000 mg kg^{-1}.

Mean blade length of tall fescue cultivars fell to 90, 88, and 53% of the control with increasing salinity (7500, 12 500, and 15 000 mg kg^{-1} of equal portions of NaCl and $CaCl_2$) (Horst & Beadle, 1984).

IV. SALINITY EFFECTS ON TURFGRASS SEED GERMINATION

The effects of salinity on a turfgrass may vary with stage of plant development. Sensitivity may be different during germination than at later stages. There is considerable evidence that turfgrasses are particularly sensitive to soil salinity during germination and early seedling growth. In a germination study, Lunt et al. (1961) found weeping alkaligrass and Alta tall fescue were most salt tolerant, while Kentucky bluegrass, creeping bentgrass, and colonial bentgrass (*Agrostis tenuis* Sibth.) were less tolerant. Sodium chloride consistently had a greater depressive effect on germination than an equivalent concentration of $CaCl_2$. Harivandi et al. (1982b) found Kentucky bluegrass to be least salt tolerant during germination and seedling stages, while Dawson red fescue was intermediate and alkaligrass was highest in salt tolerance at these growth stages. In another study (Torello & Symington, 1984), the effects of increasing media salinity on seed germination were similar for three cool-season grasses. Percentage germination remained the same over the salt concentration range of 0.017 to 0.17 mol L^{-12} NaCl after 8 d of incubation for Kentucky bluegrass and 6 d for alkaligrass and red fescue (cv. Dawson and Checker). Final total percent germination was less for the three grasses than for the controls, with the salt-tolerant red fescue cultivars and alkaligrass least affected. Within the five Kentucky bluegrasses studied, 'Ram 1' and 'Adelphi' had the highest germination percentage in the most saline media.

Total germination and days to germination are important considerations in choosing turfgrasses. Work by Horst and Taylor (1983) showed significant differences among 44 Kentucky bluegrass cultivars for germination percentage and time required to germinate in a saline media. Differences in mean percentage germination relative to the control ranged from 117% for 'Delta' to 4% for 'Bonnieblue.' When seeds of 'Fylking' Kentucky bluegrass were presoaked for 24 h in water or 100 000, 200 000 and 300 000 mg kg^{-1} NaCl solutions and then germinated in the laboratory on moistened paper, the presoaking in saline media did not affect final germination percentages (Cordukes, 1970). The length of time to complete germination increased with salinity concentration. Total germination of six perennial ryegrass cultivars was unaffected by up to 10 000 mg kg^{-1} of salinity (sea salt mixture) in the germination media, although germination rate decreased with increased salinity (Dudeck & Peacock, 1985b). The drop in germination rate was attributed to increased osmotic stress. In earlier work, Ayers (1952) found that the first increments of salinity tend to retard germination, but additional increments progressively reduce final germination percentage. Since total germination of perennial ryegrass was unaffected up to 10 000 mg kg^{-1} of salt (Dudeck & Peacock, 1985b) while mature plant top growth yields were reduced 50% at about 7500 mg kg^{-1} (Maas, 1986; Richards, 1954), perennial ryegrass appears to be more salt tolerant during germination than at later growth stages. Fiesta perennial ryegrass had the lowest germination rate (18%) and the lowest total germination rate (21%), and tied with 'Citation II' for highest total germination (97%).

Relative salt tolerance during germination and seedling growth of tall fescue cultivars have also been studied (Horst & Beadle, 1984). Germination rate as a percentage of the control averaged 75, 62, and 51% for 7500, 12 500 and 15 000 mg kg^{-1} of equal portions of NaCl and CaCl$_2$, respectively. Mean seedling survival at the end of 21 d averaged 92% of the control for seeds germinated and grown in the 7500 mg kg^{-1} treatment. 'Houndog' and a group of experimental lines exhibited enhanced germination and seedling survival. Average seedling survival declined to 83% of the control at 12 500 mg kg^{-1} and 75% of the control at 15 000 mg kg^{-1}.

Highly significant differences in percent germination between weeping and Lemmon alkaligrasses occurred in 25, 50, and 75% synthetic sea water (Table 6–1), with weeping alkaligrass showing the greater salt tolerance (Harivandi et al., 1982a). For weeping alkaligrass, germination percentages at the 0, 25, and 50% levels of sea water were not significantly different. At 75% sea water, up to 50% germination occurred. Lemmon alkaligrass had only 14% germination at 75% sea water concentration.

Even highly tolerant grasses are not immune to salt effects during germination. Certain turfgrasses, especially alkaligrass, may germinate successfully in sandy soils irrigated with highly salty water (e.g., diluted synthetic sea water) as long as the soil is kept moist enough that germination is not retarded by a combination of salt and osmotic stresses. Also, turfgrass seeds sown in saline sand can germinate after a portion of the substrate salt is leached (Harivandi et al., 1982b). This suggests that inhibited germination in highly saline conditions was partially due to osmotic stress. These results are consistent with work using seeds of halophytic plants, since seeds also failed to germinate in highly saline conditions but germinated readily when transferred from the saline environment (Macke & Ungar, 1971; Ungar, 1962).

Data from short-term screening studies such as those previously mentioned, though suggestive of general tolerance to salt stress, would lead to more accurate characterization if accompanied by data from long-term field studies carried out under a variety of conditions. Long-term field studies are lacking, and are needed to substantiate short-term studies.

V. DIAGNOSING SALINITY PROBLEMS

Salinity/sodicity in soil can vary greatly over relatively short distances. "Salt spots" that support no growth may extend into nonsaline or slightly saline areas that support normal turf growth. Spotty stands of grass and bare spots are common in soils with salinity, sodicity, or both problems. Bare spots that are covered with a white crust upon drying are typically saline; where bare spots occur without a white crust, a sodic environment is more likely (Richards, 1954).

Specific symptoms of salinity stress in turfgrasses vary (Beard, 1973; Bernstein & Hayward, 1958; Dudeck & Peacock, 1985a; Harivandi et al., 1982a, b; Harivandi et al., 1983; Hayward & Wadleigh, 1949; Hughes et al., 1975; Lunt et al., 1961; Oertli et al., 1961; Oster, 1981; Youngner et al., 1967). The first symptom of injury is reduced growth. Leaves may have narrower and stiffer blades, and can be slightly darker than normal or even blue-green in color. These symptoms are similar to those of drought stress. Reduced size and width of blades and the stiffness of leaves correlate with reduced cell size. Smaller cells may stem from a water deficit induced by high osmotic potential in the root medium. Reduction of intracellular spaces, strengthening of palisade parenchyma, and thickened cuticle, together or alone, may cause darker green color. Later, or at high salinity levels, visual symptoms including wilting can occur unless considerable water is applied. This stage is followed by irregular shoot growth. If specific ion (e.g., B) toxicity occurs, necrotic spots may develop on leaves. As salinity stress increases, shoots appear increasingly wilted and become progressively darker green. Higher salinity levels cause burning of leaf tips with the burn eventually extending downward over the entire leaf surface. At such levels, shoot growth is greatly reduced and turfgrass is stunted. As salinity stress increases, root growth is stunted with individual roots occasionally becoming enlarged. The stunted shoot growth associated with salt stress eventually results in a shallow root system. If corrective steps are not taken, grass growth over time will be minimal, shoot density will decrease, and the turfgrass stand will thin as individual plants die, leaving patchy turfgrass appearance.

Although a salinity problem can often be identified by visual symptoms alone, assessing the magnitude of the problem and identifying potential solutions is possible only after chemical analysis of representative soil samples. The analysis should determine pH and levels of soluble salts, and the relationship of Na to Ca and Mg (SAR). If B problems are suspected, soil levels of this element should be determined. These measurements can be used to determine the type and amounts of soil amendments or water needed to reclaim an affected soil. They may also help in choosing appropriate grasses for a site.

Salt content of soil can vary widely within one site, either naturally or as a result of management. It is critical that soil samples be representative of the turf area under investigation. A good sample is a composite of several different cores, each taken to a depth of at least 10 cm and from within an area uniform in regard to slope, drainage, irrigation, and fertilization. Only by conscientious sampling can the small amount of soil that is finally analyzed yield useful information.

The extent of salt uptake and its consequent effects on turfgrass growth are directly related to the salt concentration of the soil solution. Growth of most turfgrasses is usually not significantly affected by salt levels (EC_e) below 2 to 3 dS m^{-1}. In soils with salt levels of 3 to 6 dS m^{-1}, the growth of some turfgrasses is restricted; at 6 to 10 dS m^{-1} the growth of many turfgrasses is restricted; and above 10 to 15 dS m^{-1} only very salt-tolerant turfgrasses will grow. This categorization provides only the most general guidelines to the effect of salinity on turfgrass species and cultivars in their tolerance of both individual salts and total salinity. Each turfgrass must be individually evaluated in regard to a specific soil salinity.

In most cases, electrical conductivity (EC_e) values obtained from a soil test should be supplemented with measurements of pH, and B and Na (SAR or ESP) content. These factors may play indirect but important roles in turfgrass performance on saline soils. Even at soil salinity levels ordinarily not injurious to turf, injury may occur due to low or high soil pH, which can cause mineral toxicities or deficiencies. Although turfgrasses vary in pH requirements, a pH range of 5.5 to 7.0 is considered optimum for most turfgrasses.

Sodium, which often exists or accumulates in the soil as a result of irrigating with Na-laden water, does not cause direct injury to turfgrasses. Compared to other plants, turfgrasses are relatively Na tolerant. As soil ESP becomes ≥ 15, turfgrass stands may be damaged by soil physical changes that cause impermeability to water and air. (These changes may not occur, however, if the EC_w of the irrigation water exceeds 2 dS m^{-1}) (Fig. 6–1). Symptoms of reduced soil permeability include water logging, slow infiltration rates, crusting, compaction, and poor aeration. Any of these factors can accentuate problems related to high salinity.

Only after an assessment of EC_e, pH, SAR (ESP), and B content can soil and water salinity/sodicity and its potential effect on turf be accurately assessed.

VI. REDUCING SALINITY PROBLEMS

As indicated, excessively high levels of soluble salts in soil and water can create considerable difficulties for turfgrass growth. The scope of the problem, assessed by soil testing, and soil, plant, and site observations, determines the short- and long-term potential for growing quality turf on saline soils.

Common approaches to solving soil salinity problems include: (i) restricting salt contamination of a site, (ii) reducing salts by leaching, (iii) using salt-tolerant grasses, and (iv) managing the turf to counterbalance salt problems. Often a combination of these practices is required to grow turf successfully on saline sites.

A. Restricting Salt Contamination

Levels of soluble salts in water used for turfgrass irrigation may range from very low, to very high. Water of questionable quality is common in wells and streams of arid and semiarid regions. Near saline bodies of water, intrusion into aquifers and tidal action can cause contamination. In humid areas, salt problems from use of poor quality, salt-laden water are uncommon because salt solutions are dilute and natural precipitation normally removes excess salts from the root zone. For efficient irrigation management, water quality should be determined by laboratory analysis. It may be practical to blend different quality waters for irrigation, or, in the case of sodic waters, to treat water chemically with gypsum ($CaSO_4$) or other materials to lessen its SAR (Oster et al., 1984).

In arid and semiarid regions, salts normally accumulate in low-lying areas with poor surface drainage and in soils over shallow water tables. The only practical solution on severely saline sites may be to avoid landscaping with plant materials entirely. In drier climates, it is not uncommon to cap extremely saline soils with imported coarse soil, from which salts can be easily leached, before planting turf. Chemical analysis of the soil used for capping is necessary to ensure that it is indeed an appropriate medium for this purpose. Often, pure sand is used for capping highly saline soil.

Severe turf-related salt problems also result from the use of various salts for deicing traffic surfaces. Problems stemming from deicing can be reduced if materials other than NaCl are used. Calcium chloride and urea are common substitutes. Improved drainage of roadside turf sites may also lessen or prevent damage by deicing compounds. Further research into alternatives to salt as a deicing compound and new salt-tolerant turfgrasses is essential, since roadside salinity continues to be a serious problem.

Because of the relatively low application rate of lawn fertilizers, even those with a high salt index generally cause little damage to turf. Foliage desiccation may occur if soluble fertilizers are applied to wet turf. Other situations to avoid include overapplication, spilling, or washing and concentrating fertilizer in low, poorly drained areas, all of which are potential causes of salt buildup and damage to turfgrass.

B. Reducing Salts by Leaching

The primary method of correcting soil salinity is leaching salts through the root zone. The leaching fraction of irrigation plus precipitation is that portion of the waters that passes through the root zone, carrying dissolved salts with it. The smallest leaching fraction that maintains normal plant growth and development under a given set of conditions is referred to as that site's leaching requirement. In arid regions, natural precipitation may carry salts no more than a few inches or feet below the soil surface. Flooding such soils with excessive amounts of good quality water previous to turfgrass establishment may reduce the possibility of future salinity problems. In other areas, continuous or periodic leaching of the soil can provide a fairly permanent way of maintaining quality turfgrass production. The leaching requirement in these cases depends on salt content of the irrigation water and the salt tolerance of the turfgrass. Also, the soil type where turf is grown influences water movement and consequently leaching. For example, 20 cm of rainfall passing through a sandy soil can remove approximately 50% of the salts in the top 90 cm. In a clay soil, 20 cm of water would reduce salts by 50% in only the top 45 cm (Oster et al., 1984).

Where feasible, improving soil drainage should be considered before turf establishment. Surface drainage improvements made before turf installation provide long-term benefits for both water management and salt control. Subsurface drainage improvements, although fairly expensive, can be achieved by physically altering the soil with organic and inorganic amendments; installing perforated tubing; tiling and constructing gravel-filled trenches. Be cautious when adding organic material such as animal manure to the soil. Manure may contain as much as $100\ 000$ mg kg^{-1} of salt, therefore leaching after incorporation is generally required (Oster et al., 1984).

Although subsurface drainage is often considered the best method to remove salt, it may not always work well. It may fail if drain lines are too widely spaced, deep, or shallow; lie in a high water table; or lack adequate fall. Drains must be properly engineered and installed for effective salt and water removal from a turfed area.

Although saline soils cannot be reclaimed by chemical amendments, conditioners, or fertilizers, sodic soils may sometimes be reclaimed by addition of $CaSO_4$, elemental S, or sulfuric acid (H_2SO_4) (Hoffman, 1986; Oster et al., 1984; Richards, 1954) (Table 6-3). Gypsum is the material most often added to sodic soils. Sometimes naturally occurring Ca may be more than adequate to replace Na in a sodic soil. In such instances, replacement is activated by addition of S. Where native Ca is insufficient, 2240 kg ha^{-1} of $CaSO_4$ reduces the exchangeable Na percentage in a 15-cm deep sandy soil by approximately 10% (Oster et al., 1984). Once exchangeable soil Na has been replaced on the soil colloid, sufficient water must be applied to leach Na through the soil profile. Subsurface drainage must then be adequate to leach the Na and prevent the development of a shallow water table.

Good quality water is preferable to salt-laden water for leaching. Several investigators (Jury et al., 1978a, b; Reeve & Doering, 1966) have used saline water to reclaim sodic soils. Irrigation techniques influence salinity problems in turf and are as important as the water quality used in leaching. Sprinkler irrigation provides a fairly uniform distribution of water to turf and the movement of salts is uniformly downward. Light, frequent sprinkler irrigations can cause soluble salts to build rapidly in the turf root zone. This irrigation practice is particularly dangerous in dry climates, where frequent light irri-

Table 6-3. Chemical properties of various amendments for reclaiming sodic soil (Hoffman, 1986).

Amendment	Chemical composition	Physical description	Solubility in cold water	Amount equivalent to 1 kg of pure gypsum
			kg m^{-3}	kg
Gypsum	$CaSO_4 \cdot 2H_2O$	White mineral	2.4	1.0
Sulfur	S_8	Yellow element	0	0.2
Sulfuric acid	H_2SO_4	Corrosive liquid	Very high	0.6
Lime sulfur	9% Ca + 24% S	Yellow-brown solution	Very high	0.8
Calcium carbonate	$CaCO_3$	White mineral	0.014	0.6
Calcium chloride	$CaCl_2 \cdot 2H_2O$	White salt	977	0.9
Ferrous sulfate	$FeSO_4 \cdot 7H_2O$	Blue-green salt	156	1.6
Pyrite	FeS_2	Yellow-black mineral	0.005	0.5
Ferric sulfate	$Fe_2(SO_4)_3 \cdot 9H_2O$	Yellow-brown salt	4400	0.6
Aluminum sulfate	$Al(SO_4)_3 \cdot 18H_2O$	Corrosive granular material	869	1.3

gations with water containing only moderate salt levels can result in salinity problems. Subsurface irrigation does not provide for soil leaching above the water source. Upward water movement carries salts to the surface where they may accumulate (Oster et al., 1984).

The amount of water that must pass through soil to reduce soluble salts to tolerable levels depends on initial soil salinity, water application method, and soil type. Typically, 70% or more of the soluble salts present in saline, mineral soil will be removed by leaching with a depth of water equal to the depth of the soil (Hoffman, 1986; Oster et al., 1984).

Leaching is often a useful technique for easing salinity problems. On impervious soils it is usually necessary to improve drainage before attempting to leach. A second limitation to leaching involves B, which can be slightly absorbed by soil particles and is sometimes difficult to leach. Approximately twice as much water is required to remove a given fraction of B as to remove the same amount of soluble salts by continuous ponding (Oster et al., 1984). Water may contain sufficient B that an alternate water source should be sought, where wells are the irrigation source.

C. Use of Salt-Tolerant Grasses

The availability of turfgrasses with moderate to high levels of salt tolerance has increased during the last 20 yr. Research has determined the salt tolerance of commonly grown grasses, and has led to development and introduction of grasses specially adapted for salty sites (Table 6-4). Although several grasses will tolerate high salt levels, their quality may not be acceptable for all turf uses. These grasses may also be difficult to propagate or weedy in nature. It is not unusual for a desirable turfgrass species grown on a marginal soil high in soluble salts to be invaded by less desirable grasses. A com-

Table 6-4. Estimated salt tolerance of common turfgrasses.

Cool-season turfgrass		Warm-season turfgrass	
Name	Rating†	Name	Rating†
Alkaligrass (*Puccinellia* spp.)	T	Bahiagrass (*Paspalum notatum* Fluegge)	MS
Annual bluegrass (*Poa annua* L.)	S	Bermudagrass (*Cynodon* spp.)	T
Annual ryegrass (*Lolium multiflorum* Lam.)	MS	Blue grama [*Bouteloua gracilis* (H.B.K.)	MT
Chewings fescue (*Festuca rubra* L. spp. *commutata* Gaud.)	MS	Lag. ex steud.] Buffalograss [*Buchloë dactyloides* (Nutt.)	MT
Colonial bentgrass (*Agrostis tenuis* Sibth.)	S	Engelm.] Centipedegrass	S
Creeping bentgrass (*Agrostis palustris* Huds.)	MS	[*Eremochloa ophiuroides* (Munro) Hackel]	
Creeping bentgrass cv. Seaside	MT	Seashore paspalum	T
Creeping red fescue (*Festuca rubra* L. spp. *rubra*)	MS	(*Paspalum vaginatum* Swartz.)	
Fairway wheatgrass [*Agropyron cristatum* (L.) Gaertn.]	MT	St. Augustinegrass [*Stenotaphrum secundatum* (Walter) Kuntze]	T
Hard fescue (*Festuca longifolia* Thuill.)	MS	Zoysiagrass (*Zoysia* spp.)	MT
Kentucky bluegrass (*Poa pratensis* L.)	S		
Perennial ryegrass (*Lolium perenne* L.)	MT		
Rough bluegrass (*Poa trivialis* L.)	S		
Slender creeping red fescue cv. Dawson (*Festuca rubra* L. spp. *trichophylla*)	MT		
Tall fescue (*Festuca arundinacea* Schreb.)	MT		
Western wheatgrass (*Agropyron smithii* Rydb.)	MT		

† The rating reflects the general difficulty in establishment and maintenance at various salinity levels. It in no way indicates that a grass will not tolerate higher levels with good growing conditions and optimum care. The ratings are based on soil salt levels (EC_e) of: Sensitive (S) $= <3$ dS m^{-1}, moderately sensitive (MS) $=$ 3-6 dS m^{-1}, moderately tolerant (MT) $=$ 6-10 dS m^{-1}, tolerant (T) $= >10$ dS m^{-1}.

mon example is Kentucky bluegrass turf contaminated by naturally occurring alkaligrass.

Even relatively salt-tolerant grasses can have their tolerance reduced by adverse conditions. Stress caused by climatic conditions and soil characteristics other than salinity, make grasses more sensitive to salt stress. Drought stress tends to concentrate salts in the soil solution causing increased salinity stress. Although a saturated paste soil test might indicate that a grass is likely to perform suitably in a given soil, other stresses not measured by that test might reduce its performance. Because of the large number of variables under field conditions, research on salt tolerance done under closely controlled conditions in greenhouses, growth chambers, and laboratories can only provide general guidelines. Salt-tolerant grasses may provide only a temporary solution to renovating saline sites. Salt levels may eventually build to intolerable levels that exclude the growth of even the most tolerant plants, if soil drainage and precipitation are insufficient for needed leaching.

The soil salt level that a given turfgrass will tolerate varies with type of salt, environmental stresses, and management practices. Recent evidence (Dudeck & Peacock, 1985a, b; Dudeck et al., 1983; Harivandi et al., 1982a, b, 1983; Horst & Beadle, 1984; Horst & Taylor, 1983; Peacock & Dudeck, 1985b; Wu, 1981; Youngner et al., 1967) also indicates that wide differences in salt tolerance can exist inter- and intra-species. Consequently, current knowledge allows for selection of more salt-tolerant cultivars within an adapted turf species.

General guidelines to the relative salt tolerance of some of the more important turfgrasses can be established (Table 6-4). Possible differences in salt tolerance during stand establishment and maintenance are not accounted for in the classification presented here. In addition, it should be noted that published information on salt tolerances of various plants often base tolerance on salinity levels that cause reduction in growth or yield (Maas, 1986; Rhoades, 1983; Richards, 1954). With turfgrass production and management such reductions may not be of paramount concern. Consequently, the classification presented here (Table 6-4) is based on the estimated potential of grasses to produce fair quality turf under good management.

Because salinity varies within a site, grasses of various tolerance levels may be grown successfully in combination. For example, mixtures of sod forming, cool-season grasses such as Kentucky bluegrass and creeping red fescue are often mixed with more salt-tolerant perennial ryegrass and alkaligrass. Further research is needed regarding the compatibility and performance of various turfgrass mixtures, especially mixtures of sod-forming species with bunch types such as alkaligrass. Sod may be needed for vegetating saline sites. Appropriate grasses with different salinity tolerance can be grown offsite for this purpose.

It is clear that increasing salinity problems in turfgrass culture demand aggressive breeding programs and development of more salt-tolerant species and cultivars. Tissue culture and other genetic engineering techniques that have been developed and used in an attempt to improve environmental stress tolerances of other crops, would seem a natural area for turfgrass scientists to explore. Several universities' turfgrass research programs have begun using tissue culture in turfgrass breeding. A combination of cell suspension culture and pressure selection technique was used to isolate a cell line of Kentucky bluegrass that is tolerant to 0.17 mol L^{-1} of NaCl (equivalent to one-third the salinity of sea water) (Torello & Symington, 1984). Selecting for salt tolerance with the embryogenic Dawson red fescue cell line was also successful up to 0.17 mol L^{-1} of NaCl concentration. The potential may exist to use tissue culture to screen turfgrasses for tolerances to salt and other stress factors simultaneously. An obvious example would be simultaneous screening for enhanced drought and salt tolerance, since these two tolerances have been highly correlated (Levitt, 1972).

D. Managing Turfgrass to Counterbalance Salinity Problems

As discussed before, improper fertilization practices can cause turf salinity problems. Plants grown on infertile soils may appear more salt tolerant than those grown with adequate fertility. In such cases fertility, rather than salinity, is the primary limiting factor to growth (Maas, 1986). Often, proper fertilization will increase turf quality regardless of soil salinity; however, fertilizer responses will normally be more noticeable where salinity stress does not occur.

Clipping removal from a site as a means of salt removal is questionable, but the practice may be of use in reducing B levels (Oertli et al., 1961). Proper irrigation is important for managing high quality turf on salt-affected soils. Primary recommendations call for keeping the soil moist, but not wet, to prevent salt concentration in the soil solution, and watering deep enough to move salts as far as possible below the root zone.

Author's Note: Much turfgrass research has been done in controlled environments and much data exist on the response of turfgrass plants to individual salts or specific ions. Field research is needed in these same areas and in the area of correcting soil salinity.

REFERENCES

Ackerson, R.C., and V.B. Youngner. 1975. Responses of bermudagrass to salinity. Agron. J. 67:678–681.

Ayers, A.D. 1952. Seed germination as affected by soil moisture and salinity. Agron. J. 44:82–84.

Beard, J.B. 1973. Turfgrass, science and culture. Prentice-Hall, Englewood Cliff, NJ.

Bernstein, L. 1967. Quantitative assessment of irrigation water quality. Am. Soc. Test. Material Spec. Tech. Publ. 416. ASTM, Philadelphia.

Bernstein, L., and H.E. Hayward. 1958. Physiology of salt tolerance. Annu. Rev. Plant Physiol. 9:25–46.

Bresler, E., B.L. McNeal, and D.L. Carter. 1982. Saline and sodic soils. Springer Verlag, Berlin.

Brod, H.G., and H.U. Preusse. 1980. The influence of deicing salts on soil and turf cover. p. 461–468. In J.B. Beard (ed.) Proc. 3rd Int. Turfgrass Res. Conf., Munich, Germany. 11-13 July 1977. Int. Turfgrass Soc., and ASA, CSSA, and SSSA, Madison, WI.

Butler, J.D., J.L. Fults, and G.D. Sanks. 1974. Review of grasses for saline and alkali areas. p. 551–556. In E.C. Roberts (ed.) Proc. 2nd Int. Turfgrass Res. Conf., Blacksburg, VA. 19-21 June 1973. ASA and CSSA, Madison, WI.

Butler, J.D., P.E. Rieke, and D.D. Minner. 1985. Influence of water quality on turfgrasses. p. 71–84. In V.A. Gibeault and S.T. Cockerham (ed.) Turfgrass water conservation. Univ. of California Coop. Ext. Publ. 21405.

Cain, J.C. 1955. The effect of potassium and magnesium on the absorption of nutrients by apple trees in sand culture. Proc. Am. Soc. Hortic. Sci. 65:25–31.

Chetelat, R., and L. Wu. 1986. Contrasting response to salt stress of two salinity tolerant creeping bentgrass clones. J. Plant Nutr. 9:1185–1197.

Cordukes, W.E. 1970. Turfgrass tolerance to road salt. The Golf Superintendent 38(5):44–48.

Deal, E.E., and R.E. Engel. 1965. Iron, manganese, boron, and zinc: Effects on growth of Merion Kentucky bluegrass. Agron. J. 57:553–555.

Donaldson, D.R., R.S. Ayers, and K.Y. Kaita. 1979. Use of high boron sewage effluent on golf greens. Calif. Turf. Cult. 29:1-2.

Dudeck, A.E., S. Singh, C.E. Giordano, T.A. Nell, and D.B. McConnell. 1983. Effects of sodium chloide on *Cynodon* turfgrasses. Agron. J. 75:927-930.

Dudeck, A.E., and C.H. Peacock. 1985a. Effects of salinity on seashore paspalum turfgrasses. Agron. J. 77:47-50.

Dudeck, A.E., and C.H. Peacock. 1985b. Salinity effects on perennial ryegrass germination. HortScience 20:268-269.

Emmert, F.N. 1961. The bearing of ion interactions on tissue analysis results. p. 231-243. *In* W. Renther (ed.) Plant analysis and fertilizer problems. Am. Inst. of Biol. Sci., Washington, DC.

Epstein, E., J.M. Taylor, and R.L. Chaney. 1976. Effects of sewage sludge compost applied to soil on some soil physical and chemical properties. J. Environ. Qual. 5:422-426.

Greub, L.J., P.N. Drolsom, and D.A. Rohrueder. 1985. Salt tolerance of grasses and legumes for roadside use. Agron. J. 77:76-80.

Hanes, R.E., L.W. Zelozny, and R.E. Blaser. 1970. Effects of deicing salts on water quality and biota—literature review and recommended research. Highway Res. Info. Serv. Abstr. 3(4):17.

Harivandi, M.A., J.D. Butler, and P.N. Soltanpour. 1982a. Effects of sea water concentrations on germination and ion accumulation in alkaligrass. Commun. Soil Sci. Plant Anal. 13:507-517.

Harivandi, M.A., J.D. Butler, and P.N. Soltanpour. 1982b. Salt influence on germination and seedling survival of six cool season turfgrass species. Commun. Soil Sci. Plant Anal. 13:519-529.

Harivandi, M.A., J.D. Butler, and P.N. Soltanpour. 1983. Effects of soluble salts on ion accumulation in *Puccinellia* spp. J. Plant Nutr. 6:255-266.

Hayward, H.E., and C.H. Wadleigh. 1949. Plant growth on saline and alkali soils. Adv. Agron. 1:1-49.

Hoffman, G.J. 1986. Guidelines for reclamation of salt-affected soils. Appl. Agric. Res. 1:65-72.

Horst, G.L., and N.B. Beadle. 1984. Salinity affects germination and growth of tall fescue cultivars. J. Am. Hortic. Sci. 109:419-422.

Horst, G.L., and R.M. Taylor. 1983. Germination and initial growth of Kentucky bluegrass. Agron. J. 75:679-681.

Hughes, T.D., J.D. Butler, and G.D. Sanks. 1975. Salt tolerance and suitability of various grasses for saline roadsides. J. Environ. Qual. 4:465-368.

Hutchinson, F.E. 1970. Environmental pollution from highway deicing compounds. J. Soil Water Conserv. 25:144-146.

Jury, W.A., H. Frenkel, D. Devitt, and L.H. Stolzy. 1978a. Transient changes in the soil-water system from irrigation with saline water: II. Analysis of experimental data. Soil Sci. Am. J. 42:585-590.

Jury, W.A., H. Frenkel, and L.H. Stolzy. 1978b. Transient changes in the soil-water system from irrigation with saline water: I. Theory. Soil Sci. Soc. Am. J. 42:579-585.

Levitt, J. 1972. Responses of plants to environmental stresses. Academic Press, New York.

Lunt, O.R., C. Kaempffe, and V.B. Youngner. 1964. Tolerance of five turfgrass species to soil alkali. Agron. J. 56:481-483.

Lunt, O.R., V.B. Younger, and J.J. Oertli. 1961. Salinity tolerance of five turfgrass varieties. Agron. J. 53:247-249.

Maas, E.V. 1986. Salt tolerance of plants. Appl. Agric. Res. 1:12-26.

Macke, A.J., and I.A. Ungar. 1971. The effects of salinity on germination and early growth of *Puccinellia nuttalliana*. Can. J. Bot. 49:515-520.

Mdison, J.H. 1971. Principles of turfgrass culture. Van Nostrand Reinhold Co., New York.

Nowicki, Cz., J. Radwanski, and M. Lipinska. 1985. The influence of salt on turfgrass. p. 195-198. *In* F. Lemaire (ed.) Proc. 5th Int. Turfgrass Res. Conf., Avignon, France. 1-5 July. Inst. Natl. de la Recherche Agron., Paris.

Oertli, J.J., O.R. Lunt, and V.B. Youngner. 1961. Boron toxicity in several turfgrass species. Agron. J. 53:262-265.

Oster, J.D. 1981. Salinity and its management. p. 14-23. *In* W.B. Davis, and M.A. Harivandi (ed.) Water management. Proc. 1981 Calif. Golf Course Superint. Inst., Asilomar, CA. Univ. of California Coop. Ext., Davis.

Oster, J.D., G.J. Hoffman, and F.E. Robinson. 1984. Management alternatives: Crop, water and soil. Calif. Agric. 38:29–32.

Parker, G.G. 1975. The hydrogeology and problems of peninsular Florida's water resources. Proc. Fla. Turf Grass Conf. 22:13–36.

Peacock, C.H., and A.E. Dudeck. 1985a. A comparative study of turfgrass physiological responses to salinity. p. 822–829. In F. Lemaire (ed.) Proc. 5th Int. Turf. Res. Conf., Avignon, France. 1–5 July. Inst. Natl. de la Recherche Agron., Paris.

Peacock, C.H., and A.E. Dudeck. 1985b. Physiological and growth responses of seashore paspalum to salinity. HortScience 20:111–112.

Peryea, F.J., and F.T. Bingham. 1984. Reclamation and regeneration of boron in high-boron soils. Calif. Agric. 38(10):35.

Reeve, R.C., and E.J. Doering. 1966. The high salt water method for reclaiming sodic soils. Soil Sci. Soc. Am. Proc. 30:498–504.

Rhoades, J.D. 1972. Quality of water for irrigation. Soil Sci. 173:277–284.

Rhoades, J.D. 1975. Water quality assessment model. p. 151–153. In Salinity laboratory annual report for 1975. U.S. Salinity Lab., USDA-ARS, Riverside, CA.

Rhoades, J.D. 1982. Reclamation and management of salt-affected soils after drainage. p. 123–197. In Rationalization of water and soil research and management. Proc. 1st Annu. Western Provincial Conf., Lethbridge, AB. 29 Nov.–2 Dec. Province of Alberta, Canada.

Rhoades, J.D. 1983. Using saline waters for irrigation. p. 829–878. In I.P. Sentis and A.F. deAndreu (ed.) Salt affected soils of Latin America. Proc. Int. Workshop on salt affected soils of Latin America, Maracay, Venezuela. 23–30 Oct. Univ. Central de Venezuela Faculted de Agronomia, Maracay, Venezuela.

Rhoades, J.D., and L. Bernstein. 1971. Chemical, physical, and biological characteristics of irrigation and soil water. p. 141–222. In L.L. Ciaccio (ed.) Water and water pollution handbook. Vol. 1. Marcel Dekker, New York.

Richards, L.A. (ed.). 1954. Diagnosis and improvement of saline and alkali soils. USDA Handb. 60. U.S. Gov. Print. Office, Washington, DC.

Roberts, E.C., and E.L. Zykura. 1967. Effect of sodium chloride on grasses/or roadside use. Highw. Res. Rec. 193:35–42.

Rozema, J., and M. Visser. 1981. The applicability of the rooting technique measuring salt resistance in populations of Festuca rubra and Juncus species. Plant Soil 62:479–485.

Shear, C.B., H.L. Crane, and A.T. Myers. 1953. Nutrient element balance: Response of tung trees grown in sand culture to potassium, magnesium, calcium and their interactions. USDA Tech. Bull. 1085. U.S. Gov. Print. Office, Washington, DC.

Tiku, B.L., and R.W. Snaydon. 1971. Salinity tolerance within the grass species Agrostis stolonifera L. Plant Soil 35:421–431.

Torello, W.A. 1985. Salinity stress. Am. Lawn Applicator (Oct.) 85:36–38.

Torello, W.A., and A.G. Symington. 1984. Screening of turfgrass species and cultivars for NaCl tolerance. Plant Soil 82:155–161.

Ungar, I.A. 1962. The influence of salinity on seed germination in succulent halophytes. Ecology 43:763–764.

Wainwright, S.J. 1981. Plants in relation to salinity. Adv. Bot. Res. 9:221–261.

Wu, L. 1981. The potential for evolution of salinity tolerance in Agrostis stolonifera L. and Agrostis tenuis Sibth. New Phytol. 89:471–486.

Wu, L., and D.R. Huff. 1983. Characteristics of creeping bentgrass clones (Agrostis stolonifera L.) from a salinity-tolerant population after surviving drought stress. HortScience 18:883–885.

Youngner, V.B., and O.R. Lunt. 1967. Salinity effects on roots and tops of bermudagrass. J. Br. Grassl. Soc. 22:257–259.

Youngner, V.B., O.R. Lunt, and F. Nudge. 1967. Salinity tolerance of seven varieties of creeping bentgrass, Agrostis palustris Huds. Agron. J. 59:335–336.

7

Physiological Effects of Temperature Stress

J.M. DiPAOLA

North Carolina State University
Raleigh, North Carolina

J. B. BEARD

Texas A&M University
College Station, Texas

Plant temperature directly influences how efficiently its many physiological processes function. Energy transfer to and from plant surroundings governs its temperature. Radiation, transpiration, and convection greatly influence plant temperature. Radiation includes both solar and thermal sources. A turf receives solar energy directly and indirectly through reflection from clouds, nearby leaves, and other surrounding objects. Solar radiation is typically about 1.32 to 1.42 kW m^{-2} (Kreider & Kreith, 1981). Incident radiation varies depending on the time of year (earth and sun positional effects) and latitude. The water vapor content of the atmosphere can alter total incident radiation by 5 to 20%, while clouds can reduce incoming radiation by as much as 90% (Kreider & Kreith, 1981). Thermal radiation is emitted by any object that is warmer than absolute zero and occurs during both the day and night. Thermal radiation from objects with temperatures between 0 and 50 °C is only at infrared wavelengths. It is possible for the thermal radiation received by a plant to equal or exceed that of solar radiation (Gates, 1965). Plants typically reradiate 50% or more of the radiant energy they absorb (Gates, 1965).

Transpiration involves the loss of water vapor from the plant through the stomata and cuticle. This is a cooling process that significantly influences plant temperature. Thermal energy can be transferred by convection, which accounts for about 3 to 4% of the total thermal balance between a plant and its surroundings (Gates, 1965). If the leaf is warm, the air adjacent to the leaf is warmed. Its density is reduced and this layer of air will then rise. This heated air layer is then replaced with cooler air, thus establishing a circulatory movement of air that results in heat loss from the leaf. Energy transfer by conduction is minimal. Energy transfer processes between the turf and its surroundings are clearly quite dynamic (Fig. 7-1).

Copyright © 1992 ASA-CSSA-SSSA, 677 S. Segoe Rd., Madison, WI 53711, USA. *Turfgrass—Agronomy Monograph no. 32.*

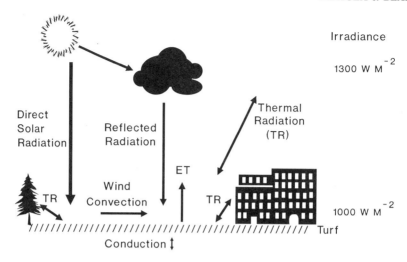

ET - Evapotranspiration

Fig. 7–1. Energy transfer between turf and its surroundings.

I. TEMPERATURE OPTIMA

A. Root and Shoot Growth

Turfgrass growth and development is restricted to a specific temperature range (Fig. 7–2). There is little biological activity above 50 °C or below 0 °C (Beard, 1973; Leopold & Kriedemann, 1975). While most active plant growth occurs between 10 and 40 °C, the optimum temperature for maximum metabolic activity or growth differs among plant species and, in some cases, among cultivars (Beard, 1973; Treshow, 1970). The optimum temperature range for cool-season turfgrass shoot growth is 15 to 24 °C, while that for warm-season turfgrass shoot growth is 27 to 35 °C (Beard, 1973; Youngner, 1961). For a given plant species, the various growth stages often have differing temperature optimums. Maximum tillering usually occurs slightly below the optimum shoot growth temperature (Beard, 1973). Zoysiagrass (*Zoysia japonica* Steud.) shoot growth, root dry weight, rhizome dry weight, internode length, and blade and stolon length were all greater at 27 °C than at 21 °C (Youngner, 1961). In any event, the maximum shoot growth temperature may not correspond with peak turfgrass performance. One can envision circumstances in turfgrass management when some loss in turf performance and quality under temperature stress is permitted to ensure a minimal level of survival. This approach could avoid the costly expense of reestablishment following periods of stress.

As might be expected, soil temperature has more influence than air temperature on turfgrass root growth (Beard, 1973; Carroll, 1943; Kinbacher, 1963). Cool-season turfgrasses maintain their best root growth at temperatures

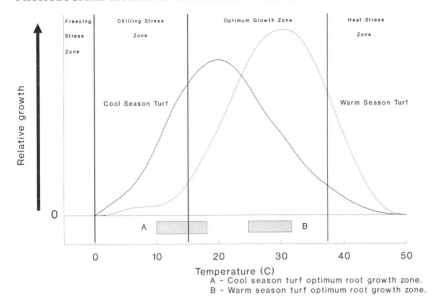

Fig. 7-2. Turf growth and temperature stress zones.

between 10 and 18 °C, while warm-season turfgrasses sustain their greatest root growth at temperatures between 24 and 29 °C (Beard, 1973; Youngner, 1961). Several cool-season turfgrasses have been observed to maintain root growth through the fall if the soil is unfrozen (Stuckey, 1941). Martin and Wehner (1987) found a negative correlation (-0.83) between the depth of annual bluegrass (*Poa annua* L.) roots and maximum soil temperature at a 10-cm depth. Bermudagrass [*Cynodon dactylon* (L.) Pers. $\times$ *C. transvaalensis* Davey] and St. Augustinegrass [*Stenotaphrum secundatum* (Walter) Kuntze] have been observed to maintain root growth during the fall at soil temperatures below 10 °C and after shoot color loss has occurred (DiPaola et al., 1982).

B. Metabolic Activity

Metabolic processes within the plant are influenced by temperature changes within the range of 10 to 40 °C. The rate of chemical reactions, gas solubility, and water uptake are all influenced by temperature. Enzyme activity and plant growth more than doubles with a 10 °C rise in temperature between 10 and 40 °C (Leopold & Kriedemann, 1975). As the temperature drops from 25 to 0 °C, the viscosity of water doubles. Uptake and transport of water by the plant becomes increasingly difficult as temperatures decrease (Treshow, 1970). Photosynthesis depends on CO_2 diffusion and enzyme activity that are greatly influenced by temperature. In most plants, photosynthesis is negligible below 10 °C and increases with temperature up to about 30 °C (Treshow, 1970; Leopold & Kriedemann, 1975). Duff and Beard (1974b) and Miller (1960) found this situation to be true for creeping bentgrass (*Agrostis palustris* Huds.). Upper temperature limits will vary with plant species, but photosynthessi in most species decreases when temperatures exceed 30 °C.

Photosynthetic rate also depends on the solubility of gases in aqueous solution within plant cells. Carbon dioxide and oxygen solubility in aqueous solution increases as temperature decreases. Carbon dioxide fixation may then be favored at lower temperatures and could result in carbohydrate reserve accumulations. Soluble carbohydrates and free-amino N accumulated in ryegrass (*Lolium* spp.) seedlings when grown continuously at 12 °C compared to 25 °C (Beevers & Cooper, 1964). Bermudagrass carbohydrates, mostly as starch, were found to increase by 23 °C during the fall (Dunn & Nelson, 1974). Rogers et al. (1975) found increased accumulation of starch and total non-structural carbohydrates in zoysiagrass during the fall. These components were found to decrease by 40% during the winter and early spring. Beevers and Cooper (1964) suggested that cooler temperatures resulted in slower respiratory activity and slowed degradation of photosynthate. Reduced respiratory activity would also lead to a lowered ATP supply necessary for continued metabolic activity. This would partially explain the accumulation of free amino N, since ATP must be available to incorporate amino acids into proteins.

C. Microclimate Influences

A discussion of temperature effects on turf would be incomplete without some mention of microclimate variation. Trees, buildings, and other objects alter the thermal balance between a turf and its surroundings (Rosenberg, 1983) (Fig. 7–3). The moderation of daily temperature extremes in the shade compared to full-sunlight areas is an example of microclimatic influences (Beard, 1973). In the northern hemisphere, slopes that face south are warmer than those facing north. This temperature difference favors the succession

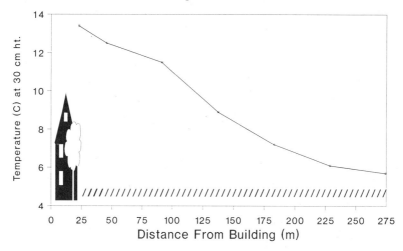

Fig. 7–3. Turf microclimate: A temperature profile. After Beard (Knochenhauer, 1934).

of cool-season turfgrass species on the north-facing slopes of an east-west roadway located in the transition zone, while warm-season species are favored on the south-facing slopes (Ward, 1969). Temperature gradients exist across relatively uniform, level surfaces like golf courses. Relatively minor differences in soil conditions and topography can result in measurable variation in canopy temperature.

II. TURFGRASS TEMPERATURE STRESS

Stress subjects the turfgrass plant to hardship. A *temperature stress* of turfgrasses occurs when they are exposed to temperatures above or below their optimum range. Each stress induces a *strain* or *injury* which results from direct or indirect physical or metabolic alterations. Using Levitt's (1980) terminology, a strain or injury is *elastic*, when it is reversible, but is termed *plastic*, when it is irreversible injury. Turfgrasses are exposed to at least three distinct types of temperature stress: (i) freezing, (ii) chilling, and (iii) heat stress (Fig. 7-4) (Levitt, 1980). *Freezing stress* occurs at temperatures at or below 0 °C. *Chilling stress* occurs at temperatures below 12 °C, but above freezing. *Heat stress* occurs at temperatures above the optimum for turfgrass growth, which is typically above 45 °C. *Low temperature stress* is a broad term encompassing freezing and chilling stress. In relative terms, warm-season turfgrass species possess excellent resistance to heat stress, but suffer significantly from low temperature stress. Cool-season turfgrass species are more resistant to low temperature stress, but perform poorly under high temperature stress when compared to warm-season species. Cool-season turf-

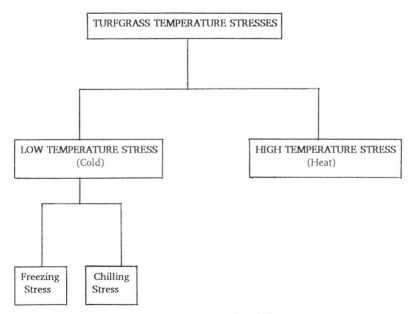

Fig. 7-4. Turfgrass temperature stresses. After Levitt (1980).

grasses are noticeably affected by low temperature stress, and warm-season turfs can be injured under high temperature stress conditions. Freezing stress of turf is often confused with *winter injury*, but the latter is a more comprehensive term that includes turf losses from low temperature stress, traffic, desiccation, soil frost-heaving and low temperature pathogens (Beard, 1973).

The plant's ability to survive temperature stress is its *resistance*. Temperature stress resistance can result from requiring a greater stress to effect a specific injury in the plant, or the plant's ability to reduce the injury experienced by a specific stress (Levitt, 1980). Turfgrass survival to temperature stress can be accomplished by several mechanisms (Fig. 7–5). *Avoidance* is plant resistance to temperature stress resulting from a prevention or reduction in the stress exposure. The exclusion of a stress so that plant

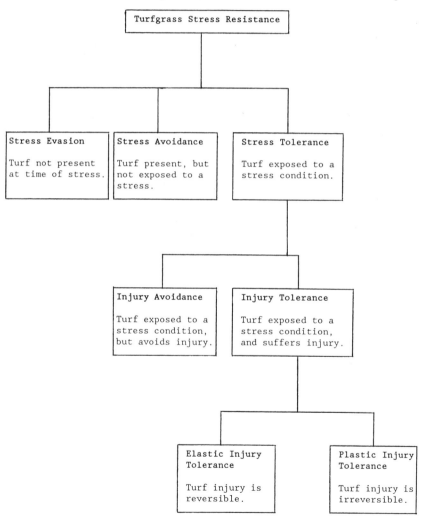

Fig. 7–5. Potential mechanisms of turfgrass stress resistance. After Levitt (1980).

tissue is warmer during low temperature or cooler during high temperature stress is an avoidance mechanism. Stress exclusion can be completely or only partially effective. Survival of warm-season turf near buildings or heating vents in cold climates is an example of stress avoidance. Cool-season turfs on the north side of buildings or slopes in warm climates often avoid heat stress. Bermudagrass is able to avoid low temperature stress by producing rhizomes within the surrounding soil. Rhizomes are located more deeply within the soil profile than crown and stolon tissues and thus are better able to avoid the low temperature stress. Early morning anthesis is considered a heat stress avoidance mechanism for rice (*Oryza sativa* L.), since floral structure are easily injured under high temperature conditions (Yoshida et al., 1981).

Tolerance is plant resistance to temperature stress resulting from the prevention or reduction in the injury of a stress (Levitt, 1980). It entails a stress experience by the plant so that tissue is cold during low temperature stress and hot during high temperature stress. Despite experiencing the stress, a tolerant plant may prevent, minimize, or repair the injury. Most turfgrasses must possess tolerance mechanisms to survive periods of temperature stress. A tolerant turfgrass could avoid the injury associated with temperature stress exposure. As a tolerance mechanism, turfs using *injury avoidance* would require greater temperature stress to produce a given injury level compared with sensitive plants. These plants must either tolerate *elastic* or *plastic* injury. The former group of plants could also be described as having avoided irreversible injury.

Strictly speaking, plants that complete their life cycle before the onset of stress conditions demonstrate *stress evasion*. These plants are neither avoidant nor tolerant, but evade stress by regeneration from seed. *Poa annua* L. subspp. *annua* is a turfgrass that employs stress evasion. This grass grows during the cooler portions of the year and produces seed to survive high temperature stress during summer. *Hardiness* is another commonly used term that typically implies tolerance or acclimation rather than stress avoidance.

Many studies concerning the temperature stress physiology of grasses have dealt with annual nonturfgrass plants such as winter cereals (Andrews et al., 1974; De La Roche et al., 1972, 1975; Metcalf et al., 1970; St. John et al., 1979). The results from such studies must be cautiously extrapolated to turfgrasses. Annual crop programs may employ planting and harvest techniques to evade stress periods, while perennial turfs must suffer injury, enter dormancy, or otherwise survive temperature stresses.

III. TURFGRASS FREEZING STRESS

Turfgrass freezing stress occurs at temperatures at or below freezing. Soil temperatures are more critical than air temperatures, since crowns, stolons, and rhizomes are located near or slightly below the soil surface (Beard, 1973; Beard & Daniel, 1965). Turf loss from freezing stress injury results in costly reestablishment, increased weed pressure, greater soil erosion, reduced use and lower aesthetic quality of the area. It has been stated that exposure to temperatures at or below freezing is a primary factor limiting the adaptation of warm-season turfgrasses to northern climates (Beard, 1973). Increased freezing stress tolerance would extend the northern limits of culture for most turfgrasses (Beard, 1973). This hypothesis assumes that other winter survival problems like desiccation, low temperature active pathogens, frost heaving, and traffic are not limiting.

Maintaining the integrity of the turfgrass crown is essential for freezing stress survival. Leaf, root, and lateral shoot regeneration occurs from the turfgrass crown the following spring (Beard, 1973). The freezing tolerance of a grass depends on the degree of injury and the region of the crown affected. The lower region of annual bluegrass crowns is more susceptible to freezing stress injury than the upper region (Beard & Olien, 1963). Such injury is likely to be exaggerated by desiccation during the late winter and early spring. At this time, the warm air above the turf can increase transpiration beyond the water uptake capability of the roots that must orginate from the injured lower region of the crown.

Freezing first occurs around the vessels and in the intercellular spaces of the shoot (Levitt, 1980). During freezing, the protoplast and cell wall contract as water moves from within the cell to the ice loci in the intercellular spaces (Stuckey & Curtis, 1938; Siminovitch & Scarth, 1938). This extracellular ice formation can split cells apart as they shrink. Once thawing begins, a surviving cell can reabsorb the intercellular water and recover its turgor, while dead cells expand to near their original shape, but the protoplast remains constricted (Levitt, 1980; Stuckey & Curtis, 1938).

A. Freezing Resistance

Freezing stress avoidance by supercooling is important to many woody plants (Levitt, 1980), but is of unknown significance to turfgrasses. Extracellular freezing results in a dehydration of the cell as water moves across the plasma membrane into the intercellular spaces (Levitt, 1980; Siminovitch & Scarth, 1938). Extracellular freezing results in a reduction in the vapor pressure in the intercellular spaces, thus drawing water from the cell. As the extracellular ice grows, the cell contracts due to water loss. The concentration of solutes within the cell increases as the water moves to the extracellular ice loci. This increased concentration of cell contents further lowers the freezing temperature of the cell. The role of water movement in enhancing freezing stress tolerance may partially explain how moderate water stress exposure often improves freezing stress tolerance (Gusta et al., 1980). The permeability of the plasma membrane is important to the cell's ability to transfer enough water to establish an equilibrium concentration and prevent intracellular freezing. Intracellular freezing occurs with rapid temperature reductions and is almost certainly lethal (Levitt, 1980; Siminovitch & Scarth, 1938; Siminovitch et al., 1978; Stuckey & Curtis, 1938). During intracellular freezing, the cytoplasm probably freezes before the vacuole (Stuckey & Curtis,

1938). Death by intracellular freezing may depend on the size of the ice crystals formed within the cell.

B. Freezing Stress Tolerance Range

Considerable variation in freezing stress tolerance exists among turf-grasses. Among the cool-season species, creeping bentgrasses and rough bluegrass (*Poa trivialis* L.) will tolerate exposure to the lowest temperatures, while perennial ryegrass is generally found to be the least tolerant (Beard, 1966; Gusta et al., 1980). Beard (1966) found that Kentucky bluegrasses (*Poa pratensis* L.) had good freezing stress tolerance, while annual bluegrass, Pennlawn red fescue (*Festuca rubra* L.), and redtop (*Agrostis alba* L.) had intermediate tolerance. The tall fescues (*Festuca arundinacea* Schreb.) and the ryegrasses were found to have the least tolerance.

Gusta et al. (1980) determined crown LT_{50} values (i.e., the temperature at which 50% of the crowns survive) for several cool-season turfgrasses (Table 7-1). Creeping bentgrass had the lowest LT_{50} value (-35 °C), followed by bromegrass (*Bromus* spp.), Kentucky bluegrasses, red fescue, alkaligrass (*Puccinellia* spp.), hard fescue (*Festuca longifolia* Thuill.), and perennial ryegrass (-5 to -15 °C). Some turfgrass species were found to have LT_{50} differences among cultivars. Among the perennial ryegrasses, common was the least tolerant ($LT_{50} = -5$ °C), while Manhattan had LT_{50} value of -15 °C. Within the Kentucky bluegrasses, Merion, Adelphi, and Nugget had LT_{50} values of -21 °C, while Windsor was found to have an LT_{50} of -30 °C. Penncross, Penneagle and Emerald creeping bentgrass all had LT_{50} values of -35 °C. It is possible for very freezing stress-tolerant turfgrasses, such as creeping bentgrass, to winterkill due to disease (e.g., snow mold), desiccation, or other factors, while less-tolerant grasses survive. The ranking

Table 7-1. Cool-season turfgrass resistance to freezing stress.

Turf	Genus	Cultivars	Crown moist.[†]	Ranking[‡]	LT_{50}[§]
		no.	%		°C
Rough bluegrass	*Poa*	--	72	Excellent	--
Creeping bentgrass	*Agrostis*	3	54–61	Excellent	-35
Bromegrass	*Bromus*	2	--	--	-30
Kentucky bluegrass	*Poa*	7	73–78	Good	-21 to -30
Canada bluegrass	*Poa*	--	--	Good	--
Colonial bentgrass	*Agrostis*	--	--	Good	--
Redtop	*Agrostis*	--	--	Good	--
Annual bluegrass	*Poa*	--	80	Medium	--
Creeping red fescue	*Festuca*	2	78	Medium	-24
Tall fescue	*Festuca*	--	74–77	Medium	--
Alkaligrass	*Puccinellia*	2	--	--	-21 to -27
Hard fescue	*Festuca*	1	--	--	-21
Perennial ryegrass	*Lolium*	11	79–81	Poor	-5 to -15
Annual ryegrass	*Lolium*	--	80	Very poor	--

† From Beard (1966). Crown Moisture in December in Michigan.
‡ From Beard (1973).
§ After Gusta et al. (1980).

of turfgrass by freezing stress tolerance can serve as a guide for turfgrass selection when freezing stress is a concern.

Gusta et al. (1980) measured electrolyte leakage following low temperature exposure, of various portions of Fylking Kentucky bluegrass plants. Using this technique, leaves were determined to have the greatest freezing stress tolerance during the mid-winter ($LT_{50} = -40\,°C$), followed by crowns ($LT_{50} = -28\,°C$), and roots and rhizomes ($LT_{50} = -20\,°C$). Dunn and Nelson (1974) found bermudagrass rhizomes to be less freezing stress tolerant than stolons. However, Rogers et al. (1975) noted that rhizomes and stolons of Meyer zoysiagrass had equivalent freezing stress tolerance. The apparent discrepancy between these two studies that involved field sampling, may be at least partly explained by differences in experimental technique. In the field, rhizomes would experience low temperature stress after stolon and crown tissue because of the buffering effects of the surrounding soil. Field sampling, as was the case in all of the above studies, could conceivably result in the comparison of rhizomes, stolons, and crown tissues that have experienced differing hardening temperature conditions. Increased freezing stress tolerance following turfgrass exposure to low temperatures has been reported for centipedegrass [*Eremochloa ophiuroides* (Munro) Hackel] (Johnston & Dickens, 1977). Soil and moisture conditions prior to sampling could impact low temperature exposure and freezing stress tolerance. This could explain the lower freezing stress tolerance of bermudagrass rhizomes compared with stolons when sampled from the field in September (Dunn & Nelson, 1974). Rogers et al. (1975) and Dunn and Nelson (1974) considered the lower portion of a sample plug of turf to be rhizome material. This sampling technique then would clearly include other plant tissues along with rhizomes. It is important to recognize that rhizomes and to a lesser extent crowns, are insulated by the surrounding soil. As the temperature declines, these structures are often able to avoid low temperature exposure. Rhizome avoidance of freezing stress was attributed to the better winter survival of young stands of vegetatively established bermudagrass, compared with seeded areas (Juska & Murray, 1974).

Considerably less is known about the freezing stress tolerance range of warm-season turfgrasses. Beard (1973) listed a relative ranking of warm-season turfgrass freezing stress tolerance. This ranking along with published LT_{50} values for warm-season turfgrasses is presented in Table 7-2. Zoysiagrass is clearly the most freezing stress tolerant with an LT_{50} of $-11\,°C$, followed by bermudagrass with LT_{50} values ranging from -5 to $-8\,°C$. Centipedegrass LT_{50} values (-6 to $-7\,°C$) would suggest that this species is more freezing stress tolerant than its zone of adaptation would indicate. Centipedegrass is not found or cultured successfully quite as far north in the USA as bermudagrass, yet the LT_{50} values for these grasses are comparable. This might be explained by reductions in centipedegrass cold tolerance following exposure to short periods (2–4 d) of warm conditions (Johnston & Dickens, 1976; Reeves & McBee, 1972).

Freezing stress tolerance differences between cultivars of warm-season turfgrasses have been reported, particularly among bermudagrass and

Table 7-2. Warm-season turfgrass resistance to freezing stress.

Common name (Genus)	Turf Species	Cultivars	Ranking[†]	LT_{50}
Zoysiagrass (*Zoysia*)	*Z. japonica*	Meyer	Medium	-11[#]
Buffalograss (*Buchloë*)	*B. dactyloides*	--	--	--
Blue grama (*Bouteloua*)	*B. gracilis*	--	--	--
Bermudagrass (*Cynodon*)	*C. dactylon* × *C. transvaalensis;*	Tifgreen Tifdwarf Midway U-3	Poor	-5 to -8[‡§]
	C dactylon	Westwood		
Manilagrass (*Zoysia*)	*Z. matrella*	--	Poor	--
Bahiagrass (*Paspalum*)	*P. notatum*	--	Very poor	--
Centipedegrass (*Eremochloa*)	*E. ophiuroides*	Oklawn Mississippi I & II Tenn. Hardy	Very poor	-6 to -7[¶]
Carpetgrass (*Axonopus*)	*A. compressus* and *A. affinis*	--	Very poor	--
St. Augustinegrass (*Stenotaphrum*)	*S. secundatum*	--	Very poor	--
Kikuyugrass (*Pennisetum*)	*P. clandestinum*	--	--	--

[†] Beard (1973).
[‡] Davis and Gilbert (1970).
[§] Dunn and Nelson (1974).
[¶] Johnston and Dickens (1977).
[#] Rogers et al. (1975).

St. Augustinegrass cultivars (Beard et al., 1980a). 'Midway' bermudagrass had superior freezing stress tolerance, while 'Pee Dee', 'Sunturf', 'Midiron', and 'Tifgreen' all were found to have excellent tolerance among the 19 cultivars of breeding lines tested. 'Texturf 1F', 'Tiffine', 'Everglades', and 'Bayshore' exhibited good tolerance, while 'Tiflawn', 'FB119', and 'Ormond' ranked poorest in freezing stress tolerance. Dunn and Nelson (1974) found 'U-3' bermudagrass to be less freezing stress tolerant than either Midway or 'Westwood', yet Beard et al. (1980a) observed equivalent tolerance between U-3 and Midway. Davis and Gilbert (1970) found Tifgreen bermudagrass had a lower LT_{50} than 'Tifdwarf.' The lower freezing stress tolerance of Tifdwarf compared to Tifgreen has been confirmed by Beard et al. (1980a).

Johnston and Dickens (1977) found equivalent survival among seven centipedegrass selections (FC-2, FC-8, Mississippi I, Mississippi II, Oklawn, P11A, and Tennessee Hardy) following exposure to $-9.7\,°C$. Beard et al. (1980b) observed the survival of seven St. Augustinegrass cultivars following their exposure to extreme cold weather. Texas common was found to have the best survival (74%), followed by Seville (53%) and Raleigh (51%). Floratam, Scotts 516, and Garrett's 141 all had $<50\%$ survival. In another Texas study, Menn et al. (1985) found Texas common and Raleigh to have equivalent cold tolerance. Additional information concerning warm-season turfgrass freezing stress tolerance differences is needed.

1. Seasonal Variation

Beard (1966) observed fluctuations in turfgrass freezing stress tolerance throughout the fall and winter. Turfgrass freezing stress tolerance was obtained and lost somewhat gradually, with peak hardiness occurring in early winter. A similar seasonal distribution of tolerance has been observed for bermudagrass (Davis & Gilbert, 1970). Gusta et al. (1980) observed that Fylking Kentucky bluegrass crown LT_{50} values rose from $-28\,°C$ in April, and to $-4\,°C$ in June. These LT_{50} values are probably sufficient to protect the turf from spring frosts. The buffering capacity of the typically moist soil during the spring further reduces the likelihood of the turf experiencing significant freezing stress despite elevated LT_{50} values. Rogers et al. (1975) found that Meyer zosiagrass freezing stress tolerance increased during the fall. The LT_{50} value decreased from $-5.6\,°C$ in September to $-11.1\,°C$ by January. Bermudagrass cold tolerance has also been found to increase during the fall (Davis & Gilbert, 1970; Dunn & Nelson, 1974). Bermudagrass LT_{50} values decreased from -2.2 in September to $-8.1\,°C$ in February (Davis & Gilbert, 1970). Johnston and Dickens (1977) maintained seven centipedegrass selections at either $22\,°C$ day/$4\,°C$ night or $31\,°C$ day/$25\,°C$ night conditions. Selections maintained under the former regime had better survival following freezing stress at $-9.7\,°C$ than those maintained at $31\,°C$ day and $25\,°C$ night conditions.

Exposure to $5\,°C$ day and $2\,°C$ night conditions for 14 d dehardened Kentucky bluegrass, such that it failed to regain its mid-winter freezing stress tolerance level (Gusta et al., 1980). Centipedegrass has been observed to

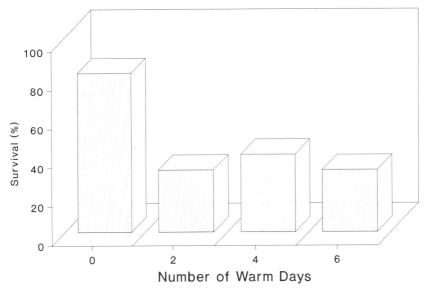

Fig. 7-6. Fluctuations in centipedegrass cold tolerance. After Johnston and Dickens (1976).

rapidly lose its cold tolerance following the exposure of hardened plants to just 2 d of favorable (greenhouse, 22–37 °C) growing conditions (Johnston & Dickens, 1976) (Fig. 7-6). In most areas of centipedegrass adaptation, it is likely that the winter season will include several warm days. When this occurs, the loss of centipedegrass turf to freezing stress would be much greater than that indicated from the data of studies that used fully hardened plants. A similar rapid loss (2–3 d) of acquired cold tolerance has been observed in St. Augustinegrass (Reeves & McBee, 1972). Both of these turfgrasses possess stolons, lateral shoots that grow above-ground. In comparison, bermudagrass and zoysiagrass have rhizomes and stolons. The former lie protected beneath the soil surface.

The above noted studies clearly demonstrate that late winter and early spring are periods of reduced turfgrass freezing stress tolerance. Thus, a turf is increasingly susceptible to injury from low temperature conditions and improperly timed cultural practices during this period. This is also a time when desiccation potential is high. Cool soils and warm winds combine to decrease the water absorption capability of the root system while the draw of water from the plant is increased. Additional studies on the interaction of cultural practices, desiccation, and freezing stress tolerance are warranted, particularly for the warm-season turfgrass species.

2. Fertility

Previous investigations, particularly on warm-season turfgrass species, have examined the influence of various fertilization regimes on winter survival, freezing stress tolerance, or both (Cook & Duff, 1976; Davis & Gilbert, 1970; Gilbert & Davis, 1971; Reeves et al., 1970; Reeves & McBee,

1972). These studies were not conclusive or in complete agreement, but they have demonstrated the importance of avoiding excess N (49 kg ha^{-1} or more) fertilization during the fall. Nitrogen applications just prior to warm-season turfgrass dormancy and around the time of the last fall mowing for cool-season turfs have been referred to as late-season fertilization. Late-season N applications have resulted in improved fall color retention and earlier spring greenup of warm- and cool-season turfs. From a nutritional standpoint, it is apparent that the warm-season turfgrass root system is capable of absorbing nutrients during portions of the fall and winter even though the aboveground shoots are browned by low temperature stress (DiPaola et al., 1982).

Unfortunately, increased N applications have also resulted in marked reductions in the winter survival and freezing stress tolerance of warm-season turfs (Gilbert, 1986; Gilbert & Davis, 1971; Palmertree et al., 1974; Reeves & McBee, 1972). Reeves et al. (1970) reported that fall N applications did not influence bermudagrass winter survival. Increased N nutrition from 1.5 to 4.3 kg ha^{-1} yr^{-1} did not adversely impact the winter survival of four bermudagrass cultivars (Juska & Murray, 1974). Winterkill is a broad term that encompasses more than freezing stress tolerance. Turf loss in the field would depend on many factors including low temperature stress. Nitrogen fertilization of turf that is at or below adequate levels would be expected to result in an improvement in stand and survival. Dunn and Nelson (1974) found that the cold-tolerant bermudagrass cultivar had lower total tissue N than those that were not tolerant.

Reductions in the freezing stress tolerance of warm-season turfgrasses following increased N fertilization is consistent with the response reported for cool-season species (Carroll, 1943; Carroll & Welton, 1939). This agreement is noteworthy with respect to warm-season turfgrasses given the inherently greater freezing stress tolerance of the cool-season species. The insulative effect of increased shoot biomass through raised cutting height or increased N fertilization has resulted in a lowering of centipedegrass winter survival (Gilbert, 1986). This response would be expected to be more severe for stoloniferous species since these lateral stems are elevated above the soil as shoot growth and thatch accumulation develops. One can reason that N induced reductions in freezing stress tolerance would be a more critical turfgrass problem for warm-season species in the northern region of their adaptation where low temperatures are experienced more frequently than in southern zones.

The deleterious effects of increased N nutrition on the freezing stress tolerance, winter survival, or both of warm-season turfgrasses has been offset by increased K nutrition (Gilbert & Davis, 1971; Palmertree et al., 1974; Reeves et al., 1970). Juska and Murray (1974) found that high (336 kg ha^{-1} yr^{-1}) K levels increased the winter survival of Arizona common and Tufcote bermudagrasses by threefold. The effects of increased K fertilization were less pronounced on the more freezing stress-tolerant bermudagrass cultivars (e.g., Midiron and Tifgreen). Recovery of bermudagrass from winter injury was best following applications of K (336 kg ha^{-1} yr^{-1}) in combination with ammonium nitrate (4.3 kg of N ha^{-1} yr^{-1}). Potassium's role in carbohydrate synthesis and translocation, protein synthesis, regulation of transpiration, and enzyme activity is likely important during the cold hardening period (Beard, 1973; MacLeod, 1965; Monroe et al., 1969; Pellet & Roberts, 1963; Walker & Ward, 1974). Beard (1986) noted that high N fertilization could impair carbohydrate redistribution in some species, and can thereby reduce freezing stress tolerance.

3. Moisture Content

Dehydrated tissues are known to withstand exposure to very low temperatures. Wheat (*Triticum aestivum* L.) seed exposed to −196 °C for 120 s germinated if the moisture content was 10.6%, while seed at 25.1% moisture failed to germinate (Lockett & Luyet, 1951). Wheat seed at <24% moisture would not freeze when exposed to −25 °C, while one-half the number of seed would freeze if the moisture content fell between 27 and 28% (Stuckey & Curtis, 1938). All seed at moisture contents above 30% froze when exposed to −25 °C. Beard (1964, 1965b, 1966; Beard & Olien, 1963) has conducted extensive studies on the freezing stress tolerance of cool-season turfgrasses. These investigations resulted in important contributions to understanding the effects of freezing stress on cool-season turfgrass species. The importance of the turfgrass crown, in particular its moisture content, on freezing stress tolerance has been documented. The tolerance of several cool-season turfgrass species was found to be inversely proportional to the crown moisture content (Beard, 1966). December crown moisture content ranged from 54% for Congressional creeping bentgrass to 85% for annual ryegrass. A similar relationship was observed by Metcalf et al. (1970) for three wheat and three barley (*Hordeum vulgare* L.) cultivar crowns. Gusta et al. (1980) found that ryegrass crowns tended to have the highest water content and the poorest freezing stress tolerance among the six genera evaluated. These researchers failed to find a clear relationship between crown moisture content and the freezing stress tolerance among cultivars.

C. Physiological Alterations

Much research has been devoted to identifying the primary site(s) of freezing injury within the cell. Many physiological processes that are affected by low temperature stress have also been monitored (Davis & Gilbert, 1970; De La Roche et al., 1975; Mayland & Cary, 1970; Rogers et al., 1977; St. John et al., 1979; Wang & Li, 1987). The cell membrane has been found to be greatly affected by low temperature stress. Alteration of membrane permeability, composition, ultrastructure, and electrical characteristics have all been observed (Wang & Li, 1987). Various organelles have also been suspected as key sites of freezing stress injury (DiPaola, 1979; Rogers et al., 1977). Some of the many physiological changes during freezing stress include increased soluble protein concentration (Davis & Gilbert, 1970), increased starch, total nonstructural carbohydrates or both (Davis & Gilbert, 1970;

Rogers et al., 1975) increased sulfhydryl content (Mayland & Cary, 1970; Paulsen, 1968), increased N content (Zech & Pauli, 1960), increased amino acid content (Paulsen, 1968), decreased hydration levels (Beard, 1966, 1973; Olien, 1964; Paulsen, 1968), increased photosynthetic activity (Rogert et al., 1977), increased amylolytic enzymes activity (Rogers et al., 1977), increased fatty acid content (De La Roche et al., 1972, 1975; DiPaola, 1979; Gerloff et al., 1966; Lyons et al., 1964), and an increased ratio of unsaturated to saturated fatty acids (De La Roche et al., 1972, 19775; DiPaola, 1979; Gerloff et al., 1966; Lyons et al., 1964; St. John et al., 1979).

1. Carbohydrate Reserves

Starch and total nonstructural carbohydrate content (TNC) of turfgrasses increases during fall hardening period (Davis & Gilbert, 1970; Rogers et al., 1975). Rogers et al. (1975) found that starch and TNC level of Meyer zoysiagrass rhizomes and stolons increased during September and remained at about 50% of dry weight through December. This increase in carbohydrates is likely a result of decreased shoot growth during the cool fall conditions while the photosynthetic rate declines more slowly. However, it is clear that there is a strong association between carbohydrate reserves and freezing stress tolerance (Davis & Gilbert, 1970). A decrease in TNC occurred after December to only 15% of dry weight by March. Rogers et al. (1975) suggested that this response indicates the use of these reserves as an energy source until renewed shoot growth occurs the following spring.

Total sugars in Meyer zoysiagrass also increased during the fall, while the concentration of reducing sugars remained steady. A similar response was observed in three bermudagrass cultivars (Dunn & Nelson, 1974). The carbohydrate levels among U-3, Midway, and Westwood bermudagrasses were roughly equivalent and failed to adequately account for the winter survival differences among cultivars. Zoysiagrass has been reported to have three times the fall carbohydrate accumulation of bermudagrass (Rogers et al., 1975; Dunn & Nelson, 1974). This may partially account for the improved winter survival of zoysiagrass compared to bermudagrass.

2. Nucleic Acid and Protein Synthesis

Concentration of total N and free amino acids in bermudagrass increased during the fall and remained level through early spring (Dunn & Nelson, 1974). Davis and Gilbert (1970) found an increased total protein concentration in bermudagrass during cold hardening. Based on electrophoretic techniques, shifts in the qualitative characteristics of rhizome proteins were also observed. Palmertree et al. (1974) found increased total soluble protein concentration in the stolons and crowns of centipedegrass during cold hardening. Accumulations of soluble proteins and alterations in protein composition have also been observed in wheat (Trunova, 1987). During hardening, winter wheat normally increases its protein concentration from 38 to 62 mg g^{-1} of dry weight, while leaves treated with the protein inhibitors cycloheximide, chloramphenicol, and actininomycin D failed to accumulate protein

(Trunova, 1987). This indicates that low temperature protein synthesis during hardening is de novo rather than the result of protein release following the degradation of tissues under stress conditions (Trunova, 1987). The above group of studies suggest that although freezing stress tolerance is accompanied by accumulation of proteins and sugar, protein accumulation alone is not always enough to improve freezing stress tolerance.

3. Membrane Alteration

Membranes are important structural components of the cell that are capable of significant environmentally induced modifications (Thompson, 1983). Phospholipids and their fatty acid portions are major components of biological membranes (Levitt, 1980). The fatty acyl chains of phospholipids can exist in a gel or liquid crystalline state depending on their phase transition temperature. This transition temperature depends, in part, on the length and degree of unsaturation of the fatty acyl chains (Vignais, 1976). Membrane rigidity is favored by the presence of long chain, saturated fatty acyl chains as components of the membrand lipids. Membranes fluidity is enhanced by the incorporation of short chain polyunsaturated fatty acyl components of the membrane lipids.

Increased membrane fluidity is a desirable trait during freezing stress conditions. A more flexible membrane system could limit or decrease membrane disruption during freezing (Mayland & Cary, 1970). Membrane fluidity is necessary to allow the protein components of the membrane to alter their shape or change position (Thompson, 1983). There is a significant correlation between membrane lipid constituents and the activity of membrane bound enzymes (Thompson, 1983). Increasing the fatty acid unsaturation level of a membrane is one method of improving membrane permeability (Levitt, 1980). Phase transition of a lipid membrane from a liquid crystalline to a solid gel state has been shown to decrease membrane permeability by as much as one-third (Levitt, 1980).

Winter wheat grown at 2 °C was found to contain considerably higher phospholipid levels compared to those grown at 24 °C. Linolenic acid (18:3) was observed to increase continually over a 37-d period at 2 °C, while 18:1 and 18:2 fatty acids concentrations decreased (De La Roche et al., 1972, 1975). In addition to altering fatty acid unsaturation, temperature stress influences the proportions of phospholipid or glycolipid classes and the sterol to phospholipid ratio of the membrane (Thompson, 1983).

4. Organelle Effects

The protoplast will typically freeze prior to the vacuole (Stuckey & Curtis, 1938). Work by Wang and Li (1987) suggests that wheat vacuoles and protoplasts remaining intact following freezing stress increased by more than 21% for acclimated compared to nonacclimated wheat leaf tissues. These authors also noted that increased linolenic acid and palmitic acid concentrations were significantly correlated with organelle freezing tolerance. Increased freezing tolerance from an elevated linolenic acid concentration was greater for the vacuole compared to the protoplast.

The chloroplasts of overwintering wheat were observed to suffer structural injury that was restored during the spring (Levitt, 1980). Working with zoysiagrass and bermudagrass, Rogers et al. (1977) found bermudagrass chloroplasts changed from an elongated shape in late summer to a globular appearance during the fall. This was compared to zoysiagrass chloroplasts which maintained a consistent shape from summer through the fall (October). The grana lamellae of nondormant zoysiagrass chloroplasts were largely intact in November, while that of bermudagrass chloroplasts were usually damaged.

D. Freeze Smothering

Freeze smothering is an appropriate term used by Levitt (1980), since oxygen deficiency and toxic gas buildup can become factors under an ice cover along with the freezing stress. Ice sheets can establish a barrier to the exchange of gases between the soil and the atmosphere. Freeze smothering has not been a major cause of winter injury to cool-season turfgrasses (Beard, 1964, 1965a,b). Considerable turf injury has been observed when the turf crowns increase in hydration level by standing in water prior to ice encasement (Beard, 1964). In this case, the injury is likely to be from freezing stress rather than freeze smothering. With reasonable drainage, most cool-season turfgrasses can tolerate as many as 60 d of ice encasement or cover (Beard, 1964, 1965a,b). Carbon dioxide and other respiratory products have been observed to accumulate for winter wheat and rye (*Secale cereale* L.) under ice sheets (Andrews & Pomeroy, 1977). Injury during ice encasement was attributed to an altered gaseous environment under the ice, rather than the damage from low temperature alone (Andrews & Pomeroy, 1977). In this work, mitochondrial structure remained intact until 21 d of ice encasement.

IV. TURFGRASS CHILLING STRESS

Chilling stress is defined as low temperature stress in the absence of freezing (Levitt, 1980). Chilling injury is observed on plants from tropical or subtropical climates when temperatures fall below 12 °C (Lyons, 1973). Exceptions do occur and include damage to flowering rice at 15 °C (Adir, 1968). Within the turfgrass species, chilling stress is predominately a concern for warm-season grasses. Many of the changes found to occur in the plant during hardening develop within the temperature zone of chilling stress. Turfgrass chilling injury has been characterized by the presence of necrotic lesions, loss of chlorophyll, reduction in photosynthetic rate, and the cessation of growth (DiPaola et al., 1981; Karbassi et al., 1971; Karnok & Beard, 1983; Ludlow & Wilson, 1970; Miller, 1960; Rogers et al., 1977; Youngner, 1959).

The differing types of chilling injuries have been described thoroughly by Levitt (1980) (Fig. 7-7). Direct chilling injury is characterized by the rapid development of symptoms within 24 h (Levitt, 1980). Soybean (*Glycine max*

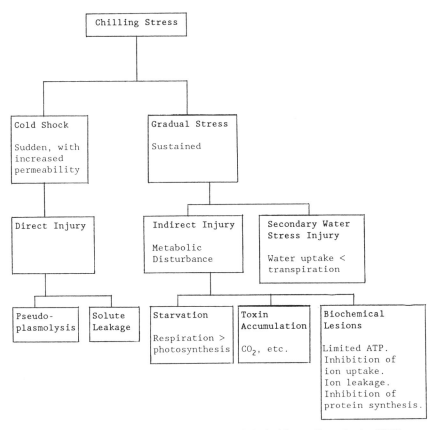

Fig. 7-7. Types of chilling injuries and their physiological bases. From Levitt (1980).

L.) injury has been observed at 2 °C after only a 5-min exposure (Bramlage et al., 1978). Such injury is too rapid to be accounted for by metabolic disturbances (Levitt, 1980). In contrast, indirect chilling injury involves the slow development of symptoms after several days exposure to stress conditions. As might be expected, intermediate plants (i.e., those that express both direct and indirect chilling injury symptoms) are known (Levitt, 1980).

A. Physiological Alteration

Chilling injury appears to involve several physiological dysfunctions including a loss in amylolytic activity (Chatterton et al., 1972; Karbassi et al., 1972; Rogers et al., 1977), decreased carbon dioxide exchange rate (Karnok & Beard, 1983; White & Schmidt, 1988, 1989), reduced net photosynthesis/dark respiration ratio (Karnok & Beard, 1981; Rogers et al., 1977; White & Schmidt, 1988) and increased photo-oxidation of chlorophyll (McWilliam & Naylor, 1967). Protection of chlorophyll from photodestruction has been shown to be one function of the carotenoid pigments within the chloroplast (Anderson & Robertson, 1960; Krinski, 1966, 1978;

McWilliam & Naylor, 1967). Leakage of K^+ ions is a commonly observed manifestation of direct chilling injury (Levitt, 1980). Corn (*Zea mays* L.) roots at 1 °C for 3 to 6 h have been observed to leak K^+ ions. Ion leakage is at first slow, followed by a rapid leakage phase that occurs concurrently with lesion appearance (Levitt, 1980). Reductions in K^+ ion uptake have been observed to occur simultaneously with increased ion leakage in barley (Levitt, 1980). The ion uptake of wheat roots at 1 °C was found to be only one-third that of controls at 25 °C, while K^+ ion loss increased by 1.5-fold (Nordin, 1977). Such alterations in ion movement likely involve changes in plant membrane characteristics.

Increases in membrane permeability due to indirect chilling injury also results in increased leakage of ions and amino acids (Levitt, 1980). Working with rice, Zhang et al. (1987) found 30 to 70% electrolyte leakage after 8 d exposure to 6 °C. These authors reported that ultra-light applications of mefluidide (3–15 mg L^{-1}) reduced electrolyte leakage, perhaps by alteration of plasma membrane properties. Light is essential for this injury and leaf bleaching to occur (Levitt, 1980; Youngner, 1959). Youngner (1959) demonstrated that chilling injury of bermudagrass involves an interaction of reduced temperatures and high light intensity. The appearance of anthocyanin pigment, particularly in those leaves at the top of the canopy, signals the start of chlorophyll loss for bermudagrass under chilling stress (DiPaola et al., 1981). The rate of chlorophyll degradation appears to be accelerated beyond the rate of chlorophyll synthesis. As day temperatures increase, however, the effects of cool night temperatures can be reduced in bermudagrass (Youngner, 1959).

1. Starvation

Chilling indirect injury due to starvation has been postulated, but unconfirmed (Levitt, 1980). Thylakoid membranes of chill-sensitive species are less able to maintain a light-induced high energy state at chilling temperatures (Melcarek & Brown, 1977). As previously noted, Rogers et al. (1977) found the grana lamellae of green zoysiagrass (chilling resistant) chloroplast were largely intact, while those of the more chilling sensitive bermudagrass were damaged during fall chilling stress conditions. Such damage and chlorophyll photo-oxidation at chilling stress temperatures could result in a much greater respiration rate than photosynthetic activity. This imbalance can be reasoned to lead to starvation, but observed cases of chilling injury occur long before plant food reserves are depleted (Levitt, 1980).

Starvation can occur in the presence of ample food reserves if such stores cannot be accessed because of translocation inhibition (Levitt, 1980). Cases of translocation inhibition under chilling conditions have been reported (Crawford & Huxter, 1977; Hilliard & West, 1970). Daily accumulations of starch in *Digitaria decumbens* disappear (and are presumably translocated) at night at optimum growth temperatures. However, such accumulations remain at 10 °C night temperatures (Hilliard & West, 1970). The inhibition of starch translocation from the chloroplasts could conceivably result in reductions in the photosynthetic rate and growth, and eventually lead to root starvation. Crawford and Huxter (1977) found a marked reduction in the soluble sugar concentration of corn roots at 2 °C. This drop in soluble sugars was accompanied by reductions in respiration and growth of the root that were reversed by exogenous applications of sugar to root tissues.

2. Biochemical Lesions

Biochemical lesions result from metabolic dysfunctions that lead to the deficiency of an essential intermediate metabolite like ATP (Levitt, 1980). Such lesions can be expected since chilling stress decreased aerobic phase respiration, which would led to a reduction in oxidative phosphorylation, and thus the plant's ATP supply. This could lead to ion leakage and protein breakdown. Unfortunately, supportive evidence of this scenario is lacking. Certain enzymes (e.g., amylase) are inhibited more than others under chilling conditions (Levitt, 1980; Rogers et al., 1977).

The inability of *Digitaria* to remove accumulated starch grains from its chloroplasts under chilling night conditions (Hilliard & West, 1970) could reflect a dysfunction of starch degrading enzymes. Amylolytic activity has been found to be very low following 10 °C night periods (Karbassi et al., 1972). Additionally, gibberellic acid (GA₃) treatment to chilled *Digitaria* has been somewhat successful as a preventive treatment of turfgrass chilling injury (DiPaola et al., 1981; Karbassi et al., 1971; Karnok & Beard, 1983). Bermudagrass photosynthetic rate under chilling was improved following GA₃ application, while St. Augustinegrass did not respond (Karnok & Beard, 1983). Gibberellic acid treatment has improved bermudagrass growth and color for about 14 d under chilling stress conditions (DiPaola et al., 1981; Dudeck & Peacock, 1985). Sachs et al. (1971) found that the systemic fungicide carboxin improved the color retention of zoysiagrass and common bermudagrass under chilling conditions. Dudeck and Peacock (1985) noted a similar response for Tifdwarf bermudagrass under chilling stress. White and Schmidt (1988) found that iron treatment (120 mg m^{-2}) increased Tifgreen net photosynthesis before, during, and after chill treatment. These authors later reported improved bermudagrass color during chilling stress following Fe treatment and a 28% increase in mean nighttime carbon exchange rate (White & Schmit, 1989).

3. Organelle Effects

Photosynthetic rate reductions during chilling have been reported and may reflect changes within the chloroplasts. Thylakoid disruption was observed in the chloroplasts of chill sensitive *Sorghum* spp. following exposure to 10 °C nights, while none was found with a chill-resistant *Paspalum* (Taylor & Craig, 1971). The ultrastructure of bermudagrass mesophyll and bundle sheath chloroplasts appeared normal after 18 h of chilling stress (Karnok & Beard, 1985), yet long-term chilling stress exposure resulted in damage to the grana lamellae (Rogers et al., 1977). Hilliard and West (1970) found that the large amounts of starch grains present within *Digitaria* chloroplasts at the end of a light period, disappeared during a 30 °C night, but remained through a 10 °C dark period. Such starch accumulation under chilling stress may partly explain previously reported cases of chloroplast swelling (Taylor & Craig, 1971), but may not fully account for chilling stress induced reductions in photosynthetic rate (Karnok & Beard, 1985; Rogers et al., 1977).

V. TURFGRASS HIGH TEMPERATURE STRESS

The upper limit for higher plant growth is normally considered to be about 45 to 55 °C (Levitt, 1980). Some higher plants, however, can survive a short-term exposure to temperatures of 60 to 65 °C (Levitt, 1980). Since the rate of ordinary chemical reactions increases with temperature, heat stress induced growth reductions must be the result of the inhibition of the plant's metabolism in some physical or chemical manner (Levitt, 1980). Krans and Johnson (1974) observed chlorosis of creeping bentgrass after a period of several days with high temperatures in the range of 35 to 45 °C. High temperature stress reduce grass shoot growth, tillering, root growth, stand density, and leaf size (Duff & Beard, 1974a; Yoshida et al., 1981). Heat stress occurs most often during mid-summer when the intensity of turf use is often maximized.

Heat stress rarely occurs under field conditions in the absence of water stress. Desiccation and pests often injure the turf during periods of sustained high temperature. Warm-season turfgrasses possess excellent heat tolerance, while heat stress is a primary factor restricting the use of cool-season turf in many areas of the USA (Wehner & Watschke, 1981). Cool-season turfgrasses are particularly susceptible to high temperature stress effects given their poor vigor and shallow root system during the heat of the summer (Beard & Daniel, 1965, 1966). Increased root mass and improved distribution profile within the soil has improved turfgrass resistance to heat-related stress (Krans & Johnson, 1974).

A. Water Stress Association

Injury from heat stress is closely associated with that of water stress (Julander, 1945; Wallner et al., 1982). Kinbacher (1962) concluded that winter oat (*Avena byzantina* K. Koch) was more tolerant to a combination of heat and water stresses than to heat stress alone. Increased transpiration due to rising temperature results in stomatal closure, thus reducing transpirational cooling and increasing leaf temperature. Syringing for the purpose of moderating canopy temperature has been investigated under summer conditions in the northeastern USA (Duff & Beard, 1966; Hawes, 1965). Duff and Beard (1966) observed a canopy temperature reduction of 1 to 2 °C which lasted 2 h following the application of 6.4 mm of water at 1200 h. Hawes (1965) found that applications of 3 mm of water between 1130 and 1500 h resulted in a canopy temperature reduction of 4 and 0.8 °C at 120 and 600 s after syringing, respectively. In North Carolina, DiPaola (1984) found bentgrass canopy temperatures in the absence of wilt were not altered 1 h after syringing regardless of the water volume (0–5.5 mm) or timing (1200, 1300, 1400, 1500, 1600 h, twice daily, 5-hourly treatments). Further research is needed concerning the influence of syringing on the internal water status of turfgrasses and the potential physiological benefits of the transient (<30 min) moderation of canopy temperature that does occur.

B. Heat Stress Duration

Unlike freezing stress, the duration of heat stress is a critical factor in the degree of plant injury sustained. Heat hardening (exposure to 39 °C for 10 d) of Kentucky bluegrass increased its killing temperature by 1 °C, yet extended the high temperature (50 °C) exposure time needed for injury by more than 1 h (Wallner et al., 1982). The duration and temperature of heat kill are related as shown below:

$$T = a - b \log D \text{ (Levitt, 1980)}$$

where
T = the kill temperature, °C;
D = exposure duration for kill, min;
a = 67.5 (Wallner et al., 1982); and
b = 10.2 (Wallner et al., 1982).

Wallner et al. (1982) found that heat killing time more clearly agreed with previously known drought resistances of turfgrasses than did the killing temperature (Table 7–3). Buffalograss [*Buchloë dactyloides* (Nutt.) Engelm.] and bermudagrass had killing times in excess of 600 min at 50 °C, while killing time for creeping bentgrass was only 144 min. This difference compared favorable with previously reported turfgrass drought resistance rankings (Beard, 1973). Tall fescue had good drought resistance, but a killing time

Table 7–3. Relationship between heat killing time, killing temperature, and drought resistance among turfgrass species. After Wallner et al. (1982).

Turf	Genus	Drought resistance[†]	Heat killing	
			Time[‡]	Temperature[§]
			min	°C
Buffalograss	*Buchloe*	Excellent	>600	61.1
Bermudagrass	*Cynodon*	Excellent	>600	59.9
Tall fescue	*Festuca*	Good	166	55.4
Red fescue	*Festuca*	Good	252	55.8
Kentucky bluegrass	*Poa*	Medium	176	54.8
Perennial ryegrass	*Lolium*	Fair	240	56.9
Creeping bentgrass	*Agrostis*	Poor	144	55.4

[†] From Beard (1973).
[‡] Estimated time at 50° C for 50% electrolyte leakage.
[§] Estimated temperature for 50% electrolyte leakage after 20 min.

of 166 min at 50 °C. Wallner et al. (1982) attributed the better drought resistance to the deep root system profile of tall fescue.

C. Study Techniques

Most researchers have found it necessary to immerse plant tissue in distilled water while imposing heat stress treatments to remove the potential confounding effects of associated water stress (Cordukes, 1977; Kinbacher, 1962; Minner et al., 1983; Wehner & Watschke, 1984). Wallner et al. (1982) found that 50% electrolyte loss occurred after only 30 min of leaf tissue exposure to 50 °C for several turfgrasses (bermudagrass, buffalograss, creeping bentgrass, Kentucky bluegrass, perennial ryegrass, red fescue, and tall fescue), while 150 min was required if the tissue was immersed in distilled water. The best separation of species heat tolerance was obtained by using heat-hardened tissue and immersing tissue during the imposition of heat stress (Wallner et al., 1982).

Wehner and Watschke (1984) studied Kentucky bluegrass, annual bluegrass, and perennial ryegrass and found that heat tolerance rankings from electrolyte leakage data failed to agree with that based on the recovery growth weight method. Conductivity tests indicated slight injury from 43 to 47 °C, while recovery weights decreased by more than 50% for all grasses evaluated.

D. High Temperature Stress Tolerance Range

Initial cool-season turfgrass high temperature stress injury has been observed at 41 to 43 °C (Wehner & Watschke, 1981). Complete kill of Kentucky bluegrass, perennial ryegrass, and annual bluegrass occurred at 47 to 49 °C. Kentucky bluegrasses were more heat tolerant than perennial ryegrasses in both field (Minner et al., 1983) and greenhouse (Wehner & Watschke, 1981) investigations. Wallner et al. (1982) examined leaf tissue electrolyte leakage from seven turfgrass species following exposure to heat stress. Bermudagrass and buffalograss had the highest heat tolerance with killing temperatures of 59.9 and 61.1 °C, respectively. Using this technique, growth chamber grown creeping bentgrass, Kentucky bluegrass, perennial ryegrass, red fescue, and tall fescue were determined to have similar killing temperatures (Table 7–3). As might be expected, the killing time at 50 °C for the warm-season turfgrasses, buffalograss, and bermudagrass, was >600 min, while that for cool-season species was <300 min (Wallner et al., 1982). Annual bluegrass was determined to be less heat tolerant than Kentucky bluegrass (Wehner & Watschke, 1981). Improved heat tolerance has been identified in 26 of 115 selections of *Poa annua* (Cordukes, 1977). Yoshida (1981) felt that the heritability of heat tolerance in rice was fairly high.

Kenblue and two experimental Kentucky bluegrass selections were more heat tolerant than Nugget or Pennstar under growth chamber (low irradiance) conditions (Watschke et al., 1970). Minner et al. (1983) found field-grown Sydsport Kentucky bluegrass to be more heat tolerant than Vantage or Pennstar (Table 7–4). However, Wehner and Watschke (1981) evaluated 22

Table 7-4. Turfgrass cultivar recovery (as a percentage of nonstressed control plant weight) following heat stress. (After Minner et al., 1983).

Turf	Cultivar	Recovery
		%
Poa pratensis	Sydsport	72.5a*
	Pennstar	66.9b
	Vantage	65.6b
Lolium perenne	Pennfine	59.9c
	Citation	58.0c
	Caravelle	56.3c

* Means followed by the same letter are not significantly different at $P = 0.5$ according to the FLSD test.

Kentucky bluegrass cultivars under greenhouse conditions, including Sydsport, Vantage, and Pennstar, and found all to be of similar heat tolerance. The compensation points of 10 Kentucky bluegrass cultivars were equivalent at 35 °C and ranged from 85 to 98 μL CO_2 L^{-1}. Such differential tolerance among cultivars between studies may reflect preconditioning effects.

Caravelle, Citation, Loretta, and Pennfine perennial ryegrasses were found to be of equivalent heat tolerance in the field (Minner et al., 1983). Under greenhouse conditions, Loretta was found to be less heat tolerant than Pennfine, Diplomat, and Citation (Wehner & Watschke, 1981). White et al. (1988) reported a high temperature requirement for 50% electrolyte leakage of 59.5 °C for Prelude and 56.5 °C for Manhattan II perennial ryegrass. As with Kentucky bluegrass cultivar heat tolerance differences between studies, the disparity between the two ryegrass reports may simply reflect preconditioning differences.

1. Seasonal Variation

Relatively, little is known concerning seasonal fluctuations in turfgrass heat tolerance. Wehner et al. (1985) found that Adelphi Kentucky bluegrass heat tolerance, measured as recovery weight, increased from May through July and then decreased from August through October. After 2 yr of field investigation, these authors reported a significant relationship between heat tolerance, and both daylength and mean low temperature. The heat tolerance for a given day was best predicted when based on mean daylength and low temperatures for the preceding 2-d period. When their regression equation is used to predict Kentucky bluegrass heat tolerance from weather records for four locations in the USA, there is a surprising degree of similarity in the curves during the summer months (Fig. 7-8).

Annual bluegrass heat tolerance in the field was found to increase from mid-spring to late spring and then remain relatively high through late summer (Martin & Wehner, 1987). Unlike Kentucky bluegrass, the best regression equation for annual bluegrass heat tolerance included mean daily maximum temperature for the two preceding days and mean total precipitation for the preceding 2 to 4 d. Divergent profiles of the seasonal heat tolerance of annual bluegrass are found across locations when this regression equation is applied

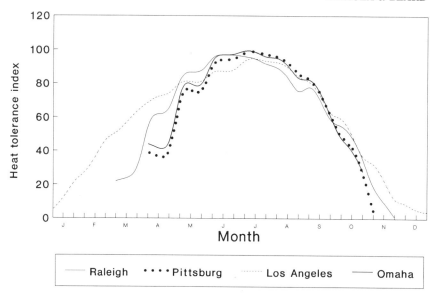

Fig. 7-8. Profile of Kentucky bluegrass heat tolerance. After Wehner et al. (1985).

to weather records (Fig. 7-9). An earlier rise in the heat-tolerance index is predicted for Raleigh, compared to the more northern sites of Omaha, NE and Cleveland, OH. The spring increase in annual bluegrass heat tolerance is predicted to be delayed until late June and July for Los Angeles, CA.

The increased heat tolerance of annual bluegrass during the late spring and summer is curious, since this period is one of prolific flowering and

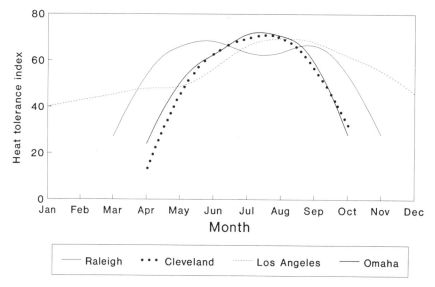

Fig. 7-9. Profile of annual bluegrass heat tolerance. After Martin and Wehner (1987).

demand for photosynthate. Loss of annual bluegrass during the late spring and summer is quite common throughout the USA. Apparently, the increased heat tolerance of this species is still insufficient compared to the high temperature stress conditions present during the late spring and summer.

2. Cultural Effects and Preconditions

Turf quality typically deteriorates during intervals of high temperature stress. Additionally, heat stress induced growth reductions limit the recuperative potential of the turf (Krans & Johnson, 1974). Management alternatives that would moderate turf quality reductions under heat stress conditions would be most welcomed by managers. Cultural programs might be conducted in anticipation of heat stress or during periods of high temperature exposure (Wehner et al., 1985). Interest would also be high for cultural strategies that would maximize recovery following periods of high temperature stress.

Watschke et al. (1972) suggested that Kentucky bluegrass heat tolerance could be improved by maximizing carbohydrate reserves through moderation of N fertility, raised cutting heights, reduced clipping frequency and syringing. The transient nature of the canopy temperature moderation through syringing has been previously discussed. Elevated levels of N have reduced Kentucky bluegrass heat tolerance in the greenhouse (Pellet & Roberts, 1963; Wehner & Watsch, 1981). In solution culture, Kentucky bluegrass had better survival following exposure to 43 to 49 °C when grown at 11 mg N kg^{-1} than 102 mg N kg^{-1} (Pellett & Roberts, 1963). Increased K fertility (63 vs. 10 mg K kg^{-1}) improved the heat tolerance of Kentucky bluegrass under a high N (102 mg N kg^{-1}) fertilization regime. Wehner and Watschke (1981) studied 22 Kentucky bluegrass cultivars, annual bluegrass, and four perennial ryegrasses and decreased heat tolerance with increased N fertilization. Turf maintained at 94.4 kg of N ha^{-1} had a mean injury score of 3.1 (5 = no injury) at 45 °C, while injury scores for that kept at 11.8 kg of N ha^{-1} remained above 3.1 until exposed to a temperature of 47 °C.

Under field conditions, the adverse impact of increased N fertilization on the heat tolerance of field grown cool-season turfgrasses had been unclear. Minner et al. (1983) found that moderate N fertilization, 98 to 196 kg of N ha^{-1} yr^{-1}, had little effect on the heat tolerance of Kentucky bluegrass and perennial ryegrass grown under field conditions. These authors noted that Carroll's (1943) finding of reduced heat tolerance with increased N was based on an unusually high fertilization rate of 245 kg of N ha^{-1}. The conclusion that Kentucky bluegrass heat tolerance is unchanged by increased but moderate (< 196 kg of N ha^{-1} yr^{-1}) levels of N fertility has also been confirmed by Wehner et al. (1985).

Given the close association of water and heat stress, irrigation management might be expected to influence turfgrass heat tolerance. Turfgrass heat tolerance is improved if the stress period is preceded by exposure to moderately hot, dry growing conditions (Julander, 1945; Levitt, 1980; Martin & Wehner, 1987). Martin and Wehner (1987) concluded that there appeared to be little potential for improving the heat tolerance of annual bluegrass through irrigation management since prior exposure to dry conditions seemed to favor enhanced stress tolerance. However, in cases where turf managers irrigate to excess, reduced irrigation frequency prior to periods of anticipated high temperature stress may well have practical importance.

Becwar et al. (1983) in studying seedling Kentucky bluegrass, perennial ryegrass, red fescue, and weeping alkaligrass [*Puccinellia distans* (L.) Parl.] found that previous exposure to water stress (25% that of well-watered turf) failed to increase in vitro heat tolerance of turfgrass leaves. These authors measured heat tolerance using an electrolyte leakage assay following exposure to 48 °C. Researchers finding a positive relationship between previous exposure to hot, dry conditions and subsequent heat tolerance typically have used recovery regrowth as a measure of high temperature stress tolerance (Julander, 1945; Levitt, 1980; Martin & Wehner, 1987; Minner et al., 1983; Wehner & Watschke, 1981). Given the short recovery periods (typically 14–28 d) for regrowth sampling, it is difficult to envision significant turf regrowth in the absence of a true heat tolerance in the previous studies. The lack of a pretreatment water stress induced enhancement of turfgrass heat tolerance in the studies of Becwar et al. (1983) may be a result of the immaturity of the turf studied. Since leaf water potential was not measured, the actual degree of water stress experienced by the turf is also somewhat uncertain. Additionally, the use of the electrolyte leakage assay on leaf tissue presumes a yet unconfirmed parallel between the heat tolerance of leaf and crown tissues. High soil temperatures have been observed to be more injurious to turfgrasses than exposure to similar air temperatures (Carroll, 1943; Kinbacher, 1963).

Minner et al. (1983) concluded that turfgrass heat tolerance was affected more by previous temperature and precipitation exposure than by modest N levels. Watschke et al. (1970) found that Kentucky bluegrass, grown in a chamber under low irradiance and moderate N nutrition, had reduced NO_3 uptake and increased foliar growth under heat stress when preconditioned at day/night temperatures of 18/10 °C compared with prior exposure to 35/20 °C. These authors concluded that preconditioning of Kentucky bluegrass with exposure to cool temperatures enhanced heat tolerance. However, Wallner et al. (1982) studied seven turfgrasses grown under chamber conditions and found that most species had increased heat tolerance following prior exposure to 38/24 °C day/night temperatures compared with a regime of 24/18 °C. Such temperature preconditioning increased the killing temperature of Kentucky bluegrass by 1 °C and delayed the killing time at 50 °C by 68 min. Depending on the turfgrass, the killing temperature increased from 0.2 to 2.0 °C following preconditioning. White et al. (1988) observed a sevenfold increase in heat stress injury to perennial ryegrass when grown at 25 °C than at 41 °C. Additionally, Duff and Beard (1974b) found leaf photosynthetic rate increased by 18 to 45% for creeping bentgrass grown under a 40/30 °C day/night temperature regime compared with a 20/10 °C preconditioning.

E. Physiological Alteration

Injury and death from exposure to high temperatures can result from at least two sources (Beard, 1973; Watschke et al., 1972). Direct heat kill results from protein precipitation and denaturation. The mechanism(s) of indirect heat injury to turf has been the subject of some debate (Beard, 1973; Duff & Beard, 1974a,b; Schmidt & Blaser, 1967; Watschke et al., 1972; Youngner & Nudge, 1968).

1. Photosynthesis

Exposure to high temperature results in a depression of turfgrass leaf photosynthetic rates (Duff & Beard, 1974b; El-Sharkawy & Hesketh, 1964). Sorghum net photosynthesis peaked at 60 mg CO_2 dm^{-2} h^{-1} at 40 °C (El-Sharkawy & Hesketh, 1964). Creeping bentgrass photosynthetic rate when grown at 20/10 °C day/night temperatures peaked at 30 °C at 81 μL O_2 cm^{-2} h^{-1} (Duff & Beard, 1974b). When exposed to 40 °C, the photosynthetic rate of creeping bentgrass decreased to 61 μL O_2 cm^{-2} h^{-1}. Photosynthetic rate was reduced from 95 μL O_2 cm^{-2} h^{-1} at 30 °C to 89μL O_2 cm^{-2} h^{-1} at 40 °C for creeping bentgrass grown under 40/30 °C day/night conditions. Watschke et al. (1972) found that those cultivars best adapted to high temperature conditions also had the highest photosynthetic rates. The optimum temperature for sorghum photosynthesis has been found to be higher for leaves with greater photosynthetic rates (El-Sharkawy & Hesketh, 1964). These results strongly suggest the importance of maintained photosynthetic capacity if maximum heat tolerance is to be maintained.

2. Carbohydrate Reserves

Heat tolerance of grasses has long been linked to the level of carbohydrate reserves within the plant (Julander, 1945). Improved bentgrass (Schmidt & Blaser, 1967) and Kentucky bluegrass (Wehner et al., 1985) performance under high temperature conditions occurred when night temperatures were cool. These authors reasoned that the cool nights permitted greater conservation of fixed photosynthate due to lower dark respiration. Researchers have found depressed carbohydrate reserves for Kentucky bluegrass grown under high temperature conditions (Baker & Jung, 1968; Watschke et al., 1970, 1972). Watschke et al. (1970) found a decrease in carbohydrate reserves from 12.7 to 9.8% of dry weight for Kentucky bluegrass shifted from 10/10 °C to 35/20 °C day/night temperature conditions. This response led these authors to conclude that prolonged periods of heat stress could result in a depletion of carbohydrate reserves. However, Duff and Beard (1974a,b) working with creeping bentgrass demonstrated that carbohydrate levels can increase by better than 50% under high temperature stress conditions despite shoot growth reductions of 36% for turf at 40/30 °C compared with turf at 20/10 °C day/night temperature regimes.

3. Protein Synthesis

Net protein synthesis in cool-season turfgrasses appears to be a heat labile process. Wehner and Watschke (1984) found the incorporation of radio-labelled leucine was reduced by 69% in plants previously exposed to 43 °C compared with those held at 27 °C. Label incorporation at 45 °C was only 10% of that for control turf at 27 °C.

Although more widely studied in animals, plants synthesize heat shock proteins in response to high temperature stress. Induction of heat shock proteins at 40 °C is quite rapid (Baszczynski & Walden, 1982; Belanger et al., 1986; Key et al., 1981, 1982; Sachs & Ho, 1986). Transcriptional level increases in certain heat shock protein genes has been observed in as little as 3 to 5 min of heat shock (Sachs & Ho, 1986). The appearance of heat shock proteins in soybean was evident within 60 min of a shift from 30 to 40 °C (Key et al., 1981). In corn, heat shock protein synthesis occurred following only 15 min at 41 °C (Baszczynski & Walden, 1982) and continued for 240 min after which a decline began as heat stress was prolonged (Key et al., 1981). Following only a brief exposure to 41 °C, heat shock proteins represented more than 15% of the total polypeptide synthesis in corn (Baszc-zynski et al., 1982). Exposure of barley aleurone layers to 45 °C resulted in a cessation of protein synthesis and death (Belanger et al., 1986). In corn, a new set of heat shock proteins are synthesized at 45 °C (Cooper & Ho, 1983).

The production of heat shock proteins is reversible since returning soy-bean (Key et al., 1981) and corn (Baszczynski et al., 1982; Kelly & Freeling, 1982) tissue to 28 °C after exposure to 40 °C resulted in a renewal of normal protein synthesis within 180 to 360 min, respectively. Clearly plants have the capacity to rapidly turn on and off the synthesis of heat shock proteins, and also turn over existing heat shock mRNAs with the return to cooler conditions.

While rapid increases in temperature to 40 °C induce heat shock protein synthesis, more gradual temperature rises of 2.5 °C h^{-1} can also result in their production. Heat shock of turf is possible in a field by several means including the sudden placement of hot metal objects (e.g., lids and cans) on the grass, the use of certain covers, or irrigation from hose or pipe lines that have been on the surface of the ground and exposed to the sun for extended periods.

It should be noted that many other stimuli could induce the production of certain heat shock proteins. These include water stress, dinitrophenols, high salt, arsenite, anaerobiosis, paraquat (Wu et al., 1988) and high ABA, ethylene, or auxin (Sachs & Ho, 1986). Heat shock proteins have been found to occur in distinct size groups (Cooper & Ho, 1983; Necchi et al., 1987; Ougham, 1987; Sachs & Ho, 1986; Vierling et al., 1986). The *large* group contain proteins that are 68 to 104 kDa in size. *Intermediate* and *small* proteins are 20 to 62 kDa and 15 to 18 kDa, respectively. The large heat shock proteins are common in animals and bacteria, while the small group is unique to higher plants. Synthesis of heat shock proteins in cereals appears to be a two or three phased process depending upon the duration of the heat stress (Cooper & Ho, 1983; Necchi et al., 1987).

Table 7-5. Heat shock protein association with cellular structures in maize. (From Cooper and Hu, 1987).

Protein	Location
HSP 29	Mitochondria
HSP 18	Plasma membrane
HSP 70	Plasma membrane
HSP 25	Endoplasmic reticulum
HSP 72	Endoplasmic reticulum
HSP 79–83	Cytosol

Heat shock proteins are thought to somehow enhance the heat tolerance of plant tissue (Key et al., 1982; Ougham, 1987; Sachs & Ho, 1986), but their identity is largely unknown (Key et al., 1981). However, the development of enhanced heat tolerance in maize seedlings can occur in the absence of heat shock protein synthesis (Bonham-Smith et al., 1987). The synthesis of these proteins was induced at the transcriptional level. Normal protein synthesis was suppressed at the translational level in soybean (Key et al., 1981), but continued in grasses under heat stress (Cooper & Ho, 1983; Sachs & Ho, 1986).

All maize tissues synthesize heat shock proteins during heat shock, with the exception of the germinating pollen (Sachs & Ho, 1986). Floral structures are known for their sensitivity to high temperature stress (Yoshida et al., 1981). In barley, heat shock resulted in a rapid induction of heat shock proteins, while the synthesis of α-amylase was suppressed (Belanger et al., 1986). More than 85% of the α-amylase mRNA sequences were destroyed within 3 h or heat shock. This loss in α-amylase was correlated with the rapid disruption of the rough endoplasmic reticulum. The cellular location of heat shock proteins in maize has been characterized (Cooper & Ho, 1987). Five heat shock proteins were found closely associated with the mitochondria, plasma membrane, endoplasmic reticulum, and cytosol (Table 7-5). In corn, Vierling et al. (1986) demonstrated that certain heat shock proteins (HSP24 kDa) were synthesized in the cytoplasm and then transported into the chloroplast.

The physiological role of heat shock proteins is currently unclear, particularly for turfgrass species. Cooper and Ho (1987) postulated a potential role for heat shock proteins in the maintenance of plant membranes during heat stress. Altschuler and Mascarenhas (1982) suggested that heat shock proteins might be needed for recovery from sudden heat shock. These proteins clearly exist in grasses and may well contribute to improved heat tolerance of the plant.

CONCLUDING REMARKS

It seems likely that in the near future, turf researchers will discover the mechanisms for enhanced temperature stress survival. This projection is partly based on the broad range of temperature stress resistance that exists among the turfgrass species. Cool-season turf species range in freezing stress tolerance (LT_{50} values) from -5 to $-35\,°C$, while that for warm-season species ranges from -6 to $-11\,°C$. Heat stress tolerance varies from excellent (buffalograss) to poor (creeping bentgrass). Comparative exploration into how some species are better able to survive temperature stress injury should help to elucidate stress resistance mechanisms.

The importance of the turfgrass crown in both practical turf management and the science of physiological temperature stress resistance must be fully recognized. Recuperative potential and the ability to reconstitute a turf following injury rests with this organ. It is increasingly evident that the mechanisms employed by the turfgrass plant to develop stress resistance differ from those in operation during stress recovery. There is a paucity of information concerning the physiological nature of turfgrasses during temperature stress recovery. Additionally, a greater understanding of secondary lateral stem development is warranted. Turf species that possess significant rhizome development survive temperature stress by avoidance due to the protective nature of the surrounding soil.

As scientists, we are only beginning to understand the mechanisms and components of turf temperature stress. Although much of the past research has fundamentally enhanced our thinking in turfgrass science, each study referenced in this chapter is a small piece of the physiological stress resistance puzzle. The challenge for future research is to bridge the gaps in our understanding and begin to couple research findings to better comprehend the physiological systems that comprise stress resistance in turfgrasses.

REFERENCES

Adir, C.R. 1968. Testing rice seedlings for cold water tolerance. Crop Sci. 8:264–265.

Altschuler, M., and J.P. Mascarenhas. 1982. The synthesis of heat-shock and normal proteins at high temperatures in plants and their possible roles in survival under heat stress. p. 321–327. *In* M.J. Schlesinger et al. (ed.) Heat shock from bacteria to man. Cold Spring Harbor Lab. Publ., Cold Spring Harbor, NY.

Anderson, I.C., and D.S. Robertson. 1960. Role of carotenoids in protecting chlorophyll from photodestruction. Plant Physiol. 35:531–534.

Andrews, C.J., and M.K. Pomeroy. 1977. Mitochondrial actively and ethanol accumulation in ice-encased winter cereal seedlings. Plant Physiol. 59:1174–1178.

Andrews, C.J., M.K. Pomeroy, and I.A. De La Roche. 1974. Changes in cold hardiness of over-wintering winter wheat. Can. J. Plant Sci. 54:9–15.

Baker, B.S., and G.A. Jung. 1968. Effect of environmental conditions on the growth of four perennial grasses. II. Response to fertility, water, and temperature. Agron. J. 60:158–162.

Baszczynski, C.L., and D.B. Walden. 1982. Regulation of gene expression in corn (*Zea mays* L.) by heat shock. Can. J. Biochem. 60:569–579.

Beard, J.B. 1964. Effects of ice, snow and water covers on Kentucky bluegrass, annual bluegrass and creeping bentgrass. Crop Sci. 4:638–640.

Beard, J.B. 1965a. Bentgrass (*Agrostis* spp.) varietal tolerance to ice cover injury. Agron. J. 57:513.

Beard, J.B. 1965b. Effects of ice covers in the field on two perennial grasses. Crop Sci. 5:139–140.

Beard, J.B. 1973. Turfgrass: Science and culture. Prentice-Hall, Englewood Cliffs, NJ.

Beard, J.B. 1966. Direct low temperature injury of nineteen turfgrasses. Quart. Bull. Mich. Agric. Exp. Stn. 48(3):377–383.

Beard, J.B. 1986. An assessment of late season nutritional strategies on C-4 warm season grasses. p. 81–98. *In* B.G. Joyner (ed.) Advances in turfgrass fertility. ChemLawn Serv. Corp., Columbus, OH.

Beard, J.B., S.M. Batten, and G.M. Pittman. 1980a. The comparative low temperature hardiness of 19 bermudagrasses. p. 21–23. *In* Texas turfgrass research. 1979–80. Texas Agric. Exp. Stn. Progr. Rep. 3835.

Beard, J.B., S.M. Batten, and G.M. Pittman. 1980b. St. Augustinegrass cultivar evaluation. p. 44–47. *In* Texas turfgrass research 1978–79. Texas Agric. Exp. Stn. PR-3677.

Beard, J.B., and W.H. Daniel. 1965. Effect of temperature and cutting on the growth of creeping bentgrass (*Agrostis palustris* Huds.) roots. Agron. J. 57:249–250.

Beard, J.B., and W.H. Daniel. 1966. Relationship of creeping bentgrass (*Agrostic palustris* Huds.) root growth to environmental factors in the field. Agron. J. 58:337–339.

Beard, J.B., and C.R. Olien. 1963. Low temperature injury in the lower portion of *Poa annua* L. crowns. Crop Sci. 3:362–363.

Becwar, M.R., S.J. Wallner, and J.D. Butler. 1983. Effect of water stress on in vitro heat tolerance of turfgrass leaves. HortScience 18:93–95.

Beevers, L., and J.P. Cooper. 1964. Influence of temperature on growth and metabolism of ryegrass seedlings. II. Variation in metabolites. Crop Sci. 4:143–146.

Belanger, F.C., M.R. Brodl, and T.D. Ho. 1986. Heat shock causes destabilization of specific mRNAs and destruction of endoplasmic reticulum in barley aleurone cells. Proc. Natl. Acad. Sci. 83:1154–1358.

Bonham-Smith, P.C., M. Kapoor, and J.D. Bewley. 1987. Establishment of thermotolerance in maize by exposure to stresses other than a heat shock does not require heat shock protein synthesis. Plant Physiol. 85:575–580.

Bramlage, W.J., A.C. Leopold, and D.J. Parrish. 1978. Chilling stress to soybeans during imbibition. Plant Physiol. 61:525–529.

Carroll, J.C. 1943. Effect of drought, temperature, and nitrogen on turfgrasses. Plant Physiol. 18:19–36.

Carroll, J.C., and F.A. Welton. 1939. Effect of heavy and late application of nitrogenous fertilizer on the cold resistance of Kentucky bluegrasses. Plant Physiol. 14:297–308.

Carter, J.L., L.A. Garrard, and S.H. West. 1973. Effect of gibberellic acid on starch degrading enzymes in leaves of *Digitaria decumbens*. Phytochemistry 12:251–254.

Chatterton, N.J., G.E. Carlson, W.E. Hungerford, and D.R. Lee. 1972. Effect of tillering and cool nights on photosynthesis and chloroplast starch in pangola. Crop Sci. 12:206–208.

Cook, T.W., and D.T. Duff. 1976. Effects of K fertilization on freezing tolerance and carbohydrate content of *Festuca arundinacea* Schreb. maintained as turf. Agron. J. 68:116–119.

Cooper, P., and T.D. Ho. 1983. Heat shock proteins in maize. Plant Physiol. 71:215–222.

Cooper, P., and T.D. Ho. 1987. Intracellular localization of heat shock proteins in maize. Plant Physiol. 84:1197–1203.

Cordukes, W.E. 1977. Growth habit and heat tolerance of a collection of *Poa annua* plants in Canada. Can. J. Plant Sci. 57:1201–1203.

Crawford, R.M.M., and T.J. Huxter. 1971. Root growth and carbohydrate metabolism at low temperatures. J. Exp. Bot. 28:917–925.

Davis, D.L., and W.B. Gilbert. 1970. Winter hardiness and changes in soluble protein fractions of bermudagrass. Crop Sci. 10:7–9.

De La Roche, I.A., M.K. Pomeroy, and C.J. Andrews. 1975. Changes in fatty acid composition in wheat cultivars of contrasting hardiness. Cryobiology 12:506–512.

De La Roche, I.A., C.J. Andrews, and M.K. Pomeroy. 1972. Lipid changes in winter wheat seedlings (*Triticum aestivum*) at temperatures inducing cold hardiness. Can. J. Bot. 50:2401–2409.

DiPaola, J.M. 1979. Fatty acid composition of turfgrass crowns and its relationship with direct low temperature hardiness. Ph.D. diss. Texas A&M Univ., College Station, TX (Diss. Abstr. 8003122, Vol. 40).

DiPaola, J.M. 1984. Syringing effects on the canopy temperatures of bentgrass greens. Agron. J. 76:951–953.

DiPaola, J.M., J.B. Beard, and H. Brawand. 1982. Key events in the seasonal root growth of bermudagrass and St. Augustinegrass. HortScience 17(5):829–831.

DiPaola, J.M., K.J. Karnok, and J.B. Beard. 1981. Growth, color and chlorophyll pigment content of bermudagrass turfs under chilling conditions as influenced by gibberellic acid. p. 527–534. *In* R.W. Sheard (ed.) Proc. 4th Turfgrass Res. Conf., Guelph, ON, Canada. 19–23 July. Int. Turfgrass Soc., Ontario Agric. Coll., Univ. of Guelph, Guelph, ON.

Dudeck, A.E., and C.H. Peacock. 1985. 'Tifdwarf' bermudagrass growth response to carboxin and GA_3 during suboptimum temperatures. HortScience 20:936–938.

Duff, D.T., and J.B. Beard. 1966. Effects of air movement and syringing on the microclimate of bentgrass turf. Agron. J. 58:495–497.

Duff, D.T., and J.B. Beard. 1974a. Supraoptimal temperature effects upon *Agrostis palustris*. I. Influence of shoot growth and density, leaf blade width and length, succulence and chlorophyll content. Physiol. Plant. 32:14–17.

Duff, D.T., and J.B. Beard. 1974b. Supraoptimal temperature effects upon *Agrostis palustris*. II. Influence on carbohydrate levels, photosynthetic rate and respiration rate. Physiol. Plant. 32:18–22.

Dunn, J.H., and C.J. Nelson. 1974. Chemical changes occurring in three bermudagrass turf cultivars in relation to cold hardiness. Agron. J. 66:28–31.

El-Sharkawy, M.A., and J.D. Hesketh. 1964. Effects of temperature and water deficit on leaf photosynthetic rates of different species. Crop Sci. 4:514–518.

Gates, D.M. 1965. Heat transfer in plants. Sci. Am. 213(6):76–84.

Gerloff, E.D., T. Richardson, and M.A. Stahmann. 1966. Changes in fatty acids of alfalfa roots during cold hardening. Plant Physiol. 41:1280–1284.

Gilbert, W.B. 1986. Centipedegrass for low maintenance areas. p. 63–66. *In* Proc. 24th Annu. North Carolina Turf. Conf., Winston-Salem, NC. 8–10 Jan. Turfgrass Counc. of North Carolina, Southern Pines.

Gilbert, W.B., and D.L. Davis. 1971. Influence of fertility ratios on winter hardiness of bermudagrass. Agron. J. 63:591–593.

Gusta, L.V., J.D. Butler, C. Rajashekar, and M.J. Burke. 1980. Freezing resistance of perennial turfgrasses. HortScience 15(4):494–496.

Hilliard, J.H., and S.H. West. 1970. Starch accumulation associated with growth reduction at low temperatures in a tropical plant. Science 168:494–496.

Hawes, D.T. 1965. Studies of the growth of *Poa annua* as affected by soil temperature, and observations of soil temperature under putting green turf. M.S. thesis. Cornell Univ., Ithaca, NY.

Johnston, W.J., and R. Dickens. 1976. Centipedegrass cold tolerance as affected by environmental factors. Agron. J. 68:83–85.

Johnston, W.J., and R. Dickens. 1977. Cold tolerance evaluation of several centipedegrass selections. Agron. J. 69:100–103.

Julander, O. 1945. Drought resistance in range and pasture grasses. Plant Physiol. 20:573–599.

Juska, F.V., and J.J. Murray. 1974. Performance of bermudagrasses in the transition zone as affected by potassium and nitrogen. p. 149–154. *In* E.C. Roberts (ed.) Proc. 2nd Int. Turfgrass Res. Conf., Blacksburg, VA. 19–21 June 1973. ASA and CSSA, Madison, WI.

Karbassi, P., L.A. Garrard, and S.H. West. 1971. Reversal of low temperature effects on a tropical plant by gibberellic acid. Crop Sci. 11:755–757.

Karbassi, P., S.H. West, and L.A. Garrard. 1972. Amylolytic activity in leaves of a tropical and a temperate grass. Crop Sci. 12:58–60.

Karnok, K.J., and J.B. Beard. 1985. The effects of chilling temperatures on the chloroplast ultrastructure of *Cynodon dactylon* as affected by gibberellic acid. Acta Agron. Acad. Sci. Hungaricae, Tomus 34(3–4):259–265.

Karnok, K.J., and J.B. Beard. 1983. Effects of gibberellic acid on the CO_2 exchange rates of bermudagrass and St. Augustinegrass when exposed to chilling temperatures. Crop Sci. 23:514–517.

Karnok, K.J., and J.B. Beard. 1981. Effects of chilling temperatures on the carbon balance of *Cynodon dactylon* and *Stenotaphrum secondatum*. p. 535–540. *In* R.W. Sheard (ed.) Proc. 4th Turfgrass Res. Conf., Guelph, ON, Canada. 19–23 July. Int. Turfgrass Soc., Ontario Agric. Coll., Univ. of Guelph, Guelph, ON.

Kelly, P.M., and M. Freeling. 1982. A preliminary comparison of maize anaerobic and heat-shock proteins. p. 315–319. *In* M.J. Schlesinger et al. (ed.) Heat shock from bacteria to man. Cold Spring Harbor Lab. Publ., Cold Spring Harbor, NY.

Key, J.L., C. Lin, E. Ceglarz, and F. Schoffl. 1982. The heat-shock response in plants: Physiological considerations. p. 329–336. *In* M.J. Schlesinger et al. (ed.) Heat shock from bacteria to man. Cold Spring Harbor Lab. Publ., Cold Spring Harbor, NY.

Key, J.L., C. Lin, and Y.M. Chen. 1981. Heat shock proteins of higher plants. Proc. Natl. Acad. Sci. 78:3526-3530.

Kinbacher, E.J. 1962. Effect of relative humidity on the high-temperature resistance of winter oats. Crop Sci. 2:437-440.

Kinbacher, E.J. 1963. Relative high-temperature resistance of winter oats at different relative humidities. Crop Sci. 3:466-468.

Krans, J.V., and G.V. Johnson. 1974. Some effects of subirrigation on bentgrass during heat stress in the field. Agron. J. 66:526-530.

Kreider, J.F., and F. Kreith. 1981. Solar energy handbook. McGraw-Hill Book Co., New York.

Krinski, N.I. 1978. Non-photosynthetic functions of carotenoids. Philos. Trans. R. Soc. London Ser. B 282:581-590.

Krinski, N.I. 1966. The role of carotenoid pigments as protective agents against photosensitized oxidations in chloroplasts. p. 423-430. In T. W. Goodwin (ed.) The biochemistry of chloroplasts. Vol. I. Academic Press, New York.

Leopold, A.C., and P.E. Kriedemann. 1975. Plant growth and development. 2nd ed. McGraw-Hill, New York.

Levitt, J. 1980. Responses of plants to environmental stresses. Vol. 1. 2nd ed. Academic Press, New York.

Lockett, M.C., and B.J. Luyet. 1951. Survival of frozen seeds of various water contents. Biodynamica 7(134):67-76.

Ludlow, M.M., and G.L. Wilson. 1970. Photosynthesis of tropical pasture plants. I. Illuminance, carbon dioxide concentration, leaf temperature and leaf vapor pressure difference. Aust. J. Biol. Sci. 24:448-470.

Lyons, J.M. 1973. Chilling injury in plants. Ann. Rev. Plant Physiol. 24:445-466.

Lyons, J.M., T.A. Wheaton, and H.K. Pratt. 1964. Relationship between the physical nature of mitochondrial membranes and chilling sensitivity in plants. Plant Physiol. 39:262-268.

MacLeod, L.B. 1965. Effect of nitrogen and potassium fertilization on the yield, regrowth, and carbohydrate content of the storage organs of alfalfa and grasses. Agron. J. 57:345-350.

Martin, D.L., and D.J. Wehner. 1987. Influence of prestress environment on annual bluegrass heat tolerance. Crop Sci. 27:579-585.

Mayland, H.F., and J.W. Cary. 1970. Chilling and freezing injury to growing plants. Adv. Agron. 22:203-235.

McWilliam, J.R., and A.W. Naylor. 1967. Temperature and plant adaptation. I. Interaction of temperature and light in the synthesis of chlorophyll in corn. Plant Physiol. 42:1711-1715.

Melcarek, P.K., and G.N. Brown. 1977. Effects of chill stress on prompt and delayed chlorophyll fluorescence from leaves. Plant Physiol. 60:822-825.

Menn, W.G., J.B. Beard, and D.S. Dahms. 1985. Turf quality evaluations for six near-release St. Augustinegrass selections and four St. Augustinegrass cultivars. p. 39-41. In Texas turfgrass research 1983-84. Texas Agric. Exp. Stn. PR-4322.

Metcalf, E.L., C.E. Cress, C.R. Olien, and E.H. Everson. 1970. Relationship between crown moisture content and killing temperature for three wheat and three barley cultivars. Crop Sci. 10:362-365.

Miller, J.V. 1960. Temperature effect on the rate of apparent photosynthesis of seaside bent and bermudagrass. Proc. Am. Soc. Hortic. Sci. 75:700-703.

Minner, D.D., P.H. Dernoeden, D.J. Wehner, and M.S. McIntosh. 1983. Heat tolerance screening of field-grown cultivars of Kentucky bluegrass and perennial ryegrass. Agron. J. 75:772-775.

Monroe, C.A., G.P. Covits, and C.R. Skogley. 1969. Effects of N and K levels on the growth and chemical composition of Kentucky bluegrass. Agron. J. 61:294-296.

Necchi, A., N.E. Pogna, and S. Mapelli. 1987. Early and late heat shock proteins in wheats and other cereal species. Plant Physiol. 84:1378-1384.

Nordin, A. 1977. Effects of low root temperature on ion uptake and ion translocation in wheat. Plant Physiol. 39:305-310.

Olien, C.R. 1964. Freezing processes in the crown of 'Hudson' barley, Hordeum vulgare (L. emend. Lam.) Hudson. Crop Sci. 4:91-95.

Ougham, H.J. 1987. Gene expression during leaf development in Lolium temulentum: Patterns of protein synthesis in response to heat-shock and cold-shock. Physiol. Plant. 70:479-484.

Palmertree, H.D., C.Y. Ward, and R.H. Pluenneke. 1974. Influence of mineral nutrition on the cold tolerance and soluble protein fraction of centipedegrass. p. 500-507. In E.C. Roberts (ed.) Proc. 2nd Int. Turfgrass Res. Conf., Blacksburg, VA. 19-21 June 1973. ASA and CSSA, Madison, WI.

Paulsen, G.M. 1968. Effect of photoperiod and temperature on cold hardening in winter wheat. Crop Sci. 8:29-32.

Pellet, H.M., and E.C. Roberts. 1963. Effects of mineral nutrition on high temperature induced growth retardation of Kentucky bluegrass. Agron. J. 55:473-450.

Reeves, S.A., and G.G. McBee. 1972. Nutritional influences on cold hardiness of St. Augustinegrass (*Stenotaphrum secundatum*). Agron. J. 64:447-450.

Reeves, S.A., G.G. McBee, and M.E. Bloodworth. 1970. Effect of N, P, and K tissue levels and late fall fertilization on the cold hardiness of Tifgreen bermudagrass (*Cynodon dactylon* × *C. transvaalensis*). Agron. J. 62:659-662.

Rogers, R.A., J.H. Dunn, and C.J. Nelson. 1975. Cold hardening and carbohydrate composition of Meyer zoysia. Agron. J. 67:836-838.

Rogers, R.A., J.H. Dunn, and C.J. Nelson. 1977. Photosynthesis and cold hardening in zoysia and Bermudagrass. Crop Sci. 17:727-732.

Rosenberg, N.J. 1983. Microclimate: The biological environment. 2nd ed. John Wiley and Sons, New York.

Sachs, M.M., and T.D. Ho. 1986. Alteration of gene expression during environmental stress in plants. Ann. Rev. Plant Physiol. 37:363-376.

Sachs, R.M., R.W. Kingberry, and J. DeBie. 1971. Retardation by carboxin of low temperature induced discoloration in zoysia and bermudagrass. Crop Sci. 11:585-586.

Schnmidt, R.E., and R.E. Blaser. 1967. Effects of temperature, light and nitrogen on growth and metabolism of 'Cohansey' bentgrass (*Agrostis palustris* Huds.). Crop Sci. 7:447-451.

Siminovitch, D., and G.W. Scarth. 1938. A study of the mechanism of frost injury to plants. Can. J. Res. 16:467-481.

Siminovitch, D., J. Singh, and I.A. De La Roche. 1978. Freezing behavior of free photoplasts of winter rye. Cryobiology 15:205-213.

St. John, J.B., M.M. Christiansen, E.N. Ashworth, and W.A. Genter. 1979. Effect of BASF 13-338, a substituted pyridazinone, on linolenic acid level and winter hardiness of cereals. Crop Sci. 19:65-69.

Stuckey, I.H. 1941. Seasonal growth of grass roots. Am. J. Bot. 28:486-491.

Stuckey, I.H., and O.F. Curtis. 1938. Ice formation and death of plant cells by freezing. Plant Physiol. 13:815-833.

Taylor, A.O., and Craig, A.S. 1971. Plants under climatic stress. II. Low temperature, high light effects on chloroplast ultrastructure. Plant Physiol. 47:719-725.

Thompson, G.A. 1983. Molecular responses of membranes to stress. p. 7-28. *In* A.C. Purvis (ed.) Molecular and physiological aspects of stress in plants. Proc. South. Sect. Am. Soc. of Plant Physiol.

Treshow, M. 1970. Environment and plant response. McGraw-Hill, New York.

Trunova, T.I. 1987. Winter wheat frost hardiness and protein synthesis at chilling temperatures. p. 43-57. *In* P.H. Li (ed.) Plant cold hardiness. Alan R. Liss, New York.

Vierling, E., M.L. Mishkind, G.W. Schmidt, and J.L. Key. 1986. Specific heat shock proteins are transported into chloroplasts. Proc. Natl. Acad. Sci. 83:361-365.

Vignais, P.M. 1976. Fluidity of mitochondrial lipids. p. 367-379. *In* L. Packes and A. Gomez-Puyou (ed.) Mitochondria bioenergetics, biogenesis and membrane structure. Academic Press, New York.

Walker, R.H., and C.Y. Ward. 1974. Influence of N and K nutrition on net photosynthesis, dark respiration, and carbohydrates in centipedegrass. p. 196-208. *In* E.C. Roberts (ed.) Proc. 2nd Int. Turfgrass Res. Conf., Blacksburg, VA. 19-21 June 1973. ASA and CSSA, Madison, WI.

Wallner, S.J., M.R. Becwar, and J.D. Butler. 1982. Measurement of turfgrass heat tolerance in vitro. J. Am. Soc. Hortic. Sci. 107:608-613.

Wang, H.C., and J.S. Li. 1987. The difference in freezing tolerance between protoplast and vacuole of wheat leaves. p. 221-228. *In* P.H. Li. (ed.) Plant cold hardiness. Alan R. Liss, New York.

Ward, C.Y. 1969. Climate and adaptation. p. 27-79. *In* A.A. Hanson and F.V. Juska (ed.) Turfgrass science. ASA, Madison, WI.

Watschke, T.L., R.E. Schmidt, and R.E. Blaser. 1970. Responses of some Kentucky bluegrasses to high temperature and nitrogen fertility. Crop Sci. 10:372-376.

Watschke, T.L., R.E. Schmidt, E.W. Carson, and R.E. Blaser. 1972. Some metabolic phenomena of Kentucky bluegrass under high temperature. Crop Sci. 12:87-90.

Wehner, D.J., D.D. Minner, P.H. Dernoeden, and M.S. McIntosh. 1985. Heat tolerance of Kentucky bluegrass as influenced by pre- and post-stress environment. Agron. J. 75:772-775.

Wehner, D.J., and T.L. Watschke. 1981. Heat tolerance of Kentucky bluegrasses, perennial ryegrasses, and annual bluegrass. Agron. J. 73:79–84.

Wehner, D.J., and T.L. Watschke. 1984. Heat stress effects on protein synthesis and exosmosis of cell solutes in three turfgrass species. Agron. J. 76:16–19.

White, R.H., and R.E. Schmidt. 1988. Carbon dioxide exchange of 'Tifgreen' bermudagrass exposed to chilling temperatures as influenced by iron and BA. J. Am. Soc. Hortic. Sci. 113(3):423–427.

White, R.H., and R.E. Schmidt. 1989. Bermudagrass response to chilling temperatures as influenced by iron and benzyladenine. Crop Sci. 29:768–773.

White, R.H., P. Stefany, and M. Comeau. 1988. Pre- and poststress temperature influence perennial ryegrass in vitro heat tolerance. HortScience 23:1047–1050.

Wu, C.H., H.L. Warren, K. Sitaraman, and C.Y. Tsai. 1988. Translational alterations in maize leaves responding to pathogen infection, paraquat treatment, or heat shock. Plant Physiol. 86:1323–1329.

Yoshida, S., T. Satake, and D.S. Mackill. 1981. High-temperature stress in rice. Int. Rice Res. Inst. Res. Paper Ser. 67.

Youngner, V.B. 1959. Growth of U-3 bermudagrass under various day and night temperatures and light intensities. Agron. J. 51:557–559.

Youngner, V.B. 1961. Growth and flowering of zoysia species in response to temperatures, photoperiods, and light intensities. Crop Sci. 1:91–93.

Youngner, V.B., and F.J. Nudge. 1968. Growth and carbohydrate storage of three *Poa pratensis* L. strains as influenced by temperature. Crop Sci. 8:455–457.

Zech, A.C., and A.W. Pauli. 1960. Cold resistance in three varieties of winter wheat as related to nitrogen fractions and total sugars. Agron. J. 52:334–337.

Zhang, L.X., P.H. Li, and M.J. Tseng. 1987. Amelioration of chilling injury in rice seedlings by mefluidide. Crop Sci. 27:531–534.

8   Shade and Turfgrass Culture

A.E. DUDECK

University of Florida
Gainesville, Florida

C.H. PEACOCK

North Carolina State University
Raleigh, North Carolina

Maintaining high-quality turf in shaded areas poses a difficult problem for every turf manager. When temperature, soil water, and mineral nutrition are adequate for rapid growth, light interception and CO_2 concentration are usually the most important growth-limiting factors. It has been estimated that 20 to 25% of all existing turfs must be maintained under some degree of shade from buildings, shrubs, or trees (Beard, 1973).

    Solar energy in the form of light is the energy source for photosynthetic activity of green-plant parts. Only a small portion of solar energy reaching the earth is used in the process of photosynthesis, 1 to 5% on a yearly basis and 3 to 10% during maximum active growth (Cooper, 1970). A minimum light intensity is needed for photosynthesis to begin. Productivity in terms of amounts of synthesized organic matter increases with increased photosynthetic irradiance up to 116 to 233 $W\ m^{-2}$. Further increases do not increase productivity of photosynthesis of cool-season grasses. In warm-season grasses, photosynthetic productivity increases to a maximum of 390 to 465 $W\ m^{-2}$. Not all warm-season grasses respond to high photosynthetic irradiance but only those belonging to panicoid and chloridoid groups (Bogdan, 1977). A listing of several grasses according to their photosynthetic capacity is presented in Table 8–1.

    Panicoid and chloridoid grasses differ from festucoid grasses in the photosynthetic process part of which is related to differences in leaf anatomy. In the grass leaf, the mesophyll consists of small, relatively uniform cells containing small chloroplasts and one or two layers of larger cells known as bundle-sheath cells that surround the conductive tissue. In warm-season grasses, the bundle-sheath cells have slightly thicker walls and contain large, linear-shaped granulated chloroplasts (Johnson & Brown, 1973). These cells are known as Kranz-type cells and turfgrasses with these have Kranz anatomy. In cool-season grasses, bundle-sheath cells have thin membraneous walls and usually contain no chloroplasts. These are known as nonKranz-type cells. Kranz cells apparently play a considerable role in photosynthesis and in pas-

Copyright © 1992 ASA-CSSA-SSSA, 677 S. Segoe Rd., Madison, WI 53711, USA. *Turfgrass—*Agronomy Monograph no. 32.

Table 8-1. Monocotyledon plants with high or low photosynthetic capacity. (After Black, 1971.)

High photosynthetic capacity monocotyledons

Andropogon scoparius Michaux	*Panicum capillare* L.
Andropogon virginicus L.	*Panicum maximum Jacq.*
Cenchrus ciliaris L.	*Panicum virgatum* L.
Cenchrus echinatus L.	*Paspalum dilatatum* Poiret
Cynodon dactylon (L.) Pers.	*Paspalum notatum* Fluegge
Cyperus esculentus L.	*Pennisetum purpureum* Schumacher
Cyperus rotundus L.	*Saccharum officinarum* L.
Dactyloctenium aegyptium (L.) Rich.	*Setaria italica* (L.) P. Beauv.
Digaria pentzii Stent	*Setaria viridis* (L.) P. Beauv.
Digitaria sanguinalis (L.) Scop.	*Sorghum bicolor* (L.) Moench
Echinochloa colona L.	*Sorghum halepense* (L.) Pers.
Echinochloa crus-galli (L.) Beauv.	*Sorghum vulgare* Pers.
Eragrostis chloromelas Steudel	*Trichachne californica* (Benth.) Chase.
Eragrostis pilosa (L.) P. Beauv.	*Trichachne insularis* (L.) Nees.
Heteropogon contortus (L.) P. Beauv.	*Tripsacum dactyloides* L.
Leptochloa dubia (H.B.K.) Nees.	*Zea mays* L.
Leptochloa fusca Kunth	

Low photosynthetic capacity monocotyledons

Agropyron repens (L.) P. Beauv.	*Lolium multiflorum* Lam.
Agrostis alba L.	*Medica mutica* Walt.
Avena sativa L.	*Oryza sativa* L.
Cyperus alternifolius gracilis L.	*Panicum commutatum* Schult.
Dactylis glomerata L.	*Phalaris arundinacea* L.
Eichhornia crassipes (C. Martins) Solms-Laub.	*Phalaris canariensis* L.
Festuca arundinacea Schreb.	*Poa pratensis* L.
Hordeum vulgare L.	*Triticum aestivum* L.

sage of products of carbon assimilation through them into conductive tissues (Bogdan, 1977).

In cool-season grasses, the photosynthetic process is the Calvin or C_3 cycle under which initial products of C assimilation are 3-carbon acids, which are further used for the formation of carbohydrates (Cooper & Tainton, 1968). In warm-season grasses with Kranz-type cells, initial products of photosynthesis are 4-carbon acids. This photosynthetic cycle is known as the C_4 pathway, which in its initial stages is usually combined with the Calvin cycle. Under the Calvin cycle, a portion of CO_2 absorbed by the leaf but not used is released back into the atmosphere. Under the C_4 cycle, CO_2 penetrates into bundle sheath cells and serves as an additional gaseous source for photosynthesis (Hatch, 1972). This probably contributes to efficiency of CO_2 utilization and water use by warm-season grasses (Berry, 1975). The C_4 pathway of photosynthesis can function under lower concentrations of CO_2 in the atmosphere than can cool-season grasses with the Calvin or C_3 pathway.

Optimum temperatures for Calvin cycle photosynthesis are 15 to 20° C, which are the optimum air temperatures for cool-season grasses. For the C_4 pathway of photosynthesis, optimum temperatures are 30 to 40° C. These are temperatures that leaves of warm-season grasses can reach under direct sunlight (Bogdan, 1977). Optimum photosynthetic irradiance for the

C_4 pathway to function is 390 to 465 W m^{-2} whereas it is only 116 to 233 W m^{-2} for the Calvin cycle of cool-season grasses. High carbon fixation in warm-season grasses can be reached only at high temperatures and high photosynthetic irradiance (Cooper, 1970). This can be up to 50 to 70 mg dm^{-2} h^{-1} of CO_2 or 30 to 50 g m^{-2} d^{-1} of dry matter; whereas, the highest rates reached in cool-season grasses are 20 to 30 mg dm^{-2} h^{-1} of CO_2 or 2 g m^{-2} d^{-1} of dry matter. The photosynthetic-respiratory balance is a critical factor in shade adaptation. Net photosynthesis must exceed respiration if the plant is to survive (Wilkinson et al., 1975). Obviously, reduced photosynthetic irradiance limits production of all grasses assuming all other growth factors are not limiting. A summary of major differences between C_3 and C_4 grasses related to photosynthetic pathway is presented in Table 8-2.

I. COMPONENTS OF SHADE

A. Light Quantity

The solar spectrum can be divided into three main regions: ultraviolet (300–400 nm), visible (400–700 nm), and the infrared (700–3000 nm). Solar radiation (SR) or short-wave radiation refers to radiation originating from the sun with wavelengths between 300 and 3000 nm. Short-wave irradiance varies from 0 at night to over 900 and 1200 mW cm^{-2} at solar noon on clear days in temperate and tropical regions, respectively. Photosynthetically active radiation (PAR) refers to radiation in the visible (400–700 nm) region. About 45% of direct SR is PAR, but when both diffuse and direct components of SR are considered, PAR is about 50% of total SR (Monteith, 1973).

Light intensity has a profound effect on plant growth and development. Photosynthetically active radiation available for plant growth varies from month to month, day to day, and from minute to minute depending on time of year, angle of sun, day length, and cloud cover (Monteith, 1978). In addition, percentage of incident PAR that is intercepted and absorbed by a turf canopy varies with kind and structure of the canopy. Photosynthetically active radiation that is absorbed by photosynthetic tissue is converted to chemical energy, which is used to fix atmospheric CO_2 into a wide variety of chemical compounds. Efficiency of this conversion depends on numerous environmental and plant factors including temperature, soil water, plant nutrition, age and health of leaves, demand for assimilate, and availability of atmospheric CO_2. Differences in evapotranspiration by turfgrass within a landscape receiving variable amounts of shade are a result of differences in energy between sites and not due to changes in the canopy itself as long as there is a complete turf cover.

B. Light Quality

In many landscapes, turfgrasses grow in close association with trees and shrubs. Trees being the dominant plant canopy reduce available light needed

Table 8-2. Anatomical, biochemical, and physiological differences between C_3 and C_4 grasses related to photosynthetic pathway. (After Jones, 1985.)

Characteristic	C_3	C_4
Leaf anatomy		
Mesophyll cells	Chloroenchyma cells of mesophyll are not usually arranged radially around the bundle sheath. More than four chlorenchymatous mesophyll cells between adjacent bundle sheaths. Large intercellular air spaces in mesophyll.	Chlorenchyma cells of mesophyll usually arranged radially around the bundle sheath. Two to four chlorenchymatous mesophyll cells between adjacent bundle sheaths. Reduced intercellular air spaces in mesophyll.
Bundle sheath cells	Bundle sheath usually double with inner thick-walled cells and outer larger parenchyma cells	Bundle sheath double (Eragrostoideae and others) or single (many Panicoideae). Inner thick-walled sheath often incomplete.
Chloroplasts	Bundle sheath and mesophyll chloroplasts usually similar in size and structure.	Bundle sheath chloroplasts often have reduced granal development, are often larger than mesophyll chloroplasts and usually accumulate large amounts of starch in the light.
Lemma anatomy	Contrasting to round, elliptical, or crescent-shaped silica cells. Trichomes often absent. Stomata large. Fewer silica cells per unit area than C_4.	Dumbbell- or cross-shaped silica cells. Trichomes present. Stomata small. More silica cells per unit area than C_3.
Enzyme responsible for CO_2 fixation:		
Mesophyll cells	RuBP carboxylase	PEP carboxylase
Bundle sheath cells	RuBP carboxylase	RuBP carboxylase
Photorespiration	Present	Absent, or greatly reduced
Maximum crop growth rate	Usually <40 g m^{-2} d^{-1}	Usually >40 g m^{-2} d^{-1}
Maximum leaf photosynthetic rate	Usually <50 mg dm^{-2} h^{-1} of CO_2	Usually >50 mg dm^{-2} h^{-1} of CO_2
CO_2 compensation rate	>20 μL CO_2 L^{-1}	<10 μL CO_2 L^{-1}
Light saturation of photosynthesis	0.2–0.25% of full sunlight	Full sunlight
Optimum temperature for growth	About 25° C	About 30° C
Day length sensitivity of flowering response	Long-day plants	Qualitative short-day or day-neutral plants

for adequate density and vigor of the turf ground cover. Few turfgrass species are well adapted for growth in reduced light environments (Beard, 1965; Wilkinson et al., 1975; Wood, 1969).

Tree canopies alter the spectral composition of available light and reduce irradiance on underlying turf for photosynthesis. Light quality is often altered to the point that adequate photosynthesis cannot take place. Both McKee (1963) and Gaskin (1965) have shown that light in shade of buildings and under tree canopies differs in spectral composition. Light on the shaded, north side of a building was higher in the blue wavelengths than light in the nonshaded areas. Spruce (*Picea* sp.), oak (*Quercus* sp.), and maple (*Acer* sp.) absorbed a large amount of blue light waves leaving what McKee termed a "red" shade. McBee (1969) found that the spectral distribution of light differed in relation to distance away from the trunk of a post oak tree (*Quercus stellata* Wang.). He postulated that leaf canopy density near the perimeter of the tree is probably thin enough to permit penetration of blue light but partially deflects and reflects longer wave lengths of light. As the canopy becomes denser, all wave lengths are inhibited to a greater degree, particularly those in the blue portion of the spectrum. He also found that warm-season turfgrass grew better under short wavelengths (< 575 nm) and suggested that acceptable turf of certain bermudagrasses (*Cynodon* sp.) could be grown in shaded areas if minimum levels of light of short wavelengths are available. McVey et al. (1969) independently confirmed this in their study. They found that 'Tifgreen' bermudagrass and 'Windsor' Kentucky bluegrass (*Poa pratensis* L.) grew acceptably at no less than 40 to 50% of full sunlight under blue light-transmitting panels in the field.

C. Microenvironment

The microenvironment conducive to disease activity was most significant in affecting grass adaptation to shade. Beard (1965) found that higher relative humidity and extended periods of dew associated with reduced light intensity produced a more succulent type of growth which encouraged disease activity. Light, moisture, or nutrient deficiencies were not key factors in grass adaptation to shade. Tree canopies alter a turf microenvironment not only by reducing light intensity but also by restricting air movement, moderating temperature extremes, and increasing the level of CO_2. Turfgrass managers should be concerned about the following factors associated with the shade environment and their effects on grass growth: (i) reduced photosynthetic irradiance that produces undesirable plant characteristics such as thinner leaves with a more delicate leaf structure and increased succulence, reduced shoot density, reduced root and shoot growth, and reduced tillering much of which is related to reduced carbohydrate availability; (ii) increased disease development caused by prolonged dews, decreased wind movement, and increased relative humidity; and (iii) increased susceptibility to turf injury from wear and environmental stress.

II. SHADE AS A STRESS FACTOR

A. Plant Growth Response

Plant growth responses have been summarized and presented as contrasts in growth responses to shade in Table 8-3.

1. Physiological

Boardman (1977) presented an excellent, in-depth discussion at the cellular level on physiological responses of plants grown under different light intensities. Overall plant response of turfgrasses when grown under low light intensities are as follows: (i) higher chlorophyll content, (ii) lower respiration rate, (iii) lower compensation point, (iv) lower carbohydrate reserve, (v) lower C/N ratio, (vi) reduced transpiration rate, (vii) higher tissue moisture content, and (viii) lower osmotic pressure (Beard, 1973). One of the most common observations in shading studies is that shaded plants become elongated, weight per unit leaf area (specific leaf weight) decreases, and leaf area per unit shoot weight (leaf area ratio) increases (Earley et al., 1966; Eriksen & Whitney, 1981; Ludlow et al., 1974). Another common observation is that shading reduces root and rhizome growth proportionately more than shoot growth. This results in an increase in the ratio of shoot weight to root or rhizome weight (Burton et al., 1959; Eriksen & Whitney, 1981; Patterson, 1980a).

Table 8-3. Contrast summary of turfgrass growth responses to shade.

Level of expresion	Growth response	
	Decreased	Increased
Anatomical	Chloroplasts	Thylakoid and grana stack
	Cuticle thickness	development
	Stomatal density	
	Vascular tissue	
Morphological	Leaf thickness	Rhoot/shoot ratio
	Leaf width	Leaf area
	Stem diameter	Leaf length
	Dry weight	Spongy parenchyma tissue
	Horizontal growth habit	Vertical growth habit
	Stolon number and total length	Plant height
	Intermode diameters	Succulence
	Shoot density	
	Rhizome growth	
Nutritional	Growth and yield, but interactions are often observed	Dark green color
	Carbohydrates	
Physiological	Photosynthesis	Tissue moisture
	Respiration rate	Lignin content
	Compensation point	
	Carbohydrate reserve	
	C/N ratio	
	Transpiration rate	
	Osmotic pressure	
	Flowering	

Also, shading may severely reduce number of leaves, tillers, and rhizomes produced by the plant (Patterson, 1980a) though under certain conditions moderate shade may increase tillering (Inosaka et al., 1977) and even shoot growth (Eriksen & Whitney, 1981; Singh et al., 1974; Wong & Wilson, 1980).

Because of reduced photosynthesis, nonstructural carbohydrate concentration usually decreases dramatically under shade (Burton et al., 1959), and in forage grasses heading may be either hastened or delayed (Inosaka et al., 1977). Burton's study also revealed a decrease in available carbohydrates and a significant increase in lignin of shaded 'Coastal' bermudagrass.

Considerable research has been done with sun and shade plants (Berry, 1975; Boardman, 1977). Bohning and Burnside (1956) measured the rate of photosynthesis in relation to photosynthetic irradiance in leaves of several dicotyledonous species of plants. Light compensation and saturation points for sun species were 9 to 13 W m^{-2} and 168 to 210 W m^{-2}, respectively. Shade species reached their light saturation point at 84 W m^{-2} with some species showing a maximum saturation as low as 34 to 42 W m^{-2}. The compensation point for shade species was approximately 4 W m^{-2}. Alexander and McCloud (1962) found that the light saturation point of isolated leaves in bermudagrass [*Cynodon dactylon* (L.) Pers.] was 210 to 252 W m^{-2}. At least 215 W m^{-2} of light were required to reach the compensation point.

2. Morphological

Solar radiant flux influences the morphological development of plants (Masterlerz, 1977). A high level of solar radiant energy promotes root development and increases the root/shoot ratio. Leaves of plants grown in full sunlight are thicker and have a smaller area than those grown in shade. A high radiant flux favors development of several layers of long palisade cells in leaves, whereas shading promotes production of leaves with more spongy parenchyma tissue. Sun leaves also have a larger number of stomata, thicker cell walls and cuticle, fewer and larger chloroplasts, and a higher ratio of internal to external leaf surface than leaves grown in shade. Generally, a high radiant flux decreases plant height but increases stem diameter and dry weight. Plants grown in shade are taller with thinner stems and lower dry weights than plants exposed to full sunlight.

Wilkinson and Beard (1974) found that leaf length of 'Merion' Kentucky bluegrass and 'Pennlawn' red fescue (*Festuca rubra* L.) increased with decreasing photosynthetic irradiance to 83 W m^{-2} while leaf length was reduced at intensities below 83 W m^{-2}. Each species had narrower leaves with successive reductions in photosynthetic irradiance. Both species had horizontal leaf angles at high photosynthetic irradiance. Red fescue remained horizontal under low photosynthetic irradiance while Kentucky bluegrass exhibited a vertical growth habit. Clipping weights of both species decreased and percent moisture increased under lower photosynthetic irradiance. Chlorophyll concentration per square decimeter decreased while chlorophyll concentration per gram increased as photosynthetic irradiance decreased.

Shoot and root production decreased under decreased photosynthetic irradiance. Red fescue, however, produced greater shoot weight than Kentucky bluegrass under the lowest levels, while the latter was superior at the highest levels. Kentucky bluegrass produced less leaf area, fewer shoots per square centimeter, and fewer tillers per plant with each decrement of lower photosynthetic irradiance, while red fescue produced equal numbers in these categories through 42 W m^{-2}. Thus, Pennlawn red fescue was superior to Merion Kentucky bluegrass at low photosynthetic irradiance only in terms of shoot growth below the cutting height or production of verdure.

Peacock and Dudeck (1981) found that shade did not affect total chlorophyll content on a leaf area or leaf weight (wet or dry) basis over six cultivars of St. Augustinegrass [*Stenotaphrum secundatum* (Walter) Kuntze]. Differences between cultivars, however, were noted for the following parameters: specific leaf weight and first, second, and third internode diameters decreased linearly, but length of the second internode increased linearly with decreased light intensity. Length of stolons was not affected by shade, but number and total stolon length were reduced.

Observations by McBee and Holt (1966) indicate that short internode length may be a useful guide in classifying bermudagrasses for shade tolerance. They postulate that as light energy is reduced, a physiological system is either activated or inhibited which results in stem elongation and a reduction in stem diameter. They also found that shaded grasses that grew poorly during the summer months improved in density and ground cover in the fall. They suggested that shading would be less detrimental if accompanied by a reduction in temperature.

Burton et al. (1959) found that Coastal bermudagrass produced roots and rhizomes at a decreasing rate as shade increased. Ludlow et al. (1974) observed a decrease in the number of tillers in some tropical grasses when subjected to shade. Conversely, tiller production depended on total radiant energy received by the plant and was independent of its duration or intensity.

Beard (1973) summarized several morphological changes caused by reduced light levels. Typical observations were noted as follows:

1. Thinner leaves with less weight per unit area.
2. Reduced leaf width.
3. Increased leaf length and plant height.
4. Reduced shoot density.
5. Longer internodes.
6. Reduced tillering.
7. Reduced stem diameter
8. Reduced appearance rate of successive leaves on the stem, and
9. More upright growth habit.

3. Anatomical

Merion Kentucky bluegrass displayed a decrease in cuticle thickness and vascular and support tissues under reduced photosynthetic irradiance; whereas Pennlawn red fescue did not (Wilkinson & Beard, 1975). Stomatal density of both species decreased under reduced light; whereas stomatal pore length did not vary with photosynthetic irradiance. Number of chloroplasts per cross-sectional unit area decreased with reduced photosynthetic irradiance for both species. Merion Kentucky bluegrass had increased thylakoid and grana stack development within individual chloroplasts at reduced photosynthetic irradiance. Chloroplast ultrastructure remained unchanged in Pennlawn red fescue. Shade adaptation of Pennlawn red fescue may be related to cuticle thickness, more developed vascular and support tissue, and chloroplast ultrastructure. Stomata and chloroplast density responses of the two species to reduced photosynthetic irradiance were similar and could not be associated with the ability of Pennlawn red fescue to provide a more desirable turf in the shade than Merion Kentucky bluegrass.

4. Nutritional

Burton et al. (1959) found that shading reduced growth and yields of Coastal bermudagrass particularly when heavily fertilized. When grown under shade, grass receiving 1800 kg of N ha^{-1} yr^{-1} showed a much greater reduction in growth and yield than that given 224 kg of N. High-N plots yielded significantly more than low-N plots under full daylight and significantly less when plants were grown under a light reduction of 71%. A particularly sharp reduction in weight was noted for rhizomes and roots. McVey et al. (1969) reported darker green turf grown under blue light. This was thought to be due to an increase in nitrogenous compounds in plant tissue as carbohydrate formation is favored at higher light intensities. Schmidt and Blaser (1967) also found that liberal N fertilization of 'Cohansey' bentgrass (*Agrostis palustris* Huds.) decreased carbohydrates and inhibited root development when grown in shade. Eriksen and Whitney (1981) confirmed that under N-deficient conditions, most yields and forage quality parameters in six tropical forage grasses were enhanced under moderate shade. The tropical grasses studied generally responded to N fertilization only under conditions of moderate to high solar radiation.

A strong interaction between light intensity and N nutrition is often observed in shading experiments. When N nutrition is low, shade can stimulate shoot dry matter yields and increase N concentration of the shoot (Eriksen & Whitney, 1981; Wong & Wilson, 1980); however, when N is abundant, increasing shade results in an almost linear decrease in shoot dry matter yield (Burton et al., 1959).

B. Environmental Stress

Beard (1973) presents an excellent discussion on environmental stresses associated with shade. In addition to lower radiation and reduced temperatures in shade, a tree canopy restricts the nocturnal cooling process by inhibiting heat loss as outgoing, long-wave radiation. The net effect is moderation of air and soil temperatures. Water transpired from tree and grass increases relative humidity under the tree canopy. In general, highest relative humidity occurs at night and decreases throughout the day. Dense ornamental plantings seriously restrict wind movement which in turn affects temperature, relative humidity, and CO_2 content under the canopy. In general, dew is less under a tree canopy, but when it does form, it remains for a longer duration than in open, turf areas.

III. SHADE ECOLOGY

A. Plant Competition

Light quality and amount of light available to a plant is reduced when it is shaded by taller plants and when it is grown at high population densities. For example, growth of weeds germinating under a grass cover is often limited by shading. Individual grass plants grown at high population densities are often smaller and more juvenile than those grown at lower populations. This is one reason tall fescue (*Festuca arundinacea* Schreb.) and overseeded grasses are often seeded at very high rates. Furthermore, high seeding rates enhance finer texture. Plants adapt to shading and competition for light in several ways. Gross structure of the plant as well as leaf morphology and biochemistry adjust to changes in light regime. This adaptation to suboptimal irradiance has been reviewed recently by Patterson (1980b).

1. Tree Roots

Tree roots can reduce the growth and vigor of most turfgrasses even when water and nutrients are maintained at optimum levels (Whitcomb, 1972). Kentucky bluegrass was more sensitive to tree root effects than was red fescue, rough bluegrass (*Poa trivialis* L.), and perennial ryegrass (*Lolium perenne* L.). Red fescue was strongly competitive growing equally well with or without tree root competition. Rough bluegrass and perennial ryegrass were intermediate. In another study, Whitcomb and Roberts (1973) further demonstrated Kentucky bluegrass rooting to be severely restricted by trees having shallow feeder roots.

2. Allelopathy

Excellent discussions on allelopathy were recently presented by Putnam and Tang (1986) and Rice (1984). Barberry (*Berberis* spp.), horse chestnut (*Aesculus* spp.), rose (*Rosa* spp.), lilac (*Syringa* spp.), viburnum (*Viburnum* spp.), fir (*Abies* spp.), and mockorange (*Philadelphus* spp.) have considerable allelopathic activity. All inhibit neighboring plants and cause soil toxicity. Barberry produces an alkaloid, berberin, which is a strong inhibitor of plant growth and development.

Tree-turfgrass allelopathic effects were first reported by Whitcomb and Roberts (1973). Silver maple (*Acer saccharinum* L.) and honeylocust (*Gleditsia triacanthos* L.) roots established prior to seeding common Kentucky bluegrass had a significant effect on the growth of Kentucky bluegrass, but the latter had no effect on tree roots. Established tree roots reduced the number of bluegrass plants established from seed but had no effect on tiller production. They hypothesized that allelopathy was involved. Fales and Wakefield (1981) studied effects of turfgrasses on establishment and growth of dogwood (*Cornus florida* L.) and forsythia (*Forsythia intermedia* Spaeth.). Both ornamental plants established poorly when planted in mature sods of Kentucky bluegrass and red fescue. Aqueous root leachates from perennial ryegrass, Kentucky bluegrass, and red fescue reduced top and root growth of forsythia. Similarly, Fisher and Adrian (1981) reported allelopathic effects of bahiagrass (*Paspalum notatum* Fluegge) on slash pine (*Pinus elliottii* var. *elliottii* Engeim.). Not only did competition from actively growing bahiagrass significantly reduce pine growth, but also dry bahiagrass mulch had an inhibitory effect. Aqueous root leachates from bahiagrass significantly reduced root, shoot, and total dry weight of pine seedlings. Similar effects from tall fescue were reported on the growth of sweetgum (*Liquidambar styraciflua* L.) (Walters & Gilmore, 1976) and black walnut (*Juglans nigra* L.) (Todhunter & Beineke, 1979).

B. Turfgrass Quality

1. Shade Adaptation

Shade adaptation of a turfgrass ground cover is influenced by a complex of microclimatical, pathological, and physiological responses. Primary factors involve: (i) reduced irradiance, (ii) tree root competition for nutrients and water, (iii) microclimate that favors disease activity, (iv) succulent grass tissue, and (v) reductions in shoot density, root growth, and carbohydrate reserves (Beard, 1965, 1973; Schmidt & Blaser, 1967; Wilkinson et al., 1975). Plants which adapt to shade environments can do so by a combination of physiological or morphological adaptations (Leopold & Kriedmann, 1975). Plants capable of shade adaptation develop a higher photochemical efficiency, which is expressed by a steeper slope in the early phases of their light response curves. Boardman (1977), however, concludes that no one factor is the primary cause of altered photosynthetic capacity. Wilkinson et al. (1975) concluded that the photosynthetic-respiratory balance is a critical factor in shade adaptation. For a plant to survive, net photosynthesis must exceed respiration. They found that Merion Kentucky bluegrass and Pennlawn red fescue responded similarly to reduced light intensity in terms of net photosynthesis, light saturation levels, and light compensation points, but these factors could not be associated with the ability of Pennlawn red fescue to provide a more desirable turf than Merion Kentucky bluegrass in shade. Dark respiration of individual plants of Pennlawn was reduced at the lowest light intensity, but dark respiration of Merion was not reduced. This response may contribute to the positive CO_2 balance of Pennlawn at reduced light intensities and thus to its shade adaptability. Gilbert and DiPaola (1985) grew pure strands, mixtures, and blends of cool-season turfgrasses under a tree canopy of deciduous trees, which reduced light levels 88%. 'Rebel' tall fescue and 'Glade' Kentucky bluegrass were superior grasses compared to other turf cultivars. Karnok and Augustin (1981) demonstrated that Glade Kentucky bluegrass (shade tolerant) exhibited a higher rate of photosynthesis under reduced light than Merion Kentucky bluegrass (shade intolerant). Glade maintained a more favorable carbon level in the shade, thus allowing for greater shoot growth. Other grasses in Gilbert and DiPaola's studies were affected by disease problems in shade caused by powdery mildew (*Erysiphe graminis* DC.) and *Pythium* complex. These disease problems are similar to that reported by Vargas and Beard (1981).

2. Disease Problems

It is generally agreed that higher relative humidity, extended periods of dew cover, and reduced photosynthetic irradiance enhances activity of certain pathogens on turf grown in shaded environments, particularly *E. graminis, Fusarium* spp., *Helminthosporium* spp., *Pythium* spp., *Rhizoctonia* spp., and *Sclerotinia* spp. (Beard, 1965, 1969; Callahan & Fribourg, 1975, p. 13–15; Chesnel et al., 1980; Gilbert & DiPaola, 1985; Fenner, 1978; Vargas & Beard, 1981; Whitcomb, 1972; Winstead & Ward, 1974). Beard (1965) lists diseases as one of the most limiting factors in growing turfgrasses under shaded conditions. Severity of any one disease was greater for grasses grown as a monoculture than for mixtures of different species. Kentucky bluegrass was able to persist better when included in a mixture with other species than when seeded alone.

C. Shade-Tolerant Turfgrasses

Most authorities agree that of the warm-season turfgrasses, St. Augustinegrass and zoysiagrass (*Zoysia* sp. Willd.) have good to excellent shade tolerance; centipedegrass [*Eremochloa ophiuroides* (Monro) Hackel] and bahiagrass have medium shade tolerance; while bermudagrass has poor shade tolerance (Barrios et al., 1986; Beard, 1973; Wood, 1969) (Table 8-4). Differences between cultivars within species, however, have been noted (Aldomares & Beard, 1980, p. 25–28; Barrios et al., 1986; McBee & Holt, 1966; Peacock & Dudeck, 1981).

Table 8-4. Relative shade tolerance of turfgrasses.

Tolerance	Grass	
	Cool-season	Warm-season
Excellent	Fine fescues	St. Augustinegrass
Good	Creeping bentgrass	Zoysiagrass
	Colonial bentgrass	
	Rough bluegrass	
	Tall fescue	
Fair	Perennial ryegrass	Bahiagrass
		Carpetgrass
		Centipdegrass
Poor	Kentucky bluegrass	Bermudagrass

Of the cool-season turfgrasses, red fescues have excellent shade tolerance; rough bluegrass, tall fescue, and creeping bentgrass have good shade tolerance; perennial ryegrass and Kentucky bluegrass have fair to poor shade tolerance, respectively (Beard, 1973; Harivandi et al., 1984; Wood, 1969) (Table 8-4). Differences between cultivars have been reported within cool-season turfgrass species also (Smalley, 1981; Wood, 1969; Wu et al., 1985). Active turfgrass breeding programs at several agricultural experiment stations as well as in private industry are developing shade-tolerant cultivars in existing and potentially new turfgrass species.

D. Modification of Shade Environments

It is possible to modify the shade environment to improve conditions for turfgrass growth (Demoeden, 1986, p. 1–2; Duble, 1985; Smith & Reike, 1986; Wilkinson, 1974). Light intensity reaching the turf can be increased by selectively pruning limbs within the tree canopy. Selective pruning is particularly effective with trees such as maples and oaks that have dense canopies. Sunflecks can be an important source of light for photosynthesis in turfs growing under shade (Evans, 1956). In general, single trees do not present a serious shade problem. Lower limbs of single trees should be pruned to a height of 3 m. This will allow for direct sunlight to reach the turf during early morning and late afternoon.

Dense shrub plantings should be thinned or selectively removed to prevent air stratification and improve wind movement. This will decrease relative humidity in the turf environment and enhance drying. If possible, plantings should be thinned or removed in relation to prevailing winds.

Before establishing turf under trees, shallow tree feeder roots should be pruned to a depth of 10 cm. Plant shade and ornamental trees that are deep rooting with open canopies. Fall establishment of cool-season grasses under deciduous trees is best. This allows for the longest period of high photosynthetic irradiance. Tree fertilization should be as deep as possible to discourage formation of shallow feeder roots.

IV. TURFGRASS CULTURAL PRACTICES UNDER SHADE

Turfgrass cultural practices must be modified in shaded areas to enhance light interception and avoid development of succulent leaf tissue. Mowing height should be raised as high as possible to provide for maximum leaf area for absorption of limited radiant energy. Increased mowing height increases depth of turfgrass rooting and helps to maintain turf density. Irrigation should be applied only when turf shows signs of stress. These are folded leaf blades, blue-gray color overall, and footprints or wheelmarked impressions due to loss of turgor. Water deeply to encourage deep rooting of the turf. Shallow, light, and frequent irrigations enhance disease activity and encourage development of shallow root systems. Excessive N fertilization should be avoided. This encourages shoot growth over root growth which places a further stress on carbohydrate reserves. Excessive N increases tissue succulence which again increases disease susceptibility and decreases abilty of turf to withstand environmental stress. Minimize traffic in shaded areas since wear tolerance is reduced. Use fungicides discriminately if disease becomes a serious problem.

It is possible that no turfgrass species will provide a suitable ground cover in shade. Fortunately, evergreen and deciduous ground covers far outnumber the choices of turfgrasses for use in shaded environments (Halfacre & Shawcroft, 1989; MacCaskey, 1982; Martin, 1983). In extreme shade, a mulch of bark, woodchips, or an inert mulching material such as pumice, rock, or gravel may be used as a ground cover in this situation.

REFERENCES

Alexander, C.W., and D.E. McCloud. 1962. CO_2 uptake (net photosynthesis) as influenced by light intensity of isolated bermudagrass leaves contrasted to that of swards under various clipping regimes. Crop Sci. 2:132–135.

Almodares, A., and J.B. Beard. 1980. Turfgrass shade research update. p. 25–28. Texas Turfgrass Res. 1978–79 Prog. Rep. 3672.

Barrios, E.P., F.J. Sundstrum, D. Babcock, and L. Leger. 1986. Quality and yield response of four warm-season lawngrasses to shade conditions. Agron. J. 78:270–273.

Beard, J.B. 1965. Factors in the adaptation of turfgrasses to shade. Agron. J. 57:457–459.

Beard, J.B. 1969. Turfgrass shade adaptation. 273–282. In R.R. Davis (ed.) Proc. 1st Int. Turfgrass Res. Conf., Harrogate, England. 15–18 July. Sports Turf Res. Inst., Bingley, England.

Beard, J.B. 1973. Turfgrass: science and culture. Prentice Hall, Englewood Cliffs, NJ.

Berry, J.A. 1975. Adaptation of photosynthetic processes to stress. Science 188:644–650.

Black, C.C. 1971. Ecological implications of dividing plants into groups with distinct photosynthetic production capacities. Adv. Ecol. Res. 7:87–114.

Boardman, N.K. 1977. Comparative photosynthesis of sun and shade plants. Ann. Rev. Plant Physiol. 28:355–377.

Bogdan, A.V. 1977. Tropical pasture and fodder plants. Longman, New York.

Bohning, R.H., and C.A. Burnside. 1980. The effect of light intensity on rate of apparent photosynthesis in leaves of sun and shade plants. Am. J. Bot. 43:577–561.

Burton, G.W., J.E. Jackson, and F.E. Knox. 1959. Influence of light reduction upon the production, persistence, and chemical composition of coastal bermudagrass (Cynodon dactylon). Agron. J. 51:537–542.

Callahan, L.M., and H.A. Fribourg. 1975. Effects of shade on stand and sod quality of selected turf and forage grasses. Tenn. Farm Home Sci. 96:13–15.

Chesnel, A., R. Croise, and B. Bourgoin. 1980. Tree shade adaptation of turfgrass species and cultivars in France. p. 431–436. In J.B. Beard (ed.) Proc. 3rd Int. Turfgrass Res. Conf., Munich, Germany. 11–13 July 1977. Int. Turfgrass Soc., and ASA, CSSA, and SSSA, Madison, WI.

Cooper, J.D. 1970. Potential production and energy conversion in temperate and tropical grasses. Herb. Abstr. 40:1–15.

Cooper, J.D., and N.M. Tainton. 1968. Light and temperature requirements for the growth of tropical and temperate grasses. Herb. Abstr. 38:167–176.

Dernoeden, P.H. 1986. Establishing and maintaining turf in shade. The agronomist. Maryland Agric. Exp. Stn. May.

Duble, R. 1985. Growing turfgrass in the shade. Fla. Turf Dig. 2(9):38.

Earley, E.B., R.J. Miller, G.L. Reichert, R.H. Hageman, and R.D. Seif. 1966. Effects of shade on maize production under field conditions. Crop Sci. 6:1–7.

Eriksen, F.I., and A.S. Whitney. 1981. Effects of light intensity on growth of some tropical forage species. I. Interaction of light intensity and nitrogen fertilization on six forage grasses. Agron. J. 73:427–433.

Evans, G.C. 1956. An area survey method of investigating the distribution of light intensity in woodlands with particular reference to sunflecks. J. Ecol. 44:391–427.

Fales, S.L., and R.C. Wakefield. 1981. Effects of turfgrass on the establishment of woody plants. Agron. J. 73:605–610.

Feldhake, C.M., J.D. Butler, and R.E. Danielson. 1985. Turfgrass evapotranspiration: Responses to shade preconditioning. Irrig. Sci. 6:265–270.

Fenner, M. 1978. Susceptibility to shade in seedlings of colonizing and closed turf species. New Phytol. 81:739–744.

Fisher, R.F., and F. Adrian. 1981. Bahiagrass impairs slash pine seedling growth. Tree Planters Notes 32:19–21.

Gaskin, T.A. 1965. Light quality under saran shade cloth. Agron. J. 57:313–314.

Gilbert, W.B., and J.M. DiPaola. 1985. Cool-season turfgrass cultivars performance in the shade. p. 265–274. *In* F. Lemaire (ed.) Proc. 5th Int. Tufgrass Res. Conf., Avignon, France. 1–5 July. Inst. Natl. de la Recherche Agron., Paris.

Halfacre, R.G., and A.R. Shawcroft. 1989. Landscape plants of the southeast. Sparks Press, Raleigh, NC.

Harivandi, M.A., W. Davis, V.A. Gibeault, M. Henry, J. Van Dam, and L. Wu. 1984. Selecting the best turfgrass. Cal. Turfgrass Cult. 34(4):17–18.

Hatch, M.D. 1972. Photosynthesis and the C_4 pathway. Div. of Plant Ind. p. 19–26. *In* Annu. Rep. 1971. CSIRO, Canberra, Australia.

Inosaka, M.O., K. Ito, H. Numaguchi, and M. Misumi. 1977. Studies on the productivity of some tropical grasses. 4. Effect of shading on heading habit of some tropical grasses. Jpn. J. Trop. Agric. 20:2365–239.

Johnson, S.C., and W.V. Brown. 1973. Grass leaf ultrastructural variations. Am. J. Bot. 60(8):727–735.

Jones, C.A. 1985. C_4 grasses and cereals. Wiley Interscience, New York.

Karnok, K.J., and B.J. Augustin. 1981. Growth and carbon dioxide flux of Kentucky bluegrass during sod establishment under low light. p. 517–526. *In* R.W. Sheard (ed.) Proc. 4th Int. Turfgrass Res. Conf., Guelph, ON, Canada. 19–23 July. Int. Turfgrass Soc., and Ontario Agric. Coll., Univ. of Guelph, Guelph, ON.

Leopold, A.C., and P.E. Kriedmann. 1975. Plant growth and development. McGraw-Hill, New York.

Ludlow, M.M., G.L. Wilson, and M.R. Heslehurst. 1974. Studies on the productivity of tropical pasture plants. 1. Effect of shading on growth, photosynthesis, and respiration in two grasses and two legumes. Aust. J. Agric. Res. 25:425–433.

MacCaskey, M. 1982. Lawns and ground covers. Horticultural Publ. Co., Tucson, AZ.

Martin, E.C. 1983. Landscape plants in design. Avi Publ. Co., Westport, CT.

Masterlerz, J.W. 1977. The greenhouse environment. John Wiley and Sons, New York.

McBee, G.G. 1969. Association of certain variations in light quality with the performance of selected turfgrasses. Crop Sci. 9:14–17.

McBee, G.G., and E.C. Holt. 1966. Shade tolerance studies on bermudagrass and other turfgrasses. Agron. J. 58:523–525.

McKee, G.W. 1963. Use of a color temperature meter to characterize light quality in the field. Crop Sci. 3:271–272.

McVey, G.R., E.W. Mayer, and J.A. Simmons. 1969. Responses of various turfgrasses to certain light spectra modifications. p. 264–272. *In* R.R. Davis (ed.) Proc. 1st Int. Turfgrass Res. Conf., Harrogate, England. 15–18 July. Sports Turf Res. Inst., Bingley, England.

Monteith, J.L. 1973. Principles of environmental physics. Edward Arnold, London.

Monteith, J.L. 1978. Reassessment of maximum growth rates for C_3 and C_4 crops. Exp. Agric. 14:1–15.

Patterson, D.T. 1980a. Shading effects on growth and partitioning of plant biomass in Cogongrass (*Imperata cylindrica*) from shaded and exposed habitats. Weed Sci. 28:735–740.

Patterson, D.T. 1980b. Light and temperature adaptation. p. 205–235. *In* J.D. Hesketh and J.W. Jones (ed.) Prediction photosynthesis for ecosystem models. Vol. 1. CRC Press, Boca Raton, FL.

Peacock, C.H., and A.E. Dudeck. 1981. Effects of shade on morphological and physiological parameters of St. Augustinegrass cultivars. p. 493–500. *In* R.W. Sheard (ed.) Proc. 4th Int. Turfgrass Res. Conf., Guelph, ON, Canada. 19–23 July. Int. Turfgrass Soc., and Ontario Agric. Coll., Univ. of Guelph, Guelph, ON.

Putnam, A.R., and Chung-Shih Tang. 1986. The science of allelopathy. John Wiley and Sons, New York.

Rice, E.L. 1984. Allelopathy. 2nd ed., Academic Press, Orlando, FL.

Schmidt, R.E., and R.E. Blaser. 1967. Effect of temperature, light, and nitrogen on growth and metabolism of 'Cohansey' bentgrass (*Agrostis palustris* Huds.). Crop Sci. 7:447–451.

Singh, M., W.L. Ogren, and J.M. Widholm. 1974. Photosynthetic characteristics of several C_3 and C_4 plant species grown under different light intensities. Crop Sci. 14:563–566.

Smalley, R.R. 1981. Tillering responses of five fine-leaf fescue cultivars to variations of light intensity. p. 487–492. *In* R.W. Sheard (ed.) Proc. 4th Int. Turfgrass Res. Conf., Guelph, ON, Canada. 19–23 July. Int. Turfgrass Soc., Ontario Agric. Coll., Univ. of Guelph, Guelph, ON.

Smith, T.M., and P.E. Rieke. 1986. Lawns in shade. Michigan Agric Exp. Stn. Bull. E-1576.

Todhunter, M.N., and W.F. Beineke. 1979. Effect of fescue on black walnut growth. Tree Planters Notes 30(3):20–23.

Vargas, J.M., and J.B. Beard. 1981. Shade environment-disease relationships of Kentucky bluegrass cultivars. p. 391–395. *In* R.W. Sheard (ed.) Proc. 4th Int. Turfgrass Res. Conf., Guelph, ON, Canada. 19–23 July. Int. Turfgrass Soc., and Ontario Agric. Coll. Univ. of Guelph, Guelph, ON.

Walters, D.T., and A.R. Gilmore. 1976. Allelopathic effects of fescue on the growth of sweetgum. J. Chem. Ecol. 2:469–479.

Whitcomb, C.E. 1972. Influence of tree root competition on growth response of four cool-season turfgrasses. Agron. J. 64:355–359.

Whitcomb, C.E., and E.C. Roberts. 1973. Competition between established tree roots and newly seeded Kentucky bluegrass. Agron. J. 65:126–129.

Wilkinson, J.F. 1974. Shade stress and turfgrass culture. p. 83–88. *In* D.P. Martin and J.F. Wilkinson (ed.) Ohio Turfgrass Conf. Proc., Columbus. 3–5 Dec. Ohio State Univ., Columbus.

Wilkinson, J.F., and J.B. Beard. 1974. Morphological responses of *Poa pratensis* and *Festuca rubra* to reduced light intensities. p. 231–240. *In* E.C. Roberts (ed.) Proc. 2nd Int. Turfgrass Res. Conf., Blacksburg, VA. 19–21 June 1973. ASA and CSSA, Madison, WI.

Wilkinson, J.F., and J.B. Beard. 1975. Anatomical responses of 'Merion' Kentucky bluegrass and 'Pennlawn' red fescue at reduced light intensities. Crop Sci. 15:189–194.

Wilkinson, J.F., J.B. Beard, and J.B. Krans. 1975. Photosynthetic respiratory responses of 'Merion' Kentucky bluegrass and 'Pennlawn' red fescue at reduced light intensities. Crop Sci. 15:165–168.

Winstead, C.W., and C.Y. Ward. 1974. Persistence of southern turfgrasses in a shade environment. p. 221–230. *In* E.C. Roberts (ed.) Proc. 2nd Int. Turfgrass Res. Conf., Blacksburg, VA. 19–21 June 1973. ASA and CSSA, Madison, WI.

Wong, C.C., and J.R. Wilson. 1980. Effects of shading on the growth and nitrogen content of green panic and siratro in pure and mixed swards defoliated at two frequencies. Aust. J. Agric. Res. 31:269–285.

Wood, G.W. 1969. Shade tolerant turfgrasses of the United States and Canada. p. 293–288. *In* R.R. Davis (ed.) Proc. 1st Int. Turfgrass Res. Conf., Harrogate, England. 15–18 July. Sports Turf Res. Inst., Bingley, England.

Wu, L., D. Huff, and W.B. Davis. 1985. Tall fescue turf performance under a tree shade. Hort-Science 20(2):281–282.

9   Effects of Traffic on Turfgrasses

ROBERT N. CARROW

University of Georgia
Griffin, Georgia

A. MARTIN PETROVIC

Cornell University
Ithaca, New York

Vehicular and foot traffic on turfgrasses can result in major damage to turf sites, especially on high use recreational areas. Traffic problems are of four general types: soil compaction, wear, rutting or soil displacement, and divoting. Soil compaction and wear are considered the most important problems and will receive the most attention in this chapter.

Soil compaction is defined as the pressing together of soil particles, resulting in a more dense soil mass with less pore space. *Wear* is the injury to a turfgrass from pressure, scuffing, or tearing directly on the turfgrass tissues. The term *traffic* is more general in nature and includes both wear and soil compaction stresses. However, some authors have used "wear" as an inclusive term for wear and soil compaction. This terminology is unfortunate since "wear" is a direct plant injury and does not directly influence soil properties. In this review, the term traffic will be used to cover wear and soil compaction stresses where both are present.

Rutting or soil displacement is the displacement of soil particles due to pressure, which results in a rut or depression. Obviously, compaction and wear can result at the same time, but the major immediate problem would be an uneven turfgrass surface. *Divots* are pieces of turf removed by the action of a golf club, polo mallet or other such object striking the sod.

All four types of traffic could occur at the same time but one form is normally the predominant stress at any one point in time. With sandy soils or soils below field capacity in moisture content, wear is the dominant injury. Soil compaction often becomes a major traffic problem on soils high in silt and clay and when heavy loads are applied. Rutting occurs primarily when excessive loads are applied to a soil above field capacity in moisture content. With a thatchy turf, divoting could be a problem.

On intense use recreational sites, these stresses are most evident and a high degree of expertise is required to maintain an acceptable quality turfgrass sward. On the other extreme, a home lawn with little traffic may exhibit few,

Copyright © 1992 ASA-CSSA-SSSA, 677 S. Segoe Rd., Madison, WI 53711, USA. *Turfgrass—Agronomy Monograph no. 32.*

if any, of these stresses. In the following pages, each type of traffic stress will be discussed in detail. Beard (1973) provides a good literature review and discussion of research results on traffic effects up to 1973.

I. SOIL COMPACTION

A. Sources of Soil Compaction

A comprehensive comparison of the effects of traffic type on the extent of soil compaction under turfgrass situations is lacking. In general, however, foot and vehicular traffic cause considerably more compaction on turfgrass sites than water droplet impact.

1. Water Droplet Impact

Water droplet impact from either rainfall or irrigation is thought to have little or no effect on soil compaction of established turfgrass sites (Beard, 1973). Howver, during the establishment period, rain droplets caused a 15% increase in bulk density of the surface 2.5 cm of soil on an unvegetated soil compared to vegetated soil (Cohron, 1971).

The degree to which water droplets cause soil compaction is a function of clay mineralogy. Soils containing expanding-lattice clay fractions when hydrated will expand, then shrink and have considerable surface cracking during the drying phase. Subsequently, the cracks of voids can be filled by surface soil reducing porosity and increasing bulk density (Cohron, 1971). Nonexpanding lattice clays are less susceptible to this form of compaction.

Rain intensity and drop size can affect the magnitude of soil compaction due to kinetic energy differences. Cohron (1971) reported that drizzle-type rain, with a precipitation rate of 7×10^{-5} mm s^{-1}, had a kinetic energy level of 2.2 Jm^{-2} h^{-1}. In comparison, a heavy intensity rain with a precipitation rate of 4.2 mm s^{-1} had 343.3 Jm^{-2} h^{-1} of kinetic energy. Thus, except for the isolated heavy intensity rainfall events, water droplet impact should have only a minor effect on soil compaction due to the minimal kinetic energy.

2. Foot Traffic

Foot and vehicular traffic are the major soil compacting forces on most recreational turfgrass sites. The degree of soil compaction created by foot traffic is influenced by the (i) speed of the traffic event (i.e., walking vs. running), and (ii) the magnitude of the compacting force that is a function of surface contact area and weight. High speed foot traffic, such as a running football player, can produce much greater compacting force than a walking person. Van Wijk et al. (1977) reported that a running athlete could exert 1.52 MPa pressure, but under static conditions, only 0.04 MPa, a 38-fold difference.

The shape and surface contact area of the shoe can have a pronounced effect on the static pressure exerted on the soil. Watson (1961) described an example of a 90-kg person wearing either football shoes or street shoes. The football shoes had a contact surface of 4.45 cm^2 corresponding to 1 MPa static pressure compared to the street shoes with 109 cm^2 of contact area and 0.04 MPa of static pressure. The 25-fold difference in compacting pressure created by the football shoe could result in a greater degree of soil compaction.

While it may be possible to apply wear to a grass without compaction, the reverse is not possible. However, in soil compaction studies, the use of a smooth power roller can minimize wear. Based on our experience, other precautions that will reduce wear are: (i) roll when the soil is most susceptible to compaction—such as near field capacity; (ii) use a roller as heavy as possible but without bruising the turf [In one study (Carrow, 1980a), the use of a water-filled power roller did not result in any apparent wear, but when the weight was increased by adding sand plus water to the power roller, wear did occur.]; and (iii) repeated passes may be necessary to achieve the desired level of compaction, but these should be put on in as short a time period as possible. After the initial compaction, less severe application can be used to maintain the compaction level. This is preferable to using repeated passes on a frequent basis.

3. Vehicular Traffic

During the forward movement of a drive wheel, there are three primary types of forces exerted on the soil, which include the following (Sloane et al., 1981): (i) the vertical force due to the dynamic load of the wheel, (ii) the sheer stress resulting from wheel slippage, and (iii) vibration transmitted from the engine through the tire. All three forces can be manipulated to some degree to minimize compaction.

The current trend away from large, heavy maintenance equipment to smaller, light vehicles to reduce soil compaction has merit (Zontek, 1983). It is commonly thought that it is possible to compensate for larger, heavier vehicles by increasing the tire diameter or width without increasing soil compaction. This is based on the belief that the actual contact pressure (weight/unit area) can be the same between vehicles, thus, no increase in compaction force. From studies done with agricultural equipment, Blackwell and Soane (1981) showed that heavy equipment with larger, wider tires did increase the depth of soil compaction compared to light vehicles with narrower tires at the same tire contact pressure.

Rapid starting, stopping, and turning which causes wheel slippage can further compact soil and to a much greater degree than by increasing the weight (load) (Davies et al., 1973). However, when wheel slippage is not occurring, increasing the tractor speed from 0.2 to 5 m s^{-1} reduced the degree of compaction by as much as 50% in the surface 5 cm of soil (Stafford & De Carvelho Mattos, 1981).

Tire tread design can also influence the soil compaction effect of vehicular traffic (Beard, 1973). Lugged or knobby type tread designs, with the same tire diameter and width, will have considerably less contact surface area, thus greater compacting pressure than smooth tires. The smooth "turf type" tire design, widely used on much of the turfgrass equipment, is an excellent example of how to minimize this type of compaction. Turf maintenance equipment with "turf type," pneumatic tires generally apply 0.03 to 0.05 MPa static pressure (van Wijk et al., 1977).

B. Distribution of Soil Compaction

Soil compaction can occur in different zones within the soil. In turfgrasses, the most common soil compaction situations would be (i) in the first few centimeters of the soil surface, (ii) surface compaction but to a depth of 20 to 40 cm, and (iii) deep in the soil profile in either a narrow or wide zone. Each of these circumstances would result in different effects on air, water, and root movement, as well as presenting unique maintenance or correctional problems.

Beard (1973) noted that the majority of compaction in turfgrass situations occurred in the top 8 cm of the soil surface, mostly in the upper 3 cm. In field studies using a smooth power roller to simulate the pressures typical of turf equipment and walking traffic, Sills and Carrow (1982) and O'Neil and Carrow (1982) found that the soil bulk densities were influenced mainly in the upper 3 cm. This type of compaction is the easiest to correct because cultivation equipment can penetrate this surface zone.

A thicker compacted layer at the surface can result from heavier traffic, such as tractors with lugged tires. Vanden Berg et al. (1957) determined the vertical stress on a soil from a rear tractor tire exerting an average pressure of 0.37 MPa. Near the surface, pressures were 0.35 MPa, but even at a 35-cm depth pressures of 0.07 MPa were detected. Such a deep zone would be expected to have more deleterious effects on plants than a shallower zone and would be more difficult to correct.

Sometimes a compacted zone can occur below the surface. For example, in housing developments the original topsoil may be stripped, construction equipment run on the subsoil, and then 8 to 20 cm of topsoil is applied on top of the compacted subsoil. This situation would restrict water percolation and turfgrass, tree, and shrub root growth. It is also the most difficult soil compaction problem to correct. In agronomic crops, a deep, compacted zone can occur just below the depth of plowing, because of pressure under the plow point. This is normally a thin zone but still restrictive to water and root movement. A similar zone may occur just below the core on shattercore (solid) tines, especially after repeated cultivations (Murphy & Rieke, 1987).

Compaction may be continuous or discontinuous over an area. For example, in row crops traffic is confined to the inter-row areas. On turfgrass recreational sites, traffic tends to be random over an area from maintenance equipment and humans. However, concentrated sites of traffic are not uncommon, such as the center area of a football field, in front of a soccer goal, in foot paths, and on golf course tees. These sites are the first to exhibit adverse effects on soils and plants from the traffic.

C. Effects of Compaction on Soil Properties

Several review articles or books have been published concerning soil physical properties and compaction effects: Arkin and Taylor (1981), Barnes et al. (1971), Barley and Greacen (1967), Carson (1974), Dexter (1988), Emerson et al. (1978), Grable (1966), and Hakansson et al. (1988). Waddington (1969) and Madison (1971) reviewed the effects of compaction on turfgrass soils and the growth of turf. A brief review will aid in understanding how compaction influences soil physical properties and turf-grass growth.

1. Bulk Density

As pressure is applied to a soil, soil aggregates are deformed and individual particles are reoriented. Total pore space declines, especially the larger pores that are important for gas and water movement and as channels for root penetration. The soil becomes more dense and the pore-size distribution is altered with fewer macropores but more micropores. Thus, compaction will influence the air-water relationship by increasing moisture retention.

2. Soil Strength

As soil particles are pressed together during compaction, cohesive forces are enhanced, particularly as the soil dries. Thus, soil strength increases upon compaction (Chancellor, 1971). This property is measured by civil engineers on a dry soil by the modulus of rupture. While the modulus of rupture is only measured on a dry soil, a property that is more directly related to root growth is penetration resistance, which can be determined at any soil moisture content and is measured by a penetrometer. A hard, compacted soil with high cohesive forces plus few large pores results in high penetration resistance and *mechanical impedance* for root growth.

3. Soil Aeration

Oxygen is consumed in the soil by plant roots and microorganisms, while CO_2 is produced from respiration by living organisms. Without adequate gas exchange between the soil and aerial atmospheres, soil O_2 becomes limiting to plant growth and CO_2 increases. Glinski and Stepniewski (1985) provide a good review of soil aeration and its effects on plants.

When a soil drains after wetting, sufficient air-filled pores are necessary for gas exchange. Many of these pores are interaggregate (between aggregates) pores in a well-aggregated soil. Destroying these interaggregate pores by compaction results in (i) reduced total porosity, (ii) fewer air-filled pores, (iii) an increase in water-filled pores (i.e., smaller pores), and (iv) disruption of pore continuity. Since O_2 diffuses through air 10^5 times faster than through water, it should not be surprising that reduced aeration is a major problem under compaction. The air-filled pores are also important for water infiltration, percolation, and root penetration.

4. Moisture Relations

Since water-filled porosity increases with compaction, total moisture content is often higher for a compacted soil at a particular matrix potential. In a loamy sand soil with poor inherent moisture-holding capacity, this could be beneficial, but with a fine-textured soil, the result is excessive moisture. The water retained often is not readily available to plants, especially at less negative potentials, since matrix forces are enhanced by compaction.

5. Infiltration and Percolation

Even a thin layer of compacted soil at the surface can greatly reduce water infiltration. Infiltration is highest through larger pores, soil cracks, root channels, and worm or insect channels. It depends on matrix and gravitational forces. Without such means of entry, infiltration occurs through the smaller pores at a much slower rate.

A compacted zone at any location in the soil will reduce water percolation and can result in a perched water table if water application or rainfall exceeds hydraulic conductivity. The combined effects of compaction on infiltration and percolation present the grower with a host of potential problems: reduced irrigation flexibility, runoff, standing water problems such as scald and intracellular freezing, dry spots, and high humidity diseases.

6. Soil Temperature

A wet, compacted soil retains more moisture than if not compacted. In order for a compacted soil to warm up in early spring, the soil matrix plus any retained water must be heated. Thus, compacted soils are slower to warm up in the spring. However, once a compacted soil is heated up, it will retain heat longer due to a greater thermal mass resulting in higher average soil temperatures in the summer.

Tables 9–1 and 9–2 contain data on soil physical properties under turfgrass situations illustrating the effects of soil compaction. Compaction results in increased bulk density, moisture retention at the higher matrix potentials, and penetrometer resistance (i.e., mechanical impedance), while total pore space, aeration porosity, and hydraulic conductivity decrease. The two major means that soil compaction results in adverse plant effects are by (i) low soil oxygen, and (ii) high mechanical impedance (Arkin & Taylor, 1981; Miller, 1986).

Table 9-1. Compaction effects on a sandy loam soil planted to perennial ryegrass (*Lolium perenne* L.) (Sills & Carrow, 1983).

Soil physical property	Compaction level		Change with compaction, %
	None	Compacted†	
Bulk density, Mg m^{-3}			
0-3 cm depth	1.27	1.34*	+5.5
3-6 cm depth	1.26	1.37*	+8.7
Moisture content by volume in 0-3 cm depth, %			
0 MPa	42.4‡	39.2*‡	−7.5
−0.010 MPa	21.4	22.1NS§	+3.2
−0.033 MPa	17.3	18.6*	+7.5
−0.100 MPa	16.0	17.6*	+10.0
Aeration porosity at 0-3-cm depth, %			
−0.010 MPa	21.0	17.2*	−18.1
−0.033 MPa	25.1	20.3*	−19.1
Penetrometer resistance, MPa			
−0.033 MPa	0.026	0.042*	+61.5

* Significant at the 5% level.

† Compaction was with a falling weight in a greenhouse study conducted in 30.5 cm I.D. PVC containers.

§ NS = not significant.

D. Factors Influencing Soil Compaction

The type of compacting force on a soil has a major influence on the degree of compaction. Primary compacting forces in turfgrass situations are water droplet impact, foot traffic, and vehicular traffic that were previously discussed in the section "Sources of Soil Compaction." Other factors that influence compactibility of a soil are soil texture, soil structure, moisture content, particle-size distribution, and plant factors.

Table 9-2. Compaction effects on saturated hydraulic conductivity of several sand-peat-soil ratios (Waddington et al., 1974).

Parts by volume†			Saturated hydraulic conductivity, cm h^{-1}	
Coarse sand	Soil	Peat	Noncompacted	Compacted
8	0	2	>144	137
8	1	1	>144	61
6	2	2	76	28
6	3	1	58	6
5	3	2	76	3
5	4	1	72	8
4	4	2	74	2
4	5	1	9	>1
0	8	2	9	>1

† Coarse sand: 95% of particles between 0.50 and 2.00 mm. Soil: silt loam; 22% sand, 59% silt, 19% clay. Peat: well-decomposed, fine-textured, reed-sedge peat.

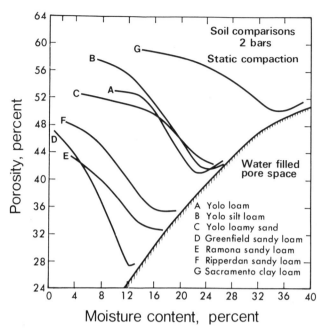

Fig. 9–1. Degree of compaction as a function of soil texture and soil moisture content (Barnes et al., 1971).

1. Soil Texture, Soil Structure, and Moisture Content

The degree of soil compaction created by traffic is a function of both soil texture and soil moisture content. This concept is illustrated in Fig. 9–1. Generally, as the soil moisture content increases a corresponding linear or exponential reduction in porosity occurs until the moisture content approaches saturation. Any further increase in moisture content results in a reduction of the compaction effect on porosity.

Many sports turf areas unfortunately are used extensively in seasons of intense rainfall. In many cases, play is initiated when the soil moisture content is at or near saturation (Gradwell, 1965). Thus, traffic at this point will have a maximum effect on soil compaction adding greatly to the difficulty of maintaining sport turf sites. Boufford and Carrow (1980) observed the effects of intense, short-term traffic on a tall fescue (*Festuca arundinacea* Schreb.) turf when the soil was at different moisture contents. Traffic at field capacity (-0.012 MPa matrix potential) resulted in the greatest increase in bulk density. At saturation (0 MPa), bulk density was not affected but the moisture release curve illustrated a marked shift from larger to smaller pores. This resulted from destroying the soil structure under saturated conditions even though no compaction occurred.

The effect of soil moisture on the degree to which a soil is compacted can be explained by the development of a diffuse double layer of charge in conjunction with particle orientation (Baver et al., 1972). At low moisture contents, there is insufficient water present for either the formation of a diffuse double layer at the soil particle interface or for particle orientation. As the soil moisture content increases, the double layer is formed and expands to create a lubricating effect between particles. Particle orientation can then occur and total pore space is reduced. At high soil moisture, the remaining pores are water-filled and further reduction in porosity can only occur if either water could be compressed or water is forced out of the pores (Harris, 1971). However, once such a puddled soil is allowed to dry, it will consolidate into a more dense mass.

While coarse-textured soils (sand) may compact, the bridging between the hard sand particles prevents the elimination of most of the larger pores. Thus, adverse effects of compaction on soil physical properties are less evident on sands than fine-textured soils (Beard, 1973). This is especially demonstrated from studies involving sand modified with varying proportions of soil and organic matter (Brown & Duble, 1975; Taylor & Blake, 1979, 1981). Taylor and Blake (1981) observed that as the sand content increased from 69 to 93%, the bulk density of the surface 5.3 cm of the mixtures decreased from 1.62 to 1.47 Mg m^{-3}. In addition, the infiltration rate, correspondingly, increased from 0.2 to 4.4 cm h^{-1}. Both responses indicate that the increasing sand content reduced the degree of compaction noted under actual golf course conditions. Once sufficient sand is present for the bridging between sand particles to occur, then sand starts to create larger pores and a relatively rigid matrix resistant to compaction is formed.

However, as illustrated in Fig. 9-1 for soils that had < 50% sand, the two soils containing the highest sand content [Greenfield (coarse-loamy, mixed, thermic Typic Haploxeralfs) and Ripperdam sandy loam soils] responded the most to compaction. This is partially a function of particle-size distribution.

2. Particle Size-Distribution

Of the major factors influencing the severity of soil compaction, much research has centered on understanding the effects of particle-size distribution on soil compactivity for sport turf sites. Numerous investigators have examined the concept that uniform particle-size distribution can minimize soil compaction (Brown & Duble, 1975; Bingaman & Kohnke, 1970; Howard, 1959; Kunze, 1956; Swartz & Kardos, 1963; Taylor & Blake, 1979, 1981; Van Dam et al., 1975; Zimmerman, 1973). After 9 yr under field conditions with traffic, Waddington et al. (1974) found that a coarse sand with a very uniform particle-size distribution had an infiltration of 7.5 cm h^{-1} compared to 1.3 cm h^{-1} for a wide particle-size distribution of a silt loam soil.

This concept is also valid for soils containing < 50% sand. As shown previously (Fig. 9-1) soil texture affected the degree of soil compaction. Figure 9-2 contains the particle-size distribution of the soils shown in Fig. 9-1. A comparison of Fig. 9-1 and 9-2 reveals that the soil having the broadest distribution of particle size resulted in the most compacted soil.

With a wide range of particle size, the spaces between particles and interaggregate pores are filled with the smaller particles. This results in a high

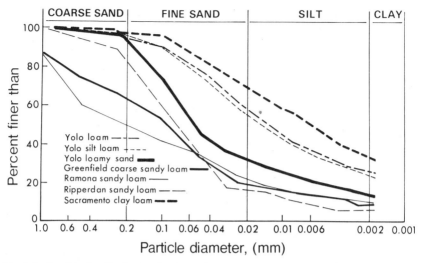

Fig. 9-2. Particle size distribution for the various soils shown in Fig. 9-1 (Barnes et al., 1971).

initial bulk density and under pressure the soil becomes a dense, compacted mass with few large pores.

3. Plant Factors

The presence of plant tissues, living or dead may influence to some degree the ability of soils to resist compaction. High proportions of turfgrass shoots, roots, and thatch can act to absorb and dissipate compacting forces (Beard, 1973). Van Wijk et al. (1977) observed that the presence of turfgrass increased the soil strength, as measured with a cone penetrometer, from 0.2 to 1.0 MPa (depending on organic matter content) over unvegetated soil. This would indicate that a considerably higher compacting force would be needed to compact turfgrass covered soil to the same degree as bare soil. This is thought to occur as a result of the root system hindering lateral displacement of soil as an object, such as a cone-shaped penetrometer probe, enters the soil. Thomas and Guérin (1981) found that a turfgrass cover reduced the degree of compaction from a studded roller over no cover. Their data suggested that tall fescue prevented compaction most, Kentucky bluegrass and perennial ryegrass intermediate, and fine fescue and timothy (*Phleum pratense* L.) least.

Other definitive studies of plant effects on soil compactibility are lacking and research is needed. However, it would be reasonable to assume that any factors which provide greater verdure should help cushion against compacting forces. Examples would be a greater shoot density and higher mowing height.

E. Effects of Soil Compaction on Turfgrasses

Madison (1971) noted that "compaction is the foremost turf problem" on recreational turfgrasses by causing an overall decline in growth, vigor, quality, and persistence. However, in many instances, compaction is not recognized as the cause of turf deterioration since compaction does not directly reduce plant activity (Trouse, 1971). Instead, soil compaction acts by affecting other factors influencing growth, such as soil aeration, soil strength, plant and soil moisture relationships, or soil temperatures (Barley & Greacen, 1967; Carson, 1974; Grable, 1966; Hakansson et al., 1988; Miller, 1986; Rosenberg, 1964; Taylor et al., 1972). Thus, compaction has been termed a *hidden stress*.

Considerable research effort has been devoted to alleviate compaction by soil modification (Waddington et al., 1974), but limited quantitative information on the physiological, anatomical, or morphological responses of turfgrasses to compaction is available in the literature. However, research conducted to simulate compacted conditions, such as research under low soil aeration, provides insight into how and why compaction affects turfgrasses.

1. Root Growth and Activity

Considerable literature has been published on the effects of compaction on plant root development and morphology (Cannell, 1977; Barley & Greacen, 1967; Taylor et al., 1972; Trouse, 1971; Arkin & Taylor, 1981). The various physiological or morphological root responses to compaction are primarily a result of reduced aeration, high soil strength, increased ethylene concentrations, altered soil water status, or interactions of these factors.

The most conspicuous rooting response to soil compaction is *altered root distribution*. Fryrear and McCully (1971) studied the root distribution of side-oats grama [*Bouteloua curtipendula* (Michx.) Torr.] subjected to compaction and observed decreased deep root growth, while surface lateral rooting increased. This illustrates the importance of examining root growth by zones in the soil in contrast to total growth. When determining root growth at 42 and 84 d after compacting a mature perennial ryegrass (*Lolium perenne* L.), O'Neil and Carrow (1983) reported a higher percentage of roots occurring in the surface 0 to 5 cm zone and a lower percentage in the 10 to 25 cm zone with increased compaction. Changes in root distribution were also reflected by the decrease in root density (mg root cm^3 soil) in the 10 to 25 cm zone with compaction. Total root weights over the 0 to 25 cm zone decreased by 20% ($P < 0.10$) at the end of the study.

Using Kentucky bluegrass (*Poa pratensis* L.), when the soil was kept moist (0 to -0.04 MPa), Agnew and Carrow (1985a) reported similar results with more surface rooting while deep rooting decreased and total root growth increased by 14% compared to uncompacted turf. When the soil was allowed to become drier (0 to -0.40 MPa), surface rooting still increased and deep rooting decreased under compaction. Total root growth decreaed by 10% relative to the uncompacted check. Under the drier irrigation regime, we attributed the reduced root growth to greater mechanical impedance.

The observation of greater surface rooting under compaction in the above studies (O'Neil & Carrow, 1983; Agnew & Carrow, 1985a) may be due to *reduced root growth (elongation) rate* in response to higher mechanical impedance. This would cause roots to accumulate at the surface instead of growing deeper into the profile. However, another explanation may be ethylene-promoted *adventitious root initiation.* Soil ethylene concentrations can be elevated under low soil aeration (Kawase, 1981). Drew et al. (1979) noted that ethylene stimulated adventitious rooting in corn (*Zea mays* L.). The situation of increased total root growth in the 0 to 25 cm root zone with all the increase in the surface 0 to 5 cm, as observed by Agnew and Carrow (1985a) under the -0.04 MPa irrigation regime, suggests that compaction stimulated surface root growth or initiation. Fryrear and McCully (1971) noted greater lateral root development under compaction of side-oats grama. Waddington and Baker (1965) observed surface root development in Kentucky bluegrass under low soil aeration. However, in all these studies soil ethylene levels were not measured. Adventitious root formation at the surface few centimeters of soil would be beneficial in allowing greater water uptake from this region.

If the degree of compaction is very high, then root growth may decline in all zones (Thurman & Pokorny, 1969; Sills & Carrow, 1983) due to the overwhelming importance of mechanical impedance. At moderate compaction, soil aeration would be the primary influence on root growth, while under heavy compaction both aeration and mechanical impedance are important. Cannell (1977) provides a good discussion of these relationships using data from several sources. Cannell (1977) noted that mild compaction may retard main root (seminal) elongation, while lateral root production is prolific. With severe compaction, the soil pore sizes are very small and soil aeration is low. Thus, both main root and lateral root growth rates may be restricted by low aeration and high soil strength.

In one study (Carrow, 1980b), *root deterioration* in the summer was enhanced by high levels of compaction. This may have been due to less favorable soil O_2 levels or higher soil temperatures, since both can enhance root maturation (Beard, 1973).

Luxmoore and Stolzy (1972) developed a mathematical model for oxygen diffusion within and into a root as influenced by various root and soil characteristics. They illustrated the importance of plant aeration, which is the O_2 used in root respiration that enters the root by intercellular spaces from the aboveground atmosphere. Plants with high *root porosities* depended less on soil aeration for root respiration, especially at increasing distances away from the root tip.

Kawase (1981) noted that root porosities of mesophytes had been shown to be increased by waterlogging. The low soil O_2 levels apparently elevate ethylene concentrations by stimulating anaerobic ethylene production while reducing ethylene diffusion out of roots. High ethylene in turn enhances cellulase activity that subsequently results in the presence of interconnected air spaces within roots (aerenchyma). Other mechanisms for aerenchyma development may also exist, such as cell death from starvation under anaerobic respiration (McPherson, 1939).

Increased root porosity of grasses is well documented under waterlogged situations (Kawase, 1981; Hook & Crawford, 1978; Miller, 1986). It would seem reasonable to assume similar results would occur under compacted conditions, where a major effect of compaction is to reduce soil aeration. Immediately after a rainfall or irrigation, compacted soils can exhibit limited aeration for long periods (O'Neil & Carrow, 1983).

Agnew and Carrow (1985a) subjected mature Kentucky bluegrass to compaction for 0, 9, and 99 d, which resulted in root porosities of 8.0, 7.2, and 13.0%, respectively, under a moist irrigation regime of -0.04 MPa. When a drier irrigation regime of -0.40 MPa was used, the resulting root porosities were 7.8, 8.9, and 25.0%, respectively. The authors attributed part of the greater root porosities under the long-term compaction (99 d) to adventitious root development in the surface 0 to 5 cm soil zone. Adventitious roots have higher porosities than do primary roots (Luxmoore & Stolzy, 1972) and initiation of adventitious surface roots is stimulated by low aeration (Kawase, 1981). Thus, their development under compacted conditions could aid grasses in acclimating to compaction (i.e., lower soil aeration) over a period of time by increasing plant aeration. Luxmoore et al. (1970) and Stolzy (1972) predicted that at least 25 to 74% of the O_2 consumed in maize root respiration was from plant aeration and may be higher in the surface roots. Also, Agnew and Carrow (1985a) noted that Kentucky bluegrass plants with the highest root porosities exhibited the highest water uptake under low soil O_2 conditions.

Schumacher and Smucker (1981) found reduced root porosities for drybean (*Phaseolus vulgaris* L.) under high mechanical impedance. They attributed this response to cellular distortions. Interestingly, they indicated that compressed cells should reduce O_2 diffusion within the root leading to higher ethylene concentrations. Greater adventitious root initiation did occur at higher mechanical impedance and was attributed to higher ethylene. Their study lasted 8 d and if carried longer, may have resulted in greater root porosities from ethylene induced aerenchyma formation. In the study of Agnew and Carrow (1985a), highest root porosities occurred under the combination of long-term compaction plus a dry irrigation regime of -0.40 MPa. This treatment would result in long periods under low aeration as well as periods where mechanical impedance would be high. Under these conditions, the higher root porosities may be due to cell wall deterioration at the high soil strengths in dry soil water contents or adventitious root formation during moist soil periods.

Root morphological alterations in addition to the ones already discussed have been observed on various plant species subjected to compaction or low soil aeration (Hook & Crawford, 1978; Arkin & Taylor, 1981; Atwell, 1988). Examples include reduced root hair development and shorter and thicker roots (Waddington & Baker, 1965). Atwell (1988) provides an excellent discussion of how root morphological changes in response to compaction can influence further root growth.

Hormonal changes may also occur, as previously indicated by the discussion on ethylene in the root system. These may result in secondary physiological or morphological responses in plants (Bradford & Yang, 1981; Kawase, 1981). Specific studies on turfgrasses and their hormonal changes with compaction have not been reported in the research literature.

Low soil aeration has been reported to cause *reduced root water uptake.* Holder and Brown (1980) observed 15 to 35% reduction in water uptake in beans as soil O_2 levels decreased from 21 to 3%. The time of exposure was important below 3% O_2 with prolonged exposure to low O_2 resulting in a substantial drop in water uptake. They attributed these responses to reduced root permeability with permeability decreasing over time of exposure.

Mechanisms controlling water uptake during periods of low O_2 were discussed by Everard and Drew (1989). They noted two ways for reduced water flux into roots to occur under anerobic conditions: (i) a reduction in the hydraulic conductivity of the radial pathway for water movement, and (ii) a decline in the osmotic component of the driving force for water flux. The initial response of a rapid decrease in water flux upon exposure to roots to low O_2 was attributed to radial resistance to flow across the plasma membranes of the root epidermis. Flow normally occurs in metabolically maintained, hydrophilic pores spanning the membrane. Under anerobic conditions, there is a complete or partial loss of this pathway. Recovery of membrane integrity normally occurs within a day due to increased root energy production from anaerobic (ethanolic) fermentation processes. This process can often provide sufficient energy for roots to maintain a viable root system until longer term adventitious roots develop or aerenchyma formation occurs. Recovery of hydraulic conductivity within 2 d of exposure to low soil O_2 can also be a result of root death with the roots acting in a wick-like manner. In this case, the improved water flux would be temporary.

On compacted sites, the turfgrasses would be subjected to long-term and repeated periods of low soil O_2, especially on frequently irrigated recreational turf. Wet wilt and scald injuries (Beard, 1973) observed in turfgrasses are probably manifestations of the water uptake—root permeability relationship. O'Neil and Carrow (1983) found some evidence for a reduced water uptake where they determined water use by soil depth after compacting a mature perennial ryegrass. For the 28 d after compaction, water uptake was reduced in the surface 0 to 5 and 5 to 10 cm zones but not in the 10- to 25-cm zone. Agnew and Carrow (1985a) observed an immediate reduction in surface water extraction after compacting a Kentucky bluegrass. In both studies, shoot growth decreased immediately after the compaction events but soil moisture levels were high. Thus, the turfgrasses apparently were not able to obtain sufficient moisture for growth under the low aeration-high moisture conditions. A plausible explanation for such an immediate response would be reduced root permeability.

In the previous discussion on turfgrass root responses to soil compaction, it is obvious that low soil aeration is a primary cause, especially for frequently irrigated, high use recreational turfgrasses. Several researchers have investigated the possibilities of a critical soil aeration level for turfgrass root growth.

One approach has been to determine the percent air-filled pore space at which O_2 appears to limit root growth. Cannell (1977) indicated that for many crops, a 10% air-filled porosity after drainage would be sufficient. Less than this value causes a discontinuity between pores that greatly reduces gaseous diffusion. Carrow (1980a) discusses how this relationship has been useful in formulating root zone mixes so as to avoid poor aeration.

A more specific relationship between soil aeration status and root growth is possible by use of O_2 diffusion rate (ODR) measurements (Letey et al., 1966). Stolzy (1972) reviewed critical ODR values for grasses and suggested that plant tolerance to low aeration would be in the order: rice (*Oryza sativa* L.) > corn > bermudagrass [*Cynodon dactylon* (L.) Pers.] > barley (*Hordeum vulgare* L.) > Kentucky bluegrass. The critical soil ODR value for many plants for root growth is 20×10^{-8} g cm^{-2} min^{-1} but may be lower for many grasses (Stolzy, 1972; O'Neil & Carrow, 1983).

O'Neil and Carrow (1983) and Agnew and Carrow (1985a) reported that soil ODR values were below the 20×10^{-8} g cm^{-2} min^{-1} for 50 to 100 h after an irrigation event on compacted sod compared to <5 hr for an uncompated turfgrass. In both studies, a reduction in deep rooting occurred while surface root growth (0–5 cm depth) increased. In contrast, van Wijk et al. (1977) reported that low ODR seldom inhibited turf growth on soccer fields since they did not observe many critical ODR levels. However, their measurements were not at specific times after water application. For accurate correlation to rooth growth, ODR values must be carefully monitored over time, especially following irrigation or a rainfall when soil aeration is the lowest.

Enhanced *root exudates* under low soil O_2 or high mechanical impedance have been reported (Smucker & Erickson, 1987). The root exudates contained ethanol, amino acids, and sugars. Such high levels of root exudates could enhance the growth of specific microorganisms as well as being a carbon drain on the plant.

2. Shoot Growth

Irrespective of whether soil compaction decreases rooting in all soil zones or just the deep root growth while surface rooting increases, the volume of soil explored by the roots for nutrient and water uptake is markedly reduced. Thus, a plant grown on compacted soil will be more susceptible to drought and high temperature stresses and be less able to recuperate if injured. Shoot growth should respond negatively to this adverse root environment, especially if stresses such as heat, drought, and pests occur.

Top growth or yield have been widely reported to be affected by compaction. However, the response highly depends upon soil texture (Rosenberg, 1964). On sands and loose, friable soils, moderate compaction can increase yield by improving soil moisture conditions. When Cuddeback and Petrovic (1985) applied compaction to *Agrostis palustris* Huds. grown on a sandy loam soil, they reported improved visual quality and reduced winter injury, while thatch level decreased. Such beneficial responses have been observed by others on sandy soils (Rosenberg, 1964). When soils are high in silt or clay, moderate to severe compaction would decrease yield. For fine-textured soils, this suggests a positive parabolic relationship between plant yield (or some other shoot response) and bulk density if a wide enough range of bulk density is used. Thus, slight compaction may enhance yield but compacting soils above a critical bulk density (unique to the particular soil and crop) would decrease yield.

Another factor that influences shoot response to compaction is the time of year or environmental conditions. For example, compacted, cool-season turfgrass may actually appear greener and be of equal or greater visual quality than a noncompacted turf in the cool periods of the year when moisture and nutrients are not limiting (Flannagan & Bartlett, 1961). However, once high evaporation demand occurs, the limited root growth or viability soon expresses itself in reduced shoot growth.

Several researchers have illustrated that traffic on turfgrasses reduces shoot growth and turf quality. However, many of these include a substantial wear component. In this section, we will discuss only those studies where compaction was known to be the predominant traffic stress.

Visual quality integrates several components with shoot density, color, and uniformity being of primary importance. Carrow (1980a) noted that visual quality decreased as bulk density increased for three cool-season grasses growing on a silt loam soil.

Part of the decrease in visual quality under compaction could be attributed to reduced *shoot density* (Cordukes, 1968; O'Neil & Carrow, 1982; O'Neil & Carrow, 1983). In contrast, Watson (1950) noted that Kentucky bluegrass plant density increased with compaction. Bourgoin and Mansat (1979) and Carrow (1980a) observed a shoot density increase for perennial ryegrass under moderate compaction. Conflicting reports on shoot density responses to compaction appear to stem from the nonlinear (parabolic) relationship between plant growth responses and bulk density (Rosenberg, 1964). In studies with a wide range in compaction stress shoot density has been shown to be reduced.

Verdure has been used as a measure of total top growth. Rimmer (1979) found that ferdure increased with slight compaction and then decreased. A decline in verdure with compaction has been reported (Carrow, 1980a; O'Neil & Carrow, 1983; Sills & Carrow, 1982). Interestingly, those studies conducted under field situations, where other compaction-induced stresses may develop, such as drought and high temperature, have revealed the strongest negative relationship between compaction and verdure.

Compaction effects on *rhizome and stolon development* have been reported. In one study (Shearman & Watkins, 1985), Kentucky bluegrasses were plugged and lateral shoot growth assessed under compacted vs. noncompacted treatments. Compaction reduced the lateral growth of most cultivars but intraspecific differences were observed. On 'Sydsport' Kentucky bluegrass, rhizome growth was 37% less under compaction (Agnew, 1984) than for uncompacted. With less top growth, total photosynthate production would decline and could be expressed as decreased lateral shoot growth.

The shoot growth parameter that appears most sensitive to compaction is leaf growth or *clipping yield*. When compaction is applied to a mature turfgrass, the vertical shoot growth rate immediately decreases (O'Neil & Carrow, 1983; Agnew & Carrow, 1985a; Sills & Carrow, 1982). Thus, clipping yield per unit of time declines. In the study by O'Neil and Carrow (1983), reduced clipping yield was apparent during the 28 d immediately following compaction. Total clipping yields were reduced by 38 and 53% for their moderate and heavy compaction treatments compared with those of the uncompacted turf.

A significant reduction in clipping occurred by the first mowing (6 d) after compaction in the investigations of O'Neil and Carrow (1983) and Agnew and Carrow (1985a) but changes in distribution of roots were not apparent for several weeks. Soil moisture was maintained between 0 and −0.04 MPa matrix potential in these studies. Thus, the lack of an adequate root system or lack of soil moisture would not account for this rapid decrease in growth. A possible explanation could be reduced moisture uptake due to a decline in root permeability as was discussed in the root growth section (Everard & Drew, 1989). Smit et al. (1989) found that reduced leaf growth under low soil O_2 was related to limited cell wall extensibility and over a longer period decreased cell division. The mechanism for low O_2 to induce leaf cell changes was not determined.

Regardless of the reason for a shoot growth reduction under compaction, the decline in shoot density, verdure, and clipping yield would produce a sod more prone to wear—the other major traffic stress. A thinner turfgrass stand in conjunction with slow growth would reduce wear tolerance. This can be observed on athletic fields or golf course greens where the rootzone mixes have been modified to minimize compaction effects. These turfgrasses can then tolerate substantially more traffic before severe thinning occurs.

3. Nutrient Uptake

Nutrient uptake and nutrient ratios in many plant species have been reported to be altered by compacted conditions (Parish, 1971; Grable, 1966; Cannell, 1977; Castillo et al., 1982; Veen, 1988). In general, the reduction in uptake under compaction appears to follow the order K > N > P > Ca > Mg, while Na uptake may increase. The reasons for these observations are not well defined but may include a combination of restricted root growth, reduced root activity, restricted mass flow of soil water, and altered soil nutrient activity and mobility. Parish (1971) provides a good discussion on how these factors may affect various nutrients on a wide number of species.

Letey et al. (1964b) monitored N, P, K, and Na uptake by 'Newport' Kentucky bluegrass under different soil aeration conditions. At <6% O_2 concentration, N, P, and K uptake declined rapidly, while Na uptake increased threefold. Similar results were found for barley (Letey et al., 1962). In contrast, Waddington and Baker (1965) found no effect of low ODR on N, P, or K content of Kentucky bluegrass. They attributed the lack of response to liberal fertilization and the development of a high concentration of surface roots.

When tall fescue (Sills & Carrow, 1982) and Kentucky bluegrass (Sills & Carrow, 1983) were subjected to different N rates and compaction levels, the percentage of N in the leaf tissues was not affected by compaction. However, compaction caused less N use per unit area of sod (mg of N/100 cm^2). N use per unit area declined by 23 to 39% under compaction relative to uncompacted treatments. Also, N recovery [(mg of N used/mg N applied) $\times$ 100] decreased by 10 to 31% when compared to a noncompacted turf. Applying more N to the compacted turf did not improve N use per unit area on the Kentucky bluegrass but N use was improved for the tall fescue. Slower shoot growth, reduced root growth, and possibly limited root permeability under the compaction treatments could restrict N uptake when determined on an area basis.

In both of these studies, compaction reduced total root growth and deep rooting (15–30 cm depth). However, when high N rates were coupled with compaction, a detrimental synergistic effect on rooting occurred. For example, compaction applied at the lower N rate caused a 13.3% reduction in total rooting but a 45% reduction at the higher N rate on the Kentucky bluegrass (Sills & Carrow, 1983). The higher N rate stimulated clipping yield and apparently resulted in less translocation of photosynthates for root growth.

These results indicate that additional N applied to an adequately fertilized, but compacted turfgrass stand could cause a marked reduction in rooting. The additional N did not entirely compensate for the adverse shoot responses under compaction and the compacted turfgrasses were less responsive to applied N than were uncompacted stands. Thus, turf managers should not attempt to use excessive N to compensate for slow-growing, thin turf if the cause for these responses is compacted soil conditions. Gore et al. (1979) found that excessive N was often deleterious on several turfgrass mixtures subjected to traffic (wear plus soil compaction).

In a paper by Kulkarni and Savant (1977), soil compaction was reported to increase root cation exchange capacity of several plants including maize. They attributed the response to higher N content in the roots and more carboxyl ($-COOH$) groups. Nitrogen content of the leaves was not reported nor were the implications of these results discussed.

4. Plant Water Use and Status

The primary concern in this section is to provide insight into how soil compaction may influence turfgrass water use once the moisture is in the soil profile. However, compaction has a major effect on whether water enters the soil (i.e., infiltration) and how much water enters in a given period.

Carrow (1981), Madison (1971), and Waddington (1969) summarized the effects of compaction on soil physical properties under turfgrass conditions and these were discussed previously in this chapter. Many of the alterations in soil physical properties adversely influence irrigation programming. For example, reduced infiltration and percolation would result in longer irrigation cycles, greater runoff, and a higher percentage of evaporation loss.

Using common bermudagrass, evapotranspiration (ET) declined under compaction (Morgan et al., 1966). Similar results have been found for perennial ryegrass (Sills & Carrow, 1983; O'Neil & Carrow, 1983) and Kentucky bluegrass (O'Neil & Carrow, 1982; Agnew & Carrow, 1985a). Evapotranspiration decreased by 28% (Sills & Carrow, 1983); 21 to 49% (O'Neil & Carrow, 1983); 20% over the season with a 3.5 to 11% reduction during the hottest period (O'Neil & Carrow, 1982); and a 21% decrease (Agnew & Carrow, 1985a). Thus, a major influence of compaction on turfgrass is a decrease in water use.

Interestingly, growers often apply more water to their compacted sites. Several reasons for this phenomenon are possible. Low infiltration rates can enhance runoff and evaporation losses; thereby making it difficult to apply larger quantities of water for deep, less-frequent irrigations. Thus, growers may resort to lighter, more frequent applications that enhance evaporative losses by maintaining a moist soil surface. The more open canopy of a compacted turf would result in a lower canopy resistance for water loss and higher incident radiation on the soil surface. Also, since compacted turfgrass is slower growing, the turf manager may unconscientiously attempt to stimulate extra shoot growth by irrigating more often. The limited rooting depth under compaction can result in water moving beyond the root system. Carrow (1986) reviewed the many ways that compaction influences water management and provided practical management solutions.

O'Neil and Carrow (1982) observed that additional water does not improve a compacted turf if it is already receiving adequate water as indicated by tensiometer readings. In fact, irrigating too frequently can result in very low ODR levels for extended periods (O'Neil & Carrow, 1983; Agnew & Carrow, 1985a). Another reason for the difference between experimental results and field water use is that the researchers used tensiometers to guide their irrigation scheduling and irrigated only when the soil water potential reached a critical level. This is in contrast to growers relying on set schedules or other techniques to estimate when to irrigate.

While compaction reduced turfgrass total water use in research studies, the specific reasons for this response are complex. Several plant and soil factors may be working simultaneously to reduce water uptake, water availability, and water loss, while other factors may actually enhance water loss. Table 9–3 lists the various mechanisms proposed or shown to influence water use on grasses under compacted conditions. The net result is a reduction in water use.

Recent research indicates that soil compaction may decrease leaf water potential. Agnew and Carrow (1985b) measured midday leaf water potentials (Ψ_L) of compacted and uncompacted Kentucky bluegrass following an irrigation event. The turfgrass subjected to compaction demonstrated lower (more negative) Ψ_L. This may have been due to lower soil ODR levels, which

Table 9-3. Suggested mechanisms for reduced water use of grasses under soil compaction.

Cause of reduced water uptake under compaction[†]	Key references
Altered root distribution; less deep root growth, and reduced volume of soil in contact with roots	Agnew & Carrow, 1985a O'Neil & Carrow, 1983 Sills & Carrow, 1983
Reduced root permeability under low soil O_2 levels.	Agnew & Carrow, 1985a Bradford & Yang, 1981 O'Neil & Carrow, 1983
Less shoot growth as exhibited by slower leaf extension rate, decreased clippings, verdure, shoot density. Less leaf area should reduce transpiration but may increase evaporation due to a lower canopy resistance.	Numerous authors—see section on shoot growth.
Reduced stomatal densities	Agnew & Carrow, 1985b
Compaction or low soil O_2 induced stomatal closure	Agnew & Carrow, 1985b Bradford & Yang, 1981 Sojka & Stolzy, 1980
Altered soil moisture retention curve; the soil water content vs. soil water potential relationship is altered.	Madison, 1971
Altered mass flow or diffusion of water to the root.	Cannell, 1977

† While many factors reduce water use of a compacted turf, water use may be enhanced by (a) low soil infiltration promoting frequent irrigation, (b) a more open caopy enhancing evaporation losses from a higher soil temperature and lower canopy resistance.

could inhibit water uptake and make the plant more susceptible to drought stress.

In this same research project, stomatal responses under uncompacted and compacted soil conditions were studied. Saturating the soil to produce low soil O_2 caused stomatal resistance to increase after 2 d. One suggested mechanism for stomatal closure under low soil aeration was that increased root resistance would lead to low Ψ_L and finally to higher stomatal resistance (Sojka & Stolzy, 1980). However, Agnew and Carrow (1985b) did not find a close relationship between Ψ_L and stomatal response. Another possible mechanism is stomatal closure induced by abscisic acid (ABA) accumulation (Schravendijk & van Andel, 1985) under low soil O_2.

As the soil water potential Ψ_s decreases, a positive relationship between Ψ_L and stomatal closure does occur (Agnew & Carrow, 1985b). Compared to uncompacted turfgrass, the compacted plants exhibited a higher stomatal resistance and a lower Ψ_L. At lower Ψ_s, the compacted grass root system is not as effective in extracting water as under noncompacted conditions; thereby, inducing a lower Ψ_L and stomatal closure.

Some evidence exists that compaction can influence stomatal density. When Kentucky bluegrass was grown under well-watered conditions, compaction caused a reduction of 27% in adaxial stomatal density but had no effect on abaxial densities (Agnew & Carrow, 1985b). Sojka and Stolzy (1980) discussed how low soil O_2 may alter stomata per unit area or size. Thus, the significance of low soil aeration or compaction-stomatal density relations needs further investigation.

Water-use efficiency (g of dry matter of crop yield/mL of ET) was not affected by compaction in the studies of Sills and Carrow (1983) and O'Neil and Carrow (1983). While compaction reduced ET in these investigations, it also reduced growth with little net effect on water-use efficiency.

5. Carbohydrate Reserves

The total nonstructural carbohydrate (TNC) reserves of turfgrasses are important for hardiness and recuperation from injury. Carrow (1980a) determined TNC levels in three cool-season grasses subjected to various compaction stresses. During the cooler portions of the year, no difference in TNC levels was noted. In midsummer, however, TNC levels declined 23 to 50% compared to the noncompacted grasses. Under greenhouse conditions (Sills & Carrow, 1983) and in a field study sampled in September (Sills & Carrow, 1982), TNC levels were similar for both uncompacted and compacted treatments. These studies would suggest that compaction may contribute to reduced TNC levels primarily when in conjunction with summer stresses. The specific reasons for reduced TNC under compaction are not determined. The data of Agnew and Carrow (1985b) showing higher stomatal diffusion resistances under compaction would indicate that photosynthesis may be partially restricted or a higher canopy temperature (see next section) may result in somewhat greater respiration rates and reduced TNC.

6. Canopy Temperatures

Since compaction influences water uptake and turf density, it seems reasonable that it may affect canopy temperatures. In a study where canopy temperatures were measured diurnally by infrared thermometry on a Kentucky bluegrass subjected to three levels of compaction, canopy temperatures were greater for the compacted turf (Agnew, 1984). Figure 9–3 illustrates diurnal data from 2 d in August with 16 August a cloudy day and 2 d after irrigation, while 19 August was clear and 5 d after irrigation. In Fig. 9–4, the 1400 h canopy temperatures are shown for 2 d after irrigation (Julian date 228 = 16 August) to 7 d after an irrigation event. The compacted grass consistently exhibited higher canopy temperatures of 0.5 °C (cloudy days) to 3.0 °C (clear days) relative to the uncompacted treatments. Similar results were also reported by Agnew and Carrow (1985b) in a greenhouse study.

Agnew (1984) and Agnew and Carrow (1985b) attributed the higher canopy temperatures primarily to reduced evapotranspiration cooling of the compacted turfgrass. Another potential cause for higher canopy temperatures could be a less dense turf allowing higher soil temperatures to occur. In the study by Agnew (1984), shoot density did decline with compaction but a reasonably dense stand still existed. By monitoring soil temperatures, he found that compaction did result in soil temperatures of 0.2 to 1.0 °C higher at the 5-cm depth. Thus, under these conditions, the reduced ability of the turf to take up water under compaction appeared to be the primary factor. If shoot density declined appreciably, however, then increased soil temperatures would be expected to contribute to greater canopy temperatures.

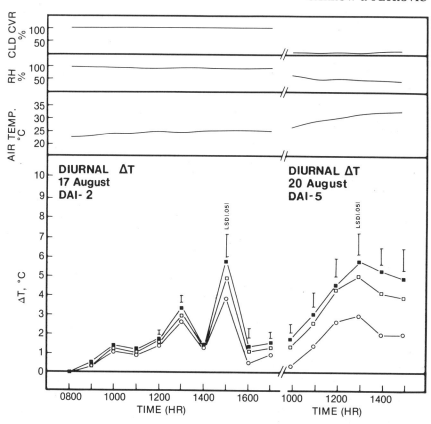

Fig. 9-3. Diurnal canopy temperatures of Kentucky bluegrass for 2 d as influenced by soil compaction (0 = no compaction, □ = 10 passes with a power roller, ■ = 20 passes with a power roller). CLD CVR = cloud cover; RH =relative humidity; T = canopy-air temperature; and DAI = days after irrigation (Agnew, 1984).

These data suggest that a compacted turfgrass would be more susceptible to indirect and direct high temperature stresses. The prolonged exposure to somewhat higher temperatures would be especially detrimental as the summer progresses, while on a very hot day, direct kill from high temperature could occur (Beard, 1973).

7. Environmental Stress Tolerance

In previous sections, it was discussed how soil compaction could predispose turfgrass to drought and high temperature stresses. Certainly, a weakened plant with low carbohydrate reserves growing in a medium with poor physical properties likely would be susceptible to environmental stresses. Stresses that may be enhanced by soil compaction plus possible reasons are listed in Table 9-4. It should be noted that these are most of the major environmental stresses occurring on turf.

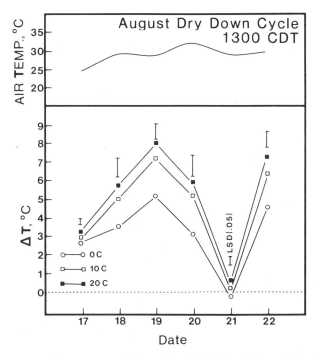

Fig. 9-4. Canopy and air temperature differentials at 1300 CDT as influenced by soil compaction. T = canopy-air temperature (Agnew, 1984).

Little data are available on compaction-stress interactions, except for drought and high temperatures. However, field observation indicates that the various stresses listed in Table 9-4 are often more prevalent on compacted sites. In a study by Thurman and Pokorny (1969), common bermudagrass grown under different compaction levels was exposed to −9.4° C and recovery determined after 21 d. Recovery decreased as compaction increased. They attributed the better recovery in the uncompacted soil to more favorable root regeneration.

Table 9-4. Environmental stresses observed in experimental or field situations to be enhanced by soil compaction and possible reasons for the response.

Environmental stress	Reasons for the stress to be induced by soil compaction
High temperature (direct and indirect)	Reduced water uptake, weakened plant, thinner turf for insulation of the crown, reduced TNC levels†
Wilt and drought	Reduced water uptake, weakened plant, low carbohydrate reserves, low infiltration, high evaporation losses, runoff
Scald and wet wilt	Poor drainage, low aeration limiting water uptake, weakened plant
Intracellular freezing	Poor drainage can promote crown hydration, weakened plant, low TNC levels for hardiness/recovery
Winter desiccation	Poor infiltration may lead to dry soils

† TNC = total nonstructural carbohydrates.

Even if soil compaction does not enhance the possibility of a particular stress on turf, it would reduce the recuperative ability of the grass once it was injured. Slow shoot growth, reduced water and nutrient uptake, and lower TNC levels would restrict recovery (Beard, 1973).

8. Disease Incidence

Specific research on compaction-turfgrass disease relations was not found in the literature. However, some diseases are more prevalent in moist microenvironments that are common for poorly drained compacted soils. Also, the light, frequent irrigation scheduling often used on compacted sites should maintain a moist microenvironment favorable for disease activity. Vargas (1981) indicated that several turfgrass diseases were more common under poor drainage, namely, *Pythium* blight, *Rhizoctonia* brown patch, *Fusarium* patch, and *Typhula* blight. An excellent review of how moist soil conditions may influence soil microorganisms has been written by Parr et al. (1981). Smucker and Erickson (1987) noted that low soil O_2 results in the accumulation of CO_2 at the root-soil interface. The elevated levels of CO_2 can stimulate growth of *Fusarium* spp. Also, root tissue injury under low soil oxygen may allow entry of soil organisms into the roots and result in enhanced infection (Everard & Drew, 1989).

Once a disease infestation occurs, the severity may be greater and recovery slower under compacted conditions. The slower growth rate and potentially lower TNC levels would inhibit recuperation. Shearman and Watkins (1985) noted this for stem rust (*Puccina* spp.) on compacted bluegrass.

9. Germination and Establishment

Normally, the soil is tilled to provide good physical conditions for establishment. Once the turfgrass is seeded or vegetatively established, compaction may occur from rainfall, irrigation, maintenance equipment, or foot traffic. Measures are often taken to reduce the potential for compaction such as mulching, restricting traffic, and using only light maintenance equipment. Trouse (1971) reviewed how soil compaction could adversely influence plant establishment on a wide variety of species. Kentucky bluegrass establishment from plugs has been found to be reduced by compaction (Shearman & Watkins, 1985).

10. Community Ecology

When compaction alters the physical properties of a soil, not all plant species are affected to the same extent. Therefore, some plants have a relative competitive advantage over other plants. For example, on sports turf sites, goosegrass [*Eleusine indica* (L.) Gaertn], knotweed (*Polygonum aviculare* L.), and annual bluegrass (*Poa annua* L.) often invade, while adjacent untrafficked areas have few of these weeds (Beard, 1973; Beard et al., 1978). These weeds invade because they can germinate and grow under low soil aeration and the desirable species deteriorate. However, this does not mean that it is the best growing condition for the particular plant. Annual bluegrass can invade a compacted turf site during cool weather due to its prolific seed-head production as openings in the desirable turfgrass stand permit seed germination and establishment. Even though the annual bluegrass can tolerate the compacted soil, it is not as healthy and vigorous as it would be in an incompacted soil. When summer stresses occur, these stands are often the first to die out.

Gore et al. (1979) subjected 16 mixtures composed of five species to traffic and no traffic treatments. With traffic, total cover of all mixtures declined but the relative proportion of *Lolium perenne* L., *Phleum pratense* L., and *Poa pratensis* L. increased, while *Festucs rubra* L. and *Agrostis tenuis* Sibth. decreased. This illustrates that compaction can influence community ecology and alter the original composition of a turfgrass stand.

F. Effects of Soil Compaction on Maintenance Regimes

Compaction can influence the turfgrass plant by affecting root growth, shoot growth, nutrient uptake, plant water use, TNC reserves, stress tolerance, disease incidence, establishment, and community ecology. These responses will dramatically impact the maintenance programs of turfgrass sites receiving compaction. Such sites cannot be adequately maintained without a high degree of expertise by the turfgrass manager, additional maintenance inputs, and extensive labor. Carrow (1981) detailed the numerous ways that a maintenance program could be altered by compaction. One area that will require more attention is practices to alleviate compaction. This is the topic of the next section.

G. Alleviation of Soil Compaction Effects

Cultural practices for preventing or alleviating soil compaction can be grouped into four categories: (i) selection of tolerant species and cultivars, (ii) traffic control and water management, (iii) cultivation practices, and (iv) soil modification. No single practice is effective but several must be combined for a successful maintenance program.

1. Turfgrass Selection

Little information is available in research literature concerning relative tolerance of species or cultivars to compaction. Much more information is printed concerning tolerance to traffic (wear plus soil compaction). Traffic tolerance will be covered in the section on wear. In this section, only those studies where soil compaction was the predominant stress will be discussed.

Carrow and Troll (1981) evaluated five species with regard to compaction tolerance (Table 9–5). Based on visual quality and percent turf cover following compaction for 56 d, the relative tolerance was perennial ryegrass = Kentucky bluegrass > tall fescue > colonial bentgrass > red fescue. In another

Table 9-5. Relative tolerance of five cool-season species to soil compaction in Massachusetts (Carrow & Troll, 1981).

Species	Visual quality† Not comp.	Comp.	Turf cover, %‡ Not comp.	Comp.
Manhattan perennial ryegrass	8.0ab§	8.0b	96a	97a
Merion Kentucky bluegrass	8.3a	8.3a	100a	100a
Kentucky-31 Tall fescue	8.0ab	7.5c	99a	94ab
Highlight Red fescue	7.6a	5.1e	97a	64c
Exeter Colonial bentgrass	8.4a	6.8d	100a	90b

† Visual quality: 9 = ideal, 1 = no live turf. Taken 8 wk after initiation of compaction treatments.
‡ Ratings taken 8 wk after initiation of compaction treatments. Compaction treatment was 12X weekly with 1X = 1 pass with smooth power roller at 1.1 kg cm^{-2}.
§ Duncan's multiple range test.

investigation, Carrow (1980a) observed that 'Pennfine' perennial rygrass and 'Baron' Kentucky bluegrass exhibited very good visual quality and turf cover when subjected to moderately heavy compaction. Both were found to be decidedly superior to 'Kentucky-31' tall fescue (Table 9-6).

While Kentucky-31 tall fescue appears to be less tolerant to compaction, it possesses other desirable characteristics important for home lawns, low-budget athletic fields, and parks in the transition zone of the USA. Its deep root system and very good drought tolerance makes it a turf easy to maintain in the summer. In contrast, Kentucky bluegrass may be more vigorous and competitive in the football season but difficult to maintain in the summer.

Table 9-6. Relative tolerance of three cool-season species to soil compaction in Kansas (Carrow, 1980a).

Species (S)	Compaction level (C)†	Visual quality‡	Turf cover§ %	Shoot density shoots 100 cm^{-2}
Kentucky blue (Baron)	0	8.5	97	208
	12X	7.6	97	174
	24X	7.2	95	188
Perennial rye (Pennfine)	0	7.9	97	184
	12X	7.1	94	242
	24X	6.9	95	198
Tall fescue (Kentucky-31)	0	7.1	94	66
	12X	5.5	76	58
	24X	4.8	61	46
LSD 0.05 (S)¶		0.8	7	27
LSD 0.05 (C)#		0.3	7	38

† Compaction treatments were 0, 12X, 24X weekly for 8 wk. 1X = 1 pass with smooth power roller at 1.1 kg cm^{-2}.
‡ Visual quality rating: 9 = ideal, 1 = no live turf. Taken after 60 d of compaction treatments.
§ Percent turf cover and shoot density ratings taken after 60 d of compaction treatments.
¶ For differences among species at the same compaction level.
# For differences between species treatments for different compaction levels.

Recent research (Shildrick & Peel, 1983; Meyer, 1983) indicates that several of the newly developed tall fescue cultivars are superior to Kentucky 31. Both of these investigations imposed traffic stresses but a major component appeared to be compaction. This illustrates that cultivars of a species can vary with respect to compaction tolerance. Another example would be the improved turf-type perennial ryegrass relative to common types where the improved types are much superior.

Relative compaction tolerances of warm-season turfgrass have received little research attention. Field observation suggests that bermudagrass and zoysiagrass (*Zoysia japonica* Steud.) have very good tolerance to compaction. Buffalograss [*Buchloë dactyloides* (Nutt) Engelm.] appears to have a high tolerance to compaction. A relatively common practice on buffalograss fairways has been to roll them, especially in the moister region of its zone of adaptation. The compacted soil results in more runoff and a less favorable condition for broadleaf or grassy weed competition. In a study involving both wear and compaction, Burton and Lance (1966) reported that 'Tiflawn' and 'Tifway' bermudagrass had better traffic tolerance than common bermudagrass.

Compaction tolerance is only one of the parameters a grower should use when selecting a species or cultivar for a high use recreational site. A high compaction tolerance does not mean a turf has a high recuperative potential once it is injured (Beard, 1973). Also, adaptation to the environmental and pest stresses of the particular region is important.

2. Traffic Control and Water Management

Repeated traffic over the same site results in a higher degree of compaction, as well as more wear (Burton & Lance, 1966). Schmidt et al. (1989) demonstrated that compaction applied in the fall was less detrimental than if applied at or just after spring greenup of 'Midiron' bermudagrass (*Cynodon* spp.). Thus, control of traffic timing, frequency, and type is an important means of the various alternatives for traffic control. Carrow (1981, 1985, 1986) presents a comprehensive discussion of how soil compaction and water management are interrelated.

3. Soil Cultivation

Alleviation of soil compaction caused by traffic can be accomplished by several methods including soil cultivation. Cultivation in terms of turfgrass management involves tillage or cultivation of the surface soil zone without destroying the turf. Methods of cultivation include coring, (hollow tine, solid tine, and drill), slicing, spiking, grooving, forking, and subaerification. Rieke and Murphy (1989) recently reviewed turfgrass cultivation research.

The basic principles involved in alleviation of compaction by cultivation centers on spatial distribution of traffic effects on soil physical properties. Traffic causes soil compaction and has its maximum effect on soil physical properties near the compacted surface and decreases linearly away from the compaction site (Dexter & Tanner, 1972; Gill, 1968). Foot and vehicular traffic on turfgrass sites causes compaction to reach a maximum about 2 cm below the soil surface and has little effect deeper than 10 cm (Beard, 1973). However, compaction has been shown to affect soil as deep as 25 cm (O'Neil & Carrow, 1983). Thus, when a cultivation tool passed through the surface zone of compacted soil, the air and water flow can be improved.

The process of using hollow tines or spoons to remove a soil core has been traditionally called *core cultivation* or sometimes referred to as aerification. There are several forms of core cultivation, namely spoon, drum, and vertical operating hollow tine (VOHT). More recently, solid tine and drill devices have been used to open a hole into the turf and soil. These have also often been called coring operations, but will be covered in a separate section, while hollow tine and spoon core cultivation will be discussed in this section.

The depth and spacing of holes created by hollow tine or spoon core cultivation varies, but generally they are not deeper than 10 cm and are spaced from 5 to 10 cm apart. The core diameter also varies from about 6 to 20 mm.

There has been limited detailed investigation into the overall effectiveness of core cultivation in alleviating soil compaction. In addition, the results to date are conflicting in that core cultivation has improved or had no effect on alleviating compaction and in several cases created more compaction.

Bryne et al. (1965) and Morgan et al. (1965) found that manually dug coring holes 2.5 cm in diameter by 15 cm deep, back-filled with coarse aggregate, substantially increased the infiltration of a compacted putting green. Morgan et al. (1965) noted that an area cored with 6-mm spoons had considerably lower infiltration rates than control plots and Byrne et al. (1965) saw no increase in infiltration rates over uncored cultivated check plots with VOHT core cultivation.

Engel and Alderfer (1967) studied the water infiltration rates for 1 yr following 10 yr of core cultivation (three times per year) with 12-mm diam. spoons to a Nixon silt loam soil (fine-loamy, mixed, mesic Typic Hapludults). They observed that the water infiltration rate was slightly (26%) increased (nonsignificant) with spoon core cultivation over the uncored plots. This research site, however, did not receive supplemental traffic except from routine maintenance operations.

On a nontrafficked, silt loam soil, Goss (1984) reported that hollow tine treatment increased infiltration when applied several times per year. Bulk density, however, increased. On a sand soil, Canaway et al. (1986) found that hollow tine coring substantially enhanced infiltration before traffic but only slightly after traffic.

Letey et al. (1964a) used several VOHT treatments on a compacted bentgrass green and measured ODR at three soil depths. Oxygen diffusion rate increased as the depth and extent of VOHT treatment increased. Also, Barber and Carrow (1985) showed improved ODR from hollow tine coring.

In a long-term field study, Waddington et al. (1974) examined the interaction of soil mixture and VOHT core cultivation under traffic on selected soil physical properties. In general, VOHT core cultivation increased infiltration of compacted soils on mixtures containing high sand volumes.

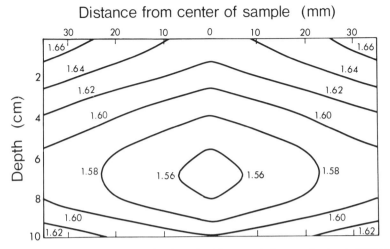

Fig. 9-5. Spatial bulk density distribution of a Metea sandy loam soil prior to VOHT core cultivation (Petrovic, 1979).

They pointed to the need to understand the cause of the poor soil physical condition. If this condition is a result of traffic compaction of the surface soil, core cultivation would improve the soil physical conditions. However, if this condition was a function of inherently inadequate physical properties, the core cultivation should have little or no beneficial effects on infiltration.

The findings of Petrovic (1979) can also help explain the lack of substantive improvement in soil physical properties following core cultivation. Results from experiments conducted under laboratory conditions without plants showed that VOHT core cultivation severely compacted the tine/soil interface compared to the uncored sample (Fig. 9-5 and 9-6). The compaction dissipated rapidly with distance away from the hole and had no effect past

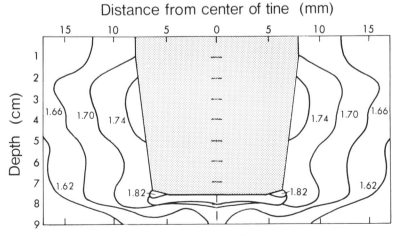

Fig. 9-6. Spatial bulk density distribution of a Metea sandy loam soil following VOHT core cultivation with a 12.6-mm diam. tine (Petrovic, 1979).

1 cm. In a companion study conducted under greenhouse conditions with Penncross creeping bentgrass (*Agrostis palustris* Huds. cv. Penncross), it was observed that this same pattern occurred and increased bulk density was noted 14 d after cultivation. However, 93 d after VOHT core cultivation, the side wall region had collapsed but the highly compacted zone of soil at the bottom of the coring hold was present. Thus, VOHT core cultivation initially compacts the soil adjacent to the coring hole.

As with any form of compaction, the degree of compaction caused by VOHT core cultivation is a function of soil texture, soil moisture, and the degree to which the soil is already compacted. Soil types more susceptible to compaction, like the silt loam soil used by Engel and Alderfer (1967), would show a greater degree of compaction caused by VOHT core cultivation. Petrovic (1979) showed that both the drier soil and initially more compacted soil resulted in less compaction from VOHT coring. Roberts (1975) also observed that VOHT core cultivation reduced water infiltration rates on a compacted clay loam soil.

Murphy (1986) and Murphy and Rieke (1987) studied the effects of hollow tine coring on a sandy loam and a loamy sand under both compacted and noncompacted conditions. Soil density decreased and aeration porosity increased after cultivation on both compacted and noncompacted soils. However, hydraulic conductivity and field measured infiltration decreased with cultivation on the noncompacted soil but were not affected on the compacted soil. There was some evidence of higher penetrometer readings just below the depth of cultivation, especially on the noncompacted soil. A short-term increase in rooting occurred within the soil immediately surrounding the core hole but rooting was consistently inhibited below the depth of tine penetration.

On a compacted sandy loam with Tifway bermudagrass, Carrow (1988) reported that hollow tine coring was most effective of five cultivation methods for reducing penetrometer resistance. After 2 yr, penetrometer resistance did increase in the zone just below the tine depth. Root growth in the 20 to 60 cm zone increased by 20 to 35% and water extraction from this zone also increased.

The long-term effects of core cultivation on compaction alleviation as influenced by soil type are uncertain. Further research is needed to examine this issue, especially in light of the results of Petrovic (1979) on persistence of compaction created by VOHT core cultivation. Also, the recent development of new cultivation methods illustrate the need for more comparative research of cultivation methods.

Conflicting results from different cultivation research investigations, as for example core cultivation effects on infiltration, may be caused by several factors: (i) cultivation effects on soils and plants can be different on compacted and noncompacted sites (Thus, studies conducted on a noncompacted soil may not yield results applicable to the same soil after compaction.), (ii) results from short-term studies may differ from long-term investigations, (iii) research conducted on a soil that resists compaction (i.e., a very sandy soil) may not be extrapolated to a finer-textured soil more prone to compaction, and (iv) cultivation treatments applied on a moist soil can have different effects than if conducted on a dry soil. Research scientists should consider these aspects when developing cultivation studies, reading the research literature, and applying their results to real world situations. The above factors could contribute to confusion in research results with any type of cultivation, not just hollow tine core aeration.

Solid tine cultivation is a recent trend and can involve tines of 8- to 40-cm length. The short tines are from 0.6- to 1.9-cm diam. and their use is often called *shattercoring*. The tines are placed on the same units used for hollow tine coring and theoretically cause a shattering action on the soil upon impact. Use of the smaller diameter tines (0.6 cm diam.) results in very little surface disruption and has been used in place of spiking on golf greens. The deeper tines (25–40 cm) are attached to a Vertidrain unit and is termed *vertidrain* cultivation.

Murphy (1986) and Murphy and Rice (1987) found that shattercoring reduced soil density and increased aeration porosity but to a lesser extent than hollow tine coring after 2 yr. In the first year, shattercoring loosened the soil better than the hollow tine operation, but penetrometer readings were higher the second year in shattercore plots. Also, a compact layer just below the tine depth was forming in the second year.

As shattercore frequency increased, Goss (1984) reported that infiltration decreased. Also, when shattercoring was applied to a noncompacted silt loam soil, bulk density increased.

While hollow tine cultivation enhanced bermudagrass rooting and water extraction on a compacted sandy loam, shattercoring did not (Carrow, 1988). In addition, shattercoring was less effective in reducing surface soil strength and caused a zone of higher penetrometer resistance just below the tine penetration depth. In this study, the solid tines would not penetrate the soil unless it was very moist. This could negate the shattering effect observed on soils where penetration can occur even when somewhat dry.

Research is limited on vertidrain cultivation but it is being widely used on sports fields in Europe and golf courses in the USA with apparent success. Boekel and Zwiers (1981) tested vertidrain cultivation on a sports field and found no loosening or any effect on infiltration, but ground cover did improve. Improved drainage by the vertidrain operation was noted by Müeller (1982). Currently, research is underway at the University of Georgia on vertidrain cultivation.

Deep drill coring is achieved by drilling holes into the soil. A commercial unit has been widely used on golf courses in the USA for the past several years. Hole depth is 25 cm with 1.6-cm diam. drills with 13-cm spacing. Some soil is brought out of the hole. Carrow (1988) found 31 to 55% better deep rooting (25- to 60-cm depth) of bermudagrass grown on a compacted soil as well as better water extraction from this zone.

Slicing cultivation normally involves the creation of a narrow triangular shaped noncontinuous slit in the soil without removing the soil. The slit is usually 5- to 10-cm deep. The slicing unit for large areas may be composed of disk or triangular shaped blades attached to a circular wheel or frame.

On many of the triplex greens mowers, slicing units can be rapidly interchanged with the reel gang unit for slicing of tees and greens. Some slicing units are able to make continuous slits. One new device has blades that are pulled through the soil and make cuts 10-cm deep at 15-cm spacings. This procedure is called *verti-slicing*.

Alleviation of surface soil compaction could be possible by slicing, but has not been well documented. Moreover, on soils with poor soil physical conditions as a result of either the inherent soil properties (soil texture) or from deep compaction created during establishment, slicing, spiking, or grooving may have little or no effect due to penetration depth.

Since the slicing operation does not involve soil removal, it is very possible that slicing would initially compact the soil at the interface of the slicing slit and soil as noted for VOHT core cultivation (Petrovic, 1979). The effectiveness of slicing in alleviating compaction caused by traffic is uncertain. In a study by Barber and Carrow (1985), slicing did not influence ODR levels. Slicing by a slit tine unit did improve infiltration on naturally sandy football pitches (Kamp, 1979). Carrow (1988), however, did not observe any positive influence on soil physical properties or turfgrass growth from slicing a compacted sandy loam soil. But, a larger slicing unit called the Aerway slicer did improve deep root growth (20–60 cm) by 53 to 120% for bermudagrass grown on a compacted sandy loam, while water extracton also increased. The Aerway slicer has only recently been used on turfgrass. The slicing tines are up to 20-cm long, 10-cm wide, and 0.8-cm thick. By design, there is a slight torque action that could help loosen the soil, which does not occur with other slicers.

The *spiking* technique was developed to alleviate surface soil compaction on areas that cannot have either extended periods of limited use or major disruption of the playing surface, such as putting greens. Spiking cultivation results in shallow, 2- to 4-cm deep, narrow holes created by solid tines. As with slicing, soil is not removed during the spiking operation. In many cases, spiking is done at weekly or biweekly intervals during the high traffic periods. Cultivation with 0.6 cm diam. solid tines at a 5 to 10 cm spacing is an alternative to spiking.

The influence of spiking on reducing the degree of soil compaction has not been extensively researched. Petrovic and Rieke (1978) studied the effects of power driven and weighted tractor-drawn spiking units on the visual quality and root growth of creeping bentgrass (*Agrostis palustris* Huds. cv. Toronto) under trafficked conditions. Spiking was done at weekly intervals during April through October. They observed that both types of spiking units markedly reduced the visual quality in late August but had little or no effect during the fall period. The root growth, however, was increased by 40% with the power driven spiking unit compared to the untreated control; whereas, the heavier tractor-drawn unit had no effect on root growth. It appears that the power-driven type spiking unit was alleviating surface soil compaction allowing for improved root growth. Engel and Alderfer (1967) observed that spiking of a putting green not receiving extensive traffic did not affect water infiltration rates but slightly increased the O_2 diffusion rates in the surface

15 cm of the soil. Zwiers (1982) reported no benefit of spiking a compacted soil. Ward (1983) reported better drainage after spiking football pitches.

Grooving is a cultivation technique in which a continuous narrow slit or groove is made in the soil to a depth that seldom exceeds 10 cm and is generally <2-cm deep. The grooves are made by rapidly rotating, vertical power-driven knives or blades spaced 2 to 8 cm apart. Grooving, sometimes referred to as vertical mowing, is most often used in a thatch control program and for renovation, but since there is penetration of the surface layer of soil, alleviation of surface soil compaction could be possible. Engel and Alderfer (1967) noted that in a study where traffic was limited, twice annual grooving reduced the water infiltration rate by 56% over the nongrooved control area. This indicates that grooving probably increased soil compaction. Further research is needed to determine the effectiveness of grooving cultivation on soil compaction.

Forking is to use a fork to punch holes into an area. Forking is useful to help improve drainage on a small area. Baker (1981) demonstrated that forking could improve infiltration from 2 mn h^{-1} to 30 to 66 mm h^{-1} on a Rugby field.

Sub-aerification is achieved by vibrating blades that penetrate up to 25-cm deep at 15- to 30-cm spacings. When the soil is somewhat dry, the vibrating action can help break up subsurface layers or a compacted soil. A reduction in penetrometer resistance after sub-aerification was noted by Boekel and Zwiers (1982) on a sports field. Müeller-Beck (1985) reported similar results. While sub-aerification units have been available for several years, only recently has interest increased. This procedure may be especially beneficial on soils with subsurface compaction or layers.

4. Soil Modification

On areas that received intensive traffic, soil modifications may be required. Good reviews of the various soil modification procedures are presented by Beard (1973, 1982), and Waddington (1969). A brief overview of the general approaches to modification will be presented.

Partial modification can be achieved by the addition of a physical amendment to the existing soil. Sand, calcined clays, peats, and other amendments are used. If partial modification is to be successful, a good topdressing-cultivation program must be followed to prevent layering. Also, proper amendments must be chosen. Even under ideal conditions, partial modification alters only the surface 5 to 8 cm (2-3 in.) of soil and positive results may not be apparent for several years.

Complete modification is done by preparing a root-zone mix that may or may not include the existing soil. Examples of well-known complete modification systems are the U.S. Golf Assoc. Green Section green and the Prescription Athletic Turf (PAT) system for green construction (Beard, 1973). Complete modification will be successful only if the components of the root-zone mix are carefully chosen, mixing is complete, and drainage is provided. While the initial cost is high, complete modification can save much money and time in future maintenance and renovation.

Another type of soil modification is the chemical soil conditioners. Examples of chemical conditioners proposed to alleviate compacted soil are: various wetting agents; materials containing algae, fungi, or bacteria polysaccharides; bituminous emulsions, polyacrylmide, polyvinyl alcohol, vinyl acetate-maleic acid copolymer (VAMA, Krilium), gypsum ($CaSO_4$), and others. Some of these materials may be useful under specific situations, but little research data is available to support any effectiveness under traffic conditions. The traffic on turf areas quickly destroys any aggregation or structure formation that may result from chemical treatment.

McGuire et al. (1978) and Petrovic (1975) evaluated the effectiveness of several chemical soil conditioners under turfgrass conditions. Without compaction, many of the conditioners improved structure and aeration, but when compaction was applied, the structure was not maintained.

H. Future Trends in Soil Compaction Research on Turfgrasses

Since soil compaction is an indirect stress, it is more difficult to study than other stresses. Researchers must monitor the whole plant-soil-atmospheric system to understand specifically how and why compaction affects plant growth and development. Very good procedures have been formulated by researchers on how to modify soils to avoid compaction. However, our understanding of how and why compaction influences turfgrasses is a more recent development and one that will require considerable research effort. Carrow and Wiecko (1989) provide an expanded discussion of future research needs in soil compaction. Four areas of research interest are needed: (i) the quantification of compaction tolerance of existing species and cultivars, (ii) the identification of morphological/physiological/anatomical responses of grasses to soil compaction and their relative importance as injury mechanisms *or* tolerance mechanisms., (iii) using the information in item (ii) we must develop more tolerant grasses, and (iv) the formulation of more effective cultural programs to prevent/minimize/alleviate compaction stress. Of special importance will be the identification of cultivation techniques and programs to alleviate compaction. The current research data base in this area is very limited (Rieke & Murphy, 1989).

II. WEAR

Wear is defined as injury to a turfgrass stand from pressure, tearing, and scuffing directly on the tissues. Thus, wear damage should be determined within a short time after the wear treatment has been imposed. If a period of several days expires between the wear treatment data and the time of measuring plant responses, the researcher may be determining the recuperative ability of the grass rather than wear tolerance. Another confounding factor evident in many "wear" studies is the presence of soil compaction due to the techniques used to impose the wear. As we have noted in the previous section, compaction will dramatically influence the degree of injury to turf and its recuperative ability. Again, if the researcher waits for several days for plant responses to develop, he may be determining compaction effects rather than wear or at best a combination of the two.

The separation of wear and soil compaction components of traffic injury is especially important when attempting to identify specific mechanisms of injury or tolerance to either of these stresses at the interspecific and intraspecific levels. Unless we can identify those characteristics that result in tolerance of a grass, breeders will not be able to screen or breed for these characteristics. As an example, Shearman and Beard (1976) found Kentucky-31 to have very good wear tolerance based on a high total cell wall content (Shearman & Beard, 1975b). This is a component that breeders could use as a selection criterion. Canaway (1981) reviewed "traffic" literature in an attempt to identify plant characteristics that imparted wear tolerance. He could find very few areas of agreement among authors primarily because the research studies most often contained both wear and soil compaction stresses but in various combinations. Thus, separation of only plant characteristics important for wear was not possible.

Attempting to evaluate both wear and compaction tolerance in a single test procedure can result in misleading information. For example, if Kentucky-31 tall fescue growing on a fine-textured soil was subjected to a studded, offset roller treatment to apply wear plus compaction, it would not perform well, even with its good wear tolerance. The reason is because Kentucky-31 has poor soil copmaction tolerance (Carrow, 1980a). Thus, a grower using this cultivar on a sand-based field where compaction is not a problem could obtain good results, while on a fine-textured athletic field, it would not perform as well.

A. Wear Studies

In this section, we will review those studies where wear was the predominant stress, while in the next section, studies with both wear and compaction (i.e., traffic) will be discussed.

Carrow and Johnson (1989) demonstrated that wear damage on turf from golf car traffic was immediate and increased with increased traffic, but with substantial wear occurring with only 15 passes in 1 d over an area. Straight line driving patterns caused much less injury than sem-circular or sharp-turn patterns.

Youngner (1961) used a wear machine that could apply scuffing, tearing, and punching types of wear. Bermudagrass, zoysiagrass, and tall fescue are species with good wear tolerance. Moderate wear tolerance was exhibited by Kentucky bluegrass, perennial ryegrass (not the turf type), creeping bentgrass (*Agrostis palustris* Huds.), and red fescue (*Festuca rubra* L.) with colonial bentgrass (*Agrostis tenuis* Sibth.) showing poor tolerance. In a second test, bermudagrass cultivars had different wear tolerances but their relative rankings varied with type of wear and mowing height at the time of treatment.

Using a wear simulator (Shearman et al., 1974) capable of applying wheel (pressure) and sled (tearing and crushing) types of wear, the best wear tolerance occurred on perennial ryegrass (turf-type), followed by tall fescue and Kentucky bluegrass (Shearman & Beard, 1975a). Intermediate to wear tolerance were red fescue and annual ryegrass (*Lolium multiflorum* Lam.), while rough bluegrass (*Poa trivialis* L.) ranked lowest. Youngner (1962) evaluated the wear tolerance of several mixtures and found that the ones containing perennial ryegrass or tall fescue were most tolerant.

In a series of studies, Shearman and Beard (1975a, b, c) were able to identify several characteristics that influenced wear tolerance at the interspecific level. Total cell wall content (percent weight basis) accounted for 78% of the variation in wear tolerance of seven species. Lignocellulose, cellulose, and lignin were less related. They also found that species with high leaf tensile strength and wide leaf width tended to have better wear tolerance (Shearman & Beard, 1975c) but no correlation was observed for verdure, shoot density, percent leaf moisture, percent relative turgidity, or load bearing strength. The lack of correlation of wear tolerance to verdure and shoot density is surprising, since Youngner (1961, 1962) had observed that closer mowing heights reduced wear tolerance. Also, the common observation of greater wear under wilted conditions suggests that percent leaf moisture should be important (Burton & Lance, 1966). Perhaps a further refinement of techniques would provide more insight into plant characteristics related to wear tolerance.

Substantial intraspecific differences in wear tolerance of bermudagrasses were reported by Beard et al. (1981). Using percent verdure at 3 d after wear treatment, they observed percent reductions in verdure from 10.7% ('Pee Dee') to 46.1% (Tiflawn). High pre-wear verdure was also correlated to better wear tolerance. Unfortunately, they did not determine any other characteristics to see how they correlated to wear tolerance. Interestingly, verdure was a good indicator of wear tolerance at the intraspecific level, while it was not at the interspecific level (Shearman & Beard, 1975c).

Bourgoin et al. (1985) investigated plant characteristics that correlated to wear tolerance of cultivars within three different species. Their research method involved imposing over several months wear plus soil compaction and only soil compaction. Thus, true wear aspects were difficult to separate from possible confounding influences of soil compaction and inherent recuperative potential. They reported that high initial (pre-wear) tillers per unit area related to wear tolerance of cultivars in all three species. Within *Lolium perenne* cultivars, higher relative water content and higher ADF (lignin and cellulose) shoot tissue content tended to be related to wear tolerance.

Wear resulted in reduced thatch thickness, clipping yields, and recuperative ability for creeping bentgrass (*Agrostis palustris* Huds.) (Kohlmeier & Eggens, 1983). Intermediate N aided recovery while deficient and excessive levels did not. When *Lolium perenne*, grown on a sand medium, was subjected to wear, turf receiving high N deteriorated at a more rapid rate than plots receiving intermediate levels (Canaway, 1984). As N increased from low to intermediate, wear tolerance also increased.

Turfgrass managers have speculated that several factors should influence wear tolerance: species, cultivar, mowing height, stand density, cultivation practices, topdressing procedure, succulence of the turf, N level, K level, and others (Shearman, 1989). However, specific data on many of these are lacking. When evaluating the influence of a particular cultural aspect (e.g., N nutrition), several precautions should be taken: (i) after the cultural treatment has been applied and the wear has been imposed, damage should be assessed immediately (i.e., 1–2 d) after the wear (This will show the wear injury.); (ii) any influence of a cultural practice should, ideally, be related back to physiological, morphological, or anatomical characteristics of the plant that relate to wear tolerance (As an example, N could be expected to influence total cell wall content, verdure, shoot density, leaf moisture content, and other aspects.); and (iii) the effects of the cultural practice on recuperation from injury should be assessed by observing regrowth after the initial injury.

The influence of golf care tire design and golf shoe design on wear of turf was reviewed by Beard (1973). Only minor differences in golf car tire tread designs on wear injury were observed by Carrow and Johnson (1989). With the same tread configuration, no difference between radial and nonradial tires on wear of Tifway bermudagrass (*Cynodon dactylon* × *C. transvaalensis*) were found. All tires did cause considerable wear damage. Also, they did not find any major differences in wear caused by two different golf car types. Gibeault et al. (1983) compared several golf shoe designs and reaffirmed that differences in wear injury do occur.

Under very intensive traffic, the physical wear tolerance of grasses can be improved by use of paver systems (Shearman et al., 1980) or other energy-absorbing systems (Wood, 1973). Using a concrete-grid system with turfgrass planted in the turf, Shearman et al. (1980) reported improved wear tolerance and beter recuperative rate for six turfgrass species. Winter survival, however, was decreased for two species. Under this paver system, wear tolerance was highest for 'Merion' Kentucky bluegrass, 'Manhattan' perennial ryegrass and Kentucky-31 tall fescue. 'Fairway' crested wheatgrass (*Agropyron cristatum* Gaertn.) and 'Highlight' chewings fescue were least wear tolerant.

B. Traffic Studies on Actively Growing Turf

Numerous studies have been conducted on turfgrasses using devices that apply both wear and soil compaction (Canaway, 1982; Evans, 1988). Such devices were developed to simulate the type of traffic found on sports fields. These studies are beneficial for determining effects of simulated traffic from a particular sport on the turf and for quantifying how management practices may alter traffic responses. However, it is difficult to formulate specific conclusions from such studies about the individual stresses of soil compaction and wear (Carrow & Wiecko, 1989). One reason is because soil type will influence the plant response. On a sandy soil, wear would be the dominant stress, while compaction would be prevalent on fine-textured soils. Thus, the exact same traffic treatment on the same species but grown on different soil types can result in much different results. Perennial ryegrass would be expected to rank well in most tests because of possessing excellent wear tolerance (Shearman & Beard, 1975a), and compaction tolerance (Carrow, 1980a), but red fescue would rank good only on sandy sites due to its poor compaction tolerance. This influence of soil type is especially a confounding factor in those studies that include several different soil types.

Another difficulty in interpreting results from traffic studies is the time frame within which data were collected. On data obtained a week or more after applying traffic treatments, the reader is often at a loss as to whether the results reflect initial wear, soil compaction expressing itself, or inherent recuperative potential of the grass. This situation is analogous to interpreting data from research investigations involving drought and high temperature stresses. While both often occur together in nature, our best approach to developing a basic understanding of these stresses comes from studies where only one stress is involved.

When evaluating the data from traffic studies, some aids in understanding the results are that: (i) the data obtained within 7 d of the first traffic application should reflect primarily wear damage; (ii) by carefully looking at how treatments were applied (i.e., all in 1 d or spread over a long period) and the soil type, one can often determine whether compaction or wear was important in the particular study. Many authors provide at least some soil physical property characterization; and (iii) to look at the particular device used to apply traffic treatments and determine its potential for wear (as well as the type of wear) and soil compaction.

Studies that used techniques where both compaction and wear were applied include: Bourgoin and Mansat (1980), Cuddeback and Petrovic (1985), Fushtey et al. (1983), Monnet (1983), Parr (1981), and Shildrick and Fuller (1983). Also, the *Journal of the Sports Turf Research Institute* (Hayes, 1989) contains several traffic-related articles in the 1978 (Vol. 54) through 1989 (Vol. 65) issues by several authors.

C. Traffic Studies on Dormant Turf

Several types of traffic-related injuries have been observed during the winter months on turfgrasses: (i) wear on dormant tissues (Schmidt, 1980) (Grasses without rhizomes are most likely to be the most seriously injured.); (ii) traffic on frozen, green leaf tissues [Beard (1973) indicated that disruption of the brittle protoplasm caused death of leaf tissues. This is a minor but unsightly injury.]; and (iii) traffic on turf where the surface few centimeters are thawed, especially if the soil is saturated can cause mechanical crown damage and disruption of the soil surface (Beard, 1965, 1975).

Research investigations on dormant wear tolerance of species and cultivars and the factors that relate to tolerance are limited. Batten et al. (1981) studied the wear injury on winter overseeded grasses established in a dormant bermudagrass. Perennial ryegrass exhibited better wear tolerance than rough bluegrass and high N reduced wear tolerance of both grasses.

D. Future Trends in Wear Research on Turfgrasses

Some of the components that relate to wear tolerance have been identified. Further elicitation of the various morphological, anatomical, and physiological aspects that make one grass more tolerant than another would be useful, especially at the intraspecific level since it is at this level that the breeder must work. Identification of key components may allow breeders to develop more wear-tolerant grasses for high traffic areas.

Quantification of the wear tolerance of currently available species, and especially cultivars to various types of wear, including wear when the turf is dormant, would be useful. Also, the specific influence of various cultural practices on wear tolerance would be beneficial, particularly if the results are related to plant morphological, anatomical, and physiological changes induced by the cultural practices. A detailed discussion of future wear research has been presented by Carrow and Wiecko (1989).

III. RUTTING AND SOIL DISPLACEMENT

A. Causes

Rutting and soil displacement are a result of compression and the physical removal of soil. Both are caused by foot and vehicular traffic on sports turf. The degree to which a turfgrass site is susceptible to rutting and soil displacement is a function of similar factors affecting soil compaction, namely soil texture, soil strength, soil moisture, and the magnitude, duration, and speed of the traffic event.

The problem of rutting and soil displacement occurs most often on wet, fine-textured soils. Soil under these conditions is susceptible to compaction that allows for ruts to develop and have a low shear strength allowing for soil displacement. Therefore, traffic events that occur under periods of high soil moisture content, typical in fall, winter, and early spring, on fine-textured soils can result in considerable rutting and soil displacement.

In addition to the previously mentioned factors, Van Wijk (1980) found that both the turfgrass root system and the magnitude of organic matter amendment of sand have a major role in rutting and soil displacement. They found that the presence of turfgrass root systems increased the penetration resistance (determined with a cone penetrometer) which resulted in less rutting and soil displacement, especially at a low soil organic matter content (2.3%). Also, they observed that increasing the organic matter content from 2.3 to 8.6% increased the penetration resistance by 7 MPa, thus causing less rutting and soil displacement. A common observation is that moist sands are more firm than when dry.

B. Prevention and Correction

Prevention of rutting and soil displacement is based on the surface soil zone being firm enough to withstand penetration. A method of determining the playability of a sports field has been suggested by Van Wijk (1980). The method involved the determination of soil strength of the surface 2 to 3 cm of soil with a 1 cm^2 base, 60 degree cone-type penetrometer. For intensively played areas (i.e., center of football fields), he found the penetration resistance had to be at least 1.4 MPa. This value was found to be highly correlated with adequate playing conditons and is independent of other soil properties.

Prevention of rutting and soil displacement is accomplished by developing a firm soil surface. Many factors can contribute to a firm soil surface, but the most prominent factors are moisture and soil texture. Drying the soil will dramatically increase the penetration resistance of fine textured soils. Therefore, providing for rapid surface and subsurface draining is important. Also, using soils high in sand that inherently have good drainage can help reduce rutting and soil displacement. The soil modification practices described under alleviation of soil compaction can be used for this purpose.

In many cases, allowing the site to adequately drain after an irrigation or rainfall prior to an athletic event can help reduce rutting and soil displacement. This, however, too often proves to be impractical due to the recreational demand on the site.

Rolling can remove minor variations in surface contours and provide a smoother surface. The practice of rolling is often used to prepare a sports turf site for intensive traffic. In this case, the soil is compacted to the point in which rutting and soil displacement cannot occur. It should be pointed out that rolling to this degree will also severely compact the soil and cause other problems as described earlier.

IV. DIVOTS AND BALL MARKS

Divots occur when a piece of sod is removed from the turfgrass stand by the force of a golf club. Beard (1973) reported that the size of the divot depended on the player, turfgrass species, and cutting height. Other factors may also be involved such as the thatch level and moisture status of the turfgrass and underlying soil.

On golf course greens, the impact of the ball can result in a ball mark where a circular soil depression and a raised area occur. If the ball mark is not repaired before the next mowing, the raised portion is removed, leaving a small dead area. Also, lifting the depressed area helps maintain a smooth putting surface.

REFERENCES

Agnew, M.L. 1984. Canopy/soil temperatures and acclimation responses of Kentucky bluegrass to soil compaction and moisture stress. Ph.D. diss. Kansas State Univ., Manhattan (Diss. Abstr. 84-28123).

Agnew, M.L., and R.N. Carrow. 1985a. Soil compaction and moisture stress preconditioning on Kentucky bluegrass. I. Soil aeration, water use, and root responses. Agron. J. 77:872–878.

Agnew, M.L., and R.N. Carrow. 1985b. Soil compaction and moisture stress preconditioning on Kentucky bluegrass. II. Stomatal resistance, leaf water potential, and canopy temperature. Agron. J. 77:878–884.

Arkin, G.F., and H.M. Taylor (ed.) 1981. Modifying the root environment to reduce crop stress. Am. Soc. of Agric. Eng., St. Joseph, MO.

Atwel, B.J. 1988. Physiological responses of lupine roots to soil compaction. Plant Soil 111:277–281.

Baker, S.W. 1981. The effect of earthworm activity on the drainage characteristics of winter sports pitches. J. Sports Turf Res. Inst. 57:9–23.

Barber, J., and R.N. Carrow. 1985. Evaluation of cultivation techniques for soil compaction. p. 114. In Agronomy abstracts. ASA, Madison, WI.

Barley, K.P., and E.L. Greacen. 1967. Mechanical resistance as a soil factor influencing the growth of roots and underground shoots. Adv. Agron. 19:1–43.

Barnes, K.K., W.M. Carleton, H.M. Taylor, R.I. Throckmorton, and G.E. Vanden Berg. (ed.) Compaction of agricultural soils. Am. Soc. of Agric. Eng., St. Joseph, MO.

Batten, S.M., J.B. Beard, D. Johns, and G. Pittman. 1981. Perennial ryegrass-rough bluegrass polystand study for winter overseeding. p. 47–51. In Texas turfgrasses research—1979–1980. Texas Agric. Exp. Stn. PR-3840.

Baver, L.D., W.H. Gardner, and W.R. Gardner. 1972. Soil physics. John Wiley and Sons, New York.

Beard, J.B. 1965. Effects of ice covers in the field on two perennial grasses. Crop Sci. 5:139–140.

Beard, J.B. 1973. Turfgrass: Science and culture. Prentice-Hall, Englewood Cliffs, NJ.

Beard, J.B. 1975. Snowmobile damage to turf. Grounds Maint. 10:52.

Beard, J.B. 1982. Turf management for golf courses. Burgess Publ. Co., Minneapolis.

Beard, J.B., S.M. Batten, and A. Almodares. 1981. An assessment of wear tolerance among bermudagrass cultivars for recreational and sports turf use. p. 24–26. In Texas turfgrass research—1979–1980. Texas Agric. Exp. Stn. PR-3836.

Beard, J.B., P.E. Rieke, A.J. Turgeon, and J.M. Vargas, Jr. 1978. Annual bluegrass (Poa annua L.)—Description, adaptation, culture, and control. Res. Rep. 352. Michigan State Univ. Agric. Exp. Stn., East Lansing.

Bingaman, D.E., and H. Kohnke. 1970. Evaluating sands for athletic turf. Agron. J. 62:464–467.

Blackwell, P.S., and B.D. Soane. 1981. A method of predicting bulk density changes in field soils resulting from compaction by agricultural traffic. J. Soil Sci. 32:51–65.

Boekel, P., adn J.S. Zwiers. 1981. Relieving sub-surface compaction in sports turf. Z. Veg. Landschafts Sports. 5(4):144–147.

Boufford, R.W., and R.N. Carrow. 1980. Effects of intense, short-term traffic on soil physical properties and turfgrass growth. Trans. Kansas Acad. Sci. 83:78–85.

Bourgoin, B., and P. Mansat. 1979. Persistence of turfgrass species and cultivars. J. Sports Turf Res. Inst. 55:121–140.

Bourgoin, B., and P. Mansat. 1980. Artificial trampling and player traffic on turfgrass cultivars. p. 55–63. In R.W. Sheard (ed.) Proc. 4th Int. Turf. Res. Conf., Guelph, ON, Canada. 19–23 July. Int. Turfgrass Soc., and Ontario Agric. Coll., Univ. of Guelph, Guelph, ON.

Bourgoin, B., P. Mansat, B. Ait Taleb, and M.H. Quaggog. 1985. Explicative characteristics of treading tolerance in Festuca rubra, Lolium perenne, and Poa pratensis. p. 235–242. In F. Lemaire (ed.) Proc. 5th Int. Turfgrass Res. Conf., Avignon, France. 1–5 July. Inst. Natl. de la Recherche Agron., Paris.

Bradford, K.J., and S.F. Yang. 1981. Physiological responses of plants to waterlogging. Hortic. Sci. 16:25–30.

Brown, K.W., and R.L. Duble. 1975. Physical characteristics of soil mixtures used for golf green construction. Agron. J. 67:647–652.

Burton, G.W., and C. Lance. 1966. Golf car versus grass. Golf Superintendent 34:66–70.

Byrne, T.G., W.B. Davis, L.J. Booker, and L.F. Werenfels. 1965. Vertical mulching for improvement of old greens. Cal. Agric. 19(5):12–14.

Canaway, P.M. 1981. Wear tolerance of turfgrass species. J. Sports Turf Res. Inst. 57:65–83.

Canaway, P.M. 1982. Simulation of fine turf wear using the differential slip wear machine and quantification of wear treatments in terms of energy expenditure. J. Sports Turf. Res. Inst. 58:9–15.

Canaway, P.M. 1984. The response of *Lolium perenne* turf grown on sand and soil to fertilizer nitrogen. I. Ground cover response as affected by football-type wear. J. Sports Turf. Res. Inst. 60:8–18.

Canaway, P.M., S.P. Isaac, and R.E. Bennett. 1986. The effects of mechanical treatments on the water infiltration rate of a sand playing surface for association football. J. Sports Turf. Res. Inst. 62:67–73.

Cannell, R.Q. 1977. Soil aeration and compaction in relation to root growth and soil management. *In* T.H. Cooker (ed.) Appl. Biol. 2:1–85.

Carrow, R.N. 1980a. Influence of soil compaction on three turfgrass species. Agron. J. 72:1038–1042.

Carrow, R.N. 1980b. Effects of different soil compaction levels on Kentucky bluegrass. p. 115. *In* Agronomy abstracts. ASA, Madison, WI.

Carrow, R.N. 1981. Soil compaction. Golf Course Manage. 49:59–62,66.

Carrow, R.N. 1985. Turfgrass-soil-water relationships. p. 85–102. *In* V. Gibeault (ed.) Turfgrass and water relations. Sod Prod. Assoc./Univ. of California, Oakland.

Carrow, R.N. 1986. Water management on compacted soil. Weeds, Trees Turf 25(3):34, 38, 40.

Carrow, R.N. 1988. Cultivation methods on turfgrass water relationships and growth under soil compaction. 1988 Turfgrass Res. Summary. U.S. Golf Assoc. Green Section, Far Hills, NJ.

Carrow, R.N., and B.J. Johnson. 1989. Turfgrass wear as affected by golf car tire design and traffic patterns. J. Am. Soc. Hortic. Sci. 114:240–246.

Carrow, R.N., and J. Troll. 1981. Management of high traffic areas. Proc. 50th Univ. of Mass. Turf Conf. 1981:1–10.

Carrow, R.N., and G. Wiecko. 1989. Soil compaction and wear stresses on turfgrasses: Future research directions. p. 37–42. *In* H. Takatoh (ed.) Proc. 6th Int. Turfgrasses Res. Conf. Tokyo. 31 July-5 Aug. Jpn. Soc. Turfgrass Sci., Tokyo.

Carson, E.W. (ed.) 1974. The plant root and its environment. Univ. Press of Virginia, Charlottesville.

Castillo, S.R., R.H. Dowdy, J.M. Bradford, and W.E. Larson. 1982. Effects of mechanical stress on plant growth and nutrient uptake. Agron. J. 74:526–530.

Chancellor, W.J. 1971. Effects of compaction on soil strength. *In* K.K. Barnes et al. (ed.) Compaction of agricultural soil. Am. Soc. of Agric. Eng., St. Joseph, MO.

Cohron, G.T. 1971. Forces causing soil compaction. *In* K.K. Barnes (ed.) Compaction of agricultural soil. Am. Soc. of Agric. Eng., St. Joseph, MO.

Cordukes, W.E. 1968. Compaction. Golf Course Superintendent 36(8):20–24.

Cuddeback, S., and A.M. Petrovic. 1985. Traffic effects on the growth and quality of *Agrostis palustris* Huds. p. 411–416. *In* F. Lemaire (ed.) Proc. 5th Int. Turfgrass Res. Conf., Avignon, France. Inst. Natl. de la Recherche Agron., Paris.

Davies, D.B., J.B. Finney, and S.J. Richardson. 1973. Relative effects of tractor weight and wheel-slip in causing soil compaction. J. Soil Sci. 24:399–409.

Dexter, A.R. 1988. Advances in characterization of soil structure. Soil Tillage Res. 11:199–238.

Dexter, A.R., and D.W. Tanner. 1972. Soil deformation induced by a moving cutting blade, and expanding tube and a penetrating sphere. J. Agric. Eng. res. 17:371–375.

Drew, M.C., M.B. Jackson, and S. Gifford. 1979. Ethylene-promoted adventitious rooting and development of cortical air spaces (aerenchyma) in roots may be an adaptive response to flooding in *Zea mays* L. Planta 147-83–88.

Emerson, W.W. et al. (ed.) 1978. Modification of soil structure. John Wiley and Sons, New York.

Engel, R.E., and R.B. alderfer. 1967. The effect of cultivation, topdressing, lime, nitrogen and wetting agent on thatch development in 1/4 inch bentgrass turf over a ten-year period. N.J. Agric. Exp. Stn. Bull. 818:32–45.

Evans, G.E. 1988. Tolerance of selected bluegrass and fescue taxa to simulated human foot traffic. J. Environ. Hortic. 6(1):10–14.

Everard, J.D., and M.C. Drew. 1989. Mechanisms controlling changes in water movement through the roots of *Helianthus annuus* L. during continuous exposure to oxygen deficiency. J. Exp. Bot. 40(210):95–104.

Flannagan, T.R., and R.J. Bartlett. 1961. Soil compaction associated with alternating green and brown stripes on turf. Agron. J. 53:404–405.

Fryrear, D.W., and W.G. McCully. 1971. Development of grass root systems as influenced by soil compaction. Range Manage. 25:254–257.

Fushtey, S.G., D.K. Taylor, and D. Fairey. 1983. The effect of wear stress on survival of turfgrass in pure stands and in mixtures. Can. J. Plant Sci. 63:317–322.

Gibeault, V.A., V.B. Youngner, and W.H. Bengeyfield. 1983. Golf shoe study II. USGA Green Sect. Rec. 21(5):1–7.

Gill, W.R. 1968. Influence of compaction hardening of soil on penetration resistance. Trans. ASAE 11:741–745.

Glinski, J., and W. Stepniewski. 1985. Soil aeration and its role for plants. CRC Press, Boca Raton, FL.

Gore, A.J.P., R. Cox, and T.M. Davies. 1979. Wear tolerance of turfgrass mixtures. J. Sports Turf Res. Inst. 55:45–68.

Goss, R.L. 1984. Aerification—A comparison of shattercore versus hollow tine. p. 46–48. In R.L. Goss (ed.) Proc. 38th Northwest Turf. Conf., Spokane, WA. 17–20 Sept. Washington State Univ., Puyallup.

Grable, A.R. 1966. Soil aeration and plant growth. Adv. Agron. 18:57–106.

Gradwell, M.W. 1965. Soil physical conditions of winter and the growth of ryegrass plants. I. Effects of compaction and puddling. N.Z. J. Agric. Res. 8:238–269.

Hakansson, I., W.B. Voorhees, and H. Riley. 1988. Vehicle and wheel factors influencing soil compaction and crop response in different traffic regimes. Soil Tillage Res. 11:239–282.

Harris, W.L. 1971. The soil compaction process. p. 9–46. In K.K. Barnes et al. (ed.) Compaction of agriculture soils. Am. Soc. Agric. Eng., St. Joseph, MO.

Hayes, P. 1989. Journal of the Sports Turf Research Institute. Vol. 1-65. Sports Turf Res. Inst., Bingley, West Yorkshire, England.

Holder, C.B., and K.W. Brown. 1980. The relationship between oxygen and water uptake by roots of intact bean plants. Soil Sci. Soc. Am. J. 44:21–25.

Hook, D.H., and R.M.M. Crawford. 1978. Plant life in anaerobic environments. Ann Arbor Sci. Publ., Ann Arbor, MI.

Howard, H.L. 1959. The resopnse of some putting green mixtures to compaction. M.S. thesis, Texas A&M Univ., College Station.

Kamp, W.A. 1979. Effects of aeration with slit tines on some soil characteristics of football pitches. Z. Veg. Landschafts Sports. 2(1):17–21.

Kawase, M. 1981. Anatomical and morphological adaptations of plants to water logging. HortScience 16:30–34.

Kohlmeier, G.P., and J.L. Eggens. 1983. Effects of wear and nitrogen on creeping bentgrass. Can. J. Plant Sci. 63:189–193.

Kulkarni, B.K., and N.K. Savant. 1977. Effect on soil compaction on root-cation exchange capacity of crop plants. Plant Soil 48:269–278.

Kunze, R.J. 1956. The effects of compaction on different golf green soil mixtures on plant growth. M.S. thesis. Texas A&M Univ., College Station.

Lewtey, J., L.H. Stolzy, N. Valoras, and T.E. Szuezkiewiez. 1962. Influence of soil oxygen on growth and mineral concentration of barley. Agron. J. 54:538–540.

Letey, J., L.H. Stolzy, O.R. Lunt, and N. Valoris. 1964a. Soil oxygen and clipping height effects on the growth of Newport bluegrass. Calif. Turf. Cult. 14:9–12.

Letey, J., L.H. Stolzy, O.R. Lunt, and V.B. Youngner. 1964b. Growth and nutrient uptake of Newport bluegrass as affected by soil oxygen. Plant Soil 20:143–148.

Letey, J., W.C. Morgan, S.J. Richards, and N. Valoras. 1966. Physical soil amendments, soil compaction, irrigation, and wetting agents in turfgrass management. III. Effect on oxygen diffusion rate and root growth. Agron. J. 58:531–535.

Luxmoore, R.J., L.H. Stolzy, and J. Letey. 1970. Oxygen diffusion in the soil-plant system. II. Respiration rate, permeability, and porosity of consecutive excised segments of maize and rice roots. Agron. J. 62:322–324.

Luxmoore, R.J., and L.H. Stolzy. 1972. Oxygen diffusion in the soil-plant system. VI. A synopsis and commentary. Agron. J. 64:725–729.

Madison, J.H. 1971. Principle of turfgrass culture. Van Nostrand Reinhold Co., New York.

McGuire, E., R.N. Carrow, and J. Troll. 1978. Chemical soil conditions effects on sand soils and turfgrass growth. Agron. J. 70:317–321.

McPherson, D.C. 1939. Cortical air spaces in the roots of *Zea mays* L. New Phytol. 38:190–202.

Meyer, W. 1983. The response of turfgrass cultivars to wear stress. p. 128. *In* Agronomy abstracts. ASA, Madison, WI.

Miller, D.E. 1986. Root systems in relation to stress tolerance. Hortic. Sci. 21(4):963–970.

Monnet, Y. 1983. Resistance d'especes, cultivars et melanges de graminees a gazon au pietinement. revue Hortic. 234:15–23.

Morgan, W.C., J. Letey, and L.H. Stolzy. 1965. Turfgrass renovation by deep aerification. Agron. J. 57:494–496.

Morgan, W.C., J. Letey, S.J. Richards, and N. Valoras. 1966. Physical soil amendments, soil compaction, irrigation, and wetting agents in turfgrass management I. Effects on compactability, water infiltration rates, evapotranspiration, and numbers of irrigation. Agron. J. 58:525–535.

Murphy, J.A. 1986. Hollow and solid tine cultivation effects on soil structure and turfgrass root growth. M.S. thesis. Michigan State Univ., East Lansing.

Murphy, J.A., and P.E. Rieke. 1987. Hollow and solid tine coring research. p. 28–33. *In* P.E. Rieke and M.T. McElroy (ed.) 57th Annu. Michigan Turf. Conf. Proc. Vol. 16., East Lansing. 12–14 Jan.

Müeller, F. 1982. NL-Maschenenbrichte. Heute: Rasenbelüftung mit Verti-Drän. Neve Landschaft 27:826–827.

Müller-Beck, K.G. 1985. Loosening of compaction in the vegetation layer of turfgrass pitches. p. 427–438. *In* F. Lemaire (ed.) Proc. 5th Int. Turfgrass Res. Conf. Avignon, France. 1–5 July. Inst. Natl. de la Recherche Agron. Paris.

O'Neil, K.H., and R.N. Carrow. 1982. Kentucky bluegrass growth and water use under different soil compaction and irrigation regimes. Agron. J. 74:933–936.

O'Neil, K.J., and R.N. Carrow. 1983. Perennial ryegrass growth, water use and soil aeration status under soil comaction. Agron. J. 75:177–180.

Parish, D.H. 1971. Effects of compaction on nutrient supply to plants. *In* K.K. Barnes et al. (ed.) Compaction of agricultural soils. Am. Soc. of Agric. Eng., St. Joseph, MO.

Parr, T.W. 1981. A population study of a sports turf system. *In* R.W. Sheard (ed.) Proc. 4th Int. Turfgrass Res. Conf., Guelph, ON, Canada. 19–23 July. Int. Turfgrass Soc., Ontario Agric. Coll., Univ. of Guelph, Guelph, ON.

Parr, J.F., W.R. Gardner, and L.F. Elliott (ed.) 1981. Water potential relations in soil microbiology. SSSA Spec. Publ. 9. SSSA, Madison, WI.

Petrovic, A.M. 1975. The effect of several chemical soil conditioners and an algal polymer on compacted soil and growth of cool season turfgrasses. M.S. thesis, Univ. of Massachusetts, Amherst.

Petrovic, A.M. 1979. The effects of vertical operating hollow time (VOHT) cultivation on turfgrass soil structure. Ph.D. diss. Michigan State Univ., East Lansing (Diss. Abstr. 80-06178).

Petrovic, A.M., and P.E. Rieke. 1978. Progress report on cultivation and gypsum studies. p. 50–68. *In* Proc. Michigan Turf. Conf., East Lansing. 12–15 Jan. Vol. 7. Michigan State Univ., East Lansing.

Rieke, P.E., and J.A. Murphy. 1989. Advances in turf cultivation. p. 49–54. *In* H. Takatoh (ed.) Proc. 6th Int. Turfgrass Res. Conf., Tokyo. 31 July–5 Aug. Jpn. Soc. Turfgrass Sci., Tokyo.

Rimmer, D.L. 1979. Effects of increasing compaction on grass growth in colliery spoil. J. Sports Turf Res. Inst. 55:153–162.

Roberts, J.M. 1975. Some influences of cultivation on the soil and turfgrass. M.S. thesis. Purdue Univ., Lafayette, IN.

Rosenberg, N.J. 1964. Response of plants to the physical effects of soil compaction. Adv. Agron. 16:181–196.

Schmidt, R.E. 1980. Winter survival of bermudagrass. Golf Course Manage. 48(10):24–26.

Schmidt, R.E., M.L. Henry, and D.R. Chalmers. 1989. Postdormancy growth of *Cynodon dactylon* as influenced by traffic and nutrition. p. 165–167. *In* H. Takatoh (ed.) Proc. 6th Int. Turf. Res. Conf., Tokyo. 31 July–5 Aug. Jpn. Soc. Turfgrass Sci., Tokyo.

Schravendijk, H.W., and O.M. van Andel. 1985. Interdependence of growth, water relations and abscisic acid level in *Phaseolus vulgaris* during waterlogging. Physiol. Plant. 63:215–220.

Schumacher, T.E., and A.J.M. Smucker. 1981. Mechanical impedance effects on oxygen uptake and porosity of drybean roots. Agron. J. 73:51–55.

Shearman, R.C. 1989. Improving wear tolerance of sports fields. Grounds Maint. 24(2):84–85, 104–106.

Shearman, R.C., and J.B. Beard. 1975a. Turfgrass wear mechanisms: I. Wear tolerance of seven turfgrass species and quantitative methods for determining turfgrass wear injury. Agron. J. 67:208–211.

Shearman, R.C., and J.B. Beard. 1975b. Turfgrass wear tolerance mechanisms. II. Effects of cell wall constituents on turfgrass wear tolerance. Agron. J. 67:211–215.

Shearman, R.C., and J.B. Beard. 1975c. Turfgrass wear tolerance mechanisms. III. Physiological, morphological, and anatomical characteristics associated with turfgrass wear tolerance. Agron. J. 67:215–218.

Shearman, R.C., J.B. Beard, C.M. Hansen, and R. Apaclla. 1974. Turfgrass wear simulator for small plot investigations. Agron. J. 66:332–334.

Shearman, R.C., E.J. Kinbacher, and T.P. Riordan. 1980. Turfgrass-paver complex for intensively trafficked areas. Agron. J. 72:372–374.

Shearman, R.C., and J.E. Watkins. 1985. Kentucky bluegrass lateral growth and stem rust response to soil compaction stress. Hortic. Sci. 20:388–390.

Shildrick, J.P., and M.P. Fuller. 1983. Effects of artificial winter wear on turfgrass swards of different age and composition. Z. Veget. Land. Sports. 6:87–94.

Shildrick, J.P., and C.H. Peel. 1983. Football-stud wear on turf-type cultivars of tall fescue. J. Sports Turf Res. Inst. 59:124–132.

Sills, M.J., and R.N. Carrow. 1982. Soil compaction effects on nitrogen use in tall fescue. J. Am. Soc. Hortic. Sci. 107:934–937.

Sills, M.J., and R.N. Carow. 1983. Turfgrass growth, N use, and water use under soil compaction and N fertilization. Agron. J. 75:488–492.

Smit, B., M. Stachowiak, and E. van Volkenburg. 1989. Cellular processes limiting leaf growth in plants under hypoxic root stress. J. Exp. Bot. 40(210):89–94.

Smucker, A.J.M., and A.E. Erickson. 1987. Anaerobic stimulation of root exudates and disease of peas. Plant Soil 99:423–433.

Soane, B.D., P.S. Blackwell, J.W. Dickson, and D.J. Painter. 1981. Compaction by agricultural vehicles: A review. II. Compaction under tyres and other running gear. Soil Soil Till. Res. 1:373–399.

Sojka, R.E., and L.H. Stolzy. 1980. Soil oxygen effects on stomatal respnse. Soil Sci. 130:350–358.

Stafford, J.V., and P. de Carvelho Mattos. 1981. The effect of forward speed on wheel-induced soil compaction: Laboratory simulation and field experiments. J. Agric. Eng. Res. 26:333–347.

Stolzy, L.H. 1972. Soil aeration and gas exchange in relation to grasses. In V.B. Youngner and C.M. McKell (ed.) The biology and utilization of grasses. Academic Press. New York.

Swartz, W.E., and L.T. Kardos. 1963. Effects of comparison on physical properties of sand-soil-peat mixtures at various moisture contents. Agron. J. 55:7–10.

Taylor, D.H., and G.R. Blake. 1979. Sand content of sand-soil-peat mixtures for turfgrass. Soil Sci. Soc. Am. J. 43:394–398.

Taylor, D.H., and G.R. Blake. 1981. Laboratory evaluation of soil mixtures for sports turf. Soil Sci. Soc. of Am. J. 45:936–940.

Taylor, J.M., M.G. Huck, and B. Klepper. 1972. Root development in relation to soil physical conditions. p. 57–77. In D. Hillel (ed.) Optimizing the soil physical environment towards greater crop yields. Academic Press, New York.

Thomas, R., and J.P. Guerin. 1981. A method of measuring quality of sports turf. p. 151–156. In R.W. Sheard (ed.) Proc. 4th Int. Turfgrass Res. Conf., Guelph, ON, Canada. 19–23 July. Int. Turfgrass Soci., and Ontario Agric. Coll., Univ. of Guelph, Guelph, ON.

Thurman, P.C., and F.A. Pokorny. 1969. The relationship of several amended soils and compaction rates on vegetative growth, root development and cold resistance of 'Tifgreen' bermudagrass. J. Am. Hortic. Sci. 94:463–465.

Trouse, A.C., Jr. 1971. Soil conditions as they affect plant establishment, root development and yield. A present knowledge and need for research. p. 225–240. In K.K. Barnes et al. (ed.) Compaction of agricultural soils. Am. Soc. Agric. Eng., St. Joseph, MO.

Van Dam, J., V.A. Gibeault, W.B. Davis, and K. Mueller. 1975. A study of three sand mixes. Calif. Turf. Cult. 25:25–27.

Vanden Berg, G.E., A.W. Cooper, A.E. Erickson, W.M. Carleton. 1957. Soil pressure distribution under tractor and implement traffic. Agric. Eng. 38:854–855, 859.

van Wijk, A.L.M. 1980. A soil technological study on effectuating and maintaining adequate playing conditions of grass sports fields. Agric. Res. Rep. 903. PUDOC, Wageningen.

van Wijk, A.L.M., W.B. Verhaegh, and J. Beuving. 1977. Grass sportsfields: Top layer compaction and soil aeration. Rasen Turf Gazon 8:47–52.

Vargas, J.M., Jr. 1981. Management of turfgrass diseases. Burgess Publ. Co., Minneapolis.

Veen, B.W. 1988. Influence of oxygen deficiency on growth and function of plant roots. Plant Soil 111:259–266.

Waddington, D.V. 1969. Soil and soil related problems. p. 80–129. *In* A.A. Hanson and F.V. Juska (ed.) Turfgrass science. Agron. Monogr. 14. ASA, Madison, WI.

Waddington, D.V., and J.H. Baker. 1965. Influence of soil aeration on the growth and chemical composition of three grass species. Agron. J. 57:253–258.

Waddington, D.V., T.L. Zimmerman, G.J. Shoop, L.T. Kardos, and J.M. Duich. 1974. Soil modification for turfgrass areas. Penn State Univ. Progr. Rep. 337.

Ward, C.J. 1983. Amenity grass-drainage review. Rep. to the Sports Council. Dep. of the Environ. through Natl. Environ. Res. Counc. Sports Turf Res. Inst., Bingley, England.

Watson, J.R., Jr. 1950. Irrigation and compaction on established fairway turf. USGA J. Turf Manage. 3(4):25–28.

Watson, J.R. 1961. Some soil physical effects of traffic. p. 1–9. *In* Proc. of 16th Am. Texas Turf Conf., College Station. Texas A&M Univ., College Station.

Wood, G.M. 1973. Use of energy-absorbing materials to permit turf growth in heavily trafficked areas. Agron. J. 65:1004–1005.

Youngner, V.B. 1961. Accelerated wear test on turfgrasses. Agron. J. 53:217–218.

Youngner, V.B. 1962. Wear resistance of cool-season turfgrasses. Effects of previous mowing practices. Agron. J. 54:198–199.

Zimmerman, T.L. 1973. The effect of amendment, compaction, soil depth and tine on various physical properties of physically modified Hagerstown soil. Ph.D. diss. Penn State Univ. (Diss Abstr. 73-24053).

Zontek, S.J. 1983. They are mowing fairways with triplex mowers and picking up the clippings, too! USGA Green Sec. Rec. 21(1):1–5.

Zwiers, J.S. 1982. De betekenis van prikrollen voor de bespeelbaarheid van grassportvelden. NSF Tech. Med. 39:16–19.

10 Soils, Soil Mixtures, and Soil Amendments

DONALD V. WADDINGTON

Pennsylvania State University
University Park, Pennsylvania

The turfgrass grower's interest in soils extends beyond the usual role of soil as a plant growth medium that provides mechanical support, essential elements, water, and O_2 to the root system. Soil properties affect plant growth and influence the utilization and maintenance of turf areas. Their effects on use and maintenance may be related to the quality of turf produced or due to more direct soil effects such as hardness of compact soils or standing water on poorly drained soil. Soils should be selected and managed to provide a suitable turf cover, maximize utilization of the turf area, and minimize problems associated with the maintenance of turfgrass. If soils do not meet these criteria, their properties may be altered by the addition of chemical and physical amendments, the use of various cultivation and construction techniques, or a combination of these methods.

I. SOIL PROFILES ON TURFGRASS AREAS

Because turfgrasses are normally established on plowed or otherwise disturbed soil, the soil profiles often differ from the typical profiles that developed during soil formation. Beard (1973), Davis (1973a), and Daniel and Freeborg (1979) have discussed root-zone systems that illustrate various profiles that may occur on turfgrass sites. The type of profile influences soil management decisions.

A. Natural Profile

A typical profile under turfgrass when little soil disturbance has occurred consists of organic (O) horizons at the surface, the Ap horizon (plow layer), and undisturbed B horizon (subsoil) beneath the Ap. Such a profile is illustrated in Fig. 10–1A. The symbols O_i, O_e, and O_a are used to designate horizons with slightly, intermediately, and highly decomposed organic matter, respectively. The thickness of the organic layer (called thatch on turf areas) depends on the age of the turf, the species and cultivar of grass, and various environmental and management factors. The Ap horizon depth (often called

Copyright © 1992 ASA-CSSA-SSSA, 677 S. Segoe Rd., Madison, WI 53711, USA. *Turfgrass—Agronomy Monograph no. 32.*

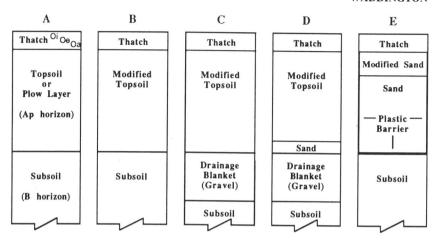

Fig. 10-1. Various soil profiles found on turfgrass areas.

the plow layer or topsoil) varies according to the previous tillage depth and any erosion losses prior to turf establishment.

B. Artificial Profiles

On highly trafficked turf areas, it is common practice to physically modify the native topsoil or use a prepared topsoil mixture. Also, some form of subsurface drainage is often used on such areas. A variety of artificial profiles (Fig. 10-1B–10-1E) can be constructed for different situations, such as golf greens or athletic fields.

In some instances a modified topsoil is placed directly on subsoil (Fig. 10-1B). Physical amendments can also be incorporated into the soil surface to create two textural layers in the topsoil. A drainage blanket of gravel or crushed rock (with or without drainage tile) is often placed beneath the topsoil to provide rapid movement of drainage water from the area (Fig. 10-1C). A coarse layer (gravel) beneath the finer topsoil creates a false water table because water will not move readily from the fine to coarse layer unless it is at a high matric potential (i.e., the water content must be at or near saturation for movement into the coarser layer to occur). The effect of this boundary layer is an increase in water retention in the soil above the coarse layer (Miller, 1964, 1969; Miller & Bunger, 1963; Dougrameji, 1965; Unger, 1971). Many fine-textured soils would be too wet under such conditions; however, with sandy soils the increased water retention is advantageous. Soil depth over a coarse layer is an important consideration, because the deeper the soil the lower the water content near the surface after excess water has drained form the system. The data of Davis et al. (1970) show this relationship for various soil mixtures. The coarser the topsoil, the shallower the depth should be to have adequate levels of water retention.

The effect of a coarse layer on increasing water retention in the soil above depends on the difference in particle size between the layers and the sharpness of the boundary between the layers (Miller & Bunger, 1963; Miller, 1964, 1969). As the particle size differential between the layers increases, the amount of water retained in the finer upper layer also increases; and more water is held above a sharp boundary rather than a mixed interface of the layers.

A sand layer is sometimes placed between the modified topsoil and the drainage blanket to restrict movement of fines from the topsoil into and through the drainage blanket (Fig. 10-1D). Such a sand layer has been included in U.S. Golf Association (USGA) Green Section specifications for putting green construction (USGA Green Section Staff, 1960, 1973; Radko, 1974), but it may not be required in all cases (Brown & Duble, 1975; Brown et al., 1980). The size of pores influences migration of soil particles. It has been suggested that to minimize movement of fines into an underlying coarse layer the diameter of coarse particles should not exceed that of the fine particles by a factor of more than five to seven (USGA Green Section Staff, 1973). The movement of silt particles through sand columns, as studied by Wright and Foss (1968), illustrates the relationship between particle size and particle movement. Fine silt (0.02–0.002 mm) completely washed through medium sand (0.5–0.25 mm), and about 25 to 50% of coarse silt (0.05–0.02 mm) was leached through a column of medium sand. Appreciable amounts of fine silt moved through fine sand (0.25–0.10 mm), but only a little movement of coarse silt occurred. The size range of fine sand is 5 to 12.5 times as large as the largest particles of fine silt, and two to five times greater than the largest coarse silt. Brown and Duble (1975) reported that particle migration from mixtures into a gravel layer was affected by the gravel size; however, little evidence of migration was found when less than one-half of the gravel was greater in size than 6.4 mm. They concluded that a sand layer is not needed to prevent migration if the majority of gravel is between 6.4 to 9.5 mm or smaller.

In some cases sands are used as growing media. Sand may be placed directly on the subgrade and tile systems (Davis, 1973b) or over a plastic barrier to increase water retention. In the Purr-Wick root-zone system (Daniel, 1978), sand is placed on a plastic liner, which has provisions for drainage and water level control. To improve nutrient retention, the surface 5 cm is modified to obtain a mixture such as 50% (volume) sand, 20% peat, 20% calcined clay, and 10% vermiculite. Thus, two horizons are present within the sand topsoil (Fig. 10-1E). Similar to the Purr-Wick system is the Prescription Athletic Turf (PAT) system used to construct athletic field playing surfaces. The PAT system includes pumps attached to the drainage system to enhance drainage during periods of intense rainfall.

Pure sand systems have also been developed by workers in California. Early work begun by Lunt (1956a,b, 1961) was continued by others (Davis et al., 1970). A tile system is placed on the subgrade, and the need for a plastic barrier is determined by textural and drainage characteristics of the subgrade. These sand systems have been used successfully for putting greens (Davis, 1973b, 1981) and athletic fields (Davis et al., 1974); however, maintenance practices must be adjusted for the sand medium used on these areas (Davis, 1983).

C. Management-Induced Profiles

Various horizontal and vertical layers can be created within root zones by management practices. Such layers are illustrated in Fig. 10–2. Topdressing practices and inadequate on-site mixing during construction are often the cause of textural layers within turf soils. On poorly drained turfgrass areas, core cultivation, slit drainage, and combinations of these practices are commonly used to alleviate compaction and improve drainage. Topdressing with sandy materials after core cultivation creates vertical channels of the topdressing material. Vertical channels or bands of gravel, sand, or other amendments may be the result of slit trenching or sand injection into grooves cut into the turf and soil (Fisher & Ede, 1974; Moreland, 1981; Baker, 1982). Networks of intersecting slit drains can be used as well as parallel drains.

An organic layer within the profile can result from thatch layers being buried by topdressing or by the addition of a soil layer as fill material. An organic soil layer is introduced with sod grown on organic soil. A textural layer can be created during sodding if the soil on the sod differs from that on the site. Thus, a porous-growing media could be sealed by a fine-textured soil deposited with sod.

Black layer, or black plug layer, is a condition that develops within the profile of some sand greens. Its occurrence is not limited to sand media, but most observations have been made on golf greens built with sand. The layer occurs under anaerobic conditions and is favored by the presence of organic matter and S. The black color has been attributed to the formation of FeS. Decline of bentgrass (*Agrostis* spp.) growing on the green is sometimes associated with black layer. The layer may exist as a 2.5- to 7.5-cm thick surface layer or as a subsurface layer with a thickness of 0.8 cm or greater. Cullimore et al. (1990) reported that black layer has a complex structure of lateral plates, columnar projections, and globular masses. Little root growth occurs in the layers, and odors associated with anaerobic soil conditions have

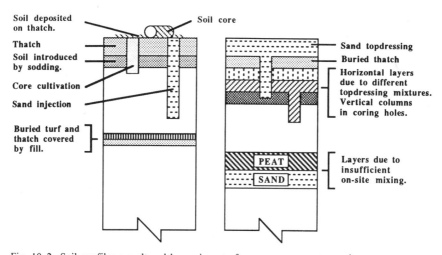

Fig. 10–2. Soil profiles are altered by various turfgrass management practices.

been noted in cases where turf is declining. In some cases, blue-gree algal species have been associated with black layer (Hodges, 1987a,b). The algae itself and mucilage produced by algae can clog soil pores to create anaerobic conditions and the algae can serve as the source of organic matter to contribute to the black layer formation. Formation of the layer has also been attributed to oxygen depletion by aerobic microbial respiration and sulfide formation by anaerobic microorganisms. Metal sulfides cause the black color, and in advanced stages of formation the metal sulfides clog pores and intensify the anaerobic condition (Berndt et al., 1987). Plugging of pores also has been attributed to the formation of biofilms by consortia of bacteria, and such biofilms may be either clear or black (Lindenbach & Cullimore, 1989; Cullimore et al., 1990). The key to black layer management appears to be water control (i.e., good drainage and judicial irrigation to avoid anaerobic conditions). Much of the published information on observations and research on black layer has been limited to articles in trade magazines and conference proceedings (Berndt et al., 1987, 1989; Berndt & Vargas, 1989; Hodges, 1987a, b, 1989; Hall, 1989).

Management-induced layers, whether intentional or unintentional, affect factors such as water movement, water retention, nutrient retention, and root growth. Therefore, they must be considered when diagnosing turfgrass problems and when planning turfgrass management programs. Even very thin layers can influence the above factors because the effects are due to the discontinuity of pore sizes at the layer interface.

D. Future Research

The effects of different textured layers, compacted layers, and hardpans in soil profiles have received considerable study outside of the turfgrass situation; however, established principles apply to turfgrass areas as well.

Several practices currently used by some turfgrass managers need to be included in future research efforts. Geotextile fabrics have been used to prevent migration of topsoil particles into underlying layers of gravel. The effectiveness of such materials for this purpose should be determined, and they should be compared to sand layers. Factors such as particle migration, clogging, and water retention effects should be studied using both fabric and sand systems. Top mix composition should be a variable in such studies. Currently, a research study is underway at the University of Tennessee in which several geotextile fabrics are being evaluated for this use (L.M. Callahan, 1989, personal communication).

In recent years, sand has been used to topdress turfgrass areas (primarily putting greens) that were constructed with finer-textured materials. Opinions have varied on the desirability of topdressing with pure sand (Madison et al., 1974; Davis, 1978; Hall, 1978; Rossi & Skogley, 1987). Research is needed on both the short- and long-term effects of this practice on soil physical properties within the sand layer as it continues to increase in depth and at the interface of the sand and the original soil material.

Research should continue on the development and properties of black layers that occur in turf soils. Several causes have been suggested, and a better understanding of layer development in the field is needed. Under natural conditions, horizon development is relatively rapid on sandy parent materials. Attempts should be made to relate black layer to processes active in soil genesis and horizon development. How does black layer relate to gleyzation and mottling in waterlogged soils, and to black mottles formed in the presence of sulfur compounds? Are some observed black layers actually illuvial accumulations of organic matter? Processes described with black layer are found in literature related to soil genesis and soil chemistry. For example, Jenny (1980, p. 166) mentioned black coloration due to S compounds in gley horizons and Stevenson (1960, p. 278) stated that reduction of SO_4 and incompletely oxidized inorganic S compounds to H_2S is relatively unimportant in well-aerated soils because under these conditions sulfides produced during decomposition of organic matter or through the reduction of inorganic S compounds are assimilated into microbial tissue or oxidized; however, under waterlogged (anaerobic) conditions S-reducing bacteria produce large amounts of sulfide, H_2S accumulates, and the bacterial activity is "conspicuous by the odor of H_2S and the blackening of soils, muds, and water through the formation of FeS." Continued research should provide answers to questions concerning this complex and variable condition.

Research results on the relationships between soil texture and depths of soil needed in various man-made profiles would be of practical use. General guidelines are used, but more specific specifications would be helpful. When availability of water in sandy soils is to be increased by the utilization of false water tables or plastic liners, inappropriate textures, depths, or both contribute to failures of such systems.

II. ORGANIC HORIZONS

The organic layer that occurs on turfgrass soils is commonly called thatch. Because thatch is such a common component of most soil profiles under turfgrass, it will be dealt with in this section as a soil-related factor that both influences and is influenced by turfgrass management.

A. Definitions

The glossary of turfgrass terms in the Proceedings of The Third International Turfgrass Research Conference (Beard, 1980) defines thatch as a loose intermingled organic layer of dead and living shoots, stems, and roots that develops between the zone of green vegetation and the soil surface; "pseudo thatch" as the upper surface layer above a thatch that is composed of relatively undecomposed leaf remnants and clippings; and "mat" as thatch that has been intermixed with mineral matter, which is a condition commonly found on greens or other areas that have been topdressed.

In the USGA Green Section "Dictionary of Golf Turfgrass Terms" (USGA, 1977), mat is defined in a different context as: "Thickly overgrown and entangled mass of vegetation. In turf, undecomposed mass of roots and stems hidden underneath green vegetation. Associated with sponginess or fluffiness in turf." Madison (1971) defined mat as a network of interlayered living stems above the ground surface. Thus differences in usage of the term mat exist within the turfgrass industry. Differences in ways individuals perceive thatch are evidenced by definitions of the USGA (1977) and Beard (1973) that have described thatch as a tightly intermingled layer. While the tenacity with which vegetative strands are intermingled would denote a tightness, the porous and compressible nature of thatch could denote a loose arrangement or structure.

B. Thatch Development, Decomposition, and Properties

The annual addition of dry organic residues on sports turf has been estimated to be 8000 kg ha^{-1}, which includes 3500 kg of roots, 2000 kg of clippings, and 2500 kg of other vegetative parts (Riem Vis, 1981). Thatch develops when a turfgrass produces surface organic matter at a rate faster than the organic matter is decomposed. Thus, any factor that influences grass growth rate or organic matter decomposition could be a factor in thatch accumulation. These factors include the species and varieties of turfgrasses, which may vary in growth rate and composition; the presence of an adequate microbial population for decomposition; environmental factors, such as water, temperature, air, and pH, that affect organic matter decomposition; and various management practices.

Thatch is composed primarily of the plant parts that are most resistant to decay. Lederboer and Skogley (1967) reported that nodes and crown tissues were most resistant to decomposition, and that sclerified vascular strands of stems and leaf sheaths were more resistant to decomposition than clippings and sloughed leaves. They also found a higher lignin content in the more resistant plant tissue. Results of Meinhold et al. (1973) showed increased thatch accumulation in 'Tifgreen' bermudagrass [*Cynodon transvaalensis* Burtt-Davis × *C. dactylon* (L.) Pers.] with increased lignin content. Duble and Weaver (1974) found a correlation between bermudagrass thatch and lignin content of the aboveground portion of turf maintained at 25 mm, but not at 6-mm cutting height. They also reported that decomposition of leaf and stem tissue was twice as fast as that of root tissue. Murray and Juska (1977) reported that clipping return to Kentucky bluegrass (*Poa pratensis* L.) turf had an effect of increasing thatch accumulation only after the thatch thickness on the area had become 12.5 mm. With less thatch, a more favorable environment favored rapid decay and little contribution of clippings to the thatch layer. Street et al. (1980) found that decomposition of 'Kentucky-31' tall fescue (*Festuca arundinacea* Schreb.) tissue decreased as tissue content of Si increased. An effect of Si was not noted with 'Pennstar' Kentucky bluegrass tissue mixed with or layered on soil.

Thatch development is favored by low soil pH. Edmond and Coles (1958) reported that after 20 yr of treatments, 25 to 32 mm of thatch had developed when ammonium sulfate use had lowered the soil pH to near 5, while on other areas having a pH near 6 thatch did not accumulate. Potter et al. (1985) reported that after 7 yr of fertilization of Kentucky bluegrass with various rates of NH_4NO_3, thatch depths of 7 and 16 mm were associated with surface 2-cm soil pH values of 5.7 and 4.6. Kock (1978), Schmidt (1978), and Smith (1979) also reported more thatch accumulation where acidifying fertilizers had lowered the soil pH. Sartain (1985) found that the acidity promoted thatch except in the presence of Ca, applied as $Ca(OH)_2$, a result that suggests that Ca may be a major limiting factor in thatch decomposition under acidic conditions. Smiley and Craven (1978) observed more thatch where fungicides had decreased pH. Liming has been shown to slow thatch development in long-term studies (Rhode Island Agricultural Experiment Station, 1957; Engel & Alderfer, 1967; Murray & Juska, 1977). Less thatch with liming could be attributed to greater microbial activity, more earthworm activity, or both.

Significant differences in thatch accumulation have been found among Kentucky bluegrass cultivars (NE-57 Technical Research Committee, 1977; Shearman et al., 1980b, 1983). Shearman et al. (1983) reported that thatch was correlated with verdure, indicating a tendency for more thatch with more vigorous cultivars. Thatch in blends approximated the average accumulation of blend components in pure stands. The thatching potential for Kentucky bluegrass cultivars was shown to vary among locations in the northeastern USA, but on the average, 'Aquila', 'A-20', 'Nugget', 'Birka', and Pennstar were among the cultivars developing the most thatch (NE-57 Technical Research Committee, 1977). In Nebraska, Nugget and Birka also ranked high in thatch development; however, A-20, Aquila, and Pennstar were among cultivars developing lower amounts of thatch (Shearman et al., 1983). Significant differences in thatch accumulation among bermudagrass cultivars have also been reported (Dunn et al., 1980; Landry & Karnok, 1985; White & Dickens, 1984).

Pesticide use has been shown to affect thatch decomposition. Fungicides may inhibit microbial decomposition of thatch, and by controlling turfgrass diseases they may be the reason for greater production of turfgrass tissue. Smiley and Craven (1978) reported fungicidal effects that accounted for a range of Kentucky bluegrass thatch depth of 2.8 to 22 mm after 3 yr of fungicide use; however, fungicides did not significantly alter microflora in the thatch and soil (Smiley & Craven, 1979). Halisky et al. (1981) also reported more thatch accumulation in Kentucky bluegrass with the use of fungicides. Over a 5-yr period, thatch development on bentgrass was favored by fungicide applications (Goss et al., 1980). Meinhold et al. (1973) observed less bermudagrass thatch accumulation where fungicides had been used. Duble and Weaver (1974) reported that applications of the fungicides fenaminosulf {sodium [4-(dimethylamino) phenyl] diazene sulfonate} and thiram (tetramethylthiuram disulfide) decreased decomposition of bermudagrass leaf tissue, but only thiram decreased decomposition of stem tissue. In more recent reports, Smiley et al. (1985) and Smiley and Fowler (1986) stated that thatch increases due to fungicides could be attributed to a greater rate of tissue production, rather than due to a reduction in tissue decomposition.

More thatch has been found on areas where the herbicides calcium arsenate (Jansen & Turgeon, 1977; Turgeon et al., 1975) and Bandane (polychlorodicyclopentadiene isomers) (Turgeon et al., 1975) were used. Although thatch accumulation was associated with a decrease in earthworm activity, the increase in thatch was attributed primarily to a reduction in microbial activity (Cole & Turgeon, 1978). Reduced earthworm activity was also associated with greater thatch accumulation where chlorinated hydrocarbon insecticides were used (Randall et al., 1972). 'Highland' dryland bentgrass (*Agrostis castellana* Boiss. & Reuter) thatch depth, after 5 yr of preemergence herbicide use, was greater with tricalcium arsenate than bensulide [O,O-diisopropyl phosphorodithioate S-ester with N-)2-mercaptoethyl) benzenesulfonamide] use (14.4 vs. 7.6 mm), and thatch depth on untreated turf (10.9 mm) was not significantly different from either herbicide treatment (Goss et al., 1980). Turgeon et al. (1974) found less thatch with some preemergence herbicidal treatments, and suggested that a reduction in growth of grasses due to the herbicides may have counteracted tendencies for thatching due to herbicide toxicity to earthworms and other soil organisms.

Hurto et al. (1980) measured physical characteristics of Kentucky bluegrass thatch and found bulk density values in the range of 0.22 to 0.63 compared to 1.06 to 1.47 g cm^{-3} for the underlying soil. The bulk density of the thatch varied depending on the amount of soil mixed with it. Thatch had more total porosity than soil, and a greater amount of macroporosity in thatch was indicated by more water being released at high matric potentials. The porous nature of thatch was illustrated by results of Taylor and Blake (1982), who found that a 30 to 40 mm layer of Kentucky bluegrass thatch slowed initial infiltration rates but did not restrict sustained infiltration rates. Times for 20 mm of water to infiltrate sand, moist thatch on sand, and dry thatch on sand were 0.36, 4.42, and 6.34 min, respectively. Danneberger (1977) reported cation exchange capacity (CEC) values of 63 and 81 cmol$_c$ kg^{-1} on thatch of 'Penncross' creeping bentgrass (*Agrostis palustris* Huds.) and 'Merion' Kentucky bluegrass, respectively. These values were high when compared to the mineral soil, which had values of 23 to 26 cmol$_c$ kg^{-1}. Because of the low bulk density of thatch (0.26 and 0.14 g cm^{-3} for the bentgrass and bluegrass, respectively), comparisons made on a volume basis indicated that fewer exchange sites were present in a given volume of thatch than an equal volume of soil. Core cultivation, reincorporation of cores into the thatch layer, vertical mowing, and combinations of these practices alter the properties of thatch layers by decreasing organic content, increasing bulk density, and decreasing CEC, although on a volume basis, exchange sites would be increased (Danneberger & Turgeon, 1986).

C. Effects of Thatch

Detrimental effects of thatch are often emphasized; however, a thin layer of thatch may add resiliency to a playing surface, increase wear tolerance, and insulate soil from temperature extremes (Beard, 1973). A thatch layer can provide greater impact absorption on turfgrass areas (Rogers & Waddington, 1990b). Such an effect could be of importance in impact type injuries from falling to turf and also to the bounce of balls used in various sporting events. Detrimental effects of excessive thatch have been associated with delayed wetting, low water retention, temperature extremes in thatch, disease and insect problems, pesticide effectiveness, foot printing, scalping, interpretation of soil test results, fertilizer movement, and seed production. The following observations are evidence of the diverse and wide-reaching effects of thatch.

Thatch may inhibit control of preemergence herbicides (Hurto et al., 1979), fungicides (Haliskey et al., 1981), and insecticides (Niemczyk et al., 1977). Degradation of preemergence herbicides benefin (N-butyl-N-ethyl-α,α,α-trifluro-2,6-dinitro-p-toluidine) and DCPA (dimethyl tetrachloro-terephthalate) was faster in Kentucky bluegrass thatch than in soil (Hurto et al., 1979). This result suggested that more frequent applications or higher rates may be required to maintain effective levels in thatchy turf. Hurto and Turgeon (1979b) observed more injury to Kentucky bluegrass from applications of benefin, oxadiazon [2-tert-butyl-4-(2,4-dichloro-5-isopropoxyphenyl)-Δ^2-1,3,4-oxadiazolin-5-one], and prosulfalin [N-[[4-(dipropylamino)-3,5-dinitrophenyl]sulfonyl]-S,S-dimethylsulfinimine] to thatchy turf than from applications on thatch-free turf. Hurto and Turgeon (1979a) reported that paraquat (1,1'-dimethyl-4,4'-bipyridinium ion) residues in thatch inhibited the establishment of perennial ryegrass (*Lolium perenne* L.), but no inhibition occurred from glyphosate [N-(phosphono-methyl) glycine] use prior to seeding. Some insecticides are bound by thatch (Niemczyk et al., 1977; Sears & Chapman, 1982; Niemczyk & Krueger, 1982) and movement to soil-inhabiting insects may be restricted. Branham and Wehner (1985) reported that thatch not only reduced downward movement of diazinon [O,O-diethyl O-(2-isopropyl-4-methyl-6-pyrimidinyl) phosphorothiote] into the soil, but also increased its degradation, which would further decrease its effectiveness for insect control.

Initial stands of overseeded cool-season grasses on bermudagrass greens were reduced when existing thatch thickness exceeded 50 mm (Ward et al., 1974). Schmidt and Shoulders (1972) also observed that thatch contributed to poor stands on overseeded greens.

Effects of thatch on fertility were noted by Nelson et al. (1980), who found greater leaching and volatilization losses of urea-N from thatch than from soil, and by Turner et al. (1978) who reported that thatch inclusion with soil samples significantly increased the soil test levels of K. Although thatch is not generally included in soil test samples (Turner & Waddington, 1978), it has been suggested that it be included because roots do absorb nutrients from thatch as well as the underlying soil (Christians et al., 1981).

Mechanical thatch removal reduced dollar spot disease (*Sclerotinia homoeocarpa*) and affected the numbers and kinds of nematodes in Kentucky bluegrass turf (Halisky et al., 1981), and reduced winter injury on 'Meyer' zoysiagrass (*Zoysia japonica* Steud.) (Dunn et al., 1981). Early greenup of bermudagrass was associated with thinner thatch layers (Dunn et al., 1980). Canode and Law (1979) reported that when thatch was reduced by burning seed fields, increases in primary tillers and the number of large tillers of Kentucky bluegrass resulted in increased seed yields.

The hydrophobic nature of dry thatch may cause runoff and slow water entry into the soil (Edmond & Coles, 1958; Taylor & Blake, 1982); however, thatch can also absorb appreciable amounts of water and prevent movement of water from irrigation or rainfall from reaching the soil (Edmond & Coles, 1958; Zimmerman, 1973). After a heavy rainfall, Edmond and Coles (1958) measured water contents of 1.73 and 0.72 kg kg^{-1} in the top and bottom, respectively, of a 25 to 32 mm thatch layer; and water content in mineral soil beneath the thatch was less than in a thatch-free soil. Zimmerman (1973) reported that the amount of water retained in bentgrass thatch ranging from 13 to 19 mm in depth was usually equal to 50% or more of the thatch depth, and there was usually more water in the thatch on compacted than on noncompacted plots. Poorly oxidized conditions in wet thatch can adversely affect turfgrass growth and increase infection by pathogenic fungi (Thompson et al., 1983). Zimmerman (1973) also reported that the maximum-minimum temperature range in August was wider in thatch than the underlying soil due primarily to higher maximum temperatures in the thatch. The thatch and air temperature maximums for a given period were nearly equal.

D. Thatch Management

Turfgrass managers may use a variety of biological and physical (mechanical) controls to prevent or remove excess thatch accumulation (Beard, 1973). Murray and Juska (1977) did not observe significant effects from several management practices on thatch accumulation during the first 5 yr of treatments. Thus, it is not surprising that some short-term studies did not show an effect of management treatments. In studies of about 90 d duration, Ledeboer and Skogley (1967) found no evidence of an influence on thatch decay from applications of lime, fertilizer, sucrose, glucose, or topdressing. In 7 mo of treatments, bermudagrass thatch was not adequately controlled by combinations of aerification, N source, liming, or topdressing (Smith, 1979). However, in a 13-yr experiment in Rhode Island, liming and topdressing with a 1:1 mixture of sandy loam soil and coarse sand decreased thatch and sponginess in turf (Rhode Island Agricultural Experiment Station, 1957). Engel and Alderfer (1967) studied the effects of various management practices on creeping bentgrass turf over a 10-yr period. Topdressing with a sandy loam soil five times per year and groove cultivation in spring and fall gave the greatest reductions in organic matter. After 7 yr, treatments of groove cultivation, liming with ground limestone at 1.22 t ha^{-1} yr^{-1}, and topdressing had thatch depths of 6, 7, and 7 mm, respectively, compared to 9 mm on the control plot. Increasing annual N application from 292 to 439 kg ha^{-1} tended to increase thatch; however, liming and topdressing with the extra N negated this effect and also gave the best quality turf. Injury from using mechanical treatments alone decreased turf quality; however, topdressing following these treatments improved quality.

In a 3-yr study on creeping bentgrass, Eggens (1980) reported that the most effective treatments for reducing thatch were coring plus vertical mowing plus topdressing and topdressing alone. Thatch accumulation was not affected by increasing N fertilization from 200 to 400 kg of N ha^{-1} yr^{-1}; however, mowing height had an effect, with 4.5 and 10.2 mm of thatch for mowing heights of 5 and 8 mm, respectively. In contrast, Landry and Karnok (1985) measured more bermudagrass thatch at 19 mm than 31 mm mowing height after 5 yr.

Murray and Juska (1977) reported that clippings contributed to Kentucky bluegrass thatch after thatch thickness had reached 12.5 mm, except on aerated and wetting agent treatment plots. Liming reduced thatch accumulation and Milorganite fertilization increased thatch. Of mechanical treatments, aeration had the least thatch, and vertical mowing and hand raking had less than the check. Increases from 100 to 200 kg of N ha^{-1} yr^{-1} (Shearman et al., 1980b, 1983) and from 147 to 244 kg of N ha^{-1} yr^{-1} (NE-57 Technical Research Committee, 1977) did not affect thatch accumulation in Kentucky bluegrass. Researchers in Rhode Island measured 25% more Kentucky bluegrass thatch accumulation at a mowing height of 38 mm than at 19 mm after 5 yr, while clipping heights of 25 and 50 mm imposed in the last 2 yr of a 5-yr study had no effect on thatch accumulation at a Virginia location (NE-57 Technical Research Committee, 1977).

Over a 2-yr period, thatch depth of *Paspalum vaginatum* was not significantly affected by cutting heights of 13 and 32 mm or annual N fertilization rates of 98, 195, 293, and 390 kg of N ha^{-1} (Henry et al., 1979). In a 23-wk study, Meinhold et al. (1973) found 30% more bermudagrass thatch at a high N fertilization rate (25 vs. 75 kg of N ha^{-1} every 2 wk), and more thatch when $(NH_4)_2 SO_4$ rather than Milorganite was the N source, reflecting growth differences from using soluble and slow-release sources. Return of clippings increased thatch depth, but a thatch weight increase was not significant. Potassium fertilization had no effect on thatch. Smith (1979) measured less bermudagrass thatch with frequent aeration, and more thatch with $(NH_4)_2 SO_4$ than $Ca(NO_3)_2$ as the N source. A lower pH was associated with $(NH_4)_2 SO_4$ use. Edmond and Coles (1958) also reported more thatch due to low pH from $(NH_4)_2 SO_4$ use. Kock (1978) reported more thatch with eight grasses when acidifying fertilizers had decreased soil pH from 5.2 to 4.0 than when pH was increased from 5.2 to 6.0 due to fertilizers with an alkaline reaction. Schmidt (1978) observed more thatch at pH 4 than pH 5. Youngner et al. (1981) reported slightly less thatch was found on the wettest of several irrigated treatments.

Dunn et al. (1981) reported that vertical slicing reduced thatch depth of zoysia by 12 to 18% each year over a 5-yr period. Mowing at 19 mm compared to 38 mm decreased thatch 13 to 25% annually. Thatch was not affected by applications of 98 or 293 kg of N ha^{-1} yr^{-1}. Ledeboer and Skogley (1967) noted more advanced decomposition of thatch on areas where soil topdressing had been used. Cooper and Skogley (1981) reported that topdressing of bentgrass greens significantly decreased thatch and the percentage organic matter in the surface 5.1 cm. Potter et al. (1985) reported that increased N fertilization increased thatch on Kentucky bluegrass turf; also associated with increased N rates were lower soil and thatch pH values and lower earthworm numbers. Weston and Dunn (1985) measured decreases in thatch on Merion Kentucky bluegrass due to verticutting and core cultivation. A combination of these practices reduced thatch more than either one alone, and the reduction was greater on unfertilized turf than that receiving 98 or 195 kg of N ha^{-1} yr^{-1}. The work of Danneberger and Turgeon (1986) showed that soil added to thatch by cultivation practices altered thatch properties.

White and Dickens (1984) used various cultural practices on bermudagrass for three seasons, and topdressing four times per year resulted in less thatch than once per year topdressing. No difference in thatch accumulation was measured between twice yearly and monthly frequencies of either core cultivation or vertical mowing. About 3 mm more thatch accumulated with activated sewage sludge used to supply 1020 kg of N ha^{-1} yr^{-1} than with NH_4NO_3 at 580 kg of N ha^{-1} yr^{-1}. Sartain (1985) reported less thatch from the use of isobutylidene diurea (IBDU) than $(NH_4)_2 SO_4$ or activated sewage sludge. In this 5-yr study, acidic soil conditions favored thatch development except in the presence of Ca, which was added as $Ca(OH)_2$ but only in a quantity sufficient to increase the soil pH from 4.0 to 4.5 in the surface 5 cm.

Carrow et al. (1987) reported that after four seasons of treatments on 'Tifway' bermudagrass, N at 98, 196, and 296 and K at 49, 98, and 196 kg ha^{-1} yr^{-1} did not influence thatch accumulation. Core cultivation once or twice per year did not reduce thatch, but vertical mowing twice per year decreased thatch by 8%. Topdressing with sand (one or two 6.4-mm applications per year) reduced thatch by 44 to 62%.

Johnson et al. (1988) measured thatch on centipedegrass [*Eremochloa ophiuroides* (Munro) Hackel] after 4 yr of treatments. Thatch, reported as percentage organic matter in thatch plugs, increased from 17% in an unfertilized check to 20% when 100-44-83 kg of kg of N-P-K ha^{-1} yr^{-1} was applied. No further increase was noted when fertilization was doubled or when K was increased to 186 or 290 kg ha^{-1}. Vertical mowing twice per year decreased thatch by 15 to 17%. Topdressing with soil (0.65-cm depth in March) caused a 48% reduction in thatch (from 25–13% organic matter).

Gibeault et al. (1976) evaluated three biological dethatching materials and found no significant reduction in thatch with their use. Sartain and Volk (1984) studied the effect of several white-rot fungi on thatch decomposition in four turfgrass species. *Coriolus versicolor* caused the largest lignin reduction in the thatch of all species. Other effects were species dependent; for example, *Phebia giganta* significantly reduced cellulose content in thatch of bermudagrass and centipedegrass but not in that of Kentucky bluegrass or St. Augustinegrass [*Stenotaphrum secundatum* (Walter) Kuntze].

Many management decisions, including the use of pesticides as mentioned earlier, have an influence on thatch. A well-planned maintenance program should use the various practices that will maintain a balance between thatch deposition and decomposition.

E. Future Research

The development and nature of thatch and the effects of thatch have been well documented by research results. Many discrepancies occur in results from research dealing with thatch management. Depending on the study, one could conclude that factors such as N fertilization, mowing height, clipping removal, core cultivation, and topdressing will or will not have an effect on thatch accumulation or removal. No doubt the duration of experiments has contributed to such divergence in conclusions. Studies have lasted from 3 mo to 13 yr. In some cases, one may question the practical significance of statistical differences due to treatments (e.g., significant differences of 2 and 3 mm in thatch depth between treated and control plots after 7 yr as reported by Engel and Alderfer, 1967). Various species and cultivars that were used in these studies may have affected results. The result that a cultivar can be classified as a high thatch producer at one location and a low producer at another is not surprising. Cultivars as well as species vary in their adaptation, and thus in their performance, at various locations.

Certainly the discrepancies in results should not be taken to imply correctly vs. incorrectly conducted studies. However, in many cases data that might have been used to interpret differences in results among studies have not been presented. Because so many factors contribute to thatch development, extra care should be taken in future research to provide detailed information about the test site. Information other than location, soil type, and grass is needed. Previously and currently used pesticides are of concern, whether the use was experimental or part of a maintenance program. All maintenance practices should be given. The thatch present at the beginning of the experiment should be indicated. Thatch and soil pH and soil nutrient levels may have a bearing on results and should be reported. Earthworm and microorganism populations may need consideration. In reporting results, researchers should take more time to discuss reasons for agreement or disagreement with previous research, provided conditions were adequately described in the previous work.

There is a need for long-term thatch management studies on both new turf stands and on existing thatchy stands of known history. Such studies could lead to a more clear understanding of how various practices work alone and interact with other practices. Ideally, such research will be designed primarily as thatch studies, and in the case of variety evaluations, fertility studies, and other similar studies, thatch characterization will be a planned measurement throughout the study rather than an afterthought at the conclusion of the study.

In some studies, the researchers may want to control certain factors to eliminate indirect effects. For instance, Potter et al. (1985) showed that increased N fertilization increased thatch and decreased soil and thatch pH and earthworms. Since previous reports had associated more thatch with both acid soils and lower earthworm populations, it is difficult to determine whether the increase due to N resulted from greater organic matter production due to more tillers and growth, from less decomposition due to a lowering of earthworm and microbial activity caused by the low pH, or both. Thus, in future research, liming could be used to eliminate the variation in pH due to N rate and appropriate chemicals could be used to control earthworms. Then thatch differences, if any, could be compared to tiller numbers, growth rate, verdure, and other plant factors that could be affected by N rate.

Most of the research does not support the commonly perceived notion that increased N fertility increases thatch. A zero rate of N has not been commonly used in N-rate studies. In cases where it was used, N fertilization usually resulted in more thatch than when no fertilization occurred. In studies where the low rate of N was about 100 kg ha^{-1} yr^{-1}, increasing the rate by factors of two or three did not result in more thatch. If overfertilization with N increases thatch, this effect is generally not supported by published results. Thatch increases have been reported where soil pH was decreased due to various N sources.

Another area deserving more research is the methodology in measuring thatch. Perhaps this factor has also contributed to some of the discrepancies in results. Thatch depth of plugs has been measured compressed and not compressed. Thatch may be stretched when samples are pulled with pluggers, thus compression corrects for this effect. However, if loose and dense thatch are produced by treatments, the compression may adversely affect the looser thatch. Thatch has also been characterized by weighing dried thatch samples and reporting as weight per unit area and by ashing dry samples and determining loss on ignition or ash content as a percentage. Also thatch weight or loss on ignition on samples taken to a uniform depth (equal volume) has been used. Based on 192 observations for organic matter dry weight and compressed thatch thickness and 152 observations for uncompressed thatch thickness in regional Kentucky bluegrass evaluations, compressed and uncompressed thatch thicknesses were significantly correlated ($r = 0.76$) as were dry weights and compressed thatch thickness ($r = 0.73$) and dry weights and uncompressed thatch thickness ($r = 0.52$) (NE-57 Technical Research Committee, 1977). Meinhold et al. (1973) reported that clipping return increased thatch depth but not thatch weight. Thus there is not always agreement among methods of measurement. The objectives and treatments should influence the choice of measurement. Thickness or organic matter weight seems appropriate where thatch has been unaltered by soil additions. However, consider a case in which soil has been worked into a thatch layer. Thatch thickness may not significantly change as the soil fills pores in the thatch; however, loss on ignition on a weight basis decreases just by the addition of the soil. In this case, loss on ignition on a volume basis (sampled to prescribed depth) would be more appropriate. If the objectives are to alter the physical properties of the organic horizon by incorporating soil, bulk density or some measure of water or air status may be more appropriate than organic content or thickness.

In the 1960s and 1970s, several products were marketed with claims that they would enhance thatch decomposition. In recent years, products with similar claims have been introduced. Although previous products were not effective, the search for an easy cure continues and products should be tested to substantiate or refute claims. Generally these products contain various combinations of plant nutrients, easily decomposed organic materials, inoculum, enzymes, and wetting agents. If decomposition of thatch is enhanced, research should be aimed at determining whether a single component or a combination is required for such activity.

Although thatch accumulation is usually discussed in terms of contributions from turfgrass species being grown, weed species could also contribute to this organic layer. Small leaves from shrubs or trees, as well as leaves cut into small pieces by mowing, can become part of this layer. The author has noted many leaflets of a honey locust (*Gleditsia triacanthos* var. *inermis*) in the thatch of a home lawn. In this case, leaves are not routinely removed and the leaflets "disappear" into the turf. The contribution of nonturfgrass sources to thatch accumulation does not appear to have been studied; however, the potential for such additions does exist in many landscaped areas. If such contributions are found to be significant, tree and shrub leaf collection and removal from turf areas, rather than chopping with mowers, could be recommended to reduce thatch accumulation.

III. MINERAL HORIZONS

The properties of mineral soil horizons are well documented, and their effects on plant growth are similar for turfgrasses and many other plants. Physical properties influence air and water relationships, soil temperature, soil strength, and anchorage of plants. Chemical properties affect the amount and availability of essential plant nutrients in the soil. Biological properties relate to organic matter and the activities of living organisms in the soil.

A. Physical Properties

The importance of having good physical properties on turf soils has been stressed for many years. In 1932, Welton (1932) wrote that "the feel of the soil is the most accurate guide" in selecting soil for putting greens. Besides their effect on plant growth, physical properties have an important impact on the use and maintenance of turf areas. Few would dispute the opinion of Ferguson (1950) that "surface compaction and poor drainage are the two greatest hindrances that are encountered in the maintenance of proper soil-moisture and soil-air conditions." Wet soils may limit both use and maintenance of turf areas; therefore, a well-drained soil is always desirable. Hard, rigid soil affects the playing surface and, depending on the sport or activity, could affect the player directly or the play of a game, such as altering the bounce of a ball. Soil strength reflects the soil's ability to resist or endure an applied force. It is influenced by bulk density and soil water content.

Besides affecting root penetration and seedling emergence, soil strength also influences the playing surface of sports fields. A low soil strength allows deformation, whereas a high strength may be too hard. The effects of bulk density and soil-water conditions on soil strength and playability of grass sports fields have been reported by van Wijk and Beuving (1975) and van Wijk (1980a, b, c). van Wijk and Beuving (1978) reported that organic matter additions were more effective than clay additions for improving soil strength of sand fields during rainy seasons. van Wijk (1981) has discussed a model that uses bulk density, matric potential, and soil strength data to predict the duration and frequency of inadequate playing conditions on fields of various top layers and subsoils.

1. Surface Characteristics on Sports Fields

Soil physical condition, alone and in combination with the turfgrass present, affects important interactions between the ball and playing surface: bounce, rolling resistance, and friction and spin; and between the player and playing surface: friction, traction, and turf shear strength; and surface stiffness, hardness, and resilience (Bell et al., 1985; Canaway, 1985). Ball bounce is commonly reported as ball bounce resilience, which is the ratio of height of bounce to height of drop. Rolling resistance is a measure of deceleration of a rolling ball, and it is usually reported as the distance a ball rolls on a surface after rolling down a ramp. Friction between a ball and the surface can cause a spin or affect the spin imparted by a player on the ball. These properties are studied using high-speed film and by measuring the bounce distance of a spinning ball released on a surface. Bell et al. (1985) used the term *friction* in association with smooth footwear and the term *traction* was applied to studded, cleated, or spiked footwear. Shear strength has been used to describe traction measured with a studded measuring apparatus. The force required to rotate or laterally pull a test plate or sole pressed onto the surface is commonly used to indicate friction, traction, and shear strength. Bell et al. (1985) described various techniques to measure these properties associated with footing. Surface stiffness is the ratio of an applied force or load to the amount of deflection of the surface, and the resilience of a surface is a measure of the energy returned to a player after contacting a surface. Impact-absorbing characteristics of surfaces are usually determined by measuring the deceleration of a falling weight when it impacts on the surface (American Society for Testing and Materials, 1978). An accelerometer attached to the weight is used to obtain the deceleration in g's, where g = acceleration due to gravity. The maximum g (g_{max}) obtained may be reported as well as duration and other characteristics of the impact curve of g over time.

Gramckow (1968) measured impact absorption and shear resistance on turf. Impact absorption was greater on sand than clay or loam, greater on moist than dry soil, greater on Tifway bermudagrass than 'Alta' tall fescue, and greater at the highest cutting height. Sand had a lower shear resistance than clay or loam soils. Interest in surface characteristics seemed to wane for a period; however, recent research has indicated a renewed interest. The Clegg Impact Soil Tester (Lafayette Instruments Co., Lafayette, IN) (Clegg, 1978), a portable apparatus used to measure maximum, or peak, deceleration, has been used to assess the quality of playing surfaces for cricket (Lush, 1985), soccer (Holmes & Bell, 1986a), and tennis (Holmes & Bell, 1986b). The acceleration signal from the Clegg Tester has been fed into a portable vibration analyzer (Bruel & Kjaer Model 2515, Bruel & Kjaer Instruments, Inc., Marlborough, MA), which provides a display of the impact curve, averaging capability for repeated measurements, and storage of impact data (Rogers & Waddington, 1990a). Henderson et al. (1990) prepared surfaces in boxes for laboratory testing of impact properties using the ASTM (1978) F355 method. Thomas and Guerin (1981) described methods for determining resiliency (displacement of surface from a constant force) and elasticity (time for compacted area to closely return to its original state) of sports turf. Results were influenced by turf species and varieties, time of the year, and growing media. Canaway and Bell (1986) described an apparatus for measuring traction and friction on playing surfaces. Zebarth and Sheard (1985) developed methods for evaluating horse racing surfaces.

Plants in the soil affect playing surface characteristics; however, the effects have varied with different soils, species, and experimental conditions. Zebarth and Sheard (1985) reported that turf roots in a sandy loam soil increased surface hardness (impact resistance) and shear resistance. Adams et al. (1985) also found that roots increased shear resistance of a sandy root zone. Henderson et al. (1990) reported that the presence of turf decreased peak deceleration on a sand and clay, but not on a silt loam, in which a more extensive root system was noted. Gramckow (1968) found a differential effect of species on both peak deceleration and shear resistance. Rogers and Waddington (1989) reported that tall fescue turf had lower peak deceleration and higher shear resistance values than bare soil. Bell et al. (1985) reviewed results of many of the studies on playing surfaces. These studies on playing surfaces show that the importance of physical properties, soil strength in particular, goes beyond their effect on plant growth. These properties also affect the playability and safety of the surface.

2. Soil Compaction

Under many conditions, aggregation and soil permeability are improved where grasses are grown. However, intensive traffic on turfgrass areas may counteract the beneficial effect of grass. When soil structure is degraded on highly trafficked areas, compacted soil conditions result. The pore size distribution is altered under such conditions, and fewer large pores exist. Thus the air and water relationships may vary considerably depending on the severity of compaction. Some of the conditions that are often associated with compaction are hard soil, crusted soil, dry spots, standing water, shallow root systems, and the presence of tolerant plants such as knotweed (*Polygonum aviculare* L.), clover (*Trifolium repens* L.), and goosegrass

[*Eleusine indica* (L.) Gaerth.]. However, the presence of one of these conditions does not always mean that compaction is the cause.

When soils are compacted, changes in physical properties are most apparent; however, chemical and biological properties also will be influenced by the changes in the soil physical condition. When soils are compacted, bulk density, heat conductivity, mechanical impedance to roots, CO_2 levels, and usually water retention increase, while air porosity, infiltration, percolation, and oxygen diffusion decrease. Such effects on turfgrass areas have been reported by Alderfer (1951), Letey et al. (1966), Morgan et al. (1966), Waddington et al. (1974), Schmidt (1980), Carrow (1980), Kavanagh and Jelley (1981), O'Neil and Carrow (1983), and Sills and Carrow (1982, 1983). Detrimental effects of compaction on turfgrass have included reductions in top and root growth, N utilization, shoot density, verdure, percentage cover, and quality (Letey et al., 1966; Valoras et al., 1966; Thurman & Pokorny, 1969; Carrow, 1980; O'Neil & Carrow, 1982, 1983; Sills & Carrow, 1982, 1983). Harper (1953) and Flannagan and Bartlett (1961) observed more white clover on compated turf areas.

Various types of pavements have been used to protect turf growing on heavily trafficked areas, with variable effects on the maintenance of good quality turf being observed (Wood, 1973; Shearman et al., 1980a). Additional information on compaction and traffic on turfgrass areas is presented in chapter 9 in this book.

3. Soil Water, Air, and Temperature

Soil texture, structure, and organic matter largely influence the pore size distribution, which in turn influences water, air, and temperature relationships. Soil water relationships are discussed in chapter 12 in this book.

a. Soil Aeration. Soil aeration refers to the process by which soil air is replaced by atmospheric air, and may be characterized by measuring O_2 and CO_2 concentrations, gaseous diffusion rates, and air porosity. Differences in plant tolerance to limiting O_2 supply have been reported by Cannon (1925), who measured root elongation of plants grown with the roots exposed to various O_2 concentrations. He noted that species that naturally occur where the soil may be puddled or water-saturated all or part of the year exhibit a greater tolerance to O_2 deficiency, and that no species requiring a high percentage of O_2 for root growth has been found to occur in areas where the substratum is saturated part of the year. For instance, bog rush (*Juncus effusus*) and water cress (*Nasturtium officinale*) were found to be tolerant of low O_2, whereas alfalfa (*Medicago sativa* L.) was not. Russell (1973) stated that rice (*Oryza sativa* L.), buckwheat (*Fagopyrum esculentum* Moench), and some willows (*Salix* sp.) grow well when the air supply in the root zone is restricted, while tomato (*Lycopersicon esculentum* Mill.), and possibly pea (*Pisum sativum* L.) and corn (*Zea mays* L.), need a very good air supply. Edminster and Reeve (1957) reported that plants normally grown on well-drained and aerated soils usually are most sensitive to low O_2 levels, and that those plants that tolerate long periods of little O_2

have special tissues in their stems and roots which conduct O_2 to the roots. Grable (1966) concluded that the diffusion of O_2 from the tops to the roots of plants was the most likely explanation for the ability of some plants to grow in waterlogged soils. Kacperska-Palacz (1962) reported that the volume of air space within grass species differs, and a larger percentage of air space is found in grasses that naturally occur in a wet environment and in deeper-rooted grasses. Agnew and Carrow (1985a) found that the porosity within Kentucky bluegrass roots was increased when turf was grown under compacted conditions, and that plants with greater root porosities were more efficient in water uptake during periods of low soil O_2 conditions. Greater surface rooting was also associated with low soil O_2.

Grasses appear to be more tolerant of poor soil aeration than many other agronomic and horticultural crops. Finn et al. (1961) grew timothy (*Phleum pratense* L.), bromegrass (*Bromus inermis* Leyss), and reed canarygrass (*Phalaris arundinacea* L.) at several soil water contents and found them to be quite tolerant of saturated soil conditions and low O_2 diffusion rates. Tolerance of O_2 diffusion rates lower than those considered critical for many crop plants has also been shown for the emergence of bermudagrass and weeping lovegrass [*Eragrostis curvula* (Shrad.) Nees] seedlings (Hughes et al., 1966) and the growth of perennial ryegrass (Gradwell, 1965; O'Neil & Carrow, 1983) and perennial ryegrass-annual bluegrass (*Poa annua* L.) turf (van Wijk, 1980c; van Wijk et al., 1977). Waddington and Baker (1965) reported that Penncross creeping bentgrass and goosegrass were very tolerant of poor soil aeration and more tolerant than Merion Kentucky bluegrass, which tolerated lower O_2 diffusion rates than those reported as critical for 'Newport' Kentucky bluegrass (Letey et al., 1964). Under high water table conditions, annual bluegrass, Kentucky bluegrass, and creeping red fescue (*Festuca rubra* L.) developed shallower root systems than tall fescue, goosegrass, perennial ryegrass, Colonial bentgrass (*Agrostis capillaris* L.), and creeping bentgrass (Waddington & Zimmerman, 1972). Davis and Martin (1949) reported that various species of *Agrostis* were exceptionally tolerant of flooding. Colonial bentgrass grown in solution culture was found to be tolerant of low O_2 contents, and grew satisfactorily at O_2 contents as low as 1 to 2 mg kg^{-1} (Engel, 1951). These results contrast those of Gilbert and Shive (1942) who observed marked decreases in soybean [*Glycine max* (L.) Merr.] growth when the O_2 content of the solution culture was 6 mg kg^{-1}. Tomato plants and oat (*Avena sativa* L.) had a higher O_2 requirement than soybean. Kurtz and Kneebone (1980) reported that the need for adequate aeration in the root zone of bentgrass increases with temperature. Oxygen diffusion rates in soil decrease following rainfall or irrigation, and Agnew and Carrow (1985a) reported that rates fell below 0.20 g cm^{-2} min^{-1} (often considered as a critical low value for root growth) for 143 h on compacted turf, but for only 26 h on uncompacted turf. Agnew and Carrow (1985b) reported that high stomatal diffusive resistance in Kentucky bluegrass caused by low soil O_2 could likely result in greater high temperature stress to the turf under flooded conditions.

Williamson and Willey (1964) reported that without surface watering tall fescue yields were about the same for water table depths of 23 and 43 cm. When 2.5 cm of surface water per week was applied, yield with a 41-cm water table was greater than with a 20-cm water table. The difference was attributed to leaching of N from the root zone. Nitrogen application helped to mask any effects of water table depth on grass yields. Willhite et al. (1965) reported that N fertilization of timothy may have compensated for unfavorable soil aeration. Waddington and Baker (1965) suggested that liberal fertilization of bluegrass, bentgrass, and goosegrass may have accounted for similar yields and chemical compositions when these grasses were grown under various soil aeration conditions. Grable (1966) concluded that the principle requirement for high yields of grasses grown in poorly aerated soils is adequate fertilization to compensate for fewer roots, less root activity, or both.

When poor aeration is the result of soil compaction, mechanical impedance may also be a factor influencing the root growth and distribution. According to Flocker et al. (1959), the slowing of metabolic processes of plants grown in compacted soil may be attributed to one or a combination of several factors, including poor water utilization, restricted nutrient uptake, lack of oxygen, accumulation of CO_2, and mechanical impedance to root penetration.

Microbial activity is also affected by soil aeration (Alexander, 1977). Good aeration is needed for rapid microbial breakdown of organic materials and also for the conversion of NH_3 and organic forms of N to the NO_3 form. Symbiotic fixation of N by legumes is favored by good aeration. Low soil oxygen supply suppresses microbial proliferation and enhances denitrification of NO_3–N.

b. Soil Temperature. Soil temperature influences plant growth and many microbial processes in the soil, including organic matter decomposition and various N transformations. Richards et al. (1952) and Troughton (1957) have reviewed the effects of soil temperature on the growth of grasses. Troughton (1957) compiled a list of optimum temperatures for root growth for various species. Optimum temperatures or ranges reported for some of the grasses were as follows: Colonial bentgrass, 13 to 21; redtop (*Agrostis alba* L.), 30; carpetgrass (*Axonopus affinis* Chase), 27 to 32; bermudagrass, 27 to 38; ryegrass, 7 to 17; dallisgrass (*Paspalum dilatatum* Poir.), 27 to 32; timothy, 13 to 21; and Kentucky bluegrass, 13 to 23 °C. Richards et al. (1952) stated that bermudagrass appears to be favored by temperatures around 35 °C, while most cool-season grasses do well in the range of 15 to 22 °C. A temperature of 27 °C appears to be unfavorable for Kentucky bluegrass root growth. High soil temperatures favor rapid maturation and eventual root loss of cool-season grasses during the summer. Stuckey (1942) reported that after about 120 d roots of Colonial bentgrass grown at a soil temperature of 27 °C had matured and some had decayed, and at 10 °C roots were still immature when those grown at 27 °C had disintegrated. Youngner and Nudge (1976) reported a sharp decrease in Kentucky bluegrass root length with an increase in soil temperature from 18 to 27 °C. This effect was greater on clipped than unclipped grass. Clipping decreased the effects of soil temperature on top growth and nonstructural carbohydrates. Beard and Daniel (1965) grew creeping bentgrass at 16, 21, 27, and 32 °C, and measured a reduction in total root production with each increase in temperature, with greater reductions at higher temperatures; however, rate of root growth was similar except at 32 °C, where a sharp decrease was noted. Beard and Daniel (1966) reported that under irrigated conditions, soil temperature was more effective than air temperature, soil moisture, and light intensity in predicting seasonal variation in creeping bentgrass root growth. Germination, seedling growth, shoot and rhizome growth, and heat and cold tolerance of grasses are also associated with soil temperatures (Beard, 1973). Hawes and Decker (1977) reported better healing of creeping bentgrass turf at 21 and 32 °C than at 10 °C.

Soil warming has been used on turf areas to provide unfrozen turf for use in winter, to melt snow, encourage grass growth, and enhance germination (McBee et al., 1968; Daniel, 1970; Escritt, 1970; Langvad, 1970; Ledeboer et al., 1971b, c; Fisher, 1974). The use of a protective plastic cover with soil heating has enhanced germination and improved turf quality and growth in early winter (Ledeboer et al., 1971b, c). Heat can be supplied by underground pipe systems circulating water or brine, buried electrical cables, or underground forced warm air. Some studies have dealt with the power requirements, soil temperature distribution, and costs of soil warming (Janson, 1970b; Ledeboer et al., 1971a; McKiel et al., 1971; Fisher, 1974).

c. Water Repellency. Water repellency is sometimes observed on turfgrass areas. Small areas exhibiting water repellency are commonly referred to as localized dry spots. This condition has been associated with dry thatch, which is slow to rewet, and water-repellent soils. Taylor and Blake (1982) reported that the time for 2 cm of water to infiltrate into sand was increased from 0.36 min to 4.42 and 6.34 min when moist and dry thatch, respectively, were present. Water-repellent soils have been observed in various regions (DeBano & Letey, 1969). Naturally occurring repellency is often associated with sandy soils and the presence of plant residues and fungi. Schantz and Piemeisel (1917) reported that mycelia of basidiomycete fungi were associated with water-repellent soils beneath fairy rings. Wilkinson and Miler (1978) and Henry and Paul (1978) have reported on the occurrence of water repellency on sandy soils of golf greens. In both cases, thatch was readily wetted and the water repellency occurred in the soil just beneath the thatch-soil interface. Miller and Wilkinson (1977) attributed the water repellency to the coating of sand grains with fulvic acid-like materials synthesized by basidiomycete hyphae. Maintaining moist soil has been suggested as the best preventive method for dry spots, and corrective action usually involves core cultivation or spiking, application of a wetting agent, and thorough watering. The use of wetting agents improves rewetting of water-repellent soils, and increases infiltration of water into such soils but has either negligible or negative effects on wettable soil (Letey et al., 1975).

B. Chemical Properties

Soil chemical properties, along with physical and biological properties, affect the amount and availability of elements in the soil. The CEC is an expression of the total amount of exchangeable cations ($cmol_c$ kg^{-1} of soil) that a soil can hold, and its value depends on the amount and kind of clay and organic matter in the soil. Thus, soil modification on turfgrass areas often changes this property.

1. Soil reaction

Soil reaction refers to the acidity or alkalinity of soil and is expressed as a pH value. The soil pH affects soil physical properties, nutrient forms and availability, toxic substances, and microbial activity. Rieke (1970) reviewed effects of pH and factors that influence it on turfgrass areas.

Plants differ in their responses to soil acidity and alkalinity, and various authors have listed optimum pH ranges for turfgrasses (Table 10-1). Palazzo and Duell (1974) reported that growth of fine fescues (*Festuca* sp.) was inversely related to pH over a range fo 4.2 to 7.6; however, Kentucky bluegrass and perennial ryegrass growth was inhibited in the most acid soils. Musser (1948) found that low acidity and high P favored increased proportions of Kentucky bluegrass in mixed Kentucky bluegrass-bentgrass turf. When pH was increased from 4.5 to 6.5, growth of annual bluegrass

Table 10-1. Optimum soil pH ranges for turfgrasses.

Common name	Optimum pH range		
	Spurway (1941)	Musser (1962)	Beard (1973)
Annual bluegrass	6.0-7.0	5.1-7.6	5.5-6.5
Canada bluegrass	6.0-7.5	5.6-7.6	5.5-6.5
Rough bluegrass	6.0-7.0	5.8-7.6	6.0-7.0
Kentucky bluegrass	5.5-7.5	6.0-7.6	6.0-7.0
Colonial bluegrass	6.0-7.0		5.5-6.5
Creeping bentgrass	6.0-7.0		5.5-6.5
Velvet bentgrass	5.5-7.0		5.0-6.0
Bentgrass		5.4-7.6	
Redtop	5.0-6.0	5.1-7.6	5.0-6.0
Creeping fed fescue	5.5-6.5	5.4-7.6	5.5-6.5
Chewings fescue	5.5-6.5	5.4-7.6	5.5-6.5
Sheeps fescue	4.5-6.0		4.5-5.5
Tall fescue	6.5-8.0	5.4-7.6	5.5-6.5
Ryegrasses	6.0-7.0	6.5-8.1	6.0-7.0
Timothy			6.0-7.0
Bahiagrass			6.5-7.6
Bermudagrass	6.0-7.0	5.1-7.1	6.0-7.0
Carpetgrass	6.0-7.0	4.7-7.1	5.0-6.0
Centipedegrass		4.0-6.1	4.5-5.5
St. Augustinegrass		6.1-8.1	6.5-7.5
Zoysiagrass		4.6-7.6	6.0-7.0
Buffalograss	6.0-7.5	6.1-8.7	
Crested wheatgrass		6.1-8.7	
Gramagrass		6.1-8.7	

improved on a loamy sand but no effect was noted on a silt loam (Juska & Hanson, 1969), while the same pH change improved growth of Kentucky bluegrass on both soil types (Juska et al., 1965). Edmond and Coles (1958) reported more *Poa* spp. encroachment into browntop (*Agrostis capillaris* L.) and chewings fescue (*Festuca rubra* subsp. *commutata* Gaud.) turf at pH 6 than at pH 5. Differences in tolerance to soil acidity also occur among cultivars within the same species. Lundberg et al. (1977) reported differences in bermudagrass cultivars, and Murray and Foy (1978) found differences in Kentucky bluegrasses and also noted that individual plants of tall fescue cultivars showed wide differences in growth at pH 4.3. When acid soils were limed to obtain a pH range of 4.1 to 7.9, acid-tolerant cultivars of Kentucky bluegrass were also most tolerant of alkaline soil but acid-tolerant tall fescue cultivars were most sensitive to alkaline soil (Murray & Foy, 1980). Kock (1978) reported that creeping red fescue and Colonial bentgrass became more aggressive when soil pH decreased to 4, while Kentucky bluegrass and timothy were favored at pH 6. Thus soil pH can be a factor in the competitiveness and persistence of turfgrasses used alone or in mixtures.

Soil reaction also influences weed populations in turf areas. Westover (1926) reported that white clover and crabgrass (*Digitaria* sp.) were favored by liming; however, Monteith and Bengston (1939) found that liming decreased crabgrass and had no effect on white clover. Edmond and Coles (1958) reported less clover with increased soil acidity. Welton and Carroll (1941) and Turner et al. (1979) observed fewer dandelions (*Taraxacum officinale* Wiggers) at low pH values.

The effects of soil pH on various N transformations within the soil are well documented. On turfgrass areas, an added component to the typical N cycle is the release of N from slow-release N sources. Bredakis and Steckel (1963) reported that the rate of N release from ureaform and natural organic fertilizers was greater at pH 6.7 than at pH 5.5, a result that illustrates the effect of soil pH on microbial decomposition of these N sources. In contrast, Basaraba (1964) and Winsor and Long (1956) reported more N release from ureaform at acidic pH values, a result that was associated with increased solubility as pH was lowered. Release of N from isobutylidene diurea (IBDU) is independent of microbial activity and was slow under alkaline soil reactions (Lunt & Clark, 1969). Hughes (1976) reported a reduction in N release from IBDU as soil pH was increased from 5.6 to 7.7. Volk and Dudeck (1976) observed toxicity to turgrass fertilized with IBDU under alkaline soil conditions.

Liming of acid soils is beneficial to the growth of most plants. Seatz and Peterson (1964) listed benefits obtained from liming soils:

1. Increased availability of plant nutrients by chemical or biological activity. Availability of N, S, P, Ca, Mg, and Mo is increased.
2. Decreased solubility of Al and Mn, which may be toxic in acid soils.
3. Improved soil structure, especially under conditions where organic matter is important in cementation and structure stability.
4. Increased root activity and better root distribution improves plant efficiency in using available nutrients and water.

The reaction rate of lime in the field is slower than in the laboratory due to poor mixing of soil and lime in the field (Adams & Pearson, 1967; Barber, 1967). Because reaction rate is affected by the degree of mechanical mixing, reaction rates would be expected to be at a minimum when lime is surface-applied to untilled soil (Adams & Pearson, 1967).

Lime moves slowly through the soil. Brown et al. (1956) reported that 2 yr after surface applications of limestone on a fine sandy loam, the 2.2 t ha^{-1} rate had affected the pH only in the upper 25 mm of soil, the 6.7, 9.0, and 18.0 t ha^{-1} rates affected the top 51 mm, and the 35.8 t ha^{-1} rate caused an appreciable change as deep as 102 mm. Longnecker and Sprague (1940) applied 2.2 t ha^{-1} of hydrated lime and ground limestone to established sod on 12 soil types, and observed a sharp rise in pH in the upper 25 mm of all soils by the end of 6 mo. Substantial changes in pH at the 51, 76, and 102 mm depths did not occur until after 30 mo. These patterns in distribution should be taken into account when sampling for pH determination. Results such as these present a good argument for the recommendation which calls for soil testing and the thorough mixing of limestone into soil prior to turfgrass establishment. Phosphorus, which also moves slowly in the soil, should receive the same treatment. The use of core cultivation prior to liming provides a means of deeper placement of liming materials on established turfgrass areas.

Materials used to increase the soil acidity include elemental S, H_2SO_4, $Al_2(SO_4)_3$, and $FeSO_4$. These materials may be used in the improvement of alkali soils in dry regions, and in humid regions they may be used to overcome the effects of overliming or to create a soil reaction more favorable to acid-loving plants (Tisdale et al., 1985). When S is used, soil conditions must be favorable for the bacterial conversion of the S to H_2SO_4, and thorough mixing with the soil is important. The acidifying effect from 32 kg of S will neutralize about 100 kg of limestone ($CaCO_3$). When S is added to established turf stands to decrease soil pH, the greatest change occurs near the soil surface, and shallow soil sampling (to 10- or 20-mm depth) should be used to monitor pH changes (Rieke, 1970). Rieke (1970) reported injury and loss of bentgrass turf from an application of 2930 kg ha^{-1} of elemental S. Attempts to create acidic conditions in soils containing free $CaCO_3$ are largely unsuccessful. If acidic conditions are desired, calcareous sands should not be used as the growing media or for soil modification. Soil acidity is also increased by the use of acid-forming N fertilizers such as NH_4NO_3, $(NH_4)_2 SO_4$, ammonium phosphates, urea, ureaform, and certain organics (Pierre, 1928, 1934; Wolcott et al., 1965). Nitrate sources of N, such as KNO_3 and $Ca(NO_3)_2$, decrease soil acidity. The acidity or basicity of a fertilizer depends on differences in plant uptake and on biological transformations of the applied cations and anions.

2. Saline and Sodic Soils

Saline and sodic soils occur in arid and semiarid areas; however, saline soils may occur near sea water in humid areas. Saline soils contain sufficient soluble salts to impair productivity, and plant growth is affected mainly by the high osmotic pressure decreasing water availability. Sodic soils (formerly alkali soils) contain sufficient exchangeable Na to adversely affect plant growth and cause poor soil structure by deflocculating the soil. Recent concern with salt problems on turf has been attributed to urbanization of areas having saline soils and the use of salts for deicing highways (Butler et al., 1974).

Plants differ in their tolerance to salt (U.S. Salinity Laboratory Staff, 1954). Bermudagrass and birdsfoot trefoil (*Lotus corniculatus* L.) have high salt tolerance, and perennial ryegrass, tall fescue, and orchardgrass (*Dactylis glomerata* L.) are representative of plants having medium salt tolerances. White clover has a low salt tolerance. Lunt et al. (1961) investigated the tolerance of five turfgrasses to salinity. 'Seaside' creeping bentgrass and Alta tall fescue were found to be more tolerant than Highland dryland bentgrass and Kentucky bluegrass. Alkaligrass [*Puccinellia distans* (L.) Parl.] was more tolerant than these common turfgrass species. The tolerance of alkaligrass to salt has been reported by others. Harivandi et al. (1982) found 'Fults' weeping alkaligrass [*P. distans* (L.) Parl.] and 'common' Lemmon alkaligrass [*P. lemmoni* (Vasey) Scribn.] superior in performance over Kentucky bluegrass, perennial ryegrass, creeping bentgrass, and creeping red fescue. Ahti et al. (1980) reported Fults weeping alkaligrass to be highly salt tolerant, and observed a wider range of tolerance to salt among fine-leaved fescues than among Kentucky bluegrass cultivars. Hughes et al. (1975) found alkaligrass to be more salt tolerant than four other grass species. Greub et al. (1985) reported that alkaligrasses [*P. distans, P. lemmoni, P. airoides* (Nutt.) Wats. and Coult.] and alkali sacaton [*Sporobolus airoides* (Torr.) Torr.] were more salt tolerant than nine other grass species.

The salinity tolerance of seven varieties of creeping bentgrass was determined by Youngner et al. (1967) The top growth of all species decreased as salinity was increased. 'Arlington,' Seaside, 'Pennlu,' and 'Old Orchard' were most tolerant. 'Congressional' and 'Cohansey' were intermediate, and Penncross was least tolerant. Seaside showed the best survival under extreme saline conditions, and the best recovery after being removed from salt conditions. Significant differences in salt tolerance have also been reported among Kentucky bluegrasses (Horst & Taylor, 1983), bermudagrasses (Dudeck et al., 1983), and seashore paspalum (*Paspalum vaginatum* Swartz) (Dudeck & Peacock, 1985).

Lunt et al. (1964) determined the tolerance of five turfgrasses to sodic conditions. Seaside bentgrass and *P. distans* had only moderate growth reduction at exchangeable Na percentages of 26 to 28%. Alta fescue, Kentucky bluegrass, and common bermudagrass had their growth reduced by one-third to one-half in this range, but only slight growth reductions occurred with 11 or 12% exchangeable Na. More detailed discussions concerning saline and sodic conditions can be found in chapter 6.

C. Biological Properties

A wide variety of living organisms are present in both the mineral and thatch portions of soil. These organisms have essential roles in many processes, including organic matter decomposition, various N and S transformations, and pesticide degradation. Nematodes and disease-causing fungi such as *Pythium*, *Fusarium*, and *Rhizoctonia* are soil inhabitants. Earthworms are perhaps the best known of the macrofauna found in soils. Earthworms mix surface organic residues and underlying soil, and their channels improve water and air movement. Earthworm casts aid in the development of good soil structure. However, earthworm casts on close-cut turf are considered objectionable from both the aesthetic and playing viewpoints. Earthworms prefer moist, medium- to fine-textured soils with high amounts of organic matter and adequate amounts of Ca. Edmond and Coles (1958) reported few earthworms under turf in an acid soil. Associated with these conditions were more thatch development, poorer soil aggregation, higher soil bulk density, and greater soil strength (penetration resistance). Potter et al. (1985) reported an increase in soil acidity and thatch, and a decrease in earthworms with increased N fertilization.

D. Future Research

Much of the previous work dealing with soil physical properties of turf areas has been related to altering these properties by soil modification. Various physical properties have been measured in turf soils; however, additional research is needed on their physiological effects on the turfgrass plants. Possibly, critical limits could be set within the wide range of soil strength, water, air, and temperature conditions found in turf soils. Soil aeration and low O_2 effects probably have received the least attention.

Recently research has involved the relationships of soil and turf conditions to the intended use of the turf area. Impact absorption and traction of sports surfaces need to be evaluated under a range of soil textures, water contents, bulk densities, and turf stands. Standard methods need to be developed to evaluate surfaces, and, eventually, performance specifications could be set for field surfaces. Research should provide information that will lead to maintenance and construction that can be used to achieve minimum performance levels or ranges.

In some cases, correction of chemical-related problems may not be feasible. Thus, research dealing with turfgrass tolerance to adverse chemical properties should continue so that better-adapted species and cultivars can be used on areas having limitations related to soil reaction, Al and other metal toxicities, salinity, sodic conditions, or low nutrient availability. There is a need for soil test calibration research to have a better basis for soil test recommendations. Such work should include both micronutrients and macronutrients.

Little research has been done on biological properties of soils used for turfgrass. Information is needed on the effect of pesticides on earthworms, microorganisms, and other nontarget life in the soil. Considering the importance of soil organisms in N transformations, organic matter decomposition, pesticide degradation, and other processes in the soil, research in these areas could contribute significantly to both management and environmental concerns.

IV. SOIL MODIFICATION

Soil modification refers to the alteration of soil properties by the addition of soil amendments. On turfgrass areas, soil modification usually refers to the addition of physical amendments such as peat or sand; however, in a wider sense, materials such as lime and fertilizer are also amendments that modify soil properties. Soil modification is used to improve soils with inherently poor physical conditions and soils that would develop unacceptable physical conditions when compacted under normal use. Thus, soil modification is an essential practice on most golf greens, athletic fields, and other intensively used turf areas. Although modification is usually aimed at changing properties of fine- and medium-textured soils, there are situations where modification of very sandy soils is desirable.

The goals of soil modification are to improve plant-soil relationships, alter the conditions on or beneath the playing surface, and minimize soil and turf management problems. Soil modification can improve soil air and water conditions so that grass growth is favored. Improved drainage and less severely compacted soils associated with modified soils can provide areas in which standing water or saturated soils will not affect the quality of play or even cause delays or cancelations in the use or maintenance of the area. When soil physical problems limit grass growth or the area's use and maintenance, management programs must be modified to cope with or correct the soil problem.

Various organic and inorganic amendments may be used to modify soil properties. The effectiveness of these amendments depends on their individual properties, the amount added, the properties of the soil to which they are added, and the uniformity of mixing with the soil.

A. Organic Soil Amendments

Peat is the most popular organic amendment used to improve soil properties. Dyal (1960) and Bethke (1988) reported that commercial peats vary considerably in water and organic matter contents, stage of decomposition, ash content, pH, and water retention. The water and organic content of peat as purchased should be of concern to the buyer from an economic standpoint. The ash content, degree of decomposition, pH, and water retention properties influence the modification effects of peat additions. Fibrous peats in any stage of decomposition are preferred over sedimentary and woody-type peats. Lucas et al. (1965) classified peats used as soil amendments into three types: (i) moss peat, which is derived from sphagnum, hypnum, and other mosses; (ii) reed-sedge peat, which is formed from reeds, sedges, marsh grasses, cattails, and other swamp plants; and (iii) peat humus, which is peat of any source that has decomposed to a point that original plant parts are not identifiable. Peats occur in various stages of decomposition, and intergrades between peat humus and the fibrous types occur. Properties of these peats and suitability for various uses are shown in Table 10-2. Although sphagnum moss peat was rated low for turf situations by Lucas et

Table 10-2. Properties and recommended uses of different peat types (Lucas et al., 1965).

Property	Sphagnum moss peat	Hypnum moss peat	Reed sedge peat		Peat humus
			Low lime	High lime	
pH	3..0–4.0	5.0–7.0	4.0–5.0	5.1–7.5	5.0–7.5
Water-holding capacity, kg kg^{-1}†	15.0–30.0	12.0–18.0	5.0–12.0	4.0–12.0	1.5–5.0
Ash content, kg kg^{-1}†	0.01–0.05	0.04–0.10	0.05–0.15	0.05–0.18	0.10–0.50
Volume wt., g cm^{-3} (lb ft^{-3})†	0.07–0.11 (4.5–7.0)	0.08–0.16 (5.0–10.0)	0.16–0.24 (10.0–15.0)	0.16–0.29 (10.0–18.0)	0.32–0.64 (20.0–40.0)
Nitrogen, g kg^{-1}†	6–14	20–35	15–30	20–35	20–35
USE:					
Soil conditioning‡	Fair	Good	Good	Good	Good
Golf green mix (10% vol.)	Poor	Good	Good	Good	Excellent
Potting soil mix (50% vol.)	Excellent	Good	Good	Good	Fair
Adding stable organic matter‡	Poor	Fair	Good	Good	Excellent

† Calculated on oven-dry basis.   ‡ Five centimeters worked into soil.

al. (1965), Blake et al. (1981) have observed no adverse effects where it has been used. Peats can improve both fine- and coarse-textured soils (Lucas et al., 1965; Sprague & Marrero, 1931). Bethke (1988) suggested that coarse-textured peat having little evidence of decomposition be used to modify fine-textured soils, and that more decomposed peats having a fine texture be used for coarser-textured soil. Peats are normally used at rates of 5 to 20% by volume. Excessive rates may allow many physical and chemical properties of the mixture to be dominated by the organic matter. Lucas et al. (1965) listed the following benefits of peat:

1. Increased moisture holding capacity of sandy soils.
2. Increased infiltration into fine-textured soils.
3. More friable and better aerated soils.
4. Decreased bulk density and improved root penetration.
5. Increased buffer capacity of soils (increased CEC).
6. Increased microbial activity.
7. Serves as a slow-release source of plant nutrients.
8. Makes certain elements, such as Fe and N, more available.

Sawdust is another organic material that can be used to modify soils (Allison & Anderson, 1951; Anderson, 1957; Bollen & Glennie, 1961; Lunt, 1955, 1961; White et al., 1959). Some beneficial changes in soil properties that have been reported are increases in humus, CEC, aggregation, moisture-holding capacity, and air porosity. An adverse effect from sawdust use is the possibility of N and P deficiencies due to immobilization of these elements by microorganisms decomposing sawdust. Fresh sawdust from some species has been shown to decrease germination and seedling growth of turfgrasses (Waddington et al., 1967); thus, it seems advisable to use weathered or composted sawdust rather than fresh material.

In some cases, sawdust or ground bark is fortified with N and composted prior to marketing as an organic amendment. Wood products may also be treated with acid, heat, and a N source. Such was the case with a lignified redwood, which was shown to be more effective than sphagnum peat for increasing oxygen diffusion (Letey et al., 1966), water movement, and resistance to compaction in amended soils (Morgan et al., 1966). Soil salinity was greater with redwood than with peat use (Valoras et al., 1966). Micronutrient binding in metallo-organic complexes can occur during decomposition of organic matter, and Albrecht et al. (1982) suggested that such reactions were involved when foliar concentrations of Fe, Cu, and Zn decreased with time when ryegrass (*Lolium multiflorum* Lam.) was grown in aged, composted hardwood bark.

Organic materials other than peats and wood products have not been used extensively on turfgrass areas. Anderson (1950–1951) has discussed some of these materials. Sprague and Marrero (1931) observed benefits from additions of well-rotted manure and spent mushroom compost, and Richer et al. (1949) reported soil improvement from mushroom compost and cocoa shells. Davis et al. (1970) evaluated nine organic amendments, including ammoniated rice hulls, an organic compost derived from sewage sludge and other organic residues, peats, and various sawdust and bark products. Shepard (1978) included sewage sludge and stalk chops from various crops in his study of the effectiveness of organic amendments.

B. Inorganic Soil Amendments

Various inorganic materials have been evaluated as amendments for improving soil physical conditions. Most are termed "coarse" amendments and are of a size and stability that effectively increase permeability in fine- and medium-textured soils. However, some may be used to increase water retention and decrease air porosity and permeability in coarse-textured soils. For example, in the modification of a loamy fine sand, vermiculite additions increased microporosity, available water, and CEC; and colloidal phosphate additions increased microporosity and CEC while decreasing air porosity and permeability (Smalley et al., 1962; Horn, 1970). Perlite increased total porosity and water retention in sandy soils and increased infiltration in fine sand and decreased it in coarse sand (Crawley & Zabcik, 1985). Clinoptilolite zeolite, a natural silicate mineral, increased water availability, CEC, and turf quality when used to amend sand (Ferguson et al., 1986). Similar effects for various amendments were reported by Davis et al. (1970). Descriptions and research references for inorganic amendments follow:

Sand. Sand is the most commonly used coarse amendment. Quartz sand is favored due to its chemical inertness and resistance to physical weathering. Sands may come from natural deposits or from crushed rock. Ideally, sands should contain little or no soft, weathered, or weakly cemented sandstone particles, easily weathered minerals or rocks, or flat particles such as mica. Sands containing limestone may impart a soil pH higher than desired. Sands are effective for increasing air porosity and water movement, but decrease water retention in modified soils. The effectiveness of sands for soil modification depends largely on the particle size distribution of the sand. The bulk density of sands depends on the particle size distribution. Values can range from 1.45 to 1.70 g cm^{-3}, with uniformly sized sands having lower values and well-graded or multicomponent sands having higher values. (Garman, 1952; Kunze, 1956; Kunze et al., 1957; Howard, 1959; McDonald, 1962; Swartz & Kardos, 1963; Juncker & Madison, 1967; Shoop, 1967; Zimmerman, 1969, 1973; Davis et al., 1970; Bingaman & Kohnke, 1970; Paul et al., 1970; Keen, 1970; Adams et al., 1971; Ralston & Daniel, 1973; Waddington et al., 1974; Schmidt, 1980; Blake, 1980).

Calcined clay. Clay materials, such as montmorillonite and attapulgite, are heated at temperatures of about 700 °C and higher to form calcined clays. Those used for soil amendments should be hard and resistant to breakdown and screened to appropriate sizes. A fine grade has been marketed for topdressing on greens. Calcined clays have a bulk density of about 0.56 g cm^{-3}. They are effective in increasing air porosity and permeability, but have had the opposite effect when added to some sands. They are very porous and hold large quantities of water, much of which is unavailable for plant use (Montgomery, 1961; Hansen, 1962; Smalley et al., 1962; Letey et al., 1966; Morgan et al., 1966; Valoras et al., 1966; Shoop, 1967; Zimmerman, 1969, 1973; Davis et al., 1970; Horn, 1970; Paul et al., 1970; Ralston & Daniel, 1973; Waddington et al., 1974).

Diatomite. Stable, lightweight granules are produced by calcining diatomite, a hydrated silica mineral derived from the remains of diatoms. It is effective in increasing air porosity and permeability. It has a bulk density of about 0.39 g cm^{-3}, and much of the water held by this porous material is unavailable to plants (Davis et al., 1970; Ralston & Daniel, 1973).

Vermiculite. Expanded particles are formed by heating mica materials at temperatures of about 760 °C. Vermiculite is very porous, has a high water-holding capacity, and ranges in bulk density from 0.07 to 0.12 g cm^{-3}. In noncompacted fine-textured soils, it increases drainage and aeration; however, it is subject to collapse from compaction on turfgrass areas. As an amendment for coarse-textured soils, it can decrease air porosity and water movement. Some grades of unexpanded vermiculite have been beneficial in modifying sandy soils (Garman, 1952; Hagan & Stockton, 1952; Smalley et al., 1962; Davis et al., 1970; Horn, 1970; Paul et al., 1970).

Perlite. This light, expanded, porous material is produced by heating siliceous, obsidian-like volcanic rock at about 980 °C. Perlite is resistant to weathering, but the brittle particles may be broken by compaction forces. Bulk density ranges from 0.10 to 0.14 g cm^{-3}. It has not been as effective as some other coarse amendments for increasing permeability in fine-textured soils, and has decreased permeability in some sands. A fine material has increased total porosity and available water in a modified soil, while a coarser grade increased total porosity and air porosity (Hagan & Stockton, 1952;

McDonald, 1962; Shoop, 1967; Zimmerman, 1969, 1973; Davis et al., 1970; Paul et al., 1970; Waddington et al., 1974; Crawley & Zabcik, 1985).

Expanded Shale. Crystallized, expanded particles are formed by calcining shale. When screened to obtain appropriate sizes, the material has been effective for increasing air porosity and infiltration rates. The material has a bulk density of about 0.95 g cm^{-3} (Schmidt, 1980).

Pumice. Pumice is a very porous volcanic rock containing about 70% silica. As a soil amendment it has increased water retention, air porosity, and permeability. A fine grade increased available water in a fine-textured soil, while a coarse grade increased total porosity and air porosity (McDonald, 1962; Davis et al., 1970; Paul et al., 1970).

Slag. Water-quenched blast furnace slag, a by-product of the steel industry, is essentially a calcium-aluminum silicate. Water quenching the molten slag produces a porous aggregate that can be used as an amendment for increasing air porosity and water movement. The bulk density is about 0.75 g cm^{-3}. Mechanical strength may be a limitation on heavily used areas. The material is basic and acts as a liming material to increase soil pH (Shoop, 1967; Zimmerman, 1969, 1973; Waddington et al., 1974; Skirde, 1978).

Sintered Fly Ash. Fly ash is a solid waste material from coal-fired power plants. It has a texture similar to a very fine sandy loam; however, when pelletized and sintered at temperatures of 1080 to 1650 °C, it can be screened to obtain coarser particles that are suitable as a soil amendment. Sintered fly ash additions have increased infiltration rates and decreased water retention in modified soils (Patterson & Henderlong, 1970).

Clinoptilolite Zeolite. A natural silicate mineral containing about 74% SiO_2 and having a porous crystaline structure. The bulk density ranges from 0.48 to 0.85 g cm^{-3} for granules between 3 and 8 mm. When properly sized, the particles can improve drainage, as well as provide increased water and nutrient retention (Ferguson et al., 1986; Ferguson & Pepper, 1987).

C. Other Amendments

Although conventional methods of soil modification on turf areas usually involve the use of physical amendments, such as the aforementioned organic and inorganic materials, chemical and biochemical amendments are sometimes recommended for improving soil physical conditions. If such amendments should increase flocculation and water stable aggregation in soils, one must still be concerned with the compactive forces on turf areas destroying aggregation. The most positive and lasting soil modification will result from physical amendments.

Gypsum ($CaSO_4$) is commonly used for improving sodic soils. Gypsum has been reported to increase aggregation and infiltration on some nonsodic soils (Rinehart et al., 1953); however, the consensus among soil scientists seems to agree with Follett et al. (1981) who stated that this amendment will not be useful for improving poor permeability due to problems of soil texture, compaction, hardpans, claypans, or high water tables.

DeBoodt (1972) discussed modifying soils with soil-conditioning chemicals that stabilize aggregation, alter soil wetting properties, and alter soil CEC. McGuire et al. (1978) reported that the use of these chemicals [bitumenous emulsions, polyacrylamides (PAM), and polyvinyl alcohol (PVA)] on compacted sand soils did not have a beneficial effect on soil physical properties, CEC, or turfgrass growth. Bitumenous emulsions caused hydrophobic conditions, less water retention, and poorer turf quality.

Various biological and biochemical products have been suggested for improving turf soils. They may contain wetting agents, easily decomposed organic materials, and other ingredients that are claimed to activate soil microbes, increase aggregation, improve water infiltration, and improve water retention. Significant crop yield responses to such products are rarely obtained (Rauschkolb et al., 1970; Weaver et al., 1974; Kelling et al., 1983). No effect was noted on soil water retention, infiltration, or other soil properties following the addition of one biochemical additive (Rauschkolb et al., 1970). On a creeping bentgrass area, application of two soil conditioners containing ferment, surface active agents, and water did not significantly influence turf yield, soil aggregation, infiltration, or water retention (D.V. Waddington, 1972, unpublished data).

D. Effects of Soil Modification on Soil Properties

Various soil properties may be altered by the addition of soil amendments. The magnitude of change is affected by amendment and soil properties as well as the amount of amendment added. Although generalities can be made concerning the effects of amendments, it may be unwise to base specifications for soil modification on generalities. Preliminary evaluation of new materials or unusual mixtures seems appropriate before large-scale use. Methods for evaluation of mixtures have been described (Ferguson et al., 1960; USGA Green Section Staff, 1973; Elrick et al., 1981). Taylor and Blake (1981) concluded that sand content was a better measure of the physical qualities of soil mixtures in the field than were physical properties of laboratory packed samples. Correlation of infiltration rate and hydraulic conductivity of compacted samples was poor: $r = 0.41$. Waddington et al. (1974) also reported rather low correlations between laboratory percolation rates and field infiltration rates in the second through fifth year of their field study: for noncompacted treatments $r = 0.22$ to 0.45, and for compacted treatments, $r = 0.56$ to 0.71. Later in this study, correlations of hydraulic conductivity, determined on 12 sand-soil-peat mixtures that were compacted when at -4 kPa matric potential, and infiltration rates on 10-yr-old compacted and compacted plus core-aerated field plots, resulted in $r = 0.76$ for the compacted plots and $r = 0.91$ for compacted plus aerated plots (D.V. Waddington, 1979, unpublished data). Blake et al. (1981) indicated that improved laboratory tests or techniques are needed to better predict field results.

Taylor and Blake (1984) reported that sand content of soil mixtures could be predicted from the properties of the sand, soil, and peat used in the mixture. Assuming that a good quality peat is used and the sand component is entirely sand and assuming bulk density values of 1.57, 1.19, and 0.16 g cm^{-3} for sand, soil, and peat, respectively, the sand content (kg kg^{-1}) can be accurately predicted in sandy mixtures by determining the sand content in the soil. Baker (1985a) mixed a sand (93.5% > 0.125 and < 0.5 mm) with 67 soils to obtain 20% < 0.125 mm in the mixtures. Considerable variation occurred in these mixtures: hydraulic conductivity ranged from 0.28 to 12.47 cm h^{-1}; total porosity, 28.2 to 47.5%; air porosity at -4 kPa matric potential, 0 to 18.5%; and shear strength, 5.1 to 26.3 kPa. Factors such as aggregation, clay content, organic matter content, and dispersibility of clay and silt in the soil component caused these variations. Baker (1985b) stated that the acceptability of soil mixtures can be based on particle size analysis (sand, loamy sand, sandy loam, and coarser sandy clay loams and loam were acceptable unless they contained high amounts of very find sand), organic matter (2-12% by weight in soil and <4-5% in final mix), and clay dispersibility.

Spomer (1980) developed a mathematical model to predict porosity and water retention in sand-soil mixtures. The model takes into consideration that soil fills macropores in sand. As a threshold proportion of added sand is passed, air porosity is formed in the mix. A threshold level for air porosity and permeability is often noted in research where a range of amendment additions has been used. McDonald (1962), using sand to modify a clay loam soil, noted a decrease in air porosity with added sand until a level of sand of 50% by volume was added. Then an increase in air porosity was noted. In modification of a silt loam soil, little change in air porosity or infiltration rate was measured until coarse amendment volumes reached 50 to 60% (Waddington et al., 1974).

The effects of soil texture and the kind and amount of organic amendments on soil modification have been shown by Sprague and Marrero (1931) and Richards et al. (1964). Sprague and Marrero (1931) used well-rotted manure, spent mushroom soil, and cultivated, raw, and moss types of peat to modify clay loam, loam, and sandy soils. The materials were added at rates equivalent to 90 and 179 t ha^{-1} (0.5 kg kg^{-1} water content), and were mixed to a 170-mm depth. All of the organic materials increased the moisture-holding capacity of each soil. The organic additions slowed water movement in the sandy soil, except with the high application rate of moss peat, and increased water movement in the clay loam. Percolation was decreased by adding the 90 t ha^{-1} rate to the loam, but the 179 t ha^{-1} rate of raw peat and moss peat increased percolation over that obtained with untreated soil. Richards et al. (1964) modified two sandy loams and a loam with additions of 30 and 60% by volume of redwood shavings, pine shavings, and peat. Increasing the organic amendment decreased bulk density, increased hydraulic conductivity, and increased the volume of water lost over the range of 0 to -30 kPa matric potential. Richer et al. (1949) reported that increased infiltration occurred on golf greens amended with cocoa shells, mushroom soil, and peat. The effects from increasing the amounts of amendments varied with the materials. As the amount added was increased from 7 to 14 and 21% by weight, the infiltration rate increased with cocoa shells, mushroom soil, and a Florida peat, but decreased with a New Jersey peat. The New Jersey peat had a higher bulk density than the Florida peat (0.56 vs. 0.25 g cm^{-3}) and caused a higher infiltration rate than the Florida peat at each level (7, 14, and 21% by weight).

The persistence of an organic additive is also important. Sprague and Marrero (1932) found that cultivated peat persisted in the soil longer than mushroom soil and well-rotted manure. They pointed out that slowly decaying materials give longer lasting physical effects and that rapidly decaying materials are important from the standpoint of nutrient release. Richer et al. (1949) reported that cocoa shells decayed more rapidly than peat, but still maintained good physical conditions with a lower soil organic matter content. This effect was attributed to greater aggregation of silt and clay brought about by the products of decomposition. Decomposition of sawdust from softwoods (Allison & Klein, 1961) was slower than that of hardwoods (Allison & Murphy, 1962), and with some tree species, sawdust decomposed more rapidly than bark (Allison & Murphy, 1963). Decomposition of sawdust was more rapid than of peat when these materials were mixed with soil (Bollen & Lu, 1957; Hornsby & Phillips, 1965; Maas & Adamson, 1972). Lucas et al. (1965) rated peat types according to their value as sources of stable organic matter as follows: peat humus (decomposed) > reed-sedge peat > hypnum moss peat > sphagnum moss peat.

Longley (1936) reported that additions of peat to lawn soils favored grass growth, and a 50-mm layer seemed better than either a 25- or 100-mm layer. The 100-mm layer created a soft and spongy soil. DeFrance (1941) also reported that peat incorporation was advantageous for turfgrass establishment. Modification of a clay subsoil with various wood by-products did not improve seedling growth rate or establishment of 'Kentucky-31' tall fescue (Metcalf & Henderlong, 1967).

In an evaluation of various forms of organic matter for soil mixtures, eight sources were added at 10% by volume to sand and seeded to Penncross creeping bentgrass (Shepard, 1978). Organic materials included Michigan peat, sphagnum peat, ground pine bark, oak sawdust, sewage sludge, corn stalk chop, cotton stalk chop, and soybean stalk chop. After 52 wk, the following observations were made for the surface 5 cm of the mixtures. Mixes with spaghnum peat, cotton chop, soybean chop, and pine bark had higher air porosity than unmodified sand. Only pine bark increased total porosity. Bulk density was decreased by additions of all amendments except Michigan peat. All significantly increased organic matter, with highest values occurring for Michigan peat, pine bark, oak sawdust, and sewage sludge. Percolation rate was decreased by additions of Michigan peat and oak sawdust, increased by soybean chop, and unaffected by the other materials. All materials increased CEC, with the highest value being for mixtures containing pine bark.

Juncker and Madison (1967) determined the moisture characteristics of sand-peat mixes. As the peat content was increased, the mixtures had a lower bulk density, held more available water, drained more rapidly at high matric potentials, and approached wilting conditions more gradually at a low matric potential. The sand had relatively uniform pore sizes, but the peat had a wider distribution of pore sizes. Larger pores associated with the peat allowed for better drainage at high soil water matric potential, giving a lower zone of saturation. Smaller pores associated with peat accounted for the gradual changes in moisture as the wilting matric potentials were approached.

The effects of several organic and inorganic physical soil amendments were reported in a series of papers by Morgan et al. (1966), Letey et al. (1966), and Valoras et al. (1966). Unamended soil and soil amended with 30% (by volume) peat, lignified redwood, and calcined clay were used in these studies. Water infiltration rates for the soil and amended soils were in the order of soil < peat < lignified redwood = calcined clay, and compactibility was in the order of soil > peat > lignified redwood > calcined clay. Compaction decreased the infiltration into unamended soil and peat amended soil, but had no effect on the other two mixes. Oxygen diffusion rates were lowest in unamended soil, next lowest in the peat mix, and highest in the lignified redwood and calcined clay mixes.

The particle size distribution of sand has been shown to influence the effectiveness of sand, and thus the amount required for modification. Swartz and Kardos (1963) added medium sand (0.5–0.25 mm) to eight soils to obtain total sand weight percentages of 30, 50, and 70. As the sand content was increased, available water decreased and air porosity and percolation rate increased. They concluded that the total sand content of a mixture to be subjected to compaction should approach 70%. The size range of 2.0 to 0.25 mm in diameter in the mixes was the dominant fraction in controlling percolation rate. Kunze (1956) concluded that sand of a uniform size, 1.0 to 0.5 mm, appeared to be most desirable for soil modification, and Kunze et al. (1957) reported that 85 to 90% sand (1.0–0.5 mm) was needed to produce desirable air porosity and permeability levels in modified Houston Black clay soil (fine, montmorillonitic, thermic Udic Pellusterts).

Lunt (1956b) reported that a desirable sand size was 0.4 to 0.2 mm, and a sand should have about 75% in this range and not more than 6 to 10% < 0.10 mm. About 85 to 90% (vol.) of such a sand should be mixed with 5 to 7.5% each of fibrous peat and well-aggregated clay to obtain a mixture resistant to compaction. Howard (1959) found that sand with 50% of the particles between 0.50 and 0.25 mm was most desirable in sand-soil-peat mixtures ranging from 5–4–1 to 8.5–0.5–1 parts by volume. In sand-organic matter mixtures, Davis et al. (1970) obtained greatest modification with uniform sands: one having 94% of the particles between 1.0 and 0.25 mm and the other having 79% between 2.0 and 0.5 mm and 94% between 2.0 and 0.25 mm. Waddington et al. (1974) reported more effective modification with a uniform coarse sand (95% between 2.0 and 0.5 mm and 80% between 1.0 and 0.5 mm) than with a concrete or mortar sand. Keen (1970) stated that at least 85% sand by volume was required to obtain optimum modification in sand-silt loam-peat mixtures. Brown and Duble (1975) reported that an optimum mixture contained 85% sand, 5% clay, and 10% moss peat, on a volume basis. Taylor and Blake (1979) reported that at least 87% sand by weight was required to provide effective modification for turfgrass growth, while also assuring an infiltration rate of at least 2.3 cm h^{-1}. Blake (1980) suggested parameters to define the quality of sand for modification, and suggested limits for fineness modulus (an index of fineness-coarseness) of 1.7 to 2.5 and for uniformity coefficient (an index of grading) of < 4. The fineness modulus is defined as the sum of the cumulative percentages of sand retained on U.S. standard sieve numbers 4, 8, 16, 30, 50, and 100 divided by 100. The uniformity coefficient (C_u) is defined as the ratio of the particle size below which 60% of the material falls to the diameter below which 10% falls (d_{60}/d_{10}). These limits support the particle size ranges and uniformity in size recommended by others. Janson (1970a) recommended that d_{60}/d_{10} of sports field soil not exceed 10 to 15, with d_{10} between 0.2 and 0.02 mm and no material greater in diameter than about 4 mm. Adams et al. (1971) recommended that sands have 90% of their weight within the range of 0.6 to 0.1 mm and have a d_{90}/d_{10} of 1.5 to 3.5

Results of research with sand sizes are reflected in the recommendations of the USGA Green Section Staff (1974), which stated that sand between 1.0 and 0.25 mm is ideal for green mixtures, and gave an acceptable range of 1.0 to 0.1 mm, with 75% ideally being between 0.50 and 0.25 mm.

Non-uniform or well-graded sands are less effective than uniform sands for modification. Lotspeich (1964) reported that multi-component sand composed of several size fractions favors compaction, and that maximum compaction occurs when the particle sizes are such as to allow tetrahedral packing with mutual contact of all grains. Larger quantities of non-uniform sand would be required to produce a given level of modification. The influence of particle size distribution on compaction of sand-soil mixtures was shown by Bodman and Constantin (1965), who observed the greatest maximum bulk density with a mixture having a sand-silty clay soil ratio of 80:20 by weight. Lower bulk densities were obtained with lower and greater amounts of added sand. Keen (1970) reported that blowing dust adds fine soil material to the surface of modified soils, and that sand additions to such areas can prevent surface sealing by the dust and plant residues.

Uniform sands of slightly smaller particle size than specified for soil modification are suitable for soil-less turf soils composed of sand alone or sand plus organic amendment. Bingaman and Kohnke (1970) reported that fine to medium sand (0.5–0.1 mm) was a satisfactory growth media for athletic turf. Davis (1973a, b) suggested that sand for sand golf greens be at least 60% 0.5 to 0.25 mm in size, 85 to 95% in the range of 1.0 to 0.10 mm, not > 8% < 0.1 mm, and not > 10% in the 2.8 to 1.0 mm range. Daniel (1972) specified a uniform sand with most particles in the 0.5 to 0.25 mm range for Purr-Wick greens; however, finer sands can be used if the depth of the sand is increased (Daniel, 1978). Coarser materials can be used in soil-less greens if they are underlain by a plastic liner to increase water retention (Ralston & Daniel, 1973). Ralston and Daniel (1973) evaluated various root-zone materials underlined with plastic. All had infiltration rates >7 cm h^{-1} and some exceeded 150 cm h^{-1}. They reported conservation of water and infrequent irrigation requirements with a fine dune sand (97% between 0.3 and 0.15 mm), diatomite, and mixtures containing sand, calcined clay, and peat. Greater water retention and less bentgrass wilt with a finer sand was also reported by Roberts (1977). Two sands evaluated by Davis et al. (1970) showed characteristics suitable for soil-less sites. One contained 39% 0.5 to 0.25 mm and 50% 0.25 to 0.1 mm particles, and the other contained 68% 0.5 to 0.25 mm and 25% 0.25 to 0.1 mm particles.

Various experiments have been conducted to evaluate and compare the effects of different inorganic soil amendments on soil physical properties. McDonald (1962) added up to 50% by volume fine (<0.84 mm) and coarse (0.84–2.00 mm) perlite, pumice, and sand to a clay loam soil to determine their effects on physical properties. Total porosity increased with additions of fine or coarse perlite or coarse pumice. Macroporosity (air porosity) increased with additions of coarse perlite or pumice, and available water increased with fine perlite or pumice additions. Additions of both coarse and fine perlite and pumice resulted in lower values for unavailable water. In mixtures prepared as slurries, sand additions decreased total porosity. Macroporosity was decreased with 15 and 30% sand, but began to increase at the 50% level; however, even at the 50% level the macroporosity value of 7.9% was still low enough to limit percolation rates. In slurried mixtures containing perlite and pumice, only the 50% coarse perlite treatment, with a value of 0.83 cm h^{-1}, exceeded a 0.10 cm h^{-1} percolation rate. In nonslurried mixtures, percolation rates for 50% additions were 46.2, 22.8, and 66.0 cm h^{-1} for coarse perlite, pumice, and sand, respectively. The author concluded that 20% or more perlite or pumice would be needed to obtain an appreciable effect on physical properties, and that coarse amendments should be used where changes in available water are not of practical importance.

Davis et al. (1970) used nine organic and eight inorganic amendments to modify five sands. Organic amendments included peats, various sawdust and bark products, an organic compost, and rice hulls, and inorganic amendments included calcined clays, diatomite, vermiculite, perlite, pumice, and a foamed plastic synthetic peat. Amendments were added in 10% increments to obtain a range of 0 to 60% by volume. Mixes were compacted and measurements were made for infiltration rate, unavailable water, and total water and air porosity in the surface 89 mm at matric potentials from 0 to -6 kPa. The results showed that the effect of an added amendment can be affected by the amount added, the type of sand to which it was added, and the soil water matric potential at which an effect is measured. Considering the interactions which may occur in response to added amendments, one should not accept generalizations as being true in all cases. For example, with a fine sand having a relatively low infiltration rate, vermiculite additions slightly decreased infiltration rates, but on a coarse sand a sharp decrease was measured. In some cases, the effect of an amendment on air porosity varied from an increase to a decrease as soil water matric potential decreased;

however, this relationship did not occur at all levels of amendment. Additions of some amendments at 10 to 20% decreased infiltration rates, while greater additions increased rates over those of sand alone. With sands predominantely in the 0.5 to 0.1 mm size range, rice hull additions tended to have no effect or increase water retention at the highest and lowest matric potentials, but at intermediate matric potentials, rice hulls decreased water retention. The greatest decrease in water retention as matric potential decreased was at high matric potentials with rice hulls added, but with the sands alone the sharpest decrease in retention occurred as the matric potential approached -5 kPa. In general, additions of the amendments increased water retention; however, organic amendments, diatomite, and calcined clay also increased unavailable water. Vermiculite and perlite had little effect on unavailable water, as did pumice on four of the five sands. Infiltration rates were usually decreased by additions of composted fine bark, composted bark humus, uncomposted bark, organic compost, peats, synthetic peat, perlite, and vermiculite. Depending on the amount added, one processed sawdust product increased infiltration in all sands, but another decreased rates on coarser sands and increased rates when added in higher amounts to fine sands. A calcined clay increased infiltration rates in coarser sands but decreased rates in fine sands. Increases in infiltration were usually associated with increases in air porosity; however, this relationship did not exist for all amendments. Perlite caused some large increases in air porosity while decreases were occurring in infiltration rates. Similar responses occurred with some sands when processed redwood sawdust was added. Although air porosity indicated increases in large pores, the large pores apparently were separated by a finer matrix of pores that inhibited water movement through the mix.

The nonconsistent effect of four inorganic and five organic amendments on the hydraulic conductivity of three sands was illustrated by the results of Paul et al. (1970). Vermiculite was consistent among the sands in its decreasing effect on permeability as the amount added was increased. Differences in response to amendments were attributed to differences in pore geometry, which is affected by particle stability of amendments as well as the particle size distribution resulting from the mixing of sand and an amendment.

Waddington et al. (1974) reported the effects of soil modification, compaction, and aeration on soil physical properties. In a 10-yr field study, three sands, two slags, calcined clay, and perlite were used to modify a silt loam soil. A coarse sand and calcined clay were most effective in increasing air porosity and infiltration. Two slags, mortar sand, and concrete sand followed in effectiveness, and perlite was the least effective of the materials studied. At least 50 to 60% coarse amendment by volume was needed to reach the threshold point where increases in air porosity and permeability were obtained. Available water decreased as sand, slag, or calcined clay content increased. Infiltration rates decreased over the years, with the greatest decreases being observed in highly modified mixtures. For example, a compacted coarse sand-soil-peat mixture of 8-1-1 decreased from the value of 60 cm h^{-1} in the first year to 2.8 cm h^{-1} in the 10th year, while a 5-4-1 mix decreased from 19.8 to 0.8 cm h^{-1}. In the final year of the study, aeration of compacted mixes had increased the infiltration rate on the 8-1-1 mix to 22.9 cm h^{-1} and the rate on the 5-4-1 mix to 3.6 cm h^{-1}. Compaction accelerated the decrease in infiltration with time, and aeration slowed it. Additions of amendments in this study were also noted to alter the fertility status of the various mixtures. Zimmerman (1969) reported that sand addition decreased CEC and soil nutrient levels in mixtures. Perlite-amended soil mixtures tended to be higher in P and N than mixtures containing more dense amendments. Nutrient levels are on a weight basis, but mixtures were made on a volume basis. Thus, when equal amounts of different amendments were compared in a mix, perlite-containing mixtures had a greater weight percentage of soil than other mixtures due to the lower bulk density of perlite. Slag amendments caused high pH and Ca levels, reflecting the chemical nature of the materials. In coarse sand-soil-peat mixtures, increasing peat from 10 to 20% at the expense of sand decreased pH and increased soil N and CEC. Increasing peat from 10 to 20% at the expense of soil decreased pH, reduced P in mixtures containing 60 and 80% sand, and increased CEC and N in 50% sand mixtures. More differences in fertility existed in original mixtures than in field samples because field plots had been limed and fertilized. In general, field samples were more fertile than original mixtures.

Smalley et al. (1962) used vermiculite, colloidal phosphate, fired clay (calcined clay), and peat to modify a loamy fine sand. All were added at a 10% by volume rate. Also included were 5% colloidal phosphate and 20% vermiculite treatments. All materials except colloidal phosphate increased total porosity. Air porosity was increased by calcined clay and peat, but decreased by colloidal phosphate and vermiculite. Hydraulic conductivity increased with calcined clay additions and decreased with the other amendments. With this sandy soil, decreased air porosity and hydraulic conductivity from vermiculite additions improved growth and quality of the bermudagrass turf maintained under putting green conditions. Horn (1970) reported the following results after this study had been conducted for 10 yr. A 150-mm mixing depth was as good as a 300-mm depth. Vermiculite additions increased capillary porosity, available water, CEC, and turfgrass quality; and a 10% addition was equal to or better than 20%. Calcined clay increased air porosity, capillary porosity, permeability, and CEC, and decreased available water and turf quality. Colloidal phosphate increased rooting depth and weight (in upper 76 mm), capillary porosity, and CEC; and decreased air porosity and permeability. Addition of 5% was better than 10%. Peat increased capillary porosity and available water, but most had oxidized after the first year. The best mixture for the first two years was one that contained 20% vermiculite, 5% colloidal phosphate, 10% calcined clay, and 10% peat, but later in the study the same mix without peat was equal in performance.

E. Future Research

Soil modification research has documented the effectiveness of many amendments, and guidelines for amendment selection and ratios of components in a soil mixture are commonly based on research findings. Laboratory testing of mixtures is also available. Much of the research in the USA has been directed toward golf greens, while in Europe more attention has been given to soccer fields. In the USA, there is increasing interest in soil modification for athletic fields, in particular football fields, where modification is aimed at improving drainage. Sand additions can provide such drainage, but they can also affect footing or traction. This aspect should not be neglected in athletic field soil research. One approach to stabilize sandy soils with interlocking mesh elements has been evaluated at Texas A&M University (Sifers & Beard, 1988; Beard & Sifers, 1990).

Many turf soils are evaluated using various laboratory tests. Tests may be as simple as a particle size analysis or more comprehensive as with the testing to meet USGA Green Section specifications. Seldom are field data taken from areas constructed using the designated soils. Field testing over several years could be used to relate field properties with laboratory results. For example infiltration rates, air porosity, and bulk density in the field could be compared to laboratory test results. Such information would allow refinement of recommendations based on future laboratory testing.

Composted sewage sludges have been suggested as substitutes for peat in soil modification. It appears that such materials will be available for many years to come. Although their organic matter contents have been lower than those of peat, they could serve as organic matter sources in soil mixtures. Research is needed to characterize these components both physically and chemically and to determine their effectiveness and longevity as soil amendments.

Other wastes and by-products are often suggested for amending soils. These also should be thoroughly evaluated prior to general use.

V. SUMMARY

A wide range of soil conditions exists on turfgrass areas. Properties of soils on these areas are often affected by construction methods and turfgrass management practices used on the area. Coarse sand or gravel layers are used beneath topsoil mixtures to increase water retention in the mixture. Plastic liners are also used to increase water retention in sandy media. Various organic amendments (usually peat) can be used to improve physical properties of both fine- and coarse-textured soils. Because many native soils do not maintain acceptable physical properties when compacted by normal use and maintenance of turf areas, sand and other coarse amendments can be used to improve permeability of these soils. The particle size distribution of these amendments largely affects their effectiveness for soil modification. Considerable research data has helped in developing guidelines for amendment selection and soil modification.

Most soil profiles consist of a surface organic layer (thatch) and mineral soil horizons. Thatch affects many aspects of turfgrass management, and its development, nature, and control have been the subject of many research studies. The mineral horizons may be natural or "man made" due to alterations by soil modification.

Soil physical properties have an effect on the playing quality of sports turf surfaces. In recent years, interest in this subject has increased. Various methods have been developed and measurements have been made to relate turf surfaces to factors such as ball bounce, ball roll, impact absorption properties, and shear resistance. Thus, turfgrass researchers have broadened their efforts to include the effects of soil properties on the utilization of turf areas as well as their effects on turfgrass growth.

Future research should help define the effectiveness of geotextile fabrics between root zone and drainage layers, various products suggested for thatch decomposition, and sewage sludge composts as soil amendments. Discrepancies in thatch research results suggest that more detailed studies are needed in the area of thatch management. Studies dealing with the effects of soil physical conditions on turfgrass physiology are needed and many contributions can be made concerning the biological properties of turf soils. Also, laboratory testing for both physical properties and fertility should be correlated with results in the field to refine recommendations.

REFERENCES

Adams, F., and R.W. Pearson. 1967. Crop response to lime in the southern United States and Puerto Rico. p. 161-206. In R.W. Pearson and F. Adams (ed.) Soil acidity and liming. Agron. Monogr. 12. ASA, Madison, WI.

Adams, W.A., V.I. Stewart, and D.J. Thornton. 1971. The assessment of sands suitable for use in sports fields. J. Sports Turf Res. Inst. 47:77-86.

Adams, W.A., C. Tanavud, and C.T. Springsguth. 1985. Factors influencing the stability of sportsturf rootzones. p. 391-399. In F. Lemaire (ed.) Proc. 5th Int. Turfgrass Res. Conf., Avignon, France. 1-5 July. Inst. Nat. de la Recherche Agron., Paris.

Agnew, M.L., and R.N. Carrow. 1985a. Soil compaction and moisture stress preconditioning in Kentucky bluegrass. I. Soil aeration, water use, and root responses. Agron. J. 77:872-878.

Agnew, M.L., and R.N. Carrow. 1985b. Soil compaction and moisture stress preconditioning in Kentucky bluegrass. II. Stomatal resistance, leaf water potential, and canopy temperature. Agron. J. 77:878-884.

Ahti, K., A. Moustafa, and H. Kaerwer. 1980. Tolerance of turfgrass cultivars to salt. p. 165-171. In J.B. Beard (ed.) Proc. 3rd Int. Turfgrass Res. Conf., Munich, Germany. 11-13 July 1977. Int. Turfgrass Soc., and ASA, CSSA, and SSSA, Madison, WI.

Albrecht, M.L., M.E. Watson, and H.K. Tayama. 1982. Chemical characteristics of composted hardwood bark as they relate to plant nutrition. J. Am. Soc. Hortic. Sci. 107:1081-1084.

Alderfer, R.B. 1951. Compaction of turf soils—some causes and effects. USGA. J. Turf Manage. 4(2):25-28.

Alexander, M. 1977. Introduction to soil microbiology. 2nd ed. John Wiley and Sons, New York.

Allison, F.E., and M.S. Anderson. 1951. The use of sawdust for mulches and soil improvement. USDA. Cir. no. 891. U.S. Gov. Print. Office, Washington, DC.

Allison, F.E., and C.J. Klein. 1961. Comparative rates of decomposition in soil of wood and bark particles of several softwood species. Soil Sci. Soc. Am. Proc. 25:193-196.

Allison, F.E., and R.M. Murphy. 1962. Comparative rates of decomposition of wood and bark particles of several hardwood species. Soil Sci. Soc. Am. Proc. 26:463-466.

Allison, F.E., and R.M. Murphy. 1963. Comparative rates of decomposition in soil of wood and bark particles of several species of pines. Soil Sci. Soc. Am. Proc. 27:309-312.

American Society for Testing and Materials. 1978. Standard test method for shock-absorbing properties of playing surface systems and materials. ANSI-ASTM F 355-78. Annual Book of ASTM Standards. Am. Soc. for Testing and Materials, Philadelphia.

Anderson, M.S. 1950-1951. Wastes that improve soil. p. 877–882. *In* Crops in peace and war. USDA Yearbook Agric., U.S. Gov. Print. Office, Washington, DC.

Anderson, M.S. 1957. Sawdust and other natural organics for turf establishment and soil improvement. USDA-ARS 41-18.

Baker, S.W. 1982. Regional variation of design rainfall rates for slit drainage schemes in Great Britain. J. Sports Turf Res. Inst. 58:57–63.

Baker, S.W. 1985a. Topsoil quality: Relation to the performance of sand-soil mixes. p. 401–409. *In* F. Lemaire (ed.) Proc. 5th Int. Turfgrass Res. Conf., Avignon, France. 1–5 July. Inst. Natl. de la Recherche Agron., Paris.

Baker, S.W. 1985b. The selection of topsoil to be used for sand-soil rootzone mixes: A review of current procedures. J. Sports Turf Res. Inst. 61:65–70.

Barber, S.A. 1967. Liming materials and practices. p. 125–160. *In* R.W. Pearson and F. Adams (ed.) Soil acidity and liming. Agron. Monogr. 12. ASA, Madison, WI.

Basaraba, J. 1964. Mineralization of urea-formaldehyde compounds at different pH levels and temperatures. Can. J. Soil Sci. 44:131–136.

Beard, J.B. 1973. Turfgrass science and culture. Prentice-Hall. Englewood Cliffs, NJ.

Beard, J.B. (ed.) 1980. Glossary of turfgrass terms. p. 507–515. *In* J.B. Beard (ed.) Proc. 3rd Int. Turfgrass Res. Conf., Munich, Germany. 11–13 July 1977. Int. Turfgrass Soc., and ASA, CSSA, and SSSA, Madison, WI.

Beard, J.B., and W.H. Daniel. 1965. Effect of temperature and cutting on the growth of creeping bentgrass (*Agrostis palustris* Huds.) roots. Agron. J. 57:249–250.

Beard, J.B., and W.H. Daniels. 1966. Relationship of creeping bentgrass (*Agrostis palustris* Huds.) root growth to environmental factors in the field. Agron. J. 58:337–339.

Beard, J.B., and S.I. Sifers. 1990. Feasibility assessment of randomly oriented, interlocking mesh element matrices for turfed root zones. p. 154–165. *In* R.C. Schmidt et al. (ed.) Natural and artificial playing fields: Characteristics and safety features. ASTM STP 1073. Am. Soc. for Testing and Materials, Philadelphia.

Bell, M.J., S.W. Baker, and P.M. Canaway. 1985. Playing quality of sports surfaces: A review. J. Sports Turf Res. Inst. 61:26–45.

Berndt, L., and J. Vargas. 1989. Sulfur, organic matter and the black layer, Part II. Golf Course Manage. 57(6):80, 83, 84.

Berndt, L., J.M. Vargas Jr., A.R. Detweiller, P.E. Rieke, and B.E. Branham. 1987. Black layer formation in highly maintained turfgrass soils. Golf Course Manage. 55(6):106–112.

Berndt, L., J. Vargas Jr., and M. Melvin. 1989. Sulfur, organic matter and the black layer. Golf Course Manage. 57(3):44, 45, 48, 50.

Bethke, C.L. 1988. A guide to the selection of peat for use in turf. Golf Course Manage. 56(3):100, 102, 103, 106, 108, 110, 112.

Bingaman, D.E., and H. Kohnke. 1970. Evaluating sands for athletic turf. Agron. J. 62:464–467.

Blake, G.R. 1980. Proposed standards and specifications for quality of sand for sand-soil-peat mixes. p. 195–203. *In* J.B. Beard (ed.) Proc. 3rd Int. Turfgrass Res. Conf., Munich, Germany. 11–13 July 1977. Int. Turfgrass Soc., and ASA, CSSA, and SSSA, Madison, WI.

Blake, G.R., D.H. Taylor, and D.B. White. 1981. Sports-turf soils: Laboratory analysis to field installation. p. 209–216. *In* R.W. Sheard (ed.) Proc. 4th Int. Turfgrass Res. Conf., Guelph, ON, Canada. 19–23 July. Int. Turfgrass Soc., Ontario Agric. Coll., Univ. of Guelph, Guelph, ON.

Bodman, G.B., and G.K. Constantin. 1965. Influence of particle size distribution in soil compaction. Hilgardia 36:567–591.

Bollen, W.B., and D.W. Glennie. 1961. Sawdust, bark, and other wood wastes for soil conditioning and mulching. For. Prod. J. 11:38–46.

Bollen, W.B., and K.C. Lu. 1957. Effect of Douglas fir sawdust mulches and incorporations on soil microbial activities and plant growth. Soil Sci. Soc. Am. Proc. 21:35–41.

Branham, B.E., and D.J. Wehner. 1985. The fate of diazinon applied to thatched turf. Agron. J. 77:101–104.

Bredakis, E.J., and J.E. Steckel. 1963. Leachable nitrogen from soils incubated with turfgrass fertilizers. Agron. J. 55:145–147.

Brown, B.A., R.I. Munsell, R.F. Holt, and A.V. King. 1956. Soil reactions at various depths as influenced by time since application and amounts of limestone. Soil Sci. Soc. Am. Proc. 20:518–522.

Brown, K.W., and R.L. Duble. 1975. Physical characteristics of soil mixtures used for golf green construction. Agron. J. 67:647–652.

Brown, K.W., J.C. Thomas, and A. Almodares. 1980. The necessity of the two-inch sand layer in greens construction. USGA Green Sect. Rec. 18(6):1-4.

Butler, J.D., J.L. Fults, and G.D. Sanks. 1974. Review of grasses for saline and alkali areas. p. 551-556. *In* E.C. Roberts (ed.) Proc. 2nd Int. Turfgrass Res. Conf., Blacksburg, VA. 19-21 June 1973. ASA and CSSA, Madison, WI.

Canaway, P.M. 1985. Playing quality, construction and nutrition of sports turf. p. 45-56. *In* F. Lemaire (ed.) Proc. 5th Int. Turfgrass Res. Conf., Avignon, France. 1-5 July. Inst. Natl. de la Recherche Agron., Paris.

Canaway, P.M., and M.J. Bell. 1986. Technical note: An apparatus for measuring traction and friction on natural and artificial playing surfaces. J. Sports Turf Res. Inst. 62:211-214.

Cannon, W.A. 1925. Physiological features of roots, with special reference to the relation of roots to aeration of the soil. Publ. 368. Carnegie Inst. of Washington, Washington, DC.

Canode, C.L., and A.G. Law. 1979. Thatch and tiller size as affected by residue management in Kentucky bluegrass seed production. Agron. J. 71:289-291.

Carrow, R.N. 1980. Influence of soil compaction on three turfgrass species. Agron. J. 72:1038-1042.

Carrow, R.N., B.J. Johnson, and R.E. Burns. 1987. Thatch and quality of Tifway bermudagrass turf in relation to fertility and cultivation. Agron. J. 79:524-530.

Christians, N.E., K.J. Karnok, and T.J. Logan. 1981. Root activity in creeping bentgrass thatch as measured by ^{32}P and ^{33}P. Commun. Soil Sci. Plant Anal. 12:765-774.

Clegg, B. 1976. An impact testing device for in situ base course evaluation. Aust. Road Res. Board Proc. 8:1-6.

Clegg, B. 1978. An impact soil test for low cost roads. p. 58-65. *In* Proc. 2nd Conf. Road Eng. Assoc. of Asia and Australia, Manila, Philippines. October. Road Eng. Assoc. of Asia and Australia, Kuala Lumpur, Malaysia.

Cole, M.A., and A.J. Turgeon. 1978. Microbial activity in soil and litter underlying bandane- and calcium arsenate-treated turfgrass. Soil Biol. Biochem. 10:181-186.

Cooper, R.J., and C.R. Skogley. 1981. An evaluation of several top-dressing programs for *Agrostis palustris* Huds. and *Agrostis canina* L. putting green turf. p. 129-136. *In* R.W. Sheard (ed.) Proc. 4th Int. Turfgrass Res. Conf., Guelph, ON, Canada. 19-23 July. Int. Turfgrass Soc., Ontario Agric. Coll., Univ. of Guelph, Guelph, ON.

Crawley, W., and D. Zabcik. 1985. Golf green construction using perlite as an amendment. Golf Course Manage. 53(7):44-52.

Cullimore, D.R., S. Nilson, S. Taylor, and K. Nelson. 1990. Structure of a black plug layer in a turfgrass putting sand green. J. Soil Water Conserv. 45:657-659.

Daniel, W.H. 1970. Soil warming in North America. p. 235-237. *In* Proc. 1st Int. Turfgrass Res. Conf., Harrogate, England. 15-18 July 1969. Sports Turf Res. Inst., Bingley, England.

Daniel, W.H. 1972. Purr-Wick root zone system for turf. Midwest Turf News and Res. Dep. of Agronomy, Purdue Univ. 40 (revised).

Daniel, W.H. 1978. Purr-Wick root zone system for turf. Midwest Turf News and Res. Dep. of Agronomy, Purdue, Univ. 40 (5th rev.)

Daniel, W.H., and R.P. Freeborg. 1979. Turf managers' handbook. Harvest Publ. Co., Cleveland, OH.

Danneberger, T.K. 1977. Edaphic properties of thatch and thatch-like derivatives in turf. M.S. thesis. Univ. of Illinois, Urbana.

Danneberger, T.K., and A.J. Turgeon. 1986. Soil cultivation and incorporation effects on the edaphic properties of turfgrass thatch. J. Am. Soc. Hortic. Sci. 111:184-186.

Davis, A.G., and B.F. Martin. 1949. Observations on the effect of artificial flooding on certain herbage plants. J. Br. Grassl. Soc. 4:63-64.

Davis, W.B., 1973a. Sands and their place on the golf course. p. 57-63.*In* The superintendent's agronomic role: Proc. 1973 Calif. Golf Course Superintendent Inst., Pacific Grove, CA. 4-9 Mar. Univ. Extension, Univ. of California, Davis.

Davis, W.B. 1973b. Examples of real solutions—the fine sand green. p. 71-79. *In* The superintendent's agronomic role. Proc. 1973 Calif. Golf Course Superintendent Inst., Pacific Grove, CA. 4-9 Mar. Univ. Extension, Univ. of California, Davis.

Davis, W.B. 1978. Pros and cons of frequent sand topdressing. Calif. Turf. Cult. 28(4):25-29.

David, W.B. 1981. Sand green construction. Calif. Turfgrass Cult. 31(1):4-7.

Davis, W.B. 1983. Problems and solutions to maintaining sand greens and playing fields. Calif. Turf. Cult. 33(1 to 4):1-2.

Davis, W.B., D.S. Farnham, and K.D. Gowans. 1974. The sand football field. Calif. Turf. Cult. 24(3):17-20.

Davis, W.B., J.L. Paul, J.H. Madison, and L.Y. George. 1970. A guide to evaluating sands and amendments used for high trafficked turfgrass. Univ. of California Agric. Ext. AXT-n 113.

DeBano, L.F., and J. Letey (ed.). 1969. Water-repellent soils. *In* Proc. Symp. on water-repellent soils, Riverside, CA. 6-10 May 1968. Univ. of California, Riverside.

DeBoodt, M. 1972. Improvement of soil structure by chemical means. p. 43-55. *In* D. Hillel (ed.) Optimizing the soil physical environment toward greater crop yields. Academic Press, New York.

DeFrance, J.A. 1941. A comparison of grasses for athletic fields and the effect on the turf of peat incorporated with the soil. Proc. Am. Soc. Hortic. Sci. 39:433-438.

Dougrameji, J.S. 1965. Soil-water relationships in stratified sands. Ph.D. thesis. Michigan State Univ., E. Landing (Diss. Abstr. 66-371).

Duble, R.L., and R.W. Weaver. 1974. Thatch decomposition in bermudagrass turf. p. 445-451. *In* E.C. Roberts (ed.) Proc. 2nd Int. Turfgrass Res. Conf., Blacksburg, VA. 19-21 June 1973. ASA and CSSA, Madison, WI.

Dudeck, A.E., and C.H. Peacock. 1985. Effects of salinity on seashore paspalum turfgrasses. Agron. J. 77:47-50.

Dudeck, A.E., S. Singh, C.E. Giordano, T.A. Nell, and D.B. McConnell. 1983. Effects of sodium chloride on *Cynodon* turfgrasses. Agron. J. 75:927-930.

Dunn, J.H., C.J. Nelson, and J.L. Sebaugh. 1980. Characterization of thatch, rhizomes, carbohydrates, and spring deadspot in twenty cultivars of bermudagrass. J. Am. Soc. Hortic. Sci. 105:653-657.

Dunn, J.H., K.M. Sheffer, and P.M. Halisky. 1981. Thatch and quality of Meyer zoysia in relation to management. Agron. J. 73:949-952.

Dyal, R.S. 1960. Physical and chemical properties of some peats used as soil amendments. Soil Sci. Soc. Am. Proc. 24:268-271.

Edminister, T.W., and R.C. Reeve. 1957. Drainage problems and methods. p. 378-385. *In* Soil. USDA Yearbook Agric., U.S. Gov. Print. Office, Washington, DC.

Edmond, D.B., and S.T.J. Coles. 1958. Some long-term effects of fertilizers on a mown turf of browntop and Chewings fescue. N.Z. J. Agric. Res. 1:665-674.

Eggens, J.L. 1980. Thatch control on creeping bentgrass turf. Can. J. Plant Sci. 60:1209-1213.

Elrick, D.E., R.W. Sheard, and N. Baumgartner. 1981. A simple procedure for determining the hydraulic conductivity and water retention of putting green soil mixtures. p. 189-200. *In* R.W. Sheard (ed.) Proc. 4th Int. Turfgrass Res. Conf., Guelph, ON, Canada. 19-23 July. Int. Turfgrass Soc., Ontario Agric. Coll., Univ. of Guelph, Guelph, ON.

Engel, R.E. 1951. Studies of turf cultivation and related subjects. Ph.D. thesis. Rutgers Univ., New Brunswick, NJ.

Engel, R.E., and R.B. Alderfer. 1967. The effect of cultivations, lime, nitrogen and wetting agent on thatch development in 1/4-inch bentgrass turf over a 10-year period. New Jersey Agric. Exp. Stn. Bull. 818:32-45.

Escritt, J.R. 1970. Soil warming in the United Kingdom. p. 241-242. *In* Proc. 1st Int. Turfgrass Res. Conf., Harrogate, England. 15-18 July 1969. Sports Turf Res. Inst., Bingley, England.

Ferguson, G.A., and I.L. Pepper. 1987. Ammonium retention in sand amended with clinoptilolite. Soil Sci. Soc. Am. J. 51:231-234.

Ferguson, G.A., I.L. Pepper, and W.R. Kneebone. 1986. Growth of creeping bentgrass on a new medium for turfgrass growth: Clinoptilolite zeolite-amended soils. Agron. J. 78:1095-1098.

Ferguson, M.H. 1950. Soil water and soil air: Their relationship to turf production. USGA J. Turf Manage. 3(3):35-36.

Ferguson, M.H., L. Howard, and M.E. Bloodworth. 1960. Laboratory methods for evaluation of putting green soil mixtures. USGA. J. Turf Manage. 13(5):30-32.

Finn, B.J., S.J. Bourget, K.F. Neilsen, and B.K. Dow. 1961. Effects of different soil moisture tensions on grass and legume species. Can. J. Soil Sci. 41:16-23.

Fisher, G.G. 1974. Heating turf by underground warm air. p. 215-220. *In* E.C. Roberts (ed.) Proc. 2nd Int. Turfgrass Res. Conf., Blacksburg, VA. 19-21 June 1973. ASA and CSSA, Madison, WI.

Fisher, G.G., and A.N. Ede. 1974. Vertical band soil additive methods for established turf. p. 281-286. *In* E.C. Roberts (ed.) Proc. 2nd Int. Turfgrass Res. Conf., Blacksburg, VA. 19-21 June 1973. ASA and CSSA, Madison, WI.

Flannagan, T.R., and R.J. Bartlett. 1961. Soil compaction associated with alternating green and brown stripes on turf. Agron. J. 53:404-405.

Flocker, W.J., J.A. Vomocil, and F.D. Howard. 1959. Some growth responses of tomatoes to soil compaction. Soil Sci. Soc. Am. Proc. 23:188–191.

Follet, R.H., L.S. Murphy, and R.L. Donahue. 1981. Fertilizers and soil amendments. Prentice-Hall, Englewood Cliffs, NJ.

Garman, W.L. 1952. The permeability of various grades of sand and peat and mixtures of these with soil and vermiculite. USGA. J. Turf Manage. 6(1):27–28.

Gibeault, V.A., R. Baldwin, J. Bivins, and D. Hanson. 1976. Evaluation of biological dethatching materials. Calif. Turf. Cult. 26(4):29–30.

Gilbert, S.G., and J.W. Shive. 1942. The significance of oxygen in nutrient substrates for plants: I. The oxygen requirement. Soil Sci. 53:143–152.

Goss, R.L., T.W. Cook, S.E. Brauen, and S.P. Orton. 1980. Effects of repeated applications of bensulide and tricalcium arsenate on the control of annual bluegrass and on quality of Highland Colonial bentgrass putting green turf. p. 247–255. In J.B. Beard (ed.) Proc. 3rd Int. Turfgrass Res. Conf., Munich, Germany. 11–13 July 1977. Int. Turfgrass Soc., and ASA, CSSA, and SSSA, Madison, WI.

Grable, A.R. 1966. Soil aeration and plant growth. Adv. Agron. 18:57–106.

Gradwell, M.W. 1965. Soil physical conditions of winter and the growth of ryegrass plants. I. Effects of compaction and puddling. N.Z. J. Agric. Res. 8:238–269.

Gramckow, J. 1968. Athletic field quality studies. Cal-Turf, Camarillo, CA.

Greub, L.J., P.N. Drolsom, and D.A. Rohweder. 1985. Salt tolerance of grasses and legumes for roadside use. Agron. J. 77:76–80.

Hagan, R.M., and J.R. Stockton. 1952. Effect of porous soil amendments on water retention characteristics of soils. USGA. J. Turf Manage. 6(1):29–31.

Hall, J.R., III. 1978. Avoid the temptation of sand topdressing. p. 9–10. In Tech turf topics (August). VPI and SU, Blacksburg, VA.

Hall, J.R., III. 1989. An agronomic perspective on black layer. Park/Grounds Manage. 42(3):20–22.

Halisky, P.M., R.F. Myers, and R.E. Wagner. 1981. Relationship of thatch to nematodes, dollar spot and fungicides in Kentucky bluegrass turf. p. 415–420. In R.W. Sheard (ed.) Proc. 4th Int. Turfgrass Res. Conf., Guelph, ON, Canada. 19–23 July. Int. Turfgrass Soc., Ontario Agric. Coll., Univ. of Guleph, Guelph, ON.

Hansen, M.C. 1962. Physical properties of calcined clays and their utilization for rootzones. M.S. thesis. Purdue Univ., W. Lafayette, IN.

Harivandi, M.A., J.D. Butler, and P.M. Soltanpour. 1982. Salt influence on germination and seedling survival of six cool season turfgrass species. Commun. Soil Sci. Plant Anal. 13:519–529.

Harper, J.C., II. 1953. Irrigation, compaction, and aeration of fairway turf. USGA J. Turf Manage. 6(4):27–31.

Hawes, D.T., and A.M. Decker. 1977. Healing potential of creeping bentgrass as affected by nitrogen and soil temperature. Agron. J. 69:212–214.

Henderson, R.L., D.V. Waddington, and C.A. Morehouse. 1990. Laboratory measurements of impact absorption on turfgrass and soil surfaces. p. 127–135. In R.C. Schmidt et al. (ed.) Natural and artificial playing fields: Characteristics and safety features. ASTM STP 1073. Am. Soc. for Testing and Materials, Philadelphia.

Henry, J.M., V.A. Gibeault, V.B. Youngner, and S. Spaulding. 1979. Paspalum vaginatum 'Adalayd' and 'Futurf,' Calif. Turf. Cult. 29(2):9–12.

Henry, J.M., and J.L. Paul. 1978. Hydrophobic soils on putting greens. Calif. Turf. Cult. 28(2):9–11.

Hodges, C.F. 1987a. Blue-gree algae and black layer. Landscape Manage. 26(10):38, 42, 44.

Hodges, C.F. 1987b. Blue-green algae and black layer. Landscape Manage. 26(11):30–31.

Hodges, C.F. 1989. Another look at black layer. Golf Course Manage. 57(3):54, 56, 58.

Holmes, G., and M.J. Bell. 1986a. A pilot study of the playing quality of football pitches. J. Sports Turf Res. Inst. 62:74–91.

Holmes, G., and M.J. Bell. 1986b. Technical note: Playing surface hardness and tennis ball rebound resilience. J. Sports Turf Res. Inst. 62:207–210.

Horn, G.C. 1970. Modification of sandy soils. p. 151–158. In Proc. 1st Int. Turfgrass Res. Conf., Harrogate, England. 15–18 July 1969. Sports Turf Res. Inst., Bingley, England.

Hornsby, A.G., and R.E. Phillips. 1965. Comparative effects of undecomposed wood residues and peat moss on growth of sudan grass. Arkansas Agric. Exp. Stn. Bull. 696.

Howard, H.L. 1959. The response of some putting-green soil mixtures to compaction. M.S. thesis. Texas A&M Univ., College Station.

Horst, G.L., and R.M. Taylor. 1983. Germination and initial growth of Kentucky bluegrass in soluble salts. Agron. J. 75:679-681.

Hughes, T.D. 1976. Nitrogen release from isobutylidene diurea: Soil pH and fertilizer size effects. Agron. J. 68:103-106.

Hughes, T.D., J.D. Butler, and G.D. Sanks. 1975. Salt tolerance and suitability of various grasses for saline roadsides. J. Environ. Qual. 4:65-68.

Hughes, T.D., J.F. Stone, W.W. Huffine, and J.R. Gingrich. 1966. Effect of soil bulk density and soil water pressure on emergence of grass seedlings. Agron. J. 58:549-553.

Hurto, K.A., and A.J. Turgeon. 1979a. Effect of thatch on residual activity of nonselective herbicides used in turfgrass renovation. Agron. J. 71:66-71.

Hurto, K.A., and A.J. Turgeon. 1979b. Influence of thatch on preemergence herbicide activity in Kentucky bluegrass (*Poa pratensis*) turf. Weed Sci. 27:141-146.

Hurto, K.A., A.J. Turgeon, and M.A. Cole. 1979. Degradation of benefin and DCPA in thatch and soil from a Kentucky bluegrass (*Poa pratensis)* turf. Weed Sci. 27:154-157.

Hurto, K.A., A.J. Turgeon, and L.A. Spomer. 1980. Physical characteristics of thatch as a turfgrass growing medium. Agron. J. 72:165-167.

Jansen, I.J., and A.J. Turgeon. 1977. Indirect effects of thatch-inducing herbicide on soil physical properties under turf. Agron. J. 69:67-70.

Janson, L.-E. 1970a. Adequate soil type for sport turfgrasses. p. 142-148. *In* Proc. 1st Int. Turfgrass Res. Conf., Harrogate, England. 15-18 July 1969. Sports Turf Res. Inst., Bingley, England.

Janson, L.-E. 1970b. Theoretical investigation of artificial heating of the topsoil. p. 243-251. *In* Proc. 1st Int. Turfgrass Res. Conf., Harrogate, England. 15-18 July 1969. Sports Turf Res. Inst., Bingley, England.

Jenny, H. 1980. The soil resource: Origin and behavior. Springer-Verlag New York, New York.

Johnson, B.J., R.N. Carrow, and R.E. Burns. 1988. Centipedegrass decline and recovery as affected by fertilizer and cultural treatments. Agron. J. 80:479-486.

Juncker, P.H., and J.J. Madison. 1967. Soil moisture characteristics of sand-peat mixes. Soil Sci. Soc. Am. Proc. 31:5-8.

Juska, F.V., and A.A. Hanson. 1969. Nutritional requirements of *Poa annua* L. Agron. J. 61:466-468.

Juska, F.V., A.A. Hanson, and C.J. Erickson. 1965. Effects of phosphorus and other treatments on the development of red fescue, Merion, and common Kentucky bluegrass. Agron. J. 57:75-78.

Kacperska-Palacz, A. 1962. (The aeration system in some grasses appearing chiefly on lowland meadows.) (In Polish.) Rocz. Nauk Roln. Ser. F 75(2):295-318.

Kavanagh, T., and R.M. Jelley. 1981. Soil atmoshpere studies in relation to compaction. p. 181-188. *In* R.W. Sheard (ed.) Proc. 4th Int. Turfgrass Res. Conf., Guelph, ON., Canada. 19-23 July. Int. Turfgrass Soc., Ontario Agric. Coll., Univ. of Guelph, Guelph, ON.

Keen, R.A. 1970. Soil modification for traffic tolerance. p. 159-160. *In* Proc. 1st Int. Turfgrass Res. Conf., Harrogate England. 15-18 July 1969. Sports Turf Res. Inst., Bingley, England.

Kelling, K.A., R.G. Hoeft, R.D. Voss, and J.B. Jones, Jr. 1983. Soil additives. Where do we stand? Solutions: J. Fluid Fert. Ind. 27(4):14, 19, 20, 22-24, 26.

Kock, L. 1978. Thatch accumulation by species and cultivars as a result of the application of alkaline and acid fertilizers under Alpine conditions of Rinn. (In German). Z. Vegetationstechnik 1:62-64.

Kunze, R.J. 1956. The effects of compaction of different golf green soil mixtures on plant growth. M.S. thesis. Texas A&M Univ., College Station.

Kunze, R.J., M.H. Ferguson, and J.B. Page. 1957. The effects of compaction on golf green mixtures. USGA J. Turf Manage. 10(6):24-27.

Kurtz, K.W., and W.R. Kneebone. 1980. Influence of aeration and genotype upon root growth of creeping bentgrass at supra-optimal temperatures. p. 145-148. *In* J.B. Beard (ed.) Proc. 3rd Int. Turfgrass Res. Conf., Munich, Germany. 11-13 July 1977. Int. Turfgrass Soc., and ASA, CSSA, and SSSA, Madison, WI.

Landry, G.W., and K.J. Karnok. 1985. Turf quality, spring greenup and thatch accumulation of several improved bermudagrasses. p. 299-305. *In* F. Lemaire (ed.) Proc. 5th Int. Turfgrass Res. Conf., Avignon, France. 1-5 July. Inst. Natl. de la Recherche Agron., Paris.

Langvad, B. 1970. Soil heating under sports turf in Sweden. p. 252-257. *In* Proc. 1st Int. Turfgrass Res. Conf., Harrogate, England. 15-18 July 1969. Sports Turf Res. Inst., Bingley, England.

Ledeboer, F.B., C.G. McKiel, and C.R. Skogley. 1971a. Soil heating studies with cool season turfgrasses. I. Effects of watt density, protective covers, and ambient environment on soil temperature distribution. Agron. J. 63:677–680.

Ledeboer, F.B., and C.R. Skogley. 1967. Investigations into the nature of thatch and methods for its decomposition. Agron. J. 59:320–323.

Ledeboer, F.B., C.R. Skogley, and C.G. McKiel. 1971b. Soil heating studies with cool season turfgrasses. II. Effects of N fertilization and protective covers on performance and chlorophyll content. Agron. J. 63:680–685.

Ledeboer, F.B., C.R. Skogley, and C.G. McKiel. 1971c. Soil heating studies with cool season turfgrasses. III. Methods for the establishment of turf with seed and sod during the winter. Agron. J. 63:686–689.

Letey, J., W.C. Morgan, S.J. Richards, and N. Valoras. 1966. Physical soil amendments, soil compaction, irrigation, and wetting agents in turfgrass-management: III. Effects on oxygen diffusion rate and root growth. Agron. J. 58:531–535.

Letey, J., J.F. Osborn, and N. Valoras. 1975. Soil water repellency and the use of nonionic surfactants. Contribution no. 154, California Water Resources Center, Univ. of California, Davis.

Letey, J., L.H. Stolzy, O.R. Lunt, and V.B. Youngner. 1964. Growth and nutrient uptake of Newport bluegrass as affected by soil oxygen. Plant Soil 20:143–148.

Lindenbach, S.K., and D.R. Cullimore. 1989. Preliminary *in vitro* observations on the bacteriology of the black plug layer phenomenon associated with the biofouling of golf greens. J. Appl. Bacteriol. 67:11–17.

Longley, L.E. 1936. Influence on grass growth of various proportions of peat in lawn soils. Proc. Am. Soc. Hortic. Sci. 34:649–652.

Longnecker, T.C., and H.B. Sprague. 1940. Rate of penetration of lime in soils under permanent grass. Soil Sci. 50:277–288.

Lotspeich, F.B. 1964. Strength and bulk density of compacted mixtures of kaolinite and glass beads. Soil Sci. Soc. Am. Proc. 28:737–740.

Lucas, R.E., P.E. Rieke, and R.S. Farnham. 1965. Peats for soil improvement and soil mixes. Michigan State Univ. Ext. Bull. 516.

Lundberg, P.E., O.L. Bennett, and E.L. Mathias. 1977. Tolerance of bermudagrass selections to acidity. I. Effects of lime on plant growth and mine spoil material. Agron. J. 69:913–916.

Lunt, H.A. 1955. The use of woodchips and other wood fragments as soil amendments. Connecticut Agric. Exp. Stn. Bull. 593.

Lunt, H.A. 1961. Improving nursery soil by addition of organic matter. Connecticut Agric. Exp. Stn. Circ. 219.

Lunt, O.R. 1956a. A method of minimizing compaction in putting greens. S. Calif. Turf. Cult. 6(3):1–4.

Lunt, O.R. 1956b. Minimizing compaction in putting greens. USGA J. Turf Manage. 9(5):25–30.

Lunt, O.R. 1961. Soil mixes and turfgrass management. S. Calif. Turf. Cult. 2(3):23–24.

Lunt, O.R., and S.B. Clark. 1969. Properties and value of 1,1-diureido isobutane (IBDU) as a long-lasting nitrogen fertilizer. J. Agric. Food Chem. 17:1269–1271.

Lunt, O.R., C. Kaempffe, and V.B. Youngner. 1964. Tolerance of five turfgrass species to soil alkali. Agron. J. 56:481–483.

Lunt, O.R., V.B. Youngner, and J.J. Oertli. 1961. Salinity tolerance of five turfgrass varieties. Agron. J. 53:247–249.

Lush, W.M. 1985. Objective assessment of turf cricket pitches using an impact hammer. J. Sports Turf Res. Inst. 61:71–79.

Maas, E.F., and R.M. Adamson. 1972. Resistance of sawdusts, peats, and bark to decomposition in the presence of soil and nutrient solution. Soil Sci. Soc. Am. Proc. 36:769–772.

Madison, J.H. 1971. Practical turfgrass management. Van Nostrand Reinhold Co., New York.

Madison, J.H., I.L. Paul, and W.B. Davis. 1974. Alternative method of greens management. p. 431–437. *In* E.C. Roberts (ed.) Proc. 2nd Int. Turfgrass Res. Conf., Blacksburg, VA. 19–21 June 1973. ASA and CSSA, Madison, WI.

McBee, G.G., W.E. McCune, and K.R. Beerwinkle. 1968. Effect of soil heating on winter growth and appearance of bermudagrass and St. Augustinegrass. Agron. J. 60:228–231.

McDonald, D.C. 1962. The effects of additions of pumice and expanded perlite on the physical properties of Taita clay loam soil. N.Z. J. Sci. 5:279–294.

McGuire, E., R.M. Carrow, and J. Troll. 1978. Chemical soil conditioner effects on sand soils and turfgrass growth. Agron. J. 70:317–321.

McKiel, C.G., F.B. Ledeboer, and C.R. Skogley. 1971. Soil heating studies with cool season turfgrasses. IV. Energy requirements for electric soil heating. Agron. J. 63:689-691.

Meinhold, V.H., R.L. Duble, R.W. Weaver, and E.C. Holt. 1973. Thatch accumulation in bermudagrass turf in relation to management. Agron. J. 65:833-835.

Metcalf, J.I., and P.R. Henderlong. 1967. Establishment and seedling growth of Kentucky 31 tall fescue on an exposed clay subsoil as influenced by fertilizers and wood by-products. Proc. West Va. Acad. Sci. 39:146-151.

Miller, D.E. 1964. Estimating moisture retained by layered soils. J. Soil Water Conserv. 19:235-237.

Miller, D.E. 1969. Flow and retention of water in layered soils. USDA-ARS Conserv. Res. Rep. 13. U.S. Gov. Print. Office, Washington, DC.

Miller, D.E., and W.C. Bunger. 1963. Moisture retention by soil with coarse layers in the profile. Soil Sci. Soc. Am. Proc. 27:586-589.

Miller, R.H., and J.F. Wilkinson. 1977. Nature of the organic coating on sand grains of nonwettable golf greens. Soil Sci. Soc. Am. J. 41:1203-1204.

Monteith, J., and J.W. Bengtson. 1939. Experiments with fertilizers on bluegrass turf. Turf Cult. 1:153-191.

Montgomery, R.H. 1961. The evaluation of calcined clay aggregates for putting green rootzones. M.S. thesis. Purdue Univ., W. Lafayette, IN.

Moreland, J. 1981. Drainage design to handle intensive football field use. Weeds, Trees, Turf 20(4):46, 48, 50.

Morgan, W.C., J. Letey, S.J. Richards, and N. Valoras. 1966. Physical soil amendments, soil compaction, irrigation, and wetting agents in turfgrass management. I. Effects of compactability, water infiltration rates, evapotranspiration, and number of irrigations. Agron. J. 58:525-528.

Murray, J.J., and C.D. Foy. 1978. Differential tolerances of turfgrass cultivars to an acid soil high in exchangeable aluminum. Agron. J. 70:769-774.

Murray, J.J., and C.D. Foy. 1980. Lime responses of Kentucky bluegrass and tall fescue cultivars on an acid, aluminum toxic soil. p. 175-183. In J.B. Beard (ed.) Proc. 3rd Int. Turfgrass Res. Conf., Munich, Germany. 11-13 July 1977. Int. Turfgrass Soc., and ASA, CSSA, and SSSA, Madison, WI.

Murray, J.J., and F.V. Juska. 1977. Effect of management practices on thatch accumulation, turf quality, and leaf spot damage in common Kentucky bluegrass. Agron. J. 69:365-369.

Musser, H.B. 1948. Effects of soil acidity and available phosphorus on population changes in mixed Kentucky bluegrass-bent turf. J. Am. Soc. Agron. 40:614-620.

Musser, H.B. 1962. Turf management. Revised ed. McGraw-Hill Book Co., New York.

NE-57 Technical Research Committee. 1977. Northeastern regional turfgrass evaluation of Kentucky bluegrass (Poa pratensis L.) 1968-1973. Pennsylvania Agric. Exp. Stn. Bull. 814.

Nelson, K.E., A.J. Turgeon, and J.R. Street. 1980. Thatch influence on mobility and transformation of nitrogen carriers applied to turf. Agron. J. 72:487-492.

Niemczyk, H.D., and H.R. Krueger. 1982. Binding of insecticides on turfgrass thatch. p. 61-63. In H.D. Niemczyk and B.G. Joyner (ed.) Advances in turfgrass entomology. ChemLawn Corp., Columbus, OH.

Niemczyk, H.D., H.R. Krueger, and K.O. Lawrence. 1977. Thatch influences movement of soil insecticides. Ohio Rep. 62:26-28.

O'Neil, K.H., and R.N. Carrow. 1982. Kentucky bluegrass growth and water use under different soil compaction and irrigation regimes. Agron. J. 74:933-936.

O'Neil, K.J., and R.N. Carrow. 1983. Perennial ryegrass growth, water use, and soil aeration status under soil compaction. Agron. J. 75:177-180.

Palazzo, A.J., and R.W. Duell. 1974. Responses of grasses and legumes to soil pH. Agron. J. 66:678-682.

Patterson, J.C., Jr., and P.R. Henderlong. 1970. Turfgrass soil modification with sintered fly ash. p. 161-171. In Proc. 1st Int. Turfgrass Res. Conf., Harrogate, England. 15-18 July 1969. Sports Turf Res. Inst., Bingley, England.

Paul, J.L., J.H. Madison, and L. Waldron. 1970. The effects of organic and inorganic amendments on the hydraulic conductivity of three sands used for turfgrass soils. J. Sports Turf Res. Inst. 46:22-32.

Pierre, W.H. 1928. Nitrogenous fertilizers and soil acidity: I. Effect of various nitrogenous fertilizers on soil reaction. J. Am. Soc. Agron. 20:254-269.

Pierre, W.H. 1934. The equivalent acidity or basicity of fertilizers as determined by a newly proposed method. J. Assoc. Offic. Agric. Chem. 17:101-107.

Potter, D.A., B.L. Bridges, and F.C. Gordon. 1985. Effect of N fertilization on earthworm and microarthropod populations in Kentucky bluegrass turf. Agron. J. 77:367-372.

Radko, A.M. 1974. Refining green section specifications for putting green construction. p. 287-297. In E.C. Roberts (ed.) Proc. 2nd Int. Turfgrass Res. Conf., Blacksburg, VA. 19-21 June 1973. ASA and CSSA, Madison, WI.

Ralston, D.S., and W.H. Daniel. 1973. Effect of porous rootzone materials underlined with plastic on the growth of creeping bentgrass (Agrostis palustris Huds.) Agron. J. 65:229-232.

Randell, R., J.D. Butler, and T.D. Hughes. 1972. The effect of pesticides on thatch accumulation and earthworm populations in Kentucky bluegrass turf. HortScience 7(1):64-65.

Rauschkolb, R., A.D. Halderman, and L. True. 1970. Evaluation of a biochemical soil additive. Agrichem. Age 13(10):6, 8.

Rhode Island Agricultural Experiment Station. 1957. Sponginess in turf. R.I. Agric. 4(1):5.

Richards, S.J., R.M. Hagan. and T.M. Mccalla. 1952. Soil temperature and plant growth. p. 303-480. In B.T. Shaw (ed.) Soil physical conditions and plant growth. Agron. Monogr. 2. Academic Press, New York.

Richards, S.J., J.E. Warneke, A.W. Marsh, and A.K. Aljibury. 1964. Physical properties of soil mixes. Soil Sci. 98:129-132.

Richer, A.C., J.W. White, H.B. Musser, and F.J. Holben. 1949. Comparison of various organic materials for use in construction and maintenance of golf greens. Pennsylvania Agric. Exp. Stn. Prog. Rep. 16.

Rieke, P.E. 1970. Soil pH for turfgrasses. p. 212-220. In Proc. 1st Int. Turfgrass Res. Conf., Harrogate, England. 15-18 July 1969. Sports Turf Res. Inst., Bingley, England.

Riem Vis, F. 1981. Accumulation and decomposition of organic matter under sports turf. p. 201-207. In R.W. Sheard (ed.) Proc. 4th Int. Turfgrass Res. Conf., Guelph, ON., Canada. 19-23 July. Int. Turfgrass Soc., Ontario Agric. Coll., Univ. of Guelph, Guelph, ON.

Rinehart, J.C., G.R. Blake, J.C.F. Tedrow, and F.E. Baer. 1953. Gypsum for improving drainage of wet soils. New Jersey Agric. Exp. Stn. Bull. 772.

Roberts, J.M. 1977. Water movement within Purr-Wick greens. Ph.D. thesis. Purdue Univ., W. Lafayette, IN (Diss. Abstr. 78-13109).

Rogers, J.N., III, and D.V. Waddington. 1989. The effect of cutting height and verdure on impact absorption and traction characteristics in tall fescue turf. J. Sports Turf Res. Inst.. 65:80-90.

Rogers, J.N., III, and D.V. Waddington. 1990a. Portable apparatus to assess impact characteristics of athletic field surfaces. p. 96-110. In R.C. Schmidt et al. (ed.) Natural and artificial playing fields: Characteristics and safety features. ASTM STP 1073. Am. Soc. for Testing and Materials, Philadelphia.

Rogers, J.N., III, and D.V. Waddington. 1990b. Effects of management practices on impact absorption and shear resistance in natural turf. p. 136-146. In R.C. Schmidt et al. (ed.) Natural and artificial playing fields: Characteristics and safety features. ASTM STP 1973. Am. Soc. for Testing and Materials, Philadelphia.

Rossi, F., and C.R. Skogley. 1987. Topdressing golf greens. p. 1-3. In URI Turfgrass Res. Rev. 18. Rhode Island Agric. Exp. Stn., Kingston.

Russell, E.W. 1973. Soil conditions and plant growth. 10th ed. Longman Group, New York.

Sartain, J.B. 1985. Effect of acidity and N source on the growth and thatch accumulation of Tifgreen bermudagrass and on soil nutrient retention. Agron. J. 77:33-36.

Sartain, J.B., and B.G. Volk. 1984. Influence of white-rot fungi and topdressings on the composition of thatch components of four turfgrasses. Agron. J. 76:359-362.

Schantz, H.L., and R.L. Piemeisel. 1917. Fungus fairy rings in eastern Colorado and their effects on vegetation. J. Agric. Res. 11:191-245.

Schmidt, R.E. 1980. Bentgrass growth in relation to soil properties of Typic Hapludalfs soil variously modified for a golf green. p. 205-214. In J.B. Beard (ed.) Proc. 3rd Int. Turfgrass Res. Conf., Munich, Germany. 11-13 July 1977. Int. Turfgrass Soc., and ASA, CSSA, and SSSA, Madison, WI.

Schmidt, R.E., and J.F. Schoulders. 1972. Winter turf development on dormant Bermudagrass as influenced by summer cultivation and winter N fertilization. Agron. J. 64:435-437.

Schmidt, W. 1978. Thatch formation as affected by fertilizers with acidifying or calcifying action, at the dry trials centre at Giessen. (In German.) Z. Vegetationstechnik 1:65-69.

Sears, M.K., and R.A. Chapman. 1982. Persistence and movement of four insecticides applied to turfgrass. p. 57-59. In H.D. Niemczyk and B.G. Joyner (ed.) Advances in turfgrass entomology. ChemLawn Corp., Columbus, OH.

Seatz, L.F., and H.B. Peterson. 1964. Acid, alkaline, saline, and sodic soils. p. 292–319. *In* F.E. Bear (ed.) Chemistry of the soil. 2nd ed. Reinhold Publ. Corp., New York.

Shearman, R.C., A.H. Bruneau, E.J. Kinbacher, and T.P. Riordan. 1983. Thatch accumulation in Kentucky bluegrass cultivars and blends. HortScience 18:97–99.

Shearman, R.C., E.J. Kinbacher, and T.P. Riordan. 1980a. Turfgrass-paver complex for intensively trafficked areas. Agron. J. 72:372–374.

Shearman, R.C., E.J. Kinbacher, T.P. Riordan, and D.H. Steinegger. 1980b. Thatch accumulation in Kentucky bluegrass as influenced by cultivar, mowing, and nitrogen. HortScience 15:312–313.

Shepard, D.P. 1978. Comparison of physical and chemical properties of commercial and indigenous forms of organic matter in golf green soil mixtures. M.S. thesis. The Univ. of Tennessee, Knoxville.

Shoop, G.J. 1967. The effects of various coarse textured material and peat on the physical properties of Hagerstown soil for turfgrass production. Ph.D. thesis. The Pennsylvania State Univ., University Park (Diss. Abstr. 67-15416).

Sifers, S.I., and J.B. Beard. 1988. Plant morphological and soil physical characterizations resulting from turfgrass root zones augmented with a randomly oriented interlocking mesh matrices. p. 156. *In* Agronomy abstracts. ASA, Madison, WI.

Sills, M.J., and R.N. Carrow. 1982. Soil compaction effects on nitrogen use in tall fescue. J. Am. Soc. Hortic. Sci. 107:934–937.

Sills, M.J., and R.N. Carrow. 1983. Turfgrass growth, N use, and water use under soil compaction and N fertilization. Agron. J. 75:488–492.

Skirde, W. 1978. Investigations on the use of blast-furnace slag in landscaping and sportsground construction. (In German.) Z. Vegetationstechnik 1:59–61.

Smalley, R.R., W.L. Pritchett, and L.C. Hammond. 1962. Effects of four amendments on soil physical properties and on yield and quality of putting greens. Agron. J. 54:393–395.

Smiley, R.W., and M.M. Craven. 1978. Fungicides in Kentucky bluegrass turf: Effects on thatch and pH. Agron. J. 70:1013–1019.

Smiley, R.W., and M.M. Craven. 1979. Microflora of turfgrass treated with fungicides. Soil Biol. Biochem. 11:349–353.

Smiley, R.W., and M. Craven Fowler. 1986. Turfgrass thatch components and decomposition rates in long-term fungicide plots. Agron. J. 78:633–636.

Smiley, R.W., M. Craven Fowler, R.T. Kane, A.M. Petrovic, and R.A. White. 1985. Fungicide effects on thatch depth, thatch decomposition rate, and growth of Kentucky bluegrass. Agron. J. 77:597–602.

Smith, G.S. 1979. Nitrogen and aerification influence on putting green thatch and soil. Agron. J. 71:680–684.

Spomer, L.A. 1980. Prediction and control of porosity and water retention in sand-soil mixtures for drained turf sites. Agron. J. 72:361–362.

Sprague, H.B., and J.F. Marrero. 1931. The effect of various sources of organic matter on the properties of soils as determined by physical measurements and plant growth. Soil Sci. 32:35–47.

Sprague, H.B., and J.F. Marrero. 1932. Further studies on the value of various types of organic matter for improving the physical condition of soils for plant growth. Soil Sci. 34:197–208.

Spurway, C.H. 1941. Soil reaction (pH) preferences of plants. Michigan Agric. Exp. Stn. Spec. Bull. 306.

Stevenson, I.L. 1960. Biochemistry of soil. p. 242–291. *In* F.E. Bear (ed.) Chemistry of the soil. 2nd ed. ACS Monogr. 160 Reinhold Publ. Corp., New York.

Street, J.R., P.R. Henderlong, and F.L. Himes. 1980. Influence of silica on chemical composition and decomposition of turfgrass tissue. p. 329–336. *In* J.B. Beard (ed.) Proc. 3rd Int. Turfgrass Res. Conf., Munich, Germany. 11–13 July 1977. Int. Turfgrass Soc., and ASA, CSSA, and SSSA, Madison, WI.

Stuckey, I.H. 1942. Influence of soil temperature on the development of Colonial bentgrass. Plant Physiol. 17:116–122.

Swartz, W.E., and L.T. Kardos. 1963. Effects of compaction on physical properties of sand-soil-peat mixtures at various moisture contents. Agron. J. 55:7–10.

Taylor, D.H., and G.R. Blake. 1979. Sand content of sand-soil-peat mixtures for turfgrass. Soil Sci. Soc. Am. J. 43:394–398.

Taylor, D.H., and G.R. Blake. 1981. Laboratory evaluation of soil mixtures for sports turf. Soil Sci. Soc. Am. Proc. 45:936–940.

Taylor, D.H., and G.R. Blake. 1982. The effect of turfgrass thatch on water infiltration rates. Soil Sci. Soc. Am. Proc. 46:616–619.

Taylor, D.H., and G.R. Blake. 1984. Predicting sand content of modified soil mixtures from sand, soil, and peat properties. Agron. J. 76:583–587.

Thomas, R., and J.R. Guerin. 1981. A method of measuring quality of sports turf. p. 151–156. In R.W. Sheard (ed.) Proc. 4th Int. Turfgrass Res. Conf., Guelph, ON., Canada. 19–23 July. Int. Turfgrass Soc., Ontario Agric. Coll., Univ. of Guelph, Guelph, ON.

Thompson, D.C., R.W. Smiley, and M. Craven Fowler. 1983. Oxidation status and gas composition of wet turfgrass thatch and soil. Agron. J. 75:603–609.

Thurman, P.C., and F.A. Pokorny. 1969. The relationship of several amended soils and compaction rates on vegetative growth, root development and cold resistance of 'Tifgreen' bermudagrass. J. Am. Soc. Hortic. Sci. 94:463–465.

Tisdale, S.L., W.L. Nelson, and J.D. Beaton. 1985. Soil fertility and fertilizers. 4th ed. Macmillan Publ. Co., New York.

Troughton, A. 1957. The underground organs of herbage grasses. Bull. 44. Commonwealth Bur. of Pastures and Field Crops. Com. Agric. Bur., Farmham Royal, Bucks, England.

Turgeon, A.J., J.B. Beard, D.P. Martin, and W.F. Meggitt. 1974. Effects of successive applications of preemergence herbicides on turf. Weed Sci. 22:349–352.

Turgeon, A.J., R.P. Freeborg, and W.N. Bruce. 1975. Thatch development and other effects of preemergence herbicides in Kentucky bluegrass turf. Agron. J. 67:563–568.

Turner, T.R., and D.V. Waddington. 1978. Survey of soil testing programs for turfgrasses. Commu. Soil Sci. Plant Anal. 9:71–87.

Turner, T.R., D.V. Waddington, and J.M. Duich. 1978. The effect of sampling depth and thatch on soil test results on turfgrass areas. Commun. Soil. Sci. Plant Anal. 9:89–104.

Turner, T.R., D.V. Waddington, and T.L. Watschke. 1979. The effect of fertility levels on dandelion and crabgrass encroachments of Merion Kentucky bluegrass. p. 280–286. In R.B. Taylorson (ed.) 1979 Proc. N.E. Weed Sci. Soc., Boston. 3–5 Jan. N.E. Weed Sci. Soc., Boston.

Unger, P.W. 1971. Soil profile gravel layers: I. Effect on water storage, distribution, and evaporation. Soil Sci. Soc. Am. Proc. 35:631–634.

U.S. Golf Association. 1977. Dictionary of golf turfgrass terms. USGA Green Section, Far Hills, NH.

U.S. Golf Association Green Section Staff. 1960. Specifications for a method of putting green construction. USGA J. Turf Manage. 13(5):24–28.

U.S. Golf Association Green Staff. 1973. Refining the Green Section specifications for putting green construction. USGA Green Sect. Rec. 11(3):1–8.

U.S. Golf Association Green Section Staff. 1974. Sand for golf courses. USGA Green Sect. Rec. 12(5):12–13.

U.S. Salinity Laboratory Staff. 1954. Diagnosis and improvement of saline and alkali soils. USDA Handb. 60. U.S. Gov. Print. Office, Washington, DC.

Valoras, N., W.C. Morgan, and J. Letey. 1966. Physical soil amendments, soil compaction, irrigation, and wetting agents in turfgrass management: II. Effects on top growth, salinity, and minerals in the tissue. Agron. J. 58:528–531.

van Wijk, A.L.M. 1980a. Soil water conditions and playability of grass sportsfields. I. Influence of soil physical properties of top layer and subsoil. Z. Vegetationstechnik 3:7–15.

van Wijk, A.L.M. 1980b. Soil water conditions and playability of grass sportsfields. II. Influence of tile drainage and sandy drainage layer. Z. Vegetationstechnik 3:16–22.

van Wijk, A.L.M. 1980c. A soil technological study on effectuating and maintaining adequate playing conditions of grass sports fields. Agric. Res. Rep. 903. Centre for Agric. Publ. and Doc., Wageningen, Netherlands.

van Wijk, A.L.M. 1981. Use of models in sports field construction research. p. 217–231. In R.W. Sheard (ed.) Proc. 4th Int. Turfgrass Res. Conf., Guelph, ON., Canada. 19–23 July. Int. Turfgrass Soc., Ontario Agric. Coll., Univ. of Guelph, Guelph, ON.

van Wijk, A.L.M., and J. Beuving. 1975. Relation between playability and some soil physical aspects of the top layer of grass sportsfields. Rasen Turf Gazon 6:77–83.

van Wijk, A.L.M., and J. Beuving. 1978. Relation between soil strength, bulk density and soil water pressure head of sandy top layers of grass sportsfields. Z. Vegetationstechnik 1:53–58.

van Wijk, A.L.M., W.B. Verhaegh, and J. Beuving. 1977. Grass sportsfields: Top-layer compaction and soil aeration. Rasen Turf Gazon 8:47–52.

Volk, G.M., and A.E. Dudeck. 1976. Abnormal color response of turf ryegrass to topdressed isobutylidene diurea. Agron. J. 68:534–536.

Waddington, D.V., and J.H. Baker. 1965. Influence of soil aeration on the growth and chemical composition of three grass species. Agron. J. 57:253–258.

Waddington, D.V., W.C. Lincoln, Jr., and J. Troll. 1967. Effect of sawdust on the germination and seedling growth of several turfgrasses. Agron. J. 59:137–139.

Waddington, D.V., and T.L. Zimmerman. 1972. Growth and chemical composition of eight grasses grown under high water table conditions. Commun. Soil. Sci. Plant Anal. 3:329–337.

Waddington, D.V., T.L. Zimmerman, G.J. Shoop, L.T. Kardos, and J. M. Duich. 1974. Soil modification for turfgrass areas. I. Physical properties of physically amended soils. Pennsylvania Agric. Exp. Stn. Prog. Rep. 337.

Ward, C.Y., E.L. McWhirter, and W.R. Thompson, Jr. 1974. Evaluation of cool-season turf species and planting techniques for overseeding bermudagrass golf greens. p. 480–495. In E.C. Roberts (ed.) Proc. 2nd Int. Turfgrass Res. Conf., Blacksburg, VA. 19–21 June 1973. ASA and CSSA, Madison, WI.

Weaver, R.W., E.P. Dunigan, J.F. Parr, and A.E. Hiltbold. 1974. Effect of two soil activators on crop yields and activities of soil microorganisms in the southern United States. Texas Agric. Exp. Stn., College Station. South. Coop. Ser. Bull. 189.

Welton, F.A., and J.C. Carroll. 1941. Control of lawn weeds and the renovation of lawns. Ohio Agric. Exp. Stn. Bull. 619.

Welton, K. 1932. Structural requisites of putting green soil. Bull. USGA Green Sect. 12(2):29–37.

Weston, J.B., and J.H. Dunn. 1985. Thatch and quality of Meyer zoysia in response to mechanical cultivation and nitrogen. p. 449–458. In F. Lemaire (ed.) Proc. 5th Int. Turfgrass Res. Conf., Avignon, France. 1–5 July. Inst. Natl. de la Recherche Agron., Paris.

Westover, H.L. 1926. Commercial fertilizers. Bull. USGA Green Sect. 6:234–242.

White, A.W., Jr., J.E. Giddens, and H.D. Morris. 1959. The effect of sawdust on crop growth and physical and biological properties of Cecil soil. Soil Sci. Soc. Am. Proc. 23:365–368.

White, R.H., and R. Dickens. 1984. Thatch accumulation in bermudagrass as influenced by cultural practices. Agron. J. 76:19–22.

Wilkinson, J.F., and R.H. Miller. 1978. Investigation and treatment of localized dry spots on sand greens. Agron. J. 70:299–304.

Willhite, F.M., A.R. Grable, and H.K. Rouse. 1965. Interaction of nitrogen and soil moisture on the production and persistence of timothy in lysimeters. Agron. J. 57:479–481.

Williamson, R.E., and C.R. Willey. 1964. Effect of depth of water table on yield of tall fescue. Agron. J. 56:585–588.

Winsor, G.W., and M.I.C. Long. 1956. Mineralization of the nitrogen of urea-formaldehyde compounds in relation to soil pH. J. Sci. Food Agric. 7:560–564.

Wolcott, A.R., H.D. Foth, J.F. Davis, and J.C. Shickluna. 1965. Nitrogen carriers: I. Soil effects. Soil Sci. Soc. Am. Proc. 29:405–410.

Wood, G.M. 1973. Use of energy-absorbing materials to permit growth in heavily trafficked areas. Agron. J. 65:1004–1005.

Wright, W.R., and J.E. Foss. 1968. Movement of silt-size particles in sand columns. Soil Sci. Soc. Am. Proc. 32:446–448.

Youngblood, V.B., O.R. Lunt, and F. Nudge. 1967. Salinity tolerance of seven varieties of creeping bentgrass Agrostis palustris Huds. Agron. J. 59:335–336.

Youngner, V.B., A.W. Marsh, R.A. Strohman, V.A. Gibeault, and S. Spaulding. 1981. Water use and turf quality of warm-season and cool-season turfgrasses. p. 251–257. In R.W. Sheard (ed.) Proc. 4th Int. Turfgrass Res. Conf., Guelph, ON., Canada. 19–23 July. Int. Turfgrass Soc., Ontario, Agric. Coll., Univ. of Guelph, Guelph, ON.

Youngner, V.B., and F.J. Nudge. 1976. Soil temperature, air temperature, and defoliation effects on growth and nonstructural carbohydrates of Kentucky bluegrass. Agron. J. 68:257–260.

Zebarth, B.J., and R.W. Sheard. 1985. Impact and shear resistance of turf grass racing surfaces for Thoroughbreds. Am. J. Vet. Res. 46:778–784.

Zimmerman, T.L. 1969. Infiltration rates and fertility levels of physically amended Hagerstown soil. M.S. thesis. The Pennsylvania State Univ., University Park.

Zimmerman, T.L. 1973. The effect of amendment, compaction, soil depth, and time on various physical properties of physically modified Hagerstown soil. Ph.D. thesis. The Pennsylvania State Univ., University Park (Diss. Abstr. 73-24053).

11

Nutritional Requirements and Fertilization

THOMAS R. TURNER

University of Maryland
College Park, Maryland

NORMAN W. HUMMEL, JR.

Cornell University
Ithaca, New York

As with any plant grown for the use or benefit of people, understanding the nutritional requirements of turfgrasses is among the most important factors in their successful culture. Inadequate soil nutrient levels, insufficiently or excessively applied nutrients, and improperly applied nutrients can each lead to problems in the general health, vigor, and quality of a turfgrass stand. As the use or quality expectations of a turfed area increase, so does the importance of adequate soil fertility and a proper fertility program. In extreme cases, poor or improper fertility can lead to the decline and eventual loss of major portions of a turfgrass stand.

In classical plant nutrition literature, 17 elements are generally considered essential for plant growth. These include: C, H, O, N, K, P, Ca, Mg, S, Fe, Mn, Zn, Cu, Mo, B, Cl, and Co. Other elements, such as Si, may be beneficial to some plants in some situations, but have not been shown at this time to be absolutely essential according to strict classical definitions. Traditionally, when plant nutritional requirements are discussed, C, H, and O are not addressed in detail since they are obtained in sufficient quantities by the plant from air and water rather than from existing soil or applications by people. Thus, the thrust of this chapter includes turfgrass responses to the remaining essential elements and other elements that, though not essential, may influence turfgrass performance. Since detailed discussions of the soil chemical reactions involved with these elements can be found in other monographs, they will not be reviewed in detail in this chapter.

I. NITROGEN

Nitrogen management is one of the more important cultural aspects in establishing and maintaining quality turfgrasses. Excluding O_2, H, and C, N is required in the largest amount of any of the 17 essential plant nutrients.

Copyright © 1992 ASA-CSSA-SSSA, 677 S. Segoe Rd., Madison, WI 53711, USA. *Turfgrass—* Agronomy Monograph no. 32.

The inherent N levels of most soils are rarely sufficient to meet the nutritional demands of quality turfgrasses. Therefore, turfgrasses usually need to be fertilized with N to maintain a desirable quality.

Nitrogen is a vital constituent of the chlorophyll molecule, amino acids, proteins, nucleic acids, enzymes, and vitamins (Epstein, 1972). Nitrogen makes up 20 to 60 g kg^{-1} of the dry matter of turfgrass plants (Butler & Hodges, 1967), depending on the species. Nitrogen concentration has also been shown to be inversely proportional to mowing height and directly proportional to N-fertilization rate (Turgeon et al., 1979).

A. Nitrogen Transformations and Losses

Nitrogen is a dynamic element and there are several avenues that exist through which N may be lost from a turfgrass system. Categorically, N may be taken up by the plant, stored in the soil or thatch, lost to the atmosphere, or lost to the groundwater.

1. Plant Uptake

There is much research documenting the uptake and efficiency of fertilizer N under field conditions. Snow (1976), using ammonium nitrate (NH_4NO_3) reported N recovery in the biomass ranging from 50 to 75% of the applied N when annual N rates were 97 kg ha^{-1}. As annual N rates were increased to 360 kg of N ha^{-1}, the biomass N recovery dropped to 20 to 54% of the applied N. Starr and DeRoo (1981), using radioactive labelled ammonium sulfate [$(NH_4)_2SO_4$] reported 30% N rcovery in the roots and shoots.

Nitrogen recovery also varies with the N source that is used. Hummel and Waddington (1981) applied several slow- and fast-release N sources to Kentucky bluegrass (*Poa pratensis* L.) turf and reported that N recovery in the clippings ranged from 15 to 52% of the applied N over a 3-yr period. Nitrogen recovery for various N sources followed a general order of: soluble source = sulfur-coated urea (SCU) > methylene urea = isobutylidene diurea (IBDU) > activated sludge > ureaform. Additional information on N recovery is discussed later in this chapter.

2. Stored in the Soil

Nitrogen applied to turf can also be tied up in unavailable forms through immobilization. Starr and DeRoo (1981) reported that 19 to 27% of labelled fertilizer ^{15}N applied to turf was immobilized as organic N in the thatch. The amount of fertilizer immobilized in the soil organic matter, including roots, was 14 to 20% of the applied N where clippings were removed and returned, respectively. The large amount of fertilizer N immobilized in the thatch suggests that the layer can sustain a highly active microbial population that could tie up a significant proportion of the fertilizer N. More research is necessary to look at N dynamics within the thatch layer to better understand the fate of fertilizer N applied to turfgrass.

3. Lost to Groundwater

Leaching losses of N from turfgrass systems not only reduces the efficiency of the applied N, but also represents a real environmental concern should nitrates (NO_3) enter the groundwater. Leaching of NO^3-N from heavily irrigated sandy mediums was reported by Rieke and Ellis (1974), Snyder et al, (1980), and Brown et al. (1977) with as much as 60% of the applied N lost through leaching in the latter study. However, the loss of NO_3-N was negligible on finer-textured soils or soil mixes (Rieke & Ellis, 1974; Brown et al., 1982). Using an unirrigated sandy loam soil as the growth medium, Starr and DeRoo (1981) reported no leaching of radioactive-labelled N from the turfgrass root zone.

These results clearly document that NO_3-N can be lost from turfgrasses grown on sandy soils. The use of slow-release fertilizers, however, has reduced or eliminated leaching losses in several studies (Rieke & Ellis, 1974; Nelson et al., 1980; Brown et al., 1982; Andre, 1986). Unfortunately, most of these studies have only monitored losses over a 2- or 3-yr period. Longer term studies may determine if a turfgrass system has a maximum N load that it can handle or retain, beyond which N would be lost through leaching. This maximum N load would be expected to be reached sooner where clippings are returned.

4. Lost to the Atmosphere

The two primary mechanisms by which fertilizer N can be lost to the atmosphere are NH_3 volatilization and denitrification. Urea is a commonly used N source for turfgrasses. Since fertilizers are surface applied on established turfgrasses, the scenario exists for appreciable volatilization where urea is used. Urease, an enzyme responsible for the hydrolysis of urea, was found to be high enough in thatch for NH_3 volatilization from urea to occur (Torello & Wehner, 1983). Nelson et al. (1980) reported that volatilization losses were 39% of the applied urea N on thatch cores compared to 5% loss from soil cores.

Several other studies have investigated NH_3 volatilization on turf. Losses ranging from 20 to 30% of the urea-N applied to several grases were reported by Volk (1959). Hargrove et al. (1977) reported losses of 3 to 10% of the applied N from NH_4NO_3 and 36 to 45% for $(NH_4)_2SO_4$ from a bermudagrass (*Cynodon dactylon* L.) sod grown on calcareous soil. In laboratory studies, Fenn and Kissell (1974) reported losses as high as 68% of the applied urea N, also on calcareous soil.

Titko et al. (1987) examined the effects of placement, temperature, and relative humidity (RH) on ammonia (NH_3) volatilization of urea applied to turfgrass. They reported higher losses from granular-applied urea than dissolved urea, except when irrigation immediately followed application. Volatilization losses from both forms increased as temperature increased from 10 to 22 °C, but there was no further difference as the temperature increased to 32.2 °C. Ammonia loss from dissolved urea applications were greater at 68% than at 31% RH, but losses from granular urea were not affected.

The high volatilization rates reported in several studies may be artifacts of the closed systems used to measure NH_3 losses, not taking into account the effects of the changed environment within the chambers. Using an aerodynamic measuring technique, Sheard and Beauchamp (1985) reported volatilization losses from urea ranging from 6.7 to 15.1% of the applied N. Volatilization losses were proportional to the time interval that existed between fertilizer application and rainfall event.

Torello et al. (1983) reported a significant reduction in volatilization losses where S-coated urea was the N source used. Losses were greater from spray-applied urea than from dry applications of prilled urea. Also, NH_3 losses were greater from methylol urea than from a ureaformaldehyde suspension.

Denitrification can occur when a soil becomes waterlogged and an anaerobic environment exists. Small additions of water to a grass sward were found to significantly increase denitrification losses, which were strongly influenced by temperature (Denmead et al., 1979). Mancino et al. (1988) found that 2 to 5% of applied N was lost as N_2O from saturated silt and silt loam soils at 22 °C. When the soil temperature was increased to 30 °C, losses ranged from 45 to 85% of the applied N. Denitrification losses were only 0.1 to 0.4% of the applied N when the soil was at 75% saturation.

B. Nitrogen Effects on Turfgrasses

Nitrogen has been shown to affect turfgrasses in several ways including color, density, shoot growth, root growth, susceptibility to diseases and environmental stress, composition of the turfgrass sward, and recuperative ability. These effects are well documented and were thoroughly reviewed by Beard (1973). This review will highlight selected articles, especially those published since the last review.

1. Establishment

While the benefits of N fertilizer in the seedbed are commonly known, they are not well documented in the literature. Hummel (1980), using several N sources, reported that 97 kg of N ha^{-1} provided darker color and more rapid establishment than 48 kg of N ha^{-1}. The most rapid establishment of Kentucky bluegrass was obtained from water soluble sources and IBDU.

Mazur and White (1983) found that the rate of establishing creeping bentgrass (*Agrostis palustris* Huds.) greens at 4 wk was significantly greater with IBDU than ureaform or urea, but not greater than S-coated urea. Poor establishment where urea was used was attributed to leaching losses on the highly permeable green.

These results demonstrate the importance of N source selection for turfgrass establishment. Turfgrasses were more rapidly established with sources that provided N in a readily available form. On highly permeable soils, however, the use of slowly available forms, with the exception of ureaform would be a preferred N source. Ureaform did not contain sufficient available N to enhance establishment in both studies.

Hubbell and Dunn (1985), however, reported that preplant ureaform applications increased zoysiagrass (*Zoysia japonica* Steud.) cover plugged into a Kentucky bluegrass sod by 10 to 20% during the first 2 yr compared to control plots or those fertilized postplant with urea. While not measured, it is possible that N efficiency was lower on the urea plots due to volatilization losses of the sod-applied urea. The warm, wet conditions that prevailed throughout the test were also conducive to rapid mineralization of ureaform N.

2. Maintenance

A N-fertility program should be designed to maintain a controlled level of available N that does not stimulate shoot growth to the extent that root growth is impaired. Root growth will increase as N levels increase above zero (Juska et al., 1955; Hylton et al., 1964; Christians et al., 1981b; Canaway, 1984). However, high levels of available N will stimulate shoot production and growth, thus limiting the quantity of stored carbohydrates available for protein synthesis. High available N has been shown to cause a distinct suppression in root growth (Juska et al., 1955; Hylton et al., 1964; Schmidt & Blaser, 1967; Zanoni et al., 1969; Watschke & Waddington, 1974, 1975; Christians et al., 1981a; Leyer & Skirde, 1980; Canaway, 1984) and nonstructural carbohydrates (Schmidt & Blaser, 1967; Zanoni et al., 1969; Watschke & Waddington, 1974, 1975).

On warm-season grasses, increased root and rhizome production on zoysiagrass has been reported with increasing N levels (Juska, 1959a). Horst et al. (1985) also reported increased root and rhizome production and improved root viability scores as N rate applied to bermudagrass increased from 0 to 48.9 kg of N ha^{-1} per growing month.

Nitrogen fertilization has been reported to improve wear tolerance of turfgrasses, up to a threshold whereby additional N will deteriorate it (Leyer & Skirde, 1980; Canaway, 1984). These researchers determined that the critical level where N favored wear tolerance on cool-season grasses fell between 200 to 300 kg of N ha^{-1} yr^{-1}.

Kohlmeier and Eggens (1983) also found that the bentgrass recovery from wear injury was improved with the application of 300 kg of N ha^{-1} yr^{-1} over 0 N, but that 600 kg of N ha^{-1} impeded recovery. Hawes and Decker (1977) also reported improved healing of bentgrass with increasing N levels.

Nitrogen applications have been shown to aid in recovery of turfgrasses from drought (Schmidt & Breuninger, 1981), herbicide injury (Johnson, 1984), winter dormancy (Christians et al., 1985), scalping (Watschke & Waddington, 1975), and centipedegrass [*Eremochloa ophiuroides* (Munro) Hackel] decline (Johnson et al., 1987).

Turfgrass tolerance to environmental stress has been shown to be influenced by N fertility. In general, excessive N levels were shown to reduce cold hardiness (Carroll & Welton, 1939; Carroll, 1943) and heat tolerance

(Pellett & Roberts, 1963) of Kentucky bluegrass turf, primarily due to the increased tissue hydration with increasing N levels. Watschke and Waddington (1975) reported that Kentucky bluegrass plants fertilized at 244 kg of N ha^{-1} wilted sooner and recovered later than at lower rates (122 kg of N ha^{-1}).

The composition of a turfgrass community may be influenced by N-fertility levels. In Kentucky bluegrass-red fescue (*Festuca rubra* L.) mixtures, Kentucky bluegrass was reported to dominate at higher N levels while red fescue was dominant at lower N rates (Juska et al., 1955). Likewise, tall fescue-Kentucky bluegrass polystands will quickly become predominately bluegrass at higher N fertility.

Adams (1980) found that the percent annual bluegrass in a polystand with perennial ryegrass had increased with N levels at three mowing heights. Eggens and Wright (1985) reported that the competitiveness of annual bluegrass in a polystand with creeping bentgrass was decreased as the percent NH_4 in a nutrient solution increased.

Several studies have shown that decreases in both dicot and monocot weeds in turf with increasing N fertility levels can be primarily attributed to increased turfgrass vigor and density (Beard, 1973; Adams, 1980; Mehnert & Madel, 1982; Johnson & Bowyer, 1982; Murray et al., 1983).

The level of available N can also influence the occurrence and severity of turfgrass diseases. Turf grown at high levels of N have been shown to be more susceptible to brown patch (*Rhizoctonia solani*) (Bloom & Couch, 1960), Ophiobulus patch (*Ophiobulus graminis*) (Goss & Gould, 1967b), leaf spot (*Helminthosporium* spp.) (Cheesman et al., 1965; Halisky et al., 1966), and pink snow mold (*Fusarium nivale*) (Madison et al., 1960; Riem, 1981).

Conversely, turf grown at low N levels have been shown to be more prone to dollar spot (*Sclerotinia homeocarpa*) (Cook et al., 1964; Markland et al., 1969; Sartain & Dudeck, 1980a), red thread (*Laetisaria fuciforme*) (Gould et al., 1967; Muse & Couch, 1965; Cahill et al., 1983; Woolhouse, 1986), take all patch (*Gaeumannomyces graminis*) (Dernoeden, 1987), and rusts (*Puccinia* spp.) (Couch, 1973).

Nitrogen has long been associated with thatch accumulation. Engel and Aldefer (1967, p. 32–45) noted increased puffiness of a creeping bentgrass green when high rates of N were applied over a period of 4 to 6 yr. Weston and Dunn (1985) reported significant increases in thatch on zoysiagrass turf as the N rate increased from 0 to 96 kg of N ha^{-1}, but there were no differences as the N rate increased to 195 kg of N ha^{-1}. Shearman et al. (1980) reported no increase in thatch accumulation on Kentucky bluegrass as N rate increased from 100 to 200 kg of N ha^{-1}. Likewise, Carrow et al. (1987) did not observe changes in thatch accumulation in a bermudagrass turf as N rate varied from 96 to 296 kg of N ha^{-1} yr^{-1}. The results of these studies suggest that the increased turfgrass vigor as N is increased from zero to a low level will result in increased biomass production. However, a threshold may exist above which increasing N levels will not significantly increase thatch accumulation.

Nitrogen effects on thatch accumulation also appear to be affected by N source. Thatch was observed to accumulate most quickly when $(NH_4)_2SO_4$

was used as the N source (Smith, 1979; Potter et al., 1985; Sartain, 1985; Spangenberg et al., 1986), due to the greater acidifying effect of this N source. More rapid accumulation of thatch on bermudagrass has been observed from activated sewage sludge than several other N sources (White & Dickens, 1984; Sartain, 1985).

These many studies have collectively shown the benefit of N fertilization on rooting, and other factors when going from a deficiency to a sufficiency level. They have also demonstrated how excess N can be detrimental. The studies fail, however, to clearly identify what the N requirements of these grasses are.

The N requirement of turfgrasses will, of course, be influenced by many factors, including species and cultivar. Gilbeault and Hanson (1980) and Dudeck et al. (1985) observed differential responses of perennial ryegrass and bermudagrass cultivars, respectively, to N rates. Cultivars of the same species were clearly shown to have different N requirements.

The N requirements of turfgrasses are also affected by edaphic conditions including soil physical properties and organic matter. Sills and Carrow (1983) reported that compaction affected tall fescue responses to N fertilization. Higher N rates were required to compensate for the detrimental effects of compaction on visual quality and shoot growth. Sills and Carrow (1983) also found that N use per unit area of perennial ryegrass turf decreased by as much as 30.5% on compacted soil. They found that applying more N to the turf grown on compacted soil did not improve the N use per unit area.

Much would be gained in our ability to predict N requirements if a reliable soil test for N existed. Besides measuring inorganic N, the test must be able to predict or estimate mineralizable organic N. Until such a test is developed, N fertilization recommendations will remain largely empirical.

The timing of N applications for maximum turfgrass performance will also be influenced by many factors, including grass species, climate, and N source. In recent years, however, the benefits of late fall fertilization have been widely acclaimed. In the 1960s, Powell et al. (1967a) increased winter rooting of creeping bentgrass where N had been applied in the late fall. Late fall fertilization was also shown to stimulate photosynthesis and carbohydrate production at temperature just above freezing with no apparent shoot growth, respiration, or carbohydrate utilization (Powell et al., 1967b). Powell et al. (1967b) further reported that desirable turf color was maintained throughout the winter and into the spring. A similar color response was reported by Christians et al. (1985) and Snyder and Schmidt (1974).

C. Nitrogen Sources

Many different sources of N are used in the turfgrass industry currently. The N sources vary considerably in their release characteristics, and these factors should be considered when fertilizer programs are developed.

There are several ways in which N sources may be classified; however, the most widely accepted means is to classify N sources as quickly available or slowly available fertilizers.

1. Quickly Available

Quickly available N sources are often called quick release, water soluble, or farm grade fertilizers, and contain N in the NO_3 or NH_4 form. Nitrate-N is immediately available for plant uptake but is also easily leached from the soil. Ammonium N is less prone to leaching but more prone to volatilization. Nitrification of NH_4 to NO_3 is fairly rapid in most soil conditions; therefore, the N from NH_4 fertilizers is also quickly used by turfgrass plants. Turfgrass plants will also take up NH_4–N, however. In fact, preferential uptake of NH_4–N over NO_3–N by perennial ryegrass was shown in simulated spring conditions (Watson, 1986). Quickly available N sources include inorganic salts, urea, and ureaformaldehyde products.

a. Inorganic Salts. Inorganic salts commonly used for turfgrass fertilization include $(NH_4)_2SO_4$, NH_4NO_3, and several ammonium phosphates. These sources are water soluble and may be applied in dry form or liquid delivery systems. They are commonly used in turfgrass fertilizer formulations rather than alone.

Application of inorganic salts to turfgrasses produced a rapid initial flush of growth of short duration (Hummel & Waddington, 1981, 1984; Waddington et al., 1985). The efficiency of inorganic salts, that is, the percentage of the applied N recovered in grass clippings, tends to be higher than slow-release N sources (Hummel & Waddington, 1981, 1984; Mehnert et al., 1984). However, most of the N is recovered in the clippings in the first 4 to 6 wk following application. Starr and DeRoo (1981), using ^{15}N-labelled $(NH_4)_2SO_4$, reported 20 to 30% of the applied N was recovered in the clippings within 3 wk. After that, the uptake of labelled N dropped to nearly zero. Inorganic salts have relatively high salt indexes, therefore, the potential for foliar burning exists with these sources (Monteith & Bengston, 1939).

b. Urea. Urea is produced by combining atmospheric N with methane to produce ammonia gas and CO_2. The ammonia is then reacted with the CO_2 under high temperature and pressure to form urea, which contains 45 to 46% N. Urea is an organic compound but water soluble.

Urea has been extensively evaluated on both warm- and cool-season turfgrasses. Characteristics of urea include a quick initial release rate of short duration (Moberg et al., 1970; Barrios et al., 1982b; Mosdell et al., 1986; Spangenberg et al., 1986; Landschoot & Waddington, 1987), and a high foliar burn potential (Moberg et al., 1970; Johnson & Christians, 1984; Spangenberg et al., 1986). An earlier section discussed that urea N was also prone to leaching and volatilization losses. These characteristics warrant that a urea-based fertilizer program be based on several light applications through the growing season.

When urea is applied to soil, the urea must be hydrolyzed in the presence of the enzyme urease to NH_4, and then nitrified to NO_3 before the N is root absorbed by the turfgrass plant in the NH_4 or the NO_3 forms. While these reactions are usually rapid, Wesely et al. (1985) found that maximum N uptake from foliar-applied urea occurred within 24 h after application. After

72 h, 31 to 61% of the applied N was recovered in verdure. Like other soluble sources, the efficiency of urea has been high, with as much as 63% of the applied N recovered in the clippings (Moberg et al., 1970).

c. Ureaformaldehyde Products. Ureaformaldehyde (ureaform, UF) is a generic name for several methylene urea polymers that are the condensation product of urea with formaldehyde (Fuller & Clark, 1947; Hays & Haden, 1966; Kaempffe & Lunt, 1967; Katy & Fassbender, 1966; Yee & Love, 1946). The initial reaction product of urea and formaldehyde is methylol urea (Fig. 11-1). Methylol urea is a water-soluble form of chemically combined formaldehyde which in many respects is similar to formaldehyde; that is, it is a strong bacteriacide.

Methylol ureas have been commercially available for turfgrass fertilization as products containing about 50% of the N from methylol urea and the rest from urea. Methylol ureas have been thoroughly evaluated for turfgrass use. Methylol ureas have produced turfgrass responses similar to other water-soluble sources; that is a rapid initial response of short duration (Spangenberg et al., 1986; Landschoot & Waddington, 1987). Methylol ureas have been shown to cause less foliar burn than other soluble sources (Johnson & Christians, 1984; Spangenberg et al., 1986).

When properly condensed, the methylol urea is converted to methylene urea polymers of various chain lengths. Ureaform products formed by this process are slow-release N sources and are discussed in that section of this chapter. The number of methylene urea polymers formed with a molecular excess of urea is five. Table 11-1 gives the molecular weight distribution of methylene ureas that may be found in a UF fertilizer.

2. Slowly Available N Sources

Called slow-release, controlled release, or water-insoluble fertilizers, slowly available N sources include those that contain N either in an insoluble form, or as a water-soluble source encapsulated in an impermeable coating.

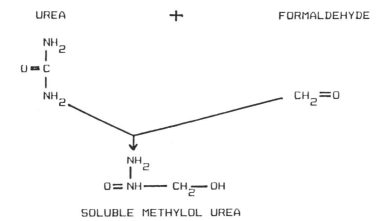

Fig. 11-1. Formation of soluble methylol urea from the reaction of urea with formaldehyde.

Table 11-1. Distribution of methylene urea polymers in a typical ureaform.

	Distribution	Mole wt.	WSN†	AI‡	Nitrification	
	%		%		%	wk
Methylene diurea	10	132	34	100	92	6–8
Dimethylene triurea	15	204	25	98	90	8–12
Trimethylene tetraurea	40	276	16	60	80	10–15
Tetramethylene pentaurea	25	348	10	35	50	12–24
Pentamethylene hexaurea	10	421	4	30	20	24–32

† Water-soluble N.
‡ Activity index = [(CWIN − HWIN)/CWIN] × 100.

Release of N from slowly available sources may involve biological or physical processes. General characteristics of slowly available N sources include low water solubility, lower salt index, and slow initial turfgrass response of longer duration than quick release sources. Slowly available N sources can be classified further as natural organics, synthetic organics, and coated materials.

a. Natural Organics. Prior to 1950, natural organics were the only slow-release N sources available to turfgrass managers. Examples of natural organic N sources include bone meal, dried blood and other waste products of the food-processing industry, activated sewage sludge, soybean meal, and cottonseed meal.

The N in natural organics is tied up in complex organic compounds that must be broken down by soil microorganisms before the N can become available to the turfgrass plants. Therefore, environmental factors that influence microorganism activity, such as soil pH, temperature, and moisture will govern N release from these materials.

Activated sewage sludges are the most common natural organic N sources used on turfgrasses. Activated sewage sludge products are made by aerobically digesting sewage sludge in aeration tanks. The sludge is inoculated with microorganisms to hasten the digestion process. The flocculated end product is withdrawn from the tanks, dried, ground, screened, and sterilized by steam (Beard, 1973) or radiation.

Milorganite is an activated sewage sludge that is widely used in the turfgrass industry. Milorganite contains 6% N, of which 92% is water insoluble. Milorganite applications to cool-season turfgrasses have produced slow initial responses, uniform growth and quality through summer months, and little evidence of N release in cooler months (Moberg et al., 1970; Hummel & Waddington, 1981; Waddington et al., 1985; Landschoot & Waddington, 1987). Nitrogen efficiency from Milorganite was reported to be in the 20 to 40% range (Moberg et al., 1970; Hummel & Waddington, 1981); higher than from ureaform, but lower than from soluble sources, IBDU, and SCU.

In warmer climates, Barrios et al. (1982a) found Milorganite to produce superior quality bermudagrass and higher yields throughout the growing season when compared to quick- and slow-release N sources. Sartain (1985) found that bermudagrass quality was not significantly influenced by N source when Milorganite was compared to ammonium sulfate and IBDU. However,

IBDU and $(NH_4)_2SO_4$ produced higher yields and N recoveries than Milorganite. An acidic soil pH in the latter study may have hindered mineralization of the organic N to a point whereby yields were significantly less than those produced by IBDU and $(NH_4)_2SO_4$. Conversely, the soil pH in the former study was 6.6 to 7.0; a range favorable to microbial activity.

Milorganite is also a source of micronutrients such as Fe, Cu, and Zn. Barrios et al. (1982a) reported increased tissue levels of these three elements when Milorganite was applied to bermudagrass. Similar results were reported by Hummel (1980) on Kentucky bluegrass.

Milorganite usage has been associated with decreased dollar spot on creeping bentgrass (Markland et al., 1969; Cook et al., 1964). While the exact mechanism of this effect is not known, it is possible that the high cadmium content of Milorganite (110 mg kg^{-1}) had a fungicidal or fungistatic effect on these pathogens. Regardless of the mechanism, the suppression of dollar spot was greater than normally observed for this disease from just N stimulation.

Applications of Milorganite to bermudagrass turf have resulted in significant reductions in plant parasitic nematode populations (White & Dickens, 1984). The authors postulated that the activated sludge may have enhanced biological control factors in the soil environment.

Other sludges have been evaluated for turfgrass fertilization as well. Waddington et al. (1985) compared several sludge materials, including Milorganite, and found few differences. Landschoot and Waddington (1987) evaluated a sludge compost and determined that it was unacceptable as a N source for turfgrasses because of an extremely slow-release rate. The variability that exists in sludge or other waste products demonstrates the need to evaluate these materials before they are commercially produced.

b. Synthetic Organics. The synthetic organic class of slowly available N sources includes ureaformaldehyde reaction products and IBDU. Both N sources are made by reacting urea with other chemicals to produce more complex compounds.

Ureaformaldehydes are the reaction products of urea with formaldehyde (Fig. 11-1 and 11-2). The initial reaction product of this reaction is methylol urea, a water-soluble N source that has been used for turfgrass fertilization. A discussion of methylol ureas can be found in the section on Quickly Available N Sources.

When property condensed, the methylol urea is converted to methylene urea polymers of various chain lengths. The number of methylene urea polymers formed with a molecular excess of urea is five. Table 11-1 gives the molecular weight distribution of methylene ureas that may be found in a ureaform fertilizer.

The percent distribution of methylene urea polymers in a UF fertilizer depends on the urea to formaldehyde molecular ratio. As the U/F ratio is increased, the distribution of shorter chained polymers such as methylene diurea and dimethylene triurea also increases (Fuller & Clark, 1947; Yee & Love, 1946). The mineralization and nitrification of UF fertilizers is

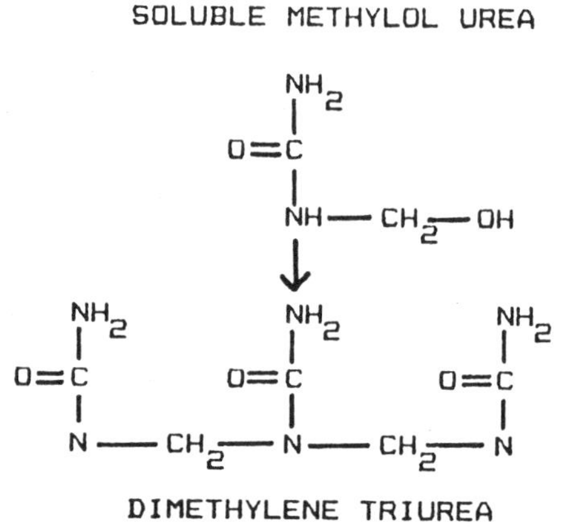

SOLUBLE METHYLOL UREA

DIMETHYLENE TRIUREA

Fig. 11-2. Formation of an insoluble ureaform polymer.

determined by the molecular size of the methylene ureas; the rate decreasing with increasing length (Hays & Haden, 1966; Katy & Fassbender, 1966).

The N from ureaform fertilizers can be classified into three fractions based on solubility (Kaempffe & Lunt, 1967). Fraction I, or the cold water soluble N (CWSN), is the portion that is soluble in water at 20 to 25 °C. This fraction consists of unreacted urea, methylene diurea, and dimethylene tri-urea. Fraction II is the portion of cold water insoluble N (CWIN) that is hot water soluble N (HWSN). This portion will dissolve in a pH 7.5 buffered phosphate solution in 30 min at 98 to 100 °C, and includes trimethylene tetraurea and tetramethylene pentaurea. Fraction III, or the hot water insoluble N (HWIN), is that portion that is not dissolved in the hot water soluble fractionation. It is composed of petamethylene hexaurea and longer chained molecules. The HWIN and CWIN are usually referred to collectively as water insoluble N (WIN).

The relative availability of WIN in a ureaformaldehyde product may be classified by its activity index (AI). The AI was defined by Katy and Fassbender (1966) as the percentage of the CWIN that is HWSN. It is assumed that this portion of the CWIN fraction will become available over a growing season.

The Association of American Plant Food Control Officials has defined ureaformaldehyde fertilizers as reaction products of urea and formaldehyde containing at least 35% N, largely as insoluble but slowly available form, with the WIN at least 60% of the total N, and the AI not less than 40%. The conventional ureaforms, such as Nitroform (Nor AM Chemical Corp., Wilmington, DE) fall within these limits. In this presentation, ureaform refers to products meeting such limits. In current trade usage, "ureaform" and "ureaform reaction" products may also apply to materials having <60% of the total as WIN, and even completely water-soluble products made by reacting urea with formaldehyde.

Ureaform produced with a 1.3:1 urea to formaldehyde ratio contains 38% N, of which 65 to 71% of the total N is WIN. Methylene-urea products produced with a 1.9:1 urea/formaldehyde ratio contains 39% N, of which 36% of the total N is WIN. Because of the high percentage of WIN in urea-form, the initial response to ureaform applications is slow (Arminger et al., 1948, 1951; Juska et al., 1970). However, the methylene urea described above has produced a rapid turfgrass response and occasionally produced a residual response that was not evident with water-soluble sources (Hummel, 1980; Landschoot, 1984).

A flowable UF (FLUF, W.A. Cleary Corp., Somerset, NJ) has been developed for use in liquid delivery systems. Produced with a 1.8:1 U/F ratio, FLUF contains 18% N of which 20 to 25% of the total N is WIN. Spangen-berg et al., (1986) found that FLUF produced a slightly slower initial response than urea, and some evidence of better residual N in the second year. Few differences, however, were significant. Landschoot and Waddington (1987) reported that initial turfgrass response to FLUF was less than urea, but residual effects were insigificant. Despite having a low WIN percentage, FLUF has been shown to be safer than soluble sources. Johnson and Christians (1984) found FLUF to have little foliar burning potential.

Microorganisms are responsible for the mineralization of ureaform N, and thus the availability of N for plant uptake (Yee & Love, 1946; Corke & Robinson, 1966; Fuller & Clark, 1947; Hays & Haden, 1966). Therefore, the availability of UF N has been slow under cool conditions (Basaraba, 1964; Slater, 1966). Wilkinson (1977) and Hummel and Waddington (1981) reported that turfgrass response to UF peaked in mid-summer as soil temperatures increased. In general, the overall performance of ureaform in cool, temperate climates has been poorer than other slow or quick-release N sources (Moberg et al., 1970; Waddington & Duich, 1976; Kavanagh et al., 1980; Hummel & Waddington, 1981, 1984; Szymczak & Lemaire, 1985; Mehnert et al., 1984; Will & Belger, 1985; Landschoot & Waddington, 1987). When applied frequently throughout the year (Spangenberg et al., 1986); or in warmer climates (Barrios et al., 1982a, b), the performance of UF was comparable to other N sources.

Mineralization of UF has also been shown to be influenced by soil moisture and pH. Watschke and Waddington (1974) and Waddington et al. (1977) observed increased response from ureaform under wet conditions. Winsor and Long (1956) and Basaraba (1964) found that the availability of UF N was greater under acidic conditions, perhaps due to the increased solubility of UF as the pH decreased. Bredakis and Steckel (1963), however, found increased mineralization of UF as the soil pH approached 7.0.

Ureaform is more typically marketed in formulations in which a portion of the N is from water-soluble sources. Killian et al. (1966) and Hummel and Waddington (1981) observed an improvement in response when UF was used in conjunction with soluble N sources in a 50:50 ratio. Wisniewski et al. (1958), however, did not find improvement in performance when ureaform made up 75% of the N in the formulation. The percent water soluble N in the latter formulation probably was insufficient to improve response over the UF alone.

Nitrogen recovery is usually low for the first year but increases in subsequent years as the accumulated N from previous year's applications becomes available (Moberg et al., 1970; Waddington et al., 1976; Hummel & Waddington, 1981).

Isobutylidene diurea is a synthetic organic, slow-release fertilizer introduced in the mid 1960s from Japan. Isobutylidene diurea is the condensation product of the reaction of urea with isobutyraldehyde (Fig. 11–3). It is a white crystalline material that is marketed in two particle sizes: coarse (0.7–2.5 mm) and fine (0.5–1.0 mm). IBDU contains 31% N of which 90% of the total N is WIN in the coarse material, and 85% of the total N is WIN in the fine material.

Release of N from IBDU is the result of hydrolysis of IBDU to urea. Unlike ureaform, the quantity of IBDU converted to urea is independent of microbial activity (Lunt & Clark, 1969). Hamamota (1966) suggested that

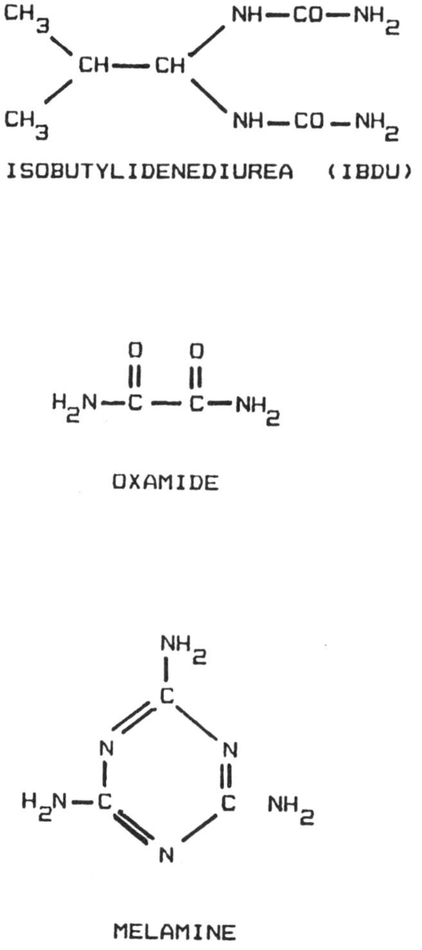

ISOBUTYLIDENEDIUREA   (IBDU)

OXAMIDE

MELAMINE

Fig. 11–3. Chemical structure of three synthetic organic N sources.

the formation of urea from IBDU is actually a two-stage process: dissolution and hydrolysis. Lunt and Clark (1969) found that this conversion of IBDU to NH_3 occurred readily under most soil conditions.

Nitrogen release from IBDU is influenced by temperature, moisture, particle size, and soil pH. Lunt and Clark (1969) reported a moderate enhancement of solubilization of IBDU at higher temperatures. Hamamota (1966) reported that 80% of IBDU N became available in 2 w at 25 °C. At 10 °C, 8 wk was required to release 80% of the IBDU N.

Hughes (1976) found that nitrification of IBDU N was greatest at pH 5.7, with a 33% reduction at pH 6.8, and a 50% reduction at pH 7.7. Lunt and Clark (1969) found IBDU to perform poorly on alkaline soils. Volk and Dudeck (1976) reported phytotoxicity to turfgrass from high rates of IBDU when applied to alkaline soil.

Hughes (1976) documented the effect of particle size on release of IBDU-N. When mixed with soil, N recovery was 75% in 10 wk for particles in the 0.6 to 0.7 mm range, 60% was recovered in 21 wk for IBDU particles in the 1.0 to 1.2 mm range, and only 50% recovery in 32 wk for those particles in the 1.7- to 2.0-mm range. Lunt and Clark (1969) reported similar results. Hydrolysis of the finer particle IBDU is quicker because of the greater surface area.

Faster initial turfgrass response to fertilization was reported for the finer grades of IBDU than coarser grades (Waddington et al., 1977; Hummel & Waddington, 1981). Wilkinson (1977), however, reported similar responses on Kentucky bluegrass from fine and coarse grades. Hummel and Waddington (1981) found that N recovery in Kentucky bluegrass clippings over a 3-yr period averaged 47% of the applied fine IBDU N compared to 37% for the coarser grade.

Responses to IBDU applications in the field have varied. A delayed or slow initial response to IBDU applications was reported by Moberg et al. (1970), Volk and Horn (1975), Waddington et al. (1977), Wilkinson (1977), Kavanagh et al., (1980), and Hummel and Waddington (1981). However, Waddington and Duich (1976) reported a quick release from IBDU applied to bentgrass greens, probably due to the incorporation of the fertilizer by core cultivation prior to and topdressing following fertilization. A quick initial response of seedling turf was also observed when IBDU was raked into the surface 2 cm of soil during seedbed preparation (Hummel, 1980). These results demonstrate the importance of moisture for the release of IBDU N. Poor initial response to IBDU on established turf is probably due to the IBDU resting in a poor moisture holding medium; that is, thatch. When the IBDU is placed in direct contact with the soil, the delayed release often observed with placement on established turf does not occur.

After the initial delay to applications on established turf, IBDU has provided very good residual response (Moberg et al., 1970; Kavanagh et al., 1980; Hummel & Waddington, 1981; Mosdell et al., 1987). Good late fall or early spring color from IBDU-treated turf was reported by Moberg et al. (1970), Waddington and Duich (1976), Wilkinson (1977), and Woolhouse (1983). Good low-temperature response from IBDU can probably be explained by the fact that release of IBDU N is independent of microbial activity. Low temperature, therefore, would have less of an effect on mineralization of IBDU than other environmental factors.

IBDU is also formulated in combination with water-soluble sources. Hummel (1980) found that a 50% IBDU-N:50% water soluble-N formulation produced better color than IBDU alone for several weeks after application, suggesting that IBDU may be better suited for fertilizer formulation than as a product by itself. With continued use of IBDU as the sole N source, the delay becomes less obvious due to the release of residual N from previous applications.

Oxamide is a synthetic organic N source still in the experimental stage of development. High production costs of oxamide have hindered its commercial production, but a review of research results indicated that it has potential for use as a N source for turfgrass. A diamide of oxalic acid (Fig. 11-3) oxamide is a white, nonhygroscopic powder with a N content of 31.8% and very low water solubility (Hauck & Koshino, 1971). The release of N is the result of hydrolysis of oxamide in the presence of the enzyme amidase (Frankenberger & Tabatabai, 1980).

The release rate of oxamide was shown to be influenced by particle size (DeMent et al., 1961; Engelstad et al., 1964; Hauck, 1964). Plant responses to very fine oxamide (<0.42 mm) have been reported to be similar to NH_4NO_3 (DeMent et al., 1961; Engelstad et al., 1964; Cantarella & Tabatabai, 1983). Landschoot and Waddington (1987), however, found slightly slower initial turfgrass response to fine (<0.25 mm) oxamide than urea. Higher color ratings and greater N uptake in the second year suggests a carryover response from previous applications. Landschoot and Waddington (1987) and Mosdell et al. (1987), both reported that coarser grades of oxamide (1-3 mm) resulted in much slower initial turfgrass response to fertilization, but longer residual response than the finer grades.

The availability of oxamide N was also reported to be influenced by soil pH (DeMent et al., 1961). Nitrogen recovery was found to be greater on limed soil (pH 7.5) than on unlimed soil (pH 5.2).

Placement will influence mineralization of oxamide and N availability. Lower N recovery has been reported from surface-applied oxamide than with incorporated oxamide (34 vs. 72%), presumably due to increased volatilization losses (Engelstad et al., 1964).

Turfgrass response to oxamide has most closely resembled that produced by IBDU, that is, a delayed response to fertilization with good residual (Landschoot & Waddington, 1987; Mosdell et al., 1987).

Melamine is a synthetic organic fertilizer that is produced by reacting urea with itself under high temperature and pressure in the presence of NH_3 until a six-member ring with three C and three N is formed. An amine group is bonded to the carbons in the ring (Fig. 11-3), forming a product with a N analysis of 67% that is sparingly water soluble.

The release of N from melamine is due to microbial degradation. Hauck and Stephenson (1964) reported that melamine appears to act as a bacteriacide, inhibiting the enzyme systems involved in the initial breakdown of the triazine ring. In incubation studies, they found that only 17% of melamine N was nitrified in 24 wk.

In field studies, Terman et al. (1964) reported that the response of bermudagrass to melamine was equal or slightly better than ureaform. Mosdell et al. (1987) evaluated melamine on Kentucky bluegrass turf and found that the nitrification was slow. Poor overall turf quality as reflected by a large number of dates in which color was unacceptable also reflected the very slow mineralization of melamine.

c. Coated Materials. Coated N sources are made by coating urea or other soluble N sources with an impermeable or semipermeable coating. The coatings prevent the wetting of the soluble N sources so that the release of N from the final product is delayed. The release of N may depend on the degradation of the coating, or controlled by the physical make up of the coating. The two most common forms of coated fertilizers include SCU and resin-coated urea (RCU).

Sulfur-coated urea is made by spraying atomized molten S on preheated urea granules or prills. The S coating provides an insoluble barrier that prevents the immediate dissolution of urea. As the S solidifies on the urea, however, pinholes, cracks, and other defects occur in the coating. Usually the S coating is then sealed with a thin coating of wax of a combination of polyethylene and heavy weight oil. A conditioner (diatomaceous earth) is added to decrease stickiness and to make the product hydrophilic. The final product contains 32 to 38% N, 13 to 22% S, 2 to 3% sealant, and about 2% conditioner. The sealant and conditioner are absent from some SCU products.

The slow release of N from SCU results from differences in the time periods required for individual granules to begin releasing urea through their pores. Scheib and McClellan (1976) found that pinhole capillary pores are the most common defect in S coatings and appear to be the principal path for the release of urea from these products. The mechanism of slow release from a SCU product has both diffusion controlled and defect-initiated components acting simultaneously. The gross release of a SCU is an overall average of the behavior of many individual granules.

Allen et al. (1971) and Scheib and McClellan (1976) recognized that the coating thickness is an important variable controlling dissolution, but this relationship also involves a consideration for coating uniformity. The effective coating thickness is only equal to the thinnest areas of the coating.

Variation that exists in the S coating of SCU products is responsible for the uniform, sustained release of N from these products. Jarrell et al. (1979) suggested that three classes of granules exist in a typical SCU product. Class I granules have unobstructed holes or cracks in the coating that enable urea to be released as soon as the granule is wetted. Class II granules have defects in the S coating that are plugged with a sealant. This class of granules would release urea when the sealant is degraded. Class III granules are those that have no defects in the S coating. These granules are the longest lasting, with the release of urea dependent on the degradation of the sealant or the S coating.

A laboratory 7-d dissolution rate (DR) is used to characterize SCU materials. The 7-d DR is the amount of SCU N that will dissolve in water at 38 °C in a 7-d period. Typical values for commercially available SCU products range from 25 to 35%; however, one product with a S only coat has a value of about 65%.

Hummel and Waddington (1984) compared two SCU sources with different DRs, but manufactured by the same process. They found that the DR was a good indicator of expected plant response in the first year. They reported that 60 to 80% of the SCU-25 N (25% 7-d DR) had released within 8 wk after application, compared to only 38 to 53% of the SCU-11 (11% 7-d DR) releasing within this time. As a result, the overall turfgrass response to an 11% material was much lower than a 25% material. However, by the third year, sufficient N carryover had resulted on plots treated with the SCU-11 that the differences in response were smaller than in the first year. In another study, Hummel and Waddington (1981) found that turfgrass response to an SCU product with a S only coat and a 7-d dissolution rate of 83% closely resembled that of $(NH_4)_2SO_4$, and was much faster releasing than SCU with a dissolution rate of 25.

There are many variables that control the release of SCU N in the field, including coating characteristics and environmental factors. Jarrell and Boersma (1979, 1980) have developed mathematical models for predicting N release from SCU as affected by these variables.

The release of N from SCU is influenced by coating thickness and particle size. Waddington and Turner (1980) compared SCU materials with similar dissolution rates but different coating methods. They found that the N release was quicker for S plus wax coating than for a S only coat, due to the thicker S coating required in the latter product to obtain the same DR.

Sulfur-coated ureas are available in different particle sizes. Advantages to using smaller particle sizes include: better coverage due to more particles per unit area; better size for blending; and reduced mower damage and pickup.

As the particle size of a material to be coated decreases, the surface area per unit weight of fertilizer to be coated incrases. Therefore, applying the S at the same rate by weight to a fine and coarse urea would result in the coarse product having a thinner coat, thus a faster release rate (Allen et al., 1971; Allen & Mays, 1971; Rindt et al., 1968).

The increased surface area of finer grade materials may also increase the rate at which the coating degrades. Hummel and Waddington (1986) compared regular and fine SCU materials with similar DRs, and found that the fine materials released N significantly faster. Thus, when coating methods and particle sizes are varied, the 7-d dissolution rate may not be a good indicator of field response.

Allen et al. (1971), Oertli (1973), Prasad (1976), and Hashimoto and Mullins (1979) found that the dissolution of SCU was temperature dependent, the release rate increasing with increasing temperatures. These results suggest that there may be a need for heavier S coatings when SCU is used in tropical or subtropical conditions.

Dawson and Akratanakul (1973) and Prasad (1976) found that N release from SCU increased with decreasing soil water tension. A soil moisture variable probably explains why Allen et al. (1971) and Prasad (1976) found that the release of N from SCU was faster when mixed with soil than when surface applied. In flooded soils, however, release of SCU was shown to be much slower than in aerated soils (Giordano & Mortvedt, 1970).

Soil pH has been shown to only slightly effect N release from SCU. Giordano and Mortvedt (1970) and Hashimoto and Mullins (1979) reported that liming the soil increased N release from SCU; however, the effect was slight. Hummel (1982) found no effect of soil pH on release rate within the range of 6 to 8. Oertli (1973) also reported no pH effects in solution culture.

Soil microbes have been shown to have a slight effect on SCU release. The inclusion of a microbicide in the wax coating was shown to slightly decrease the rate of release of SCU (Rindt et al., 1968). Hummel (1982) reported less SCU release in fumigated soil, and a nonsignificant trend toward more rapid release on soil previously treated with SCU.

Early evaluations found SCU to be an effective slow-release N source for bermudagrass fertilization (Allen et al., 1971; Mays & Terman, 1969a; Rindt et al., 1968) and tall fescue (Mays & Terman, 1969b). Woolhouse (1973, 1974) reported that two applications of an SCU prill produced a high-quality turf similar to that produced by multiple applications of $(NH_4)_2SO_4$. Volk and Horn (1975) found that a SCU with a 9% dissolution rate gave more favorable results than IBDU, ureaform, and activated sewage sludge. On creeping bentgrass, Waddington and Duich (1976) found the response to SCU to be intermediate between IBDU and ureaform. Hummel and Waddington (1981) found that two applications of SCU produced superior quality turf more uniformly through the season than several other slow and quick release N sources.

Turfgrass management practices have been shown to influence SCU performance. Tractor and mower traffic were found to cause pellet breakage and fertilizer burn where a high rate of a SCU prill was applied to a bentgrass fairway (D.V. Waddington, 1974, unpublished data). Mowing may also be a factor when SCU is applied to close cut turf due to pellet pickup and removal (Gowans & Johnson, 1973). Woolhouse (1974) reported that 17 to 21% of the applied SCU was removed from turf mowed at 5 mm. Hummel (1986), however, found that fertilizer pickup was 5% of the applied N or less when S-coated feed grade urea was applied to bentgrass turf mowed at 4 mm.

Resin-coated ureas (RCU) are a class of N sources that include two products: Agriform and Escote. Agriform fertilizers are resin-coated fertilizer products manufactured by Osmocote primarily for the nursery and greenhouse industries. Agriform fertilizers available for the turfgrass market have been evaluated for fertilization of creeping bentgrass turf. Besemer (1963) reported that resin-coated fertilizer applied to creeping bentgrass turf every 12 to 16 wk would give a performance similar to monthly applications of soluble sources. Gowans and Johnson (1973) reported 8 mo of acceptable quality turf was produced from a single application of a resin-coated urea. Waddington and Duich (1976) however, showed that three applications of Agriform resin-coated fertilizer were necessary to maintain acceptable quality bentgrass turf through the season.

Escote RCUs are made by spraying a thin plastic coating onto a urea prill. Talcum is added to the process to alter the physical characteristics of the coating. More specifically, the amount of talc added during production will influence the pore size and number on the coating. Therefore, RCUs of well defined and reproducible release rates may be made. The final product contains 41% N.

The exact mechanism of release is not documented, but it has been suggested that the release of N is the result of a "controlled" osmosis of water into the pellet. The fertilizer pellet will swell until the internal pressure either causes the pellet to crack open, release the urea, or forces the urea solution back out through the pores.

Hummel (1989) evaluated four Escote RCUs with release rates of 70, 100, 150, and 270 d. Turfgrass response closely correlated to the release rate, that is, the 70-d material produced the most rapid response of shortest duration. The 270-d material proved to be too slow to produce acceptable quality turf from two annual applications. Single spring applications of the 100- to 150-d materials produced acceptable quality turf throughout most of the season.

Studies conducted in Georgia on centipedegrass [*Eremochloa ophiuroides* (Munro.) Hack.] also found that release N from RCU to be closely related to the designated release rate as the release from an RCU 100 was significantly quicker than a RCU 200 (Carrow & Johnson, 1989). The RCU-100 produced a response similar to that produced by SCU.

D. Nitrification and Urease Inhibitors

Other means of improving the efficiency of N fertilizers includes using chemicals that control the microflora involved in N transformations, keeping the N in more stable forms. Nitrification inhibitors are chemical compounds that prevent the biochemical process of oxidation of NH_4 to NO_3-N. Keeping N in the NH_4-N form can be advantageous under conditions that would favor NO_3-N loss by either leaching or denitrification. Nitrification inhibitors, therefore, keep the applied N in a stable form until the nitrification inhibitor activity ceases.

Two nitrification inhibitors that inhibit NH_4-N oxidation by *Nitrosomonas* bacteria have been evaluated on turf. Nitrapyrin [2-chloro-6-(trichloromethyl)pyridine] is a nitrification inhibitor marketed as N-Serve that has been successfully used in agronomic crops. Waddington et al. (1975), however, found no significant advantage to using nitrapyrin in combination with a liquid application of a soluble fertilizer. The high volatility of nitrapyrin, and the inability for soil incorporation probably explains its failure to work on sod.

Dicyandiamide (DCD) is a low volatility nitrification inhibitor that contains 66% N, so it can be included in formulations as a N source as well as a nitrification inhibitor. Landschoot (1984) evaluated several combinations of DCD with $(NH_4)_2SO_4$ on Kentucky bluegrass turf. He concluded that there was little advantage to using DCD as a N source alone, or in combination with $(NH_4)_2SO_4$. Release of N was extremely slow from DCD.

Spangenberger et al. (1986) evaluated a 3.2% DCD + $(NH_4)_2SO_4$ combination and a 4.6% DCD + urea combination, and compared them to $(NH_4)_2SO_4$ and urea alone. While some color and yield differences were observed, they concluded that there was little advantage to including DCD in the formulation. Similar comparisons were made by Mosdell et al. (1986), with the same conclusions.

Like nitrapyrin, the failure of DCD to inhibit nitrification in turf may be due to volatilization. Although DCD is less volatile than nitrapyrin, the data presented by Landschoot (1984) suggests some form of N loss. Where DCD was used alone as a N source, initial turfgrass color was much poorer than that produced by a DCD combination with $(NH_4)_2SO_4$. There was, however, some evidence of release of DCD N later in the year, suggesting some nitrification inhibition. Waddington et al. (1989) obtained similar results, but also observed significant turfgrass injury from DCD when applied in warm temperatures (25 °C) that was attributed to ammonia volatilization.

Urease inhibitors theoretically improve the efficiency of urea N by preventing or reducing volatilization losses. They do so by inhibiting urease activity, thereby reducing urea hydrolysis. Phenylphosphorodiamidate (PPD) is a strong urease inhibitor that was evaluated on turf (Joo & Christians, 1986). They found trends in clipping yields that suggested reduced NH_3 volatilization losses where PPD was applied with urea. In another study, Joo et al. (1987) found that PPD and N-butyl phosphorothiaic triamid (NBPT) reduced NH_3 loss when combined with liquid urea applications to Kentucky bluegrass turf.

Cationic materials in combination with urea are believed to reduce the rate at which urea hydrolyzes. In greenhouse and laboratory studies, Fenn et al. (1982) reported reduced NH_3 losses where urea was applied in combination with Ca and K salts. Joo and Christians (1986a) investigated this concept on turf. Using low concentrations of magnesium chloride with urea, their results suggested a slight reduction in NH_3 volatilization. However, they reported that Mg may increase the phytotoxicity of fertilizer solutions in times of environmental stress. Further studies by Joo and Christians (1986a) showed that the measured loss of NH_3 was less where K and Mg salts were combined with urea than where urea was applied to turf alone.

II. POTASSIUM

The roles of K in plant nutrition have been studied in a wide variety of species for scores of years. Although not directly associated with the molecular structure of any plant constituents, K has been determined to be an essential element in numerous plant functions, such as photosynthesis, carbohydrate and protein formation, water relationships, and enzymatic activity.

A. Levels in Turfgrass Plants

Despite not being involved in the direct molecular structure of any plant constituent, K is second to N in the amounts required by turfgrass plants, excluding C, H, and O. Wide ranges of tissue K have been reported and reflect differences in turfgrass species and varieties (Butler & Hodges, 1967; Waddington & Zimmerman, 1972; Mehall et al., 1983; Turner & Waddington, 1983), fertilization practices (Waddington et al., 1978; Turner, 1980; Watschke et al., 1977; Sartain & Dudeck, 1980b), and time of sampling (Mehall et al., 1983; Waddington & Zimmerman, 1972; Hall & Miller, 1974).

The wide differences found in tissue K make the interpretation of tissue levels for purposes of diagnosing deficiencies difficult. For example, Waddington and Zimmerman (1972) measured average percentage tissue K levels of 35.8, 36.8, 44.8, 38.6, 43.1, 35.9, and 43.5 g kg^{-1} for annual bluegrass (*Poa annua* L.), Kentucky bluegrass, colonial bentgrass (*Agrostis tenius* Sifth.), creeping bentgrass, tall fescue (*Festuca arundinacea* Schreb.), creeping red fescue (*Festuca rubra* L.), and perennial ryegrass (*Lolium perenne* L.), respectively. All grasses received the same management. In comparing 15 Kentucky bluegrass cultivars, tissue K varied from as much as 25.7 g kg^{-1} for 'Enmundi' to 20.8 g kg^{-1} for 'Parade' and 'Sydsport'. In this same study, K tissue content for Emundi ranged from as low as 17.6 to as high as 33.5 g kg^{-1} for a single season.

Despite these evident problems in using tissue levels as a diagnostic tool, attempts have been made to establish sufficiency ranges. For Kentucky bluegrass forage, Martin and Matocha (1973) classified values < 15 g kg^{-1} as deficient, values between 16 and 20 g kg^{-1} as critical, values between 20 and 24 g kg^{-1} as adequate, and values > 30 g kg^{-1} as high. For annual and perennial ryegrass forage, they classified values < 21 g kg^{-1} as deficient, values between 26 and 30 g kg^{-1} as critical, values between 30 and 35 g kg^{-1} as adequate, and values > 45 g kg^{-1} high. Lunt et al. (1964) associated a minimum K value of 10 g kg^{-1} with maximum yield of Kentucky bluegrass. Walker and Pesek (1967) associated a value of 17.4 g kg^{-1} of K with maximum bluegrass forage growth, with this value being dependent on the P level. Waddington et al. (1978) obtained creeping bentgrass tissue K levels as low as 5.8 g kg^{-1} of K, with some chlorosis occurring, whereas no chlorosis was observed on this date on plots with 10.4 g kg^{-1} tissue of K. Turner (1980) found no deficiency symptoms on perennial ryegrass, creeping red fescue, nor Kentucky bluegrass with tissue levels of 29.0, 18.1, and 19.0 g kg^{-1} of K, respectively.

In an attempt to summarize existing information, Jones (1980) suggested a sufficiency range of 10.0 to 25.0 g kg^{-1} (Table 11-2). He emphasized, however, that these ranges were not equally applicable to all situations.

Table 11-2. Elemental tissue content sufficiency ranges and common turfgrass deficiency symptoms.

Element	Tissue content sufficiency range (Jones, 1980)	Deficiency symptoms
N	27.5–35.0 g kg^{-1}	General yellow-green or chlorotic color. Older leaves initially go off color and dieback from tip. Shoot density and tillering decrease.
P	3.0–5.5 g kg^{-1}	Leaves progress from dark green to purplish to reddish purple color. Stand may appear wilted and exhibit poor spring green-up and growth.
K	10.0–25.0 g kg^{-1}	Older leaves exhibit yellowing first, followed by dieback at top and then along leaf margin. Early spring chlorosis observed.
Ca	5.0–12.5 g kg^{-1}	Younger leaves exhibit symptoms first, with reddish brown color along leaf margins.
Mg	2.0–6.0 g kg^{-1}	Older leaves turn red to cherry red along margins.
S	2.0–4.5 g kg^{-1}	Similar to N deficiency although mid-vein may remain green.
Fe	35–100 mg kg^{-1}	Younger leaves exhibit symptoms first, typically an interveinal chlorosis—leaves may appear almost white under severe deficiency.
Mn	25–150 mg kg^{-1}	Interveinal chlorosis of younger leaves. Necrotic spots may develop on leaves.
Zn	20–55 mg kg^{-1}	Stunted leaves. Some chlorosis. Puckered leaf margins.
Cu	5–20 mg kg^{-1}	Tips of younger leaves dieback. May get white-tip. Growth may be stunted.
B	10–60 mg kg^{-1}	Reduced growth and stunting.
Mo	Not known	Similar to N deficiency. May get some interveinal chlorosis.
Cl	Not known	Not commonly observed in turf.

B. Effects on Turfgrass Establishment

The role of K during the establishment phase of turfgrass has never been shown to be as critical as might be expected for an element found in such relatively high tissue concentrations. Published information is lacking. Responses observed, however, have tended to be more dramatic with the warm-season grasses compared to cool-season grasses. Juska (1959a) found a highly significant positive response to K applications during the establishment of 'Meyer' zoysiagrass for topgrowth and for stolon growth and spread. He further stated that adequate K was necessary for rapid establishment of zoysia. Fry and Dernoeden (1987), however, observed little benefit in the establishment of zoysia from plugs when K was applied to soil having moderate initial soil K levels.

Although critical soil K levels must certainly exist for turfgrass establishment, little research has been conducted to determine or document these levels. In studying the K effects on the establishment from seed of several cool-season turfgrass species, Turner (1980) found few beneficial and some detrimental effects from K applications, even on soil with K levels as low as 70 kg of K ha^{-1} soil. In fact, at very high rates of K application using muriate of potash, severe seedling injury resulted from high soluble salt levels created by these applications. In an establishment study using Kentucky bluegrass sod, Turner (1980) found no beneficial effects from K applications on sod rooting, despite low soil levels of 96 kg of K ha^{-1} soil.

C. Effects on Turfgrass Maintenance

Contrary to establishment, numerous reports have been made on the effects of K applications for the maintenance of turf. Types of responses reported include growth; disease incidence and weed encroachment; tolerances to environmental stress and wear; as well as general aesthetic quality.

The effect of K on turfgrass growth after establishment has been mixed. With warm-season grasses, the growth response to K is generally species dependent, with centipedegrass having relatively high requirements compared to bermuda or zoysia (Pritchett & Horn, 1966). Keisling (1980) found that the initiation of new bermudagrass rhizomes and longevity of existing rhizomes on a low K soil were directly related to increasing K applications. With cool-season grasses, seemingly conflicting results often are reported. On closely clipped bentgrass, Bell and DeFrance (1944) found increasing K increased weight of accumulated roots. Juska et al. (1965) reported greater stimulation of root growth than top growth by K additions. Pellet and Roberts (1963) obtained greater Kentucky bluegrass foliar growth in sand culture with high K; however, Monroe et al. (1969) obtained less growth of Kentucky bluegrass in sand culture with very high K and found the N/K balance could be important, although most growth parameters were increased by moderate K additions. In sand culture studies, Christians et al. (1979) found that more K was needed to maximize bluegrass and bentgrass quality than to maximize tissue production. In continuing field experiments with putting green bentgrass, Waddington et al. (1972) obtained some growth response to K additions in the first 4 yr of applications, but generally obtained little or no response compared to plots receiving no K (soil level 52 kg of K/ha^{-1}) from the sixth year on (Waddington et al., 1978). In a series of soil test calibration studies on soil low to very low in K, Turner (1980) found that topgrowth of creeping red fescue and Kentucky bluegrass was not affected by K applications, whereas perennial ryegrass was affected on only 33% of the dates measured.

Growth response differences by bluegrass and bentgrass to K levels may be due to their ability to use soil K. Potassium uptake at low levels of soil K has been shown to be closely correlated with root cation exchange capacity, with bentgrass having a stronger attraction and uptake of K than bluegrass (Gray et al., 1953). Colby and Bredakis (1966) questioned the value of soil tests for determining the need of K fertilization of bentgrass species due to the strong capacity of bentgrasses to use K from mineral sources in the soil.

The direct and indirect effects of K applications on factors affecting overall turfgrass quality are more important than their inconsistent effects on turfgrass growth. Perhaps more than any other factor affecting turfgrass quality, researchers have attempted to relate disease incidence to fertilization practices, such as timing and rate of application as well as nutrient interactions. While much information is available on the relationship between disease incidence and N fertility, less is available regarding soil K levels and K applications.

Incidence of several diseases, however, has been related to K applications. Leaf spot disease of bermudagrass has been shown to be much more severe where soil K has been kept low (Evans et al., 1964; Juska & Murray,1974). On soils low in K, however, no relation was found between leaf spot and K applications to Kentucky bluegrass (Turner, 1980).

Dollar spot of bermudagrass was reported by both Horn (1970) and Juska and Murray (1974) to be reduced by K applications; although Horn (1970) found the degree to be source and rate dependent. Carrow et al. (1987) reported somewhat less dollar spot of 'Tifway' bermudagrass with 49 kg of K ha^{-1} than at higher rates. Johnson et al. (1987) found no benefit in reducing this disease on Tifway bermudagrass from using rates of 50 to 300 kg K ha^{-1}. Markland et al. (1969) reported that increased bentgrass foliage K reduced dollar spot incidence, although Waddington et al. (1978) did not find any significant effect of K additions on dollar spot incidence of bentgrass, despite a range of soil K of 52 to 245 of K ha^{-1} and a range of tissue K of 17.4 to 26.3 g kg^{-1} K. In the same test, Waddington et al. (1978) found an increase in brown patch with increasing K. Fusarium patch was reported to be decreased by K when low rates of N were applied but had no effect at higher N rates (Brauen et al., 1975). Goss and Gould (1968), however, reported that the addition of K in the absence of P generally increased the incidence of fusarium patch. Goss (1969) also related reduced incidence of red thread and take-all patch to K applications. Goss and Gould (1967a) stated that a K deficiency and high N treatments can cause an accumulation of nonprotein N and unused carbohydrates, with the resulting high concentration of sugars and nitrates being a favorable media for growth of disease organisms. Turner (1980), however, found no effect of K applications on red thread incidence of either perennial ryegrass or creeping red fescue despite low soil K levels. Cahill et al. (1983) also found K applications to have little influence on red thread of perennial ryegrass.

Potassium plays a role in drought and heat tolerance, and especially cold tolerance of warm-season grasses. Decreases in winter injury or increases in winter hardiness due to increased K levels have been reported for bermudagrass (Adams & Twersky, 1960; Alexander & Gilbert, 1963; Gilbert & Davis, 1971; Juska & Murray, 1974) and for centipedegrass (Palmertree et al., 1974). Beard and Rieke (1966) stated that turfgrass winter survival was at a maximum when K rates were about one-half that of the N rate. Cook and Duff (1976), however, did not find substantial effect of K on freezing tolerance of tall fescue, nor was any effect on the winter injury of perennial ryegrass found by Turner (1980).

High N coupled with high K was shown by Pellet and Roberts (1963) to give better heat resistance to Kentucky bluegrass than high N and low K. Waddington et al. (1978) found that bentgrass wilting was more severe where no K had been applied; however, DiPaola and Engel (1976) found no important benefit from K applications on the desiccation resistance of bentgrass. Escritt and Legg (1970) reported that on plots receiving only N and P, no K deficiency was observed until after 20 yr, when decreased drought resistance was observed. Schmidt and Breuninger (1981) found that the recovery of Kentucky bluegrass turf from summer drought was enhanced by K fertilization. This K fertilization effect was further enhanced when coupled with P fertilization.

Other specific turfgrass responses to K include weed encroachment and wear tolerance. Waddington et al. (1978) reported an increase of *Poa annua* encroachment into bentgrass as soil K increased from 52 to 245 kg of K ha^{-1} due to K fertilization, possibly due to an improvement in the heat and drought tolerance of this species, which is generally poor. Other weeds, such as crabgrass (*Digitaria* spp.) and dandelion (*Taraxacum officinales*), have also been shown to moderately increase as K applications increase (Monteith & Bengtson, 1939; Turner, 1980; Turner et al., 1979; Hansen, 1970). These relationships are often complex, however, and may depend on levels of other nutrients.

In wear-tolerance studies, Shearman and Beard (1975) reported bentgrass wear tolerance improved significantly with annual K additions in the range of 270 to 360 kg ha^{-1}. Hawes and Decker (1977) found no significant effect of K on healing potential of bentgrass; however, initial soil K levels were high. Carrow et al. (1987) found no influence of K on reducing the injurious effects of coring and verticutting of bermudagrass, nor was recovery from injury hastened.

Several studies have evaluated K effects on general quality and color. Carrow et al. (1987) reported that 49 kg of K ha^{-1} provided better color and density of Tifway bermudagrass than did higher rates. Johnson et al. (1987) did not find any enhancement of Tifway bermudagrass visual quality, however, within the range of 50 to 300 kg of K ha^{-1}, nor was thatch accumulation affected (resulting soil K concentrations from these applications ranged from 70–136 kg ha^{-1}). Barrios and Jones (1980), however, found no effect of K applications on the quality of bermudagrass. Both zoysia and bermuda have exhibited poorer color and early spring performance when no K was applied (Sturkie & Rouse, 1967). Waddington et al. (1978) noted early spring chlorosis of bentgrass on K-deficient soil, which lasted 10 to 14 d. No chlorosis occurred on plots that received K. Turner (1980) noted virtually no visual quality improvements in perennial ryegrass, creeping red fescue, nor Kentucky bluegrass, despite K applications being made to soils low in K. Christians et al. (1979) found that as the K level increased, less N was needed for maximum turfgrass quality. They concluded from this study that K may play a more important role in maintenance of turf quality than previously thought, with the N/K balance of particular importance.

III. PHOSPHORUS

The roles of P in plant nutrition have been well defined and are numerous. Of key importance is its essential role in energy transformations.

Phosphorus is required for photosynthesis, the interconversion of carbohydrates, fat metabolism, oxidation reactions, and as a component of genetic material such as nucleic acids.

A. Levels in Turfgrass Plants

Phosphorus is generally required in substantially smaller amounts in turfgrass than either N or K. As with K, wide ranges in tissue P have been reported in turfgrasses, which makes interpretation of these values difficult for diagnostic purposes.

Waddington and Zimmerman (1972) measured average tissue P levels of 5.7, 5.6, 5.3, 7.6, 6.4, 5.4, and 7.1 g kg^{-1} for annual bluegrass, Kentucky bluegrass, colonial bentgrass, creeping bentgrass, tall fescue, creeping red fescue, and perennial ryegrass, respectively. Butler and Hodges (1967) found tissue P values from as low as 2.0 g kg^{-1} for Meyer zoysia to as high as 5.1 g kg^{-1} for 'Kentucky-31' tall fescue, while two bluegrass varieties differed by 1.8 g kg^{-1} tissue P. During a 1-yr period, tissue P, averaged over 15 Kentucky bluegrass varieties, ranged from a low of 1.0 g kg^{-1} dry weight to a high of 4.4 g kg^{-1} dry weight (Mehall et al., 1983).

Attempts have been made to establish sufficiency ranges for tissue P. Based on a review of literature, Martin and Matocha (1973) outlined approximate sufficiency ranges for tissue P for cool-season forage grasses. For Kentucky bluegrass, values <1.8 g kg^{-1} were considered deficient, from 2.4 to 3.0 g kg^{-1} were critical, from 2.8 to 3.6 g kg^{-1} were adequate, and values >4.0 g kg^{-1} were considered high. For annual and perennial ryegrass values <2.8 g kg^{-1} were deficient, from 2.8 to 3.4 g kg^{-1} were critical, from 3.6 to 4.4 g kg^{-1} were adequate, and >5.0 g kg^{-1} were high. Values ranging from 1.2 to 2.4 g kg^{-1} of P were found in healthy bluegrass by Oertli (1963). Lunt et al. (1964) reported a minimum tissue P level of 4 g kg^{-1} was associated with maximum yield of 'Newport' Kentucky bluegrass. Maximum yield of Kentucky bluegrass was associated with a value of 2.5 g kg^{-1} by Walker and Pesek (1967), although this value depended on tissue P levels. On a soil with only 27 kg ha^{-1} of P, average creeping bentgrass tissue P levels of 5.0 g kg^{-1} were obtained, with no deficiency noted nor growth response occurring as tissue P increased to 8.4 g kg^{-1} due to P applications (Waddington et al., 1978). Turner (1980) noted no growth-related deficiencies for perennial ryegrass, creeping red fescue, nor Kentucky bluegrass with associated tissue P levels of 4.8, 3.3, and 2.0 g kg^{-1}, respectively. Jones (1980) suggested a sufficiency range for turfgrass tissue P of 3.0 to 5.5 g kg^{-1} (Table 11-2). These sufficiency ranges may, however, need to be adjusted for time of sampling. Hall and Miller (1974) found that 74% of the 'Merion' Kentucky bluegrass clipping samples taken in July and September which had <3.6 g kg^{-1} of P could be related to yields <50% maximum. In November, only 60% of the samples that had <2.3 g kg^{-1} of P could be related to yields <50% maximum.

B. Effects on Turfgrass Establishment

Contrary to effects measured with K, P plays a critical role in the establishment of cool-season turfgrasses from seed and warm-season grasses from vegetative material. In the vegetative establishment of zoysiagrass, a significant top, root, and stolon growth response to P additions was obtained by Juska (1959a) on a soil extremely low in P. He concluded that adequate P was necessary for rapid establishment of zoysiagrass. Wood and Duble (1976) found that P affected St. Augustinegrass growth most during the first 8 wk of establishment. At 8 wk, coverage on plots receiving little or no P averaged <50% whereas plots receiving P averaged 73% coverage. After 8 wk, the P rate had little effect on rate of coverage. On a soil high in P, however, Fry and Dernoeden (1987) found little benefit from P applications in the establishment of Meyer zoysiagrass from plugs.

Responses to P additions to the seedbeds of cool-season grasses are among the most critical and dramatic in turfgrass fertility. Juska et al. (1965), adding P to soil before seeding cool-season turfgrass species, reported increased top and root growth, although root weights tended to decrease at very high P rates. Westfall and Simmons (1971) found that on low P soils, P applications substantially increased Kentucky bluegrass seedling density. Nitrogen, applied without P, did not improve seedling growth and development while reducing root weights; however, when soil P was adequate, N applied alone increased the rate of seedling development, and improved turfgrass quality. On P-deficient soils, McVey (1967) found a Kentucky bluegrass seedling growth response to extremely low rates of P applications.

Turner (1980), in an attempt to provide soil test calibration data for turfgrass establishment, performed a series of studies relating the establishment of several cool-season turfgrass species to different rates of applied P on several soils. In summarizing these series of studies, he stated that initial soil P levels of 67 kg ha^{-1} were not sufficient for rapid turfgrasses establishment. Increasing soil P levels to 80 to 157 kg ha^{-1} resulted in the most satisfactory and rapid establishment. Higher P rates resulted in little additional benefit during the establishment phase. Differences in stand density were generally observed to begin 3 to 4 wk after germination, presumably as seed P had been used. On soil with existing initial soil P levels of 175 kg ha^{-1}, no increase in the rate of establishment was obtained from seedbed P applications, indicating no added P is needed for establishment of turfgrass on soil with initial P levels this high. Christians et al. (1981b) reported that the establishment rate of Kentucky bluegrass seeded on soil with P levels of 33 kg ha^{-1} increased up to applied P rates of 5.4 kg ha^{-1} annually.

Species and varieties may differ in their response to seedbed P applications. Juska et al. (1965) reported that the top growth of Merion Kentucky bluegrass increased more rapidly and to a higher level with increasing establishment P rates than common Kentucky bluegrass. An interaction occurred with P additions and soil pH. At a pH of 6.5, bluegrass and red fescue total plant growth showed little response to P applications; however, at pH 4.5, bluegrass plant growth increased with P additions while red fescue was still unaffected. King and Skogley (1969), however, did not find any effect from seedbed P applications on the subsequent species composition of a Kentucky bluegrass-red fescue mixture. Turner and Waddington (1983) evaluated monostands of chewings fescue, Kentucky bluegrass, and perennial ryegrass established on the same soil. Response of these turfgrass species to seedbed P applications was similar; however, the magnitude and duration of ground cover and quality response by the chewings fescue was less than for the other two species. Soil P levels were thus considered to be less critical for establishing chewings fescue.

The effect of depth of P incorporation into the seedbed has also been studied. King and Skogley (1969) compared surface P applications, incorporation to a 10-cm depth, and three-fourths incorporated and one-fourth surface applied in the establishment of a seeded Kentucky bluegrass-red fescue mixture. In a fall seeding, initial results were best with surface applications and the three-fourths to one-fourth placement, although differences diminished with time. In a spring seeding, P placement made no difference. Turner (1980) found that P raked into the surface 1.2 cm resulted in similar establishment response as higher P rates incorporated to a depth of 11 cm. However, potential long-term effects from incorporation vs. surface application of P during seeding were not studied. In an effort to enhance establishment rates of tall fescue and Kentucky bluegrass by placing P in closer proximity to germinating seed, Hathcock et al. (1984), studied the effect of coating seed with fertilizer materials. When seed was coated with treble superphosphate, little or no germination occurred, apparently due to very high H-ion concentrations as this P source went into solution around the seed. Beneficial effects were measured when dicalcium phosphate was used in the seed coating.

Long-term benefits from P applications to the seedbed have been observed. Turner et al. (1979) found that 6 yr after establishment, spring greening was enhanced by the original seedbed P applications and crabgrass encroachment was reduced. After 9 yr, the seedbed P applications resulted in greater top growth and reduced dandelion encroachment. Watschke et al. (1977) reported that a growth response of Kentucky bluegrass was still apparent 5 yr after seedbed applications of P.

Few studies have been reported relating soil P applications to the establishment of an area with sod. Turner (1980) measured the rooting strength of Kentucky bluegrass sod 6 and 36 wk after placement of sod. No differences in strength of rooting were found due to P applications to the sodbed, despite very low initial soil P levels. Watschke et al. (1977), however, reported that results with Kentucky bluegrass indicated that P enhanced rooting of sod plugs. Also, the magnitude of P absorption measured in the surface 1.3 cm of soil exemplified the need for P near the surface for optimum turfgrass establishment.

C. Effects on Turfgrass Maintenance

Although numerous types of turfgrass responses to maintenance applications of P have been described, responses have generally not been as dramatic as N and K. Growth responses to P applications have been inconsistent. Although P additions caused an increase in top growth, root growth, and tillering of Italian ryegrass (Hylton et al., 1965), several researchers have found little influence of P on turfgrass growth. Pritchett and Horn (1966) stated that warm-season turfgrasses in general show little growth response to P applications. Robinson et al. (1976) found no influence of P applications to a New Zealand browntop-New Zealand chewings fescue lawn mixture for verdure, root weights, or tiller numbers. In a sand culture, P had little influence on Kentucky bluegrass or creeping bentgrass growth (Christians et al., 1979). Waddington et al. (1978) found little influence of P on topgrowth of bentgrass putting green turf, even when soil P was low. Turner (1980), in a series of soil test calibrations studies, found little influence of P on the growth of perennial ryegrass, Kentucky bluegrass, or creeping red fescue, despite low soil P levels. Hall and Miller (1974), however, did find increased Kentucky bluegrass growth with P applications to a soil that was very low in soil P.

Some growth problems may occur at high rates of P applications using a solution culture. Menn and McBee (1970) found that high P levels caused a suppression of bermudagrass growth. Bell and DeFrance (1944) reported that large amounts of P may reduce bentgrass root accumulation. Phosphorus was also reported by Holt and Davis (1948) to decrease bentgrass root weights when a complete fertilizer was compared to one without P, although foliar coverage was increased. Phillips and Webb (1971) suggested excessive P rates may accentuate micronutrient problems.

Turfgrass color and visual quality responses to maintenance applications of P have been observed by several researchers. Waddington et al. (1978) observed that creeping bentgrass receiving P applications was often a lighter green color than when not fertilized with P. Turner (1980) noted a darker green color of Kentucky bluegrass on a very low P soil where no P was applied. Small additions of P resulted in a lighter but healthier green color. He also observed similar results on a Kentucky bluegrass-perennial ryegrass mixture. On this site, lack of K applications accentuated the dark green color. The darker green color on these turfs not receiving P applications was not judged to be preferable to the lighter green color of P treated turf. Despite these color differences, little influence was observed on the visual quality of turf. On soils low to very low in P, visual quality of stands of perennial ryegrass, Kentucky bluegrass, and creeping red fescue was negligibly influenced by P applications over a 2-yr period (Turner, 1980). Christians et al. (1979) found little influence of P applications on the visual quality of bentgrass.

Sturkie and Rouse (1967) observed similar color patterns with P applications on zoysia and bermudagrass. Both species became lighter green as P rates increased. However, they also found that high rates of P caused chlorosis of zoysia in early spring and late fall. Christians et al. (1981a) also found that at very high rates of P applications, Kentucky bluegrass quality and tissue chlorophyll content decreased, possibly due to adverse effects on Mg or Fe uptake and metabolism.

Although general turfgrass quality has not been shown to be dramatically affected by P applications, the incidence of several diseases that could periodically affect quality have been influenced by P. Kentucky bluegrass turf fertilized with N and P, N and K, or especially N, P, and K was less diseased with stripe smut (*Ustilago striiformis*) than turf fertilized with N alone (Hull et al., 1979), although they stated that this effect might be modified by the availability of soil P and K. Goss and Gould (1968) reported that on a soil where P was not low, incidence of fusarium patch was decreased by P at lower N rates, although at higher N rates, P had little effect. Goss (1969) also stated that P applications may have a significant effect on the control of take-all patch, and may interact with S applications in this disease's control (Davidson & Goss, 1972). Goss (1969) also stated that N, P, and K additions interact on the incidence of red thread; however, Cahill et al. (1983), observing perennial ryegrass, and Turner (1980), observing perennial ryegrass and creeping red fescue, did not find any influence of P applications on red thread incidence. Bloom and Couch (1960) found increased severity of brown patch under high N with normal P and K nutrition, but stated that increases in P and K could offset the increased susceptibility. Dollar spot incidence of creeping bentgrass did not appear to be affected greatly by P rates (Waddington et al., 1978), although somewhat lower incidence was found where no P was applied. Turner (1980) reported no influence of P on the incidence of dollar spot on perennial ryegrass, or on the incidence of leaf spot on Kentucky bluegrass.

Phosphorus may also influence heat, cold, and drought tolerance of turfgrasses, but usually not to nearly the degree that N or K do. Gilbert and Davis (1971) found that the addition of P improved the cold tolerance of bermudagrass as long as N and K were in adequate supply. However, Palmertree et al. (1974) did not find any effect of P on the cold hardiness of centipedegrass.

Phosphorus appears to interact with other nutrients in the heat and drought tolerance of cool-season grasses. When temperatures and N levels were high, Pellet and Roberts (1963) reported that high P rates can cause further deterioration of Kentucky bluegrass. Also, Goss (1963) reported better bentgrass putting green quality in the hotter months on turf receiving no P, but better quality in the cooler months where P was applied. However, Schmidt and Breuninger (1981) found that P strongly affected the recovery of Kentucky bluegrass from summer drought. Adequate soil P levels were considered imperative for rapid Kentucky bluegrass recovery from drought, particularly when it had been liberally fertilized with N. Keen (1969) has stated that when water is limiting, small additions of P may considerably improve utilization of the limited water available.

A unique situation arises with annual bluegrass and P applications. In most situations, annual bluegrass is considered a weedy grass and its control and diminishment is desirable. In some situations, however, annual bluegrass is the predominant species and it is managed for maximum survival. In either case, P nutrition can play a major role.

Encroachment of annual bluegrass into desired species has been related to P additions. Waddington et al. (1978) found an increase in annual bluegrass in bentgrass putting green turf as soil P increasd from 27 to 210 kg ha^{-1} as a result of P fertilization. Goss et al. (1975) found that P applications increased annual bluegrass encroachment into bentgrass at all levels of applied N, with the greatest infestation occurring at moderate N levels. Some of this encroachment of annual bluegrass, which has poor heat and drought tolerance compared to bentgrass, may be due to improved drought resistance. Escritt and Legg (1970) reported that P additions contributed to the drought resistance of annual bluegrass. A common herbicidal means of controlling annual bluegrass is the use of calcium arsenates; however, Carrow and Rieke (1972) stated that high P may reduce the rate of arsenates used by *Poa annua*, thus decreasing control by this chemical method.

Dest and Allinson (1981) studied P and N applications on a putting green turf that was 95% annual bluegrass and thus being managed to obtain maximum annual bluegrass survival. Phosphorus applications as compared to no P increased both the density and survival of annual bluegrass. They also found that P applications should be adjusted upwards with increasing rates of applied N to maximize survival. These studies make it apparent that P nutrition in its relation to annual bluegrass survival must be carefully considered in situations where annual bluegrass is either likely to be a weed problem or is the predominant desired species.

Other effects of P nutrition have also been reported. Hansen (1970) reported that N applied without P or K resulted in higher weed populations than a fertilizer with N, P, and K; however, the application of P or K alone without N substantially increased weed infestation. Turner (1980) reported a moderate reduction in crabgrass infestation of creeping red fescue as P rates increased. Pritchett and Horn (1966) stated that parasitic nematode infestation of turfgrass roots decreased as P additions increased, even with adequate initial soil P levels. Escritt and Legg (1970) reported that P additions reduced moss invasions into annual bluegrass.

IV. CALCIUM

Calcium is the known component of one enzyme, amylase, and is a cofactor of several other enzymes. It is a major component of the middle lamella of cell walls and thus becomes important in the mechanical strength of tissues. Calcium plays a strong role in meristematic activity.

Levels of Ca in turfgrass tissue tend to be similar to P. Waddington and Zimmerman (1972), measuring tissue levels of turfgrass species grown under identical conditions, reported average Ca tissue contents of 6.4, 5.6, 6.6, 6.2, 5.0, 4.9, and 6.0 g kg^{-1} for annual bluegrass, Kentucky bluegrass, colonial bentgrass, creeping bentgrass, tall fescue, creeping red fescue, and perennial ryegrass, respectively. Butler and Hodges (1967) reported greater variations among turfgrass species, with tissue values of 2.7, 3.6, 5.1, 3.9, 4.9, 3.6, 2.9, and 3.8 g kg^{-1} being determined for Kentucky bluegrass,

Merion Kentucky bluegrass, perennial ryegrass, creeping red fescue, tall fescue, colonial bentgrass, Meyer zoysia, and bermudagrass, respectively. As is the case with several elements, tissue Ca can vary significantly throughout the season. Tissue Ca levels of Kentucky bluegrass during one growing season ranged from a low of 8.2 to a high of 14.7 g kg^{-1} (Hall & Miller, 1974). Jones (1980) suggested a turfgrass sufficiency range for tissue Ca of 5.0 to 12.5 g kg^{-1}.

Demonstrated turfgrass responses to applications of Ca have been few. Most responses that some may attribute to Ca applications are in fact responses to changes in soil reaction caused by Ca-containing materials such as Ca-oxide, Ca-hydroxide, calcitic limestone, or dolomitic limestone. Nittler and Kenny (1971) found wide differences in Kentucky bluegrass cultivar tolerance to low Ca, with 'Arista', 'Fylking', 'Cougar', 'Zwartburg', and 'Pennstar' more tolerant than 'Newport', 'Windsor', 'Nugget', and 'Delta'. In nutrient solution studies, Moore et al. (1961) found that susceptibility of colonial bentgrass to pythium blight was greater when Ca was deficient. In a further study, they found that pectolytic-enzyme activity in leaves of bentgrass was greater under low Ca nutrition (Moore & Couch, 1968). These enzymes were reported to be involved in the blighting by pythium of bentgrass leaves.

V. MAGNESIUM

Magnesium is a component of the chlorophyll molecule and the most common activator of enzymes, particularly those concerned with energy metabolism. Nearly all enzymes that act on phosphorylated substances have Mg as a cofactor.

Tissue levels of Mg in turfgrasses tend to be somewhat lower than Ca and P levels. Tissue Mg values of 2.0, 1.6, 2.1, 2.2, 3.0, 1.7, and 1.9 g kg^{-1} were measured in annual bluegrass, Kentucky bluegrass, colonial bentgrass, creeping bentgrass, tall fescue, creeping red fescue, and perennial ryegrass, respectively, by Waddington and Zimmerman (1972). Somewhat more variation among turfgrass species were determined by Butler and Hodges (1967). Tissue Mg values reported were 1.6, 3.2, 3.2, 2.4, 3.5, 2.5, 1.3, and 2.5 g kg^{-1} for Kentucky bluegrass, Merion Kentucky bluegrass, perennial ryegrass, creeping red fescue, tall fescue, colonial bentgrass, Meyer zoysiagrass, and bermudagrass. Hall and Miller (1974) found significant variation in Kentucky bluegrass tissue Mg throughout the growing season, ranging from a low of 2.4 to a high of 4.6 g kg^{-1}. Jones (1980) suggested a turfgrass sufficiency range for tissue Mg of 2.0 to 6.0 g kg^{-1}.

Few studies have directly related Mg applications to turfgrass response. Kamon (1974), however, did assess the relative Mg requirements of three warm-season grass species grown in sand culture. The severity of deficiency symptoms were greatest for zoysiagrass, followed by centipedegrass and was least for bermudagrass, although the initial rate of appearance of Mg deficiency was in the opposite order. With zoysiagrass, leaf length, shoot length, and shoot weight were increased by various rates of added Mg in the sand culture; however, root length and root weight were not affected by Mg additions. On soil with Mg levels of 134 kg ha^{-1}, no growth response of bermudagrass or perennial ryegrass was noted in response to Mg applications (Sartain & Dudeck, 1980b). Although no visual deficiency symptoms were observed, Walker and Ward (1974) measured low Mg absorption by centipedegrass receiving high K fertilization. Decreased net photosynthesis measured under this high K fertilization was believed to be due to the low tissue Mg levels.

VI. SULFUR

Sulfur is a constituent of several amino acids, including cystine, cysteine, and methione, and thus is a constituent of numerous proteins. Coenzymes such as thiamine, biotin, and coenzyme A contain S, and the sulfate ion activates some enzymes.

Tissue levels of S in turfgrasses have not been commonly reported. However, Waddington et al. (1978) measured S tissue values of creeping bentgrass ranging from 2.6 to 4.0 g kg^{-1}, depending on time of sampling during the growing season. A range of 2.97 to 4.24 g kg^{-1} were reported (Goss et al., 1979) in bentgrass tissue, depending on level of N, P, K, and S fertilization. Love (1962) reported that 1.5 g kg^{-1} tissue S was adequate for creeping bentgrass and creeping red fescue. Jones (1980) suggested a turfgrass sufficiency for tissue S of 2.0 to 4.5 g kg^{-1}.

Growth responses to S applications have been demonstrated by Goss et al. (1979). Under high N fertility, bentgrass growth was increased by 71% when S was applied compared to no S applications. Using S rates ranging from 0 to 224 kg ha^{-1}, Brauen et al. (1975) also observed color enhancement of bentgrass with S applications. An interaction was observed as well with N applications. High rates of N application resulted in poorer color when no S was applied, yet significantly improved color occurred at intermediate and high rates of S application.

Relationships between disease incidence and S applications have also been observed. Fursarium patch incidence of bentgrass decreased with increasing rates of S application, with no disease evident when the highest rates of S were applied (Brauen et al., 1975). Davidson and Goss (1972) reported that S-containing compounds were most effective in the control of take-all patch of bentgrass, although Dernoeden (1987) did not find S alone to be effective in this disease's control.

Sulfur applications may help reduce annual bluegrass encroachment into bentgrass putting greens, but the response is highly dependent on N fertility (Goss et al., 1975). The highest S rate used, 168 kg ha^{-1} annually, reduced annual bluegrass populations at all levels of N fertility, whereas at low rates of S application annual bluegrass levels increased with increasing N. In this same study, it was observed that no black algae was present in S-treated turf, although bentgrass that received no S had high amounts of algae.

VII. MICRONUTRIENTS

Seven elements are classified as micronutrients in plant nutrition literature: Fe, Mn, Zn, Cu, B, Mo, and Cl. These elements, although critical and essential for plant growth and survival, are termed micronutrients due to the relatively small quantities required by plants compared to the other eight essential elements. Until recent years, few research studies had been conducted relating turfgrass performance to deficiencies and applications of these nutrients. Several factors in the last 15 yr, however, including the growth of the lawn care industry and the increased use on golf courses of putting green and tee mixtures that have very high sand contents, have led to greater attention being focused on the micronutrients, particularly Fe. Despite this, there is still a great need for further research to pinpoint conditions and situations where applications of micronutrients to turfgrass may be beneficial, as well as those situations where detrimental effects may occur.

Plant tissue testing has been the most promising method of determining potential micronutrient deficiencies of turfgrasses. As with the macronutrients, however, a variety of factors may influence tissue levels measured and the subsequent interpretation of these levels for diagnostic purposes, including turfgrass species and varieties (Waddington & Zimmerman, 1972; Butler & Hodges, 1967) and time of sampling (Waddington & Zimmerman, 1972; Hall & Miller, 1974). Based on current information, however, Jones (1980) attempted to establish micronutrient tissue sufficiency ranges for turfgrasses where practicable.

Micronutrient deficiency symptoms are listed in Table 11–2. However, deficiency symptoms are often obscure and may vary with species, the degree of the deficiency, and whether other deficiency, biotic, or abiotic problems exist. Thus, making visual observations of micronutrient deficiencies are often difficult and sometimes unreliable.

A. Iron

Iron is probably the most important micronutrient in practical terms in regard to turfgrass performance. It has thus been the focus of the greatest amount of turfgrass micronutrient research, although most of the information available today is still in the form of observations or unpublished research. Iron is essential in chlorophyll synthesis, as a constituent of several heme and nonheme enzymes and carriers, and may play a role in nucleic acid synthesis.

Tissue Fe levels of different turfgrass species grown under identical conditions differ dramatically. Waddington and Zimmerman (1972) reported average tissue Fe concentrations of 135, 107, 204, 170, 127, 111, and 162 mg kg^{-1} for annual bluegrass, Kentucky bluegrass, colonial bentgrass, creeping bentgrass, tall fescue, creeping red fescue, and perennial ryegrass, respectively. Butler and Hodges (1967) reported even greater differences, with tissue values of 102, 189, 934, 266, 354, 179, 203, and 1066 mg kg^{-1} for Kentucky bluegrass, Merion Kentucky bluegrass, perennial ryegrass, creeping red fescue, Kentucky-31 tall fescue, colonial bentgrass, Meyer zoysiagrass, and bermudagrass. During a 1-yr period, tissue Fe in colonial bentgrass ranged from a low of 106 to a high of 362 mg kg^{-1} (Waddington & Zimmerman, 1972). Jones (1980) established a general sufficiency range of 35 to 100 mg kg^{-1} for turfgrasses.

Conditions that may induce Fe deficiencies are varied. Soils that have a high pH, have very high P levels, are calcareous, or are inherently very low in Fe, such as a sandy soil, may cause deficiencies. Iron deficiency may be amplified by high growth rates casued by N applications or by excessive levels of other metal ions. Cold and wet soils, particularly in spring, when growth rates tend to be high, may also induce an Fe deficiency. Understanding the cause of the deficiency can thus be important in taking the appropriate corrective measures. Conversely, understanding the conditions under which an Fe deficiency is most likely to occur is a valuable diagnostic tool.

Kurtz (1981) found that several zoysiagrass varieties exhibited greater Fe uptake at a soil pH of 5.5 than at a soil pH of 7.5. Ryan et al. (1975) were able to alleviate Fe deficiency of common bermudagrass grown on calcareous soil through application of sulfuric acid. Thus, maintaining a soil pH below 7.0 should help minimize some Fe-deficiency problems.

Some potential exists for minimizing Fe-deficiency problems, where soil conditions or management practices may favor such deficiencies, through the selection of Fe-efficient turfgrasses. Kurtz (1981) found substantial differences among zoysia cultivar selections in their ability to use available Fe. Harivandi and Butler (1980) and McCaslin et al. (1981) have found differences in Fe chlorosis among Kentucky bluegrass and bermudagrass varieties as well. Thus, further identification and selection of varieties exhibiting greater tolerance to low- available Fe levels may be beneficial for regions in the country where such problems are prevalent.

The application of Fe, however, has historically been the most common and practical means of correcting Fe deficiencies. Deal and Engel (1965) reported that low rates of Fe application to Kentucky bluegrass under low fertility produced a rapid increase in green color that lasted 4 to 5 wk. A slight improvement continued for up to 16 wk. Sod density was increased, and root weights were increased 25 wk after application of 1.1 kg ha^{-1} of Fe. Top growth was not generally affected by these Fe applications. Minner and Butler (1984) reported that Kentucky bluegrass color improved with applications of $FeSO_4$ up to a rate of 49 kg ha^{-1} of Fe. They also found that the initial production of acceptable color could be achieved at much lower rates with Fe chelates compared to $FeSO_4$. Snyder and Schmidt (1974) found that applications to creeping bentgrass of Fe in combination with N, compared to N alone, enhanced appearance, chlorophyll content, and early spring growth, while offsetting the injurious effect of heavy fall-winter N applications. Recovery from winter desiccation was also improved with Fe applications. In comparing Fe sources, they determined that chelated Fe produced a better root system than $FeSO_4$.

Due to the color enhancement achieved with Fe applications without a concommitent increase in topgrowth, recent attention has been given to

Fe applications as a partial replacement for N and in situations where no apparent Fe deficiencies exist. Yust et al. (1984) investigated means of enhancing the color of Kentucky bluegrass in lieu of excessive N fertilization. They found that color enhancement due to Fe applications at rates of 1.1, 2.2, and 4.5 kg of Fe ha^{-1} lasted for several weeks to several months depending on the weather following application. When cool wet periods followed application, color enhancement due to Fe applications without N lasted only 2 to 3 wk. When cool dry periods followed application, color enhancement lasted several months. Iron chelate, compared to $FeSO_4$, at the 2.2 kg ha^{-1} rate, produced the best overall results. Combining Fe with 25 kg of N ha^{-1} produced color equal to 49 kg of N ha^{-1}. They concluded that combining Fe with N can result in acceptable turfgrass color with lower rates of N.

Due to the relatively small actual quantities of micronutrients needed by turfgrass plants, the potential for creating detrimental effects or toxicities strongly exists, both through overapplication or complex interactions with other essential elements. Deal and Engel (1965) reported severe discoloration, burning, and inhibition of rhizome formation of Kentucky bluegrass from the application of 56 kg of Fe ha^{-1}. Under high fertility, all Fe rates investigated adversely affected sod density for 10 wk. Yust et al. (1984) observed no serious injury (considered foliar dieback) to Kentucky bluegrass from Fe applications of up to 17.7 kg ha^{-1}. A blackish green color appeared on turf treated with Fe applications of 4.5 to 17.7 kg ha^{-1}; however, it generally recovered within 2 wk. Although foliar toxicity was observed at Fe rates above 17.7 kg ha^{-1}, no permanent damage was caused.

Carrow et al. (1988b) stated that the controlling factor that determines which Fe rate should be used for lawn applications is initial phytotoxicity and not long-term benefits. They found centipedegrass phytotoxicity for a particular rate of Fe was affected by N levels and the air temperature on the day of application. They summarized their findings as follows:

1. If applied to centipedegrass on a moderately warm day (21–33 °C), the maximum acceptable Fe rate was 2.0 kg ha^{-1} in combination with 0 or 9.8 kg of N ha^{-1}. Up to 39.0 kg of N ha^{-1} could be applied without any Fe before N-induced toxicity occurred.

2. If applied on a very hot day (28–37.5 °C), only 0.73 kg of Fe ha^{-1} could be applied with 12.2 kg of N ha^{-1} without objectionable phytotoxicity. The maximum N rate under these conditions was 24.2 kg of N ha^{-1} before N-induced toxicity occurred.

3. The 2.0 kg of Fe ha^{-1} rate provided positive visual quality and color responses for up to 35 d after treatment, whereas, the 0.73 kg of Fe ha^{-1} rate improved color for only 22 d after treatment.

B. Manganese

Manganese serves in plant nutrition as an activator of numerous enzymes, particularly oxidation-reduction reactions, and as a constituent of one known enzyme. It is involved in chlorophyll synthesis and plays a role in photosynthesis.

The amount of Mn found in turfgrass tissue is typical of most micronutrients. Waddington and Zimmerman (1972) measured average Mn levels of 250, 154, 414, 339, 434, 185, and 304 mg kg^{-1} for annual bluegrass, Kentucky bluegrass, colonial bentgrass, creeping bentgrass, tall fescue, creeping red fescue, and perennial ryegrass, respectively. Butler and Hodges (1967) reported Mn tissue levels of 18, 48, 73, 54, 71, 83, 29, and 57 mg kg^{-1} for Kentucky bluegrass, Merion Kentucky bluegrass, perennial ryegrass, creeping red fescue, tall fescue, colonial bentgrass, Meyer zoysiagrass, and bermudagrass, respectively. A great deal of tissue Mn variation can occur throughout the year. Waddington and Zimmerman (1972), for example, found tissue Mn in creeping bentgrass to vary from a low of 163 mg kg^{-1} to a high of 391 mg kg^{-1} in one season. Jones (1980) suggested a sufficiency range of 25 to 50 mg kg^{-1} for turfgrasses.

As with most of the micronutrients, few observations of turfgrass responses to Mn have been noted. Deal and Engel (1965) reported that Mn applications to Kentucky bluegrass did not affect clipping yields, but lower rates stimulated root growth and improved color for about 4 wk when fertility levels were low. Sod density improved for about 5 wk. No toxicity symptoms developed with rates as high as 84 kg ha^{-1} of Mn. Christians et al. (1981a) reported in a study on N and K effects on bentgrass that at higher N, tissue growth decreased somewhat with K additions. They hypothesized that a N–K induced Mn deficiency may have been the cause. Tissue Mn was measured at 33 mg kg^{-1}.

C. Zinc

Zinc is a component of several enzymes, including several dehydrogenases such as alcohol dehydrogenase, lactic dehydrogenase, and malic dehydrogenase. Zinc may play a role in auxin synthesis.

Tissue Zn levels are generally lower than Fe or Mn. Waddington and Zimmerman (1972) measured average tissue Zn levels of 78, 52, 70, 61, 50, 54, and 57 mg kg^{-1} for annual bluegrass, Kentucky bluegrass, colonial bentgrass, creeping bentgrass, tall fescue, creeping red fescue, and perennial ryegrass, respectively. Butler and Hodges (1967) reported tissue levels of 19, 45, 52, 30, 47, 50, 35, and 34 mg kg^{-1} of Zn for Kentucky bluegrass, Merion Kentucky bluegrass, perennial ryegrass, creeping red fescue, tall fescue, colonial bentgrass, Meyer zoysiagrass, and bermudagrass, respectively. Turner (1980) measured tissue Zn levels of 30.6, 31.5, and 22.3 mg kg^{-1} for perennial ryegrass, creeping red fescue, and Kentucky bluegrass, respectively. Jones (1980) suggested a sufficiency range of 20 to 55 mg kg^{-1} for turfgrasses.

Zinc effects on turfgrasses have not been studied in detail. Deal and Engel (1965) reported that growth rate, color, and sod density of Kentucky bluegrass were not affected by Zn applications. However, root growth was stimulated by an application of Zn at a rate of 5.6 kg ha^{-1}, while rhizome growth was strongly inhibited by an application of 28 kg ha^{-1}. Wu et al. (1981) found differences in bermudagrass cultivars to tolerance of excessive Zn levels. At a solution concentration of 50 mg kg^{-1} of Zn, 'Santa Ana' and 'Tifgreen' exhibited no reduction in root growth whereas Tifway and 'Tifdwarf' showed substantial reduction. When Zn concentration was increased to 200 mg kg^{-1}, root growth of Tifway and Tifdwarf was seriously inhibited, whereas the other two cultivars exhibited injury levels similar to these two at 50 mg kg^{-1}.

D. Copper

Copper is a component of numerous enzymes. These include ascorbic acid oxidase, lactase, polyphenol oxidase, and cytochrome oxidase. Tissue levels of Cu are generally very low. Average tissue Cu levels of 26, 25, 31, 35, 23, 25, and 24 mg kg^{-1} were measured for annual bluegrass, Kentucky bluegrass, colonial bentgrass, creeping bentgrass, tall fescue, creeping red fescue, and perennial ryegrass, respectively (Waddington & Zimmerman, 1972). Tissue Cu levels of 35.5, 25.5, 37.6, 20.5, 34.0, 18.7, 17.5, and 43.0 mg kg^{-1} were found in Kentucky bluegrass, Merion Kentucky bluegrass, perennial ryegrass, creeping red fescue, tall fescue, colonial bentgrass, Meyer zoysiagrass, and bermudagrass, respectively (Butler & Hodges, 1967). Levels of 8.0, 8.4, and 7.3 mg kg^{-1} tissue Cu were reported by Turner (1980) for perennial ryegrass, creeping red fescue, and Kentucky bluegrass. A turfgrasses sufficiency range of 5 to 20 mg kg^{-1} was suggested by Jones (1980).

Although published information on Cu is lacking, turfgrass deficiencies appear to be rare. Toxicities to turfgrass, although rare, may be of more concern. In nutrient solution, Wu et al. (1981) showed root injury to bermudagrass at solution concentrations above 0.25 mg kg^{-1} of Cu. Tolerances of bermudagrass cultivars to Cu were Tifgreen > Tifdwarf > Santa Ana > Tifway.

E. Boron

The precise role of B in plant nutrition has yet to be determined. It is believed to play a role in carbohydrate metabolism.

The amount of B required by turfgrass plants is extremely small. Waddington and Zimmerman (1972) determined average levels of 36, 16, 26, 30, 22, 26, and 24 mg kg^{-1} of B for annual bluegrass, Kentucky bluegrass, colonial bentgrass, creeping bentgrass, tall fescue, creeping red fescue, and perennial ryegrass, respectively. Butler and Hodges (1967) reported levels of 6, 9, 14, 6.5, 9, 6, 6, and 9.5 mg kg^{-1} for Kentucky bluegrass, Merion Kentucky bluegrass, perennial ryegrass, creeping red fescue, tall fescue, colonial bentgrass, Meyer zoysiagrass, and bermudagrass, respectively. Turner (1980) obtained levels fo 9.4, 9.2, and 7.9 mg kg^{-1} for perennial ryegrass, creeping red fescue, and Kentucky bluegrass, respectively. Jones (1980) suggested a B-sufficiency range of 10 to 60 mg kg^{-1} for turfgrasses; however, Turner (1980) noted no deficiency symptoms for the reported values of < 10 mg kg^{-1}.

Deal and Engel (1965), using B application rates of 1.7 and 8.4 kg ha^{-1} on Kentucky bluegrass, observed a rapid increase in color for 5 wk after application when fertility levels were low. Root growth was stimulated and sod density was also increased for approximately 5 wk. Under high levels of fertility, however, the higher B rate resulted in a pale green turf for 13 wk, with leaf tip death occurring.

On soils with excessive B levels, species selection may be critical for successful turfgrass growth. Oertli et al. (1961) determined that sensitivity to excess B is related to B uptake rates by turfgrass plants. Accumulation of B, and thus injury, was in the order: creeping bentgrass > perennial ryegrass > 'Alta' fescue > Kentucky bluegrass > zoysiagrass > bermudagrass. Toxicity occurred as a tip burn, appearing most severe on older leaves. They stated that clipping will remove excess B accumulating in leaf tips and, when practical, increasing frequency of clipping may permit turfgrasses to tolerate higher B levels.

F. Molybdenum

Molybdenum is a component of several enzymes, including nitrogenase and nitrate reductase. It is thus required for normal assimilation of N in plants.

Smaller amounts of Mo are required by plants than any other essential element. Butler and Hodges (1967) reported tissue Mo levels of 1.77, 3.35, 8.45, 2.72, 4.05, 2.25, 1.77, and 8.20 mg kg^{-1} for Kentucky bluegrass, Merion Kentucky bluegrass, perennial ryegrass, creeping red fescue, tall fescue, colonial bentgrass, Meyer zoysiagrass, and bermudagrass, respectively. Jones (1980) stated that tissue-sufficiency levels for Mo in turfgrasses are not known at this time.

G. Chlorine

The role of chlorine in plant nutrition is not well defined. No enzymes of other essential organic compounds contain Cl as a constituent, however, it appears that Cl may act in conjunction with one or more enzymes of photosystem II of photosynthesis. Although responses of other crops have been described, deficiency symptoms or beneficial responses of turfgrasses to Cl have not been reported. As such, tissue sufficiency ranges for turfgrasses have not been established.

VIII. NONESSENTIAL ELEMENTS

Several elements that are nonessential for the growth and survival of turfgrasses nevertheless can play a role in turfgrass performance. Generally their effects are detrimental and occur when levels are excessive. Sodium is the most common example of a nonessential element that may adversely affect turf, and is discussed in detail in chapter 6 by Harivandi et al.

Aluminum, particularly under acid soil conditions below a pH of 5.0, can become toxic to turfgrass plants. Sensitivity to Al toxicity by turfgrass species and varieties were evaluated by Murray and Foy (1978). Thirty-five Kentucky bluegrass, 15 fineleaf fescue, and 6 tall fescue varieties were compared. Major differences in growth due to changes in soil pH and thus Al availability were found among varieties of all species. Comparing four bermudagrass cultivars, Wu et al. (1981), showed tolerance to Al in the order of Tifway > Tifgreen > Santa Ana > Tifdwarf. Differences in the four cultivars were also shown for tolerance to excessive levels of another metal, chromium. Both studies suggest excellent potential for the selection and development of cultivars that have greater tolerances to excessive metal levels in the soil.

Differences in species tolerance to excessive levels of a nonessential element have been used to advantage in the case of arsenic. Annual bluegrass shows greater sensitivity to arsenic toxicity than bentgrass, and thus arsenates have been used to selectively control annual bluegrass in bentgrass turfs (Beard et al., 1978). Turgeon et al. (1975) reported that repeated arsenate applications to Kentucky bluegrass turf resulted in higher wilting tendency, higher disease incidence, shallower rooting, and increased thatch development.

The effect of silicon on the growth and water absorption of three turfgrass species were evaluated by Street et al. (1981). Clipping yields of Kentucky-31 tall fescue, Pennstar Kentucky bluegrass, and common bermudagrass were unaffected by silica applications. Average tissue silica concentrations for tall fescue, bluegrass, and bermudagrass leaf blades were 23.9, 36.6, and 24.0 g kg^{-1}, respectively, for the lower rate of silica application. For the higher rate of application, values were 41.4, 61.0, and 38.5 g kg^{-1}. The amount of water transpired by Kentucky bluegrass was reduced by 10.2 to 17.5% over the study period by the high rate of silica application. They concluded that in field conditions, however, silicon would not appear to have any important role in fertilization programs.

IX. SOIL REACTION

The effect of soil reaction on turfgrass performance has been reported in numerous studies. The reasons for these responses may be numerous but are often unelucidated or are not precisely known, and are beyond the scope of this chapter. However, they may include (i) direct effects, such as H-ion toxicity, increased or decreased availability of essential elements, and increased availability of nonessential elements, such as Al which may become toxic, and (ii) indirect effects, such as changing the microbiological environment and thus their populations. These microbiological changes may in turn affect turfgrass performance through their effect on disease incidence, thatch decomposition, and N conversion reactions and thus N availability to the turfgrass plant.

Soil reaction changes may be brought about through numerous means. Increases in soil acidity may be due to material applications of humans, such as NH_4-based N fertilizers and S or S-containing pesticides, or by natural processes, such as thatch and organic matter decomposition. Decreases in soil acidity may be brought about by the addition of liming materials or continued use of irrigation water having a basic reaction. The mechanisms of these reactions and the characteristics and comparisons of various liming and acidifying agents, as well as the effects on nutrient availability and uptake, have been reviewed in detail in other monographs.

Various turfgrass responses to differences in soil reaction have been reported, although not to the extent that might be expected based on the importance given to it in general plant nutrition literature. Turfgrass species have been reported to have somewhat different optimal ranges of soil reaction. Musser (1950) reported that the soil reaction ranges for good growth of zoysiagrass, bermudagrass, centipedegrass, and St. Augustinegrass were 4.5 to 7.6, 5.1 to 7.1, 4.0 to 6.1, and 6.1 to 8.1, respectively. For creeping red fescue, chewings fescue, tall fescue, and bentgrass, he reported an optimal range of 5.4 to 7.6. He further reported optimal ranges for Kentucky bluegrass, annual bluegrass, roughstalk bluegrass (*Poa trivialis* L.), and ryegrasses of 6.0 to 7.6, 5.1 to 7.6, 5.7 to 7.6, and 5.5 to 8.1. Although these values certainly have some broad validity, actual optimal ranges for overall turfgrass performance and quality are probably of a much narrower range for each species.

Growth and establishment responses to differences in soil reaction have been shown, but also vary considerably. Juska (1959a) reported on the influence of liming Meyer zoysiagrass. Substantial increases in root, stolon, and topgrowth occurred as soil pH was increased by liming from 4.7 to 6.1 if N was applied as well. If N was not applied, this change in soil reaction had little effect. No detrimental effect occurred with increases in soil pH to 8.0, with stolon growth actually being further encouraged. Lundeberg et al. (1977) found that bermudagrass grown as forage on strip mine spoil with a pH of 2.9 exhibited increases in root growth and yields as liming raised the pH to 3.8, but liming to a higher pH caused no further increase in yield and reduced root yields. They concluded that bermudagrass could tolerate very acid conditions and that the toxicity of certain elements rather than the direct effect of low pH limits bermudagrass growth.

Several reports of differences in growth of cool-season turfgrass species due to changes in soil reaction have been made. Murray and Foy (1980) reported that tall fescue was much more tolerant of acid soil than Kentucky bluegrass. In another report (Murray & Foy, 1978), they found that tall fescue had greater sensitivity to soil acidity than fine-leaved fescues, with greater tall fescue growth occurring at a soil pH of 5.7 than 4.3. Although fine-leaved fescue also exhibited increased growth at the higher pH, the majority of cultivars had adequate growth at 4.3 soil pH. Juska et al. (1965) also found that red fescue performed better than Kentucky bluegrass at a soil pH of 4.5, although both performed better at a pH of 6.5. Root, rhizome, and clipping yields were higher at the higher pH. Juska and Hanson (1966) reported greater root yields of annual bluegrass on a loamy sand with a pH of 6.5 vs. 4.5, although they found no difference on a silt loam. Palazzo and Duell (1974) reported that Kentucky bluegrass varieties produced maximum growth in a pH range of 6.0 to 6.5, perennial ryegrass at 6.0 to 6.4, and tall fescue at 6.0 to 7.0. All of these species decreased in growth above a pH of 7.0. Contrary to other reports, red fescue growth was found to decrease as the pH increased from 4.2 to 7.6 due to limestone applications. Turner (1980) found little positive or negative growth effect from liming established stands of perennial ryegrass, creeping red fescue, and Kentucky bluegrass grown on soil with initial soil pH of 5.6, 6.0, and 5.1, respectively. Turner et al. (1979) found greater growth and tiller density of Merion Kentucky bluegrass at a soil pH of 5.6 than on the same soil limed to a pH of 6.4. In a series of soil test calibration studies for turfgrass establishment, Turner (1980) reported that liming on soils with initial soil pH of 5.8 and 6.3 reduced growth of Kentucky bluegrass and perennial ryegrass, respectively, in the initial month of growth. This reduction in growth was attributed to reduced P availability. After the first month of growth, however, seedbed applications of limestone had little further growth effects.

Due to species differences in preferred soil reaction, proportion of species in turfgrass mixtures could be affected by soil pH. Musser (1948) found the proportion of Kentucky bluegrass in a Kentucky bluegrass-bentgrass turf was higher under low acidity, with bentgrass showing a wide range of tolerance to soil pH.

Within a given species, cultivars may show substantial differences in response to soil pH levels. Murray and Foy (1980) compared 12 Kentucky bluegrass cultivars at soil pH levels of 4.4 up to 7.6. Only six cultivars produced measurable growth at a pH of 4.4. Liming to raise soil pH to 5.0 substantially increased growth of all cultivars. Yields of most cultivars reached a maximum at a pH of 5.7 and declined at pH 7.6, although maximum yield for acid-tolerant cultivars ranged from 5.7 to 7.6. Their results indicated that acid-tolerant Kentucky bluegrass cultivars would not be at a disadvantage over nonacid tolerant cultivars under nonacid soil conditions. Tall fescue cultivars responded in different degrees to liming as well. With ranges of soil pH from 4.1 to 7.9, yield of all seven cultivars increased substantially as soil reaction approached neutrality and then decreased as soil became alkaline. Maximum yields were obtained at a soil pH of 6.7 for all cultivars except 'Kenhy', which had a maximum yield at a pH of 5.5. Although no deficiency symptoms were observed, the decreases in yield were suggestive of reduced availability of one or more micronutrients.

Relationships between soil reaction and various diseases have been reported. Ledeboer and Skogley (1967) found greater incidence of dollar spot on bentgrass when 2440 kg of limestone ha^{-1} was applied than when none was applied; however, Couch and Bloom (1960) and Turner (1980) reported no influence of pH or liming on dollar spot of bentgrass or perennial ryegrass, respectively. Bloom and Couch (1960) found an interaction between N levels and pH on brown patch severity of bentgrass, with pH having an influence when N was moderate to high but not when N was low. Turner (1980) found decreases in red thread incidence of perennial ryegrass with two limestone applications of 3050 kg ha^{-1} on a soil with a pH of 5.6, although lower rates of applications had little influence. Couch (1973) stated that plant response to a pathogen is a complex interaction between pH and other nutrient levels and that response cannot be predicted based solely on pH conditions.

Other turfgrass responses to liming that have been reported include thatch accumulation, weed encroachment, and visual quality. Kentucky bluegrass thatch, which can affect turfgrass quality in several ways, has been reduced by maintaining a pH of 7 and applying limestone in the spring and fall (Murray & Juska, 1977). Sartain (1985) reported substantially reduced bermudagrass thatch accumulation at a soil pH above 5.0 than below 4.0, with the least thatch on soil with a pH of 4.5. Smith (1979) found that liming in combination with other management practices did not adequately control bermudagrass thatch on a putting green and Ledeboer and Skogley (1967) found no effect of limestone applications on thatch decomposition.

Sartin (1985) reported that *Poa annua* encroachment during the cool season into bermudagrass increased from 0 to 63% as soil pH increased from 5.0 to 5.8. It appeared that the incidence of *Poa annua* and *Stellaria media* in bermudagrass during the cool-season growth period could be minimized by maintaining the soil pH between 4.5 and 5.0. Turner et al. (1979) reported less dandelion encroachment into Merion Kentucky bluegrass on soil with a pH of 5.6 than on soil limed to pH 6.4.

Despite these previously described turfgrass responses to soil reaction and liming, few reports have been made on their effects on general visual quality. Sartain (1985) observed no difference in bermudagrass visual quality with a range of soil pH from 3.5 to 5.8, with all turf having acceptable quality. Turner (1980) on soils with initial pH of 5.6, 6.0, 5.1, and 6.5, reported virtually no beneficial nor detrimental effects from limestone applications to established stands of perennial ryegrass, creeping red fescue, Kentucky bluegrass, and Kentucky bluegrass, respectively. Visual quality, however, may be indirectly affected by soil reaction due to the effects of N release from some N sources. For example, release of N from IBDU has been reported to be reduced substantially at a pH of 7.7 comapred to 5.7 (Hughes, 1976). Nitrogen recovery from oxamide, however, has been reported greater at a soil pH of 7.5 than 5.2 (DeMent et al., 1961). Thus, the overall effect of soil reaction and liming on turfgrass quality becomes a complex issue, with species, cultivars, soil texture, N source applied, and pest problems prevalent all influencing optimum soil pH levels.

X. FUTURE TURFGRASS FERTILITY RESEARCH NEEDS

Although a vast number of fertility studies have been conducted since the 1930s, there are still areas of limited information and seemingly conflicting results. The complexity of turfgrass performance in relation to fertility levels and fertilizer applications reflect differences in climate; turfgrass species and cultivar requirements; inherent soil physical and chemical conditions;

management factors such as irrigation, mowing heights, and clipping removal; intensity of use; and prevalent disease and weed problems. As new problems develop, such as the "black layer" problem of golf course putting greens, the nutritional relationships involved must continue to be studied on an individual basis. However, there are still relatively broad areas of fertility relationships in turfgrass management that warrant further investigation. Among the more important are the following:

1. Turfgrass Soil Test Calibration Studies—Turner (1978) showed a wide disparity existed among turfgrass soil-testing laboratory recommendations for fertilizer and limestone recommendations in the early 1970s. Although advances have been made in the last 10 yr, there is still a great need on a regional basis for determining and relating turfgrass response to different levels of applied nutrients on soils with varying inherent soil fertility levels as determined by soil tests. These calibration studies need to be conducted for different turfgrass species under several types of management and use situations.

2. Micronutrient Studies—There is an increase in use on golf courses of high sand content mixtures that may be prone to micronutrient problems. With the increase, there is often indiscriminate applications of micronutrients by turfgrass professionals in a variety of situations. Much more information is needed on the potential conditions where micronutrient applications may be either beneficial or detrimental and on the optimum rates, sources, timing, and methods of application.

3. Nutrient Interactions—As has been described, the response to a given element often depends on existing soil levels and on the rates of application of other elements. Numerous studies are still needed to elucidate these interrelationships, particularly among micronutrients and between micronutrients and various levels of a given macronutrient. Refinement of tissue analysis sufficiency ranges reflecting these interrelationships is needed as part of this line of investigation.

The difficult question arises as to what parameters should be used as standards of evaluation for these aforementioned areas of research needs. Although growth parameters should be measured, these alone provide a poor guidelines to overall turfgrass performance and should be a minor component of evaluation procedures in these studies. Much greater emphasis should be placed on (i) the biochemical and physiological effects, such as water use rates, of nutrient applications and interactions, and (ii) the subsequent effect of these biochemical and physiological changes on field observations of various components of turfgrass quality, such as drought tolerance or disease resistance. Also, with the increasing demand in all phases of the turfgrass industry for improved integrated pest management programs, emphasis in these suggested studies needs to be directed as well towards the interaction with other turfgrass management practices in reducing or minimizing potential pest problems.

REFERENCES

Adams, W.A. 19890. Effects of nitrogen fertilization and cutting eight on the shoot growth, nutrient removal and turfgrass composition of an initially perennial ryegrass dominant sports turf. p. 343–350. *In* J.B. Beard (ed.) Proc. 2nd Int. Turfgrass Res. Conf., Munich, Germany. 11–13 July 1977. Int. Turfgrass Soc., and ASA, CSSA, and SSSA, Madison, WI.

Adams, W.E., and M. Twersky. 1960. Effect of soil fertility on winter killing of coastal bermudagrass. Agron J. 52:325–326.

Allen, S.E., C.M. Hunt, and G.L. Terman. 1971. Nitrogen release from sulfur-coated ureas as affected by coating weight, placement and temperature. Agron. J. 63:529–533.

Allen, S.E., and D.A. Mayas. 1971. Sulfur-coated fertilizers for controlled release: Agronomic evaluation. J. Agric. Food Chem. 19:809–812.

Alexander, P.M., and W.B. Gilbert. 1963. Winter damage to bermuda greens. Golf Course Rep. 31(9):50–53.

Andre, W. 1986. Nitrate emissions from turf cover based on DIN 18035 T4 after application of various fertilizers. Rasen Turf Gazon 17:38–43.

Arminger, W.H., K.S. Clark, F.O. Lundstrom, and A.E. Blair. 1951. Ureaform: greenhouse studies with perennial ryegrass. Agron. J. 43:123–127.

Arminger, W.H., I. Forbes, Jr., R.E. Wagner, and F.O. Lundstrom. 1948. Ureaform—a nitrogenous fertilizer of controlled availability: Experiments with turfgrasses. Agron. J. 40:342–356.

Barrios, E.P., and L.G. Jones. 1980. Some influences of potassium nutrition on the growth and quality of Tifgreen bermudagrass. J. Am. Soc. Hortic. Sci. 105:151–153.

Barrios, E.P., L.G. Jones, K.L. Koonce, and L.P. Leger. 1982a. Fertilizing 'Tifgreen' bermudagrass golf greens in Louisiana. Louisiana State Univ., Bull. 734.

Barrios, E.P., L.G. Jones, K.L. Koonce, and L.P. Leger. 1982b. Influence of certain nitrogen fertilizers on quality and growth of lawn grasses in Louisiana. Louisiana Agric. Exp. Stn. Bull. 739.

Basaraba, J. 1964. Mineralization of urea-formaldehyde compounds at different pH levels and temperatures. Can. J. Soil Sci. 44:131–136.

Beard, J.B. 1973. Turfgrass: Science and culture. Prentice-Hall, Englewood Cliffs, NJ.

Beard, J.B., and P.E. Rieke. 1966. The influence of nitrogen, potassium, and cutting height on the low temperature survival of grasses. p. 34. *In* Agronomy abstracts. ASA, Madison, WI.

Beard, J.B., P.E. Rieke, J.A. Turgeon, and J.M. Vargas. 1978. Annual bluegrass (*Poa annua* L.): Description, adaptation, culture, and control. Michigan State Univ. Agric. Exp. Stn. Rep. 352.

Besemer, S.T. 1963. A comparison of resin-fertilizer with non-coated soluble fertilizers on bentgrass putting green turf. Calif. Turfgrass Cult. 13(1):3–5.

Bell, R.S., and J.A. DeFrance. 1944. Influence of fertilizers on the accumulation of roots from closely clipped bentgrasses and on the quality of the turf. Soil Sci. 58:17–24.

Bloom, J.R., and H.B. Couch. 1958. Influence of the pH, nutrition, and soil moisture on the development of large brown patch. Phytopathology 48:260.

Bloom, J.R., and H.B. Couch. 1960. Influence of environment on diseases of turfgrass. 1. Effect of nutrition, pH, and soil moisture on *Rhizoctonia* brown patch. Phytopathology 50:532–535.

Brauen, S.E., R.L. Goss, C.J. Gould, and S.P. Orton. 1975. The effects of sulphur in combinations with nitrogen, phosphorus, and potassium on color and Fusarium patch disease of Agrostis putting green turf. J. Sports Turf Res. Inst. 51:83–91.

Bredakis, E.J., and J.E. Steckel. 1963. Leachable nitrogen from soils incubated with turfgrass fertilizers. Agron. J. 55:145–147.

Brown, K.W., R.L. Duble, and J.C. Thomas. 1977. Influence of management and season on fate of N applied to golf greens. Agron. J. 69:657–671.

Brown, K.W., J.C. Thomas, and R.L. Duble. 1982. Nitrogen source effect on nitrate and ammonium leaching and runoff losses from greens. Agron. J. 74:947–950.

Butler, J.D., and T.K. Hodges. 1967. Mineral composition of turfgrasses. HortiScience 2:62–63.

Cahill, J.V., J.J. Murray, N.R. O'Neill, and P.H. Dernoeden. 1983. Interrelationships between fertility and red thread fungal disease of turfgrass. Plant Dis. 67:1080–1083.

Canaway, P.M. 1984. The response of *Lolium perenne* (perennial ryegrass) turf grown on sand and soil to fertilizer nitrogen. II. Above-ground biomass, tiller numbers and root biomass. J. Sports Turf Res. Inst. 60:19–26.

Cantarella, H., and M.A. Tabatabai. 1983. Amides as sources of nitrogen for plants. Soil Sci. Soc. Am. J. 47:599–603.

Carroll, J.C. 1943. Effects of drought, temperature, and nitrogen on turfgrasses. Plant Physiol. 18:19–36.

Carroll, J.C., and F.A. Welton. 1939. Effects of heavy and late applications of nitrogenous fertilizers on the cold resistance of Kentucky bluegrass. Plant Physiol. 14:297–308.

Carrow, R.N., and B.J. Johnson. 1989. Evaluation of slow-release nitrogen carriers on centipedegrass. Hortic. Sci. 24(2):277–279.

Carrow, R.N., and P.E. Rieke. 1972. Soil factors affecting arsenic toxicity on *Poa annua*. p. 24–29. *In* J.M. Vargas (ed.) 42nd Annu. Michigan Turfgrass Conf. Proc., East Lansing. 19–20 Jan. Michigan State Univ., East Lansing.

Carrow, R.N., B.J. Johnson, and R.E. Burns. 1987. Thatch and quality of Tifway bermudagrass in relation to fertility and cultivation. Agron. J. 79:524–530.

Carrow, R.N., B.J. Johnson, and R.E. Burns. 1988a. Centipedegrass decline and recovery as affected by fertilizer and cultural treatments. Agron. J. 80:479–486.

Carrow, R.N., B.J. Johnson, and G.W. Landry, Jr. 1988b. Centipedegrass response to foliar application of iron and nitrogen. Agron. J. 80:746–750.

Cheesman, J.H., E.C. Roberts, and L.H. Tiffany. 1965. Effects of nitrogen level and osmotic pressure of the solution on incidence of *Puccinia graminis* and *Helminthosporium sativum* infection in 'Merion' Kentucky bluegrass. Agron. J. 57:599–602.

Christians, N.E., K.L. Diesburg, and J.L. Nus. 1985. Effects of nitrogen fertilizer and fall topdressing on the spring recovery of *Agrostis palustris* Huds. ('Penncross' creeping bentgrass) greens. p. 459–467. *In* F. Lemaire (ed.) Proc. 5th Int. Turfgrass Res. Conf., Avignon, France. 1–5 July. Inst. Natl. de la Recherche Agron., Paris.

Christians, N.E., D.P. Martin, and K.J. Karnok. 1981a. The interrelationship among nutrient elements applied to calcareous sand greens. Agron. J. 73:929–933.

Christians, N.E., D.P. Martin, and K.J. Karnok. 1981b. The interaction among nitrogen, phosphorus, and potassium on the establishment, quality and growth of Kentucky bluegrass (*Poa pratensis* L. 'Merion'). p. 341–348. *In* R.W. Sheard (ed.) Proc. 4th Int. Turfgrass Res. Conf., Guelph, ON, Canada. 19–23 July. Int. Turfgrass Soc., and Ontario Agric. Coll., Univ. of Guelph, Guelph, ON.

Christians, N.E., D.P. Martin, and J.F. Wilkinson. 1979. Nitrogen, phosphorus, and potassium effects on quality and growth of Kentucky bluegrass and creeping bentgrass. Agron. J. 71:564–567.

Colby, W.G., and E.J. Bredakis. 1966. The feeding power of four turf species for exchangeable and nonexchangeable potassium. p. 35. *In* Agronomy abstracts. ASA, Madison, WI.

Cook, R.N., R.E. Engel, and S. Bachelder. 1964. A study of the effect of nitrogen carriers on turfgrass disease. Plant Dis. Rep. 48:254–255.

Cook, T.W., and D.T. Duff. 1976. Effects of K fertilizers on freezing tolerance and carbohydrate content of *Festuca arundinacea* Schreb. maintained as turf. Agron. J. 68:116–119.

Corke, C.T., and J.B. Robinson. 1966. Microbial decomposition of various fractions of ureaformaldehyde. Nature (London) 211:1202–1203.

Couch, H.B. 1965. Effect of nutrition and pH on turfgrass disease incidence. p. 44. *In* Agronomy abstracts. ASA, Madison, WI.

Couch, H.B. 1973. Diseases of turfgrasses. 2nd ed. Robert E. Kreiger Publ. Co., Huntington, NY.

Couch, H.B., and J.R. Bloom. 1960. Influence of environment on diseases of turfgrasses. II. Effect of nutrition, pH, and soil moisture on Sclerotinia dollar spot. Phytopathology 50:761–763.

Davidson, R.M., Jr., and R.L. Goss. 1972. Effects of P, S, N, lime, chlordane, and fungicides on ophiobolus patch disease of turf. Plant Dis. Rep. 56(7):565–567.

Dawson, M.D., and W. Akratanakul. 1973. SCU—The effect of soil temperature and moisture. Sulfur Inst. J. 9:14.

Deal, E.D., and R.E. Engel. 1965. Iron, manganese, boron, and zinc: Effects on growth of Merion Kentucky bluegrass. Agron. J. 57:533–555.

DeMent, J.D., C.M. Hunt, and G. Stanford. 1961. Hydrolysis, nitrification and nitrogen availability of oxamide, as influenced by particle size. J. Agric. Food Chem. 9:453–456.

Denmead, O.T., J.R. Freney, and J.R. Simpson. 1979. Studies of nitrous oxide emission from a grass sward. Soil Sci. Soc. Am. J. 43:726–728.

Dernoeden, P.H. 1987. Management of take-all patch of creeping bentgrass with nitrogen sulfur, and phenyl mercury acetate. Plant Dis. 71:226–229.

Dest, W.M., and D.W. Allinson. 1981. Influence of nitrogen, and phosphorus fertilization on the growth and development of *Poa annua* L. (Annual bluegrass). p. 325–332. *In* R.W. Sheard (ed.) Proc. 4th Int. Turfgrass Res. Conf., Guelph, ON, Canada. 19–23 July. Int. Turfgrass Soc., and Ontario Agricl Coll., Univ. of Guelph, Guelph, ON.

DiPaola, J.M., and R.E. Engel. 1976. Desiccation resistance of *Agrostis palustris* Huds. under various levels of nitrogen and potassium. p. 76–89. *In* R.E. Engel (ed.) 1976 Rutgers Turfgrass Proc. Rutgers Univ., New Brunswick, NJ.

Dudeck, A.E., C.H. Peacock, and T.E. Freeman. 1985. Response of selected bermudagrasses to nitrogen fertilization. p. 495–504. *In* F. Lemaire (ed.) Proc. 5th Int. Turfgrass Res. Conf., Avignon, France. 1–5 July. Inst. Natl. de la Rcherche Agron., paris.

Eggens, J.L., and C.P.M. Wright. 1985. Nitrogen effects on monostands and polystands of annual bluegrass and creeping bentgrass. HortScience. 20:109–110.

Engel, R.E., and R.B. Aldefer. 1967. The effects of cultivation, topdressing, lime, nitrogen, and wetting agent on thatch development in 1/4-inch bentgrass turf over a ten-year period. 1967 Report on Turfgrass Research at Rutgers Univ., NJ. Rutgers Univ. Agric. Exp. Stn. Bull. 818.

Engelstad, O.P., C.M. Hunt, and G.L. Terman. 1964. Response of corn to nitrogen in oxamide and ammonium nitrate in greenhouse experiments. Agron. J. 56:579–582.

Epstein, E. 1972. Mineral nutrition of plants: Principles and perspectives. John Wiley and Sons, New York.

Escritt, J.R., and D.C. Legg. 1970. Fertilizer trials at Bingley. p. 185–190. *In* Proc. 1st Int. Turfgrass Res. Conf., Harrogate, England. 15–18 July 1969. Sports Turf Res. Inst., Bingley, England.

Evans, E.M., R.D. Rouse, and R.T. Godauskas. 1964. Low soil potassium sets up coastal for a leaf spot disease. Highlts. Auburn, AL. Agric. Exp. Stn. Agric. Res. 11:(2).

Fenn, L.B., and D.E. Kissel. 1974. Ammonia volatilization from surface applications of ammonium compounds on calcareous soils. II. Effects of temperature and rate of ammonium nitrogen application. Soil Sci. Soc. Am. Proc. 38:206–210.

Fenn, L.B., J.E. Mathocha, and E. Wu. 1982. Substitution of ammonium and potassium for added calcium in reduction of ammonia loss from surface-applied urea. Soil Sci. Soc. Am. J. 46:771–776.

Fitts, J.W., and W.L. Nelson. 1956. The determination of lime and fertilizer requirements of soils through chemical tests. Adv. Agron. 8:241–282.

Frankenberger, W.T., Jr., and M.A. Tabatabai. 1980. Amidass activity in soils: I. Method of assay. Soil Sci. Soc. Am. J. 44:282–287.

Fry, J.O., and P.H. Dernoeden. 1987. Growth of zoysiagrass from vegetative plugs in response to fertilizers. J. Am. Soc. Hortic. Sci. 112(2):286–289.

Fuller, W.H., and K.G. Clark. 1947. Microbiological studies on urea-formaldehyde preparations. Soil Sci. Soc. Am. Proc. 12:198–202.

Gilbeault, V.A., and D. Hanson. 1980. Perennial ryegrass mowing quality and appearance in response to three nitrogen regimes. p. 39–43. *In* J.B. Beard (ed.) Proc. 3rd Int. Turfgrass Res. Conf., Munich, Germany. 11–13 July 1977. Int. Turfgrass Soc. and ASA, CSSA, and SSSA, Madison, WI.

Gilbert, W.B., and D.L. Davis. 1971. Influence of fertility ratios on winter-hardiness of bermudagrass. Agron. J. 63:591–593.

Giordano, P.M., and J.J. Mortvedt. 1970. Release of nitrogen from sulfur-coated urea in flooded soil. Agron. J. 62:612–614.

Goss, R.L. 1963. Response of bentgrass putting green turf to various ratios of N, P, and K. p. 118. *In* Agronomy abstracts. ASA, Madison, WI.

Goss, R.L. 1969. Some inter-relationships between nutrition and turf disease. p. 351–361. *In* Proc. 1st Int. Turf Res. Conf., Harrogate, England. 15–18 July. Sports Turf Res. Inst., Bingley, Yorkshire.

Goss, R.L., S.E. Brauen, and S.P. Orton. 1975. The effects of N, P, K, and S on *Poa annua* L. in bentgrass putting green turf. J. Sports Turf Res. Inst. 51:74–82.

Goss, R.L., S.E. Brauen, and S.P. Orton. 1979. Uptake of sulfur by bentgrass putting green turf. Agron. J. 71:909–913.

Goss, R.L., and C.J. Gould. 1967a. The effect of potassium on turfgrass and its relationship to turfgrass diseases. p. 52. *In* Agronomy abstracts. ASA, Madison, WI.

Goss, R.L., and C.J. Gould. 1967b. Some interrelationships between fertility levels and *Ophiobolus* patch disease in turfgrasses. Agron. J. 59:149–151.

Goss, R.L., and C.J. Gould. 1968. Some interrelationships between fertility levels and Fusarium patch disease on turfgrasses. J. Sports Turf Res. Inst. 44:19-26.

Goss, R.L., and C.J. Gould. 1971. Some interrelationships between fertility levels and corticium red thread disease of turfgrasses. J. Sports Turf Res. Inst. 47:48-53.

Gould, C.J., V.L. Miller, and R.L. Goss. 1967. Fungicidal control of red thread disease of turfgrass in western Washington. Plant Dis. Rep. 51:215-219.

Gowans, K.D., and E.J. Johnson. 1973. Nitrogen source in relation to turfgrass establishment in sand. Calif. Turfgr. Cult. 23:9-13.

Gray, B., M. Drake, and W.G. Colby. 1953. Potassium competition in grass-legume associations as a function of root exchange capacity. Soil Sci. Soc. Am. Proc. 17:235-239.

Halisky, P.M., C.R. Funk, and R.E. Engel. 1966. Melting-out of Kentucky bluegrass varieties by *Helminthosporium vagans* as influenced by turf management practices. Plant Dis. Rep. 50:703-706.

Hall, J.R., and R.W. Miller. 1974. Effect of phosphorus, season and method of sampling on foliar analysis of Kentucky bluegrass. p. 155-171. *In* E.C. Roberts (ed.) Proc. 2nd Int. Turf. Res. Conf., Blacksburg, VA. 19-21 June 1973. ASA and CSSA, Madison, WI.

Hamamota, M. 1966. Isobutylidene diurea as a slow acting nitrogen fertilizer and the studies in this field in Japan. Proc. No. 90. The Fertilizer Soc., London.

Hansen, R. 1970. Turf fertilizer trials at Weihenstephan. p. 200-203. *In* Proc. 1st Int. Turfgrass Res. Conf., Harrogate, England. 15-18 July 1969. Sports Turf Res. Inst., Bingley, England.

Hargrove, W.L., D.E. Kissel, and L.B. Fenn. 1977. Field measurement of ammonia volatilization from surface applications of ammonium salts to a calcareous soil. Agron. J. 69:473-476.

Harivandi, M.A., and J.D. Butler. 1980. Iron chlorosis of Kentucky bluegrass cultivars. Hortic. Sci. 15:496-497.

Hashimoto, I., and R.C. Mullins. 1979. Dissolution of sulfur-coated urea in soil: I. Wax sealed sulfur-coated urea. Soil Sci. Am. J. 43:1165-1168.

Hathcock, A.H., P.H. Dernoeden, T.R. Turner, and M.S. McIntosh. 1984. Tall fescue and Kentucky bluegrass response to fertilizer and lime seed coatings. Agron. J. 76:879-883.

Hauck, R.C. 1964. New nitrogen fertilizers. Commer. Fert. Plant Food Ind. 108:23-66.

Hauck, R.C., and M. Koshino. 1971. Slow-release and amended fertilizers. p. 455-494. *In* R.A. Olson et al. (ed.) Fertilizer technology and use. 2nd ed. SSSA, Madison, WI.

Hauck, R.D., and F.E. Stephenson. 1964. Nitrification of triazine nitrogen. J. Agric. Food Chem. 12:147-151.

Hawes, D.T., and A.M. Decker. 1977. Healing potential of creeping bentgrass as affected by nitrogen and soil temperature. Agron. J. 69:212-214.

Hays, J.T., and W.W. Haden. 1966. Soluble fraction of ureaforms - nitrification, leaching and burning properties. J. Agric. Food Chem. 14:339-341.

Holt, C.C., and R.L. Davis. 1948. Differential responses of Arlington and Norbeck bentgrasses to kinds and rate of fertilizers. Agron. J. 40:282-284.

Horn, G.C. 1970. Potassium fertilizers for Tifway bermudagrass. p. 204-211. *In* Proc. 1st Int. Turfgrass Res. Conf., Harrogate, England. 15-18 July 1969. Sports Turf Res. Inst., Bingley, England.

Horst, G.L., A.A. Baltensperger, and M.D. Firkner. 1985. Effects of N and growing season on root-rhizome characteristics of turf-type bermudagrasses. Agron. J. 77:237-242.

Hubbell, G.P., and J.H. Dunn. 1985. Zoysiagrass establishment in Kentucky bluegrass using growth retardants. J. Am. Soc. Hortic. Sci. 110:58-61.

Hughes, T.D. 1976. Nitrogen release from isobutylidene diurea: Soil pH and fertilizer particle size effects. Agron. J. 68:103-106.

Hull, R.J., N. Jackson, and C.R. Skogley. 1979. Influence of nutrition on stripe smut severity in Kentucky bluegrass turf. Agron. J. 71:553-555.

Hummel, N.W., Jr. 1980. Evaluation of slow-release nitrogen sources for turfgrass fertilization. M.S. thesis. The Pennsylvania State Univ., University Park.

Hummel, N.W., Jr. 1982. Evaluation of sulfur-coated urea for fertilization of turfgrasses. Ph.D. thesis. The Pennsylvania State Univ., University Park (Diss. Abstr. 82-18908).

Hummel, N.W., Jr. 1986. Evaluation of elite sulfur-coated urea for bentgrass fertilization. p. 19. *In* N.W. Hummel, Jr. (ed.) 1986 Cornell Turfgrass Research Report. Cornell Univ., Ithaca, NY.

Hummel, N.W., Jr. 1989. Resin-coated urea evaluation for turfgrass fertilization. Agron. J. 81:290-294.

Hummel, N.W., Jr., and D.V. Waddington. 1981. Evaluation of slow-release nitrogen sources on 'Baron' Kentucky bluegrass. Soil Sci. Soc. Am. J. 45:966-970.

Hummel, N.W., Jr., and D.V. Waddington. 1984. Sulfur-coated urea for turfgrass fertilization. Soil Sci. Soc. Am. J. 48:191–195.

Hummel, N.W., Jr., and D.V. Waddington. 1986. Field dissolution of sulfur-coated ureas in turfgrass. HortScience 21:1155–1156.

Hylton, L.O., Jr., A. Ulrich, D.R. Cornelius, and K. Okhi. 1965. Phosphorus nutrition of Italian ryegrass relative to growth, moisture content, and mineral constituents. Agron. J. 57:505–508.

Hylton, L.O., D.E. Williams, A. Ulrich, and D.R. Cornelius. 1964. Critical nitrate levels for growth of Italian ryegrass. Crop Sci. 4:16–19.

Jarrell, W.M., and L. Boersma. 1979. Model for the release of urea by granules of sulfur-coated urea applied to soil. Soil Sci. Soc. Am. J. 43:1044–1050.

Jarrell, W.M., and L. Boersma. 1980. Release of urea by granules of sulfur-coated urea. Soil Sci. Soc. Am. J. 44:418–422.

Jarrell, W.M., G.S. Pettygrove, and L. Boersma. 1979. Characterization of the thickness and uniformity of the coatings of sulfur-coated urea. Soil Sci. Soc. Am. J. 43:602–605.

Johnson, B.J. 1984. Influence of nitrogen on recovery of bermudagrass (*Cynodon dactylon*) treated with herbicides. Weed Sci. 32:819–823.

Johnson, B.J., and T.H. Bowyer. 1982. Management of herbicide and fertility levels on weeds and Kentucky bluegrass turf. Agron. J. 74:845–850.

Johnson, B.J., R.N. Carrow, and R.E. Burns. 1987. Thatch and quality of Tifway bermudagrass turf in relation to fertility and cultivation. Agron. J. 79:524–530.

Johnson, S.J., and N.E. Christians. 1984. Fertilizer burn comparisons of concentrated liquid fertilizers applied to Kentucky bluegrass turf. J. Am. Soc. Hortic. Sci. 109:890–893.

Jones, J.R., Jr. 1980. Turf analysis. Golf Course Manage. 48(1):29–32.

Joo, Y.K., and N.E. Christians. 1986a. The measurement of ammonia volatilization from turfgrass areas as treated with surface-applied urea. p. 135. *In* Agronomy abstracts. ASA, Madison, WI.

Joo, Y.K., and N.E. Christians. 1986b. The response of Kentucky bluegrass turf to phenylphosphorodiamidate (PPD) and magnesium (Mg + +) applied in combination with urea. J. Fert. Issues 3:30–33.

Joo, Y.K., N.E. Christians, and J.M. Bremner. 1987. Effect of N-(n-butyl) thiophosporic triamide (NBPT) on growth response and ammonium volatilization following fertilization of Kentucky bluegrass (*Poa pratensis* L.) with urea. J. Fert. Issues 4(3):98–102.

Juska, F.V. 1959a. Response of Meyer zoysia to lime and fertilizer treatments. Agron. J. 51:81–83.

Juska, F.V. 1959b. Evaluation of cool-season turfgrasses. Park Maint. 12:18–20.

Juska, F.V., and A.A. Hanson. 1966. Nutritional requirements of *Poa annua* L. p. 35. *In* Agronomy abstracts. ASA, Madison, WI.

Juska, F.V., A.A. Hanson, and C.J. Erickson. 1965. Effects of phosphorus and other treatments on the development of red fescue, Merion, and common Kentucky bluegrass. Agron. J. 57:75–78.

Juska, F.V., A.A. Hanson, and A.W. Hovin. 1970. Growth response of 'Merion' Kentucky bluegrass to fertilizer and lime treatments. Agron. J. 62:25–27.

Juska, F.V., and J.M. Murray. 1974. Performance of bermudagrass in the transition zone as affected by potassium and nitrogen. p. 149–154. *In* E.C. Roberts (ed.) Proc. 2nd Int. Turfgrass Res. Conf., Blacksburg, VA. 19–21 June 1973. ASA and CSSA, Madison, WI.

Juska, F.V., J. Tyson, and C.M. Harrison. 1955. The competitive relationships of Merion Kentucky bluegrass as influenced by various mixtures, cutting heights and levels of nitrogen. Agron. J. 47:513–518.

Kaempffe, G.K., and D.R. Lunt. 1967. Availability of various fractions of urea-formaldehyde. J. Agric. Food Chem. 15:967–971.

Kamon, Y. 1974. Magnesium deficiency in zoysiagrass. p. 145–148. *In* E.C. Roberts (ed.) Proc. 2nd Int. Turfgrass Res. Conf., Blacksburg, VA. 19–21 June 1973. ASA and CSSA, Madison, WI.

Katy, S.E., and C.A. Fassbender. 1966. Biodegradability of urea-formaldehyde and related compounds. J. Agric. Food Chem. 14:336–338.

Kavanagh, T., T.P. Cormican, and P. Newburn. 1980. Suitability of urea-based slow release nitrogen fertilizers for turfgrass. Sci. Hortic. 31:89–93.

Keen, R.A. 1969. Turfgrass under semi-arid and arid conditions. p. 130–150. *In* A.A. Hanson and F.V. Juska (ed.) Turfgrass science. Agron. Monogr. 14. ASA, Madison, WI.

Keisling, T.C. 1980. Bermudagrass rhizome initiation and longevity under differing potassium nutritional levels. Commun. Soil Sci. Plant Anal. 11:629–635.

Killian, K.C., O.J. Attoe, and L.E. Englebert. 1966. Urea-formaldehyde as a slowly available form of nitrogen for Kentucky bluegrass. Agron. J. 58:204–206.

King, J.W., and C.R. Skogley. 1969. Effect of nitrogen and phosphorus placements and rates on turfgrass establishment. Agron. J. 61:4–6.

Kohlmeier, G.P., and J.L. Eggens. 1983. The influence of wear and nitrogen on creeping bentgrass growth. Can. J. Plant Sci. 63:189–193.

Kurtz, K.W. 1981. Use of 59 Fe in nutrient solution cultures for selecting and differentiating Fe-efficient and Fe-inefficient genotypes in zoysiagrass. p. 267–275. In R.W. Sheard (ed.) Proc. 4th Int. Turfgrass Res. Conf., Guelph, ON, Canada. 19–23 July. Int. Turfgrass Soc., and Ontario Agric. Coll., Univ. of Guelph, Guelph, ON.

Landschoot, P.J. 1984. Comparison of nitrogen fertilizers of Kentucky bluegrass turf. M.S. thesis. The Pennsylvania State Univ., University Park.

Landschoot, P.J., and D.V. Waddington. 1987. Response of turfgrass to various nitrogen sources. Soil Sci. Soc. Am. J. 51:225–230.

Ledeboer, F.B., and C.R. Skogley. 1967. Investigations into the nature of thatch and methods for its decomposition. Agron. J. 59:320–323.

Leyer, C., and W. Skirde. 1980. Effects of nitrogen fertilizer levels and wear tolerance of sports turf. Z. Veget. Landsch. Sports. 3:25–31.

Love, J.R. 1962. Mineral deficiency symptoms on turfgrass. I. Major and secondary nutrient elements. Wis. Acad. Sci. Arts Lett. 51:135–140.

Lundeberg, P.E., O.L. Bennett, and E.L. Mathias. 1977. Tolerance of bermudagrass selections to acidity. I. Effects of lime on plant growth and mine spoil material. Agron. J. 69:913–916.

Lunt, O.R., and S.B. Clark. 1969. Properties and value of 1,1 diureido isobutane (IBDU) as a long-lasting nitrogen fertilizer. J. Agric. Food Chem. 17:1269–1271.

Lunt, O.R., V.B. Youngner, and P.H. Khadr. 1964. Critical nutrient levels in Newport bluegrass. p. 106. In Agronomy abstracts. ASA, Madison, WI.

Madison, J.H., L.H. Petersen, and T.K. Hodges. 1960. Pink snowmold on bentgrass as affected by irrigation and fertilizer. Agron. J. 52:591–592.

Mancino, C.F., W.A. Torello, and D.J. Wehner. 1988. Dinitrification losses from Kentucky bluegrass sod. Agron. J. 80:148–153.

Markland, F.E., E.C. Roberts, and L.R. Frederick. 1969. Influence of nitrogen fertilizers on Washington creeping bentgrass Agrostis palustris Huds. II. Incidence of dollar spot Sclerotinia homeocarpa, infection. Agron. J. 61:701–705.

Martin, W.E., and J.E. Matocha. 1973. Plant analysis as an aid in the fertilization of forage crops. p. 393–426. In L.M. Walsh and J.D. Beaton (ed.) Soil testing and plant analysis. SSSA, Madison, WI.

Mays, D.A., and G.L. Terman. 1969a. Response of coastal bermudagrass to nitrogen in sulfur-coated urea, urea, and ammonium nitrate. Sulfur Inst. J. 5:7–10.

Mays, D.A., and G.L. Terman. 1969b. Sulfur-coated urea and uncoated soluble nitrogen fertilizers for fescue forage. Agron. J. 61:489–492.

McCaslin, B.D., R.F. Samson, and A.A. Baltensperger. 1981. Selection for turf-type bermudagrass genotypes with reduced iron chlorosis. Commun. Soil Sci. Plant Anal. 12:189–204.

Mazur, A.R., and C.B. White. 1983. Mineralization of N from several sources and establishment of 'Penncross' creeping bentgrass on putting green media. Agron. J. 75:977–982.

McVey, G.R. 1967. Response of seedlings to various phosphorus sources. p. 53. In Agronomy abstracts. ASA, Madison, WI.

McVey, G.R. 1968. How seedlings respond to phosphorus. Weeds Trees Turf 7(6):18–19.

Mehall, B.J., R.J. Hull, and C.R. Skogley. 1983. Cultivar variation in Kentucky bluegrass: P and K nutritional factors. Agron. J. 75:767–772.

Mehnert, C., and F. Madel. 1982. The influence of reduced nitrogen application on plant population, grass clippings yield and mineral deficiencies in ordinary turf. Rasen Turf Gazen 13:28–33.

Mehnert, C., G. Voigtlander, and F. Madel. 1984. Effects of fertilizer N from on N uptake by turf. Z. Veget. Landsch. Sports. 7:17–23.

Menn, W.G., and G.G. McBee. 1970. A study of certain nutritional requirements for Tifgreen bermudagrass (Cynodon dactylon × C. transvaalensis.) utilizing a hydroponic system. Agron. J. 62:192–194.

Minner, D.D., and J.D. Butler. 1984. Correcting iron deficiency of Kentucky bluegrass. Hortic. Sci. 19:109–110.

Moberg, E.L., D.V. Waddington, and J.M. Duich. 1970. Evaluation of slow-release nitrogen sources on Merion Kentucky bluegrass. Soil Sci. Soc. Am. Proc. 34:335-339.

Monroe, C.A., G.D. Coorts, and C.R. Skogley. 1969. Effects of nitrogen-potassium levels on the growth and chemical composition of Kentucky bluegrass. Agron. J. 61:294-296.

Monteith, J., and J.W. Bengston. 1939. Experiments with fertilizers on bluegrass turf. Turf Cult. 1(3):153-191.

Moore, L.D., and H.B. Couch. 1968. Influence of calcium nutrition on pecolytic and cellulolytic enzyme activity of extracts of Highland bentgrass foilage blighted by *Pythium ultimum*. Phytopathology 58:833-838.

Moore, L.D., H.B. Couch, and J.R. Bloom. 1961. Influence of nutrition, pH, soil temperature, and soil moisture on pythium blight of Highland bentgrass. Phytopathology 51:578.

Mosdell, D.K., W.H. Daniel, and R.P. Freeborg. 1986. Evaluation of dicyandiamide-amended fertilizers on Kentucky bluegrass. Agron. J. 78:801-806.

Mosdell, D.K., W.H. Daniel, and R.P. Freeborg. 1987. Evaluation of oxamide as a slow-release nitrogen source on Kentucky bluegrass. Agron. J. 79:720-725.

Murray, J.J., and C.D. Foy. 1978. Differential tolerances of turfgrass cultivars to an acid soil high in exchangeable aluminum. Agron. J. 70:769-774.

Murray, J.J., and C.D. Foy. 1980. Lime responses of Kentucky bluegrass and tall fescue cultivars on an acid, aluminum-toxic soil. p. 175-184. *In* J.B. Beard (ed.) Proc. 3rd Int. Turfgrass Res. Conf., Munich, Germany. 11-13 July 1977. Int. Turfgrass Soc., and ASA, CSSA, and SSSA, Madison, WI.

Murray, J.J., and F.V. Juska. 1977. Effect of management practices on thatch accumulation, turf quality, and leaf spot damage in common Kentucky bluegrass. Agron. J. 69:365-369.

Murray, J.J., D.L. Klingman, R.G. Nash, and E.A. Woolson. 1983. Eight years of herbicide and nitrogen fertilizer treatments on Kentucky bluegrass (*Poa pratensis*) turf. Weed Sci. 31:825-831.

Muse, R.R., and H.B. Couch. 1965. Influence of environment on diseases of turfgrasses. IV. Effect of nutrition and soil moisture on *Corticium* red thread of creeping red fescue. Phytopathology 55:507-510.

Musser, J.B. 1948. Effects of soil acidity and available phosphorus on population changes in mixed Kentucky bluegrass-bent turf. Agron. J. 40:614-620.

Musser, H.B. 1950. Turf management. McGraw-Hill Book Co., New York.

Nelson, K.E., A.J. Turgeon, and J.R. Street. 1980. Thatch influence on mobility and transformation of nitrogen carriers applied to turf. Agron. J. 72:487-492.

Nittler, L.W., and W.J. Kenny. 1971. Cultivar differences among calcium deficient Kentucky bluegrass seedlings. Agron. J. 64:73-75.

Oertli, J.J. 1963. Nutrient disorders in turfgrass. Calif. Turfgrass Cult. 12:17-19.

Oertli, J.J. 1973. Effect of temperature microbial activity, salinity, and pH on the release of nitrogen of sulfur-coated urea. Z. Pflanzenernaehr. Boedenkd. 134:227-236.

Oertli, J.R., O.R. Lunt, and V.B. Youngner. 1961. Boron toxicity in several turfgrass species. Agron. J. 53:262-265.

Palazzo, A.J., and R.W. Duell. 1974. Responses of grasses and legumes to soil pH. Agron. J. 66:678-682.

Palmertree, H.D., C.Y. Ward, and R.H. Pluenneke. 1974. Influence of mineral nutrition on the cold tolerance and soluble protein fraction of centipedegrass. p. 500-507. *In* E.C. Roberts (ed.) Proc. 2nd Int. Turfgrass Res. Conf., Blacksburg. VA. 19-21 June 1973. ASA and CSSA, Madison, WI.

Pellett, R.M., and E.C. Roberts. 1963. Effects of mineral nutriton on high temperature induced growth retardation of Kentucky bluegrass. Agron. J. 55:474-476.

Phillips, A.B., and J.R. Webb. 1971. Production, marketing and use of phosphorus fertilizers. p. 271-310. *In* R.A. Olson et al. (ed.) Fertilizer technology and use. SSSA, Madison, WI.

Pocklington, T.E., J.D. Butler, and T.K. Hodges. 1984. Color variations of creeping bentgrass cultivars as related to iron and chlorophyll. Hortic. Sci. 9:62-63.

Potter, D.A., B.L. Bridges, and F.C. Gordon. 1985. Effect of N fertilization on earthworm and microarthropod populations in Kentucky bluegrass turf. Agron. J. 77:367-372.

Powell, A.J., R.E. Blaser, and R.E. Schmidt. 1967a. Effect of nitrogen on winter root growth of bentgrass. Agron. J. 59:529-530.

Powell, A.J., R.E. Blaser, and R.E. Schmidt. 1967b. Physiological and color aspects of turfgrasses with fall and winter nitrogen. Agron. J. 59:303-307.

Prasad, M. 1976. Release of nitrogen from sulfur-coated urea as affected by soil moisture, coating, weight, and method of placement. Soil Sci. Soc. Am. J. 40:134-136.

Pritchett, W.L., and G.C. Horn. 1966. Fertilization fights turf disorders. Better Crops Plant Food 50(3):22–25.

Rieke, P.E., and B.G. Ellis. 1974. Effect of nitrogen fertilization on nitrate movements under turfgrass. p. 120–130. *In* E.C. Roberts (ed.) Proc. 2nd Int. Turfgrass Res. Conf., ASA, Madison, WI.

Riem, V.F. 1981. Fusarium patch disease in relation to nitrogen fertilization. Z. Veget. Landsch. Sports. 4:33–35.

Rindt, D.W., G.M. Blouin, and J.B. Getsinger. 1968. Sulfur coating on nitrogen fertilizer to reduce dissolution rate. J. Agric. Food Chem. 16:773–778.

Robinson, G.S., K.K. Moore, and J. Murphy. 1976. Effects of mowing height and frequency, rolling and phosphate level on the quality of fine turf. J. Sports Turf. Res. Inst., 52:77–84.

Ryan, J., J.L. Stroehlein, and S. Miyamoto. 1975. Sulfuric acid applications to calcareous soils: Effects on growth and chlorophyll content of common bermudagrass in the greenhouse. Agron. J. 67:633–637.

Sartain, J.B. 1985. Effects of acidity and N source on the growth and thatch accumulation of 'Tifgreen' bermudagrass and on soil nutrient retention. Agron. J. 77:33–36.

Sartain, J.B., and A.E. Dudeck. 1980a. Influence of N fertilization on the utilization of nutrients by bermudagrass and overseeded ryegrass turfgrasses. Proc. Fla. State Hortic. Soc. 92:364–367.

Sartain, J.B., and A.E. Dudeck. 1980b. Yield and nutrient accumulation of Tifway bermudagrass and overseeded ryegrass as influenced by applied nutrients. Agron. J. 74:488–491.

Scheib, R.M., and G.H. McClellan. 1976. Characteristics of sulfur texture on SCU. Sulfur Inst. J. 12:2–5.

Schmidt, R.E., and R.E. Blaser. 1967. Effect of temperature, light, and nitrogen on growth and metabolism of 'Cohansey' bentgrass (*Agrostis palustris* Huds.) Crop Sci. 7:447–451.

Schmidt, R.E., and J.M. Brueninger. 1981. The effects of fertilization on recovery of Kentucky bluegrass turf from summer drought. p. 333–340. *In* R.W. Sheard (ed.) Proc. 4th Int. Turfgrass Res. Conf., Guelph, ON, Canada. 19–23 July. Int. Turfgrass Soc., and Ontario Agric. Coll., Univ. of Guelph, Guelph, ON.

Sheard, R.W., and E.G. Beauchamp. 1985. Aerodynamic measurement of ammonia volatilization from urea applied to bluegrass-fescue turf. p. 549–556. *In* F. Lemaire (ed.) Proc. 5th Int. Turfgrass Res. Conf., Avignon, France. 1–5 July. Inst. Natl. de la Recherche Agron., Paris.

Shearman, R.C., and J.B. Beard. 1975. Influence of nitrogen and potassium on turfgrass wear tolerance. p. 101. *In* Agronomy abstracts. ASA, Madison, WI.

Shearman, R.C., E.J. Kinbacher, T.P. Riordan, and D.H. Steinegger. 1980. Thatch accumulation in Kentucky bluegrass as influenced by cultivar, mowing and nitrogen. HortScience 15:312–313.

Sills, M.J., and R.N. Carrow. 1982. Soil compaction effects on nitrogen use in tall fescue. J. Am. Soc. Hortic. Sci. 107(5):934–937.

Sills, M.J., and R.N. Carrow. 1983. Turfgrass growth, N use, and water use under soil compaction and N fertilization. Agron. J. 75:488–492.

Slater, R.A. 1966. The evaluation of several nitrogen fertilizer formulations on Merion Kentucky bluegrass. M.S. thesis. The Pennsylvania State Univ., University Park.

Smith, G.S. 1979. Nitrogen and aerification influence on putting green thatch and soil. Agron. J. 71:680–684.

Snow, J.T. 1976. The influence of nitrogen rate and application frequency and clipping removal on nitrogen accumulation in a Kentucky bluegrass turf. M.S. thesis. Cornell Univ., Ithaca, NY.

Snyder, G.H., E.D. Burt, and J.M. Davidson. 1980. Nitrogen leaching in bermudagrass turf: Daily fertilization vs. tri-weekly conventional fertilization. p. 185–193. *In* J.B. Beard (ed.) Proc. 3rd Int. Turfgrass Res. Conf., Munich, Germany. 11–13 July 1977. Int. Turfgrass Soc., and ASA, CSSA, and SSSA, Madison, WI.

Snyder, V., and R.E. Schmidt. 1974. Nitrogen and iron fertilization of bentgrass. p. 176–185. *In* E.C. Roberts (ed.) Proc. 2nd Int. Turfgrass Res. Conf., Blacksburg, VA. 19–21 June 1973. ASA and CSSA, Madison, WI.

Spangenberg, B.G., T.W. Fermanian, and D.J. Wehner. 1986. Evaluation of liquid-applied nitrogen fertilizers on Kentucky bluegrass turf. Agron. J. 78:1002–1006.

Starr, J.L., and H.C. DeRoo. 1981. The fate of nitrogen fertilizer applied to turfgrass. Crop Sci. 21:531–536.

Street, J.R., P.R. Henderlong, and F.L. Himes. 1981. The effect of silica rates on the growth, silica deposition, and water absorption among three turfgrass species. p. 259–268. *In* R.W. Sheard (ed.) Proc. 4th Int. Turfgrass Res. Conf., Guelph, ON, Canada. 19–23 July. Int. Turfgrass Soc., Ontario Agric. Coll., Univ. of Guelph, Guelph, ON.

Sturkie, D.G., and R.D. Rouse. 1967. Response of zoysia and Tiflawn bermuda to P and K. p. 54. *In* Agronomy abstracts. ASA, Madison, WI.

Szymczak, E., and F. Lemaire. 1985. Effect of four ternary fertilizers containing slow-release nitrogen and timing of application on *Lolium perenne* L. turf. p. 533–549. *In* F. Lemaire (ed.) Proc. 5th Int. Turfgrass Res. Conf., Avignon, France. 1–5 July. Inst. Natl. de la Recherche Agron., Paris.

Terman, G.L., J.D. DeMent, C.M. Hunt, J.T. Cope, Jr., and L.E. Ensminger. 1964. Crop responses to urea and urea pyrolysis products. J. Agric. Food Chem. 12:151–154.

Titko III, S., J.R. Street, and T.J. Logan. 1987. Volatilization of ammonia from granular and dissolved urea applied to turfgrass. Agron. J. 79:535–540.

Torello, W.A., and J.D. Wehner. 1983. Urease activity in Kentucky bluegrass turf. Agron. J. 75:654–656.

Torello, W.A., J.D. Wehner, and A.J. Turgeon. 1983. Ammonia volatilization from fertilized turfgrass stand. Agron. J. 75:454–456.

Turgeon, A.J., R.P. Freeborg, and W.N. Willis. 1975. Thatch development and other effects of preemergence herbicides in Kentucky bluegrass turf. Agron. J. 67:563–565.

Turgeon, A.J., G.G. Stone, and T.R. Peck. 1979. Crude protein levels in turfgrass clippings. Agron. J. 71:229–232.

Turner, T.R. 1980. Soil test calibration studies for turfgrasses. Ph.D. diss. The Pennsylvania State University, University Park (Diss. Abstr. 80-24499).

Turner, T.R., and D.V. Waddington. 1978. Survey of soil testing programs for turfgrasses. Commun. Soil Sci. Plant Anal. 9(1):71–87.

Turner, T.R., and D.V. Waddington. 1983. Soil test calibration for establishment of turfgrass monostands. Soil Sci. Soc. Am. J. 47:1161–1166.

Turner, T.R., D.V. Waddington, and T.L. Watschke. 1979. The effect of fertility levels on dandelion and crabgrass encroachment of Merion Kentucky bluegrass. p. 280–286. *In* R.B. Taylorson (ed.) Proc. Northeastern Weed Science Soc. Vol. 33, Boston. 3–5 Jan. Evans Printing Co., Salisbury, MD.

Volk, G.M. 1959. Volatile loss of ammonia following surface application of urea to turf or bare soils. Agron. J. 51:745–749.

Volk, G.M., and A.E. Dudeck. 1976. Abnormal color response of turf ryegrass to topdressed isobutylidene diurea. Agron. J. 68:534–536.

Volk, G.M., and G.C. Horn. 1975. Response curves of various turfgrasses to applications of several controlled-release nitrogen sources. Agron. J. 67:201–204.

Waddington, D.V. 1986. Characteristics and responses to sulfur-coated urea, IBDU, and oxamide nitrogen fertilizers. p. 17–40. *In* B.J. Joyner (ed.) Advances in turfgrass fertility. ChemLawn Corp., Columbus, OH.

Waddington, D.V., and J.M. Duich. 1976. Evaluation of slow release nitrogen fertilizers on 'Pennpar' creeping bentgrass. Agron. J. 68:812–815.

Waddington, D.V., J.M. Duich, and T.R. Turner. 1977. Turfgrass fertilization with isobutylidene diurea and ureaform. p. 319–334. *In* R.L. Goulding (ed.) Proc. 1977 Controlled Release Pesticide Symp., Oregon State Univ., Corvallis.

Waddington, D.C., P.J. Landschoot, and N.W. Hummel, Jr. 1989. Response of Kentucky bluegrass turf to fertilizers containing dycyandiamide. Commun. Soil Sci. Plant Anal. 20:2149–2170.

Waddington, D.V., E.L. Moberg, and J.M. Duich. 1972. Effects of N source, K source, and K rate on soil nutrient levels and the growth and elemental composition of Penncross creeping bentgrass, *Agrostis palustris* Huds. Agron. J. 64:562–566.

Waddington, D.V., E.L. Moberg, J.M. Duich, and T.L. Watschke. 1976. Long-term evaluation of slow release nitrogen sources on turfgrass. Soil Sci. Soc. Am. J. 40:593–597.

Waddington, D.V., and T.R. Turner. 1980. Evaluation of sulfur-coated urea fertilizers on 'Merion' Kentucky bluegrass. Soil Sci. Soc. Am. J. 44:413–417.

Waddington, D.V., T.R. Turner, J.M. Duich, and E.L. Moberg. 1978. Effect of fertilization on 'Penncross' creeping bentgrass. Agron. J. 70:713–718.

Waddington, D.V., T.R. Turner, and J.M. Duich. 1985. Evaluation of turfgrass fertilizers on Kentucky bluegrass. The Pennsylvania State Univ., Agric. Exp. Stn. Progr. Rep. 386.

Waddington, D.V., T.R. Turner, and J.M. Duich. 1975. Responses of cool-season turfgrasses to liquid applications of fertilizer. The Pennsylvania State Univ. Agric. Exp. Stn Progr. Rep. 350.

Waddington, D.V., and T.L. Zimmerman. 1972. Growth and chemical composition of eight grasses grown under high water table conditions. Commun. Soil Sci. Plant Anal. 3(4):329–337.

Walker, W.M., and J. Pesek. 1967. Yield of Kentucky bluegrass (*Poa pratensis*) as a function of its percentage of nitrogen, phosphorus, and potassium. Agron. J. 59:44–47.

Walker, R.H., and C.Y. Ward. 1974. Influence of N and K nutrition on net photosynthesis, dark respiration, and carbohydrates in centipedegrass. p. 196–208. *In* E.C. Roberts (ed.) Proc. 2nd Int. Turfgrass Res. Conf., Blacksburg, VA. 19–21 June 1973. ASA and CSSA, Madison, WI.

Watschke, T.L., and D.V. Waddington. 1974. Effect of nitrogen source, rate, and timing on growth and carbohydrates of 'Merion' Kentucky bluegrass. Agron. J. 66:691–696.

Watschke, T.L., and D.V. Waddington. 1975. Effect of nitrogen fertilization on the recovery of 'Merion' Kentucky bluegrass from scalping and wilting. Agron. J. 67:559–563.

Watschke, T.L., D.V. Waddington, D.J. Wehner, and C.L. Forth. 1977. Effect of P, K, and lime on growth, composition, and ^{32}P absorption by Merion Kentucky bluegrass. Agron. J. 69:825–828.

Watson, C.J. 1986. Preferential uptake of ammonium nitrogen from soil by ryegrass under simulated spring conditions. J. Agric. Sci. (Cambridge) 107:171–177.

Wesely, R.W., R.C. Shearman, and E.J. Kinbacher. 1985. Foliar N-uptake by eight turfgrasses grown in controlled environment. J. Am. Soc. Hortic. Sci. 110:612–614.

Westfall, R.T., and J.A. Simmons. 1971. Germination and seedling development of Windsor Kentucky bluegrass as influenced by phosphorus and other nutrients. p. 52. *In* Agronomy abstracts. ASA, Madison, WI.

Weston, J.B., and J.H. Dunn. 1985. Thatch and quality of 'Meyer' zoysia in response to mechanical cultivation and nitrogen fertilization. p. 449–458. *In* F. Lemaire (ed.) Proc. 5th Int. Turfgrass Res. Conf., Avignon, France. 1–5 July. Inst. Natl. de la Recherche Agron., Paris.

White, R.H., and R. Dickens. 1984. Thatch accumulation in bermudagrass as influenced by cultural practices. Agron. J. 76:19–22.

Wilkinson, J.F. 1977. Effect of IBDU and UF rate, date and frequency of application on 'Merion' Kentucky bluegrass. Agron. J. 69:657–661.

Will, H., and E.U. Belger. 1985. Results of five years of research with slow-release fertilizers for turf receiving wear. Z. Vegetat. Landsch. Sports. 8:57–63.

Winsor, G.W., and M.I.C. Long. 1956. Mineralization of the nitrogen of urea-formaldehyde compounds in relation to soil pH. J. Sci. Food Agric. 7:560–564.

Wisniewski, A.J., J.A. DeFrance, and J.R. Kolbett. 1958. Results of ureaform fertilization on lawn and fairway turf. Agron. J. 50:575–576.

Wood, J.R., and R.L. Duble. 1976. Effects of nitrogen and phosphorus on establishment and maintenance of St. Augustinegrass. Texas Agric. Exp. Stn. PR-3368C.

Woolhouse, A.R. 1973. An assessment of the effectiveness of a slow-release nitrogen fertilizer on sports turf. J. Sports Turf Res. Inst. 49:8–20.

Woolhouse, A.R. 1983. An investigation of the effectiveness of IBDU as a slow-release source of nitrogen. J. Sports Turf. Res. Inst. 59:93–102.

Woolhouse, A.R. 1974. Further assessment of the effectiveness of a slow-release nitrogen fertilizer on sports turf. J. Sports Turf. Res. Inst. 50:34–46.

Woolhouse, A.R. 1986. The assessment of perennial ryegrass cultivars for susceptibility to red thread disease. J. Sports Turf Res. Inst. 62:147–152.

Wu, L., D.R. Huff, and J.M. Johnson. 1981. Metal tolerance of bermudagrass cultivars. p. 35–40. *In* R.W. Sheard (ed.) Proc. 4th Int. Turfgrass Res. Conf., Guelph, ON, Canada. 19–23 July. Int. Turfgrass Soc., and Ontario Agric. Coll., Univ. of Guelph, Guelph, ON.

Yee, J.Y., and K.S. Love. 1946. Nitrification of urea formaldehyde reaction products. Soil Sci. Soc. Am. Proc. 11:389–392.

Yust, A.K., D.J. Wehner, and T.W. Fermanian. 1984. Foliar application of N and Fe to Kentucky bluegrass. Agron. J. 76:934–938.

Zanoni, L.J., L.F. Michelson, W.G. Colby, and M. Drake. 1969. Factors affecting carbohydrate reserves of cool-season turfgrasses. Agron. J. 61:195–198.

12   Water Requirements and Irrigation

W. R. KNEEBONE

2491 N. Camino De Oeste
Tucson, Arizona

D. M. KOPEC AND **C. F. MANCINO**

University of Arizona
Tucson, Arizona

Water available to turfgrasses from rainfall and soil storage is rarely synchronized with plant needs in either time or quantity. Water problems vary from absolute desiccation to submersion and correction of these problems must be addressed by judiciously applied irrigation or drainage. The priority of irrigation as a component of turfgrass management ranges from an absolute essential for grass survival in arid climates to luxury, "cosmetic" applications in areas of high rainfall. Judicious application of irrigation water requires uniform application at rates sufficient to meet the needs of the particular turfgrass situation. Besides a well-designed and operated irrigation system, there are other parameters essential to this process. These include the infiltration rate of the soil, the evapotranspiration (ET) potential, the water requirement of the turfgrass as determined by ET rates, and the level of turfgrass performance chosen. This chapter will address itself to water requirements, direct and indirect measurement thereof, and factors which affect them.

I. WATER REQUIREMENT

Several terms have been used in studies of water use by crop plants. Use of the term *water requirement*, particularly by agricultural engineers, is "the amount of water from rainfall and irrigation necessary to meet specific production or performance needs." The priority use of the term water requirement, particularly by agronomists, is that given by Briggs and Shantz (1913) in which water requirement is measured in terms of units of water per unit of crop harvested. *Water use efficiency* in crops has been discussed in terms of water per unit production, for example, Dobrenz et al. (1969b) or in terms of production per unit water (Pendleton, 1965; Frank et al., 1987). Under both definitions, efficiency can come from high production or low consumptive water use, but preferably both. In general, the term water re-

Copyright © 1992 ASA-CSSA-SSSA, 677 S. Segoe Rd., Madison, WI 53711, USA. *Turfgrass—Agronomy Monograph no. 32.*

quirement encompasses many facets of turfgrass water use physiology, which must be understood to link the proper research technique to meet the specific research objective. To delineate the different approaches to studying turfgrass water requirements, some definitions need to be discussed.

Turfgrass water use rate is defined as the total amount of water needed for plant growth which includes water lost by the transpiration and evaporation from soil and plant surfaces. Water use rates are expressed in terms of inches or millimeters per day and referred to as ET.

Water requirement and water use efficiency by turfgrass are determined in relation to performance and quality standards, rather than yield standards (Shearman, 1985). The water requirement of turf becomes the water required to meet a performance standard rather than a production standard. Stated in this way, the term also implies that it is a minimum value that will vary with the type of turf used or required. The turf water use rate may be influenced by soil moisture availability, the degree of water demand, by the atmosphere, and by cultural management practices. Complex interactions often occur between the plant's ability to dissipate its solar heat load and the available soil moisture. This is referred to as soil-plant-atmosphere continuum (SPAC) (Carrow, 1985).

The term *drought* can have various meanings among scientists, turf managers, and lay personnel. This text will use those terms set forth by the Crop Science Society of America. Drought is defined as "a condition caused by a period of dry weather, sufficiently prolonged to cause plant damage and water supply shortages, usually defined as a cumulated precipitation deferring from normal, accompanied by above-normal atmospheric evaporated demands." *Drought resistance* is a general term encompassing mechanisms in which plants withstand periods of dry weather. These mechanisms are comprised of *drought avoidance* and *drought tolerance.*

Drought avoidance is "the ability of a plant to avoid tissue-damaging water deficits even while growing in a drought environment favoring the development of water stress." A positive tissue water balance is thus maintained and excludes the stress. Drought avoidance may be a function of increased root depth and root water uptake properties, and reduced ET. Evapotranspiration reductions may be due to reduced surface area (leaf area), alteration of leaf properties that influence radiation interception and heat load dissipation, stomatal regulation to conserve water, and leaf surface properties such as epidermal hair and wax.

Drought tolerance is the ability of a turf to endure low (more negative) water potentials caused by drought. Drought-tolerance mechanisms include osmoregulation and desiccation tolerance achieved via protoplasm resistance. These terms demonstrate the different mechanisms of how plants can react to a drought environment.

The need for water conservation in turfgrass management while avoiding drought stress is universal in areas of both high rainfall or desert regions. Considerations of turfgrass water requirements should be "what are the minima required by a turfgrass for the performance level desired?" A corollary might be, "how much performance can be obtained from a given amount of water?'' These approaches necessitate different experimental approaches to answer such questions (e.g., measuring water use under nonlimiting soil moisture conditions, or measuring plant responses under increasing or preselected soil moisture [or simulated] stress levels). The application and limitations of such experimental methods will be discussed in the appropriate sections of this chapter.

To start, the basic factors affecting turfgrass water use rate will be reviewed: (i) evaporative demand of the air surrounding the sward; (ii) the quantity and quality of the water with which the sward is supplied; and (iii) transpiration and evaporation levels typical of the specific type of sward and soil in response to evaporative demands.

II. EVAPORATIVE DEMAND AND WATER USE

The driving force for evaporative demand is solar radiation. Amounts and effectiveness of solar radiation are functions of climate, season, altitude, and latitude. The energy from solar radiation can be absorbed or dissipated in many ways, one of which is by the latent heat of evaporation (transpiration). The first consideration in determining water requirements is to establish basic patterns of evaporative demand and determine how that demand is translated into ET losses from turf whose water use is not restricted in any other way. Having established a potential (or reference) evaporative demand, the factors can be considered which limit or change ET at given levels of demand.

Literature is extensive on crop water use and methods for its estimation or measurement (Doorenbos & Pruitt, 1975; Gay, 1981; Teare, 1984). Most presentations start with evaporative demand as basic. An obvious measurement of evaporative demand is to expose a free water surface and measure water loss. Probably the method for which most data are available is the U.S. Weather Service Class A Pan. This is 122-cm in diameter and 25-cm deep supported 15 cm above the ground (Doorenbos & Pruitt, 1975). If conditions for the pan site are closely matched with those for the crop, the *correlation* between pan loss and consumptive water use will approach unity. Consumptive use, however, is usually *less* than evaporative losses from Class A Pans, varying from 50 to 90% with stage of growth, crop, and other modifying factors. It is important to know if pan evaporimeters use the Class A standards. If not, then Pan reference values may be seriously biased, usually upwards.

Ordinary wash tubs have been successfully used in farm fields in Montana to schedule irrigations. The tubs are exposed in the field to rainfall and irrigation. Irrigations are made whenever the water level drops below a predetermined point and ends when it reaches standard levels (Westeson & Hanson, 1981). Handreck (1979) in Australia recommended use of metal waste-baskets or half oil drums as evaporimeters for adjusting turfgrass irrigation. He stated that irrigation levels as low as 25% of evaporative losses could sustain turf.

The well-known Penman estimates for water use were derived as a means of calculating loss from a free water surface (Penman, 1948). This method is an equation combining energy balance and mass transfer principles. Data required for the Penman model include wind speed, net radiation, temperature and vapor pressure deficits (VPD). The Penman equation is based on sound theoretical principles. Local calibration of the Penman model is often necessary because daily patterns of wind, temperature, VPD and net radiation are represented as a single numerical ET value. The need for local calibration increases if VPD and solar radiation are estimated from other measured environmental data, resulting in some new accommodation of the wind function of the equation. The Penman model is applicable to humid and dry climates alike for estimating a potential (reference) ET.

A once widely used estimate of evaporative demand in the western USA is that proposed by Blaney and Criddle (1962). Evaporative demand is determined using monthly average temperatures and the percentage of the annual daylight hours occurring in that month. They derived a generalized estimate of water use, which was adjusted by a crop coefficient to fit the particular crop and its development stage. Quackenbush and Phelan (1965) adjusted the original Blaney-Criddle formula to estimate turfgrass use and a well-known series of estimates of potential irrigation needs across the continental USA was derived and published by the Toro Company (Anonymous, 1966) using this formula. Madison (1971) took the Toro data one step further and published a map with a series of isosiccative lines drawn from the tabular Toro data. Borelli et al. (1981) published a compendium of Blaney-Criddle crop coefficients for turfgrasses which were based on actual water use measured at several western locations exhibiting generally dry climates.

The Jensen-Haise equation is more precise than the Blaney-Criddle procedure and much simpler than the Penman method yet derives values very close to Penman over time (Al-Nakshabandi, 1983). This formula is an empirical method of estimating reference ET that has been used by irrigation engineers throughout the west. The model relates reference ET to solar radiation and temperature using alfalfa as a reference crop (Jensen & Haise, 1963). The model does not take wind speed into account and is, therefore, subject to considerable error under highly advective conditions. This model is best used for periods that span a minimum of 5 d or so. For a thorough review of ET and atmospheric models (see Rosenberg, 1983a, b).

Jensen-Haise estimates are presented in daily public radio announcements and are available from a "hotline" number in Denver, CO, to provide the public with data upon which to base their watering programs (Anonymous, 1982) as part of a community water conservation effort. A similar effort to provide the public with water requirement estimates and enhance water conservation, is the provision in the Phoenix area of a charted wheel that sets watering levels according to maximum temperatures (Kopec et al., 1986). Under Arizona summer conditions, correlations of temperatures with measured water requirements for bermudagrass are very high ($r = 0.88$). Kim (1983) found lower, but still highly significant values in Texas, under more humid conditions.

The Arizona Meteorological Network (AZMET) is a university-sponsored system that provides the public with reference ET values. A "turf hot line" is available for users in the Phoenix area for obtaining turfgrass water use on a daily basis. Extensive research is underway devising crop coefficients (actual/Reference ET) (Kc) for bermuda and ryegrass turf in that state (Kopec et al., 1988).

Both the modified Penman equation and a pan evaporimeter were used to calculate Kc values for Kentucky bluegrass (*Poa pratensis* L.), perennial ryegrass (*Lolium perenne* L.), and red (*Festuca rubra* L.) and sheeps (*F. ovina* L.) fescue in Rhode Island (Aronson et al., 1987a). They found that Kc values were different among the four cool-season species, and that Penman-based estimates were less variable than Pan-based Kc values.

Doorenbos and Pruitt (1975) provide ways for practical, local adjustment of data for four methods of estimate. Each method was aimed at calculating potential water loss from a reference crop similar to a turf. Their reference is "the rate of ET from an extended surface of 8 to 15 cm tall green grass cover of uniform height, actively growing, completely shading the ground and not short of water." The four methods used were: Blaney-Criddle, Penman, net radiation, and Class A Pan. Estimates of reference crop water requirements following the Dorrenbos and Pruitt (1975) procedures should normally give values equal to or greater than those for a typical turfgrass situation. Such estimates would provide guidelines for irrigation system design and capacity.

Penman values are adjusted by a crop coefficient (Kc) to estimate actual potential ET losses from the particular crop involved. For example, Shearman and Pederson (1986) found an average Kc of 0.88 for Kentucky bluegrass turf in Nebraska. Most estimates of evaporative potenital require some sort of Kc adjustment to meet specific situations and Kc values will obviously vary (Doorenbos & Pruitt, 1975; Borelli et al., 1981). Kneebone and Pepper (1982) surveyed available data relating turf water use to Class A evaporative pan losses and found Kc pan values ranging from 50 to 90%. It is important to realize that a Kc value is a fractional percentage of a base (reference) value. Base values must be determined on a local basis to determine actual water requirements (e.g., using mini-lysimeters or other methods).

Automated meteorological-agricultural networks in Nebraska (Rosenberg et al., 1983a), California (Snyder et al., 1985), and Arizona (Kopec et al., 1988) use forms of the Penman equation to provide daily crop water use estimates. The turfgrass irrigation industry now markets weather stations that calculate reference ET on site. The estimates are then capable of being used for automatic irrigation scheduling. Correction values for soil and turfgrass type, soil compaction level, plant type and shade factors can be assigned from station to station. With this information, station times are manipulated to restore adequate soil moisture based on the reference ET and the factors mentioned above.

The availability and use of evaporative potential information from meteorological and Class A Pan data, is certain to increase. Locally developed research-based crop coefficients from this information, will enhance water conservation because different Kc values can be expected for different turfgrass species and cultural management factors.

Deficit irrigation refers to some fractional level of irrigation made in response to some reference water use estimate, such as Class A Pan, Penman, or some other reference determination or estimate. The maximum (or base) standard may be determined by measuring ET directly from well-watered turf using small weighing lysimeters (Feldhake et al., 1984; Dry & Butler, 1989b). Deficit irrigation treatments often include both deficit irrigation replacement levels and irrigation timing variables (days between irrigations). Caution must be used when interpreting data because it varies depending upon the species or cultural practices used.

Replacement of soil water (regardless of the deficit level) saturates some portion of the soil profile from the surface downwards. Even deficit irrigations that provide "shallow" applications of water re-wet a substantial part of the fibrous root zone, where much of the water uptake occurs. Therefore, both drought avoidance and drought tolerance mechanisms may be operating at some time between irrigations. The measurement of actual "water use" during deficit irrigation experiments may be of academic interest only, especially when mini-lysimeters are used (which can be restricted in root volume). Field evaluation of soil moisture depletion during a deficit irrigation study may be of greater applied value, since one can better monitor soil moisture changes with depth, and levels of soil moisture stress occur gradually as compared to a smaller confined soil system (e.g., small lysimeter or pots). The choice of an experimental unit should be based on the research objective.

III. OTHER FACTORS AFFECTING WATER USE

A. Soil Moisture

In a sense, water use by turfgrass can be compared with a pump (solar radiation) at one end of a casing (the plant) and the aquifer (soil moisture in the root zone) at the other. All three affect the volume delivered (the transpiration stream). Water lost by direct evaporation from soil surfaces can be viewed similarly, with the plant as conduit replaced by soil capillarity. Water cannot be pumped from a dry well nor can it be pumped from a well without a power source. For this reason, all standard procedures to estimate potential water use include the proviso that sufficient water is available (soil moisture at or above field capacity). When soil moisture is high, water use is primarily a function of evaporative demand (pump capacity) and estimates based upon that demand are estimates of maximum water use. As soil moisture becomes less than field capacity, water use becomes more and more a function of moisture availability. The plant can also interact with both evaporative demand and soil water potential to affect the transpiration stream, for example, stomatal regulation (drought avoidance).

Many studies have shown that water use is directly related to available soil water (Madison & Hagan, 1962; Doss et al., 1962; Kneebone & Pepper, 1982, 1984; Hang & Miller, 1983). In 1965, Quackenbush and Phelan suggested that water savings could be made with little loss in turf quality by allowing short periods of water stress between irrigations. Relatively few workers have evaluated quality along with water use rate at less than optimal water regimes. Available data indicate that major savings in water use can often be made with only minor losses in quality. This is particularly true where the water stress is compensated for by providing other inputs. An early example is a study conducted in Israel by Mantell (1966) with kikuyu grass (*Pennisetum clandestinum* Hochst ex Chiov.). He set up a series of irrigation regimes ranging from 5 to 30-d intervals between replenishments to field capacity. He found that quality of N-fertilized grass irrigated at 25-d intervals was equivalent to that of unfertilized grass irrigated at 5-d intervals, with water savings of 45%. A more recent study by Danielson et al. (1981) with Kentucky bluegrass measured water use when the soil was irrigated to 100% field capacity and to various lesser percentages. Irrigation to 80% field capacity reduced quality only 10% while reducing consumptive use 20%. Quality was drastically reduced at watering levels below 70%, but rapidly recovered when watered fully.

Studies at the University of California South Coast Field Station with Bermudagrass (*Cynodon dactylon* L. Pers.), St. Augustinegrass [*Stenotophrum secundatum* (Walter) Kuntze.], tall fescue (*Festuca arundinacea* Schreb.), and Kentucky bluegrass involved a series of soil and Class A Pan-based irrigation treatments comparable to irrigation done by local turfgrass managers (Youngner et al., 1981). One treatment involved summer irrigation at 87% of evaporation from a sunken pan. Three others were controlled by tensiometers maintained at 0.015, 0.035, and 0.055 MPa for cool-season grasses. In all cases, the treatment with the highest soil moisture tension used the least water. There were no significant differences in turf-quality ratings among treatments for bermudagrass or St. Augustinegrass but a 56% water savings for the 0.065 MPa tensiometer treatment was realized. The lowest tensiometer treatment reduced quality of Kentucky bluegrass but there were no significant differences among the others, again with substantial differences in water applied. Augustin et al. (1981) have shown similar savings in Florida using tensiometer based irrigations with little loss of turf quality when compared with homeowner timed settings.

Further California studies (Gibeault et al., 1985; Meyer et al., 1985) irrigated several turfgrasses at 100, 80, and 60% of ET values estimated from modified Class A Pan data. Reducing water applications to 80% ET decreased quality ratings only 3% for the cool-season species and 5% for the warm-season species (Meyer et al., 1985). Even at 60% of ET, bermudagrass quality was better than acceptable and not significantly different from bermudagrass at 100% of ET. As might be expected from their higher water use rates, quality of the cool-season grasses was significantly reduced at the 60% of required ET irrigation. Water application rates at 100% of calculated ET were 78% of Class A Pan losses for the cool-season grasses and

66% for warm-season species. These ratios correspond with those found by Kneebone and Pepper (1982) in Arizona studies where water was not limited.

Available data show that carefully managed deficit irrigation is at least a means toward potential savings in water with relatively small losses in quality of turf. Hazards from over-watering may be of greater importance than potential quality losses from lower levels of irrigation (as one example, the 100% watering level in the California study led to undesirable increases in weeds in the cool-season turf) (Gibeault et al., 1985). It should be noted that these experiments were conducted with minimal traffic. Research is warranted to determine the effects of trafficking in conjunction with irrigation variables.

Several factors enter into the relationship between water supplied and water used by grass. At optimal soil moisture levels, plants retain full turgor under all but the most extreme conditions of evaporative demand. With reductions in soil moisture, turgor is progressively reduced and two things happen. One of these is a closing of stomatal guard cells which is a drought avoidance mechanism. This reduces water loss, conserving remaining soil reserves. It also reduces CO_2 entry and hence photosynthesis and growth. In most turfgrass situations where wear is not extreme, excess growth is undesirable. Mildly reduced top growth also has the effect of allowing roots to partition available photosynthates and thus encourages deeper rooting. Deeper and more extensive rooting, if soil temperatures are not limiting, allows exploitation of more stored soil moisture and because of the greater reservoir reduces the potential degree of water stress at any stage between irrigations (drought avoidance).

B. Mowing

Evaporation or transpiration increases as surface area increases. Increased mowing height and amount of top growth can be expected to increase water use, since increased leaf area enhances potential transpiration loss. It also changes the geometry of the plant canopy surface, making it rougher (allowing for more turbulent gas exchange between the canopy and bulk air), causing less boundary layer resistance, and increasing the capacity for absorbing advective heat. A secondary effect of increased top growth is an increase in root growth. This beneficial response results in a greater soil water source to exploit.

Most data on the effect of mowing height on water use are with cool-season grasses. Madison and Hagan (1962) found that moisture extraction over a 2-yr period from the top 50 cm of soil by Kentucky bluegrass mowed at 2.5 cm was 15% greater than the same grass mowed at 1.25 cm. Mowing at 5 cm increased water use by 27% over the 1.25-cm height. Root growth was also greater.

Shearman and Beard (1973) studied water use by 'Penncross' creeping bentgrass (*Agrostis palustris* Huds.) in a growth chamber. Increasing the mowing height from 0.7 to 2.5 cm increased the water use rate by 50%. Mowing at 12.5 cm resulted in an additional 37% moisture loss when compared with the 2.5-cm height. This same study also showed that water use could be increased by 41% when mowing frequency was increased from biweekly to six times per week. Feldhake et al. (1983) found a 15% increase in water use by Kentucky bluegrass mowed at 5 cm when compared with Kentucky bluegrass mowed at 2 cm. However, the turf maintained at the higher height of cut showed only a small decrease in visual quality when a 37% irrigation defict was used when compared to well watered controls. In contrast, quality of the shorter turf decreased sharply when a 27% irrigation deficit was exceeded. All the turf tested had similar root systems due to the limiting nature of the containers they were grown in. The authors concluded that heat stress caused the decrease in visual quality because of the inability of the shorter turf to dissipate heat effectively. Elevated canopy temperatures had been measured during this study. The same conclusion was reached in related research (Feldhake et al., 1984). Fry (1989b) reported a 6% increase in ET for both *Poa annua* and Penncross creeping bentgrass maintained at 12 mm as opposed to a 6 mm mowing height using small bucket lysimeters.

Biran et al. (1981) found that raising the mowing height from 3 to 6 cm increased water use over a 6-wk period by 29% for 'Alta' tall fescue (*Festuca arundinaceae* Schreb.) and 25% for 'Pennfine' perennial ryegrass. Permanent increases in plant growth and chlorophyll content were also observed. Increasing mowing height on the warm-season grasses 'Emerald' zoysiagrass (*Zoysia japonica × tenuifolia*) and 'Suwanee' bermudagrass resulted in a small and temporary increase in growth and water use. Within the warm-season grass species, Kim and Beard (1984) reported that low N-requiring grasses {such as zoysiagrass (*Zoysia* sp.), buffalograss [*Buchloë dactyloides* (Nutt.) Engelm.], and centipedegrass [*Eremochloa ophiuroides* (Munro) Hackel]} showed increased ET rates at optimum heights of cut. In contrast, the ET response rate of grasses responsive to increased N levels such as bermudagrass and seashore paspalum (*Paspalum vaginatum* Swartz.) were more sensitive to N fertility level than to mowing height.

Pederson (1985) found that the ET rates of cool-season grasses increased with mowing height. These grasses tend to have vertical leaf orientations and high leaf extension rates. Kim (1983, 1987) found that grasses with horizontal leaf orientations and limited leaf extension rates used less water than their opposites under suboptimal or optimal growing conditions (height and fertility). Thus, type of grass, mowing height, and fertility practices all must be taken into consideration when trying to reduce ET by manipulating cultural practices.

Mowing frequency and mower sharpness can affect water use. Shearman and Beard (1973) found the water use of Penncross creeping bentgrass increased by 15% as mowing frequency increased from 1 to 12 times every 14 d. Immediately after mowing there is a temporary increase in water loss from the cut leaf ends that is aggravated by shredding, tearing, or bruising caused by dull blades. This, however, is a transient effect and only a small portion of the total water use. It becomes more important where mowing is very frequent, as on a golf green.

Steinegger et al. (1983) have shown that Kentucky bluegrass, mowed with a sharp mower actually had an increased total water use of 20 to 30%

when compared to turf mowed with a dull mower blade. The reduced water use of turf mowed with a dull mower, however, was actually associated with a reduction in shoot density ($r = 0.88$), verdure ($r = 0.93$), and less growth, ultimately resulting in less evaporative surface area.

After reviewing available research data, Shearman (1985) concluded that frequent mowing with sharp mowers at modest mowing heights offered the best compromise of mowing effects on water use and turf quality while maximizing water conservation and turf performance.

C. Fertilization

Any cultural practice that increases leaf surface area, internode length, and vertical leaf extension rate should also increase water use. Nitrogen fertilization increases shoot growth and we would expect increases in water use under higher N regimes. In a study by Danielson et al. (1981), Kentucky bluegrass receiving "adequate" N used 10% more water than unfertilized grass over all levels of irrigation tested. Shearman and Beard (1973) found that preconditioning 'Penncross' creeping bentgrass with four levels of N (0, 50, 250, and 500 mg L^{-1}) resulted in a corresponding increase in water use. Leaf width, shoot density, and shoot growth increased with increasing N levels and these morphological changes were positively correlated ($r \geq 0.80$) with water use rates. Water use was negatively correlated ($r = -0.98$) with stomatal density that decreased as N increased. Excessive N levels (1500 mg of N L^{-1}) reduced shoot density, shoot growth, and water use rates.

Feldhake et al. (1983, 1984) showed that Kentucky bluegrass grown under a deficient N level (4 kg of N 1000 m^{-2} yr^{-1}) had lower ET levels than when N was applied at 4 kg of N 1000 m^{-2} mo^{-1}). This was attributed to the slower growth rate and lighter green color (which reflected energy) of the N-deficient turfgrass. Thirteen percent more water was used at the higher N rate. Kim (1983) examined the influence of different cultural practices on the ET rate of nine warm-season turfgrasses. When turf was maintained under optimum N fertilizer levels (125–500 g are^{-1} growing mo^{-1} depending on the turf species) higher ET rates were observed than when under limiting N conditions. Seven of these grasses showed significant increases in vertical leaf extension rates at their optimum N level. He felt that mowing height was more important in determining the ET rates of grasses with a low N requirement and growth response to N than for grasses that were very responsive to N fertility. He contrasted the low N-requiring grasses zoysia, buffalograss, and centipedgrass with the high N-requiring bermudagrasses and seashore paspalum.

Soil compaction may affect ET more than N source or N rates. Sills and Carrow (1983) reported that N applied to Pennfine perennial ryegrass growing on a compacted soil had little effect on ET. However, water use efficiency (g of tissue g of water^{-1}) was increased. Soil compaction may affect ET more than the N carrier treatments and N rates applied.

Nitrogen fertilization of creeping bentgrass golf greens during times of heat stress can materially reduce root growth because carbohydrate reserves, otherwise available for maintenance of roots, are diverted for increased shoot growth. Drought stress may be observed under these conditions because the impaired root system cannot provide enough soil water to replace that lost to the atmosphere by transpiration. Shorter roots may reduce potential water use because of a reduction in the available soil water reservoir. In reality, shorter roots have the net effect of increasing the irrigation requirement because of the need to maintain moisture in the upper 5 to 10 cm of surface soil where the roots are located.

Although the following discussion does not directly pertain to turf water use, it does point out that the influence of macronutrients on turf quality, growth, and physiological response to drought stress is an interactive one. The same probably can be said for their influence on turfgrass water use. There is a great demand for further research in this area.

At this time, research data are limited concerning the influence of P and K on the water requirements of turfgrass. Potassium fertilization increases drought, heat, cold, and disease resistance. The mechanisms are not well understood. Potassium increases root production (Marklund & Roberts, 1967) which, in and of itself, may increase the available soil water reservoir but also the potential consumptive water use of turf. Waddington et al. (1978) reported that K applications decreased the incidence of wilting in Penncross creeping bentgrass. Work at Nebraska with 'Fylking' Kentucky bluegrass, also showed that wilting decreased with increasing K levels (Shearman, 1982). Turf receiving increased levels of K had increased turgor pressure that contributed to better wear tolerance (Shearman & Beard, 1975). Schmidt and Breuninger (1981) found K applications aided in the recovery of drought-stressed Kentucky bluegrass. However, Christians et al. (1981) showed that the response of Kentucky bluegrass to K was dependent upon the other nutrients applied. For example, when high K (10.8 kg are^{-1}) was applied with high N or P applications turfgrass quality was reduced. High K levels in combination with low N or P levels improved turfgrass quality.

The influence of P on turfgrass drought tolerance or avoidance is not well understood. As mentioned previously, its effects may be interactive with N and K. Schmidt and Breuninger (1981) found that P aided in the recovery of Kentucky bluegrass from drought but its effects were interactive with N. For cotton (*Gossypium hirsutum* L.), P has also been shown to influence the leaf water potential at which stomates close by apparently increasing sensitivity of the guard cells to abscisic acid (Radin, 1984). Phosphorous-deficient plants showed decreased leaf conductance at a greater leaf water potential than P-adequate plants. Suboptimal N levels also increased stomatal sensitivity to exogenous ABA in cotton (Radin & Hendrix, 1988).

D. Soil Compaction

Typical observable effects of compaction on turfgrass growth are reductions in both shoot and root growth. Obviously both effects should reduce potential water use of turf by limiting the size of the exploitable soil reservoir on one end and by reducing the transpiring surface on the other. Detailed studies by O'Neil and Carrow (1983) with 'Derby' perennial ryegrass under three compaction levels showed average water use per day of 1.01, 0.63, and 0.32 cm during the last 20 d of an experiment with no compaction, moderate compaction, and heavy compaction, respectively. There was no significant difference in water use efficiency (g of tissue g of water^{-1}) because of the reduced growth associated with compaction. There was no significant difference in total root weight among compaction levels but there was a change in proportions of total roots at different soil levels. The amount of roots in the 0 to 5 cm level actually increased at the heaviest level of compaction. Since water use decreased, this suggests that root efficiency in water uptake was limited by the low oxygen diffusion rates (ODR) found at high compaction levels. A later study, by Agnew and Carrow (1985) found the same increased shallow rooting, but also showed that ODR levels were below those critical for plant growth. In another study with Pennfine perennial ryegrass, Sills and Carrow (1983) found a 28% reduction in water use in compacted soil associated with a 30% reduction in clipping yields.

As O'Neil and Carrow (1983) observed, typical watering practices by turfgrass managers on compacted areas involve frequent light waterings to compensate for low infiltration rates and shallow roots. With reduced top growth this means increased runoff potential and evaporation losses from soil surfaces that may more than compensate for the reduced water use by the grass and may mean a net increase in irrigation under actual field conditions.

E. Growth Regulators

Any chemical contributing to the development of a short, compact turfgrass with low vertical leaf extension rates should also reduce ET (Kim & Beard, 1983). Plant growth regulating (PGR) chemicals such as maleic hydrazide and chlorflurenol (methyl-2-chloro-9-hydroxyfluorene-9-carboxylate, methyl-9-hydroxyfluorene-9-carboxylate) reduce cell division in the meristemic region. Reduction of cell elongation is typical of growth regulators such as mefluidide. However, the influence of these PGRs and others on the water requirements of turf is not conclusive at this time.

Johns and Beard (1982) reduced the growth of St. Augustinegrass and bermudagrass with flurprimidol. Consumptive water use was reduced by up to 29% when compared with untreated checks. A significant reduction in leaf area index was also found. In another study (Borden & Campbell, 1985), the water requirement of paclobutrizol and Mon-4621 treated zoysia was reduced 22%. Decreased growth was also observed.

Doyle and Shearman (1985) tested the effects of growth regulators on Kentucky bluegrass turf. Evapotranspiration was initially lowered by the chemicals tested, but amidichlor, flurprimidol, and mefluidide-treated turf exhibited increased ET rates 35 to 42 d after treatment because of enhanced turfgrass growth following the growth suppression period. Watschke (1976) showed that suppression of Kentucky bluegrass growth with several growth retardants was sometimes followed by a "flush" of growth which was greater than the growth of untreated controls. Metsulforon methyl and sulfometuron methyl also increased turf growth from 8 to 18 wk after application (Rogers et al., 1987).

Soluble N fertilizers reduced initial chemical phytotoxicity of some PGRs and decreased growth suppression while increasing posttreatment growth (Watschke, 1979). A flush of growth either as a rebound from growth suppression by growth regulating chemicals or stimulation by N fertilizers applied to alleviate chemical phototoxicity might increase the consumptive water requirement of the treated turfgrass once the growth retardants effect ends.

The short-term effect of reduced turfgrass shoot growth due to PGR applications appears to be a reduction in water use. However, the long-term water use rate may not be any lower (or may actually be higher) if: (i) an extended increase in shoot growth occurs following cessation of the treatment; (ii) N applications are made to the turf to mask phytotoxic effects of the PGR; (iii) the plant becomes more susceptible to environmental stress due to direct or indirect effects of the PGR; and (iv) a reduction in root growth due to decreased shoot growth results in a need for a more frequent irrigations to prevent drought stress.

F. Abscisic Acid

Abscisic acid (ABA) prevents stomatal opening and promotes stomatal closure (Bidwell, 1974). Little research has been done, when compared to many other crops, to study the factors influencing ABA production, release, translocation, and influence on stomates in turfgrasses. Kim (1987) demonstrated 4.0, 7.6, and 1.6-fold increases in endogenous ABA levels in bahiagrass (*Paspalum notatum* Fluegge), bermudagrass and St. Augustinegrass, respectively, following 13 d of drought. Evapotranspiration rates have been shown to be low for bahiagrass, low to medium for bermudagrass, and high for St. Augustinegrass.

Although application to large turfgrass areas is economically prohibitive, ABA reduced transpiration rates in Texas studies of Penncross creeping bentgrass and 'Tifway' bermudagrass by 59 and 12%, respectively (Stahnke, 1981). Bermudagrass had a 23% reduction in growth. In contrast, Libscomb and Welterlen (1986) and Rose et al. (1986) found no transpiration reduction from cool- or warm-season turfgrass sods treated with ABA. Conflicting results on the influence of abscisic acid on water use are not unusual. Leaf age, N and P nutrition, kinetin levels and previous exposure to water stress have all been found to influence stomatal response to ABA (Radin & Hendrix, 1988; Radin, 1984). Changes in apoplastic pH, as a result of tissue dehydration, may also allow for the release of endogenous ABA from mesophyll cells (Hartung et al., 1988).

G. Anti-transpirants

Anti-transpirants work in several ways: (i) Chemicals such as hexaoctadecanol, cetyl-alcohol and steryl-alcohol reduce transpiration by forming a mono-molecular layer located at the water-air interface in the leaf mesophyll which reduces transpirational loss of water; (ii) The metabolic inhibitors phenylmercuric acetate (PMA) and dodecenylsuccinic acid (DSA) prevent stomatal opening; and (iii) Wax and oil emulsions prevent water loss by completely covering the leaf surface with a film.

Oertli (1963) worked with steryl-alcohol and cetyl-alcohol. He found that transpiration could be decreased in barley seedlings but was accompanied by decreased dry matter production. Phytotoxic effects were observed. Atsatt and Bliss (1963) found that spray application (112 kg ha^{-1}) of hexaoctadecanol (HO) to Kentucky bluegrass seed beds not only promoted germination by preventing water loss from the soil, but resulted in a greater amount of plant cover 30 d following treatment. They also observed a flush of growth 2 mo following HO application. The researchers attributed this to increased soil N availability resulting from an apparent stimulation of microbial activity. They concluded that this chemical might be beneficial in large-scale turf production. Roberts and Lage (1965) increased the growth (dry weight) of Kentucky bluegrass by addition of cetyl-stearyl-octadecanol to applied nutrient solutions. These alcohol compounds, however, are too costly to apply to large areas of turf, making their commercial use unlikely.

Wax and oil emulsions reduce photosynthesis and transpiration due to increased diffusive resistance (Slatyer & Bierhuizen, 1964). Reduced photosynthetic activity over prolonged periods of time could result in decreased shoot and root growth. This would be unacceptable in turfgrass situations where high shoot density, a deep root system and a high recuperative potential from injury, disease and wear are necessary. Another problem associated with these chemicals is in obtaining a uniform film covering of the leaf surface (Gale & Hagan, 1966; Shearman, 1985).

Phenylmercuric acetate and DSA have some promise as turfgrass anti-transpirants. Davenport (1966, 1967) found PMA and DSA to be effective in reducing transpirational water loss from creeping red fescue and colonial bentgrass (*Agrostis tenuis* Sibth). For fescue, the duration and extent of anti-transpirational effects and chemical phytotoxicity were related to PMA application rate. An optimum concentration of $10^{-3.5}$ M PMA resulted in a 20% reduction in water loss and only a 2% reduction in dry weight. DSA was just as effective, less phytotoxic, and less of a hazard to the environment than PMA. Mancino et al. (1987) found that a $10^{-3.5}$ M DSA solution did not discolor 'Belle' perennial ryegrass nor reduce clipping yield and soluble leaf sugar levels. At Texas A&M, a mixture of decenylsuccinic acid and Aqua-Gro reduced the water requirement of Penncross creeping bentgrass by 30% without visual injury (Stahnke, 1981).

Concern has been expressed over the effects of reduced stomatal opening on plant photosynthesis. Research has shown that photosynthesis is reduced to a much lesser extent than transpiration when metabolic inhibitor anti-transpirants are applied to corn (*Zea mays* L.) (Shimshi, 1963a), sorghum [*Sorghum bicolor* (L.) Moench] (Fuehring, 1973), tobacco (*Nicotiana tobacum* L.) (Shimshi, 1963b), and cotton (*Gossypium hirsutum* L.) (Slatyer

& Bierhuizen, 1964). This reinforces the likelihood that some anti-transpirants would not adversely influence turfgrass quality.

H. Stomatal Characteristics

Kim (1987) presented a major examination of the stomatal characteristics of 11 major warm-season turfgrasses. Stomata of bermudagrass were sunken, wax protected, and closed rapidly following the onset of drought stress. These grasses had low ET rates under both drought stressed and nondrought stressed conditions. A high degree of wax accumulation was associated with low ET rates of buffalograss and zoysiagrass. Bahiagrass had high ET rates under nonstressed conditions, but very low ET rates when stressed. This was attributed to rapid stomatal closure. The stomates of centipedegrass and St. Augustinegrass were not protected by wax and reopened during drought stress. This was also confirmed by Peacock and Dudeck (1984) for St. Augustinegrass. These two grasses have high ET rates under both drought stressed and nondrought stressed conditions.

Stomatal characteristics are an obviously important factor in the control of transpiration. However, canopy resistance and turbulent air exchange resistance may be more critical in determining ET rates than stomatal or leaf resistance. Johns et al. (1983) found the former from two to four times more important than the latter in St. Augustinegrass water use under nonstress conditions. Dobrenz et al. (1969a) found significant differences in stomate density among genotypes of blue panicgrass (*Panicum antidotale* Retz.), but could show no relationship between stomate density and transpiration levels or water-use efficiency. Kramer (1983) states that the relative importance of stomatal characteristics is subject to complex interactions with many factors and is difficult to assess. Kneebone and Pepper (1982) and Kim (1983) showed high ET rates for tall fescue and St. Augustinegrass which Kim associated with lower canopy resistances resulting from such factors as low shoot density, high leaf surface area, and rapid vertical leaf extension rate. Zoysiagrass and bermudagrass did not exhibit these characteristics and had low to medium rates of ET. These factors make the use of plant growth regulating compounds more feasible in terms of reducing turfgrass water use than do chemicals which simply block or close stomates. This is true so long as these chemicals do not decrease shoot density or cause a flush of posttreatment growth.

IV. SPECIES AND CULTIVARS

Where direct comparisons have been made, cool-season (C_3) grasses have used more water than warm-season (C_4) grasses, in most cases by a significant margin (Tovey et al., 1969; Biran et al., 1981; Danielson et al., 1981; Youngner et al., 1981; Kneebone & Pepper, 1982; Kim, 1983; Gibeault et al., 1985; Kim & Beard, 1988). Water use differences among species with C3 and C4 types have also been demonstrated (Biran et al., 1981; Youngner et al., 1981; Kim & Beard, 1983; Aronson et al., 1985; Gibeault et al., 1985; Kim & Beard, 1988).

In a 2-yr field study comparing seeded bermudagrass to 'Tifgreen' and 'Santa Ana' at two management levels, Kneebone and Pepper (1982) found no significant differences among them in water use, all using water within a rather narrow range. Biran et al. (1981) measured significantly greater water use by 'Suwanee' bermudagrass than Santa Ana, just as common St. Augustinegrass did when compared with a dwarf selection. In both cases, however, a much greater growth habit difference existed than normally is found among turfgrass cultivars. Grasses used in this study were subject to tremendous advection as experimental units were grown aboveground level.

Kim (1983, 1987) and Kim and Beard (1988) found significant differences in water used by turf-type bermudagrasses, but rankings were not always the same under different culture management regimes. Under uniform cultural management conditions (3.8-cm mowing height and 12.5 kg of N ha^{-1} biweekly) ET rates were similar for Tifgreen, 'Tifway' and 'Arizona Common' bermudagrasses for two or three ET measurement periods. Turfgrass water use rates during the other measurement period were within 10% of each other (Kim & Beard, 1988). Significant ET rate differences were observed among the 12 species or cultivars tested, and within the zoysiagrasses ('Meyer' and 'Emerald Zoysia'). Tall fescue, the only cool-season grass tested, had the highest ET rate. In this study, a calcined clay was the growing medium and soil moisture not limited. They attributed low ET rates with high canopy resistances (reduced transfer of water vapor to the surrounding atmosphere) caused by high shoot density, relatively horizontal leaf angle, low leaf area, and a slow vertical leaf elongation. However, actual leaf areas were not determined in that study.

With cool-season grasses, Schmidt and Everton (1985) demonstrated significantly higher water use for 'Adelphi' Kentucky bluegrass when compared with four other cultivars under two N and two irrigation regimes. The four other cultivars did not differ significantly from each other. Kopec and Shearman (1987) demonstrated significant differences in ET rates and water requirements among cultivars of tall fescue under Nebraska field conditions. In that experiment, 30-cm deep lysimeters with identical soil bulk densities were allowed to transpire over several 4- to 5-d periods in the field. Volumetric water content was shown to influence ET rate between cultivars as the ratio of actual ET to Atmospheric Reference ET changed with the fraction of available moisture. Generally, 'Kenhy' and 'Kentucky-31' had higher ET rates than the four other cultivars. Water use rates and volumetric water contents could not however, fully explain variable degrees of wilting, as cultivars varied in this response, regardless of growth habit.

In a greenhouse study, Aronson et al. (1987b) monitored gravimetric water loss of Kentucky bluegrass, perennial ryegrass, red and sheeps fescue relative to that of a well watered (reference) Kentucky bluegrass turf. The ET rates of all grasses were unaffected by decreasing available soil moisture until a soil water potential of -50 to -80 KPa was reached. At that point the "relative evapotranspiration" (actual/well watered Kentucky bluegrass) decreased with soil moisture stress. Below − 60 KPa, chewings fescue (*Festuca rubra* L.) sustained the highest relative ET. Plant water potentials decreased by 50 to 75% when − 80 KPa was reached for Kentucky bluegrass and perennial ryegrass, while both red and chewings fescue remained relatively constant until − 400 KPa was achieved. Decreasing visual quality estimates were observed with decreased ET rates for perennial ryegrass and Kentucky bluegrass, but both fescues maintained acceptable quality.

To date, results from water use comparisons of cultivars have not been as promising as breeders would prefer, but the premise that improved cultivars exhibiting a capacity for improved drought avoidance or tolerance can be developed still appears valid and much work is underway toward this specific goal. A great deal of information is still needed to select breeding criteria that will meet this goal. Texas studies have shown that leaf orientation and leaf extension rates are important (Kim & Beard, 1988). However, other studies, such as that by Dernoeden and Butler (1979), with Kentucky bluegrass, have been unable to specify the criteria to be used. A quantifiable drought mechanism reaction of a specific turfgrass-plant (genotype) in a competitive population (sward) may not be identical to that of single spaced plants. This has yet to be demonstrated in detail for cross-pollinated turfgrass species, which are often highly heterozygous. Selection for heat tolerance in perennial ryegrass is evidenced in the fact that cultivars exhibit differential heat tolerance in overseeding trials, with some perennating year round in hot desert climates. Given that many apomictic Kentucky bluegrass and most of the warm-season grasses are vegetative propagules of the same genotype, drought avoidance or tolerance studies conducted on single plants may be more applicable to a turf managed sward.

V. LEVEL OF PERFORMANCE DESIRED

As the foregoing discussion has indicated, management practices that reduce water use are usually those that also reduce growth. Where growth requirements are mimimal and only minimal growth is encouraged, large water savings can be made as well as savings in mowing and other management inputs. Examples would be in open park areas or golf course roughs. Where considerable wear is expected, such as on athletic fields and fairways, one must manage to replace that wear with new growth. This requires more irrigation water. Growth per unit of water is highest with rapid growth and relatively high water levels. A third category of high water cost occurs where lushness and uniformity are part of the required turfgrass performance. Landscaping of resorts and hotels is a high water cost category. Golf greens require high water levels to maintain uniform dense growth. In both of these cases, it is nevertheless probable that present watering procedures are excessive and near equivalents in quality could be produced with less water. Many more turfgrass problems occur because too much water is applied than occur as a result of too little. These include diseases, weeds, compaction, and anaerobic soil conditions.

VI. PROCEDURES IN MEASURING WATER USE

A. Soil Moisture Content

One must have some means for determining available soil water. Crude estimating procedures such as squeezing soil samples in the hand or inserting a rod or screwdriver, can be effective in experienced hands. Experienced managers also gauge soil moisture by turf conditions. There are, however, more precise instrumental procedures.

Measuring changes in soil water content over time is the most widely used method of determining turfgrass water use. Measurement of soil water content can be performed by gravimetric, volumetric, neutron scattering, gamma-ray attenuation, time domain refractometry, and other methods. Knowing how much water is applied from rainfall or irrigaiton, or by monitoring soil moisture at appropriate intervals and depths, one can determine how much water is used by turfs or lost to runoff and deep percolation.

Water content is determined gravimetrically by taking soil from the effective rootzone, weighing, oven drying, and then re-weighing. The difference in weight is the water content on a weight (gravimetric) basis. Erie et al. (1965) monitored consumptive water use of a bermudagrass lawn in Mesa, AZ over several years by gravimetric determinations, which yielded realistic soil moisture depletion values. Other procedures for measuring soil moisture content are calibrated using gravimetric means at some point. The advantages and disadvantages of this and other methods of measuring soil moisture content are listed in Table 12–1.

When the specific volume of the soil sampled is known, volumetric water content can be determined by multiplying the soil bulk density by the gravimetric water content. Volumetric water contents are reported directly, or used to calculate soil water depth. This information is also used for developing soil moisture retention curves. Volumetric soil moisture content is preferred strongly over mere gravimetric determinations because it removes soil textural differences.

The neutron probe method determines water content as a function of H reception of "fast" thermal neutrons from an emitting source. Hydrogen molecules (mostly from water) alter neutrons from the source emitter. The rate of return of slow neutrons traveling back to the detector is inversely related to the soil water content. Neutron scattering requires calibration on different soils (usually by gravimetric means), but allows frequent non-destructive sampling at the same location once this is done. It does not provide accurate estimates of soil moisture at depths of 15 cm or less because neutrons may escape from the soil into the atmosphere. It is probably best used for turfs with higher mowing heights and deep root systems. Kopec (1985) used the neutron probe technique to show that tall fescue clones exhibited drought avoidance by deep soil moisture depletion. Clones differed in soil moisture depletion and visual wilting during an imposed soil drought in 1984. Devitt and Miller (1988) used a neutron probe to calculate salt and

Table 12-1. Measurement techniques for determining turfgrass water use (evapotranspiration, ET).

Type of measurement	Advantage	Disadvantage
	Direct measurement	
Soil core/probe	Ease of operation	Destructive sampling Labor intensive
Microlysimeters	Ease of operation Repetition through multiple experimental units	Labor intensive Can have restricted root system
Drainage lysimeters	Capable of achieving large surface areas, soil volumes, and depths	Lag response time may be excessive
	Indirect measurement	
Gypsum blocks	Accurate below −0.2 MPa Can be left in place for long periods Can be used to activate irrigations	Sensitive to salinity Requires soil calibration Point measurement only
Tensiometer	Accurate for moist soils (0 to −0.08 MPa) Can be used to activate irrigation	Requires considerable field maintenance
Thermal dissipation sensors	Measures moisture content by heat dissipation rate of soil moisture content Accurate over wide temperature range	Cost Require heating time for reading
Neutron probe	Nondestructive	Requires licensing for use Required calibration Not for soil depths <15 cm Radiation hazard
Gamma-density probe	Nondestructive Allows for surface measurements	Requires licensing Influenced by plant water content Radiation hazard
Thermo-couple psychrometers	Accurate Applicable to wide range of soil types Measured total water potential	Calibration required Expensive Temperature sensitive Deteriorates in soil
Time domain reflectometry (TDR)	Provides volumetric water content	Experimental/ developmental phase

soil moisture stress together in a subsurface turf irrigation trial using saline water in Nevada.

Gamma-ray attenuation is also a nondestructive method of determining soil moisture. It provides surface measurements, but is influenced by moisture in the turf vegetation. Augustin and Snyder (1985) found that although turf and thatch influenced moisture readings, moisture in the upper soil layers had the greatest influence on gauge readings. Gamma-ray attenuation and neutron scattering present potential radiation hazards and hence must be used with caution.

Time domain refractometry is an experimental method for determining soil moisture. This unit measures the di-electric constant of the soil which is measured between two parallel stainless steel rods inserted into the soil (Topp et al., 1980). The integrated value over the length of the rod is measured. This allows for precise measurements within a narrow band of soil depth but allows measurements to be made near the soil surface where large root densities are found. This is a real advantage over other methods. Likewise, rods installed at a 45° angle or horizontally yield average soil moisture estimates for the depth of soil spanned by the rods. The unit determines soil moisture contents regardless of temperature, soil types, soil bulk density, and salt content. Its use to date by turf scientists has been limited and centered on instrument development. Improved instrumentation will increase the dependability of Time Domain Refractometry units available. The cost is similar to that of a neutron probe ($5000.00) and there is no radiation hazard. For a review of application technique, see Topp et al. (1984) and Topp and Davis (1985).

B. Lysimeters

A lysimeter is a container providing a closed system in which plants are grown, to which water and nutrients can be added, and by means of which the fate of the latter two can be ascertained. Two general types, each with various subtypes, have been used to measure water use. These are weighing lysimeters and percolation lysimeters. Weighing lysimeters can be as simple as pots that are weighed at various intervals under different water regimes. A somewhat more complicated (but still simple) system is that used by Danielson et al. (1981) where field performance was evaluated by lysimeters made of large PVC pipe inserted into PVC cylinders set into turf grown under various management practices. Similar methods were used by Kim (1983), Feldhake et al. (1983, 1984), Kopec (1985), and Fry and Butler (1989a, b) where lysimeters were lifted and weighed at regular intervals.

Construction of mini-lysimeters and the use of root zone medium are important considerations. If the objectives of the research are to determine potential or maximum water use rate (ET), then lysimeters which have a depth of approximately 20 cm or so can be used. Either a calcined clay or a fine silica sand can be used. These materials offer a minimum of water perching and have adequate soil moisture-holding capacity. These mini-lysimeters can be made from PVC pipe (Kopec & Shearman, 1987), or by simply using either standard 2- or 3-gallon nursery pails that are painted white to avoid heat transfer into the lysimeter which would elevate ET.

Taller lysimeters have been used (Kopec & Shearman, 1987) that allow greater root growth. These can be used for time-series induced drought studies, where root-related drought avoidance mechanisms can be studied relative to ET. To simulate a true field-type situation, either lysimeters with intact soil cores or packed to field bulk density are used. These lysimeters can approach weights of 40 kg, depending on depth, and are thus labor intensive and realistically only a few experimental units can be monitored.

Drainage is an additional factor warranting due consideration. Commercially available nursery containers, when filled with calcined clay or fine silica sand afford suitable drainage from the drainage ports in the casting itself. PVC lysimeters, which offer increased soil depth options, require special drainage features. Early models used a simple drain plug (large test tube stoppers) inserted into the base (Feldhake et al., 1983). An improved design (Rogowsky & Jacoby, 1977) uses large chamfered holes in the lysimeter base. Overlaying these outlets is a porous fabric cloth that protrudes through the holes. The soil is then packed into the lysimeter, producing soil knob extrusions for drainage when the lysimeter is in contact with the underlying soil. After drainage (gravitational water) has been occurred, a plastic catch basin can then be inserted over the base of the lysimeter and sealed with tape. Therefore, subsequent water loss is from ET only.

When constructing and placing lysimeters in the field, the lysimeter itself should fit into a liner with minimum clearance between the two. The lining material should have minimal heat transfer properties, and not be steel or metal. A "rim" effect can cause significant bias when using mini-lysimeters. Therefore, the lysimeter (and liner) should be of minimal thickness. It is critical that the lysimeters be placed at soil level in the field, and the vegetation not be allowed to exceed the radius of the lysimeter edge, which results in erroneous ET values for a given unit of area. Every effort should be made to align the field and lysimeter turf canopies edgewise to best estimate the true ET.

Percolation lysimeters are also containers of various sizes designed in such a way that water can be added to the top and leachates can be collected from the bottom. The difference between the amount of water added and the leachate obtained is the amount of water lost from the surface or remaining in the soil. Water use measurements by Kneebone and Pepper (1984) were made using this method. These lysimeters are best used for weekly water use, since lag times are evident in response to irrigation and drainage. A variant of the percolation lysimeter is one that uses measured subirrigation. Krans and Johnson (1974) used Mariott siphons to deliver water to the bottom of lysimeters in which creeping bentgrass was grown at different water table levels. Instead of a differential between added water and percolation water, the consumptive water use was measured by disappearance from the siphon container. Kneebone and Pepper (1982) also used this technique. Percolation lysimeters have the advantage in that a larger surface area is represented, a limitation when using smaller mini-lysimeters. They are, however, subject to advection when below surface alleyways are included to accommodate a service area for the Mariott siphon containers.

A variant of the standard percolation lysimeter is the buried microlysimeter described by Drake et al. (1980) and used to evaluate leachates under turf. By measuring water applied to an equivalent surface area above the microlysimeter and measuring leachates collected from it, an estimate of water used by the turf can be derived.

C. Growth Chambers

With plants growing in a closed system, transpiration can be measured by comparisons of the moisture content of incoming air to that of air leaving the chamber. Augustin and Karnok (1983) described such a system.

Johns et al. (1983), following earlier studies by Linacre (1972), estimated ET by St. Augustinegrass from resistance to sensible heat flux density. They measured canopy temperatures under full illumination and after abrupt shading. They concluded that such a procedure could be used effectively under field conditions.

Reicosky (1981) described a portable chamber in which vapor pressure differences over a 30 to 60-s time span from placement in the chamber can be used to calculate ET. The system has proved reliable with crops and might well be adaptable to turfgrass studies.

Some limitations of growth chamber conducted ET work include border effects, low light levels and lack of controlled windspeed, making a small scope of inference not necessarily applicable to field conditions. However, growth chambers offer control of variables that are not normally achieved under field conditions. Therefore, the advantage of growth chambers is the capability of investigating one or two effects as constants.

D. Canopy Temperatures

Turf research interest exists in plant-based stress detection using infrared thermometry (IRT). Infrared thermometry measures canopy or canopy-air temperatures that can be analyzed with additional variables to determine plant stress through transpirational efficiency. Since transpiration is a cooling process, unstressed turfs have lower canopy temperatures, and as soil water becomes limited or other limits to transpiration occur, canopy temperatures rise. Thus, IRT offers stress detection through both integration of both soil and aerial environments. Kneebone and Pepper (1979) found that at equivalent soil moistures, differentials in transpiration levels could be distinguished between turfgrass species by using a hand-held infrared thermometer. Tall fescue, St. Augustinegrass, and bermudagrass were evaluated. Danielson et al. (1981) found that surface temperatures of Kentucky bluegrass increased up to 1.66 °C with each 10% decrease in ET.

Various models for detecting plant water stress by canopy temperature sensing exist. Jackson et al. (1977) measured canopy-air temperatures and ET for wheat (*Triticum aestivum* L.). They found an empirical relationship between ET, net radiation, and canopy-air temperature.

Jackson et al. (1977) developed the stress-degree-day (SDD) concept. This index involves midday canopy temperatures that are summed until a specified level is reached to require irrigation. Idso et al. (1981) developed the crop water stress index (CWSI) that was intended to normalize SDD for environmental changes in vapor pressure gradient. Critical point modelling (CPM) was developed as an irrigation model. It calls for irrigation when measured canopy-air temperature is greater than the predicted degree value. Geiser et al. (1982) used the CPM model on corn which provided water savings when compared to other methods of irrigation scheduling.

Empirical model studies conducted with bermudagrass turf at the University of Arizona showed that the empirically based CWSI model gave inconsistent estimates over a range of water-stressed conditions, and that the empirical model was correlated to net radiation (Jalali-Farahani et al., 1986). Solving for predicted canopy-air temperatures with the same turf data using a surface energy balance equation gave ET estimates within 13% of measured values (Slack et al., 1986).

Throssell et al. (1987) developed indices for the SDD, CWSI-empirical, and CPM on Kentucky bluegrass. When used for irrigation scheduling, these models resulted in 112, 140, and 210 mm of water applied, respectively, during a 24-d drought. Tensiometer scheduling required 98 mm. Visual quality was better for the CWSI and CPM treatments due to the higher amounts of water applied and number of application events.

Canopy temperature sensed by infrared sensing to date has been used more successfully as a research tool than for irrigation scheduling. The empirical CWSI models developed for turfs have produced low R^2 values (Throssell et al., 1987) and can change with season and location (R.N. Carrow, 1988, personal communication). This probably is due to a reliance of the mathematical model on solar radiation. The CWSI concept was devised under arid conditions. However, under similar conditions for bermudagrass turf, the energy balance model seems more appropriate. This model requires additional measurements of net radiation and wind speed along with the vapor pressure deficit and canopy and ambient air temperatures. Commercial development of portable IRT units is currently in the research and development phase, with the anticipation that either portable-hand held or fixed head sensors will more accurately determine turf stress index values and be capable of activating irrigation solenoids.

Temperature sensed stress models are limited in the fact that drought avoidance (stomatal regulation) would increase canopy temperature levels, while the turf may or may not be severely stressed for long periods of time. The major advantage of remotely sensed canopy temperatures are that the measurements are nondestructive, and can cover a large surface area (depending on field of view angle and subsampling of areas).

E. Tensiometers

Among the simplest of instruments used to determine soil moisture tension is the tensiometer. A water-filled system is in equilibrium with soil moisture through a porous connection, usually a ceramic cup. As soil moisture tension increases, water is drawn from the system and the resulting suction (negative pressure) directly read on a gauge. The gauge itself can be wired to switch irrigation on or off and such controls have been widely used. Since tensiometer accuracy is best below 80 centibar (0.08 MPa) tension and the maximum range is from 0 to 1 bar (0–0.1 MPa) tensiometers are useful only under fairly moist conditions. Moisture tensions in the root zone of growing turf are, however, ordinarily in this range.

Augustin et al. (1981) estimated ET of St. Augustinegrass from tensiometer readings and irrigation records. A study by Busch and Kneebone (1966) used mercury tensiometers to determine the beginning and end of irrigations measured through city water meters, which provided a cumulative summary of water used by each plot served. Their limitations were moderate maintenance and they served as point measurements, which read a small volume of soil.

F. Resistance Blocks

Since water conducts electricity, decreases in soil water content are coupled with increased resistance to current flow. Resistance blocks made of porous materials with wires at either end make use of this principal. The blocks are buried at appropriate depths and become permeated with moisture at a similar tension to that of the surrounding soil. Resistance is measured by connecting the wires through a wheatstone bridge. Readings must be calibrated for the given soil with actual soil moisture (usually gravimetrically). Deterioration of the block or changes in the ionic content of the soil water will affect the resistance readings. The advantage of block studies is the capacity for measuring higher tensions (up to 2 MPa). Like tensiometers, they are limited by being a point measurement, and are more applicable for research than for irrigation scheduling, especially in nonhomogeneous soils.

G. Thermocouple Psychrometers

Thermocouple psychrometers depend upon extremely accurate readings of very small differences in relative humidity within a soil. As with wet and dry bulb comparisons in air, they measure temperatures at two thermocouple junctions (one wet, one dry) in cells in equilibrium with soil-air moisture. The wet junction is created by cooling to dew point levels by passing a current through it. Major use has been in soil moisture research, quite often by hand-fashioned equipment, but commercial units are available. Response covers as wide a range as that of the resistance blocks with great precision. Readings must also be calibrated to known soil moisture conditions for given soils.

Another type of sensor under development and use measures heat dissipation from a point source in ceramic blocks in equilibrium with soil water. Heat dissipation varies with water content and readings can be computer-translated into levels of soil water potential or used to control irrigation at set levels (Phene et al., 1981).

VII. TYPICAL WATER REQUIREMENT LEVELS

Beard (1973) compiled an extensive review of literature pertaining to water use by turfgrasses published before 1970 and updated in 1985 (Beard,

1985). He stated that typical water use rates vary from 2.5 to 7.5 mm d^{-1} with maxima as high as 12 mm d^{-1}. A review by Kneebone (1981) of studies in western states on several grasses over a range of climates and seasons showed average use rates ranging from 1.9 to 9.8 mm d^{-1}. Maximum water use measured in a 2-yr study at Tucson, AZ was by tall fescue which averaged 12 mm d^{-1} over a 3-wk period in 1978 (Kneebone & Pepper, 1979). This, however, was with a fixed water table which probably limited uptake to some extent. Later studies by the same workers (Kneebone & Pepper, 1984) demonstrated that bermudagrass turf could use up to 8 mm d^{-1} as a yearlong average when watered at excessive rates (364 mm wk^{-1}). Maximum daily rates in that study were 25 mm d^{-1} and included a large advective heat component. It is probable that much of the excess loss was from soil surface moisture. Al-Nakshabandi (1983) measured maximum water use by bermudagrass to be 11.23 mm d^{-1} in July in the country of Kuwait. This was more than calculated from atmospheric models and he also postulated advective heat effects. The advective heat component is one that many turf areas face since they are often adjacent to open areas such as parking lots, streets and buildings, and open soils that are heat sinks and dissipators. To date almost all water use data on turfgrass have been determined under semiarid or arid climates. Comparable data from humid climates are needed.

Since absolute values for water requirements vary over a wide range, it is difficult to prescribe values in terms of mm d^{-1} or wk^{-1}. Statements such as "provide an inch a week" can be fallacious in either direction. If available data are compared with Class A Pan evaporation, one finds that many of the climatic and locational differences are smoothed out and typical turfgrass water requirements range from 55 to 80% Class A Pan evaporation. Warm-season grasses normally use from 55 to 65% and cool-season grasses from 65 to 80% typical pan evaporation during the major growing season. In spite of the very high water use values found at Tucson under excessive irrigation, pan coefficients for bermudagrass water requirements have varied from 55 to 65% over a range of irrigation levels and conditions. Tifgreen bermudagrass watered twice each week at 100% Class A pan evaporation during an entire season at Tucson used 63% of the applied water (W.R. Kneebone, 1984, unpublished data).

As with any generalized statement, there are exceptions. In the case of pan coefficients for turf, there is a tendency for relatively high values during periods of low evaporative demand and low water use. Eight of 12 values cited by Kneebone (1981) show this trend.

Difference in pan coefficients between seasons or levels of evaporative demand may relate to differences in proportions of active and passive water uptake by roots. During periods of high demand, most of the water absorbed by the roots is the result of a difference in water potential and is a mass flow phenomenon. At very low evaporative demand, much of the water uptake is active due to osmotic potential differences, and can induce a pressure gradient from roots to leaves that is independent of external conditions. During periods of low evaporative demand, soil moisture levels are normally high. Soil temperatures during cool periods of low evaporative demand are often also high compared to leaf and air temperatures, adding a possible energy gradient to the root-shoot water flow. For a discussion of passive and osmotic flow, see Kramer (1983). The relative importance of "root pressure" and mass flow phenomena to water use vary with the environment whether under humid or arid conditions. One would expect osmotic potentials to be of much greater relative importance in humid areas.

Penman-derived reference ET estimates are approximately 70% of Class A Pan evaporation. As with any research where a reference or crop coefficient is used, it is essential to disclose the method for determining reference ET and how the crop coefficient was derived.

VIII. SUMMARY

A. Turfgrass Water Use

Because supplies are limited in amount or costly, water for turfgrass irrigation must be used efficiently. This requires irrigation systems capable of uniform delivery to the turf in appropriate amounts and the ability to determine what water and management inputs relate to a realistic minimum water use.

Reviews of studies to date indicate that at any given location and time, water use by cool-season grasses will range from 65 to 80% of Class A evaporative pan losses while warm-season grasses are in the range of 55 to 65%. Typical water use rates vary from 2.5 to 7.5 mm d^{-1} with maximum values as high as 12 mm d^{-1}.

Although evaporative demand can be slightly modified by such environmental factors as slope, aspect, and air drainage, the principal means for minimizing water use involve standard cultural management practices. The range in pan constants given in the previous paragraph represents a large potential for conservation. Deficit irrigation, modified fertilizer regimes, frequent mowing to produce a lower, more uniform canopy and the appropriate choice of species and cultivars provide means for water conservation. Recent research efforts have demonstrated differences between cultivars of the same species in both cool- and warm-season turfgrasses for ET. Programs have begun to investigate the components of drought reactions of turfgrasses to gain insight into drought avoidance and drought tolerance mechanisms. This forthcoming information may allow plant breeders to develop turfs that respond favorably to specific management programs which will use less water than current irrigation management schemes. Use of anti-transpirants has not, to date, been effective in lowering water use and studies of the relatively low contribution (25%) of stomatal loss to water use help to explain this. Cost is also a major factor. Growth regulators do have potential for water saving as the preceding discussion of minimum growth for any degree of performance suggests.

B. Research Considerations

Turfgrass water use is a complex interaction of atmospheric, plant and soil phenomena. Investigations in any one of these areas would generally require control of the other two. These restraints generally make an unreal scenario for complete explanation of the mechanisms incurred in drought or water use related research, especially under field conditions. Usually, plant and soil parameters can be measured together. Researchers should describe the general conditions under which experiments are conducted, to avoid confounding interpretations and better identify objectives with mechanistic responses, whenever possible.

The degree of "available" soil moisture for turf can vary tremendously with soil type, depth, and texture. The concept of conducting turf water use research under nonlimiting soil moisture conditions is certainly different from research where drought tolerance is concerned. In this manner, it is important to decide which mechanisms and physiological responses should be monitored relative to the experimental objectives.

New methods and technologies for determining plant and soil water stress are being evaluated as irrigation tools. These include the use of new soil moisture sensors that are combinations of ceramic and electrical sensors, capable of activating irrigation valve solenoids. Measurement of soil moisture by TDR may be a useful tool in turfgrass water use research. Remote sensing of turfgrass canopy temperatures is already used for conducting research, and hopefully applications for irrigation scheduling will be developed as the technology improves.

The concept of estimating an atmospheric demand for water vapor is not new, but employment of energy based models is becoming more acceptable, since advances in instrumentation have occurred. Considerable research has been undertaken to determine the relationship between actual turf water use and Ref ET. These relationships may be used to schedule irrigation amounts in the future.

More research is needed to identify the interaction of canopy structure with atmospheric conditions as it relates to turf water use. Since certain cultural management factors can affect canopy structure and growth, they too, can affect water use.

Research is needed to relate the physiological responses associated with water use, coupled with a better understanding of morphological parameters that affect water use rate. These activities need to be coordinated and conducted using sound techniques to meet the water use challenges the turf industry will face nationally.

REFERENCES

Agnew, M.L., and R.N. Carrow. 1985. Soil compaction and moisture stress preconditioning in Kentucky bluegrass. I. Soil aeration, water use, and root responses. Agron. J. 77:872–878.

Al-Nakshabandi, G.A. 1983. The potential evapotranspiration of short grass (*Cynodon dactylon*) as related to the estimated potential evaporation and evapotranspiration from meteorological data in the coastal region of Kuwait. J. Arid Environ. 6:33–38.

Anonymous. 1966. Rainfall—evapotranspiration data for 342 climate zones in the United States. The Toro Co., Minneapolis.

Anonymous. 1982. The water wise way to a healthier hardier lawn. Office of Community Affairs, Denver Water Department, Denver.

Aronson, L.J., A.J. Gold, J.L. Cisar, and R.J. Hull. 1985. Water use and drought response of cool-season turfgrasses. p. 113. *In* Agronomy abstracts. ASA, Madison, WI.

Aronson, L.J., A.J. Gold, R.J. Hull, and J.L. Cisar. 1987a. Evapotranspiration of cool-season turfgrasses in the humid northeast. Agron. J. 79:901–904.

Aronson, L.J., A.J. Gold, and R.J. Hull. 1987b. Cool season turfgrass response to drought stress. Crop Sci. 27:1261–1266.

Atsatt, P.R., and L.C. Bliss. 1963. Some effects of emulsified hexaoctadeconal on germination, establishment and growth of Kentucky bluegrass. Agron. J. 55:533–537.

Augustin, B.J., G.H. Snyder, and E.O. Burt. 1981. Turfgrass irrigation water conservation using soil moisture sensing devices. p. 139. *In* Agronomy abstracts. ASA, Madison, WI.

Augustin, B.J., and K.J. Karnok. 1983. A controlled environment system for turfgrass research. Agron. J. 75:306–308.

Augustin, B.J., and G.H. Snyder. 1985. Measuring turfgrass soil moisture with a surface nuclear gauge. p. 113. *In* Agronomy abstracts. ASA, Madison, WI.

Beard, J.B. 1973. Turfgrass science and culture. Prentice Hall, Englewood Cliffs, NJ.

Beard, J.B. 1985. An assessment of water use by turfgrasses. p. 45–60. *In* V.A. Gibeault and S.T. Cockerham (ed.) Turfgrass water conservation. Publ. 21405. Univ. of California, Riverside.

Bidwell, R.G.S. 1974. Plant physiology. Macmillan Publ. Co., New York.

Biran, I., B. Brando, I. Bushkin-Harav, and E. Rawitz. 1981. Water consumption and growth rate of 11 turfgrasses as affected by mowing height, irrigation frequency, and soil moisture. Agron. J. 73:85–90.

Blaney, H.F., and W.D. Criddle. 1962. Determining consumptive use and irrigation water requirements. USDA-ARS Tech. Bull. 1275. U.S. Gov. Print. Office, Washington, DC.

Borden, P., and R.W. Campbell. 1985. Water use of growth regulator-treated 'Meyer' zoysiagrass during establishment. p. 113. *In* Agronomy abstracts. ASA, Madison, WI.

Borelli, J., L.O. Pochop, W.R. Kneebone, I.L. Pepper, R.E. Danielson, W.E. Hart, and V.B. Youngner. 1981. Blaney-Criddle coefficients for western turfgrasses. J. Irrig. Drainage Div. Proc. Am. Soc. Civ. Eng. 107:333–341.

Briggs, J.L., and H.L. Shantz. 1913. The water requirements of plants. I. Investigation in the great plains in 1910 and 1911. USDA Bur. Plant Ind. Bull. 284. U.S. Gov. Print. Office, Washington, DC.

Busch, C.D., and W.R. Kneebone. 1966. Subsurface irrigation with perforated plastic pipe. Trans. ASAE 9:100–101.

Carrow, R.N. 1985. Soil/water relationships in turfgrass. p. 87–102. *In* V.A. Gibeault and S.T. Cockerham (ed.) Turfgrass water conservation. Univ. of Calif. Coop. Ext. Publ. 21405.

Christians, N.E., D.P. Martins, and K.J. Karnok. 1981. The interactions among nitrogen, phosphorus, and potassium on the establishment, quality, and growth of Kentucky bluegrass (*Poa pratensis* L. 'Merion').

Danielson, R.E., C.M. Feldhake, and W.E. Hart. 1981. Urban lawn irrigation and management practices for water saving with minimum effect on lawn quality. Complete Rep. Office of Water Res. and Technol. Proj. No. A-043-Colo., Fort Collins, CO. U.S. Dep. of the Interior, Washington, DC.

Davenport, D.C. 1966. Effects of phenylmercuric acetate on transpiration and growth of small plots of grass. Nature (London) 212:801–802.

Davenport, D.C. 1967. Effects of chemical anti-transpirants on transpiration and growth of grass. J. Exp. Bot. 18:332–337.

Dernoeden, P.H., and J.D. Butler. 1979. Relation of various plant characters to drought resistance of Kentucky bluegrass. Hortic. Sci. 14:511–512.

Devitt, D.A., and W.M. Miller. 1988. Subsurface drip irrigation of bermudagrass with saline water. Appl. Agric. Res. 3:133–143.

Dobrenz, A.K., L.N. Wright, A.B. Humphrey, M.A. Massengale, and W.R. Kneebone. 1969a. Stomate density and its relationship to water-use efficiency of blue panicgrass (*Panicum antidotale* Retz.). Crop Sci. 9:354–357.

Dobrenz, A.K., L.N. Wright, M.A. Massengale, and W.R. Kneebone. 1969b. Water use efficiency and its association with several characteristics of blue panicgrass (*Panicum antidotale* Retz.) clones. Crop Sci. 9:213–216.

Doorenbos, J., and W.O. Pruitt. 1975. Guidelines for predicting crop water requirements. Irrigation and Drainage Paper 24. FAO, Rome.

Doss, B.D., O.L. Bennette, D.A. Ashley, and H.A. Weater. 1962. Soil moisture regime effect on yield and evapotranspiration from warm season perennial forage species. Agron. J. 54:239–242.

Doyle, J.M., and R.C. Shearman. 1985. Plant growth regulator effects on evapotranspiration of a Kentucky bluegrass turf. p. 115. *In* Agronomy abstracts. ASA, Madison, WI.

Drake, R.J., I.L. Pepper, G.V. Johnson, and W.R. Kneebone. 1980. Design and testing of a new microlysimeter for leaching studies. Agron. J. 72:397–398.

Erie, L.J., O.F. French, and K. Harris. 1965. Consumptive use of water by crops in Arizona. Univ. of Arizona Agric. Exp. Stn. Bull. 169.

Feldhake, C.M., R.E. Danielson, and J.D. Butler. 1983. Turfgrass evapotranspiration. I. Factors influencing rate in urban environments. Agron. J. 75:824–830.

Feldhake, C.M., R.E. Danielson, and J.D. Butler. 1984. Turfgrass evapotranspiration. II. Responses to deficit irrigation. Agron. J. 76:85–89.

Frank, A.B., R.E. Barker, and J.D. Berdahl. 1987. Water use efficiency of grasses grown under controlled and field conditions. Agron. J. 79:541–544.

Fry, J.D., and J.D. Butler. 1989a. Water management during tall fescue establishment. Hortic. Sci. 24:79–81.

Fry, J.D., and J.D. Butler. 1989b. Annual bluegrass and creeping bentgrass evapotranspiration rates. Hortic. Sci. 24:268–271.

Fuehring, H.D. 1973. Effect of anti-transpirants on yield of grain sorghum under limited irrigation. Agron. J. 65:348–350.

Gale, J., and R.M. Hagan. 1966. Plant anti-transpirants. Ann. Rev. Plant Physiol. 17:269–282.

Gay, L.W. 1981. Potential evapotranspiration for deserts. *In* D.D. Evans and J. Thames (ed.) Water in desert ecosystems. Dowden, Hutchinson, and Ross, New York.

Geiser, K.M., D.C. Slack, E. Allred, and K.W. Stange. 1982. Irrigation scheduling using crop canopy-air temperature differentials. Trans. ASAE 25:689–694.

Gibeault, V.A., J.L. Meyer, V.B. Youngner, and S.T. Cockerham. 1985. Irrigation of turfgrass below replacement of evapotranspiration as a means of water conservation: Performance of commonly used turfgrasses. p. 347–356. *In* F. Lemaire (ed.) Proc. 5th Int. Turfgrass Res. Conf., Avignon, France. 1–5 July. Inst. Natl. de la Recherche Agron., Paris.

Handreck, K.A. 1979. When should I water? (Discovering Soils No. 8). Rellim Tech. Publ., Adelaide, Australia.

Hang, A.N., and D.E. Miller. 1983. Wheat development as affected by deficit, high frequency sprinkler irrigation. Agron. J. 75:234–239.

Hartung, W., J.W. Radin, and D. Hendrix. 1988. Abscisic acid movement into the apoplastic solution of water-stressed cotton leaves. Plant Physiol. 86:908–913.

Idso, S.B., R.D. Jackson, P.J. Pinter, Jr., R.J. Reginato, and J.L. Hatfield. 1981. Normalizing the stress degree day parameter for environmental variability. Agric. Net. 24:45–55.

Jackson, R.D., R.J. Reginato, and S.B. Idso. 1977. Wheat canopy temperature: A practical tool for evaluating water requirements. Water Resour. Res. 13:651–656.

Jalali-Farahani, H., D.C. Slack, A.D. Matthias, and D.M. Kopec. 1986. Crop water stress parameters for turfgrass and their environmental stability. Trans. ASAE Paper No. 86-2595. Am. Soc. Agric. Eng., St. Joseph, MI.

Jensen, M.E., and H.R. Haise. 1963. Estimating evapotranspiration from solar radiation. J. Irrig. Drainage Div. Proc. Am. Soc. Civ. Eng. 89(IR4):15–41.

Johns, D., and J.B. Beard. 1982. Water conservation—A potentially new dimension in the use of growth regulators. Texas Turfgrass Res. 1982 Prog. Rep. 4040.

Johns, D., J.B. Beard, and C.H.M. Van Bavel. 1983. Resistances to evapotranspiration from a St. Augustinegrass turf canopy. Agron. J. 75:419–422.

Kim, K.S. 1983. Comparative evapotranspiration rates of thirteen turfgrasses grown under both non-limiting soil moisture and progressive water stress conditions. M.S. thesis. Texas A&M Univ., College Station.

Kim, K.S. 1987. Comparative drought resistance mechanisms of eleven major warm-season turf grasses. Ph.D. diss. Texas A&M Univ., College Station (Diss. Abstr. 87-20914).

Kim, K.S., and J.B. Beard. 1983. Comparative ET rates of eleven major warm season turfgrasses grown under both uniform and optimal cultural regimes. p. 127. *In* Agronomy abstracts. ASA, Madison, WI.

Kim, K.S., and J.B. Beard. 1984. The effects of nitrogen fertility level and mowing height on the evapotranspiration rates of nine turfgrasses. Texas Turfgrass Res. Prog. Rep. 4269–4289.

Kim, K.S., and J.B. Beard. 1988. Comparative turfgrass evapotranspiration rates and associated plant morphological characteristics. Crop Sci. 28:328–331.

Kneebone, W.R. 1981. Water conservation research. Golf Course Manage. 49:35–40.

Kneebone, W.R., and I.L. Pepper. 1979. Water requirements for urban lawns. Arizona Project Completion Rep. OWRT Proj. No. B-035-WYO. Part I.

Kneebone, W.R., and I.L. Pepper. 1982. Consumptive water use by sub-irrigated turfgrasses under desert conditions. Agron. J. 74:419–423.

Kneebone, W.R., and I.L. Pepper. 1984. Luxury water use by bermudagrass. Agron. J. 76:99–1002.

Kopec, D.M. 1985. Tall fescue soil moisture depletion, evapotranspiration and growth parameters. Ph.D. thesis. Univ. of Nebraska, Lincoln (Diss. Abstr. 85-26596).

Kopec, D.M., P.W. Bronw, D.C. Slack, C.F. Mancino, and L.F. Salo. 1988. Desert turfgrass crop coefficients. p. 153. In Agronomy abstracts. ASA, Madison, WI.

Kopec, D.M., W.R. Kneebone, I.L. Pepper, and C.F. Mancino. 1986. Consumptive water use model for desert turfgrass. p. 109. In Agronomy abstracts. ASA, Madison, WI.

Kopec, D.M., and R.C. Shearman. 1987. Evapotranspiration of tall fescue turf. HortScience 23:300–301.

Kramer, P.J. 1983. Water relations of plants. Academic Press, New York.

Krans, J.V., and G.V. Johnson. 1974. Subirrigation and fertilization of bentgrass during prolonged heat stress. p. 527–533. In E.C. Roberts (ed.) Proc. 2nd Int. Turfgrass Res. Conf., Blacksburg, VA. 19–21 June 1973. ASA and CSSA, Madison, WI.

Linacre, E.T. 1972. Leaf temperatures, diffusion resistances, and transpiration. Agric. Meteorol. 10:365–382.

Lipscomb, SH., and M.S. Welterlen. 1986. Effects of wetting agents and anti-transpirants on rooting of Kentucky bluegrass. p. 136. In Agronomy abstracts. ASA, Madison, WI.

Madison, J.H. 1971. Principles of turfgrass culture. Van Nostrand Reinhold Co., New York.

Madison, J.H., and R.M. Hagan. 1962. Estimation of soil moisture by Merion bluegrass (*Poa pratensis* L. 'Merion') turf, as affected by irrigation frequency, mowing height and other cultural operations. Agron. J. 54:157–160.

Mancino, C.F., H. Bassiriad, D.M. Kopec, and W.B. Miller. 1987. Influence of antitranspirants on turfgrass growth and physiology. p. 137. In Agronomy abstracts.

Mantell, A. 1966. Effect of irrigation frequency and nitrogen fertilization on growth and water use of a Kikuyugrass lawn (*Pennisetum clandestinum* Hochst ex Chiov.). Agron. J. 58:559–561.

Marklund, F.E., and E.C. Roberts. 1967. Influence of varying nitrogen and potassium levels on growth and mineral composition of *Agrostis palustris* Huds. p. 53. In Agronomy abstracts. ASA, Madison, WI.

Meyer, J.L., V.A. Gibeault, and V.B. Youngner. 1985. Irrigation of turfgrass below replacement of evapotranspiration as a means of water conservation: Determining crop coefficient of turfgrasses. p. 357–364. In F. Lemaire (ed.) Proc. 5th Int. Turfgrass Res. Conf., Avignon, France. 1–5 July. Inst. Natl. de la Recherche Agron., Paris.

Oertli, J.J. 1963. Effects of fatty alcohols and acids on transpiration of plants. Agron. J. 55:137–138.

O'Neil, K.J., and R.N. Carrow. 1983. Perennial ryegrass growth, water use, and soil aeration status under soil compaction. Agron. J. 75:177–180.

Peacock, C.H., and A.E. Dudeck. 1984. Physiological response of St. Augustinegrass to irrigation scheduling. Agron. J. 76:275–279.

Pederson, M.J. 1985. Evapotranspiration rates of cool season turfgrass species. M.S. thesis. Univ. of Nebraska, Lincoln.

Pendleton, J.W. 1965. Increasing water use efficiency by crop management. p. 236–258. In W.H. Pierre et al. (ed.) Plant environment and efficient water use. ASA and SSSA, Madison, WI.

Penman, H.L. 1948. Natural evaporation from open water, bare soil, and grass. Proc. R. Soc. London Ser. A 193:120–146.

Phene, C.J., J.L. Fouss, T.A. Howell, S.H. Patton, M.W. Fisher, J.O. Bratcher, and J.L. Rose. 1981. Scheduling and monitoring irrigation with the new soil matric potential sensor. p. 91–105. In Proc. Am. Soc. Agric. Eng. Irrig. Scheduling Conf., ASAE Publ. 23-81. Am. Soc. Agric. Eng., St. Joseph, MI.

Quackenbush, T.H., and J.T. Phelan. 1965. Irrigation water requirements of lawns. J. Irrig. Drain. Div. Am. Soc. Civ. Eng. 91:11–19.

Radin, J.W. 1984. Stomatal responses to water stress and to abscisic acid in phosphorus-deficient cotton plants. Plant Physiol. 76:392–394.

Radin, J.W., and D.L. Hendrix. 1988. The apoplastic pool of abscisic acid in cotton leaves in relation to stomatal closure. Planta 174:180–186.

Reicosky, D.C. 1981. A research tool for evapotranspiration measuements for model validation and irrigation scheduling. p. 74–80. In Proc. Am. Soc. Agric. Eng. Irrig. Scheduling Conf., ASAE Publ. 23-81. Am. Soc. Agric. Eng., St. Joseph, MI.

Roberts, E.C., and D.P. Lage. 1965. Effects of an evaporation retardant, a surfactant, and an osmotic agent on foliar and shoot development of Kentucky bluegrass. Agron. J. 57:71–74.

Rogers, J.N., E.M. Miller, and J.W. King. 1987. Growth retardation of bermudagrass with metsulfuron methyl and sulfometuran methyl. Agron. J. 79:225–229.

Rogowsky, A.S., and E.L. Jacoby, Jr. 1977. Assessment of water loss patterns with microlysimeters. Agron. J. 69:419–424.

Rose, D.L., D.C. Smith, J.M. DiPaola, W.B. Gilbert, and A.H. Bruneau. 1986. Dormant transplanting of bermudagrass sod. p. 138. In Agronomy abstracts. ASA, Madison, WI.

Rosenberg, N.J., B.L. Blad, and S.B. Verma. 1983b. Microclimate: The biological environment. 3rd ed. Wiley Interscience, New York.

Rosenberg, N.J., K.G. Hubbard, J.M. Norman, R.J. Supolla, and T.L. Thompson. 1983a. A demonstration and evaluation of the use of climate information to support irrigation scheduling and other agricultural operations. Center for Agric. Meteorology and Climatology Progress Rep. No. 83-1. Inst. of Agriculture and National Resources, Univ. of Nebraska, Lincoln.

Schmidt, R.E., and J.M. Breuninger. 1981. The effects of fertilization on recovery of Kentucky bluegrass turf from summer drought. p. 333–340. In R.W. Sheard (ed.) Proc. 4th Int. Turfgrass Res. Conf., Guelph, ON, Canada. 19–23 July. Int. Turfgrass Soc., Ontario Agric. Coll., Univ. of Guelph, Guelph, ON.

Schmidt, R.E., and L.A. Everton. 1985. Moisture consumption of Kentucky bluegrass (Poa pratensis L.) cultivars. p. 373–379. In F. Lemaire (ed.) Proc. 5th Int. Turfgrass Res. Conf., Avignon, France. 1–5 July. Inst. Natl. de la Recherche Agron., Paris.

Shearman, R.C. 1982. Nitrogen and potassium influence on Kentucky bluegrass turf. Univ. of Nebraska. 7th Annu. Turfgrass Field Day. Dep. Hortic. Publ. 82-2. p. 67–69.

Shearman, R.C. 1985. Turfgrass culture and water use. p. 61–70. In V.A. Gibeault and S.T. Cockerham (ed.) Turfgrass water conservation. Univ. of California, Riverside. Publ. 21405.

Shearman, R.C., and J.B. Beard. 1973. Environmental and cultural pre-conditioning effects on the water use rate of Agrostis palustris Huds. cultivar 'Penncross.' Crop Sci. 13:424–427.

Shearman, R.C., and J.B. Beard. 1975. Influence of nitrogen and potassium on turfgrass wear tolerance. p. 101. In Agronomy abstracts. ASA, Madison, WI.

Shimshi, D. 1963a. Effect of chemical closure of stomata on transpiration in varied soil and atmosphere environments. Plant Physiol. 38:709–712.

Shimshi, D. 1963b. Effect of soil moisture and phenylmercuric acetate upon stomatal aperture, transpiration, and photosynthesis. Plant Physiol. 38:713–721.

Sills, M.J., and R.N. Carrow. 1983. Turfgrass growth, N use, and water use under soil compaction and N fertilization. Agron. J. 75:488–492.

Slack, D.C., H.J. Farahani, D.M. Kopec, and A.D. Matthias. 1986. Predicting turfgrass evapotranspiration from canopy temperature. Trans. ASAE Paper 86-2521. 1986 Winter meetings, Chicago. 16–19 Dec. Am. Soc. Agric. Eng., St. Joseph, MI.

Slatyer, R.O., and J.F. Bierhuizen. 1964. The influence of several transpiration suppressants on transpiration, photosynthesis and water-use efficiency of cotton leaves. Aust. J. Biol. Sci. 17:131–146.

Snyder, R.L., W.O. Pruitt, D.W. Henderson, and A. Dong. 1985. California irrigation management system final report. Univ. of California, Davis Land, Air, and Water Resources Paper 10013.

Stahnke, G.K. 1981. Evaluation of anti-transpirants on creeping bentgrass and bermudagrass. M.S. thesis. Texas A&M Univ., College Station.

Steinegger, D.H., R.C. Shearman, T.P. Riordan, and E.J. Kinbacher. 1983. Mower blade sharpness effects on turf. Agron. J. 75:479–480.

Teare, J.D. (ed.). 1984. Crop-water relations. John Wiley and Sons, New York.

Throssell, C.N., R.N. Carrow, and G.A. Milliken. 1987. Canopy temperature based irrigation scheduling indices for Kentucky bluegrass turf. Crop Sci. 27:126–131.

Topp, J.C., J.L. Davis, and A.P. Annan. 1980. Electromagnetic determination of soil water content: Measurements in coaxial transmission lines. Water Resour. Res. 16:574–582.

Topp, G.C., J.L. Davis, W.G. Bailey, and W.D. Zebchuk. 1984. The measurement of soil water content using a portable TDR hand probe. Can. J. Soil Sci. Rev. 64:313–321.

Topp, G.C., and J.L. Davis. 1985. Measurement of soil water content using time-domain reflectometry. J. Soil Sci. Am. 49:19–24.

Tovey, R., J.S. Spencer, and D.C. Muckell. 1969. Turfgrass evapotranspiration. Agron. J. 61:863–867.

Waddington, D.V., T.R. Turner, J.M. Duich, and E.L. Moberg. 1978. Effect of fertilization on 'Penncross' creeping bentgrass. Agron. J. 70:713–718.

Watschke, T.L. 1976. Growth regulation of Kentucky bluegrass with several growth retardants. Agron. J. 68:787–791.

Watschke, T.L. 1979. Penn State tests reveal growth regulator pros and cons. Weeds Trees Turf 18(8):32.

Westesen, G.L., and T.L. Hanson. 1981. Irrigation scheduling using wash tub evaporation pans. Proc. Am. Soc. Agric. Eng. Irrig. Scheduling Conf. ASAE Publ. 23-81:144–149.

Youngner, V.B., A.W. Marsh, R.A. Strohman, V.A. Gibeault, and S. Spaulding. 1981. Water use and quality of warm-season and cool-season turfgrasses. p. 251–257. In R.W. Sheard (ed.) Proc. 4th Int. Turfgrass Res. Conf., Guelph, ON, Canada. 19–23 July. Int. Turfgrass Soc., and Ontario AGric. Coll., Univ. of Guelph, Guelph, ON.

13 Energy Conservation and Efficient Turfgrass Maintenance

PHILIP BUSEY

University of Florida
Fort Lauderdale, Florida

JOHN H. PARKER

Florida International University
Miami, Florida

The maintenance of turfgrass is a labor and energy/resource intensive process. In addition to its esthetic and recreational benefits, turf provides environmental benefits such as heat dissipation and control of soil erosion and dust. The purpose of this chapter is to develop an understanding of the ways that turfgrasses can be managed to minimize the energy and economic costs while sustaining the benefits. This understanding will help managers who compare practices and results, make optimum decisions to minimize costs and maximize benefits, and thereby conserve energy and other resources. Although the focus is on energy savings, energy-efficient practices will also, in general, provide significant environmental and economic benefits.

Turfgrass maintenance requires significant nonrenewable energy, and this is our immediate concern. World production of oil and gas, which provide about 75% of the U.S. energy, is expected to peak by the end of the 20th century (Anonymous, 1980). While the discovery of new reserves is expected to extend this resource throughout the 21st century, the supply will be increasingly strained, and rapidly rising prices are anticipated. Recent concerns regarding acid rain and global warming also increase the need to reduce fossil fuel consumption. These trends will have a major impact on all economic and technologic activities, including turfgrass maintenance.

Turfgrass maintenance practices (mowing, watering, and fertilizing) can best be looked at as input variables in an environmental system. This viewpoint is valuable because realistic improvements in maintenance efficiency (i.e., the ratio of benefits to costs) will involve the integration of practices in the total landscape. The environmental viewpoint is important also because it facilitates an understanding of the benefits of turfgrass. Farmers have for centuries recognized that grass in the landscape helps hold the earth together as no other vegetation type can do. Rights-of-way managers have identified the utility and safety benefits of turfgrass on easements and road shoulders. Grasses can increase by several times the soil shearing resistance, which in-

Copyright © 1992 ASA-CSSA-SSSA, 677 S. Segoe Rd., Madison, WI 53711, USA. *Turfgrass—Agronomy Monograph no. 32.*

creases the potential stability of shallow soils on steep slopes (Waldron & Dakessian, 1982). Hydrologists have recognized the infiltration benefits of pervious lawns (Fig. 13–1), which reduce runoff (Mattraw & Sherwood, 1977). Finally, the esthetic and recreational uses of turfgrass have been recognized in a variety of integrated landscapes, which bring together other vegetation types and inert objects, as well as buildings and people (Roberts & Roberts, 1989). The benefits of turfgrass are one component of the efficiency equation.

A popular presentation of turfgrass is as a visual amenity maintained at great expense and effort (e.g., Raasch, 1983; Tasker, 1981). There is a

Fig. 13–1. Pervious turf area designed for infiltration. Stormwater runoff from a paved parking area is directed through interrupted curbing to collect in a turf-covered catchment area. Conservation benefits of turfgrass ecosystems are one of the numerators in the maintenance efficiency relationship. Broward Mall, Plantation, FL.

general image of the besieged homeowner who is enslaved behind the mower, or is occupied destroying weeds and insects to achieve a lawn as green as the neighbor's. Cooperative Extension Service recommendations instruct us to replace high-maintenance turf with ground cover, to save energy (Pivorunas et al., 1982), although no data is presented. These portrayals of the excesses of turfgrass, and its ultimate futility, are but one side of a sociological divergence. Persons to whom the lawn is an important resource may reasonably spend considerable money and energy towards achieving a small increment in turf quality. Those with different priorities may consider a lower maintenance level and a lower turf quality to be adequate, or may choose some other vegetation system.

These sociological portrayals indicate a need for studying efficient turfgrass management because: (i) people should always strive to reduce the use of nonrenewable energy, and other costs; (ii) the benefits of turfgrass are poorly understood; and (iii) little factual information is available, for either costs or benefits. What makes turfgrass an appealing target for analysis and energy conservation practices is that throughout the USA it is an extensive system that is relatively well defined and somewhat homogeneous. Efficiency improvements can potentially result in major savings in energy. Also pertinent is that natural swards exist which provide some of the benefits of turfgrass, but do not require nonrenewable energy. How have grasses gone from having been self-sustaining parts of the natural ecosystem to becoming major consumers of fossil fuel?

In keeping with the trend in society, turf research and development has emphasized improvements in the technologies of fertilization, irrigation, mowing, and pest control, with little consideration of the impacts on energy use. These developments have made energy-intensive technologies more available and more widely used. Golf course greens are mowed more closely than in previous decades. The residential power mower, which was uncommon in the 1950s, is commonplace today. Petroleum-based synthetic pesticides, unavailable before the 1940s, are widely used today. Plastic irrigation components have made automatic lawn sprinkling obtainable for persons who previously watered their lawn by hand or not at all. Without these technologies, presumably we would have the rougher, grassy fields of our ancestors, but we would use much less fossil fuel. Alternatively, now that energy-intensive technologies are available, we must understand how to use them in the most judicious, efficient manner possible. This chapter will attempt to show how simple approaches will accomplish that goal, and result in large savings in energy and other resources, while maintaining the benefits of turfgrass.

I. TURFGRASS AS AN ENERGY SINK

Although turfgrass is a renewable energy resource, the energy produced is often small compared with the nonrenewable energy used to grow it. Energy required to maintain turfgrass is more than the "direct" energy (e.g., gasoline or diesel fuel) which is used to operate the lawnmower and other equipment. Manufactured fertilizers, pesticides, and some soil amendments are produced via energy intensive materials and processes. Irrigation water, particularly if it has been municipally treated or pumped from great depths or across long distances, is quite energy consumptive (Parker, 1982). The process of constructing lawn maintenance equipment and tools is energy intensive. Labor used in maintenance also has an energy component. This includes the energy required to feed, clothe, and house the persons who mow the turf. These are examples of "indirect energy." The total energy (direct and indirect) in producing goods and services is called *embodied energy* (Costanza, 1980). It is an important facet in the cost of growing turfgrass.

The determination of the various energy costs of turfgrass management explicitly illustrates the fact that turf management practices are tied by economic linkages to coal fields, petroleum wells, and other limited, nonrenewable sources of energy. The advantage of using an energy measure (instead of a dollar measure) of turfgrass cost lies in the potential for stability. Economic processes such as mowing, fertilizer manufacture, and fuel combustion will continue to cost about the same amount of energy, regardless of economic conditions, if these processes were done in approximately the same manner from year to year. Dollar costs, on the other hand, can vary with economic conditions, and can vary with the availability of nonrenewable energy. The dollar costs of some processes that have relatively high embodied energy (e.g., fertilization) are sensitive to fluctuations in energy supply.

Economic studies provide a quantitative basis for calculating energy used in turfgrass. Energy intensity, the ratio of units of energy to dollars, can be used as a basis of conversion from dollars to energy units, and vice versa. Energy intensity values are high for economic sectors (e.g., the petroleum industry) that have a high component of direct energy, as well as for other sectors (e.g., fertilizer production) which are closely linked to other energy intensive sectors. The energy intensity of turfgrass, which would be measured in watt-hours per dollar (or other energy equivalents) is a blend of the energy intensities of its various components. Energy intensity of various sectors is specific only to a particular time (e.g., a year), and the effects of inflation influence the energy intensity of different sectors differently.

As an example, dollar expenditures (Table 13–1) were determined for various turfgrass maintenance components in the state of Florida in 1974 (Anonymous, 1976). Energy intensities for economic sectors associated with turf maintenance items have been calculated (R.C. Fluck, 1979, personal communication) from energy analysis (Bullard et al., 1978). When dollar expenditures were multiplied by energy intensities, the result was that 2271 W h m^{-2} yr^{-1} were used to maintain turfgrass in Florida in 1974. Coincidentally, this value compares closely to one obtained earlier by process analysis (Falk, 1976) for a cool-season turf ecosystem in California: 2169 W h m^{-2} yr^{-1}. Falk's study considered mainly direct energy. For example, the only labor energy that he considered was metabolic energy. The indirect energy (e.g., that needed to clothe and shelter the laborer) was not considered,

Table 13-1. Comparison of energy requirements for turfgrass maintenance practices in Florida and California.

| Input | Florida, 1974 | | | California, 1973 |
	1974 dollars	Energy intensity	Rate†	Rate‡
	10^6	10^3 BTU $\$^{-1}$	— W h m^{-2} yr^{-1} —	
Fuel and oil	25.3	341.8§	685.5	478.7
Equipment purchased	118.5	49.4	464.7	--
Fertilizer	33.7	111.9	299.2	135.9
Water	38.3	81.7	248.2	1488.6
Service company fees	58.8	24.7	115.2	—
Wages and salaries	110.8	9.3	81.4	(51.6)¶
Insect and nematode control	7.9	111.7	70.7	--
Lawn waste disposal	10.3	81.7	67.1	--
Equipment maintenance	18.5	31.6	46.5	--
Topsoil, sand cover, etc.	6.7	82.5	43.8	--
Multipurpose chemicals	4.8	111.7	42.5	--
Weed controls	3.8	111.7	33.7	--
Disease controls	2.8	111.7	24.9	--
Other costs	4.4	51.4	17.9	--
Lime and soil conditioner	0.6	296.0	14.8	--
Annual grass seed	1.9	42.4	6.4	--
Sod (for existing turf)	1.7	30.2	4.0	--
Other seed	0.7	42.4	2.5	13.7
Thatch removal and aeration	1.0	26.1	2.0	--
Plugs, etc. (existing turf)	0.1	30.2	0.1	--
Total	450.6	63.5	2270.6	2168.5

† Based on dollars × energy intensity; Florida 1974 turf area was 369 000 ha; BTU = 0.2929 Wh.
‡ California lawn was 110 m^2 (Falk, 1976); energy units were converted as Kcal = 1.163Wh.
§ Assumes 70% gasoline at 297.9 10^3 BTU $\$^{-1}$ and 30% diesel at 444.3 10^3 BTU $\$^{-1}$.
¶ Includes only direct (metabolic) energy of labor.

nor was the embodied energy of other inputs, for example, lawn mowing equipment or pesticides. Falk's study was based on a home lawn maintained by its occupant, and it was not unreasonable to ignore the nonmetabolic costs of maintenance. Some measure of equipment purchase or depreciation would have been desirable, however. The energy due to irrigation in the California study was quite high. This nearly offset the gaps in different methods of estimation, explaining why Florida and California were comparable.

In the Florida example there was a vast range (Fig. 13-2) of turf costs per unit area for different property classes. Golf courses were high in both dollars and watt-hours, which would be expected on the basis of their high intensity of use and demanding standards. Apartments (including condominiums) were high, in both economic and energy costs. Turfgrass energy costs for single family homes were high, while economic costs were near the mean for other turf areas. The homes (Fig. 13-2) resulted in an outlier from the regression of other property classes. This illustrates a higher energy intensity of home lawn turf (2.06 10^4 W h dollar^{-1}) compared with all other turf areas (1.22 10^4 W h dollar^{-1}). The average across all classes was 1.86 10^4

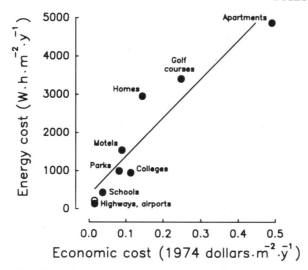

Fig. 13–2. Relationship of energy cost (watt-hours per square meter per year) and economic cost (1974 dollars per square meter per year) for Florida turfgrass property classes.

W h dollar^{-1}. This may be compared with the average energy intensity for all goods and services (1.51 10^4 W h dollar^{-1}) to show that turfgrass in Florida was 23% higher in energy intensity than the U.S. economy as a whole.

The efficient use of fossil fuel in the maintenance of turfgrass is becoming increasingly important. Energy consumed for this purpose means that less is available to grow food, heat and cool houses, and transport goods. Also, the cost of fuels has become a significant aspect of the total cost of growing turfgrass. As dwindling supplies of nonrenewable energy increase in price, turfgrass managers compete economically with other users of energy. The resulting increase in costs can be severely limiting to the commercial turfgrass manager who depends on large machinery and large amounts of fertilizers and pesticides to produce quality turf. The resulting increase in costs could be even more limiting to the homeowner who, as we have shown, may grow an even more energy-intensive product than other turf property classes. While addressing the long-term exhaustion of fossil fuels, there are vivid examples in the short-term of worldwide energy problems. Demand for oil is inelastic in the short-term, and prices quadrupled in 1973 to 1974 (Eden et al., 1981). The increased prices for natural gas and petroleum since 1973 have especially impacted two energy-intensive components of growing turfgrass—fertilizers and pesticides. For example, the price of ammonia more than doubled between 1973 and 1974 (Fluck & Baird, 1980). Ammonia is used in the manufacture of most N sources used in turfgrass fertilizers, explaining why fertilizer prices rose rapidly in response to reduced availability of energy.

Many observers expect petroleum and natural gas resources to become less available and even more expensive in the near future and effectively vanish as fuel sources by the mid-21st century. This will impact on highly mechanized operations—golf courses and sod farms—but will also affect home lawns and parks. At a time when technology is improving the control and precision by which quality turf is managed, many desirable new tools will become more difficult to purchase and use. Some consumers may respond by reducing the size of their turfgrass areas and, in some cases, may eliminate then entirely. Subsequently we will show that such an approach does not necessarily reduce total energy consumption.

II. PRACTICES FOR ENERGY CONSERVATION

The first step in evaluating ways to improve energy efficiency in turfgrass management is to categorize maintenance practices and identify those that are energy intensive. It appears that mowing, watering, and fertilization account for about 75% of all accountable expenditures, if we may assume that fuel and equipment costs are for mowing (Table 13–1). An overstatement based on this assumption may be offset by a prorated portion of indirect energy items (e.g., service company fees and wages) that also should be attributed to mowing, watering, and fertilization. Pest control might account for only 5% of turf energy costs, although pest control also has a share of labor-related energy costs.

The next step in evaluating ways to improve energy efficiency is to determine the effect of reducing or redirecting energy intensive practices on turfgrass benefits (Roberts & Roberts, 1989). Energy conservation practices, which provide the most energy savings with the least reduction in benefits, will be the most useful. Table 13–2 summarizes some energy-conserving turfgrass maintenance practices. A qualitative approach is favored in this discussion, although limited quantitative data are presented.

In some cases, reductions in energy use may have positive or negative side-effects. For example, using reduced amount of fertilizers and pesticides may minimize the risk of those substances leaching into the groundwater. However, failure to fertilize adequately, and failure to apply pesticides against acute pest problems, may lead to turf loss. This, in turn, may possibly lead to the loss of soil by erosion and increased levels of sediment in waterways. Even thin turf will have greater potential for run-off than dense, healthy turf.

A. Mowing

Mowing is usually a large energy-consuming practice in turfgrass culture but is fundamental to healthy turf. Fuel energy and equipment purchase, which we assume is primarily related to mowing, represented 1150 W h m^{-2} yr^{-1}, or about 50% of total energy cost in the Florida survey (Table 13–1). In Great Britain, mowing represented 66% of economic costs of turf maintenance (Rorison, 1980). Fuel and oil alone represented 919 W h m^{-2} yr^{-1} for home lawns in Florida. Process analysis resulted in a measurement of total primary energy to mow typical Florida home lawn turfgrasses with a gasoline rotary mower (Fluck & Busey, 1988). Values were 10.6 W h m^{-2} for St. Augustinegrass [*Stenotaphrum secundatum* (Walt.) Kuntze] and 35.8

Table 13–2. Representative turfgrass energy conservation practices.

Major activity	Practice	Energy conservation and environmental benefits	Potential negative impacts
Mowing	Appropriate mower selection (size, type, and options)	Reduced power requirements, reduced energy to throw clippings, less stalling	None anticipated, except increased labor effort for push-type mowers
	Reduced mowing frequency	Reduced mowing energy	Stalling, weeds, higher power requirements
Edging	Softer, less straight, "mowable" edges	Significantly reduced edging requirements	Less manicured look
Fertilization	Reduced N application	Reduced mowing, pesticide, and irrigation requirement; reduced groundwater contamination	Weeds, unhealthy turf
	Appropriate nutrient ratio and formulation	Healthy turf, more even growth pattern	Extra expense for some slow-release formulations
Irrigation	Proper design, pipe sizing	Higher uniformity and efficiency	Extra capital outlay
	Less frequent irrigation	Reduced water consumption, less mowing and fertilizing, increased drought avoidance	Less green appearance at times, loss of turf
Pest management	Monitoring	Early diagnosis provides greater opportunities in control alternatives	Extra time and expense required to monitor
Turfgrass installation	Select adapted cultivars	Appropriate to local climate and resistant to pest, reduced pesticide use	Feasible mostly in new installations

W h m^{-2} for thick bahiagrass (*Paspalum notatum* Flügge), per cutting. This included the relatively small component of indirect energy required for processing petroleum into fuel. If it is assumed that these values extended across 26 cuttings per year, the resulting 276 to 931 W h m^{-2} yr^{-1} would bracket the survey calculations of 919 W h m^{-2} yr^{-1}.

That the process of mowing can be potentially more efficient is clear when we consider how little energy is actually involved in cutting. A study of agricultural mowing found that the energy required to cut grass leaf blades was only 2 to 14% of the total energy needed to operate a rotary mower (McRandal & McNulty, 1978). The remainder of the energy was needed to propel leaf blades and cover inefficiencies in motors and mowing parts. In the Florida study, an average of 3.0 W h m^{-2} direct input energy was required for electric mowing of different grasses under various management levels (Fluck & Busey, 1988). Only 0.3 W h m^{-2} energy was required to cut and move cut grass blades. A higher multiplication factor was used to account for the additional primary energy used in electric power production, compared with gasoline (3.90 vs. 1.22), but total primary energy consumption of electric powered mowing was still only about one-half that for gasoline.

An obvious energy-conserving approach is to reduce the frequency of mowing. However, frequent mowing is necessary to maintain density, an important factor contributing towards several benefits (recreation, conservation, and esthetics). An important function of mowing turf is the control of weeds. Infrequently mowed turf may become dominated by ephemeral weedy and woody species. Haley et al. (1985) also documented a greater buildup of thatch with less-frequent mowing of Kentucky bluegrass (*Poa pratensis* L.). This was attributed to increased clumping that resulted in a slower microbial decomposition.

A problem associated with less-frequent mowing is that when the turf and weeds are allowed to grow excessively between mowings and it is difficult to get through, the mower will tend to choke and will require frequent restarting. Engine efficiency may be further impaired by consequent overheating, loss of lubricant, wear on moving parts, and damage to the mower. Although unmown grasses may provide good cover on some embankments, in general, reducing the frequency of mowing may result in reductions in the esthetic and environmental benefits of turfgrass and should be pursued with caution. Taller mown Kentucky bluegrass has an increased tendency to accumulate thatch (Shearman et al., 1980). Significant reductions in the frequency of mowing can best be accomplished by decreasing turfgrass growth rates by reductions in fertilization and watering or by the use of growth regulators as discussed later.

Adjustments in mowing frequency should be made in appropriate response to seasonal growth rate variations. A general rule of never mowing more than about one-third of the blade height will resolve most mowing frequency situations. Even in a subtropical climate such as southern Florida, there is wide variation in mowing interval requirement. However, turfgrass is often mowed on a regular, periodic schedule. Lawn cutting contracts often provide a regular interval of mowing throughout the year. This would cause excessive growth between mowings in some months, and unnecessary mowings during other months. Golf course greens are often mowed on a daily basis, and frequent mowing appears to encourage higher plant populations and reduced grain (Madison, 1962), both desirable objectives.

Another factor in mowing energy is equipment selection and maintenance. Purchase of equipment (primarily mowers) accounted for more than 20% of turf energy in Florida (Table 13-1). It is important to match mowing equipment to the size of the area and turfgrass density. By selecting adequately sized equipment that will properly do the job, energy will be saved. Excessively large equipment will burn more fuel and have unnecessarily large indirect energy, particularly in the form of energy of manufacture. Maintaining proper engine tuning, and adjustment of governor control to partial settings (but sufficient for cutting power requirements) can improve fuel efficiency (Hunt, 1968). One must be cautious in this approach, so that torque demands do not exceed the design capabilities, and thus overload the drive train or the pistons.

About three-fourths of mowing energy is attributable to motor losses, drive train losses, and moving air (Fluck & Busey, 1988) which are closely associated with engine speed. Direct cutting energy per unit area can be reduced by using sharpened blades. One study (Steinegger et al., 1983) showed a 22% increase in gasoline consumption with dull mower blades. Significant energy is used in propelling cut leaf blades. As would be expected, mowing wet grass uses considerably more energy than mowing dry grass (Fluck & Busey, 1988).

Reel-type mowers use less energy than rotary mowers because shearing of grass stems is three times as efficient as inertia cutting (O'Dogherty & Gale, 1991) and because reel mowers do not propel leaf blades as much as do rotary mowers. However, there are restrictions. Reel-type mowers cannot cut very tall grass and they require more specialized sharpening than do rotary mowers. The rapid elongation of seedheads in some turfgrass species precludes the use of reel-type mowers. Flail-type mowers use 1.4 to 2.9 W h m^{-2} energy, compared to 2.8 to 3.9 W h m^{-2} for rotary (horizontal) mowers (Hunt, 1968), but can result in large reductions in turf quality and density (Johnson et al., 1987). One method for making the mowing process more efficient is the use of mowers that use less energy such as "push" mowers or non-self-propelled mowers. Although the size of the potential energy savings is not known, the exercise benefit of these mowers is apparent. An energetically determined recommendation to use one type of mower over another would depend upon the compatibility of such a plan with other considerations, such as type of grass, labor, and size of the operation.

B. Edging

In turfgrass management, the maintenance of edges and borders is more energy intensive per unit area than is mowing large areas. This activity is a potential source of pollution as the use of herbicides for edging increases.

In both instances (mechanical and chemical edging), modifications in edge design may yield significant reductions in maintenance energy costs.

With regard to labor time, a study at Utah Technical College (Van Zomeren, 1983) obtained a rate for lawn edging (vertical trimming) of 400 linear feet per hour, compared with 22 000 to 65 000 $ft^2 h^{-1}$ for mowing, depending on mower type. Trimming using a walk-behind, 24-in. wide, mower occurred at 4500 linear feet per hour. Evidently, part (but not necessarily all) of this activity was attributable to mowing around borders and edges. The edging in the Utah study was performed only one-half as frequently as mowing and trimming, but the total annual time for edging and trimming was 2900 h compared to 4520 h for mowing. Thus, 39% of all labor time was for edging and trimming, and this was largely attributable to borders, trees, and other obstacles, rather than open turf areas. In some cases, this may be an acceptable allocation of resources, considering the important function of accented walkways, flower beds, trees, and shrubbery in complementing turfgrass. Whenever high maintenance edges are used as esthetic features, they should be given prominent locations, as they add greatly to total cutting time (and potential energy expenditure).

An approach to reduce the energy to maintain turfgrass edges is to move away from the sharply edged, carefully manicured look. With less cleanly cut vertical profiles between turf and ornamental beds, requirements for edging decrease. The resultant esthetic appearance may match the mechanically edged border, with significant energy savings. In some cases where turfgrass interfaces with pavement, noninvasive turfgrass species might be used to reduce or eliminate the need for edging. Warm-season grasses provide fewer examples in this area than do cool-season grasses, but centipedegrass [*Eremochloa ophiuroides* (Munro) Hack.] would qualify as a less invasive warm-season species.

Some borders, if appropriately designed, may be edged by using a mower. This may be facilitated by using slightly elevated pavements, or other solid barriers, along the borders. Some mowers have sufficient vacuum to pull leaf blades in from such barriers. Irregular border materials such as rocks and wooden posts that hinder the use of mowers should be avoided in this situation. Sharp angles, particularly for inside corners (e.g., where sidewalks intersect), are to be particularly avoided, because they necessitate special equipment). Another method for mower edging involves border plants (e.g., ferns) which cascade down onto the turf. This will potentially shade out weeds that would otherwise penetrate the shrub bed, and it will allow for the underpass of a mower deck, thereby eliminating the need for edging. Also, trees can be clustered, and incorporated into shrub or ground cover beds, rather than isolated in the midst of the turf, so that they will not contribute to edging and trimming requirements. A secondary benefit from this approach is the deposition of fallen leaves among the shrubbery or ground cover, where they will act as a beneficial mulch, instead of falling onto the turf, where they would often have to be picked up. Other considerations (e.g., appearance, shade tolerance, fire hazard) will help decide whether this is feasible.

Finally, more extensive use of heavy mulching at borders may reduce energy consumption, not only through reduced requirements for edging but also due to fewer future requirements for fertilization and watering in those areas. It should be noted that expensive mulch that has been transported long distances may be energy intensive (Parker, 1982), thus local sources (e.g., wood chips) are preferred. In these various methods for reducing energy maintenance inputs for edging, care must be taken to ensure that the edges do not become weedy and thus a source of inoculum for weed dispersal into the turf area.

C. Nutrition

Fertilizers contain substantial primary energy costs and have greater than twice the value of energy per dollar than that for farm machinery (Fluck & Baird, 1980). Reducing annual applications of fertilizer may contribute directly to overall energy savings, both in fertilizer energy and energy of application. Secondary reductions in energy use can also occur. When fertilizer rate is increased, most other energy maintenance costs increase in response to a more rapid turf growth rate. Fluck and Busey (1988) showed that mowing energy for bermudagrass increased linearly with increasing N fertilization rate. This can be viewed as a partial association of increased growth rate. For example, Shearman and Beard (1973) observed for creeping bentgrass (*Agrostis palustris* Huds.) increased water use rates, and increased shoot density and shoot growth rates, at increased N nutrition levels. Wilting of St. Augustinegrass turf has been observed to occur more frequently when it receives 30 g N m^{-2} yr^{-1} compared with 10 g N m^{-2} yr^{-1} (P. Busey, 1987, unpublished data). However, in instances of turf establishment, high rates of fertilization may be required to achieve a stand offering greater competition to weeds.

One method for reducing fertilizer requirements is to return clippings to the turf, thereby recycling much of the required nutrients. Over 4 yr of returning turf clippings in a cool-season grass mixture, an additional 4 g of N m^{-2} was accumulated through the return of clippings (Starr & DeRoo, 1981). Significantly improved quality ratings were observed when clippings were returned, in Kentucky bluegrass and bermudagrass [*Cynodon dactylon* (L.) Pers.] (Haley et al., 1985; Johnson et al., 1987). In the Kentucky bluegrass study, this effect was most notable under lower rates of fertilization (Haley et al., 1985). Return of clippings was shown to have no significant contribution to thatch development in Kentucky bluegrass (Beard, 1976). It should be noted that the energy savings due to reductions in fertilization requirements may be offset by the fact that, if clippings are not collected, more frequent mowings may be required for esthetic reasons. Haley et al. (1985) also evaluated the use of mulching mowers designed to finely chop clippings before returning them to the turfgrass. In general, turfgrass quality ratings were reduced by the mulching mower, because of the problem of clippings sticking together. Thatch buildup was reduced, however, by the use of the mulching mower, compared to a nonmulching mower.

Many home lawnmowers are sold with grass catchers as a standard feature, and on those models side discharge equipment is an option that must be specially ordered. Home lawnmowers vary in the uniformity of distribution of clippings not bagged (Anonymous, 1984), which may determine whether or not clippings return is acceptable. The collection of yard wastes, including turfgrass clippings, is a major component of municipal solid waste, and should be avoided wherever possible.

Climate and soil affect nutrient retention. Normally the rate, timing, and other aspects of fertilization highly depend on specific conditions. Timing of fertilizer application should consider three points: (i) fertilizer will be most effectively taken up during active root growth periods; (ii) some nutrients will be lost by leaching, denitrification, and volatilization, and at high rates of application there may be a disproportionately greater net loss; and (iii) greater losses due to volatilization and leaching will tend to occur during warm weather or as a result of heavy rainfall or irrigation. An energy conserving plan for lawns is to fertilize in the spring and the fall, and to reduce summer fertilization. For cool-season grass areas, the turf is not in such active growth in the summer. For warm-season grass areas, summers are often hot and wet, the potential for nutrient leaching is great, and the grass is already growing too fast. Warm-season grass growth will tend to tax the capacity of mowing equipment during such periods, which can be exacerbated by excessive fertilizer application. Warm-season grasses show severe springtime root browning following cool ($< 10\,°C$) soil temperatures (DiPaola et al., 1982) which can make fertilizer application inappropriate at that time. Special grass mixtures can be affected by fertilization timing. For example, June fertilization of a zoysiagrass (*Zoysia japonica* Steud.)-bluegrass mixture encouraged 63 to 75% zoysiagrass, depending on mowing height, while October fertilization encouraged only 5 to 27% zoysiagrass (Engel, 1974).

A method of application that releases nutrients slowly so that they are more fully used by the turfgrass will minimize volatilization and excessive flushes of growth. Slower release fertilizer not only allows for reduced leaching, but also reduced frequency of application, which can result in lower labor costs. In bermudagrass turf in Florida, from 0.1 to 5.5% of applied N was leached from various slow-release sources, which compared with 9.3% leaching from a water-soluble source, $Ca(NO_3)_2$ (Snyder et al., 1981). Under extreme conditions (low field capacity and high irrigation), 35 to 55% of the applied N was lost by leaching, when soluble N was used (Snyder et al., 1980). However, the increased cost of slow-release nutrients must also be considered. The energy cost of formulating these special products may offset other energy savings, except where application costs are high, or excessive leaching is anticipated. Fertigation (fertilization through the irrigation system) is another method for providing a uniform pattern of N availability, and it has been shown to reduce leaching losses (Snyder et al., 1980).

Proper availability of nutrients can promote healthy, manageable turf. Deficiencies in poorly mobile micronutrients (e.g., Fe) are made temporarily worse by high N rates (Wallace & Lunt, 1960). In Florida, bahiagrass often exhibits a noticeable Fe chlorosis during the spring, and this can be exacerbated by high N fertilization (Horn, 1963). Lower rates of N application should help alleviate such problems, and including micronutrients in the fertilizer mix may be an inexpensive (often temporary) way of promoting healthy turf. Iron may enhance turf color, but generally should not be used as a substitute for N (Schmidt & Snyder, 1984). However, at pH 7.7 Kentucky bluegrass showed no response from N alone, but showed a high response from several Fe treatments, regardless of whether N was applied (Minner & Butler, 1984). Depending upon the cation exchange capacity and other considerations such as continued solubilization of Ca, ammoniacal-N fertilizer will lower soil pH and may be more appropriate than application of micronutrients for the correction of deficiencies (Snyder et al., 1979).

Estimates of the primary energy cost for N varies from 5 to 10 times the primary energy cost of P and K (Fluck & Baird, 1980). Therefore, a lower marginal increase in turf value per unit of P or K would easily justify the addition of P and K rather than extra N. Phosphorus and K are also believed to promote healthy root growth, and some persons have presumed that luxuriant application rates of P and K may be beneficial. More research is needed on the possible substitutability of less energy intensive nutrients.

D. Watering

As mentioned earlier, irrigation water, particularly that supplied from municipal water treatment processes, is quite energy intensive. Parker (1982) found that for a typical residential landscape in Florida, more energy was used for irrigation than for fertilization. In Falk's (1976) study of a residential lawn in California, 69% of the estimated turfgrass energy was attributed to irrigation. Consequently, reducing the volume of irrigation water used can reduce energy consumption. Other approaches, such as reduced pumping head, improved pumping plant performance, and operating away from periods of peak electrical demand may be feasible in some situations. Potential energy savings for sprinkler irrigation systems range between 10 and 45% (Giley, 1983). Two areas for large, controllable savings by the turfgrass manager are reduced net irrigation amount and improved irrigation efficiency.

The transpiration potential of turgid, photosynthesizing grass leaf blades is relatively inflexible. Turfgrass wilts when it does not receive sufficient rainfall or irrigation to meet transpiration needs. Wilting of turf is often esthetically unacceptable, plus it is a forerunner of dormancy or death. An energy conservation practice is to wait to irrigate until the turfgrass shows *early* signs of wilting. Some species (e.g., bahiagrass), are capable of wilting and avoiding drought injury by undergoing an extended dormancy. Thus, in some climates, the turfgrass manager can successfully postpone irrigation for extended periods, or forego it altogether. In practice, turfgrass managers, particularly homeowners, often irrigate excessively. In southern New Mexico, homeowners applied about 40% more water than estimated requirements (Cotter & Chavez, 1979). This was despite the fact that up to 50% of the landscape areas were in some instances covered with mulching rock or xerophytic plants. Delayed irrigation can substantially increase the likelihood of natural rainfall providing a large proportion of evapotranspiration requirements. Automatic, tensiometer soil moisture sensing devices have been shown to reduce 74% of bermudagrass irrigation, compared with daily timed irrigation (Augustin & Snyder, 1984). Although equivalent color ratings were generally obtained from both irrigation strategies, the best dry-season ratings were obtained from a combination of daily timed irrigation in conjunction with a slow-release fertilizer source.

Irrigation which exceeds transpiration needs (after subtracting for rainfall) is not only wasteful due to percolation and run-off but also causes fertilizer leaching. (In some alkaline and saline areas, percolation is needed to leach away solutes.) Excessive irrigation can cause a shift to water-loving weeds, such as sedges. Excessive irrigation has been shown to cause bermudagrass turf to become a luxury user, to the extent that 71% more ET was observed at high rates of irrigation compared with low rates of irrigation (Kneebone & Pepper, 1984).

Less frequent irrigation may encourage deeper root growth (Madison & Hagan, 1962) and might thereby increase the drought avoidance of turfgrass. This is supported by data from several species that showed that irrigation at a higher soil moisture tension contributed to a shallower effective rooting depth (Doss et al., 1960). By contributing to a deeper root system, and thus a greater available soil moisture reserve, such "drought conditioning" may reduce the net irrigation requirement. Mowing practices can affect turf water use. Although mowing with a dull blade should be discouraged on other bases (e.g., increased fuel consumption), it was shown to reduce water use rates by 55% (Steinegger et al., 1983).

Irrigation systems should be designed for even water distribution. However, for most systems, to irrigate all areas adequately, an excessive amount of water is applied to some areas. Irrigation managers should carefully diagnose their systems for uniformity. The uniformity coefficient, calculated as 100 minus the average (percentage) deviation of irrigation applications at individual locations from their overall mean, is generally 70 to 85% or higher (Pair et al., 1975). Factors such as sprinkler geometric pattern, overlap, pressure, and wind speed can affect this efficiency greatly. While wind speed is assuredly corruptive to sprinkler distribution patterns, other reasons against daytime irrigation are popular overstatements. Direct evaporation from wet foliage is not important, and evaporation and wind drift losses are estimated to range from 2 to 8% (Christiansen & Davis, 1967).

As with mower selection, irrigation pumps and other components should be chosen to properly supply the needs of turf areas. Excess capacity may be needed to compensate for future uncertainties (e.g., fluctuating water tables, changes in sprinklers). However, large systems can be properly designed with several pumps of different sizes, so that the appropriate pumping capacity will be available as needed. Other improvements, such as low-pressure heads and variable frequency drive (VFD) pump motor control have been shown to reduce irrigation energy requirements (Whalen, 1988).

Subsurface irrigation is an effective means to reduce potential evaporative losses but may have attendant problems of nonuniform distribution in sand soil (Snyder et al., 1973) and clogging of drain tile pores (Stewart et al., 1965). In addition to the considerable cost of installing such a system, some mechanical operations (e.g., deep aerification and sod harvesting) are impeded.

In arid lands, the competition for water is intense. Scarce water resources in some areas are pumped from great depths and across long distances, resulting in even larger than normal energy inputs for irrigation water. Under these energy-intensive conditions, additional water-conserving techniques such as water recycling within the turf system (leachate) and within other components of the society (using sewage effluent) are cost effective. A problem with leachate, particularly in arid regions, is high salt buildup. On the other hand, the use of "grey" water (e.g., secondary sewage effluent) has proven to be safe and effective in many communities.

E. Pesticides and Growth Regulators

The manufacture of pesticides (herbicides, insecticides, fungicides, and nematicides) requires the highest energy per weight among all agricultural inputs. In some cases, more than 120 W h g^{-1} is sequestered in producing active ingredients of pesticides, although 30 to 80 W h g^{-1} is most common (Fluck & Baird, 1980). In comparison with pesticides, the energy value of N in fertilizers is generally 10 to 20 W h g^{-1}. After the active ingredient is formulated, the total sequestered energy can be greater. In one example, a pesticide requiring 56 W h g^{-1} for the active ingredient and mixed one part pesticide to four parts oil base at 12.5 W h g^{-1} will sequester 106 W h g^{-1} a.i. (Fluck & Baird, 1980).

The relatively high energy of pesticides is offset somewhat by the fact that pesticides are highly active biologically. Only a few kilogram or less of pesticides per hectare are usually required, so their impact per unit of sequestered energy is large. In fact, herbicides have occasionally received use in row crops as a means of reducing energy-demanding tillage operations.

As pesticides become more selective, the soundness of their use in the landscape becomes more apparent. Rachel Carson (1960) pointed out this fact, "The success of selective spraying for roadside and right-of-way vegetation, where it has been practiced, offers hope that equally sound ecological methods may be developed for other vegetation programs for farms, forests, and ranges—methods aimed not at destroying a particular species but at managing vegetation as a living community." This is an example of how turfgrass practices, by applying an energy-efficient approach to land management, can contribute ecological understanding to agriculture as a whole.

In this context, in some extensive turf systems (e.g., highway roadsides) growth regulators have been used successfully to reduce the mowing requirements and reduce transpiration. Where such products are effective in reducing the growth of weeds as well as turf, their potential for reducing turf energy expenditures for maintenance is promising. More long-term research on the effect of growth regulators is needed, because of the observed effects of these products on restricting root growth (Elkins et al., 1977).

However, when pesticides (insecticides, especially) are used in an intensive prevention strategy (as is done by some lawn care companies), their associated energy costs may exceed those of any other component in turfgrass maintenance (Parker, 1982). Nontarget effects of pesticides are another cost of turfgrass maintenance that should be considered. These effects can include: human exposure, exposure of other organisms, and leaching and runoff into other environments. Turfgrass thatch is an effective filter for several pesticides. More than 90% of all recoverable residues of several insecticides were shown to remain in the thatch, 91 d after application (Niemczyk et al., 1988).

III. STRATEGY FOR ENERGY CONSERVATION

Approaches have been suggested for the reduction of energy expended in specific turfgrass maintenance programs. A recurring element in this discussion has been that practices are interrelated, both to other practices and the benefits derived from turfgrass. Turfgrass inputs and outputs obviously form a system, and a general approach is needed. The means to reduce energy use is not to simply postpone or to stop a practice. Such an approach may force more inputs in terms of other practices, or may so greatly reduce the benefits of the turf that efficiency is actually reduced.

Although a systems model might possibly be developed, most scientific evidence that would be used in such a model is so limited in space and time, and is so restricted in the number of variables, as to be of minimal help at the present time. Turfgrass managers are often confronted with an existing turf installation, and will seek immediate benefits from a strategic approach. Practical, day-to-day energy savings will come from following strategies that describe decision opportunities, although each embraces only a small part of the total turf equation. At the same time, there is considerable need for scientific testing and development in the following areas, and this should assist in translating results across climatic and use zones.

A. State the Objectives and Acceptance Standards

The numerator in an efficiency relationship is an index of output: "How well does a process provide benefit?" In driving an automobile, kilometers driven is the numerator. For turfgrass, a complex biological system providing social and esthetic benefits, it is difficult to define a quantitative scale of possible benefits. Busey and Burt (1979) attempted to show the relationship of benefits to costs, for several turfgrasses, but no units of benefit were given. Turf managers must deal with the qualitative concept of acceptability. Is it green enough? Does it play well enough? Does the turf adequately protect the highway embankment from erosion?

One must first state the pattern of use and the objectives for a turf area. Turfgrass objectives are usually site-specific, and this further supports the qualitative concept of an acceptance standard. A greens-type turf installed along highway roadsides might provide acceptable erosion control benefits, but the excellent putting characteristics of such a turf would not be of value in that location. Analysis of the objectives of turf must also deal with other conditions of the site, including the indirect detrimental effects of maintenance practices. If required maintenance activities for a turfgrass harm desirable trees and shrubs, then that turf system might be unacceptable. Obviously, this cannot be predicted until after maintenance inputs and approaches are considered, and so a feedback approach would be needed.

By writing down specific thresholds of acceptability, and the standard for measuring them, the turfgrass manager can simplify some of the problems of cost-benefit analysis. Several tools have been used for measuring turfgrass quality, and most of them are visual. For example, Feldhake et al. (1984) used banded color reference cards as a visual aid.

A confounding factor in evaluating the potential impacts on turfgrass objectives of improvements in energy efficiency is that turfgrass maintenance, at least in the residential sector, is an enjoyable and beneficial activity for some people. Even if the consumer were to accept slightly lower esthetic benefits from turfgrass to achieve significant energy savings, how many potentially healthful hours of exercise would be lost? (This is offset by the fact that some people may be allergic or respond negatively to mowing, dust,ultraviolet exposure, and pesticides.) The reduction in turfgrass maintenance that would be a savings for the local parks department might be of uncertain value to the homeowner who has time and who benefits from mowing the grass.

B. Describe the Resources and Maintenance Needs

An important part of describing the resources is to state the overall characteristics of climate, soils, species, and cultivar of turfgrass that are currently present. This will help the turf manager and outside evaluators understand the circumstances for maintenance, and will be helpful whenever major changes (e.g., renovation or replanting) are considered.

A trial budget is needed, and component activities should be compared according to their frequencies, areas covered, performance standards, and alternatives. This appraisal must consider equipment, supplies, and personnel needs. A budget serves both as a planning tool and a method of system control. Planning is important in making sure that resources are procured at reasonable cost and are available when needed. System control occurs because a budget can help provide a regular flow of inputs and a basis for altering the rate of flow.

C. Establish Action Thresholds and Regular Monitoring

All specific practices that have been discussed (mowing, fertilization, watering, and pest control) should have particular thresholds for action. By having pre-stated rules, (e.g., "mow when leaf blades are 50% taller than the height of cut"), energy can be saved in several ways. First, practices can be potentially withheld until their application is optimum. Secondly, some degree of organization can be incorporated, which will help the management process.

Much of the development of decision-making rules for landscape plants has come from entomology, where the concept of economic injury level (EIL) has been used (Raupp et al., 1988). A regular program of monitoring and inspection may uncover problems (e.g., diseases, insects) at an early stage, and early treatment can prevent the problem from becoming serious. In some cases, such as excessive soil moisture, the problem may be very obvious, but the solution may not be easy. Other problems, such as weeds, may only be aftereffects from fundamental causes such as turf damage by nematodes or insects. If maintenance is directed only towards removing existing weeds, then it is possible that the turf will remain weak and weeds will again become a problem.

The objective in frequent inspection and follow-up is to be able to allocate resources early enough for them to have optimum effect. Some turfgrass problems cannot be diagnosed immediately, or even if they can be, their importance may not be immediately known. Therefore the turfgrass manager must be adequately assured that the corrective measures will be effective. If that cannot be known, and if the cost of making an incorrect diagnosis and selecting an appropriate solution are significant, probably the best things to do are:

1. Consult with someone else who has a similar problem.
2. Consult with a specialist who deals with that particular kind of problem.
3. Try out your own solution on a small scale, leaving matched untreated areas that can be compared to the treated areas.

D. Identify and Carefully Regulate Energy Amplifiers

Certain practices in one area increase energy costs in other areas. For example, in dense, established turf, high rates of fertilizer use increase mowing energy requirement and increase the frequency of turfgrass wilt. Fertilization practices should be watched very carefully, to ensure that they are appropriate for maintaining turfgrass health and adequate vigor, but are not contributing to luxuriant growth. Nitrogen response is frequently observed as a "greening up" of the turf, and although this may be dramatic and satisfying to see in the short term, it can be a waste of energy in several areas.

Close mowing is another potential amplifier of turf energy costs. Close mowing increases the necessary frequency of mowing, contributes to shallow rooting and vulnerability to root pathogens, and can reduce available photosynthates. The dangers of close mowing must be carefully balanced with practical benefits (e.g., playing quality).

E. Eliminate Obvious Waste

Resource analysis and monitoring may reveal some turfgrass management practices and conditions that provide only minimal benefit, or may be harmful to the turfgrass, and should be eliminated. Any input which is added beyond the point of maximum response may possibly be deleterious. Treatments that are applied improperly may fail to accomplish their objectives, and thereby be wasted. Specific examples follow:

1. Scalping the turfgrass, causing loss of stand and weed invasion.
2. Distribution of clippings to sidewalks, requiring their subsequent removal.
3. Watering while it is raining, causing wastage of water and energy.
4. Misdirection of irrigation to pavements, endangering bicyclists.
5. Broken sprinkler heads not repaired, causing water waste, erosion and liability.
6. Application of herbicidal guard rail treatment to large turf areas, causing loss of turf.
7. Application of N to luxuriant turf, causing invasion by insects.
8. Applying a fungicide with a floodjet nozzle, causing loss of product, and no disease control.

F. Proper Timing

There are critical processes in turfgrass maintenance (e.g., care of seedlings during establishment) for which proper timing is crucially important. Timing, which has been mentioned in the context of all practices, is an example of a "strategic" approach that costs nothing (except knowledge of when to do it) and can provide long-term benefits.

IV. DESIGN FOR ENERGY CONSERVATION

Initial design is a potential source of long-term savings in turf energy use. Design considerations have been mentioned specifically under several practices (e.g., mowing and irrigation), but it is important to be familiar with several overriding ideas of energy efficiency in turfgrass.

A. Elimination of Turfgrass

Some reports on landscape energy conservation recommend that turfgrass areas be replaced with other landscape elements (e.g., trees or shrubs). Landscape alternatives to irrigated turf were esthetically accepted in a xeric climate (Thayer, 1982), although several energy factors (installation cost, mowing energy, and weed control) were not considered. Pivorunas et al. (1982) recommended that ground cover be planted in lieu of turfgrass, to reduce energy maintenance costs, but without any comparative analysis. One study (Parker, 1982) analyzing the replacement of turfgrass with shrubs and trees found that higher energy expenditures would actually result *unless* drought- and disease-resistant species were used. Water management officials have recommended the replacement of turfgrass with gravel to reduce evapotranspiration (Anonymous, 1978) but secondary impact (e.g., heat buildup) were not considered.

The meager evidence available suggests that turfgrass is often more efficient in the use of resources than its immediate alternatives. In one study (Van Zomeren, 1983), annual hours for turf maintenance were 8178 for 8.09 10^6 ft^2, or 1.0 h 1000 ft^{-2}. Annual hours for tree and shrub maintenance (including leaf removal from turf areas) were 3243, but the combined area involved was not given. Comparing the stated area in shrubs (208 000 ft^2) with maintenance time for shrub beds (2400 h) results in 11.5 h per thousand square feet, which is far less efficient than the 1.0 h per thousand square feet for turf. In xeric situations such as Arizona, luxuriant turfgrass may not be an appropriate cover for amenity areas, but would offer recreational benefits for limited, intensively managed play areas. In contrast, in humid situations such as southern Florida, turfgrass offers reduced exposure to mosquitoes (*Aedes albopictus*), and serves as an alternative to the costly succession of woody exotic vegetation that plagues public easements. The native sawgrass (*Cladium jamaicense* Crantz) which was present in this region has an evapotranspiration rate of 1.74 m yr^{-1}, exceeding that of one Florida turfgrass, bahiagrass, 1.37 m yr^{-1} (Clayton, 1949, cited by Shih, 1981). Thus, in humid regions, turfgrass could conserve water better than some native vegetation. It is more difficult to compare evapotranspiration rates of turfgrasses with trees, simply because it has been difficult to develop accurate, area-based determinations of tree evapotranspiration. Where ecological communities are compared, "Under similar climatic conditions, forests . . . transpire appreciably more than grasslands. . . ." (Larcher, 1980).

Thus, evidence shows that, in some cases, tree cutting, destruction of native vegetation, and its replacement with unlimited turf areas would conserve water. The point that is missing in the preceding comparison is that turfgrass provides unique benefits, while trees also provide unique benefits, and usually trees and turf together offer benefits greater than either one by itself. For different ecological and use situations, a variety of vegetation types will be most appropriate. In any case, a narrow view of the use or nonuse of turfgrass would be unsound. Turfgrass appears in some cases to be relatively more efficient in maintenance expenses on an area basis than other vegetation types, although there is generally a lack of adequate data.

Scientific evidence shows that for millennia, grasses controlled erosion, built the soil, and provided diverse habitats, with zero input of fossil energy. Sociological factors may be an important component in the public perception of turfgrass and its popular portrayal. Socioeconomic factors and lot sizes were cited in several studies as factors in maintenance intensity of lawns and gardens, in reactions to lawn maintenance, and in enforced neighborhood conformity (Schmid, 1975). Sociological factors may also be involved behind the publicly endorsed viewpoint (in some instances) that reduction of turfgrass areas will lead to a reduction in energy costs, when in fact there is no general evidence to show that this is true.

B. Turfgrass Placement

When the turf area is installed or redeveloped, the following parameters should be considered:

1. Climate and microclimate.
2. Soil conditions and topography.
3. Preexistent traffic patterns, and other environmental conditions and obstructions.

Each of these factors will assist in anticipating potential problems, and in making broad changes in maintenance needs. For example, if there is already a well-worn trail between the cafeteria and the dormitory, a walkway should be established along that route. This would alleviate excessive damage to the turf, and allow for the efficient movement of many persons. If an area is generally too wet for equipment and traffic, a more appropriate type of vegetation may be considered. Examples include rushlike species or a willow (*Salix* sp.) or some other nonturf species that will grow well and compete with weeds. If that is unacceptable, either from a safety or a design point of view, then the topography or drainage conditions could possibly be altered to alleviate the wetness problem. If the area is a sloped bank, then making the slope more gentle may make it easier to use turf equipment.

An important design consideration with regard to energy conservation and turfgrass usage is the potential impact on the consumption of energy used for air conditioning buildings. Planting turfgrass next to a building reduces soil and adjacent air temperatures compared with bare soil (Beard & Johns, 1985; Johns & Beard, 1985). The decreased convective heat transfer to a typical building in Texas, surrounded by turf, compared with bare soil, was 1.46×10^6 W h mo^{-1}. This amounted to 6.54×10^3 W h m^{-2} mo^{-1} savings of cooling energy when prorated over the 223-m^2 turf area. As pointed out earlier, 2.2×10^3 W h m^{-2} yr^{-1} was the turfgrass maintenance energy required in both California and Florida. Thus 1 yr's maintenance energy is <1 mo's savings in cooling energy resulting from use of turf. Even larger savings would be expected when the turf was compared with asphalt or concrete. Other studies (Parker, 1981, 1983; De Walle, 1983; Parker, 1987) have indicated that trees and shrubs placed near buildings are much more effective than turf for reducing building air conditioning requirements.

The use of these vegetative elements immediately adjacent to buildings does not necessarily eliminate the use of turfgrass in those areas. It should be noted, however, that if the area is going to be significantly shaded by buildings or vegetation, it will be important to plant shade-tolerant turfgrass species. If the tree canopies are only moderately thick, or are high enough, to allow some sunlight to reach the ground for significant periods of time, some turfgrasses can be used. In fact, shading by a moderate tree canopy may reduce other turfgrass maintenance energy requirements. Less sunlight means less evapotranspiration of the turfgrass will occur, and less frequent watering of turfgrass will generally be required. Water use has been shown to increase linearly with radiation, where shade was controlled artificially (Feldhake et al., 1983). Additional reductions in water use might occur due to factors present in association with natural tree shade, for example, lower wind speed, higher humidity, and lower air temperature. Unfortunately, competition with tree roots may in some cases offset the reduced evapotranspiration of the turf. Tree roots can in some instances exert a greater influence on growth response of turf than is explainable based only on light level, moisture, and nutrient competition (Whitcomb, 1972).

The energy savings associated with designs that reduce the use of sharp edges and borders has already been addressed. In a strategic sense, such a reduction requires a different design concept, and would possibly require a softer, more natural appearance for other landscape elements. This approach is made more difficult by small-sized properties, which increase the edge effects on turf areas, and the impact of rectangular edges on design of sprinkler systems and mowing pattern. Small properties are more conducive to negative interaction among landscape elements (e.g., shading, leaf removal, differential herbicide sensitivity, trimming, and edging requirements).

C. Turfgrass Selection

The main consideration in the placement and selection of turf is whether a particular turfgrass will grow well with little care, that is, is it appropriate for the site? For different regions, there is usually a pragmatically tested group of turfgrass cultivars or species that are resistant to local stresses. New cultivars are occasionally developed that are superior in resistence and year-round vigor and which provide acceptable turfgrass qualities. Host plant resistance is a documented trait of some new cultivars. This can be an energy-saving characteristic, because it can mean that the cultivar will be grown with minimal use of pesticides. Other examples of improved adaptation, in such traits as drought-resistance or shade-tolerance have been shown to exist. Unfortunately, we are not aware of research that has shown differences in mowing energy requirement.

Most development has apparently resulted in varieties requiring higher inputs. For example, in Kentucky bluegrass, the common types appeared to be naturally better adapted to dry conditions, compared to improved types (Dernoeden & Butler, 1978). There may be economic justification for emphasizing the breeding of grasses for intensively managed areas where maintenance costs are highest, and emphasizing management techniques in semi-natural swards and situations that cost little to maintain (Humphreys, 1980).

Breeding can potentially save energy, where it improves the quality and public acceptability of adapted low-maintenance plant materials, thereby extending their use into medium-maintenance areas. Such an approach may be more appropriate, in many cases, than attempting to bring about environmental adaptations that have not been accomplished in millions of years of natural selection.

D. Research

Research is the ultimate design process for saving energy. For various reasons, little research has been done on energy-conserving turf maintenance practices. What may be effective in one turfgrass situation may not be feasible elsewhere. What may seem like a good practice to one person may be inappropriate to another. Priorities also vary with property sizes and use patterns. As environmental variables vary, so too does the ease with which turfgrass is maintained.

Much turfgrass literature is dominated by studies of the effects of fertilization rates on turfgrass appearance, and the effectiveness of various chemicals in controlling a particular insect, disease, or weed. Some studies have begun and ended within a total span of a few weeks or months, during which the indirect environmental impacts might not have been apparent. Although this addresses pesticide efficacy, environmental impacts are important, and cannot easily be considered in such a time span. In the past, funding for efficacy studies has been more readily available than for environmental studies. Thus there is much room for improvement in the comprehensiveness and significance of turfgrass research.

The interaction between various energy maintenance inputs indicates that they should be studied jointly. In fact, this has not been typical. Research which integrates agronomy, entomology, ecology, and the various other "ologies" is more difficult, and sometimes less conclusive, than simple, single-variable approaches.

Research and education on energy-conserving turfgrass maintenance is needed, but significant progress will be made only when a systems approach is applied. More fundamental research is needed to understand the functioning of turfgrass ecosystems so that appropriate experimental models can be devised and tested. When experimental models are tested, representative sample units should be used. In testing turfgrass recommendations, in some cases the appropriate sample unit should be a whole turfgrass installation, not just the traditional field plot (Busey, 1981). The study population would be all such installations to which the practice would be applied. Studies of older established turf systems should also be made. It is noteworthy that some older lawns in good health have had only minimal maintenance. Others with minimal maintenance are of poor quality. An analysis of these established lawns, including any documentation of relevant information such as the stratigraphy of thatch distribution, and the annual records of maintenance practices, may reveal valuable lessons for the energy-efficient management of younger turfgrass systems.

V. CONCLUSION

Cultural uses of grasses occurred before fossil fuel was a source of energy. The hoofed mammal had been a mower, a weed controller, and an applicator of fertilizer. When the lawn mower was substituted for the hoofed mammal, turfgrass energetics was bound to become a consideration. Lawn legislation also emerged in some communities, requiring that a lawn be installed before a certificate of occupancy would be issued, and establishing specific standards for upkeep. Lawn legislation recognized and reinforced the widespread notion that lawns provided benefits, although scientists still struggle with a quantification of those benefits.

Turfgrass research and education responded to the demand for lawns, particularly in cultures derived out of northern Europe and eastern Asia. Research provided knowledge of turfgrass response to specific inputs. Technology followed, though with little consideration of energy costs or of secondary ecological consequences. More stringent turfgrass performance expectations led to supplemental irrigation, artificial fertilization, and pesticide use. Pesticides introduced new areas for potential concern. Beneficial insects and microorganisms became nontarget casualties, and in some cases their removal from the turf ecosystem may have increased a dependence on the continued use of pesticides.

Almost everything that has been done has increased energy usage, while improving turfgrass quality. This has been done for the benefit of people, and not because turfgrass is by nature demanding of high-energy inputs. When we consider that persons in free market economies attempt to make beneficial exchanges, we see that turfgrass has been a part of the energy flow, neither a source nor a sink. "From an ecological perspective, markets can be viewed as an efficient energy allocation device that humans have developed to solve the common problem facing all species—survival" (Costanza, 1980).

When we consider the components of turfgrass maintenance, we also see that we have a real problem—and an opportunity. Fossil fuel will not be plentiful in the future. Energy-intensive products used to maintain turfgrass will be much less available, yet the demand for turfgrass will likely be greater than ever. Softer paths must be sought to provide the riches of turf.

These future paths are towards the ecological understanding of turfgrass, as well as related natural systems. Turfgrass managers can already use basic ideas that derive from understanding the growth of the turfgrass plant—as described elsewhere in this book—but also by writing down objectives, resources, and obvious wastes in turfgrass maintenance. By looking at turfgrass as a resource to be managed—a process, not a product—we can more easily see the interactions that enable us to conserve energy while preserving a healthy environment.

REFERENCES

Anonymous. 1976. Florida turfgrass survey 1974. Florida Dep. of Agric. and Consumer Serv., Tallahassee.

Anonymous. 1978. Landscaping: Water conservation. South Florida Water Manage. District, West Palm Beach, FL.

Anonymous. 1980. Energy in transition, 1985-2010. Natl. Acad. Sci. Natl. Res. Counc. Committee on Nuclear and Alternative Systems. W.H. Freeman and Co., San Francisco.

Anonymous. 1984. Self-propelled lawnmowers. Consumer Rep. 49(no. 6, June):321-326.

Augustin, B.J., and G.H. Snyder. 1984. Moisture sensor-controlled irrigation for maintaining bermudagrass turf. Agron. J. 76:848-850.

Beard, J.B. 1976. Clipping disposal in relation to rotary lawn mowers and the effect of thatch. J. Sports Turf Res. Inst. 52:85-91.

Beard, J.B., and D. Johns. 1985. The comparative heat dissipation from three typical urban surfaces: Asphalt, concrete, and a bermudagrass turf. Texas Turfgrass Research—1985. Texas Agric. Exp. Stn. Prog. Rep. 4329.

Bullard, C.W., P.S. Penner, and D.A. Pilati. 1978. Energy analysis: Handbook for combining process and input-output analysis. Resour. Energy 1:267-313.

Busey, P. 1981. Turfgrass field plot methods: An overview. p. 157-164. In R.W. Sheard (ed.) Proc. 4th Int. Turfgrass Res. Conf., Guelph, ON, Canada. 19-23 July. Int. Turfgrass Soc., and Ontario Agric. Coll., Univ. of Guelph, Guelph, ON.

Busey, P., and E.O. Burt. 1979. Turf, energy, and the environment. Proc. Fla. State Hortic. Soc. 92:224-227.

Carson, R. 1962. Silent spring. Fawcett Publ. Greenwich, CT.

Christiansen, J.E., and J.R. Davis. 1967. Sprinkler irrigation systems. p. 885-904. In R.M. Hagan, et al. (ed.) Irrigation of agricultural lands. Agron. Monogr. 11. ASA, Madison, WI.

Clayton, B.S. 1949. Water control investigation, report of progress. Project 89. Univ. of Florida Agric. Res. Educ. Ctr., Belle Glade.

Costanza, R. 1980. Embodied energy and economic valuation. Science 210:1219-1224.

Cotter, D.J., and F. Chavez. 1979. Factors affecting water application rates on urban landscapes. J. Am. Soc. Hortic. Soc. 104:189-191.

De Walle, D.R., G.M. Heisler, and R.E. Jacobs. 1983. Forest home sites influence heating and cooling energy. J. For. 81:84-88.

Dernoeden, P.H., and J.D. Butler. 1978. Drought resistance of Kentucky bluegrass cultivars. HortScience 13:667-668.

DiPaola, J.M., J.B. Beard, and H. Brawand. 1982. Key events in the seasonal root growth of bermudagrass and St. Augustinegrass. HortScience 17:829-831.

Doss, B.D., D.A. Ashley, and O.L. Bennett. 1960. Effect of soil moisture regime on root distribution of warm season forage species. Agron. J. 52:569-572.

Eden, R., M. Posner, R. Gending, E. Crouch, and J. Stanislaw. 1981. Energy economics. Cambridge Univ. Press, Cambridge, Great Britain.

Elkins, D.M., J.W. Vandeventer, and M.A. Briskovich. 1977. Effect of chemical growth retardants on turfgrass morphology. Agron. J. 69:458-461.

Engel, R.E. 1974. Influence of introgen fertilization on species dominance in turfgrass mixtures. p. 104-111. In E.C. Roberts (ed.) Proc. 2nd Int. Turfgrass Res. Conf., Blacksburg, VA. 19-21 June 1973. ASA and CSSA, Madison, WI.

Falk, J.H. 1976. Energetics of a suburban lawn ecosystem. Ecology 57:141-150.

Feldhake, C.M., R.E. Danielson, and J.D. Butler. 1983. Turfgrass evapotranspiration. I. Factors influencing rate in urban environments. Agron. J. 75:824-830.

Feldhake, C.M., R.E. Danielson, and J.D. Butler. 1984. Turfgrass evapotranspiration. II. Responses to deficit irrigation. Agron. J. 76:85-89.

Fluck, R.C., and C.D. Baird. 1980. Agricultural energetics. AVI Publ. Co., Westport, CT.

Fluck, R.C., and P. Busey. 1988. Energy for mowing turfgrass. Trans. ASAE 31:1304-1308.

Gilley, J.R. 1983. Energy utilization and management in irrigation. p. 31-59. In D. Hillel (ed.) Advances in irrigation. Vol. 2. Academic Press, New York.

Haley, J.E., D.J. Wehner, T.W. Fermanian, and A.J. Turgeon. 1985. Comparison of conventional and mulching mowers for Kentucky bluegrass maintenance. HortScience 20:105-107.

Horn, G.C. 1963. Yellowing of turfgrasses. Fla. Turf-grass Assoc. Bull. 10(1):1-5.

Humphreys, M.O. 1980. Grass breeding objectives, principles, and potentials. p. 57–67. *In* I.H. Rorison and R. Hunt (ed.) Amenity grassland: An ecological perspective. John Wiley and Sons, Chichester, Great Britain.

Hunt, D. 1968. Farm power and machinery management. Iowa State Univ. Press, Ames.

Johns, D., and J.B. Beard. 1985. A quantitative assessment of the benefits from irrigated turf on environmental cooling and energy savings in urban areas. Texas Turfgrass Research—1985. Texas Agric. Exp. Stn. Prog. Rep. 4329.

Johnson, B.J., R.N. Carrow, and R.E. Burns. 1987. Bermudagrass turf response to mowing practices and fertilizer. Agron. J. 79:677–680.

Kneebone, W.R., and I.L. Pepper. 1984. Luxury water use by bermudagrass turf. Agron. J. 76:999–1002.

Larcher, W. 1980. Physiological plant ecology. Springer-Verlag, Berlin.

Madison, J.H. 1962. Mowing of turfgrass. III. The effect of rest on seaside bentgrass turf mowed daily. Agron. J. 54:252–253.

Madison, J.H., and R.M. Hagan. 1962. Extraction of soil moisture by Merion bluegrass (*Poa pratensis* L. 'Merion') turf, as affected by irrigation frequency, mowing height, and other cultural operations. Agron. J. 54:157–160.

Mattraw, H.C., Jr., and C.B. Sherwood. 1977. Quality of storm-water runoff from a residential area, Broward County, Florida. J. Res. U.S. Geol. Surv. 5:823–834.

McRandal, D.M., and P.B. McNulty. 1978. Impact cutting behavior of forage crops. II. Field tests. J. Agric. Eng. Res. 23:329–338.

Minner, D.D., and J.D. Butler. 1984. Correcting iron deficiency of Kentucky bluegrass. HortScience 19:109–110.

Niemczyk, H.D., Z. Filary, and H. Krueger. 1988. Movement of insecticide residues in turfgrass thatch and soil. Golf Course Manage. 56:22, 26.

O'Dogherty, M.J., and G.E. Gale. 1991. Laboratory studies of the dynamic behaviour of grass, straw and polystyrene tube during high-speed cutting. J. Agric. Eng. Res. 49:33–57.

Pair, C.H., W.W. Hinz, C. Reid, and K.R. Frost (ed.) 1975. Sprinkler irrigation. The Irrigation Assoc., Silver Springs, MD.

Parker, J.H. 1981. Uses of landscaping for energy conservation. Report for the Governor's Energy Office of Florida. Office of the Governor, State of Florida, Tallahassee.

Parker, J.H. 1982. An energy and ecological analysis of alternate residential landscapes. J. Environ. Syst. 11:271–288.

Parker, J.H. 1983. Landscaping to reduce energy used in cooling buildings. J. For. 81:82–84.

Parker, J.H. 1987. The use of shrubs in energy conservation plantings. Landscape J. 6:132–138.

Pivorunas, D.J., R.J. Black, and D. Burch. 1982. Ground covers for energy conservation— South Florida. Univ. of Florida Coop. Ext. Serv. Energy Info. Fact Sheet EI-53.

Raasch, C. 1983. Annual battle of the lawn is on again. USA Today (May 2) 1983:1–2A.

Raupp, M.J., J.A. Davidson, C.S. Koehler, C.S. Sadof, and K. Reichelderfer. 1988. Decision-making considerations for aesthetic damage caused by pests. Bull. Entomol. Soc. Am. 34:27–32.

Roberts, E.C., and B.C. Roberts. 1989. Lawn and sports turf benefits. The Lawn Inst., Pleasant Hill, TN.

Rorison, I.H. 1980. The current challenge for research and development. p. 3–10. *In* I.H. Rorison and R. Hunt (ed.) Amenity grassland: An ecological perspective. John Wiley and Sons, Chichester, Great Britain.

Schmid, J.A. 1975. Urban vegetation. Dep. Geog. Res. Paper 161. Univ. of Chicago, Chicago, IL.

Schmidt, R.E., and V. Snyder. 1984. Effects of N, temperature, and moisture stress on the growth and physiology of creeping bentgrass and response to chelated iron. Agron. J. 76:590–594.

Shearman, R.C., and J.B. Beard. 1973. Environmental and cultural preconditioning effects on the water use rate of *Agrostis palustris* Huds., cultivar Penncross. Crop Sci. 13:424–427.

Shearman, R.C., E.J. Kinbacher, T.P. Riordan, and D.H. Steinegger. 1980. Thatch accumulation in Kentucky bluegrass as influenced by cultivar, mowing, and nitrogen. HortScience 15:312–313.

Shih, S.F. 1981. Evapotranspiration as related to climatic factors in south Florida. Fla. Sci. 44:109–118.

Snyder, G.H., E.O. Burt, and G.J. Gascho. 1979. Correcting pH-induced manganese deficiency in bermudagrass turf. Agron. J. 71:603–608.

Snyder, G.H., E.O. Burt, J.S. Rogers, and K.L. Campbell. 1973. Theory and experimentation for turf irrigation from multiple subsurface point sources. Soil Crop Sci. Soc. Fl. 33:37–41.

Snyder, G.H., E.O. Burt, and J.M. Davidson. 1980. Nitrogen leaching in bermudagrass turf: Daily fertigation vs. tri-weekly conventional fertilization. p. 183–193. In J.B. Beard (ed.) Proc. 3rd Int. Turfgrass Res. Conf., Munich, Germany. 11–13 July 1977. Int. Turfgrass Soc., and ASA, CSSA, and SSSA, Madison, WI.

Snyder, G.H., E.O. Burt, and J.M. Davidson. 1981. Nitrogen leaching in bermudagrass turf: Effect of nitrogen sources and rates. p. 313–324. In R.W. Sheard (ed.) Proc. 4th Int. Turfgrass Res. Conf., Guelph, ON, Canada. 19–23 July. Int. Turfgrass Soc., and Ontario Agric. Coll., Univ. of Guelph, Guelph, ON.

Starr, J.L., and H.C. DeRoo. 1981. The fate of nitrogen fertilizer applied to turfgrass. Crop Sci. 21:531–536.

Steinegger, D.H., R.C. Shearman, T.P. Riordan, and E.J. Kinbacher. 1983. Mower blade sharpness effects on turf. Agron. J. 75:479–480.

Stewart, E.H., E.O. Burt, and R.R. Smalley. 1965. Subirrigation of turf. Proc. Florida Turf-Grass Manage. Conf. 13:153–159.

Tasker, G. 1981. Save water and stay cool by getting rid of your grass. The Miami Herald (6), 7 June 1981:H-1.

Thayer, R.L., Jr. 1982. Public response to water-conserving landscapes. HortScience 17:562–565.

Van Zomeren, R. 1983. Data collecting: It pays off. Park Maintenance 36(11):10–12.

Waldron, L.J., and S. Dakessian. 1982. Effect of grass, legume, and tree roots on soil shearing resistance. Soil Sci. Soc. Am. J. 46:894–899.

Wallace, A., and O.R. Lunt. 1960. Iron chlorosis in horticultural plants, a review. Proc. Am. Soc. Hortic. Sci. 75:819–841.

Whalen, B. 1988. VFD control. Golf Course Manage. 56(2):36, 38, 42, 44, 48.

Whitcomb, C.E. 1972. Influence of tree root competition on growth response of four cool season turfgrasses. Agron. J. 64:355–359.

14 Integrated Pest Management

ARTHUR H. BRUNEAU

North Carolina State University
Raleigh, North Carolina

JOHN E. WATKINS

University of Nebraska
Lincoln, Nebraska

RICK L. BRANDENBURG

North Carolina State University
Raleigh, North Carolina

Turf pests include any biotic organism that adversely affects the production, function, or quality of turfgrass (Turgeon, 1985). Weeds, plant pathogens, insects, and nematodes make up the major pest problems associated with turf. Certain vertebrates, mites, and viruses may also become pests of turf. Pest control is of concern to most professional turfgrass managers and home dwellers (Sturgeon & Jackson, 1980; O'Neill, 1985; McEwen & Madder, 1986; Owens, 1986; Colbaugh, 1987; Hall, 1987) attempting to achieve and sustain an aesthetically pleasing, functional, and comfortable environment along with recreational enjoyment. Annual expenditures of $190 million for chemical lawn care pest control products alone indicates the importance placed on having injury-free turf from pests (Colbaugh, 1987). Improved, cost effective pest control strategies are necessary due to budgetary constraints, environmental concerns, government regulations, reduced availability and effectiveness of pesticides, pesticide resistance and greater public concern.

Integrated Pest Management (IPM) is a pest management system that incorporates various control tactics to keep pests from reaching injurious levels, while minimizing the effect on humans and the environment (Fig. 14–1). It is promoted as a means of effectively maintaining pests at subeconomic or acceptable levels.

I. HISTORY OF INTEGRATED PEST MANAGEMENT

Integrated Pest Management is the result of a continuing evolution in pest management (Smith et al., 1976; Sill, 1982; Owens, 1986). Several of the methods presently used in IPM were available and widely used in the

Copyright © 1992 ASA-CSSA-SSSA, 677 S. Segoe Rd., Madison, WI 53711, USA. *Turfgrass—* Agronomy Monograph no. 32.

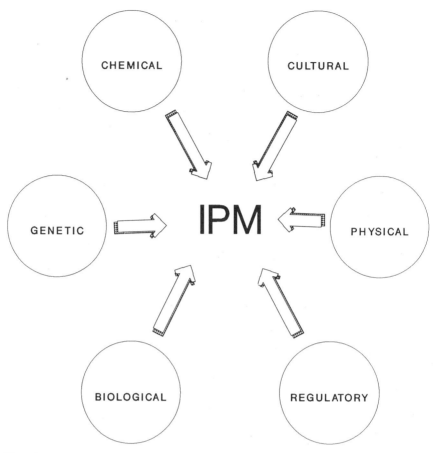

Fig. 14–1. Integrated Pest Management (IPM) uses all available control tactics to keep pests from reaching injurious levels, while minimizing the effect on man and the environment.

late 19th and early 20th centuries (Glass, 1976; Flint & van den Bosch, 1981). They included natural, chemical, mechanical and cultural control techniques, as well as host resistance. Musser (1962), in his textbook entitled *Turf Management* discussed the use of various cultural practices for control of weeds and diseases. The integration of these techniques were sometimes employed by managers; however, control was considered an end unto itself rather than a component of the crop production system (Smith et al., 1976). These methods worked well on small areas with minimal inputs but proved unsatisfactory as agriculture intensified and plants with narrow gene pools became more abundant (Glass, 1976).

In addition, managers and crop protection specialists often emphasized single tactic (usually chemical) approaches to pest control that were ineffective (Smith et al., 1976; Flint & van den Bosch, 1981). Emphasis was placed on the damaging pest with little concern about the effects these approaches had on the environment and other potential pests (Smith et al., 1976; Flint

& van den Bosch, 1981) or the cultural practices contributing to increased pest activity. Eradication (usually not an economically viable option) rather than management of pests was preferred in most instances (Musser, 1962).

Dissatisfaction with the pest control practices of the 1940s led most crop protection specialists to look toward the "miracle" synthetic, organic pesticides as a means of control (Flint & van den Bosch, 1981). Pesticides such as 2,4-D (2,4-dichlorophenoxy) acetic acid; silvex (2-(2,4,5-trichlorophenoxy) proprionic acid); chlordane (1,2,4,5,6,7,8,8-octachlor-2,3,3a,4,7,7a-hexahydro-4,7-methanoindane); dieldrin ((1R,4S,4aS,5R,6R,7S,8S,8aR)-1,2,3,4,10,10-hexachloro-1,4,4a,5,6,7,8,8a-octahydro-6,7-epoxy-1,4:5,8-dimethanonanapthalene); aldrin ((1R,4S,4aS,5S,8R,8aR)-1,2,3,4,10,10-hexachloro-1,4,4a,5,8,8a-hexahydro-1,4:5,8-dimethanonapthalene; heptachlor (1,4,5,6,7,8,8-heptachloro-3a,4,7,7a-tetrahydro-4,7-methanoindene); and DDT (dichloro diphenyl trichloroethane) were heavily promoted in the 1950s and 1960s (Musser, 1962; Fleming, 1976). These pesticides were inexpensive, easy to use, long lasting and provide a broad spectrum of control (Musser, 1962; Furtick, 1976; Flint & van den Bosch, 1981; Pfadt, 1985). Eradication was considered achievable and in some instances, desirable (Flint & van den Bosch, 1981). Engel and Ilnicki (1969) stated that "Eradication of weeds will become more commonplace with the development of better herbicides." This shift away from ecological considerations toward more chemical control was reported to have begun in the 1920s and continued until the mid-1960s (Smith et al., 1976; Flint & van den Bosch, 1981; Pfadt, 1985).

Unfortunately, this chemical dependency led to ecological problems that were largely ignored until the 1960s. These included increasingly poorer control of target organisms, a reduction of beneficial insects and natural enemies of turf pests, resurgence of certain pests, phytotoxic effects on crops, and hazards to people's health directly and indirectly by damage to the environment (Madison, 1971; Smith et al., 1976; Flint & van den Bosch, 1981; Reinert, 1982a; Pfadt, 1985).

Examples of single tactic pest management practices along with short-sighted usage of gene pools and production techniques are evident in turfgrass culture. The widespread use of single cultivars of Kentucky bluegrass (*Poa pratensis* L.) in the 1960s and 1970s that possessed narrow gene pools eventually resulted in damaging outbreaks of stripe smut [*Ustilago striiformis* (West.) Niessl.] and rust (*Puccinia* spp.). In addition, the production of succulent turfgrass growth through poor irrigation and fertilization practices has been reported to enhance pest problems (Madison, 1971; Beard, 1973; Owens, 1986; Colbaugh, 1987).

The environmental issue came under public scrutiny in the early 1960s with the release of Rachel Carson's best seller, *Silent Spring* (Carson, 1962; Madison, 1971). Her book was followed by a report released in 1963 by the President's Science Advisory Committee entitled the *Use of Pesticides* which addressed concerns regarding potentially harmful effects of these compounds on beneficial plants and animals (PSAC, 1963). Recommendations included assessment of pesticide levels in men and the environment; development of safer pest control methods; revision of laws pertaining to pesticide use and

Fig. 14–2. Legislation concerning posting and prenotification laws indicate a new interest in pesticides and their uses.

public education. The President's directive of 1972 entitled "Message on Environmental Protection," resulted in a national effort to develop pest (primarily insect) management programs that not only protect the nation's food supply but also people and the environment (Smith et al., 1976). This directive promoted funding of an interdisciplinary, interagency research project referred to as the "Huffaker IPM Project," which emphasized the systems approach to pest management (ESCOP, 1979).

These events hastened the development of the pest management concept. Crop protection specialists were shifting from the unilateral, single tactic approach of pest control to a more ecological based, systematic approach in which various control measures were integrated into an overall management program. Turf managers and home owners could no longer afford the luxury of relying solely on the use of pesticides to solve their lawn pest problems. Broad spectrum, long residual pesticides were becoming less available due to regulation, environmental concerns by the public, liability coverage, and higher costs (Turgeon, 1981; Metcalf, 1987; Casey & Prostak, 1987). Developmental costs for each new pesticide approached $45 million in 1984 (Metcalf, 1987). In addition, a recent public opinion poll found that many people perceive pesticides to be a higher risk to people than can be substantiated by research (Barrons, 1987). Chemophobia has become a new word in the vocabulary of the public. The fear of what is synthetic vs. what is natural has resulted in recent scares over pesticide use, especially in the turf setting. While this has become an emotional issue, many facts support the argument that properly applied pesticides to the turf proved to be of minimal risk to people. Future education of the public on the absence of risks in turf management, as compared to everyday risks from exposure to "natural" products is a must. Legislation concerning posting and prenotification laws and the special reviews underway on certain turfgrass pesticides indicate a new interest in pesticides and their use on turf (Fig. 14–2).

II. INTEGRATED PEST MANAGEMENT

The term *integrated pest management* as we now know it began with Smith and Allen in 1954 (Smith et al., 1976) and Bartlett in 1956 (Pfadt,

1985) who described "integrated control" as an ecologically based system that used biological and chemical approaches to control. Smith and Reynolds (1965) later broadened the definition to include all pest control measures (Smith et al., 1976). Geier and Clark proposed the term *pest management* in 1961 for programs that were designed around the biology of the pest (Smith et al., 1976). *Management* was preferred because it implied that pests were not to be eradicated, but rather managed based on ecologically sound principles (Smith et al., 1976; CAST, 1982). There may be situations where total control is necessary and others where a level of pest damage is tolerable (Bingham, 1981). Clearly, eradication is not always necessary (Madison, 1971; Vargas, 1981).

A number of authors and associations have continued to expand and refine the IPM concept (Bottrell, 1979; CAST, 1982; Pfadt, 1985; Owens, 1986). Integrated Pest Management is presently considered as a multidisciplinary, ecologically based pest management system. It optimizes natural mortality factors through the systematic and balanced use of all environmentally, economically, and socially compatible control methods in attempting to keep potential pests from reaching unacceptable levels (Flint & van den Bosch, 1981; CAST, 1982; Owens, 1986).

III. THE PHILOSOPHY AND PRINCIPLES OF INTEGRATED PEST MANAGEMENT

The presence of an organism in an agroecosystem or managing unit does not in itself constitute a pest problem (ESCOP, 1979; Pfadt, 1985). Organisms inhabiting an agroecosystem are only classified as pests if human needs and values dictate. Species do not determine pest status (Flint & van den Bosch, 1981). For example, certain broadleaved weeds may be objectionable on a putting green but tolerable or even preferred in a natural or parklike setting. Organisms become pests when intolerable levels are reached as determined by person's assessment (Flint & van den Bosch, 1981; Owens, 1986).

Pests can be categorized as primary pests, organisms that are most likely to reach unacceptable levels; occasional pests, organisms that infrequently reach unacceptable levels; and potential pests, organisms that rarely reach unacceptable levels (ESCOP, 1979). Potential pests are usually present in turf at nondamaging levels (Potter, 1986). However, reductions in natural enemies, a decrease in turf vigor, environmental stress, and other factors can cause potential pests to reach unacceptable levels (Flint & van den Bosch, 1981; Colbaugh, 1987; Tashiro, 1987; Watschke, 1987).

Turf managers can develop one of three viable strategies for the management of turfgrass pests (Glass, 1976). They include prevention, or once the pest is present, eradication and containment. The intent with each is to use all available control measures in a single integrated system. The system attempts to maximize natural control forces such as plant resistance or natural enemies of the pest with minimal disruption to the agroecosystem. The system is implemented only when unacceptable turf injury is imminent (Glass, 1976; Sawyer & Casagrande, 1983). Prevention is often the choice when managing diseases such as Pythium blight (*Pythium* spp.) or noxious annual grasses such as goosegrass [*Eleusine indica* (L.) Gaertn.]. Eradication may be necessary when pests invade high maintenance or intensively used areas where the pest tolerance level is zero. The presence of a single broadleaf weed in a putting green can adversely affect ball roll and play. Containment is the preferred strategic approach to pest management (CAST, 1982; Turgeon, 1985). Containment is often the least disruptive to the desirable features of the agroecosystem and the best way to ensure the continuation of beneficial organisms and natural enemies of turf pests (Pfadt, 1985). Pest management strategies must be flexible enough to allow for redirection and refinement as agroecosystems change (Flint & van den Bosch, 1981; Pfadt, 1985).

Accurate monitoring of pests and natural enemies can determine the stage at which initial injury occurs, and the "threshold" level at which pest management measures should be implemented (Flint & van den Bosch, 1981; Pfadt, 1985). Defining this "esthetic or economic injury level" and "economic or action threshold level" is one of the major tasks facing turf managers and turf protection specialists (Potter, 1986). It depends upon the needs and desires of the turf manager, the producer and the end user, as well as the environment and the type and condition of the turfgrass being grown (Potter, 1986; Tashiro, 1987). Unfortunately, we still lack many of the thresholds needed to make wise management decisions. The development of predictive models and disease detection kits are two innovative methods being brought into practical use. Computer programs, useful as decision aids and identification tools, are being developed at both universities and in private industry to expedite decision-making processes and select the optimum management approach.

Because pest management is only one of several components to be considered in the overall management program, the authors prefer the term "Integrated Plant Management" instead of Integrated Pest Management. This approach takes into account environmental, cultural, economic, and sociological considerations in the management of the host plant as a means of managing the pest(s). For this reason, the acronym IPM will henceforth refer to Integrated Plant Management. The presence of a pest may indicate that the management program needs altering or refining. For example, mowing Kentucky bluegrass too short in the summer favors weed encroachment (Jagschitz & Ebdon, 1985). The application of a herbicide may provide short-term relief, but as long as the turf is improperly cut, weeds will continue to be a problem.

IPM differs from traditional chemically dependent pest control in that it is a process rather than a reaction (Owens, 1986). It should be sufficiently flexible to be useful in the urban environment where there is a diversity among turfgrasses being grown and management practices (Owens, 1986). As new pest problems arise and periodic influxes of biotic and abiotic stresses occur, the pest management program in place must be modified to meet the new challenge (Flint & van den Bosch, 1981).

The interdisciplinary approach unique to IPM, along with the monitoring of pests and beneficial organisms, provides a greater awareness of the agroecosystsem by managers (Smith et al., 1976). This awareness helps to prevent the use of control measures that could result in pest resurgence due to the destruction of natural predators. It also minimizes the possibility of incorrect diagnosis which is common with unilaterally designed control measures (Smith et al., 1976; Flint & van den Bosch, 1981).

While IPM encourages a balanced use of several management methods (Flint & van den Bosch, 1981; Pfadt, 1985), there is no assurance that there will be a reduction in the amount of pesticides applied (CAST, 1982). In some instances the amount of pesticide used may increase. The use of environmentally safe, short residual pesticides may result in more frequent applications but pose less risk to people and the environment. Integrated Pest Management considers pesticides an integral part of the total management program to be used only when necessary and in a judicious manner (Pfadt, 1985; Tashiro, 1987).

IV. TURF INTEGRATED PEST MANAGEMENT AS A SYSTEM

Knowledge is the cornerstone to any successful IPM program. Familiarization with the turf being grown, the pests likely to be a problem, and the biotic and abiotic forces that may impact both the pest and the turfgrasses being maintained is essential in preventing pests from reaching unacceptable levels (ESCOP, 1979; Flint & van den Bosch, 1981; Pfadt, 1985). It is difficult, if not impossible, for the turf manager to develop an efficient and effective IPM strategy if this information is unavailable (Fig. 14-3).

A. Turfgrass Considerations

Turf characteristics, stage of development, degree of vigor and management requirements are important considerations when developing a pest management strategy. Turfgrass species and cultivars can differ in their response to various pests and pesticides (Beard, 1973; Vargas, 1981; Funk & Ahmad, 1983; Turgeon, 1985; Tashiro, 1987). In a study by Lindgren et al. (1981), 38 cultivars of Kentucky bluegrass responded differently to density and visual injury from the bluegrass billbug (*Sphenophorus parvulus* Gyllenhal). Resistance can also play an important role in reducing disease incidence (Couch, 1973; Vargas, 1981; Smiley, 1983).

In contrast, certain turfgrass species may limit available management practices. Sethoxydim is detrimental to bahiagrass (*Paspalum notatum* Fluegge) but is safe to use on fully established centipedegrass [*Eremochloa ophiuroides* (Munro) Hackel] (Lewis & DiPaola, 1985). Turfgrass species and cultivars that produce excessive thatch levels can restrict the effectiveness of certain insecticides (Potter, 1986; Niemczyk, 1987; Niemczyk & Krueger, 1987; Niemczyk et al., 1987; Tashiro, 1987). In an experiment designed to trace the downward movement of recoverable residues in turfgrass thatch

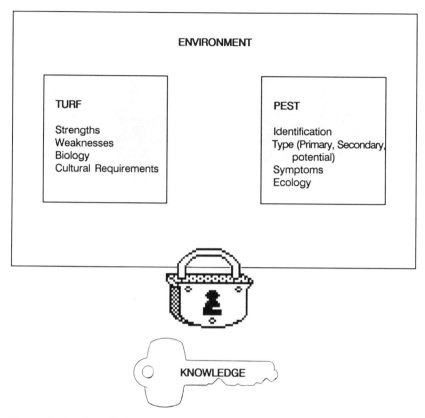

Fig. 14-3. Knowledge is the key to a successful IPM program.

and underlying soil, at least 90% of residues of all insecticides tested remained in the thatch 91 d after treatment despite immediate post-treatment irrigation (Niemczyk et al., 1987). Recent studies have shown that preirrigation can enhance scarab grub control. The preirrigation promotes movement of the grubs nearer to the soil surface while enhancing insecticide movement into the soil following the posttreatment irrigation (Villani & Wright, 1988a). Since turfgrasses vary in their performance over diverse environmental conditions, planting of blends or mixtures instead of a single cultivar has been widely recommended to broaden the basis of pest or disease resistance and enhance season-long turf performance (Smiley, 1983).

The stage of development and condition of the turfgrasses being grown will influence the degree of susceptibility to a pest and its tolerance to certain pesticides. Immature turf is susceptible to seedling diseases caused by *Pythium* and *Rhizoctonia* spp. (Smiley, 1983). An example of pesticide intolerance is with sethoxydim that cannot be applied to newly planted centipedegrass stolons for crabgrass control without the potential for causing phytotoxicity.

Cultural practices such as mowing, watering, liming and fertilizing significantly effect turf vigor (Beard, 1973). Vigorous, healthy turf is one of the best defenses against pest injury (Turgeon, 1985). Active turf growth may effectively prevent the establishment of annual weedy grasses (Hummel & Neal, 1987), and usually withstands higher population levels of root-feeding insects (Tashiro, 1987). For example, crabgrass that requires high light intensity for seed germination is less of a problem under higher cutting heights and adequate fertilization (Jagschitz & Ebdon, 1985). Turf vigor can be significantly affected by climatic, biotic, and edaphic factors (Beard, 1973).

Turfgrass fertilization and watering have been shown to influence populations of southern chinch bugs (Reinert & Kerr, 1973), bermudagrass stunt mite (*Eriophyes cynodoniensis* Sayed) (Butler, 1963; Johnson, 1975) and two-lined spittlebugs [*Prosapia bicincta* [Say]] (Cobb, 1985) and annual bluegrass (*Poa annua* L.).

The ability to affect turfgrass disease incidence and severity by altering management practices of the host plant is also well documented (Couch, 1973; Vargas, 1981; Smiley, 1983). Mowing, thatch accumulation, irrigation practices, fertilizers, and soil reaction have been shown to influence disease incidence and injury (Smiley, 1983). Halisky et al. (1981) observed a higher incidence of dollar spot (*Sclerotinia homoeocarpa*) in heavily thatched turf compared to mechanically dethatched areas. Turf, improperly mowed or fertilized, will be more susceptible to leaf spot caused by *Drechlera* spp. (Colbaugh, 1987).

These examples demonstrate the importance of correct diagnosis and host familiarity (ESCOP, 1979; Flint & van den Bosch, 1981). By knowing the management requirements of a turf, the manager can develop an optimum cultural program (Madison, 1971). Knowledge of the host plant will also help determine which pests should be monitored (Flint & van den Bosch, 1981).

B. Environmental Considerations

Familiarization with the environment in which the turf is being grown, and how the host plant and major pests interact in this environment are of prime importance in developing an IPM strategy (Flint & van den Bosch, 1981).

Abiotic factors causing injury to turfgrass fall into the major categories of chemical, physical, and mechanical (Smiley, 1983). Examples of chemical injury are misapplied pesticides, animal urine, deicing salts, excess fertilizer, nutrient deficiencies, air pollutants, and chemical spills. Hail, lightning, early or late frosts, drought, and soil compaction are examples of physical factors. Mower injury, scalping and wear from traffic are examples of mechanical injury. Abiotic injury can sometimes be incorrectly diagnosed as pest injury (Tashiro, 1987) (Fig. 14-4).

Turf vigor can be significantly affected by climatic, biotic, and edaphic factors (Beard, 1973). Environmental factors influence the abundance and extent of injury caused by pests. Chinch bugs (*Blissus* spp.) and sod web-

Fig. 14–4. Frost damage on bermudagrass can be mistaken for pest damage.

worms (*Crambus* spp.) are most injurious during high temperature and moisture stress (Tashiro, 1987). In contrast, nematode injury is favored by mild-to-warm soil temperatures (Smiley, 1983) and soils that are low in nutrients and water-holding capacity. Plant disease develops only when environmental conditions are conducive for the disease (Couch, 1973; Smiley, 1983). Damage from copper spot (*Gloecoercospora sorghi*) is greatest on infertile, acid soils (Smiley, 1983), while powdery mildew is most severe in shaded areas (Smiley, 1983). Environmental factors can also have an impact on beneficial organisms associated with the agroecosystem. Warm, moist weather is required before the fungus *Beauveria bassiana* (Balsamo) Vuill. can reduce populations of chinch bug (Tashiro, 1987). Milky disease (*Bacillus popilliae* Dutky and *B. lentimorbus* Dutky), a natural pathogen of the Japanese beetle, performs poorly in New England because cold temperatures inhibit growth of the bacteria (Fleming, 1968; Tashiro, 1987).

Environmental factors can affect the performance and toxicity of pesticides. Soil texture, cation exchange capacity, and moisture; sunlight; precipitation; and temperature can affect the performance of herbicides (Madison, 1971) and insecticides. Preemergence herbicides lose their effectiveness quicker when conditions are conducive for microbial growth, the primary means of degradation. Microbial activity and preemergence degradation is highest when the soil is warm, moist, and well aerated (Shurtleff et al., 1987). High adsorptive rates of fine-textured clay soils may require increased rates of pree-mergence herbicides compared to sandy soils (Shurtleff et al., 1987). The potential for vapor drift of certain herbicides such as high volatile esters of 2,4-D increases as temperature increases.

C. Pest Considerations

Familiarization with the signs and symptoms of primary, occasional, and potential turf pests helps the turf manager distinguish between impor-tant and unimportant pest problems. Periodic monitoring of pest activity will help determine the optimum management strategy.

An understanding of the biology and ecology of major turf pests will help determine the best method to monitor their presence (Flint & van den Bosch, 1981; O'Neill, 1985; Tashiro, 1987). The life cycle of the pest will determine when and where it is likely to be a problem, and when it is more vulnerable to control measures (Tashiro, 1987) (Fig. 14–5). Vulnerability is most often associated with the juvenile stage of many weeds and insects (Beard, 1973; Tashiro, 1987). A knowledge of pest biology can also contrib-ute to more effective application of pesticides. As example, insecticides ap-plied in liquid form for the control of surface feeding insects should not be watered into the soil, whereas insecticides applied for the control of soil ac-tive insects should be thoroughly drenched into the soil to provide effective control (Bruneau et al., 1985).

The timing of control measures is a key issue that must be addressed by turf managers (ESCOP, 1979; Potter, 1986). Management decisions and practices should be implemented before turf pests reach unacceptable levels. The pest density or disease severity level where this first occurs is referred to as the "aesthetic or economic injury level." With turf culture, aesthetics and sociological factors can often take priority over economic considerations (Owens, 1986; Potter, 1986). This is especially true in the urban setting (Flint & van den Bosch, 1981; Owens, 1986; Potter, 1986). The pest or disease lev-el at which the decision is made to introduce control measures is referred to as the "control action threshold" (Flint & van den Bosch, 1981). Correct determination and proper interpretation of these levels is necessary to en-sure effective and efficient pest management (Flint & van den Bosch, 1981). Unfortunately, very few injury and threshold levels have been determined for turfgrass insects (Potter, 1986), weeds, and diseases. The threshold and tolerance levels reported for turf insects are subject to interpretation by the turf manager (Potter, 1986; Tashiro, 1987). Turf species, turf vigor, time of year, level of maintenance, environmental conditions, and the manager's or homeowner's perception of acceptable injury are some of the factors in-fluencing development of these levels (Flint & van den Bosch, 1981; Potter, 1986; Tashiro, 1987). Despite these problems, general turf insect threshold levels provided in the literature in combination with field experience can prove useful in formulating an IPM strategy. Reinert (1982b) reduced insecticide applications for southern chinch bug (*Blissus insularis* Barber) by 90% while

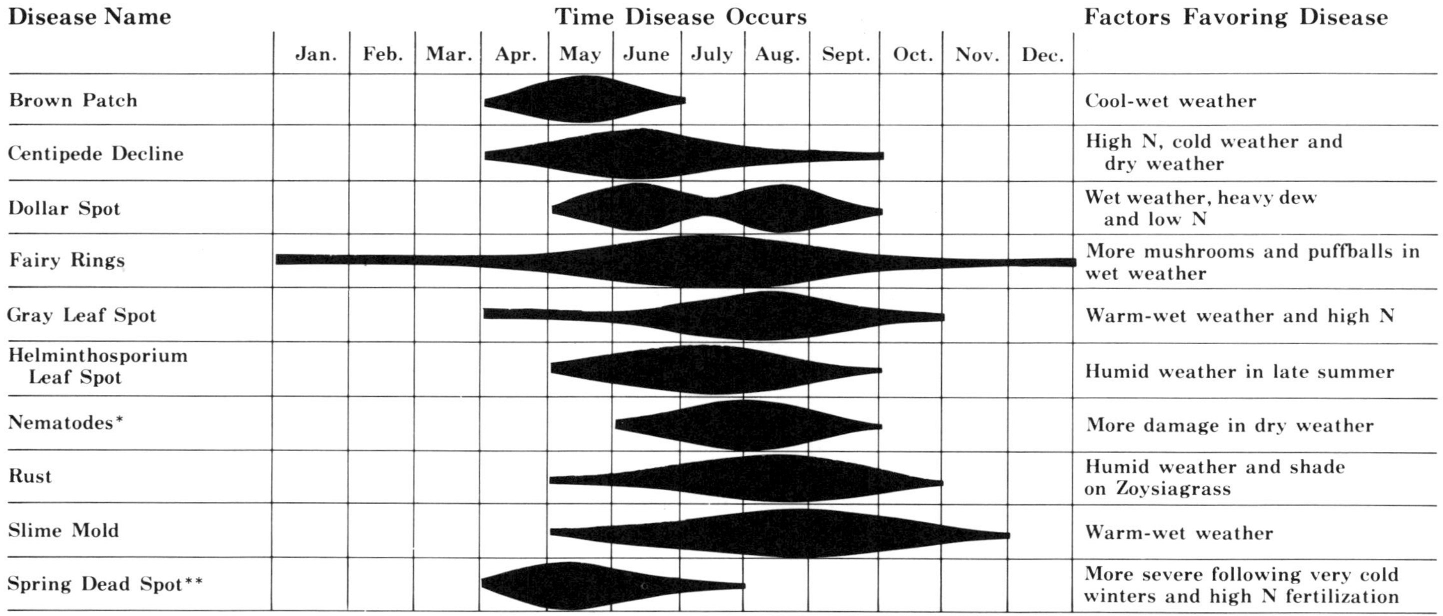

Disease Name	Time Disease Occurs	Factors Favoring Disease
Brown Patch	May–June (peak)	Cool-wet weather
Centipede Decline	May–Sept.	High N, cold weather and dry weather
Dollar Spot	May–Aug.	Wet weather, heavy dew and low N
Fairy Rings	Apr.–Dec.	More mushrooms and puffballs in wet weather
Gray Leaf Spot	Apr.–Sept.	Warm-wet weather and high N
Helminthosporium Leaf Spot	May–Sept.	Humid weather in late summer
Nematodes*	June–Sept.	More damage in dry weather
Rust	May–Sept.	Humid weather and shade on Zoysiagrass
Slime Mold	Mar.–Nov.	Warm-wet weather
Spring Dead Spot**	Mar.–July	More severe following very cold winters and high N fertilization

* Have soil samples assayed for nematodes to determine if nematodes are a problem.

** Apply effective fungicide at high rate in the fall (October 15 to November 15) to areas that had the disease the previous spring.

Fig. 14–5. Activity chart for diseases of warm-season grasses (bermudagrass, zoysiagrass, centipedegrass, and St. Augustinegrass) (Bruneau et al., 1985).

producing acceptable St. Augustinegrass [*Stenotaphrum secundatum* (Walter) Kuntze] turf when he based treatment on a specific threshold level.

Periodic monitoring of pests and beneficial organism population levels, of pest signs, symptoms and stage of development, and periodic observation and assessment of turf quality are the primary means of gathering necessary data to make pest management decisions (ESCOP, 1979; Flint & van den Bosch, 1981; Pfadt, 1985). Monitoring involves systematic sampling to measure either the pest density or damage (Flint & van den Bosch, 1981). Systematic monitoring is also used to develop a data base for predictive models, identify resistant hosts, determine the effect of control measures on beneficial organisms, determine injury and threshold levels of various pests and beneficial organisms and to alert researchers and managers to other organisms not being monitored (Flint & van den Bosch, 1981; Hartman & Ascerno, 1981).

To detect infestations of turf pests, the manager must identify the grasses being maintained and become familiar with their strengths, weaknesses, and requirements; know what the turf looks like when it is healthy; and be familiar with the biology, ecology, signs, and symptoms of pests and diseases (Bruneau et al., 1985). Familiarization with these factors along with a knowledge of the environmental-host-pests or disease interactions will help to determine the best method of monitoring (Flint & van den Bosch, 1981). Frequent turf inspection and accurate diagnosis can result in early pest detection and reduced turf injury (Reinert, 1982b; Tashiro, 1987).

Experience and training are important requisites to proper diagnosis (Smiley, 1983) during monitoring. Frequency and intensity of inspection will depend upon the situation. It is unnecessary and impractical for lawn care applicators to monitor each lawn daily; however, golf course superintendents should inspect their turf on a frequent and regular basis.

A thorough review of the techniques used to detect and identify turf pests are discussed by Tashiro (1987) and Smiley (1983). An aspirator is useful in collecting small mobile insects that are found on the grass or soil surface. An aerial or sweep net can be used to catch flying insects or insects on leaf blades (Tashiro, 1987). Soil insects can be detected by examining the roots, stems, and surrounding soil (Bruneau et al., 1985) (Fig. 14–6). Use of a sod cutter or cup cutter have proven useful when monitoring soil-inhabiting insects (Tashiro, 1987). Chinch bugs can be detected by flotation (Tashiro, 1987). Irritants such as pyrethrins and household detergent have been effective in verifying the presence of surface-feeding insects such as sod webworms (Pyralidae), armyworms, and cutworms (Noctuidae) as well as some soil insects such as mole crickets (*Scapteriscus* spp.) (Fig. 14–7). The Berlese funnel has been effective in sampling populations of billbug (*Sphenophorus* spp.) adults, chinch bugs, webworms, cutworms, and mites (Acarina) (Niemczyk, 1981). Pitfall traps have been used to monitor adult billbugs, chinch bugs, and other crawling insects in turf (Niemczyk, 1981) and soil (Lawrence, 1982). Visual counts of the green June beetle [*Cotinis nitida* (Linnaeus)], May-June beetles (*Phyllophaga* spp.), and Japanese beetle (*Popillia japonica* Newman) on host plants have been used to predict threshold

Fig. 14-6. (*Above*) Larval excrement and silken tunnels suggest sod webworms. (*Below*) Weak,
   easily drought-stressed bluegrass plants that break readily at or near the crown are indicative
   of bluegrass billbug damage.

populations (Tashiro, 1987). Light traps have been used to monitor flight
activity of sod webworms (Tolley & Robinson, 1986) and masked chafers
(Potter, 1981). The use of degree days can sometimes be used to predict when
susceptable stages of the pests are present (Tolley & Robinson, 1986).

   In turf pathology, correct identification of the specific pathogens may
be difficult. The most easily identified turf diseases are the rusts, smuts, and

Fig. 14-7. Periodic monitoring and sampling of pest activity will help determine the optimum management strategy. (*Above*) Taking visual counts of insects. (*Below*) Use of household detergents to flush surface-feeding insects.

powdery mildew (Smiley, 1983). Classical symptoms as described in identification keys are not always evident. More than one organism may be present that confounds the diagnosis or the expected symptoms may not be present because of unusual weather or cultural practices. Therefore, correct diagnosis depends upon symptoms observed in the field and a clinical analysis of samples (Vargas, 1981; Smiley, 1983). Devices that measure spore populations and environmental conditions conducive to disease development are helpful in decision making (Turgeon, 1981). Recent development of immunoassey techniques can assist in making a rapid and accurate diagnosis of certain turf diseases (Miller et al., 1987). These are marketed as turf disease detection kits for on-site diagnosis of diseases such as Pythium blight (*Pythium* spp.), brown patch (*Rhizoctonia* spp.), and dollar spot.

Weed identification can often be accomplished in the field with the aid of a good identification key. The inflorescence is sometimes necessary for the identification of certain plants. This may require that a specimen be brought into a greenhouse and allowed to flower.

When the pest reaches the control action threshold level as determined by monitoring, additional integrated management tactics are implemented. The agroecosystem is continually monitored to ensure that the tactics implemented are effective and to follow the response of other potential pests (Flint & van den Bosch, 1981; Pfadt, 1985).

V. AVAILABLE TACTICS

IPM programs rely on six basic approaches or tactics for plant protection. These include: (i) regulatory, (ii) genetic, (iii) cultural, (iv) biological, (v) physical, and (vi) chemical. These must be integrated into a management program that fits the turf area and purpose.

A. Regulatory

Certification of seed and plant material, quarantines; and elimination of noxious weeds or alternate hosts of plant pathogens are examples of regulatory procedures that can minimize the spread of pests from one location to another (Shurtleff et al., 1987). Certified seed and vegetative material must meet certain minimum standards regarding the absence of pests. The standards are set by state or federal regulatory agencies (Anonymous, 1983). Some states require that certain cultivars be grown to be eligible for certification (Turner & Dernoeden, 1990). Seed labeling informs the buyer of the percent of "other crop" and weed seed in a given seed lot (Beard, 1973). Quarantines have been used to limit distribution of certain turfgrass insects such as the Japanese beetle and the European chafer [*Rhizotrogus* (Amphimallon) *majalis* (Razoumowsky)] (Tashiro, 1987).

B. Genetic

Use of improved, adapted grasses is one of the most effective (Vargas, 1981; Turgeon, 1985; Tashiro, 1987) and ecologically sound ways to manage turf pests (Flint & van den Bosch, 1981). This practice is compatible with other management tactics. Many consider insect and disease resistance the ultimate goal in plant protection even though it is expensive and time consuming to develop (Tashiro, 1987). A reduction in labor, equipment, and pesticide costs can be expected when resistant turfgrasses are grown (Reinert, 1982a; O'Neill, 1985). Turfgrasses adapted to a climatic region are less susceptible to environmental stress and, thus, less prone to pest attack (O'Neill, 1985). The incorporation of compatible cultivars into blends and mixtures is suggested to minimize disease incidence over a wide range of environmental and cultural conditions (Turgeon, 1981; Smiley, 1983). Adapted cultivars enhance overall turf vigor and its recuperative capacity following pest injury (Tashiro, 1987).

Many of the improved turfgrasses currently in use have been bred for tolerance or resistance to major pests (Vargas, 1981; Smiley, 1983). The benefit of planting multiple-disease resistant grasses has been well documented (Vargas, 1981; Shurtleff et al., 1987), and the planting of cultivars that exhibit resistance to the major diseases found in a certain area is encouraged (Madison, 1971; O'Neill, 1985).

Although a relatively new area, breeding turfgrasses for insect resistance is increasing (Tashiro, 1987). Reinert (1982a), in reviewing host resistance in turfgrasses to insects and mites, listed environmental concerns, insect resurgence, and resistance to insecticides as the major thrusts stimulating interest in developing insect-resistant turfgrasses. Turfgrasses exhibit differential responses to armyworms (Quisenberry & Wilson, 1985); billbugs (Funk et al., 1985); chinch bugs (Lynch et al., 1987); mites (Johnson, 1975); spittlebugs (Stimmann & Taliferro, 1969; Taliferro et al., 1969); scales (Olton, 1973); greenbug (Jackson et al., 1981); and webworms (Reinert & Busey, 1983). Resistance appears to be due to several factors including greater tolerance to feeding or reduced levels of infestation (Tashiro, 1987). Accomplishments have been slow because of the absence of acceptable techniques for screening germplasm and the need for greater interdisciplinary efforts among researchers (Reinert, 1982a). Insect resistance of turfgrasses can be overcome. This was demonstrated when the southern chinch bug, *Blissus insularis* Barber, was able to feed and reproduce on St. Augustinegrass previously identified as being resistant (Busey & Center, 1987).

There are no reports of weed-resistant turfgrass cultivars to date; however, the use of improved, adapted grasses has been shown to reduce the potential for weed encroachment (Madison, 1971; Funk, 1981; Turgeon, 1985). Herbicide-tolerant turfgrass cultivars are being developed that should allow for more selective control of weed problems (Funk, 1981).

C. Cultural

Cultural practices influence a turf's susceptibility and recovery from pest attack and injury. It also affects the pest's ability to develop and compete with the host plant (Couch, 1979; Smiley, 1983; Shurtleff et al., 1987). Many pests can be kept at nondamaging levels if the cultural practices favor growth of the grass rather than that of the insect or pathogen (Turgeon, 1985). Poor management produces a weak turf that is more vulnerable to insect, nematode, or disease injury (Turgeon, 1981; Potter, 1986; Shurtleff et al., 1987; Colbaugh, 1987).

Mowing turf at the proper frequency and height are important in maintaining healthy plants (Beard, 1973). Mowing below the proper height for a given turfgrass species can result in a weakened, thin turf that is suceptible to weed encroachment and disease (Madison, 1971; Turgeon, 1985). Crabgrass (Beard, 1973; Jagschitz & Ebdon, 1985) and certain diseases such as *Drechslera* spp. (Smiley, 1983) are enhanced by mowing turf too short (Fig. 14-8). Leaves in infrequently mowed turf act as a food base for plant pathogens (Smiley, 1983) and as a hiding place for pests. The severed edge of leaf tips are major avenues for pathogen infection (Smiley, 1983), thus, higher cutting frequency and dull mower blades may enhance disease severity (Vargas, 1981).

Certain diseases such as Pythium blight and dollar spot (Smiley, 1983), and weed seed (Beard, 1973) can be spread by mowing wet turf. Mowers should be washed before each use and the turf only cut when it is dry. Unfortunately, there are situations, such as with putting greens, that require frequent mowing even when the foliage is wet.

Proper watering reduces the potential for disease development (Vargas, 1981), weed encroachment (Beard, 1973), and insect damage (Tashiro, 1987). Irrigating deeply (15–20 cm) but infrequently promotes deeper rooting and a healthier turf (Beard, 1973). Light, frequent irrigation encourages a shallow root system, compaction from traffic, increases susceptibility to pests and reduces environmental stress tolerance (Beard, 1973; Smiley, 1983; Potter, 1986). Irrigation schedules should be designed to minimize the length of time that foliage remains wet with free water. Most foliar pathogens require 6 to 8 h of free moisture on the leaf surface for spore germination and infec-

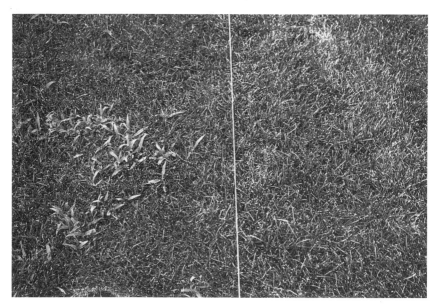

Fig. 14–8. Crabgrass invades a Kentucky bluegrass cultivar mowed at 1.9 m (*left*) but is absent when the cultivar is mowed at 3.8 cm (*right*).

tion (Vargas, 1981; Smiley, 1983). Saturated soils due to overwatering or poor drainage can intensify the activity of certain plant pathogens such as *Pythium* and *Fusarium* spp. that tolerate low oxygen levels (Smiley, 1983). Goosegrass and knotweed (*Polygonum aviculare* L.) are often found growing in compacted, wet areas (Beard, 1973).

Early detection of insect injury is difficult when the turf is experiencing drought stress (Tashiro, 1987). Dry soils can promote pest problems (Colbaugh & Engleke, 1985; Smiley, 1983) and usually need supplemental irrigation for recovery (Potter, 1986).

Meeting the nutritional needs of the turf is necessary for optimal growth and the ability of a turf to resist or recover from pest injury (Smiley, 1983; Shurtleff et al., 1987; Tashiro, 1987). Specific nutrient requirements are best determined with a soil test (Emmons, 1984). Nutrient imbalances and improper timing of fertilizer application can weaken turfgrasses and predispose them to pest problems (Smiley, 1983; Shurtleff et al., 1987). Red sorrel (*Rumex acetosella* L.) is often associated with infertile, acid soils. Excessive N fertilization increases outbreaks of diseases caused by Pythium blight, brown patch, leaf spot, and certain insects whereas a N-deficient turf is more susceptible to rusts, dollar spot, and crabgrass encroachment. Other nutrients such as K, P, Ca, and Mg have been shown to increase disease severity (Smiley, 1983).

Excessive thatch is a haven for turfgrass insects (Tashiro, 1987); reduces pesticide effectiveness (Hurto et al., 1979) and selectivity (Hurto & Turgeon, 1979); and is a favorable environment (Madison, 1971) and energy source (Shurtleff et al., 1987) for plant pathogens. Thatch may influence pesticide choice as some pesticides bind tightly to the organic matter (Table 14-1). Incompatible soil reactions, deficient nutrient levels, repeated applications of pesticides, and continuously wet turf promote thatch development (Smiley, 1983). On the other hand, grass selection as well as core cultivation in combination with topdressing and verticutting will discourage thatch buildup (Beard, 1973; Shearman et al., 1980).

Turf cultivation, especially core aerification, is beneficial in alleviating the effects of soil compaction by producing healthy plants and reducing the amount of moisture present. Pythium blight (Madison, 1971) and knotweed (Turgeon, 1985) are pests that suggest the presence of compacted soils.

Table 14-1. Water solubility of insecticides and their binding characteristics on turfgrass thatch. (From Tashiro, 1987.)

Insecticide	Water solubility, insecticides applied	Units of thatch required to bind 50%
	ppm[†]	
Chlorpyrifos (Dursban)	<1	4
Diazinon	40	75
Isazophos (Triumph)	150	300
Trichlorfon (Dylox, Proxol)	120 000	500 +
Bendiocarb (Turcam)	40	640 +

† Obtained from manufacturer's technical data; mg L^{-1} = ppm.

D. Physical

Some examples of physical approaches to pest management are sanitary practices, steam sterilization, mechanical traps, noise devices, drainage, poling, washing of equipment, and removal of plant material (Beard, 1973; Marsh & Bertholf, 1986; Shurtleff et al., 1987). Cleaning of equipment and clothing prior to entering a noninfested area may reduce the spread of pests such as weed seeds, plant pathogens, and small insects (Potter, 1986). Unfortunately, this is impractical for most turf areas. Soil heat treatment can reduce the potential for weed infestation by killing seed present in the soil (Beard, 1973). Mechanical traps, sound repellents, fences, and netting have been successful in controlling certain vertebrates such as moles, rodents, and birds (Marsh & Bertholf, 1986). The pruning and removal or careful placement of landscape plants can improve air movement over a turf area and thus reduce the duration of leaf wetness and drifting of snow. Both of these contribute to disease development (Bruneau et al., 1985).

E. Biological

The use of natural enemies to control turf pests is thought by some advocates to be one of the most important considerations in pest management (Flint & van den Bosch, 1981; Klein, 1987) and most appealing to the general public. Biological control involves introducing natural enemies (antagonists, parasites, and predators) or promoting those already present in the turf (Flint & van den Bosch, 1981; Shurtleff et al., 1987). However, some researchers believe that the biological control measures available for use in managing turfgrass pests are extremely limited (Potter, 1986; Shurtleff et al., 1987). A turf manager must be willing to accept a measure of damage until a resident population of the parasite or predator reaches an acceptable level. The use of natural enemies has been limited due to their host specificity, as well as their sensitivity to pesticides and adverse weather conditions (Shurtleff et al., 1987; Tashiro, 1987). Lengthy time periods must often pass before control is achieved. Despite these shortcomings, agriculturalists and commercial interests are taking a serious look at biological control agents because of their potential effectiveness, relative safety, and appeal to the general public. Potential biological control agents include nematodes, bacteria, fungi, viruses, protozoa, predators, and parasitoids (Kamm & McDonough, 1979; Ferron, 1981; Finney, 1981; Henry, 1981; Klein, 1982; Ahmad & Funk, 1983; Georgis, 1987; Klein, 1987; Pye, 1987; Shetlar, 1987; Isenhour, 1988) as well as allelopathic plants (Shurtleff et al., 1987). The use of the commercially available *Bacillus popilliae* bacterium that infects Japanese beetle grubs has been one of the most effective biocontrol programs on turf (Fleming, 1968). This bacterium causes a disease in white grubs called *milky disease*. However, it does not control all species of white grubs and takes several years to effectively reduce grub populations. It is ineffective north of New York City because of its sensitivity to cold temperatures and is indirectly affected by insecticides due to the decline in host population (Tashiro, 1987). Compared to registered insecticides, it is expensive, in short supply, and difficult to apply (Shetlar, 1987). Success has been achieved in culturing the bacterium on artificial media. This will make it easier to produce and market and possibly result in the release of strains of *Bacillus popilliae* that are effective against other scarab larvae.

Emphasis is now being directed toward the use of endophytic fungi to control certain insects in turf (Funk et al., 1983; Hurley et al., 1984; Funk et al., 1985; Ahmad et al., 1985, 1986; Kirfman et al., 1986). Perennial ryegrass cultivars containing endophytic fungi (*Acremonium* and *Epichloe* spp.) have exhibited resistance to sod webworms (Hurley et al., 1984) and billbugs (Ahmad et al., 1986). Cultivars of red fescue (*Festuca rubra* L.), hard fescue (*Festuca longifolia* Thuill.), and perennial ryegrass (*Lolium perenne* L.) have shown resistance to the hairy chinch bug (*Blissus leucopterus hirtus* Montandon) (Funk et al., 1985). The discovery of endophyte-enhanced resistance to several important turf insects should encourage the development and maintenance of cultivars having this unique form of biological control (Funk et al., 1983). Efforts are underway to determine if endophytes can be transferred to other grass species.

Researchers are also looking at entomogenous nematodes of the genera *Neoaplectana, Steinernema*, and *Heterorhabdites* (Georgis, 1987; Kard et al., 1988; Villani & Wright, 1988b) for the control of scarab larvae, northern masked chafer (*Cyclocephala borealis* Arrow), Japanese beetles, mole crickets (*Scapteriscus* spp.), and cutworms (Pye, 1987; Shetlar, 1987; Shetlar et al., 1988b). Desirable characteristics of entomogenous nematodes include wide host range, tolerance to environmental stress, rapid response, the ability to grow on artificial media, no evidence of insect immunity and environmental safety (Georgis, 1987). Unlike microbial pathogens, nematodes are not subject to government registration, but are difficult to keep viable during shipment, storage, and application (Georgis, 1987). However, they may be susceptible to insecticides applied for the management of other pests. In addition, specific irrigation requirements may be necessary for optimal establishment (Shetlar et al., 1988b).

Care must be taken to ensure that other pest management approaches complement the natural enemies and beneficial organisms present (Flint & van den Bosch, 1981). This is not always possible in the urban setting due to different user attitudes (Potter, 1986). Use of pesticides that are the least detrimental will help ensure the most benefit derived from those natural enemies present (Tashiro, 1987). Many areas for the enhancement of natural controls are under development, but additional research is still necessary (Daar, 1987).

F. Chemical

Pesticides are one of the more necessary, frequently used and beneficial approaches available to the turf manager (Madison, 1971; Flint & van den Bosch, 1981; Turgeon, 1985; Tashiro, 1987). Pesticides have and will continue to be a popular means of effectively managing a pest problem (Glass, 1976; Goss, 1981).

Despite the advances made in the area of nonchemical control, there are many instances where pesticides are the only effective control measure (Smiley, 1983; Tashiro, 1987). Preventive rather than curative fungicide programs are often preferred for the control of diseases on high value turf (Vargas, 1981). The use of preemergence herbicides is preferred over the use of postemergence herbicides because fewer applications are required and there is less risk of phytotoxic injury to the turf (Turgeon, 1985).

Turf managers, service support groups, and homeowners rely heavily on pesticides for pest prevention and control (Bennett et al., 1983; Shetlar, 1987). Approximately 90% of the homeowners use pesticides in and around their homes (McEwen & Madder, 1986). This is significant since 60% of all turf is found in the home lawn setting (Welterlin, 1987) and most homeowners are poorly trained in the proper use of pesticides (Brown et al., 1987). The intensity (amount per unit area) of pesticide use appears to be highest in urban settings (McEwen & Madder, 1986). Expenditures for lawn care pesticides approached $190 million in 1988 with most of that occurring in and around large cities (Colbaugh, 1987). This trend is expected to continue.

Sole reliance on chemical control often leads to problem situations (Wood, 1986). Problems associated with pesticide use include drift to nontarget areas, phytotoxicity, hard-to-clean equipment, and difficulty in product storage and disposal (Madison, 1971) (Fig. 14-9).

Pesticides can also have an effect on the turfgrass directly. Grass plots treated with heavy rates of chlordane were observed to experience visual drought symptoms earlier than untreated turf. This has been observed to continue for 5 yr after application (Engel & Callahan, 1967). Thatch develop-

Fig. 14-9. Misapplication of a pesticide can result in turf loss.

ment through overuse of pesticides that adversely affect microbial decomposition of thatch has also been documented (Niemczyk, 1974). Fungicides can increase thatch and disease development by suppressing beneficial organisms (Smiley, 1983). Repeated use of long residual herbicides can affect future management decisions and may result in the encroachment of difficult-to-control weeds (Madison, 1971).

Resistance of insects, plant pathogens, weeds, and rodents to various pesticides has been documented (Flint & van den Bosch, 1981). Nearly 500 species of arthropods have demonstrated resistance to insecticides with some exhibiting multiple resistance to an entire group of insecticides (Metcalf, 1987). The resistance of the southern chinch bug to high rates of chlorpyrifos and diazinon is one classic example of insect resistance (Reinert, 1982b). Insecticide resistance had also been noted for bluegrass billbugs (Niemczyk & Frost, 1978). Japanese beetles (Niemczyk & Lawrence, 1973), European chafers (Tashiro et al., 1971) and a southwestern June beetle (*Phyllophaya crinita*) (Frankie & Hamman, 1972). Fungicide resistance was first demonstrated by the development of cadmium-resistant strains of dollar spot fungi in the 1960s (Vargas, 1981). The problem of fungicide resistance has been magnified due to the widespread use of specific mode of action fungicides like the benzimidizoles that has allowed the development of new strains (Vargas, 1981). Sanders (1987) stated that this is the major problem facing individuals involved with chemical disease control. Sanders (1987) investigated reduced-rate fungicide mixtures in an attempt to delay fungicide resistance and enhance cost effectiveness; however, care must be taken to avoid sublethal doses that may actually accentuate resistance (Reinert, 1982b).

The ability of pests to tolerate the effects of certain pesticides is the result of natural selection through the repeated and frequent use of the same pesticide (Flint & van den Bosch, 1981). Turfgrass managers often increase the frequency or dosage of pesticides when confronted with the problem of resistance, thus failing to realize that they are in effect accelerating this natural selection process (Flint & van den Bosch, 1981; Reinert, 1982b). Alternating pesticides has been discussed as a way of delaying or avoiding pesticide resistance (Smiley, 1983; Fickle, 1985); however, there is little available evidence to support the merits of this concept (Sanders, 1987; Tashiro, 1987). There are few reports of herbicide-resistant turfgrass weeds, but the potential for such problems exists. Watschke (1985) reported that goosegrass had exhibited resistance to some trifluralin herbicides. Reducing the aesthetic expectations for turf may also reduce the need for pesticide applications. In addition, spray water pH may alter the effectiveness and the residual activity of a pesticide (Shetlar et al., 1988a).

The effect of pesticides on nontarget organisms has been well documented. Cockfield and Potter (1983, 1984) observed that a single application of chlorpyrifos greatly reduced the ability of predators to ingest the eggs of the sod webworm (*Crambus* and *Pediasia* spp.). It also reduced populations of many groups of predaceous arthropods for at least 3 wk. Herbicides may increase or decrease the disease incidence by altering the root and shoot metabolism of the turf (Smiley, 1981). Hodges (1980) reported that

Fig. 14–10. Root inhibition of centipedegrass following the application of a preemergence herbicide.

applications of 2,4-D, MCPP, and dicamba increased leaf spot severity (*Drechslera sorkiniana*) on Kentucky bluegrass. Several preemergence herbicides have been shown to inhibit turf root growth and can affect sod establishment (Shearman et al., 1979) (Fig. 14–10). Insecticides can indirectly affect

Fig. 14–11. Slime mold can be physically rather than chemically controlled by brushing, mowing, or washing the turf.

Table 14-2. Toxicity of technical grades of turfgrass insecticides. (From Tashiro, 1983.)

	LD_{50} mg/kg[†]	
Common name	AO[‡]	AD
Propyl thiopyrophosphate	890–1700	3830
Carbaryl[§]	500–850	4000
Trichlorfon	560–630	2000
Diazinon	300–400	455–900
Chlorpyrifos	97–276	500–2000
Isazophos	60–200	200–700
Bendiocarb[§]	40–156	510–800
Ethoprop	61	26
Isofenphos	28–38	188
Fensulfothion	2–11	3–30

† LD_{50} mg/kg = lethal dose, kills 50% of a test animal group, usually white rats. mg/kg = equivalent to 1 part chemical to a million parts test animal weight.
‡ AO = acute oral. AD = acute dermal. Acute refers to a single dose response, as opposed to successive sublethal doses fed or applied over a long period of time.
§ Carbamate insecticides; all others are organophosphate insecticides.

the microbial balance in the soil by suppressing saprophytic and parasitic insects that feed on microorganisms (Smiley, 1981). Unfortunately, few researchers are trying to develop compatible biological control/pesticide strategies (Smiley, 1981; Flanders, 1986).

Pesticides are an integral part of any pest management measure (Madison, 1971). Care should be taken to prevent the onset of multiple resistance by incorporating nonchemical approaches whenever possible (Reinert, 1982a) (Fig. 14-11). Specific, nonpersistent pesticides should be used only when necessary to supplement an agronomically sound turf management program (Madison, 1971; Turgeon, 1981; Reinert, 1982a). When chemical control is justified, turf managers should take these precautions to select a safe yet effective pesticide (Table 14-2); follow label directions; be aware of proper application techniques and rates; treat only those areas in need; and use action thresholds when available (Tashiro, 1987; Pfadt, 1985; Madison, 1971; Turgeon, 1985).

VI. IMPLEMENTATION STRATEGIES

Urban environments, with their diversity of plant species, unique ecological niches, and socioeconomic pressures, are some of the most complex of the agroecosystems (Short et al., 1982). Since urban pest ecosystems are heavily influenced by human activities, the development and implementation of urban pest management programs presents an exciting challenge (Owens, 1986). Many of these challenges are sociological and lie outside the realm of applied biology, ecology, or agronomics. The biological aspects are closely interwoven with the attitudes and expectations of the clientele.

Ravlin and Robinson (1985) surveyed the attitudes and knowledge of homeowners in Virginia and determined the feasibility of implementing an insect pest management program for turfgrass. Their objectives were to determine the level and type of residential turf maintenance, homeowner knowledge of common turf pests and diseases, where homeowners were obtaining information on lawn care and pest control, homeowners' willingness to pay for lawn maintenance and pest management, and the prospects of implementing an IPM program for urban lawns.

Almost 80% of the homeowners surveyed were unsatisfied with the present condition of their lawn (Ravlin & Robinson, 1985). This was consistent with findings reported by Smith and Gill (1987) in initiating an IPM program in Montgomery County, Maryland. Residents expressed interest in the program because they felt their present pesticide program was not cost-effective and because they were concerned some of their pesticide applications were not needed. In the Ravlin and Robinson (1985) survey, homeowner knowledge of the biotic and abiotic factors of lawn care and pest control was limited to a few key pests. Roughly one-third of those surveyed stated the best method of turfgrass insect control was the application of insecticides, while only 24% believed both chemical and nonchemical methods afforded the best control.

The majority of homeowners surveyed related property values, in part, to the quality of the landscape, and most were willing to pay some amount for lawn maintenance. In their opinion, informed homeowners were requesting an explanation on the nature of the damage before applying pesticides. This points to a need for the more biologically oriented approach provided in the IPM philosophy. It also points out that considerations other than pest efficacy (such as toxicity) should be considered in such a program.

The success of any IPM program, rural or urban, depends on clientele acceptance (Ravlin & Robinson, 1985; Stoner et al., 1986; Frisbie & McWhorter, 1986). Poe (1981) states that the characteristic of IPM programs is a demand for both interdisciplinary and multidisciplinary teamwork. Team members include horticulturists and agronomists who integrate production practices with the plant protection component provided by plant pathologists, entomologists, nematologists, and weed scientists to achieve crop management. Outlying disciplines such as engineering, biometeorology, wildlife, communications, and computer science all contribute to the development and successful implementation of IPM programs. The dynamic nature of an urban crop system requires periodic assessment of pest activity (Poe, 1981) and timely delivery of pest or plant management information (Short et al., 1982) for successful implementation.

Shurtleff et al. (1987) have identified six basic principles of turfgrass IPM. The principles are to identify the pests, define the turf management unit or agroecosystem, develop reliable monitoring techniques, establish economic and density thresholds, evolve descriptive and predictive models, and develop an effective and economical pest management strategy. Most turfgrass management texts (Turgeon, 1985) or turfgrass pest texts (Couch, 1973; Vargas, 1981; Shurtleff et al., 1987) present chapters on general turfgrass IPM and management of specific turfgrass pests and diseases. In general, these chapters concentrate on the basic areas of regulatory, genetics and breeding, cultural, and chemical.

The selective use of pesticides remains the front line of defense against turf pests (Shurtleff et al., 1987). When pesticides are applied in conjunction with sound management practices, their use will usually be reduced. Turf managers should keep accurate records of pest or disease occurrences and chemical applications. These records can be used in monitoring indicator areas and accurately timing pesticide applications when economic thresholds are reached. Turf records may provide insight into apparent control failures using pesticides. As homeowners and turf managers become more aware of the philosophy of IPM, they will be less dependent on chemicals as rescue treatments for pest or disease problems.

Frisbie and McWhorter (1986) and Poe (1981) pointed out that there are several features, regardless of crop, that are common requisites in the implementation of an IPM program. These include developing clear objectives for the IPM program, involving academic and theoretical approaches using systems models to forecast potential pest or disease outbreaks (The use of systems models in turfgrass IPM is still in its infancy.), monitoring pest and disease levels using field scouting methods, collecting basic research data to be used to synthesize crop system components into an integrated unit and show interrelationships among the various components, i.e., host, pest, environment, etc., conducting pilot demonstrations to determine the feasibility of the IPM program, and evaluating test plots to demonstrate cost-effectiveness of the program.

Hellman et al. (1982) and Short et al. (1982) used many of the IPM criteria just discussed to develop and implement two highly successful turfgrass IPM programs. Short et al. (1982) initiated an urban IPM study in Florida for the purpose of evaluating a monitoring system of pest management and turfgrass culture. The study was conducted on residential lawns in Gainesville, Fort Lauderdale, and Orlando. Twenty lawns in each city were involved. Ten at each location were maintained under normal management and prevention programs while another 10 received approved cultural practices and the IPM monitoring program. Pesticide applications were reduced by as much as 90% for the IPM lawns at all locations during the 2-yr study period. No visible difference was noted between the preventatively sprayed lawns and the IPM lawns. Short et al. (1982) concluded that cultural practices and monitoring of pests and beneficial arthropods, diseases, and weeds are the most important aspects of pest management for turfgrass.

Hellman et al. (1982) reported on a highly successful urban ornamental and turfgrass IPM program in Maryland. Like the Florida study, they used residential lawns as the focus of their program. The IPM package consisted of a three-level organizational structure. Level I consisted of state extension specialists serving as resource personnel and the Insect and Plant Diagnostic Clinic serving as a pest/disease identification source for Level II. Level II was made up of county extension agents, scout supervisors, or private consultants. These individuals made recommendations based on information obtained at Level III. Level III consisted of the residences being monitored. Each yard was scouted weekly from late May to mid-August. The cost to the homeowner over the 14-wk period ranged from $30 to $50 for lot sizes of <0.1 to 0.3 ha, respectively. Development of a reliable monitoring program was a critical step in implementing the program. The implementation phase consisted of developing detailed landscape maps of each residence, collecting preseason soil samples to make fertilizer and, if needed, nematicide recommendations, scouting yards on a weekly basis, and developing annotated landscape maps and newsletters on a weekly basis. Each week cooperators received an IPM community newsletter and a landscape map showing the location of pests and recommended control options. The final phase consisted of a post-program survey to determine cooperator acceptance and possible changes in ornamental and turf management methods. Results of the questionnaire showed that 98% of the participants were satisfied with the program's structure, cost, and scouting methods. Eighty percent of the cooperators followed 75 to 100% of the IPM recommendations and were inclined toward cultural rather than chemical recommendations. Strong points of the program were scout/homeowner relations, landscape maps, weekly newsletter, and information packets provided to each participant.

One of the most critical components to such IPM programs is adequate scout training. It is difficult for a first year scout to detect early symptoms of a pest problem if their only experience has been in training sessions with photographs and slides. Educating and maintaining well-trained scouts is essential to effective programs in turf. The use of videotapes, laboratory samples, and cultures of pests help by permitting a more accurate representation of what will be encountered in the field.

The future of turfgrass IPM, and IPM in general, will depend upon clientele acceptance, development of useful modeling systems, and the training of knowledgeable IPM professionals. Unfortunately, the impetus for academic IPM programs is losing momentum (Haning, 1987). Federal and state funding has remained level of declined in the early 1980s. IPM is not recognized as a true discipline and few true interdisciplinary courses are offered. Many states lack the staff needed to address the research and extension issues in turfgrass IPM. In entomology, there are critical needs for the development of threshold levels that will be useful under various environmental and turf situations. There is also a strong need to develop predictive models that will reduce our dependency on preventive treatments. Our understanding of many insect pests is still quite limited (ground pearls, bermudagrass scale, billbugs, etc.) and additional research is clearly needed. The development of strong interdisciplinary IPM curricula will provide incentive for future professionals to implement new, more sophisticated, yet practical, IPM programs. While economic advantages of IPM may at times be marginal, the sociological and environmental benefits of judicious pesticide use are strong justification for continued implementation. Both homeowners (Cooper et al., 1987) and golf course superintendents (Grant & Faubel, 1987) perceive the advantages to this approach. The IPM philosophy has played a vital role in urban and rural agriculture for a long time and will continue to be a key factor of the good life we have come to take for granted.

REFERENCES

Ahmad, S., and C.R. Funk. 1983. Bluegrass billbug (Coleoptera: Curculionidae) tolerance of ryegrass cultivars and selections. J. Econ. Entomol. 76:414–416.

Ahmad, S., S. Govindarajan, C.R. Funk, and J.M. Johnson-Cicalese. 1985. Fatality of house crickets on perennial ryegrass infected with a fungal endophyte. Entomol. Exp. Appl. 39:183–190.

Ahmad, S., J.M. Johnson-Cicalese, W.K. Dickson, and C.R. Funk. 1986. Endophyte resistance in perennial ryegrass to the bluegrass billbug, *Sphenophorus parvulus* (Coleoptera: Curculionidae). Entomol. Exp. Appl. 41:3–10.

Anonymous. 1983. Oregon certified seed handbook. Oregon State Univ., Corvallis.

Barrons, K.C. 1987. How risky are pesticides? Sci. Food Agric. 5(1):Jan. Reprint ISSN 0738-9310.

Beard, J.B. 1973. Turfgrass: Science and culture. Prentice Hall, Englewood Cliffs, NJ.

Bennett, G.W., E.S. Runstrom, and J.A. Weiland. 1983. Pesticide use in homes. Bull. Entomol. Soc. Am. 29(1):31.

Bingham, S.W. 1981. Effects of broadleaf herbicides on bermudagrass golf greens. p. 377–390. *In* R.W. Sheard (ed.) Proc. 4th Int. Turfgrass Res. Conf., Guelph, ON, Canada. 19–23 July. Int. Turfgrass Soc., and Ontario Agric. Coll., Univ. of Guelph, Guelph, ON.

Bottrell, D.R. 1979. Integrated pest management. Council on Environmental Quality. U.S. Gov. Print. Office, Washington, DC.

Brown, W.M., Jr., W.S. Crenshaw, and C. Rasmussen-Dykes. 1987. Urban IPM education and implementation: Implications for the future. Am. Chem. Soc. (Preprints of papers) 27(2):549–553.

Bruneau, A.H., J.M. DiPaola, W.B. Gilbert, W.M. Lewis, L.T. Lucas, and R.L. Robertson. 1985. Turfgrass pest management: A guide to major turfgrass pests and turfgrasses. North Carolina Agric. Ext. Serv. Publ. AG-348.

Busey, P., and B.J. Center. 1987. Southern chinch but (Hemiptera: Heteoptera: Lygaeidae) overcomes resistance in St. Augustinegrass. J. Econ. Entomol. 80:608–611.

Butler, G.D., Jr. 1963. The biology of the bermudagrass eriophyid mite. Ariz. Agric. Exp. Stn. Rep. 219:8–13.

Carson, R. 1962. Silent spring. Crest Books, New York.

Casey, C.A., and D.J. Prostak. 1987. Integrated pest management of ornamentals in New Jersey. Am. Chem. Soc. (Preprints of papers) 27(2):545–546.

Council for Agricultural Science and Technology. 1982. Integrated pest management. Rep. 93. CAST, Ames, IA.

Cobb, P.P. 1985. Two-lined spittlebugs on southern turf. ALA (Am. Lawn Appl.) 6(5):62–63.

Cockfield, S.D., and D.A. Potter. 1983. Short-term effects of insecticidal applications on predaceous arthropods and oribatid mites in Kentucky bluegrass turf. Environ. Entomol. 12:1260–1264.

Cockfield, S.D., and D.A. Potter. 1984. Predation on sod webworm eggs as affected by chlorpyrifos application to Kentucky bluegrass turf. J. Econ. Entomol. 77:1542–1544.

Colbaugh, P.F. 1987. Turfgrass management practices and their influence on pests. Am. Chem. Soc. (Preprints of papers) 27(2):632–633.

Colbaugh, P.F., and M.C. Engelke. 1985. An environmental genetics model for turfgrass improvement: Pathological aspects. p. 119–125. *In* F. Lemaire (ed.) Proc. 5th Int. Turfgrass Res. Conf., Avignon, France. 1–5 July. Inst. Natl. de la Recherche Agron., Paris.

Cooper, R.J., P.J. Vittum, and P.C. Bhowmik. 1987. Urban lawn IPM: Results of a pilot program. Am. Chem. Soc. (Preprints of papers) 27(2):543–544.

Couch, H.B. 1973. Diseases of turfgrass. 2nd ed. Kreigger Publ. Co., New York.

Couch, H.B. 1979. Relationhsip of management practices to the incidence and severity of turfgrass diseases. p. 65–72. *In* Advances in turfgrass pathology. B.G. Joyner and P.O. Larsen (ed.) Harcourt Brance Jovanovich, Duluth, MN.

Daar, S. 1987. Integrated pest management for the lawn care industry: New, less toxic product opportunities. Am. Chem. Soc. (Preprints of papers) 27(2):722–724.

Emmons, R.D. 1984. Turfgrass science and management. Delmar Publ., Albany, NY.

Engel, R.E., and L.M. Callahan. 1967. Merion Kentucky bluegrass response to soil residue of pre-emergence herbicides. Weeds 15:128–130.

Engel, R.E., and R.D. Ilnicki. 1969. Turf weeds and their control. p. 240–287. *In* A.A. Hanson and F.V. Juska (ed.) Turfgrass science. Agron. Monogr. 14. ASA, Madison, WI.

Experiment Station Committee on Organization and Policy. 1979. Integrated pest management. A program of research for the state agricultural experiment stations and the colleges of 1890. NCSU Press, Raleigh, NC.

Ferron, P. 1981. Pest control by the fungi *Beauveria* and *Metahizium*. p. 465–482. *In* H.D. Burges (ed.) Microbial control of pests and plant diseases 1970–1980. Academic Press, London.

Fickle, J.S. 1985. Rotational fungicide programs for turf. Grounds Maint. 20(11):42–45.

Finney, J.R. 1981. Potential of nematodes for pest control. p. 603–620. *In* H.D. Burges (ed.) Microbial control of pests and plant diseases 1970–1980. Academic Press, London.

Flanders, R.V. 1986. Potential for biological control in urban environments. p. 95–127. *In* G.W. Bennett and J.M. Owens (ed.) Advances in urban pest management. Van Nostrand Reinhold Co., New York.

Fleming, W.E. 1968. Biological control of the Japanese beetle. USDA Tech. Bull. 1383.

Fleming, W.E. 1976. Integrating control of the Japanese beetle—A historical review. USDA-ARS Tech. Bull. 1545.

Flint, M.L., and R. van den Bosch. 1981. Introduction to integrated pest management. Plenum Press, New York.

Frankie, G.W., and P.J. Hamman. 1972. The white grub problems in Texas turfgrass. Texas A&M Univ. Agric. Ext. Serv. Entomol. Notes 12:1–2.

Frisbie, R.E., and G.M. McWhorter. 1986. 3.6 Implementing a statewide pest management program for Texas, U.S.A. p. 234–262. *In* J. Palti and R. Aushers (ed.) Advisory work in crop pest and disease management. Springer-Verlag, New York, New York.

Funk, C.R. 1981. Perspectives in turfgrass breeding and evaluation. p. 3–10. *In* R.W. Sheard (ed.) Proc. 4th Int. Turfgrass Res. Conf., Guelph, ON, Canada. 19–23 July. Int. Turfgrass Soc., and Ontario Agric. Coll., Univ. of Guelph, Guelph, ON.

Funk, C.R., and S. Ahmad. 1983. The bluegrass billbug: Susceptibility of bluegrass to damage. New York State Turfgr. Assoc. Bull. 117:842–843.

Funk, C.R., P.M. Halisky, M.C. Johnson, M.R. Siegel, A.V. Stewart, S. Ahmad, R.H. Hurley, and I.C. Harvey. 1983. An endophytic fungus and resistance to sod webowrms: Association in lolium perennel. Bio/Technology 1(2):189–191.

Funk, C.R., P.M. Halisky, S. Ahmad, and R.H. Hurley. 1985. How endophytes modify turfgrass performance and response to insect pests in turfgrass breeding and evaluation trails. p. 137–145. *In* F. Lemaire (ed.) Proc. 5th Int. Turfgrass Res. Conf., Avignon, France. 1–5 July. Inst. Natl. de la Recherche Agron., Paris.

Furtick, W.R. 1976. Implementing pest management programs: An international perspective. p. 29–38. *In* J.L. Apple and R.F. Smith (ed.) Integrated pest management. Plenum Press, New York.

Georgis, R. 1987. Nematodes for biological control of urban insects. Am. Chem. Soc. (Preprints of papers) 27(2):816–821.

Glass, E.H. 1976. Pest management: Principles and philosophy. p. 39–50. *In* J.L. Apple and R.F. Smith (ed.) Integrated pest management. Plenum Press, New York.

Goss, R.L. 1981. Establishment and management of turfgrasses. p. 97–103. *In* R.W. Sheard (ed.) Proc. 4th Int. Turfgrass Res. Conf., Guelph, ON, Canada. 19–23 July. Int. Turfgrass Soc., and Ontario Agric. Coll., Univ. of Guelph, Guelph, ON.

Grant, F., and G.L. Faubel. 1987. Present assessment of needs of the golf turf industry as related to pesticide and the control of pests. Am. Chem. Soc. (Preprints of papers) 27(2):455–457.

Halisky, P.M., R.F. Myers, and R.E. Wagner. 1981. Relationship of thatch to nematodes, dollar spot and fungicides in Kentucky bluegrass turf. p. 415–420. *In* R.W. Sheard (ed.) Proc. 4th Int. Turfgrass Res. Conf., Guelph, ON, Canada. 19–23 July. Int. Turfgrass Soc., Ontario Agric. Coll., Univ. of Guelph, Guelph, ON.

Hall, J.R. 1987. Impact of quality turfgrass management programs upon urban environmental quality. Am. Chem. Soc. (Preprints of papers) 27(2):539–540.

Haning, B.C. 1987. Integrated pest management (IPM) courses and curricula: regaining momentum. Plant Dis. 71(2):197–198.

Hartman, J., and M. Ascerno. 1981. Monitoring methods in urban IPM. p. 144–146. *In* G.L. Worf (ed.) Proc. Urban integrated pest management workshop. The Natl. Coop. Ext., Dallas. 16–18 Nov. Univ. of Wisconsin, Madison.

Hellman, J.L., J.A. Davidson, and J. Holmes. 1982. Urban ornamental and turfgrass integrated pest management in Maryland. p. 31–38. *In* H.D. Niemczyk and B.G. Joyner (ed.) Advances in turfgrass entomology. Hammer Graphics, Piqua, OH.

Henry, J.E. 1981. Natural and applied control of insects by protozoa. Ann. Rev. Entomol. 26:49–73.

Hodges, C.F. 1980. Postemergence herbicides and pathogenesis by Drechslera sorokiniana on leaves of *Poa pratensis*. p. 101–112. *In* B.G. Joyner and P.O. Larson (ed.) Advances in turfgrass pathology. Harcourt Brace Jovanovich, Duluth, MN.

Hummel, N., and J. Neal. 1987. Turfgrass IPM program: Reducing the need for preemergence herbicides through proper fertilization of Turf: A demonstration. New York State Turfgrass Assoc. Bull. 131:1239.

Hurley, R.H., C.R. Funk, R.W. Duell, and W.A. Meyer. 1984. Registration of Repell perennial ryegrass. Crop Sci. 24:997.

Hurto, K.A., A.J. Turgeon, and M.A. Cole. 1979. Degradation of benefin and DCPA in thatch and soil from a Kentucky bluegrass (*Poa pratensis* L.) turf. Weed Sci. 27(2):154–157.

Hurto, K.A., and A.J. Turgeon. 1979. Effect of thatch on residual activity of nonselective herbicides used in turfgrass renovation. Agron. J. 71:66–71.

Isenhour, D.J. 1988. Interactions between two Hymenopterous parisitoids of the fall armyworm (Lepidoptera: Noctuidae). Environ. Entomol. 17(3):616–620.

Jackson, D.W., K.J. Vessels, and D.A. Potter. 1981. Resistance of selected cool and warm season turfgrasses to the greenbug (*Schizaphul graminuos*). Hortic. Sci. 16:558–559.

Jagschitz, J.A., and J.S. Ebdon. 1985. Influence of mowing, fertilizer and herbicide on crabgrass infestation in red fescue turf. p. 699–704. *In* F. Lemaire (ed.) Proc. 5th Int. Turfgrass Res. Conf., Avignon, France. 1–5 July. Inst. Natl. de la Recherche Agron., Paris.

Johnson, F.A. 1975. Bermudagrass mite, *Eriophyes cynodoniensis* Sayed (Acarina: Eriophyidae) in Florida with reference to its injury symptomology, ecology, and integrated control. Ph.D. Diss. Univ. of Florida, Gainesville (Diss. Abstr. 36/08B, p. 3759).

Kamm, J.A., and L.M. McDonough. 1979. Field tests with the sex pheromone of the cranberry girdler. Environ. Entomol. 8:773–775.

Kard, B.M.R., F.P. Hain, and W.M. Brooks. 1988. Field suppression of three white grub species (Coleoptera: Scarabaeidae) by the Entomogenous Nematodes *Steinernama Fettiae* and Heterohabditis *heliothidis*. J. Econ. Entomol. 82:1033–1039.

Kirfman, G.W., R.L. Brandenburg, and G.B. Garner. 1986. Relationship between insect abundance and endophyte infestation level in tall fescue in Missouri. J. Kans. Entomol. Soc. 59(3):552–554.

Klein, M.G. 1982. Biological suppression of turf insects. *In* H.D. Niemczyk and B.G. Joyner (ed.) Advances in turfgrass entomology. Hammer Graphics, Piqua, OH.

Klein, M.G. 1987. Suppression of white grubs with microorganisms and attractants. Am. Chem. Soc. (Preprints of papers) 27(2):814–815.

Lawrence, K.O. 1982. A linear pitfall trap for male crickets and other soil arthropods. Fla. Entomol. 65:376–377.

Lewis, W.M., and J.M. DiPaola. 1985. Tolerance of Eremochloa ophiuroides, *Paspalum notatum* and *Festuca arundinacea* to herbicides. p. 717–725. *In* F. Lemaire (ed.) Proc. 5th Int. Turfgrass Res. Conf., Avignon, France. 1–5 July. Inst. Natl. de la Recherche Agron., Paris.

Lindgren, D.T., R.C. Shearman, A.H. Bruneau, and D.M. Schaaf. 1981. Kentucky bluegrass cultivar response to bluegrass billbug (*Sphenophorus parvulus* Gyllenhal). Hortic. Sci. 16(3):339.

Lynch, R.E., S. Some, I. Dicko, H.D. Wells, and W.G. Monson. 1987. Chinch bug damage to bermudagrass. J. Entomol. Sci. 22:153–158.

Madison, J.H. 1971. Practical turfgrass management. Van Nostrand Reinhold Co., New York.

Marsh, T.B., and J.K. Bertholf. 1986. Importance of sanitation. p. 51–68. *In* G.W. Bennett and J.M. Owens (ed.) Advances in urban pest management. Von Nostrand Reinhold Co., New York.

McEwen, F.L., and D.J. Madder. 1986. Environmental impact of pesticide use. p. 25–50. *In* G.W. Bennett and J.M. Owens (ed.) Advances in urban pest management. Van Nostrand Reinhold Co., New York.

Metcalf, R.L. 1987. Impact of insecticide resistance upon long term prospects for insect control. Am. Chem. Soc. (Preprints of papers) 27(2):347–349.

Miller, S.A., G.D. Grothaus, F.P. Petersen, J.H. Rittenburg, and R.K. Lankow. 1987. Detection and monitoring of turfgrass pathogens by immunoassay. Am. Chem. Soc. (Abstr. of Papers) 194(Aug.):249.

Musser, H.B. 1962. Turf management. McGraw-Hill, New York.

Niemczyk, H.D. 1974. Section 6 abstract—New turf problem(s): resistance to chlordane in the Japanese beetle and attendant thatch. p. 424-425. *In* E.C. Roberts (ed.) Proc. 2nd Int. Turfgrass Res. Conf., Blacksburg, VA. 19-21 June 1973. ASA and CSSA, Madison, WI.

Niemczyk, H.D. 1981. Destructive turf insects. HDN Books, Wooster, OH.

Niemczyk, H.D. 1987. The influence of application timing and posttreatment irrigation on the fate and effectiveness of isotemphos for control of Japanese beetle (Coleytera: Scarabacidae) larvae in turfgrass. J. Econ. Entomol. 80:465-470.

Niemczyk, H.D. and H.R. Krueger. 1987. Persistence and mobility of isazofos in turfgrass thatch and soil. J. Ecol. Entomol. 80:950-952.

Niemczyk, H.D., Z. Filary, and H. Krueger. 1987. Movement of insecticide residues in turfgrass thatch and soil. Am. Chem. Soc. (Preprints of papers) 27(2):443.

Niemczyk, H.D., and C. Frost. 1978. Insecticide resistance found in Ohio bluegrass billbugs. Ohio Rep. 63(2):22-23.

Niemczyk, H.D., and K.O. Lawrence. 1973. Japanese beetle: Evidence of resistance to cyclodiene insecticides in larvae and adults in Ohio. J. Econ. Entomol. 66:520-521.

O'Neill, N.R. 1985. Disease management technology and strategies. p. 57-62. *In* F. Lemaire (ed.) Proc. 5th Int. Turfgrass Res. Conf., Avignon, France. 1-5 July. Inst. Natl. de la Recherche Agron., Paris.

Olton, G.S. 1973. Considerations of turfgrass varieties in the management of insect pests. p. 30-33. *In* W.R. Kneebone (ed.) Proc. Arizona Turfgrass Conf., Tucson. 4-5 Apr. Univ. of Arizona, Tucson.

Owens, J.M. 1986. Urban pest management: Concept and context. p. 1-12. *In* G.W. Bennett and J.M. Owens (ed.) Advances in urban pest management. Van Nostrand Reinhold Co., New York.

Pfadt, R.E. 1985. Fundamentals of applied entomology. Macmillan Publ. Co., New York.

Poe, S.L. 1981. An overview of integrated pest management. Hortic. Sci. 16(4):501-516.

Potter, D.A. 1981. Seasonal emergence and flight of northern and southern masked chafers in relating to air and soil temperature and rainfall patterns. Environ. Entomol. 10:793-797.

Potter, D.A. 1986. Urban landscape pest management. p. 219-252. *In* G.W. Bennett and J.M. Owens (ed.) Advances in urban pest management. Van Nostrand Reinhold Co., New York.

PSAC. 1963. Use of pesticides. U.S. Gov. Print. Office, Washington, DC.

Pye, A.E. 1987. Using a cold adapted beneficial nematode Neoaplectana carpoccapsae to control soil pest insects. Am. Chem. Soc. (Preprints of papers) 27(2):826-827.

Quisenberry, S.S., and H.K. Wilson. 1985. Consumption and utilization of bermuda grass by fall armyworm (Lepidopleia: Noctuidae). Environ. Entomol. 12:1837-1840.

Ravlin, F.W., and W.H. Robinson. 1985. Audience for residential turf grass pest management programs. Bull. ESA 31(3):45-50.

Reinert, J.A. 1982a. A review of host resistance in turfgrasses to insects and acarines with emphasis on the southern chinch bug. p. 3-12. *In* H.D. Niemczyk and B.G. Joyner (ed.) Advances in turfgrass entomology. Hammer Graphics, Piqua, OH.

Reinert, J.A. 1982b. Southern chinch bug resistance to insecticides: A method for quick diagnosis of chlorpyrifos (OP) resistance and alternate controls. Fla. Turfgrass Proc. 30:64-78.

Reinert, J.A., and P. Busey. 1983. Resistance of bermudagrass selections to the tropical sod webworm (Lepidoptera: Pyralidae). Environ. Entomol. 12:1844-1845.

Reinert, J.A., and S.H. Kerr. 1973. Bionomics and control of lawn chinch bugs. Bull. Entomol. Soc. Am. 19:91-92.

Sanders, P.L. 1987. Reduced-rate fungicide mixtures to delay fungicide resistance in pathogen populations. Am. Chem. Soc. (Preprints of papers) 27(2):446.

Sawyer, A.J., and R.A. Casagrande. 1983. Urban pest management: A conceptual framework. Urban Ecol. 7:145-157.

Shearman, R.C., E.J. Kinbacher, and D.H. Steinegger. 1979. Herbicide effects on sod transplant rooting of three Kentucky bluegrass cultivars. HortScience 14(3):282-283.

Shearman, R.C., E.J. Kinbacher, T.P. Riordan, and D.H. Steinegger. 1980. Thatch accumulation in Kentucky bluegrass as influenced by cultivar, mowing, and nitrogen. Hortic. Sci. 15:312-313.

Shetlar, D.J. 1987. Use of entomogenous nematodes for control of turfgrass infesting insects. Am. Chem. Soc. (Preprints of papers) 27(2):822-825.

Shetlar, D.J., P.R. Heller, and P.D. Irish. 1988a. Turfgrass insect and mite manual. The Pennsylvania Turfgrass Counc., Lemont, PA.

Shetlar, D.J., P.E. Suleman, and R. Georgis. 1988b. Irrigation and use of entomogerons nematodes, *Neooplectaur* spp. and *Heterorhabditis helisthides* (Rhabditidae: Steinernematidae and Heterorhabditidae), for control of Japanese beetle (Coleoglera: Scarabaeidae) grubs in turfgrass. J. Econ. Entomol. 81:1318–1322.

Short, D.E., J.A. Reinert, and R.A. Atilano. 1982. Integrated pest management for urban turfgrass culture—Florida. p. 25–30. *In* H.D. Niemczyk and B.G. Joyner (ed.) Advances in turfgrass entomology. Hammer Graphics, Piqua, OH.

Shurtleff, M.C., T.W. Fermanian, and R. Randell. 1987. Controlling turfgrass pests. Prentice-Hall, Englewood Cliffs, NJ.

Sill, Jr., W.H. 1982. Plant protection: An integrated interdisciplinary approach. Iowa State Univ. Press, Ames.

Smiley, R.W. 1981. Nontarget effects of pesticides on turfgrasses. Plant Dis. 65:1117–1123.

Smiley, R.W. 1983. Compendium of turfgrass diseases. Am. Phytological Soc., St. Paul.

Smith, D., and S. Gill. 1987. Anatomy of an IPM program. Landscape Manage. 26(8):46–50.

Smith, R.F., J.L. Apple, and D.G. Bottrell. 1976. The origins of integrated pest management concepts for agricultural crops. p. 1–16. *In* J.L. Apple and R.F. Smith (ed.) Integrated pest management. Plenum Press, New York.

Smith, R.F., and H.T. Reynolds. 1965. Principles, definitions and scope of integrated pest control. p. 11–17. *In* D.F. Waterhouse (ed.) Proc. FOA Symp. on Integrated Pest Control, Rome. 11–15 Oct. FAO, Rome.

Stimmann, M.W., and C.M. Taliaferro. 1969. Resistance of selected accessions of bermudagrass to phytotoxemia caused by adult two-lined spittlebugs. J. Econ. Entomol. 62:1189–1190.

Stoner, K.A., R.J. Sawyer, and A.M. Shelton. 1986. Constraints to the implementation of IPM programs in the U.S.A.: A course outline. Agric. Ecosystems Environ. 17:253–268.

Sturgeon, Jr., R.V., and K.E. Jackson. 1980. Diseases and nematodes. p. 293–302. *In* J.B. Beard (ed.) Proc. 3rd Int. Turfgrass Res. Conf., Munich, Germany. 11–13 July 1977. Int. Turfgrass Soc., and ASA, CSSS, and SSSA, Madison, WI.

Taliaferro, C.M., D.B. Leuck, and M.W. Stimmann. 1969. Tolerance of Cynodon clones to phytotoxemia caused by the two-lined spittlebug. Crop Sci. 9:765–766.

Tashiro, H. 1987. Turfgrass insects of the United States and Canada. Cornell Univ. Press, Ithaca, New York.

Tashiro, H., K.E. Personius, D. Zinter, and M. Zinter. 1971. Resistance of the European chafer to cyclodiene insecticides. J. Econ. Entomol. 64:242–245.

Tolley, M.P., and W.H. Robinson. 1986. Seasonal abundance prediction of sod webworm (Lepidophera: Pyralidae) adult emergence in Virginia. J. Econ. Entomol. 79:400–404.

Turgeon, A.J. 1981. Turfgrass pest management. p. 351–368. *In* R.W. Sheard (ed.) Proc. 4th Int. Turfgrass Res. Conf., Guelph, ON, Canada. 19–23 July. Int. Turfgrass Soc., Ontario Agric. Coll., Univ. of Guelph, Guelph, ON.

Turgeon, A.J. 1985. Turfgrass management revised edition. Reston Publ. Co., Reston, VA.

Turner, T.R., and P.H. Dernoeden. 1990. Turfgrass cultivar recommendations for Maryland Agricultural Extension Service. Turf mimeo no. 77:1–7.

Vargas, Jr., J.M. 1981. Management of turfgrass diseases. Burgess Publ. Co., Minneapolis.

Villani, M.G., and R.J. Wright. 1988a. Use of radiography in behavioral studies of turfgrass-infesting scarab grub species (Coleoptera: Scarabeidae). Bull. Entomol. Soc. Am. 34:132–144.

Villani, M.C., and R.J. Wright. 1988b. Entomogenous nematodes as biological control agents of European chafor and Japanese beetle (Coleoptera: Scarabeidae) larvae infesting turfgrass. J. Econ. Entomol. 81:484–487.

Watschke, T.L. 1985. Turfgrass weed control and growth regulation. p. 63–80. *In* F. Lemaire (ed.) Proc. 5th Int. Turfgrass Res. Conf., Avignon, France. 1–5 July. Inst. Natl. de la Recherche Agron., Paris.

Watschke, T.L. 1987. Cultural weed control in turfgrass. p. 634. *In* G.W. Bennett and J.M. Owens (ed.) Advances in urban pest management. Van Nostrand Reinhold Co., New York.

Welterlin, M.S. 1987. Current trends in pesticide use for turfgrass management. Am. Chem. Soc. (Preprints of papers) 27(2):450.

Wood, F.E. 1986. Nonpesticidal components essential to pest management. p. 129–162. *In* G.W. Bennett and J. Mowers (ed.) Advances in urban pest management. Van Nostrand Reinhold, New York.

15 Turfgrass Management Operations

S. T. COCKERHAM

University of California, Riverside
Riverside, California

J. A. VAN DAM

University of California Cooperative Extension
San Bernardino, California

Any organization that is complex enough to perform various functions, has an individual or group that produces the product for which the organization was formed. A manufacturer makes a thing, a theater company gives a performance, and a maintenance staff provides a service. Within the organization, marketing, administration, distribution, and others support the department that performs that work of production—operations.

Turfgrass Management Operations is the functional entity, or group, in an organization that actually performs the work in the maintenance of a turfgrass installation. Mowing, fertilization, irrigation, and spraying depend greatly upon the operations manager's knowledge of turfgrass science, but also, require attention to the management of resources. There are scientific techniques and concepts that have been developed, in the field of Operations Research, which can greatly reduce the confusion and frustrations inherent in managing maintenance.

Operations Research seeks a better understanding of work and productivity by using scientific measurements and analyses. By definition, Operations Research involves the application of scientific method by interdisciplinary teams to problems involving control of organized (man-machine) systems so as to provide solutions which best serve the purposes of the organization as a whole (Ackoff & Sasieni, 1968).

I. TURFGRASS MANAGEMENT OPERATIONS SYSTEMS

A system is a collection of interrelated elements whose whole is greater than the sum of the parts. A single element accomplishes nothing by itself. When the different parts of a system work together, a synergism is achieved where the output of the system is greater than the sum of the individual contributions (Schroeder, 1981).

Copyright © 1992 ASA-CSSA-SSSA, 677 S. Segoe Rd., Madison, WI 53711, USA. *Turfgrass*—
Agronomy Monograph no. 32.

When "Turfgrass Management Operations", as an entity, is viewed as a transformation system, or a system to transform inputs, such as labor, energy, and materials into a product or service, the decision-making process is greatly facilitated. When viewing the system in such a manner, it becomes particularly useful in problem identification and formulation.

A business organization is a system. Its parts are the functions primarily of marketing, operations, and finance. Operations as an entity can also be viewed as a system. Its major components or parts are the functions of production, maintenance, and management. The Turfgrass Management Operations System is illustrated in Fig. 15-1. The components are independent as well as interdependent. In Turfgrass Management Operations, production is the direct activities of maintaining the site; maintenance involves the care of the equipment and supplies inventory; while management includes supervision, planning, and budgeting. Personnel is considered to be a significant part of the supervision function.

The systems approach to problem solving helps define the boundaries and identify the parts of operations that are affected by a decision. Criteria for operations decisions are generally cost, quality, dependability, and flexibility.

The cost criterion is important and can be equated to efficiency. All relevant costs must be considered. A lathe is either on or off. It is normally run a fixed number of hours per day. Costs are computed on that basis. Not so with people. Two different people, each being paid the same rate, may "run" varying hours and with varying outputs, thus making costing difficult (McDonald & Stromberger, 1969).

While the quality criterion for operations decisions is concerned with the degree of the service provided, it is influenced by decisions about budgets, equipment, personnel, ownership values, and management's approach taken toward quality control. Quality in the care of a turf site or a landscape is

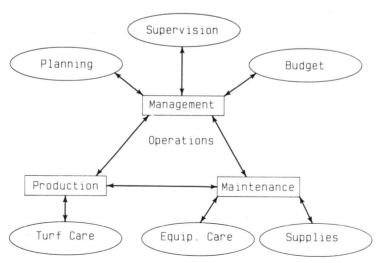

Fig. 15-1. Turfgrass Management Operations System.

equally difficult to measure or quantify. However, by using the ownership values as guidelines, such things as height of cut, frequency of mowing, pruning, edging, litter removal, and similar cultural practices can be forecast and measured.

Dependability is also affected by various management decisions, including those involving equipment, personnel, and scheduling. It can be measured as a percentage of promises met, number of complaints, downtime of equipment, or similar activities. In contrast, flexibility involves the ability of operations to make changes in schedules, programs, and techniques, as well as to make timely adjustments to changing conditions and situations.

Perhaps, one of the most important considerations in the management decision process involves tradeoffs. Make or buy, lease or purchase, quality vs. speed, more personnel vs. increased overtime, and others are matters that require some sort of compromise. Tradeoffs are made among the decision criteria of cost, quality, dependability, and flexibility. These criteria should serve as the basis for evaluating tradeoff decisions and for choosing a particular alternative.

To effectively use a systems approach for making administrative decisions in Turfgrass Management Operations, the overall goals and objectives of the facility's landscape must be established and agreed upon. These goals and objectives are determined by ownership values and influenced by the specific site characteristics.

II. OWNERSHIP VALUES

The concept of ownership values must be recognized, understood, and accepted for they fix the parameters of present and future maintenance needs. All of the demands of the landscape are basic to the expectations of the ownership and, thus, determine the ownership values.

The most significant factor in determining the management of a landscape site is the intended use. Goals and objectives of the owner must be identified. The owner is the controlling unit and may be a private individual, a firm, an institution, an organization, or a government agency.

Goals and objectives are expected to become the demands, both aesthetic and athletic, that activities will eventually make on the site. Based upon these demands, the owner must define a set of values to establish the degree of maintenance intensity that will be required. This degree of intensity and attendant expenditures are key factors in developing a maintenance program.

The function of a facility influences the choice of the turf quality (Fig. 15-2). Highway roadsides are at the low end of the quality scale since erosion control is the primary function of the turf. No one is expected to play on this grass and people only view it at highway speeds. In contrast, golf greens have very high quality demands in playability and aesthetics. The costs of maintenance per square foot reflects the quality requirements.

Home lawns are shown to reflect a mid-quality level. However, if the goals and objectives of the owner of a large, luxury apartment complex is

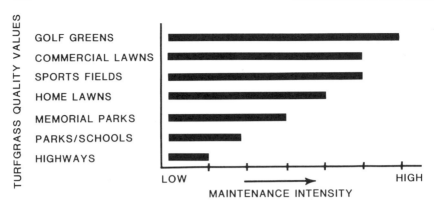

Fig. 15-2. Relationship of turfgrass quality values to maintenance intensity.

to rent to wealthy individuals, the management intensity of that commercial lawn would more than likely be quite high. Conversely, low resource level would respectively reflect lower quality levels of maintenance.

III. PREPLANNING REQUIREMENTS

Before program development can occur, specific data must be collected by inventorying the site, designating equipment, personnel, supplies, and similar resources. Most of the currently accepted scientific methods for planning use the concepts of computer modeling (Hussain & Hussain, 1981). In these techniques, the program is developed using actual information and the various components are moved around to get the most efficient fit, much as in a game of chess. This same concept can be accomplished "on the job", but at great cost in time and money. Thus, applications of business planning models can save considerable time and expense compared to trial and error on the job.

A. Inventory

Site inventory includes the number, type, and location of plant materials, as well as, dimensions of the area of nongrowing use areas such as walks, streets, and parking lots, and growing areas such as beds, ground covers, turf, shrubs, trees, and other ground cover plantings. Drawings are then made of the entire facility, or existing drawings are corrected to the current "as-built" configuration.

Facility resources inventory includes the skills level and availability of labor; available quantities of supplies and materials; and the capital and operating budgets. The latter may be developed as the maintenance program begins to take form. All data are then entered into the computer for further analyses.

B. Sectoring

Following the identification and determination of the physical characteristics, the facility is divided into convenient management sectors. A common division is based upon function, such as mowing, irrigating, fertilizing, and spraying. Geographic areas and specific maintenance requirements (e.g., front lawns vs. play areas or trees/shrubs vs. turf) are also common methods for sectoring. In large facilities, it is not unusual to use combinations of these methods.

C. Task Identification

In turfgrass and landscape maintenance, there are a number of tasks or jobs that must be performed. These tasks must be identified and listed as a part of the planning process. Such cultural practices as mowing with large or small mowers, mowing with powered or push mowers, irrigation, trim, edge, fertilize, renovate, and spray are all separate jobs and are to be scheduled separately.

D. Budgeting

In management, dollars follow people. This means that the key to controlling costs in an organization is control of labor-hours. Management's tool for monitoring labor expenditures is the labor budget which is periodically reviewed during the budget period.

The Turf Management Operations labor budget begins with the estimation of the number of people required for the tasks. In the budget segment shown in Table 15–1, the organization intends to retain the two irrigators for the entire year. Realizing that irrigation needs will vary, the manager forecasts the hours per week per person that will be needed in each month. From that point, the calculations are straightforward to arrive at the monthly and annual labor costs for irrigation.

The labor requirements for each task are evaluated. In the example, the need for mower operators varies throughout the year. The budget shows the expected month for hiring and laying off as well as the hours per week per person. Again, the bottom line is the cost per month. The salaried people are considered to be fixed labor costs as opposed to the variable labor costs of the other employees. Salary increases and overtime can change the costs during the year. Overtime for salaried people is estimated and calculated just as the variable labor in the other budget segments.

Supplies and other costs are budgeted just as labor. The input is forecast and the cost calculated. For example, it is decided to apply 250 kg/ha of fertilizer in April and again in September on a site that contains 5 ha of turf. There wll be 1250 kg of fertilizer needed in each of those months. With the fertilizer price at $200/t, the cost will be $250/mo.

$$(1250 \text{ kg fertilizer}/1000 \text{ kg/t}) \times (\$200/t) = \$250$$

Other supplies are budgeted in a similar manner.

Table 15-1. Example of a segment of a turfgrass management operations labor budget.

Description	Jan.	Feb.	Mar.	Apr.	May	June	July	Aug.	Sept.	Oct.	Nov.	Dec.	Total
wk/mo	4	4	5	4	4	5	4	4	5	4	4	5	
Irrigation[†]													
People	2	2	2	2	2	2	2	2	2	2	2	2	
h/(wk person)	35	35	40	44	44	50	50	50	50	44	40	35	
h/(mo person)	140	140	200	176	176	250	200	200	250	176	160	175	
$/h	6.25	6.25	6.25	6.25	6.25	6.25	6.25	6.25	6.25	6.25	6.25	6.25	
$/(mo person)	875	875	1250	1100	1100	1562.5	1250	1250	1562.5	1100	1000	1093.75	$14 018.75
$/mo	1750	1750	2500	2200	2200	3125	2500	2500	3125	2200	2200	2187.5	$28 037.50
Mowing[‡]													
People	2	2	3	3	4	4	3	3	3	3	3	2	
h/(wk person)	35	35	40	44	44	44	44	44	40	40	40	35	
hr/(mo person)	140	140	200	176	176	220	176	176	200	160	160	175	
$/h	6	6	6	6	6	6	6	6	6	6	6	6	
$/(mo person)	840	840	1200	1056	1056	1320	1056	1056	1200	960	960	1050	$12 594.00
$/mo	1680	1680	3600	3168	4224	5280	3168	3168	3600	2880	2880	2100	$37 428.00
Field supervisor[§]													
People	1	1	1	1	1	1	1	1	1	1	1	1	
Salary/mo	1800	1800	1800	1800	1800	1800	1800	1800	1800	1800	1800	1800	$21 600.00
Total operations													
Labor	5230	5230	7900	7168	8224	10205	7468	7468	8525	6880	6680	6087.5	$87 065.50

[†] Illustrates a constant labor force with work hours varying with demand.
[‡] Illustrates fluctuating labor requirement varying with work demand.
[§] Illustrates fixed costs with salaried personnel.

Since labor is the largest budget item, and the easiest of which to lose control, it is extremely important to apply considerable thought and effort to making accurate projections.

IV. ANALYTICAL TECHNIQUES FOR SYSTEMS MANAGEMENT

Operations research has provided many techniques that use statistics in management decisions. Combined with the systems approach, which helps define the parameters for the decision, these techniques are valuable tools for a turf manager.

A. Work Measurement and Performance Standards

Planning and budgeting for Operations require information about the time needed to complete the various tasks. Management usually identifies these times as standards for performance by or for the personnel of the organization. To accurately determine standards, work must be measured in an equitable manner.

In 1911, Frederick W. Taylor published a paper in which the use of a stop watch was introduced as a means of measuring work and determining performance standards. This technique has been controversial and a point of friction between labor and management. However, in the process of using work measurement to improve efficiency, managers identified poor work conditions as contributing to inefficiency, which led to upgrading those conditions (Taylor, 1911).

A performance standard defines the amount of time that should be required for work executed under certain conditions. Average time to complete work is not used because it reflects the amount of time taken and not what should have been taken. Standards can be "tight" if used for incentives or "loose" if used for production capacity.

In determinating standards, both quality and quantity must be considered (Lowry et al., 1940). In modern management techniques, time studies are often used with employee input to set standards. For a service organization, such as a turfgrass management facility, quality control consists of employee attitude and performance and is, overall, the equivalent of product quality control for a manufacturer (Hostage, 1975).

Labor inputs in a landscape maintenance vary significantly from one type of plant material to another (Van Dam et al., 1981). In Table 15–2, the labor hours per year required to maintain 100 m^2 of specific plants in a landscape ranged from 1.49 h for ivy (*Cissus* spp.) to 51.28 h for creeping fig (*Lolium perenne* L.) with 3.81 h needed for a mixed or general turf. Labor requirements for trees also varied widely, according to species, as shown in Table 15–3. It is advisable to develop similar labor data for a given facility since much of the work is site specific. This type of data is required and used to establish performance standards.

Table 15-2. Labor inputs per year by type of ground cover.

Type of plant	h/100 m^2
Ground covers	
Creeping fig (*Ficus pumila* L.)	51.28
Annuals	26.48
Baby tears (*Helxine soleirolii*)	19.51
Iris (*Iris* spp.)	8.92
African daisy (*Arctotis* spp.)	8.64
Algerian ivy (*Hedera canariensis* L.)	5.02
Gazania (*Gazania ringens*)	4.09
Jasmine (*Jasminum* spp.)	3.53
Lily-of-the-Nile [*Agapanthus africanus* (L.)]	2.32
Bellflower (*Campanula* spp.)	2.14
Cissus (*Cissus* spp.)	1.49
Turfgrass	
Perennial ryegrass (*Lolium perenne* L.)	8.83
Bermudagrass [*Cynodon dactylon* (L.)]	7.25
Kentucky bluegrass (*Poa pratensis* L.)	4.74
General turf	3.81

Table 15-3. Labor inputs per year by type of tree.

Type of tree	Avg. h/tree
Acacia (*Acacia* spp.)	3.76
Maidenhair tree (*Gingko biloba* L.)	2.87
Oak (*Quercus* spp.)	2.81
Ficus spp.	2.06
Fern pine (*Podocarpus elongata*)	1.93
Cypress (*Cupressus* spp.)	1.40
Evergreen pear (*Pyrus kawakami*)	1.09
Crabapple (*Malus* spp.)	1.06
Sycamore (*Platanus* spp.)	0.98
Avocado (*Persea americana* Miller)	0.91
Pine (*Pinus* spp.)	0.90
Southern magnolia (*Magnolia grandiflora* L.)	0.70
Jacaranda (*Jacaranda acutifolia*)	0.66
Citrus	0.59
Palm (*Phoenix* spp.)	0.49
Deodar cedar (*Cedrus deodara*)	0.45
Eucalyptus spp.	0.41
Camphor tree [*Cinnamomum camphora* (L.)]	0.36
Redwood (*Sequoia* spp.)	0.33
Crape myrtle (*Lagerstoemia indica*)	0.10
Birch (*Betula* spp.)	0.09
Alder (*Alnus cordata*)	0.08
Sweetgum (*Liquidamber styraciflua* L.)	0.02

B. The Normal Curve

Statisticians have determined that any time a sample of 30 or more people or units are selected randomly, and are examined for any one characteristic that can be measured on a continuous scale, there are a few individuals that are very low on this characteristic and a few that are very high which, obvi-

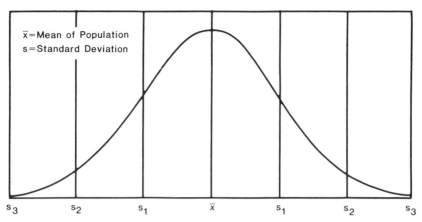

Fig. 15-3. Normal curve.

ously, leaves the majority to fall somewhere in between (Crocker et al., 1984). An important point is that most will be near the average and there will be about the same number at either extreme.

With analysis of large numbers of such samples, a curve could be drawn showing the frequency distribution that characteristically occur. Curves would be bell-shaped. The distribution has become called a normal distribution which is shown as a bell-shaped curve known as the "normal curve" (Fig. 15-3).

The normal curve is the basis for much of statistical theory. In statistics, a sample is mathematically analyzed to determine where it fits on the normal curve. The analyst then knows what the probability is for a value of a characteristic to occur in the population. A population is a statistical term defined as the larger group from which a sample is taken and can be anything not just people. For example, a hectare of Kentucky bluegrass turf could be studied as a sample representing the population of all turf of that species grown in a certain area.

Statisticians have divided the base of the normal curve into six approximately equal parts, with three parts on either side of the mean. Each division is called a standard deviation (SD). Those to the left of the mean represent items that have less of the characteristic and those to the right have more. The mean of the sample is found by summing the values of the characteristics and dividing by the number of items measured. The mean becomes the middle of the curve.

In practice, the line of the curve is of less importance, to the statistician, than the area under the curve, which represents the population. The area under the curve one standard deviation to each side of the mean is 68.27% of the total area, two standard deviations is 95.45%, and three equals 99.73%. Those percentages also relate to the probability of a characteristic occurring within the population (Hamburg, 1977).

The standard deviation is calculated by first summing all of the measurements, of a sample, and dividing by the number of items to determine the mean as shown in Eq. [1] (Snedecor, 1967).

$$\bar{x} = (SX)/n \qquad [1]$$

where
$\bar{x}$ = mean,
X = individual measurement,
SX = sum of the measurements,
n = number of items.

This mean is subtracted from each measurement to get the deviation from the mean (Eq. [2]).

$$x_i = X - \bar{x} \qquad [2]$$

where x_i = individual deviation from the mean.

These deviations are squared, summed, and divided by the number of items for the variance (Eq. [3]).

$$s^2 = (Sx_i/n) \qquad [3]$$

where s^2 = variance.

The square root of the variance is the SD (Eq. [4]).

$$s = \sqrt{s^2}. \qquad [4]$$

A normal curve and SD can be useful in turfgrass operations. An example, would be developing a performance standard for mowing of a large lawn. The lawn area would be observed for eight mowings and the following numbers were recorded in minutes per 0.01 ha:

Time per mowing, min/0.01 ha X	Mean $\bar{x}$	$(X - \bar{x})$	$(X - \bar{x})^2$
14	10	4	16
13	10	3	9
12	10	2	4
10	10	0	0
9	10	−1	1
8	10	−2	4
7	10	−3	9
7	10	−3	9
80			52

$\bar{x} = 80/8 = 10$
$s^2 = 52/8 = 6.5$
$s = \sqrt{6.5} = 2.55$

The sample of eight mowings, at one per week, is used to represent the population, which would be all the mowings of that site. An analysis of the sample is used to forecast that there is an 84.14% probability that the lawn will be mowed in 12.55 min or less.

By adding one SD to the right side to the total for the left the probability is found. Since the mean is in the center, there is 50% of the area under the curve on each side. The manager is not concerned about the low end as speedy mowings are bonuses, while the high end is for conservative planning. One SD to the right of the mean is 34.14%, therefore, the probability is 50% plus 34.14 or 84.14%.

Most managers would be quite satisfied if they were assured that an operational decision had an 84.14% chance of being right. In turf research, a scientist would insist upon at least 95% probability of accuracy and, in many cases, 99% is desired.

Performance standards could be set using the mean and the SD as shown in the example. If more confidence is required, the range could be taken from two SDs. That would imply that nearly 98% of the time the lawn would be mowed in 10 plus 2.55 plus 2.55 or 15.10 min. This could be the "loose" standard, as discussed in the previous section, and one SD could be the "tight" standard.

C. Experience Curve

In Turfgrass Management Operations, new sites are frequently added for maintenance or new people are added to the personnel roster. Performance standards may be well established or an individual in the organization may simply use his judgement and past experience to estimate time requirements. In either case, planning and budgeting are performed for the new work. Regardless of what process is used, rather large errors in time estimates can occur when the job is performed. These errors are due to a variety of causes.

One source of error is improvement in efficiency as experience is gained. Most people realize that the amount of time required to perform a task or group of tasks diminishes with repetition. A worker can perform a task better the second time, and each succeeding time he performs it. Turf managers may not be aware that the improvement pattern can be predicted because of its regularity. Nor are they aware that such patterns can apply, not only to individual performance, but also to the performance of groups and organizations as well.

This improvement from repetition generally results in a reduction of manhour requirements and, consequently, a reduction in operating costs. From research, the pattern of this improvement has been quantified in the experience curve sometimes called the *learning curve* or the *improvement curve*. The relationship upon which the curve is based is that each time the output quantity doubles, the unit labor-hours are reduced at a constant rate (Reuter, 1979).

Table 15-4. Unit factor for improvement ratios at three improvement rates (i.e., 70, 80, 90%)

Unit†	Improvement ratios		
	70%	80%	90%
1	1.0000	1.0000	1.0000
2	0.7000	0.8000	0.9000
3	0.5682	0.7021	0.8462
4	0.4900	0.6400	0.8100
5	0.4368	0.5956	0.7830
8	0.3430	0.5120	0.7290
10	0.3058	0.4765	0.7047
16	0.2401	0.4096	0.6561
24	0.1949	0.3595	0.6169

† Number of times an activity is repeated.

This can be shown with an example in which 1000 labor-hours, or 13 employees working 9.6 8-h days, are required to perform the landscape maintenance tour of a new site for the first time. If it is assumed that the constant improvement rate is 80%, determined using work measurement techniques, then it can be forecast that the second tour requires only 80% as many labor-hours as the first or 800 labor-hours. The fourth tour would require 80% of the second or 640 labor-hours and the eighth 80% of the fourth, and so on until the improvement was so small as to be meaningless.

To obtain the labor-hours experience values, tables have been developed that give the factor for each work tour or unit of production at various improvement ratios at three improvement rates. Table 15-4 gives the unit factors for improvement ratios at three improvement rates. The unit factor for the selected unit (work tour) is multiplied by the original number of man-hours to determine the required number of hours for that work tour.

The points determined by the relationship of labor-hours to work tours or units produced can be plotted on a graph. Plotted on standard arithmetic paper, the curve in Fig. 15-4 shows a rapid initial decline that levels off. The flattening of the curve indicates when the job will become routine and each tour will take more or less the same amount of time (Johnson et al., 1972).

D. Weighted Estimation of Activity Times

In estimating the time to complete any task, whether for routine maintenance or for a specific project, it is often useful to estimate more than one time for each activity to allow for uncertainty. A common technique is to estimate the most optimistic time, the most realistic time, and the most pessimistic time, then mathematically give more weight or emphasis to the realistic time. Equation [5] represents a weighted estimate of the times, based upon statistical theory.

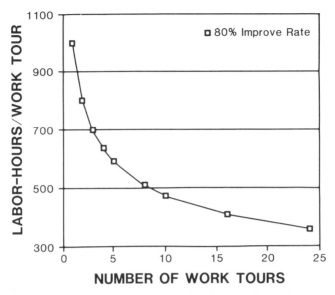

Fig. 15-4. Experience curve for labor-hour reduction for care of turf sites.

$$T_E = (a + 4m + b)/6 \qquad [5]$$

where
T_E = estimated time,
a = most optimistic time,
m = most realistic time, and
b = most pessimistic time.

For example, given the size of a park, a job is estimated to require 8 d. If all proceeds as expected and there are no problems, it could take as little as 4 d. If breakdowns of key equipment occur, it could take as many as 15 d. The weighted compromise estimated time would be:

$$T_E = [4 + 4(8) + 15]/6 = 8.5 \text{ d} \qquad [6]$$

This method is particularly useful if it is inconvenient to make complete plans for each of the three time estimates, but it is still desirable to consider the uncertainty of the most realistic estimate (Byrd, 1974).

E. Investment Analysis

The purchase of an asset, such as a piece of equipment or a building, is an investment by the firm or organization. For the organization, this is often quite a significant expenditure, requiring a great deal of thought, as well as use of whatever analytical tools available for the decision.

In business, the analysis of potential cash flows is used to compare various alternatives. In this instance, cash flow refers to either the additional revenue brought in by the investment or the cash savings to be realized. Cash flows are projected for several periods, usually months or years, ending with what might be considered the life of the investment.

For example, the purchase of a self-propelled mower would be the investment. The cash flows would be the earnings or savings for each year ending at 5 yr. The net cash flow streams for each year can then be discounted to present values or the return on investment capital can be computed. Revenues generated by the investment are estimated by forecasting as most pessimistic, most likely, and most optimistic. In facilities where Turfgrass Management Operations would not be dealing with revenue, the budgetary savings generated by the investment would be used. The forecasting procedure allows for analysis of the risk of each alternative. Most good spreadsheet software can be used for these analyses.

Integral to all of the financial analytical tools is the concept of the "time value of money." This refers to the theory that a dollar received now is worth more than a dollar received in the future. Disregarding things like inflation, price increases, or the uncertainty of receiving the dollar in the future, today's dollar could be drawing interest and be worth a dollar plus the interest. Discounting is the mathematical procedure to calculate the value of future dollars in present terms using a given interest percentage. The discount rate is simply the interest rate and is often called the *cost of capital*, the rate the organization must pay for its money. For large financially stable firms, the cost of capital may be the "prime" interest rate. For the public sector, the cost of capital could be the interest paid on bond issues.

Analyses of the costs of investments in assets, to be used in Turfgrass Management Operations, can be made using techniques such as Net Present Value (NPV), Internal Rate of Return (IRR), and payback.

1. Net Present Value

Net present value uses the cost of capital to find the present value of the future cash flows and makes a comparison with the cost of the investment. In the calculation, if the NPV is a positive number, the investment would payoff for the organization. The mathematics may seem somewhat complex (Eq. [7]), but most small, handheld electronic financial calculators are programmed to calculate NPV (Schall & Haley, 1980).

NPV = present value of future cash flows − initial cost

$$[CF_1/(1 + k)] + [CF_2/(1 + k)^2] + \ldots + CF_n/(1 + k)^n - I \qquad [7]$$

where
CF_1 = cash flow in period 1,
CF_2 = cash flow in period 2, etc.,
I = initial cost,
k = cost of capital, and
n = number of last period.

For example, the initial cost of a certain mower is $15 000 and it is estimated that this particular unit will save $3900/yr in labor and operating costs for 5 yr. In addition, the organization can borrow money at a 9% interest rate for its cost of capital. Therefore,

$$NPV = [3900/(1 + 0.09)] + [3900/(1 + 0.09)^2] + \ldots$$

$$+ [3900/(1 + 0.09)^5] - 15\,000 = 169.64. \qquad [8]$$

The NPV is positive; therefore, the investment would benefit the organization. The same analysis would be calculated for the most pessimistic and most optimistic scenarios. For example, as it may relate to a maintenance mower with a useful life pessimistically estimated to be fewer years or the annual cash flow to be less.

A common forecast will show uneven cash flows, such as what might happen if operating costs were expected to increase, decreasing savings, for each year the mower ages. The NPV is calculated in exactly the same manner for uneven cash flows.

2. Internal Rate of Return

Internal rate of return finds the discount rate, associated with the investment, and compares that rate with the cost of capital. The actual analysis discounts the cash flows of the investment to NPV of zero. The resulting discount rate is the rate expected to be earned on an investment. If that rate is greater than the cost of capital, the investment will be worthwhile to the organization.

The mathematics require almost a trial and error procedure. In Eq. [9], r value is continuously substituted or discounted until the NPV is zero. This is accomplished on readily available financial calculators or computer software by the use of loops that repeatedly make the substitution until the correct result is found. It is a difficult computation to do by hand (Schall & Haley, 1980).

$$IRR = [CF_1/(1 + r)] + [CF_2/(1 + r)^2] + \ldots$$

$$+ [CF_n/(1 + r)^n] - I = 0 \qquad [9]$$

where
   IRR = internal rate of return = 0, and
    r = rate which discounts to an NPV of zero.

Using the same example with initial cost of $15 000, cash flows of $3900 per period, and a 9% cost of capital, the IRR computes to be 9.43%. The IRR analysis also shows the investment to be worthwhile, because the IRR is greater than the cost of capital.

In the discussion of the NPV and IRR, it was assumed that the asset would not have any value at the end of the last cash flow period. Realistically, nearly every asset would have some salvage value. This can be considered in the calculations by adding the estimated salvage value to the last cash flow as if the asset were sold in the last year.

3. Payback Period

One of the most common methods of evaluating an investment is the calculation of the payback period. In this technique, the future cash flows are estimated and divided into the investment cost to get the time required to pay off the investment as shown in Eq. [10] (Schall & Haley, 1980).

Payback period = (Investment required/Annual cash flow)

$$= \$15\,000/(\$3900/yr) = 3.8 \text{ yr.} \tag{10}$$

A more accurate estimate of payback period begins by using the time value of money by computing the future value of the investment as shown in Eq. [11]. This can be simplified by using Future Value tables or a financial calculator.

$$F_n = P(1 + r)^n \tag{11}$$

where
F = future value of the initial investment after n interest periods,
P = initial investment, and
r = interest rate.

$$F_{5\,yr} = \$15\,000\,(1 + 0.09)^5 = \$23\,079.36 \tag{12}$$

The future value of the initial investment is then divided by the annual cash flow to get the payback period as shown in Eq. [13].

Payback period

= (Future value of investment required/Annual cash flow)

$$= \$23\,079.36/(\$3900/yr) = 5.9 \text{ yr.} \tag{13}$$

In this example, the payback period exceeds the 5-yr estimated useful life of the mower. If this analysis were the only one used, there should be questions raised as to the potential value of the asset to the organization. By having calculated both, the NPV and the IRR, the manager has two analyses that indicate that the investment would be worthwhile and one, payback with future value, that raises a red flag. This is why these analyses should be used merely as tools. They are not final decision makers, but do help reduce uncertainty.

V. PROCESS DESIGN

Process design is often used to track various operations used in producing a product. In turfgrass management, which is a service, the design of the process of maintaining a landscape site could proceed much as that found in manufacturing.

A. Process Flow

One of the significant decisions to be made in process design is the process flow. Process flow is the sequence of operations used to achieve selected results. In turfgrass management, operations is the accumulation of tasks such as mowing, aerifying, and edging, into one term or functional group. The process flow provides operations with the foundation for scheduling those tasks. There are three types of process flows: project, line, and intermittent.

Project flow is generally used in operations that are not continuous in nature, such as landscape construction. For the most part, turfgrass management is continuous. Often, there are construction projects, such as sprinkler system renovation or cart path installation, that could be planned using project flow.

Line flow was conceived for the continuous and repetitive assembly line tasks. Therefore, it fits the regularity of turfgrass maintenance operations. It is characterized by a linear sequence of operations used to produce the service.

For line flow to be effective, the procedures must be well standardized and must actually flow from one operation to the next in a prescribed sequence. For example, in maintenance of a football field after the Sunday game, an assembly line approach can be used to organize the process flow for the week leading to the next game (Fig. 15–5). Cleanup is followed by irrigation, then mowing, sweeping, aeration, dragging, sweeping, irrigating,

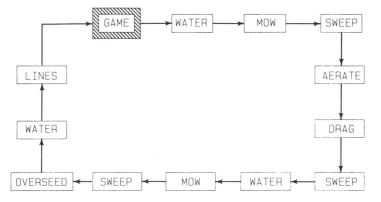

Fig. 15–5. Line flow of turfgrass management tasks on a football field beginning after a game to prepare for the next.

mowing, sweeping, overseeding, irrigating, painting lines, and numbers. Routine maintenance is programmed into a flow.

In designing for line flow, individual tasks should be balanced so that one task does not delay the next. Even though this type of flow tends to be quite efficient, it is very inflexible. The tasks, therefore, must ideally be in one given order and routinely performed.

Intermittent flow is characterized by work performed in batches at recurring intervals. In this case, equipment and labor are organized into work units by similar skill or equipment. Only the work units required will flow to the job. For example, a city may have several grounds crews each having the equipment and capability of doing nearly everything. A crew would tour a park and mow, edge, spray, fertilize, sweep, and prune shrubs. This would be a batch type of operation.

Intermittent operations are extremely flexible, but they tend to compromise efficiency. Further, the wide flexibility often leads to problems in controlling schedules, and quality so that they are often justified solely when the volume of work is low or customized in nature.

B. Linear Programming

Linear programming supports scheduling decisions that include assignment of variable resources to jobs or tasks to be completed and are each different in performance time and complexity. It assists managers in reaching a sound factual decision through mathematical formulations of operations/scheduling problems (Schroeder, 1981).

Linear programming can be used, in Turfgrass Management Operations, to determine the one allocation of resources that minimizes or maximizes some numerical quality, such as cost, profit, labor-hours, and turfgrass growth rate, out of many possible alternatives. Resources can include such items as space, time, personnel, finances, and equipment. Linear programming can weigh and analyze each of the various resource alternatives, allowing the manager to consider only the best choices. This is a tremendous aid in making decisions.

The algebraic procedure, used for solving a linear programming problem, is an analytical technique beyond the scope of this discussion. There are software programs available for personal computers that provide turfgrass managers the capability and opportunity to use this valuable management tool.

The most significant use of linear programming for a turf manager would be in scheduling. In the field of turfgrass management, shortages in the resources of people, equipment, and time are the rule rather than the exception. This inevitably places a heavy demand for the efficient use of them. Scheduling can be a laborious process of trial and error, especially for a large facility or organization. Linear programming is particularly useful for applications, as in scheduling where several problems must be solved simultaneously. The use of linear programming could readily increase the efficiency of that process (Agrawal & Heady, 1972).

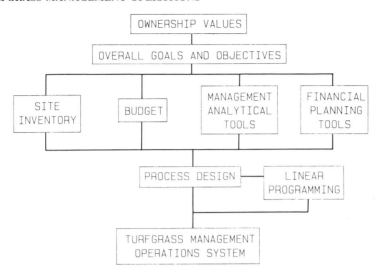

Fig. 15-6. Using process design to develop a Turfgrass Management Operations System based upon Ownership Values.

C. Turfgrass Management

The Turfgrass Management Operations System is developed by using process design. The procedure begins with the Ownership Values and the inherent goals and objectives of the owner (Fig. 15-6). The functional units considered for the development to reach the ownership goals and objectives are: (i) the site inventory and budget, (ii) the management analytical tools; and (iii) the financial planning tools. Process design, using linear programming is used to arrive at the best Turfgrass Management Operations System.

The decision-making process begins with problem definition, moves through the generation, evaluation, and choice of alternatives, and ends with implementation (Schroeder, 1981). Although the sequence is a logical order, events normally occur simultaneously, such as might arise in the generation and evaluation of alternatives using the management analytical tools and financial-planning tools. The actual implementation of the Turfgrass Management Operations System occurs following the process design stage. Linear programming is applied in the process design stage for development and later in the management activities as another important tool.

VI. RESEARCH ON TURFGRASS OPERATIONS

Operations research has been conducted primarily on manufacturing processes, although there is increasing work being done in the service industry. Some tried-and-true techniques have been adapted to maintenance, but maintenance does not always fit neat assembly line formula. When compounded by living plants, weather, diseases, traffic, aesthetics, and the other demands of the landscape, the unpredictability of the operations is significant.

Even with all of the unforeseen problems, it is still possible to develop better management tools. The needs are many. What system would be the most efficient for running a golf course, a sod farm, a landscape maintenance operation (private or public sector), or a cemetary? How can the inputs of energy, materials, labor, and capital be maximized? Research in operations decision making, materials requirements planning systems, job design, quality control systems, work measurement, and productivity for turfgrass management is wide open.

Few turfgrass researchers have the background or the interest to conduct operations research. It may be necessary to consider developing interactions with business and management faculty. The turfgrass industry is maturing and the time has come for the scientific community to consider the real world of turfgrass managers struggling to complete their tasks while meeting new technological, governmental, and agronomic challenges.

VII. SUMMARY

The concept of ownership values is intrinsic to the maintenance of any turf or landscape site. What does the owner want? The ownership goals and objectives are basic to the demands made on the landscape. Maintenance intensity of the site will be determined by these ownership values.

In establishing a turfgrass management program, a site inventory must be taken. The inventory is used to determine available resources and accumulate various data on the specific site. Then the site is divided into maintenance sectors and maintenance tasks are identified.

Turf maintenance is carried on by Turfgrass Management Operations, an entity within the organization. This entity works as a system with the parts being production, maintenance, and management. Production is the actual turf care provided, while maintenance within the operations concept is concerned with equipment care and the supplies inventory. The third and remaining part of the system is management that involves supervision, planning, and budgeting. The criteria for operations decisions are cost, quality, dependability, and flexibility.

To aid in decision making, Operations Research has developed several analytical techniques.

1. Work measurement and the setting of performance standards provide data for use in the planning of personnel scheduling.

2. The normal curve, based upon statistically normal distribution can be used by turfgrass managers in developing performance standards. By computing the SD of the time measurements, the manager will have confidence in the standards set, due to the probability of occurrence.

3. Experience curves are useful in determining time required to complete maintenance of a turf site from the first time to the point when the job becomes routine.

4. Weighting of activity times is also a procedure for estimating turf-grass management task completion time. The most realistic forecast is combined with the most optimistic and most pessimistic. Each forecast is weighted, with the most realistic weighted the heaviest. The method reduces the effects of uncertainty about the forecast by providing a single most-effective time to use for planning purposes.

In planning and forecasting, the technique of combining the weighting of activity times, where the most optimistic time, the most realistic time, and the most pessimistic time are combined with the most realistic time weighted over the other two. This is intended to provide one most effective time for planning purposes, yet reducing the effects of uncertainty about the forecast.

5. Capital budgeting techniques include: NPV, IRR, and Payback. The best use of the scarce financial resource is determined by comparing the savings or revenue generated by a piece of equipment, or other asset, to the purchase price spread out over the useful life.

6. Process flow is the determination of the movement of the personnel through the various turf management tasks in an efficient manner. The actual scheduling of the tasks can be aided by the use of a computer and linear programming.

The Turfgrass Management Operations System is developed using the techniques of process design. This brings us back to the use of operations for the management of a turfgrass site, where the chapter began.

Not all of the management tools discussed are applicable to all turfgrass facilities. Some of the analytical techniques developed for decision making in systems management can be helpful in turfgrass management decisions. With all of that, the fact does remain that efficiency and quality in workmanship are not easily put into numbers. An employee's pride in the organization he/she works for and enthusiasm for his/her job are still among the most fundamental components to success.

REFERENCES

Ackoff, R.L., and M.W. Sasieni. 1968. Fundamentals of operations research. John Wiley and Sons, New York

Agrawal, R.C., and E.O. Heady. 1972. Operations research methods for agricultural decisions. The Iowa State Univ. Press, Ames.

Byrd, J., Jr. 1975. Operations research models for public administration. Lexington Books, D.C. Heath and Co., Lexington, MA.

Crocker, O.L., S. Charney, and J.S.L. Chiu. 1984. Quality circles: A guide to participation and productivity. New Am. Library, New York.

Hamburg, M. 1977. Statistical analysis for decision making. Harcourt Brace Jovanovich, New York.

Hostage, G.M. 1975. Quality control in a service business. Harv. Business Rev. 53:4. 98–106.

Hussain, D., and K.M. Hussain. 1981. Information processing systems for management. Richard D. Irwin, Homewood, IL.

Johnson, R.A., W.T. Newell, and R.C. Vergin. 1972. Operations management: A systems concept. Houghton-Mifflin Co., New York.

Lowry, S.M., H.B. Maynard, and G.J. Stegemerten. 1940. Time and motion study and formulas for wage incentives. McGraw-Hill Book Co., New York.

McDonald, H.E., and T.L. Stromberger. 1969. Cost control for the professional service firm. Harv. Business Rev. 47:1. 109–121.

Reuter, V.G. 1979. Using graphic management tools. J Systems Manage. 30:6–17.

Schall, L.D., and C.W. Haley. 1980. Introduction to financial management. McGraw-Hill Book Co., New York.

Schroeder, G.W. 1981. Operations management: Decisoin making in the operations function. McGraw-Hill Book Co., New York.

Snedecor, G.W. 1967. Statistical methods. Iowa State College Press, Ames.

Taylor, F.W. 1911. Shop management. Harper and Brothers Publ., New York.

Van Dam, J., J. Mamer, and W. Wood. 1981. Labor requirement analysis for landscape maintenance. Leaflet 21232. Div. of Agric. Sci., Univ. of California, Berkeley.

16 Plant Growth Regulators and Turfgrass Management

T. L. WATSCHKE

Penn State University
University Park, Pennsylvania

M. G. PRINSTER

Chemlawn Research & Development
Douglasville, Georgia

J. M. BREUNINGER

Dow/Elanco
Sacramento, California

Altering the growth rate of turfgrass through exogenous applications of various chemicals has been a research endeavor of turfgrass scientists for more than 40 yr. In most situations, the vertical development of a turfgrass sward does not improve the quality of the stand (aesthetically or functionally). However, the removal of this unneeded foliar growth results in substantial maintenance expense primarily in the form of labor, equipment, and fuel. Certainly, the cosmetic result of high-quality mowing is important. However, if mowing "stripes" are not a part of the requirement for aesthetic acceptability, then chemical growth suppression would be acceptable in principle.

Chemicals that are specific enough to only suppress vertical foliar growth and not development at any other meristem are not currently available. Since the middle 1940s, several chemicals have been researched for their potential as turfgrass growth regulators (PGR). Among these chemicals were B-995, phosphon, ethrel, maleic hydrazide, chlorflurenol, gibberellins, and kinins. Beard reviewed these materials in 1973, while more recently, reviews of growth regulation in turfgrass science has been done by Elkins (1983) and Watschke (1985). It is apparent from these reviews that chemical suppression of turfgrass growth cannot be accomplished without negatively impacting the ability of treated turf to recover from any form of stand loss. The ability of turfgrasses to recover from injury albeit from pests, environment, or physical abuse, is one of the most important attributes they possess. To decrease the inherent recovery capability of a grass by applying growth-suppressing chemicals can only be done with the full realization of the consequences.

Copyright © 1992 ASA-CSSA-SSSA, 677 S. Segoe Rd., Madison, WI 53711, USA. *Turfgrass—Agronomy Monograph no. 32.*

As a result, the use of growth-suppressing chemicals has not been widespread in the turfgrass industry, but rather has been practically restricted to use in areas where turf injury is not likely to be severe and esthetic quality is not of paramount concern (such as roadsides).

Several researchers (Danneberger & Street, 1986; DiPaola et al., 1985; Field & Whitford, 1982; McCarty et al., 1985; Morre, 1983; Moore & Tautvydas, 1986; Schmidt & Bingham, 1977; Shearing & Batch, 1982) concur that the characteristics of the ideal chemical growth regulator application for roadsides would:

1. Inhibit inflorescence elongation and development and suppress the vertical foliar growth of treated grass through a long window of application.
2. Cause no objectionable phytotoxicity or discoloration of turf.
3. Allow or enhance lateral shoot growth (rhizomes, stolons, and tillers) to maintain sward density and recovery.
4. Permit or enhance the root growth of the treated grass plants.
5. Cause similar effects on numerous grass species.
6. Control or suppress the growth and development of undesirable plant species, especially the highly noticeable broadleaf weeds and brush.

Recently, DiPaola (1987) published a summary of turfgrass growth regulators based primarily on his research in North Carolina. Included in his summary are: materials, trade names, manufacturers, site of uptake, application rate changes, turfgrass responses including tolerances and toxicity rating (two rates), and other pertinent comments. Most trade publications regularly feature PGR articles that are prepared by those turfgrass scientists that have active PGR research programs.

I. CATEGORIZATION OF TURFGRASSES AND SITES

To discuss the practicality of growth regulator use, it is necessary to categorize or classify turfgrass areas. Kaufmann (1986a) recently developed a classification scheme as a means to describe four levels of management. His highest level of management, class A, included frequent mowing, fertilization, pest control, and often used irrigation. Class B had frequent mowing with occasional weed control and fertilization. Class C consisted of infrequent mowing with occasional weed control. Class D cannot be considered to be turf management as it had no mowing with only occasional brush and weed control. Examples of class A areas would be golf greens, tees and fairways, sportsfields, high-quality home lawns, and improved sections of industrial grounds, parks, sod farms, and some cemeteries. Examples of class B areas would be industrial grounds, parks, most cemeteries, golf course rough areas, and most home lawns. Examples of class C areas would be roadsides and class D areas would include guard rails, railroad and utility rights-of-way, and any other areas where total vegetation control is often the objective.

II. CLASSIFICATION OF PLANT GROWTH REGULATORS

Kaufmann (1986a) and Watschke (1985) categorized available products as Types I and II growth regulators. Type I compounds can inhibit or suppress the growth and development of susceptible grass species. These growth-inhibiting compounds are foliar absorbed and can rapidly stop cell divison and differentiation in meristematic areas; whereas, growth-suppressing compounds are crown and root absorbed and allow for some initial growth. Type II growth regulators suppress grass growth through the interference of gibberellin biosynthesis, thus reducing cell elongation and subsequent plant organ expansion (Kaufmann, 1986b).

A. Type I Growth Regulators

1. Inhibitors (Type I)

The following table shows plant growth regulators that inhibit or stop growth and development.

Common name	Trade name(s)	Manufacturer
Maleic hydrazide	Slo-gro, MH-30	Uniroyal
Chlorflurenol	Maintain CF-125	Uniroyal
Mefluidide	Embark	PBI Gordon

Maleic hydrazide (MH) [1,2-dihydro-3,6-pyridazine-dione] was introduced as a growth regulator for turf in the early 1950s. A rate of 4.48 kg a.i./ha was recommended for the foliar supression and seedhead inhibition of cool-season grasses in rough and semi-rough areas (Elkins, 1983).

Maleic hydrazide is foliarly absorbed. Uptake is slow and compounded by decreased leaf cell turgidity when associated with drought stress. This compound acts as a uracil anti-metabolite and is not readily metabolized within plant tissue. In the vascular system, MH is readily translocated to the growing points, especially downward. Maleic hydrazide suppresses turf by inhibiting cell division in shoots, buds, and roots (Danneberger & Street, 1986; Street, 1980), thus causing excessive thinning and root loss (Freeborg & Daniel, 1981; Duell, 1980; Wakefield & Fales, 1977). Billot and Hentgen (1974) suggested MH achieved seedhead suppression through the inhibition of reproductive tiller development. Severe injury and color loss has also been observed with the use of MH (Elkins, 1974; Elkins & Suttner, 1974; Foote & Himmelman, 1967; Freeborg & Daniel, 1981; Pennucci & Jagschitz, 1985), especially during periods of drought stress (Danneberger & Street, 1986; Shearing & Batch, 1982).

Because the primary activity of MH is to inhibit cell division, it must be applied prior to inflorescence initiation. Applications made after the window of activity will result in drastically reduced seedhead inhibition (Naylor & Davis, 1950). Researchers have described this window as being short (Foote & Himmelman, 1971), and highly unpredictable (Stich et al., 1978; White et al., 1970). Inconsistent results and injury have prevented widespread use of maleic hydrazide among grassland operators (Beard, 1985; Johnston & Faulkner, 1985; Shearing & Batch, 1982).

Maleic hydrazide has little activity on broadleaf species and should be used in combination with a broadleaf herbicide for total vegetation management (Chappell & Hipkins, 1982; Foote & Himmelman, 1967, 1971). Jagschitz et al. (1978), Stich et al. (1978) and Chappell et al. (1977) noted the addition of 2,4-D [(2,4-dichlorophenoxy) acetic acid], dicamba (3,6-dichloro-o-anisic acid), mecoprop {2-[(4-chloro-otolyl)oxy]propionic acid}, or silvex [2-(2,4-5-trichlorophenoxy)propionic acid] to MH applications did not alter the efficacy of the growth retardant.

Chlorflurenol (methyl-2-chloro-9-hydroxyfluorene-9-carboxylate, methyl-9-hydroxy fluorene-9-carboxylate) was introduced in the 1960s. Like MH, it provides foliar growth suppression and inhibits inflorescence development of susceptible cool-season grass species. Chlorflurenol can also inhibit or retard the growth of herbaceous broadleaf and woody species and seedling grasses at rate between 2.24 and 3.36 kg a.i./ha (Elkins, 1983). Combinations of MH (3.36 kg a.i./ha) plus chlorflurenol (1.12 kg a.i./ha) have been recommended for consistent multispecies sward suppression (Elkins, 1983).

Chlorflurenol, a foliarly and root-absorbed compound, moves freely throughout the plant to areas of meristematic activity and accumulates in roots, shoots, and buds (WSSA Herbicide Handbook, 1983). Growth and development is subsequently stopped or slowed as cell division is inhibited.

Chlorflurenol has been reported to cause unacceptable injury to turfgrasses (Elkins, 1974; Freeborg & Daniel, 1981) and has a short window of application to achieve seedhead inhibition (Beard, 1985). Like MH, the use of chlorflurenol has been limited due to unpredictable efficacy, and intolerable injury and stand loss associated with its use on cool-season grasses (Beard, 1985; Johnston & Faulkner, 1985; Watschke, 1979b; Fales et al., 1976; Wakefield & Dore, 1974).

Mefluidide {N-[2,4-dimethyl-5-[[(trifluoromethyl)-sulfonyl] amino] phenyl] acetamide} was commercially introduced in 1978 as a seedhead and foliar suppressant for use in rough turf areas (Elkins, 1983; Johnston & Faulkner, 1985). Activity has been observed on both warm- and cool-season grass species (Beard, 1985), but season-long seedhead control is achieved with applications to cool-season grasses only (Anonymous, 1983).

Mefluidide is foliarly absorbed and, unlike MH and chlorflurenol, exhibits little translocation to other leaf organs, roots, and lateral growth meristems (Field & Whitford, 1982; WSSA, 1983). Nielson and Wakefield (1975) observed far less root and rhizome suppression with mefluidide than with MH and MH plus chlorflurenol. McWhorter and Wills (1978), through radioactive carbon tracing, found that the absorbed mefluidide remained in the treated lamina with little export.

Penetration of leaf tissue occurs most readily at basal leaf sheaths and leaf axils (WSSA, 1983) and because of limited movement, uniform spray coverage and distribution is essential (Anonymous, 1983). Uptake is complete within 4 to 6 h after application (Tautvydas, 1983) and by 96 h 90%

of the absorbed material is not yet metabolized (Field & Whitford, 1983). Activity of this compound occurs at the leaf base where cell division and elongation occur (Anonymous, 1983) causing reduced sheath extension and canopy height. Mefluidide also causes uncontrolled cell division in reproductive apices, which distorts stem extension and impairs seedhead development (Field & Whitford, 1982).

The most of action of mefluidide is not completely understood. Wilkenson (1982) stated that it may act to inhibit gibberillic acid (GA) biosynthesis and subsequent cell elongation. Truelove et al. (1977) however, concluded that since the growth retarding action of mefluidide could not be reversed with applications of exogenous GA, there was additional activity on plant growth. Reportedly, retardation occurs by inhibited cell division and meristematic activity of responsive plant areas that come into contact with this compound (WSSA, 1983). Elkins (1983) emphasized that lower concentrations of mefluidide that inhibit cell elongation will not inhibit cell division, and that cell division is inhibited by higher concentrations.

Applications of mefluidide should be restricted to green, actively growing grass. Mowing the sward 4 to 5 d before or after the application will provide a sustained mowed appearance (Field & Whitford, 1982). Timing of mefluidide applications is critical for optimal seedhead control. Application should be at least 14 d before seedhead emergence, with the application window being broader than that of MH and chlorflurenol (Elkins, 1983).

Several researchers (Watschke, 1976, 1979b; Chappell et al., 1977; Schott et al., 1977; Fales et al., 1976) reported that mefluidide caused unacceptable phytotoxicity on fine-textured species and suggested that its use be limited to rough turf areas. Watschke (1978) and Chappell et al. (1977) reported that mefluidide caused injury on tall fescue; whereas, Warmund et al. (1980) and Wakefield and Fales (1977) reported no phytotoxicity on this species. Mefluidide-induced injury has been reported to be greater than that caused by MH and chlorflurenol (Wehner, 1980) and more injury has generally been noted when treated turf was environmentally stressed (Duell et al., 1977; Schott et al., 1977). Suppressed tiller and rhizome formation and subsequent stand density losses of cool-season grasses from applications of mefluidide have been observed (Dernoeden, 1984; Elkins et al., 1977; Fales et al., 1976; Field & Whitford, 1982; Nielson & Wakefield, 1975; Wakefield & Fales, 1977).

2. Growth Suppressors (Type I)

The following chemicals suppress growth but growth continues at a reduced rate.

Common name	Trade name(s)	Manufacturer
EPTC	Shortstop	Stauffer
Amidochlor	Limit	Monsanto

EPTC (*S*-ethyl dipropylthiocarbamate), has been marketed for seedhead inhibition and growth suppression of tall fescue (*Festucs arundinacea* Schreb.) on roadsides. Leaf expansion was reportedly not affected by applications of EPTC (Chappell, 1985; Link et al., 1981).

Chappell (1983), Chappell and Hipkins (1982) and Link et al. (1981) found that EPTC effectively reduced seedhead density and suppressed seedhead height of tall fescue. Chappell (1985) observed EPTC will suppress seedheads when the developing inflorescence is between 0 to 15 cm at application time. When the seedhead reaches 12 to 15 cm, the ability of EPTC to prevent further development is drastically reduced. For comparison, mefluidide did not suppress seedheads after they reached 7 to 8 cm in length. Chappell (1985) concluded the window of activity of EPTC was 6 to 8 wk and that mefluidide had a shorter window for efficacy.

Beard (1985) reported that EPTC was absorbed by the roots of tall fescue. Danneberger and Street (1986) stated, however, the site of uptake could possibly be the root but was still unknown. EPTC was categorized by Kaufmann (1986a) as a growth suppressor rather than an inhibitor. Growth is permitted but at a slowed rate. The slowed growth is partially due to the time it takes for root absorption to occur, and partially due to the mode of action. EPTC interrupts the biosynthesis of GA or gibberillin-like substances of sensitive species, and it reduces the ability of tissue to respond to exogenous GA (Donald, 1981; Donald et al., 1979; Wilkenson & Ashley, 1979).

EPTC caused no foliar injury or discoloration of tall fescue and sometimes enhanced foliar quality when compared to untreated grass (Chappell, 1983; Chappell & Hipkins, 1982; Link et al. 1981). McElroy (1984), however, observed injury to Kentucky bluegrass (*Poa pratensis* L.) from both high and low rates of EPTC. Farwell (1986) stated that if applications are made before spring green-up, or if chemical distribution is not uniform, then discoloration can occur. He also noted stressful growing conditions would cause thinning of swards treated with EPTC. Fine-textured turf species have been injured by this compound (Danneberger & Street, 1986).

Danneberger and Street (1986) claimed that EPTC provides weed suppression due to its herbicidal origin. Others reported no broadleaf control with this compound alone, but that season-long vegetation maintenance could be obtained when EPTC was applied in combination with dicamba (Farwell, 1986; Chappell, 1983; Chappell & Hipkins, 1982).

Amidochlor [*N*-|(acetylamino) methyl]-2-chloro-*N*-(2,6-diethyl-phenyl) acetamide) was commercially introduced to the turf growth regulator market in 1985. This compound has been observed to inhibit seedhead development and suppress foliar growth of cool-season grasses by 50% for 6 wk (Kaufmann et al., 1983; Sandbrink et al., 1983; Stehling et al., 1983). Kretzmer and Kaufmann (1985) observed 4 to 5 wk of activity on tall fescue. Amidochlor is recommended for use on low to medium maintenance turf area.

Kaufmann (1986b) reported that amidochlor reduces the vertical growth rate of the crown meristems, and that root and intercalary leaf meristems were not affected. Kaufmann (1986b) referred to amidochlor as a grass growth suppressor as its root-absorbed characteristics and mode of action work to initially slow grass growth and later inhibit it. Kaufmann et al. (1983) had previously stated that granular and spray applications that did not reach the crowns or root systems by irrigation or rainfall would not be effective. This characteristic of amidochlor will probably limit its use on roadsides due to unpredictable rainfall and the deep-rooted nature of many roadside grass species.

Sandbrink et al. (1983) stated that applications made too early in the spring would delay grass green-up for approximately 4 wk. Bhowmik (1984) observed variable phytotoxicity in experiments during two consecutive years, but noted that amidochlor had no adverse effects on turf recovery. Stehling et al. (1983) observed no phytotoxicity associated with applications of amidochlor on cool-season grasses, even at rates up to 16.8 kg/ha. Bhowmik (1984) and Stehling et al. (1983) observed turf-quality improvements and increased growth 6 wk after application when growth supression subsided.

Seedhead inhibition associated with amidochlor has been shown to be somewhat variable from season to season (Bhowmik, 1984). McElroy (1984) and Sandbrink et al. (1983) observed the window of application of amidochlor to be approximately 4 wk long with applications being made prior to seed-head elongation.

Kretzmer and Kaufmann (1985) observed no enhancement of grass tiller-ing with the use of amidochlor. They also found that root weights were not significantly reduced at the time coinciding with foliar suppression. Bhowmik (1987b) observed no reduction in root length or weight after three consecutive years of amidochlor treatments.

3. Herbicide (Type I) Growth Regulators

Herbicide Type I growth regulators are compounds possessing post-emergence herbicidal activity that have also been shown to inhibit the growth and development of turfgrasses at sublethal rates. These compounds are characterized as having an extremely narrow margin of safety and misappli-cations resulting in overdose can cause severe injury or death to grass stands (Kaufmann, 1986a). Chemicals that are in this category are listed in the following table.

Common name	Trade name(s)	Manufacturer
Glyphosate	Roundup	Monsanto
Chlorsulfuron	Glean, Telar	DuPont
Sulfometuron methyl	Oust	DuPont
Metsulfuron methyl	Ally, Escort	DuPont
Fluazifop-butyl	Fusilade	IDI
Sethoxydim	Poast	BASF
Imidazolinone	Event	American Cyanamid

Glyphosate [N-(phosphonomethyl) glycine] was originally developed as a nonselective herbicide. At reduced rates, this compound has been shown to provide growth suppression and seedhead inhibition of some grass species [orchardgrass [*Dactylis glomerata* L.), tall fescue) (Facteau et al., 1985; Dickens & Turner, 1984; Rosemond et al., 1984). Glyphosate is foliarly absorbed and readily translocated throughout the entire plant and acts to inhibit certain metabolic enzymes (WSSA, 1983).

Lewis et al. (1985) found that glyphosate adequately suppressed tall fescue seedheads while maintaining acceptable stand density. Dickens and Turner (1984), however, observed that glyphosate rates high enough to inhibit seedheads also caused unacceptable phytotoxicity on tall fescue. Glyphosate has been shown to be an ineffective seedhead inhibitor (Brenner et al., 1985) and foliar suppressant for perennial ryegrass (*Lolium perenne* L.) (Brundage & Williams, 1985; Regan & William, 1985), but did provide adequate foliar suppression of orchardgrass (Facteau et al., 1985). Rosemond et al. (1984) stated that low dose applications of glyphosate provided adequate seedhead suppressions and foliar growth reduction to bahiagrass (*Paspalum notatum* Fluegge) for 45 to 60 d and that sequential applications greatly extended the suppressions period.

Chlorsulfuron {2-chloro-*N*-[(4-methoxy-6-methyl-1,3,5-triazin-2-yl) aminocarbonyl]-benzenesulfonamide}, metsulfuron{methyl 2-[[[[(4-methoxy-6-methyl-1,3,5-triazin2-yl)-amino] carbonyl]-amino] sulfonyl] benzoate} and sulfometuron methyl {Methyl 2-[[[[(4,6-dimethyl-2-pyrimidinyl) amino] carbonyl] amino] sulfonyl] benzoate} belong to the sulfonyl urea family of herbicides These compounds are foliar and root absorbed (Ross & Lembi, 1985), a characteristic desirable for consistant efficacy under variable weather conditions (Shearing & Batch, 1982). Sulfonyl urea herbicides show activity on numerous broadleaf and grass species at extremely low rates and are readily translocated throughout plants to prevent growth by inhibiting meristematic activity in shoot and root tips (Ross & Lembi, 1985).

Chlorsulfuron has activity on most broadleaf weeds and some annual grasses (Murray & Klingman, 1983; Ross & Lembi, 1985; WSSA, 1983). Tall fescue has been shown to be quite sensitive to this compound (Christians & Nans, 1984; Christians, 1985; Larocque & Christians, 1985; Maloy & Christians, 1985, 1986; McElroy, 1984), but apparently it can be used with some margin of safety (Morre & Tautvydas, 1986). This compound displays synergistic activity when applied in combination with mefluidide (Morre & Tautvydas, 1986; McElroy, 1984). DiPaola et al. (1985) and Dickens and Turner (1984) observed that sulfometuron methyl and metsulfuron methyl were effective for seedhead inhibition of tall fescue. DiPaola et al. (1985) reported that these compounds caused injury to tall fescue below the minimum acceptable level and that metsulfuron methyl caused thinning, especially at higher rates.

Sethoxydim {2[1-(ethoxyimino)butyl]-5-[2-(ethylthio)propyl]-3-hydroxy-2-cyclohexen-1-one} is a herbicide developed to eradicate grassy weeds in broadleaf crops, but has been shown to suppress grass growth at reduced rates (Brenner et al., 1985; Wiles & Williams, 1985). Sethoxydim is rapidly absorbed through the foliage and readily translocated throughout the plant. Activity in grass occurs at the meristematic regions (WSSA, 1983) causing death to the growing points at recommended herbicidal rates (Ross & Lembi, 1985).

Fluazifop-butyl {RS butyl 2-[-4-(5-trifluoromethyl-2-pyridol oxy) phenoxy] propinoate} is a selective postemergence grass herbicide. Very low rates of this compound have been shown to provide growth retardant activity on grasses (Regan & William, 1985; Brenner et al., 1985; Wiles & Williams, 1985; WSSA, 1983). Fluazifop-butyl is quickly absorbed through leaf surfaces and translocated to rhizomes and stolons of perennial grasses (WSSA, 1983). This compound has similar activity as sethoxydim (Ross & Lembi, 1985).

Imidazolinone [5-ethyl-2-(4-isopropyl-4-methyl-5-oxo-2-imidazolin-2-yl) nictotinic acid] has pre-acid postemergence herbicide activity on many annual and perennial grasses and has been shown to provide foliar growth and seedhead suppression of cool-season grasses (Bhowmik, 1985, 1987a; Prinster & Watschke, 1986; Prinster, 1987). Others have not found significant growth suppression of cool-season species (Pennucci & Jagschitz, 1985). Herbicide Type I materials have been extensively evaluated on warm-season grasses. Lewis et al. (1987) found that bahiagrass seedheads could be suppressed by May applications of ACP 1900 at 78 g a.i. ha^{-1}, MH at 4.5 kg ha^{-1}, and sulfometuron at 22 g a.i. ha^{-1}. Gonzalez et al. (1984) reduced mowing and controlled many weeds in bahiagrass and bermudagrass [*Cynoden dactylon* (L.) Pers.] along roadsides in Alabama, Georgia, and Louisiana. Flanagan and Peacock (1986) found that sethoxydim, sethoxydim plus mefluidide, EPTC, and EPTC plus dicamba consistently suppressed bahiagrass with acceptable turf quality along Florida roadsides. Turner and Dickens (1984) compared sulfometuron applications made in November, February, April, and July on bahiagrass in Alabama. July application was too injurious while November resulted in <50% growth supression. April application date provided the best seedhead suppression and more than 50% growth suppression.

Link and Atkins (1983) also found that April applications of sulfometuron methyl provided the best seedhead suppression of bahiagrass. In the more southern parts of the southeastern USA, sequential applications of PGRs appears to improve results (Gonzalez et al., 1984), while DiPaola et al. (1984c) found sequential treatments on bahiagrass in North Carolina to be unnecessary.

B. Type II Growth Regulators

Type II growth regulators act to suppress grass growth but not to inhibit it. These compounds interfere with gibberellin biosynthesis, thus reducing cell elongation and subsequent plant organ expansion (Kaufmann, 1986b; Watschke, 1985).

Common name	Trade name(s)	Manufacturer
Flurprimidol	Cutless	Elanco
Paclobutrazol (PP-333)	Scott's TGR	ICI

Flurprimidol {α-(1-methylethyl)-α-[4-(trifluoro-methoxy) phenyl] 5-pyrimidine-methanol} has been shown to provide extended foliar suppression on cool-season grasses (Welterlan & Nash, 1984; Freeborg, 1983; Dernoeden, 1982; Watschke, 1981). Brueninger et al. (1983) observed 12 wk of canopy suppression with tall fescue in an orchard situation.

Beard (1985) and Batten (1983) described flurprimidol as primarily a root-absorbed compound with some foliar absorption. Dernoeden (1984), Welterlan and Nash (1984), and Watschke (1981) noted foliar suppression caused by this compound was not noticed as rapidly as some of the foliar-absorbed products, but that it did suppress growth for up to 3 wk longer (Dernoeden, 1984; Hurto, 1981; Watschke, 1981; Wehner, 1980). Once absorbed, this compound acts to inhibit the production of GA, thus retarding cell elongation (Kaufmann, 1986b; Batten, 1983). Suppression caused by this chemical can be reversed by applications of exogenous GA (Brueninger, 1984).

Flurprimidol has been shown to increase the density of treated stands of Kentucky bluegrass (Dernoeden, 1982, 1984; Watschke, 1981). Dernoeden (1984), Brueninger et al. (1983), and Symington et al. (1982) observed enhanced tillering of some grasses as lateral growth was permitted but at a much-reduced rate. Batten (1983) reported that flurprimidol-treated grass had dramatically shortened internodes and leaves that were shortened and in clusters, thus causing a witch's broom effect. Freeborg (1983) stated that flurprimidol caused improved root systems. Dernoeden (1984) found a positive correlation between enhanced root weights and increased tiller density.

Flurprimidol has little efficacy on seedhead inhibition (Freeborg, 1983; McElroy et al., 1983; Symington et al., 1982; Hurto, 1981; Watschke, 1981; Wehner, 1980) and has been shown to actually enhance the seedhead production of Kentucky bluegrass after several years of application (Dernoeden, 1984). Seedhead heights were reduced as culm lengths were shortened (McElroy et al., 1983; Link et al., 1981; Watschke, 1981). Brueninger et al. (1983) and Freeborg (1983) observed that turf treated with flurprimidol had improved color compared to untreated. Sawyer et al. (1983), Dernoeden (1982), and Symington et al. (1982) noticed some injury but considered it to be acceptable.

Flurprimidol has been observed to provide suppression of broadleaf species within treated areas (Danneberger & Street, 1986; Welterlen, 1984; Murray & Klingman, 1983). Kaufmann (1986b) stated that the anti-gibberellic mode of action of flurprimidol can suppress internode elongation of all plants. Flurprimidol has also been observed to provide weed suppression in areas where it has improved grass stand density and subsequently deterred the invasion of annual grasses (Dernoeden, 1984). Some researchers contend that this compound provides possible pre-emergence activity on *Digiteria* spp. (Sawyer et al., 1983; Dernoeden, 1982).

Paclobutrazol (PPP-333), {(2RS,3RS)-1-(4-chlorophenyl)-4,4-dimethyl-2-1,2,4,-triazol-l-yl) penta-n-3-ol] is a compound of differing chemical nature, but possessing many similar type activities to those induced by flurprimidol (Kaufman, 1986b; Batten, 1983; McElroy et al., 1983; Sawyer et al., 1983; Symington et al., 1982; Link et al., 1981; Watschke, 1981, 1985). Paclobutrazol, however, has been shown to cause longer suppression of Kentucky bluegrass than flurprimidol (Watschke, 1981). Both compounds have been shown to increase photosynthate partitioning into tillers from Weeks 2 to 4 following application of Kentucky bluegrass (Branham & Hanson, 1986).

Uptake of this paclobutrazol is primarily through the roots, and rainfall following application will enhance activity. Foliar uptake is almost nonexistant (Barrett & Bartuska, 1982). Once in the plant, paclobutrazol acts to inhibit gibberellin biosynthesis, by blocking the oxidation of Kaurene to Kaurenoic acid (Dalziel & Lawrence, 1984; Johnston & Faulkner, 1985). Noticeable retardation is slow but lasts for greater periods of time than many foliar-absorbed growth regulators (Shearing & Batch, 1982, 19779). Paclobutrazol acts to reduce leaf and culm elongation of treated grasses. Hence, seedheads are significantly shortened (Shearing & Batch, 1982, 1979), but are not totally inhibited (McElroy et al., 1983; Symington et al., 1982; Link et al., 1981; Watschke, 1981). Brueninger et al. (1983) realized a savings of 12 mowing cycles during a 14-wk suppression period on tall fescue in an orchard situation.

Paclobutrazol can cause the stems and stolons of treated grass to become thicker and more prostrate and rosette-like in growth habit (Batten, 1983; Shearing & Batch, 1979, 1982). Enhanced tillering and subsequent increased seedhead and sward density have also been observed (Wiles & Williams, 1985; Brueninger et al., 1983; Shearing & Batch, 1979, 1982). It was noted that finer turf species were suppressed better than the deeper rooted coarse-textured species and that a population shift in favor of the coarse species could occur. Higher rates of paclobutrazol are needed to provide adequate suppression to the coarse species (Johnston & Faulkner, 1985; Shearing & Batch, 1979, 1982).

Treated areas initially tended to be discolored by applications of paclobutrazol (Johnston & Faulkner, 1985; Brueninger et al., 1983; Sawyer et al., 1983; Symington et al., 1982). Johnston and Faulkner (1985) and Shearing and Batch (1979, 1982), however, observed darker green foliage 3 to 4 wk after application. Researchers have reported the ability of paclobutrazol to retard the growth of dicotyledonous species (Shearing & Batch, 1982). Sawyer et al. (1983) noted probable preemergence control of *Digitaria* spp. with the use of this compound.

C. Comparisons and Combinations

The foliar absorbed, inhibitor-type (Type I) growth regulators usually provide immediate, yet relatively short-lived foliar suppression of grasses. The inhibition of grass inflorescences is their most desirable feature for roadside applications. Unfortunately, they usually lack activity to suppress or inhibit the growth of broadleaf species that commonly invade low-maintenance swards. The root absorbed, growth retardant (Type II) compounds, however, provide a longer duration of foliar suppression of grasses and can also suppress the growth of dicots. They do not, however, inhibit seedheads. Ideally, treatments using Type I growth inhibitors in combination with Type II growth retardants could provide optimal vegetation control as the biological activity of each type is complementary. Combination treatments could potentially suppress a wider range of grass and broadleaf species, and thus provide a more consistant sward appearance (Johnston & Faulkner, 1985; Shearing & Batch, 1982).

Tautvydas (1983) reported synergistic activity between mefluidide and Type II growth regulators. McElroy et al. (1983) also noted synergism between amidochlor and Type II growth regulators. Applications of these combinations greatly extended the duration of growth suppression than when Type I compounds were applied alone (Pennucci & Jagschitz, 1985; Sawyer & Wakefield, 1984).

McCarty et al. (1985), DiPaola et al. (1984b), and Shearing and Batch (1982) reported excellent seedhead suppression and foliar retardation of cool-season grasses when treatments included mefluidide and a Type II growth retardant. Shearing and Batch (1982) concluded that rates of either compound could be reduced to achieve desired results and that the window of application for seedhead inhibition could be extended with the combined application. Johnson (1989) found that combinations of paclobutrazol plus mefluidide (1.1 plus 0.4 kg a.i. ha^{-1}, respectively) and combinations of flurprimidol plus mefluidide (1.1 plus 0.4 kg a.i. ha^{-1}, respectively) provided good seedhead suppression of tall fescue in Georgia if applied any time during March.

Research with PGRs on bermudagrass has included applications of Type I, herbicide Type I, Type II and various combinations. Wu et al. (1976) applied MH, mefluidide, etheton, and chlorflurenol and reduced growth up to 50%, but generally caused injury too severe for home lawns. In California, Hield et al. (1979) reduced growth of bermudagrass for 28 d with mefluidide at 1.12 kg ha^{-1}, but growth suppression was accompanied by discoloration. In North Carolina, Deal (1983) found that MH and flurprimidol reduced growth of common bermudagrass when applications were made in spring or summer.

More recently, sulfometuron methyl and metsulfuron methyl have been evaluated for growth suppression of bermudagrass (Brede, 1984; Rogers et al., 1987; King & Rogers, 1986). These authors concluded that sequential applications (10 plus 10 g ha^{-1} of each in May followed by 20 plus 20 g ha^{-1} of each in June, and 30 plus 30 g ha^{-1} of each in July) could reduce bermudagrass growth by 70% and control most weeds. Although such a sequential approach would be costly, mechanical mowing would practically be eliminated with only slight discoloration. Johnson (1988) sequentially applied flurprimidol on bermudagrass and found that four applications at 0.2 kg ha^{-1} at 3-wk intervals provided more suppression than a single application at 0.8 kg ha^{-1}.

III. LIMITATIONS FOR USE

A. Phytotoxicity

Quality loss, exhibited as foliar injury and discoloration, can be attributed directly to the phytotoxic effects PGR chemicals may have on susceptible grass plants at rates required to achieve desired growth suppression (Elkins et al., 1974). Kaufmann (1986a) reported that improper applications to sensitive turf often leads to phytotoxicity. Foliar injury and discoloration has been observed as tip burn and necrosis (Bhowmik, 1987; DiPaola et al., 1985), leaf blade chlorosis and subsequent stand yellowing (Morre & Tautvydas, 1986), blue-green cast (Dernoeden, 1984), foliar bleaching and leaf tip reddening (Carrow & Johnson, 1990). It has been noted that moisture stress can enhance the degree of discoloration (DiPaola et al., 1985; Freeborg, 1979). Schmidt and Bingham (1977) stated that lack of soil moisture can increase the concentration of available chemical to grass plants, thus enhancing its activity on root and top growth.

Injury and discoloration can lead to an eventual decline in the health of treated grass plants. Mathias et al. (1971) noted that the carbohydrate reserves of several grass species were significantly reduced where foliar injury had occurred. Watschke (1976), however, observed an initial conservation of carbohydrates when plant growth was chemically suppressed. Later in the study, discoloration prevented photosynthesis and total nonstructural carbohydrates were depleted. This phenomenon intensified as reapplication compounded foliar discoloration.

Discoloration precludes the use of growth regulators on many highly visible, highly managed amenity turf areas (Watschke, 1976; Elkins et al., 1974). A slight degree of phytotoxicity is probably acceptable on highway rights-of-way where these chemicals have found widespread use (Duell, 1985). When possible, injury must be minimized as these low maintenance turf areas often undergo stress throughout the year (Danneberger & Street, 1986).

Several researchers (McCarty et al., 1985; DiPaola et al., 1985; Welterlen, 1984; Watschke, 1979c; Jacschitz, 1976; Nielson & Wakefield, 1975; Wakefield & Dore, 1974) observed improved foliar quality when N-containing fertilizers were introduced into the growth suppression program. However, Sawyer et al. (1983) reported enhanced discoloration if N fertilizer was applied before growth regulators, but N applied following a PGR decreased injury. Foliar iron eliminated loss of green color on centipedegrass [*Eremochloa ophiurodes* (Munro) Hackel] from PGR application but did not influence the degree of leaf tip reddening from one PGR (Carrow & Johnson, 1990).

Watschke (1976) concluded that if suppressed grass stands were not allowed to initiate regrowth, then ultimately sward appearance could become more unsightly than the initial foliar discoloration. Hence, a successful PGR application can decrease sward quality by preventing the foliar replacement of the grass. As older leaves naturally senesce, the prolonged foliar suppression of treated plants prevents foliage replacement to a degree required to sustain sward greenness. A thinner, coarser, and off-colored grass stand develops and the thinner canopy allows the senesced foliage, thatch, and soil to be more visible. Continual foliar replacement of healthy, untreated turf would prevent this condition from occurring (Freeborg, 1983; Shearing & Batch, 1979, 1982; Link et al., 1981; Wakefield & Dore, 1974). Kaufmann (1986a) also supported the role of natural senescence in delayed quality loss of turfgrass areas treated with PGRs. He further reported that the speed of natural leaf senescence in cool-season grasses increased greatly in reproductive tillers. He noted that PGR applications during and just after seedhead elongation consistently resulted in severe turf quality loss in species or varieties having a high number of reproductive tillers.

Several researchers noted initial stand losses from applications of growth regulators (Wehner, 1980; Watschke et al., 1977; Fales et al., 1976; Wakefield & Dore, 1974). Initial thinning can dissipate after several months and be unnoticeable the following season (Dernoeden, 1984; Watschke, 1979c). Schmidt and Bingham (1977) and Watschke (1976) observed increased seedhead numbers in the season following a growth regulator application. They concluded that this was due to enhanced tillering following the recovery of a suppressed canopy. Repeated annual applications can cause the most severe stand losses and are not advised (Danneberger & Street, 1986; Dernoeden, 1984; Watschke et al., 1977). Danneberger and Street (1986) and McElroy (1984) emphasized the importance and function of maintaining stand density in relation to turf/soil stability to prevent erosion, especially on steep embankments typical of roadsides.

Freeborg (1979) stated that the ideal grass growth regulator would effectively reduce leaf and stem elongation while permitting or enhancing the production of tillers, rhizomes, stolons, and roots. Thus, mowing requirements would be decreased without sacrificing a vigorous and dense stand of turf.

Reduced foliar replacement and retarded lateral growth caused by growth regulators can be compounded by unfavorable environmental conditions, disease and insect damage, and other stress factors resulting in decreased turf density and quality (Beard, 1985; Freeborg, 1983; McElroy, 1984). Season-long suppression is undesirable as grass plants need to grow to rejuvenate themselves, thus replacing stress-induced canopy loss (Danneberger & Street, 1986; Beard, 1985). Prolonged growth inhibition would prevent rapid stand recovery.

B. Pest Problems

Disease is more severe on retarded grass plants when compared to nontreated plants because reduced growth rate and recuperative potential prevents turf from masking disease-blighted leaves (Danneberger & Street, 1986; Watschke, 1976, 1979b). Incidences of red thread (*Laetisaria fuciformis*), dollar spot (Sclerotinia homoeocarpa F. Bennett), helminthosporium leaf spot (*Bipolaris* and *Drechsclera* spp.), rust (*Puccinia* spp.), and striped smut (*Ustilago striiformis*) have been reported to be more prevalent on retardant treated grass (Dernoeden & Wehner, 1981; Watschke, 1976, 1979b; Watschke et al., 1977; Elkins & Suttner, 1974; Elkins et al., 1974; White et al., 1970).

Low maintenance turf areas, typical of roadsides are easily invaded by undesirable weeds (Danneberger & Street, 1986). Sward density loss and reduced turf vigor as a result of PGR applications reduce grass competitiveness and encourage weed encroachment, thus further reducing the quality of these low maintenance swards (Dernoeden, 1984; McElroy, 1984; Dernoeden & Wehner, 1981). Elkins et al. (1974) found that weed infestations were sometimes directly proportional to the amount of density loss. Ideally, the introduction of PGRs into mowing management schemes should lengthen the interval between mowings. Decreased mowing pressure though, would allow weed populations to become more prominant in the roadside (Shearing & Batch, 1979; Stich et al., 1978). Dernoeden (1982, 1984) and Dernoeden and Wehner (1981) observed that smooth crabgrass [*Digitaria ischaemum* (Schreb.)] invaded void areas that resulted from thinning due to PGR use. Willis and Yemm (1966) noticed an increased percentage of broadleaf weeds after several consecutive years of growth regulator usage.

It has been shown that many available PGRs are compatible with common broadleaf herbicides (e.g., 2,4-D, dicamba, mecoprop, and silvex) (Jagschitz et al., 1978; Stich et al., 1978; Chappell et al., 1977). Morre and Tautvydas (1986) noticed occasional antagonism with the combination of 2,4-D and mefluidide, which resulted in reduced seedhead inhibition. Boeker (1970) observed enhanced foliar retardation with mixtures of broadleaf herbicides and MH. Stich et al. (1978) and Willis and Yemm (1966) observed that some foliar and seedhead suppression was caused by broadleaf herbicide applications alone.

C. Root Growth

Stunted roots resulting from PGR use would be deleterious to the ability of the sward to maintain itself, especially during heat and drought stress (Shearing & Batch, 1982). Retarded root renewal would prevent adequate water and mineral uptake required to sustain grass plants (Field & Whitford, 1982). It has been observed, however, that a chemically reduced grass canopy has significantly reduced transpiration and water use, thus allowing the turf to better withstand droughty conditions (Doyle & Shearman, 1985; Watschke, 1979b, 1981).

Research concerning the relationship of PGRs and their effects on rooting is inconsistent, even when identical experiments were performed two consecutive years (Freeborg & Daniel, 1981). Results of studies involving various turfgrass species have shown the following: roots were not affected but resumed growth before the foliage (Wakefield & Fales, 1977); the duration of root suppression mirrored that of the foliage (Wakefield & Dore, 1974); or prolonged root suppression may (Schmidt & Bingham, 1977) or may not (Dernoeden, 1984) be detectable the following year. Field and Whitford (1982) observed little inhibited root growth until 8 wk after treatment, at which time reduced leaf area and photosynthetic assimilation capacity severely inhibited root growth.

Wakefield and Fales (1977) and Nielson and Wakefield (1975) noted post-suppression flushes in root growth at 7 to 9 wk after treatment. Kaufmann et al. (1983) concluded that root growth may be enhanced as a result of aboveground suppression. Kaufmann (1986a), Beard (1985), Hagman (1983), and Batten (1983) stated that late spring applications of mefluidide can improve the ability of annual bluegrass to tolerate summer drought stress through shoot suppression and subsequent enhanced rooting. Cooper et al. (1987) has documented root growth and annual bluegrass quality as a result of mefluidide-wetting agent applications.

Soper (1958) noted that as the ratio of vegetative tillers to reproductive and flowering tillers increased, there was a greater survival of ryegrass plants (*Lolium* spp.) to summer drought stress. He attributed this to a greater number of retained or initiated roots on the grass plants with more vegetative tillers. Cooper et al. (1985) observed that the carbohydrate level of annual bluegrass roots was significantly increased for 3 wk when seedheads were chemically suppressed. Petrovic et al. (1985) concluded that chemical inhibition of seedheads in *Poa annua* L. could reduce root system deterioration and subsequent summer decline.

Generally, researchers have found that PGRs cause root renewal interference (Schmidt & Bingham, 1977) even if it is temporary (McCarty et al., 1985; Wakefield & Fales, 1977; Wakefield & Dore, 1974; Fales et al., 1976). Schmidt and Bingham (1977) suggested that prolonged root growth inhibition was due to either a chemical residual in the soil or the chemical caused a sustained effect on root development.

D. Swards of Mixed Species

Low maintenance swards typical of roadside areas tend to be of diverse and dynamic botanical composition. Lawn grasses established as vegetative cover for roadsides are invaded by grass and broadleaf species growing on land adjacent to rights-of-way as native species tend to reclaim disturbed areas (Landers, 1981).

Chemical mowing strategies must consider the effects of PGRs on all plant species to sustain a consistent and uniform sward appearance similar to that provided by conventional mowing (Shearing & Batch, 1982). Freeborg (1983) stated that the use of growth regulators on multispecies swards can cause surface irregularities due to the differential growth suppression of each species. He compared this response to a selective herbicide in that sward populations will change as the competitive ability of some species are reduced while others are not. Danneberger and Street (1986) and Shearing and Batch (1979) concluded that the untidy appearance of a differentially suppressed sward can result in the need for mowing sooner than desired, which may defeat the reason for using a growth retardant in the first place.

Although the flowering of cool-season grasses generally occurs in late spring (Sandbrink et al., 1983) inconsistencies in seedhead suppression among species in these swards by certain PGR applications have been noted (Morre & Tautvydas, 1986; Duell et al., 1977). Thus, as grass species vary in their inflorescence development, they also have varied seedhead suppression responses to PGR applications. Duell et al. (1977) suggested preparing seed mixes of grass species with known corresponding seedhead development rates for use on areas that are to be chemically treated with PGRs.

McElroy (1984) noted that growth regulator responses differed between fine- and coarse-textured species in that seedhead suppression was less consistently affected in the coarse-textured species. Tall fescue and perennial ryegrass generally have been more difficult to suppress and less susceptible to injury than Kentucky bluegrass and other intensively managed turfgrasses (Danneberger & Street, 1986; Welterlan & Nash, 1984; Watschke, 1979c).

Willis and Yemm (1966) observed significant population increases of red fescue and Kentucky bluegrass and a marked decline in coarse and clumped species due to repeated annual applications of MH. Elkins and Kitowski (1972) and Shearing and Batch (1979) also noted that MH caused greater phytotoxicity on coarse-textured rather than fine-textured cool-season species. Conflicting results were reported by Duell et al. (1977) in that MH caused greater stand loss on fine fescues (*Festuca ruba* L.) than on tall fescue. Elkins et al. (1974) observed that chlorflurenol caused greater growth suppression of tall fescue than Kentucky bluegrass.

Willis and Yemm (1966) attributed these differing textural responses to the fact that coarse, wider bladed species intercepted more foliarly absorbed spray. They also reported that grass species with exposed growing points may have more dramatic responses from applications of MH than rhizomatous grass species whose underground buds would be suppressed only through adequate translocation. Shearing and Batch (1982) described species' response differences to root-absorbed compounds. They stated that the shallower rooting habits of fine-textured grasses allowed them to intercept more of the growth retarding chemical, thus allowing the lesser suppressed, deeper rooted, coarse-textured species to dominate. Inconsistent suppression has been found to occur within similar textured species with applications of MH and mefluidide (Duell, 1980; Wakefield & Dore, 1974). Buettner et al. (1976) and Watschke (1979b) detected growth regulator differences even among varieties of Kentucky bluegrass.

E. Effects of Applications for Consecutive Years

No adverse effects were found for single spring applications for three consecutive years for amidochlor, mefluidide, or ethephon applied to a red fescue-Kentucky bluegrass sward (Bhowmik, 1987b). Dernoeden (1984) reported that two annual applications of ethephon, flurprimidol, or mefluidide over a 4-yr period did not adversely affect tiller or root recuperative potential for a Kentucky bluegrass-red fescue stand. The aforementioned PGRs, however, elicited adverse effects that could limit their continuous use in a turf.

F. Post-Suppression Responses

Enhanced foliar greenness as PGR effects wear off of treated areas has been reported by several researchers (Bhowmik, 1987a; McElroy, 1984; Chappell, 1983; Batten, 1983; Freeborg, 1979; Watschke, 1979b, 1978). Improved color is a desirable attribute of growth regulator usage, however, an enhanced foliar appearance of a sward may not necessarily reflect its overall quality (McElroy, 1984).

Rapid growth flushes following foliar suppression have also been observed (Cooper et al., 1985; Watschke, 1976, 1979b; Watschke et al., 1975; Parups & Cordukes, 1977; Mathias et al., 1971). Shearing and Batch (1982) and Watschke (1979b) stated that this foliar growth stimulation was short lived, lasting only 5 to 6 wk. Excelerated growth after a period of chemical suppression, may negate mowing savings experienced earlier in the season.

IV. IMPLEMENTATION OF GROWTH REGULATOR USE

Current mowing operations provide an aesthetically pleasing, uniform, and natural sward surface. The practicality of the use of chemical vegetation management lies in the extent to which alteration in the visual appearance of the turfgrass will be acceptable for the realized advantages (Shearing & Batch, 1979; Fales et al., 1976). Shearing and Batch (1979) stated that changes in sward appearance induced by the use of plant growth regulators is most easily accepted in rough turf situations where aesthetic standards are low.

A. Roadsides: Seedhead and Foliar Suppression

Along roadside grass management strategies, such as the introduction of chemical regardants, should provide results more economical than those realized through conventional mowing. The opportunity to replace mowing of grass by applications of plant growth regulators appears to have several advantages. Decreasing the number of seasonal mowings offers much potential for cost savings in fuel as energy inputs of one chemical application can replace inputs required for several conventional mowings. Equipment purchase and maintenance costs savings could also be realized. Turfgrass growth regulators use may also reduce man-hours spent mowing hazardous, uneven, and often steep embankments, around signs and other obstructions, and small islands of turf at interchanges and between lanes (Field, 1983).

Morre and Tautvydas (1986) realized effective vegetation management with a single growth regulator spray application for less than, or equivalent to the cost of one mowing cycle. DiPaola et al. (1985) estimated mowing costs of $6 to $12/ha and reported that current growth regulator applications would cost between $5 and $8/ha and reduce mowing needs by 50%. Johnson (1981) realized savings of $10 to $18/ha by reducing required mowings from five to six per season to only one or two mowings. A cost comparison conducted by 3M Company revealed that the cost of chemical regulation of a difficult-to-mow area was approximately equivalent to the cost of two mowing/trimming operations (Anonymous, 1983). Hence, if more than two mowing/trimming procedures would be required, then chemical maintenance would become less expensive.

Another benefit from reduced spring mowing is increased availability of manpower during a demanding time of the year. Growth regulators also slow grass growth at a time of the year when the rainy season is at its peak, thus causing problems in the scheduling of conventional mowing operations (White et al., 1970).

The suppression of grass seedhead production along roadsides is extremely important. Allowed to develop, seedheads detract from roadway safety by hindering the line-of-sight of motorists and being a fire hazard (DiPaola et al., 1985). Freeborg (1983) and Elkins and Suttner (1974) stressed the importance of seedhead inhibition in chemical vegetation management by stating that partial or complete inflorescence development suppression would eliminate the need for their removal, thus saving at least one mowing and reducing the subsequent straw that can smother turf. McCarty et al. (1985) concluded that shortened culms resulting from chemical suppression are less objectionable and would reduce the need for mechanical removal. Morre and Tauvydas (1986) and Morre (1983) stated that the highest priority of growth regulators on roadsides is to suppress inflorescences. Even a few escapes would detract from the esthetics of the roadside.

McElroy (1984) emphasized the importance of seedhead suppression by describing how grass blades attain a certain height and then lodge. After lodging, continued blade elongation is unnoticeable and has little to no effect on sward appearance. Unsuppressed seedheads reduce aesthetic quality and can impair visibility throughout the spring and summer. Baker (1983), however, maintained that lodged grass plants provide an acceptable unmowed appearance and can be beneficial by providing protection against soil erosion, and by reducing evaporation of soil moisture.

White et al. (1970) stated that the philosophy of growth retardant use is not to completely eliminate foliar grass growth and the need for mowing. Beard (1973) concurred by stating that growth-regulating chemicals should only slow the growth of turf rather than to completely inhibit it. Chemical mowing should suppress shoot growth for a consistant and defined period of time after which growth would fully resume (DiPaola et al., 1985; Schmidt & Bingham, 1977; Beard, 1973). Danneberger and Street (1986) contend that growth suppression should last at least 5 to 6 wk to realize a significant reduction in the number of mowings.

B. Timing of Growth Regulator Applications

Optimal growth regulator timing for cool-season grasses, or the window of application, is that period of time in the spring when maximum beneficial effects of the chemical retardant can be realized. Kaufmann et al. (1984) and McElroy (1984) stated that this period begins in the spring when growth regulator applications can no longer delay normal spring green-up and the window terminates when applications fail to successfully suppress seedhead production. Applications made before or after this period of time would not improve sward quality and may not reduce mowing. Practical use of growth retardants for extensive highway right-of-ways would require a product with a relatively long window of application to accommodate the logistics of application (Beard, 1985; Saywer & Wakefield, 1985).

Timing of applications of plant growth regulators is critical for obtaining maximum seedhead inhibition. Success of an application depends upon the condition of the plant with respect to seedhead development stage. Chappell (1985), DiPaola et al. (1985), Billot and Hentgen (1974), and Chailakhyan (1968) concluded that the progression of inflorescence development varied with soil and air temperature from season to season, and that calendar dates for growth regulator applications were not reliable management indicators. Hence, dependable measures of seedhead development must be used to ensure proper application timing. Recently, Danneberger et al. (1987) determined the lowest effective rate and proper timing of mefluidide application for seedhead suppression of *Poa annua* L. based on growing degree days (GDD). Using a base temperature of 13 °C, application rates of 0.4 kg ha^{-1} applied between 15 and 30 GDD gave excellent seedhead suppression.

Elkins (1974) and Naylor and Davis (1950) stated that greater seedhead suppression resulted when chemical treatments were applied prior to apical meristem elongation and seedhead emergence. DiPaola et al. (1984b) found that optimal growth regulator timing for tall fescue was after spring green-up and seedhead initiation but prior to a canopy height of 20.3 to 22.9 cm. During this time, the developing inflorescence is contained within the sheath and is approximately 2.5 to 3.7 cm in length and about 2 wk from emergence. They found that applications made during this 2-wk interval (when seedhead lengths had grown beyond 3.7 cm) resulted in decreased seedhead inhibition of tall fescue.

Chappell (1985) noted a drastic reduction in seedhead inhibition when developing tall fescue inflorescences elongated to 12.0 to 15.0 cm, or even 7.0 to 8.0 cm depending upon the chemical used. DiPaola et al. (1983) and Kaufmann et al. (1984) found similar results when applying MH at differing stages of inflorescence elongation. The greatest tall fescue seedhead suppression was achieved by applications made when seedheads were 4.2 cm long or less. Percent seedhead suppression was reduced when applications were made when inflorescneces were 9.3 cm and even greater reduction occurred at lengths of 22.2 and 31.1 cm.

C. Plant Growth Regulator Use and Management Classification

Kaufmann (1986a) discussed the PGR use by turfgrass management classification interaction. He concluded that the use of growth regulators on class A turf was extremely small and very specialized. For example, mefluidide has been used successfully for seedhead suppression on golf course fairways that are predominately annual bluegrass. Seedhead suppression results in improved playing conditions and aesthetic quality and has been observed to improve summer stress tolerance. Cooper et al. (1987) concluded that mefluidide applications which provided good seedhead suppression, also prevented root decline in flowering annual bluegrass. Although not labeled for applications to creeping bentgrass (*Agrostis palustris* Huds.), it appears that very low rates can be applied to putting greens contaminated with annual bluegrass and seedhead suppression can be accomplished without significant injury to the bentgrass. Mefluidide is routinely used for growth control around markers in highly maintained cemeteries without decreasing quality any more than a common line trimmer.

Type II growth regulators (paclobutrazol and flurprimidol) have been used successfully on golf course fairways to reduce annual bluegrass and increase cover of more desirable species, particularly creeping bentgrass (Shoop et al., 1986). Although creeping bentgrass is suppressed in vertical foliar development, stolon growth continues after treatment. Flurprimidol has also been shown to have some preemergence activity on both annual bluegrass and creeping bentgrass (Gaussoin & Branham, 1987), thus potentially limiting bentgrass overseeding at or near treatment time when rates of 0.56 kg ha^{-1} or greater are used. Conversely, growth of annual bluegrass is severely suppressed. This differential growth suppression of a species in a mixed grass stand provides the golf course superintendent with a unique tool with which to manipulate plant competition.

The use of growth regulators on class A areas will probably remain specialized. Very little loss of aesthetic quality can be tolerated, and the need to maintain recuperative potential will always be paramount. Obviously, class A areas receive substantial recreational use and wear tolerance of chemically suppressed turf is not desirable (Brueninger & Watschke, 1982).

Both Type I and II growth regulators can be used on areas that Kaufmann (1986a) classified as class B. However, with the exception of most industrial grounds and cemeteries, the other examples of class B areas receive too much traffic. Brueninger and Watschke (1982) found that regardless of the PGR type used, treated golf course roughs did not tolerate traffic as well as that of nontreated areas. This study demonstrated the importance of being able to antidote the growth-suppressing properties of type II chemicals with applications of gibberellins.

Class C turf, since it is usually only mowed two or three times per year and is rarely abused through use, is that class of turf where growth regulators have been used most widely and successfully. The most commonly treated area in class C is turf grown along highways.

Grass species provide a relatively fast, easy, and inexpensive means to vegetatively prevent soil erosion and stabilize roadbanks. The low growth habit of grass species provides for safe, unobstructed recovery zones adjacent to lanes of travel. Turf also provides a natural, esthetically pleasing landscape for motorists.

In the 1950s, the U.S. highway system began to evolve into what is now the U.S. Interstate highway system. During this time, right-of-way passages were expanded from 20.1 m to at least 91.4 m, with median strips of variable width (Young & Hatten, 1983). In 1979, it was estimated that upon completion of the national system of interstate and scenic highways, more than 400 000 ha would be added to the existing 1 million ha of roadside areas. Newly constructed right-of-way areas are between 60 and 75% unpaved. These exposed areas of soil should immediately be stabilized vegetatively to prevent soil erosion. Roadside vegetation that is not established or maintained properly can lead to premature highway deterioration (Baker, 1983).

Gilbert (1969) described the environment of the roadside and the many unfavorable conditions that endogenous species could encounter. These conditions would include the following: "poorer growing media, heavy surface flows of water from the roadway, concentrations of (deicing) salt, concentrations of wet snow resulting in ice sheets and smothering, rapid and extreme changes in temperature resulting from nearness of surfaced areas, and high and variable winds from passing vehicles." Numerous micro-ecosystems typifying roadsides merit sowing of diverse grass species so that one or more components of the mix will survive the situations encountered (Duell et al., 1977).

Tall fescue is the most widely adapted cool-season turfgrass and seed is relatively inexpensive and germinates quickly (DiPaola et al., 1985). Hence, tall fescue has been established in many locations in the USA to stabilize roadbanks and enhance the overall safety and aesthetics of highway right-of-ways (Buckner & Bush, 1979).

Once tall fescue is established, vegetative bud regeneration can perpetuate the turf stand indefinitely (Buckner & Bush, 1979). Thus, maintenance requirements are minimal with mowing being the only procedure performed on an annual basis. Unfortunately, tall fescue can exhibit vigorous foliar growth (especially in the spring) and it is capable of producing an abundance of seedheads, thus possessing some undesirable traits for low maintenance roadside situations. Kaufmann (1986a) stated that cool-season grasses produce up to one-half their total annual foliar growth during a 6-wk period in the spring.

Tall fescue has a tough, wide blade that contributes to excessive mowing energy costs (Baker,1983). Elkins (1974) stated that it may require two or more mowings for removal of grass seedheads, which are unsightly and can obstruct motorists' vision. The number of additional mowings required for a given site varies with stand vigor, density, and growth habit of invading woody and herbaceous species, and its proximity to urban areas where higher esthetic standards are desired. Though of limited acreage, these higher maintenance areas may require up to 12 annual mowings (Elkins, 1974).

Due to the obvious suitability fit for growth regulator use along roadsides, considerable research has been conducted which has led to the adoption of management strategies involving their use in many states. Although Type I and Herbicide I, and Type II PGRs can all be used on class C areas, herbicide Type I have an extremely narrow rate range, and thus, a narrow margin of safety. Many different combinations of growth regulator types have been evaluated on roadsides with varying degrees of success. Currently, no chemical possesses all the attributes required to be a panacea growth regulator for roadsides. The seedhead suppressing characteristics of Type I PGRs are needed, the longevity and tiller stimulation characteristics of Type II PGRs are needed, and the weed control characteristics of herbicide Type I PGRs are desirable. As a result, researchers are currently evaluating combinations of growth regulator types, and herbicide tank mixes that provide seedhead and growth suppression, weed control, and minimal injury.

The addition of broadleaf herbicides to any given growth regulator application has been recommended by numerous researchers. Many growth regulators have little to no efficacy on broadleaf species whose uninhibited growth is quite noticeable as they extend beyond the suppressed canopy (Chappell, 1983; Chappell & Hipkins, 1982; Elkins et al., 1974; Farwell, 1986; Foote & Himmelman, 1971, 1967; Jagschitz et al., 1978; Stich et al., 1978; White et al., 1970; Willis & Yemm, 1966). Morre (1981) concluded that seasonal mowings for the state of Indiana could be reduced from five to three with a cost savings of $300 000 per year, solely through proper weed management. He found consecutive fall-spring applications of 2,4-D significantly reduced annual, biennial, and perennial broadleaf weeds. Late germinating weeds can also become a problem later in the season. Though cost effectiveness associated with chemical growth suppression would be reduced, this situation could be resolved for annual grassy weeds (and some broadleaf species) through the addition of a preemergence herbicide (Morre & Tautvydas, 1986).

Some growth regulators (e.g., chlorflurenol, flurprimidol, and paclobutrazol) possess the ability to not only suppress the growth of grass, but also the growth of broadleaf species within the treated sward (Welterlen, 1984; Elkins, 1983; Murray & Klingman, 1983; Shearing & Batch, 1982). Sulfonyl urea herbicides can also act as grass growth retardants while controlling broadleaf and some grassy weeds (Kaufmann, 1986b). Hence, successful chemical vegetation management and improved sward appearance would be realized through reduced mowing and weed control (Stich et al., 1978).

The growth supression of warm-season grasses along roadsides is best accomplished by the use of herbicide Type I chemicals. Warm-season grasses have shown considerably better tolerance than cool-season grasses to these materials.

Class D areas most commonly treated with herbicide Type I growth regulators as total vegetation control is often the objective. In such cases, bare ground can be acceptable, at least for a period of time. Ideally, vegetation control of class D areas should not result in the movement of the chemical used to surrounding sites.

V. PLANT GROWTH REGULATOR RESEARCH IN TURFGRASS MANAGEMENT

A. Emphasis Based on Projected Use

Most of the research on PGRs in academic situations is conducted with the ultimate user in mind. Therefore, two broad categories of research have evolved; determining the utility of PGRs for use in areas of low maintenance (primarily roadsides and similar situations), and determining the utility of PGRs for use in fine turf (primarily home lawns and golf courses).

In either category, the term utility is meant to include the more common forms of PGR evaluation; seedhead suppression, phytotoxicity, growth suppression, timing of application, and regrowth, but also includes the evaluation of the impact of other management factors, such as pest control and fertility. Occasionally, PGR research is conducted to evaluate the effects of traffic, method of application, and compatibility with other chemicals. In-depth research on morphological responses, stand conversions in mixed populations, and physiological-metabolic responses to PGR applications has not been persued extensively. Research on PGR effects on photosynthesis, respiration, transpiration, carbohydrate partitioning, and other physiological responses is beginning to be published more frequently, and continued emphasis is required to bring a much better understanding of plant-PGR responses. As more is published and research is continued, the full utility of existing PGR chemistry can be realized.

Little early chemical screening research is conducted at universities. Generally, screening is conducted in the industry sector, with university cooperators becoming involved after promising compounds have been identified in the greenhouse. Sometimes, a year of field evaluation "in-house" by industry is also conducted before releasing the compound to university cooperators. Consequently, the more basic research associated with chemical development is conducted primarily by scientists in industry rather than academia.

Another area of research that is conducted by scientists in industry and academia is to determine the utility of older chemistry in combination with new. More often than not, combining chemistry has led to synergistic responses that are confusing, frustrating, and can take months or years to sort out.

As the number of scientists involved in PGR research continue to grow and industry emphasis continues to be in development of new compounds, the opportunity to conduct meaningful PGR research in turfgrass science will grow regardless of the setting.

B. Emphasis Based on Chemical Development

Most agrichemical companies have discovery groups that identify PGRs. Since 1975, more new compounds have been released for evaluation than at any other time. As more ways are developed to suppress plant growth, the synthesis of new compounds will continue to be supported. As researchers develop management strategies that can accommodate certain types of compounds, their commercial utility will grow.

Much has been written about the attributes of the "ideal" growth regulator for turf, but the practicality of synthesizing such a compound is extremely difficult. Consequently, chemistry must be fitted to use. For example, it is not necessary to interrupt the biosynthesis of gibberellin if the intent is to suppress seedhead development. Synthesis of new compounds will be targeted toward attaining specific plant responses for use with particular management situations. The challenge for turfgrass researchers will be to develop those management systems that best use PGRs. To accomplish such a task may require innovative changes in traditional management practices. However, the potential for PGRs to provide a net gain in the overall quality of turfgrass sites exists, and as chemicals continue to be developed research will find the best solutions for their use.

C. Evaluation, Interpretation, and Publication

Over time, the techniques used to evaluate PGRs in turfgrass science have evolved and certain of them are widely accepted. Most scientists evaluate seedhead suppression using visual estimates, while some record seedhead numbers; both methods have been published. Vertical growth is commonly measured by several methods involving a ruler or other incremental device. Generally, a lightweight disc of various types fitted around a graduated rod have been used. The disc is dropped down the rod and comes to rest on top of the turf canopy for which the height is being determined. Regardless of method, there has been excellent concurrence among researchers as to which rates and formulations of particular compounds suppress growth more than others. The most significant problem associated with height measurements appears to be interference by seedheads when the measurement is being taken. A clear definition of parameter being measured must always be made, such as distinguishing between canopy height and seedhead height.

Quality or appearance ratings are subjective and are made up of several components. Therefore, most researchers are now using a rating system that includes all of the components that go into the final quality score. By presenting or publishing results in such a manner, confusion can be eliminated as to why a particular numerical rating has been assigned to a treatment at any given time during the evaluation period. For example, if the presence of seedheads causes the appearance of the stand to be rated low for quality (as is often the case for the untreated control) then the fact that seedheads are responsible for the low rating should be known. In the same experiment, a chemical treatment may be causing discoloration, which could result in the same numerical quality rating as the control, but for a different reason.

A uniform system for evaluating and reporting phytotoxicity is needed. The injury resulting from application of PGRs is usually described as leaf tip die-back, discoloration of leaf blades, or thinning. Much of the time, individual compounds will differ in the type of injury that they cause. The exact nature of the injury must be reported and any reference to thinning must include data for stand density or cover before and after PGR treatment. Too often, a compound is identified as one that thins the turf (an observation made by comparing treated vs. nontreated turf). If the compound significantly suppresses growth (particularly tillering) then the nontreated sward will appear denser over time, but the compound did not thin the stand that was present at application. The fact that tillering has been suppressed should not be considered ideal, but to report that a treatment "thinned the turf" is incorrect in the example cited.

Evaluation of disease incidence in PGR-treated turf is generally made and reported in a consistent manner. Leaf-blighting diseases are usually the most troublesome on PGR-treated turf. When growth is suppressed, new leaves cannot emerge to "heal" the stand and disease severity appears worse than where PGRs were not used. A visual reduction in turf color in treated vs. nontreated turf appears to be the most practical method of determining whether a PGR actually enhanced disease injury. Rating a diseased, PGR-treated sward lower than untreated turf for overall appearance is a result of the inability of suppressed turf to rapidly replace injured leaves with new foliage.

Encroachment by weeds is somewhat more difficult to interpret. Obviously, plant competition plays a significant role in weed invasion and therefore, turfgrass treated with a PGR is less able to compete. As reported earlier in this chapter, plant competition may also be successfully manipulated through the use of PGRs (creeping bentgrass vs. annual bluegrass). Generally, Type I PGRs have little impact on the germination or growth of most weeds. Therefore, annual grasses readily invade treated turf and cause the quality of the stand to decrease more than untreated turf where competition has not been affected. Competition by broadleaf weeds is also enhanced when the stand has been treated with a Type I PGR. Interpretation of the efficacy of preemergence herbicides used in conjunction with Type I PGRs must take into consideration the role that plant competition plays in untreated plots. The same interpretation difficulty can occur when evaluating the efficacy of broadleaf weed control materials.

Basic research projects in turf involving PGRs generally employ standardized techniques. Measurement of various physiological parameters (Photosynthesis, respiration, and transpiration) of PGR-treated plants requires a precision that can best be accommodated with sophisticated instrumentation. This commonality ensures that results can be reproduced from location to location. Reproducibility is further enhanced by the fact that the most basic PGR research is conducted in controlled environments.

D. Future Research

The potential for PGR use is significant and as more diverse chemistry is developed and as management strategies are devised that accommodate their use, they will become more universely accepted as management tools. Therefore, future PGR research in turfgrass science will be very broadly based. The necessity for applied, consumer-oriented evaluation type research will continue. Emphasis will be placed on "fitting" PGRs into existing management programs and to develop new and innovative management programs that focus on the utility of PGRs. Future research must resolve the pest management problems that continue to constrain PGR use, particularly disease and weed control. As new chemistry is developed the trend appears to be the synthesis of low dose, high activity compounds that will require additional research in the area of delivery system technology. Future emphasis should also be placed on more basic research to provide the fundamental understanding of plant response so that interpretation of growth responses can be enhanced.

For the foreseeable future, industry and academia appear to be committed to allocating significant resources to PGR research. Interest at the graduate level continues to be strong, which will ensure a continuity of emphasis and effort in the years ahead.

REFERENCES

Anonymous. 1983. Embark 2-S. Plant growth regulator. Customer Product Performance Manual. Agricultural products/3M, St. Paul.

Baker, R.F. 1983. Roadside vegetation: Implementation of fine fescue grasses. Transp. Res. Rec. 913:23–28.

Barrett, J.E., and C.A. Bartuska. 1982. PP-333 effects on the stem elongation dependent on site of application. HortScience 17:737–738.

Batten, S.M. 1983. Growth regulators — New tools for the '80's? USGA Green Sec. Rec. 21(3):1–3.

Beard, J.B. 1973. Turfgrass: Science and culture. Prentice-Hall, Englewood Cliffs, NJ.

Beard, J.B. 1985. Effect of growth regulators on turf. Grounds Maint. 20(6):66.

Bhowmik, P.C. 1984. Effects of growth retardants on turfgrass. Proc. NEWSS 38:315–320.

Bhowmik, P.C. 1985. Duration of turfgrass growth suppression with growth retardants. Proc. NEWSS 39:266.

Bhowmik, P.C. 1987a. Response of three cool-season turfgrass species to ACP-1900. Proc. Plant Growth Regul. Soc. Am. 11:341–346.

Bhowmik, P.C. 1987b. Response of a red fescue—Kentucky bluegrass turf to three consecutive annual applications of amidochlor, mefluidide, and ethephon. Weed Sci. 35:95–98.

Billott, C., and A. Hentgen. 1974. Effect of growth regulators on certain turfgrasses. p. 463–473. In E.C. Roberts (ed.) Proc. 2nd Int. Turfgrass Res. Conf., Blacksburg, VA. 19–21 June 1973. ASA and CSSA, Madison, WI.

Boeker, P. 1970. Growth control. p. 464–468. In J.R. Escritt (ed.) Proc. 1st Int. Turfgrass Res. Conf., Harrogate, England. 15–18 July 1969. Sports Turf Res. Inst., Bingley, England.

Branham, B.E., and K.U. Hanson. 1986. Effects of synthetic plant growth regulators on carbohydrate partitioning in Kentucky bluegrass. Proc. Plant Growth Regul. Soc. Am. 10:224.

Brede, A.D. 1984. Plant growth regulators on bermudagrass turf. Proc. South. Weed Sci. Soc. 37:271.

Brenner, L.K., C. Garbacik, and R.D. Williams. 1985. Chemical mowing with postemergence herbicides-1984. p. 19–22. In L. Brundage and R.D. William (ed.) Living mulch report. Oregon State Univ., Corvallis.

Brueninger, J.M. 1984. Growth regulation of cool season turfgrass. Ph.D. thesis. The Pennsylvania State Univ., University Park.

Breuninger, J.M., and T.L. Watschke. 1982. Effects of growth retardants, traffic, and nitrogen on fine fescue. p. 139. In Agronomy abstracts. ASA, Madison, WI.

Breuninger, J.M., T.L. Watschke, and L.D. Tukey. 1983. Effect of PP-333 and flurprimidol (EL-500) on tall fescue in an apple orchard. Pros. NEWSS 37:372–375.

Brundage, L., and R.D. William. 1985. Chemical mowing with postemergence herbicides-1985. p. 23–24. In L. Brundage and R.D. William (ed.) Living mulch report. Oregon State Univ., Corvallis.

Buettner, M.R., R.D. Ensign, and A.A. Boe. 1976. Plant growth regulator effects on flowering of Poa pratensis L. under field conditions. Agron. J. 68:410–413.

Carrow, R.N., and B.J. Johnson. 1990. Response of centipedegrass to plant growth regulator and iron treatment combinations. Appl. Agric. Res. 5(1):21–26.

Chailakhyan, M.K. 1968. Biochemistry and physiology of plant growth substances. The Runge Press, Ottawa, ON.

Chappell, W.E. 1983. Eptam as a growth inhibitor. Grounds Maint. 18(4):94.

Chappell, W.E. 1985. Effect of EPTC (S-ethyl dipropyl thiocarbamate) on seed formation in *Festuca arundinacea*. p. 745–747. *In* F. Lemaire (ed.) Proc. 5th Int. Turfgrass Res. Conf., Avignon, France. 1–5 July. Inst. Natl. de la Recherche Agron., Paris.

Chappell, W.E., J.S. Coartney, and M.L. Link. 1977. Plant growth regulators for highway maintenance. Proc. South. Weed Sci. Soc. 30:300–305.

Chappell, W.E., and P.L. Hipkins. 1982. Further studies on grass seedhead inhibition with EPTC and other growth inhibitors. Proc. South. Weed Sci. Soc. 35:266.

Christians, N.E. 1985. Response of Kentucky bluegrass to four growth retardants. J. Am. Hortic. Sci. 110:765–769.

Christians, N.E., and J. Nan. 1984. Growth retardant effects on three turfgrass species. J. Am. Hortic. Sci. 109:45–47.

Cooper, R.J., A.J. Koski, J.R. Street, and P.R. Henderlong. 1985. Influence of spring mefluidide on the carbohydrate status of *Poa annua* L. p. 115. *In* Agronomy abstracts. ASA, Madison, WI.

Cooper, R.J., P.R. Henderlong, J.R. Street, and K.J. Karnok. 1987. Root growth, seedhead production, and quality of annual bluegrass as affected by mefluidide and a wetting agent. Agron. J. 79:929–934.

Dalziel, J., and D.K. Lawrence. 1984. Biochemical effects of kaurene oxidase inhibitors, such as paclobutrazol. Monogr. 11. Br. Plant Growth Regulator Group.

Danneberger, T.K., B.E. Branham, and J.M. Vargas. 1987. Mefluidide applications for annual bluegrass seedhead suppression based on degree-day accumulation. Agron. J. 79:69–71.

Danneberger, T.K., and J.R. Street. 1986. PGR's for highway turf. Weeds, Trees Turf 25(6):40.

Deal, D.L., Jr. 1983. Common bermudagrass growth, dormancy, winter hardiness, and spring green-up following selected GA$_3$ and growth retardant applications. M.S. thesis. North Carolina State Univ., Raleigh.

Dernoeden. P.H. 1982. Effects of growth retardants applied three successive years to a Kentucky bluegrass turf. Proc. NEWSS 36:336–343.

Dernoeden, P.H. 1984. Four-year response of a Kentucky bluegrass-red fescue turf to plant growth retardants. Agron. J. 76:807–813.

Dernoeden, P.H., and D.J. Wehner. 1981. Effects of a reapplication of growth retardants in a two year study on Kentucky bluegrass. Proc. NEWSS 35:312–321.

Dickens, R., and D.L. Turner. 1984. Suppression of inflorescence development in tall fescue. p. 149. *In* Agronomy abstracts. ASA, Madison, WI.

DiPaola, J.M. 1987. Plant growth regulators. Lawn Servic. 4:18–22.

DiPaola, J.M., W.B. Gilbert, and W.M. Lewis. 1983. Tall fescue response to growth retardant treatment as influenced by inflorescence development. p. 125. *In* Agronomy abstracts. ASA, Madison, WI.

DiPaola, J.M., W.B. Gilbert, and W.M. Lewis. 1984a. Growth retardant phytotoxicity and shoot inhibition on immature tall fescue. p. 150. *In* Agronomy abstracts. ASA, Madison, WI.

DiPaola, J.M., W.B. Gilbert, and W.M. Lewis. 1985. Selection, establishment, and maintenance of vegetation along North Carolina's roadsides. Final Report to North Carolina Dep. of Transportation.

DiPaola, J.M., W.M. Lewis, and W.B. Gilbert. 1984b. Tall fescue and bahiagrass growth regulator trials. Crop Sci. Dep., Raleigh, NC, Res. Rep. 100.

DiPaola, J.M., W.M. Lewis, and W.B. Grant. 1984c. Roadside growth retardant research update. Proc. 23rd Ann. North Carolina Turfgrass Conf.

Donald, W.W. 1981. EPTC effects in the lettuce (*Lactuca sativa*) hypocotyl bioassay for gibberellins. Weed Sci. 29:490–499.

Donald, W.W., R.S. Fawcett, and R.G. Harvey. 1979. EPTC effects on corn (*Zea mays*) growth and endogenous gibberellins. Weed Sci. 27:122–127.

Doyle, J.M., and R.C. Shearman. 1985. Plant growth regulator effects on evapotranspiration of Kentucky bluegrass turf. p. 115. *In* Agronomy abstracts. ASA, Madison, WI.

Duell, R.W. 1980. Responses of turfgrasses to chemical retardants and other management factors. Proc. NEWSS 34:381.

Duell, R.W. 1985. Turfgrass quality and phytotoxicity affected by growth retardants. p. 749–751. *In* F. Lemaire (ed.) Proc. 5th Int. Turfgrass Conf., Avignon, France. 1–5 July. Inst. Natl. de la Recherche Agron., Paris.

Duell, R.W., R.M. Schmitt, and S.W. Cosky. 1977. Growth retardant effects on grasses for roadsides. p. 311–323. *In* J.B. Beard (ed.) Proc. 3rd Int. Turfgrass Res. Conf., Munich, Germany. 11–13 July. Int. Turfgrass Soc., ASA, CSSA, and SSSA, Madison, WI.

Elkins, D.M. 1974. Chemical suppression of tall fescue seedhead development and growth. Agron. J. 66:426–429.

Elkins, D.M. 1983. Growth regulating chemicals for turf and other grasses. *In* L.G. Nickell (ed.) Plant growth regulating chemicals, Vol. II. CRC Press, Boca Raton, FL.

Elkins, D.M., and T.L. Kitowski. 1972. Chemical growth retardants may eliminate the need for mowing. Crops Soils 24:12–13.

Elkins, D.M., and D.L. Suttner. 1974. Chemical regulation of grass growth. I. Field and greenhouse studies with tall fescue. Agron. J. 66:487–491.

Elkins, D.M., J.A. Tweedy, and D.L. Suttner. 1974. Chemical regulation of grass growth. II. Greenhouse and field studies with intensively managed turfgrasses. Agron. J. 66:492–497.

Elkins, D.M., J.W. Vandeventer, and M.A. Briskovich. 1977. Effect of growth retardants on turfgrass morphology. Agron. J. 69:458–461.

Facteau, T., D. Burkhart, and R. McAllister. 1985. Chemical mowing of Mid-Columbia orchardgrass-1985. p. 26. *In* L. Brundage and R.D. William (ed.) Living mulch report. Oregon State Univ., Corvallis.

Fales, S.L., A.P. Nielson, and R.C. Wakefield. 1976. Top growth and root growth response of red fescue to growth retardants. Proc. NEWSS 30:334–339.

Farwell, B.J. 1986. The suppression of seedhead formation in tall fescue with EPTC. Proc. NEWSS 40:127.

Field, R.J. 1983. The chemical retardation of grass growth. Outlooks Agric. 12(3):111–118.

Field, R.S., and A.R. Whitford. 1982. Effect of simulated mowing on the translocation of mefluidide in perennial ryegrass (*Lolium perenne* L.) Weed Res. 22:177–181.

Flanagan, M.S., and C.H. Peacock. 1986. Effects of plant growth regulators on bahiagrass. Fl. Tech. Res. Bull. 1986:67–72.

Foote, L.E., and B.E. Himmelman. 1967. Vegetation control along fence lines with maleic hydrazide. Weed Sci. 15:38–41.

Foote, L.E., and B.E. Himmelman. 1971. Maleic hydrazide as a roadside grass retardant. Weed Sci. 19:86–90.

Freeborg, R.P. 1979. Need for growth regulators accentuated by rising costs. Weeds, Trees Turf 18(8):25.

Freeborg, R.P. 1983. Growth regulators. Weeds, Trees Turf 21(6):46.

Freeborg, R.P., and W.H. Daniel. 1981. Growth regulation of *Poa pratensis* L. p. 477–486. *In* R.W. Sheard (ed.) Proc. 4th Int. Turfgrass Res. Conf., Guelph, ON, Canada. 19–23 July. Int. Turfgrass Soc., Ontario Agric. Coll., Univ. of Guelph, Guelph, ON.

Gaussoin, R.E., and B.E. Branham. 1987. Annual bluegrass and creeping bentgrass germination response to flurprimidol. HortScience 23:441–442.

Gilbert, W.B. 1969. Turfgrass establishment on roadsides. p. 583–591. *In* Proc. 1st Int. Turfgrass Res. Conf., Harrogate, England. 15–18 July. Sports Turf Res. Inst., Bingley, England.

Gonzales, F.E., R.L. Atkins, and G.C. Brown. 1984. Sultometuron methyl, rate and timing studies on bermudagrass and bahiagrass roadside turf. Proc. South. Weed Soc. 37:272–274.

Hagman, J. 1983. Double-edged sword. Weeds, Trees Turf 22(6):52–54.

Hield, H., S. Hemstreet, V.A. Gibeault, and V.B. Youngner. 1979. Warm season turf growth control with Embark. Calif. Agric. 33:15–16.

Hurto, K.A. 1981. Effects of EL-500 on a Kentucky bluegrass: Red fescue turf. Proc. NEWSS 35:331–335.

Jagschitz, J.A. 1976. Response of Kentucky bluegrass to growth retardant chemicals. Proc. NEWSS 30:327–333.

Jagschitz, J.A., J.D. Stich, and R.C. Wakefield. 1978. Effect of growth retardants on cool-season lawngrasses. Proc. NEWSS 32:318.

Johnson, B.J. 1988. Influence of nitrogen on the response of 'Tifway' bermudagrass (*Cynodon dactylon* to flurprimidol). Weed Technol. 2:53–58.

Johnson, B.J. 1989. Response of tall fescue (*Festuca arundinacea*) to plant growth regulator application dates. Weed Technol. 3:408–413.

Johnson, W.D. 1981. Chemical roadside vegetation management program in North Carolina. Trans. Res. Rec. 805:20–21.

Johnston, D.T., and J.S. Faulkner. 1985. The effects of growth retardants on swards of normal and dwarf cultivars of red fescue. J. Sports Turf Res. Inst. 61:59–64.

Kaufmann, J.E. 1986a. Growth regulators for turf. Grounds Maint. 21(5):72.

Kaufmann, J.E. 1986b. The role of PGR science in chemical vegetation control. Proc. Plant Growth Regul. Soc. Am. 13:2–14.

Kaufmann, J.E., J.J. Sandbrink, and S.J. Stehling. 1984. Chemical regulation of the annual life-cycle of perennial cool-season grasses. p. 152. *In* Agronomy abstracts. ASA, Madison, WI.

Kaufmann, J.E., J.J. Sandbrink, S.J. Stehling, and P.S. Thibodeau. 1983. Efficacy of six plant growth regulators on Michigan roadside grasses. p. 128. *In* Agronomy abstracts. ASA, Madison, WI.

King, J.W., and J.N. Rogers, III. 1986. Bermudagrass growth suppression with sulfomefuron methyl and metsulfuron methyl. Arkansas Farm Res. 35:4.

Kretzmer, K.A., and J.E. Kaufmann. 1985. The effect of limit growth regulator on several growth parameters of three cool-season turfgrasses. p. 118. *In* Agronomy abstracts. ASA, Madison, WI.

Landers, R.Q. 1981. Management of roadside vegetation: Some principles from range science. Transp. Res. Rec. 805:20–21.

Larocque, D.J., and N.E. Christians. 1985. Selective control of tall fescue in Kentucky bluegrass with chlorsulfuron. Agron. J. 77:86–89.

Lewis, W.M., J.M. DiPaola, A.H. Bruneau, and W.B. Gilbert. 1987. Regulation of turfgrass seedheads along roadsides. Proc. Plant Growth Regul. Soc. Am. 11:384.

Lewis, W.M., J.M. DiPaola, W.B. Gilbert, and A.H. Bruneau. 1985. Growth retardant evaluations on tall fescue and bahiagrass roadsides. p. 118. *In* Agronomy abstracts. ASA, Madison, WI.

Link, M.L., and R.L. Atkins. 1983. Control and suppression of warm season grasses to reduce mowing on highway rights-of-way. Proc. South. Weed Sci. Soc. 36:310–312.

Link, M.L., W.E. Chappell, P.L. Hipkins, and D.S. Ross. 1981. The use of growth inhibitors for seedhead inhibition in rough turf in 1979. Proc. South Weed Sci. Soc. 34:215–220.

Maloy, B.M., and N.E. Christians. 1985. Effect of chlorsulfuron on several cool-season grasses. p. 118. *In* Agronomy abstracts. ASA, Madison, WI.

Maloy, B.M., and N.E. Christians. 1986. Tolerance of tall fescue and Kentucky bluegrass to chlorsulfuron under field conditions. Weed Sci. 34:431–434.

Mathias, E.L., O.L. Bennett, G.A. Jung, and P.E. Lundberg. 1971. Effects of two growth regulating chemicals on yield and water use of three perennial grasses. Agron. J. 63:480–483.

McCarty, L.B., J.M. DiPaola, W.M. lewis, and W.B. Gilbert. 1985. Tall fescue response to plant growth retardants and fertilizer sources. Agron. J. 77:476–480.

McElroy, M.T. 1984. Evaluation of selected plant growth regulators for use on highway roadside turfs. M.S. thesis. Dep. of Agron., Michigan State Univ., Ann Arbor.

McElroy, M.T., P.E. Rieke, S.L. McBurney, and J.E. Kaufmann. 1983. Efficacy of six plant growth regulators on Michigan roadside grasses. p. 128. *In* Agronomy abstracts. ASA, Madison, WI.

McWhorter, C.G., and G.D. Wills. 1978. Factors affecting translocation of 14-C mefluidide in soybeans (*Glycine max*), common cocklebur (*Xanthium pensylvanicum*) and johnsongrass (*Sorghum halepense*). Weed Sci. 26:382–388.

Morre, D.J. 1981. Influence of research and development on roadside management. Transport. Res. Rec. 805:11.

Morre, D.J. 1983. New program of chemical mowing along Indiana roadsides. Transport. Res. Rec. 913:16–18.

Morre, D.J., and K.J. Tautvydas. 1986. Mefluidide, chlorsulfuron, 2,4-D, surfactant combinations for roadside vegetation management. J. Plant Growth Regul. 4:189–201.

Murray, J.J., and D.L. Klingman. 1983. Growth regulators, nitrogen levels, and herbicides on turf. Proc. NEWSS 37:371.

Naylor, A.W., and E.A. Davis. 1950. Maleic hydrazide as a plant growth regulator. Bot. Gaz. 112:112–126.

Nielson, A.P., and R.C. Wakefield. 1975. Effects of growth retardants on the top growth and root growth of turfgrasses. Proc. NEWSS 29:403–408.

Parups, E.V., and W.E. Cordukes. 1977. Growth of turfgrasses as affected by Atrinal and Embark. HortScience 17:737–738.

Pennucci, A., and J.A. Jagschitz. 1985. The effect of growth retardants on four lawn grasses. Proc. NEWSS 39:260–265.

Petrovic, A.M., R.A. White, and M. klingerman. 1985. Annual bluegrass growth and quality as influenced by treatments of growth retardants and wetting agents. Agron. J. 77:670.

Prinster, M.G. 1987. Chemical growth regulation of tall fescue (*Festuca arundinacea* Schreb.) on Pennsylvania roadsides. M.S. thesis. Agronomy Dep., The Pennsylvania State Univ., Univesity Park.

Prinster, M.G., and T.L. Watschke. 1986. Effects of growth regulators on tall fescue. Proc. NEWSS 40:126.

Regan, R., and R.D. Williams. 1985. Chemical suppression of a perennial ryegrass in nursery stock. p. 27-28. *In* L. Brundage and R.D. Williams (ed.) Living mulch report. Oregon State Univ., Corvallis.

Rogers, III, J.N., E.M. Miller, and J.W. King. 1987. Growth retardation of bermudagrass and metsulfuron methyl and sulfometuron methyl. Agron. J. 79:225-229.

Rosemond, J.M., D.D. Baird, and C.G. Erickson. 1984. Plant growth suppression properties and potentials of glyphosate. *In* Agronomy abstracts. ASA, Madison, WI.

Ross, M.A., and C.A. Lembi. 1985. Applied weed science. Burgess Publ. Co., Minneapolis.

Sandbrink, J.J., J.E. Kaufmann, S.J. Stehling, and P.S. Thibodeau. 1983. Application timing of MON-4620 on cool-season grasses. p. 130. *In* Agronomy abstracts. ASA, Madison, WI.

Sawyer, C.D., and R.C. Wakefield. 1984. Timing of growth retardant application on a turfgrass mixture. Proc. NEWSS 38:309.

Sawyer, C.D., and R.C. Wakefield. 1985. Spring growth period for effective application of growth retardants on turf. Proc. NEWSS 39:267.

Sawyer, C.D., R.C. Wakefield, and J.A. Jagschitz. 1983. Evaluations of growth retardants for roadside turf. Proc. NEWSS 37:372-375.

Schmidt, R.E., and S.W. Bingham. 1977. Chemical growth regulation of 'Baron' Kentucky bluegrass. Agron. J. 69:995-1000.

Schott, P.E., H. Will, and H. Nolle. 1977. Turfgrass growth reduction by means of a new plant growth regulator. p. 325-328. *In* J.B. Beard (ed.) Proc. 3rd Int. Turfgrass Res. Conf., Munich, Germany. 11-13 July. Int. Turfgrass Soc., ASA, CSSA, and SSSA, Madison, WI.

Shearing, S.J., and S.J. Batch. 1979. PP-333 — Field trials to control growth of amenity grasses. p. 87-97. *In* D.R. Clifford and J.R. Lenton (ed.) Recent developments in the uses of plant growth retardants. Monogr. 4. British Plant Growth Regulator Group,

Shearing, S.J., and S.J. Batch. 1982. Amenity grass retardation — Some concepts challenged. p. 467-483. *In* J. McLaren (ed.) Chemical manipulation of crop growth and development. Butterworth Sci., London.

Shoop, G.J., R.H. Hoefer, and D.G. Ortega. 1986. Flurprimidol (EL-500) growth regulator effect on bentgrass fairways in the northeast. Proc. NEWSS 40:131.

Soper, K. 1958. Effects of flowering on the root system and summer survival of ryegrass. N.Z. J. Agric. Res. 33:329-340.

Stehling, S.J., J.E. Kaufmann, J.J. Sandbrink, and P.S. Thibodeau. 1983. Range of application rates on MON-4620 for efficacy, safety and uniform turfgrass response. p. 130. *In* Agronomy abstracts. ASA, Madison, WI.

Stich, J.D., R.C. Wakefield, and J.A. Jagschitz. 1978. Combinations of growth retardants and broadleaf herbicides for roadside turfgrasses. Proc. NEWSS 32:328-331.

Street, J.P. 1980. Growth regulators for turf — Selection and use. Grounds Maint. 15(4):16.

Symington, A.G., L.E. Craker, and K.A. Hurto. 1982. Comparison of growth retardants on Kentucky bluegrass. Proc. NEWSS 36:344.

Tautvydas, K.G. 1983. Synergistic growth retardation of grasses with mefluidide/PGR combinations. p. 51-56. *In* Proc. 10th Annu. PGRSA Meeting.

Truelove, B., D.E. Davis, and C.G. Pillai. 1977. Mefluidide effects on growth of corn (*Zea mays*) and the synthesis of protein by cucumber (*Cucumis sativas*) cotyledon tissue. Weed Sci. 25:360.

Turner, D.L., and R. Dickens. 1984. Sulfometuron-methyl tolerances in 'Pensacola' bahiagrass. Proc. South. Weed Sci. Soc. 37:275.

Wakefield, R.C., and A.T. Dore. 1974. Growth control for highway turf. p. 569-576. *In* E.C. Roberts (ed.) Proc. 2nd Int. Turfgrass Res. Conf., Blacksburg, VA. 19-21 June 1973. ASA and CSSA, Madison, WI.

Wakefield, R.C., and S.L. Fales. 1977. Effects of growth retardants on the shoot and root growth of roadside turfgrasses. p. 303-309. *In* J.B. Beard (ed.) Proc. 3rd Int. Turfgrass Res. Conf., Munich, Germany. 11-13 July. Int. Turfgrass Soc., ASA, CSSA, and SSSA, Madison, WI.

Warmund, M., C. Long, and J. Vesecky. 1980. Response of stressed turfgrass to growth regulators. North Central Weed Control Conf. 35:123-124.

Watschke, T.L. 1976. Growth regulation of Kentucky bluegrass with several growth retardants. Agron. J. 68:787-792.

Watschke, T.L. 1978. Growth retardation of tall fescue in a trellised apple orchard. Proc. NEWSS 32:318.

Watschke, T.L. 1979a. Effects of mefluidide and MH on tall fescue. Proc. NEWSS 33:320–323.

Watschke, T.L. 1979b. Growth retardation of 'Merion' and 'Pennstar' Kentucky bluegrass. Proc. NEWSS 33:303–307.

Watschke, T.L. 1979c. Penn State tests reveal growth regulator pros and cons. Weeds, Trees Turf 18(8):32.

Watschke, T.L. 1981. Effects of four growth retardants on two Kentucky bluegrasses. Proc. NEWSS 35:322–330.

Watschke, T.L. 1985. Turfgrass weed control and growth regulation. p. 63–80. *In* F. Lemaire (ed.) Proc. 5th Int. Turfgrass Res. Conf., Avignon, France. 1–5 July. Inst. Natl. de la Recherche Agron., Paris.

Watschke, T.L., D.V. Waddington, and C.L. Forth. 1975. Growth regulation of tall fescue. Proc. NEWSS 29:397–402.

Watschke, T.L., D.J. Wehner, and J.M. Duich. 1977. Initial and residual effects of growth regulators on a 'Pennstar'-'Fylking' Kentucky bluegrass blend. Proc. NEWSS 31:378–389.

Wehner, D.J. 1980. Growth regulation of Kentucky bluegrass and tall fescue. Proc. NEWSS 31:378–389.

Welterlen, M.S. 1984. Tall fescue growth and color responses to fall applied plant growth regulators and nitrogen. p. 150. *In* Agronomy abstracts. ASA, Madison, WI.

Welterlen, M.S., and A.S. Nash. 1984. Effects of MON-4621 and MON-4624 on Kentucky bluegrass and tall fescue turf. Proc. NEWSS 38:307–308.

White, D.B., D. Heng, T.B. Bailey, and L. Foote. 1970. Chemical regulation of growth in turfgrass. p. 481–497. *In* Proc. 1st Int. Turfgrass Res. Conf., Harrogate, England. 15–18 July 1969. Sports Turf Res. Inst., Bingley, England.

Wiles, L., and R.D. William. 1985. Grass suppression screening trials — 1984. p.15. *In* L. Brundage and R.D. William (ed.) Living mulch report. Oregon State Univ., Corvallis.

Wilkenson, R.E. 1982. Mefluidide inhibition of sorghum growth and gibberellin precursor biosynthesis. J. Plant Growth Regul. 1:85–94.

Wilkenson, R.E., and D. Ashley. 1979. EPTC induced modificaation of gibberellin biosynthesis. Weed Sci. 27:270–274.

Willis, A.J., and E.W. Yemm. 1966. Spraying of roadside verges: Long-term effect of 2,4-D and maleic hydrazide. Proc. Br. Weed Control Conf., 8th 2:505–510.

Weed Science Society of America. 1983. Herbicide handbook. Weed Sci. Soc. of Am., Champaign, IL.

Wu, C., H.R. Myers, P.W. Santelmann. 1976. Chemical retardation of bermudagrass turf. Agron. J. 68:949–952.

Young, H.E., and D.B. Hatton. 1983. Right-of-way forestry. Trans. Res. Rec. 913:14–16.

17 Field Research

C. RICHARD SKOGLEY AND CARL D. SAWYER

University of Rhode Island
Kingston, Rhode Island

Agronomist M. A. Carleton (1907) stated that "Agronomy as a science investigates anything and everything concerned with field crops and this investigation is supposed to be made in a most thorough manner, just as would be done in any other science." Ball (1916) noted that it has been necessary for experiments in agronomy to turn from the gross aspect to minute detail to solve some of its problems. He observed that empirical knowledge was being supplemented by fundamental information as a result of organized research and improvement in its techniques.

The design of field experiments and the proper interpretation of results have been of concern to agronomists for many years as both were recognized as being critical to research. Today, information on these subjects is voluminous, but not by chance. When the American Society of Agronomy (ASA) was founded in 1907, field research was still largely done in an empirical and primitive manner.

An early concern of the Society membership was the lack of standardization in experimental method. Within a few years of founding, a five-member committee of the society, chaired by A.T. Wiancko (1924), was named and charged with recommending standards for field experimentation. The committee report was presented at the annual meeting in 1923 and was published in 1924. The report contained recommended standards for field experiments dealing with both soil fertility and crop production.

Other agronomists made early contributions to improvement in field plot design (Worthen, 1928; Garber, 1931). We currently have excellent standards and procedures for performing and interpreting agronomic research as a result of these studies and those of many other agronomists and statisticians through the years. Examples of the continued emphasis on research methods are the chapters included in the ASA monograph *Methods of Soil Analysis, Part I, Physical and Mineralogical Methods*, (Dixon, 1986; Kempthorne & Allmaras, 1986; Petersen & Calvin, 1986), and papers published in agronomic and horticultural journals (e.g., Chew, 1976; Nelson & Rawlings, 1983).

While turfgrass is not a crop, as usually defined, the nature of research in the commodity is generally similar to that of other agronomic crops. The following discussion refers specifically to field research but is also applicable to greenhouse and laboratory trials. Turfgrass research experimental tech-

Copyright © 1992 ASA-CSSA-SSSA, 677 S. Segoe Rd., Madison, WI 53711, USA. *Turfgrass—Agronomy Monograph no. 32.*

niques have been refined and standardized by numerous investigators. The purpose of this chapter is to provide a brief general description of selected field research techniques with supporting references. We cannot provide detailed methodology for each technique within the scope of this chapter and the reader is referred to the references for specific details.

I. CHARACTERISTICS OF A WELL-PLANNED EXPERIMENT

Field plot design deals with the factors necessary for properly planned agricultural field experiments. These factors are: size, shape, and arrangement of plots as experimental units, together with the effects of the units on each other; the number of replications; the field layout of the experiment; and the method of statistical interpretation of data.

Little and Hills (1978) stated that "statistical science helps the researcher design his experiment and objectively evaluate the resulting numerical data." They presented three "R's" of experimentation.

1. *Replicate.* This is the only way you will be able to measure the validity of your conclusions from an experiment.
2. *Randomize.* Statistical analysis depends upon the assignment of treatments to plots in a purely objective, random manner.
3. *Request help.* Ask for help when in doubt about how to design, execute, or analyze an experiment.

These authors also listed several characteristics essential for proper experimental objectives. Among them are:

1. *Simplicity.* Keep the selection of treatments and the experimental arrangement as simple as possible, and consistent with experimental objectives.
2. *Degree of precision.* There should be a high degree of probability that the experiment will be able to measure treatment differences with the precision desired. An appropriate design with sufficient replication is implied.
3. *Absence of systematic error.* Planning must ensure that experimental units receiving one treatment differ in no systematic way from those receiving another treatment so unbiased estimates of each treatment effect can be obtained.
4. *Range of validity of conclusions.* Conclusions should have a wide range of validity. Repeating an experiment would increase the range of validity of conclusions that might be drawn. A factorial set of treatments is another way for increasing the range of validity of an experiment.
5. *Calculation of the degree of uncertainty.* All experiments have some degree of uncertainty as to the validity of conclusions. An experiment should be designed so it is possible to calculate the probability of obtaining the observed results by chance alone.

II. PROCEDURE FOR EXPERIMENTATION

Little and Hills (1978) also listed and described several considerations that should be carefully thought through to assure success in experimentation. Among the most important considerations were:

1. Definition of the problem.
2. Statement of objectives.
3. Selection of treatments.
4. Selection of experimental material.
5. Selection of experimental design.
6. Selection of the units for observations and the number of replications.
7. Control of the effects of the adjacent experimental units on each other.
8. Consideration of data to be collected.
9. Outlining statistical analysis and summarization of results.

In addition to these stated concerns for preparing a research project they provided good suggestions on the following:

1. Conducting the experiment.
2. Analyzing data and interpreting results.
3. Preparing a complete, readable, and correct report of the research.

III. FIELD EXPERIMENT CONSIDERATIONS

A. Site Selection

There are several important considerations when selecting a site for field experiments. The soil of the research site should be similar in texture, structure, and internal drainage to the local area, region, or state in which the research results would be used. The soil within the experimental location should be uniform in physical and chemical properties and have no recent history of unlike past cropping or management treatments. An area with a slight slope to permit good surface drainage is preferred. The area should be uniformly exposed to sunlight and wind and removed from the influence of other vegetation. Availability of irrigation is highly desirable for many types of research with turfgrasses.

B. Turf Establishment

Late summer and early autumn is generally the most efficient time to establish cool-season grasses on research areas. Warm-season grasses are generally established at the beginning of the growing season. The availability of irrigation will help to ensure rapid and uniform establishment with either type of grass.

Establishing plots, whether by seeding or vegetative methods, involves good soil preparation, adjustment of soil pH and fertility, if appropriate,

Fig. 17-1. Seeding small plots by hand. Care must be taken to distribute seed evenly over the entire plot, and prevent blowing or tracking of seed from one plot to the next.

and grading and firming the soil. A quality seedbed with a smooth, finished surface that permits uniform seed distribution is important. Use of a soil sterilant prior to seeding or vegetative establishment may prove beneficial. If weeds and normal soil microbial populations are desired, sterilants should not be used.

Small plot seeding is generally done by hand (Fig. 17-1). Individual grasses or mixtures are weighed, bagged, and numbered for each plot according to a field plan. Plots are seeded individually, ideally when there is little wind so that seed is not blown to adjacent plots. Light wooden or metal frames, made to plot size, with the sides and ends covered with plastic, can be used as wind screens when seeding.

Seeding may be done with carefully calibrated mechanical drop spreaders on large plot areas. Spreaders may be calibrated quite accurately with a box fabricated of metal, plastic, or other material, that is hung below the spreader gate. The spreader is filled with seed or other products to be calibrated, pushed for a measured distance, and the material in the box is collected and weighed. Spreader settings can be adjusted until the desired rate of seed or other material is determined. Alternatively, delivery rate can be determined for a range of spreader settings and a calibration curve constructed by plotting delivery rate vs. spreader setting. Walking speed affects application rate and should be monitored during treatment application.

C. Plot Size, Shape, and Marking

Plot size is a major consideration with field research although there are no standard dimensions. The nature of the data to be collected, the treatments to be imposed, and the maintenance equipment required or available for use are major factors governing size. In addition, the area available and the available labor and funding may influence plot size and number of treatments.

Turfgrasses are perennial plants and daily, weekly, or monthly management operations over a period of several years are generally required to obtain reliable research results. For these reasons, field research with turfgrasses is expensive. Detailed planning of plot size and experimental layout is necessary for developing the most efficient, yet productive experimental design.

A plot size of 1 by 2 m is frequently used for variety or mixture evaluation, fertilizer studies, and pesticide evaluations where subjective data such as quality score, color, and phytotoxicity are to be obtained. This plot size is often adequate even where objective evaluations are to be made. If plant or soil samples must be removed routinely, larger plots may be required.

Individual plots need not be separated from adjacent plots by borders. Plot integrity can be maintained if care is taken when establishing the plots and during treatment application. If plots must be separated, it can be done after establishment by periodic use of a power lawn edger or by banding a narrow strip between plots with a nonselective-type herbicide. Narrow bands of a contrasting, noncreeping grass, such as fine fescue (*Festuca* spp.) or perennial ryegrass (*Lolium perenne* L.) may be seeded between plots during trial establishment to maintain individual plot integrity. Depressions or bare ground between plots that could interfere with mowing or disrupt surface water movement must be avoided.

The overall plot outline or dimensions can be established after the seedbed has been prepared or following turfgrass establishment. Accurately located corners are variously marked and should be semipermanent, easy to locate, and unobtrusive to mowers and maintenance equipment. The simplest types are wood, plastic, or metal stakes. To maintain visibility of the corners, vegetation at the stake location can be controlled with a nonselective herbicide sprayed inside a coffee can with both ends removed. Pins at least 15 cm in length with thin, metallic, or plastic square plates or round discs secured to the top are frequently used. Concrete markers made in round quart oil containers and set in holes made with a putting green cup cutter make good corner markers.

Metal pins or large nails placed at the correct spacing around the circumference of the test area subdivide the experimental area into individual plots. Heavy string or twine run from end-to-end and side-to-side and secured to the pins or nails outlines the individual plots.

Plot marking can be similar to that for seeding new trials when cultural or pesticide studies are to be imposed on established grasses. If frequent applications are to be made on close-cut turf, grooves cut with an edger give a semipermanent outline. On higher-cut turf, various athletic field line painters can be used if the paint will not affect research results. These paints will last through several mowings.

D. Treatments and Maintenance

Treatment application is often made by hand to small, individual plots after accurately weighing or measuring the product to be applied. Jars with holes in the lids can be used for hand spreading. Small amounts of material insufficient for uniform hand application may be diluted with dry sand or other inert material of similar size and density. Liquids can be diluted with water and applied with a sprayer or sprinkling can.

The maintenance program should be planned prior to the initiation of the research trial. Mowing height and frequency should be established and the schedule maintained faithfully. Maintenance materials such as fertilizers, topdressings, and pesticides should be applied accurately, and rate and time of application documented. Dry materials are best applied with calibrated drop spreaders. Liquids may be applied as sprays using carefully calibrated sprayers.

If the area is to be irrigated, application should be scheduled to avoid moisture stress yet not be excessive. Soil moisture sensors such as tensiometers or moisture blocks may provide the best accuracy in determining water requirements.

E. Data Collection

Turfgrass stands are perennial and the quality of stand often changes from year to year depending on seasonal weather, management practices, and maturity. With many field experiments, treatments are not applied until the stands are fully developed. Data collection during the first growing season may be frequent if the objectives deal with factors such as seedling establishment rate or preemergence weed control. In variety evaluation, emphasis is often placed on characteristics of mature turf; however, rapidity of turf maturation also provides valuable information.

Stand and quality changes may be subtle, but over time the influence of management and environment on the turfgrass community can be major. It is widely agreed that experiment duration should be several years. Members of the Northeastern Turfgrass Research Committee consider 5 yr to be a minimum period for many experiments, particularly variety and mixture studies, soil modification trials, and most management experiments.

Frequency of evaluation or data collection will vary according to the nature of the experiment. The test protocol should indicate the planned frequency. In cultivar or species mixture trials, subjective measurements of turfgrass quality are perhaps the most frequently used evaluation. Quality ratings are commonly recorded at least once each month during the growing season. Ideally, this is done about the same date each month. Other data, such as winter color, spring green-up, disease incidence, and insect injury should be recorded at the appropriate time and may only be done once or a few times per season. Evaluations or measurements must be made as specified in the project plan.

IV. FIELD RESEARCH TECHNIQUES

A. Subjective Data

Turfgrass quality cannot be measured in the same manner as other agricultural crops. The quality of turfgrass verdure is not measured by yield, color, or nutritive value of fruit or forage. Rather, quality is a measure of aesthetic appeal, durability, density, ease of establishment and maintenance, and perhaps, longevity or hardiness. Resistance to or tolerance of diseases and insects is also a desirable quality of turfgrasses. The most widely used and accepted method of recording quality data is the visual quality rating system. This visual method of rating or scoring takes into consideration the color, density, and uniformity of a stand, or overall appeal, as judged by the evaluator. Turfgrass specialists working with various grasses routinely see wide ranges of quality from thin, open, off-color stands to vigorous, green, dense swards. One becomes aware of the very best stand possible for each of the various grasses and use situations that are under study. This top quality needs to be fixed in the mind of a researcher as it is upon this level that quality scoring is based.

The quality scale is generally based on the values nine to one with nine representing the very best possible rating a stand can receive while one would indicate a completely dead or dormant stand. Researchers have agreed to use only whole numbers when scoring turfgrass quality in national and regional research trials. This simplifies computer entry of the large amount of data generated in these trials. Many researchers use half-numbers when taking quality ratings for their own studies.

The visual method of taking various data on turfgrass quality has long been a subject of concern and discussion among turfgrass agronomists. The Northeastern Turfgrass Research Committee members, meeting once or twice annually since 1962, have demonstrated and agreed that subjective quality ratings are valid when taken by experienced researchers. At a June, 1975 Northeast Regional meeting, turfgrass researchers held a workshop on standardization of data collection. Each of 14 evaluators was assigned a code number before going to the field to rate quality, density, percent ground cover, color, and leaf spot on 14 entries in the 1972 regional Kentucky bluegrass (*Poa pratensis* L.) trial located at Beltsville, MD. Ground cover was rated on a scale of 0 to 100%. Other variables were rated using a 1 to 9 scale with 9 indicating the maximum for quality, density, darkness of green, and resistance to leaf spot (*Drechslera* spp. and *Bipolaris* spp.). Results were analyzed statistically, summarized, and returned to evaluators for discussion on the following day. Results were discussed and it was concluded that in general there was agreement among evaluators although not all used the same part or range of the scale in rating. Correlation of ratings between evaluators showed this to be true except for color. The group returned to the field plot area to discuss several nonconformities in rating among the evaluators. It should be noted that at least 12 of the 14 researchers were experienced in field data collection.

The analysis of variance was significantly different due to entry and evaluator. There was also a significant interaction. The ranges of correlation coefficients between ratings of two evaluators were as follows:

Quality	$r = 0.86$ to 0.99
Density	$r = 0.55$ to 0.99
Ground cover	$r = 0.66$ to 1.00
Color	$r = 0.00$ to 0.96
Leaf spot	$r = 0.67$ to 0.98

With quality ratings, most evaluators were quite uniform although different parts of the rating scale were used. There were wider differences in assessment of density as some evaluators concentrated on general plant appearance while others actually ran their hands over the turf to get a feel for tiller density. The data for percent groundcover was fairly uniform although one evaluator appeared to have made an error. Color ratings were uniform for the better varieties in the trial but varied considerably for the entries having the lowest quality rating. It appeared that some evaluators did not distinguish between genetic color of the entry and the discoloration caused by leaf spot disease. Color data should be taken when no disease symptoms are present. Ratings for leaf spot were quite uniform.

The average ratings for quality, density, percent ground cover, color, and leaf spot, and the range of rating among the 14 evaluators participating in the exercise are shown in Table 17-1.

Horst et al. (1984) reported poor consistency with various visual quality ratings for studies in Texas and Oregon. They did not indicate the experience level of their evaluators, however.

Quality ratings of a turfgrass plot will change greatly during a season. Quality scores may be as low as two or three as the grasses come out of winter dormancy. During peak growing periods of spring or autumn, they may rate near or at the top of the scale. A seasonal average turf score of six to seven is often considered a requirement for a high-quality grass. It is necessary to keep the full scale in mind when recording quality ratings, always reflecting on the highest quality stand of grass required for a perfect score of nine.

The following suggestions should aid in the process of recording subjective data such as quality, color, or injury. First, have an assistant to record the figures or use a small cassette recorder to record values because it is difficult to readjust the eyes to observe the grass plots after adjusting them to a light-colored recording sheet. Repeated eye adjustment to the reflection from a score sheet can make careful observation of the grasses difficult. The eyes must be focused intently on the grasses without distraction if meaningful ratings are to be obtained. Second, conduct the evaluations on cloudy days when shadows and reflections within the grass stand are minimized. Research plots should be arranged in a trial so they can be rated when standing at the south side of the plot. Subtle differences are more readily observed when the sun is at the back of the recorder. It is best to do the visual rating from mid-morning to early afternoon while the sun is at its highest point. In early and late season especially, long shadows make it difficult to take

Table 17-1. Average ratings and range of ratings of Kentucky bluegrass cultivars scored by 14 evaluators at a 1975 Northeastern Regional Turfgrass Research Committee workshop on subjective evaluations.

Entry no.	Quality Avg.	Quality Range	Density Avg.	Density Range	Ground cover Avg.	Ground cover Range	Color Avg.	Color Range	Leafspot Avg.	Leafspot Range
4	5.6 cd*	4.3–6.3	6.2 c-f	5.3–7.7	87ab	72– 95	6.5 abc	5.3–8.0	6.1 cd	5.0–7.0
10	5.7 cd	5.0–6.3	6.3 c-f	5.7–7.7	87 ab	73– 93	5.9 b-e	4.7–67	6.0 cd	4.7–7.0
15	7.1 ab	6.3–8.3	7.1 a-d	5.3–8.7	95 a	89–100	6.4 abc	5.0–7.7	7.6 ab	6.3–8.7
17	1.5 f	1.0–2.3	1.9 h	1.3–3.7	17 e	11– 28	4.3 f	1.0–7.3	2.1 g	1.0–4.3
19	6.5 abc	5.0–7.7	6.8 b-f	5.3–9.0	93 ab	83–100	6.3 a-d	5.0–7.3	6.8 abc	5.7–7.7
30	4.5 de	3.3–5.7	6.0 def	4.0–7.7	81 bc	67– 94	4.9 ef	3.7–6.7	5.1 de	3.7–7.0
34	7.2 ab	6.7–8.0	7.6 ab	6.7–8.3	96 a	92–100	7.1 a	5.7–8.7	7.6 ab	6.0–8.3
48	6.4 abc	5.3–7.3	7.4 abc	6.3–9.0	94 ab	88–100	5.8 b-e	5.0–6.3	6.3 bcd	5.0–8.3
52	6.0 bc	3.7–6.7	5.8 ef	3.3–9.0	84 abc	32– 98	6.8 ab	5.7–8.0	7.2 abc	6.0–8.3
58	7.1 ab	6.3–8.3	8.1 a	7.0–9.0	96 a	92–100	6.6 ab	5.0–7.7	7.3 abc	5.0–8.3
75	4.3 e	3.3–4.7	5.6 f	4.7–6.7	74 c	60– 90	5.4 e-f	3.7–7.0	4.2 ef	3.0–5.3
80	3.6 e	2.7–4.3	4.4 g	3.3–6.7	60 d	48– 72	5.2 def	2.7–7.0	3.8 f	2.7–4.7
86	7.4 a	6.3–9.0	6.9 a-e	4.0–9.0	95 a	90–100	7.4 a	6.3–8.7	7.9 a	6.7–8.7
92	7.1 ab	6.3–8.0	7.2 abc	6.3–8.0	94 ab	81–100	6.9 ab	6.0–8.0	7.3 abc	5.7–8.7

* Means within a column followed by the same letter are not significantly different at the 5% level using Duncan's Multiple Range Test.

Fig. 17–2. It is helpful to outline plots with string prior to rating.

good ratings. Treatment differences are usually more apparent prior to mowing, because mowing direction can cause different reflective patterns within
the turf. It is often helpful to outline plots with pins and string prior to rating
(Fig. 17–2). If more than one individual will be responsible for plot evaluation, those involved should work together frequently to ensure uniformity
in their ratings.

Score sheets that represent the layout of the trial, with a square or rec-
tangle representing each plot, simplify field data collection. Each square on
the sheet is numbered in sequence and each replication designated. Noting
plot size and outside dimensions of the total trial on the recording sheet aids
in marking the study for data collection. Treatment information must be
omitted from the score sheet to reduce the possibility of personal bias.

Permanent record books must be maintained in which the raw data from
each observation are recorded. Data may also be recorded on tape and entered into a computer although permanent hand records do have value.

Cameras are valuable tools for turfgrass researchers. A camera can
record what the human eye has observed and put it on record for future reference. A good quality 35-mm single lens reflex camera is required for field
researchers. A 28- or 35-mm wide angle lens can be used to advantage in
taking pictures of plots.

B. Objective Data

1. Color

Several techniques have been used to quantify turfgrass color.

a. Chlorophyll Indices. Madison (1960) and Madison and Andersen (1963) used a chlorophyll index based on chlorophyll content (mg of chlorophyll dm^{-2}) of aboveground tissue sampled immediately after mowing. Johnson (1974) used a similar procedure, however chlorophyll was extracted from dried clippings. The chlorophyll index correlates well with turfgrass color response to fertilizer treatments, however, it may not distinguish differences between mowing, irrigation, or shading practices (Madison & Andersen, 1963; Mantell & Stanhill, 1966).

b. Light Sensitive Instruments. A Se photocell and light meter held 1 m above turf were used by Mantell and Stanhill (1966) to measure light reflectance. Correlations between light reflectance, visual ratings, leaf chlorophyll content, and plant density were highly significant. A disadvantage to the method is that it depends upon full sunlight near midday. Birth and McVey (1968) used a single-beam spectrophotometer to develop a two-wavelength reflectance ratio as an index of turf color. The instrument is independent of external light and results were highly correlated with visual ratings. More recently, Kavanagh et al. (1985) evaluated the Hunter Colour Difference Meter, an instrument used elsewhere in science and industry, for color analysis of clippings. The meter was found to be useful in quantifying color differences between cultivars and treatments.

c. Color Charts. Color charts such as those used in soil classification (Nickerson Color Fan; Munsell Color Co., Inc., 10 East Franklin St., Baltimore, MD 21230) have been used to describe turf color (Beard, 1973; Butler, 1963). Feldhake et al. (1984) used cards painted with green and tan bands about the width of a grass blade to help in rating turf growing in lysimeters. Proportions of green and tan on the cards varied in 10% increments from 100% tan (dead turf) to 100% green.

Objective evaluation of turf color minimizes experimental error due to differences between locations, seasons, and observers; however, the methods are more time consuming and costly than visual ratings.

2. Density

Counting the number of shoots per unit area is a method used for determining density. Turfgrass stands are usually sufficiently uniform that relatively small quadrat or sample sizes may be used. The number of subsamples counted from each treatment and replication depends upon the precision required and time available for counting. Determination of sample and quadrat size is discussed in many plant ecology texts (e.g., Greig-Smith, 1964; Kershaw, 1973; Mueller-Dombois & Ellenberg, 1974). If nondestructive sampling is required, counting is usually done with randomly placed quadrats in the field. Plot size is generally sufficient to allow plugs to be taken.

Brede and Duich (1982) compared three round sampling tools (35, 51, and 102 mm inside diam.) with the Noer profile sampler (13 by 76 mm). Population estimates in Kentucky bluegrass were similar for all four tools when loose tillers cut by the sampler but remaining on the sampled area were counted. Although variability was somewhat greater with the Noer sampler, the row of tillers was easier to count.

3. Species Counts in Mixed Stands

Species composition of mixtures can be estimated visually in quadrats or whole plots where color, growth habit, and texture are distinct for each species. Point quadrat methods have been used to count species in mixed stands (Engel & Trout, 1980; Leasure, 1949; Mahdi, 1951). Mahdi and Stoutemyer (1953) found point quadrats to be inadequate while studying population shifts in dense lawns. They used a 2.5-cm diam. soil sampling probe to take plugs that were later separated by species and counted. Identification errors were minimized with the use of a binocular microscope. Brede and Duich (1984) used a Noer profile sampler to obtain plugs for plant counts, noting that species identification and counting could proceed from one end of the rectangular plug to the other.

4. Plot Cover

Plot cover is usually estimated visually for whole plots or in randomly dropped quadrats of appropriate size. Cover may be quantified using the point-quadrat method. Although time-consuming compared to visual estimates, the method is useful in determining cover by different species in a mixed stand (Levy & Madden, 1933). An optical point quadrat frame was developed by Laycock and Canaway (1980) and was used to measure cover on athletic fields (Canaway et al., 1986).

5. Establishment Rate

Timely, repetitive estimates of cover and density provide information on rate of establishment of seedings. Brede (1987) developed an isolated plot technique for studying growth and survival of grass seedlings in the field.

6. Yield

Turf response to such factors as fertility treatments, growth regulators, and cultural practices is frequently measured by comparing clipping weights. Small areas, such as turf growing in lysimeters, must be clipped by hand while mowers may be used for larger plot research. Reel-type mowers give a cleaner, more uniform cut than rotary mowers and are preferred as research tools. A rotary mower or sickle-bar must be used where growth is excessive or mowing is deliberately delayed, as in growth regulator tests. Cloth bags may be fitted to rotary mower chutes to collect yield samples.

7. Verdure

The living grass aboveground is affected by fertility and cultural treatments. Verdure is obtained by hand clipping stems and leaves after a uniform mowing. Madison (1962) removed 102-mm diam. cores from plots, sheared shoots, and returned cores.

8. Thatch

Thatch content is determined by measuring the thickness of the layer or by determining organic matter content. Thatch depth may be measured directly from plugs (Duble & Weaver, 1974; Shearman et al., 1983). Sampling variability may be reduced by removing shoots and soil from samples and compressing the sample with a weight while measuring thatch thickness (Cooper & Skogley, 1981; Fermanian et al., 1985; Spangenberg et al., 1986). Thatch may be oven dried to a constant moisture level and ashed for an expression of organic matter content. Thatch organic matter content is the dry weight less the remaining mineral weight from a given sample volume (Carrow et al., 1987; Johnson et al., 1987; Landry & Karnok, 1985; Murray & Juska, 1977). This method is appropriate where soil has been incorporated into the thatch layer.

Instruments have been developed to estimate thatch depth by comparing differences in compression of turf surfaces with different bearing pressures (Volk, 1972; White & Dickens, 1984). The "thatch meters" permit rapid, nondestructive sampling in the field; however, results are not consistently correlated with thatch depth.

9. Seedheads

Seedheads may be counted in the field with appropriate quadrats. Alternatively, the seedheads may be clipped, stored, and counted at some later date. Clipping is advantageous with poly-stands where it is less tedious and there is less chance of error when seedheads can be separated by species.

10. Sod Strength

Sod strength has been measured as the force required to pull sod pieces apart. Rieke et al. (1968) constructed a device for applying force to a sod strip clamped securely at one end while having the other end clamped in a movable frame. The weight of sand poured at a constant rate into a container attached to the movable frame was recorded when the turf separated. The technique is useful in evaluating species, varieties, blends, mixtures, and management practices in sod production (Hall et al., 1985; Rieke et al., 1968). Jagschitz (1980) used a similar device, powered by an electric motor, to evaluate development and rooting of Kentucky bluegrass (*Poa pratensis* L.) sod treated with herbicides (Fig. 17-3). Burns and Futral (1980) used an Instron Universal Testing Instrument (Model 1130, Instron Corp., Canton, MA) to measure sod strength. The instrument is costly but frequently used by agencies or university departments involved with materials testing. An advantage to the Instron is that it produces a printout of the breaking pattern and sod elongation.

11. Sod Rooting

King and Beard (1969) developed a technique for measuring the force required to lift transplanted sod vertically from the rooting medium. Sod

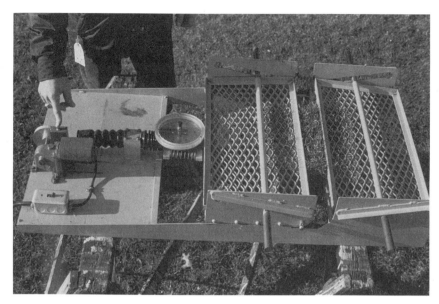

Fig. 17–3. Device for measuring sod strength. Indicator on dial in center records maximum force required to tear apart sod piece clamped in frames. (Courtesy John Jagschitz.)

pieces were placed in 30- by 30-cm frames having fiberglass screen bottoms and allowed to root for a designated period of time. A block and tackle arrangement was used to apply force to lift the frame. Bingham (1974) used a similar procedure to evaluate the effect of selected herbicides on rooting of sod.

Ledeboer et al. (1971) and Jagschitz (1980) measured rooting of 10 cm diam. plugs cut from treated areas with a putting green cup cutter. A wire ring with a cross-bar was placed beneath each sod plug as it was transplanted to a nearby untreated area. After rooting, plugs were lifted with a maximum weight indicator scale by attaching a wire hook to the cross-bar under the plug (Fig. 17–4).

12. Root Production

Field study of root production is limited by the laborious task of separating roots from soil. If not done carefully, significant loss of sample may occur. Also, growth rate is difficult to measure in the field. For these reasons, much of the research on turfgrass roots is conducted in transparent containers, rhizotrons, or in sand or solution cultures.

Root samples are usually obtained from soil cores. Core diameter and number of samples will depend on root density and the level of precision required. Roots are washed free of soil over a screen by immersing or using a fine water spray (Bourgoin et al., 1985; Dudeck et al., 1985; Goss & Law, 1967; Powell et al., 1967). Numerous automated devices have been constructed for washing roots of plants other than turf, some of which may be useful in turfgrass research (Bohm, 1979; Smucker et al., 1982). Once washed,

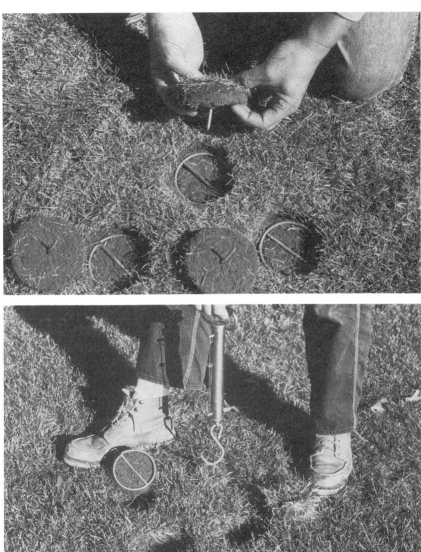

Fig. 17–4. *Top*. Measurement of sod rooting. Plugs cut from treated sod are placed over wire rings. Nails mark center of plug. *Bottom*. To measure rooting, nail is removed, a hook inserted through nail hole and attached to ring, and a maximum recording scale used to record force necessary to uproot plug. (Courtesy John Jagschitz.)

roots are usually oven dried and weighed; however, Willard and McClure (1932) noted the importance of ashing samples to obtain true root weight and reduce variability.

The effect of growth retardants and herbicides on root growth has been measured by transplanting plugs of treated turfgrass to beds of sand (Fales et al., 1976; Jagschitz, 1980; Nielsen & Wakefield, 1975). The plugs were carefully dug at intervals from 3 to 10 wk after transplanting and roots were washed free of sand, dried, and weighed.

The dense, fibrous nature of turfgrass roots makes direct measurement of root length laborious and time consuming. Bohm (1979) has reviewed methods of measuring root length, and Reicosky et al. (1970) have compared several methods using soybean [*Glycine max* (L.) Merr.] roots. Peacock and Dudeck (1985) estimated total length of St. Augustinegrass [*Stenotaphrum secundatum* (Walter) Kuntze] roots washed from 5 cm diam. by 15-cm long soil samples. They used a line-intercept method that Newman (1966) developed. Parr et al. (1984) used a modified line-intercept method (Tennant, 1975) to estimate root length of ryegrasses cut at different heights. Voorhees et al. (1980) described a technique for measuring root length using a computer-controlled digital scanning microdensitometer.

Rhizotrons allow continuous, nondestructive observation of roots under field conditions. Bohm (1979) and Huck and Taylor (1982) have reviewed designs, construction details, and investigative techniques used in rhizotrons. Turfgrass research has been conducted with rhizotrons at Texas A&M Univ., College Station (DiPaola & Beard, 1976; Sifers et al., 1985), Ohio State Univ., Columbus (Karnok & Kucharski, 1982), The Univ. of Georgia, Athens (K.J. Karnok, 1988, personal communication), and The Univ. of Nebraska, Lincoln (Shearman & Barber, 1987).

Monitoring roots through the glass or plastic windows of a rhizotron provides qualitative information such as root color, direction of growth and root-branching patterns. Methods of measuring root length, density, and growth rate have been reviewed by Bohm (1979) and Huck and Taylor (1982). A binocular microscope coupled with a movie camera has been used to observe and record details of root growth and morphology, and soil microflora and fauna (Karnok & Kucharski, 1982). Root observation cells also function as lysimeter units at the Ohio State facility, allowing measurement of evapotranspiration and collection of leachates. Rhizotrons are actually laboratories constructed in the field at great expense. Relatively inexpensive minirhizotrons have been developed for viewing root growth under field conditions. Branham et al. (1986) used 5.1-cm diam. plastic tubes inserted through the soil profile to monitor growth of Kentucky bluegrass roots. Roots were viewed with a camera lowered into the tube (Fig. 17–5). Bohm (1979) and Upchurch and Ritchie (1983) have described similar systems.

13. Wear Tolerance

Several simulators have been developed to evaluate turfgrass wear from crushing, scuffing, or tearing (Bourgoin & Mansat, 1981; Dudeck & Burt, 1975; Shearman et al., 1974; Shildrick, 1974; Youngner, 1961). Wear tolerance of cultivars, species, or mixtures is determined by percent cover or visual estimates following treatment, or by choosing a wear end point. Youngner (1961) and Shearman et al. (1974) defined the end point to be the number of simulator revolutions to reach a point where all leaf blades were removed, leaving only stems and bare ground.

Shearman and Beard (1975a, b, c) investigated mechanisms involved in wear tolerance and compared four methods of evaluating wear: (i) visual rating of wear injury, (ii) percent total cell wall content, (iii) percent verdure, and (iv) percent chlorophyll/unit area remaining after wear treatment. Percent verdure, the verdure of injured turf divided by verdure of uninjured turf multiplied by 100, was the preferred method for quantitatively evaluating wear-tolerance differentials.

14. Putting Green Speed

Indices for the effects of cultural treatments on golf greens are the trueness and distance of ball roll (Beard, 1973). Mechanical putters (Monteith, 1929) and, more recently, inclined plane devices (Batten et al., 1981; Radko, 1980) have been used to measure ball roll.

15. Temperature

Measuring the temperature component of the turfgrass microclimate has been facilitated by small thermocouple sensors. Thermocouples produce an electrical signal permitting the use of electronic recording devices capable of storing large amounts of data. Welterlen and Watschke (1981) have discussed techniques for thermocouple placement and automation of temperature measurements.

Hand-held infrared thermometers have been used to measure canopy temperatures of turfgrasses (Feldhake et al., 1983; Throssell et al., 1987). Roberts (1986) used a dial-type thermometer with 3-mm diam. probe to measure temperatures beneath protective covers placed on dormant turf.

16. Carbon Fixation and Translocation

Most physiological research on turfgrass is conducted in the laboratory, greenhouse, or growth chamber where factors affecting physiological processes can be controlled and where analytical equipment is nearby. In recent years, however, equipment has been developed so that basic research can be conducted in the field. The most commonly used methods for studying photosynthetic activity employ an infrared gas analyzer (IRGA) to measure CO_2 flux.

Photosynthetic CO_2 exchange rates (CER) of turfgrass communities have been determined by placing a transparent chamber over the sward (Fig. 17–6) and monitoring changes in CO_2 concentration of the atmosphere within the chamber for several minutes (Mehall et al., 1984; Peacock & Dudeck, 1984; Spokas & Cooper, 1987). Air within the chamber is circulated with a fan. Air samples may be pumped continuously through the IRGA, or may be sampled with syringes and the CO_2 content analyzed by passing through an IRGA in the laboratory (Boote et al., 1980).

When plants are exposed to light, the CER reflects apparent photosynthesis, the CO_2 assimilated by the turf less CO_2 released by the plants, thatch, and soil. After obtaining the light CER, Peacock and Dudeck (1984) covered

Fig. 17–5. Minirhizotron. Video camera housed in cylinder (A) is lowered into plastic tubes inserted into turfgrass rootzone (B). Photos C and D illustrate root growth between 19 and 26 Aug. 1986. (Courtesy Bruce Branham.)

the chamber with a light-proof white cover to obtain the CER of dark respiration (plants and soil). Gross photosynthesis was determined as the sum of apparent photosynthesis and dark respiration. Such measurements do not account for photorespiratory CO_2 release that can represent a significant error under conditions favoring photorespiration (high light and elevated temperature).

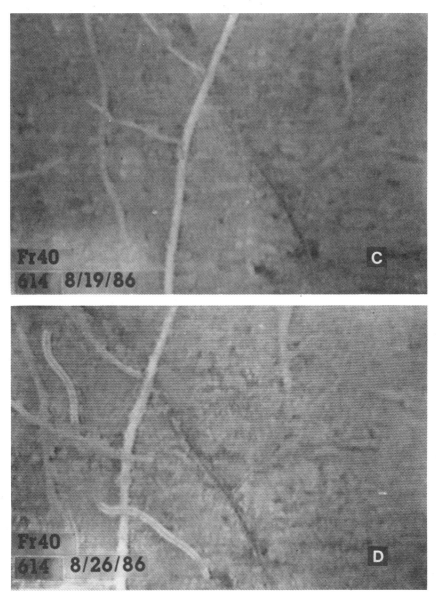

Fig. 17–5. Continued.

Hull (1976) has described a radioactive tracer technique for following the distribution of photoassimilated C. Turf under a 15-cm diam. bell jar was exposed to 5.6×10^{11} Bq of $^{14}CO_2$ for 15 min. A 10-cm diam. plug was harvested from the treated turf 2 to 96 h after treatment. Shoot and root fractions were separated, freeze dried, ground, and assayed for ^{14}C. Photosynthate partitioning was expressed as percent distribution of recovered radioactivity within the various grass fractions (leaf blades, leaf sheaths and stems,

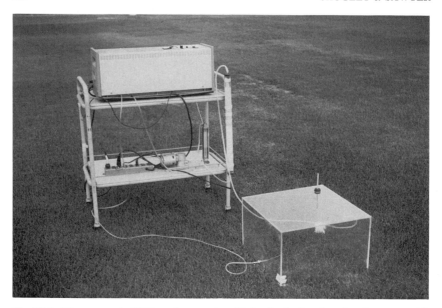

Fig. 17–6. Measurement of CO_2-exchange rates. Air in plastic chamber placed over sward is circulated through infrared gas analyzer (*top shelf*) by pump (*bottom shelf*). (Courtesy Richard Hull.)

rhizomes and roots) (Hull, 1987). Photosynthate flux through plant organs and metabolic pools was estimated based on changes in specific activity (counts min^{-1} mg^{-1} material) with time (Hull & Smith, 1974).

17. Soil Moisture and Evapotranspiration

Turfgrass water use can be monitored in the field by several or a combination of methods. Measurements of evapotranspiration (ET) are involved.

Soil moisture content can be determined directly by the gravimetric method or indirectly by the use of gypsum blocks with resistance meter, tensiometer, or neutron probe. With the gravimetric method, the soil is weighed, dried for 24 h at 105 °C, and weighed again to determine its moisture content (Gardner, 1986). Although the gravimetric method is precise, obtaining soil samples is time consuming, may be limited by plot size, and there is a time delay while waiting for samples to dry.

There is a considerable range in cost, labor, and sensitivity of methods for measuring soil moisture. Advantages and limitations of these methods have been discussed in detail by Cassell and Klute (1986) and Gardner (1986).

Weighing lysimeters (Feldhake et al., 1983; Aronson et al., 1985) are frequently used in the field to measure ET. These are variously sized buckets or containers of soil containing established grasses that are set into field plots with the surface flush with the surrounding soil surface. The buckets can be removed at desired intervals and weighed to determine evapotranspirational losses. Solar radiation, relative humidity, temperature, and wind speed are the most important climatic variables influencing ET. Formulas such as the modified Penman equation (Dunn & Leopold, 1978) are used to predict reference ET on the basis of these climatic factors.

18. Nutrient Uptake by Turf

Nutrient analysis of clippings is used to compare sources, rates, and time of application of fertilizers, particularly N fertilizers. Clippings are easily obtained through normal plot maintenance practices and are available throughout the growing season. Hummel and Waddington (1981) evaluated 24 slow-release sources of N by obtaining dry weight yields and N content of 'Baron' Kentucky bluegrass clippings. Nitrogen uptake was expressed as a percentage of N applied per year. Nutrient recovery by plants is normally determined by subtracting uptake in an untreated control plot from that in treated plots. If a control is not included, the nutrient removed by the plant should be referred to as uptake rather than recovery.

Similar techniques have been used to calculate weekly and seasonal removal of major plant nutrients (Wray, 1974), and to compare Kentucky bluegrass cultivar variation in P and K nutrition (Mehall et al., 1983).

19. Nutrient Leaching

The fate of nutrients not taken up by turfgrasses is monitored by sampling soils and soil solutions. Attention has been focused on N, particularly NO_3, which is readily carried out of the plant root zone with the potential for leaching into groundwater. Rieke and Ellis (1974) sampled the soil profile of plots at 2-wk intervals. Leaching of NO_3 was observed by determining NO_3 concentrations in 0 to 15, 15 to 30, 30 to 45, and 45 to 60 cm increments of soil samples.

Leaching losses are also determined by analysis of soil solutions. Leachate samples have been obtained by applying suction to lysimeter tubes placed in the soil (Hesketh et al., 1986; Snyder et al., 1980, 1981), by applying suction to the base of soil lysimeters (Dowdell & Webster, 1980; Starr & DeRoo, 1981; Starr et al., 1978), and by collecting gravitational flow from drains installed in plots (Brown et al., 1982; Duble et al., 1978; Mitchell et al., 1978).

Leaching of NO_3 from Kentucky bluegrass root zones have also been determined by placing ion exchange resin bags about 40 cm below the soil surface (Petrovic & Hummel, 1985).

20. Nitrogen Volatilization

Volatilization loss of N as NH_3 can be significant following surface application of urea. Freney et al. (1983) reviewed factors affecting NH_3 volatilization. Few field investigations of N volatilization have been conducted. Volk (1959) trapped NH_3 in an inverted dish containing a pad saturated with 10% H_2SO_4. Ammonia was determined by washing the pad in a beaker, adding alkali, distilling and titrating. McInnes et al. (1986) and Sheard and Beauchamp (1985) noted that enclosure techniques create atypical microenvironments that may result in inaccurate estimates of NH_3 loss.

Sheard and Beauchamp (1985) used an aerodynamic diffusion method to estimate NH_3 flux from an application of urea to turf. Ammonia gas collector flasks and sensitive anemometers were mounted on a mast. Ammonia flux was estimated from measurements of air movement and NH_3 concentration. Strong diurnal changes in the flux of NH_3 were observed.

V. SUMMARY

We have presented information on planning and performing field research, not including pesticide studies, with turfgrasses. Generally, we presented a method briefly and provided references for more detail as to other research methods. Excellent techniques have been developed for doing field research. New methods or refinements of traditional techniques are constantly being developed. Researchers are encouraged to keep abreast of these innovations by regular review of *Agronomy Journal, Crop Science, HortScience*, and other research journals that deal with turfgrass science. Also, many research reports not involving turfgrass may present research methods that are applicable to turfgrass situations.

REFERENCES

Aronson, L.J., A.J. Gold, J.L. Cisar, and R.J. Hull. 1985. Water use and drought responses of cool-season turfgrasses. p. 113. *In* Agronomy abstracts. ASA, Madison, WI.

Ball, C.R. 1916. Some problems in agronomy. J. Am. Soc. Agron. 8:337–343.

Batten, S.M., J.B. Beard, D. Johns, A. Almodares, and J. Eckhardt. 1981. Characterizations of cool-season turfgrasses for winter overseeding of dormant bermudagrass. p. 83–94. *In* R.W. Sheard (ed.) Proc. 4th Int. Turfgrass Res. Conf., Guelph, ON, Canada. 19–23 July. Int. Turfgrass Soc., and Ontario Agric. Coll., Univ. of Guelph, Guelph, ON.

Beard, J.B. 1973. Turfgrass: Science and culture. Prentice-Hall, Englewood Cliffs, NJ.

Bingham, S.W. 1974. Influence of selected herbicides on rooting of turfgrass sod. p. 372–377. *In* E.C. Roberts (ed.) Proc. 2nd Int. Turfgrass Res. Conf., Blacksburg, VA. 19–21 June 1973. ASA and CSSA, Madison, WI.

Birth, G.S., and G.R. McVey. 1968. Measuring the color of growing turf with a reflectance spectrophotometer. Agron. J. 60:640–643.

Bohm, W. 1979. Methods of studying root systems. p. 1–188. *In* W.D. Billings et al. (ed.) Ecological studies. Vol. 33. Springer-Verlag New York, New York.

Boote, K.J., J.W. Jones, G.H. Smerage, C.S. Barfield, and R.D. Berger. 1980. Photosynthesis of peanut canopies as affected by leaf-spot and artificial defoliation. Agron. J. 72:247–252.

Bourgoin, B., and P. Mansat. 1981. Artificial trampling and player traffic on turfgrass cultivars. p. 55–63. *In* R.W. Sheard (ed.) Proc. 4th Int. Turfgrass Res. Conf., Guelph, ON, Canada. 19–23 July. Int. Turfgrass Soc., and Ontario Agric. Coll., Univ. of Guelph, Guelph, ON.

Bourgoin, B., P. Mansat, B. Aittaleb, and M.H. Ouaggag. 1985. Explicative characteristics of treading tolerance in *Festuca rubra, Lolium perenne* and *Poa pratensis*. p. 235–244. *In* F. Lemaire (ed.) Proc. 5th Int. Turfgrass Res. Conf., Avignon, France. 1–5 July. Inst. Natl. de la Recherche Agron., Paris.

Branham, B.E., A.J.M. Smucker, J. Ferguson, P.E. Rieke, and J.A. Murphy. 1986. Examining the turfgrass root zone with minirhizotrons. p. 131. *In* Agronomy abstracts. ASA, Madison, WI.

Brede, A.D. 1987. Isolated plot technique for studying seedling growth of turfgrasses. Agron. J. 79:5–8.

Brede, A.D., and J.M. Duich. 1982. Cultivar and seeding rate effects on several physical characteristics of Kentucky bluegrass turf. Agron. J. 74:865–870.

Brede, A.D., and J.M. Duich. 1984. Establishment characteristics of Kentucky bluegrass-perennial ryegrass turf mixtures as affected by seeding rate and ratio. Agron. J. 76:875–879.

Brown, K.W., J.C. Thomas, and R.L. Duble. 1982. Nitrogen source effect on nitrate and ammonium leaching and runoff losses from greens. Agron. J. 74:947–950.

Burns, R.E., and J.G. Futral. 1980. Measuring sod strength with an Instron Universal Testing Instrument. Agron. J. 72:571–572.

Butler, J. 1963. Some characteristics of the more commonly grown creeping bentgrasses. p. 23–25. Illinois Turfgrass Conf. Proc.

Canaway, P.M., L. Carr, R.A. Bennett, and S.P. Isaac. 1986. The effect of renovation on the ground cover of swards of eight turfgrass species grown on sand and soil and subjected to football-type wear. J. Sports Turf Res. Inst. 62:118–132.

Carleton, M.A. 1907. Development and proper status of agronomy. J. Am. Soc. Agron. 1:17–24.

Carrow, R.N., B.J. Johnson, and R.E. Burns. 1987. Thatch and quality of Tifway bermudagrass turf in relation to fertility and cultivation. Agron. J. 79:524–530.

Cassell, D.K., and A. Klute. 1986. Water potential: Tensiometry. p. 563–594. In A. Klute (ed.) Methods of soil analysis. Part 1. 2nd ed. Agron. Monogr. 9. ASA and SSSA, Madison, WI.

Chew, V. 1976. Comparing treatment means: A compendium. HortScience 11:348–357.

Cooper, R.J., and C.R. Skogley. 1981. An evaluation of several topdressing programs for *Agrostis palustris* Huds. and *Agrostis canina* L. putting green turf. p. 129–136. In R.W. Sheard (ed.) Proc. 4th Int. Turfgrass Res. Conf. Guelph, ON, Canada. 19–23 July. Int. Turfgrass Soc., and Ontario Agric. Coll., Univ. of Guelph, Guelph, ON.

DiPaola, J.M., and J.B. Beard. 1976. Development of a turfgrass rhizotron at Texas A&M. p. 114–117. In Proc. of the 31st Annual Texas Turfgrass Conf.

Dixon, W.J. 1986. Extraneous values. p. 83–90. In A. Klute (ed.) Methods of soil analysis. Part 1. 2nd ed. Agron. Monogr. 9. ASA and SSSA, Madison, WI.

Dowdell, R.J., and C.P. Webster. 1980. A lysimeter study using nitrogen −15 on the uptake of fertilizer nitrogen by perennial ryegrass swards and losses by leaching. J. Soil Sci. 31:65–75.

Duble, R.L., J.C. Thomas, and K.W. Brown. 1978. Arsenic pollution from underdrainage and runoff from golf greens. Agron. J. 70:71–74.

Duble, R.L., and R.W. Weaver. 1974. Thatch decomposition in bermudagrass turf. p. 445–451. In E.C. Roberts (ed.) Proc. 2nd Int. Turfgrass Res. Conf., Blacksburg, VA. 19–21 June 1973. ASA and CSSA, Madison, WI.

Dudeck, A.E., and E.O. Burt. 1975. Effects of simulated golf traffic on the establishment and performance of several overseeded turfgrasses. Fla. Turf 8:3–5.

Dudeck, A.E., C.H. Peacock, and T.E. Freeman. 1985. Response of selected bermudagrasses to nitrogen fertilization. p. 495–504. In F. Lemaire (ed.) Proc. 5th Int. Turfgrass Res. Conf., Avignon, France. 1–5 July. Inst. Natl. de La Recherche Agron., Paris.

Dunn, T., and L.B. Leopold. 1978. Water in environmental planning. Freeman and Co., San Francisco.

Engel, R.E., and J.R. Trout. 1980. Seedling competition of Kentucky bluegrass, red fescue, colonial bentgrass, and temporary grasses. p. 379–390. In J.B. Beard (ed.) Proc. 3rd Int. Turfgrass Res. Conf., Munich, Germany. 11–13 July 1977. Int. Turfgrass Soc., and ASA, CSSA, and SSSA, Madison, WI.

Fales, S.L., A.P. Nielsen, and R.C. Wakefield. 1976. Top growth and root growth response of red fescue to growth retardants. Proc. Northeast Weed Sci. Soc. 30:334–339.

Feldhake, C.M., R.E. Danielson, and J.D. Butler. 1983. Turfgrass evapotranspiration. I. Factors influencing rate in urban environments. Agron. J. 75:824–830.

Feldhake, C.M., R.E. Danielson, and J.D. Butler. 1984. Turfgrass evapotranspiration. II: Responses to deficit irrigation. Agron. J. 76:85–89.

Fermanian, T.W., J.E. Haley, and R.F. Burns. 1985. The effects of sand topdressing on a heavily thatched creeping bentgrass green. p. 439–448. In F. Lemaire (ed.) Proc. 5th Int. Turfgrass Res. Conf., Avignon, France. 1–5 July. Inst. Natl. de la Recherche Agron., Paris.

Freney, J.R., J.R. Simpson, and O.T. Denmead. 1983. Volatilization of ammonia. p. 1–32. In J.R. Freney and J.R. Simpson (ed.) Gaseous loss of nitrogen from plant-soil systems. Nijhoff/Junk, The Hague.

Garber, R.J. 1931. A method of laying out experiment plots. J. Am. Soc. Agron. 23:286–293.

Gardner, W.H. 1986. Water content. p. 493–544. In A. Klute (ed.) Methods of soil analysis. Part 1. 2nd ed. Agron. Monogr. 9. ASA and SSSA, Madison, WI.

Goss, R.L., and A.G. Law. 1967. Performance of bluegrass varieties at two cutting heights and two nitrogen levels. Agron. J. 59:516–518.

Greig-Smith, P. 1964. Quantitative plant ecology. 2nd ed. Butterworths, London.

Hall, J.R., L.H. Taylor, and J.F. Shoulders. 1985. Sod strength and turfgrass quality of Kentucky bluegrass cultivars, blends and mixtures. p. 807–820. In F. Lemaire (ed.) Proc. 5th Int. Turfgrass Res. Conf., Avignon, France. 1–5 July. Inst. Natl. de la Recherche Agron., Paris.

Hesketh, E.S., R.J. Hull, and A.J. Gold. 1986. Estimates of nitrate-nitrogen leached from a Kentucky bluegrass turf. p. 134–135. In Agronomy abstracts. ASA, Madison, WI.

Horst, G.L., M.C. Engelke, and W. Meyers. 1984. Assessment of visual evaluation techniques. Agron. J. 76:619–622.

Huck, M.G., and H.M. Taylor. 1982. The rhizotron as a tool for root research. Adv. Agron. 35:1–33.

Hull, R.J. 1976. A carbon-14 technique for measuring photosynthate distribution in field grown turf. Agron. J. 68:99–102.

Hull, R.J. 1987. Kentucky bluegrass photosynthate partitioning following scheduled mowing. J. Am. Soc. Hortic. Sci. 112:829–834.

Hull, R.J., and L.M. Smith. 1974. Photosynthate translocation and metabolism in Kentucky bluegrass turf as a function of fertility. In E.C. Roberts (ed.) Proc. 2nd Int. Turfgrass Res. Conf., Blacksburg, VA. 19–21 June 1973. ASA and CSSA, Madison, WI.

Hummel, N.W., Jr., and D.V. Waddington. 1981. Evaluation of slow-release nitrogen sources on 'Baron' Kentucky bluegrass. Soil Sci. Soc. Am. J. 45:966–970.

Jagschitz, J.A. 1980. Development and rooting of Kentucky bluegrass sod as affected by herbicides. p. 227–235. In J.B. Beard (ed.) Proc. 3rd Int. Turfgrass Res. Conf., Munich, Germany. 11–13 July 1977. Int. Turfgrass Soc., and ASA, CSSA, and SSSA, Madison, WI.

Johnson, B.J., R.N. Carrow, and R.E. Burns. 1987. Bermudagrass turf response to mowing practices and fertilizer. Agron. J. 79:677–680.

Johnson, G.V. 1974. Simple procedure for quantitative analysis of turf color. Agron. J. 66:457–459.

Karnok, K.J., and R.T. Kucharski. 1982. Design and construction of a rhizotron-lysimeter facility at the Ohio State University. Agron. J. 74:152–156.

Kavanagh, T., D. O'Beirne, and T.P. Cormican. 1985. Use of the Hunter colour difference meter for colour evaluation in turfgrass experiments. p. 255–262. In F. Lemaire (ed.) Proc. 5th Int. Turfgrass Res. Conf., Avignon, France. 1–5 July. Inst. Natl. de la Recherche Agron., Paris.

Kempthorne, O., and R.R. Allmaras. 1986. Errors and variability of observation. p. 1–30. In A. Klute (ed.) Methods of soil analysis. Part 1. 2nd ed. Agron. Monogr. 9. ASA and SSSA, Madison, WI.

Kershaw, K.A. 1973. Quantitative and dynamic plant ecology. 2nd ed. Am. Elsevier Publ. Co., New York.

King, J.W., and J.B. Beard. 1969. Measuring rooting of sodded turfs. Agron. J. 61:497–498.

Landry, G.W., and K.J. Karnok. 1985. Turf quality, spring greenup and thatch accumulation of several improved bermudagrasses. p. 299–305. In F. Lemaire (ed.) Proc. 5th Int. Turfgrass Res. Conf., Avignon, France. 1–5 July. Inst. Natl. de la Recherche Agron., Paris.

Laycock, R.W., and P.M. Canaway. 1980. A new optical point quadrat frame for the estimation of cover in close-mown turf. J. Sports Turf Res. Inst. 56:91–92.

Leasure, J.K. 1949. Determining the species composition of swards. Agron. J. 41:204–206.

Ledeboer, F.B., C.R. Skogley, and C.G. McKiel. 1971. Soil heating studies with cool-season turfgrasses. III: Methods for the establishment of turf with seed and sod during the winter. Agron. J. 63:686–689.

Levy, E.B., and E.A. Madden. 1933. The point method of pasture analysis. N.Z. J. Agric. 46:267–279.

Little, T.M., and F.J. Hills. 1978. Agricultural experimentation. John Wiley and Sons, New York.

Madison, J.H. 1960. The mowing of turfgrass. I: The effect of season, interval, and height of mowing on the growth of seaside bentgrass turf. Agron. J. 52:449–452.

Madison, J.H. 1962. Turfgrass ecology. Effects of mowing, irrigation, and nitrogen treatments of Agrostis palustris Huds., 'Seaside' and Agrostis tenuis Sibth., 'Highland' on population, yield, rooting and cover. Agron. J. 54:407–412.

Madison, J.H., and A.H. Andersen. 1963. A chlorophyll index to measure turfgrass response. Agron. J. 55:461–464.

Mahdi, Z. 1951. The point quadrat method for analyzing the composition of turf. S. Calif. Turf Cult. 1:4.

Mahdi, Z., and V.T. Stoutemyer. 1953. A method of measurement of populations in dense turf. Agron. J. 45:514–515.

Mantell, A., and G. Stanhill. 1966. Comparison of methods for evaluating the response of lawn grass to irrigation and nitrogen treatments. Agron. J. 58:465–468.

McInnes, K.J., R.B. Ferguson, D.E. Kissel, and E.T. Kanemasu. 1986. Field measurements of ammonia loss from surface applications of urea solution to bare soil. Agron. J. 78:192–196.

Mehall, B.J., R.J. Hull, and C.R. Skogley. 1983. Cultivar variation in Kentucky bluegrass: P and K nutritional factors. Agron. J. 75:767–772.

Mehall, B.J., R.J. Hull, and C.R. Skogley. 1984. Turf quality of Kentucky bluegrass cultivars and energy relations. Agron. J. 76:47–50.

Mitchell, W.H., A.L. Morehart, L.J. Cotnoir, B.B. Hesseltine, and D.N. Langston, III. 1978. Effect of soil mixtures and irrigation methods on leaching of N in golf greens. Agron. J. 70:29–35.

Monteith, J. 1929. Testing turf with a mechanical putter. Bull. USGA Green Sect. 9(1):3–6.

Mueller-Dombois, D., and H. Ellenberg. 1974. Aims and methods of vegetation ecology. John Wiley and Sons, New York.

Murray, J.J., and F.V. Juska. 1977. Effect of management practices on thatch accumulation, turf quality and leaf spot damage in common Kentucky bluegrass. Agron. J. 69:365–369.

Nelson, L.A., and J.O. Rawlings. 1983. Ten common misuses of statistics in agronomic research and reporting. J. Agron. Educ. 12:100–105.

Newman, E.I. 1966. A method of estimating the total length of root in a sample. J. Appl. Ecol. 3:139–145.

Nielsen, A.P., and R.C. Wakefield. 1975. Effect of growth retardants on the top growth and root growth of turfgrasses. Proc. Northeast Weed Sci. Soc. 29:403–409.

Parr, T.W., R. Cox, and R.A. Plant. 1984. The effects of cutting height on root distribution and water use of ryegrass (*Lolium perenne* L. S23) turf. J. Sports Turf Res. Inst. 60:45–53.

Peacock, C.H., and A.E. Dudeck. 1984. Physiological response of St. Augustinegrass to irrigation scheduling. Agron. J. 76:275–279.

Peacock, C.H., and A.E. Dudeck. 1985. Effect of irrigation interval on St. Augustinegrass rooting. Agron. J. 77:813–815.

Petersen, R.G., and L.D. Calvin. 1986. Sampling. p. 33–51. *In* A. Klute (ed.) Methods of soil analysis. Part 1. 2nd ed. Agron. Monogr. 9. ASA and SSSA, Madison, WI.

Petrovic, A.M., and N.W. Hummel. 1985. Nitrogen source effects on nitrate leaching from late fall nitrogen applied to turfgrass. p. 120. *In* Agronomy abstracts. ASA, Madison, WI.

Powell, A.J., R.E. Blaser, and R.E. Schmidt. 1967. Effect of nitrogen on winter root growth of bentgrass. Agron. J. 59:529–530.

Radko, A.M. 1980. The U.S.G.A. Stimpmeter for measuring the speed of putting greens. p. 473–476. *In* J.B. Beard (ed.) Proc. 3rd Int. Turfgrass Res. Conf., Munich, Germany. 11–13 July 1977. Int. Turfgrass Soc., and ASA, CSSA, and SSSA, Madison, WI.

Reicosky, D.C., R.J. Millington, and D.B. Peters. 1970. A comparison of three methods for estimating root length. Agron. J. 62:451–453.

Rieke, P.E., J.B. Beard, and C.M. Hansen. 1968. A technique to measure sod strength for use in sod production studies. p. 60. *In* Agronomy abstracts. ASA, Madison, WI.

Rieke, P.E., and B.G. Ellis. 1974. Effects of nitrogen fertilization on nitrate movements under turfgrass. p. 120–130. *In* E.C. Roberts (ed.) Proc. 2nd Int. Turfgrass Res. Conf., Blacksburg, VA. 19–21 June 1973. ASA and CSSA, Madison, WI.

Roberts, J.M. 1986. Influence of protective covers on reducing winter desiccation of turf. Agron. J. 78:145–147.

Sheard, R.W., and E.G. Beauchamp. 1985. Aerodynamic measurement of ammonia volatilization from urea applied to bluegrass-fescue turf. p. 549–557. *In* F. Lemaire (ed.) Proc. 5th Int. Turfgrass Res. Conf., Avignon, France. 1–5 July. Inst. Natl. de la Recherche Agron., Paris.

Shearman, R.C., and J.F. Barber. 1987. Turfgrass rhizotron construction and design. p. 139. *In* Agronomy abstracts. ASA, Madison, WI.

Shearman, R.C., and J.B. Beard. 1975a. Turfgrass wear tolerance mechanisms: I. Wear tolerance of seven turfgrass species and quantitative methods for determining wear injury. Agron. J. 67:208–218.

Shearman, R.C., and J.B. Beard. 1975b. Turfgrass wear tolerance mechanisms: II. Effects of cell wall constituents on turfgrass wear tolerance. Agron. J. 67:211-215.

Shearman, R.C., and J.B. Beard. 1975c. Turfgrass wear tolerance mechanisms: III. Physiological, morphological, and anatomical characteristics associated with turfgrass wear tolerance. Agron. J. 67:215-218.

Shearman, R.C., J.B. Beard, C.M. Hansen, and R. Apaella. 1974. Turfgrass wear simulator for small plot investigations. Agron. J. 66:332-334.

Shearman, R.C., A.H. Bruneau, E.J. Kinbacher, and T.P. Riordan. 1983. Thatch accumulation in Kentucky bluegrass cultivars and blends. HortScience 18:97-99.

Shildrick, J.P. 1974. Wear tolerance of turfgrass cultivars in the United Kingdom. p. 23-34. In E.C. Roberts (ed.) Proc. 2nd Int. Turfgrass Res. Conf., Blacksburg, VA., 19-21 June 1973. ASA and CSSA, Madison, WI.

Sifers, S.J., J.B. Beard, and J.M. DiPaola. 1985. Spring root decline (SRD): Discovery, description and causes. p. 777-788. In F. Lemaire (ed.) Proc. 5th Int. Turfgrass Res. Conf., Avignon, France. 1-5 July. Inst. Natl. de la Recherche Agron., Paris.

Smucker, A.J.M., S.L. McBurney, and A.K. Srivastava. 1982. Quantitative separation of roots from compacted soil profiles by the hydropneumatic elutriation system. Agron. J. 74:500-503.

Snyder, G.H., E.O. Burt, and J.M. Davidson. 1980. Nitrogen leaching in bermudagrass turf: Daily fertigation vs. tri-weekly conventional fertilization. p. 185-193. In J.B. Beard (ed.) Proc. 3rd Int. Turfgrass Res. Conf., Munich, Germany. 11-13 July 1977. Int. Turfgrass Soc., and ASA, CSSA, and SSSA, Madison, WI.

Snyder, G.H., E.O. Burt, and J.M. Davidson. 1981. Nitrogen leaching in bermudagrass turf: Effect of nitrogen sources and rates. p. 313-324. In R.W. Sheard (ed.) Proc. 4th Int. Turfgrass Res. Conf., Guelph, ON. 19-23 July. Int. Turfgrass Soc., and Ontario Agric. Coll., Univ. of Guelph, Guelph, ON.

Spangenberg, B.G., T.W. Fermanian, and D.J. Wehner. 1986. Evaluation of liquid-applied nitrogen fertilizers on Kentucky bluegrass turf. Agron. J. 78:1002-1006.

Spokas, L.A., and R.J. Cooper. 1987. Relationships between plant growth regulator induced phytotoxicity and Kentucky bluegrass photosynthesis. p. 139. In Agronomy abstracts. ASA, Madison, WI.

Starr, J.L., and H.C. DeRoo. 1981. The fate of nitrogen fertilizer applied to turfgrass. Crop Sci. 21:531-536.

Starr, J.L., H.C. DeRoo, C.R. Frink, and J.Y. Parlange. 1978. Leaching characteristics of a layered field soil. Soil Sci. Soc. Am. J. 42:386-391.

Tennant, D. 1975. A test of a modified line intersect method of estimating root length. J. Ecol. 63:995-1001.

Throssell, C.S., R.N. Carrow, and G.A. Milliken. 1987. Canopy temperature based irrigation scheduling indices for Kentucky bluegrass turf. Crop Sci. 27:126-131.

Upchurch, D.R., and J.T. Ritchie. 1983. Root observations using a video recording system in mini-rhizotrons. Agron. J. 75:1009-1015.

Volk, G.M. 1959. Volatile loss of ammonia following surface application of urea to turf or bare soils. Agron. J. 51:746-749.

Volk, G.M. 1972. Compressibility of turf as a measure of grass growth and thatch development on bermudagrass greens. Agron. J. 64:503-506.

Voorhees, W.B., V.A. Carlson, and E.A. Hallauer. 1980. Root length measurement with a computer-controlled digital scanning microdensitometer. Agron. J. 72:847-851.

Welterlen, M.S., and T.L. Watschke. 1981. Techniques for thermocouple placement and the automation of temperature measurements in the microenvironment of Kentucky bluegrass. Agron. J. 73:808-812.

White, R.H., and R. Dickens. 1984. Thatch accumulation in bermudagrass as influenced by cultural practices. Agron. J. 76:19-22.

Wiancko, A.T., S.C. Salmon, A.C. Arny, H.H. Love, and C.A. Mooers. 1924. Report of committee on standardization of field experiments. J. Am. Soc. Agron. 16:1-15.

Willard, C.J., and G.M. McClure. 1932. The quantitative development of tops and roots in bluegrass with an improved method of obtaining root yields. J. Am. Soc. Agron. 24:509-514.

Worthen, E.L. 1928. Symposium on 'field experiments.' J. Am. Soc. Agron. 20:421-425.

Wray, F.J. 1974. Seasonal growth and major nutrient uptake of turfgrasses under cool, wet conditions. p. 79-88. In E.C. Roberts (ed.) Proc. 2nd Int. Turfgrass Res. Conf., Blacksburg, VA. 19-21 June 1973. ASA and CSSA, Madison, WI.

Youngner, V.B. 1961. Accelerated wear tests on turfgrasses. Agron. J. 53:217-218.

18 Controlled Environment Research Methods for Turfs

JAMES B. BEARD

Texas A&M University
College Station, Texas

The objective of this chapter is to discuss our current state of knowledge concerning the preparation of turfs for botanical and physiological experiments in the glasshouse, growth chamber, or laboratory. The success of the experiment depends to a great extent on proper plant culture. It is especially important for a turf as it is a relatively complex plant community that is intimately interfaced with the soil biological system. Detailed discussions of specific qualitative and quantitative assessments of individual plant organs, tissues, or cells will not be discussed. Rather references will be listed for published comprehensive reviews or discussions of methodology for specific botanical and physiological assessments.

The importance of pursuing investigations on whole plant turf communities cannot be over emphasized. While individual plants should be studied in much detail to simplify initial concepts, it is inevitably necessary that the specific botanical or physiological responses concerned be assessed within the complex plant community of a turf. Furthermore, while the development of a basic understanding of key botanical and physiological processes and systems from a mechanistic standpoint necessitates investigations under glasshouse, controlled environment growth chamber, and laboratory simulation conditions, final resolution of practical problems still necessitates confirmation through field experiments, the methodology of which is addressed in chapter 17 by Skogley and Sawyer in this book.

Due to realistic restraints on the length of this chapter, it was not possible to review all methods that have been used in botanical and physiological studies of turfgrasses. Rather emphasis is placed on the major types of methodology used in the propagation, culture, and preparation of turfs prior to and during the course of an investigation. While this author has developed or modified many of the approaches outlined in the chapter, not all the methods discussed herein have been personally evaluated. Rather the author has relied on selected sources from original publications in several cases. No integration of methods is attempted in this chapter, as this varies greatly depending on the particular experiments involved and should fall within the realm of specific responsibilities of the individual investigators. Thus, this chapter addresses specific methodologies individually with emphasis on the

Copyright © 1992 ASA-CSSA-SSSA, 677 S. Segoe Rd., Madison, WI 53711, USA. *Turfgrass—* Agronomy Monograph no. 32.

unique aspects of a complex turf community. It should be recognized that the methodology used in the culture and preparation of turfs for specific qualitative and quantitative assessments may vary among turfgrass species and even among cultivars. Thus, preliminary comparative methodology experiments may need to be conducted on a specific species or cultivar before an investigation is initiated.

It is the author's hope that the information assembled in this chapter will provide a sound basis from which new investigators in the turf research field can develop proper methodology quickly and, hopefully, will improve upon the methodology as new instrumentation and concepts evolve.

I. PLANT MATERIALS PREPARATION

The preparation of individual plants for specific experiments is relatively simple compared to the preparation complexities of a turfgrass community (Fig. 18-1). Not only must a proper balance of shoot density, leaf area, and rooting that is representative of field conditions be ensured, but also the allied balance of soil flora and fauna must be considered in some cases. Failure to recognize the importance of proper preparation of turfs for botanical and physiological experiments may lead to serious confounding of effects involved in quantitative measurements. This is particularly true in the case of growth, plant water relations, photosynthesis, and carbohydrate studies.

Fig. 18-1. Propagation of a diverse range of turfs for experimentation. (Courtesy of J.B. Beard, Texas A&M University.)

A. Plant Material Source

It is vital that the seed or vegetative plant material used in certain studies is uniform from a genetic standpoint. This can be a substantial problem with many widely available sources of turfgrass seeds, such as common Kentucky bluegrass (*Poa pratensis* L.), Arizona common bermudagrass (*Cynodon dactylon* L. Pers.), and Georgia common centipedegrass [*Eremochloa ophiuroides* (Munro) Hackel], and may be impossible for species where some cultivars are polycross progenies.

In studies where only a single cultivar for each of one or more species is involved, it may be important to select a cultivar that is widely used. Typically, such cultivars have been more completely described from an experimental standpoint, which can be important. In addition, certified seed or vegetative planting stock of these cultivars is more readily available and hopefully will be available for an extended period. Thus, other researchers who wish to repeat an experiment or expand on the basic experiment can do so using the same plant material from a trueness-to-type genetic standpoint. It is also important to document the presence or absence of any endophyte in the species/cultivar being used.

Once propagation from a finite source has been initiated, it is important that vegetative increases be conducted using a root-zone substrate that has been fumigated to prevent the introduction of off-type plants. In addition, sanitary measures must be practiced to avoid off-type plant contamination from adjacent external sources. Such sources may include seed disseminated from nearby cultivars or strains of the same species or from vegetative nodes disseminated during mowing of turfs. It is important to thoroughly clean the mowing unit before changing from one genotype to the next. Complete isolation in a separate room or growth chamber may be necessary for some experiments.

1. Seed

In the case of seed, it is essential that it be obtained from a fully documented certified seed source, and maybe even from the breeder. Further, the amount obtained should be of sufficient quantity so the same seed source can be used throughout the duration of the investigation. The latter provides continuity from one experiment to the next. On receipt of the seed, it is important to record the certifying agency, seed lot number, origin of seed lot, purity, and germination with testing date. It also is important to obtain seed of the highest purity possible. Finally, proper seed storage conditions in terms of a cool temperature ($<5\,^{\circ}$C) and low humidity ($<50\%$) must be used, especially for an extended series of experiments that may require more than a 1-yr duration.

2. Sprigs

With certain turfgrass species and cultivars, propagation is only practiced by vegetative methods, such as sprigging. For many types of experiments this is actually the preferred method of propagation in order to ensure maximum genetic trueness to type. Considerable variability occurs within cultivars of some seeded species, such as tall fescue (*Festuca arundinacea* Schreb.). Thus, selecting an individual plant for a treatment could be risky. More replications may be required. Another option to eliminate variability is to propagate individual tillers from a maternal plant. In some cases it may be important that propagation be initiated from a single meristematic node or even a single cell.

3. Mature Sod

Certain investigations dictate the use of mature, ecologically stable turfs of at least 4- to 5-yr old. Typically, a turfgrass community does not reach a reasonably stable shoot density and equilibrium age among plants until after the first full year. In the case of biological stresses, certain disease and insect problems may not appear until the turf is from 4- to 5-yr old. Frequently, it is not practical to establish a turf and wait the length of time required to develop a mature turf before the experiments can be initiated. Thus, the common procedure is to collect representative sod samples from fully established, field-grown sites, such as an allied turfgrass field research laboratory. If the experiment dictates that the soil can not be washed from the sod, it is best if the root zones are comparable on the field propagation site and in the experimental containers.

Where a genetically uniform monostand is desired, it is important that the sod collected be from a source where adequate precautions have been taken to avoid contamination with off-type plants. Sources of such contamination may be external to a plot as well as introduced in the original planting due to failure to use certified planting stock with assured trueness to type from a genetic standpoint. In situations where establishment has been from seed of a species with varying degrees of cross fertilization, over time there is the possibility for genetic drift or segregation into distinct genotypes. This is particularly true for strongly stoloniferous or rhizomatous species where one aggressive genotype may become dominant. The genotype that dominates may vary depending on the cultural practices employed and the differential tolerances to environmental stresses and pests that occur in a specific climate. Therefore, a 5-yr-old mature sod may be drastically different genetically from the original planting.

4. Sanitary Practices

Upon receipt of vegetative plant material, and even seeds, the sample should be thoroughly inspected, along with any accompanying soil, for undesirable parasitic fungi, viruses, bacteria, insects, mites, or nematodes that may have contaminated either the plant material or the soil associated with the root zone. One can minimize the chance of confounding from these potentially negative biological stresses by taking these simple sanitary steps with the aid of the appropriate plant pathologist and/or entomologist.

B. Propagation Containers

The actual container surface area, rooting volume, and depth selected may vary significantly depending on the experimental objectives and on the particular turfgrass species and cultivar to be used. There are certain basic criteria that must be considered in the selection of containers for propagation of turfs: wall contaminants/phytotoxicity, surface area, size, depth, drainage, wall transparency, handling ease, structural strength, and life span.

1. Wall Contaminants/Phytotoxicity

The walls of some containers may contain contaminates that interfere with certain types of experiments. Included are essential elements that interfere with nutrient responses as well as elements or organic compounds that are phytotoxic. Contaminates can be critical in adversely affecting nutritional studies, especially essential micronutrients in nutrient deficiency experiments. For example, many metallic containers are a source of micronutrients. Also, ceramic containers may concentrate excessive levels of Mg in the root-zone medium. Containers with walls that are relatively inert or safe include glass, Styrofoam, and walls coated with Teflon.

The container should not possess any inorganic elements or organic compounds that may be phytotoxic to either the roots or shoots. For example, large-diameter PVC pipe cut into sections and capped are useful containers for certain types of root investigations (Fig. 18–2). New PVC pipe contains organic compounds on its surface that may be toxic to grass roots. Fortunately, weathering in the field over a period of months, especially when regular-

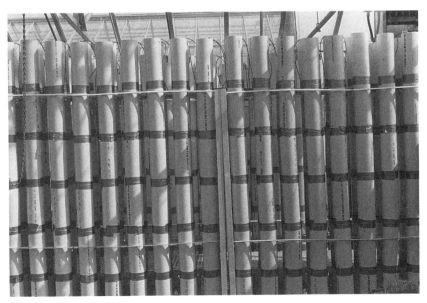

Fig. 18–2. A root column assembly, involving 120 cm long by 15-cm diam. PVC pipe, used in turfgrass investigations. (Courtesy of J.B. Beard, Texas A&M University.)

ly exposed to moisture or preferably submerged in water, will eliminate the potential phytotoxicity problem.

Phytotoxicity is a potential problem for certain types of containers where the material is quite permeable or absorptive. This is a particular problem in experiments where pesticides, inorganic elements, and organic compounds are applied at regular intervals, since certain container construction materials may accumulate these compounds over time to the point that phytotoxicity occurs. Also, the absorption on container walls of elements or organic compounds that are experimental treatments may affect their detection in experiments where their levels are being monitored.

If there is any doubt about container phytotoxicity, an initial methodology experiment should be conducted to compare the potential phytotoxicity from the type of container being considered vs. a container which is known to be free of phytotoxicity problems. Containers known to contain impurities that are potential problems may be used for certain types of studies if lined with polyethylene. Special care must be taken to avoid puncturing the plastic liner. In addition, it is important that the plastic liner containing the rooting medium and allied root system be held in a fixed position, as movement may damage or even sever delicate components of in situ root systems.

2. Size

The components of size in container selection include upper soil surface area for plant propagation and root zone volume, especially depth. The size of the container selected may vary greatly depending on the type of experiment to be conducted. It may range from containers of only 5 cm in diameter or square sides at the top to 30 cm or more. Small-diameter containers of 5 to 7.5 cm, such as Conetainers, are typically used in the propagation of individual plants through the initial tillering stage, before transplanting the shoot and intact root system into a larger container for the actual experiment (Fig. 18–3). Where a representative turfgrass community must be developed for a specific experimental objective, the shoot coarseness and stand density must be taken into consideration when selecting the container in terms of upper soil surface area available. Turfs that possess rather coarse-textured shoots with wide leaves of 3 + mm and a low shoot density of <100 dm^{-2} will require a large surface area of at least 180 cm^2, with 320+ cm^2 preferred, to form a representative turfgrass community. For example, a St. Augustinegrass [Stenotaphrum secundatum (Walter) Kuntze] turf will require a much larger surface area than a zoysiagrass (Zoysia matrella L. Merr.) turf.

3. Depth

The depth of the container can be extremely important in many types of turfgrass studies. Because water must be at zero tension to drain from containers, shallow containers typically will maintain a higher water content when irrigated regularly. Both the type of mix and depth of root zone can be varied to modify the amount of water retained (White & Mastalerz, 1966).

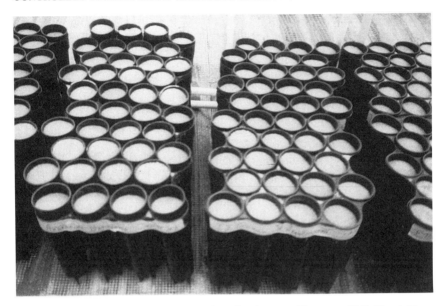

Fig. 18–3. Conetainers used in the propagation of turfgrasses. (Courtesy of J.B. Beard, Texas A&M University.)

Most medium- and fine-textured soils are poor choices for shallow containers. Experiments at Texas A&M Univ. of S. Sifers and J. Beard compared the response of various *Cynodon* cultivars when grown as turfs in a 6-cm deep flat-type propagation container vs. a container of 30 cm in depth each containing a medium-textured sand with 10% by volume peat humus. There were striking variations in both the quantity and length of lateral shoot growth produced under the two distinctly different container depths. The shallow container produced atypical shoot-growth responses. In addition, shallow flat-type containers present an increased potential for water stress and an accelerated loss of nutrients via leaching even under relatively controlled conditions. Although shallow, flat containers can be used for the vegetative increase of plant material to be planted for specific experiments, for many types of turf experiments it is desirable to select a container with a minimum rooting depth of 20 cm, with 30 cm preferred. As a general rule, most warm-season turfgrasses require a deeper rooting container than the cool-season species.

4. Drainage

Except where a closed soil system, such as for nutrient or water balance studies, is an important strategy in the planned experiment, it is important to provide adequate openings at the base of the container to ensure drainage of excess gravitational water. Containers are available with only one hole in the bottom, or with multiple holes where better drainage is needed. Clay pots lose moisture more rapidly than plastic pots, and therefore may require fewer openings for drainage. In closed systems, excessive soil water can be prevented by regular weighing to determine the water requirements.

5. Wall Transparency

The sides of the container should be composed of an opaque material or painted with an opaque coating. This will eliminate light transmission through the walls of the container to the extent that root growth characteristics are altered.

6. Handling Ease

There are experiments that require frequent movement of the turfed containers, such as for weighing, where weight and bulkiness considerations must be taken into account. The need to lift and move a large number of containers on a regular basis may restrict both the size of the container and type of root zone medium selected in terms of its bulk density. A specialized mechanical lifting and handling apparatus may need to be devised for large, heavy containers.

7. Structural Strength

The structural strength of a container relative to the weight of the root-zone medium contained within is important where frequent handling is required. Unfortunately, increased structural strength may also add to the container weight as well as the cost.

8. Life Span

Many glasshouse and growth chamber environments involve temperature and moisture conditions that subject the container to severe weathering stresses. Thus, it is important to ensure that the projected life span of the container exceeds the planned duration of the experiment.

C. Root Zone Media

Certain studies necessitate the use of an intact soil profile dug from a representative field site. However, in most studies practicality dictates that the root-zone medium used in glasshouse, growth chamber, and laboratory simulation experiments be a modified substrate. The root-zone medium selected is dictated by the objectives of the investigation, the methodology employed, and the types of data collected. The root-zone media discussed herein encompass those most commonly used, but this does not imply that there are no other satisfactory media for certain turfgrass studies. For certain types of investigations the root-zone mix should be fumigated, or in some cases even sterilized, prior to planting to eliminate negative confounding by parasitic organisms. An adequate supply of the root-zone mix should be prepared and stockpiled to meet the requirements for a series of experiments within a study.

Each root-zone medium should be fully characterized from both a chemical and a physical standpoint prior to initiation of an experiment (Horwitz, 1970; Klute, 1986; Page, 1982). Soil with a hydrophobic, alkaline, saline, sodic, B, heavy metal, or pesticide residue problem should be avoided, unless that dimension is an essential aspect of the experiment. During the course of the experiment, it may be important to regularly characterize the soil matric potentials of container soils via gypsum block, tensiometer, or soil psychrometer techniques.

The use of a fractionated decomposed organic matter source, such as peat humus, with a pH of 5.5 to 7.5 can be an effective component in rootzone mixes where a quantitative assessment of the root system is not required. In fact, it offers the advantages of enhanced water retention, especially near the soil surface, improved nutrient retention, and decreased weight per unit volume that can be important where frequent lifting of containers is involved. The use of a decomposed or undecomposed organic matter source as part of the root-zone mix should not be attempted where separation of the rooting medium from the roots is desired. The fine grass roots tend to grow into and through the organic matter particles and similar open rooting media, such as fritted clay. A portion of the roots are broken off and retained within the rooting media when attempting to separate roots from the rooting media.

1. Sand

Where roots are to be assessed in terms of biomass, depth, number, vitality, or root hair characterization, the use of a 100% washed, screened, silica sand is advantageous. A sand particle size distribution meeting the Texas Method specifications (Beard, 1982) is often needed (Table 18–1). Sand is a desirable root zone medium because it is easily separated from the roots by gentle washing with minimum damage to the delicate roots and root hairs of turfgrasses. A sand of the proper particle size distribution may also be desired from the standpoint of providing favorable drainage and aeration for plant growth. When selecting the sand, it is important that it be a silica sand, rather than a calcarious sand. The latter typically contains a high calcium carbonate fraction that adversely affects the substrate pH. Nutrition experiments are best accomplished in a silica sand substrate because of its inert status. As an added precaution the silica sand may be washed with distilled water.

Table 18–1. Texas guidelines for sand particle size distribution. (Adapted with the permission of Macmillan Publishing Company from *Turf Management for Golf Courses* by James Beard. Copyright © 1982 by The United States Golf Association.)

Gravel >2 mm	Very coarse sand, 1–2 mm	Coarse sand, 1.0–0.5 mm	Medium sand, 0.5–0.25 mm	Fine sand, 0.25–0.10 mm	Very fine sand, 0.10–0.05 mm	Silt and clay, <0.05 mm
Maximum 3%	Maximum 7%		Maximum 78% Minimum 25%			Maximum 3% clay 5% sand
Maximum Not more than 10% of total		Desired range 65% minimum 75% optimum		Maximum Not more than 25% of total, preferably 10% of total		Maximum Not more than 5% of total

Table 18-2. Summary of physical and chemical specifications for the Texas Method of root zone modification. (Adapted with the permission of Macmillan Publishing Company from *Turf Management for Golf Courses* by James Beard. Copyright © 1982 by The United States Golf Association.)

Physical and chemical parameters	Root-zone mix specification	
	Ideal	Acceptable†
Sand particle-size distribution	See Table 18-1	See Table 18-1
Sand shape/composition	Sharp, silica	Sharp, silica
Organic matter	<10% mineral ash; decomposed	<10% mineral ash; decomposed
Root-zone mix specifications, compacted:		
Infiltration rate for compacted root zone	10–15 cm h^{-1}	8–25 cm h^{-1}
Porosity	40–55% by volume	40–55% by volume
Bulk density	1.4 g cm^{-3}	1.2–1.6 g cm^{-3}
Water retention capacity	18% by weight	12–25% by weight
Soil reaction	5.5–7.5 pH	5.5–7.5 pH

† Specifications represent the minimums and maximums.

2. High-Sand Mix

A high sand root zone medium, such as the Texas Method specifications (Beard, 1982), should be considered where a more buffered root zone than 100% sand is desired, as it is less vulnerable to potentially dramatic shifts in soil reaction, nutrient level, and biological activity. In this case, soil and decomposed organic matter fractions are included along with the sand in component percentages that meet detailed specifications for the compacted root zone mix (Table 18–2). The result is improved water-retention characteristics, cation exchange capacity (CEC), and pH stability, while retaining the favorable water movement and aeration characteristics of a 100% sand root zone.

3. Light-Weight Mix

Light-weight root-zone mixes are desirable for certain types of turfgrass studies where quantitative root assessments are not involved and mechanical strength is not an issue. They are particularly useful for large increases of vegetative materials. Three of the more popular mix systems have been developed at Univ. of California (Baker, 1957) and Cornell Univ. (Boodley & Sheldrake, 1963).

The California light-weight mix typically involves a combination of sphagnum peat moss, medium to fine sand and calcium + dolomitic limestone, plus a specific mix of fertilizers (Table 18-3). A main goal in its development was to minimize disease problems.

The Peat-lite Mixes A and B of Boodley and Sheldrake (1963) are characterized by excellent nutrient and water-holding capacity, light weight, and minimal disease problems. Peat-lite Mix A contains sphagnum peat moss and vermiculite, plus dolomitic limestone, superphosphate, and a complete fertilizer of N–P–K; while Peat-lite Mix B contains perlite as a substitute for vermiculite, plus dolomitic limestone, superphosphate and a complete fer-

Table 18-3. Specifications to make 0.75 m^3 (1.0 yd^3) of three light weight root-zone mixes.

Mix component	California IC mix	Cornell Peat-Lite A	Cornell Peat-Lite B
Shredded German or Canadian sphagnum peat moss	0.38 m^3 (13.5 ft^3)	0.38 m^3 (13.5 ft^3)	0.38 m^3 (13.5 ft^3)
Fine sand, 0.5-0.05 mm	0.38 m^3 (13.5 ft^3)	--	--
No. 2 Vermiculite, Horticultural Grade	--	0.38 m^3 (13.5 ft^3)	--
Horticultural perlite	--	--	0.38 m^3 (13.5 ft^3)
Ground limestone, perferably dolomitic	3.3 kg (7.5 lb)	4.5 kg (10 lb)	4.5 kg (10 lb)
Calcium limestone	1.1 kg (2.5 lb)	--	--
Superphosphate, 20% powdered	1.1 kg (2.5 lb)	1.1 kg (2.5 lb)	1.1 kg (2.5 lb)
5-10-5 fertilizer	--	5.4 kg (12 lb)	7.2 kg (16 lb)
Potassium nitrate	113 g (4 oz)	--	--
Potassium sulfate	113 g (4 oz)	--	--

Note: If the peat moss is very dry, it is advisable to add a small amount of water sufficient to reduce dust problems.

tilizer of N-P-K (Table 18-3). A peat-light mix should be maintained in a moist condition as it is quite difficult to rewet once allowed to dry out.

Fertilizer additives can be adjusted according to the particular turfgrass needs. Mixing of the ingredients can be accomplished in a rotary tumbler such as a small concrete mixer. Water should be added slowly during the mixing process and prior to the addition of the fertilizer. A total mixing duration of 15 min is generally satisfactory. Numerous modifications of these three types of light weight mixes are used in turfgrass research (Table 18-4).

Table 18-4. Specifications to make 0.75 m^3 (1.0 yd^3) of peat-light root zone mix for turfgrass propagation. (Modified from Boodley and Sheldrake, 1963.)

Mix component	Quantity	
Sphagnum moss peat, fluffed†	0.38 m^3	(13.5 ft^3)
No. 2 horticultural grade vermiculite	0.38 m^3	(13.5 ft^3)
Water—pH near 7, nonsaline, nonsodic	47.0 L	(12.5 gal)
Dolomite lime	5.6 kg	(12.3 lb)
10-4.4-8.3 fertilizer (N-P-K)	3.2 kg	(7.1 lb)
Sequestrene 138 Fe (iron chelate)	35.0 g	
or		
Sequestrene 330 Fe (iron chelate)	21.0 g	
Micronutrient concentrate (described below)	236.0 mL	
To make 1 L of micronutrient concentrate:		
Copper sulfate (CuSO$_4$·5H$_2$O)	14.0 g	
Zinc sulfate (ZnSO$_4$·7H$_2$O)	6.0 g	
Manganese sulfate (MnSO$_4$·H$_2$O)	4.0 g	
Boric acid (H$_3$BO$_3$)	14.0 g	
Add water to make 1 L		

† A cubic foot of baled peat equals approximately 1.5 ft^3 of loose peat. A reduction in volume occurs during mixing.

4. Soils

In studies where specific local or regional problems are being addressed rather than basic concepts, it may be important to select a soil representative of the problem area. Be sure an adequate supply of the representative soil is obtained and stockpiled to meet the needs of all individual experiments planned during the investigation.

5. Fritted Clay

Use of 100% fritted clay is particularly important in the case of evapotranspiration investigations where the root system component will not be quantitatively assessed (Johns et al., 1981, 1983; van Bavel et al., 1978). A fritted clay root-zone medium ensures the most repeatable soil water potential (ψW) following gravitational drainage that is so critical as the base reference point in water balance studies using minilysimeters.

6. Solution Culture

The solution culture method of plant culture for research has advantages over a soil root-zone medium in that it is possible to maintain a constant water potential, an adequate dissolved oxygen level in the root zone environment, and constant nutrient availability. The propagation of individual plants in solution culture is advantageous in that it removes the confounding effects of the soil community, nutrient availability, and interplant root competition. Accordingly, individual plant solution culture has been used successfully in turfgrass nutrient deficiency symptom investigations (Love, 1962) and where the propagation of individual grass plants of a very uniform nature is needed for subsequent physiological studies (Howard & Watschke, 1984). A technique has also been developed for solution culture studies of a turfgrass community (Pellett & Roberts, 1963; Roberts & Lage, 1965). In this system, a cultural lid system was developed for the establishment of the turfgrass community upon the solution culture.

There is no solution culture composition that is optimal for all grass species or cultivars or even for all stages of plant growth and the time of year. One of the most widely used nutrient solutions involves a quarter to half strength modified Hoagland's solution (Hoagland & Arnon, 1950) (Table 18-5). Aeration and agitation are particularly important in solution culture. Aeration is typically via either perforated plastic tubes or aeration stones. The rate of aeration is usually in the range of 8 to 10 mL m^{-3} s^{-1}. The solution culture should also be changed at least weekly to avoid significant shifts in nutrient levels or salinity.

An alternative to a full water culture system where the roots are submerged in a nutrient solution involves a nutrient culture in an inert substrate. Materials that have been used include distilled water washed sand or gravel, plus perlite, vermiculite, or various combinations of these materials. In this system, the nutrient solution is generally applied in excess quantities into the containers so that there is a substantial flushing of the nutrient solution out through the bottom of the container.

Table 18-5. Guidelines to prepare a nutrient solution for experimental use involving distilled water and chemically pure salts. (Adapted from Hoagland & Arnon, 1950.)

Solution	Molarity	Compound (pure salt)	Quantity added
			cc L^{-1} dH$_2$O
1	1 M	KH$_2$PO$_4$, potassium, orthophosphate, di H	1
	1 M	KNO$_3$, potassium nitrate	5
	1 M	Ca(NO$_3$)$_2$, calcium nitrate	5
	1 M	MgSO$_4$, magnesium sulfate	2

To the above solution add solutions "a" and "b" below. First "a" at 1.0 cc L^{-1}, then "b" at 1.0 cc L^{-1}.

			g L^{-1} dH$_2$O
a		H$_3$BO$_3$, boric acid	2.86
		MnCl$_2$·4H$_2$O, manganese chloride	1.81
		ZnSO$_4$·7H$_2$O, zinc sulfate	0.22
		CuSO$_4$·5H$_2$O, copper sulfate	0.08
		H$_2$MoO$_4$·H$_2$O, molybdic acid	0.09
b		FeC$_4$H$_4$O$_6$, iron tartrate	0.5%

Finally, adjust pH to approximately 6.0 by adding 0.1 N H$_2$SO$_4$.

D. Planting

The planting rate, placement depth, and relative position on the soil surface must be uniform across all containers, especially where the establishment rate is an important component of an experiment.

1. Seeding

For seedings, the same number of pure live seeds should be used. The simplest way to ensure a uniform planting depth is to seed onto a level surface followed by topdressing with a fixed quantity of root-zone mix distributed uniformly over the surface. This procedure avoids disruption in seed placement across the soil surface, which may occur if an attempt is made to randomly mix the seed into the soil following its placement on the surface.

2. Sprigging

In the case of vegetative sprigging, a wooden or metal template whose perimeter is slightly smaller than the inside dimensions of the container can be used. A series of fixed V-shaped protrusions can be placed on the underside of the template such that when pressed onto the surface root zone it imprints a uniform series of furrows into which the vegetative sprigs can be placed. Additional root-zone mix can then be topdressed over the sprigs in the furrows up to the soil surface.

3. Sodding

When transplanting sod into containers, it is extremely important to harvest all sod at the same soil depth to ensure uniform positioning of the soil surface relative to the top perimeter and base of the container. Equally important is to harvest the sod at as shallow a depth as possible and still retain the sod strength needed for transplanting. The shallower the harvest depth, the more rapid transplant rooting will occur. Harvesting closely mowed turfs at soil depths of 2 cm or thicker may greatly delay transplant rooting and subsequent initiation of the experiment (Beard, 1973).

E. Irrigation

The evapotranspiration demand upon turfgrasses grown in a glasshouse environment in certain climatic regions can be exceptionally high at times. Dependency on timely manual watering of key experiments conducted in the glasshouse or for turfs being prepared for critical laboratory studies can frequently lead to disastrous results. The installation of an automated irrigation system is a far more reliable, cost-effective approach.

The overhead sprinkler/mist irrigation systems are best adapted for use on turfs in glasshouses. In contrast, drip and subsurface irrigation systems are more commonly used in growth chambers and stress simulation chambers. The irrigation system must be pressurized to ensure constant flow to all areas. If the pressure is derived from a domestic system, it may be necessary to install a pressure regulator valve if the pressure varies significantly throughout a 24-h period.

1. Overhead Sprinkler System

A typical irrigation system for a glasshouse with 112-cm wide benches (Fig. 18–4) is described as follows: choose either a three or six station con-

Fig. 18–4. View of a typical mist system used in the automatic irrigation of turfs in a research glasshouse. (Courtesy of J.B. Beard, Texas A&M University.)

troller connected via electric control lines to two to six electric adjustable valves. The multi-station controller may consist of an electric clock or a solid state unit, with the latter being more flexible and reliable. A multi-program controller allows variable irrigation frequencies for individual groups of containerized plant material depending on the establishment stage, propagation method, root-zone mix and depth, turfgrass species, or water requirement of the experiment being conducted. For variable irrigation frequencies, it is advisable to select an electronic rather than a mechanical or electromechanical controller, as run times of the latter two are quite variable while those of the electronic controller are precise. The controller should always have a battery backup so in the event of a short-term power loss, the program is retained rather than reverting to a default or to no program. A 24-V supply system and three-wire grounded circuits for all components are advisable under wet conditions for safety from electrical shock. The valves allow adjustment in water pressure from 70 to 345 kPa.

The water distribution lines with appropriate fittings are positioned lengthwise down the center of each bench. Typically, a 1.3-cm diam., class 315 PVC pipe is adequate. Tees are positioned at intervals along the piping to ensure head-to-head coverage, with 1.3-cm diam. risers extending upwards to a height of 0.5 to 1 m, depending on the height of the containers and allied turf canopy involved. A typical spray/mist nozzle will deliver a low angle spray at a rate of 5 to 10 L h^{-1} depending on water pressure, with an adjusted radius of up to 120 cm.

An overhead spray/mist system not only functions as a supplemental water source, but also aids in controlling other canopy microenvironmental parameters, such as atmospheric moisture content and temperature. Weekly maintenance of the irrigation system is particularly important in ensuring application uniformity. Not only is the spray/mist highly dependent upon operating pressure, but also on the nozzle capacity and spray pattern type. Nozzles should be examined at least weekly with cleaning and adjustment accomplished as needed.

The irrigation frequency practiced on established turfs may be daily, especially with shallow containers. The interval between irrigations may be as frequent as every 1 to 2 h, during the establishment phase from either seed or vegetative propagules. Critical initial propagation via excised vegetative plant parts may require misting for 20 to 40 s every 1 to 10 m.

2. Drip System

A drip emitter irrigation system may be used for certain types of investigations, such as those involving elongated columns typically used in rooting investigations (Fig. 18–5) or when the foliage must remain dry. As with the sprinkler irrigation system, drip system components will include a controller with time clock as previously described, appropriate electrical valves as needed, and distribution lines. The drip system is adaptable to the incorporation of an injection system for fertilizers and systemic fungicides and insecticides. The emitters must be stablized in the center of the container. A

Fig. 18-5. View of a typical drip system used in the automatic irrigation of turfs in a research glasshouse. (Courtesy of J.B. Beard, Texas A&M University.)

nontoxic anchor should be positioned on the end of the emitter to hold the tube in place and prevent backflow of salts and media into the tube. Soil displacement that interferes with surface rooting may be a problem, especially during the turf-establishment phase as well as with individual plants. Appropriate precautions may be needed to provide mechanical stabilization of the soil surface using a permeable, nontoxic material.

3. Subirrigation

A third method of irrigation that is effective in certain types of investigations involves subirrigation. Subirrigation must be designed to include proper aeration and regular water replacement that minimizes (i) anaerobic conditions and the accumulation of resultant toxic organic compounds, (ii) the accumulation of potentially toxic soluble salts, and (iii) disease development. Subirrigation may be intermittent or continuous. A regular water replacement schedule should be followed, the minimum being weekly. Aeration is essential.

4. Water Quality

It is important to use a quality water source when irrigating turfs being prepared for critical experiments, such as nutritional studies. The irrigation water may be from a distilled, deionized, or tap water source. The quality of the water source should be analyzed initially and monitored periodically during an investigation. Special considerations include objectionable levels

Fig. 18-6. Manual clippers being used to cut grass leaves from turfs growing in containers in a glasshouse. (Courtesy of J.B. Beard, Texas A&M University.)

of soluble salts, Fe, Na, B, carbonates, bicarbonates, and heavy metals. If the water quality is unacceptable and an alternate source is not available, it may be necessary to remove the objectionable component via either high-volume distillation, a reverse osmosis system, or an oxidizing system. Reverse osmosis is typically more economical where relatively high volumes of water are required.

F. Mowing

The most basic practice in the culture of turfs is mowing. To achieve a comparable leaf area and biomass among turfs from container to container, it is vital to ensure that the soil surface is positioned at the same height relative to the upper rim of the container. In this regard, it is important that steps be taken to ensure soil settling before turf establishment onto the root-zone mix within the container. Placement of the root-zone mix in the container followed by irrigation for 7 to 10 d will minimize settling problems. It is not possible to achieve a comparable mowing height and resultant uniform leaf area and biomass among containers without establishing the same soil surface heights above the container base and below the container rim.

1. Clippers

Defoliation can be accomplished by the use of manual or electric clippers that may have a clipping collection device attached (Fig. 18-6). Manual or electric clippers used for mowing turfs have an advantage in that they do not necessitate lifting the containers. It is commonly practiced for general vegetation removal of excessive leaf growth during increases of plant material. Unfortunately, this approach is very poor in terms of simulating the actual mowing operation in the field, such as with mechanically powered reel mowers. The uniformity in height of cut using manual or electric clippers can be improved if a metal ring or device of similar nature that matches the perimeter shape of the container can be set on the rim to establish a fixed reference height. The clippers are then operated from this fixed perimeter height across the turf thereby producing a more uniform height of cut for the turf both within the container and among containers. Even using this technique, it is not possible to accurately simulate the mowing uniformity and resultant leaf area and biomass produced by a standard turf mower, such as the reel unit described in the following paragraph.

2. Reel Mower

Where experiments involve assessment of a representative turfgrass community, it is important that the mowing technique simulate the operation as typically accomplished in the field. This is particularly important in studies involving evapotranspiration, photosynthesis, respiration, and carbohydrate relationships. In other words, a simulated mower device is essential for any experiment where canopy density, biomass, or leaf area strongly influence the parameter of interest. One of the more common units involves the modification of a reel mower in which an electric motor is attached via a series of pulleys and belts to the center drive shaft of a reel. A hydraulic-driven greensmower cutting unit is desirable, as it is small in size and offers good precision. The hydraulic drive allows ease of control and safety as belts, pulleys, and chains are eliminated. The actual mower unit is constructed on a fixed base above a movable shelf that is mounted via rollers on a fixed track (Fig. 18-7). Individual pots and containers are placed on the shelf at the proper height. The shelf is then pushed, from the underside, forward into the bedknife to accomplish the mowing operation. The mower position height above the movable shelf may be adjustable, as is the height of the turf and associated container above the shelf. This facilitates mowing at a diversity of turf heights and container depths. It is essential that appropriate protective safety devices be developed for the modified mower.

Another approach is to mount the mower on a track system via rollers such that it can be moved across the length of a bench mowing the grasses at a fixed height. The containerized turfs are placed underneath at a fixed height. This latter approach is more typically used where a large number of containerized turfs require the same cutting height, such as chemical screening. The mower may be equipped with a removable catcher for use in studies where clipping collection is desired.

Fig. 18-7. A fixed mounted, electrically powered reel mower with movable shelf underneath used for mowing turfs grown in containers of variable depths. (Courtesy of J.B. Beard, Texas A&M University.)

G. Fertilization

Maintenance of a continuous, uniform nutritional status in turfs growing in containers is an important dimension in the preparation of turfs prior to initiation of specific experiments. First the quantities of essential elements present in the root zone medium and irrigation water should be determined by chemical tests prior to initiation of the experiment. At the same time, a pH analysis of the root zone medium should be made and adjustments accomplished as needed to ensure plant nutrient availability.

The design of certain experiments may call for the use of a specific fertilizer or individual nutrient carrier to be incorporated into the root zone. However, for the broad array of experiments where differential nutrient levels are not a component in the treatment design of a study, the more common approach is liquid fertilization via either foliar feeding or soil drench. The liquid fertilization method is particularly useful in studies where the root zone is composed of a high sand content and thus has minimal nutrient retention. Uniform distribution of dry fertilizers over a turf canopy growing in small containers is difficult to achieve.

1. Liquid Fertilization

The fertilization program may range from foliar feeding at 3- to 5-d intervals to drench fertilization at 7- to 14-d intervals. The specific application frequency varies depending on the amount of irrigation water being applied and the allied quantity of water moving through and draining out of the soil profile per unit of time. The concentration of the nutrient mix used also varies with the particular grass species, development stage, growth rate, and degree of environmental stress, especially temperature, existing during the growing period.

A formula and procedure for mixing of a stock nutrient solution has been developed by Hoagland and Arnon (1950) which has been used with good success in certain types of turf studies (Table 18–5). This Hoagland's modified nutrient solution is typically applied at one-fourth to one-half strength as a soil drench. Researchers may need to use technical grade fertilizer salts, instead of fertilizer grade that may contain impurities, especially for nutritional experiments. Commercial sources of nutrient preparations for foliar feeding are available and can be effectively used in the general culture of turfs for many types of experiments. Each manufacturer provides literature concerning the concentrations and use of these foliar feeding solutions.

2. Nutrient Injection

A nutrient injection system may be used as part of an automatic irrigation system, especially for drip irrigation of small surface area turfed containers. Commercially available proportioner injectors may be effectively used, rather than the large supply tanks that have been developed by some investigators in the past. The proportioner injects a concentrated nutrient solution, or stock, automatically as the water flows through the injector. A standard ratio of 1:100 to 1:200 may be used. Equipment is available with ratios up to 1:1000 and a tank capacity up to 95 L. The diluted nutrient solution should be sampled and analyzed periodically to ensure nutrient injection at the specified rate. The practice of nutrient injection at each irrigation cycle is not advised due to the potential for salt buildup. A separate controller system or a bypass line should be designed and installed such that water alone can be applied as necessary to ensure leaching of salts through the root zone. Also, be sure to install a backflow preventer.

H. Pest Management

A primary concern in turf preparation for detailed botanical and physiological studies involves the prevention of disease, insect, virus, nematode, and mite injury. The general rule is to minimize pesticide use for controlled botanical and physiological investigations, with only selected use as dictated by the threat of serious turf loss.

1. Sanitary Practices

The basic approach is to follow sanitary practices in the selection of plant material sources and processing the root-zone mix. Even with these precautions, the potential for introduction of problem pests always exists where turfs propagated in the field are transplanted into the glasshouse or growth chamber. In transplanting sods from cooler field sites to a warmer growth chamber or glasshouse, the rapid development of a Rhizoctonia blight (*Rhizoctonia solani* Kuhn.) problem frequently occurs on several species. Mite problems are particularly difficult to eliminate from glasshouses on a long-term basis. Thus, regular fumigation with a compound nontoxic to the grass species, such as nicotine sulphate applied at 30-d intervals, is usually a sound practice to follow.

2. Diseases, Insects, and Mites

Pest damage to turfs being grown in small containers can be rapid and devastating to an experiment. Mite problems develop on turfgrass species in glasshouse/growth chamber conditions that are rare in the field. A timely corrective pesticide application when the problem first appears is preferred to a preventive treatment program whenever feasible. Where a rapidly evolving pest problem is anticipated, use of the appropriate pesticide on a preventive basis may be important. It is generally advisable for the pesticide selected to be (i) readily biodegradable to nonphytotoxic components, (ii) have a short residual persistence, and (iii) have minimal effect on the soil flora and fauna and especially on the grass root system. One must always be alert to unwanted turfgrass responses from a specific pesticide application. For example, some fungicides produce nontarget growth regulatory effects that may alter the parameter of interest in the study. Most notable are the compounds triadimefon and fenarimol that influence the leaf area index. Furthermore, sensitivity among turfgrass species exists in terms of the nontarget effects.

3. Weeds

Turfgrass weed problems that develop in containers are best controlled by manual removal. This approach avoids potential phytotoxic effects to turfgrasses from using either post- or preemergent herbicides. The label of the herbicide may indicate selectivity to certain turfgrass species or cultivars. Still, it may have more subtle phytotoxic effects that alter the morphological development or physiological processes of the grass to the extent that it will confound key botanical and physiological studies.

II. CONTROLLED ENVIRONMENT METHODOLOGY

In conducting controlled environment experiments, it is essential that they can be interpreted in relation to real turf conditions in the field. This is only possible if the controlled environment accurately represents the field environment. The primary physical factors that control turfgrass botanical and physiological responses in the natural environment are: (i) quantity, quality, and duration of photosynthetically active and total short- and long-wave radiation, (ii) temperature, (iii) atmospheric water vapor concentration, (iv) turbulence of the air, (v) atmospheric gas composition, (vi) water potential of the root zone, and (vii) mineral concentration of the soil solution.

There are numerous advantages to conducting certain types of experiments in controlled-environment facilities. First and foremost is the ability to grow uniform plants for a diversity of botanical, physiological, and biochemical studies. Also it is valuable for experiments where the objective is to control a multiplicity of environmental components while varying one component to interpret the specific plant responses without confounding from other environmental parameters, as occurs under field conditions. This approach can be used for investigations where the objective is to determine the normal growth range, and the supra- and suboptimal levels that induce plant stress and eventually death, for individual environmental parameters.

In interpreting the results of controlled environment investigations, it must be recognized that most plant responses are nonlinear and that individual environmental parameters are highly interactive and affected by fluctuations of other environmental parameters. An approach to proper interpretation of the nonlinear, interactive nature of the environmental parameters is to combine results of controlled environment studies with computer simulation models of plant responses to the environment (van Bavel & McCree, 1975).

A. Environmental Monitoring

Controlled environment facilities vary greatly among research centers in terms of size, shape, and inherent design features such as direction of air flow and extent of mixing, surface reflectivity, and the ability to control CO_2 concentration. Variations in external atmospheric carbon dioxide levels and pollutants, such as ozone and peroxyacetyl nitrate, in the buildings where controlled environment facilities are housed may be significant. Thus, monitoring of key environmental parameters prior to and during the course of an investigation is vital. Proper description of the environment within a controlled environment facility also enhances the interpretation of results among researchers. In addition, detailed measurements of environmental parameters must be made over time to ensure that the environment within the controlled environment facility is representative of normal field environments.

The primary components of an environmental monitoring system are the sensors and recorder system. Investigators should know the instruments, their principles of operation, and the basic techniques for both the exposure of sensors and recording of data. Common sources of error in environmental monitoring include sensors not compatible with the recording system, sensors not properly exposed, sensors not electrically isolated, and sensors not calibrated correctly or often enough. Detailed discussions of this subject can be found in the following:

1. *Environmental Instrumentation* by Fritschen and Gay (1979).
2. *Controlled Environment Guidelines for Plant Research* edited by Tibbitts and Kozlowski (1979).
3. *Instrumentation for Environmental Physiology* edited by Marshall and Woodward (1985).

Measurements may be described in terms of accuracy and precision. Accuracy refers to a measurement that is consistent with reality; while precision refers to the repeatability of measurements with any instrument. Turfgrass researchers should be most concerned with measuring the true value of a particular environmental parameter to ensure valid interpretation of plant responses. Error also is of concern in environmental measurements, and encompasses both systematic and random dimensions. Most environmental-monitoring devices should be properly calibrated before initiation of the study. The subsequent frequency of calibration needed to ensure accuracy of the instrument will depend on the particular unit and should be according to the manufacturer's guidelines. In many cases, calibration is best done by the manufacturer.

The monitoring of controlled environment facilities should include the following components: radiation, temperature, atmospheric water vapor, wind speed, and atmospheric CO_2 level. Each of the five components will now be discussed and guidelines for monitoring environmental parameters in controlled environment facilities used for turfgrass investigations presented (Table 18–6).

1. Radiation

The radiation measurements selected must relate to the types of plant growth experiments being conducted. Radiation is measured as energy that is being transferred in the form of an electromagnetic wave. The sun or other radiation sources initiate a radiant flux that is transferred through space onto a surface where it is absorbed, reflected or transmitted by the receiving surface, which in itself acts as a second radiation source. In the case of controlled environment growth chambers, not only the lamp source, but the chamber walls and lamp surface, can act as reflectors and secondary radiation sources that influence the available radiant flux.

There is a spectral dimension to radiation measurement. Plants are responsive to different lamps with varying spectra outputs (Tibbitts & Kozlowski, 1979). In certain plant experiments, the radiation measurements should include a definitive spectral range that is known to influence the particular plant response being studied. Electromagnetic radiation which elicits biological response is generally that with wavelengths between 300 and 3000 nm (short-wave radiation). The shorter the wavelength, the greater the energy possessed by a particle of light, a photon. Hence, there are two methods by which plant scientists measure light intensity, the radiometric and photometric methods.

The radiometric method attempts to measure the irradiance or total energy of short-wave radiation incident upon a surface irrespective of wavelength. Such measurements are of utility when describing the radiant heat load incident upon a surface. Irradiance is expressed as watts of energy per square meter ($W\ m^{-2}$) or as joules per square meter per second ($Jm^{-2}\ s^{-1}$). Net radiation is equal to the radiant energy incident on a surface minus the upward energy from that surface.

Table 18-6. Suggested guidelines for monitoring environmental parameters in controlled environmental facilities used for turfgrass investigations.

Environmental parameter	Unit(s)	Sensor or sampling location	Study monitoring time(s)
Radiation			
Short-wave irradiance, 300–3000 nm	$W\ m^{-2}$	Top of turf canopy; sampled over plant-growing area at start	Start
Photosynthetic photon flux density (PPFD), 400–700 nm	$\mu mol\ m^{-2}\ s^{-1}$	Top of turf canopy; sampled over plant-growing area at start	Start and end; biweekly if longer than 14 d
Spectral irradiance, 300–3000 nm	$W\ m^{-2}\ nm^{-1}$	Top of turf canopy; in center of growing area at start	Start
Temperature			
Air	°C	Top of turf canopy; sampled over plant-growing area at start	Hourly over duration
Turf canopy	°C	Vertical center of canopy	Hourly over duration
Soil	°C	10 cm below soil surface; center of container	Hourly over duration
Atmospheric water vapor	vapor pressure, $k\ Pa$† or rel. hum., % or dew point temp., °C or absolute hum., $g\ m^{-3}$	Top of turf canopy; or center of growing area	Hourly over duration
Wind speed	$m\ s^{-1}$	Top of turf canopy; obtain maximum and minimum over plant growing area	Start and end; take 10 successive readings at each sampling
Atmospheric carbon dioxide level	$mmol\ m^{-3}$ $\mu L\ L^{-1}$	Top of turf canopy	Hourly over duration

† 0.1 k Pa = 1 mb.

The photometric method involves measurement of the concentration of photons incident on a surface irrespective of energy, the photon flux density (McCree, 1981). This is of particular interest to persons studying photochemical events initiated by absorption of photons. Photometric measurements are expressed as micromoles of photons per square meter per second (μmol m^{-2} s^{-1}). This method is most frequently utilized by persons studying photosynthesis. However, only radiation with wavelengths between 400 and 700 nm are involved in photosynthesis. Thus, photosynthetic photon flux density (PPFD) is a measure of photon concentration with wavelengths between 400 and 700 nm (McCree, 1973).

There is a diverse range of instruments available for radiometry measurements. Regardless of the type of radiation sensor, it is important to select a site that is free of obstructions both above or below the sensor to eliminate shadows.

Short-wave irradiance (300–3000 nm) can be measured with a conventional pyranometer placed in a horizontal position immediately above the turf canopy. This instrument uses thermal detectors that are of a nonselective nature. An inverted pyranometer can be used for measuring the surface albedo of a turf canopy.

The PPFD sensors are much smaller than many pyranometers, thereby allowing a more intimate positioning with the turf canopy. The precision of measurements with radiometric instruments is in the order of $\pm 1\%$. However, the accuracy in terms of capability to measure in known absolute units is far less. For example, PPFD sensors might have an accuracy agreement among several different units of $\pm 10\%$ (McCree, 1981).

There are certain types of studies where radiation measurements involve a net radiometer. Most net radiometers will include all wavelengths between 300 and 60 000 nm; longwave radiation being the component between 3000 and 60 000 nm, or the upper cutoff of the individual instrument. For turfs having an extensive surface area, assessments with a net radiometer are best made via a controlled sweep over the area at a fixed horizontal plane above the turf canopy.

Finally, there is a photoperiod dimension to radiation measurement. Photoperiod has a regulatory influence on plants via a key pigment system. The regulatory effects include seed germination, flowering, and vegetative development such as leaf unfolding/unrolling, mesocotyl elongation, and growth habit. However, photoperiod is not simply the number of hours of radiation received per day. It also involves the photosynthetic response to the total quantity of radiation received per day. For example, 12 h at 300 μmol m^{-2} s^{-1} cannot be compared with 16 hrs at 300 μmol m^{-2} s^{-1}, as the total radiation received is different as well as the number of hours of radiation. Equivalents would be 12 h at 400 μmol m^{-2} s^{-1} and 16 h at 300 μmol m^{-2} s^{-1}.

2. Temperature

Conceptually temperature measures the thermal energy level of a body (e.g., plant, soil, and air). Temperature affects the rates of biochemical reac-

Table 18-7. Relative comparisons of electrical temperature sensing elements. (From Environmental Instrumentation by L.J. Fritschen and L.W. Gay, Springer-Verlag.)

Characteristic	Thermocouple	Resistance element	Thermistor
		Electrical temperature sensor	
Physical size	Small	Large	Small
Wire size	Small to large	Very small	Very small
Signal	0.04 mV °C^{-1}	Up to 100 mV °C^{-1} with proper bridge	250–500 mV °C^{-1} with proper bridge
Stability	Excellent	Fair to excellent	Good
Linearity	Slightly nonlinear	Slightly nonlinear	Very nonlinear
Interchangeability	Excellent	Good	Poor
Sensing at a point	Excellent	Poor	Excellent
Power source	None	Required	Required
Series arrangement	Easy	Easy	No
Parallel arrangement	Easy	Need to match sensors	Need to match sensors
Temperature reference	Required	No	No

tions, plant metabolism, growth, and development. Supra- and suboptimal temperatures restrict growth and at their extremes become lethal to plants. Temperature also influences saturated vapor pressure and vapor pressure deficit, that in turn affect evapotranspiration rates.

Selection of the temperature sensor and design of the allied monitoring system depend on the objectives of the measurements. Measurement locations typically include air temperature above the turf canopy, air temperature within the turf canopy, and root substrate temperature at a 10-cm depth. In addition, assessment of actual canopy temperatures or even individual leaf temperatures are sometimes required.

The three main types of temperature sensors are the thermocouple, resistance detector, and thermistor, which are described in Table 18-7. Resistance elements must be calibrated individually and require a precision power supply. Thermistors, which are semiconductors of ceramic materials, also must be calibrated individually. While they may yield larger sensitivity, they have greater nonlinearity and tend to have problems. Their accuracy for many types of turf experiments is typically ±2°C.

For most turf situations, the thermocouple is simplest, most reliable, lowest cost, rugged, easy to install, and compatible with most measuring and recording systems. A thermocouple is basically two dissimilar metals welded together that generates an electromotive force (emf). The junction and any exposed wire of soil-bound thermocouples should have a protective coating to prevent corrosion of the metals and thus alteration of the temperature response characteristics. The thermocouple (e.g., approximately 0.5 mm diam. Cu-constantan) is connected via two wire leads to a remote electronic measuring device. Only a single thermocouple requires calibration if the thermocouples are constructed from the same single spool of premium wire. Junctions are mechanically strongest if welded with silver solder. Double-insulated wire should always be used.

Shielding from radiation is required in the case of air temperature thermocouple sensors. The shielding may be constructed of clay plates or concentric tubes whose upper surface is constructed of aluminized Mylar or a white paint coating. In contrast, the bottom of the outer shield and support arm should be constructed of a polished metal, such as stainless steel. In addition to being shielded from radiation, thermocouples for sensing air temperature should be ventilated via an aspirated device providing air movement of more than 0.5 m s^{-1}.

The insertion of a temperature sensor into a soil profile should be at the prescribed depth into undisturbed soil or into a representative position in the case of turfed containers with a modified root substrate. Thermocouples should be inserted horizontally into an undisturbed plane from an opening in the turf canopy or soil. A soil sampler can be used to produce a 5 to 10 cm diam. hole to the desired depth. A pointed rod is then placed horizontally into the cavity at the desired depth and pushed into the soil. It is then removed and the thermocouple inserted into the opening previously made by the small pointed rod of a comparable diameter.

It is difficult to measure leaf canopy temperatures with the previously described sensors because of the inability to achieve intimate contact with the leaves while at the same time avoiding direct radiation exposure. The introduction of low cost infrared thermometry was a major breakthrough in quantitatively assessing turf canopy temperatures. Light weight, portable infrared thermometers are available that include direct, simultaneous, digital readouts. As with any instrumentation periodic calibration is critical.

3. Atmospheric Water Vapor

There has been a tendency in past research with controlled environment facilities to ignore the potential effects of atmospheric water vapor content on plant response. Measurement of atmospheric water vapor is commonly accomplished via psychrometers (percent relative humidity), dew point sensors (dew point temperature, °C), or infrared analyzers (g m^{-3}). Relative humidity is the ratio of the actual vapor pressure of water in an air sample of known temperature to its saturation vapor pressure at that same temperature, expressed as a percentage. In reporting measurements of relative humidity, it is also absolutely essential to report the air temperature. Dew point, or more specifically the dew point temperature (°C), is defined as the temperature at which air becomes saturated with water vapor, when the air sample is cooled at a constant pressure. The capacity of air to hold water vapor or saturation vapor pressure increases rapidly as temperature increases and approximately doubles for every 10 °C rise in temperature in the normal range of turfgrass growth. The preferred measurement is dew point temperature because of the greater accuracy in both sensing and controlling atmospheric humidity.

Where the objective of a study involves environmental parameters other than the atmospheric water vapor content, the controlled environment growth chamber facility should be maintained at an atmospheric water vapor content within a reasonable range for growth. Extremes involving either excessive or a severe deficiency in atmospheric water vapor should be avoided unless it is part of the basic experimental design. For example, saturation deficits of <0.3 kPa should be avoided. Also, relative humidities above 90% at a temperature of 25 °C during the daylight period are not advisable. Not only is this condition less than favorable for turfgrass growth, but there is a substantially increased potential for disease. For most turfgrass investigations where a specific humidity level is not required, the saturation deficit should be maintained between 0.5 and 1 kPa. For reference, the comparable relative humidity range would be 65 to 85% at a 25 °C temperature. Controlled environment growth chamber facilities with atmospheric water vapor control should be able to maintain ± 0.1 to 0.16 kPa of vapor pressure at 25 °C, which is ± 3 to 5% relative humidity. Unfortunately, many growth chambers do not accurately maintain relative humidities above 75 to 80% at 25 °C. Within a given situation, saturation deficits should not differ by more than 0.5 kPa among treatments in investigations where atmospheric water vapor effects are not under evaluation.

The assessment of atmospheric water vapor content is most commonly accomplished via psychrometers. The sensor should be shielded and the wet bulb aspirated at 2 m s^{-1}. Regardless of the sensor selected, it must be meticulously maintained and thus positioned where readily accessible for inspection and cleaning, as contamination is a great concern with psychrometer sensors. It is important to ensure that the sensor is properly calibrated. It also is important to use different sensors for the control and record functions in controlled environment growth chamber facilities to properly monitor the control system.

Other sensors available include the lithium chloride dew cell and Pope cell electrical resistance sensor. The lithium chloride dew cell is particularly effective at dew points below 5 °C and above 35 °C. It does require a power source. The Pope cell electrical resistance sensor, which involves a sulfonated polystyrene ion exchange substrate, has a nonlinear response and thus is of marginal utility unless the sensor output is electronically linearized and temperature compensated. An infrared gas analyzer is one of the more accurate instruments for measuring atmospheric water vapor, but is a bulky, complex, and costly approach that is best used as a periodic reference check of other sensors.

4. Wind Speed

The velocity of air movement which herein will be referred to as wind speed is an important factor influencing key quantitative plant responses under controlled environment chamber conditions. Wind speed is typically expressed in meters per second (m s^{-1}). The rates of photosynthesis and evapotranspiration are particularly sensitive to the wind speed. The rates of carbon dioxide and water vapor movement are controlled by a gradient established between the internal cavity of open stomata and the adjacent external atmosphere. A thick boundary layer and upper stratification typically occur that adversely affects this gradient unless adequate wind speed is maintained.

Quantitative assessment of wind speed is typically accomplished by an instrument known as the anemometer. The sensor used in wind speed measurement should be small, rugged, and possess a low starting speed, plus a linear response to a wide range of velocities. Also, the anemometer should generate an electrical signal that is suitable for transmission and recording.

There are basically two types of instruments utilized to assess wind speed over turfs, which involve either the dynamic pressure or the thermal cooling action of winds. The most commonly used type of dynamic pressure instrument involves a moving or rotating pressure area such as a cup anemometer. The second commonly used type of action which involves the cooling effect of wind is the hot-wire anemometer.

The cup type anemometer is widely used due to its sensitivity and simplicity. It consists of a set of cups attached to the end of horizontal radial arms extending from a hub. A three-cup arrangement is the most commonly used design. The wind exerts a drag force on the cups causing a wheel assembly to rotate around a vertical shaft with the speed of rotation being a function of the wind speed. Hand held three-cup anemometers are available for use where short-term, periodic checks of wind speed are to be accomplished.

The thermal anemometers are based on the measurement of convective heat loss from a heated sensing element to the surrounding fluid. A hot-wire anemometer is typically constructed with a heat sensing element of 0.013- to 0.13-mm wire. Criteria in wire type selection include ruggedness and stability to electrical, thermal and chemical influences. Platinum is frequently used. These characteristics make the hot-wire anemometer fragile and easily contaminated. Thus, it is best used for periodic, short term monitoring of wind speeds adjacent to the turf canopy. The preferred mode of operation of the hot-wire anemometer is the constant temperature system, if solid state circuitry is used.

Finally, the anemometer should be positioned as close to the turf canopy as possible and as far away from its mast or support as possible. The mounting for the anemometer should be rigid enough to eliminate vibration and also should be oriented in a vertical position.

5. Atmospheric Carbon Dioxide

Carbon dioxide (CO_2) is essential for plant growth. Yet the CO_2 level is seldom monitored in most controlled environment research facilities where turfgrasses are studied. In many plant growth chambers the amount of new air introduced from an external origin is unknown and may not exceed 10% by volume per minute. The CO_2 level in controlled environment research facilities should be in the 320 and 350 mg kg^{-1} range. The rate of turfgrass growth declines as the CO_2 level decreases below this level; with growth ceasing near the compensation point. The warm-season turfgrasses are capable of absorbing CO_2 at levels down to 7 to 8 mg kg^{-1}, whereas cool-season turfgrasses will usually not absorb CO_2 at levels below 50 mg kg^{-1} (Krans et al., 1979). This is because of the distinctly different compensation points for CO_2 utilization between the C_4 warm-season perennial turfgrasses and the C_3 cool-season perennial turfgrasses. Carbon dioxide monitoring and injection are usually required for controlled environment growth chambers where warm-season turfgrasses are being studied.

Ambient CO_2 levels are typically maintained by gas injection from tanks. The level is typically monitored by a continuous flow infrared gas analyzer with associated monitor controls and flow meters. The CO_2 can be either periodically or continuously fed from pressure-regulated commercial CO_2 bottles into the controlled environment growth chamber. The highest P.C. or commercial grade CO_2 should be used, plus a line filter to remove any air pollutants emanating from the CO_2 bottles.

B. Environmental Simulation Chambers

There are a broad range in types of controlled environmental growth facilities that have been used in plant research, including turfgrass investigations (Langhans, 1978). Prior to 1975, most of the controlled environmental research facilities used in turfgrass research were characterized by quite low light intensities in the photosynthetically active spectrum, many are still in use. Typically, the atmospheric water vapor content, wind speed and atmospheric CO_2 level within the chamber are not monitored or controlled during turfgrass studies, even today. Failure to recognize these potential problems may easily lead to plant responses that are not representative of the intended simulated environment.

1. Controlled Environment Plant Growth Chambers

A plant growth chamber has been described as simply an artificially lighted, insulated box in which the temperature- and humidity-controlled air is circulated. Actually, there is a diverse range in commercially prefabricated types of plant growth chambers as well as in specially designed built-in controlled environment chambers or rooms. The environmental conditions simulated vary greatly depending on the original design, with the particular environmental profile capabilities being dictated by the types of investigations planned.

In planning controlled environment growth chambers for turfgrass research it is important to avoid chambers with too low a radiant load, particularly in the photosynthetically active range (McCree, 1984). An adequate radiation load in the photosynthetically active range as well as adequate wind speed horizontally across the turf are particularly critical in studies involving photosynthesis, respiration, biomass production, and evapotranspiration (van Bavel, 1970). The suggested performance characteristics for a quality environmental plant growth simulator to be used in turfgrass investigations are presented in Table 18–8. Existing chambers with unacceptably low radiant loads can frequently be retrofitted with higher radiant load light sources, such as metal halide lamps. Heat dissipation via a shallow, recirculating water barrier below the lamps may be necessary in this case, if the compressor capacity of the chamber is not adequate. Whether or not the chamber meets the specifications of a quality growth simulation chamber for turfgrasses,

Table 18–8. Suggested performance characteristics of an environmental simulator for turfgrass investigations.

Environmental parameter	Technical specifications
Radiant load	0.5 kW m^{-2} with photoperiod control
PAR load	200 W m^{-2} with photoperiod control
Photon flux	800 μmol m^{-2} s^{-1} with photoperiod control
Air temperature	5 to 40 °C ± 1 °C with diurnal control
Dewpoint temperature	3 to 35 °C ± 1 °C
Wind speed	1.2 m s^{-1} with horizontal flow over canopy
CO_2 level	300–350 mg kg^{-1} using outside air
	100–500 mg kg^{-1} using CO_2 injection
	(only during light period)

Note: A. Low dewpoints are hard to obtain and control at high temperatures.
B. Use of outside air to maintain CO_2 level can give air-conditioning problems as about 10 air transfers per hour are needed. The alternative, CO_2 injection and control, is technically complex and expensive.

it is important that the chamber environment be monitored following the specifications presented earlier in Table 18–6.

2. Cold Stress Simulation Chamber

Specially designed cold stress simulation chambers can be used very effectively in turfgrass investigations (Beard, 1966). Relatively low cost modifications can be made in a 0.64 m^3 chest-type home freezer involving the installation of an EPR valve on the compressor, two elevated racks within the chamber on which turfed containers are placed, and sufficient space at both ends for air circulation provided by a 15-cm diam. fan driven by a 0.17-hp motor positioned outside the chamber (Fig. 18–8). The latter is re-

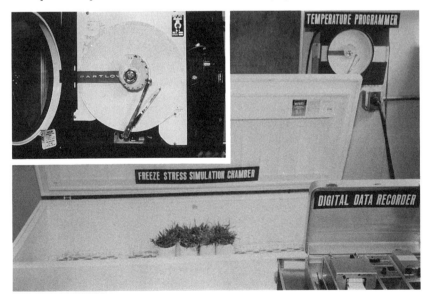

Fig. 18–8. Low temperature stress simulation chamber with controller on upper right plus closeup insert on upper left. (Courtesy of J.B. Beard, Texas A&M University.)

quired to provide uniform temperature distribution throughout the chamber. The chamber controller is designed to slowly drop the temperature over a specified range determined by the shape of a cam placed on a temperature recorder wired to control a micro-heat source placed in the base of the chamber in the form of two 60-W light bulbs. Such chambers have proven effective for low temperature stress simulation. Such short-term low temperature stress exposures do not require a radiant load.

3. Heat/Water Stress Simulation Chamber

The controlled simulation of either heat or water stress unfortunately may involve confounding between the two stresses because of their close interaction both in the field and in less explicitly controlled environmental simulations. A sound approach is to develop a simulation chamber in which the heat stress both external and internal to the entire plant is imposed under an atmospheric moisture content approaching 100% as close as possible. By the same token, in any simulated environment where the atmospheric moisture content is distinctly different from the soil moisture content it creates an internal plant gradient from the roots to the leaves that results in differential water stress within the plant. For these reasons, explicit controls of both moisture and temperature levels are important during heat and water stress simulations in chambers.

One approach to heat stress simulation in a chamber is to control temperature to the desired level while maintaining the atmospheric moisture level as close to 100% as possible (Fischer, 1967). Individual plants with soil washed

Fig. 18–9. Heat stress simulation chamber, with mount for individual whole plants shown in insert on lower right. (Courtesy of J.B. Beard, Texas A&M University.)

from the roots are then suspended in the wind stream where the moisture content and temperature of the tissue are allowed to come into equilibrium with the external atmosphere (Fig. 18-9). A similar approach (Fig. 18-10) has been used in turfgrass community investigations (John et al., 1981, 1983).

4. Glasshouse

Originally the glasshouse was constructed to ensure the survival of plants during winter periods. The use of glasshouses has become important in turf research, particularly in the north, where there is a need to maximize research activities throughout the year.

Modern glasshouses for research purposes require temperature control via automatic ventilators and shades, fan and tubular distribution, and evaporatively cooled air. Some sophisticated investigations involving explicit temperature control require a mechanical refrigeration system. This approach is limited to small experimental glasshouse facilities.

Radiant loads in glasshouses are quite important and may become a significant problem, particularly in northern areas of short days and low irradiances. Supplemental lighting of the glasshouse is required under these conditions. It also is important to ensure maximum light transmission via use of large glass panels in the original design and also by reducing the number of overhead structures such as pipes, electrical conduits, and structural supports that cause shading. Transmission is also maximized by regular cleaning of the glass surfaces. Photoperiod control of greenhouses is typically accomplished by (i) black cloth shading to obtain shorter days than normal

Fig. 18-10. Water/heat stress simulation chamber for turfs. (Courtesy of J.B. Beard, Texas A&M University.)

or (ii) by use of low-intensity artificial light to interrupt the dark period to induce long day effects.

III. BOTANICAL, PHYSIOLOGICAL, AND ANALYTICAL METHODOLOGY

As indicated in the introduction, it is not possible to address all methodologies involved in botanical and physiological studies of turfgrasses in this chapter. However, representative publications summarizing a range of methodologies that are useful in turfgrass research are presented in this section. This is not an all encompassing summary, but rather provides some key references from which a researcher can build upon to develop the best possible research methodology for solving a particular problem. In many cases, a technique must be evaluated on turfgrasses using known quantities to determine if it is sufficiently accurate from an analytical standpoint, or what modifications in the technique are required to make it applicable, for the particular turfgrass species being investigated.

I. Plant Botanical Methodology

  A. Plant Collection and Herbarium Preservation

    1. Jones, S.B., and A.E. Luchsinger. 1986. Plant systematics. Chapter 8, Specimen preparation and herbarium management. McGraw-Hill Book Co., New York. 512 p.

  B. Taxonomy and Classification

    1. Gould, F.W., and R.B. Shaw. 1983. Grass systematics. 2nd ed. Texas A&M Univ. Press, College Station. 382 p.
    2. Hitchock, A.S., and A. Chase. 1950. Manual of the grasses of the United States. 2nd ed. USDA Misc. Publ. 200. 1051 p.
    3. Hubbard, C.E., and J.C.E. Hubbard. 1984. Grasses. 3rd ed. Penguin Books, Harmondsworth, England. 476 p.
    4. Terrell, E.E., S.R. Hill, J.H. Wiersema, and W.E. Rice. 1986. A checklist of names for 3,000 vascular plants of economic importance. 2nd ed. USDA Agric. Handb. 505. 241 p.
    5. Tutin, T.G., D.M. Heywood, D.A. Valentine, S.M. Walters, and D.A. Webb (ed.). 1980. Flora Europaea. Vol. 5. Cambridge Univ. Press, Cambridge, England.
    6. Voss, E.G., et al. (ed.). 1983. International code of botanical nomenclature. Reg. Veg. 111:1–472.

II. Plant Physiological Methodology

  A. Physiological/Biochemical Separations/Radiochemistry

    1. Cooper, T.G. 1977. The tools of biochemistry. John Wiley and Sons, New York. 423 p.

B. Water Interrelationships

    1. Jones, H.G. 1983. Plants and microclimate: a quantitative approach to environmental plant physiology. Cambridge Univ. Press, Cambridge, England. 323 p.

    2. Kirkham, M.B. 1985. Techniques for water-use measurements of crop plants. HortScience 20:993–1001.

    3. Kramer, P.J. 1983. Water relations of plants. Academic Press, New York. 489 p.

    4. Spomer, L.A. 1985. Techniques for measuring plant water. HortScience 20:1021–1027.

C. Photosynthesis/Respiration

    1. Sestak, Z., J. Catsky, and P.G. Jarvis. 1971. Plant photosynthesis production. A manual of methods. The Hague, Nijhoff/Junk. 819 p.

D. Carbohydrate Metabolism

    1. Chaplin, M.F., and J.F. Kennedy. 1986. Carbohydrate analysis, a practical approach. IRL Press Limited, Oxford, England. 228 p.

    2. Smith, D. 1969. Removing and analyzing total nonstructural carbohydrates from plant tissue. Wisconsin Agric. Exp. Stn. Res. Rep. 41. 11 p.

E. Nitrogen Metabolism

    1. Bremner, J.M., and C.S. Mulvaney. 1982. Total nitrogen. p. 595–622. In A.L. Page (ed.) Methods of soil analysis. Part 2. 2nd ed. Agron. Monogr. 9. ASA and SSSA, Madison, WI.

    2. Nelson, D.W., and L.E. Sommers. 1973. Determination of total nitrogen in plant material. Agron. J. 65:109–112.

F. Plant Hormones

    1. Mitchell, J.W., and G.A. Livingston. 1968. Methods of studying plant hormones and growth-regulating substances. USDA-ARS Agric. Handb. 336. U.S. Gov. Print. Office, Washington, DC. 140 p.

    2. River, L., and A. Crozier. 1987. Principles and practice of plant hormone analysis. Vols. 1 and 2. Academic Press, New York. 401 p.

G. Tissue Culture/Cell Biology

    1. Bhojwani, S.S., and M. Razdan. 1983. Plant tissue culture theory and practice. Elsevier Publ. Co., New York. 502 p.

H. Histology/Microscopic Techniques

    1. Berlyn, G.P., and J.P. Miksche. 1976. Botanical microtechnique and cytochemistry. The Iowa State Univ. Press, Ames. 326 p.

III. Plant Analysis Methodology

    A. Tissue Chemical Analysis

        1. Horwitz, W. (ed.). 1984. Official methods of analysis. 14th ed. Assoc. of Official Analytical Chemists, Washington, DC. 1141 p.

    B. Roots

        1. Böhm, W. 1974. Methods of studying root systems. Springer-Verlag, Berlin. 188 p.

        2. Shuurman, J.J., and M.A.J. Goedewaagen. 1971. Methods for the examination of root systems and roots. PUDOC, Wageningen, Netherlands. 86 p.

IV. Soil Analytical Methodology

    A. Physical

        1. Klute, A. (ed.). 1986. Methods of soil analysis. Part 1. 2nd ed. Agron. Monogr. 9. ASA and SSSA, Madison, WI.

    B. Chemical

        1. Anonymous. 1969. Diagnosis and improvement of saline and alkali soils. 2nd ed. USDA Agric. Handb. 60. U.S. Gov. Print. Office, Washington, DC. 160 p.

        2. Page, A.L. (ed.). 1982. Methods of soil analysis. Part 2. Chemical and microbiology properties. 2nd ed. Agron. Monogr. 9. ASA and SSSA, Madison, WI. 1159 p.

    C. Biological

        1. Page, A.L. (ed.). 1982. Methods of soil analysis. Part 2. Chemical and microbiology properties. 2nd ed. Monogr. 9. ASA and SSSA, Madison, WI. 1159 p.

ACKNOWLEDGMENT

There have been more than 100 graduate students, research associates, and postdoctoral fellows over the past 30 yr who have made contributions to the development of the procedures and criteria discussed in this chapter. Further, the critical inputs of R. L. Green, D. H. Smith, S. I. Sifers, J. L. Heilman, W. G. Menn, and C.H.M. van Bavel during preparation of the manuscript are appreciated.

REFERENCES

Baker, K.F. 1957. The U.C. system for producing healthy container-grown plants. Univ. of California Agric. Exp. Stn. Manual 23.

Beard, J.B. 1966. Direct low temperature injury of nineteen turfgrasses. Quarterly Bull. Michigan Agric. Exp. Stn. 48:377–393.

Beard, J.B. 1973. Turfgrass: Science and culture. Prentice-Hall, Englewood Cliffs, NJ.

Beard, J.B. 1982. Turf management for golf courses. Macmillan Publ. Co., New York.

Boodley, J.W., and R.W. Sheldrake. 1963. Artificial soils for commercial plant growing. New York State College Agriculture, Cornell Univ. Agric. Ext. Bull. 1104.

Fischer, J.A. 1967. An evaluation of high temperature effects on annual bluegrass (*Poa annua* L.). M.S. thesis. Michigan State Univ., East Lansing.

Fritschen, L.J., and L.W. Gay. 1979. Environmental instrumentation. Springer-Verlag New York, New York.

Hoagland, D.R., and D.I. Arnon. 1950. The water-culture method for growing plants without soil. Univ. Calif. Agric. Exp. Stn. Cir. 347.

Horwitz, W. (ed.). 1970. Official methods of analysis. 14th ed. Assoc. Official Analytical Chemists, Washington, DC.

Howard, H.F., and T.L. Watschke. 1984. Hydroponic culture of grasses for physical experiments. Crop Sci. 24:991–992.

Johns, D., J.B. Beard, and C.H.M. van Bavel. 1983. Resistances to evapotranspiration from a St. Augustinegrass turf canopy. Agron. J. 75:419–422.

Johns, D., C.H.M. van Bavel, and J.B. Beard. 1981. Determination of the resistance to sensible heat flux density from turfgrass for estimation of its evapotranspiration rate. Agric. Meteorol. 25:15–25.

Karnok, K.J., and J.B. Beard. 1983. Effects of gibberellic acid on the CO_2 exchange rates of bermudagrass and St. Augustinegrass when exposed to chilling temperatures. Crop Sci. 23:514–517.

Klute, A. (ed.). 1986. Methods of soil analysis. Part I. Physical and mineralogical methods. Agron. Monogr. 9. ASA, Madison, WI.

Krans, J.V., J.B. Beard, and J.F. Wilkinson. 1979. Classification of C_3 and C_4 turfgrass species based on CO_2 compensation concentration and leaf anatomy. HortScience 14:183–185.

Langhans, R.W. (ed.). 1978. A growth chamber manual. Comstock Publ. Assoc., Ithaca, NY.

Love, J.R. 1962. Mineral deficiency symptoms of turfgrass. I. Major and secondary elements. Wis. Acad. Sci., Arts Lett. 51:135–140.

McCree, K.J. 1973. A rational approach to light measurements in plant ecology. Cur. Adv. Plant Sci. 3:39–43.

McCree, K.J. 1981. Photosynthetically active radiation. p. 41–35. *In* O.L. Lange et al. (ed.) Physiological plant ecology. I. Vol. 12A. Springer-Verlag, Berlin.

McCree, K.J. 1984. Radiation levels in growth chambers fitted with high intensity discharge lamps, with or without thermal barriers. Crop Sci. 24:816–819.

Marshall, B., and F.I. Woodward (ed.). 1985. Instrumentation for environmental physiology. Cambridge Univ. Press, New York.

Page, A.L. (ed.). 1982. Methods of soil analysis. Part II. Chemical and microbiology properties. Agron. Monogr. 9. ASA, Madison, WI.

Pellett, H.M., and E.C. Roberts. 1963. Effects of mineral nutrition on high temperature induced growth retardation of Kentucky bluegrass. Agron. J. 55:473–476.

Roberts, E.C., and D.P. Lage. 1965. Effects of an evaporation retardant, a surfactant, and an osmotic agent on foliar and root development of Kentucky bluegrass. Agron. J. 57:71–74.

Shearman, R.C., and J.B. Beard. 1973. Environmental and cultural preconditioning effects on the water use rate of *Agrostis palustris* Huds., cultivar Penncross. Crop Sci. 13:424–427.

Tibbitts, T.W., and T.T. Kozlowski. 1979. Controlled environment guidelines for plant research. Academic Press, New York.

van Bavel, C.H.M. 1970. Towards realistic simulation of the natural plant climate. p. 441–446. *In* R.O. Slatyer (ed.) Plant response to climate factors. UNESCO, Paris.

van Bavel, C.H.M., R. Lascano, and D.R. Wilson. 1978. Water relations of fritted clay. Soil Sci. Soc. Am. J. 42:657–659.

van Bavel, C.H.M., and K.J. McCree. 1975. Design and use of phytotrons in crop productivity studies. Phytotronic Newsl. 10:16–22.

White, J.W., and J.W. Mastalerz. 1966. Soil moisture as related to "container capacity". Proc. Am. Soc. Hortic. Sci. 89:758–765.

Wilkinson, J.F., J.B. Beard, and J.V. Krans. 1975. Photosynthetic-respiratory responses of 'Merion' Kentucky bluegrass and 'Pennlawn' red fescue at reduced light intensities. Crop Sci. 15:165–168.

19

Research Methods and Approaches to the Study of Diseases in Turfgrasses

G. L. SCHUMANN

University of Massachusetts
Amherst, Massachusetts

H. T. WILKINSON

University of Illinois
Urbana, Illinois

Turf can be broadly defined as grass species that are mowed closely and managed for their aesthetic and functional qualities (Beard, 1982; Vengris, 1973). The primary objective of turfgrass pathologists has been to develop strategies to manage diseases that reduce turf quality. Generally, these strategies have been directed at the pathogens and have met with only partial success. Turfgrass pathology is a complex field of study. There are numerous turfgrass species and cultivars, and many of these grasses are grown in widely differing climatic regions. Since the mid-1960s, it has become increasingly popular to blend different cultivars of a single species in addition to the common practice of mixing species in the same turf. The highly variable nature of turf complicates our ability to understand the development of its diseases. Similarly, the options available for turf management are as variable as the different grass species used in turf, further complicating the process of disease development and control.

Generally, the pathogens that produce problematic turfs are capable of effectively adapting to these complex variables. This adaptation can be demonstrated by the different symptoms of a single disease over a considerable geographic area. For example, in Illinois there is a distance of more than 700 km from the northern to the southern boundary. The appearance and severity of brown patch (caused by *Rhizoctonia solani* Kuehn) in bentgrasses (*Agrostis* spp.) during the summer months can range from small patches that last for only a few weeks in northern areas to large expanding patches that last for months in the south. Similarly, take-all patch [*Gaeumannomyces graminis* (Sacc.) Arx & D. Olivier var. *avenae* (E.M. Turner) Dennis] of creeping bentgrass (*A. palustris* Huds.) forms patches in the eastern, central, and northwestern states of the USA, but the severity, symptoms, and frequency of disease vary greatly. In approaching the study of turfgrass disease, it is important to realize the limitations of interpreting data from one experimental study for application to different turf species or different geographical areas.

Copyright © 1992 ASA-CSSA-SSSA, 677 S. Segoe Rd., Madison, WI 53711, USA. *Turfgrass—Agronomy Monograph no. 32.*

Because most grass species used for turf are perennial plants and most of the pathogens that attack them are ubiquitous, it is unreasonable to assume that pathogens can or should be eliminated. Most turf species and their parasites have coexisted for many years without one eliminating the other. The association of a particular parasite with a grass plant is not a sufficient basis for suggesting that it caused a disease observed in the turf. In general, disease problems develop due to changes in cultural practices, unusual weather conditions, or the genetic constitution of the grass plant. In such circumstances, parasitic microorganisms may realize an advantage and become pathogens capable of causing disease. Many microorganisms exist in a turf as parasites or saprophytes and cause no obvious disease symptoms until conditions allow them to act pathogenically. Disease in turfgrass usually develops because of imbalances in the turf ecosystem. For example, excessive growth due to N can predispose turf to infection by leaf blighting fungi [e.g., *Bipolaris sorokiniana* (Sacc. ex Sorokin) Shoemaker, *Drechslera poae* (Baudys) Shoemaker]. Low N levels predispose turf to dollar spot (*Lanzia* spp. and *Moellerodiscus* spp.) and red thread [*Laetisaria fuciformis* (McAlpine) Burdsall] disease. Excessive water or humidity and warm night temperatures are conducive to *Pythium* spp. and *Rhizoctonia* spp. activity and result in blighted turf. This scenario is complicated by the fact that there are more than 12 species of *Pythium* and several species of *Rhizoctonia* that can attack turf. Their relative activities in an unbalanced turf ecosystem are unclear at this time.

Highly maintained turfgrass may be considered to be an unbalanced ecosystem because of mowing, irrigation, dethatching, fertility, and other cultural practices. Disease outbreaks that occur due to the imbalances have led to the dependence on fungicides to reduce pathogen populations. Economic and environmental pressures are directing turfgrass pathologists to investigate better methods of maintaining resident microbial populations and managing pathogen activities in turf at levels that will ensure aesthetically or functionally acceptable turf.

This chapter describes the current research methods and approaches to understanding how disease develops in turf and suggests alternative approaches for this endeavor. By understanding disease development, pathogen management can be approached most effectively. Current research directions in turfgrass pathology emphasize diagnosis and etiology, epidemiology, and disease management through biological controls, cultural practices, and chemical amendments.

Etiologic studies have focused on the determination of pathogenicity of a microbial species on a single grass plant. Koch's postulates continue to be the guiding principle used to determine if an isolated microbe is a pathogen of turfgrass. This is a valid and useful approach, but falls short of a complete understanding of how and why disease develops in a population of grass plants. For example, *Fusarium* spp. are routinely isolated from Kentucky bluegrass (*Poa pratensis* L.) exhibiting severe patch disease symptoms. Although the disease was subsequently named Fusarium blight (Couch & Bedford, 1966), the original report did not include recreation of field symptoms after inoculation with *Fusarium* spp. *Magnaporthe poae* Landschoot & Jackson (summer patch) and *Leptosphaeria korrae* J. Walker & A.M. Sm. (necrotic ring spot) are ectotrophic (growing on the outer surface of roots) root pathogens of Kentucky bluegrass, and there are substantial data to support their ability to initiate a field epidemic (Landschoot & Jackson, 1987; Wilkinson & Kane, 1988). Presently, the epidemic development of summer patch and necrotic ring spot in Kentucky bluegrass is still incompletely understood.

Turfgrass pathology currently addresses both pathogenesis and epidemiology in turf. Pathogenesis refers to the stages of interaction between one pathogen and a single plant that result in disease; epidemiology refers to the interaction of a pathogen population with a plant population over a period of time as influenced by the environment (Fry, 1982; Zadoks & Schein, 1979). Pathogenesis helps define disease potential, while epidemiology considers the more complex nature of the whole turf ecosystem.

Turf is a perennial population of plants that are highly adaptive to their environment (Etter, 1951). The growth of grass leaves, roots, crowns, stolons, and rhizomes is controlled by the interaction of the environment and the physiology of grass cells. Pathogens are also well adapted for survival in a variable environment and can derive nutrients from grass plants. Unlike many other cultivated plants, the spatial density of grass and its vegetative rejuvenation produce a dense population of genetically nearly identical plants in which epidemiology is complex. While the initial stages of turf disease research must examine turf using the couplet: one plant/one pathogen, research must then move to the epidemiology of disease in the complex turf ecosystem. Besides the traditional focus on disease diagnosis and etiology, turfgrass pathology research now includes an emphasis on epidemiology and the development of integrated management of turf pathogens using cultural, chemical, and biological approaches.

I. ETIOLOGY

A. Introduction

The disease triangle symbolizes the interaction of the pathogen and the host plant as modified by the environment. The development of many turf diseases is based on a complex etiology that usually cannot be explained using the simple disease triangle or modified disease triangle (Zadoks & Schein, 1979). The etiology of a turf disease is a composite of numerous subprocesses each nested in a larger process. The basic process of disease etiology is pathogenesis. Because pathogenesis occurs far more often than significant disease symptoms appear in turf, the question then arises: how many grass plants in a turf must display symptoms before it should be described as diseased? The answer is related to the epidemiological development of disease. Thus, the complete etiology of a turf disease involves both the study of pathogenesis (one plant, one host) and of epidemiology (pathogen population, plant population).

The perennial nature of turfgrass increases the complexity of disease etiology. Many turf pathogens, including fungi, nematodes, viruses, and bacteria, can be described as perennial co-inhabitants of the turf ecosystem. The introduction of new cultivars, changes in cultural practices, new chemical amendments or revised application schedules, and use of various grass species in different environments all contribute to the continuing need for careful attention to disease etiology. Some general references are useful starting points for disease diagnosis and pathogen identification, but should be used for preliminary information, not always as a first and final opinion (Barron, 1968; Rossman et al., 1987; Shurtleff et al., 1987; Smiley, 1983; Smith et al., 1989; Vargas, 1981). Turf managers quickly find that turf diseases frequently do not match the classical symptoms found in identification manuals. Disease epidemics in turfgrass are often a result of complex interactions involving numerous abiotic stresses and more than one pathogen. The pathogens may include more than one species of a single genus, as in Pythium blight, or less closely related fungi, as in red thread and pink patch (*Limonomyces roseipellis* Stalpers & Loerakker) (Kaplan & Jackson, 1983) diseases that often occur together.

B. Disease Diagnosis and Identification

Diagnosis of a turfgrass disease by the symptoms on a single plant can be difficult because many pathogens cause similar symptoms. When symptomatology is combined with microscopic examination of infected plants for signs of the causal agent(s), an accurate diagnosis is more likely. Characteristic mycelium, spores, or fruiting bodies of pathogenic fungi may be present. This is especially true after incubation in a moist chamber for 12 to 48 h to encourage growth of the pathogen on plant surfaces and production of reproductive structures. Numerous references describe the symptoms and signs of turf diseases, and these should be consulted (Shurtleff et al., 1987; Smiley, 1983; Smith et al., 1989).

It is common to find several potential pathogens as well as secondary invaders and saprophytes in any diseased turf sample. The challenge of obtaining an accurate diagnosis then lies in determining the primary causal agent, that is, the pathogen that was responsible for initiating the disease. Information about the agronomic and disease history of the site, recent environmental records, cultural practices, and chemical applications are important in determining the primary disease agent. A badly deteriorated sample is usually impossible to diagnose due to the number of contaminating organisms present. The primary causal agent may no longer be active in advanced stages of disease.

The presence of a known pathogen in a sample with "typical" disease symptoms may conclude the diagnosis in many situations. Further evaluation may be required where, for instance, the turf has failed to respond to recommended chemical treatments. Diagnosis may then require that the pathogen be isolated from the diseased turf, but the isolation of a pathogen does not conclusively prove that the organism caused the epidemic. Isolation and identification may often be accomplished quickly, but for some problems, such as the patch diseases caused by ectotrophic fungi, final diagnosis may take months. The diagnostician must decide whether such a detailed diagnosis is warranted. It may also be useful to isolate the pathogen to confirm a field diagnosis of an epidemic. For example, in disease resistance trials it is important that the pathogen for which resistance is sought is, in fact, present in the trials. Disease situations that do not fit typical symptoms, pathogen descriptions, or disease development may lead to new and important areas of research.

C. Pathogen Isolation and Identification

As described above, accurate disease diagnosis sometimes requires that the pathogen be isolated from the plant tissue. This is also a requirement of Koch's postulates for proof of pathogenicity. In some cases, turfgrass pathogens are obligate parasites that are difficult or impossible to grow in culture, so that the requirements of Koch's postulates must be modified. Examples include downy mildew/yellow tuft [*Sclerophthora macrospora* (Sacc.) Thirumalachar, C.G. Shaw, and Narasimhan], powdery mildew (*Erysiphe graminis* DC. ex Merat), and the rusts (mostly *Puccinia* and *Uromyces* spp.). In most cases, however, the fungi that infect turfgrasses are quite easily isolated and grown in pure culture on standard nutrient media. The techniques and media for such procedures have been well described (Dhingra & Sinclair, 1985; Tuite, 1969).

Because some fungi may change genetically or lose pathogenicity after repeated subculturing, it is useful to maintain original cultures in long-term storage as a reference collection. Newly described or unusual fungi and cultures from newly described diseases should be deposited with the American Type Culture Collection or the Commonwealth Mycological Institute for access by other researchers and to preserve important research cultures that might be inadvertently lost in an individual laboratory. Bacteria can often be preserved by simply transferring them into sealable vials of sterile water or by maintaining cultures at low temperatures (H.T. Wilkinson, 1989, personal communication). Agar plugs from cultures of *Pythium* spp. may also be maintained in sterile water vials (P. Sanders, 1988, personal communication). Some *Pythium* spp. must be maintained at room temperature to preserve viability. Most fungal cultures may be maintained on nutrient media in refrigerators if they are transferred to fresh media several times per year. Foliar isolations are generally begun using standard techniques of surface disinfestation (Tuite, 1969). A surfactant such as Tween 20 is usually necessary to sufficiently wet grass blade surfaces. Fungi that must be isolated from crowns and roots that are in an advanced state of decay and contaminated with soil microorganisms may require a period of washing in running water. Ectotrophic fungi associated with patch diseases may be sensitive to the commonly used disinfestant NaClO, but can be successfully isolated from tissue disinfested with $AgNO_3$ (Juhnke et al., 1984).

Many fungal parasites can be cultured on standard media such as potato dextrose agar (PDA) or corn meal agar (CMA). Media amendments of lactic acid, to lower pH, or selected antibiotics help reduce the growth of bacteria and some fungal species during initial isolations. Since several pathogens are slow growing and easily overrun by other fungi, initial culture on water agar may allow isolation of the pathogen. Selective media will also improve chances of successfully isolating the desired pathogen free from contaminants. A number of selective media are found in the literature for the isolation of turfgrass pathogens. These include media for *Gaeumannomyces*-like fungi, *Fusarium* spp., and *Pythium* spp. (Burr & Stanghellini, 1973; Juhnke et al., 1984; Nelson et al., 1983). A selective medium for *Pythium aphanidermatum* (Edson) Fitzp. (Burr & Stanghellini, 1973) has been reported, and a modification of that medium has also been described (Sanders, 1984).

Accurate identification of fungi usually involves production of reproductive structures. While some fungi sporulate freely in culture, many do not. Various media and environmental requirements are necessary for production of spores and fruiting structures. Temperature and light quality, intensity, and duration are generally important environmental factors. This is particularly true for production of teleomorphs (sexual structures). Media and environmental conditions to induce sporulation are described in several books (Nelson et al., 1983; Sivanesan, 1987; Smiley, 1983; Sutton, 1980; VanDer Plaats-Niterink, 1981). Specific information on the identification of turfgrass pathogens in culture is also available (Barron, 1968; Hagan, 1980; Schmitthenner, 1980; Shurtleff et al., 1987; Smiley, 1983; Smith, 1980a; Smith et al., 1989).

Inclusion of sterile host material, such as leaf blades, roots, or thatch, in natural media may be necessary for successful isolation and may also increase formation of reproductive structures (Wilkinson, 1987a; Worf & Stewart, 1986). While this procedure may take months to accomplish, it is often necessary for accurate identification and to distinguish fungi for which the anamorphs (asexual stages) are similar or identical. For example, many fungi maintain an ectotrophic habit in the rhizosphere. Some have been found to be pathogenic, but many are not aggressive enough to cause noticeable damage. There are at least four known ectotrophic fungal pathogens of turf. *Gaeumannomyces graminis* var. *avenae* (take-all patch) and *L. korrae* (necrotic ring spot) are homothallic and form perithecia and pseudothecia (sexual fruiting bodies), respectively, after colonizing grass roots in axenic culture (Worf & Stewart, 1986). *Magnaporthe poae* (summer patch) and *G. incrustans* (Landschoot & Jackson) (zoysia patch) are heterothallic and will form perithecia only when paired with an opposite mating type in the presence of organic material (Landschoot & Jackson, 1989a,b; Wilkinson, 1988). While these techniques make it relatively easy to isolate a "pathogenic fungus" from a turf, it remains much more difficult to prove that it was the primary causal agent of an epidemic. Recently, *Gaeumannomyces*-like fungi have also been associated with root diseases of warm-season grass species (Elliott & Landschoot, 1991).

Other morphological features, such as clamp connections on mycelium, hyphal diameter, and septal structure may be important for fungal identification (Martin & Lucas, 1984; Smith, 1980b.). Several *Rhizoctonia* spp. and *Rhizoctonia*-like fungi are associated with turfgrass. They may be differentiated using nuclear stains to determine if cells are binucleate, tetranucleate, or multinucleate (Burpee, 1980; Martin, 1987). Within species, test strains are used to determine relatedness based on the ability of two hyphae to anastomose (fuse) (Martin & Lucas, 1984). In addition, other characteristics (e.g., colony morphology) are used to differentiate isolates of this pathogen group (Mordue et al., 1989). The relative roles of various *Rhizoctonia* spp. and strains as pathogens of turfgrasses have not been completely elucidated.

Important features other than the morphology of the mycelium and reproductive structures are useful in the description and identification of fungal isolates. These include color in culture, presence or absence of sclerotia (survival structures composed of a mass of hyphae), aerial hyphae, radial growth of mycelium, growth as measured by dry weight of mycelium, and cardinal temperatures (minimum, maximum, and optimum) for growth in culture. These parameters may be important in identifying genetic strains or races that are morphologically indistinguishable, especially in fungi in which it is difficult to induce formation of reproductive structures.

The use of highly specific serological techniques (e.g., ELISA and monoclonal antibodies) for detection and identification of turf pathogens holds great promise for certain applications. Commercial immunoassay kits are currently available for detection of fungal pathogens responsible for brown patch, dollar spot, and Pythium blight (Rittenberg et al., 1988). Monoclonal antibodies for detection of *L. korrae*, the pathogen associated with necrotic ring spot, have also been produced (Nameth et al., 1990; Shane & Nameth, 1988). Such assays may be useful for rapid qualitative and gross quantitative monitoring of pathogens in turf, since some pathogens may be detectable before symptoms appear. Applications include research uses in epidemiology and diagnosis, as well as applied uses such as fungicide recommendations and evaluation of disease forecasting models (Miller & Martin, 1988; Shane, 1988).

Careful biological studies must accompany the development of immunoassays to determine if all pathogenic strains will be detected. It is likely that pathogenic species may vary considerably according to location. To choose an antigenic determinant general enough to detect all important pathogenic strains, while specific enough not to detect nonpathogenic strains, requires extensive testing. Once reliable antibodies are available, immunoassays have several advantages over the time-consuming isolation techniques described above. Immunoassay results are usually rapid, and pathogens may be identified by technicians with little experience in identification of microorganisms. In addition, it may be possible to detect differences between pathogens that lack distinct morphological characteristics. This procedure will be particularly useful for fungi that cause similar symptoms such as various leaf-spot diseases and patch diseases caused by ectotrophic fungi. Another advantage is the possibility of detecting the pathogen presymptomatically for more effective application of fungicides. The assays may also be useful in conjunction with disease-forecasting models based on environmental conditions to determine if the pathogen population is at a threshold level requiring management. The determination of a threshold pathogen population is complicated in the simplest interactions involving one pathogen and one plant species. The complexity of a turf ecosystem will require extensive epidemiological studies to accurately interpret immunoassay results.

Bacterial and viral pathogens of turfgrasses are known but are much less common than fungal pathogens. Many bacteria are easily isolated using standard methods, but several fastidious bacteria and mycoplasma-like organisms are associated with turfgrass diseases of 'Toronto' creeping bentgrass and bermudagrass (*Cynodon* spp.). Isolation and study of such pathogens involves specialized techniques (Dhingra & Sinclair, 1985). Specialists experienced with such pathogens should be consulted for advice. A few viruses are turf pathogens, but the specialized techniques used in plant virology are beyond the scope of this chapter. Most turf pathologists seek the advice of virologists when a viral disease requires study.

The role of nematodes remains an area of controversy in turf pathology. Nematodes are obligate parasites and may be found on or in the roots of any grass plant growing in natural soil. Nematodes of many genera are turfgrass parasites. Some species are endoparasites, but most are ectoparasites that feed on grass roots without entering the plant. Isolation and identification of nematodes in turf require a sample of the roots and surrounding soil to a depth of at least 10 cm. Samples must be kept cool and moist until delivery to a diagnostic laboratory to prevent death and desiccation of the nematodes. Because nematodes are found in the soil and roots of all turfgrasses, it is necessary to sample areas that are symptomatic as well as nearby areas that do not show obvious damage. The relative populations of nematodes in the two samples will help estimate the role of the nematode population in the damage. A subsample of combined soil from the area of interest will most accurately reflect the resident nematode population.

Nematodes may be isolated from soil samples using standard techniques (Dropkin, 1989; Zuckerman et al., 1985). Weighed soil samples should be used, and the nematodes identified and counted from several subsamples of the resulting isolation. Low numbers of individuals from some genera can cause as much damage as high numbers of nematodes of other genera. Timing of sampling is also important. Nematode populations may be minimal when damage is most evident. Populations are often highest when grass is most vigorous and environmental conditions are optimal for growth. Monitoring throughout a season may be necessary to draw accurate conclusions about the role of nematodes in damaged turf (Zuckerman et al., 1985). As with all turf diseases, the interaction of nematode populations with other pathogens, such as root-infecting fungi, is complex and deserves more study (Riedel, 1980).

D. Proof of Pathogenicity

In addition to the isolation of a pathogen in pure culture, Koch's postulates require that disease symptoms be recreated following inoculation with the isolated pathogen. In turfgrass ecosystems, this concept may represent an oversimplification of the real-world environment. In many cases, the appearance of typical field symptoms requires a combination of environmental stresses involving nutrients, temperature, moisture, and a complex interaction among pathogens, hosts, and other microorganisms. Establishment of the causal agent of a turf disease has often been done by inoculating a single pathogen on healthy grass growing in a relatively sterile environment such as sand culture. In addition, proof of pathogenicity has sometimes been based on apparent infection by the isolated microorganism rather than development of epidemic symptoms that occur in the field. Because proof of pathogenicity is such an important component of the preliminary study of new or unusual diseases, this area of research deserves careful consideration.

In many areas of turfgrass research, inoculation is necessary to ensure adequate pathogen pressure and uniformity among treatments of a single experiment or between experiments. This can be useful for greenhouse/growth chamber experiments as well as field plots. Application of a quantifiable inoculum can produce relatively uniform infection that can be useful for comparison of treatments. Application of these results to natural infection must be done with caution because of the artificial nature of the pathogen "pressure."

Inoculum of obligate parasites must be produced on host tissue. Rust urediniospores are generally easy to harvest, quantify, and inoculate in an aqueous suspension on plants to be tested (Rose-Fricker et al., 1986). Evaluation of St. Augustinegrass [*Stenotaphrum secundatum* (Walter) Kuntze] for resistance to *S. macrospora* (downy mildew/yellow tuft) can be accomplished by flooding the test plants and adding infected leaves from which zoospores are produced to cause infections (Toler et al., 1983).

Inoculum in the form of conidia (asexual spores) may be produced on culture media or autoclaved leaves. After removal from the nutrient sources, the spores are applied as an aqueous suspension sprayed onto the foliage. A surfactant can increase the inoculum efficiency. This form of inoculum can be quantified with a hemocytometer (Tuite, 1969), a Sedgwick-Rafter counting chamber (Larsen et al., 1981), or other counting device and adjusted to the desired concentration. It is generally best to initially collect the conidia in as little water as possible and then dilute the spores to a specific concentration.

The desired concentration may be relatively low in a pathogenicity experiment or progressively higher in breeding cycles for disease resistance. In a pathogenicity test, the concentration of inoculum is kept reasonably low to determine if an individual propagule can cause infection and disease. High concentrations of inoculum may overload a plant's natural defenses and produce artificial symptoms. In greenhouse screening for resistance to *B. sorokiniana*, 30 000 spores/mL in a 0.5% PDA slurry was effective in eliminating all but 1% of the test plants when held at 48 h in a moist chamber at 24 to 28 °C (Vargas et al., 1980). Inoculum levels above and below that level were not useful. As the breeding cycles continued and resistance levels increased, inoculum levels were raised to maintain sufficient disease pressure.

Accurate identification of the pathogen is critical in pathology research. Equally important are the purity of an isolate and its physiologic state. Repeated subculturing of fungi in agar or liquid media can result in reduction or loss of aggressiveness or pathogenicity. The pathogenicity and aggressiveness of an isolate can be maintained or restored by periodic inoculation and reisolation of the fungus from a host plant. There is no general schedule for the "shelf-life" of fungal isolates, but pathogenicity testing is an important component of any study using pathogens maintained in culture for some time.

For research objectives, especially host/parasite interactions, it is important to apply inoculum that is genetically uniform. Single spore cultures may be used as a source of relatively uniform inoculum. For fungi that do not sporulate easily, single hyphal tip cultures may be initiated. Although less genetically uniform than single spore or hyphal tip cultures, single sclerotial cultures have also been used in some research (Jacobs & Bruehl, 1986). Most of these methods do not ensure that all nuclei are identical. Some nematological studies may also require that single nematodes of known identity be used as inoculum. The inability to maintain many species of plant-parasitic nematodes in axenic culture has hindered studies of host/parasite interactions of nematodes on turfgrass (Dropkin, 1989).

The form of inoculum should be carefully selected to meet the objectives of the research. For instance, oospores may be the predominant survival structure of *Pythium* spp. in climates with cold winters. Infested soil and thatch may be air dried to reduce other forms of the fungus to accurately reflect the overwintering inoculum for experiments (Hall et al., 1980). Likewise, colonized seed will predominantly consist of mycelium, and therefore, provide the epidemiological form of *Pythium*. The ectotrophic fungi associated with diseases of several different grass species survive and infect plants from mycelium-colonizing plant debris. The use of colonized seeds provides an excellent form of inoculum. This form of inoculum can also be adjusted to different concentrations for experimental purposes (Wilkinson et al., 1985).

It is often necessary to modify environmental conditions to establish disease in growth chamber or field situations. Unless methodology has been reported, the important parameters for establishing pathogenesis must be determined experimentally and under controlled conditions. Care must be taken that controlled and repeatable methods are developed that will ensure disease development. Most techniques are developed first for single plants or pot cultures. The application of these methods to established field plots often results in failure. Several foliar pathogens can be handled with reasonable ease in the field because they can be placed at the infection court, and the required canopy moisture can be controlled through irrigation or artificial covers (Sanders & Cole, 1986).

The climatic and edaphic conditions that predispose grass to disease are complex because they affect the physiology of both host and pathogen. Turfgrasses are dynamic plants with intricate hormonal controls and numerous meristematic tissues. Many stresses can predispose a turf to attack by primary colonists and subsequent secondary colonists. Physical stresses can predispose the turf to disease. For example, heat-stressed and wounded turf, created by mowing, is more susceptible to *Curvularia lunata* (Wakk.) Boedijn (Muchovej & Couch, 1987).

For several important diseases such as Pythium blight, brown patch, and dollar spot, sterile grain such as rye (*Lolium perenne* L.) or oats may be inoculated with the respective pathogens. The colonized seeds are then used to inoculate potted grass plants or turf field plots. The inoculum can be scattered either whole or fragmented into turf (Sanders & Cole, 1986). The efficiency of the inoculum is increased by placing it at the infection court and protecting it from climatic exposure. For example, *Rhizoctonia*-colonized seeds can be fragmented and slit into a turf using a commercially available slit seeder (H.T. Wilkinson, 1989, personal communication). This technique ensures that the pathogen is near the infection court and protected from desiccation or exposure. Pathogens may also be applied with sand, clay, or diatomaceous earth impregnated with molasses as a nutrient medium (Dhingra & Sinclair, 1985).

Soil-borne pathogens are more difficult to establish in field turf. One successful method used in studying seedling blights is to fumigate the soil with CH_3Br prior to infesting the soil with the pathogens and seeding the turf (Wilkinson et al., 1985). Limited success has been reported for infesting turf with seed grains colonized by some soil-borne pathogens. Whole oat grains colonized by *M. poae* or *G. graminis* var. *avenae* can be used effectively to inoculate seedlings or sod of Kentucky bluegrass or creeping bentgrass, respectively. In both situations, the inoculum must be in close contact with the roots. The tremendous "biological buffer" associated with turf minimizes the success of artificial infestations. Equally ineffective is the reliance on natural infestations that cannot be accurately predicted and controlled. Too often evaluation of germplasm for disease resistance has relied on natural infestation of pathogens that were not documented or quantified.

Nutrient levels are often important in establishing disease in field plots. For instance, red thread and dollar spot plots are generally maintained at low N levels while brown patch and *Pythium* plots receive higher levels of N fertility to increase disease. The form of N added to soil can affect the pH, which in turn can affect the pathogenesis of certain fungi. *Gaeumannomyces* spp. are ectotrophic and sensitive to the pH of the rhizosphere (Smiley & Cook, 1973). Ammonium-N results in suppression of take-all disease whereas NO_3-N does not and may even enhance disease (Huber et al., 1968; MacNish, 1980; Trolldenier, 1982). Nilsson (1969) reported that N sources can alter a grass rhizosphere by as much as two pH units, but these effects may be moderated by the lime content of a soil. Not all fungi are affected similarly by pH changes. *Fusarium* pathogenesis was reported to be enhanced by NH_4-N and suppressed by NO_3-N (Smiley, 1975). A complete discussion of the complex interactions of nutrients, pH, and disease is beyond the scope of this chapter, but remains significant in turfgrass pathology research. Prior to conducting research, turf should be conditioned by using the management program that will be applied throughout the experimental period. The period of conditioning should be determined experimentally as well. When conducting field experiments, as much information as possible should be recorded concerning soil type, pH, edaphic conditions, nutrient levels, climatic conditions, all management practices including irrigation, aeration, fertilization, pest control, and production and application of inoculum. This allows more appropriate comparison with other studies.

E. Host-Parasite Interactions

Host-parasite interactions involve the recognition and response activities that occur during the association of host and parasite. Parasites include all organisms that intimately associate with grass plants and derive their nutrients from them. For example, viruses, nematodes, bacteria, and many fungi form intimate associations; some fungi do not (Smiley, 1983). The slime molds that colonize the surface of grass leaves associate epiphytically with the grass plant but do not parasitize it. In contrast, rusts or endophytic fungi form an intimate association with the living protoplasm of grass plant cells. Other parasitic fungi derive nutrients from dead and dying host cells following infection.

Formation of an association between two organisms is a genetically controlled process mediated by the environment. An understanding of how grass plants respond to organisms in their environment is useful for developing effective pathogen control strategies. Most often, the pathologist studies this process from the perspective of the pathogen. The process for establishing a pathogenic association is referred to as pathogenesis. It can be divided into several stages: (i) inoculation, (ii) penetration, and (iii) infection and colonization.

Using this concept, important research questions can be defined and answered more succinctly. For example, the resistance of plants to fungal pathogenesis can be described by the nature of the resistance mechanism at the time of inoculation. Disease resistance mechanisms may be either pre-existing (present before inoculation) or active (functional after inoculation) (Russell, 1981). Breeding for disease resistance can be improved if the effective mechanism of resistance to a pathogen can be identified and studied experimentally. For example, the pre-existing condition of lignin or fungitoxic compounds in plant cell walls may present physiological barriers to infection (Hartley et al., 1976, 1978). An active mechanism of resistance is the rapid deposition of cell wall compounds at the site of penetration. For example, callose and lignin have been reported to be deposited at the inner wall surface following the initiation of penetration by foliar pathogens (Bracker & Littlefield, 1973; Friend, 1976). Resistance can involve both pre-existing and active physical and chemical mechanisms. This information can be used to assist plant breeders in the development of grass plants with greater resistance.

The interaction between endophytes and turfgrasses should be studied to determine how these fungi establish their intimate association with perennial ryegrass and tall fescue (*Festuca arundinacea* Schreb.). That understanding might facilitate the inoculation of endophytes to other grass species which has so far been impossible.

The interaction between a parasite and a grass plant is the most basic process in turfgrass pathology. By dissecting this process and then reconstructing it, our ability to manage pathogens and diseases will be greatly improved. There are conceptual models and descriptions of approaches for the study of host-parasite interactions (Bateman, 1978). Since the specialty of turfgrass pathology is relatively new, few turfgrass diseases have been studied using these approaches. Host-parasite interactions in other crops subject to infection by pathogens related to those that cause disease in turf are a rich resource for turf pathologists.

F. Disease Severity Ratings

Evaluation of disease severity is a source of controversy and difficulty in almost all areas of plant pathology including turfgrass pathology (Horsfall & Cowling, 1978). One must try to balance the time required against the accuracy of the evaluation. The complexity of evaluation methods must be justified by the desired results.

Disease severity can be evaluated from one grass plant or a sward of grass plants. Generally, turf diseases reduce the vigor of a plant or cause necrosis of tissues. In seed production, the impact of disease can be readily measured in terms of seed yield. The health or vigor of turf is usually evaluated on its aesthetic appearance, rate of leaf extension, and root/rhizome mass.

It is extremely important to recognize the specific symptoms of a disease. These can only be determined by studying single plants. In a turf epidemic, the symptoms associated with the primary pathogen may actually result from a complex of events that include pathogenesis. For example, in Illinois, *M. poae* parasitizes and causes necrosis on Kentucky bluegrass roots starting at a soil temperature about 20 °C, but the symptoms of summer patch often do not appear for many weeks when soil temperatures can be 30 °C (H.T. Wilkinson, 1988, personal communication). It is also unclear if symptoms of the summer patch epidemic are solely produced by the pathogenesis of *M. poae*. Evaluation of disease severity should include examination of plant tissues not directly colonized by the pathogen. This is especially true for the evaluation of diseases caused by soil-borne fungi.

The National Turfgrass Evaluation Program focuses on epidemic symptoms and uses a rating system of one to nine to facilitate comparisons between test locations (USDA-ARS, 1989). In recent volumes of the *Fungicide and Nematicide Tests* published by the American Phytopathological Society, fungicide efficacy evaluations are reported using similar rating scales that vary depending on the disease. Epidemic evaluations of *Pythium* blight, brown patch, and dollar spot disease severity are rated as percentage of turf area with foliar symptoms. At lower levels of disease, the number of dollar spot foci per plot are recorded. Diseases such as red thread may be rated as the percent of turf blighted and also include a quality rating of the turfgrass.

Pythium root rot has been evaluated as the number of infected plants in a random set of 25 plants or the percent area of blighted turf per unit area. Downy mildew/yellow tuft was similarly evaluated as the number of infected tufts in a measured area (Jackson, 1980). Leaf-spot evaluations range from the number of lesions on 50 random grass blades to the estimated percent of turf thinning due to melting out or crown rot (Johnston, 1988). If the disease to be evaluated results from a natural infestation and the identity of the leaf-spot pathogen is important, as in a germplasm screening, some leaves must be harvested and the pathogen identified in the laboratory (Tuite, 1969).

Disease severity in an area does not always reflect the severity of disease in terms of a single plant. Not all plants in a turf epidemic are infected or affected to the same degree. For example, the "frog-eye" pattern of a summer patch epidemic reflects different degrees of fungal colonization (H.T. Wilkinson, 1988, unpublished data). Rhizoctonia brown patch symptoms will change in intensity on a daily and yearly basis. These changes are likely due to environmental influences.

Disease ratings may include incidence or severity. In a turfgrass sward, large numbers of individual plants exist in a small area. Therefore, a measure of diseased area is recorded more often than the number of individual plants with symptoms. In evaluation of genetic resistance, however, individual plant evaluation is important. Researchers have tested the visual assessment methods and found many to be inaccurate (Sherwood et al., 1983). When the percent of an individual leaf area covered by spots was reproduced on paper and weighed, the visual evaluations generally overestimated the amount of diseased area (Sherwood et al., 1983). As epidemiological methods become more sophisticated, the disease assessment of turfgrass should become more precise. Because leaves are small and precise counting or measuring by humans is tedious and time consuming, more sophisticated and mechanized methods will be necessary. Optical scanning to determine differences in area may be adaptable for disease severity evaluation.

Data collected in disease severity evaluations must answer the research question being addressed. This involves both an understanding of disease etiology and proper experimental design. One must also be able to interpret the significance of disease severity in terms of turf performance. For instance, leaf spots may be evaluated as the number of spots per blade or by measuring the relative size of the spots. In genetic resistance evaluation, the size of the spots may more accurately reflect resistance than the number of spots (Zeiders, 1987). The percent of necrotic foliage in a plot is sometimes rated using the Horsfall-Barratt rating scale or a modified Cobb scale (Horsfall & Cowling, 1978). The accuracy necessary depends on the detail in which the investigator wishes to understand the disease and if the intent is to investigate the details of host-parasite interaction or some broader questions of epidemiology.

Diseased plants that have severely blighted foliage, crowns, or roots can be washed, dried, and weighed to determine the impact of disease (Hodges & Coleman, 1985). For example, in the study of nematode dynamics and their effect on root mass, nematode population density and blade clipping weight can be collected (Zuckerman et al., 1985). Root weights should more directly reflect nematode pathogenesis than clipping weight because roots are directly colonized by the pathogen. Smiley and Giblin (1986) determined that root cortical death could be evaluated to measure the amount of damage from an ectotrophic fungus. Cortical death could be differentiated from cellular browning by nuclear-staining techniques to determine if cells were still viable. Worf and Stewart (1986) evaluated roots of Kentucky bluegrass plants infected with *L. korrae* using a rating system that considered root discoloration and growth reduction. Both approaches are much more revealing than a topical rating of the turf quality.

II. EPIDEMIOLOGY

A. Introduction

The epidemiology of plant diseases has evolved rapidly and become relatively sophisticated in the last 25 yr (Rotem, 1988; Zadoks & Schein, 1979). Plant disease epidemics are always complicated by the interactions of the host plant, the pathogen, and all the other organisms present in the ecosystem as modified by the climatic and edaphic variables. Disease progress curves have been used to describe these epidemics using mathematical models to develop epidemiological theories and for use in disease forecasting. The epidemiology of turfgrass diseases is particularly complex because of the perennial nature of turf and enormous numbers of individual plants in the system. Most turf epidemics have been studied only at relatively superficial levels, but epidemiology is currently one of the most active areas of research in turfgrass pathology.

B. Parameters for the Study of Turf Epidemics

A turf epidemic is a biological process (a series of temporally and spatially related events) while symptoms are an instantaneous display of that epidemic. The study of an epidemic requires a reconstruction of the events that preceded symptom development. For example, in the case of summer patch in annual bluegrass (*Poa annua* L.) and Kentucky bluegrass, the amount of soil moisture and heat during spring and summer may indicate whether the epidemic will develop and how severe it will be (Wilkinson & Wagner, 1986; Kackely et al., 1990a,b,c).

Monitoring epidemic development requires that important field data be collected. The commencement of symptoms, the ontogeny of symptoms, and the frequency of symptomatic areas are important aspects of the turf history. The pattern, number, density, spatial arrangement, and size of diseased areas, as well as the nutrient status and age of the turf must be recorded. Instantaneous data describing the physical environment at the time of observation and preceding symptom appearance should be collected. Proximity to nearby physical objects such as buildings, drainage, vegetation, and stress patterns, prevailing air movement, and soil texture and stratification in the upper 10 cm of the soil, collectively, add important clues to the epidemic diagnosis. Temporal data should be recorded for soil moisture, soil temperature, pesticide and fertilizer amendments, and cultivation practices. Close examination of the turf will yield data on the number of grass species or variants, the relative development of symptoms in different grass species or cultivars, the susceptibility of the turfgrasses, the general vigor, color, and root/rhizome density. The above data are collected prior to examining a single grass plant, because these are the parameters that potentially could predispose the turf to the epidemic development of a disease.

The spatial arrangement of the symptomatic turf is important in epidemiology because it is the most readily observable response by the plant population to the activities of the pathogen population. Both the density of symptomatic plants and the nature of the interface between plants with symptoms and those without are important. Unfortunately, the severity and characteristics of an epidemic often depend on the density of susceptible hosts. For example, in a turf composed of annual bluegrass alone, a summer patch epidemic develops symptoms of nearly circular patches with a fairly distinct border. In turf composed of a mixture of annual bluegrass and other grass species, symptomatic plants may form irregular arcs or appear in a diffuse pattern (Wilkinson & Wagner, 1986). Many turf diseases, such as dollar spot and brown patch, have been named for the symptoms that appear on golf putting greens. Symptoms may be quite different on higher cut turfs and different grass species.

C. Evaluating Disease Progress

The objective of evaluating a disease epidemic is to discern how two or more populations of organisms interact over time. An epidemic is a complex of processes often too intertwined to study as a single unit. A better approach to evaluating an epidemic is to define the individual components and then attempt to combine the components to synthesize an epidemic (Zadoks & Schein, 1979).

Disease severity is an instantaneous measure of disease, but not a sufficient measure of an epidemic. To measure epidemic development, the initial morphology of the host plant must be known and quantified so that its change over time can be recorded. The instantaneous population of a pathogen is not enough to determine the potential for epidemic disease development. The turf population responds to a multitude of stimuli. Both management practices and climatic factors are complex stimuli that are intense and variable. The research necessary to define and quantify these stimuli is difficult. Often, the results of such research have been useful only on a regional basis. For example, the population dynamics of nematodes in southern turfs has received considerable attention (Heald & Inserra, 1988; Tarjan & Busey, 1985), but the data have not been applicable for understanding the pathology of nematodes in northern turfs.

It is beyond the scope of this chapter to explain the theoretical approaches to researching the epidemiology of plant diseases, but other references can serve as a starting place (Rotem, 1988). Plant disease epidemiology has recently been one of the most active areas of research in plant pathology. The benefits from approaching the study of turfgrass diseases as epidemics should be profound in terms of disease management.

An understanding of disease progress in turf epidemics has led to the development of mathematical models of the epidemics. Some models are created to help discern where necessary information is missing and lead to new areas of research. Disease models may be simplified, after critical stimuli are identified, and used for the practical application of disease forecasting and management. By attempting to link measurable levels of stimuli to disease outbreaks or severity, researchers may help turf managers to anticipate potential epidemics and apply appropriate disease-management practices.

Extensive research is needed to develop a sound and reliable model of a disease epidemic. A model must be understood both in terms of its capabilities and limitations. An anthracnose forecasting model has been developed that is based on daily mean temperatures and hours of leaf wetness, which are used to calculate a severity index (Danneberger et al., 1984). This index was only developed after research determined that the production and inoculation of conidia was governed by these climatic stimuli and that the conidia were responsible for new infections. Infection requirements were determined by placing healthy pots of annual bluegrass in holes in the field and managing them in the same way as the surrounding field turf. Each week the pots were replaced, and the removed pots of grass were examined for infection by *Colletotrichum graminicola* (Ces.) G.W. Wils. The severity index was calculated using a regression model based on the environmental data and disease severity. As with all forecasting systems, the model had to be validated by field testing that compared severity values and disease progress.

Disease forecasts have also been developed for Pythium blight on turf. The model of Nutter et al. (1983) is driven by two stimuli: maximum and minimum daily temperatures and the length of time the relative humidity is $\geq 90\%$. As the model is field tested, adjustments can be made to determine the influence of other management practices or the relative frequency of the more than 12 species of *Pythium* known to infect grasses. This model presently neglects complicating factors important in turf management that should be evaluated as potentially important stimuli. Shane (1988) recently evaluated this model and another by Hall et al. (1980) using antibody immunoassays. The technique allowed rapid and gross quantitative determination of pathogen populations at the early stages of epidemic development that could be useful in refinement of this model if the population of *Pythium* can be related to the epidemic potential.

As with most preliminary models, these may not be predictive outside the tested temperature range and do not consider the complicating factors of different biotypes of the fungus or host plant and effects of N fertility or other management practices. The turf disease models currently described are good preliminary attempts, but to be more useful, these models require the integration of other stimuli and good disease progress databases. Because the objective of practical turf pathology is to maintain a uniform and symptomless sward of grass plants, a disease model must be more effective and reliable than the subjective evaluation by a turf manager. Generally, disease models must predict the potential for epidemic development.

III. DISEASE MANAGEMENT

A. Introduction

With the advent of new knowledge and concepts for turfgrass epidemics, it should be possible to identify and integrate those management practices that will suppress disease. The integration of agronomic and horticultural practices and disease management strategies is a current challenge for turfgrass researchers. While the goal of turfgrass epidemiology is to explore and explain the pathogenic processes, disease management strategies must be developed to suppress them.

B. Biological Control

The potential for biological control of plant diseases is commonly discussed among plant pathologists, but successful examples are only beginning to be considered for the practical management of a wide range of plant diseases. Biological control can be defined as a reduction of inoculum or inhibition of pathogenesis accomplished by or through one or more organisms other than humans. This includes antagonism, competition, parasitism, and genetic resistance.

Research to develop biologically based management of various turfgrass stresses has achieved some success, but the scope of this research needs to be expanded. Most research has focused on the genetic improvement of grass species against abiotic stresses. Grass plants are selected for their esthetic qualities and growth characteristics. Germplasm that results in high-quality turf is then field evaluated for, among other traits, disease resistance. Field testing is useful for determining the spatial range of use for a genotype, but to adequately evaluate disease resistance, sufficient pathogen pressure must be applied at all geographic areas where evaluations are made. The selection of disease-resistant germplasm is discussed further in the next section.

Potential biological controls using microorganisms comprise a wide range of practices including: (i) application of weakly or nonpathogenic strains of pathogenic species; (ii) application of competitive or antagonistic saprophytic microorganisms; or (iii) manipulation of the environment to favor competitors/antagonists over the pathogens (Cook & Baker, 1983). The success of biocontrol is usually related to understanding the ecology of the microbial community present in the potential phytosphere. Numerous environmental manipulations and applications of organisms to suppress disease have shown great promise in laboratory and greenhouse experiments, but often give inconclusive or disappointing results in field experiments because the complex ecological relationships were not sufficiently explored.

Research on biological control of turf diseases has included several of the approaches listed above, and most work is relatively recent. As in nearly all plant disease situations, studies of turf diseases provide considerable evidence for the potential success of biological controls. The perennial nature of most turfgrass environments assures the presence of resident pathogen populations as well as competitors or antagonists. Despite the continual presence of turf pathogens, disease is generally seasonal or sporadic depending on the specific pathogens involved. Successful pathogenesis and epidemic development occur primarily in conducive environmental conditions when the ecosystem is unbalanced and favors the pathogen.

While part of this phenomenon is certainly related to increased host susceptibility or pathogen activity, a significant component must be related to the activity of the microbial community to which the pathogen belongs and with which the plant interacts. Laboratory and growth chamber experiments suggest that many pathogens are potentially active as disease agents at a much wider range of environmental conditions than are observed in the field based on symptom appearance. In addition, experimental determination of the host range of various turfgrass pathogens frequently does not reflect the more limited host range commonly observed in the field. Disease development would probably be more frequent and widespread without the resident microbial populations that colonize grass plants.

Further evidence for the role of competitors/antagonists in disease suppression is provided by the increase of certain diseases following the application of fungicides. Broad-spectrum fungicides that decrease resident fungal populations may increase thatch accumulation, and have been reported to increase certain diseases (Dernoeden & McIntosh, 1990; Dernoeden et al., 1990; Smiley, 1981; Smiley & Craven, 1979). The use of more narrow-spectrum fungicides has also been reported to increase disease severity caused by fungi insensitive or less sensitive to the activity of those fungicides (Smiley, 1981).

Some aspects of turfgrass management impede the use of biological controls. The relatively low economic damage thresholds on turf such as golf putting greens are a severe limitation. Low cut, highly maintained turf is so easily damaged that the degree of protection provided by manipulation of microbes may not be sufficient. The complex nature of many turf diseases may make successful biological control more difficult as well. Several diseases involve a complex or succession of organisms resulting in complicated ecological problems for study.

The use of antagonists to suppress plant disease generally requires an organism that: (i) is stimulated by the same conditions as the pathogen; (ii) acts in a timely manner so that the pathogen is inhibited; (iii) successfully competes to ensure an interaction with the pathogen; and (iv) is capable of co-survival in association with the pathogen (Cook & Baker, 1983). While not impossible, it is unlikely that an organism would be an effective antagonist if it were eliminated by the pathogen. Microbial control is a balancing act. Just as disease results from an unbalanced ecosystem, biological control acts to balance the ecosystem. This presents a formidable challenge for the use of microbial control for turfgrass because elimination of the symptoms of an epidemic is the expected level of control. In turf management, a combination of biological, chemical, and cultural practices may be necessary to achieve acceptable control. The benefits from microbial control could still be significant.

The simplest approach to develop biological control of a plant pathogen is to look for a specific species or strain of an organism from the field that might be competitive or antagonistic to a pathogen (Cook & Baker, 1983). Much has already been written about such an approach, and recommendations usually include two guidelines. First, it has been suggested that potential biocontrol agents are more likely to be found in an area in which disease is less severe than would be expected based on the environment and previous disease activity. In such a "suppressed disease" site, some resident organisms might be effectively reducing the pathogen's ability to cause disease (Cook & Baker, 1983; Dhingra & Sinclair, 1985).

Several methods have been suggested as preliminary means of detecting the presence of potential biological control agents in soil or plant tissue (Dhingra & Sinclair, 1985). Once the presence of such organisms has been detected, it is necessary to determine if the general resident population is also contributing to the suppressiveness or if a specific antagonist/competitor is the main effector. If specific organisms are detected and isolated, culture plates containing various isolates paired with pathogens can be used to determine relative growth rates, competitiveness, antagonism, and antibiotic production. Confirmation of antibiotic production is usually accomplished using cell-free filtrates. Hyperparasitic organisms can sometimes be detected by placing mycelial mats or pathogen cultures grown on retrievable supports in soil. Later, the mycelia can be examined for mycoparasitism, and potential biocontrol agents can be isolated.

The second guideline for isolation of potential biocontrol agents is that organisms isolated from plant surfaces as opposed to bulk soil are more likely to survive and compete successfully. The use of such organisms has been described for biological control of several turfgrass diseases. Binucleate strains of *Rhizoctonia* are commonly isolated from turfgrass although they are apparently either weakly or nonpathogenic. Application of these strains successfully reduced brown patch, caused by multinucleate species, in the field (Burpee & Goulty, 1984). Induced host resistance or competition for leaf exudates or space were suggested as probable mechanisms of disease suppression. While disease suppression was significant, the availability of highly effective fungicides makes the use of such a biological control less likely for acceptance on putting greens where turf can be rapidly and severely damaged. Application of binucleate, *Rhizoctonia* fungi may be more appropriate on lawns or other higher cut and less-maintained turfgrass where economic damage thresholds are higher, and disease is less likely to be severe.

Because snow mold is generally poorly controlled with fungicides, the use of cultural practices and potential biological controls to manage this disease complex has received more attention. Gray snow mold was reduced through the application of sclerotia of *Typhula phacorrhiza* (Reichard:Fr) Fr., a saprophytic fungus of the same genus as the snow mold pathogens *T. incarnata* Fr. and *T. ishikariensis* Imai var. *ishikariensis* (Årsvoll & Smith) (Burpee et al., 1987). Inoculation of turf with the competitor resulted in colonization of the turf tissue by the competitor and reduced colonization by the pathogen. Since biological control was most successful in field plots containing only natural inoculum rather than artificially inoculated plots, the importance of the pathogen population is uncertain. The biocontrol fungus can be formulated into pellets that facilitate application to turfgrass in the fall to prevent winter colonization by pathogenic *Typhula* spp. and perhaps other snow mold fungi (Burpee et al., 1987).

The potential for biological control of fairy rings was demonstrated when mycelial rings intersected naturally in turfgrass (Smith, 1980b; Wilkinson, 1987a,b). When two rings of the same species intersected they often eliminated further mycelial growth, a phenomenon that was called *extinction* (Smith, 1980b). When different species intersected, the results varied. The mycelial rings sometimes caused mutual (bilateral) extinction, sometimes only one ring was affected (unilateral extinction), and sometimes neither ring showed any apparent interaction. Laboratory studies of the interactions of these fungi in culture suggest that the interactions may involve competition, antagonism, or antibiosis (Smith & Rupps, 1978). While not usually parasitic on turfgrass, fairy ring fungi can cause damage in turf primarily from the dense, hydrophobic mycelial mat in the soil beneath the turf. Where soil removal or fumigation is not desired or economically feasible, the soil may be tilled so that the mycelia of fungi may antagonize each other at many loci, thus preventing the establishment of new fairy rings (Smith, 1980b).

While introduction of "mycofungicides" or specific competitive strains has potential in many disease situations, it may be more appropriate to consider the manipulation of resident populations of microorganisms in turfgrass disease management. This is particularly true for root and crown pathogens. Considerable research has focused recently on ectotrophic fungi responsible for patch diseases. These soil-borne fungi generally grow slowly and also are poor saprophytic competitors in soil. They apparently become significant pathogens when turfgrass is stressed. This type of situation seems to present good possibilities for manipulation of competitors/antagonists because slight changes in the microbial balance may determine the difference between weak parasitism and pathogenesis.

Some preliminary research suggests that daily watering, which keeps thatch and upper soil layers moist, can reduce necrotic ring spot patch development (Melvin et al., 1988). Laboratory analysis suggests that bacteria and actinomycete populations increase under such conditions. Other experiments are currently being conducted to determine if microbial populations may serve as general antagonists of turf diseases (H.T. Wilkinson, 1989, personal communication). Additions of compost as topdressing or application of specific bacterial strains isolated from turf are being investigated for biocontrol of turf diseases. Research results are just beginning to be published (Nelson & Craft, 1991a,b,c,d; Sanders & Soika, 1991; Soika & Sanders, 1991).

One commercial product, Clandosan 618, has been marketed for biological control of nematodes on turfgrass. It consists of chitin-protein and urea. The technical bulletin for this product suggests that the product has no direct adverse effects on plant-parasitic nematodes but, rather, stimulates the growth of antagonistic microorganisms. A 1989 report in "Biological and Cultural Tests for Control of Plant Diseases" found no reduction of *Tylenchorhynchus* population on annual bluegrass maintained at putting green height when chitin was applied (Wick, 1989).

Other traditional biological control agents, such as *Trichoderma* spp. have been investigated for use in turf-disease management, but little field research has been reported. Literature from other crop systems suggests that successful selection of agents will come from isolation of organisms adapted to potential infection sites of various pathogens (Cook & Baker, 1983). Thus, rhizosphere or phylloplane "competence" will be an important factor in the successful adaptation and maintenance of organisms for biological control in these zones. Biological control agents will be most successful when introduced and maintained through careful environmental control, cultural practices such as appropriate fertility management, mowing, and irrigation, and use of mixtures and blends of improved turfgrasses with increased genetic disease resistance. A major benefit of investigations into biocontrol is that they often lead to a better understanding of the microbial ecology of turfgrass, which may lead to better turfgrass disease management. It is obligatory that a biological control system integrate fully into the cultural management of turf if it is to be effective.

C. Genetic Resistance to Disease

An important area of emphasis in turfgrass improvement is the selection of cultivars that have resistance to disease. Breeding for disease resistance is a complex and important research area that cannot be discussed fully here, but there are several important aspects that should be mentioned. The study of disease resistance may be divided into various components including: (i) resistance based on the genetic inheritance of individual cultivars, (ii) resistance based on population genetics of blends and mixtures, and (iii) resistance based on improved stress tolerance (e.g., cold, heat, drought, and shade).

The selection of the Kentucky bluegrass cv. Merion is an important historical example of genetic resistance to disease. Since the development of Merion, newly released Kentucky bluegrass cultivars must be equal or, preferably, superior to Merion's level of resistance to leaf spot and melting out disease. The reports of the National Turfgrass Evaluation Program frequently list the resistance of new cultivars to various diseases although most of these ratings are based on undocumented natural infestations rather than deliberate inoculations. The complexity of disease resistance is well demonstrated in the reports, however.

Considerable variability in disease resistance is reported from test sites across the USA. This variability may be somewhat predictable for diseases associated with certain stresses such as drought or heat stress, soil type, or pH differences. Some variability is also probably due to different species, biotypes, or races of the pathogens in different geographic areas. Plant breeders have always struggled with the apparently limitless ability of pathogen populations to adapt to new plant population genotypes. In many crops, diseases caused by powdery mildew, rust, smut, and *Phytophthora* spp. are perpetual problems because of the relentless appearance of new races of these fungi capable of infecting new host germplasms.

Newly discovered, or at least newly reported, diseases seem to appear quickly in widespread areas, perhaps due to efficient transport of pathogens by humans. Another possible cause is the widespread planting of popular turf cultivars, which increases the selective pressure on pathogen populations to adapt. The increased use of new turfgrass genotypes resistant to certain important diseases may also result in the development of disease problems as seen in the increase of necrotic ring spot and summer patch in Kentucky bluegrass cultivars with improved resistance to leaf spot/melting out.

Selection of disease-resistant genotypes in turfgrasses may be improved by a better understanding of the biochemical interactions between the pathogen and the grass plant. For example, Mathias et al. (1981) reported a seasonal relationship between polyphenol levels and leaf spot activity on Kentucky bluegrass. Production of phenolic compounds as biochemical-resistance factors has been studied in numerous plant/pathogen relationships. While many factors affect this complex interaction, there is a possibility of finding some quantifiable biochemical resistance factors that can be used in breeding selections.

Some problems in disease resistance selection are the reproductive limitations associated with the turfgrasses themselves. This aspect of a breeding program is discussed in another chapter, but it should be reiterated that breeding programs require genetic resources, an ability to produce a variety of genotypes for selection, and a means to maintain the genetic integrity after the selections have been made. Apomixis, where it exists in turfgrasses, is useful because it reduces genetic hybridization, thus maintaining desired genetic constitution.

The use of tissue culture as a solution to some previous breeding problems holds promise, but it has not been developed fully (Boyd & Dale, 1986). The production of somaclonal variants or artificially mutated cells could increase the frequency of discovering resistance genes. Combined with rapid in vitro pathogenicity tests and subculturing of the resistant plants, the rate of producing potentially more resistant plants could be increased. This is especially attractive for improving resistance against soil-borne pathogens that are difficult to establish and slow to develop in the field. The science of whole cell and tissue culture is well developed (Gamberg & Wetter, 1975; Larkin & Scowcroft, 1981; Vasil, 1984) but its application to turfgrasses will require some modification (Lowe & Conger, 1979; McDonnell & Conger, 1984). One perpetual problem with turfgrasses is the physically small size of embryogenic and meristematic tissues. Because these tissues have a small volume to surface area ratio, they are susceptible to necrosis during disinfestation.

Certain pathogens produce toxins that may be used as parameters for pathogenicity. Some pathogens produce toxins that result in expanding leaf lesions with colored or zonate borders (Daub, 1984). Since purified toxins will cause necrotic symptoms, tissue-cultured germplasm can be treated with these toxins to estimate resistance levels. This type of system is generally simpler than managing both a living pathogen and a living plant.

Unfortunately, not all pathogens produce toxins, but other pathogen attributes may be used to simplify germplasm selection. For example, most soil-borne pythiaceous fungi must attach their infective propagules to the plant root or rhizome before penetration can occur. The ability to attach to a plant can be readily discerned by combining infective propagules and host tissue in vitro and observing the frequency of attachment. The use of modern techniques for improving disease resistance will increase as our knowledge of basic pathogenesis advances. Resistance to pathogenesis does not always translate to resistance to field epidemic development, however, and should not be substituted for it.

Breeding programs must evaluate various genotypes for their reaction to many important diseases. Resistance to one disease is not necessarily related to resistance or susceptibility to another, but sometimes there is genetic linkage of reactions to different diseases. While this has not been sufficiently studied in turfgrasses, it must be considered in breeding programs. Turfgrass breeding is further complicated by the agronomic requirements of acceptable cultivars. Highly resistant cultivars that do not possess desirable qualitative traits such as color or leaf texture will not be acceptable.

Standard methods of germplasm evaluations involve greenhouse or field testing by rating individual plants grown from seed or vegetative propagation. Vargas et al. (1980) published a summary of such selection methods. Usually outdoor evaluations must be repeated for several years to determine effects of variable environmental conditions. Selection of resistance to diseases that occur primarily in mature turfs can require many years of field observation.

Promising genotypes may then be crossed using various breeding methods, such as recurrent selection, to increase the level of genetic resistance in the progeny. Methods of exposure to pathogens using artificial inoculations must be developed that will appropriately select levels of resistance that are useful in subsequent breeding crosses. When only low levels of resistance exist in the germplasm, care must be taken to keep inoculum levels low enough to detect what resistance there is. Toler et al. (1983) determined that accessions of St. Augustinegrass are best evaluated for resistance to *S. macrospora* (downy mildew/yellow tuft) in natural infestations rather than through artificial inoculations because of this problem.

There are few reports on the inheritance of resistance to pathogens in turfgrasses. Rose-Fricker et al. (1986) studied the effects of plant maturity and segregation patterns of resistance to stem rust in perennial ryegrass. The results suggested that since seedlings were more susceptible than adult plants, selections for resistance would be more successful if mature plants were used. As in rust systems in other crops, quantitative multigenic resistance was identified. For pathogens that produce many races, the use of polygenic resistance is considered more stable and durable. While not usually demonstrating an immune response, such "slow rusting" may be highly effective in turfs in preventing or reducing spore production and epidemic development.

The use of blends and mixtures in turfgrasses holds great promise for improved genetic resistance to diseases. Different turfgrass species are subject to different disease problems and may be susceptible to different races or strains of pathogens that infect many turfgrass species. By increasing the genetic diversity of the turfgrass ecosystem, severe epidemics that destroy large turfgrass areas may be avoided. This practice is particularly useful in lower maintenance turfs such as lawns, cemeteries, and playgrounds. There have been few studies of disease epidemics in blends and mixtures. Watkins et al. (1981) reported that blends of Kentucky bluegrass cultivars developed stem rust equivalent to the average disease-resistance levels of the cultivars when grown in a pure stand. They demonstrated that inclusion of susceptible cultivars in a blend reduced the overall population level of resistance and should be avoided. A number of theoretical papers have been published on the use of cultivar mixtures and epidemic development (Ostergaard, 1983).

Turf is particularly amenable to blending, mixing, and frequent over-seeding to establish genetic diversity to increase population disease resistance. One concern is that turfgrass mainly propagates vegetatively once established. In a blend, the cultivars present will compete, and those best suited for the growing conditions will dominate, thus reducing genetic diversity. This is probably less true for blends of bunch grasses than creeping types. Both the spatial and temporal effects of blending and mixing should be evaluated thoroughly.

Vargas and Beard (1981) demonstrated that melting-out resistance as evaluated in full sunlight could not be extrapolated to reactions in shaded conditions. Variable disease reactions by different cultivars suggest that complex resistance mechanisms are involved. Thus, cultivars selected for lawns and other uses that may include shaded conditions should be evaluated under these conditions to determine disease resistance.

The current emphasis on selections for turfgrasses that are drought-tolerant, slow growing, and require less N fertility will alter disease reactions as well. The diseases commonly associated with slow-growing, N-deficient turf, such as dollar spot, red thread, and rust, may well become the predominant disease problems of these new cultivars. From a disease stand-point, an advantage of turfgrass culture compared to other crops is that main-tained turf is mowed frequently and diseased foliar tissue is continually replaced with healthy blades. If this process is slowed, the epidemiology of a number of important diseases may be altered significantly.

D. Cultural Practices

Turf pathologists often recommend a set of cultural practices along with fungicide recommendations to mitigate particular turf diseases. The role of cultural management practices and the incidence and severity of turfgrass diseases has been reviewed (Couch, 1980). He included a discussion of the impact of nutrition and pH, soil moisture, cutting height, and thatch on disease. While the general effect of nutrition and soil pH on turfgrass physi-ology and disease development is familiar for the major diseases, the details are not known in many cases (Watkins & Westerholt, 1991). A recent study of the interrelationship of fertility and red thread examined N, K, and Ca levels in leaf tissue in field plots relative to red thread disease (Cahill et al., 1983).

The impact of cultural practices such as mowing height and clipping removal continues to evoke controversy in the research community. While most pathologists would agree that it should be useful to remove clippings during foliar disease outbreaks, there is not compelling evidence that the im-provement in the health of the turf compensates for the removal of this im-portant nutrient source. Research to investigate such a question must consider, among other factors, the mode of spore dispersal.

In a recent study, three modes of spore trapping were used to determine how spore dispersal occurred in Kentucky bluegrass infected by *D. poae* (Nutter et al., 1982). The first was a commonly used spore sampler in plant pathology, the Rotorod spore sampler, in which a slide, greased with sili-cone, is used to trap airborne spores which are then counted under a micro-scope (Dhingra & Sinclair, 1985). A Kramer-Collins spore sampler was used to determine periodicity of spore production, also by using silicone greased slides that are replaced each day. Volumetric air samples deposit bands of spores on the slides after set time periods. The third method used to evalu-ate spore dispersal consisted of live plant traps of susceptible Kentucky bluegrass cultivars in pots. The study indicated that conidial trapping was minimal at heights above 7 cm and that mowing played a major role in spore dispersal.

In another study, Hagan and Larsen (1985) examined inoculum sources and seasonal and diurnal periodicity of airborne conidia in Kentucky bluegrass. Conidia of *D. poae* were recovered from thatch and leaf litter using a mineral oil flotation technique. Conidia were trapped simlarly to the previous study using the Kramer-Collins spore trap for diurnal trapping. A volumetric continuous Burkard spore trap was used for seasonal trapping data. Leaf litter was found to be a much more important source of inoculum than thatch. Airborne conidia increased as the relative humidity decreased after 0800 h and was highest from 1200 to 1600 h. In both studies, leaf spot and melting out decreased substantially after conidial production was reduced. Conidial production peaks before the melting out stage and, thus, fungicide applications would be most effective during conidial production rather than in the later stages of disease. Since most conidial production comes from detached leaf litter, collection of clippings during leaf-spot disease outbreaks may be useful in reducing more advanced disease problems. These studies evaluated only one fungal pathogen on Kentucky bluegrass although other studies have examined similar diseases on other turf species.

Moisture dynamics in turf are important to disease development. Leaf wetting and canopy humidity play a major role in disease caused by foliar pathogens and also affect the natural antagonists (Fry, 1982; Zadoks & Schein, 1979). Soil moisture content and periodicity of wetting and drying often control the activities of both the plant roots/rhizomes, pathogens, and nonpathogens that exist in the rhizosphere. In turfgrass pathology, it is important to understand how the root responds to changes in soil moisture availability and how soilborne pathogens respond to both the potential energy of the soil moisture and the physiological state of roots in that environment.

Cultural practices remain the most complex means of disease management and may lose effectiveness when individual aspects are dissected out for study. A single factor such as the addition of N may affect pH and may increase thatch development, which may stress turf plants or allow pathogens to multiply or survive more easily. Several important areas that deserve more study are the direct effects of nutrients and pH on pathogens, on the competitive thatch microorganisms that indirectly affect pathogens, and on the turfgrass plants.

E. Chemical Amendments

Fungicides are intensively used in the management of highly maintained turfgrass. Most major universities evaluate fungicides in cooperation with the agrichemical manufacturers. This practice can provide excellent information on their performance in considerably different environments. Standard methods for such evaluations have been described for greenhouse and field trials (Sanders & Cole, 1978, 1986). Useful discussions of some problems to consider in field screening have also been published (Cole & Sanders, 1980; Hickey, 1986). Examples of methods used for routine screening are also published annually by the American Phytopathological Society in *Fungicide and Nematicide Tests*.

Efficacy research methods depend on the type of disease that is to be managed (foliar or crown/root infecting), the type of fungicide that is to be applied (protectant or systemic), its formulation, and method of application. Specific application details that must be considered include: formulations, adjuvants, calibration, dilutions, rate, pH, frequency of application, uniformity of application, and compatibility with other compounds. Recent research has focused on efficacy, application method, mode-of-action of new fungicides, management of newly described diseases and resistance problems.

Understanding the interaction of the fungicide with the host, the fungus, and the environment is imperative. The poor performance of fungicides to control soilborne pathogens has been due to a lack of understanding of the interaction of the chemicals with soil, roots, and other subterranean plant parts as well as incomplete information about etiology of turfgrass epidemics themselves. For example, several sterol biosynthesis-inhibiting chemicals were described as effective in controlling ectotrophic fungi that cause patch diseases although it is unclear how and when the patch epidemics develop or when sterol-inhibiting fungicides should be used. The result has been a tremendous application of chemicals into the environment with disappointing disease control.

The use of narrow spectrum fungicides has complicated turfgrass management. Narrow spectrum fungicides will control one or only a few pathogens, but another pathogen(s) may respond by causing more severe disease than it normally would. This phenomenon could reflect a reduction of microbial competitors by the fungicide. Researchers initially screen fungicides at various concentrations for toxic effects on pathogens by using chemical-amended culture media (Sanders et al., 1983). The same method may be used to observe the effects of chemical mixtures and estimate the ability of a pathogen population to develop tolerance or resistance to a fungicide. This method is useful for gross efficacy screening, but it is not a substitute for greenhouse and field testing.

It is important to determine the mode-of-action and fate of fungicides in turfgrass. For instance, fosetyl-Al [aluminum tris (O-ethyl phosphonate)] was previously thought to stimulate biochemical resistance in plant tissue because the compound was not directly fungitoxic in fungicide-amended culture media (Sanders et al., 1983). A recent study has determined that a breakdown product of the chemical was fungitoxic and fosetyl-Al-resistant strains of *Phytophthora* spp. could be produced and identified in the laboratory (Fenn & Coffey, 1988). Mutants of *P. aphanidermatum* resistant to both metalaxyl and fosetyl-Al were obtained following exposure of a metalaxyl-resistant field isolate to a chemical mutagen in laboratory experiments (Sanders et al., 1990). Greenhouse pot studies demonstrated that the strains were resistant to both fungicides and showed virulence equal to that of the parental isolate on creeping bentgrass.

In vitro screening of fungicides may include not only inhibition of growth on fungicide-amended media, but observation of morphological effects on the fungus. Germ tubes from spores may swell and burst. Hyphal growth may be stunted or otherwise abnormal. Punja et al. (1982) screened fungicides for their ability to inhibit eruptive and hyphal germination of sclerotia and control *Sclerotium rolfsii* Sacc. (southern blight) in California.

Iprodione [3-(3,5-dichlorophenyl)-N-(1-methylethyl)2,4-dioxo-1-imada-zolidinecarboxamide] is reported to have both protective and systemic/post-infection activity in turfgrass (Danneberger & Vargas, 1982). To determine the duration of fungitoxic activity, turf plants in pots were treated with the recommended fungicide application and then inoculated with conidia of *Drechslera sorokiniana* (Sacc.) Subram. & Jain (now *Bipolaris sorokiniana*) at varying times from 0 to 40 h with maintenance mowing every 2 d and reinoculation every 4 d for the 20-d length of the experiment (Danneberger & Vargas, 1982). To determine postinfection effects, the plants were inoc-ulated, and fungicide was applied at varying times from 6 to 72 h after inoculation. Lesions were counted, sporulation was induced, and viability of the resulting conidia was tested by inoculation on healthy plants. Basi-petal or acropetal movement of the fungicide was demonstrated by dipping either roots or leaf tips in a range of concentrations of the fungicide and observing leaf spot development after inoculation with conidia.

In studies of diseases that may not produce distinct symptoms, it may be desirable to perform histological studies. Bruton et al. (1986) examined St. Augustinegrass after exposure to metalaxyl [N-2,6-dimethylphenyl)-N-(methoxyacetyl)-alanine methyl ester], an oomycete-specific fungicide, and inoculation with zoospores of *S. sclerospora* (downy mildew/yellow tuft). They fixed and stained the tissue and examined it for the presence of myceli-um and any histological abnormalities that might have been caused by the systemic fungicide. They used the absence of mycelium in inoculated plants that were later sprayed with metalaxyl as evidence of eradicative action of the fungicide.

Anecdotal evidence of unusual disease outbreaks following certain fun-gicide applications may lead to more detailed research. Kackley et al. (1989) recently reinvestigated benomyl [methyl-1(butylcarbamoyl)-2-benzimidazo-lecarbamate] enhanced growth of a basidiomycete that causes superficial fairy rings on turf. Smith et al. (1970) had reported that the fungus tolerated high levels of benomyl in amended culture medium and growth was stimulated at 0.5 and 1.0 mg/L. The fairy ring problem had only been described on turf that had been treated with benomyl. Kackley et al. (1989) described a technique that determines if growth inhibition on fungicide-amended media is due to fungitoxic or fungistatic effects. Plugs of mycelium from fungicide-amended media from each fungicide concentration were placed on non-amended culture media to determine if growth would resume or be stimu-lated. No direct stimulatory effects were noted, and disease was also reported on newly established areas with no previous fungicide history. Smith et al. (1970) suggested alternative explanations that the fungicide was more toxic to possible competitors or antagonists than the pathogenic basidiomycete.

The occurrence and management of resistance to fungicides is discussed in a recent publication (Delp, 1988). Fungicide resistance has been reported for several important turf fungicides including metalaxyl, iprodione, and the benzimidazoles (Chastagner & Vassey, 1982; Detweiler et al., 1983; Sanders, 1984). Fungicide resistance in the field is usually first noticed as a poor response to or complete failure of a chemical application. Careful evaluation is necessary to determine if the cause of the problem is actually resistance, an application problem, or perhaps enhanced microbial degradation of the compound on the site.

Many of the research methods required for such a detailed study are similar to those used in pesticide fate work and often require cooperation with a chemist. A simple bioassay of isolates on media amended with a dilution series of the fungicide may identify the existence of resistance. Successful greenhouse inoculation of plants protected with a fungicide and inoculated with isolates suspected of being resistant is additional confirmation. Cross-resistance against closely related chemicals, when they exist, should also be investigated. This has practical applications for fungicide use and also presents further evidence that fungicide resistance is the cause of the chemical failure.

An area of research that deserves special attention is the appropriate recommendations of fungicide use to prevent resistance. Metalaxyl-resistant strains of *Pythium* spp. on golf courses in Pennsylvania are still present more than 5 yr after the last application of metalaxyl (Sanders & Soika, 1988). Benzimidazole-resistant fungal strains also seem relatively fit and, as with phenylamides, single gene resistance in the fungus population may allow sudden chemical failure (Delp, 1988).

The question of resistance to the sterol biosynthesis inhibitors (SBIs) is more complicated (Delp, 1988). Resistance appears to be multigenic, which would result in a gradual chemical failure that could be overcome by increased concentration of application. Persistence of resistant strains may vary depending on the chemical. Mode-of-action studies are not complete enough to recommend alternation or mixing within this group, but it appears that cross-resistance may not occur between all SBI fungicides. Because this group is currently the source of almost all new fungicides for turfgrass diseases, this area requires emphasis in research.

Researchers of fungicide-resistance problems debate the best way to delay or prevent fungicide resistance. Most recommendations involve alternation or mixing of resistance-prone fungicides. Because the risk of resistance problems seems great in a perennial plant population that receives frequent applications during a growing season, the recommendation for mixing turf fungicides also is controversial. Some fungicide combinations involve a broad-spectrum protectant and a more specific systemic chemical. Other mixtures contain two systemic chemicals. If both chemicals in a mixture are used at full rate, the cost may be prohibitive. Thus, researchers have experimented with mixtures in which components are applied at reduced rates (Sanders et al., 1985). This has been strongly criticized by some, and recommended by others. Little field research is available as evidence.

IV. SUMMARY

Turf can be one of the most pesticide-intensive crop systems. Much environmental and economic pressure exists to manage turf diseases more effectively and with fewer chemical inputs. Turfgrass pathology research is approaching this need from many different directions. Our understanding of the identity and etiology of the pathogens that cause important turf diseases has improved tremendously in the past 20 yr. In addition, the advent of modern plant epidemiology has led to more sophisticated approaches to understanding the development of epidemics in turf within a single growing season and from year to year. Physiological studies of turf diseases are beginning to offer new approaches in the accurate assessment of disease severity, so that experimental data can be interpreted appropriately. These same studies are improving the selection of effective and durable disease-resistant genotypes for future turfgrasses. Research in all these areas has improved the practical recommendations for turfgrass disease management. Management is becoming more complex as it attempts to integrate biological, chemical, and cultural practices into an effective program for the maintenance of a stable, balanced, and healthy turf ecosystem.

ACKNOWLEDGMENT

The authors would like to thank Drs. N. Jackson, R.T. Kane, P.J. Landschoot, M.C. Shurtleff and D.V. Waddington for their reviews and comments during the preparation of this chapter and Mrs. Nancy David for her valued and patient technical editorial skills.

REFERENCES

Barron, G.L. 1968. The genera of hyphomycetes from soil. Williams and Wilkins, Baltimore.

Bateman, D.F. 1978. The dynamic nature of disease. p. 53–83. *In* J. Horsfall and E. Cowling (ed.) Plant disease. Vol. III. Academic Press, New York.

Beard, J.B. 1982. Turf management for golf courses. Burgess Publ. Co., Minneapolis.

Boyd, L.A., and P.J. Dale. 1986. Callus production and plant regeneration from mature embryos of *Poa pratensis* L. Plant Breed. Rev. 97:246–254.

Bracker, C.E., and L.J. Littlefield. 1973. Structural concepts of host-pathogen interfaces. *In* R.J.W. Byrde and C.V. Cutting (ed.) Fungal pathogenicity and the plant's response. Academic Press, New York.

Bruton, B.D., R.W. Toler, and M.P. Grisham. 1986. Preventative and curative control of downy mildew of St. Augustinegrass by metalaxyl. Plant Dis. 70:413–415.

Burpee, L.L. 1980. Identification of *Rhizoctonia* species associated with turfgrass. p. 25–28. *In* P.O. Larsen and B.G. Joyner (ed.) Advances in turfgrass pathology. Harcourt Brace Jovanovich Co., Duluth, MN.

Burpee, L.L., and L.G. Goulty. 1984. Suppression of brown patch disease of creeping bentgrass by isolates of nonpathogenic *Rhizoctonia* spp. Phytopathology 74:692–694.

Burpee, L.L., L.M. Kaye, L.G. Goulty, and M.B. Lawton. 1987. Suppression of gray snow mold on creeping bentgrass by an isolate of *Typhula phacorrhiza*. Plant Dis. 71:97–100.

Burr, T.J., and M.E. Stanghellini. 1973. Propagule nature and density of *Pythium aphanidermatum* in field soil. Phytopathology 63:1499–1501.

Cahill, J.V., J.J. Murray, N.R. O'Neill, and P.H. Dernoeden. 1983. Interrelationships between fertility and red thread fungal disease in turfgrass. Plant Dis. 67:1080–1083.

Chastagner, G.A., and W.E. Vassey. 1982. Occurrence of iprodione-tolerant *Fusarium nivale* under field conditions. Plant Dis. 66:112–114.

Cole, H., Jr., and P.O. Sanders. 1980. Fungicide evaluation from a university viewpoint. p. 127–132. *In* P.O. Larsen and B.G. Joyner (ed.) Advances in turfgrass pathology. Harcourt Brace Jovanovich Co., Duluth, MN.

Cook, R.J., and K.F. Baker. 1983. The nature and practice of biological control of plant pathogens. Am. Phytopathol. Soc., St. Paul.

Couch, H.B. 1980. Relationship of management practices to the incidence and severity of turfgrass diseases. p. 65–72. In P.O. Larsen and B.G. Joyner (ed.) Advances in turfgrass pathology. Harcourt Brace Jovanovich Co., Duluth, MN.

Couch, H.B., and E.R. Bedford. 1966. Fusarium blight of turfgrasses. Phytopathology 56:781–786.

Danneberger, T.K., and J.M. Vargas, Jr. 1982. Systemic activity of iprodione in *Poa annua* and postinfection activity for *Drechslera sorokiniana* leafspot management. Plant Dis. 66:914–915.

Danneberger, T.K., J.M. Vargas, Jr., and A.L. Jones. 1984. A model for weather-based forecasting of anthracnose on annual bluegrass. Phytopathology 74:448–451.

Daub, M.E. 1984. A cell culture approach for the development of disease resistance: Studies on the phytotoxin cercosporin. Hortic. Sci. 19:382–387.

Delp, C.J. (ed.) 1988. Fungicide resistance in North America. Am. Phytopathol. Soc., St. Paul.

Dernoeden, P.H., and M.S. McIntosh. 1990. Disease enhancement and turfgrass quality as influenced by fungicides. Phytopathology 80:975.

Dernoeden, P.H., L.R. Krusberg, and S. Sardanelli. 1990. Fungicide effects on *Acremonium* endophyte, plant-parasitic nematodes, and thatch in Kentucky bluegrass and perennial ryegrass. Plant Dis. 74:879–881.

Detweiler, A.R., J.M. Vargas, Jr., and T.K. Danneberger. 1983. Resistance of *Sclerotinia homeocarpa* to iprodione and benomyl. Plant Dis. 67:627–630.

Dhingra, O.D., and J.B. Sinclair. 1985. Basic plant pathology methods. CRC Press, Boca Raton, FL.

Dropkin, V.H. 1989. Introduction to plant nematology. 2nd ed. John Wiley and Sons, New York.

Elliott, M.L., and P.J. Landschoot. 1991. Fungi similar to *Gaeumannomyces* associated with root rot of turfgrasses in Florida. Plant Dis. 75:238–241.

Etter, A.G. 1951. How Kentucky bluegrass grows. Ann. Mo. Bot. Gard. 38:293–375.

Fenn, M.E., and M.D. Coffey. 1988. Quantification of phosphonate and ethyl phosphonate in tobacco and tomato tissues and significance of the mode of action of two phosphonate fungicides. Phytopathology 79:76–82.

Friend, J. 1976. Lignification in infected tissue. In J. Friend and D.R. Threlfall (ed.) Biochemical aspects of plant-parasite relationships. Academic Press, London.

Fry, W.E. 1982. Principles of plant disease management. Academic Press, New York.

Gamberg, O.L., and Wetter, L.R. 1975. Plant tissue culture methods. In O.L. Gamberg and L.R. Wetter (ed.) Publ. Natl. Counc. of Canada, Prairie Regional Lab., Saskatoon, SK.

Hagan, A.L. 1980. Isolation, identification, taxonomy of *Drechslera* and *Bipolaris* species on turfgrasses. p. 89–96. In P.O. Larsen and B.G. Joyner (ed.) Advances in turfgrass pathology. Harcourt Brace Jovanovich Co., Duluth, MN.

Hagan, A.K., and P.O. Larsen. 1985. Source and dispersal of conidia of *Drechslera poae* in Kentucky bluegrass turf. Plant Dis. 69:21–24.

Hall, J.J., P.O. Larsen, and A.F. Schmitthenner. 1980. Survival of *Pythium aphanidermatum* in golf course turfs. Plant. Dis. 64:1100–1103.

Hartley, R., E.C. Jones, and T.M. Wood. 1976. Carbohydrates and carbohydrate esters of ferulic acid released from cell walls of *Lolium multiforum* by treatment with cellulolytic enzymes. Phytochemistry 15:305.

Hartley, R., P.J. Harris, and G.E. Russell. 1978. Degradability and phenolic components of cell walls of wheat in relation to susceptibility to *Puccinia striiformis*. Ann. Appl. Biol. 88:153.

Heald, C.M., and R.N. Inserra. 1988. Effects of temperature on infection and survival of *Rotylenchulus reniformis*. J. Nematol. 20:356–361.

Hickey, K.D. (ed.) 1986. Methods for evaluating pesticides for control of plant pathogens. Am. Phytopathol. Soc., St. Paul.

Hodges, C.F., and L.W. Coleman. 1985. *Pythium*-induced root dysfunction in secondary roots of *Agrostis palustris*. Plant Dis. 69:336–340.

Horsfall, J.G., and E.G. Cowling. 1978. Pathometry: The measurement of plant disease. p. 119–136. In J.G. Horsfall and E.B. Cowling (ed.) Plant disease: An advanced treatise. Vol. II. Academic Press, New York.

Huber, D.M., C.G. Painter, H.C. McKay, and D.L. Peterson. 1968. Effect of nitrogen fertilization on take-all of winter wheat. Phytopathology 58:1470–1472.

Jackson, N. 1980. Yellow tuft. p. 135–137. *In* P.O. Larsen and B.G. Joyner (ed.) Advances in turfgrass pathology. Harcourt Brace Jovanovich Co., Duluth, MN.

Jacobs, D.L., and G.W. Bruehl. 1986. Saprophytic ability of *Typhula incarnata, T. idahoensis,* and *T. ishikariensis.* Phytopathology 76:695–698.

Johnston, S.A. (ed.) 1988. New Fungicide and Nematicide Data Committee, Fungicide and nematicide tests. Vol. 43. Am. Phytopathol. Soc., St. Paul.

Juhnke, M.E., D.E. Mathre, and D.C. Sands. 1984. A selective medium for *Gaeumannomyces graminis* var. *tritici.* Plant Dis. 68:233–236.

Kackley, K.E., P.H. Dernoeden, and A.P. Grybauskas. 1989. Effect of fungicides on the occurrence and growth *in vitro* of basidiomycetes associated with superficial fairy rings in creeping bentgrass. Plant Dis. 73:127–130.

Kackley, K.E., A.P. Grybauskas, and P.H. Dernoeden. 1990a. Growth of *Magnaporthe poae* and *Gaeumannomyces incrustans* as affected by temperature-osmotic potential interactions. Phytopathology 80:646–650.

Kackley, K.E., A.P. Grybauskas, R.L. Hill, and P.H. Dernoeden. 1990b. Influence of temperature-soil water status interactions on the development of summer patch in *Poa* spp. Phytopathology 80:650–655.

Kackley, K.E., A.P. Grybauskas, P.H. Dernoeden, and R.L. Hill. 1990c. Role of drought stress in the development of summer patch in field-inoculated Kentucky bluegrass. Phytopathology 80:655–658.

Kaplan, J.D., and N. Jackson. 1983. Red thread and pink patch disease of turfgrasses. Plant Dis. 67:159–162.

Landschoot, P.J., and N. Jackson. 1987. A *Magnaporthe* sp. with a *Phialophora* conidial state causes summer patch disease of *Poa pratensis* L. and *P. annua* L. Phytopathology 77:1734.

Landschoot, P.J., and N. Jackson. 1989a. *Gaeumannomyces incrustans* sp. nov., a root-infecting hyphopodiate fungus from grass roots in the United States. Mycol. Res. 93:55–58.

Landschoot, P.J., and N. Jackson. 1989b. *Magnaporthe poae* sp. nov., a hyphopodiatge fungus with a *Phialophora* anamorph from grass roots in the United States. Mycol. Res. 93:59–62.

Larkin, P.J., and W.R. Scowcroft. 1981. Somaclonal variation—A novel source of variability from cell cultures for plant improvement. Theor. Appl. Genet. 60:197–214.

Larsen, P.O., A.K. Hagan, B.G. Joyner, and D.A. Spilker. 1981. Leaf blight and crown rot of creeping bentgrass, a new disease caused by *Drechslera catenaria.* Plant Dis. 65:79–81.

Lowe, K.W., and B.V. Conger. 1979. Root and shoot formation from callus cultures of tall fescue. Crop Sci. 19:397–400.

MacNish, G.C. 1980. Management of cereals for control of take-all. J. Agric. West Aust. 21:48–51.

Martin, B. 1987. Rapid tentative identification of *Rhizoctonia* spp. associated with diseased turfgrasses. Plant Dis. 71:47–49.

Martin, S.B., and L.T. Lucas. 1984. Characterization and pathogenicity of *Rhizoctonia* spp. and binucleate *Rhizoctonia*-like fungi from turfgrasses in North Carolina. Phytopathology 74:170–175.

Mathias, J.K., C.L. Mulchi, and J.R. Hall, III. 1981. The seasonal relationship between polyphenol level and *Helminthosporium* disease activity on Kentucky bluegrass. p. 397–404. *In* R.W. Sheard (ed.) Proc. 4th Int. Turfgrass Res. Conf., Guelph, ON, Canada. 19–23 July. Int. Turfgrass Soc., and Ontario Agric. Coll., Univ. of Guelph, Guelph, ON.

McDonnell, R.E., and B.V. Conger. 1984. Callus induction and plantlet formation from mature embryo explants of Kentucky bluegrass. Crop Sci. 24:573–578.

Melvin, B.P., J.M. Vargas, Jr., and W.L. Berndt. 1988. Biological control of necrotic ring spot of *Poa pratensis.* Phytopathology 78:1503.

Miller, S.A., and R.R. Martin. 1988. Molecular diagnosis of plant disease. Ann. Rev. Phytopathol. 26:409–432.

Mordue, J.E.M., R.S. Currah, and P.D. Bridge. 1989. An integrated approach to *Rhizoctonia* taxonomy: Cultural, biochemical and numerical techniques. Mycol. Res. 92:78–90.

Muchovej, J.J., and H.B. Couch. 1987. Colonization of bentgrass turf by *Curvularia lunata* after leaf clipping and heat stress. Plant Dis. 71:873–875.

Nameth, S.T., W.W. Shane, and J.C. Stier. 1990. Development of a monoclonal antibody for detection of *Leptosphaeria korrae,* the causal agent of necrotic ringspot disease of turfgrass. Phytopathology 80:1208–1211.

Nelson, E.B., and C.M. Craft. 1991a. Introduction and establishment of strains of *Enterobacter cloacae* in golf course turf for the biological control of dollar spot. Plant Dis. 75:510–514.

Nelson, E.B., and C.M. Craft. 1991b. Suppression of brown patch with top-dressings amended with composts and organic fertilizers, 1989. p. 90. *In* W.F. Wilcox (ed.) Biological and cultural tests for control of plant diseases. Vol. 6. Am. Phytopathol. Soc., St. Paul.

Nelson, E.B., and C.M. Craft. 1991c. Suppression of dollar spot with top-dressings amended with composts and organic fertilizers, 1989. p. 93. *In* W.F. Wilcox (ed.) Biological and cultural tests for control of plant diseases. Vol. 6. Am. Phytopathol. Soc., St. Paul.

Nelson, E.B., and C.M. Craft. 1991d. Suppression of red thread with top-dressings amended with composts and organic fertilizers, 1989. p. 101. *In* W.F. Wilcox (ed.) Biological and cultural tests for control of plant diseases. Vol. 6. Am. Phytopathol. Soc., St. Paul.

Nelson, P.E., T.A. Toussoun, and W.F.O. Marasas. 1983. *Fusarium* species, an illustrated manual for identification. The Pennsylvania State Univ. Press, University Park.

Nilsson, H.C. 1969. Studies on root and foot rot diseases of cereals and grasses. I. On resistance to *Ophiobolus graminis* Sacc. Lanbruks. Annaler 35:275–807.

Nutter, F.W., Jr., H. Cole, Jr., and R.D. Schein. 1982. Conidial sampling of *Drechslera poae* from Kentucky bluegrass to determine role of mowing in spore dispersal. Plant Dis. 66:721–723.

Nutter, F.W., H. Cole, Jr., and R.D. Schein. 1983. Disease forecasting system for warm weather *Pythium* blight of turfgrass. Plant Dis. 67:1126–1128.

Ostergaard, H. 1983. Predicting development of epidemics on cultivar mixtures. Phytopathology 73:166–172.

Punja, Z.K., R.G. Grogan, and T. Unruh. 1982. Chemical control of *Sclerotium rolfsii* on golf greens in northern California. Plant Dis. 66:108–111.

Riedel, R.M. 1980. Nematode problems of northern turfgrasses. p. 59–62. *In* P.O. Larsen and B.G. Joyner (ed.) Advances in turfgrass pathology. Harcourt Brace Jovanovich Co., Duluth, MN.

Rittenberg, J.R., F.P. Petersen, G.D. Grothaus, and S.A. Miller. 1988. Development of a rapid, field usable immunoassay format for detection and quantitation of *Pythium, Rhizoctonia*, and *Sclerotinia* spp. in plant tissue. Phytopathology 78:1516.

Rose-Fricker, C.A., W.A. Meyer, and W.E. Kronstad. 1986. Inheritance of resistance to stem rust (*Puccinia graminis* subsp. *graminicola*) in six perennial ryegrass (*Lolium perenne*) crosses. Plant Dis. 70:678–681.

Rossman, A.Y., M.E. Palm, and L.J. Spielman. 1987. A literature guide for the identification of plant pathogenic fungi. Am. Phytopathol. Soc., St. Paul.

Rotem, J. 1988. Experimental techniques in plant disease epidemiology. Springer-Verlag, Berlin.

Russell, G.E. 1981. Plant breeding for pest and disease resistance. 2nd ed. Butterworths, Boston.

Sanders, P.L. 1984. Failure of metalaxyl to control *Pythium* blight on turfgrass in Pennsylvania. Plant Dis. 68:776–777.

Sanders, P.L., M.D. Coffey, G.D. Greer, and M.D. Soika. 1990. Laboratory-induced resistance to fosetyl-Al in a metalaxyl-resistant field isolate of *Pythium aphanidermatum*. Plant Dis. 74:690–692.

Sanders, P.L., and H. Cole, Jr. 1978. Greenhouse procedures for evaluation of turfgrass fungicides. p. 25–27. *In* E.I. Zehr (ed.) Methods for evaluating plant fungicides, nematicides, and bactericides. Am. Phytopathol. Soc., Minneapolis.

Sanders, P.L., and H. Cole, Jr. 1986. *In vivo* fungicide screening on field-grown turfgrasses. p. 244–247. *In* K.D. Hickey (ed.) Methods for evaluating pesticides for control of plant pathogens. Am. Phytopathol. Soc., St. Paul.

Sanders, P.L., W.J. Houser, and H. Cole, Jr. 1983. Control of *Pythium* spp. and *Pythium* blight of turfgrass with fosetyl aluminum. Plant Dis. 67:1382–1383.

Sanders, P.L., W.J. Houser, P.J. Parish, and H. Cole, Jr. 1985. Reduced-rate fungicide mixtures to delay fungicide resistance and to control selected turfgrass diseases. Plant Dis. 69:939–943.

Sanders, P.L., and M.D. Soika. 1988. Metalaxyl resistance frequency in overwintering populations of *Pythium aphanidermatum* from metalaxyl control failure sites. Phytopathology 78:1510.

Sanders, P.L., and M.D. Soika. 1991. Biological control of Pythium blight, 1990. p. 99. *In* W.D. Wilcox (ed.) Biological and cultural tests for control of plant diseases. Vol. 6. Am. Phytopathol. Soc., St. Paul

Schmitthenner, A.F. 1980. *Pythium* species: Isolation, biology, and identification. p. 33–36. *In* P.O. Larsen and B.G. Joyner. (ed.) Advances in turfgrass pathology. Harcourt Brace Jovanovich Co., Duluth, MN.

Shane, W.W. 1988. Evaluation of *Pythium* blight prediction models using an antibody-aided detection technique. Phytopathology 78:1612.

Shane, W.W., and S.T. Nameth. 1988. Monoclonal antibodies for diagnosis of necrotic ring spot of turfgrass. Phytopathology 78:1521.

Sherwood, R.T., C.C. Berg, M.R. Hoover, and K.E. Zeiders. 1983. Illusions in visual assessment of *Stagnospora* leaf spot of orchardgrass. Phytopathology 73:173–177.

Shurtleff, M.C., T.W. Fermanian, and R. Randell. 1987. Controlling turfgrass pests. Reston, Prentice-Hall, Englewood Cliffs, NJ.

Sivanesan, A. 1987. *Graminicolous* species of *Bipolaris, Curvularia, Drechslera, Exserohilum*, and their teleomorphs. Mycological Papers No. 158. CAB Int. Mycological Inst., Surrey, England.

Smiley, R.W. 1975. Forms of nitrogen and the pH in the root zone and their importance to root infections. p. 55–62. *In* G.W. Bruehl (ed.) Biology and control of soil-borne plant pathogens. Am. Phytopathol. Soc., St. Paul.

Smiley, R.W. 1981. Nontarget effects of pesticides on turfgrasses. Plant Dis. 65:17–23.

Smiley, R.W. 1983. Compendium of turfgrass diseases. Am. Phytopathol. Soc., St. Paul.

Smiley, R.W., and R.J. Cook. 1973. Relationship between take-all of wheat and rhizosphere pH in soils fertilized with ammonium vs. nitrate-nitrogen. Phytopathology 63:882–890.

Smiley, R.W., and M.M. Craven. 1979. Microflora of turfgrass treated with fungicides. Soil Biol. Biochem. 11:349–353.

Smiley, R.W., and D.E. Giblin. 1986. Root cortical death in relation to infection of Kentucky Bluegrass by *Phialophora graminicola*. Phytopathology 76:917–922.

Smith, A.M., B.A. Stynes, and K.J. Moore. 1970. Benomyl stimulates growth of a Basidiomycete on turf. Plant Dis. Rep. 54:774–775.

Smith, J.D. 1980a. Snow molds of turfgrasses: Identification, biology and control. p. 75–80. *In* P.O. Larsen and B.G. Joyner (ed.) Advances in turfgrass pathology. Harcourt Brace Jovanovich Co., Duluth, MN.

Smith, J.D. 1980b. Fairy rings: Biology, antagonism, and possible new control methods. p. 81–85. *In* P.O. Larsen and G. Joyner (ed.) Advances in turfgrass pathology. Harcourt Brace Jovanovich Co., Duluth, MN.

Smith, J.D., N. Jackson, and A.R. Woolhouse. 1989. Fungal diseases of amenity turf grasses. 3rd ed. E. & F. N. Spon, London.

Smith, J.D., and R. Rupps. 1978. Antagonism in *Marasmius oreades* fairy rings. J. Sports Turf Res. Inst. 54:97–105.

Soika, M.D., and P.L. Sanders. 1991. Effects of various nitrogen sources, organic amendments, and biological control agents on turfgrass quality and disease development, 1990. p. 91. *In* W.F. Wilcox (ed.) Biological and cultural tests for control of plant diseases. Vol. 6. Am. Phytopathol. Soc., St. Paul.

Sutton, B.C. 1980. The coelomycetes. Commonwealth Mycological Inst., Surrey, England.

Tarjan, A.C., and P. Busey. 1985. Genotypic variability in Bermudagrass damage by ectoparasitic nematodes. HortScience 20:675–676.

Toler, R.W., B.D. Bruton, and M.P. Grisham. 1983. Evaluation of St. Augustinegrass accessions and cultivars for resistance to *Sclerophthora macrospora*. Plant Dis. 67:1008–1010.

Trolldenier, G. 1982. Influence of potassium nutrition and take-all on wheat yield in dependence of inoculum density. Phytopathol. Z. 103:340–348.

Tuite, J. 1969. Plant pathological methods for fungi and bacteria. Burgess Publ., Minneapolis.

U.S. Department of Agriculture-Beltsville Agricultural Research Center. 1989. National Turfgrass Evaluation Program. USDA-ARS, Beltsville Agric. Res. Ctr., Beltsville.

VanDer Plaats-Niterink, A.J. 1981. Monograph of the genus *Pythium*. Studies in Mycology No. 21. Centraalbureau voor Schimmelcultures, Baarn, Netherlands.

Vargas, J.M., Jr. 1981. Management of turfgrass diseases. Burgess, Minneapolis.

Vargas, J.M., Jr., and J.B. Beard. 1981. Shade environment-disease relationships of Kentucky bluegrass cultivars. p. 391–396. *In* R.W. Sheard (ed.) Proc. 4th Int. Turfgrass Res. Conf., Gudlph, ON, Canada. 19-23 July. Int. Turfgrass Soc., and Ontario Agric. Coll., Univ. of Guelph, Guelph, ON.

Vargas, J.M., Jr., K.T. Payne, A.J. Turgeon, and R. Detweiler. 1980. Turfgrass disease resistance-selection, development, and use. p. 179–182. *In* P.O. Larsen and B.G. Joyner (ed.) Advances in turfgrass pathology. Harcourt Brace Jovanovich Co., Duluth, MN.

Vasil, I.K. (ed.) 1984. Cell culture and somatic cell genetics of plants. *In* I.K. Vasil (ed.) Laboratory procedures and their applications. Vol. 1. Academic Press, New York.

Vengris, J. 1973. Lawns. 2nd ed. Thomson Publ., Fresno, CA.

Watkins, J.E., R.C. Shearman, J.A. Houfek, and T.P. Riordan. 1981. Response of Kentucky bluegrass cultivars and blends to a natural stem rust population. Plant Dis. 65:345-347.

Watkins, J.E., and S.R. Westerholt. 1991. Effect of nitrogen level and cutting height on brown patch severity, 1990. p. 97. *In* W.F. Wilcox (ed.) Biological and cultural tests for control of plant diseases. Vol. 6. Am. Phytopathol. Soc., St. Paul.

Wick, R.L. 1989. Effect of Milorganite and chitin on stunt nematode populations under putting green conditions. p. 76. *In* W.F. Wilcox (ed.) Biological and cultural tests for control of plant diseases. Vol. 4. Am. Phytopathol. Soc., St. Paul.

Wilkinson, H.T. 1987a. Association of *Trechispora alnicola* with yellow ring disease of *Poa pratensis*. Can. J. Bot. 65:150-153.

Wilkinson, H.T. 1987b. Yellow ring on *Poa pratensis* caused by *Trechispora alnicola*. Plant Dis. 71:1141-1143.

Wilkinson, H.T. 1988. Etiology and epidemiology of zoysia patch in *Zoysia japonica*. Phytopathology 78:1613.

Wilkinson, H.T., J.R. Alldredge, and R.J. Cook. 1985. Estimated distances of infection of wheat roots by *Gaeumannomyces graminis* var. *tritici* in soils suppressive and conducive to take-all. Phytopathology 75:557-559.

Wilkinson, H.T., and R.T. Kane. 1988. The relatedness of patch causing fungi in the midwest. Phytopathology 78:1612-1613.

Wilkinson, H.T., and R.E. Wagner. 1986. Etiology of *Poa* patch. Phytopathology 76:1057.

Worf, G.L., and J.S. Stewart. 1986. Necrotic ring spot disease of turfgrass in Wisconsin. Plant Dis. 70:453-458.

Zadoks, J.C., and R.D. Schein. 1979. Epidemiology and plant disease management. Oxford Univ. Press, Oxford.

Zeiders, K.E. 1987. Leaf spot of indiangrass caused by *Colletotrichum caudatum*. Plant Dis. 71:348-350.

Zuckerman, B.M., W.F. Mai, and M.B. Harrison. 1985. Plant nematology laboratory manual. Univ. of Massachusetts Agric. Exp. Stn., Amherst.

20   Methods of Research in Turfgrass Entomology

ROGER H. RATCLIFFE

USDA-ARS
West Lafayette, IN

Insects and mites make up the major group of arthropod pests of turfgrasses. Although mites are not insects, their feeding habits, size, and environmental niches are similar enough to many insect species to be grouped among the pest organisms discussed in this chapter. Within this large pest complex, there are species that feed on all parts of the plant, including roots, stolons, rhizomes, and foliage. There also are many nonpest species of arthropods present in turfgrasses (Streu, 1973). This nonpest complex includes predators and parasites of pest species, and many organisms that inhabit, but do not feed on the plant. Streu (1973) proposed an invertebrate food web in a typical turfgrass ecosystem to explain the interaction of arthropods and grasses. The development of research methods to control turfgrass pests, therefore, must also take into consideration these organisms, and the effect that pest-control measures will have on them.

The influence of management practices on pest species and their control also must be considered when developing research methods. Factors such as turfgrass species, fertilizer application rate and timing, mowing height, irrigation, and pesticide usage can influence pest population either beneficially or detrimentally (Arnold & Potter, 1987; Cockfield & Potter, 1983). Turfgrasses that are maintained in a vigorous, steadily growing condition can withstand higher pest populations than poorly maintained stands, and will be able to recover once control measures are applied (Tashiro, 1987). These factors need to be considered when designing experiments.

Sound research methods for evaluating all types of pest suppression should be developed and integrated to every extent possible. This review will be of value in enhancing this process. In the following discussion, research methods are grouped according to various chemical or biological approaches to suppressing turfgrass pests, but it will be obvious to the reader that there is considerable overlap among groups in the application of methods.

No attempt will be made to review the biology of the pest species discussed in this chapter. Many of the references cited contain this information and should be readily available. Of particular interest are publications by Bowen et al. (1980), Bruneau et al. (1981), Niemczyk (1981), Shetler et al. (1983), and Tashiro (1987) which contain many excellent photographs and descriptions of pest species and their management.

Copyright © 1992 ASA-CSSA-SSSA, 677 S. Segoe Rd., Madison, WI 53711, USA. *Turfgrass—* Agronomy Monograph no. 32.

I. INSECTICIDE EVALUATION

Insecticides provide the major means of suppressing economically important turfgrass pests, although several problems have arisen from their continuous use or overuse. The impact of multiple applications of pesticides over several seasons can be cumulative, resulting in pest resurgence, insecticide resistance and other changes, such as plant species succession and plant growth response (Streu, 1969, 1973). Judicious use of insecticides or acaracides, in combination with nonchemical (pesticide) methods of suppressing pest populations will greatly reduce the incidence of many of these problems. However, the continuing development and evaluation of new and safer insecticides and acaracides is needed to effectively manage economically important pests when nonchemical methods are not available, or are not sufficiently effective to provide adequate control without chemicals.

A. Field Evaluation

1. Field Characteristics and Experimental Design

Plot size and location, and the experimental design used in evaluating insecticide treatments have varied with specific test conditions. In most tests, however, plot size has ranged from about 3 by 3 m to 6 by 6 m, and treatments have been arranged in a randomized complete block design with four to six replications. Plots of this size can be sampled and resampled at periodical intervals without causing undue injury to the turf. Treatments should include an untreated control and insecticide standard, where possible. Alleyways are desirable to prevent pesticide contamination when applying treatments, but are not always feasible. Larger plot size may be advantageous at times. Reinert (1983b) found that some insecticide treatments appeared less effective in small plot tests against the southern chinch bug (*Blissus insularis* Barber) because insects readily migrated from heavily damaged untreated plots into small-treated areas. Better control was obtained with the same insecticide when half lawn plots were used. Crocker and Simpson (1981) confined small field plots (186 cm^2) within an open-ended metal cylinder to prevent migration of southern chinch bugs, and suggested that this method could be used as a preliminary field screening test for insecticide activity. Tashiro and Personius (1970) used whole lawn plots to reduce the influence of adult bluegrass billbug (*Sphenophorus parvulus* Gyllenhal) migration on evaluation of insecticides. Lawrence and Niemczyk (1976) and Weaver and Hacker (1978) applied treatments for control of the black turfgrass ataenius [*Ataenius spretulus* (Haldeman)] and Japanese bettle (*Popillia japonica* Newman) to entire golf course fairways and left an untreated area at the end of each fairway or in the rough as a control.

Plots need to be located where natural infestations of the pest species are sufficient to provide accurate comparisons of treatments, although it may be possible to supplement natural populations with artificial infestations at times (Pass, 1966). Often areas need to be sampled prior to conducting tests to determine whether pest populations are of sufficient level or uniformity to provide good test conditions (Shread, 1953; VanDerSchaaf & Tashiro, 1975). This information can be used to group treatments within blocks according to similar infestation levels to reduce variation within replications (Reinert, 1974, 1977). Test plots have been located on home lawns (Pass, 1966; Reinert, 1982b, 1983b), golf course greens, fairways and roughs (Ali & Garcia, 1987; Brandenburg & Hertl, 1987; Heller & Kellogg, 1987a,b; Reinert & Cromroy, 1981; Reinert, 1979; Tashiro & Straub, 1973; Weaver & Hacker, 1978), city parks (Butler & Stroehlein, 1965), tennis courts (Cameron & Johnson, 1971), cemeteries (Gambrell et al., 1968), sod farms (Reinert & Cromroy, 1981), and experiment station or university turf areas (Heller & Kellogg, 1987c; Pass, 1966; Reinert, 1974, 1983a). Plots should be maintained according to standard practices for the areas under study (golf courses, home lawns, etc.) and records should be kept on weather conditions, thatch conditions, soil type and pH, turfgrass species and cultivar, mowing practices, fertilizer, lime and herbicide applications, irrigation, and rainfall prior to and following treatment, and incidence of pest resistance. Reinert (1982b), located test plots in lawns with a history of severe southern chinch bug injury, despite chemical treatment, to evaluate resistance to organic phosphate insecticides. Entomologists conducting research on cool-season turfgrass insect pests in the north central and northeastern USA developed standard procedures for evaluating insecticides in field trials and reporting results (H.D. Niemczyk, 1987, personal communication; S.R. Swier, 1988, personal communication). Recommended procedures dealt with four areas, including: (i) information on field conditions at the time of application or sampling to be recorded in materials and methods; (ii) form in which data would be presented; (iii) interpretation of results; and (iv) minimum standards for plot size, post-treatment sampling interval, and sample size. Details of the recommendations are as follows:

I. Conditions at time of application or sampling to be included in materials and methods.
    A. Soil. Characteristization (CEC; % silt, clay, and sand); pH of the top 7.5 cm; % organic matter; moisture (weight/weight); and temperature at 2.5 and 7.5 cm.
    B. Site History. Past lime, fertilizer, and pesticide use (at least insecticide use in the past 12 m); topography (general description, % slope, if significant).
    C. Turf. Vigor (general description); wet or dry foliage; composition (% grass species, weed content); height of cut; thatch depth; verbal description of density; pH.
    D. Methods of Application. Date of application and evaluation; actual time and duration of application; equipment used; pH of spray water, irrigation water, or spray mix, if possible; amount per plot (in volume/92.9 m^2 [1000 ft^2]) with a maximum of 18.9 L (5 gallon)/92.9 m^2; and posttreatment irrigation (amount, time delay after application).

E. Weather. Air temperature; wind (velocity, direction); relative humidity; cloud cover; precipitation (24 h pretreatment and 24 h posttreatment, at least, and extended records, if known).

F. Insect Activity (pretreatment counts). Location (depth in soil, distribution); species (% composition); number per unit area; stages (% of total in each stage); verbal description of appearance (milky disease, fungi, and nematodes).

II. Data for reports. Include raw data, or at least names for each replication, list standard error after mean; state whether data were transformed (and method) prior to analysis, report results of analysis of variance (ANOVA) and multiple range test (state test used); report data as insects per sample unit (or unit area) and % control; label all tables so that they can stand alone.

III. Report conclusions. Include interpretation of results and any unusual occurrences; note phytotoxic responses (if occurring, rate 0–100% with verbal description of symptoms and date of observation).

IV. Minimum standards for plot size, posttreatment sampling interval, and sample size per plot.

Insect	Plot size	Postreat interval	Sample size (per plot)
Grubs	4.6 m^2 (50 ft^2)	28 d	0.2 m^2 (2 ft^2) or at least four observations from 10.6 cm (4.25 in.) plugs
Green June Beetle	9.3 m^2 (100 ft^2)	Morning after and variable	Dead/0.4 m^2 (4 ft^2) retreat with carbaryl and count dead/0.4 m^2
Chinch bugs	2.3 m^2 (25 ft^2)	7 d	Two 20 cm (8 in.) diam. samples (5 min flotation, treat each equally)
Billbugs	4.6 m^2 for larvae; 37.2 m^2 (400 ft^2) for adults	14 d	Five 10.6-cm plugs
Black turfgrass ataenius	4.6 m^2	7 d	Five 10.6-cm plugs
Cutworms	Variable	Morning after and longer depending on mode of action	Active burrow counts, larval counts/unit area
Webworms	Variable	Morning after and longer depending on mode of action	0.1-m^2 (1 ft^2) frame Two frames/plot
Greenbugs	Variable	2 d	One 10.6-cm plug, Berlese extraction
Mites	2.3 m^2	2 d	Two 10.6-cm plug, Berlese extraction
Annual bluegrass weevil	9.3 m^2	14 d	Five 10-6-cm plugs

2. Application Methods

Insecticides have been applied in water as emulsifiable concentrates and wettable powders, or as dusts, granules, or in various baits. The most common methods of applying the various formulations will be discussed briefly, but no attempt will be made to include details of specific types of equipment, equipment calibration, application rates, spray volume, and pressure, etc. because of space limitations. This information can be found in many of the references cites in this section and in publications by Neal (1974), Niemczyk (1981), Streu (1974), Tashiro (1982), and Van Dam and Cudney (1980). Sprayer calibration and various types of research sprayers also are discussed in chapter 21 in this book (Johnson and Murphy).

In small plots, liquid formulations often have been applied with a watering can in a sufficient volume of water to provide thorough coverage of the plot area at the desired rate of application (Reinert, 1977; Tashiro et al., 1977; Vittum, 1985). This has been accomplished by applying premeasured amounts to each plot in two passes at right angles to each other (Pass, 1964; Tashiro et al., 1982). Liquids also have been applied with hand-operated compressed air sprayers (Crocker & Simpson, 1981; Reinert, 1983b), small power sprayers (Butler et al., 1963; Jefferson & Eads, 1952), tractor-mounted sprayers (Lawrence, 1981; Pass, 1966), or lawn pesticide sprayers attached to a garden hose (Crocker, 1981). It has generally been recommended that insecticide sprays applied for control of soil-inhabiting insects be watered in immediately after application to maximize control (Niemczyk, 1981). However, recent research has shown that this action may not be as necessary as previously thought (Niemczyk, 1987). Insecticide sprays applied for control of thatch-inhabiting insects, such as chinch bugs, may need irrigation following application, depending upon the volume of water applied at treatment (Reinert, 1977). Plots sprayed for control of stem- or leaf-inhabiting insects or mites should not be irrigated or mowed for 24 to 48 h after application to allow time for contact activity and consumption of foliage by insects (Niemczyk, 1981).

Granular insecticides have been applied to small plots with hand-held shakers made with a glass jar with perforated lid (Murdoch & Mitchell, 1975; Vittum, 1985), hand-operated fertilizer spreaders (Cameron & Johnson, 1971; Pass, 1964), or with either drop or broadcast-type lawn fertilizer spreaders (Lawrence, 1981; Tashiro et al., 1977). Dunbar and Beard (1975) mixed a granular insecticide with sifted sand to provide better distribution by lawn spreader. Granules have been applied to larger plots with a tractor-mounted broadcast spreader (Lawrence, 1981) and, at times, have been incorporated into the soil after application with a rototiller (Fiori et al., 1972). Granular insecticides should be applied when foliage is dry and should be watered in as soon as possible to move the insecticide off the granules and into the thatch or soil. Insecticide dusts have been applied with a hand shaker (Reinert, 1979) and a knapsack puff duster (Tuttle & Butler, 1961).

Baits have been evaluated primarily for mole cricket (*Scapteriscus* spp.) control. The successful use of baits depends upon proper timing of application, attractiveness of baits from a distance, palatability of the bait, and the effectiveness of toxicants (Kepner, 1984). In field tests, baits have been applied by hand to standard-size plots (Koehler & Short, 1976) or to soil contained in 19-L plastic buckets, to evaluate activity against mole crickets (Green et al., 1984). Drainage holes in the bottom of buckets were covered with 18-mesh screen to prevent escape of mole crickets, and they were buried in the ground to within 2.5 cm of the top. Pots were capped with an 18-mesh screen after application of baits and introduction of mole cricket adults.

3. Measuring Insecticide and Acaricide Performance

The number of samples taken per plot, sampling patterns, and the frequency of sampling of plots to evaluate chemical performance will vary with the objectives of the study, insect or mite species being studied, and the chemicals or formulations applied. Liquid applications to control foliar feeding insects generally have been evaluated within 1 to 7 d after treatment (Crocker & Simpson, 1981; Reinert, 1982b) and then on weekly or biweekly intervals (Mitchell & Murdoch, 1974). Treatments applied for control of soil-inhabiting insects have been evaluated over much longer periods of time (Vittum, 1985), especially when residual activity of the chemical was being evaluated (Tashiro et al., 1982). Spring or summer treatments during the period of grub activity have been evaluated in 1 to 3 wk following application to determine initial kill, or on a 4, 6 to 8 wk interval to determine effectiveness or residual activity. Generally, summer applications directed at young grubs have been evaluated in the fall when grubs are large enough to be readily found and soil moisture is adequate for proper sampling and examination. Counts on longer-term studies have been taken for a 9- to 12-mo period or longer.

Chemical efficacy in field trials has been evaluated by sampling plots and counting insects, or by visually estimating the amount of injury in plots due to insect or mite feeding. Feeding injury has been estimated by scoring plots for damage on a numerical scale (Butler & Stroehlein, 1965; Tashiro et al., 1977), by scoring regrowth of individual terminals (Reinert & Cromroy, 1981), or by estimating the percentage of the plot that showed visual symptoms of damage (Cameron & Johnson, 1971; Murdoch & Mitchell, 1978). Damage usually was rated by two or three observers independently, and scores were averaged to provide a single value for each plot. Visual ratings have usually been assigned on a 1 to 5 or 0 to 10 basis, where the lowest value indicated normal or undamaged turf and the highest value indicated severe damage or death of the turf. Butler and Stroehlein (1965) also used turfgrass quality, as determined by the density of the grass, as a method for measuring efficacy. Density was measured with a capacitance meter (Turner, 1961).

Sampling methods will only be described briefly, since these are covered in greater detail under Diagnostic Methods (section IV). Insects feeding on aboveground parts of plants, such as chinch bugs (*Blissus* spp.), greenbugs [*Schizaphis graminum* (Rodani)], and sod webworms, usually have been sampled by flotation or drench methods (Jefferson & Eads, 1952; Kerr, 1956;

Reinert, 1973), or by sweep net (Niemczyk & Moser, 1982), although sod webworms and greenbugs, also were collected in sod and soil samples (Niemczyk & Moser, 1982; Pass, 1965). Greenbugs were extracted from samples in Berlese funnels placed under heat for 24 h. Grass webworm [*Herpetogramma licarsisolis* (Walker)], and lawn armyworm [*Spodoptera mauritia* (Boisduval)], populations also have been estimated from the number of insects counted under plywood boards placed in plots overnight (Murdoch & Mitchell, 1975). Eriophyid mites have been counted from grass samples collected from plots and examined either in the laboratory (Tuttle & Butler, 1961; Reinert & Cromroy, 1981) or in the field (Butler et al., 1963), while winter grain mites [*Penthaleus major* (Duges)] have been collected in pit-fall traps (Streu & Gingrich, 1972) or from sod samples (Streu & Niemczyk, 1982) and populations estimated from subsamples examined in the laboratory. Chinch bug, greenbug, sod webworm, and armyworm counts have been expressed as the number of insects per 0.1 m^2 (1 ft^2). Eriophyid mite counts have been expressed as the number per gram of grass or as percentage of mite-free stems. Winter grain mite counts were grouped into four classifications based on the number of mites in a measured subsample.

Root-feeding insects usually have been counted by examining samples of sod and soil taken from plots with a cupcutter, soil auger, or spade. However, mole crickets have been sampled by counting dead or moribund insects on the soil surface (Koehler & Short, 1976) or with a soap flush applied to the plot (Short & Koehler, 1979). The latter method is the easiest and most economical (Hudson, 1984). When mole cricket tests were conducted in pots (Green et al., 1984), mortality was determined by recording and removing dead crickets from the soil surface, and then sifting through soil contents to determine the number of moribund or living crickets beneath the surface. Although the sample size and number of samples collected per plot may vary with the particular trial and pest species, insect counts should be expressed on a per unit basis (usually insects per 0.1 m^2) for uniformity.

Insecticide efficacy has also been expressed as percent reduction of insects in treated plots in relation to the untreated control, adjusted on the basis of Abbott's formula (Abbott, 1925) for mortality in the control based on pretreatment and posttreatment counts (Taylor, 1987). Taylor (1987) discussed the importance of proper understanding and application of statistical methods when analyzing data from field tests, and cautioned that changes in distribution of target pests caused by reductions in abundance may result in incorrect inferences from statistical analyses.

B. Laboratory Evaluation

Insecticide activity has been evaluated in the laboratory against a number of turfgrass insect pests, either by exposing them to treated foliage or soil, or by treating the insects directly with sprays or topical applications. Each of these methods will be described briefly. Laboratory tests require a dependable source of insects to provide the numbers and developmental stages needed to conduct accurate experiments. Insects can either be collected from the field and maintained as needed, or reared in the laboratory or green-house. Many of the references cited in this section, and the section on labora-tory methods to evaluate plants for resistance, describe methods for rearing and maintaining insects.

1. Bioassays

Bioassay methods have been used to evaluate insecticide resistance in insect populations (Dunbar & Beard, 1975; Lawrence et al., 1977; Tashiro et al., 1971), the influence of rainfall on insecticide activity (Lawrence et al., 1973), residual activity of insecticides (Fiori et al., 1972), insecticide activity and persistence in relation to soil type and moisture content (Harris & Hitchon, 1970; Tashiro & Kuhr, 1978), and the influence of formulation on insecticide effectiveness (Tashiro & Kuhr, 1978). Many of the bioassay methods have been developed for soil-inhabiting insects, particularly larvae of the Japanese beetle, European chafer [*Rhizotrogus majalis* (Razou-mowsky)] (see references cited above), and oriental beetle (*Anomala orien-talis* Waterhouse) (Dunbar & Beard, 1975). Bioassay methods also have been reported for bluegrass billbug larvae and adults (Tashiro & Personius, 1970; Tashiro et al., 1977) and mole crickets (Green et al., 1984; Kepner & Yu, 1987).

When evaluating insecticides against soil-inhabiting insects, chemicals generally have been applied in the laboratory to soil, or soil and peat or muck mixtures, either by spraying them on the soil surface or by incorporation by mixing. Soil samples collected from insecticide-treated field plots also have been evaluated for residual activity in the laboratory (Gambrell, 1953). The following methods have been used in bioassays with white grubs and bill-bugs. Soils were screened before treatment to achieve uniformity in particle size and remove debris. Treated soils were placed in wooden or metal trays, metal tins, clay or plastic pots, or clear plastic containers during tests. Soils were seeded with white clover (*Trifolium repens* L.) and various grasses (usual-ly ryegrass [*Lolium* sp.] and redtop [*Agrostis alba* L.]) to provide food for Scarabaeid grubs and with ryegrass as food for bluegrass billbug larvae. Short sections of ryegrass stems and leaves were placed on the soil surface as food for bluegrass billbug adults exposed to treated soil (Tashiro & Personius, 1970). Containers with soil were infested with known numbers of either eggs, larvae (usually third instar) or adults. Mortality and condition of larvae was checked at various exposure intervals by gently screening the soil in pots and removing dead larvae. An inexpensive and rapid method to screen Japanese beetle larvae from soil to check mortality, was described by Klein and Lawrence (1972). In mole cricket bioassays to evaluate toxicants, attractants, and feeding stimulants in baits, adult females were exposed to baits applied to moist sand in plastic cups (Green et al., 1984; Kepner & Yu, 1987). Cups were capped following introduction of the female. Mortality of crickets on or below the sand surface was recorded after 72 h. Kepner and Yu (1987) also tested feeding stimulants on mole crickets by an agar plug asay method.

Insecticide activity in soils has also been evaluated in bioassays using *Drosophila melanogaster* (Fleming et al., 1962), the common field cricket [*Acheta pennsylvanicus* (Burmeister)], and adult picture-winged flies [*Chaetopsis debilis* (Loew)], (Harris & Hitchon, 1970) as test organisms.

Bioassays have been conducted with foliar feeding insects by exposing them to foliage either sprayed with, dipped or immersed in insecticide solutions in water (Pas, 1966; Reinert & Niemczyk, 1982; Reinert & Portier, 1983; Tashiro & Personius, 1970). Foliage has also been treated in the field with insecticides (Lawrence et al., 1973) and a feeding deterrent (Ladd et al., 1978), and exposed to Japanese beetle adults in the laboratory. Treated foliage and insects have been held in 475-mL ice cream cartons lined with filter paper (sod webworm larvae), plastic petri dishes (southern chinch bug adults), or plastic pots (Japanese beetle adults). Mortality counts were taken at 24 or 72 h following exposure to evaluate toxicity of chemicals. Ladd et al. (1978) evaluated feeding deterrency by scoring leaves for the amount of defoliation after 24 to 48 h.

2. Spray Tower

Laboratory tests to evaluate insecticide activity have been conducted by spraying insects in a Potter Spray Tower (Potter, 1952). This equipment permits application of chemicals in the laboratory wihout contaminating the area with insecticide vapors. Research on turfgrass insects has been conducted with a modified version of the Potter Spray Tower, as described by Harris and Mazurek (1964). This method has been used to evaluate insecticide activity or insecticide resistance in the Japanese beetle (Niemczyk, 1975; Niemczyk & Lawrence, 1973), black turfgrass ataenius (Niemczyk & Dunbar, 1976), bluegrass billbug (Niemczyk & Frost, 1978), and southern chinch bug (Reinert & Niemczyk, 1982). One percent stock solutions of test insecticides were prepared from analytical or technical-grade materials using a mixture of acetone and olive oil (19:1 v/v) as the solvent. Treatments were replicated two or three times and 10 adult insects were treated in each replication. Insects were anesthetized with carbon dioxide (Japanese beetle, black turfgrass ataenius), or with ether (southern chinch bug), and then placed ventral side up on filter paper in 9-cm petri dishes in the spray tower. Replicates were sprayed with 5 mL of each insecticide in concentrations of 0.001, 0.01, 0.1, and 1%. The same number of insects were sprayed only with the solvent to serve as checks. Generally, 12 s were allowed for delivery of the insecticide and 18 s for settling. Following spraying, insects were removed from the petri dish and placed in a paper cup and provided with 5% honey water on rolled dental cotton stapled to the inside of the cup. The cup was covered with a glass petri dish cover and placed in a room maintained at $26 + 1.5\,°C$ and $40 + 7\%$ relative humidity (RH). Dead and moribund insects were recorded at 24 and 48 h following treatment and data were corrected for check mortality (ca. 5%) by using Abbott's formula.

3. Topical Application

Precise measurements of insecticide activity have been made by applying known quantities of technical or analytical grade chemicals to insects topically. Chemicals have been dissolved in an organic solvent, such as acetone, and applied in microliter quantities with a micro-applicator equipped with a 25 to 50 μL syringe. Various micro-applicators have been described (Baker, 1986; Kuhr et al., 1972; Ladd et al., 1984). Anywhere from 1 to 5 μL of material have been applied per insect, usually to the dorsal surface of the thorax of larvae (Ahmad & Das, 1978; baker, 1986) and to the ventral surface of the thorax, between the first pair of legs, of adults (Ng & Ahmad, 1979). Usually, 30 to 60 insects have been treated with each dose of insecticide, divided into five to six replications of 10 insects per dosage rate (Baker, 1986; Dunbar & Beard, 1975; Kuhr et al., 1972; Ng & Ahmad, 1979). With Japanese beetle, European chafer, and oriental beetle, the larvae were held in individual cups, or trays with separate cells, containing soil and grass mixtures, following treatment. Grubs were observed at regular intervals posttreatment, up to 14 d, for mortality and toxicological signs (Ahmad & Das, 1978; Kuhr et al., 1972). Ng and Ahmad (1979) held adult beetles in batches of 10 in 475-mL cups prior to treatment, and following treatment transferred them to cups containing a dental wick with 5% honey water stapled to the inside wall. Cups were capped with clear platic lids. Cameron and Johnson (1971) and Tashiro et al. (1977) held treated *Listronotus* adults in aerated plastic petri dishes containing two or three stems or leaves of annual bluegrass (*Poa annua* L.) and moist filter paper.

In all tests, controls have been included to monitor mortality in untreated or solvent-treated insects. Percent mortality of treated and control insects were compared. Mortality data were corrected by Abbott's formula and subjected to probit analysis to plot dosage/mortality regressions (Finney, 1971). The LD 50 and LD 90 values (i.e., lethal dose required to kill 50 and 90% of the population, respectively) were expressed in microgram chemical per insect. Tashiro et al. (1977) also evaluated insecticide activity by rating the amount of feeding by adults 48 h after treatment.

Ladd (1966, 1968, 1970) used similar methods for evaluating chemosterilant activity on Japanese beetle adults.

3. Variables

Laboratory and field methods developed to evaluate variables which influence insecticide efficacy in the field, such as adsorption (binding) by thatch, soil moisture and pH, and insecticide degradation, have been reported by a number of workers. Most recent studies were reported by Niemczyk (1987), Niemczyk and Chapman (1987), Niemczyk and Krueger (1987), and Villani and Wright (1988a). Factors associated with the distribution and persistence of organophosphate insecticides in thatch and soil have been reviewed by Niemczyk and Krueger (1982), Sears and Chapman (1982), and Tashiro (1982). In field trials, plot design, insecticide application methods, and methods used to collect grubs or grass, thatch or soil samples were similar to those described previously for field evaluation of insecticides. In the laboratory, however, sod and soil samples have been divided into layers, or subsamples, to provide material for residue analyses. Subsamples have consisted of surface vegetation, including green and dead tissues, the surface 1 to 1.3 cm of soil, and the succeeding 2.5 to 5.1 cm of soil (Sears & Chapman, 1982; Tashiro, 1982). For studies on adsorption of insecticides by thatch (Niemczyk & Krueger, 1982), 20-mm diam. core samples of thatch were removed from plots. Thatch was shredded and a range of thatch-water concentrations were prepared by adding varying amounts of thatch to a series of 25-ml flasks containing 10 mL of distilled water. Methods of applying insecticide to thatch-water samples and for preparing insecticide, water, and thatch slurries for extraction and analysis were also described by Niemczyk and Krueger (1982). Methods for analyzing insecticides in grubs, grass, thatch, and soil samples were described by Sears and Chapman (1982), Tashiro (1982), and Niemczyk (1987), and methods to evaluate enhanced degradation of an insecticide were described by Niemczyk and Chapman (1987). Enhanced degradation of the insecticide isofenphos (O-ethyl-O-(2-isopropoxy-carboyl)-phenyl isopropylphosphoramidothioate) in soils previously treated with this material was demonstrated by Niemczyk and Chapman (1987).

Villani and Wright (1988a) used a radiographic technique (Villani & Gould, 1986) to study the influence of soil moisture and temperature on grub movement and insecticide behavior in laboratory tests. Studies were conducted in plexiglass arenas (35 by 5 by 43 cm) filled with sieved loamy sand soil (organic matter, 2.4%; soil pH 6.9). Arenas were seeded with about 3 g of a mixture of grasses (49% red fescue [*Festuca rubra* L.], 19% Kentucky bluegrass [*Poa pratensis* L.], 15% perennial ryegrass [*Lolium perenne* L.], 14% chewings fescue [*F. rubra commutata* Gaudichaud-Beaupre], and 3% other species), and held at 20 °C with a 12:12 L/D photoperiod for 7 to 10 wk. In some tests, field-collected turfgrass sod that had been washed to remove most of the soil was placed on top of each arena. Each arena was then infested with 10 third instar grubs of one of four species (European chafer, Japanese beetle, oriental beetle, and northern masked chafer [*Cyclocephala borealis* Arrow]), with a total of 30 grubs of each species. Grubs were placed on the soil surface and allowed to dig down. Grubs that did not dig into the soil within 1 h were replaced. Within 48 h after infestation the arenas were placed in continuous darkness at 20 °C for the duration of the test. Arenas were x-rayed at different intervals after infestation or insecticide treatment. Details of the x-ray system and processing methods used to make radiographs were reported by Villani and Gould (1986) and Villani and Wright (1988a). By this technique Villani and Wright (1988a) documented species-specific differences in grub response to changes in soil moisture and temperature. Their research demonstrated the importance of examining the interaction of soil insect behavior, the soil physical environment, and insecticide movement and persistence in developing effective management tactics in turfgrass.

II. HOST PLANT RESISTANCE

Insect resistant cultivars have been developed for many crops (Painter, 1951), but this method of pest suppression has been greatly neglected in turfgrass breeding (Reinert, 1982a). However, the value of insect-resistant turfgrass cultivars was demonstated with the development and release of 'Floratam' (Horn et al., 1973) and subsequent release of 'Floralawn' (Dudeck et al., 1986) St. Augustinegrass [*Stentotaphrum secundatum* (Walter) Kuntze], which are resistant to the southern chinch bug. In spite of the lack of development of insect and mite-resistant turfgrass cultivars, several methods for screening or evaluating plants for resistance have been reported. Most of these methods were developed to evaluate plants for genetically controlled sources of resistance. More recently, however, research has been reported on evaluation of cool-season grasses for insect resistance enhanced by endophytic fungi (Funk et al., 1985; Pottinger et al., 1985). The endophyte-enhanced resistance reported to date has primarily involved fungi belonging to the genus *Acremonium*, and has been reported in tall fescue (*Festuca arundinacea* Schreb.), perennial ryegrass, and various fine leaf fescues (*Festuca* spp.) (Funk et al., 1985; Saha et al., 1986; Siegel et al., 1985). Many of the same or similar methods have been used to evaluate genetically controlled and endophyte-enhanced resistance. However, Funk et al. (1985) point out the need to differentiate between the types of resistance during research, to make optimum use of both sources in developing resistant cultivars. Methods for detecting the presence of the fungus in plant material have been described by Siegel et al. (1985). Plants being evaluated for resistance need to be examined for the presence of the fungus to determine whether resistance was genetically controlled or endophyte-enhanced.

Research methods are broadly grouped under screening or field evaluation. Screening methods include those developed to initially evaluate plants for resistance and to re-evaluate selections from previous laboratory, greenhouse, or field tests. These methods are applied primarily in laboratory and greenhouse tests, although plants have been screened for resistance in field cages (Murdoch & Tashiro, 1976; Reinert & Busey, 1983, 1984). Laboratory facilities, and greenhouses to a lesser extent, can be used to control conditions that may adversely affect selection for resistance in the field. Although it is extremely important to evaluate resistant plant selections under field conditions, often it is difficult to screen for resistance in the field because of the inability to control numerous factors (including the availability of the test insect) which influence the expression of resistance. Laboratory facilities have included reach-in or walk-in type environmental growth chambers or rooms, or other areas where environmental conditions such as temperature, relative humidity, photoperiod, or light intensity could be controlled. Such facilities offer the opportunity to conduct research on a year-around basis if plants and pest species can be maintained in adequate numbers (Ratcliffe & Murray, 1983). Greenhouses are less adaptable for controlled tests, but have been modified to provide more precise control of temperature and photoperiod (Leuck et al., 1968a).

A. Screening Methods

Test methods have varied depending upon the crop and pest species, the number of plants to be tested, and the plant age and insect growth stage used in the test. There are advantages and disadvantages to most test methods, and the method adopted for a specific pest, or pest complex, may be the one that offers the best compromise between accuracy in assessing resistance and the ability to test an adequate number of plants to properly classify germplasm sources for resistance. Tests have been conducted with growing plants, either as seedlings or more mature (older) plants, or with excised plant parts such as leaves, stems, and stolons. Seedling tests can be used to evaluate large numbers of plants in a relatively short time, and often with much less manpower. However, selected seedlings must be retested to ascertain the presence or level of resistance in older plants and often to determine the nature of resistance in individual plants. Excised plants or plant parts have been used to evaluate resistance, but care must be taken to confirm resistance in the growing plant. These and other factors must be considered when evaluating the usefulness of the methods described herein for screening grasses for resistance to specific insect and mite species.

1. Seedling Methods

Seedling test methods have been used to evaluate greenbug resistance in Kentucky bluegrass, and Canada bluegrass [*Poa compressa* (L.)] (Kindler et al., 1983; Ratcliffe & Murray, 1983), fall armyworm [*Spodoptera frugiperda* (J.E. Smith)], resistance in bermudagrass [*Cynodon dactylon* (L.)], and pearl millet [*Pennisetum typhoides* (Brum.) Staph & C.E. Hubb] (Lueck, 1970; Lueck et al., 1968a,b), and endophyte-enhanced resistance to Argentine stem weevil [*Listronotus bonariensis* (Kuschel)] in perennial ryegrass (Stewart, 1985). Grasses have been seeded at a known density in rows or blocks in flats or pots, and evaluated at various ages or size depending upon the grass species and test objectives. Kindler et al. (1983) evaluated bluegrasses in greenhouse tests at 1 and 6 wk postemergence, and Ratcliffe and Murray (1983) in the laboratory at 4 wk postemergence. Lueck et al. (1968a,b) tested bermudagrass and pearl millet selections in the greenhouse when 7.5 to 10 cm and 4 to 5 cm tall, respectively. Stewart (1985) tested perennial ryegrass seedlings when 1-cm tall.

In greenbug tests, seedlings have been infested with mixtures of nymphs and adults at rates of two to three insects per plant. Bermudagrass and pearl millet seedlings have been infested with either fall armyworm eggs or first instar larvae at rates calculated to give from 5 000–10 000 larvae per flat (61 by 40 by 8 cm), depending upon the test. Perennial ryegrass seedlings were infested at a rate of 50 adults per pot (30 by 25 by 10 cm). The relative resistance or susceptibility of seedling grasses has been evaluated by several methods. Ratcliffe and Murray (1983) and Stewart (1985) expressed resistance on the basis of percent seedling survival, while Kindler et al. (1983) and Leuck et al. (1968a,b) used a visual scoring system of 1 to 9 or 1 to 10 to rate feeding injury by fall armyworm and greenburg, respectively. Leuck et al. (1968a,b) also classified accessions scored 1 to 3 as resistant (R), 4 to 6 as intermediate (I), and 7 to 9 as susceptible (S). Leuck (1970) evaluated resistance on the basis of fall armyworm survival and development. Susceptible and resistant controls (when available) should be interspersed in flats or pots to provide comparisons (Leuck et al., 1968a; Stewart, 1985).

2. Older Plant Methods

Resistance in several turfgrass species, to a wide range of insect and mite pests, has been evaluated in laboratory and greenhouse tests on older plants. Test selections have been established in the greenhouse by seeding in pots or other containers such as peat blocks (Ratcliffe, 1982), by collecting plugs from plants in field plots or nurseries and transplanting them into pots in the greenhouse (Ahmad et al., 1985, 1987; Carter & Duble, 1976; Taliaferro et al., 1969). Plants have been tested under choice or no-choice conditions to measure tolerance, nonpreference, or antibiosis (Painter, 1951) to one or more stages of the insect. Baker et al. (1981) evaluated tolerance to feeding by hairy chinch bug (*B. leucopterous hirtus* Montandon) adults on Kentucky bluegrass cultivars by caging plants within cylindrical plastic tubes that were divided in half longitudinally. This arrangement provided conditions whereby selections grown in the same pot could be tested in the presence or absence of the insect, and tolerance could be measured by comparing differences in plant response under the two conditions.

Various methods have been developed to measure nonpreference resistance in older plants. In tests for greenbug resistance, Jackson et al. (1981) placed pots seeded to different turfgrass species together in large metal flats in the greenhouse. Spaces between pots were filled with moist Pro-mix, which was covered with fine screened soil to permit movement of greenbugs between pots. After each pot was infested with greenbugs, the flat (replication) was covered with a plexiglass and screen cage. Resistance was measured by taking insect counts at various intervals post-infestation. Taliaferro et al. (1969) used a similar method for evaluating nonpreference to the twolined spittlebug [*Prosapia bicincta* (Say)], in bermudagrass accessions. Plugs of several hundred accessions were collected from a field nursery and transplanted into flats in the greenhouse. Twelve entries were placed in each flat, including 'Coastal' bermudagrass for comparison. Flats were placed on greenhouse benches within screen-wire cages during the infestation period and were subsequently rated for spittlebug injury. Barker et al. (1983, 1984) compared feeding and oviposition nonpreference by the Argentine stem weevil to endophyte-infected and endophyte-free plants under choice and no-choice conditions. Adult weevils were placed on infected and uninfected plants caged either alone or together in a screenhouse. Weevils were removed after 96 h and tillers were examined for feeding scars and eggs as a measure of resistance.

Tests to evaluate antibiosis or feeding nonpreference under no-choice conditions were reported for the southern chinch bug (Carter & Duble, 1976), the hairy chinch bug (Ratcliffe, 1982), the greenbug (Johnson et al., 1985;

Ratcliffe & Murray, 1983), and for the house cricket (*Acheta domesticus* L.) and southern armyworm (*Spodoptera eridania* Cramer) (Ahmad et al., 1985, 1987). Usually, entire plants have been caged for infestation, however, Ratcliffe and Murray (1983) caged greenbug adults on individual leaves in small plastic snap-on cages, to ensure recovery of all living and dead aphids. Cages used to confine entire plants have usually been plastic or plexiglass cylinders with cloth, plastic, or wire screening on tops or sides to provide ventilation and access for adding insects. Cages were sealed by forcing the base into the soil within the pot. Ratcliffe (1982) sealed the base of plants grown in peat blocks with plaster of Paris to anchor the cage and prevent escape of hairy chinch bug nymphs.

Resistance in older plants has been measured by recording actual feeding injury (defoliation) on plants (Barker et al., 1983) or by scoring feeding injury on a numerical scale (Carter & Duble, 1976; Ratcliffe & Murray, 1983; Taliaferro et al., 1969), and by measuring the effect of resistance on insect survival and development. Barker et al. (1983) and Ahmad et al. (1985, 1987) also dissected insects to determine the effect of resistance on the reproductive state of females or the gross morphology of internal organs. See Field Cage Methods (section II.A.4), where whole plants also were used.

3. Excised Plant Methods

Excised leaves, stems, and stolons have been used extensively in tests to evaluate insect and mite resistance in turfgrasses. Southern chinch bug resistance in St. Augustinegrass (Crocker et al., 1982; Reinert, 1974; Reinert & Dudeck, 1974; Reinert et al., 1980, 1981) and fall armyworm resistance in bermudagrass (Combs & Valerio, 1980a) has been evaluated on excised terminal stolons. In tests with the southern chinch bug, stolons were wrapped in moist cotton and placed in inflated plastic bags with chinch bugs to evaluate resistance (Reinert & Dudeck, 1974). Bermudagrass or centipedegrass [*Eremochloa ophiuroides* (Munro) Hackel] foliage was held in vials (Combs & Valerio, 1980a) or placed on moist filter paper in various sized petri dishes (Combs & Valerio, 1980b; Lunch et al., 1983; Quisenberry & Wilson, 1985; Wiseman et al., 1982) to evaluate feeding and oviposition nonpreference and antibiosis to the fall armyworm. Sod webworm resistance has been evaluated in Kentucky bluegrass selections on excised leaves placed on moist paper in petri dishes (Buckner et al., 1969). Endophyte enhanced resistance to aphids (Johnson et al., 1985), fall armyworm (Clay et al., 1985; Hardy et al., 1985), and Argentine stem weevil (Barker et al., 1983; Gaynor et al., 1983; Pottinger et al., 1985) has been successfully studied on excised stems, leaf blades or leaf sheaths of perennial ryegrass and tall fescue held on moist filter paper in petri dishes. Excised stolons of bermudagrass have been used to evaluate resistance to bermudagrass mite (*Eriophyes cynodoniensis* Sayed) by extending cut ends of sprigs through a hole in the test container into a Hoagland's solution in a pan below (Reinert et al., 1978). Excised leaves of perennial ryegrass, Kentucky bluegrass, chewings red fescue, and bentgrass (*Agrostis* sp.) have been held on moist filter paper in petri dishes to evaluate resistance to the winter grain mite [*Penthaleus major* (Duges)] (Streu & Gingrich, 1972).

Feeding and oviposition nonpreference under choice conditions has been evaluated by placing leaf blades or sheaths, and stems within the test arena in either an alternating (Johnson et al., 1985), criss-cross (Hardy et al., 1985), or random pattern (Reinert et al., 19798; Wiseman et al., 1982). Single leaves, or multiple pairs of leaves and stems have been used when material was confined in petri dishes. Tests to evaluate nonpreference or antibiosis under no-choice conditions have been conducted similarly by confining insects on excised material from individual selections.

Resistance in excised plant material has been measured by many of the same methods used for evaluating resistance in rooted plants. Feeding or oviposition nonpreference under choice conditions has been measured by counting insects (aphids) probing, or feeding on, or under, leaves at various intervals post infestation (Buckner et al., 1969; Gaynor et al., 1983; Hardy et al., 1985; Johnson et al., 1985; Wiseman et al., 1982), by scoring feeding injury on tillers or leaves on a numerical scale (Barker et al., 1983; Buckner et al., 1969; Gaynor et al., 1983; Hardy et al., 1985; Wiseman et al., 1982), by classifying selections on the basis of number of plants living and the number and percent of plants showing symptoms (Reinert et al., 1978), and by counting the number of eggs and egg clusters and the area of placement of clusters of eggs on stem terminals (Combs & Valerio, 1980a; Reinert & Dudeck, 1984). Under no-choice conditions, resistance has been measured on the basis of its effect on insect survival and development, ovipositional response, and feeding injury on plant material. Parameters used to measure the effects of resistance on insect development have included size (length and weight) and development time of immature and adult stages, fecundity of females (eggs per female, number of eggs per day, incubation period, oviposition period in days, and percent viability of eggs), and longevity of adults. Lynch et al. (1983) and Quisenberry and Wilson (1985) used a host suitability index to provide a quantitative measure of the cumulative effects of resistance on fall armyworm larvae. The effect of feeding injury on excised material has been evaluated chemically by determining chlorophyll loss in St. Augustinegrass stolons injured by southern chinch bug (Reinert & Dudeck, 1974).

Laboratory screening methods using artificial diets to evaluate endophyte-enhanced insect resistance in turfgrasses have been reported by Gaynor et al. (1983), Prestidge et al. (1985), and Prestidge and Gallagher (1985).

4. Field Cage Methods

Murdoch and Tashiro (1976) and Reinert and Busey (1983) screened bermudagrass, centipedegrass, or St. Augustinegrass for resistance to the grass webworm and the tropical sod webworm (*Herpetogramma phaeopteralis* Guenee), respectively, in outdoor screened cages. Reinert and Busey (1984) screened selections of bahiagrass (*Paspalum notatum* Fluegge), bermudagrass, centipedegrass, St. Augustinegrass, and zoysiagrass (*Zoysia japonica* Steud.) for resistance to mole crickets in tank cages. In tests with webworms, grasses were grown in the greenhouse and transferred to the cages for exposure to adults. Grasses were arranged in a randomized complete block design and replicated within the cage. Moths were introduced into cages at a constant rate and removed after 1 or 5 d. Murdoch and Tashiro (1976) measured oviposition nonpreference by counting the number of eggs in each pot after one night's exposure to moths. Following exposure to adults, grasses were removed from the outdoor cage and placed either in the laboratory or greenhouse to evaluate larval resistance. This was accomplished by caging pots individually and recording larval-feeding injury and survival. Feeding injury was measured by scoring damage to each grass on a numerical scale. Larval survival was measured by counting the number of adults emerging from each pot. In tests with mole crickets (Reinert & Busey, 1984), adults were placed in cages, and after a period of weeks, resistance or tolerance in grasses was evaluated on the basis of damage caused by feeding or uprooting by adults. Damage estimates were made by measuring shoot growth.

B. Field Evaluation

Many of the field plot methods described for insecticide tests can be applied to studies designed to evaluate insect and mite resistance in turfgrasses. Plots generally have ranged in size from about 1 to 3 m by 2 to 8 m, with entries arranged in a randomized complete block design with three to six replications. When available, resistant and susceptible controls should be included in field trials (Shearman et al., 1983). The field evaluation of turfgrasses for insect and mite resistance usually depends upon natural infestations of the pest species. However, natural populations often vary in level from year to year, and can change rapidly under unfavorable climatic conditions (Ratcliffe, 1982), thus making it difficult to consistently evaluate resistance to some pest species in the field. It may be possible to artificially infest plots with field-collected insects (Carter & Duble, 1976; Pass, 1966) or manage pest species in the field to increase numbers for research purposes (Reinert, 1976) to reduce this problem.

As noted for insecticide field tests, plots should be managed uniformly and according to standard practices for the grass in the test area. In addition to measuring differences in resistance among plant selections in the field, it also may be useful to measure morphological differences which may influence the expression of resistance. Carter and Duble (1976) measured internode length, stem diameter, and blade length and width of St. Augustinegrass selections prior to infesting plots with southern chinch bugs, and Bruton et al. (1983) tried to correlate stolon and stigma color, to determine the influence of grass morphology on insect selection of plants.

Resistance has been measured in the field by scoring plots or plants for feeding injury and sampling plots and counting insect numbers. Sampling methods described for insecticide evaluation in field trials have been used in field tests to evaluate plant resistance. When samples are taken several times during the season, different areas of the plot should be sampled on successive dates to minimize plot damage and disturbance of insects (Ratcliffe, 1982).

Visual estimates of resistance in turfgrass selections have been made by rating insect injury in plots on a numerical scale, as described for insecticide field tests, or by percentage green turf. These methods have been used to evaluate resistance to the bluegrass billbug in Kentucky bluegrass (Ahmad & Funk, 1982; Kindler & Kinbacher, 1975; Lindgren et al., 1981; Shearman et al., 1983), to sod webworm in Kentucky bluegrass and perennial ryegrass (Buckner et al., 1969; Pass et al., 1965), and to bermudagrass mite in bermudagrass (Butler, 1961). Visual ratings have been assigned on a 1 to 5, 1 to 9, or 0 to 100% basis, where the lowest value indicated little or no injury (or most green turf) and the highest value indicated severe injury or death of the plants (or least green turf). In addition to visual estimation of feeding injury by bermudagrass mites on bermudagrass, Butler and Kneebone (1965) also rated plants for resistance by feeling by hand for distorted growth associated with mite feeding.

C. Current Programs

Reinert (1982a) reviewed the status of plant resistance programs on insects and mites in turfgrasses. Since that time, progress has been made in identifying sources of resistance in Kentucky bluegrass to the greenbug (Kindler et al., 1983; Ratcliffe & Murray, 1983) and additional sources of resistance to the southern chinch bug in St. Augustinegrass (Reinert et al., 1986), mole crickets in several warm-season grasses (Reinert & Busey, 1984), and the fall armyworm in bermudagrass (Lynch et al., 1983). In addition, three perennial ryegrass cv. Pennant (Funk et al., 1983), Repell (Hurley et al., 1984), and Citation II (Meyer et al., 1987) have been released with endophyte-enhanced resistance to billbugs and sod webworms. In spite of this progress, however, there still is the need for greatly increased emphasis on development of insect and mite-resistant turfgrass germplasm and cultivars, as noted by Reinert (1982a). For instance, relatively little effort has been placed on selection for resistance to root-feeding insects, and especially to white grubs. However, research in New Zealand on the grass grub [*Costelytra zealandica* (White)] indicates that more intensive efforts in this area may lead to progress (Farrell & Sweney, 1974). The development of cultivars with a combination of genetically controlled and endophyte-enhanced resistance holds considerable promise as a means of providing a much broader range of pest control by use of resistant cultivars. With the availability of present research methods, and the development of new methods, significant progress should be possible if support for such programs increases. To date, there has been insufficient support at state and federal research levels (see Niemczyk, 1982) to make optimum use of the information now available.

III. BIOLOGICAL SUPPRESSION

Biological suppression of turfgrass pests has been accomplished with pathogens, parasites and predators, and by the use of chemical attractants to lure insects to various types of traps. Biological suppression plays an important part in the management of turfgrass pests (Klein, 1982). Various research methods developed in conjunction with biological suppression efforts will be reviewed briefly in this section. Further information on this topic can be found in reviews by Fleming (1968, 1976), Klein, (1982), and Sailer (1984).

A. Microbials

1. Bacteria

The most widely known of the microbials used against insect pests of turf is the milky disease of Japanese beetle larvae. This disease is caused primarily by bacteria of *Bacillus popilliae* Dutky and has been used extensively in much of the eastern USA for suppression of the Japanese beetle (Klein, 1982). This bacterium, or related strains or species, also attack many other scarabaeid larvae (Dutky, 1941; Klein, 1982), including such important pests as the northern masked chafer, southern masked chafer [*C. immaculata* (Oliver)], oriental beetle, European chafer, and black turfgrass ataenius. However, extensive research has been conducted only on microbial suppression of the Japanese beetle, although this approach probably would be useful in suppressing other white grubs (Warren & Potter, 1983).

Methods for preparing spore suspensions and inoculum of *B. popilliae* have been reported by White and Dutky (1940), Beard (1944), and Warren and Potter (1983). In the laboratory, grubs have been infected with spore suspensions by injection, or in feeding tests by exposing them to soil containing spores. Apparatus and methods used to inject grubs have been described by Beard (1944), Hall et al. (1968), Tashiro and White (1954), and Warren and Potter (1983). Third instar larvae generally have been used for injection studies, although Warren and Potter (1983), tested activity on first, second, and third instar larvae. Uninjected grubs and grubs injected with distilled water have been used as controls. Feeding tests have been conducted by placing larvae in soil containing known concentrations of spores, or in field-collected soil previously treated with spores. Control groups have consisted of grubs held in soil mixed with the carrier only, or untreated soil (Tashiro & White, 1954; Warren & Potter, 1983). Injected larvae have been held individually for observation after treatment, while groups of 10 to 25 larvae have been used in feeding tests. In feeding tests, grubs have been confined in soil seeded to grass or grass-clover mixtures, as described in insecticide bioassays. The incidence of disease (percent infection) has been used to evaluate microbial activity since infection with milky disease is synonymous with eventual grub death (Warren & Potter, 1983). Percent infection of grubs has been corrected for control by using Abbott's formula and dosage/infectivity regression lines have been determined by probit analysis (Finney, 1971; SAS Institute, 1982).

Methods simlar to those described in the previous sections have been used for sampling grubs from the field to determine microbial infection (Dunbar & Beard, 1975; Polivka, 1956; Tashiro & White, 1954). The number of grubs per square meter and the incidence of disease has been determined from each sample. Soil samples also have been taken to determine the presence of the inoculum from earlier field applications (Ladd & McCabe, 1967). Bacterial activity in previously treated soils was evaluated in the laboratory by exposing healthy larvae to the soil, as described above for feeding tests. Spore concentrations were estimated in the soil samples by comparing the milky disease mortalities obtained with those recorded after incubating larvae in graded concentrations of spores in soil.

Inoculum has been applied to field plots in living, infected larvae (White, 1940), or as spore suspensions in ground larvae (Tashiro & White, 1954) or dusts (Polivka, 1956; Warren & Potter, 1983). Plot size has ranged from about 4.6 to 7.6 m^2. Inoculum has been applied by treating areas within plots with spores, either by hand or hand-operated corn planter (Fleming, 1968; Polivka, 1956). The standard method of distribution is to apply the dust in a grid at 1.2- to 3.1-m intervals with one level teaspoon (about 30 g) per spot (Klein, 1982)

Bacillus thuringiensis Berliner is a bacterium that is effective against many lepidopterous pests. Hall (1954) described methods used in conducting laboratory and greenhouse experiments with *B. thuringiensis* (B.t.) on the western lawn moth [*Tehama bonifatella* (Hulst)]. In the laboratory, B.t. dusts or sprays were applied to larvae in petri dishes supplied with fresh grass clippings for food. In the greenhouse, larvae were tested on Kentucky bluegrass grown in flats. Water suspensions of B.t. were sprayed on the flats. Larvae were retrieved for determining mortality by applying a weak pyrethrum solution to the flats. Commercial preparations of B.t. are available and can be applied like conventional insecticides; therefore, methods applied for evaluating conventional insecticides would be applicable for evaluating B.t. activity in the field. Care must be taken, however, because B.t.-treated larvae may remain moribund for several days and could be recorded as live larvae by conventional soap and pyrethroid drench methods.

2. Fungi

Fungi in the genera *Beauveria* and *Metarrhizium* have been evaluated for biological suppression of turfgrass insects (Klein, 1982). These fungi produce either white- or green-fuiting bodies, which arise on the exterior of the insect, forming a thick covering. An early attempt to control the chinch bug [probably *Blissus leucopterus leucopterus* (Say.)], in Kansas with *Beauveria bassiana* (Balsamo) Vuillemin was unsuccessful, but drew attention to the potential use of these organisms in biological suppression efforts (Coppel & Mertins, 1977). Ramoska (1984) and Ramoska and Todd (1985) conducted tests with *B. bassiana* against the chinch bug in the laboratory. Methods for growing the fungus in pure culture and harvesting conidia for inoculation were described. Chinch bug adults were inoculated with dry conidia in petri dishes by gently shaking the dish to ensure full coverage of insects. Adults were removed from the dish immediately after inoculation and placed in environmental chambers to evaluate infection when insects fed on various host plants or artificial diet, or went without food. The liquid diet and feeding stations used were described by Dreyer et al. (1981) and Ramoska and Todd (1985). Control treatments consisted of insects treated with heat-inactivated fungus. Conidia dosage was determined by washing a sample of insects from each inoculated group in 1 mL of a 0.5% Tween 20 sterile water solution. The number of conidia in the sample was counted with a hemocytometer. Hall (1954) also evaluated activity of *B. bassiana* against eggs and first to fifth instar larvae of *T. bonifatella* in the laboratory and greenhouse. Methods for holding and treating eggs and larvae were similar to those described for evaluating activity of B.t. Reinert (1978) evaluated the effect of *B. bassiana* on the southern chinch bug by confining field-infected insects for several days with healthy specimens in the laboratory. The fungus was readily transferred and was pathogenic on all stages of the southern chinch bug. Kamm (1973) collected cranberry girdler [*Chrysoteuchia topiaria* (Zeller)] larvae from the field and held them in stinder dishes lined with moist blotter paper to evaluate *B. bassiana* infection. *Beauvaria bassiana* is currently being produced and tested by several commercial firms as a potential microbial insecticide (Storey & Gardner, 1987).

3. Microsporidia

The microsporidian, *Nosema locustae* Canning, is a protozoan that has been used in the biological suppression of grasshoppers and crickets. This organism has been used primarily for suppression of grasshoppers on range grasses, however. See Henry (1981) and references cited therein for information on research methods. Liu and McEwen (1977) described research with a *Nosema* spp. attacking the hairy chinch bug. Identifications were made by examining more than 700 insects collected from the field. Methods for preparing and examining specimens were described, and a new species, *N. blissi*, was proposed.

B. Parasites and Predators

Klein (1982) used the term parasitoid, rather than parasite, when describing various organisms which suppress turfgrass pests. Coppel and Mertins (1977) define a parasitoid as "an insect parasite of an arthropod: parasitic only in its immature stages, destroying its host in the process of its development, and free-living as an adult." Most of the parasites of turfgrass pests fit this description of a parasitoid, therefore this term is used in the following discussion of research methods except when discussing parasitic nematodes.

1. Parasitoids

One of the early attempts to suppress the Japanese Beetle was conducted with parasitoids in the genus *Tiphia* (Klein, 1982). Fleming (1968) and King et al. (1951) described explorations in Asia associated with collections of these and other parasitoids of the Japanese beetle. Balock (1934) and King and Parker (1950) conducted research with the spring *Tiphia* (*T. vernalis* Rohwer), a larval parasitoid introduced into the USA in 1924. Methods for colonizing this species, making field releases and recaptures of adults, and sampling grub populations to determine rates of parasitism were described. King and Parker (1950) emphasized the importance of releasing adult *Tiphia* in areas favorable to both the host (grubs) and the adult stage of the parasitoid. Such areas included parks, golf courses, and cemeteries where sod would remain relatively undisturbed for long periods, and where there was shaded foliage where the adult *Tiphia* could find food. Ladd and McCabe (1966) reported that subsequent surveys showed little success in retaining this parasitoid in the field, although initial efforts to establish it were considered successful by King and Parker (1950).

Castner (1984) and Castner and Fowler (1984) reviewed research conducted with *Larra bicolor* F., a parasitoid wasp of mole crickets. Mole crickets for parasitization studies were found by searching the ground for surface galleries or signs of damage. Specimens were collected by using detergent flushes, linear pit-fall traps, digging, or by operating sound traps. Adult parasitoids were monitored by searching the blossoms of flowers upon which they fed. Hunting female wasps were located by scanning the soil surface during morning hours in mole cricket infested areas. Captive wasps were maintained, except during feeding or experiments, in individual stoppered glass test tubes, and stored in an ice chest to provide a cool, dark environment. Mole crickets were placed into the test tube for parasitization, after which they were confined individually in 20-dram clear, snap-cap vials, half filled with damp, sterilized sand. Mole crickets were fed every 4 to 5 d and examined 10 to 14 d and 20 to 24 d post-parasitization for parasitoid development. Parasitoid development was judged unsuccessful if the wasp larvae died while the host lived, or if no noticeable increase in larval size occurred between the first and second examinations.

Reinert (1972a, 1978) and Mailloux and Streu (1979) collected adults of the chinch bug egg parasitoid (*Eumicrosoma benefica* Gahan) in flotation samples and reared the parasitoid from hairy chinch bug or southern chinch bug eggs collected in the same samples. Reinert (1972a) held insects and debris in jars in the laboratory following collections, and removed, sexed, and counted the *Eumicrosoma* adults as they crawled from the debris. Behavior of the parasitoid on the host was described by Reinert (1972a).

Research on the introduction of, and efforts to establish parasitoids of the Rhodesgrass mealybug [*Antonia graminis* (Maskell)], was reviewed by Dean et al. (1979). Methods for laboratory rearing the parasitoids *Anagyrus antoninae* Timberlake and *Neodusmetia sangwani* (Rao) were described by Riherd (1950) and Dean et al. (1961). Dean and Schuster (1958) developed a technique for measuring percentage of parasitism by the parasitoid, *N. sangwani*, on the Rhodesgrass mealybug, and evaluated its effectiveness under caged and uncaged conditions in the field. Research methods used in rearing and colonizing several other species of parasitoids were described by Dean and Schuster (1958), Dean et al. (1961), and Schuster (1965). Dean et al. (1979) reported that *N. sangwani* was instrumental in suppressing the Rhodesgrass scale in Texas.

2. Nematode Parasites

Two types of nematodes have been established as important natural control agents for turfgrass pests (Klein, 1982). Members of the first type, which are in the family Mermithidae, are very long (20 cm +) and can be easily seen in the body of insects. Klein et al. (1976) reported the first finding of a mermithid parasite of Japanese beetle larvae, and identified it as *Psammomermis* sp. closely resembling the species *P. korsakowi*. Nematodes were collected from Japanese beetle grubs sampled from various locations in Connecticut, New York, and Vermont. Grubs collected in October were held in cold storage until January, and then placed at 27 °C for nematode emergence. Those collected in April were held at 27 °C until parasites emerged. Nematodes emerged from fall and spring-collected grubs in March and May, respectively. Nematodes in the family Steinernematidae, and Heterorhabitidae make up the second group of parasites. These are microscopic in size and kill their host in conjunction with a bacterium, *Xenorhabdus* spp. (Bedding, 1981). Fleming (1968) reviewed methods used to evaluate *Steinernema glaseri* (Steiner) in numerous tests conducted by different workers in the 1930s and 1940s against Japanese beetle grubs. In these tests, nematodes were either sprayed on plots in a water suspension, which was followed by a rinse to remove them from the foliage, or were applied in suspension in shallow holes dug in the turf. Holes were about 10 cm square and spaced at 1.5-m intervals in the plot. Turf was replaced in the holes following treatment. The availability of commercially produced parasitic nematodes (Bedding, 1981, 1984; Sailer, 1984) now makes it possible to evaluate the effectiveness of these organisms in field trials much like conventional insecticides. Villani and Wright (1988b) and Heller and Kellogg (1987a) applied suspensions of *Heterorhabditis heliothidis* (Khan, Brooks and Hirshmann) with a watering can or CO_2 sprayer to evaluate activity against European chafer or Japanese beetle grubs. Villani and Wright (1988b) applied nematodes at the rate of $310/cm^2$ ($2000/in^2$) in 11.4 L of water to the center 3.7 m^2 of 3- by 3-m plots to evaluate control of European chafer and Japanese beetle larvae. Following treatment, plots were irrigated (equivalent of 0.6 cm of rain) by sprinkler. Plots were sampled 47 to 48 d after treatment. Four 0.9 m^2 samples were taken from the center 3.7 m^2 in each of the four compass directions. Grub species were identified in the field and larvae were categorized as either alive (healthy and moribund larvae were considered alive) or dead. Heller and Kellogg (1987a) applied nematodes at the rate of 2 billion/ha (5 billion/acre) to 1.8- by 2.7-m plots. Following treatments, plots were irrigated with 0.6 cm of water. Plots were sampled for Japanese beetle larvae 30 d after treatment by taking three 0.9 m^2 samples/plot. Villani and Wright (1988b) also evaluated the efficacy of nematode applications against European chafer grubs in the laboratory. Nematodes were applied to pots (15 by 10 by 8 cm) containing grubs at rates of 0, 19.4, 33.8, 77.5, 155, and 310/cm^2 in 9.5 mL of water. Depending upon test, nematode efficacy was assessed at 12, 18, 20, and 25 d after treatment. Larvae were classified as alive or dead, and dead larvae were dissected, and the presence or absence of nematodes was noted. Observations were also made on the color of larvae (i.e., whether they were reddish in color, characteristic of infection with the symbiotic bacteria associated with *H. heliothidis*). Wright et al. (1988) reported tests with Steinernematid and Heterorhabitid nematodes for control of European chafer and Japanese beetle larvae in potted yew.

3. Vertebrate Predators

Vertebrate predators, such as birds, skunks, and moles, supress turfgrass pest populations, but generally do not provide a feasible method of biological control because of the damage which results from their searching and feeding activities (Niemczuk, 1981). Kamm (1973) studied the effects of bird feeding on sod webworm larval populations from mid-September until late November by taking samples in a field of Kentucky bluegrass infested with nearly mature larvae. Larvae which had not constructed hibernacula were extracted from samples with a Berlese funnel, while larvae and prepupae in hibernacula were extracted by dissecting the crowns of plants. Kamm (1973) estimated that birds reduced populations by more than 80%.

4. Invertebrate Predators

Various methods have been reported for studying invertebrate predators of turfgrass pests. Crocker and Whitcomb (1980) observed naturally occurring *Geocoris* spp. (big-eyed bugs) throughout a 3-yr period on a number of crops, including common bermudagrass. They monitored predator activity by watching individual insects at distances not greater than about 1 m, for up to about 2 h each. They set a minimum criteria for feeding as prolonged, visually confirmed penetration of the prey with the beak. The Rhodesgrass scale was listed among the pests preyed upon by these species. Reinert (1978) collected predators of the southern chinch bug from St. Augustinegrass lawns either by hand aspiration or by flotation. Predators were dipped from flotation samples and either counted and returned to the plot, or placed in glass jars for return to the laboratory. In the laboratory, individual predators were confined with the life stages of the chinch bugs on stolons of St. Augustinegrass and placed in either glass stinder dishes or plastic petri dishes fitted with vented lids. The quantity of prey consumed by two of the predators, *Geocoris uliginosus* and *Pagasa pallipes* Stal., was determined by confining individual adults of each species with fifth-instar chinch bugs in stinder dishes. Five chinch bug nymphs were confined with each predator daily for 5 d, and the number fed upon daily was recorded. Reinert

(1978) recorded six hemipterans, one dermapteran, several ant species, and a spider as predators of the southern chinch bug.

Cockfield and Potter (1983, 1984) sampled predaceous insect, mite, and spider populations in a Kentucky bluegrass lawn in studies to determine the short-term effects of insecticide applications on predaceous arthropods. Research was conducted on 10- by 10-m plots with a 3-m buffer zone between plots. Arthropods were sampled with pit-fall traps, which were located at least 2.5 m from the plot edge. Traps were left uncovered to permit weekly mowing. Ethylene glycol was placed in traps as a killing agent. Collections from pit-fall traps were rinsed with water on a 40-mesh screen and transferred to 75% ethanol (ETOH) for storage until counting. Arthropods were identified to family based on adults only, except for spiders. In studies to determine the effect of an insecticide application on egg predators, Cockfield and Potter (1984) conducted both field and laboratory tests. The activity of egg predators was evaluated by placing eggs, which were glued lightly onto black filter paper in petri dishes, in the plots. Ten dishes of five eggs each were placed in small depressions and level with the soil surface in each plot. An opaque disc was supported above each dish to shield the eggs from rain and direct sun. One dish in each plot was covered to exclude predators to confirm that eggs had not hatched during the exposure period. After 48 h, the number of eggs remaining in the dish were counted and missing eggs were assumed eaten by predators. Further observations were made on egg predation by placing unglued eggs in petri dishes in plots. Any predator seen eating or carrying away an egg was collected and returned to the laboratory where egg consumption was recorded over a 48-h period.

C. Attractants

The use of food-type lures and sex phermones to attract and trap one or both sexes of turfgrass pest species is another approach to biological suppression. Such traps could be used to directly reduce the number of adults or disrupt mating. The use of physical methods to attract insects, such as light traps, is discussed along with other survey methods. There is a large volume of literature available on chemical attractants of turfgrass pests, particularly for the Japanese beetle. Reviews have been published on research with Japanese beetle attractants by Fleming (1969, 1976), Klein (1981), Klein et al. (1981), and Ladd and Klein (1982). Tashiro et al. (1970) reviewed research on chemicals evaluated as attractants for the European chafer. In addition to the Japanese beetle and European chafer, sex pheromones have been identified from the northern and southern masked chafer (Potter, 1980) and species of sod webworms (Banerjee, 1969; Kamm, 1982), armyworms (Kamm et al., 1982a), and cutworms (Steck et al., 1979). In spite of the large amount of research conducted, however, there have been relatively few field trials that have evaluated the use of attractants in mass trapping programs to suppress turfgrass pest populations.

Hamilton et al. (1971) maintained a mass trapping program to control Japanese beetles on Nantucket Island, Massachusetts in 1965 to 1967. The efficiency of traps baited with food-type lures was tested in an isolated infested area for about 100 d of adult activity each year. Traps were suspended about 1.2 m above the ground and spaced about 30 to 60 m apart in areas where Japanese beetles were present or suspected of being present. Japanese beetle control was estimated by determining the reduction or increase in captures per trap each season, since larval populations were too light to make accurate counts. The number of beetles captured was determined by counting every fifth trap in each area, generally on a 7- to 10-d period. In this trial, populations of Japanese beetle adults were reduced by at least 50% by the 3 yr of trapping, but no information was available on the effect on grubs.

Gordon and Potter (1985) used a combination of food-type and pheromone lures to determine what effect season-long use of traps would have on Japanese beetle grub populations in turf. They placed traps in various locations around potted grape plants, which in turn, were located on either a golf course or in home lawns. Sites for treatments within these locations were assigned to blocks and within blocks were randomly assigned one of four plant and trap combinations based on location (upwind or downwind) and distance (3.1 or 9.3 m) of traps from plants. The control consisted of a plant without a trap. Plants and traps were oriented according to the prevailing wind direction. Within an experiment, plants were rotated among sites within blocks at regular intervals and beetle counts were taken on plants at each change. Cumulative defoliation was determined to the nearest 10% by averaging the estimates of two independent observers. Collection bags were placed at each rotation and returned to the laboratory for beetle count. Soil samples were taken from around each trap in August to establish grub density. Two sod and soil cores (15.5-cm diam. 5 cm deep) were removed at 1-m intervals, out to 7 m from the trap, in both windward and leeward directions. In these tests, defoliation was nearly always greater on plants with a trap present, but grub populations were not significantly altered in the vicinity of traps. Lauren (1979) also reported that many mass trapping trials with the grass grub in New Zealand were unable to show any effect on larval populations, although adult populations were reduced.

Between 1982 and the present, considerable research has been reported on evaluation of Japanese beetle traps to test the effect of various lures or combinations of lures, lure enhancers, wick area, trap color, and trap height on trapping efficiency. Klostermeyer (1985) also compared the effectiveness of commercial and homemade traps. The most effective of the Japanese beetle lures has been a combination of the food-type lures, phenethyl propionate + eugenol + geroniol (PEG), in a ratio of 3:7:3, with the pheromone Japonilure (Ladd et al., 1981). These lures placed in white traps were subsequently reported to be the best choice for maximizing captures of Japanese beetle adults (Ladd & Klein, 1986). Traps containing only food-type lures seem to be the most effective when placed 28 to 56 cm above the ground (Ladd & Klein, 1982). In most evaluations, Ellisco traps (Schwartz, 1968) have been used and have been suspended about 1 m above the ground (Gordon & Potter, 1985; Ladd & Tew, 1983; McGovern & Ladd, 1984). Field trials have generally used a randomized complete block design with treatments replicated four to six times. Treatments within blocks have been spaced and 5 to 8 m apart, and blocks have been separated by about 10 m (Ladd, 1986a, Ladd & Klein, 1986; McGovern & Ladd, 1984). Traps have been exposed for various intervals, and usually changed every 2 to 3 d. Trap catches have been returned to the laboratory to make or estimate counts (based on subsamples) and determine sex ratio of adults. Laboratory methods for evaluating sugars as feeding stimulants for the Japanese beetle have been described by Ladd (1986b).

Attractants for the grass grub have been evaluated in the field by placing baits in small jars or on polystyrene strips in the center of open tin traps, 30 by 33 by 10 cm in size, and containing about 2 L of water (Lauren, 1979). Baited traps were placed in randomized blocks located over an about 2.5-ha pasture, and were spaced about 15 to 20 m apart in blocks.

Potter (1980) evaluated traps baited with either adult northern and southern masked chafers or solvent rinses prepared from females of the two species. Standard Ellisco traps were used and treatments were compared with the Japanese beetle lure, phenethyl butyrate-eugenol 9:1. Traps were hung at ground level from steel supports and positioned 3 m apart. Trap placement was randomized and replicated four times. Traps were set out 0.5 h before sunset and the catch was emptied at 2300 h and again at dawn. Female solvent rinses were bioassayed by pipetting them onto shallow 30-mm diam. stainless steel dishes that were placed in the bait wells of traps. Traps were charged shortly before dusk and set out along with controls.

Research has been reported with various sod webworm species to evaluate traps baited with female and male moths or synthetic sex attractants (Kamm, 1982). Traps used to confine moths in the field were made of 3.78 L ice cream cartons from which lids and bottoms were removed (Banerjee, 1969). The inside of the carton was smeared with Stickem and the bait. Moths were confined in screen cages 3.8 cm long by 3.8 cm in diameter which were suspended by wire in the trap. Traps were stapled to wooden stakes and placed 0.6 m above the ground. Traps were placed randomly at about 3.1- to 4.6-m intervals each evening, 1.5 to 2 h after sunset. Moths caught in the traps were counted, sexed, and removed each morning. Kamm and McDonough (1979, 1980) and Kamm et al. (1982b) evaluated sod webworm pheromone and related compounds by exposing them on rubber septa in pheromone traps (Pherocon 1 C) that were suspended from stakes at a height just above the grass (for the cranberry girdler) or 40 to 50 cm above the grass (for the western lawn moth). Traps were placed at least 20 m apart in a randomized design. Replicates were placed 100 m apart. Baits were exposed in the field for 2 to 4 or 6 to 8 d depending upon the test, and were re-randomized daily. Females, and extracts from the abdominal tips of females, also were tested in the Pherocon 1 C traps. Females were confined in screen wire cages that were impregnated on small nylon bags of sand and suspended in the traps. Kamm (1982) stated that results with the cranberry girdler suggest that disruption of mating might be achieved on many species of sod webworm by using four to eight strategically located pheromone evaporators attached to a fence or shrubs of the average home lawn. Kamm et al. (1982a) used similar methods to evaluate pheromones for the armyworm. *Pseudaletia unipuncta* (Haworth), in either commercial ryegrass seed fields or in an abandoned golf course. Pherocon 1 C traps were suspended just above the canopy of the grass. Kamm and McDonough (1980) and McDonough et al. (1982) describe methods used in evaluating sex attractants against male sod webworm moths in the laboratory by electroantennogram analysis.

IV. DIAGNOSTIC METHODS

A. Survey Methods

A more detailed description of survey methods, which are reviewed briefly in this section, can be found in many of the references cited in this chapter. Publications by Niemczyk (1981) and Tashiro (1987) are particularly useful, since they include photographs or sketches of many of the sampling devices.

1. Light Traps

Black-light (BL) traps have been used to survey adult stages of many turfgrass pests, including the moths of webworms, armyworms, and cutworms, and adults of scarabaeid beetles. Beetles attracted to BL traps include the black turfgrass ataenius, Asiatic garden beetle (*Maladera castaneus* (Arrow)], European chafer, northern and southern masked chafers, and May or June beetles (*Phyllophaga* spp.) (Tashiro, 1987). None of the turf-damaging stages of pests are attracted to light traps, however. Light traps usually are equipped with a 15-W fluorescent BL lamp, baffles, and a funnel and receptacle supported on a tripod. Baffles are located at right angles to the lamp and insects that are attracted to the radiation strike the baffles and are deflected into the funnel and receptacle. The receptacle is charged with a volatile insecticide to kill insects quickly and preserve their natural appearance. Several factors may influence the effectiveness, and therefore, design and use of light traps. These include trap placement (height aboveground, location in respect to vegetation, direction in which faced), time of exposure, trap size, shape, color, lamp type, and the differences in response of sexes within species to these variables. Tashiro et al. (1967) found that BL traps with a peak radiation of 3650 A were the most attractive to European chafer adults and that traps placed adjacent to trunks of large trees caught more than those in open areas. Traps placed near the ground were generally most effective in collecting *Cyclocephala* and *Phyllophaga* adults (Chandler et al., 1955; Riegel, 1948; Stone, 1986) and collected more males than females (Lim et al., 1979). However, Roberts (1963) was able to greatly increase the number of *Cyclocephala* females caught by placing traps about 2 to 3 m above the ground. Black-light traps placed 1 m above ground were most effective in attracting males of the buffalograss webworm (*Surattha indentella* Kearfott) while gravid females were collected only at ground level

(Sorensen & Thompson, 1984). The time of peak flight activity differed between the webworm males and females in all species studied, but flight activity for the two sexes was similar in species (Banerjee, 1967; Sorensen & Thompson, 1984). Ultraviolet light traps and mercury light traps have been used to attract flying mole crickets (Ulagaraj, 1975).

A disadvantage of the light trap as a monitoring device is its lack of specificity in attracting insects. This can result in the collection of large numbers of extraneous insects. This problem can be reduced, however, by modifying traps to exclude larger insects than the species desired, or to permit small species to escape through screened areas in the receptacle (Tashiro et al., 1967). Frequent examination and collection of catches also will reduce the time required to sort extraneous insects.

2. Pheromone Traps

Pheromone-baited traps have been used to survey adult populations of turfgrass pests, as discussed in the section on biological supression. The specificity of sex attractants enhances the usefulness of pheromone traps for this purpose. Standard Japanese beetle traps baited with pheromones have been used for monitoring most scarabaeid adults. Commercially produced pheromone traps, such as the Pherocon 1 C trap and Sector trap, have been used for monitoring sod webworm adult populations (Kamm, 1982). Pheromones used for the sod webworm are commonly formulated on plastic strips or rubber septa and remain effective for from several weeks to months depending on chemical structure of the pheromone. Kamm (1982) discussed the practicality of using pheromone traps for monitoring various types of turfgrass pests. Methods used in operating pheromone traps are discussed in the section on biological suppression.

3. Pit-Fall Traps

Two types of pit-fall traps have been used for monitoring turfgrass pests. The conventional trap is made of three plastic cups with the upper, interior cup modified to act as a funnel to direct captured specimens into the collection cup (Niemczyk, 1981; Tashiro, 1987). Alcohol, or some other preservative, or water is usually placed in the collection cup. The trap is placed in a hole which is about the diameter and depth of the exterior cup so that the lip of the cup is located at the soil-thatch level. A linear pit-fall trap was designed for collecting mole crickets (Lawrence, 1982) and is useful in collecting other arthropods (Tashiro, 1987). The trap consists of a piece of PVC pipe, 7.6 cm in diameter and 2.5 m long, a 19-L plastic pail, and a 3.78-L plastic jug. A 2.5 cm-wide slot is cut lengthwise in the pipe with a 5-cm section left uncut at each end and at the mid-point for reinforcement. One end of the pipe is capped and the other end extends through holes in the side of the pail and jug so that it terminates inside the jug. Drainage holes are drilled in the bottom of the pail and jug. The trap is placed in the soil so that the pipe with the open side up, is at, or very slightly below the soil level, and the pail with jug is imbedded in the ground (see illustration in Lawrence,

1982 or Tashiro, 1987). Cannibalistic insects such as mole crickets can be separated by placing about 1 cm of soil inside the pipe and plastic jug. Insects which fall into the pipe eventually work their way into the jug.

Pit-fall traps should be emptied daily, if possible. Small shelters have been placed over traps to protect them from rainfall, however, these must be removed prior to mowing when traps are located in turf plots. When numerous small arthropods are collected, numbers can be estimated rather than counted in total. When monitoring winter grain mite populations with pit-fall traps, Streu and Gingrich (1972) estimated population density by the following method. Contents of each trap collecting jar (130 mL with about 50 mL of alcohol) were standardized to about 20 mL by either removing or adding alcohol. One-milliliter aliquots were placed in a petri dish containing alcohol and a filter paper ruled with lines about 6 mm apart. Mite populations were estimated under a stereomicroscope using an index system in which 0 = no mites present per 1-mL aliquot; 1 = 1 or 2; 2 = 3-10; 3 = 11-40; 4 = 41 and over. Three aliquots were counted from each trap. Actual numbers trapped were estimated by counting the mites in 3 one-mL aliquots/sample. Means were calculated from nine counts/treatment.

4. Flotation and Drench Methods

Chinch bugs and associated predators and parasitoids have been collected and counted by flotation. Various size open-ended metal cans or cylinders, usually ranging from 0.06 to 0.1 m^2, are forced into the turf and filled with water to accomplish this. Counts are taken of insects surfacing in 7 to 10 min. Either total chinch bugs are counted during this period, or, when populations are very dense, counts > 100 can be counted as 100 (Reinert, 1972b). Mailloux and Streu (1979) modified this method to enable collection of chinch bug eggs as well as nymphs and adults. Insects and thatch are loosened with a stream of water applied under pressure to grass enclosed in a steel cylinder 40 cm long and 17.2 cm in diameter. This provides a sampling surface of 232 cm^2. Thatch and insects are washed out of the cylinder through a pipe that is fixed at a 45 degree angle in the side and 13 cm from the top of the cylinder. This material is placed in ethyl alcohol and centrifuged to separate insects from the thatch. The sediments are then rinsed with tap water over a 100-mesh screen to remove the alcohol, and centrifuged again in a sugar solution. The supernatant is removed and examined and insect stages counted. Liu and McEwen (1979) used another modification of the flotation method to sample hairy chinch bug populations when developing sequential sampling methods. They used a heavy steel square (15 by 15 cm, and 15 cm deep) for sampling, and observed the number of insects surfacing in 15 min, or longer, if chinch bugs continued to surface.

Drench methods can be used to force Lepidoptera larvae, mole crickets, billbug adults, and chinch bugs to the surface of sod or soil (Tashiro, 1987). Either dilute solutions of pyrethrins or liquid dishwashing detergent can be used. The concentration of the irritant, volume of water applied, and the size of the area sampled have varied among tests, but the general method has been the same. Drenches are applied and counts are taken of surfacing insects for 10 min. Tashiro et al. (1983) found that 0.25% detergent (10 mL per 4 L of water) and 0.0015% pyrethrins (1 mL per 4 L) applied to 1860 cm^2 (2 ft^2) of turf in 15 L of water was the most efficient method for sampling grass webworm larvae. Reinert (1976) applied 0.946 L of 0.02 to 0.03% pyrethrins plus piperonyl butoxide on 0.37 m^2 (4 ft^2) of turf when sampling for grass and sod webworms. Matheny (1981) drenched about 1.5 m^2 of soil with 0.01% pyrethrin solution to collect mole crickets. Following application of irritants, plots should be observed continuously, since insects forced to the surface will re-enter within the 10 min counting time (Tashiro et al., 1983). Hudson (1984) considered the drench (soil flush) method the best for comparing mole cricket populations between locations or over time.

5. Soil Samples

Soil sampling for root-feeding insects is the most destructive of the methods used for surveying turfgrass pest populations. The least disruptive method of examining turf for grubs is to cut the sod loose on three sides and turn back the cut area like a flap (Tashiro, 1987). A sod cutter quickly and uniformly cuts turf so that subunits can be examined. A golf course cup cutter also is a useful tool for sampling, and if plugs are replaced after sampling, damage to the turf is minimal. If samples are returned to the laboratory, plugs cut from other areas can be used to fill the holes. To maintain uniformity in depth among samples, it is more desireable to use a sod cutter or cup cutter than a spade. The standard cup cutter takes a sample of sod and soil 10.8 cm (4.25 in.) in diameter (Tashiro, 1987). To convert the number of insects found per sample to the number per square foot, multiply by a factor of 10.15 (Niemczyk, 1981). Because of the scattered nature of grub infestations, samples of at least 0.1 m^2 (1 ft^2) should be taken per plot. Samples for white grubs have generally been taken to a depth of 10 to 12.5 cm (5–6 in.). Sampling plans for the Japanese beetle and *Phyllophaga* spp. have been reported by Guppy and Harcourt (1973) and Ng et al. (1983a,b).

6. Other Methods

Sound-trapping stations have been used to collect flying mole crickets (Dong & Beck, 1982; Ulagaraj, 1975; Walker, 1982; Walker & Fritz, 1983). Cricket adults are attracted to the highly amplified synthetic or recorded calls of male mole crickets that are emitted from speakers located over collection receptacles. Crickets lured to the traps have been caught in collection jars or on 1.5 m-diameter wading pools half-filled with water. Sound traps are most effective during the flight seasons in spring and fall. Walker et al. (1983) used this method to monitor mole crickets across Florida.

Grass webworms and lawn armyworms have been sampled from under boards (30.5 by 61 by 1.3 cm thick) placed in turf plots, as described for field evaluation of insecticide applications. However, Tashiro et al. (1983) subsequently reported that drench methods were about three times more effective in collecting these insects than boards.

B. Identification Methods

Color photographs and descriptions found in various publications, as noted in the introduction, can be used as aids in identifying these insects or mites until one becomes familiar with them. In some species, such as sod webworms, both adult and immature stages may be difficult to identify, and may require the assistance of experts familiar with those groups of insects. It is important to confirm the identity of any such species when conducting research.

Fortunately, there are fairly recognizable differences among some commonly found species which otherwise would be more difficult to separate. Larvae of the scarabaeid pests, which are very similar in general appearance, and often overlap in the field, can be separated by the pattern of spines, hairs, and bare spaces, called the raster, which are found on the ventral area of the last abdominal segment. Rastral patterns can be examined easily under a microscope, or in the field, under good illumination, with a hand lens of 10 × magnification or stronger. Many general texts on turfgrass or scarabaeid pests contain sketches of the rastral patterns for the common grubs. Tashiro (1987) pictures patterns for *Aphodius* spp., Asiatic garden beetle, black turfgrass ataenius, green June beetle [*Cotinis nitida* (L.)], European chafer, May or June beetle, Japanese beetle, Oriental beetle, and northern and southern masked chafers.

Two frequently found species of mole crickets, the southern mole cricket (*Scapteriscus acletus* Rehn and Hebard), and tawny mole cricket (*S. vicinus* Scudder) can be separated by the tibial dactyls on the foreleg. In the tawny mole cricket, the two dactyls are separated by a V-shaped space narrower than their width. In the southern mole cricket, the space is wider and U-shaped. This difference is illustrated in the article by Tashiro (1987).

Many references to particular species of insects or mites, or collections of preserved specimens are also good sources of information. It is helpful to make collections to provide aids to people working on turfgrass pest problems, particularly when multiple disciplinary research is involved.

V. SUMMARY

Numerous laboratory, greenhouse, and field research methods have been developed for studying insect and mite pests of turfgrasses. Many additional methods have been devised, but are only in various stages of publication. Methods reviewed in this chapter include those developed to (i) evaluate insecticide or acaracide activity and efficacy in the laboratory and field; (ii) evaluate the potential of pathogens, parasites, predators, and semiochemicals as biological suppressants; (iii) select and evaluate grasses for insect and mite resistance; and (iv) survey arthropod populations to evaluate suppression methods and monitor population levels. More detailed descriptions of these methods, and methods for rearing and maintaining turfgrass pests for laboratory or field research, can be found in the numerous references cited.

For those working in turfgrass entomology, these methods provide an excellent resource to draw upon for ideas, techniques, or approaches to apply in their own research. It is anticipated that greater awareness of the methodology available, will not only lead to its greater use, but also further refinement and improvement. This in turn should provide new methods and approaches for managing turfgrass pests more efficiently and safely.

REFERENCES

Abbott, W.S. 1925. A method of computing the effectiveness of an insecticide. J. Econ. Entomol. 18:265–267.

Ahmad, S., and Y.T. Das. 1978. Japanese beetle grub: Dosage-mortality response and symptoms of poisoning following treatments with chlorpyrifos and dieldrin. J. Econ. Entomol. 71:939–942.

Ahmad, S., and C.R. Funk. 1982. Susceptibility of Kentucky bluegrass cultivars and selections to infestations of and injury by the bluegrass billbug (Coleoptera: Curculionidae). J. N.Y. Entomol. Soc. 90:31–43.

Ahmad, S., S. Govindarajan, C.R. Funk, and J.M. Johnson-Cicalese. 1985. Fatality of house crickets on perennial ryegrasses infected with a fungal endophyte. Entomol. Exp. Appl. 39:193–190.

Ahmad, S., S. Govindarajan, J.M. Johnson-Cicalese, and C.R. Funk. 1987. Association of a fungal endophyte in perennial ryegrass with antibiosis to larvae of the southern armyworm, *Spodoptera eridania*. Entomol. Exp. Appl. 43:287–294.

Ali, A.D., and J. Garcia. 1987. Cutworm control in creeping bentgrass, California 1986. No. 377. Insect. Acar. Tests 12:317.

Arnold, T.B., and D.A. Potter. 1987. Impact of a high-maintenance lawn-care program on nontarget invertebrates in Kentucky bluegrass turf. Environ. Entomol. 16:100–105.

Baker, P.B. 1986. Responses of Japanese and oriental beetle grubs (Coleoptera: Scarabaeidae) to bendiocarb, chlorpyrifos, and isofenphos. J. Econ. Entomol. 79:452–454.

Baker, P.B., R.H. Ratcliffe, and A.L. Steinhauer. 1981. Tolerance to hairy chinch bug feeding in Kentucky bluegrass. Environ. Entomol. 10:153–157.

Balock. J.W. 1934. The status of *Tiphia vernalis* Rohwer, an imported parasite of the Japanese beetle, at the close of 1933. J. Econ. Entomol. 27:491–496.

Banerjee, A.C. 1967. Flight activity of the sexes of crambid moths as indicated by light-trap catches. J. Econ. Entomol. 60:383–390.

Banerjee, A.C. 1969. Sex attractants in sod webworms. J. Econ. Entomol. 62:705–708.

Barker, G.M., R.P. Pottinger, and P.J. Addison. 1983. Effect of tall fescue and ryegrass endophytes on Argentine stem weevil. p. 216–219. *In* Proc. 36th N.Z. Weed and Pest Control Conf., Palmerston North, NZ. 9–11 Aug. New Zealand Weed and Pest Control Soc., Palmerston North, NZ.

Barker, G.M., R.P. Pottinger, and P.J. Addison. 1984. Effect of *Lolium* endophyte fungus infections on survival of larbal Argentine stem weevil. N.Z. J. Agric. Res. 27:279–281.

Beard, R.L. 1944. Susceptibiity of Japanese beetle larvae to *Bacillus popilliae*. J. Econ. Entomol. 37:702–708.

Bedding, R.A. 1981. Low cost in vitro mass production of *Neoaplectana* and *Heterorhabditis* species (Nematoda) for field control of insect pests. Nematologica 27:109–114.

Bedding, R.A. 1984. Large scale production, storage, and transport of the insect-parasitic nematodes *Neoaplectana* app. and *Heterorhabditis*. Ann. Appl. Biol. 101:117–120.

Bowen, W.R., F.S. Morishita and R.O. Oetting. 1980. Insect and related pests of turfgrass. p. 31–39. *In* W.R. Bowen (ed.) Turfgrass pests. Univ. California., Div. Agric. Sci. Publ. 4053.

Brandenburg, R.L., and P.T. Hertl. 1987. Southern mole cricket control on Bermudagrass fairways, North Carolina, 1986. No. 378. Insect. Acar. Tests 12:317–318.

Bruneau, A.H., D.P. Bishop, R.C. Shearman, and R.E. Roselle. 1981. Integrated pest management, a common sense approach to turfgrass insect damage prevention and control. Nebraska Coop. Ext. Ser. EC 81-2138.

Bruton, B.D., R.W. Toler, and J.A. Reinert. 1983. Combined resistance in St. Augustinegrass to the southern chinch bug and the St. Augustine decline strain of Panicum mosaic virus. Plant Dis. 67:171–172.

Buckner, R.C., B.C. Pass, P.B. Burrus, II, and J.R. Todd. 1969. Reaction of Kentucky bluegrass strains to feeding by the sod webworm. Crop Sci. 9:744–746.

Butler, G.K., Jr. 1961. Variations in response of bermudagrass strains to eriophyid mite infestations. Ariz. Agric. Exp. Stn. Rep. 203:15–19.

Butler, G.D., Jr., and W.R. Kneebone. 1965. Variations in response of bermudagrass varieties to bermudagrass mite infestations with and without chemical control. Ariz. Agric. Exp. Stn. Rep. 230:7–10.

Butler, G.D., Jr., and J.L. Stroehlein. 1965. The use of diazinon and fertilizers for reducing bermudagrass mite damage and promoting grass growth. J. Econ. Entomol. 58:783–784.

Butler, G.D., Jr., J.L. Stroehlein, and L. Moore. 1963. The control of the bermudagrass eriophyid mite. Ariz. Agric. Exp. Stn. Rep. 219:14–25.

Cameron, R.S., and N.E. Johnson. 1971. Biology and control of turfgrass weevil, a species of Hyperodes. New York State Coll. Agric., Cornell Univ. Ext. Bull. 1226.

Carter, R.P., and R.L. Duble. 1976. Variety evaluations in St. Augustinegrass for resistance to the southern lawn chinch bug. Texas Agric. Exp. Stn. Prog. Rep. PR-3374C.

Castner, J.L. 1984. Suitability of Scapteriscus Spp. mole crickets [Ort.:Gryllotalpidae] as hosts of Larra bicolor [Hym.:Sphecidae]. Entomophaga 29:323–329.

Castner, J.L., and H.G. Fowler. 1984. Distribution of mole crickets (Orthoptera; Gryllltalpidae; Scapteriscus) and the mole cricket parasitoid Larra bicolor (Hymenoptera: Sphecidae) in Puerto Rico. Fla. Entomol. 67:481–484.

Chandler, L., J.G. Taylor, and H.O. Deay. 1955. Phyllophaga collected at light traps in Indiana (Scarabaeidae: Coleoptera). Proc. Indiana Acad. Sci. 65:149–158.

Clay, K., T.N. Hardy, and A.M. Hammond, Jr. 1985. Fungal endophytes of grasses and their effects on an insect herbivore. Oecologia 66:1–5.

Cockfield, S.D., and D.A. Potter. 1983. Short-term effects of insecticidal applications on predaceous arthropods and oribatid mites in Kentucky bluegrass turf. Environ. Entomol. 12:1260–1264.

Cockfield, S.D., and D.A. Potter. 1984. Predation on sod webworm (Lepidoptera: Pyralidae) eggs as affected by chlorpyrifos application to Kentucky bluegrass turf. J. Econ. Entomol. 77:1542–1544.

Combs, R.L., Jr., and J.R. Valerio. 1980a. Oviposition by the fall armyworm on four varieties of bermudagrass. J. Ga. Entomol. Soc. 15:164–167.

Combs, R.L., Jr., and J.R. Valerio. 1980b. Biology of the fall armyworm on four varieties of bermudagrass when held at constant temperatures. Environ. Entomol. 9:393–396.

Coppel, H.C., and J.W. Mertins. 1977. Biological insect pest suppression. Springer-Verlag, Berlin.

Crocker, R.L. 1981. White grub management in Texas turfgrasses. p. 69–77. In Texas turfgrass research — 1979–80. Texas Agric. Exp. Stn. Consolidated PR-3846.

Crocker, R.L., and C.L. Simpson. 1981. Pesticide screening test for the southern chinch bug. J. Econ. Entomol. 74:730–731.

Crocker, R.L., and W.H. Whitcomb. 1980. Feeding niches of the big-eyed bugs Geocoris bullatus, G. Punctipes, and G. uliginous (Hemiptera: Lygaeidae: Geocorinae). Environ. Entomol. 9:508–513.

Crocker, R.L., R.W. Toler, and C.L. Simpson. 1982. Bioassay of St. Augustinegrass lines for resistance to southern chinch bug (Hemiptera: Lygaeidae) and to St. Augustine decline virus. J. Econ. Entomol. 75:515–516.

Dean, H.A., and M.F. Schuster. 1958. Biological control of Rhodes-grass scale in Texas. J. Econ. Entomol. 51:363–366.

Dean, H.A., M.F. Schuster, and J.C. Bailey. 1961. The introduction and establishment of Dusmetia sangwani on Antonina graminis in south Texas. J. Econ. Entomol. 54:952–954.

Dean, H.A., M.F. Schuster, J.C. Boling, and P.T. Riherd. 1979. Complete biological control of Antonina graminis in Texas with Neodusmetia sangwani (a classic example). Bull. Entomol. Soc. Am. 25:262–267.

Dong, N., and H.W. Beck. 1982. Mark-release of sound-attracted mole crickets: flight behavior and implications for control. Fla. Entomol. 65:531–538.

Dreyer, D.L., J.C. Reese, and K.C. Jones. 1981. Aphid feeding deterrents in sorghum. J. Chem. Ecol. 7:272–283.

Dudeck, A.E., J.A. Reinert, and P. Busey. 1986. Floralawn St. Augustinegrass. Florida Agric. Exp. Stn. Cir. S-327.

Dunbar, D.M., and R.L. Beard. 1975. Status of control of Japanese beetle and oriental beetles in Connecticut. Conn. Agric. Exp. Stn. New Haven Bull. 757:1–5.

Dutky, S.R. 1941. Susceptibility of certain scarabaeid larvae to infection by type A milky disease. J. Econ. Entomol. 34:215–216.

Farrell, J.A.K., and W.J. Sweney. 1974. Plant resistance to the grass grub *Costelytra zealandica* (Coleoptera: Scarabaeidad). II. Screening for resistance in grasses. N.Z. J. Agric. Res. 17:63–67.

Finney, D.J. 1971. Probit analysis. 3rd ed. Cambridge Univ. Press, New York.

Fiori, B.J., H. Tashiro, G.L. Mack, G.R. Fryer, and M. Mckoy. 1972. European chafer: noncyclodiene insecticides for control of grubs. J. Econ. Entomol. 65:1686–1689.

Fleming, W.E. 1968. Biological control of the Japanese beetle. USDA Tech. Bull. 1386. U.S. Gov. Print. Office, Washington, DC.

Fleming, W.E., 1969. Attractants for the Japanese beetle. USDA Tech. Bull. 1399. U.S. Gov. Print. Office, Washington, DC.

Fleming, W.E. 1976. Integrating control of the Japanese beetle—Ahistorical review. USDA Tech. Bull. 1545.

Fleming, W.E., L.B. Parker, W.W. Maines, E.L. Plasket, and P.J. McCabe. 1962. Bioassay of soil containing residues of chlorinated hydrocarbon insecticides with special reference to control of Japanese beetle grubs. USDA Tech. Bll. 1266:1–44.

Funk, C.R., C.J. Peterson, S. Ahmad, and J.P. Rutkai. 1983. Registration of 'Pennant' perennial ryegrass. Crop Sci. 23:183.

Funk, C.R., P.M. Halisky, S. Ahmad, and R.H Hurley. 1985. How endophytes modify turfgrass performance and response to insect pests in turfgrass breeding and evaluation trials. p. 137–145. *In* F. Lemaire (ed.) Proc. 5th Int. Turfgrass Res. Conf., Avignon, France. 1–5 July. Inst. Natl. de la Recherche Agron., Paris.

Gambrell, F.L. 1953. Control of the European chafer, *Amphimallon majalis* Raz. in turf. J. Econ. Entomol. 46:761–765.

Gambrell, F.L., H. Tashiro, and G.L. Mack. 1968. Residual activity of chlorinated hydrocarbon insecticides in permanent turf for European chafer control. J. Econ. Entomol. 61:1508–1511.

Gaynor, D.L., D.D. Rowan, G.C.M. Latch, and S. Pilkington. 1983. Preliminary results on the biochemical relationship between adult Argentine stem weevil and two endophytes in ryegrass. p. 220–224. *In* Proc. 36th N.Z. Weed and Pest Control Conf., Palmerston North, NZ. 9–11 Aug. New Zealand Weed and Pest Control Soc., Palmerston North, NZ.

Gordon, F.C., and D.A. Potter. 1985. Efficiency of Japanese beetle (Coleoptera: Scarabaeidae) traps in reducing defoliation of plants in the urban landscape and effect on larval density in turf. J. Econ. Entomol. 78:774–778.

Green, M.E., E.L. Matheny, and S.J. Yu. 1984. Laboratory and field techniques for evaluating mole cricket (Orthoptera: Gryllotalpidae: *Scapteriscus*) baits. J. Ga. Entomol. Soc. 19:151–156.

Guppy, J.C., and D.G. Harcourt. 1973. A sampling plan for studies on the population dynamics of white grubs, *Phyllophaga* spp. (Coleoptera: Scarabaeidae). Can. Entomol. 105:479–483.

Hall, H.H., G. St. Julian, and G.L. Adams. 1968. Observations on the infection of Japanese beetle larvae with *Bacillus popilliae*. J. Econ. Entomol. 61:840–843.

Hall, I.M. 1954. Studies of microorganisms pathogenic to the sod webworm. Hilgardia 22:535–565.

Hamilton, D.W., P.H. Schwartz, Jr., B.G. Townshend, and C.W. Jester. 1971. Effect of color and design of traps on captures of Japanese beetles and bumble bees. J. Econ. Entomol. 64:430–432.

Hardy, T.N., K. Clay, and A.M. Hammond, Jr. 1985. Fall armyworm (Lepidoptera: Noctuidae): A laboratory bioassay and larval preference study for the fungal endophyte in perennial ryegrass. J. Econ. Entomol. 78:571–575.

Harris, C.R., and J.L. Hitchon. 1970. Comparison of the toxicity to insects of certain insecticides applied by contact and in the soil. J. Econ. Entomol. 57:698–702.

Heller, P.R., and S. Kellogg. 1987a. Summer control of Japanese beetle grubs on a golf course fairway in Mifflin Co., PA, 1986. No. 383. Insect. Acar. Tests 12:320–321.

Heller, P.R., and S. Kellogg. 1987b. Spring control of Japanese beetle grubs on a golf course rough in Johnston, PA, 1986. No. 385. Insect. Acar. Tests 12:321–322.

Heller, P.R., and S. Kellogg. 1987c. Spring control of bluegrass billbug on Kentucky bluegrass plots at University Park, PA, 1986. No. 382. Insect. Acar. Tests 12:319–320.

Henry, J.E. 1981. Natural and applied control of insects by protozoa. Ann. Rev. Entomol. 28:49–73.

Horn, G.C., A.E. Dudeck, and R.W. Toler. 1973. Floratam St. Augustinegrass a fast growing new variety for ornamental turf resistant to St. Augustine decline and chinch bugs. Univ. Florida Agric. Exp. Stn. Circ. S-224.

Hudson, W.G. 1984. Biology of the pest mole crickets: Other behavior, damage and sampling. p. 16–21. *In* T.J. Walker (ed.) Mole crickets in Florida. Univ. Florida Agric. Exp. Stn. Bull. 846.

Hurley, R.H., C.R. Funk, R.W. Duell, and W.A. Meyer. 1984. Registration of 'Repell' perennial ryegrass. Crop Sci. 24:997.

Jackson, D.W., K.J. Vessels, and D.A. Potter. 1981. Resistance of selected cool and warm season turfgrasses to the greenbug (*Schizaphis graminum*). HortScience 16:558–559.

Jefferson, R.N., and C.O. Eads. 1952. Control of sod webworms in Southern California. J. Econ. Entomol. 45:114–118.

Johnson, M.C., D.L. Dahlman, M.R. Siegel, L.P. Bush, G.C.M. Latch, D.A. Potter, and D.R. Varney. 1985. Insect feeding deterrents in endophyte-infected tall fescue. Appl. Environ. Microbiol. 49:568–571.

Kamm, J.A. 1973. Biotic factors that affect sod webworms in grass seed fields in Oregon. Environ. Entomol. 2:94–96.

Kamm, J.A. 1982. Use of insect sex pheromones in turfgrass management. p. 43–46. *In* H.D. Niemczuk and B.G. Joyner (ed.) Advances in turfgrass entomology. Chemlawn Corp., Columbus, OH.

Kamm, J.A., and L.M. McDonough. 1979. Field tests with the sex pheromone of the cranberry girdler. Environ. Entomol. 8:773–775.

Kamm, J.A., and L.M. McDonough. 1980. Synergism of the sex pheromone of the cranberry girdler. Environ. Entomol. 9:795–797.

Kamm, J.A., L.M. McDonough, and R.. Gustine. 1982a. Armyworm (Lepidoptera: Noctuidae) sex pheromone: Field tests. Environ. Entomol. 11:917–919.

Kamm, J.A., L.M. McDonough, and C.L. Smithhisler. 1982b. Sex attractant for *Protagrotis obscura*,, a pest of grass grown for seed. Environ. Entomol. 11:118–120.

Kepner, R.L. 1984. Chemical control of mole crickets: Baits. p. 42–46. *In* T.J. Walker (ed.) Mole crickets in Florida. Univ. Florida. Agric. Exp. Stn. Bull. 846.

Kepner, R.L., and S.J. Yu. 1987. Development of a toxic bait for control of mole crickets (Orthoptera: Gryllotalpidae). J. Econ. Entomol. 80:659–665.

Kerr, S.H. 1956. Chinch bug control on lawns in Florida. J. Econ. Entomol. 49:83–85.

Kindler, S.D., and E.J. Kinbacher. 1975. Differential reaction of Kentucky bluegrass cultivars to the bluegrass billbug, *Sphenophorus parvulus* Gyllenhal. Crop Sci. 15:873–874.

Kindler, S.D., R. Staples, S.M. Spomer, and O. Adeniji. 1983. Resistance of bluegrass cultivars to biotypes C and E greenbug (Homoptera: Aphididae). J. Econ. Entomol. 76:1103–1105.

King, J.L., and L.B. Parker. 1950. The spring *Tiphia*, an imported enemy of the Japanese beetle. USDA. Bur. Entomol. Plant Quar. E-799.

King, J.L., L.B. Parker, and H.J. Willard. 1951. Status of imported parasites of the Japanese beetle in 1950. USDA Bur. Entomol. Plant Quar., Insect Pest Surv. Spec. Suppl. (1951, No. 5). (mimeogr.).

Klein, M.G. 1981. Mass trapping for suppression of Japanese beetles. p. 183–190. *In* E.R. Mitchell (ed.) Management of insect pests with sociochemicals. Plenum Publ. Corp., New York.

Klein, M.G. 1982. Biological suppression of turf insects. p. 91–100. *In* H.D. Niemczyk and B.G. Joyner (ed.) Advances in turfgrass entomology. Chemlawn Corp., Columbus, OH.

Klein, M.G., and K.O. Lawrence. 1972. Japanese beetle: An inexpensive apparatus to manipulate medium and larvae during screening of insecticides. J. Econ. Entomol. 65:1516–1518.

Klein, M.G., W.R. Nickle, P.R. Benedict, and D.M. Dunbar. 1976. *Psammomermis* sp. (Nematoda: Mermithidae): A new nematode parasite of the Japanese beetle, *Popillia japonica* (Coleoptera: Scarabaeidae). Proc. Helminthol. Soc. Wash. 43:235–236.

Klein, M.G., J.H. Tumlinson, T.L. Ladd, Jr., and R.E. Doolittle. 1981. Japanese beetle (Coleoptera: Scarabaeidae): Response to synthetic sex attractant plus phenethyl propionate: Eugenol. J. Chem. Ecol. 7:1–7.

Klostermeyer, L.E. 1985. Japanese beetle (Coleoptera: Scarabaeidae) traps: Comparison of commercial and homemade traps. J. Econ. Entomol. 78:454–459.

Koehler, P.G., and D.E. Short. 1976. Control of mole crickets in pasturegrass. J. Econ. Entomol. 69:229–232.

Kuhr, R.J., J.L. Schohn, H. Tashiro, and B.J. Fiori. 1972. Dieldrin resistance in European chafer grub J. Econ. Entomol. 65:1555-1560.

Ladd, T.L., Jr. 1966. Egg viability and longevity of Japanese beetles treated with tepa, apholate, and metepa. J. Econ. Entomol. 59:422-425.

Ladd, T.L., Jr. 1968. The permanent and cumulative effect of tepa-induced sterility in male Japanese beetles. J. Econ. Entomol. 61:1058-1059.

Ladd, T.L., Jr. 1970. Screening of candidate chemosterilants against the Japanese beetle. J. Econ. Entomol. 63:458-460.

Ladd, T.L., Jr. 1986a. Enhancement of lures for Japanese beetles (Coleoptera: Scarabaeidae) by eugenol and japonilure. J. Econ. Entomol. 79:405-409.

Ladd, T.L., Jr. 1986b. Influence of sugars on the feeding response of Japanese beetles (Coleoptera: Scarabaeidae). J. Econ. Entomol. 79:668-671.

Ladd, T.L., Jr., M. Jacobson, and C.R. Buriff. 1978. Japanese beetle: Extracts from neem tree seeds as feeding deterrents. J. Econ. Entomol. 71;810-813.

Ladd, T.L., Jr., and M.G. Klein. 1982. Trapping Japanese beetles with synthetic female sex pheromone and food-type lures. p. 7-64. In A.F. Kydonieus and M. Beroza (ed.) Insect suppression with controlled release pheromone systems. Vol. 2. CRC Press, Boca Raton, FL.

Ladd, T.L., Jr., and M.G. Klein. 1986. Japanese beetle (Coleoptera: Scarabaeidae) response to color traps baited with phenethyl propionate + eugenol + geraniol (3:7:3) and japonilure. J. Econ. Entomol. 79:84-86.

Ladd, T.L., Jr., M.G. Klein, and J.H. Tumlinson. 1981. Phenethyl propionate = eugenol + geraniol (3:7:3) and Japonilure: A highly effective joint lure for Japanese beetles. J. Econ. Entomol. 74:665-667.

Ladd, T.L., Jr., and P.J. McCabe. 1966. The status of Tiphia vernalis Rohwer, a parasite of the Japanese beetle, in southern New Jersey and southeastern Pennsylvania in 1963. J. Econ. Entomol. 59:480.

Ladd, T.L., Jr., and P.J. McCabe. 1967. Persistence of spores of Bacillus popilliae, the causal organism of Type A milky disease of Japanese beetle larvae, in New Jersey soils. J. Econ. Entomol. 60:493-495.

Ladd, T.L., Jr., and J.E. Tew. 1983. Attraction of honey bees (Hymenoptera: Apidae) to traps baited with lures for Japanese beetles (Coleoptera: Scarabaeidae). J. Econ. Entomol. 76:769-773.

Ladd, T.L., Jr., J.D. Warthen, Jr., and M.G. Klein. 1984. Japanese beetle (Coleoptera: Scarabaeidae): The effects of azadirachten on the growth and development of the immature forms. J. Econ. Entomol. 77:903-905.

Lawrence, K.O. 1981. Japanese beetle: Control of larvae with isofenphos. J. Econ. Entomol. 74:543-545.

Lawrence, K.O. 1982. A linear pitfall trap for mole crickets and other soil arthropods. Fla. Entomol. 65:376-377.

Lawrence, K.O., M.G. Klein, and T.L. Ladd, Jr. 1973. Adult Japanese beetles: Evaluation of insecticides for control. J. Econ. Entomol. 66:477-479.

Lawrence, K.O., T.L. Ladd, Jr., and W.F. Kwolek. 1977. Japanese beetles: Quantitative determinations of larval resistance to chlordane in Ohio. J. Econ. Entomol. 70:209-210.

Lawrence, K.O., and H.D. Niemczyk. 1976. Japanese beetle: Control of larvae in turf with fensulfothion. J. Econ. Entomol. 69:35-36.

Lauren, D.R. 1979. Controlled release formulations for phenols: Use as sex attractant lures for the grass grub beetle. Environ. Entomol. 8:914-916.

Leuck, D.B. 1970. The role of resistance in pearl millet in control of the fall armyworm. J. Econ. Entomol. 63:1679-1681.

Leuck, D.B., C.M. Taliaferro, R.L. Burton, G.W. Burton, and M.C. Bowman. 1968a. Fall armyworm resistance in pearl millet. J. Econ. Entomol. 61:693-695.

Leuck, D.B., C.M. Taliaferro, G.W. Burton, R.L. Burton, and M.C. Bowman. 1968b. Resistance in bermudagrass to the fall armyworm. J. Econ. Entomol. 61:1321-1322.

Lim, K.P., K.M. Toohey, W.N. Yule, and R.K. Stewart. 1979. A monitoring program for the common June beetle, Phyllophaga anxia (Coleoptera: Scarabaeidae), in southern Quebec. Can. Entomol. 111:1381-1387.

Lindgren, D.T., R.C. Shearman, A.H. Bruneau, and D.M. Schaaf. 1981. Kentucky bluegrass cultivar response to bluegrass billbug, Sphenophorus parvulus Gyllenhal. HortScience 16:339.

Liu, H.J., and F.L. McEwen. 1977. *Nosema blissi* sp. n. (Microsporida: Nosematidae) a pathogen of the chinch bug, *Blissus leucopterus hirtus* (Hemiptera: Lygaeidae). J. Invert. Pathol. 29:141–146.

Liu, J.H., and F.L. McEwen. 1979. The use of temperature accumulations and sequential sampling in predicting damaging populations of *Blissus leucopterus hirtus*. Environ. Entomol. 8:512–514.

Lynch, R.E., W.G. Monson, B.R. Wiseman, and G.W. Burton. 1983. Bermudagrass resistance to the fall armyworm (Lepidoptera: Noctuidae). Environ. Entomol. 12:1837–1840.

Mailloux, G., and H.T. Streu. 1979. A sampling technique for estimating hairy chinch bug (*Blissus leucopterus hirtus* Montandon: Hemiptera: Lygaeidae) populations and other arthropods from turfgrass. Ann. Entomol. Soc. Quebec 24:139–143.

Matheny, E.L., Jr. 1981. Contrasting feeding habits of pest mole cricket species. J. Econ. Entomol. 74:444–445.

McDonough, L.M., J.A. Kamm, D.A. George, C.L. Smithhisler, and S. Voerman. 1982. Sex attractant for the western lawn moth, *Tehama bonifatella* Hulst. Environ. Entomol. 11:711–714.

McGovern, T.P., and T.L. Ladd, Jr. 1984. Japanese beetle (Coleoptera: Scarabaeidae) attractant: Tests with eugenol substitutes and phenethyl propionate. J. Econ. Entomol. 77:370–373.

McGovern, T.P., B. Fiori, M. Beroza, and J.C. Ingangi. 1970. Propyl 1,4-benzodioxan-2-carboxylate, a new attractant for the European chafer. J. Econ. Entomol. 63:168–171.

Meyer, W.A., C. Rose-Fricker, B.L. Rose, and C.R. Funk. 1987. Registration of 'Citation II' perennial ryegrass. Crop Sci. 27:815–816.

Milner, R.J. 1976. Laboratory evaluation of the pathogenicity of *Bacillus popilliae* var. *rhopaea*, the agent of milky disease in *Rhopaea verreauxi* (Coleoptera: Scarabaeidae). J. Invert. Pathol. 28:185–190.

Mitchell, W.C., and C.L. Murdoch. 1974. Insecticides and their application frequency for control of turf insects in Hawaii. Down to Earth 30:17–23.

Murdoch, C.L., and W.C. Mitchell. 1975. Insecticides and their application schedules for control of lawn caterpillars (*Spodoptera maurita acronyctoides* Guenee and *Herpetogramma licarsisalis* Walker) in Hawaii. J. Am. Soc. Hortic. Sci. 100:684–688.

Murdoch, C.L., and W.C. Mitchell. 1978. Application frequency of various insecticides for control of the grass webworm in bermudagrass turf. J. Econ. Entomol. 71:337–338.

Murdoch, C.L., and H. Tashiro. 1976. Host preference of the grass webworm, *Herpetogramma licarsisalis* to warm season turfgrass. Environ. Entomol. 5:1068–1070.

Neal, J.W., Jr. 1974. A manual for determining small dosage calculations of pesticides and conversion tables. Entomol. Soc. Am., College Park, MD.

Ng, Y.-S., and S. Ahmad. 1979. Resistance to dieldrin and tolerance to chlorpyrifos and bendiocarb in a northern New Jersey population of Japanese beetle. J. Econ. Entomol. 72:698–700.

Ng, Y.-S., J.R. Trout, and S. Ahmad. 1983a. Spatial distribution of the larval populations of the Japanese beetle in turfgrass. J. Econ. Entomol. 76:26–30.

Ng, Y.-S., J.R. Trout, and S. Ahmad. 1983b. Sequential sampling plans for larval populations of the Japanese beetle (Coleoptera: Scarabaeidae) in turfgrass. J. Econ. Entomol. 76:251–253.

Niemczyk, H.D. 1975. Status of insecticide resistance in Japanese beetle in Ohio. J. Econ. Entomol. 68:583–584.

Niemczyk, H.D. 1981. Destructive turf insects. Gray Print. Co., Fostoria, OH.

Niemczyk, H.D. 1982. The status of USDA-SEA-AR and U.S. University input of professional personnel to turfgrass entomology—1980. p. 127–132. *In* H.D. Niemczyk and B.G. Joyner (ed.) Advances in turfgrass entomology. Chemlawn Corp., Columbus, OH.

Niemczyk, H.D. 1987. The influence of application timing and post treatment irrigation on the fate and effectiveness of Isofenphos for control of Japanese beetle (Coleoptera: Scarabaeidae) larvae in turfgrass. J. Econ. Entomol. 80:465–470.

Niemczyk, H.D., and R.A. Chapman. 1987. Evidence of enhanced degradation of Isofenphos in turfgrass thatch and soil. J. Econ. Entomol. 80:880–882.

Niemczyk, H.D., and D.M. Dunbar. 1976. Field observations, chemical control, and contact toxicity experiments on *Ataenius spretulus*, a grub pest of turf grass. J. Econ. Entomol. 69:345–348.

Niemczyk, H.D., and C. Frost. 1978. Insecticide resistance found in Ohio bluegrass billbugs. Ohio Rep. (2) (March-April):22–23.

Niemczyk, H.D., and H.R. Krueger. 1982. Binding of insecticides on turfgrass thatch. p. 61–64. *In* H.D. Niemczyk and B.G. Joyner (ed.) Advances in turfgrass entomology. Chemlawn Corp., Columbus, OH.

Niemczyk, H.D., and H.R. Krueger. 1987. Persistence and mobility of Isazofos in turfgrass thatch and soil. J. Econ. Entomol. 80:950–952.

Niemczyk, H.D., and K.O. Lawrence. 1973. Japanese beetle: Evidence of resistance to cyclodiene insecticides in larvae and adults in Ohio. J. Econ. Entomol. 66:520–521.

Niemczyk, H.D., and J.R. Moser. 1982. Greenbug occurrence and control on turfgrasses in Ohio. p. 105–112. *In* H.D. Niemczyk and B.G. Joyner (ed.) Advances in turfgrass entomology. Chemlawn Corp., Columbus, OH.

Painter, R.H. 1951. Insect resistance in crop plants. Kansas Univ. Press, Lawrence.

Pass, B.C. 1964. Effectiveness of insecticides against white grubs in bluegrass lawns. J. Econ. Entomol. 57:1002–1003.

Pass, B.C. 1965. Influence of some cyclodiene insecticides on sod webworm populations. J. Econ. Entomol. 58:586–587.

Pass, B.C. 1966. Control of the sod webworms, *Crambus teterrellus*, *C. trisectus*, and *C. mutabilis*, in Kentucky. J. Econ. Entomol. 59:19–21.

Pass, B.C., R.C. Buckner, and P.R. Burrus, II. 1965. Differential reaction of Kentucky bluegrass strains to sod webworms. Agron. J. 57:10–11.

Polivka, J.B. 1956. Effectiveness of milky disease in controlling the Japanese beetle in Ohio. J. Econ. Entomol. 49:4–6.

Potter, C. 1952. An improved laboratory apparatus for applying direct sprays and surface films, with data on the electrostatic charge on atomized spray fuids. Ann. Appl. Biol. 39:1–27.

Potter, D.A. 1980. Flight activity and sex attraction of northern and southern masked chafers in Kentucky turfgrass. Ann. Entomol. Soc. Am. 73;414–417.

Pottinger, R.P., G.M. Barker, and R.A. Prestidge. 1985. A review of the relationships between endophytic fungi of grasses (*Acremonium* spp.) and Argentine stem weevil (*Listronotus bonariensis* (Kuschel)). p. 13–17. *In* R.B. Chapman (ed.) Proc. 4th Australasian Conf. on Grassl. Invert. Ecol. Caxton Press, Canterbury.

Prestidge, R.A., and R.T. Gallagher. 1985. Lolitrem B — A stem weevil toxin isolated from *Acremonium*-infected ryegrass. p. 38–40. *In* Proc. 38th N.Z. Weed and Pest Control Conf. Weed and Pest Control Soc., Palmerston North, NZ.

Prestidge, R.A., D.R. Lauren, S.G. Van Der Zijpp, and M.E. DiMenna. 1985. Isolation of feeding deterrents to Argentine stem weevil in cultures of endophytes of perennial ryegrass and tall fescue. N.Z. J. Agric. Res. 28:87–92.

Quisenberry, S.S., and H.K. Wilson. 1985. Consumption and utilization of Bermudagrass by fall armyworm (Lepidoptera: Noctuidae) larvae. J. Econ. Entomol. 78:802–824.

Ramoska, W.A. 1984. The influence of relative humidity on *Beauveria bassiana* infectivity and replication in the chinch bug, *Blissus leucopterous*. J. Invertebr. Pathol. 43:389–394.

Ramoska, W.A., and T. Todd. 1985. Variation in efficacy and viability of *Beauveria bassiana* in the chinch bug (Hemiptera: Lygaeidae) as a result of feeding activity on selected host plants. Environ. Entomol. 14:146–148.

Ratcliffe, R.H. 1982. Evaluation of cool season turfgrasses for resistance to the hairy chinch bug. p. 13–18. *In* H.D. Niemczyk and B.G. Joyner (ed.) Advances in turfgrass entomology. Chemlawn Corp., Columbus, OH.

Ratcliffe, R.H., and J.J. Murray. 1983. Selection for greenbug (Homoptera: Aphididae) resistance in Kentucky bluegrass cultivars. J. Econ. Entomol. 76:1221–1224.

Reinert, J.A. 1972a. New distribution and host record for the parasitoid *Eumicrosoma benefica*. Fla. Entomol. 55:143–144.

Reinert, J.A. 1972b. Control of the southern chinch bug, *Blissus insularis*, in South Florida. Fla. Entomol. 55:231–235.

Reinert, J.A. 1973. Sod webworm control in Florida turfgrass. Fla. Entomol. 56:333–337.

Reinert, J.A. 1974. Control of the southern chinch bug and sod webworm in Florida turfgrass-effect of water rate and formulation of Dursban insecticide. Down Earth 30:10–13.

Reinert, J.A. 1976. Control of sod webworms (*Herpetogramma* spp. and *Crambus* spp.) on bermudagrass. J. Econ. Entomol. 69:669–672.

Reinert, J.A. 1977. Field biology and control of *Haplaxius crudus* on St. Augustinegrass and Christmas palm. J. Econ. Entomol. 70:54–56.

Reinert, J.A. 1978. Natural enemy complex of the southern chinch bug in Florida. Ann. Entomol. Soc. Am. 71:728–731.

Reinert, J.A. 1979. Response of white grubs infesting bermudagrass to insecticides. J. Econ. Entomol. 72:546–548.

Reinert, J.A. 1982a. A review of host resistance in turfgrasses to insects and Acarines with emphasis on the southern chinch bug. p. 3–12. *In* H.D. Niemczyk and B.G. Joyner (ed.) Advances in turfgrass entomology. Chemlawn Corp., Columbus, OH.

Reinert, J.A. 1982b. Carbamate and synthetic pyrethroid insecticides for control of organiophosphate resistant southern chinch bugs (Heteroptera: Lygaeidae). J. Econ. Entomol. 75:716–718.

Reinert, J.A. 1983a. Field experiments for insecticidal control of sod webworms (Lepidoptera: Pyralidae) in Florida turfgrass. J. Econ. Entomol. 76:150–153.

Reinert, J.A. 1983b. Southern chinch bug resistance to insecticides, a method for quick diagnosis of chlorpyrifos (OP) resistance, and alternate controls. p. 64–78. *In* Proc. Fla. Turfgrass Conf., Orlando, FL. 3–6 Oct. 1982. Florida Turfgrass Assoc., Orlando.

Reinert, J.A., B.D. Bruton, and R.W. Toler. 1980. Resistance of St. Augustinegrass to southern chinch bug and St. Augustine decline strain of Panicum mosaic virus. J. Econ. Entomol. 73:602–604.

Reinert, J.A., and P. Busey. 1983. Resistance of bermudagrass selections to the tropical sod webworm (Lepidoptera: Pyralidae). Environ. Entomol. 12:1844–1845.

Reinert, J.A., and P. Busey. 1984. Biological control of mole crickets: resistant varieties. p. 25–40. *In* T.J. Walker (ed.) Mole crickets in Florida. Univ. Florida Agric. Exp. Stn. Bull. 846.

Reinert, J.A., P. Busey, and F.G. Bilz. 1986. Old world St. Augustinegrass resistant to the southern chinch bug (Heteroptera: Lygaeidae). J. Econ. Entomol. 79:1073–1075.

Reinert, J.A., and H.L. Cromroy. 1981. Bermudagrass stunt mite and its control in Florida. Proc. Fla. State Hortic. Soc. 94:124–126.

Reinert, J.A., and A.E. Dudeck. 1974. Southern chinch bug resistance in St. Augustinegrass. J. Econ. Entomol. 67:275–277.

Reinert, J.A., A.E. Dudeck, and G.H. Snyder. 1978. Resistance in bermudagrass to the bermudagrass mite. Environ. Entomol. 7:885–888.

Reinert, J.A., and H.D. Niemczyk. 1982. Insecticide resistance in epigeal insect pests of turfgrass. II. southern chinch bug resistance to organophosphates in Florida. p. 77–80. *In* H.D. Niemczyk and B.G. Joyner (ed.) Advances in turfgrass entomology. Chemlawn Corp., Columbus, OH.

Reinert, J.A., and K.M. Portier. 1983. Distribution and characterization of organophosphate-resistant southern chinch bugs (Heteroptera: Lygaeidae) in Florida. J. Econ. Entomol. 76:1187–1190.

Reinert, J.A., R.W. Toler, B.D. Bruton, and P. Busey. 1981. Retension of resistance to the southern chinch bug and St. Augustine decline in mutants of 'Floratom' St. Augustinegrass. Crop Sci. 21:464–466.

Riegel, G.T. 1948. Sex and the altitude of flight in *Cyclocephala* (Coleoptera: Scarabaeidae). Ill. Acad. Sci. Trans. 41:113–115.

Riherd, P.T. 1950. Biological notes on *Anagyrus antoninae* Timberlake (Hymenoptera-Encyrtidae) and its host *Antonina graminis* (Maskell) (Homoptera—Coccidae). Fla. Entomol. 33:18–22.

Roberts, R.J. 1963. Improved methods for obtaining and rearing first-instar *Cyclocephala immaculata* larvae for experimentation. J. Econ. Entomol. 56:538–540.

Roelofs, W.L., D.W. Pulver, K.C. Feng, and F.L. Gambrell. 1967. Attractancy tests with chromatographed European chafer extracts. J. Econ. Entomol. 60:869–870.

Saha, D.C., J.M. Johnson-Cicalese, P.M. Halisky, M.I. Van Heemstra, and C.R. Funk. 1987. Occurrence and significance of endophytic fungi in the fine fescues. Plant Dis. 71:1021–1024.

Sailer, R.I. 1984. Biological control of mole crickets: Natural enemies. p. 23–32. *In* T.J. Walker (ed.) Mole crickets in Florida. Univ. Florida Agric. Exp. Stn. Bull. 846.

SAS Institute. 1982. SAS user's guide: Statistics. SAS Inst., Cary, NC.

Schuster, M.F. 1965. Studies on the biology of *Dusmetia sansgwani* (Hymenoptera: Encyrtidae). Ann. Entomol. Soc. Am. 58:272–275.

Schwartz, P.H., Jr. 1968. Distribution of released Japanese beetles in a grid of traps. J. Econ. Entomol. 61:423–426.

Sears, M.K., and R.A. Chapman. 1982. Persistence and movement of four insecticides applied to turfgrass. p. 57–60. *In* H.D. Niemczyk and B.G. Joyner (ed.) Advances in turfgrass entomology. Chemlawn Corp., Columbus, OH.

Shearman, R.C., D.M. Bishop, D.H. Steinegger, and A.H. Bruneau. 1983. Kentucky bluegrass cultivar and blend response to bluegrass billbug. HortScience 18:441–442.

Shetler, D.J., P.R. Heller, and P.D. Irish. 1983. Turfgrass insect and mite manual. Pennsylvania Turfgrass Counc., Bellefonte.

Short, D.E., and P.G. Koehler. 1979. A sampling technique for mole crickets and other pests in turfgrass and pasture. Fla. Entomol. 62:282–283.

Shread, J.C. 1953. Isodrin, endrin and lindane for grub control in turf. J. Econ. Entomol. 46:357–359.

Siegel, M.R., G.C.M. Latch, and M.C. Johnson. 1985. *Acremonium* fungal endophytes of tall fescue and perennial ryegrass: Significance and control. Plant Dis. 69:179–183.

Sorensen, K.A., and H.E. Thompson. 1984. Light trap response of the buffalograss webworm, *Surattha indentella* Kearfott (Lepidoptera: Pyralidae), in Kansas. J. Kans. Entomol. Soc. 57:719–722.

Steck, W.F., E.W. Underhill, M.D. Chisholm, and J.R. Byers. 1979. Sex attractants for *Agrostis venerabilis* and *Euxoa albipennis* based on (Z)-5-Decenyl Acetate and (Z)-7-Dodecenyl Acetate. Environ. Entomol. 8:1126–1128.

Stewart, A.V. 1985. Perennial ryegrass seedling resistance to Argentine stem weevil. N.Z. J. Agric. Res. 28:403–407.

Stone, J.D. 1986. Time and height of flight of adults of white grubs (Coleoptera: Scarabaeidae) in the southwestern United States. Environ. Entomol. 15:194–197.

Storey, G.K., and W.A. Gardner. 1987. Vertical movement of commercially formulated *Beauveria bassiana* conidia through four Georgia soil types. Environ. Entomol. 16:178–181.

Streu, H.T. 1969. Some cumulative effects of pesticides in the turfgrass ecosystem. Proc. Scotts Turfgrass Res. Conf. I. Entomology 1:53–59.

Streu, H.T. 1973. The turfgrass ecosystem: Impact of pesticides. Bull. Entomol. Soc. Am. 19:89–91.

Streu, H.T. 1974. A manual of conversion tables, equivalents, and dosage calculations. New Jersey Agric. Exp. Stn. Circ. 608.

Streu, H.T., and J.B. Gingrich. 1972. Seasonal activity of the winter grain mite in turfgrass in New Jersey. J. Econ. Entomol. 65:427–430.

Streu, H.T., and H.D. Niemczyk. 1982. Pest status and control of winter grain mite. p. 101–104. *In* H.D. Niemczyk and B.G. Joyner (ed.) Advances in turfgrass entomology. Chemlawn Corp., Columbus, OH.

Taliaferro, C.M., D.B. Leuck, and M.W. Stimmann. 1969. Tolerance of *Cynodon* clones to Phytotoxemia caused by the two-lined spittlebug. Crop Sci. 9:765–766.

Tashiro, H. 1982. Distribution and persistence of chlorpyrifos and diazinon in soil when applied to turf. p. 53–56. *In* H.D. Niemczyk and B.G. Joyner (ed.) Advances in turfgrass entomology. Chemlawn Corp., Columbus, OH.

Tashiro, H. 1987. Turfgrass insects of the United States and Canada. Cornell Univ. Press, Ithaca, NY.

Tashiro, H., M. Beroza, T.P. Mcgovern, and N. Green. 1970. Chemicals evaluated as European chafer attractants. USDA-ARS 33-130.

Tashiro, H., and W.E. Fleming. 1954. A trap for European chafer surveys. J. Econ. Entomol. 47:618–623.

Tashiro, H., S.I. Gertler, M. Beroza, and N. Green. 1964. Butyl sorbate as an attractant for the European chafer. J. Econ. Entomol. 57:230–233.

Tashiro, H., J.G. Hartsock, and G.G. Rohwer. 1967. Development of blacklight traps for European chafer surveys. USDA Tech. Bull. 1366. U.S. Gov. Print. Office, Washington, DC.

Tashiro, H., and R.J. Kuhr. 1978. Some factors influencing the toxicity of soil applications of chlorpyrifos and diazinon to European chafer grubs. J. Econ. Entomol. 71:904–907.

Tashiro, H., C.L. Murdoch, and W.C. Mitchell. 1983. Development of a survey technique for larvae of the grass webworm and other Lepidopterous species in turfgrass. Environ. Entomol. 12:1428–1432.

Tashiro, H., C.L. Murdoch, R.W. Straub, and P.J. Vittum. 1977. Evaluation of insecticides on *Hyperodes* sp., a pest of annual bluegrass turf. J. Econ. Entomol. 70:729–733.

Tashiro, H., and K.E. Personius. 1970. Current status of the bluegrass billbug and its control in western New York home lawns. J. Econ. Entomol. 63:23–29.

Tashiro, H., K.E. Personius, D. Zinter, and M. Zinter. 1971. Resistance of the European chafer to cyclodiene insecticides. J. Econ. Entomol. 64:242–245.

Tashiro, H., T.D. Spittler, and E. Greco. 1982. Laboratory and field evaluation of isofenphos for scarabaeid grubs (Coleoptera: Scarabaeidae) control in turfgrass. J. Econ. Entomol. 75:906-913.

Tashiro, H., and R.W. Straub. 1973. Progress in control of the turfgrass weevil, a species of *Hyperodes*. Down Earth 29:8-10.

Tashiro, H., and R.T. White. 1954. Milky diseases of the European chafer. J. Econ. Entomol. 47:1087-1092.

Taylor, R.A.J. 1987. On the accuracy of insecticide efficacy reports. Environ. Entomol. 16:1-8.

Turner, F., Jr. 1961. Density measurements for evaluating turfgrass. Ariz. Agric. Exp. Stn. Rep. 203:20-21.

Tuttle, D.M., and G.D. Butler, Jr. 1961. A new eriophyid mite infesting bermudagrass. J. Econ. Entomol. 54:836-838.

Ulagaraj, S.M. 1975. Mole crickets: Ecology, behavior, and dispersal flight (Orthoptera: Gryllotalpidae: *Scapteriscus*). Environ. Entomol. 4:265-273.

Van Dam, J., and D. Cudney. 1980. Measurements, calculations, and preparing the sprayer. p. 5-9. *In* W.R. Bowen (ed.) Turfgrass pests. Univ. California Div. Agric. Sci. Publ. 4053.

VanDerSchaaf, P., and H. Tashiro. 1975. Control of Japanese beetle and European chafer grub with Dursban insecticide. Down Earth 31:9-13.

Villani, M.G., and F. Gould. 1986. Use of radiographs for movement analysis of the corn wireworm, *Melanotus communis* (Coleoptera: Elateridae). Environ. Entomol. 15:462-464.

Villani, M.G., and R.J. Wright. 1988a. Use of radiography in studies of scarab grub (Coleoptera: Scarabaeidae) behavior and management in turfgrass. Bull. Entomol. Soc. Am. 34:132-144.

Villani, M.G., and R.J. Wright. 1988b. Entomogenous nematodes as biological control agents of European chafer and Japanese beetle (Coleoptera: Scarabaeidae) larvae infesting turfgrass. J. Econ. Entomol. 81:484-487.

Vittum, P.J. 1985. Effect of timing of application on effectiveness of isofenphos, isazofos, and diazinon on Japanese beetle (Coleoptera: Scarabaeidae) grubs on turf. J. Econ. Entomol. 78:172-180.

Walker, T.J. 1982. Sound traps for sampling mole cricket flights (Orthoptera: Gryllotalpidae: *Scapteriscus*). Fla. Entomol. 65:105-110.

Walker, T.J., and G.N. Fritz. 1983. Migratory and local flights in mole crickets, *Scapteriscus* spp. (Gryllotalpidae). Environ. Entomol. 12:953-958.

Walker, T.J., J.A. Reinert, and D.J. Schuster. 1983. Geographical variation in flights of the mole cricket, *Scapteriscus* spp. (Orthoptera; Gyrllotalpidae). Ann. Entomol. Soc. Am. 76:507-517.

Warren, G.W., and D.A. Potter. 1983. Pathogenicity of *Bacillus popilliae* (*Cyclocephala* strain) and other milky disease bacteria in grubs of the southern masked chafer (Coleoptera: Scarabaeidae). J. Econ. Entomol. 76:69-73.

Weaver, J.E., and J.D. Hacker. 1978. Bionomical observations and control of *Ataenius spretulus* in West Virginia. West Virginia Agric. For. Exp. Stn. Curr. Rep. 72.

White, R.T. 1940. Survival of type A milky disease of Japanese beetle larvae under adverse field conditions. J. Econ. Entomol. 33:303-306.

White, R.T., and S.R. Dutky. 1940. Effect of the introduction of milky diseases on populations of Japanese beetle larvae. J. Econ. Entomol. 33:306-309.

Wiseman, B.R., R.C. Gueldner, and R.E. Lynch. 1982. Resistance in common centipedegrass to the fall armyworm. J. Econ. Entomol. 75:245-247.

Wright, R.J., M.G. Villani, and F. Agudelo-Silva. 1988. Steinernematid and Heterorhabditid nematodes for control of larval European chafers and Japanese beetles (Coleoptera: Scarabaeidae) in potted yew. J. Econ. Entomol. 81;152-157.

21 Turfgrass Weed Science Research Methods

B. J. JOHNSON AND T. R. MURPHY

Georgia Experiment Station
Griffin, Georgia

Turfgrass weed science research methods are similar to those employed in agronomic crops. The principles are similar even though modification of procedures may be needed for turfgrass research. Reading of weed science literature and selected references cited in this chapter will assist the researcher concerned with turfgrass weed science.

I. RESEARCH METHODS AND PROCEDURES

A. Experimental Design and Analysis

1. Design of Experiments

Correct design and statistical analysis of data are important in conducting a valid experiment. Before an experiment can be properly designed, the following factors must be considered: (i) formulation of a hypothesis that provides a tentative explanation or solution, (ii) planning an experiment to objectively test the hypothesis, (iii) careful observation and collection of data, and (iv) interpretation of the experimental data. Statisticians should be consulted when in doubt about how to design, execute, or analyze an experiment. Little and Hills (1978) discussed numerous experimental plot designs that can be adapted to turfgrass herbicide experiments. A given design should be determined by types of treatment. For example, if two herbicides at each of five rates were applied in all possible combinations, a factorial treatment arrangement could be used in a randomized complete block design. Another example includes herbicides applied at different dates of treatment. The treatments in this experiment could be arranged in a split-plot design with whole plots as herbicide treatments included in a randomized complete block and subplots as dates of treatments randomized within whole plots. In this arrangement, various herbicides were applied at selected times during a 3-yr period (Johnson, 1982a). In a different split-plot arrangement, herbicide treatments were used in a randomized complete block with subplots as frequency of treatment being stripped across all whole plots (Johnson, 1982b). Frans

Copyright © 1992 ASA-CSSA-SSSA, 677 S. Segoe Rd., Madison, WI 53711, USA. *Turfgrass—Agronomy Monograph no. 32.*

et al. (1986) have given the procedures for various field plot evaluations, plot designs, and statistical treatments. In all instances, an appropriate experimental design should be selected prior to treatment applications. If help is needed, it is more desirable to consult with a statistician during planning stages, rather than waiting until after data collection.

2. Field Experimentation

A field experiment initiated for weed control must be conducted in an area contaminated with uniform stand of weeds, although studies on toxicity of herbicides to desired turf species could be done in the absence of weeds. The weed population in the control area can be encouraged by various turfgrass management practices. For example, crabgrass (*Digitaria* spp.) seed can be encouraged to germinate by low mowing height, low fertility (to reduce turfgrass competition), and light frequent watering. The weedy area should have a natural weed population or be seeded with weed seed. Seeding should be done well in advance of the treatments to permit development of an adequate population. For preemergence herbicide experiments, it is often necessary to select the test site during the previous year while weeds are actively growing. However, for postemergence herbicide experiments, sites can be selected just prior to postemergence treatments. In a postemergence experiment, a weak weed population may be substituted when a good weed population is not present. In areas with variable weed populations, weed counts or ground cover ratings should be made for each plot at the time of postemergence treatments.

Weed seed may not germinate after planting. The variation in germination may occur from poor seed quality, improper handling of seed after harvest, or poor management practices after seeding. The best methods for seeding into established turf are groove seeding or broadcast seeding followed by grooving and vertical mowing to ensure that some seed-to-soil contact occurs. The mechanical disturbance of the turf during the overseeding with weeds may also serve to temporarily weaken turf to allow weed establishment. After overseeding, maintain the grass at a low cutting height and water frequently. Information on weed seed germination and establishment may be found in a handbook published by the Weed Science Society of America (Anderson, 1968).

The size of turfgrass field plots may vary from 0.9 by 1.5 m to 1.5 by 3 m or larger. Plots must be large enough to obtain a representative sampling of the weed population. Boom sprayers or drop spreaders may require at least a 3-m length plot and the width should be considered in selecting plot size. An appropriate plot width should be selected that will minimize the spray overlap between plots.

3. Greenhouse and Growth Chamber Experimentation

Soil mixture, water usage, pot size, temperature, and other environmental factors must be carefully considered when turfgrass experiments are conducted in the greenhouse and growth chamber. Soil media may differ, but it is usually a sandy loam (Appleby & Somabhi, 1978), silt loam, or mixture of sandy loam with peat (Salazar & Appleby, 1982a), or sandy loam with sand (Frick et al., 1978). Layers of different media may also be used if only a limited amount of soil is available. The lower layer in the container may be either a washed quartz sand or sandy loam soil. Different soil types (Salazar & Appleby, 1982b) and soils taken from field plots (Smith & Callahan, 1969) have been applied at a depth of 2.5 to 3.5 cm over the lower layers of media. The layered soil media technique should only be used for bioassay and soil residue studies where it is assumed that all soil-herbicide interactions would occur in the top layer. Greenhouse potting mixes with an abnormally high organic matter content may affect the normal activity of soil-applied herbicides. A representative field soil would be preferable to greenhouse potting mixes for soil-active herbicide investigations. With foliar active herbicides, greenhouse potting mixes would be suitable (Frans et al., 1986).

Methods of watering greenhouse turfgrass pots are important in maintaining optimum growing conditions (Lavy, 1971). Subirrigation of pots will tend to move soluble herbicides and other solutes to the soil surface. Excessive movement of water-soluble materials can be minimized by alternating surface watering and subirrigation. Burnside (1982) developed a design for greenhouse benches and pots to minimize movement of soluble herbicides. His design was four 0.8-cm legs added to the bottom of polyethylene pots to improve drainage after either subirrigation or surface watering. The holes in the pots were covered with paper discs to prevent soil loss during watering or drainage. These pots were placed on a flat, level greenhouse table with a 3-cm hinged side around the edges and was covered with 2-mil polyethylene sheeting to facilitate water retention when the sides were in the up position during subirrigation and subsequent drainage of water when the sides were down.

Greenhouse temperatures should be adjusted to best growing conditions for each turfgrass species. A range of 18 to 24 °C was used for cool-season grasses (Salazar & Appleby, 1982a, b). Temperatures of 25 to 35 °C have been used for bermudagrass [*Cynodon dactylon* (L.) Pers.] (Jordan, 1977). Depending upon the time of year, supplemental light may be required for normal turfgrass growth and development.

In the growth chamber, temperature, humidity, and light can be regulated more precisely than in the greenhouse. However, because of the smaller size of growth chambers, only a limited number of treatments can be conducted at one time. Thus, it is often necessary to replicate controlled environment studies in time, space, or both.

4. Data Collection and Analysis of Results

No single factor is more important than obtaining good reliable data from the turf herbicide experiment. Care should be taken to select and properly use methods of data collection that will eliminate as much sampling or rating variability as possible. Methods for statistical analysis vary according to the experimental design (Little & Hills, 1978). The question often asked is, how frequently should an experiment be rated? The frequency will depend on several factors such as whether the experiment contains preemergence or postemergence herbicides and if it is for weed control or turf tolerance. Although weed control ratings for the preemergence herbicide control of crabgrass may vary due to location, ratings made once from 11 to 16 wk after treatment and again anytime from 20 to 26 wk after treatment provide an effective estimate of crabgrass control (Johnson, 1976a). In this case, the earlier ratings would represent early weed control and the later ratings would represent full-season weed control. When postemergence herbicides are used, control ratings should begin within 1 to 3 wk after treatment and continue at biweekly intervals until the weeds no longer show treatment effects.

The timing of turfgrass-tolerance phytotoxicity ratings also varies with preemergence and postemergence herbicides. When preemergence herbicides are applied to dormant warm-season grasses in early spring, tolerance ratings should be made during turfgrass greenup in April or May and at monthly intervals during spring and summer (Johnson, 1978). For postemergence herbicides, turfgrass-tolerance ratings should be made 1 wk after treatment and repeated at weekly intervals until the grass fully recovers (Johnson, 1976b). In instances where the turfgrass has been killed or the injury prevents complete recovery, ratings should be made at times that will reflect the maximum phytotoxic effect of the herbicide.

5. Collecting Weed Control Data

Field, greenhouse, and growth chamber experiments should be repeated in time, space, or both to improve the reliability of the data. Field experiments are commonly conducted at the same time each year for two to three consecutive years to estimate the effects of climatic differences on treatment results. Herbicides should be applied to the same plots each year if the objective of the experiment is to estimate the effect of continued applications for a long period on weed control (Johnson, 1982a) or turfgrass tolerance (Johnson, 1978). In short-term experiments, the experimental site location may need to be changed each year to ensure a uniform weed infestation.

Lewis and Klingman (1963) reported on three evaluation methods for taking weed control data in bermudagrass turfgrass. Following are the methods that were used:

1. Visual ratings based on 0 to 100 where 0 = no control and 100 = complete control.
2. Actual weed counts in number per m^2.
3. Weight of harvested weeds per m^2.

Regardless of the evaluation method, the ranking of each herbicide treatment was similar. Visual ratings were easy, rapid, and a precise method for taking weed control data in bermudagrass turfgrass.

Hamill et al. (1977) also reported that weed counts, weed weights, and rating systems were the most commonly used methods for collecting weed control data. However, they expanded the rating system to include a rapid technique for evaluating the control of individual weed species in small plot experiments that complements other data to provide accurate and complete assessment of herbicide performance. Their methods were taken from field crops but could be adapted to turfgrass. The 0 to 10 rating system procedures are as follows:

1. Rate the entire plot area for control of broadleaf or grass weeds using a 0 to 10 scale, where 0 = complete weed cover and 10 = absence of weeds.
2. Record percentage by area that each weed species contributes to broadleaf or grass weed cover.
3. Calculate the percentage of the plot area that is covered by each individual species according to:

$$[100 - 10(a)] \, (b/100) = c$$

where

a = broadleaf or grass weed control rating,

b = observed percent contribution by area of individual weed species to the total weed cover, and

c = percent cover of plot area by individual broadleaf or grass species.

A broadleaf weed rating, $a = 3.8$ is equivalent to 38%. The percentage of ground covered by broadleaf weeds is $[100 - 10(3.8)] = 62\%$, the first term of equation.

Using the method of Hamill et al. (1977), a hypothetical example is presented for a multi-species broadleaf weed control evaluation in turfgrass.

1.   1.6% corn speedwell (*Veronica arvensis* L.)
2. 55.8% henbit (*Lamium amplexicaule* L.)
3.   3.3% parsley-piert [*Alchemilla arvensis* (L.) Scop.]
4. 36.6% common chickweed [*Stellaria media* (L.) Vill.]
5.   0.6% hop clover (*Trifolium aureum* Pollich)
6.   2.6% lawn burweed [*Soliva pterosperma* (Juss.) Less.]

Since the total ground cover for broadleaf weeds was 62%, the cover provided by each species was:

1.   1.0% corn speedwell
2. 34.6% henbit
3.   2.0% parsley-piert
4. 22.7% common chickweed
5.   0.4% hop clover
6.   1.6% lawn burweed

The same procedure can be used for grass weeds.

Several visual scales are used for weed control ratings. Some of the scales are: 1 to 5, 0 to 9, 1 to 9, 0 to 10, and 0 to 100. The investigator must define the response range of the scale. Normally, the low number represents no control and the high number represents complete control. The 0 to 100 and 0

Table 21-1. The 0 to 100 rating system. (Adapted from Frans et al., 1986.)

Rating	Description of main categories	Detailed description	
		Weed control	Turfgrass phytotoxicity
0	No effect	No weed control	No turfgrass stand reduction or injury
10	Slight effect	Very poor weed control	Slight turfgrass discoloration or stunting
20		Poor weed control	Some turfgrass discoloration, stunting, or stand loss
30		Poor to deficient weed control	Turfgrass injury more pronounced, but not lasting
40	Moderate effect	Deficient weed control	Moderate injury, turf usually recovers
50		Deficient to moderate weed control	Turfgrass injury more lasting, recovery doubtful
60		Moderate weed control	Lasting turfgrass injury, no recovery
70	Severe effect	Weed control somewhat less than satisfactory	Heavy turfgrass injury and stand loss
80		Satisfactory to good weed control	Turfgrass nearly destroyed, a few surviving plants
90		Very good to excellent weed control	Only occasional live turfgrass plants left
100	Complete effect	Complete weed destruction	Complete turfgrass destruction

to 10 scales are probably the most commonly used because they can easily be converted to percentages (Table 21-1). Little (1985) suggested that when percentage data are collected, it is often necessary to use the arcsin transformation for statistical analysis. A general rule for deciding when to use the arcsin transformation is that it should be used if the range of observed percentages is >40% around the middle of the scale, or >20% near the end of the scale.

In some instances, weed control data must be taken as percent ground cover of each weed species where 0 = complete control (Johnson, 1982a). This was necessary when a herbicide such as oxadiazon {3-[2,4-dichloro-5-(1-methylethoxy)phenyl]-5-(1,1-dimethylethyl-1,3,4-oxadiazol-2-(3*H*)-one} controlled 95 to 100% of annual bluegrass (*Poa annua* L.), corn speedwell, and hop clover but did not have activity on wild parsnip (*Pastinaca sativa* L.) and thymeleaf sandwort (*Arenaria serpyllifolia* L.). Since wild parsnip and thymeleaf sandwort were present at a low percentage of the total weed population prior to oxadiazon treatment, the rapid increase in population of these weeds after oxadiazon treatments resulted in a major shift in total weed population. Another example of ground cover weed ratings are postemergence experiments when an increase in weeds occurs and estimates were made at the time of treatment. By using a cover rating, the population for each plot can be adjusted to the change in untreated plots to get the initial adjusted stand.

Weed control ratings of greenhouse experiments can be determined by estimated plant injury where 0 = no injury to 100 = complete kill, or by harvesting the weeds from the greenhouse pots at soil level and reporting either fresh or dry weights (Appleby & Somabhi, 1978). O'Sullivan and Kossatz (1982) reported on a weed control rating scale of 0 to 9 where 0 = no injury in a greenhouse experiment. In addition, they cut off weed shoots at the soil surface 48 h after treatment and rated shoot regrowth on a 0 to 9 scale at 4 wk following shoot removal. Fresh weed weights were also determined from the regrowth. Roots were washed and weights were determined. The results from the injury rating scale and weight of weed regrowth from herbicide treatment were similar.

6. Collecting Turfgrass Tolerance Data

In turfgrass establishment, herbicide residues may exist on an area from previous applications or as applications made to the seedbed. In either case, tolerance methods that can be used during establishment of turfgrasses include percentage ground cover, number of seedlings after seeding, and number of injured or dead grass plants after sprigging. In some instances, visual growth ratings based on 0 = no growth to 100 = complete uniform turf growth may be desirable to determine the response of newly planted turf to herbicide treatments.

Response of established turfgrasses to herbicide treatments has been determined by recording clipping weights, tiller counts, visual ratings, and root weights. Clipping weights have been used less than other measurements within the last 20 yr. Visual ratings for turf quality or discoloration have been widely used, but no standards have been established. The various visual scales for turf-quality ratings include 1 to 5 (1 = no effect and 5 = complete browning), 1 to 9 (1 = no injury and 9 = turf complete necrosis), 0 to 10 (0 = complete browning and 10 = optimum turf conditions), 1 to 10 (1 = total discoloration and 10 = no discoloration), and 0 to 100 (0 = total discoloration and 100 = complete uniform or green turf). Quality or early spring growth ratings may be expressed as a percentage relative to the untreated check plots. Christians (1982) estimated the tolerance of four Kentucky bluegrass (*Poa pratensis* L.) cultivars to preemergence herbicides by removing plugs from field-treated plots and placing plugs in the greenhouse. During a 7-wk period, regrowth from plugs was cut and weighed.

Turfgrass density ratings based on percentage ground cover where 0 = no sod and 100 = complete uniform sod cover, can also be used to determine response of turfgrasses to herbicide treatments. Mahdi and Stoutemyer (1953) reported density measurement from a 2.5-cm plug that was removed from the turf with a soil sampling tube. Each single stem separated was counted as one plant. Sod tensile strength can be determined by force uniformly applied by means of sand or steel weights to a moveable platform (Turner & Dickens, 1987), using a winch, or by a method developed by Burns and Futral (1980), using an Istron universal testing instrument.

Fig. 21-1. Root development of bermudagrass was measured by the force required to uproot the grass previously planted. (Courtesy of S.W. Bingham.)

Root measurements are necessary in some tolerance studies because herbicides will reduce or inhibit root development (Johnson, 1980; Bingham & Hall, 1985). Root growth ratings can be determined from samples taken from field plots (Johnson, 1980) or from samples removed from treated field plots and placed in a greenhouse for a given period (Christians, 1982). Roots are cut off below the thatch, oven dried, and weighed for estimates of root growth. The degree of root development over a given period can be measured by force required to uproot 'Merion' Kentucky bluegrass (King & Beard, 1969) or bermudagrass (Bingham & Hall, 1985) sod (Fig. 21-1). Root growth of turfgrasses can also be determined utilizing a rhizotron as reported by Sifers et al. (1985) or by area measurement system using a high resolution camera (Barnett et al., 1987).

B. Analytical Techniques for Determining Herbicide Concentration and Fate in Plants and Soils

Technological advances in weed control depend upon pertinent field, greenhouse, growth chamber, and laboratory investigations. These types of investigations are equally important; however, research on the behavior of herbicides in plants and soils can generally be more precisely conducted in the laboratory. Most of the instrumentation and analytical techniques are adapted to both plant and soil investigations on herbicide behavior.

1. Extraction and Clean-up

Two crucial steps required for the accurate chemical analysis of plant and soil samples are extraction and clean-up (Weete, 1986). Efficient extraction depends upon the chemical and physical properties of the substrate and the herbicide. Additionally, a suitable solvent system must be selected that will extract the herbicide. Extraction methods are specific for the herbicide and the subsequent method of analysis. Banks and Robinson (1984) described methods for the extraction of oryzalin [4-(dipropylamino)-3,5-dinitrobenzene-sulfonamide] from soil. Bestman et al. (1987) outlined a procedure for the aqueous extraction of chlorsulfuron {2-chloro-N-[[(4-methoxy-6-methyl-1,3,5-triazin-2-yl)amino]carbonyl]benzenesulfonamide} from flax (*Linum sativum* L.), field pennycress (*Thlaspi arvense* L.), and wheat (*Triticum aestivum* L.). This aqueous procedure averaged 94% efficiency for the extraction of ^{14}C-chlorsulfuron.

Organic extracts of plant tissue and soil contain mixtures of substances that can interfere with subsequent analysis (Weete, 1986). Ramsteiner and Hörmann (1979) reported that the use of a strong cation-exchange resin, a polyacrylamide adsorption resin, and a styrenedivinylbenzene gel filtration column was an effective clean-up procedure for the high performance liquid chromatography (HPLC) analysis of atrazine [6-chloro-N-ethyl-N'-(1-methylethyl)-1,3,5-triazine-2,4-diamine], simazine (6-chloro-N,N'-diethyl-1,3,5-triazine-2,4-diamine), propazine [6-chloro-N,N'bis(1-methylethyl)-1,3,5-triazine-2,4-diamine], and terbuthylazine [4-*tert*. butylamino-4-chloro-6-(ethylamino)-s-triazine] residues in plant tissues.

2. Spectrophotometric Methods

Use of spectrophotometric instruments has improved the accuracy of determining herbicide properties and their concentrations in solutions. The majority of herbicides presently being used (85%) are aromatic organic chemicals which can be placed in a solvent and analyzed by spectrophotometric methods. Nonaromatic herbicides must be chemically converted before they can be analyzed by this technique. Weber (1986a) discussed the principles of and methods for the spectrophotometric analysis of herbicides. Banks and Merkle (1979) reported that spectrophotometric determinations of the chlorophyll content of large crabgrass [*Digitaria sanguinalis* (L.) Scop.] and other annual grasses could be used in a bioassay to determine fluridone [1-methyl-3-phenyl-5-[3-trifluoromethyl)phenyl]-4(1H)-pyridinone] concentration in soil.

3. Chromatographic Methods

Chromatography is a term that describes a variety of methods used for the separation of components in a mixture. Chromatography involves the use of a mobile phase—a gas or liquid solution of the compounds to be separated, and a stationary phase—a solid material coated on a glass plate or packed in a column, or a liquid coated on an inert support packed in a column or on the inside wall of a column (Weete, 1986). Components of the mixture are separated by the interaction of the compounds with the stationary phase. Weete (1986) presented a list of references for the chromatographic methods employed in the analysis of the various herbicide families.

Column chromatographic techniques are widely used for the separation (extraction, clean-up, or both) of compounds in large quantities. Weete (1986) discussed the principles of the four basic types of chromatography— adsorption, ion-exchange, partition, and exclusion. Thin-layer chromatography (TLC) is a widely used and inexpensive chromatographic method for herbicide residue analysis. All four basic types of chromatography can be applied to TLC, but the most common type is adsorption chromatography (Weete, 1986). With the use of TLC, Hurto et al. (1979) found that selected preemergence herbicides degraded more rapidly in thatch of Kentucky bluegrass turfgrass than in soil.

Gas-liquid chromatography (GLC) is a commonly used chromatographic method for quantitative herbicide residue analysis. Weete (1986) reported that theoretically any mixture could be separated into individual components by GLC if it is volatile, or could be converted to a volatile derivative, and is thermostable. Methods, types, and the sensitivities of the various detectors used in GLC have been outlined by Weete (1986). Zimdahl et al. (1984) used GLC techniques to investigate the role of time, temperature, and soil moisture on the soil degradation of pendimethalin [N-(1-ethylpropyl)-3,4-dimethyl-2,6-dinitrobenzenamine]. They reported that GLC analysis was more accurate than an oat (*Avena sativa* L. 'Sole') bioassay in predicting the soil half-life of pendimethalin. Banks and Merkle (1979) used GLC to detect fluridone residues in soil-leaching experiments.

High performance liquid chromatography is a precise, quantitative technique used for herbicide residue analysis. Improved detector sensitivity, and the analysis of thermally labile and nonvolatile herbicides that are not suited for GLC analysis have increased the use of HPLC in recent years (Weete, 1986). Additionally, HPLC is a nondestructive technique and effluent can be collected for further analysis. The HPLC was used for the determination of atrazine, simazine, propazine, and terbuthylazine residues in plant tissue (Ramsteiner & Hörmann, 1979) and to study the soil degradation of MSMA (monosodium salt of MAA) (Akkari et al., 1986).

4. Radioisotope Methods

Radioactive labeled-herbicides, in which the position of the nuclide is known, are widely used in analysis of herbicide residues in plant and soil systems (Corbin & Swisher, 1986). Radiochemical assay techniques include autoradiography, liquid scintillation spectrometry, and Geiger-Muller counting methods (Corbin & Swisher, 1986; Eastin, 1986). Autoradiography is a qualitative method used to determine the location and relative amounts of a nuclide. Autoradiography is commonly used in herbicide absorption and translocation studies (Eastin, 1986; Baradari et al., 1980; Schultz & Burnside, 1980; Whitwell et al., 1980; Peterson & Swisher, 1985; Wills & McWhorter, 1985). Liquid scintillation spectrometry is used to quantify the percent distribution of the radioactive isotope. Advantages of liquid scintillation spectrometry are: (i) sample preparation is simple and convenient, and (ii) efficiency (80–90% of the beta particles emitted from ^{14}C can be detected) (Eastin, 1986). Using liquid scintillation spectrometry, Whitwell et al. (1980) investigated the role of temperature, relative humidity, and light on the adsorption and translocation of ^{14}C-glyphosate [N-(phosphonomethyl)glycine] by common bermudagrass. Liquid scintillation spectrometry was also used to study the soil degradation of ^{14}C-pendimethalin, ^{14}C-trifluralin [2,6-dinitro-N,N-dipropyl-4-(trifluoromethyl)benzenamine] and ^{14}C-oryzalin (Nelson et al., 1983). The Geiger-Muller counter technique may also be used to quantify the amount of radioactive herbicides in plant and soil systems (Corbin & Swisher, 1986). Reviews of radiochemical assay methods used in weed science research were presented by Corbin and Swisher (1986).

C. Research Methods for Studying Herbicide Activity in Plants

Physiological investigations into the mode of action of herbicides is a prerequisite to the continued understanding of the behavior of herbicides in plants. Ashton and Crafts (1981) defined mode of action as "the sum total of anatomical, physiological, and biochemical responses that make up the total phytotoxic action of a chemical, as well as the physical (location) and molecular (degradation) fate of the chemical in the plant." Ashton and Crafts (1981) identified absorption and translocation, molecular fate, biochemical responses, and growth and plant structure as the four major subdivisions of mode of action of a given herbicide.

1. Absorption and Translocation

Adsorption and translocation studies are conducted by applying a radioactive herbicide as a foliage treatment, a root treatment through nutrient solution, or as a root treatment through soil or sand (Eastin, 1986). For foliage treatments, after a plant has reached a desired growth stage, the radioactive herbicide is applied to the designated plant part (leaf, stem, etc.) in a lanolin ring, lanolin paste, or micropipette. Root treatments involve growing the plant in a nutrient solution, sand, or soil that contains the radioactive herbicide. After a suitable period has elapsed, plants are harvested and herbicide absorption and translocation is determined by autoradiography, liquid scintillation spectrometry, or Geiger-Muller counting techniques. In autoradiography, plants or plant parts are pressed, freeze-dried, and placed adjacent to x-ray film for 2 to 4 wk (Eastin, 1986). Autoradiographic techniques showed that ^{14}C-chlorflurenol (2-chloro-9-hydroxy-9H-fluorene-9-carboxylic acid) was translocated in the apoplast and symplast of Canada thistle [*Cirsium arvense* (L.) Scop] (Baradari et al., 1980). Schultz and Burnside (1980) showed that ^{14}C-2,4-D [(2,4-dichlorophenoxy)acetic acid] and ^{14}C-glyphosate were translocated in the symplast of hemp dogbane (*Apocynum cannabium* L.). Both liquid scintillation spectrometry and Geiger-Muller counting techniques have been used to quantify the amounts of radioactive herbicide absorption and translocation (Corbin & Swisher, 1986; Eastin, 1986).

2. Molecular Fate

Herbicide selectivity is due in large part to the ability of tolerant plants to degrade or metabolize a herbicide to nonphytotoxic compounds. A review of the techniques used to study the molecular fate of herbicides in plants is beyond the scope of this chapter. Eastin (1986) discussed the applicability of radioactive herbicide use in molecular fate investigations. Campbell and Penner (1985) used silica gel TLC, autoradiography, and liquid scintillation spectrometry to detect nine metabolites of sethoxydim {2[1-(ethoxyimino) butyl]-5-[2-(ethylthio)propyl]-3-hydroxy-2-cyclohexen-1-one} in selected monocotyledonous and dicotyledonous plants.

3. Biochemical Responses

Herbicides are known to interfere with photosynthesis, respiration, oxidative phosphorylation, RNA synthesis, protein synthesis, lipid synthesis, and many other biochemical reactions (Ashton & Crafts, 1981). Truelove and Davis (1986) discussed use of the manometric techniques utilizing the Warburg apparatus and the Gilson Differential Respirometer for determinations of photosynthesis and respiration by measuring oxygen production and uptake, respectively. Photosynthetic carbon dioxide absorption can also be determined by an infrared gas analyzer (IRGA) (Truelove & Davis, 1986). Yang and Bingham (1984) used an IRGA and determined that the net photosynthesis of goosegrass [*Eleusine indica* (L.) Gaertn.] was inhibited at lower rates of metribuzin [4-amino-6-(1,1-dimethylethyl)-3-(methylthio)-1,2,4-triazin-5(4H)-one] than those required for a similar reduction in various bermudagrass cultivars. St. John (1986) has outlined methodology for studying the effects of herbicides on lipid metabolism.

4. Growth and Plant Structure

Morphological, anatomical, and cytological investigations can provide valuable information on the effect of a herbicide on plant growth and structure (Ashton & Crafts, 1981). Additionally, these studies can provide clues as to which physiological and biochemical plant processes are affected. Utilizing light and electron microscopy, Vaughn and Koskinen (1987) showed that trifluralin and two herbicidally active trifluralin metabolites inhibited mitosis at prometaphase in trifluralin-susceptible but not in trifluralin-resistant goosegrass biotypes.

D. Research Methods for Studying Herbicide Activity in Soils

1. Bioassay

A herbicide bioassay is a method to determine the concentration of a chemical in the soil with a living organism. Herbicide-sensitive plant species are used to qualitatively or quantitatively determine the presence of a specific herbicide. Bioassays may be conducted for soil or aqueous suspensions. Either type would include a comparison of indicator plants growing in the untreated and the herbicide-treated soil or aqueous suspension. Depending upon the bioassay, either individual plant part or total plant response may be measured (Lavy & Santelmann, 1986). Individual plant part responses include determinations of (i) root and shoot elongation, (ii) cell multiplication and abnormality, and (iii) chlorosis or necrosis of a specific plant part. Barrett and Lavy (1984) measured stem twisting and chlorosis of tall fescue to determine oxadiazon soil residues. Total plant responses include (i) growth inhibition (height, width, etc.), (ii) chlorosis or necrosis, and (iii) wet or dry plant weights. Mazur et al. (1969) described how a bioassay could be used to detect residues of preemergence herbicides with both the soil and aqueous suspension methods. Lavy and Santelmann (1986) have given a complete, detailed outline on bioassay procedures.

2. Adsorption

Adsorption to soil colloids affects the mobility and degradation characteristics of herbicides. Herbicides that are tightly bound to soil colloids may not be available to control weeds, have limited soil mobility, and may not be susceptible to soil degradation mechanisms (Ross & Lembi, 1985). In contrast, herbicides that are weakly bound to soil colloids may be readily leached and subject to microbial and other soil degradative processes. The availability of herbicides in the soil to control weeds is determined by the type and quantity of soil colloids, the chemical properties of a specific herbicide, the amount of soil moisture, and other environmental conditions (Ross & Lembi, 1985). Herbicide adsorption measurements are usually determined in aqueous soil suspensions. Known weights of a liquid (the herbicide solution) and a solid (the soil constituent) are mixed, allowed to equilibrate at a given temperature, and the resulting change in the herbicide concentration in the equilibrated solution is determined (Weber, 1986b). This method can be used to determine herbicide adsorption by soils, clay minerals, soil organic matter, and organic matter fractions. Dao and Lavy (1978) investigated the role of temperature, soil moisture and electrolyte concentration on the adsorption of atrazine. Goetz et al. (1986) investigated the effects of soil pH on the adsorption of imazaquin {2-[4,5-dihydro-4-methyl-4-(1-methylethyl)-5-oxo-1H-imidazol-2-yl]-3-quinolinecarboxylic acid} and showed that as the pH of a Lucedale fine sandy loam (fine-loamy, siliceous, thermic Rhodic Paleudults) increased from 5.8 to 6.6 the imazaquin concentration in soil solution increased from 47 to 100%. Weber (1986b) described methods and procedures for determining the adsorption mechanisms of herbicides to clay minerals.

3. Mobility

The vertical movement of a herbicide in soil is important in determining its efficacy, selectivity, and potential for groundwater contamination

(Weber et al., 1986). Herbicide mobility is influenced by rainfall, soil type, and the relative affinity of the herbicide for soil colloids. Methods used for determining the mobility of herbicides include the use of soil columns, soil TLC plates, and soil thick-layer trays (Weber et al., 1986). Soil TLC plates are coated with a fine silty soil matrix and the movement of herbicides is determined in a manner similar to that used with silica gel TLC plates. Goetz et al. (1986) used soil TLC plates to compare the mobility of imazaquin, atrazine, and metribuzin. Wu and Santelmann (1975) compared the relative effectiveness of soil TLC plates, soil thick-layer trays, and slotted soil columns for herbicide mobility investigations. Italian ryegrass (*Lolium multiflorum* Lam.) was used as the bioassay species for the soil thick-layer tray and slotted soil column methods. All methods provided reliable estimates of the mobility of four herbicides. The primary advantage of soil thick-layer trays and slotted soil columns was that these methods did not require the use of radioactive herbicides as did the soil TLC method. Weber et al. (1986) described procedures for the uses of natural and hand-packed soil columns in herbicide mobility investigations. Mobility investigations have been conducted to determine the rate of herbicide leaching among different soil types (Weber & Peeper, 1982), and to determine the distribution of a herbicide within a soil profile (Weber & Whitacre, 1982).

4. Degradation

Rapid herbicide degradation is desirable so that residues do not accumulate in the environment, but may be detrimental if the herbicide does not persist long enough to control weeds for the desired time period. Herbicide degradation processes include photodegradation, biodegradation, and chemical degradation (Ross & Lembi, 1985). Savage and Jordan (1980) investigated the role of sunlight and other factors on the soil surface persistence of trifluralin, pendimethalin, and fluchloralin [*N*-(2-chloroethyl)-2,6-dinitro-*N*-propyl-4-(trifluoromethyl)benzenamine]. Herbicides were extracted with a hexane/acetone (3:1) extract, and residues were determined by GLC. Utilizing this technique, these authors showed that the soil surface persistence of these herbicides was less when exposed to direct sunlight than when protected by an artificial shade cover.

Herbicide biodegradation is investigated by measuring herbicide persistence in microbial sterile and nonsterile soils. Soils are sterilized by autoclaving, fumigation, gamma irradiation, or by treating with microbial inhibitors (Skipper et al., 1986a). Biodegradation is considered to be the difference between herbicide persistence in sterile vs. nonsterile soils. Skipper et al. (1986a) outlined methods for the use of a soil perfusion apparatus, soil biometer flasks, and degradative plasmids in soil microorganisms in studying the biodegradation of herbicides. Soil biometer flasks are commonly used and enable the investigator to use ^{14}C-labeled herbicides. Herbicide biodegradation is determined by trapping evolved $^{14}CO_2$ in a KOH or NaOH solution and analyzing an aliquot by liquid scintillation spectrometry. Utilizing this technique, Skipper et al. (1986b) showed that ^{14}C-butylate [*S*-ethyl bis(2-methyl-propyl)carbamothioate] was degraded more rapidly in soils that had been treated with butylate for 2 or 7 yr than in soils that had no history of previous butylate treatment. Unless both sterile and nonsterile soils are utilized, the exact contribution of biodegradative and chemodegradative processes cannot be determined (Nelson et al., 1983).

Herbicide persistence in the soil may also be investigated by removing soil samples from treated field plots and subsequent analysis by GLC, HPLC, and soil bioassay techniques. Weber (1986b) presented procedures for sampling soils that will be used in chemical or bioassay analysis.

II. MANAGEMENT OF FIELD RESEARCH PLOTS

The management of turfgrass field plots for weed science research is important to maintain optimum growth conditions for both the turfgrass and weeds. In general, turfgrass management practices that encourage weed growth will be needed. Some of the practices are closer mowing, light frequent irrigation, vertical mowing, coring, and thatch control.

A. Cultural Requirements

1. Herbicide Residues

Residual effects of herbicides can greatly influence weed research. When preemergence herbicides are applied for weed control, it is necessary to have residual activity to provide control over a period of time. Weed seeds begin to germinate as the herbicides lose residual activity. To prevent weed seed germination, herbicides must be reapplied to the area either during the initial year of treatment or during the following year. However, repeated herbicide treatment can increase turfgrass injury to both warm- and cool-season grasses (Callahan, 1972; 1976).

Residual activity from applications of preemergence herbicides can be a disadvantage when present on areas scheduled for turfgrass planting or renovation for new experiments. For example, siduron [N-(2-methylcyclohexyl)-N'-phenylurea] can be safely applied to most of the newly planted cool-season grasses, but not to most newly planted warm-season grasses (Lewis & Gilbert, 1966). Many preemergence herbicides can injure newly sprigged warm-season grasses (Johnson, 1975) (Fig. 21–2). Grasses may recover slowly, especially when selected herbicides are applied at higher rates. Turfgrass growth may be greater at the end of the first growing season in plots treated with preemergence herbicides than in untreated plots because weed competition was eliminated.

Another disadvantage in residual activity of preemergence herbicides may occur when they are fall-applied for winter weed control in warm-season grasses that are overseeded with cool-season grass species. In most instances, herbicides must be applied two to three months in advance of overseeding, otherwise poor seed germination and severe injury to newly planted grasses

Fig. 21–2. Most preemergence herbicides will severely injure newly planted turfgrass. Light-colored bare spots on right plot were caused by treating Tifway bermudagrass with DCPA; plot on left was not treated.

may occur. When an area has recently been treated with a preemergence herbicide and must be overseeded or replanted with a different species, activated charcoal can deactivate selected herbicides (Jagschitz, 1968). The rate of charcoal needed to deactivate herbicides is 112 kg ha^{-1} for each 1.12 kg ha^{-1} of herbicide residue present (Monaco et al., 1986). It should be emphasized that charcoal in the soil will decrease preemergence activity of soil-active herbicides for several months.

2. Thatch

Thatch is an accumulation of living and decomposing organic material that often serves as the principal medium for turfgrass roots and other plant parts. Thatch layers develop when addition of organic matter to the soil surface exceeds the rate of decomposition. Accumulation of thatch is undesirable and should be controlled in turfgrass species to maintain a good uniform turf.

Hurto et al. (1979) reported that benefin [N-butyl-N-ethyl-2,6-dinitro-4-(trifluoromethyl)benzenamine] and DCPA (dimethyl 2,3,5,6-tetrachloro-1,4-benzene dicarboxylate) persisted for a shorter period of time in thatch than in soil. Higher rates or more frequent applications of these herbicides may be needed for season-long weed control in thatchy turfs. Hurto and Turgeon (1979) found that when thatchy Kentucky bluegrass was treated with benefin and oxadiazon in the spring more turfgrass injury occurred during periods of summer stress than when the same herbicides were applied to thatch-free grass.

3. Rehabilitation of Turf Areas

The length of time required to rehabilitate a turf area following completion of a herbicide study will depend on herbicides used, length of study, soil type, organic matter, climatic conditions, and other factors (Weed Science Society of America, 1989). Generally, postemergence herbicides persist in the soil for a shorter time than preemergence herbicides.

In Rhode Island, Mazur et al. (1969) reported that preemergence herbicides applied for more than 1 yr on the same plot did not result in herbicide accumulation in the soil. There appeared to be no accumulation of bensulide {O,O-bis(1-methylethyl) S-[2-[(phenylsulfonyl)amino]ethyl] phosphorodithioate} or DCPA in the depth ranges tested when multiple applications were compared with a single annual application. When bensulide was applied as granular and emulsifiable concentrate formulations for four annual treatments in Virginia (Bingham & Schmidt, 1967), residues from the granular formulation were found in the soil 11 mo after the final treatment, whereas, the emulsifiable concentrate formulation had completely dissipated in the same period.

Since many postemergence herbicides generally have limited activity in soil, the test area can be used the following year after an experiment is completed. However, when preemergence herbicides are used, it may be necessary to skip one or more years after completion of an experiment before a new experiment is initiated on the same area.

B. Herbicide Application

1. Herbicide Formulations

Precise, uniform application of a herbicide is essential for acceptable estimation of weed control and turfgrass tolerance. Most herbicides are diluted with an inert carrier to aid in the uniform application of small amounts of chemical per plot. Herbicides are generally applied either as a spray in water or broadcast dry as granules. Sprayable herbicides are formulated as water-soluble liquids, emulsifiable concentrates, or wettable powders, which when added to a liquid carrier form true solutions, emulsions, or suspensions, respectively. The dry-type herbicides are impregnated on carriers such as clay, sand, vermiculite, and finely ground plant parts such as corncobs.

2. Dry Application

The application of granules to small turfgrass plots can be made by a hand shaker jar, or with a drop-type fertilizer spreader. Regardless of the herbicide applicator, care should be taken to ensure a uniform distribution of the granules. Skips are shown in Fig. 21–3 from uneven application of granular herbicide applied for annual bluegrass in dormant bermudagrass with a drop-type spreader. To increase the bulk and improve spreading uniformity when the chemical is applied by hand, select a material such as calcined clay, corncobs, vermiculite, or sand with size and density that matches the

Fig. 21–3. Uneven granular herbicide application with a drop-type spreader. The dark streaks were skips.

herbicide formulation. Because slight speed deviations can vary the rate of granular herbicide application with a drop spreader, the chemical should be applied at the same speed as when calibrating the spreader. Calibration of a drop-spreader can be made by fastening a pan to the underside of the spreader and collecting the herbicide while operating the spreader over a known area. Calibration of a spinner spreader can be checked by placing pans on the soil surface and collecting the amount of herbicide applied during a calibration run. Wolf and Edmisten (1986) reported that accurate application of solutions from sprayers and granules from spinner spreaders requires a known constant speed of travel. They found that a commercially available pocket-size audio metronome was a useful tool to maintain a desired speed. When a spreader is used, it is important to calibrate before the use of each herbicide at each date of treatment. A rotary-type spreader can be used for granular application in large plots providing fine powdery active ingredients do not settle out, resulting in an uneven application. When a rotary-type spreader is used, it must be calibrated and this can be done by using boxes to check the granular herbicide as shown in Fig. 21–4. Granular herbicides can be applied to small plots with a hand-held gravity flow-type spreader (PBI/Gordon Corp., Kansas City, MO) with swath width adjustable from 5 to 91 cm.

Fig. 21-4. Calibration of rotary-type spreader can be checked by placing boxes on the soil surface and collecting the amount of herbicide applied during a calibration run.

3. Liquid application

Sprayers have been described for research plots, greenhouse, and laboratory experiments (Wiese, 1986). However, most sprayers have several essential characteristics in common:

1. A tank or container is used to hold liquid spray material until it is dispensed.
2. An energy source to discharge the liquid spray material from a container toward the target area. The energy source is usually provided by gas under pressure or a mechanically driven pump.
3. Various types of pressure regulators and gauges are utilized to control the pressure and discharge volume from the tank.
4. A boom and system of nozzles or openings are necessary to distribute the spray materials as small droplets evenly over soil or plant surface.

4. Research Sprayers

Following is a discussion of various research sprayers.

a. Carbon Dioxide-Powered Sprayer. The CO_2-powered sprayer is designed for use on small field plots and greenhouse pots (Buchholtz, 1950; Lillie, 1961; Wiese, 1986). The sprayer can either be operated as a back pack or bicyle type (a wheeled sprayer so named because it utilizes bicycle wheels

Fig. 21–5. Operation of a back pack sprayer.

to support the spraying apparatus). The operation of a back pack sprayer is shown in Fig. 21–5. Spray tanks and fittings are made of stainless steel or brass to minimize corrosion. Separate tank and boom assemblies may be desirable to avoid contamination.

The advantages of the back pack sprayer include the following:

1. Compact and easy to handle.
2. Ideal to use for spraying small plots with no alleys, and
3. Chemicals can be changed rapidly without contamination.

The only disadvantage in using the back-pack sprayer is that the walking speed must be calibrated and maintained at a constant rate. However, the sprayer can be calibrated by spraying similar water volume over some area until the researcher is confident of uniformity in speed. The speed can also be calibrated using an audio metronome timer that emits an audible signal at one second intervals (Regehr & Eastburn, 1980; Wolf & Edmisten, 1986).

The CO_2 bicycle sprayer is pushed by hand and operated similarly to the CO_2 back-pack sprayer. One advantage in the use of a bicycle sprayer over the back-pack sprayer is that a speedometer can be mounted on the bicycle sprayer. The speedometer will help reduce any error in walking speed. A disadvantage in the use of the bicycle sprayer is more time may be required to spray small plots. The bicycle sprayer has been popular because the various components to build it are commercially available.

b. Air-Pressure Sprayer. The air pressure sprayer can be a hand or bicycle-type sprayer and is used for small field plots and greenhouse pots (Kasasean, 1964). One version utilizes a stainless steel pneumatic air tank adapted with pressure gauge, shut-off valve, and 0.95-L high density polyethylene bottle. The plastic bottle serves as a spray container and the metal spray tank is the source of compressed air.

c. Logarithmic Sprayer. A logarithmic sprayer applies a decreasing rate of herbicide along the length of a plot and it is useful for preliminary herbicide screening. During logarithmic spraying, the main spray canister is both the diluent and compressed air container. With special attachments, a small polyethylene bottle is clipped to the main canister and inverted after filling. The diluent flows from the main canister into the plastic bottle where it flows into the spray boom. The method of calibrating logarithmic sprayers is reported by Wiese (1986).

d. Laboratory Sprayer. Shaw and Swanson (1952) reported that as little as 2 mL of liquid can be applied correctly to a 10-cm pot with a special type lab sprayer. This sprayer is good for applying herbicides where a small quantity of chemical is available or to test plants and soils in physiological studies. When a sprayer is not available, small amounts of liquid herbicide can be mixed with 25 mL of water and applied to the soil of each container.

A large laboratory sprayer was reported for applying herbicides in laboratory and greenhouse by Bouse and Bovey (1967). The spray table has drain pans, adjustable height plant supporting tray, exhaustion, activated charcoal filter system, and variable speed spray cart on an overhead track with a control panel. The speed of the cart can be changed with a variable speed drive unit on an electric motor. Excess herbicide should be disposed as approved by local environmental regulations.

e. Electrostatic Sprayer. Anantheswaran and Law (1979) reported that electrostatic spraying can be successfully used to improve droplet deposition onto turfgrass-type planar targets. The deposition achieved onto the flat targets utilizing charged spray at -6 A in conjunction with the dielectric-barrier type electrostatic precipitator was improved 3.6 times as compared with uncharged spray. The presence of an electrostatic precipitator in the form of a polyethylene sheet above the spray cloud also acts as a protection for the charged spray cloud from the effects of crosswinds.

f. Atomizer Sprayer. A hand-held atomizer sprayer can be used to spray individual turfgrass pots grown in greenhouses or growth chambers.

5. Sprayer Calibration

Flat fan tip nozzles (80° or 110°) are recommended for broadcast spraying in turfgrass. Flood jet nozzles are not recommended for turfgrass because they do not give uniform deposition of the spray. Calibration is simply adjusting the sprayer to apply the desired rate of solution. It is imperative to correctly apply the desired rate of herbicide. The sprayer must move at a constant speed to apply the chemical evenly and accurately. It must also operate at a constant pressure. Each nozzle must be the same size, clean, and set at the correct height.

There are many ways to calibrate a sprayer (Wiese, 1986). However, a small plot sprayer can be calibrated accurately as follows:

$$60\ 000\ 000/[(BW)\ (S)\ (Vol.)] = s/L$$

where
$$\begin{aligned}
60\ 000\ 000 &= \text{constant}\\
BW &= \text{width between nozzles in cm}\\
S &= \text{speed in m/min}\\
Vol. &= \text{spray volume in L/ha.}
\end{aligned}$$

Example for calibrating sprayer using 45.7-cm spacing between nozzles, 53.6 m/min speed, and 187 L of water per ha as solution rate.

$$60\ 000\ 000/[(45.7\ cm \times 53.6\ m)/(min \times 187\ L/ha)]$$

$$= 60\ 000\ 000/458\ 060 = 131\ s/L$$

To calculate milliliters applied per second, convert L to ml, and determine the inverse:

$$1000/131 = 7.63\ ml/s$$

$$7.63\ ml/s \times 60\ s = 458\ ml/60\ s$$

To prevent herbicide spray overlap in field plots, shields can be placed on the sides of each plot while spraying. When shields are not used, the outer perimeter of a plot must be deleted from the evaluations if overlapping occurred. For example, when a 1.5-m width plot is sprayed, ratings should only be made from the center 1.2 m of the plot.

6. Spray Volume

Spray volume is not critical to the activity of most herbicides provided a good spray cover is obtained during application. An exception occurred with glyphosate (Buhler & Burnside, 1983; Jordan, 1981). The activity of glyphosate was less when the chemical was applied to selected weeds in spray volumes of 95 L/ha (10 gallon/acre) or higher than at lower spray volumes [24 (2.5 gallon/acre) and 48 L/ha (5 gallon/acre)].

Because spray volumes are usually not a problem for herbicide evaluation, a volume should be selected that will provide good uniform spray coverage without runoff. A volume of 375 L/ha (40 gallon/acre) has generally been accepted by most turfgrass researchers as a standard volume.

III. FUTURE RESEARCH NEEDS

Current weed control programs are largely based on management practices that promote a dense turfgrass stand, and on the use of herbicides. Increased public concern on the use of pesticides, particularly in an urban environment, indicates a need to develop weed control methods that are not based on large quantities of herbicide inputs. Possible areas of research are: identification of turfgrass species and cultivars that are competitive with weeds, especially during establishment; investigations on the biology (germination requirements, growth patterns, and shade tolerance) of turfgrass weed species; and the effects on turfgrass maintenance practices on the growth and development of weeds. Additionally, research on the potential of registered herbicides to contaminate water either by leaching or lateral flow needs to be conducted for the various turfgrass species. Leaching studies are commonly conducted in the absence of a plant cover. The effect of turfgrass leaves, stems, roots, and thatch on the downward and lateral movement of herbicides through soil needs to be investigated.

Plant pathogens have shown potential for selective weed control in various row crops (Phatak et al., 1987) and need to be investigated for potential use in turfgrasses. Plant tissue culture techniques have been instrumental in the development of chlorsulfuron- and sulfometuron {2[[[[(4,6-dimethyl-2-pyrimidinyl)amino]carbonyl]amino]sulfonyl]benzoate acid} resistant tobacco (*Nicotiana tobacum* L.) (Chaleff & Ray, 1983) and glyphosate-resistant petunia (*Petunia* spp.) (Shah et al., 1986). The development of herbicide-tolerant and -resistant turfgrass species may be possible through plant tissue culture techniques.

IV. SUMMARY

In this chapter, we have presented research methods for conducting herbicide studies with turfgrasses under field, greenhouse, and laboratory conditions. We did not go into detailed discussion, but chose to give short descriptions and literature references to other sources which present the research methods in greater detail. In most instances, a statement was included on how the methods were related to turfgrass research. It is the responsibility of the individual researcher to use appropriate, established research methods, be innovative in the development of new methods, or modify standard methods to the specific needs for a given turfgrass herbicide research program.

ACKNOWLEDGMENT

The authors thank J.F. Miller for his contribution and assistance.

REFERENCES

Akkari, K.H., R.E. Frans, and T.L. Lavy. 1986. Factors affecting degradation of MSMA in soil. Weed Sci. 34:781–787.

Anantheswaran, R.C., and S.E. Law. 1979. Electrostatic spraying of turfgrass. USGA Green Sect. Rec. 17(6):1–4.

Anderson, R.N. 1968. Germination and establishment of weeds for experimental purposes. Weed Science Society of America Handbook. W.F. Humphrey Press, Geneva, NY.

Appleby, A.P., and M. Somabhi. 1978. Antagonistic effect of atrazine and simazine on glyphosate activity. Weed Sci. 26:135–139.

Ashton, F.M., and A.S. Crafts. 1981. Introduction. p. 1–6. In F.M. Ashton and A.S. Crafts (ed.) Mode of action of herbicides. 2nd ed. John Wiley and Sons, New York.

Banks, P.A., and E.L. Robinson. 1984. The fate of oryzalin applied to straw-mulched and non-mulched soils. Weed Sci. 32:269–272.

Banks, P.A., and M.G. Merkle. 1979. Soil detection and mobility of fluridone. Weed Sci. 27:309–312.

Baradari, M.R., L.C. Haderlie, and R.G. Wilson. 1980. Chlorfurenol effects on absorption and translocation of dicamba in Canada thistle (Cirsium arvense). Weed Sci. 28:197–200.

Barrett, R., and T.L. Lavy. 1984. Effects of soil water content on oxadiazon dissipation. Weed Sci. 32:697–701.

Barnett, C.E., R.A. White, A.M. Petrovic, and G.L. Good. 1987. An automated apparatus for measuring root length. HortScience 22:140–144.

Bestman, H.D., M.D. Devine, and W.H. Vanden Born. 1987. Extraction and separation of chlorsulfuron and its metabolites from treated plants. Weed Sci. 35:22–26.

Bingham, S.W., and R.E. Schmidt. 1967. Residue of bensulide in turfgrass soil following annual treatments for crabgrass control. Agron. J. 59:327–329.

Bingham, S.W., and J.R. Hall, III. 1985. Effects of herbicides on bermudagrass (Cynodon spp.) sprig establishment. Weed Sci. 33:253–257.

Bouse, L.F., and R.W. Bovey. 1967. A laboratory sprayer for potted plants. Weeds 15:89–91.

Buhler, D.D., and O.C. Burnside. 1983. Effect of spray components on glyphosate toxicity to annual grasses. Weed Sci. 31:124–130.

Buchholtz, K.P. 1950. A carbon dioxide powered sprayer for small plots. Agron. J. 42:614.

Burns, R.E., and J.G. Futral. 1980. Measuring sod strength with an instron universal testing instrument. Agron. J. 72:571–573.

Burnside, O.C. 1982. Greenhouse benches and pots designed to facilitate subirrigation. Weed Sci. 30:450–452.

Callahan, L.M. 1972. Phytotoxicity of herbicides to a Penncross bentgrass green. Weed Sci. 20:387–391.

Callahan, L.M. 1976. Phytotoxicity of herbicides to a Tifgreen bermudagrass green. Weed Sci. 24:92–98.

Campbell, J.R., and D. Penner. 1985. Sethoxydim metabolism in monocotyledonous and dicotyledonous plants. Weed Sci. 33:771–773.

Chaleff, R.S., and T.B. Ray. 1983. Herbicide-resistant mutants from tobacco cell cultures. Science 223:1148–1151.

Christians, N.E. 1982. Preemergence herbicide effects on four Kentucky bluegrass cultivars. HortScience 17:911–912.

Corbin, F.T., and B.A. Swisher. 1986. Radioisotope techniques. p. 265–276. In N.D. Camper (ed.) Research methods in weed science. 3rd ed. South. Weed Sci. Soc., Champaign, IL.

Dao, T.H., and T.L. Lavy. 1978. Atrazine adsorption on soil as influenced by temperature, moisture control, and electrolyte concentration. Weed Sci. 26:303–308.

Eastin, E.F. 1986. Absorption, translocation, and degradation of herbicides by plants. p. 277–289. In N.D. Camper (ed.) Research methods in weed science. 3rd ed. South. Weed Sci. Soc., Champaign, IL.

Frans, R., R. Talburt, D. Marx, and H. Crowley. 1986. Experimental design and techniques for measuring and analyzing plant responses to weed control practices. p. 29–46. *In* N.D. Camper (ed.) Research methods in weed science. 3rd ed. South. Weed Sci. Soc., Champaign, IL.

Frick, K.E., R.D. Williams, and R.F. Wilson. 1978. Interactions between *Bactra verutana* and the development of purple nutsedge (*Cyperus rotundus*) grown under three temperature regimes. Weed Sci. 26:550–553.

Goetz, A.J., G. Wehtje, R.H. Walker, and B. Hajek. 1986. Soil solution and mobility characterization of imazaquin. Weed Sci. 34:788–793.

Hamill, A.S., P.B. Marriage, and G. Friesen. 1977. A method for assessing herbicide performance in small plot experiments. Weed Sci. 25:386–389.

Hurto, K.A., and A.J. Turgeon. 1979. Influence of thatch on preemergence herbicide activity in Kentucky bluegrass (*Poa pratensis*) turf. Weed Sci. 27:141–146.

Hurto, K.A., A.J. Turgeon, and M.A. Cole. 1979. Degradation of benefin and DCPA in thatch and soil from a Kentucky bluegrass (*Poa pratensis*) turf. Weed Sci. 27:154–157.

Jagschitz, J.A. 1968. Use of charcoal to deactivate herbicide residues in turfgrass seedbeds. Proc. Northeast. Weed Sci. Soc. 22:401–408.

Johnson, B.J. 1975. Minimal herbicide treatments on the establishment of four turfgrasses. Agron. J. 67:786–789.

Johnson, B.J. 1976a. Herbicides for seasonal weed control in turfgrasses. Agron. J. 68:717–720.

Johnson, B.J. 1976b. Turfgrass tolerance and weed control with methazole and metribuzin. Weed Sci. 24:512–517.

Johnson, B.J. 1978. Response of zoysia (*Zoysia* spp.) and bermudagrass (*Cynodon dactylon*) cultivars to herbicide treatments. Weed Sci. 26:493–497.

Johnson, B.J. 1980. Root growth of southern turf cultivars as affected by herbicides. Weed Sci. 28:526–528.

Johnson, B.J. 1982a. Frequency of herbicide treatments for summer and winter weed control in turfgrasses. Weed Sci. 30:116–124.

Johnson, B.J. 1982b. Simazine formulation treatments on control of winter weeds in bermudagrass turf. Agron. J. 74:881–886.

Jordan, T.N. 1977. Effects of temperature and relative humidity on the toxicity of glyphosate to bermudagrass (*Cynodon dactylon*). Weed Sci. 25:448–451.

Jordan, T.N. 1981. Effects of diluent volumes and surfactant on the phytotoxicity of glyphosate to bermudagrass (*Cynodon dactylon*). Weed Sci. 29:79–83.

Kasasean, L. 1964. An easily made, inexpensive, multipurpose, experimental sprayer. Weed Res. 4:256–260.

King, J.W., and J.B. Beard. 1969. Measuring rooting of sodded turfs. Agron. J. 61:497–498.

Lavy, T.L. 1971. Soil moisture status and herbicide mobility in pots under differing subirrigation systems. North Cent. Weed Control Conf. Res. Rep. 28:26–28.

Lavy, T.L., and P.W. Santelmann. 1986. Herbicide bioassay as a research tool. p. 201–217. *In* N.D. Camper (ed.) Research methods in weed science. 3rd ed. South. Weed Sci. Soc., Champaign, IL.

Lewis, W.M., and G.C. Klingman. 1963. Three evaluation methods for taking weed control data in bermudagrass turf. Proc. South. Weed Conf. 16:105–109.

Lewis, W.M., and W.B. Gilbert. 1966. The effect of siduron on crabgrass and goosegrass control and the establishment of five warm-season and three cool-season turfgrasses. Proc. South. Weed Conf. 19:150–154.

Lillie, D.T. 1961. A carbon dioxide pressured portable field sprayer. Weeds 9:491–492.

Little, T.M. 1985. Analysis of percentage and rating scale data. HortScience 20:642–644.

Little, T.M., and F.J. Hills. 1978. Agricultural experimentation. John Wiley and Sons, New York.

Mahdi, Z., and V.T. Stoutemyer. 1953. A method of measurement of populations in dense turf. Agron. J. 45:514–515.

Mazur, A.R., J.A. Jagschitz, and C.R. Skogley. 1969. Bioassay for bensulide, DCPA, and siduron in turfgrass. Weed Sci. 17:31–34.

Monaco, T.J., A.R. Bonannu, and J.J. Baron. 1986. Herbicide injury: Diagnosis, causes, prevention, and remedial action. p. 399–428. *In* N.D. Camper (ed.) Research methods in weed science. 3rd ed. South. Weed Sci. Soc., Champaign, IL.

Nelson, J.E., W.F. Meggit, and D. Penner. 1983. Fractionation of residues of pendimethalin, trifluralin, and oryzalin during degradation in soil. Weed Sci. 31:68–75.

O'Sullivan, P.A., and V.C. Kossatz. 1982. Influence of picloram on *Cirsium arvense* (L.) Scop. control with glyphosate. Weed Res. 22:251–256.

Peterson, P.J., and B.A. Swisher. 1985. Absorption, translocation, and metabolism of ^{14}C-chlorsulfuron in Canada thistle. Weed Sci. 33:7–11.

Phatak, S.C., M.B. Callaway, and C.S. Vavrina. 1987. Biological control and its integration in weed management systems for purple and yellow nutsedge (*Cyperus rotundus* and *C. esculentus*). Weed Tech. 1:84–91.

Ramsteiner, K.A., and W.D. Hörmann. 1979. High-pressure liquid chromatographic determination of hydroxy-*s*-triazine residues in plant material. J. Agric. Food Chem. 27:934–938.

Regehr, D.L., and R.P. Eastburn. 1980. Audible timer for hand-carried plot sprayers. Weed Sci. 28:690–691.

Ross, M.A., and C.A. Lembi. 1985. The soil system and weed control. p. 89–106. *In* M.A. Ross and C.A. Lembi (ed.) Applied weed science. Burgess Publ. Co., Minneapolis.

St. John, J.B. 1986. Effects of herbicides on lipid metabolism. p. 345–358. *In* N.D. Camper (ed.) Research methods in weed science. 3rd ed. South. Weed Sci. Soc., Champaign, IL.

Salazar, L.C., and A.P. Appleby. 1982a. Germination and growth of grasses and legumes from seeds treated with glyphosate and paraquat. Weed Sci. 30:235–237.

Salazar, L.C., and A.P. Appleby. 1982b. Herbicidal activity of glyphosate in soil. Weed Sci. 30:463–466.

Savage, K.E., and T.N. Jordan. 1980. Persistence of three dinitroaniline herbicides on the soil surface. Weed Sci. 28:105–110.

Schultz, M.E., and O.C. Burnside. 1980. Absorption, translocation, and metabolism of 2,4-D and glyphosate in hemp dogbane (*Apocynum cannabium*). Weed Sci. 28:13–20.

Shah, D.M., R.B. Horsch, H.J. Klee, G.M. Kishore, J.A. Winter, N.E. Tumer, C.M. Hironaka, P.R. Sanders, C.S. Gasser, S. Aykent, N.R. Siegel, S.G. Rogers, and R.T. Fraley. 1986. Engineering herbicide tolerance in transgenic plants. Science 233:478–481.

Shaw, W.C., and C.R. Swanson. 1952. Techniques and equipment used in evaluating chemicals for their herbicidal properties. Weeds 1:352–365.

Sifers, S.I., J.B. Beard, and J.M. DiPaola. 1985. Spring root decline (SRD): Discovery, description and causes. p. 777–788. *In* F. Lermaire (ed.) Proc. 5th Int. Turfgrass Res. Conf., Avignon, France. 1–5 July. Inst. Natl. de la Recherche Agron., Paris.

Skipper, H.D., J.G. Mueller, V.L. Ward, and S.C. Wagner. 1986a. Microbial degradation of herbicides. p. 457–475. *In* N.D. Camper (ed.) Research methods in weed science. 3rd ed. South. Weed Sci. Soc., Champaign, IL.

Skipper, H.D., E.C. Murdock, D.T. Gooden, J.P. Zublena, and M.A. Amakiri. 1986b. Enhanced herbicide biodegradation in South Carolina soils previously treated with butylate. Weed Sci. 34:558–563.

Smith, G.S., and L.M. Callahan. 1969. The response of Kentucky bluegrass to soil residual of preemergence herbicides. Weed Sci. 17:13–15.

Truelove, B., and D.E. Davis. 1986. The measurement of photosynthesis and respiration using whole plants or plant organs. p. 325–344. *In* N.D. Camper (ed.) Research methods in weed science. 3rd ed. South. Weed Sci. Soc., Champaign, IL.

Turner, D.L., and R. Dickens. 1987. Atrazine effects on tensile strength of centipedegrass sod. Agron. J. 79:39–42.

Vaughn, K.C., and W.C. Koskinen. 1987. Effect of trifluralin metabolites on goosegrass (*Eleucine indica*) root meristems. Weed Sci. 35:36–44.

Weber, J.B. 1986a. Herbicide analysis and chemical property determinations using spectrophotometric determinations. p. 247–264. *In* N.D. Camper (ed.) Research methods in weed science. 3rd ed. South Weed Sci. Soc., Champaign, IL.

Weber, J.B. 1986b. Soils, herbicide sorption and model plant-soil systems. p. 155–188. *In* N.D. Camper (ed.) Research methods in weed science. 3rd ed. South. Weed Sci. Soc., Champaign, IL.

Weber, J.B., and T.F. Peeper. 1982. Mobility and distribution of buthidazole and metabolites in four leached soils. Weed Sci. 30:585–588.

Weber, J.B., L.R. Swain, H.J. Strek, and J.L. Sartori. 1986. Herbicide mobility in soil leaching columns. p. 189–200. *In* N.D. Camper (ed.) Research methods in weed science. 3rd ed. South. Weed Sci. Soc., Champaign, IL.

Weber, J.A., and D.M. Whitacre. 1982. Mobility of herbicides in soil columns under saturated and unsaturated-flow conditions. Weed Sci. 30:579–584.

Weed Science Society of America. 1989. Herbicide handbook. Weed Sci. Soc. of Am., Champaign, IL.

Weete, J.D. 1986. Herbicide analysis by chromatographic techniques. p. 219–245. *In* N.D. Camper (ed.) Research methods in weed science. South. Weed Sci. Soc., Champaign, IL.

Whitwell, T., P. Banks, E. Basler, and P.W. Santelmann. 1980. Glyphosate absorption and translocation in bermudagrass (*Cynodon dactylon*) and activity in horsenettle (*Solanum carolinense*). Weed Sci. 28:93–96.

Wiese, A.F. 1986. Herbicide application. p. 1–27. *In* N.D. Camper (ed.) Research methods in weed science. 3rd ed. South. Weed Sci. Soc., Champaign, IL.

Wills, G.D., and C.G. McWhorter. 1985. Effect of inorganic salts on the toxicity and translocation of glyphosate and MSMA in purple nutsedge (*Cyperus rotundus*). Weed Sci. 33:755–761.

Wolf, D.D., and K.L. Edmisten. 1986. Uniform travel speed for manually propelled sprayers and spreaders. Agron. J. 78:211–212.

Wu, C.-H., and P.W. Santelmann. 1975. Comparison of different soil leaching techniques with four herbicides. Weed Sci. 23:508–511.

Yang, Y.-S., and S.W. Bingham. 1984. Effects of metribuzin on net photosynthesis of goosegrass (*Eleusine indica*) and bermudagrass (*Cynodon* spp.). Weed Sci. 32:247–250.

Zimdahl, R.L., P. Catizone, and A.C. Butcher. 1984. Degradation of pendimethalin in soil. Weed Sci. 32:408–412.

22 Breeding Improved Turfgrasses

GLENN W. BURTON

Coastal Plain Station
Tifton, Georgia

The living green carpet called *turf* is the product of one or more genotypes interacting with an environment generally altered by management. Genotype, environment, and management influence and limit turf quality. Frequently to grow better turf, the environment must be improved by introducing drain tile, removing huge shade trees, watering, liming, and fertilizing. Much of turf management is an alteration of the environment to favor the genotype desired. Cutting heights and frequencies and disease and insect control measures are dictated by the genotypes selected and their use. The best turf is realized when genotype, environment, and management are balanced.

Frequently, the balance required for good turf can be most easily and economically achieved by changing the genotype to more nearly fit the existing environment. Substituting carpetgrass (*Axonopus affinis* Chase) for bermudagrass [*Cynodon* spp. (L.)] in low, wet areas will eliminate the need for drain tile. Planting a shade-tolerant grass, like St. Augustinegrass [*Stenotaphrum secundatum* (Walter) Kuntze] can save trees that would have to go if bermudagrass were used. By choosing centipedegrass (*Eremochloa ophiuroides* (Munro) Hackel), a homeowner can avoid the expense of insecticide treatments required to control chinchbug on a St. Augustinegrass lawn. These genotypes differ so greatly that taxonomists classify them into different genera.

Generally, much variability between genotypes can be found or created within a species. Manipulating this variability to develop improved cultivars within a species is the responsibility of the geneticist and plant breeder. Given adequate support, he can develop improved cultivars that will be in better balance with the existing environment and materially reduce management costs. Breeding the weed-resistant 'Tifway' bermudagrass solved many of the weed problems associated with common bermudagrass turf and saved millions of dollars required for weed control in common bermudagrass turf (Burton, 1960). Developing 'Tifdwarf' bermudagrass, with a putting green quality comparable to bentgrass, has helped to satisfy the insatiable demand for better putting greens in areas unsuited to bentgrass culture (Burton & Elsner, 1965). Insect-resistant cultivars could save homeowners the millions spent annually for insecticides to control these pests.

Copyright © 1992 ASA-CSSA-SSSA, 677 S. Segoe Rd., Madison, WI 53711, USA. *Turfgrass—Agronomy Monograph no. 32.*

The monetary support for turfgrass breeding has been limited. Some of the current improved turfgrass varieties were developed as byproducts of pasture and forage grass breeding. Many were picked out of nature's breeding basket by keen observers whose main job was not plant breeding. Very few originated in well-supported plant breeding programs. Yet, the ever-expanding turfgrass industry ranks among the top agricultural enterprises in the USA. Strong, strategically located turfgrass breeding programs, organized with adequate interdisciplinary assistance, would pay good dividends in terms of better turf.

I. GENERAL REQUIREMENTS

To be classed as a turfgrass, a species must be able to make a green, dense, wear-tolerant carpet when mowed. More specifically, the ideal turfgrass should be tolerant of drought and frost injury to remain green for long periods. To extend its area of usefulness, it should be able to withstand both high and low temperatures.

To reduce mowing requirements and give a better appearance when neglected, the perfect turfgrass should have a low growth habit. If our dream of a turfgrass that requires no mowing is ever realized, it will most certainly be with a low-growing species that produces few, if any, seedheads.

The turfgrass breeder will always endeavor to make his improved varieties pest resistant. Among the many pests he must consider will be the pathogens, insects, and nematodes parasitic on the grass. He will achieve improved weed resistance by increasing the density of the new variety, but as he does, he may add to the problems of thatch and insect control. Herbicide tolerance will be highly important, particularly if chemicals will be needed to control weeds.

In most instances, low forage yields will be sought. Notable exceptions will be cultivars planted along roadsides, where they must compete with weeds under an infrequent mowing regime. Here, vigorous cultivars, more like pasture and hay types, will be more successful.

Although turfed areas are frequently planted only "once in lifetime," ease of propagation cannot be overlooked. Damaged turf must be repaired. Establishment costs, directly related to ease of propagation, will influence the extent to which a new turfgrass cultivar will be used to plant new areas or replace less satisfactory types. Improving ease of establishment without sacrificing other desired traits will always improve the species and increase its use.

Seedheads detract from the appearance of turf. Grasses, like bahiagrass (*Paspalum notatum* Flügge) that produce tall, rapidly growing culms throughout the summer, may have to be mowed twice a week to maintain a smooth turf. If mowing is delayed, seeds are frequently scattered into adjacent lawns, where they may develop into serious weeds. If the grass must be propagated by seed, good seed yields will be required. If vegetative propagation is practicable, complete elimination of seedheads will improve the appearance of the turf and will help to prevent its spread into areas where it is not wanted.

II. GERMPLASM SOURCES

Good germplasm is essential for successful turfgrass breeding. Like gold, it is "where you find it" and it is not easy to find.

Turfed areas that have been in turf for many years frequently yield cultivars that prove to be rare gems. This is particularly true where the turf was originally established from seed of a heterozygous variety. Most of the superior vegetatively propagated creeping bentgrass (*Agrostis stolonifera* L.) cultivars, such as 'Arlington', 'Cohansey', and 'Congressional', were discovered on golf greens where their superiority under golf green management allowed them to reach noticeable proportions (Hanson, 1959). 'Tiflawn' bermudagrass was first selected for turf plot evaluation because it had survived in a neglected space-plant nursery, where hundreds of sister hybrids had disappeared (Burton & Robinson, 1951). Differences in disease reaction and mode of reproduction have been observed among regional collections of Kentucky bluegrass (*Poa pratensis* L.) (Hanson & Juska, 1965). The germplasm for practically all of the new cool-season grass cultivars (> 100) was collected from superior patches of turf on golf courses and lawns.

Introductions from foreign countries offer an excellent source of turfgrass germplasm. Most of the species used for turf in the USA are not native to this country. Their greatest diversity is most likely to occur near their centers of origin or in secondary centers, where they have hybridized with indigenous material. Likewise, plants resistant to disease and insect pests are most likely to be found close to their original home. Bermudagrass, for example, originated in Africa and genes for resistance to the disease, insect, and nematode pests of common bermudagrass have likewise come from that continent. Genes for winterhardiness that are needed to extend the range of adaptation of a species are more likely to occur at high altitudes or farther from the equator than the species' center of origin. In 1966, the author found the most winterhardy bermudagrasses in Berlin, Germany and the Alps of north Italy.

Frequently, related species or even genera can supply characteristics not available in the natural variants of a turfgrass. Brought together by hybridization, the desirable traits of the parent species may complement each other and give rise to hybrid varieties superior to either parent. Most of the improved bermudagrass varieties, such as 'Tifgreen' and Tifway, are F_1 hybrids between *Cynodon dactylon* L. Pers. and diploid *Cynodon transvaalensis* Burtt-Davy. The latter species imparts fineness, softness, and increased density to the triploid hybrid (Burton, 1960, 1964). The sterility that usually occurs in species hybrids poses no serious problem if vegetative propagation is practicable.

III. BREEDING METHODS DETERMINED BY MODE OF COMMERCIAL PROPAGATION

A. Vegetative Propagation

A vegetatively propagated turfgrass greatly facilitates its genetic improvement. Breeding such species requires only that a superior plant be developed. Progeny testing to ascertain the performance of succeeding generations can be omitted, and the time required to produce a superior variety can be reduced accordingly.

Interspecific and intergeneric hybridization, usually beset with sterility problems, may be freely used because seed for propagation is not needed. The sterility of such hybrids prevents pollen shed and helps to keep them restricted to the areas where planted. Nonpollen-shedding bermudagrass triploids, such as Tifway, have been particularly attractive to people allergic to bermudagrass pollen.

The reduction or elimination of seedheads can become a major objective in breeding vegetatively propagated turfgrasses, and few genetic changes could do more to lower maintenance costs and improve turfgrass appearance.

Vegetative propagation simplifies the description and identification of the new cultivar. At present, only vegetatively propagated grass cultivars may be patented. Purity of the new grass can be maintained with less effort. Only a wall or a few feet of space are required to isolate one vegetatively propagated grass from another.

B. Seed Propagation

Seed propagation usually reduces turfgrass establishment costs. It is essential for the development of turf from bunch grasses and is highly desirable for the establishment of turf from slow-spreading, rhizomatous species.

Breeding superior seed-producing turfgrass cultivars is much more difficult and time-consuming than the genetic improvement of vegetatively propagated species. In both instances, plants with the desired turf characteristics must be selected and tested. If the new cultivar is to be seed-propagated, however, it must produce good seed yields in the seed-producing area. Since the environment in the seed-growing area is usually different from that in the breeding or use area, seeding habits of new cultivars must be studied where the seed will be grown.

If the seed-propagated selections reproduce sexually, they must be progeny tested in spaced-plant nurseries and close-seeded plots. Possible genetic shifts, resulting from growing seed in a different environment, must be ascertained and avoided if significant.

Seedhead elimination or reduction cannot be a breeding objective in seed-propagated cultivars. It may be achieved, in some instances, by developing photoperiod-sensitive cultivars that flower and produce seed in the seed-producing area, but remain vegetative where grown for turf. Near the equator in South America, where a uniform 12-h day is experienced, certain varieties of bahiagrass rarely produce seedheads and are considered excellent turf-grasses. Given a 13- to 14-h day, these grasses seed profusely throughout the long-day season. Although generally propagated vegetatively at the equator, these bahiagrass varieties could be planted with seed harvested in regions that have a longer day.

IV. BREEDING METHODS DETERMINED BY MODE OF REPRODUCTION

Efficient plant breeding requires a knowledge of the mode of reproduction of the material to be improved. An understanding of the cytogenetic relationships between the members of the one or more species involved will also greatly facilitate the genetic improvement program.

The first step in any well-organized plant breeding program is the collection of germplasm. This involves bringing together members of a species and closely related species to maximize the diversity of the turfgrass to be improved.

A systematic survey and classification of the germplasm collection might well be the next step. An examination of a small, spaced-plant progeny of each accession can throw much light on its mode of reproduction. A spaced planting of a selfed progeny will also suggest how important characters in a selected plant are inherited.

Chromosome numbers should be counted as soon as possible. Genome relationships, particularly between species to be hybridized, should be established. Self- and cross-fertility relationships should be determined. To get the breeding work underway, however, such studies should first be confined to the most promising plants, the ones to be involved in the first breeding efforts.

A. Asexual Reproduction

Vegetative propagation of turfgrasses by sprigs may be considered one type of asexual reproduction. The genetic improvement of vegetatively propagated grasses merely requires the collection or creation of variable plants that must be tested to identify the superior individuals.

Apomixis is another form of asexual reproduction that occurs in a number of grasses. *Poa bulbosa*, an example of vegetative apomixis, develops small, seed-like bulbils in its flowering panicles instead of seeds. These bulbils may be used to propagate the grass. Apospory, a form of agamospermy, in which maternal tissue differentiates to form seed embryos, is the type of apomixis generally encountered in grasses. Because the word "apomixis" has usually been used instead of "apospory" to describe this phenomenon in grasses, apomixis will be used in that context for the remainder of this chapter.

Because apomixis allows for vegetative reproduction of a genotype through its seed, it combines the advantages of vegetative and seed propagation. 'Merion' bluegrass discovered by Joseph Valentine on the Merion Golf Club in Ardmore, PA, in 1936 is >96% apomictic. Thus, apomixis fixed its excellent turf characteristics including resistance to leaf spot disease caused by *Drechslera poae* (Bandys) Shoem. and permitted the propagation of Merion by seed. Progressive seed growers in the Pacific Northwest since 1950 have produced more than 70 million lb of Merion seed for North America and millions of additional pounds for Europe and other areas (Funk, 1980).

Although apomixis is heritable, the genetic mechanisms whereby it is transmitted from parent to offspring are not well understood. Burton and Forbes (1960) found evidence that apomixis in tetraploid bahiagrass was controlled by a single recessive gene in the homozygous (nulliplex) condition. Taliaferro and Bashaw (1966) reported that apomixis in buffelgrass (*Cenchrus ciliaris* L. Link) occurs in plants with the genetic constitution, *Aa-bb*. They postulated the genetic constitution of a naturally occurring sexual plant to be *AaBb*, where gene *B* conditions sexuality and is epistatic to gene *A*, which controls apomixis. Even when the mode of inheritance is not understood, apomixis may be used to facilitate turfgrass improvement as exemplified in Merion Kentucky bluegrass (Hanson, 1959).

A uniform spaced progeny from open-pollinated seed suggests that the parent plant is either highly self-pollinated or reproduces by apomixis. The existence of apomictic reproduction may be confirmed by examining embryo sacs of the accession. If the origin of asexual embryo sacs can be established cytologically or if multiple embryo sacs are produced, the uniform progeny can be attributed to apomixis.

If apomixis is facultative, as in Kentucky bluegrass, most apomictic plants will produce some sexual offspring that will differ from the parent plant. Improvement by selection within progeny of such plants may be possible (Brittingham, 1943).

If apomixis is of the obligate type that occurs in many warm-season grasses, such as the tetraploid bahiagrasses, sexual offspring will not be produced (Bashaw, 1962; Burton & Forbes, 1960). Seedlings from obligate apomictic plants are exactly like their female parent regardless of the male parent used to produce the seed. Somatic mutation, natural or induced, will create a low frequency of changes but attempts to select superior plants in the seedling progeny of a grass that reproduces by obligate apomixis have not been fruitful (Bashaw, 1962; Burton, 1962; Burton & Forbes, 1960).

Grasses that reproduce by apomixis (particularly the obligate type) may best be improved by hybridizing apomictic males with sexual female plants (Bashaw, 1962; Burton & Forbes, 1960). This technique allows the male parent to contribute half of the hybrid's germplasm, just as if it were sexual. Some of the hybrids from such matings will be apomictic in the F_1 or F_2 generation, depending on the genetic constitution of the sexual female parent. If propagation by apomixis is intended, the mode of reproduction of hybrid offspring must be tested. If a plant is apomictic, it will give rise to a uniform progeny. Five spaced plants from open-pollinated seed will usually classify the mode of reproduction of a single plant where obligate apomixis is involved. Only those selections that reproduce by apomixis need be evaluated for turf qualities.

B. Sexual Reproduction

Grasses that reproduce sexually, such as creeping red fescue (*Festuca rubra* L.), tall fescue (*Festuca arundinacea* Schreb.), perennial ryegrass (*Lolium perenne* L.), and common bermudagrass, are usually further classified with reference to the amount of cross-pollination that occurs in nature. Grasses that are naturally self-pollinated generally give rise to uniform offspring that are like their parents. Although a few chance hybrids between such plants may occur, selection within seedling offspring is not likely to be very fruitful. Self-pollinated grasses are usually improved by mating plants that carry different desired traits. Selection in advanced generations for the combination of traits sought may, after five or six generations give rise to reasonably homozygous plants that will breed true.

Naturally cross-pollinated grasses are usually heterozygous. If they are self-fertile, variable progeny can be produced by selfing selected plants. The loss in vigor, generally associated with inbreeding and frowned upon in forage crop improvement, may be desirable in turfgrasses (Dudeck & Duich, 1967).

Naturally cross-pollinated grasses are well suited to population breeding methods, such as mass selection. Actual procedures may vary from roguing out a few undesirable plants in a spaced planting before flowering to removing a few superior plants to an isolated area for seed production.

Frequently, such grasses carry a self-incompatibility mechanism that causes individual plants to be self-sterile but cross-fertile (Burton & Hart, 1967). Superior seed-propagated F_1 hybrids can be produced in such grasses by interplanting vegetatively two or more self-sterile, cross-fertile clones in isolated seed-production fields (Burton & Hart, 1967). 'Penncross' creeping bentgrass seed, as purchased on the market, comes from seed fields planted to three vegetatively propagated clones of creeping bentgrass (Hanson, 1959). The clones are heterozygous and the commercial Penncross seed, a mixture of the three possible crosses between three clones, gives rise to a variable population. The frequency of vigorous hybrid plants carrying the traits of the selected parent clones is great enough that golf greens planted with Penncross have usually been better than those seeded to other bentgrasses. Harvested seed only from fields planted to the three selected clones ensures against population drift and guarantees that Penncross seed will always contain essentially the same genotype frequencies. However, not all golf greens planted to Penncross bent can be expected to look the same when 10-yr old. Genotypes surviving on one green may be quite different from those surviving on another green in a different environment.

V. TECHNIQUES FOR CREATING VARIATION

A search for naturally occurring variants offers one of the most fruitful methods of acquiring the variable germplasm essential for a successful breeding program. Plants that have been able to survive and increase enough to be noticeable must possess many of the traits required of superior turfgrasses. Most of today's turfgrass cultivars originated in this way. If not worthy of increase themselves, they may be most valuable as parents in a breeding program. A very good clone of common bermudagrass, selected by greenskeeper, W.G. Thomas from the fourth green of the Charlotte Country Club, Charlotte, NC, became one of the parents of the highly successful Tifgreen bermudagrass (Tifton 328) (Burton, 1964).

Inbreeding heterozygous, sexually reproducing plants offers a particularly promising method of developing desirable variation in turfgrasses. Genes for dwarfness, short culms, and seedlessness are usually recessives that rarely appear or survive in cross-pollinated populations. Genes for pest resistance may also be recessive. A search of large, spaced plant nurseries planted to selfed progeny of selected heterozygous plants provides a good opportunity to find superior turfgrass types. If too much vigor is lost from inbreeding, some of it may be recovered by intermating unrelated plants with similar turf characteristics.

Hybridization is one of the most common methods used to create variation in plants. When hybrids are made, the F_1 is usually more vigorous but otherwise intermediate to the parents in most characteristics, except for those controlled by dominant genes. The F_2 generation will generally include plants ranging from the extremes of one parent to the other for most of the traits considered, and will provide new combinations of characteristics not seen in the parent and F_1 plants. If the parents are heterozygous, a large F_2 generation from a number of F_1 plants of the cross may be expected to contain dwarfs and other recessive characters not seen in either parent. Intraspecific hybrids will be easiest to make and can be advanced to the F_2 generation without difficulty.

Interspecific and intergeneric hybrids are more difficult to make than intraspecific ones, and will usually give rise to sterile F_1 hybrids. If the hybrids have superior turf characteristics and can be propagated vegetatively, their sterility may be an asset, as in the case of the triploid bermudagrass hybrids. If the hybrids are not superior as turfgrasses, cannot be commercially propagated by vegetative means, or both of these cases apply, an effort to advance them another generation should be made. Where the parents contribute different genomes, doubling the chromosome number of the F_1 hybrids may lead to the development of a fertile amphidiploid. If the chromosomes in the F_1 hybrid pair with a high frequency, doubling of the chromosome number to increase fertility is much less likely to succeed. Backcrossing the F_1 hybrid to one or both parents may yield a few seeds and produce useful variants. The possibility of developing vegetative hybrids by crossing sterile interspecific or intergeneric hybrids with another stoloniferous or rhizomatous species should not be overlooked.

Mutagenic agents will create variation as they increase mutation frequencies. At optimum dosages, chemical and radiation mutagenic agents are about equally effective in increasing mutation frequency. Generally, however, treatment with radiation, such as x-rays or thermal neutrons, results in chromosome breakage and rearrangement and reduces seed set. Mutagenic agents, such as ethyl methane sulfonate, do not cause noticeable chromosome aberrations and, consequently, affect seed set very little (Burton & Powell, 1966). Thus, chemical mutagenic agents may be preferred if seed production of the treated material is desired. If, however, sterility to eliminate pollen and facilitate control is a desirable characteristic in vegetative material, heavy radiation would be the recommended treatment.

Because most induced mutants behave as recessives and since paired loci are rarely affected by a single treatment, M_1 plants from treated seed may show comparatively few mutations, particularly if the treated seeds were homozygous. Such material must be advanced to the M_2 generation by selfing to permit full expression of the mutagenic-agent effects. Mutagen-treated heterozygous seeds will give rise to much greater variation in the M_1 generation because destruction of the dominant gene at any heterozygous locus allows the associated recessive to be expressed.

Creating variation in apomictic material is most difficult, particularly if obligate apomixis is involved. Where sexual female plants are lacking, treatment with mutagenic agents is about the only known method for increasing variability. Hanson and Juska (1962) treated seed of the facultative apomictic Merion Kentucky bluegrass with thermal neutrons to increase the number of aberrant plants up to 11-fold. Although most of the mutants were inferior to the parents, a few had turf potential. Most of their mutants tested in the M_3 generation were apomictic.

Most plants that reproduce by apomixis are highly heterozygous. Treatment of such germplasm with mutagenic agents will give rise to many mutant or off-type plants in the M_1 generation (Burton & Jackson, 1962). Carrying these mutants to the M_2 generation, generally gives uniform progeny like the mutant parent which is proof that the mutant is also apomictic. Sometimes M_2 progenies are variable, but there will usually be more than one plant of each variant. When these variants are advanced to the M_3 generation, they give uniform progeny to prove that they are also apomictic. Thus, variations that sometimes appear in certain M_2 progeny are due to sectoring in the M_1 generation, where several mutant sectors in one plant contribute seed for the M_2 test.

There is no evidence to prove that apomictic plants can be made sexual by treatment with mutagenic agents. Thus, induced mutants of apomictic plants may be expected to continue to breed true by apomixis. Since most induced mutants are likely to be inferior to their apomictic parents, literally thousands of spaced plants from treated seed should be examined in a breeding program designed to improve the turf qualities of an apomictic grass by mutagen treatment.

Many of our superior fruits, such as the 'Delicious' apple (*Malus domestica* Borkh.) arose as bud mutations in vegetative material. There is good reason to believe that Tifdwarf bermudagrass originated as a natural mutant in the vegetative stolons of Tifgreen, a sterile triploid (Burton & Elsner, 1965).

Exposing dormant rhizomes of the sterile triploid Tif bermudagrass species hybrids to 7000 to 9000 gamma rays has been an effective procedure for the creation of variation (Powell et al., 1974). Out of 158 mutants have come 'Tifway II', similar to Tifway in appearance but with greater frost and pest resistance and 'Tifgreen II', superior to Tifgreen in nematode and mole cricket resistance and persistence under low maintenance (Burton, 1982).

In recent years, tissue culture has been studied as a means of creating diversity and improving a wide variety of plant species. Among the turfgrasses receiving attention has been Penncross creeping bentgrass, the most widely used grass on golf greens (Blanche et al., 1986; Krans et al., 1982). The main objective of Krans and his staff was the development of cultivars better adapted to the southeastern USA. In their research, somatic callus (a mass of undifferentiated plant cells) was developed from mature Penncross caryopses by a series of tissue culture treatments. The resulting stock callus cultured in special media {that included 2,4-D [(2,4-dichlorophenoxy)acetic acid]} produced plantlets and plants that "were similar to seeded plants." Plants developed from tissue culture, frequently called *somaclones*, are being evaluated for turf purposes.

VI. TECHNIQUES FOR SELFING AND CROSSING

Genetic improvement, except for vegetative mutation, must be preceded by floral induction and seed production. Hybridization is greatly facilitated when the parents can be made to flower at the same time. Floral induction is subject to both genetic and environmental control. Frequently, grasses native to the tropics fail to flower when moved to areas with summer days longer than 12 h. Reducing the daily photoperiod to 12 h will usually bring such grasses into flower. Every species and genotype has an optimum photoperiod that must be known and simulated if genotypes are to be made to flower.

Hill or row plantings produce more heads and flower for a longer period than dense plantings. Removing dead winter growth with a spring fire will increase seedhead formation in bahiagrass several fold. Adequate fertilization, particularly with N, can induce heavy, prolonged flowering in a starved, nonflowering grass sod. Temperature has a significant effect on floral induction in most species.

Age affects floral induction in some grasses. The female parent for Tiflawn bermudagrass was a dwarf *Cynodon dactylon* seedling that failed to produce any seedheads until the sod was 3-yr old. The variety, No Mow bermudagrass, planted at Tifton, GA, in the spring of 1965, failed to flower until 1967, when it produced a great profusion of seed stalks. Thus, the turfgrass breeder will do well to study the floral behavior of his breeding stocks to learn how to bring them into flower at will.

Selfing requires that grass flowers be isolated from all foreign pollen. Enclosing heads in bags before anthesis begins has been the method generally used to self most grasses. Selfing bags must be porous enough to allow for moisture and gaseous interchange but tight enough to prevent pollen penetration. Bags made from glassine or kraft paper, sealed with waterproof glue, have usually met these requirements. In addition, individual bags must be small enough and light enough to keep from breaking the stalks bearing the bagged heads. The culms of many turfgrasses are so fragile that supports for the bags must also be provided. Where many heads flower over a short period, it may be desirable to enclose the entire plant in a large glassine or parchment bag.

If only a few plants are to be selfed, isolation may be found in the windows of offices and laboratories. This requires that heads to be selfed must be moved to these rooms, which can be easily accomplished with potted plants. Seed stalks of many grasses will flower and produce seed if they are cut close to the soil surface just prior to anthesis, placed immediately in tap water, and kept in the water until mature. Many heads can be placed in a bottle of water, which in turn, is located in a window where the heads will receive some light. Although seed set is frequently two to three times less and seed size is smaller than in normal field plantings, the procedure has been effective with bermudagrass and bahiagrass.

Diecious grasses such as buffalograss [*Buchloë dactyloides* (Nutt.) Engelm.] can be easily hybridized by pollinating flowers on female plants with pollen from male plants. Selfing such grasses will require the isolation of the occasional plant that bears both male and female flowers or by brother-sister or parent-offspring mating.

Hand emasculation of grass florets is a tedious, time-consuming procedure that may be necessary to produce hybrids but should be avoided wherever possible. Basically, hand emasculation involves the removal of the three anthers in each grass floret without allowing them to shed any pollen. It may be most easily accomplished at the time the florets open and begin to exsert their anthers during normal anthesis. At this stage, the anthers will dehisce naturally and shed pollen easily unless great care is exercised. Creating a dense, artificial fog will delay anther dehiscence and make the anther walls less likely to fracture when removed with tweezers (Burton, 1948).

Anthesis in many species is light-stimulated and temperature influenced. Flowering may be delayed in grasses that flower soon after sunrise by keeping them in a dark chamber. If it is necessary to delay flowering several hours beyond the normal time, lowering the temperature in the dark chamber to 4 to 10 °C will be desirable. Reduced temperature may be used to slow down the normal rate of anthesis to facilitate emasculation and increase the time during which florets can be emasculated.

Male-sterility, as it makes emasculation unnecessary, greatly facilitates crossing procedures. Genetic male-sterility, usually controlled by a recessive gene, is useful in developing hybrids that are to be advanced to the F_2 generation for selection because the F_1 is usually fertile. Cytoplasmic male-sterility, of value in a commercial F_1 hybrid breeding program, poses problems in the production of hybrids to be carried to the F_2 generation for the selection of new recombinants. If the male parents, crossed with cytoplasmic male-sterile plants, fail to carry fertility-restorer genes, the F_1 hybrids will be sterile and cannot be advanced to the F_2 generation. Both mechanisms will give rise to either F_1 or F_2 plants that cannot be selfed.

Male-sterility may be temporarily created in several grasses by altering the environment of the flowering culms. Immersing heads several days before anthesis in hot water at 43 to 48 °C for 1 to 5 min has generally rendered grasses male-sterile. Low temperatures, around 0 °C, have also caused male-sterility. Coastal bermudagrass has on occasion produced only sterile anthers shortly before the first killing frost in the fall.

Generally, the greatest seed set results if emasculated or male-sterile grasses are pollinated at the time that pollination normally occurs. A group of heads from the male parent ready to flower, placed in a bottle of water, will supply an excellent source of pollen. This may be collected in a bag and dusted on the male-sterile florets. It is frequently simpler and more effective, however, to place the bouquet of heads from the male parent in close proximity to the female heads. These may be enclosed with the heads of the female in a bag or may be isolated with the heads of the female in the windows of offices, as suggested for inbreeding.

Self-incompatibility allows for the production of hybrids without emasculation simply by bringing together two self-sterile, cross-fertile genotypes in the flowering stage. Bundles of culms ready to flower, placed in bottles of water, can be paired in isolation to create hybrids. Shaking the heads each morning will favor pollen movement and increase the number of hybrids produced. This is an excellent technique for producing polycrosses.

Mutual pollination consists of bringing together heads of two self-sterile, cross-fertile plants in isolation during anthesis. Pairing in isolation equal numbers of flowering culms in bottles of water offers one of the best ways of making hybrids by this technique. Obviously, the method depends largely on chance to create hybrids. If there are no incompatibilities and if the number of pollen grains and florets are similar for both parents, half of the seeds should be hybrids and the other half should be selfs. This method is easy and will allow for the production of many more hybrids than could be produced by hand emasculation. If the parent plants possess noticeably different characteristics, if the hybrid seeds are kept separate by female parents, and if selfed progeny of each parent are space planted along with the hybrid progeny, it should be quite easy to identify the hybrid plants. If the plants hybridized are heterozygous, the selfed plants will generally be less vigorous than the hybrids. Incorporation of a recessive marker gene, such as white stigma color in bahiagrass where normal stigma color is red, will verify chance hybrids produced by the mutual-pollination technique.

VII. SELECTION

Success of a plant breeder is determined in no small measure by his ability to identify and isolate the superior plants in a large, variable population. To facilitate the first operation, individual seedlings started in the greenhouse are usually space planted far enough apart to allow each to express its characteristics with a minimum of competition. Weeds must be controlled, and fumigation with methyl bromide before planting or spraying with herbicides immediately after planting (and as frequently thereafter as needed) will save much labor in this phase of the operation. The amine salt of 2,4-D, applied at a rate of 1 to 2 kg of acid equivalent per ha immediately after planting and at monthly intervals therefore, usually gives excellent control of most weeds. Using 2,4-D to control weeds also permits an evaluation of the tolerance of the seedlings to this commonly used herbicide.

Locating the space planting on coarse, deep sand will help to screen the population for root-system development. Only those plants with deep, extensive root systems will be able to make good growth on such soils.

Where resistance to a specific disease is sought, it may be possible to inoculate and screen the seedlings for disease resistance in flats while they are still in the greenhouse. Generally, a grass resistant to a disease in the seedling stage will retain the resistance throughout its life cycle. This technique may also be used in breeding for insect and nematode resistance.

Generally, the most promising plants can be removed from a spaced planting at the end of one or two seasons of observation. It would be well, if possible, however, to leave the space planting without care for several years thereafter to observe persistence when plants are neglected. Occasional mowing may be required to reduce excess top growth and weeds and facilitate observations. It is not uncommon for one or more superior plants to appear after such treatment.

Space plantings will not supply all the information needed to prove the worth of a new turfgrass. Small plots, managed as the turf will be maintained by the ultimate user, are needed to appraise the turf properties of promising spaced plants. If the new variety will ultimately be propagated vegetatively, the test plots can be established in this way. Since rate of spread is an important characteristic in a new grass, this information can be obtained as the plots are established. It will be important to establish each plot with comparable sprigs located in the same way if relative ratings are to have significance.

VIII. CULTIVAR DEVELOPMENT, EVALUATION, AND RELEASE

Developing cultivars from selections that will always be propagated vegetatively is a comparatively simple operation. Many superior traits of the selection such as pest resistance will have been established in the original screening procedure. Progeny tests will not be required. Establishment methods must be developed and vegetative increase for replicated plot testing will be required. Yields of planting stock should be ascertained. If the new variety is to be marketed as sod, its sod-producing characteristics should be assessed. Final evaluation should be made in replicated plots.

Developing cultivars from apomictic selections requires an additional assessment of their seed-producing ability in the region where the seed will be produced commercially. If the selection is a facultative apomict, the percent of sexual plants and their effect on the turf obtained when the seed is planted must be determined. Finally enough seed for replicated plot tests must be produced.

Of the cool-season turfgrasses, only Kentucky bluegrass reproduces in part by apomixis. All others, the fescues, ryegrasses, and bentgrasses are cross-pollinated, heterozygous, sexual, seed-propagated species. Most varieties of these grasses used before 1980 were composites, produced by mixing together several superior naturally occurring clones (Meyer, 1982). These were frequently intermated by the breeder and with no progeny testing were named and sent to the Pacific Northwest for commercial seed production. Some cultivars such as Penncross creeping bentgrass were produced from carefully tested clones that were increased and interplanted vegetatively in isolated seed fields. All commercial seed of some varieties had to be harvested from such fields. For other varieties seed so produced was classed as breeders seed that could be increased only two or three generations. Such restrictions limited varietal drift and added consistency to a variety's performance.

Most improved varieties of cool-season grasses released in recent years have been synthetics produced by intermating several superior clones (Funk, 1980). Many of these clones were good turf types to which disease resistance had been added by backcrossing (Meyer, 1982). The development of synthetic varieties can be improved by subjecting superior clones to a selfed progeny test. The performance of these clones in a spaced-plant progeny test of each single cross in a diallel involving them will help to identify the best components for a new synthetic. Obviously, seed production as well as important turf characteristics must be considered. 'Penneagle' creeping bentgrass is an excellent example. This outstanding disease-resistant putting green grass is the product of the careful evaluation of parent material for 15 yr (Duich, 1979). Finally seed of the synthetic generation (Syn 2 or Syn 3) to be used for commercial turf should be produced for replicated plot tests.

Most synthetics are produced by intermating three or more heterozygous clones selected for the turf qualities desired. Clones with finer leaves and shorter culms are used to produce the turf-type tall fescues. That only two may be used successfully is demonstrated in the recent release of the winterhardy seed-propagated 'Guymon' bermudagrass (C.M. Taliaferro, 1982, mimeographed unpublished data). Guymon is an advanced generation derived from interpollinating two very winterhardy heterozygous clones—PI 263302 from Yugoslavia and 12156 collected near Guymon, OK. Its greater winterhardiness will permit it to be grown 5° lat (560 km) further north than commercial seed-propagated bermudagrass.

Plot tests should be located on uniform soil and receive uniform management throughout the test period. Seeding rates comparable to commercial rates should be used. Square plots, ranging from 1 to 3 m^2 in size, will usually be adequate. New selections should be replicated at least twice, and if there are many entries it will be desirable to replicate the checks a number of times. Since the best varieties currently available must be surpassed by any new entry, the best varieties should be included in the test as checks.

This will permit at all times a direct comparison between currently available varieties and any new selection.

Management should simulate that generally given grasses that the new varieties may replace. Grasses bred for golf greens must be mowed daily at heights of 3 to 6 mm. They must be top-dressed with soil as golf greens are. Their tolerance of the chemicals (fertilizers, insecticides, herbicides, and nematicides) used in golf green maintenance must be established. If they must be overseeded with winter grass in regular practice, test plots must also be overseeded. Grasses that show promise for more than one use need to be managed as for each potential use. Making a management variable, such as mowing height or fertilizer rate, a part of the selection-evaluation test by splitting each plot with the management treatments may be a desirable practice.

The criteria used for the evaluation of spaced plants and plots of selected plants will include those characteristics listed under General Requirements (section I.) at the beginning of this chapter. Practically all criteria used to evaluate turfgrass selections require or permit visual appraisal. Color, perhaps one of the most important turf characteristics, is difficult to measure with machines but can be classified visually. Injury due to drought, frost, chemicals, disease, or insects will change turf color. Thus, a comparative color rating of a group of turfgrass genotypes, from 1 to 5 or 1 to 10, made at monthly intervals with additional ratings after frosts, etc. will indicate which genotypes were most pleasing to the eye and least affected by adversity. Rate of establishment, ground cover, and sod density can likewise be easily described with a relative rating system that gives the densest plots at rating of 1 and the least dense plots at rating of 10. Weed resistance may be easily described by a visual rating that gives weed-free plots at rating of 1 and the weediest plots a score of 10. Forage yield, an important measurement in forage breeding, is generally unimportant in turfgrasses except that it be low and this can be estimated visually. Even stolon length, plant height, and seedhead abundance, characters that can be measured, can be more rapidly classified with a visual rating system.

Giving the most desirable plants a rating of 1 for each trait described greatly simplifies an overall summary of the observations that will apply to a group of plants. Thus, the clones with the lowest average rating over a testing period will generally be the best. Ratings for color and sod density should be taken at least once a month. In addition, ratings should be taken at any other time that differences due to treatment or environment occur. Artificial shades, placed over different grasses, furnish the best method for appraising their shade tolerance (Burton & Deal, 1962). Wear resistance, important for fairways, playgrounds, etc. can be appraised by rating plots subjected to uniform golf-cart traffic (Burton & Lance, 1966) or wear machines constructed for this purpose. Precision and accuracy in rating may be improved by training, by rating the plots or plants two or three times whenever ratings are made, or by averaging ratings made by two or more people. Where plots are replicated, ratings may be analyzed statistically.

Regional and interregional tests add replication to local tests and indicate the area in which each grass is adapted. Bulletin 814 entitled "Northeastern Regional Turfgrass Evaluation of Kentucky Bluegrasses (*Poa pratensis* L.) 1968–1973" (NE-57 Technical Research Committee, 1977) is a good example of the type of information obtained from regional tests being carried out with major turf species in the USA. Bulletin 814 gives examples of location × cultivar interactions. The National Turfgrass Evaluation Program (sponsored by USDA-ARS, Beltsville, MD and the Maryland State Turfgrass Council, with Jack Murray and Kevin Morris as coordinators) has published a number of progress reports giving results of national tests with various species.

Rainfall, one of the major regional differences, is frequently compensated for by artificial watering. Thus, grasses adapted at Tifton, with 50 in. of rain, also do very well in Arizona, with <5 in. of natural rainfall. As a matter of fact, superior humid-region grasses frequently do even better in arid sections when watered because of more sunshine and less of the high humidity that favors the development of plant diseases. Conversely, grasses adapted to dry climates may carry susceptibility to diseases that are not evident until they are tested in humid areas. 'Sunturf' bermudagrass which is extremely susceptible to rust is an excellent example. Thus, there is a much greater need for regional and interregional tests to set latitudinal limits for new varieties than to establish their longitudinal adaptation. Cool-season grasses have a southern limit due to summer heat and plant diseases, and winter cold determines how far north a tropical grass may be dependably grown. Thus interregional tests, located north and south of the breeding center, will usually be worth much more than east and west tests. Drainage, irrigation, soil modification, and fertilization can usually overcome soil differences experienced in different regions. Since turf can usually bear the costs of these soil amendments, regional tests to appraise soil-type adaptation are not too important.

There is no substitute for ultimate user evaluation. He must be pleased if the new grass is to succeed. Tifgreen (Tifton 328) was given this kind of test by several golf course superintendents before it was released. Unfortunately, such tests frequently lead to premature release. Generally, new grass varieties that are consistently superior for at least 3 yr in well-replicated tests at one location where they are exposed to major diseases and insects, will have wide adaptation in the same longitudinal regions and will please the ultimate user.

Cultivar release procedures must protect the cultivar, ensure its continued purity, and provide for its intended use by the public. Protection can be provided under the provisions of the Plant Variety Protection Act or by registration by the Crop Science Society of America. Vegetatively propagated cultivars can be patented.

To ensure continued purity, the fields in which the new variety is to be increased must be free of seeds or plants of other varieties of the same species. These can usually be eliminated by fumigating the soil with methyl bromide prior to planting. This treatment will also eliminate most weeds and hasten the establishment of the variety. Although expensive, methyl bromide fumigation may be a good investment. If the variety reproduces sexually and is seed propagated, isolation to prevent outcrossing with other varieties must be adequate. State seed certification programs can greatly facilitate the selection and supervision of growers for new cultivars particularly those released "only to qualified certified growers."

Only as improved varieties are used can the cost of their development be justified. Thus the potential consumer must be informed of the merits of an improved turf grass. Descriptions of the new grass in turf and garden journals and on radio, television, and turf conference programs will help to "sell" the public release. Exclusive release varieties may enjoy the added advantage of advertising. Ideally, the release procedure should recognize the breeder and his/her employer and maximize the benefits the public can realize from using a better turfgrass.

REFERENCES

Bashaw, E.C. 1962. Apomixis and sexuality in buffelgrass. Crop Sci. 2:412–415.

Blanche, Fe.C., J.V. Krans, and G.E. Coats. 1986. Improvement in callus growth and plantlet formation in creeping bentgrass. Crop Sci. 26:1245–1248.

Brittingham, W.H. 1943. Type of seed formation as indicated by the nature and extent of variation in Kentucky bluegrass and its practical implications. J. Agric. Res. 67:225–264.

Burton, G.W. 1948. Artificial fog facilitates *Paspalum* emasculation. J. Am. Soc. Agron. 40:281–282.

Burton, G.W. 1951. The adaptability and breeding of suitable grasses for the Southeastern states. Adv. Agron. 3:197–241.

Burton, G.W. 1960. Tifway bermudagrass. USGA J. Turf Manage. 13(3):28–30.

Burton, G.W. 1962. Conventional breeding of dallisgrass, *Paspalum dilatatum* Poir. Crop Sci. 2:491–494.

Burton, G.W. 1964. Tifgreen (Tifton 328) bermudagrass for golf greens. USGA Green Sect. Rec. 2(1):11–13.

Burton, G.W. 1982. The Tif-turf bermudas. Parks Recreation Resourc. 1(9–10):9–12.

Burton, G.W., and E.E. Deal. 1962. Shade studies on Southern grasses. Golf Course Rep. 30(8):26–27.

Burton, G.W., and J.E. Elsner. 1965. Tifdwarf—a new bermudagrass for golf greens. USGA Green Sect. Rec. 2(5):8–9.

Burton, G.W., and I. Forbes, Jr. 1960. The genetics and manipulation of obligate apomixis in common bahiagrass (*Paspalum notatum*). p. 66–71. *In* Proc. 8th Int. Grassl. Congr., Redding, Berkshire, England. Alden Press, Oxford, Great Britain.

Burton, G.W., and R.H. Hart. 1967. Use of self-incompatibility to produce commercial seed-propagated F_1 bermudagrass hybrids. Crop Sci. 7:524–527.

Burton, G.W., and J.E. Jackson. 1962. Radiation breeding of apomictic prostrate dallisgrass, *Paspalum dilatatum* var. *pauciciliatum*. Crop Sci. 2:495–497.

Burton, G.W., and C. Lance. 1966. Golf car versus grass. Golf Course Super. 34(1):66–70.

Burton, G.W., and J.B. Powell. 1966. Morphological and cytological response of pearl millet, *Pennisetum typhoides,* to thermal neutron and ethyl methane sulfonate seed treatments. Crop Sci. 6:180–182.

Burton, G.W., and B.P. Robinson. 1951. The story behind Tifton 57 bermuda. Southern Turf Foundation Bull., p. 3–4, Spring issue.

Dudeck, A.E., and J.M. Duich. 1967. Preliminary investigations of the reproduction and morphological behavior of several selections of Colonial bentgrass, *Agrostis tenuis* Sibth. Crop Sci. 7:605–610.

Duich, J.M. 1979. Penneagle creeping bentgrass. USGA Green Sect. Rec. 17(4):8–10.

Funk, C.R. 1980. Perspectives in turfgrass breeding and evaluation. p. 3–10. *In* R.W. Sheard (ed.) Proc. 4th Int. Turfgrass Res. Conf., Guelph, ON, Canada. 19–23 July 1981. Int. Turfgrass Soc., and Ontario Agric. Coll., Univ. of Guelph, Guelph, ON.

Hanson, A.A. 1959. Grass varieties in the United States. USDA-ARS Agric. Handb. 170. U.S. Gov. Print. Office, Washington, DC.

Hanson, A.A., and F.V. Juska. 1962. Induced mutations in Kentucky bluegrass. Crop Sci. 2:369–371.

Hanson, A.A., and F.V. Juska. 1965. The characteristics of *Poa pratensis* L. clones collected from favorable and unfavorable environments. p. 159–161. *In* Proc. 9th Int. Grassl. Congr., São Paulo, Brazil. Dep. of Animal Production of the Sec. of Agric., São Paulo, Brazil.

Krans, J.V., V.T. Henning, and K.C. Torres. 1982. Callus induction, maintenance and plantlet regeneration in creeping bentgrass. Crop Sci. 22:1193–1197.

Meyer, W.A. 1982. Breeding disease-resistant cool-season turfgrass cultivars for the United States. Plant Dis. 66:341–344.

NE-57 Technical Research Committee. 1977. Northeastern regional turfgrass evaluation of Kentucky bluegrass (*Poa pratensis* L.), 1968–1973. Pennsylvania Agric. Exp. Stn. Bull. 814.

Powell, J.B., G.W. Burton, and J.R. Young. 1974. Mutations induced in vegetatively propagated turf bermudagrasses by gamma radiation. Crop Sci. 14:327–332.

Taliaferro, C.M., and E.C. Bashaw. 1966. Inheritance and control of obligate apomixis in breeding buffelgrass, *Pennisetum ciliare*. Crop Sci. 6:473–476.

SUBJECT INDEX